Webster's New World
Dictionary of
Media and
Communications

RICHARD WEINER

Webster's New World
New York   London   Toronto   Sydney   Tokyo   Singapore

First Edition

Copyright © 1990 by Richard Weiner

 Webster's New World

Simon & Schuster, Inc.
15 Columbus Circle
New York, New York 10023

WEBSTER'S NEW WORLD and colophons are registered trademarks
of Simon & Schuster, Inc.

DISTRIBUTED BY PRENTICE HALL TRADE SALES

Manufactured in the United States of America

1 2 3 4 5 6 7 8 9

Library of Congress Cataloging-in-Publication Data

Weiner, Richard.
   Webster's New World dictionary of media and communications /
Richard Weiner.
     p. cm.
   ISBN 0-13-969759-4
   1. Mass media—Dictionaries. 2. Communication—Dictionaries.
I. Title.
P87.5.W45 1990
302.23'03—dc20

90-31012
CIP

ACKNOWLEDGMENTS

It seems that all lexicographical projects turn out to be much more time-consuming than anyone ever contemplates. I have learned that a specialized dictionary is an intense labor of love by an individual who combines intellectual curiosity, research ingenuity, and writing skill with a patient devotion to simple, hard work. Nonetheless, a dictionary would not be possible without the generous help of many friends and colleagues.

Many trade and professional associations, particularly those that agreed to become members of the Editorial Advisory Board, provided invaluable trade glossaries and other materials. I also met and spoke with dozens of professionals in these fields and conducted extensive research, including visits to many libraries. My own collection of reference books now numbers several hundred.

I am pleased to thank the following organizations that joined the Editorial Advisory Board:

American Advertising Federation
American Institute of Graphics Arts
American Newspaper Publishers Association
American Society of Newspaper Editors
Broadcast Music Inc.
Cabletelevision Advertising Bureau
Direct Marketing Association
International Association of Business Communicators
International Communications Industries Association
International Exhibitors Association
National Association of Broadcasters
Newspaper Advertising Bureau
Outdoor Advertising Association of America
Radio Advertising Bureau
Specialty Advertising Association International
Videotex Industry Association

I am indebted to those anonymous librarians at the New York Public Library and other libraries with whom I consulted in person and by phone. My most-used single source was *Webster's New World Dictionary, Third College Edition.*

I especially appreciate the help of Yvonne Egertson, librarian of the American Newspaper Publishers Association. Several communications associations stated that they could not participate, lest their participation be considered an official endorsement of the book, but they provided glossaries and other materials. Obviously I am responsible for all of the definitions.

I appreciate the encouragement of Robert Markel and of my family, particularly my wife, Florence Weiner. Many colleagues suggested words. I also was aided by many typists and other assistants, especially Phyllis Scheiner and Zena Bernstein. The editors and staff at Simon & Schuster were indispensable, especially, Charles Levine, publisher; Philip Friedman, general editor; Lisa Wolff, production editor; and the two copy editors, Susan Joseph and Tobie Sullivan.

FOREWORD

From my early childhood, I have had a special interest in communication words. My father was a printer. I worked on student newspapers in elementary school, high school, and college and also worked at a radio station. I have been in the public relations field since the early 1950s. During this time, I wrote seven public relations books, conducted several college courses in public relations, and gave hundreds of lectures, developing in the process an extensive vocabulary in the media and communications fields.

From 1968 to 1986, while operating my own public relations firm, Richard Weiner, Inc., in New York, once or twice a week I sent memos to the staff (which grew close to 100 people) covering new techniques in advertising, market research, publishing, and related fields, as well as public relations. Seeing these memos accumulate, a colleague, Jon Weisberg, suggested that I compile a glossary for use by our staff, clients, and others.

That's how this dictionary began. It started in 1981, as a glossary and primer for people in public relations. It quickly proliferated into what probably is the most extensive collection of words in a variety of media and communication fields—including advertising, book production, broadcasting, computers and computer graphics, direct marketing, exhibitions, film, graphic arts, journalism, library science, mail, marketing, market research, newspapers, photography, printing, public relations, publishing, radio, recording, sales promotion, telecommunications, telephone, television, theater, typography, videotex, and writing.

I hope that readers may want to peruse this book just for pleasure and that they will enjoy the show-biz slang, the colorful words in graphic arts, and the other sections of interest to general viewers, listeners, and readers. Note, for example, the terms that start with China or Japan; the origin of the shopping mall; why newsprint turns yellow; types of headlines; and all the other information that may appear in textbooks or elsewhere, though perhaps not presented as cogently, in this first omnibus dictionary covering the wide range of contemporary communications fields.

INTRODUCTION

We live in a media and communications society.

Over four million people in the United States are employed full time in communications, including over one and a half million in printing and publishing and over a million in broadcasting, film, newspapers, and other publications. Over 600,000 people work in the telephone industry alone and another 100,000 each work in photography, public relations, and advertising. And beyond these, several million people in sales and marketing each day call upon their colleagues in advertising, market research, promotion, and public relations. The language of the media and communications makes up a vital network of meaning in today's workplace.

Even children learn such words as *commercial, fast forward, color bars, jingle, tape, theme song,* and *VCR*—television terms involving advertising, programming, or technology.

Everywhere we go we encounter media terms. At the theater we may hear references to *flies, catwalks,* and *scrim.* In TV listings we read abbreviations such as *TBA, rep, r,* and *cc.*

Even capable professionals use words whose precise meaning eludes them, such as *ADI, aliasing, anti-aliasing, A-roll, B-roll, circular, cume, frequency, reach,* and *residual*—all common terms in advertising. Many of the terms in communications and media have forgotten origins. For example, *circular* derives from *circulate.* That's why a flyer, poster, or other printed item circulated by mail or carrier is dubbed a circular.

In outdoor advertising, there are similarities and differences among *billboard, board, bulletin, display, panel, poster,* and *sign.* In graphic arts, a *mat* is not *matte. Calendered paper* is not used for *calendars.* The *Carterfone decision* is unrelated to Jimmy Carter. Some common words, too, have acquired different definitions in various communications fields, such as *character, continuity, cut, field, frame,* and *plot.*

Perhaps the greatest strengths of this book are the definitions of hundreds of things you probably know about without being able to name correctly. For example, you might not know that the theatrical classified advertisements listed alphabetically in major city dailies are called *ABC's*—different from the *stacked ads.* You have seen *agony columns, Academy leaders* (the numbers appearing on the screen before the movie starts), a *bug* printed on booklets produced by union labor, and the *A-hed* in *The Wall Street Journal;* but did you know their proper names?

Many of the terms in this book are not found in any general dictionary, and some do not appear even in specialized dictionaries or reference books. You are unlikely to find *crow quie* (not the same as *coquille board*), *intermission dropout, mouse type, non-repro blue,* or *standby guest* defined elsewhere.

Whether you are a professional in the media and communications fields or a lay person, you will find this dictionary *all up, big time,* a *blockbuster, boffo, on the button,* a *keep,* a *magnum opus, socko,* and *wammo.* So take it away, this is a *wrap.*

technical creative cost, such as that for writers, directors, producers, and performers, but not technical expenses and labor (*below-the-line costs*) The two together are called *negative cost*. In motion pictures and broadcasting, the people who do above-the-line work are called *staff*; those who do below-the-line work are called *crew*.

above the rod referring to a library catalog card out of its file box

ABP AMERICAN BUSINESS PRESS

abr. abridged; abridgment

abrasion [photography] a fine defect on the surface of processed film, whereas a *scratch* may be a defect that penetrates to the base

abrasion resistance in papermaking, the degree to which paper can withstand scuffing

abridgment condensed form, as of a book, with the original contents, style, and intent retained, though with the text reduced in length An abridgment is not the same as an ABSTRACT, DIGEST, SUMMARY, or SYNOPSIS.

A-B rolling [film] an editing technique in which odd-numbered scenes are placed on one reel (A-roll) of film or tape and even-numbered scenes are placed on the other reel (B-roll) In TV, the editing to produce a composite master film or tape is facilitated with two projectors or videotape machines and a video switcher. It is also called *checkerboarding*.

ABS international telex abbreviation for *absent subscriber, office closed*

absolute address in computer storage, a location that is permanently assigned an identification number by the computer manufacturer

absorbency the property of a substance to take in sound, light, liquid, or other matter *Absorption* is the penetration of one substance into another.

absolute film a "pure" (absolute) film, one that is abstract and not narrative, such as a pattern of moving lines or shapes produced by a computer or other device; also called *abstract film*

absorption [printing] the first stage in ink drying

a-b split 1 [advertising] a research technique in which different advertisements for the same product or service appear in alternate copies of the same issue of a publication or in alternate envelopes in a direct mailing 2 [market research] a technique in which a RANDOM SAMPLE of names are separated into two groups of equal size, with names alternately assigned to each group Research results from the two groups then can be compared.

A-B stereo a method of recording in which two omnidirectional microphones are placed several feet apart in front of the sound source in order to produce stereophonic sound; also called SPACED MICROPHONE STEREO

abstract 1 a summary 2 [journalism] the first paragraph of an article, containing the word count of the full story and the computer retrieval number

abstract film ABSOLUTE FILM

abstract mark a logo or symbol that has no obvious visual relationship to the item it represents; see also ARBITRARY MARK

abstract set a set, as on a TV news program, that has a neutral background

A-B text a direct comparison of the sound/picture quality of two projectors or other audiovisual equipment The comparison is made by playing one projector and then the other.

AC or A/C ADULT CONTEMPORARY

AC or A.C. author's correction; see AUTHOR'S ALTERATION (AA)

ACA ASSOCIATION OF CANADIAN ADVERTISERS, INC.

Academy aperture the standard size of a 35mm aperture plate of film printers and projectors It yields an ASPECT RATIO (of width to height) of 1.33 to 1, called the *Academy ratio* or *standard ratio*. See ACADEMY OF MOTION PICTURE ARTS AND SCIENCES.

Academy Awards annual prizes, called *Oscars*, presented by the ACADEMY OF MOTION PICTURE ARTS AND SCIENCES, for achievement in several categories of filmmaking

Academy leader an eight-second numbered strip of film that precedes the first picture frame in a reel of film

Academy mask a device that obstructs a portion of the aperture of a film camera, in order to establish a screen size ratio of 1.33 to 1 The mask is no longer used with today's wide screens. See ACADEMY OF MOTION PICTURE ARTS AND SCIENCES.

Academy of Motion Picture Arts and Sciences an organization in Beverly Hills, CA, of film producers, performers, and technicians Usually referred to as the *Academy*, it publishes the *Academy Players Directory*, a listing of over 5,000 actors and actresses, with photos and credits commonly used for casting. The Academy establishes various standards for the film industry (see ACADEMY APERTURE, ACADEMY LEADER, ACADEMY MASK, ACADEMY ROLL-OFF) and presents the OSCAR AWARDS.

Academy roll-off [film] a device to reduce high frequencies on soundtracks, to protect the sound system in theaters It is not used with the DOLBY SOUND SYSTEM. See ACADEMY OF MOTION PICTURE ARTS AND SCIENCES.

ACB ADVERTISING CHECKING BUREAU

accelerated aging in papermaking, a technique of artificially aging paper to predict its longevity

accelerated montage [film] a series of shots, each shorter or faster-paced than the preceding one A technique to heighten tension; it is not the same as *parallel montage*, in which two scenes are cross-cut or interspersed, although the intent of the two techniques is the same.

accelerator [photography] the alkali added to the developer to activate it and increase its function

accent a characteristic pronunciation; a distinctive feature; a mark above, below, adjacent to, or through a letter to indicate pronunciation or emphasis Here are nine common accents (if you know all these names, you are probably a crossword puzzle genius or a professional typesetter). Other accent marks are listed under PUNCTUATION MARKS.

> *acute* é
> *angstrom* å
> *cedilla* ç
> *centered point* ȧ
> *circumflex* ă
> *diaresis* (*umlaut*) ö
> *grave* è
> *macron* (long vowel) ā
> *tilde* ñ

A *floating accent* is an individual accent mark, separate from the character it modifies (the *base character*). In computerized typesetting, a *floating accent piece* is one that has a zero width so that it can appear centered in relation to the base character. A *pre-positioned accent* also has a zero width but is in a predetermined horizontal position relative to the base character, not necessarily centered.

accent face [printing] a typeface that is considerably different from and contrasts with the characters (letters) of other typefaces used in the same work

acceptability [advertising] the willingness of the media to utilize advertising or programming material

acceptance angle [photography] the minimum angle of a camera, in relation to the subject, that provides sufficient light for a specific scene; the angle at which light rays strike the photocell of an exposure meter See ANGLE OF ACCEPTANCE.

access 1 availability or approachability, as of media people to public relations practitioners or government officials to media people 2 [computers] Data stored on magnetic tape is available in *sequential access*. Data stored on disks is available in *random access*. 3 [videotex] the number of frames requested by a user

access channel a local-use channel of a cable TV system It includes public-access channels (reserved for community use) as well as commercial channels.

access code [telephone] the digit or digits used by a caller to place a connection, such as 9 for a local trunk or 8 for long distance

accessing the entering into or the extracting of information from a computer *Immediate access* or *direct access* (sometimes called *random access*) is the ability of a computer to enter (store) or obtain (retrieve) data directly from the memory area, without delay, while other data is processed. *Parallel access* or *simultaneous access* is the process of obtaining or storing data when the required time is dependent on the simultaneous transfer of all elements of a requested word or data. *Serial access* is the process of obtaining or storing data by scanning previously acquired data to determine the current location in storage and the sequential or consecutive transmission of data to or from storage.

access journalism a style of writing used by political reporters, columnists, and others that relies on information from interviews with, or access to, government officials, celebrities, and other sources

accession an item added, such as a document or a painting, by a library, museum, or other collection or repository; the process of adding such an item An *accession number* is a consecutive numeral assigned to each item as it is added; *accession order* is the sequence of the addition; *accession record* (also called, in libraries, *accession book*, *accession catalog*, or *accession file*) is the listing of the items, arranged in the order in which they were added, with information about each.

access period [television] a time period (7:30–8:00 P.M. E.S.T.) returned to the local stations by the networks under a 1970 Federal Communications Commission ruling, to provide communities with the opportunity for more local programming Though no longer a requirement, the access period has become a PRIME TIME for local stations.

access time [computers] the interval between the time at which data are requested from a storage unit to the time delivery, such as the appearance of the data on the screen, begins, or simply the time needed by a data storage unit to receive or produce information

accidental sampling a survey research method that relies on chance For instance, passersby in a shopping mall or on a street are approached and an interview is requested.

accordion fold 1 a paper in which two or more parallel creases have been made; called a *concertina fold* in the United Kingdom 2 [printing] two or more parallel folds that open like an accordion An *accordion insert* is a leaflet or other item that has a zigzag fold and is bound into or inserted in a publication or used as an enclosure.

account a calculation, record, exploration, or report; a business or organization that is a customer or client of an advertising or similar agency *On account* indicates partial payment or purchase on credit; the slang phrase *on the money*, in contrast, means exact or precise.

accountability responsibility by an individual or firm for the manner in which advertising, public relations, or other funds have been spent

accountable mail mail that requires the signature of the addressee upon receipt, such as certified or registered mail

account executive (AE) a person in an advertising agency or other firm who maintains contact with the client and usually does the basic work, assisted by an *assistant account executive* and managed by an *account supervisor* or *account group supervisor*; often called *account exec*

account group employees in an advertising agency or company department who work on a specific client's campaign Within the group may be an *account executive* and other levels of staff, such as an *account supervisor.*

account opener a gift or inducement offered by a bank to a customer to deposit money—that is, to open an account

Accredited Public Relations (APR) a title given to members of the PUBLIC RELATIONS SOCIETY OF AMERICA who pass an examination and meet other standards

Accrediting Council on Education in Journalism and Mass Communications a journalism education association in Lawrence, KS; formerly called the *American Council on Education for Journalism*

acct. account

accumeter [book production] a device that applies glue (*accumeter gluer*) to the spine or water (*accumeter moistener*) to wet the paper and provide a better fold

accumulated audience the total number of individuals reached by a broadcast or publication over a specified period of time; also called *cumulative audience* (*cume*) and sometimes called *unduplicated audience, net unduplicated audience,* or *reach* When the data refer to households instead of to individuals, the term used is *accumulated households.*

accumulator [computers] a register that stores a quantity of data, the place in the memory where additions and subtractions are made during a procedure; the arithmetically combined data are transferred before each new procedure

ACD associate creative director; AUTOMATIC CALL DISTRIBUTOR

ace [theater] a spotlight with a 1,000-watt bulb

ACE AMERICAN CINEMA EDITORS

ACE Awards annual awards of the NATIONAL CABLE TELEVISION ASSOCIATION for innovative cable TV programming

A certificate Adult certificate, a designation given by the BRITISH BOARD OF FILM CENSORS to movies that may be seen by children under 16 only when accompanied by a parent or guardian

ACES AUTOMATED CAMERA EFFECTS SYSTEM

acetate a salt of acetic acid; a term commonly used for *cellulose acetate* Because it is non-flammable, as compared to nitrate film, acetate film is called *safety film.* As a transparent thin plastic, acetate is the base of motion picture film and a type of phonograph record; in clear or translucent sheet form, it is used as an overlay on graphics and reproduction proofs. *Frosted acetate* or *prepared acetate* is a plastic sheet with one side matted (less smooth) so that adhesives, ink, paint, or other materials can be applied to it. An *acetate medium* is commonly added by artists to water-based paints to increase the paints' adhesion to acetate film or other glossy surfaces. *Acetate paints*, which generally contain acrylic (an acid derived from glycerol), are frequently used in film animation. *Acetate ink* is a thin, flexible, transparent film (not liquid and not really ink) made of cellulose acetate and also used in film animation. The animation is drawn on the acetate ink (called *cels*), which then is placed over background art and photographed one frame at a time. *Acetate records* were breakable and preceded vinyl records.

acetate sleeve a transparent plastic sheath for the protection of items, such as color transparencies

A channel the left-side band of a two-channel audio system

achromatic without color In the *achromatic color* printing process, black ink is substituted for a colored ink to create gray tones. This is also called *gray component replacement.*

acid-free stock paper that has little or no sulfuric or other acid or other destructive ingredients remaining after the manufacturing process

acknowledgment (ack., ackl.) recognition; an expression of thanks, as on an *acknowledgment page* of a book; an indication that a message has been received or transmitted

ACN A. C. NIELSEN COMPANY

A copy [journalism] a term for the part of a news story written in advance, with later material to follow; sometimes called *10-add* material because it is added to the top, or lead, of an article; also called *A matter* The *A* stands for *advance*. The term is sometimes hyphenated.

ACORN the acronym for *A Classification of Residential Neighborhoods*, a system used by a market research company, CACI, of Arlington, VA, in which households in the United States and United Kingdom are grouped by socioeconomic characteristics

acoustic coupler [telecommunications] a device with a standard telephone as a MODEM input or interface

acoustics the science of sound, especially its transmission; the qualities of a room or other area that determine how clearly sounds can be transmitted or heard in it An *acoustician* is an expert in sound. An acoustic musical instrument, such as an *acoustic guitar*, is not electronic. Acoustic musicians and singers perform without electronic instruments or accessories.

acoustic suspension [recording] a type of loudspeaker system that utilizes an airtight sealed enclosure

acoustic tile a wall or floor covering that absorbs sounds

acpt. acceptance

acquisition an unfinished work, such as a manuscript, that has been purchased by a publisher, studio, or other organization that intends to produce the work; also, a published book or other finished work purchased by a library or other institution An *acquisitions editor* or *acquiring editor* reviews manuscripts or other works for potential publication or other production. An *acquisitions librarian* is responsible for ordering or purchasing items, such as periodicals.

ACR audio cartridge; automatic carriage return (on a typewriter)

acronym a coined word, formed from the letters of a series of words, such as *laser* (from *l*ight *a*mplification by *s*timulated *e*mission of *r*adiation) An acronym is not necessarily the same as an *abbreviation* (as of an association name or other phrase), which is not pronounced as a word.

across mike referring to the technique of speaking sideways to a microphone, rather than directly into it, to reduce hissing, popping, and explosive sounds

across-the-board a program or commercial scheduled at the same time each day, generally Monday through Friday; also called *strip*

across the grain [printing] at right angles (90 degrees) to the direction in which the majority of fibers in paper being manufactured are aligned; also called *against the grain*

acrylic paint a type of fast-drying, water-soluble paint that contains acrylic (an acid derived from glycerol), used in film animation to produce smooth colors on acetate film (called *cels*) A major manufacturer of acrylic paint is Cartoon Colors, Culver City, CA.

act **1** a major division of a play, opera, or other dramatic work Most plays have two or three acts, generally separated by an intermission. A one-act play is known as a *one-acter*. In a variety program, such as at a nightclub, each performer or group is called an *act*, as is the performance itself. A person who plays a role or performs is an *actor* (man or woman) or *actress* (woman). **2** to perform; *to act all over the place:* to overact, or to exaggerate a role

ACT ANTI-COMET TAIL GUN; ACTION FOR CHILDREN'S TELEVISION

AC-T ADVERTISING CONTROL FOR TELEVISION, an advertising testing service of McCollum/ Spielman, a market research company in Great Neck, NY

act break **1** a scene change that indicates a shift in the action of a plot In TV, a commercial break often is inserted during an act break. **2** the interval between acts of a play; an intermission A backstage sign generally indicates to the performers and crew the time of an act break and the number of minutes it will take.

act curtain a curtain on a theater stage that is opened or raised at the beginning and closed or lowered at the end of each act of a play or other performance

actg. acting

acting referring to a work adapted for performance on the stage, such as an *acting script* or an *acting edition*, which contains the text, BOOK, or script as well as indications for entrances, exits, and other stage directions

actinic light [photography] short wavelength rays in the violet and ultraviolet parts of the spectrum that produce chemical changes, as in photosensitive materials *Actinic opacity* refers to the degree of imperviousness to actinic light. *Actinic transmission* is the conveying of *actinic radiation*, such as by a photographic emulsion.

action **1** a director's call to begin performing or to start filming The *action track* is the picture part of a film or tape. **2** a series of events and episodes in a dramatic or literary work *Rising action* precedes the CLIMAX of a plot; *falling action* follows the climax.

action call [theater] a CURTAIN CALL in which the performer remains in character with the gestures of the part

action cue [theater] a visual cue, involving physical movement rather than speech

action cutting [film] the instantaneous shifting from one shot to the next, generally achieved by overlapping the action on successive shots, by using two cameras (one for each shot) in simultaneous operation or by editing

action device [direct marketing] an item designed to persuade a consumer to take some specific action, such as to remove a *Yes* or *No* stamp and paste it on a card; also called *involvement device*

action field the area that is actually being filmed or taped by the camera

Action for Children's Television (ACT) a non-profit group in Newtonville, MA, established in 1971 to upgrade children's TV programs

Action News a style of TV newscasting that emphasizes fast-paced realism; sometimes called *Eyewitness News* Techniques include telecasting from the newsroom (or a set that looks like a newsroom), team coverage by reporters and newscasters, often informally dressed, and intercutting or fast mixing of live reports and newsfilm or tape.

action outline a description of the major sequences or scenes in a script to be filmed or taped

action paper a treated paper that produces copies without carbon paper

action print only (APO) the instruction to make a film print without sound (an *action print*)

action properties objects actually handled by performers, as distinct from *still props*; also called *action props*

action shot [film] a shot in which the camera follows the movement or action; also called *follow shot*, *moving shot*, or *tracking shot*

action still a photograph enlarged from a frame of a motion picture; also called *frame enlargement* It is not the same as a *production still*, a photograph taken with a STILL camera during production.

action track the picture part of a film or tape

action viewer a viewfinder attached to a film camera or used separately to locate a camera position (where the camera should be pointed) for a sports event or for other action

actives 1 [marketing] customers on a list who have made purchases within a prescribed time period, such as one year; subscribers whose subscriptions have not expired 2 [radio] listeners who call a station to make programming requests or who participate in contests or call-in programs

actor-manager an actor who also manages the theater group in which he appears, a dual position that was common in 19th-century England

actor proof a theatrical script that is extremely likely to be successful, regardless of any ineptness of the performers

Actors' Equity Association an AFL-CIO union, based in New York, of about 30,000 professional actors and actresses Members are issued *Equity cards*; producers of professionally staged plays hire an *Equity cast* in accordance with *Equity scale* (the Equity payment schedule) and regulations.

ACTS AMERICAN CHRISTIAN TELEVISION SYSTEM

act-tune a musical composition played between the acts of a play, common in the 16th and 17th centuries in England

actual the real, final cost of a program or project, as opposed to the projected cost

actuality a live or taped news report broadcast from the scene, containing the voice(s) of the newsmaker(s) as well as of the reporter

actual line focus [theater] the technique of arranging performers in a play in one or two lines so that the viewer is likely to focus on the principal performer, positioned at the front of the line or at the intersection of the two lines It differs from *visual line focus*, in which the other performers direct their attention to the principal performer.

act well a play or show that is relatively easy to perform

acutance [graphic arts] the degree of sharpness of an image, as measured by a densitometer, which indicates the density change in different areas

acute accent a mark (´) above a vowel to show quality, length, or stress and after a syllable to show stress

ACV ALL-COMMODITY VOLUME

ad advertisement; ADVERTISING

AD or **A.D.** *anno Domini* (Latin, "*in the year of the Lord*"), a designation sometimes used on tombstones and cornerstones or as a formal method of dating, to indicate a year (as in A.D. 1954); ART DIRECTOR; ASSISTANT DIRECTOR; ASSOCIATE DIRECTOR

adage an old saying that has been popularly accepted as a truth

Ad Age short for *Advertising Age*, a tabloid published weekly by Crain Communications, Chicago It is the largest-circulation publication in the advertising field.

ad alley old slang for *advertising* or *advertising industry*; see also ALLEY

adaptation   the changing of literary matter from one medium to another, such as the basing of a movie script on a novel

ad curtain   a painted drop (an OLIO), often on rollers, hung onstage in theaters (particularly vaudeville, in the 19th and early 20th centuries), on which advertisements were painted; also called *advertisement curtain, ad drop,* or *advertisement drop*

add.   **1** ADDENDUM   **2** [journalism] addition, a term indicating material to be added to copy already written   Pages or sections to be added are numbered *add 1, add 2, add 3,* and so on. Copy written in advance (*A copy*) sometimes is called *10-add.*

added scenes   [film, television] scenes added to a production after the principal photography has been completed

added value   [marketing] extra benefits of a product or service, such as delivery, financing, information by telephone, and warranty

addendum   supplementary material placed at the end of a book or other publication, or inserted as a separate sheet (such as a list of corrections)   The plural is *addenda.*

additional copy   [journalism] a notation, as on a manuscript, that more articles are available if needed

additional period   [telephone] the time after the initial period (such as three minutes) of a telephone call, used to measure charges in excess of the basic rate

additive primaries   [film] the primary colors—red, yellow, and blue—when they are combined   When lights of these colors are mixed, the result is the suggestion of white light.

additive printer   a printer for color film (also called *additive color printer*) that combines lights of red, yellow, and blue (ADDITIVE PRIMARIES), using one lamp (with *light values*) or three lamps

additive process   **1** [film] a technique of producing white light by projecting and overlapping lights of red, yellow, and blue (ADDITIVE PRIMARIES)   **2** [photography] a method of printing from a color negative using red, yellow, and blue filters

add-on sale   [marketing] the sale of a related item, such as accessories or supplies for an appliance   If it is unwarranted or excessive, the transaction is called *loading.*

address   **1** [computers] the location on a disk or in the memory within which a specific piece of information is stored, the number assigned to that location, or any part of an instruction that directly or indirectly specifies the location   An *absolute address* is permanently assigned to a specific memory location or device in the com-

puter. Addresses are stored in an *address register,* and their location is *addressable* (accessible) by use of an *address part* (a portion of an instruction word that specifies an address). The *address format* is the arrangement of the address parts of an instruction. The *instruction address* is the address used to select an instruction.   **2** [telephone] a complete telephone number, including the area code

addressability   [television] the ability of a cable TV operator to control a converter in a subscriber's home   *One-way addressability* functions from the operator to the subscriber; *two-way addressability* includes communication from the subscriber to the operator. An *addressable system* is a cable TV system with addressability.

addressable converter   a device attached to a TV set to permit access to pay-per-view or other special programs or channels

address book   a book of addresses, generally arranged alphabetically by name, such as a small booklet kept by an individual   Some telephone companies and others publish telephone directories arranged by address (called an *address book, address directory,* or *reverse phone directory*) instead of by name. A *new address book* is a directory of new subscribers of telephone service, generally individuals or companies that have recently moved.

addressee   a person or entity that receives mail; the party to whom the mail is addressed (by the mailer or addresser)

address track   the outermost border or one of the outer tracks, such as one of the audio tracks, of a videotape   It contains cueing information, to be used in editing or perhaps in broadcast transmission; for instance, the address track may provide audio or visual time or other information not to be heard by the home viewer.

ADDY   an award for outstanding national and local advertisements and advertising campaigns, presented by the AMERICAN ADVERTISING FEDERATION

adhesive binding   a bookbinding method in which the pages are glued to the spine, instead of being stitched or attached in other ways; also called *perfect binding*

ad hoc network   [broadcasting] a group of stations that is formed for a special purpose, such as the showing of *Nicholas Nickleby* or other one-time TV programs or series   *Ad hoc* is Latin for "for this."

ADI   AREA OF DOMINANT INFLUENCE

ad interim copyright   the temporary registration of materials for copyright protection, pending acceptance and full registration

adjacency 1 [broadcasting] a commercial or program preceding or following another on a radio or TV station or network, or the time period itself 2 [printing] in computerized typesetting, the condition in which two adjacent characters (letters or numbers) are spaced too close together

adjustment a settlement, usually involving the lowering of price, as when an advertisement was improperly published or broadcast

ad lib an unscripted, spur-of-the-moment, extemporaneous, improvised comment, remark, or speech; an instruction in a script or sheet of music to improvise; to improvise The term is from the Latin *ad libitum*, meaning ''it pleases.''

adlux [photography] a black-and-white transparency

admonitory head [journalism] a headline with the subject omitted, such as an exclamatory phrase

adnorm a term used by the research firm of Starch INRA Hooper, of Mamaroneck, NY, to indicate the amount of readership exposure an advertisement receives in a specific publication The measurement is based on characteristics of the publication, the size of the advertisement, and other factors that then provide a basis for comparison with similar advertisements.

ad-noter a term used by Starch INRA Hooper of Mamaroneck, NY, to designate a reader who claims to have noticed a specific advertisement

ADO [television] Ampex Digital Optics, a SPECIAL EFFECTS device made by the Ampex Corporation, Redwood City, CA

adoption the selection, by a school, department of education, or other agency, of a book in a course or school system

ADP AUTOMATIC DATA PROCESSING

ad-pub advertising and publicity, a combination of functions sometimes found at theatrical companies, who may employ an *ad-pub chief*

ADR AUTOMATIC DIALOGUE REPLACEMENT

ad retention a measurement of SIMMONS Market Research Bureau, New York, that indicates the percentage of readers of a publication who remember the advertising in the current issue

ADRMP AUTOMATIC DIALER RECORDED MESSAGE PLAYER

ADT AVERAGE DAILY TRAFFIC

AdTel a marketing service based on store scanner data and other information, conducted by BURKE MARKETING, of Cincinnati, OH

adult contemporary a format of radio stations that emphasizes current popular music but not hard rock

adv. advertising

advance 1 a news release, or a print or broadcast report, about a forthcoming event Publicity material sometimes may be used prior to the event unless it includes the designation *Hold for release.* 2 payment to an author prior to publication (called *advance on royalties* or *advance against royalties*), or any other prepayment

advance bound galleys [book production] a set of uncorrected galley proofs (typeset manuscript on long sheets) bound within a plain paper cover (generally with title and other information on the front) *Advance sheets* are unbound galleys.

advance card [marketing] a postcard or letter sent to inform the recipient that there will be a subsequent mailing, such as a questionnaire, sweepstakes entry form, or sales promotion

advance copy a book, magazine, or other publication sent prior to the regular shipping or prior to the publication date

advance dating an invoicing method in which credit is extended to a customer by setting the payment in the future, possibly several months later (in which case the practice is called *season dating* or *seasonal dating*)

advance order a sale made prior to the availability of a book or other product

advance premium a gift given to a customer in anticipation of future purchases

Advance Publications one of the country's largest media companies Headquartered in New York, it is privately owned by the Newhouse family and publishes the Newhouse Newspapers (the *Newark Star-Ledger* and others), *Parade* (the world's biggest Sunday supplement), *The New Yorker* magazine, and Condé Nast Publications (*Vogue* and other magazines). Advance also owns many cable TV systems.

advance ratings a preview of the ratings of a radio or TV program or station, provided by phone by an audience-survey company to a client

advergram a telegram that is a sales solicitation or advertisement

adverprop advertising propaganda; advertising that proselytizes or promotes an ideology, cause, or concept

advert British slang for *advertisement*

advertisee the recipient of a message from an advertiser, or the audience of an advertisement

advertiser-supported network a radio or TV network whose programs are free to listeners or viewers and that raises revenues by broadcasting commercials from advertisers Noncommercial stations and/or pay services, in contrast, seek funds from listeners and viewers.

Cable TV also includes advertiser-supported networks, such as CABLE NEWS NETWORK.

advertising the use of paid media to sell products or services or to communicate concepts and information by a sponsor or advertiser PUBLICITY, on the other hand, sometimes is called *free advertising* in that the source of the publicity does not purchase the time or space from the media (the services of professional publicity agents, of course, are not free). Some media, such as outdoor billboards, are available only or mostly to advertisers. Other media, such as newsletters, usually are not available to advertisers. In its broadest sense, PUBLIC RELATIONS incorporates all forms of communications, including advertising.

As a marketing process directed to prospective customers or other audiences, advertising generally involves purchase of time or space in a medium and thus is characterized as *controlled*, whereas publicity is not necessarily directed at potential purchasers. The industry itself also is called *advertising*, as is the end product, the *advertisement* or *ad*. The organization responsible for the process is called an *advertising department* or *advertising agency*.

advertising allowance money paid by a manufacturer or wholesaler to a retailer for advertising (by the retailer) of the product. The fee may be in the form of a deduction in the amount the retailer pays for the merchandise, rather than a direct payment to the retailer. Advertising allowance is a form of PROMOTIONAL ADVERTISING.

advertising banner a headline, usually in a newspaper or magazine, under which advertisements are grouped by category, such as antique dealers or country inns

Advertising Checking Bureau (ACB) a company in New York that monitors the advertising in every daily newspaper and many weekly newspapers in the United States. Copies of ads are sent to advertisers as a service to newspaper publishers, who do not then have to send proof that the ads were in fact published.

Advertising Council, Inc. a nonprofit organization in New York that approves and helps to conduct national public service advertising campaigns for nonprofit organizations; commonly called *Ad Council*

advertising cycle the stages in the life cycle of a product or campaign, such as the *pioneering stage* (testing and introduction), *competitive stage* (national rollout and move to maturity), and *retentive stage* (including possibly the product plateau or decline); also called *marketing cycle*

Advertising Hall of Fame See AMERICAN ADVERTISING FEDERATION.

Advertising Information Services Inc. a New York company, owned by about 20 major advertising agencies, that views tapes of prime-time network TV programs prior to broadcast and sends descriptions of their content to the agencies. Potential problems in the programs then are sent by the agencies to sponsors, or potential sponsors, of the programs.

advertising pages the number of pages of advertisements in a publication for a single issue or over a period of time, such as one year. Fractions of pages are added together, so that the total number represents the entire advertising content, expressed as pages. The *advertising content* (the portion of a publication devoted to advertising) may be expressed as the total number of lines (linage) or as a percent of contents.

advertising provider (AP) an advertiser who pays to display advertisements on a VIDEOTEX system

advertising quadrangle a concept of the four elements of communication: the sender (the advertiser), the message, the medium (print, broadcast), and the receiver. Similarly, in MARKETING, the quadrangle is the sponsor, the product, the channel of distribution, and the prospect.

Advertising Register a directory of advertisers and their agencies. Because of its red cover, it often is called the *Red Book*. The formal name is *Standard Directory of Advertisers*, published by the NATIONAL REGISTER PUBLISHING COMPANY, Wilmette, IL.

Advertising Research Foundation (ARF) a nonprofit organization of advertisers and advertising agencies. Based in New York, it conducts research and publishes the *Journal of Advertising Research*.

advertising rule a line set by a publication to separate adjacent advertisements on a page, particularly if the ads do not have ruled borders

advertising specialty a useful or decorative item used for advertising, such as a cap, T-shirt, key chain, matchbook, pen, or other common or novel product. It is generally low in cost and given away free, and thus it differs from a PREMIUM, which usually is not free. Common categories are calendars, writing instruments, and wearables. Advertising specialties generally are imprinted with an identification of or a message from the advertiser or donor. They are sometimes incorrectly called *advertising novelties*.

Advertising Specialty Institute (ASI or A.S.I.) a company in Philadelphia that assigns four-digit numbers (*ASI numbers*) to specialty advertising to simplify identification of the supplier

advertising weight the amount of advertising devoted to a specific advertising campaign, expressed in various ways, such as cost, size of audience, or RATING POINTS

advertorial an advertisement in editorial style It can occupy a page or less, or several pages—for example, as a supplement (in a newspaper or magazine) with advertising copy that resembles articles

advocacy advertising the use of purchased media time or space for the persuasive presentation of a concept or a viewpoint, rather than for the selling of a specific product or service

advt. advertisement

adWatch a monthly survey of consumer awareness of advertising, conducted by *Advertising Age* and SRI Research Center Inc. Consumers are asked, by telephone, to name the advertising that first comes to mind of all advertising seen or heard in the previous 30 days.

Ad Week a major publication in the advertising field, based in New York and published weekly in four regional editions

a.e. or **AE** ACCOUNT EXECUTIVE (as in an agency); assistant editor; associate editor

AEA ACTORS' EQUITY ASSOCIATION

aeration [printing] the use of an air stream to separate paper sheets as they are fed into a printing machine

aerial older word for *antenna*

aerial photography film and broadcasting made from a helicopter or other aircraft, resulting in an *aerial shot* (if made from atop a crane, a *crane shot*) An *aerial image*, in contrast, reflects a special-effects technique in which a real image is focused in the air, instead of on a surface. An *aerial image animation stand* is a camera support that produces a midair image, so that a cartoon character or other animated image can be filmed over live action.

aerogramme lightweight paper that folds into a self-envelope, with preprinted postage It can be purchased from the Postal Service for sending by air mail to countries outside North America.

AF or **A.F.** AUDIO FREQUENCY

AFC AUTOMATIC FREQUENCY CONTROL

affidavit [broadcasting] a notarized record of commercial and public service announcements aired by a station, listing broadcast date and time, provided to advertisers; also called *affidavit of performance*

affiliate **1** a company or organization united with or operated in association with another **2** [broadcasting] a station that contractually agrees to carry programs of the network with which it is affiliated The station may be owned by the network but generally is independently owned. A *primary affiliate* is a station that carries all or most of its programs from one network; a *secondary affiliate* or *part-time affiliate*, in a small market, may carry all three major networks (AMERICAN BROADCASTING COMPANY, COLUMBIA BROADCASTING SYSTEM, NATIONAL BROADCASTING COMPANY) or be an independent station with a relatively small amount of network programs. Abbreviated *affil.*

affective fallacy the error of judging a work (particularly a literary work) on the basis of its emotional impact (or other results) rather than on qualities of the work itself The term was coined by W. K. Wimsatt, Jr., and M. C. Beardsley in their 1954 book, *The Verbal Icon*. It is not the same as *intentional fallacy*, which is the error of judging a work by the alleged intentions of the author(s) or other creator(s).

affinity group a collection of individuals who have a common interest, background, or other similarity or link

AFIS AMERICAN FORCES INFORMATION SERVICE

AFP AGENCE FRANCE-PRESSE

AFRT AMERICAN FORCES RADIO AND TELEVISION See AMERICAN FORCES INFORMATION SERVICE.

AFRTS AMERICAN FORCES RADIO AND TELEVISION SERVICE See AMERICAN FORCES INFORMATION SERVICE.

AFRTS-PC AMERICAN FORCES RADIO AND TELEVISION SERVICE—PROGRAMMING CENTER See AMERICAN FORCES INFORMATION SERVICE.

aft. afternoon; the end of a piece of tape

AFT AUTOMATIC FINE TUNING

aftermarket the demand for goods or services, such as repairs, accessories, or replacements, related to a previous purchase Aftermarkets are common in the automotive field.

afternoon bath British film slang for an urgent order for same-day, rather than overnight, development (bath) of film

afterpiece a short play, usually a comedy, presented after a full-length play, particularly a tragedy, in England and other countries in the 18th century

afterword an epilogue

AFTRA AMERICAN FEDERATION OF TELEVISION AND RADIO ARTISTS

AGAC American Guild of Authors and Composers See SONGWRITERS GUILD OF AMERICA.

against the grain [printing] paper folded or cut at right angles to the direction of most of the fibers (the GRAIN); also called *across the grain*

agate **1** a size of type (about 5½ points) commonly used in newspaper classified advertising—real estate and employment ads, for instance There are 72 points to an inch; agate (also called *ruby*) type is the smallest-size type generally used. *Agate half measure*, half a column line, is a style sometimes used for lists of names. **2** a hard, semiprecious stone used in burnishing, such as hand tooling of a book

Agate Club an organization in Chicago composed of advertising representatives of print media

agate line a unit of measurement of a publication, generally a newspaper An agate line represents $1/14$ of an inch of a column; thus, there are 14 agate lines to the inch. For example, an advertisement or an article that is 3 columns wide and 5 inches deep consists of 210 agate lines. The number of columns in a newspaper page varies considerably, as does the width of the column, so that the exact size may vary when expressed as agate lines, though this is the generally accepted basic measurement of newspaper advertising space. The cost per agate line, referred to as the *agate line rate* or *open line rate*, is an essential part of the RATE CARD of a newspaper.

AGB See PERGAMON/AGB PLC.

AGC AUTOMATIC GAIN CONTROL

agcy. agency

age cycle the age of individuals in a group; a span of ages set up as an aid in collecting or analyzing data Government census data groups consist of individuals in categories such as *under 30, 30 to 39,* and *40 to 49.* Most marketers classify data by a different set of age cycles: *under 25, 25 to 34, 35 to 44, 45 to 54, 55 to 64,* and *over 64.*

Agence France-Presse (AFP) a major international news service, headquartered in Paris

agency **1** a government department or organization that administers an area of public policy **2** a private group or organization that provides operations or services for others, such as *advertising agency, employment agency, literary agency, public relations agency,* or *sales promotion agency* A staff member who represents clients sometimes is called an AGENT. The agent or agency generally operates on a commission, with some exceptions, such as a public relations agency. The standard advertising agency commission is 15 percent of the gross rate for print and broadcast media and $16^{2}/3$ percent for out-of-home (outdoor and transit) media An *agency network* is a group of affiliated agencies.

agency of record (AOR) an advertising agency that places the advertising with media for a client using more than one agency and/or advertising not created by the AOR

agent an individual or a member of an organization (generally called an AGENCY) who performs services on behalf of others (clients or customers), such as an *insurance agent* or a *literary agent* The term *agent* sometimes may signify *agency;* in the solicitation of periodical subscriptions, a subscription agency (such as PUBLISHERS CLEARING HOUSE) often is called an *agent.*

agent reinstate the reactivation by an AGENT of previously cancelled periodical subscriptions, generally because payment was received or an error was rectified; also called *agency reinstate* or *agent's reinstatement*

agent's clearance one or more orders obtained by an AGENT; also called *agent's order*

agitation [photography] the movement of chemicals over the film and paper in the developing and fixing stages

agitprop an activity or agency to agitate or propagandize, from the Department of Agitation and Propaganda (Odtel Agitasi i Propagandy), established in the Soviet Union in 1920

agony column a series of classified advertisements in a newspaper announcing missing individuals, pets, and other personal losses and problems It is not the same as an *advice column* or other editorial material.

agt. AGENT; agreement

AGVA AMERICAN GUILD OF VARIETY ARTISTS

A-hed a headline style usually consisting of a three-line major headline and a three-line minor headline; used by *The Wall Street Journal* The A-hed generally is used for a feature story, often on the lighter side, and appears on page 1, column 4, below the daily chart. The headlines are surrounded on each side by vertical ruled lines below the chart and are separated by a centered row of three asterisks; thus, the ruled lines and the asterisks somewhat resemble a square capital *A.*

A house a movie theater that shows first-run films, in a more attractive atmosphere than at a B HOUSE

AIA Association of Industrial Advertisers, the former name of BUSINESS AND PROFESSIONAL ADVERTISERS ASSOCIATION

AICP ASSOCIATION OF INDEPENDENT COMMERCIAL PRODUCERS

AIDA acronym for the four general goals of advertising: to obtain *a*ttention, *i*nterest, *d*esire, and *a*ction

AIDCAS process an expansion of the AIDA process, with six steps in the reaction of an individual to a sales presentation: *a*ttention, *i*nterest, *d*esire, *c*onviction, *a*ction, and *s*atisfaction

aided recall a technique for determining how well a test respondent who has been aided by prompting with hints or clues remembers an advertisement

AIGA AMERICAN INSTITUTE OF GRAPHIC ARTS

AIOD AUTOMATIC IDENTIFICATION OF OUTWARD DIALED CALLS

AIO inventory a collection of PSYCHOGRAPHICS: *attitudes, interests,* and *opinions* of individuals; also called *AIO profile*

air **1** the medium for radio and TV broadcasting A station or program, when broadcast, is *on the air.* **2** [graphic arts] open or white space within a print layout

airable suitable for use on a radio or TV station (uncommon slang)

air bell [photography] an undeveloped spot on a film negative or print It is caused by a trapped air bubble resulting from improper AGITATION of the chemical solutions used in development.

airbrush or **air brush** a technique used in a photographic laboratory to correct HALFTONES, obtain graduated tone effects, or eliminate or minimize parts of a photograph or other art It can be used, generally with an abrasive-like pumice, to remove blemishes and edit out parts of a photo. Though *airbrushing* can be done in various ways, the basic technique uses a small pressure cylinder (an *airbrush gun*) that sprays watercolor pigment by means of compressed air.

air check an audio or video transcription or recording, made from an actual broadcast, of a radio or TV commercial or program Technically, a typed transcript is not an air check, although it sometimes is called that.

air date the time of a broadcast

air-drying in papermaking, a method of using hot air to dry moist paper and produce a hard finish

air gap the space between the playback heads of a tape recorder

air master a print of a film or a tape from broadcast use; also called *air print*

airplay the broadcast of a record or tape One measurement of a hit recording is the number of airplays it receives.

airport mail facility (AMF) a U.S. Postal Service facility at or near an airport; also called *airmail field*

air ready describing a commercial, program, or other material completed and available for broadcast use

AIRS ARMY INFORMATION RADIO SERVICE

air show a TV program as actually broadcast; if taped, the final edited version

airtime or **air time** the scheduled day or period of a broadcast, described by the beginning time; the length of an actual broadcast of a program or segment, such as an interview

air-to-air filming or taping of one moving aircraft from another

airwaves the medium through which broadcasting signals are transmitted; their pathways through the air

aisle **1** a passageway for people, as in an exhibition hall, store, or theater An *aisle seat* in a theater is the seat adjacent to the aisle, occupied by an *aisle-sitter* (sometimes a critic, who can make a quick exit to write a review). **2** To *knock 'em in the aisles* or *lay 'em in the aisles* (referring to a comedy) is to be so funny that the audience (figuratively) falls in the aisles laughing.

aisle display [marketing] a point-of-purchase bin or other display unit at the end of an aisle of a supermarket or at another high-traffic location of a store

aisle jumper an overhead wire in a store, displaying banners, flags, pennants, or other point-of-purchase signs

aka or **a.k.a.** also known as, a term indicating an alias or pseudonym; for example, Anna Mary Robertson, *aka* Grandma Moses

ALA AMERICAN LIBRARY ASSOCIATION

A-lamp a low-wattage lamp with a short neck, commonly used on stage; also called *A, A-type,* or *A-type lamp*

alarum an archaic spelling of *alarm,* as in *alarums and excursions,* used as a literary phrase for pleasurable, provocative writing

albertype [photography] a print made by a gelatin process, more commonly called a COLLOTYPE

Albion press a heavy, hand-operated printing press, used to make wood or linoleum cuts Albion is an old poetic name for England.

album **1** a book with blank pages for mounting items, or a book already printed and consisting of an anthology, a collection of photos, or another literary or artistic collection **2** a long-playing record or tape, or a set of records, tapes, or printed materials

albumin or **albumen** a protein found in egg white and other substances Because of its properties (water-solubility, coagulation by heat), albumin is used in making plates used in LITHOGRAPHY, especially for book printing. *Albumen paper* was a printing paper with egg whites added to the white base to enhance the highlights of the photographic prints; it was invented by Louis Blanquart-Evrard (1802–72); a French photographer.

album-oriented radio (AOR) a station that broadcasts record albums

album-oriented rock (AOR) a rock-music format of some radio stations

album paper paper (generally black and 80-pound or another heavy weight) used in photograph and other albums

ALC automatic level control   See AUTOMATIC GAIN CONTROL.

Aldine a typeface named after Aldus Manutius (also known as Aldo Manuzio), a publisher (1450–1515) in Venice *Aldine italic* is a fine-quality ROMAN type used for display. The term *aldine* also refers to printer's ornaments, such as the dolphin and anchor used by Aldus as his mark. *Aldine bindings* are morocco with gilt decoration. An *Aldine book* is one printed by the Manutius family.

aleatory of or depending on chance In film and TV, an *aleatory technique* is used for interviews, documentaries, and other nonscripted productions. See also PERFORMANCE ART.

A-level title a major film, carried by all home video retail outlets

alfalfa theatrical slang for a *false beard*

algorithm 1 any special method of solving a problem, particularly arithmetic 2 [printing] A *justification algorithm* is the procedure or routine to compute the number of characters needed to fill a line.

aliasing defects that produce jagged edges on graphic images ANTI-ALIASING is a process to remove the jagged edges. *Visual aliasing* also refers to STROBING or to the *wagon-wheel effect* (an illusion of backward or forward movement). *Audio aliasing* is the production of unwanted audio signals. An *anti-aliasing filter* removes these signals, which often are introduced in the conversion of analog to digital signals, as with compact disks.

alibi copy a duplicate of an actual broadcast script retained by a station; a duplicate of a news release or other material (with client-approval signature) kept on file by an agency

alienation effect a response to a film, play, or other work, in which the audience remains intellectually separate from the action In a work of SURREALISM, for instance, the audience may be emotionally moved but is still aware that the events depicted are unreal. The concept was called *estrangement effect* by the German playwright Bertolt Brecht (1898–1956).

alignment 1 [printing] the arrangement of type so that the bottom of the characters are in a straight line or the pages are precisely juxtaposed with each other In *base alignment* all the characters "sit" on the same line, even if they are of different styles or sizes. *Nonalignment* of characters may be intentional (called *bounce*) or unintentional. 2 [graphic arts] the arrangement or positioning of type and illustra-tions in a layout, such as vertical and/or horizontal alignment

alive 1 a news release, article, or other material that remains available for publication 2 *keep alive:* an instruction to retain something in the active file or to have something readily available, such as scenery that is not put in DEAD STORAGE

alla breve hurriedly played music in which the half note, rather than the two quarter notes, receives the beat; from the Italian, "according to the BREVE." Popular musicians call this CUT TIME.

all along [book production] a hand-sewn binding style in which the thread is passed through the fold and around every cord or tape along the length of each section of the book In contrast is *two along* binding, in which the sewing alternates cords or tapes. All along also is called *one sheet on* or *one on*.

all-channel tuning the ability of a TV set to receive all assigned channels (channels 2–83)

all-commodity volume (ACV) [marketing] the total number of items in a product category sold in a specific area for a specific time period The distribution or sales of a brand is expressed as a percentage of the ACV market for a four-week or other period.

all-day newspaper a newspaper with editions printed in the morning and the afternoon

Allefex a machine used in movie theaters to produce various SOUND EFFECTS during a silent film

allegation a statement offered without proof; an assertion that may be true but must be proved or supported with evidence In journalism and areas of communications, the words *allege* and *alleged* should be used to indicate that proof is not being offered.

allegory a story illustrating a truth or an idea In an allegory, a symbolic character or event can be interpreted to represent a moral principle.

alley a narrow street or passageway In printing plants, special sections, such as an *ad alley*, are devoted to particular types of work.

Alliance of Motion Picture and Television Producers (AMPTP) an organization in Sherman Oaks, CA, of major film- and TV-producing companies that handles contract negotiations and labor relations, such as in the 1988 strike by the Writers Guild of America

alligator slang for a metal spring-clamp with serrated jaws used to attach lights and other items; also called a *gator grip* or *bear trap* It is used by gaffers (electricians) and called a *gaffer grip*. The spring-loaded clamp has serrations along the edges and resembles the jaws of an alligator. *Alligator clips* are used as terminals for the end of cables or wires to connect oscilloscopes and other equipment.

alliteration the repetition of an initial sound, generally a consonant, in two or more adjacent (or nearby) words, such as in a line of poetry; also called *head rhyme*

all in [printing] an indication that all proofs of typeset material have been returned by the client

all in hand 1 [journalism] newspaper jargon indicating that all the copy has been composed, or set in type, and the presses are ready to roll—a synonym for *put to bed* 2 [printing] an indication that all copy is being typeset

allocation [marketing] distribution or scheduling according to a plan, or the allotment of a product in limited quantities to designated customers; also called ALLOTMENT Allocation is common in outdoor advertising because of the limited number of prime locations.

all other [newspapers] a phrase to indicate all circulation not in the primary market area

allotment 1 [broadcasting] the allocation by the Federal Communications Commission of a carrier frequency to radio stations (AM allotment to AM stations, FM allotment to FM stations) 2 [outdoor advertising] the number of POSTER PANELS in a SHOWING, or the number offered for sale in a market (the *market allotment*)

all-over style [book production] use of a pattern on the entire front or back cover of a book's binding, instead of just in the center and/or corner

allowance See ADVERTISING ALLOWANCE.

all points addressable [computers] the ability to display each PIXEL individually

all points bulletin (APB) an alarm used by police to alert all personnel and monitored by news media

all published in regard to a series of books in which one or more intended volumes were not printed, a term referring to the volumes actually published

all rights an arrangement by which a publisher or other purchaser receives the entire income from the current and any subsequent use, such as an adaptation to another medium, of an article, play, or other work

all rights reserved a statement in a book or other item, generally on the copyright page, indicating that any reproduction requires the consent of the owner of the copyright

all singing, all dancing version a flashy, glamorized modification of a product or service

all up [printing] an indication that all copy has been typeset

allusion an indirect reference, generally to a familiar person, creative work, or historical incident

almanac a yearly publication with data, ranging from astrological, weather, and other forecasts to encyclopedic information

alpha alphabetical In telephone directories, alpha refers to a listing. Alpha and omega are the first and last letters in the Greek alphabet; the term means first and last, as in a series.

alpha and omega the beginning and the end, from the first and the last letters of the Greek alphabet

alphabet the letters of a language arranged in order; also, a system of characters, signs, or symbols to indicate letters or speech sounds In typography, *alphabet length* is the horizontal measurement (generally expressed in points, units of about $1/72$ of an inch) of the total width of the lowercase characters (letters) of a typeface.

Alpha-Beta-Gamma tests the three stages in testing a new computer program or other product Alpha testing occurs in the laboratory; then Beta takes place at a test site under actual operating conditions; Gamma is a more extensive examination made if the Beta test is inconclusive.

Alpha Epsilon Rho—The National Broadcasting Society an honorary organization primarily of students and others in broadcasting It is located at the College of Journalism, University of South Carolina, Columbia, and was formerly called *Alpha Epsilon Rho*.

alphageometric [computers] referring to the creation of text and graphic displays by the use of a common data transmission code for character generation and primitive geometric shapes to construct graphic images

alphaglyph a mark around a letter or letters to form a picture or design representing the product or service of the company or organization

alphameric referring to alphabetic characters (letters) plus punctuation marks and other conventional characters and symbols

alphamosaic [computers] referring to the creation of text and graphic displays by the insertion of dots on the screen to form mosaiclike images

alphanumeric referring to numerical characters and other conventional characters and symbols

Alpha Repertory Television Service (ARTS) a defunct cable system, owned by Hearst ABC Video Services, that transmitted cultural programming in the evening

alterations See AUTHOR'S ALTERATION (AA).

alternate [theater] a performer who takes turns with another performer in the same role, perhaps appearing on matinees or a few times each week; generally an UNDERSTUDY An *alternating cast* sometimes performs instead of the regular cast.

alternate-bundles run [marketing] a technique in which two versions of an advertisement, usually in a magazine, are printed and then commingled in one bundle for mailing in the same geographic area, so that the effectiveness of the two advertisements can be compared

alternate characters [printing] multiple versions of the same letter, or other character in a typeface, such as *italic* (slanting), *swash* (with curved flourishes), or other variations, generally set consecutively on a type style sheet

alternate-operator services companies other than Bell that provide telephone operator services, as at hotels and privately owned pay phones in bars and elsewhere

alternate-position lines [graphic arts] a technique used in engineering and other mechanical drawings, consisting of two dashes interrupting the flow of a continuous line, to indicate a missing part or for other reasons; also called *phantom lines*

alternate routing [telephone] a system of sending a call over another route when the first-choice route is not available *Automatic alternate routing* is the automatic switching of a call to other routes.

alternate sponsorship advertising by two or more organizations that share a radio or TV program or other time period

alternate weeks (A/W) an instruction for an advertisement to be run every other week

alternative press nontraditional, unconventional publications that offer a variation from the mainstream media; formerly called *underground press* or *underground media*

alternative publisher a regional, specialized, or other "small" publisher

alternative television artistic, public-service, counterculture, and other types of innovative programs; the video counterpart of ALTERNATIVE PRESS

alternative theater experimental or offbeat plays, performed off-off-Broadway in New York, at art festivals, or at theater clubs and other artistic sites; called *fringe theatre* in the United Kingdom

alternative title a subtitle, generally following the main title and preceded by *or*

altruistic display a window or other display of products or advertisements from companies that have not paid for the promotion and are receiving a "free ride"

alum potassium aluminum sulfate and other sulfates of aluminum, chromium, and iron, used in photography, printing, and other fields as clarifiers, hardeners, or purifiers This chemical is also used in the form of a *styptic pencil*, as an astringent to stop bleeding from shaving. Other aluminum compounds common in printing are *alumina* or *aluminum oxide* (an abrasive for graining plates), *aluminum sulfate* (used in papermaking), and *alumina hydrate* (ink extender).

AM 1 AMPLITUDE MODULATION **2** a term for a morning newspaper; also spelled *A.M.* or *a.m.*

AMA 1 AMERICAN MARKETING ASSOCIATION **2** automatic message accounting; see AUTOMATIC IDENTIFICATION OF OUTWARD-DIALED CALLS

amateur a nonprofessional An *amateur operator* is a radio operator who is licensed by the Federal Communications Commission and colloquially called a *ham* or a *ham operator.*

amatory publications books or other materials pertaining to love, particularly sexual

A-matter [printing] material typeset in advance of the balance or main portion of a publication, such as a special section of a newspaper or book

ambassador the highest-ranking diplomatic representative appointed by a country to represent its interests abroad In nongovernmental terms, a *goodwill ambassador* is a special representative, such as a spokesperson on behalf of a company or an organization.

Amberlith a trademarked brand of amber- or orange-colored acetate, used in offset lithography, manufactured by the Ulano Company, Brooklyn, NY The transparent film is used to prepare OVERLAYS for color separation mechanicals or artwork mounted on boards. Another commonly used film is *Rubylith.*

ambience or **ambiance** the special or distinctive atmosphere surrounding a person or place

ambient surrounding *Ambient,* or *overall, light* is directed around rather than at the subject. *Ambient noise* is background or existing sounds at a location. *Ambient air* (or *air*) is the sound of a movie set or other location at its normal quiet level, as distinct from absolute silence.

ambiguity a word or statement that has two or more possible meanings, in a context that does not make clear which interpretation is intended

ambrotype an early type of photograph consisting of a glass negative backed by a dark surface so as to appear positive, made by the collodion process invented in the mid-nineteenth century by Frederick Scott Archer (1813–57), an English photographer; see COLLOTYPE

ambush marketing a method of participating in an event by circumventing the official promoter or sponsor and thus competing with the sponsor, who may be a business competitor

AMC automatic message counting See AUTOMATIC IDENTIFICATION OF OUTWARD-DIALED CALLS.

AME associate MANAGING EDITOR

American Academy and Institute of Arts and Letters an organization in New York of distinguished artists, writers, and composers, with membership limited to 250 individuals Formed by a merger of the American Academy of Arts and Letters and the National Institute of Arts and Letters, it presents annual awards.

American Advertising Federation (AAF) an organization, in Washington, DC, of advertisers and advertising agencies, clubs, and suppliers, as well as others in advertising It presents the annual ADDY Award for excellence in national and local advertisements and advertising campaigns, and it sponsors the Advertising Hall of Fame.

American Association for Public Opinion Research an organization in Princeton, NJ of over 1,000 individuals in opinion polling and social research

American Association of Advertising Agencies (AAAA) an organization, in New York, of major advertising agencies Together, they place over three-quarters of all advertising in the United States. The 4As, as the organization is generally called, has developed various industry standards, including the wording of contracts used by most agencies, as well as by nonmembers, such as for purchasing local radio and TV spots (*AAAA Spot Contract*).

American Book Awards annual awards for literary excellence presented by the Before Columbus Foundation, based at the University of Washington in Seattle and formerly presented by the ASSOCIATION OF AMERICAN PUBLISHERS; see NATIONAL BOOK AWARDS

American Booksellers Association (ABA) a major organization, founded in 1900 and based in New York, of over 5,000 retail bookstores Its annual convention is a significant event in the publishing field.

American Broadcasting Company (ABC) one of the major radio and TV networks, based in New York The youngest of the Big Three (COLUMBIA BROADCASTING SYSTEM and NATIONAL BROADCASTING COMPANY are the other two), ABC was formed in 1943. It owns radio and TV stations, provides programming to affiliated stations, and is in other communication fields, including publishing. The parent company is Capital Cities/ABC Inc.

American Business Press (ABP) a New York-based association of business publications whose circulation is audited, or tabulated

American Christian Television System a cable network in Fort Worth, TX

American Cinema Editors (ACE) an elite group, based in Los Angeles, of about 250 motion picture and TV film editors The membership designation, *ACE*, appears on screen credits. ACE annually presents the Eddie Awards.

American Composers Alliance an organization in New York of about 300 concert music composers It presents the Laurel Leaf Awards to individuals and organizations.

American envelope an envelope that is about 4 inches wide, narrower than a EUROPEAN ENVELOPE

American Federation of Musicians of the United States (AFM) an AFL-CIO union of about 300,000 musicians Formerly called the *American Federation of Musicians*, it is located in New York.

American Federation of Television and Radio Artists (AFTRA) an AFL-CIO union of about 40,000 broadcasting workers Located in New York, near the offices of the major networks, it is the primary organization of broadcast talent. Performers who appear in TV and radio commercials are required to be members of this union and/or other unions. However, spokespersons and others who are retained by public relations practitioners for talk shows and other radio and TV programs are not required to be union members, since they are generally not paid for their services. AFTRA was formerly called *Federation of Television and Radio Actors and Actresses*.

American Forces Information Service the unit of the U.S. Department of Defense that operates the *American Forces Radio and Television Service (AFRTS)*, a joint Army, Navy, and Air Force operation established during World War II as the *Armed Forces Radio Service (AFRS)* AFRTS is a network of broadcast stations at U.S. military sites (formerly called *Armed Forces Radio and Television*). The *American Forces Radio and Television Service Programming Center (AFRTS–PC)*, in Los Angeles, provides radio and TV programs to U.S. military facilities throughout the world.

American Guild of Musical Artists (AGMA) a union of ballet and modern dancers, opera singers, and stage managers of dance and opera groups Its offices are in New York, near Lincoln Center.

American Guild of Variety Artists (AGVA) an AFL-CIO union in New York of about 5,000 circus, nightclub, and other performers

American Institute of Graphic Arts (AIGA) an organization in New York of art directors, graphics designers, printers, and others in the graphic arts

American Library Association an organization in Chicago of librarians and others involved and interested in libraries

American Marketing Association (AMA) an organization in Chicago of about 30,000 individuals in marketing and market research

American National Dictionary for Information Processing Systems (ANDIPS) a reference guide published by the American National Standards Committee of the COMPUTER AND BUSINESS EQUIPMENT MANUFACTURERS ASSOCIATION, in Washington, DC

American National Standards Institute (ANSI) an organization in New York that sets standards for computer, communications, and other equipment; formerly called AMERICAN STANDARDS ASSOCIATION (ASA)

American Newspaper Publishers Association (ANPA) the major organization of the newspaper business, with about 1,400 members, mostly daily newspapers in the United States and Canada, as well as some nondailies, and newspapers elsewhere Founded in 1887, it is located in Reston, VA.

American Publicists Guild See PUBLICISTS GUILD.

American Public Radio (APR) a nonprofit source, in St. Paul, MN, of programming for public radio stations Programs include *A Prairie Home Companion*. APR is not the same as NATIONAL PUBLIC RADIO.

American Research Bureau (ARB) See ARBITRON RATINGS COMPANY.

American Sign Language (ASL) a system of hand signals for communication with the deaf

American Society of Association Executives (ASAE) a major organization in Washington, DC of executive directors and other high-level managers of trade associations and professional and membership organizations

American Society of Cinematographers (ASC) an organization in Hollywood, CA of directors of film and TV photography The initials *ASC* or *A.S.C.* appear after members' names in film credits.

American Society of Composers, Authors and Publishers (ASCAP) an organization in New York that licenses the music created by members for broadcast and other performances A similar, more recently founded organization is BMI.

American Society of Journalists and Authors (ASJA) an organization in New York of freelance nonfiction writers

American Society of Magazine Editors (ASME) an organization in New York of top editors of major magazines ASME presents annual awards—in the form of replicas of Alexander Calder's *Elephant* sculpture—administered by the Columbia University Graduate School of Journalism.

American Society of Magazine Photographers (ASMP) an organization in New York of over 3,000 professional photographers The name was changed in 1981 to ASMP, THE SOCIETY OF PHOTOGRAPHERS IN COMMUNICATIONS, in recognition of the work of its members in various media.

American Society of Newspaper Editors (ASNE) an organization, in Reston, VA, of over 900 editors at U.S. and Canadian daily newspapers It was founded in 1922.

American Society of Picture Professionals an organization in New York of photographers, archivists, and others who work with still photographs

American Standards Association (ASA) the former name of an organization in New York that sets standards for equipment, such as photography film and paper For instance, a low ASA number indicates slow speed. The name was changed in 1982 to AMERICAN NATIONAL STANDARDS INSTITUTE (ANSI), but the well-known *ASA index* still is used to rate speed or light sensitivity of photographic materials.

American Standard Code for Information Exchange (ASCII) a computer language that facilitates information exchange between different types of communications equipment A widely used data transmission system, it achieves compatibility between devices by assigning code combinations for all characters. The acronym is pronounced ASK-ee. See also EXTENDED BINARY CODED DECIMAL INTERCHANGE CODE.

American Standard Code for Information Interchange (ASCII) [videotex] a presentation system that displays only text and is accessible to most personal computers, word processors, and terminals

American Television & Communications Corporation (ATC) one of the largest operators of cable TV systems, with over four million subscribers Owned by Time Inc., in New York, it includes Manhattan Cable TV.

American Theater Wing a nonprofit organization in New York that provides live theatrical performances at hospitals and other institutions Its activities include the development of the STAGE DOOR CANTEENS in World War II and the presentation of TONY AWARDS to theatrical performers and others.

American Women in Radio and Television (AWRT) an association in Washington, DC of women who work in all areas of broadcasting

AMF AIRPORT MAIL FACILITY

amidol a colorless crystalline compound used in photography as a developer

ammonia a colorless, pungent gas *Ammonium hydroxide* is a solution of ammonia gas in water, commonly used as a caustic in industry, including photography and printing. *Ammonium bichromate*, used in the graphic arts, consists of red crystals that become light-sensitive when mixed with albumin or other organic solutions. The *ammonia* (or *diazotype*) *process* is a dry method of developing, using ammonia fumes, to produce an *ammonia print* or *diazo print*. Ammonia systems, which use ammonia gas in the development of WHITEPRINT copying machines, are anhydrous (using ammonia without water, though water is added from a separate source) or aqueous (using ammonia mixed with water).

AMOL AUTOMATED MEASUREMENT OF LINEUPS

amp an audio amplifier, particularly one used for electronic musical instruments

ampersand the sign for *and* (&) The origin is *per se*, Latin for *in* or *by itself*, so the rather long phrase was *and per se and*. Called *short and*.

amphibole a doubtful meaning or AMBIGUITY, particularly as the result of imprecise grammar or double meaning Pronounced AM-fih-bowl, it is also called *amphibology*.

amplitude modulation (AM) the encoding of a carrier wave (such as the sound waves or audio signals of a radio station) by variation of its amplitude, or power (not its frequency) AM carrier waves are capable of traveling considerably greater distances than FREQUENCY MODULATION (FM) waves, depending on the power (up to 50,000 watts), location, transmitter height, and atmospheric conditions.

AMPTP ALLIANCE OF MOTION PICTURE AND TELEVISION PRODUCERS

AM station a station that broadcasts with an amplitude-modulated signal An *AM signal* is a long, direct radio wave that travels the earth's surface, whereas a frequency-modulated (FM) signal is a straight broadcast signal that travels only as far as the horizon. Thus, an FM station has a smaller broadcast geographic area but is received with less static or interference. There are about 4,900 commercial AM radio stations in the United States, ranging from 540 to 1600 megahertz on the dial.

ana 1 a suffix indicating sayings, writings, anecdotes, or facts of or about a person, place, or other subject, such as *Americana* Sometimes *i* is added for euphony, as in *Johnsoniana*. 2 a word for a collection of anecdotes, reminiscences, and other material about a person

ANA ASSOCIATION OF NATIONAL ADVERTISERS

anabasis a literary term that refers to the rising of an action to its CLIMAX The ancient Greeks used the word *anabainein*, from which *anabasis* derives, to describe a military expedition to overthrow a king.

anacoluthon a change from one grammatical construction to another, within the same sentence, as a rhetorical device or as an error; pronounced an-aca-LOO-thon

anaglyph a photograph of one subject made up of two slightly different views in contrasting colors, so that it appears three-dimensional when viewed through corresponding color filters, a process called *anaglyphic 3-D* or *anaglyph process*

analog a method of data storage and transmission by continuous or wavelike signals or pulses of varying (greater or lesser) intensity; in contrast to DIGITAL transmission (on or off) Analog is the traditional transmission method of voice (such as by telephone), as well as of computer data. *Analog-to-digital conversion* (*AID*) is the conversion of an analog signal into its equivalent digital signal.

analogy a similarity suggested between basically dissimilar things An analogy using the word *like* or *as* is a *simile*.

analysis of variance [marketing] the process of determining the difference between the actual costs of production and the commonly accepted standard costs; also called by the acronym *ANOVA* and *variance analysis*

analytic survey a study of a segment of a population (a finite group) to determine causes of behavior or to obtain other conclusions; a study that analyzes and explains a condition, including its origin or causes, and its effect, as compared to a DESCRIPTIVE SURVEY, which is a collection of data The process of careful analysis, testing, or experimentation within the segment is commonly used in agricultural, medical, and other scientific research.

anagram a word or phrase made from another by transposing or rearranging the letters (such as *dial* and *laid*)

anamorphic pertaining to differences in optical magnification For example, CINEMASCOPE uses an anamorphic lens in its film camera to compress a wide-angle image onto standard film and then expands the image when projecting it on a wide screen.

anapest in poetic meter or rhythm, a word or words consisting of two unstressed syllables followed by a stressed syllable

anaphora the repetition of a word or words in successive clauses or sentences, a rhetorical device used by such speakers as Winston Churchill, John F. Kennedy, and Jesse Jackson

anastrophe the reversal of the conventional order of the parts of a sentence, such as a verb before a noun, as in *came the dawn* This literary device is no longer commonly used.

anchor 1 [broadcasting] the key narrator of a newscast or other program; also called *anchorman* or *anchorwoman* Two or more individuals sharing these functions are *co-anchors*. A *local anchor* works at a local station; a *network anchor*, at a network. Specialized newscasters include *sports anchor*, *weather anchor*, and *weekend anchor*. A *field anchor* reports from a studio outside the studio headquarters. 2 [journalism] editorial or advertising matter that remains the same from issue to issue

anchor listing [telephone] an entry in the classified directory that includes a line referring the reader to a nearby display advertisement

ancillary map a small supplementary or secondary map located inside (an *inset map*) or outside the main or larger map

ANDIPS AMERICAN NATIONAL DICTIONARY FOR INFORMATION PROCESSING SYSTEMS

and sign See AMPERSAND.

ANDY the annual awards of the Advertising Club of New York, to agencies and individuals in all media, including Best of Show

anecdote original, little-known, entertaining facts of history; a short entertaining account of a happening, often personal or biographical An *anecdotist* is a person who tells or collects anecdotes. The adjective *anecdotal* refers to an anecdote or a person or thing that is full of anecdotes; *anecdotic* and *anecdotical* generally refer to a person.

angel an investor in a business, particularly a show

angle the place, position, direction, or aspect from which an object is presented to view; the slant or point of view of an article, news release, or advertising campaign Actually, there can be a difference between *angle* and *slant*. *Angle* is the point of view from which something is written, the peg on which the story is based, whereas *slant* has a connotation of bias. Thus a crime story may be written from the angle of the victim's family but with a slant in favor of or against the victim.

angled poster an outdoor advertising sign that can be seen by traffic in one direction only A

parallel poster, in contrast, is positioned parallel to the traffic flow.

angle of acceptance the maximum deviation from the standard perpendicular position of a microphone or a camera at which sound or light still is effectively transmitted

angle of approach [film] the angle of the camera; also called *angle of vision* Since the camera lens represents the audience's eyes, the angle of approach is the angle from which the audience views a film.

angle of view [photography] the determination of covering power, area covered, or focal length of a lens relative to the film size; also called *angular field*

angle of vision See ANGLE OF APPROACH.

angle on an instruction to change the angle or position of a camera, to take a different shot of the same scene; also called *another angle*

angle shot [photography] deviation from the standard position, such as a camera shot taken from the side, often to distort or foreshorten the picture

angled structure in outdoor advertising, a structure that is angled so that one end is set back more than six feet from the other end, to increase visibility in the approaching line of traffic If there is more than one structure in the FACING, the one closest to the approaching line of traffic is called the *outside panel* or *angled end* (*AE*), and the other panel or panels are called *angled* (*A*) or *inside panels*. An *angled single* (*AS*) is an angled structure with no other adjacent panels.

angstrom one hundred-millionth of a centimeter, a unit of measurement of the length of light waves, used in printing and photography

ANI AUTOMATIC NUMBER IDENTIFICATION

Anik a Canadian broadcast satellite

aniline a colorless, oily organic chemical (derived from benzene), used in varnishes and other products, including synthetic dyes (*aniline dyes*) for printing

animadversion an adverse criticism, or the act of criticizing unfavorably; from the Latin *animus*, a feeling of strong ill will To *animadvert* is to comment adversely.

animal impersonator a performer who appears as an animal, common in ancient Greek and Roman as well as Elizabethan and other theater

animal sized referring to paper that has been hardened, or sized, with glue or gelatin made from animal remains

animated graphics system (AGS) a technique to electronically alter a video image

animatic a "rough" of a TV commercial, resembling an animated cartoon, produced on film or videotape from drawings that show the stages in the STORYBOARD An animatic generally is prepared by an advertising agency, at the agency or in an animation studio, to show the advertiser the concept. A rough synchronized soundtrack usually is added; if it isn't, the film is called a *silent animatic.*

animation the process of creating static figures that appear to move and seem alive, such as cutouts, drawings, or puppets filmed a frame at a time, each slightly different in a sequence Various processes in art, film, photography, and other fields are used in animation, resulting in phrases such as *animation layout* (a plan for each scene, with colors, camera placement, and other details) and *animation zoom* (a ZOOM effect). An *animated caption* consists of cards that are moved to provide a flow of information, such as credits. An *animated title* uses graphics techniques to provide the illusion of movement. *Direct animation* is produced without a camera, such as by *cel animation,* which involves painting on cels (transparent sheets of celluloid). An *animation camera* photographs individual drawings or objects on a table (an *animation stand*) to produce an *animated cartoon,* an *animated commercial,* or other forms of animation. An *animation disk* (also called an *animation board* or *animation bed*) is a revolving circular plate mounted on a drawing table. An *animation cycle* is the repeated photographing of a series of drawings. *Computer animation* is the use of a computer to produce artwork (*computer graphics*) previously done by hand (*conventional animation*) and includes *shape animation, cycle animation* (repetitive actions), *character animation,* and *special effects animation.*

animator an artist who produces animation drawings, or the person in charge of an animation production

anisomorphic characteristic of something that does not have the same (*iso*) form (*morph*), such as a language with a format that is not parallel to that of another language

ankle to leave or quit; a verb coined by the trade publication *Variety*

anncr. announcer

annex [publishing] a section added to a document and bound with it; an update, revision, or other publication, sometimes placed in a pocket inside a law text or other book The pocket generally is inside the back cover and is usually called *pocket part.*

Annie Oakley a pass or free ticket of admission to a theater The ticket is punched with one or more holes to indicate to any recipient that it cannot be purchased or exchanged for a refund. The term comes from the pseudonym of Phoebe Ann Mozee Butler (1860–1926), a woman renowned for her shooting skill, as the ticket punches resemble bullet holes. An *Oakley holder* is a person with a free ticket.

anniversary number a special issue of a newspaper or other publication, commemorating an anniversary; also called *anniversary issue*

anniversary plan an employee relations program in which employees receive a gift or acknowledgment on the anniversary of their employment

annotation an explanatory note, sometimes made in the margin of a book or other work A symbol for an annotation is │ .

announcement a printed notice or a message during a broadcast It may be paid (*commercial announcement*) or free (*public service announcement*), perhaps made by a performer (*announcer*) in an *announcer's booth* (small studio).

announcer booth [broadcasting] a small area from which off-camera announcements or commentary can be made

annual a publication issued once a year, such as a yearbook

annual average daily traffic (annual ADT) in outdoor advertising, the number of vehicles passing a site in a 24-hour period Several counts are taken during a year, in order to provide an average daily count (*average daily traffic*).

annual report a report of the preceding year's activities Publicly owned companies send annual reports, including financial statements, to all shareholders, in accordance with requirements of the Securities and Exchange Commission; nonprofit organizations send them to members, contributors, and other entities. In the United Kingdom, the slang word is the *annuals.*

anodize to put an oxide film (such as on an offset printing plate) by an electrolytic process in which the metal recipient serves as the anode (a positively charged electrode)

anon. anonymous

anonym a person whose name is not known; also, an assumed name, or *pseudonym*

ANOVA ANALYSIS OF VARIANCE

ANPA AMERICAN NEWSPAPER PUBLISHERS ASSOCIATION

ANR AUDIO NEWS RELEASE

ans. answer

ANSI AMERICAN NATIONAL STANDARDS INSTITUTE

answer back any identifying code indicating receipt of a message or signal via Telex or other carriers

answer print the master composite of video and audio of a film, which includes editing, music, and mixing; also called *approval print, check print, first answer print, trial composite,* or *trial print* With the correction of color and other final changes, the answer print is completed into a *release print.* In home video, the *master print* is made from the answer print, and mass copies then are made individually from the *video master.*

answer song a song based on a previous one, akin to a sequel designed to recapture the success of the original, generally by the same composer and lyricist

ant. antenna

antagonist an adversary or opponent, such as a villain in a play or another character who competes with the PROTAGONIST, the hero or heroine

antenna a metallic device for sending or receiving electromagnetic waves, formerly common on rooftops, now built into radio and TV sets for receiving The origin of the term is the sensory appendages on the heads of insects and other animals.

antenna farm the location for the transmitting antennas for most or all of the TV stations in an area; sometimes also a cluster of radio transmitters In New York City, most of the antennas are atop one of the buildings of the World Trade Center.

anthology a collection of works by one or more authors, selected by an *anthologist* or compiler

anthropomorphism the attribution of human form or characteristics to a nonhuman, as an animal, a god, or an inanimate object

antihalation backing [photography] a dye (*antihalation dye*) on the base side of film to prevent light from bouncing back through the base and exposing the emulsion; also called *antihalation coating* The opaque coating (generally gray) sometimes is enhanced in its light absorption by a black layer (*a rem-jet backing*) or an *antihalation undercoating.*

antepenult the third syllable from the end of a word, such as *rith* in *arithmetic Antepenultimate* refers to anything third from the end; *penultimate,* second from the end or next to last (the syllable is called a *penult*). A final syllable is an *ultima.*

ante proscenium [theater] in front of the PROSCENIUM, or stage *Anteproscenium lights* (called *ap, AP,* or *ante-pro lights*) are on the auditorium or audience side of the proscenium.

anthem a religious song; a song of patriotism or devotion, such as the "Star-Spangled Banner" or other national songs A popular song (such as

one by the Beatles) sometimes is referred to as the anthem of a specific period or generation.

anti-aliasing [computers] the removal of the jagged edge line (*stairstep effect*) that sometimes appears on graphic images The technique, sometimes incorrectly called *aliasing,* involves the use of intermediate intensities to soften the sloped lines. An *alias* is an unwanted signal and, in signal transmission, *aliasing* is the effect of such a spurious signal.

antiabrasion coating [photography] a coating on the base side of film to reduce damage from scratching or other abrasion

anticlimax in literary or dramatic works, the descent from a preceding rise (CLIMAX), such as a sudden drop from a high level of importance or dignity An anticlimax can have a humorous or ironical effect.

anti-comet tail gun (ACT) a device in a TV camera tube to reduce or eliminate streaks, called *comets*

antiground noise [film] an electronic system that reduces the surface noise of optical sound film, so that a silent sequence will have no hum from the film itself

antihero a PROTAGONIST (hero or heroine) who does not have the traditional appearance or qualities associated with the role, such as a character in a play who is antisocial or unattractive

Antiope a French TELETEXT system

antiphon a hymn, psalm, or other work composed for responsive chanting or singing in alternating parts An *antiphonary* is a collection of antiphons, especially a book of responsive prayers. *Antiphonal chanting* generally is recited in alternation. Antiphony is the opposition of sounds or a harmony produced by this.

antiqua early roman typefaces, such as those used in 12th-century Italian manuscripts

antique a type of paper with a natural or cream-white color

antique-finish paper nonglossy stock with a soft or rough fluffy surface, used primarily for typeset material, such as book and cover papers

antistrophe a stanza of the second system in poems with contrasting or parallel stanza systems; pronounced an-TIS-tro-fee The antistrophe follows the *strophe,* as in a Greek play in which the chorus answers the previous strophe, or stanza.

antithesis in oratory and rhetoric, the use of parallel or consecutive images or examples that contrast sharply

antonomasia the use of an epithet (such as *Deep Throat*) or a title (such as *Your Honor, Mr. President*) instead of a name to refer to an individual; the use of a symbolic proper name instead of a common noun or an actual name (such as *Don Juan* instead of *seducer*, *Chairman of the Board* to refer to Frank Sinatra, or *Judas* to refer to a treacherous person)

antonym   a word that has the opposite meaning of another word

a/o   account of

A/O   AXIS OF ORIENTATION

AOG   arrival of goods, an invoice notation that the DISCOUNT period does not begin until the customer receives the merchandise; also called *receipt-of-goods* (*ROG*)

AOR   agency of record; ALBUM-ORIENTED RADIO; ALBUM-ORIENTED ROCK

AOS or **A.O.S.**   ALTERNATE-OPERATOR SERVICES

AOT   [journalism] any old time; to be used at will

a.p.   AUTHOR'S PROOF

AP   ADVERTISING PROVIDER; ASSOCIATED PRESS

A-page   an additional page inserted in the numbered pages of a text   For example, a page inserted between pages 5 and 6 would be labeled 5-A or 5-a; a second added page would be 5-B or 5-b.

apathetic shopper   [marketing] a customer who rarely makes comparisons and buys in one store, mall, or convenient location   Other categories of retail customer are ECONOMIC SHOPPER, ETHICAL SHOPPER, and PERSONALIZING SHOPPER.

APB   ALL POINTS BULLETIN

APC or **apc**   wire service jargon for *appreciate*

AP-Dow Jones   the combined news service of the ASSOCIATED PRESS and DOW JONES, based in New York   The service produces the *AP-Dow Jones Economic Report* (outside the United States), *AP-Dow Jones/Telerate* (a worldwide service, in conjunction with Telerate Systems Incorporated, that provides AP-Dow Jones news wires on a 24-hour retrieval basis on video display terminals), and *AP-Dow Jones/Quotron* (an interactive information service, outside the United States).

ape   an imitator or mimic, such as a performer who steals material from another

aperture   an opening, such as the adjustable opening of a lens to control the amount of light entering a camera   The *designated aperture* (also called *rated aperture* or *working aperture*) is the maximum diameter of the lens diaphragm as measured through the front lens element. The insertion of a lens extender or other device between the lens and the camera body changes the designated aperture to an *effective aperture.*

aperture card   a card with one or more holes, or apertures, to hold frames of microfilm; also called *image card*

apex   **1** the highest point   **2** [printing] the joining of stems at the uppermost parts of letters, such as the top of *A* or the upper part of the middle of *W*

apheresis or **aphaeresis**   the dropping of a letter or letters at the beginning of a word, a technique used by poets and other writers   The omission may be indicated by an apostrophe, as in *'tween* for *between*, but sometimes the shortened word becomes so common that it is written without the apostrophe, as in *though* for *although* or *special* for *especial*.   *Aphesis* is the loss of a short, unaccented vowel at the beginning of a word, a type of apheresis, such as *cross* for *across.*

aphorism   a brief statement of a principle or general truth, often clever or witty; a maxim

APME   ASSOCIATED PRESS MANAGING EDITORS

APO   ACTION PRINT ONLY; ARMY POST OFFICE

apochromatic lens   [photography] a lens that has been color-corrected to prevent distortion of the image and the occurrence of refracted colors along its edge

apocope   the cutting off or dropping of the last letter, syllable, or sound of a word, often indicated by an apostrophe, as in *jus'* for *just*   The verb is to *apocopate*, and the shortening process also is called *apocopation.*

apocryphal   of doubtful authorship; not genuine   The *Apocrypha* were various biblical writings rejected by the Roman Catholics and others as inauthentic.

apogee   **1** the highest or furthest point; the opposite of *perigee*   **2** the point at which an orbiting communications satellite is farthest from the earth   **3** in a literary or dramatic work, the CLIMAX

apologue   a fable

apophasis   an artful rhetorical device in which the speaker includes a topic by denying that it will be mentioned or implicitly asserts a point that he or she explicitly is denying   The technique is sometimes used by lawyers and political candidates.

aposiopesis   a sudden breaking off of a thought in the middle of a sentence, either intentionally or unintentionally, perhaps as the result of stress or emotion

apostrophe   a mark, ', consisting of a comma adjacent to the top of the next letter, that indicates an omitted letter or letters, as in a contraction (*can't* for *cannot*, or *it's* for *it is*), the possessive case (*John's car*, *men's car*), or the plural of individual numbers or letters (*dot the i's*)   The term, from the Greek *apostrophos*, meaning "averted," is also used as a figure of speech, in a poem, play, or other work, in which the speaker addresses an absent person. In order to identify an apostrophe in a manuscript, editors sometimes use an arrow, as in it↓s.

apotheosis the glorification of a person or thing; the raising of a person to the status of a god

apothegm a short, pithy saying

appeal in newspapers and other periodicals, a front-page or other reference, generally boxed or highlighted, to an article on a subsequent page

appearing size [printing] the size or value of the capital letters in a font (the alphabet in one type style and size), about two-thirds of the POINT size

appendix a collection of supplementary material, generally at the end of a book (plural is *appendixes* or *appendices*)

applause approval, commonly expressed by clapping An *applause meter* in a broadcast studio measures the sound volume of the applause, and it also can be used to intensify the sound or provide *canned applause* (the recorded sound of applause for a taped or filmed program). *Applause mail* is fan mail commending a program or performer.

apple box a small box or platform to elevate a performer; also called *riser* An apple box is generally 24 inches long, 14 inches wide, and 8 inches high. A *half-apple* is generally 4 inches high, and a *pancake* is 2 inches high.

applications program a computer program for a special purpose

appointment television a process in which TV viewers plan to view specific programs, as if they were making appointments on their weekly calendars, a habit that was common in the 1940s among listeners of network radio programs and in the 1950s among audiences of network TV programs

appositive a word phrase or clause that is in apposition to (explains) a noun, generally set off by commas, dashes, or parentheses, as in "My wife, Florence, is a writer"

approach 1 in outdoor advertising, the distance at which a panel can be seen Classifications are *long approach* (visible to slow and fast traffic from the longest distance), *medium approach*, *short approach*, and *flash approach* (shortest distance). 2 [film] a command from the director for the camera operator to move the camera closer to the subject

approval plan [publishing] the system in which books are provided by a publisher to a library on a *blanket order* basis, but with returns permitted In general, items purchased *on approval* may be returned for full refund or credit.

APR 1 Accredited Public Relations, a title given to members of the PUBLIC RELATIONS SOCIETY OF AMERICA who pass an examination and meet other standards 2 AMERICAN PUBLIC RADIO

apron 1 a covering or protective shield of a machine, such as a printing press 2 a part of a stage, in front of the arch 3 the open area in a store with bins or other free-standing fixtures 4 the lattice or other decorative finish at the bottom of an outdoor display unit 5 the top or original copy of a set of sales slips or invoices, or the leader sheet preceding the first sheet in a continuous form, such as invoices or other consecutively numbered items 6 a blank space on a printed sheet to allow for folding and binding, such as at the edge of a FOLDOUT

APW Play Report a daily bulletin summarizing the actual publication, or pickup (*play*), of the ASSOCIATED PRESS World Service

apx approximately; AVERAGE PAGE EXPOSURE

AQH AVERAGE QUARTER HOUR RATING

aquarium [film] a colloquialism for the glass-enclosed room in which sound mixing is done

aquatint [graphic arts] an ETCHING process in which spaces (instead of lines) are treated with acid to produce the effect of a wash drawing or watercolor; also the etched print itself

AR ANNUAL REPORT

arabesque an elaborate design, often on book covers, generally an interlaced pattern in the style of early Arabian designers

Arabic numerals the figures *1, 2, 3, 4, 5, 6, 7, 8, 9,* and *0,* which originated in India; contrasted with ROMAN numerals (*I, II, III,* and so on)

ARB American Research Bureau See ARBITRON RATINGS COMPANY.

arbitrary mark a trademark that is a standard word with no specific connotation or description of the product An example is *Dial* soap; in contrast, the name *Ivory* soap describes the product's color. See also ABSTRACT MARK.

Arbitron Ratings Company a firm in New York that measures the size of broadcast audiences Formerly called *American Research Bureau, Inc.,* it is famous for its use of an automatic electronic meter device (called *Arbitron,* a name loosely based on the original corporate name) attached to the TV sets of a sample of viewers. *Arbitron Information on Demand* (*AID*) provides clients with spot measurement data on TV audiences in over 200 markets. Radio reports are provided for more than 2,200 counties in the United States, based on diaries maintained by over 600,000 listeners. An *Arbitron market,* called an AREA OF DOMINANT INFLUENCE (ADI), is a cluster of counties representing TV markets. Founded in 1949, Arbitron was acquired in 1967 by Control Data Corporation, Minneapolis, MN. It is part of the Arbitron Company, which includes SAMI.

arc 1 [film, photography] a high-intensity light, generally with a carbon filament (called *carbon arc light* or *carbon arc*) The arc- (arch-) shaped flame between two adjacent electrodes connected to a powerful source of electricity is the lighting agency in the light. An *arc follow spot* is an arc spotlight that focuses on or follows a performer. *Arc out* is an instruction to move a dolly on a curve away from the action. It is also an instruction to a performer to move on a curved path in front of the camera. 2 [printing] any curved stroke other than a BOWL 3 [journalism] the line of progression, resembling a curved path, in a story 4 a mini-series within a regularly scheduled program; such as a two-parter, a three-parter, or several episodes with the same plot

arch a point-of-purchase display that goes over an aisle; also, the ceiling of a display that spans an aisle or another area

archaic belonging to an earlier period; old-fashioned *Archaism* refers to the use of archaic words or techniques, or to an archaic word or technique itself. Archaisms, such as *thou* instead of *you*, sometimes are used in poetry or as literary devices.

Arches paper a type of top-quality, 100-percent rag watercolor paper, used by artists Sometimes called *D'Arches paper*, it is made by the Arjomarie paper mill in Arches, France, and is imported into the United States by Special Papers, Inc., of Wilton, CT.

archetype a prototype, the original pattern, or model, from which all other things of the same kind are made; a perfect example of a type or group; any of several innate ideas or patterns in the psyche, expressed in dreams or in such creative works as art and film as basic symbols or images, a concept developed by Swiss psychologist Carl Jung (1875–1961); pronounced AR-kuh-tipe An image that evokes a strong sense of primitive experience is called an archetype. *Archetypal criticism* is the study of such patterns and images, and a film or other work incorporating these patterns has an *archetypal structure.*

arch flat [theater] a flat, or piece of scenery, with an arched opening

archival copy all the issues of a periodical for a year, or another period of time, with the advertising pages removed, bound in one volume

archival paper stock that is acid-free and thus resists disintegration

archival print [film] a print specially made to last for many years, of higher quality than a standard RELEASE PRINT; also called *archival release print*

archive [computers] 1 a storage area *Archiving* is the storage process. 2 to store

archives a place where public records, documents, and other materials are kept, or the materials themselves An *archivist* is in charge of archival material. *Archival quality* is the ability of a document, particularly a copy, to maintain legibility over a period of years.

arcing a curved movement, as in the circular motion of a TV pedestal camera, for which the instructions are *arc left* and *arc right*

arc of fashion the general pattern of acceptance of a fashion item among different types of customers: *early accepters, early followers, general accepters,* and *laggards*

area [theater] a part of the stage in relation to an actor's right or left as he or she faces the audience A large stage is divided into nine areas: *down right, down center, down left, right center, center, left center, up right, up center,* and *up left.*

area code a three-digit code, preceding the seven-digit telephone number, designating telephone numbers in a specific geographical section, such as 212 and 718 for New York City The first digit is a number from 2 through 9; the second digit generally is 1 or 0.

area composition the technique of typesetting directly in the proper position on a layout, rather than pasting typeset copy onto a board

Area of Dominant Influence (ADI) the geographic boundaries of TV markets For example, the New York City ADI includes 22 counties, with about 9 percent of U.S. households that own TVs. *Sales and Marketing Management* and other magazines, as well as market research companies, have various criteria for designating major market areas, including population and geography. The term *ADI* was coined by the ARBITRON RATINGS COMPANY to indicate the cluster of counties in which TV stations have a greater share of viewing households than those from any other area. Thus, an *ADI rating* is the percent of people viewing a specific TV program. The A. C. NIELSEN COMPANY has a similar concept called DESIGNATED MARKET AREA (DMA).

area probability sample [market research] the selection, based on geographical considerations, of a group that is representative of a population to be studied in a survey

A-reel the first reel in a two-reel tape (tape-to-tape) system or a film system; also called *A-wind* The second reel (*B-reel*) is the pickup.

arena the central part of an ancient Roman amphitheater; a place or building for an exhibition or event (such as a *boxing arena* or a *sports arena*) An *arena theater* has a central stage (arena *stage*) surrounded by the audience. The open style of performing in such a theater sometimes is called *arena acting*.

are you decent? [theater] a question commonly asked when knocking on a dressing room door, meaning "Are you dressed? May I come in?"

ARF ADVERTISING RESEARCH FOUNDATION

argentine [theater] a shiny thin piece of metal affixed to a flat, or piece of scenery, to simulate window glass; from the French for "silver"

argot the specialized vocabulary, or jargon, of people who are in the same work or have other similar interests; often a secret slang, as among thieves or beggars; from the French word for "beg" The pronunciation generally is anglicized: AR-gut.

arm [printing] the part of a letter that projects horizontally, such as the top of a *t*, or diagonally, as the top diagonal of a *K* or both diagonals of a *Y*

armature a supportive framework that sculptors use in modeling (shaping the form); also, the flexible skeleton of a puppet or an animation model

armorply an outdoor advertising sign constructed of wood covered with metal The word derives from armor and plywood.

armpit [journalism] a narrow headline under a wide headline

Army Information Radio Service (AIRS) an agency in Washington, DC that provides programming to radio stations at U.S. Army sites

Army Post Office (APO) a U.S. military (Army and Air Force) post office outside the continental United States

A-roll [television] the primary material, as opposed to *B-roll* In film and tape editing, alternate scenes are arranged on two reels (A-roll and B-roll) and then assembled.

arrangement an adaptation of a musical composition for instruments or voices other than those for which the work was originally written; the alteration of a work to fit the style of a particular orchestra or singer Such changes are done by an *arranger*.

array a regular grouping, such as elements arranged in rows or data arranged in sequential classes

Arriflex a commonly used 35mm film camera, made by Arnold and Richter, of West Germany, and generally called *Arri* The company also makes 16mm cameras.

arrow 1 [printing] a symbol to indicate direction, position, or change of location, such as a designation to move copy up or down in a layout 2 [broadcasting] an instruction in a script

for an announcer to raise or lower the voice level, depending on the direction of the arrow

The position of an arrow indicates the following:
- → forward, to the right, next, yields or becomes
- ← backward, to the left, preceding
- ↑ up, raise, increase
- ↓ down, lower, decrease
- ↝ a communications link

arrowgraph a diagram in which the relationships of items are indicated with arrows; also called *association map*

arrowhead an indicator, shaped like an arrowhead, used at the end of a line to point out an item or for other reference, such as to indicate the derivation of a word

ARS AUTOMATIC ROUTE SELECTION

art a design, drawing, illustration, painting, photograph, rendering, sketch, or other visual material used alone or to accompany text material; also called *artwork*

art. ARTICLE

art and mechanical (A and M) [graphic arts] a PASTEUP or completed layout (a mechanical) with the accompanying photos, drawings, or other artwork

art card a cardboard (generally 11″ × 14″) with a dark background and light letters (though it may be black letters on a white background) As used in television, it contains credits and other information and is mounted on an easel in front of a TV camera.

art director one who creates and executes artwork, in an art or design studio or art department of a company or agency An art director is not necessarily a *fine artist* (someone who paints, draws, sculpts, or performs other works of art) or a commercial artist, but rather someone who supervises in a variety of fields, including the graphic arts. In TV, an art director is the supervisor of the art department or is the production designer. In film, an art director is more commonly called *production designer* (formerly called *set designer*). The *assistant art director* is responsible for building scale models of the sets. In an opera house or other enterprise, the *artistic director* is in charge of such matters as the selection of works to be performed, and not the business or overall management.

Art Directors Club a national organization of art directors of advertising agencies and related companies and organizations Located in New York, it presents annual awards.

art film a film with aesthetic merit, not one produced primarily for commercial reasons In the mid-20th century, art films (often foreign, dubbed or captioned) were shown in small theaters (see ART HOUSE) and sometimes were commercially successful.

art gum a soft eraser used by artists to clean—for instance, to remove smudges, which are attracted to its crumbly residue (it is sometimes called a *soap eraser* because of this cleaning action)—and to erase pencil lines

art house a small theater that shows films of artistic merit (see ART FILM) There still are a few such theaters, particularly in big cities and campus communities.

article a usually short, complete piece of nonfiction writing, such as a news or feature story in a newspaper or magazine

artist and repertoire (A&R) a show-business term for the person in charge of talent (performers) and the works they perform

artist's assistant in the performing arts, particularly opera, the individual who is a personal helper to the star performers by providing such amenities as escorting them (the artists) from the dressing room to the stage

artist's board heavy paper, or paperboard, generally white, used by artists; also called *illustration board* It ranges from about 8-ply to 30-ply (heavy).

artist's proof a proof, or trial impression, of an ENGRAVING, generally with a small design, sketch, or other identifying mark (a *remarque*) and the signature of the artist in the margin

art-lined envelope an envelope with a lining of fine paper, usually colored or patterned

artotype a print made by a gelatin process, more commonly called *collotype*

art paper heavy paper with a smooth finish, used in artwork It is produced by coating with a substance such as casein and is purchased in art supply stores.

arts imaginative endeavors including the visual and performing arts Composers, musicians, performers, and writers are artists.

ARTS ALPHA REPERTORY TELEVISION SERVICE

Arts and Entertainment a cable network based in New York

ARV The American (Standard) Revised Version of the Bible

arty ostentatious or affectedly artistic

Artype a trademarked brand of acetate lettering (TRANSFER TYPE); a sheet of transparent plastic with characters that are transferred to a surface The term now generically refers to all types of transfer commonly used by artists.

ASA AMERICAN STANDARDS ASSOCIATION

ASAE AMERICAN SOCIETY OF ASSOCIATION EXECUTIVES

asap as soon as possible; pronounced A-sap

Asbestos going up a warning to performers that the fire curtain (made of asbestos) is being raised and the performance will begin in five minutes

ASC AMERICAN SOCIETY OF CINEMATOGRAPHERS

ASCAP AMERICAN SOCIETY OF COMPOSERS, AUTHORS AND PUBLISHERS

ascender the part of a lowercase letter that rises above its *x-height*, or its main body The letters *b*, *d*, *f*, *h*, *k*, *l*, and *t* have ascenders that rise above the *waist line* (top of the main body) to the *ascender line* (top of the letter). Not all ascenders rise to the same height; for example, the top of the *t* in most typefaces is lower than the tops of other ascenders.

ASCII AMERICAN STANDARD CODE FOR INFORMATION EXCHANGE

ASCIL AMERICAN STANDARD CODE FOR INFORMATION INTERCHANGE

ascription the assignment of a quality to another, as something that may be deduced In market research, *extended cell ascription* is the extension, transfer, or assignment of data from one study to another.

A section the first section of a newspaper, the main news section

aseptic packaging a packaging system in which juices and other food products are flash-heated, sterilized, and then rapidly cooled and tightly sealed in paper bottles and other containers (generally boxlike packages) that do not require refrigeration and have a long shelf life; also called *aseptics* The process was developed by Tetra Pak, a Swedish company.

A series a system of sizes of stock paper, used in Europe, with rectangular sheets in the same proportion of short side to long side Sizes between the A sizes are called the *B series*.

asgmt. ASSIGNMENT

ashcan a large, 1,000-watt carbon ARC floodlight

ash content an indication of the nonfibrous content of a sheet of paper (made from wood, rags, or other fibrous material), determined by weighing a sample before and after combustion (to produce ash)

ASI AUDIENCE STUDIES INC.

ASI or **A.S.I.** ADVERTISING SPECIALTY INSTITUTE

aside dialogue spoken by a performer in an undertone but intended to be heard

A side the more important side of a popular record A *double A side* has a hit song on both sides.

A-sign two advertising panels, joined at the top (akin to an *A*), often used on the sidewalk in front of a store or theater

as is [sales promotion] a description on a product tag or an invoice or in a catalog indicating that the item may be imperfect, incomplete, or defective, that "what you see is what you get"

ASJA AMERICAN SOCIETY OF JOURNALISTS AND AUTHORS

ASL AMERICAN SIGN LANGUAGE

ASME AMERICAN SOCIETY OF MAGAZINE EDITORS

ASMP AMERICAN SOCIETY OF MAGAZINE PHOTOGRAPHERS

ASNE AMERICAN SOCIETY OF NEWSPAPER EDITORS

aspect ratio the ratio of width to height of a film when projected on a screen It was formerly standardized at 1.33 to 1 (or 4 to 3) and called ACADEMY APERTURE. Because wide-screen formats, such as Cinemascope and Panavision, have considerably greater ratios (such as 2.55 to 1), there are technical difficulties in projecting wide-screen films on TV screens.

asperity a roughness or harshness, such as an imperfection in the surface of magnetic tape

ASR AUTHORIZED SELLING REPRESENTATIVE

assembled view a drawing or photograph of an object or equipment that shows the components assembled, as opposed to an EXPLODED VIEW, in which the parts are shown separately

assemble edit [television] the recording of all tracks (audio, video, cue, and control) simultaneously It is different from INSERT EDIT.

assembly the first phase of film editing, in which the sequences are converted, or put together, according to the order of the script; also called *stringout Assembly dailies* consist of the film footage from one day's shooting placed in proper sequence for immediate viewing the next day.

assembly language a low-level computer programming language that uses mnemonics, or memory devices, to approximate the machine code NUMERIC INSTRUCTIONS, in contrast, are machine language.

assembly sheet [book production] a set of instructions for a job, such as page sequence and positioning of printed materials

assign to designate, appoint, allot, ascribe, or transfer In language, an assign is a word or words to which meaning is designated (assigned), though the speaker or writer may not know the origin or full meaning; for example, a person may refer to another as a dodo, which means dull or stupid, though the origin of the word is the dodo, an extinct bird with rudimentary wings that were useless.

assignment 1 [broadcasting] the designation by the Federal Communications Commission of the holder of a radio or TV frequency or of a broadcast license 2 [journalism] the designation of a photo or writing task by an editor The *assignment editor* is the person at a publication or broadcast station who is in charge of assigning reporters or broadcasters to attend or cover a specific event. The daily assignments are listed in an *assignment book* (print media) or on an *assignment board* (broadcasting), or instructions may be given on an *assignment sheet*. A reporter without a regular assignment is a *general-assignment reporter* or *assignment reporter*, attached to the *assignment desk*. A request from a publicist to a publication or station to cover an event is called an *assignment memo* or a *tip sheet*.

assistant director (AD) [film] the assistant to the director, responsible for considerable preproduction tasks (including the development of the shooting schedule) Like a STAGE MANAGER, the AD often conducts rehearsals and directs crowd scenes and other background action. On the set, the AD calls for "quiet on the set" and gives the order for the cameras to roll, followed by the call from the DIRECTOR for action to begin. In large productions, there also is a *second assistant director* and a *third assistant director*, who report to the *first assistant director* or assistant director.

assistant stage manager the assistant to the stage manager of a theatrical work, who sometimes also is the prompter

assn. association

assoc. associate; association

Associate Creative Director (ACD) a deputy CREATIVE DIRECTOR in an advertising agency

associated [market research] the percentage of readers, listeners, or viewers who remember an advertisement (or portion of it) as well as the advertiser

associate director [television] the assistant to the DIRECTOR He or she generally sits next to the director in the control room and is the voice most frequently heard on the headsets by the TECHNICAL DIRECTOR, camera operators, and others involved in the production.

Associated Press (AP) a news-gathering cooperative founded in 1848 and headquartered in New York It is the world's largest wire service, with members all over the world. The AP transmits to thousands of print and broadcast media. The exact name is *The Associated Press.*

Associated Press Managing Editors an organization in New York of managing editors or other top editors from about 1,000 newspapers that are members of the ASSOCIATED PRESS

associational editing [film, television] the placement, together or consecutively, of two scenes that are in opposition, contrast, or another relationship; also called *relational editing*

associationist attitudes beliefs based on linkage (association) with other beliefs and values

association map a diagram or graph showing the relationships of items, generally with the use of arrows; also called *arrowgraph*

Association of American Publishers a major organization, in New York, of book publishers

Association of American University Presses an organization, in New York, of about 100 publishing divisions of colleges and universities

Association of Canadian Advertisers, Inc. (ACA) an organization of major advertisers, in Toronto

Association of Independent Commercial Producers (AICP) a trade association in New York that developed a cost summary used as the standard bid form by many film and videotape producers Entries on the form indicate the estimated and/or actual costs for pre-production time, WRAP, rehearsal, BUILD/STRIKE, studio shoot, and location, and other direct and indirect expenses.

Association of Independent Television Stations, Inc. an organization of nonnetwork TV stations, located in Washington, DC

Association of Industrial Advertisers (AIA) former name of the BUSINESS AND PROFESSIONAL ADVERTISERS ASSOCIATION

Association of National Advertisers (ANA) an organization in New York of about 500 major national and regional advertisers Its annual meeting is one of the key conventions in the advertising field.

Association of Theatrical Press Agents and Managers (ATPAM) an AFL-CIO union in New York of about 600 theatrical publicists and managers Broadway shows sometimes list in their *playbills* a credit for the *ATPAM apprentice manager.*

assonance the repetition of identical or similar vowel sounds in a series of words An example is the recurrence of *a* and *u* sounds in the first line of Samuel Taylor Coleridge's "Kubla Khan": In X*a*nad*u* did K*u*bl*a* Kh*a*n.

asst. assistant

assumptive close a sales technique in which the salesperson starts to write the order or wrap the product without specifically confirming that the customer has agreed to the purchase

asterisk a starlike symbol (*) commonly used in printing, particularly to indicate footnotes, references, or omissions The omission of vulgar words sometimes is written as a series of symbols, such as */#/*, and is referred to as *blank-blank*. Several asterisks sometimes are placed to the left of (preceding) an important

digit, a procedure called by computer operators *asterisk protection.*

as told to an article or book, usually autobiographical, produced by a writer from conversations with the subject (often a celebrity), who may be featured as the ostensible author of the as-told-to work

astonisher [printing] an exclamation mark (!)

as to press referring to final, corrected color proofs; a term used in GRAVURE PRINTING

asymmetrical public relations an unbalanced two-way flow of communication, in which an organization attempts to persuade its publics with little input from them

asynchronism 1 the failure to occur at the same time or frequency; also called *out of sync* 2 [telecommunications] a variable time interval between each successive character, during which the transmission is slower than SYNCHRONISM or BISYNCHRONISM

ATB all (telephone) trunks busy

ATC AMERICAN TELEVISION & COMMUNICATIONS

A-team the first team, also called *first string* In film, this consists of the on-camera performers and not the STAND-INS.

Athena Awards the annual awards for outstanding advertisements in newspapers, presented by the NEWSPAPER ADVERTISING BUREAU The award is a sculptured relief of Athena, the Greek goddess of wisdom and creativity.

atlas a book of maps; also, a book or other publication with tables, charts, illustrations, and data on a specific subject or subjects, such as an astronomy atlas In Greek mythology, Atlas was a giant who was compelled to support the heavens on his shoulders. Early books of maps showed, on the cover or the front page, Atlas supporting the earth. An *atlas folio* is a large book, about 25 inches high.

atmosphere (atmos.) tone or mood, ambience; sound and visual effects to create a mood; a group of extras in a film or other work

atmospheric effects specialist [film] an expert in simulating fog, rain, smoke, storms, and other weather conditions

atomic bomb wipe [film, television] a transition in which a scene is slowly moved up on the screen (suggesting an atom bomb cloud) as it is replaced by another scene

ATPAM ASSOCIATION OF THEATRICAL PRESS AGENTS AND MANAGERS

at rise the position of the performers onstage when the curtain goes up

att. 1 attached 2 attention, as in *Att:* (followed by the name of the person receiving the letter or other item)

attached mail first-class mail accompanying other mail, such as an envelope containing an invoice pasted on the outside of a carton or package (the *host piece*) or inserted inside it As long as the attached mail is incidental, the postage rate is that of the host piece, which may be fourth-class mail.

attachment supplementary material not bound within the main text of a book or other publication

attack comedy a comic style that features obscenities, insults, and other aggressive or confrontational behavior

attempted call a telephone call that was not completed—for instance, because of a busy signal

attentioner a note on British news wire service copy to alert an editor about an obscenity or anything else that may be objectionable

attenuation dilution, such as the reduction in strength of electrical energy (achieved with an *attenuator*), sound, or color (via *attenuated filters* or *color-compensating filters*)

attitude the feelings of a person or of a group toward a subject, developed as a result of previous influences An *attitude study* is a survey of such feelings, which can be quantified on an *attitude scale*. The degree of resistance to change in attitude is called *attitude intensity*. An inwardly held attitude often is expressed outwardly as an *opinion.*

attraction [film] a theatrical movie, such as a *coming attraction* (a movie to be shown), *current attraction*, or *feature attraction* (full-length movie)

attribute mapping a marketing technique to identify new products or new uses for existing products by listing qualities, or attributes, and then seeking *attribute space* (ways of marketing the qualities)

attribution the designation of a person quoted in a written or broadcast article or story; also, the source of information A news medium, such as a wire service or the specific publication or station that originated a story, may be named as the source.

ATW American Theater Wing

au. author

AU, Au, or **au** [publishing] author, used as an editing notation in a question addressed to the writer of a manuscript

audience a group of spectators, listeners, viewers, or readers of a performance, program, or work AVERAGE AUDIENCE is a number or rating calculated by the A. C. Nielsen Company and other research services, based on specific conditions.

audience accumulation the addition of new audiences to a publication, television program, or other medium, as successive issues or broadcasts are produced

audience composition the number or percentage or characteristics (demographics) of the men, women, children, or other groups of viewers or listeners of a specific TV or radio program or station; also called *audience comp, audience profile*, or *profile*

audience dress rehearsal [theater] a performance with an audience, before a show officially opens; also called *audience dress*

audience duplication the number or percent of individuals or households exposed more than once to the same message through the same medium (publication or broadcast) or different media over a measured period of time

audience flow the extent to which listeners or viewers remember the events on a radio or TV show from one program to another

audience format a type of programming on a station (generally radio, which is more segmented than noncable TV), to appeal to specific listeners; examples are country, mellow, news, religious, and rock Here are a few initials of audience formats:

AC	ADULT CONTEMPORARY
BB	BIG BAND
CHR	CONTEMPORARY HIT RADIO
CL	CLASSICAL
EZ	EASY LISTENING (mellow music)
MOR	MIDDLE-OF-THE-ROAD
NT	NEWS/TALK

audience holding index a minute-by-minute or other detailed analysis of the number of listeners or viewers of a program

audience participation telephone call-ins or other involvement by listeners or viewers of a performance or program or by people in the studio (a *studio audience*)

audience proof a theatrical production that is very likely to be successful

Audience Studies, Inc. (ASI) a TV advertising testing service, in Los Angeles It conducts surveys in which audiences in a theater view and rate commercials. The parent company, *ASI Market Research*, is located in New York and operates TV advertising testing systems in many cities. To ASI a program is to use the services of Audience Studies, Inc.

audience turnover a measurement of the frequency with which the audience of a radio or TV program changes over a period of time; specifically, the ratio of the net unduplicated CUMULATIVE AUDIENCE over several time periods to the average audience of one time period; also, the number of announcements required to reach half of a station's cumulative audience in a specific time period. It is also called *turnover* or *T/O*.

Audilog a television-viewing diary used in households participating in surveys of the A. C. NIELSEN COMPANY It was discontinued in 1987.

Audimeter an electronic device installed by the A. C. NIELSEN COMPANY in TV households in some markets to monitor and record TV set usage With the introduction of the PEOPLE METER, the Audimeter is not as widely used as previously.

audio the sound portion of a broadcast, film, tape, or other medium *Audio*, from the Latin *audire*, meaning "to hear," literally means "I hear."

audio billboard [radio] an identification at the beginning of an audio tape, including a brief description of the event recorded, the name of the reporter, and the number of the TAKE

audio book a recorded reading of a book or other material

audio conferencing a telephone call linking three or more parties, formerly called a *conference call* and now considered to be the simplest form of TELECONFERENCING

audio disk a phonograph record of any speed and type, played on an *audiodisk player* (a *record player*) or an *audioplayer* (a device that plays but does not record) Specifically, an audio disk is a compact record (4 to 7 inches in diameter and 1 millimeter thick) on which sound is recorded with a BINARY CODE in a series of microscopic pits in the aluminum coating. A laser beam in the disk player reconverts the sound. Digital sound reproduction is extremely accurate, and audio disks are virtually permanent, though they still are considerably more expensive than conventional records or tapes.

audio frequency band the spectrum of sound waves that can be heard, about 20 to 20,000 HERTZ; also called *audio frequency waveband*

audio mixer a sound engineer at an *audio control panel* or console; a device that combines sound from two or more sources

audio news release a tape sent to radio stations by a publicity source

audio operator [television] the person responsible for the technical quality of a program's sound The audio operator works in a control room or an audio room and communicates by headset with the *assistant audio operator* and others on the floor of the studio.

audiotape a magnetic strip on which are recorded electrical signals that can be converted to sound The audiotape is stored on a reel (*audiotape reel*) in a cassette (*audiocassette* or *audi-*

otape cassette) or in a cartridge (*audiocartridge* or *audiotape cartridge*). An *audiotape deck* or *tape deck*, which includes the tape transport but not the amplifiers and speakers, is a device for recording and/or playing back sounds. An *audiotape player* plays back but cannot record, whereas an *audiotape recorder* or *tape recorder* can record and play back the sound on the tape.

audiotex a computerized telephone service that enables callers of a local, 800, or other number to respond to a recorded message Callers press buttons on a touchtone phone to receive additional information or to be connected to a live operator. Some voice information services of this type include advertising.

audio/video (AV) sound and sight, as in a script with the text of the dialogue and a description of the accompanying visual action

audiovisual materials films, filmstrips, and other items that use sound and sight, particularly as teaching aids

audit an examination aimed at evaluating specific aspects in or services of an organization, such as an *advertising audit*, a *communications audit*, or a *public relations audit*

Audit Bureau of Circulations (ABC) a nonprofit organization formed in 1914 by the merger of the Advertising Audit Association and the Bureau of Verified Circulations It is now based in Schaumburg, IL. ABC provides verified, standardized statements of circulation of member publications. Subscribers include advertisers, advertising agencies, and publishers of newspapers and other periodicals in the United States and elsewhere; most paid-circulation, large-circulation magazines and daily newspapers are members of ABC. In 1982, ABC introduced audits of subscriber lists of cable networks. The issue of a publication whose circulation has been verified by the organization is called an *ABC issue*; a publisher's statement provided by the organization is known as an *ABC statement*. An affiliate, *Audit Bureau of Marketing Services*, audits mailing lists and other services outside of the ABC membership.

audited publication a newspaper, magazine, or other publication whose actual circulation is verified by an independent auditing service, such as AUDIT BUREAU OF CIRCULATIONS

audition a tryout or trial performance An *open audition* is open to any applicants.

auditorium main a master electrical switch or control for all lighting in a theater or hall except the emergency and aisle lights

Audit Report an analysis of the circulation of a member publisher of the AUDIT BUREAU OF CIRCULATIONS

Audits & Surveys Inc. one of the world's largest market research companies, located in New York Services include a Retail Census of Product Distribution outside the United States and a National Total Market Audit of about 40,000 retail outlets in the United States.

audit stub the portion of a ticket retained by a theater (or other organization) for accounting or auditing

auds audiences; auditoriums

augmented product a basic product with added value or benefits, such as new features

Auntie somewhat derogatory, though affectionate, slang term for the British Broadcasting Corporation (BBC)

aura an atmosphere or quality that seems to emanate from a person or thing The adjective, *aural*, refers more generally to the sense of hearing, or receiving through the ear.

auteur a filmmaker, generally a director, noted for creativity and a personal style; from the French word for *author*

auth. authentic; author; authorized

authenticator a British fact checker or researcher, particularly in film

author a writer In the broadest sense, an author is the creator of any work; legally, an author is the creator of any copyrightable work, including art, music, and computer software. *Author, author!* is the call from the audience on the opening night of a play for the playwright to take a curtain call.

author ID the biographical identification of the writer of an article in a magazine, newspaper, or other publication The name is sometimes surrounded by lines in an *author ID box.*

authorization code numbers and/or letters activated by a user to gain access to a system or service, such as long-distance telephone service

authorized selling representative (ASR) an agency appointed by a publisher, particularly of telephone directories, to sell advertising in a publication

author's alteration (AA) a revision made by the writer or customer after copy has been set in type; also called *author's correction (AC)* Since the revisions are not the result of errors by the typesetter or printer, the charges for AA's, which can be considerable, are passed onto the customer. *Author's corrections—old copy job (AC-OC)* refers to a new version or edition of a previously printed work in which the former text is retained with new material added or revisions made by the author.

author's copies complimentary books (generally six copies) given by a publisher to the author

author's correction See AUTHOR'S ALTERATION.

author's discount a special discount (such as 20 to 40 percent off the list price) provided to an author on his or her books by the publisher

author's edition one or several volumes of the complete works of an author, or an edition authorized by the author; also called *complete works* or *uniform edition*

Authors Guild a national business organization, located in New York, of writers and editors Members also belong to the *Authors League of America*, a larger organization at the same address with playwrights and other types of writers.

author's information form biographical data and answers to questions, provided by an author (generally of a book) to the publisher, for use in book jacket copy and publicity

author's night a theatrical performance in which a part of the receipts are given to the playwright No longer practiced, it was common in the 17th and 18th centuries, when the third night of a production often was a benefit performance for the playwright.

author's proof (a.p.) a copy of galleys, or long sheets of typeset manuscript, made for the author

auto-answer automatic operation, such as the capability of a telephone facsimile machine, word processor, Teletype, or other equipment to receive information while unattended

autoassembly [television] automatic editing for a commercial or program, usually using time code numbers entered into an editing computer

autochrome a black-and-white negative that is tinted, or colored, by hand

autocue See TELEPROMPTER.

autodialer a device that automatically dials a telephone number; sometimes called a *repertory dialer* The user can program telephone numbers and then call them by pushing a single button.

autograph an individual's signature An *autographed copy* or *autographed edition* is a work signed by the author or artist.

autokerning [printing] the automatic reduction of unwanted space between characters (letters or numbers); see KERNING

autolithography printing from material that is drawn by hand directly on a lithographic stone or plate

Automated Camera Effects System (ACES) a computerized method of filming animation frames, developed by the Walt Disney organization

automated measurement of lineups (AMOL) [broadcasting] an electronic method used by the A. C. Nielsen Company to decipher the codes transmitted by the networks to identify to their stations the programs in their lineups, or schedules

automatic answering   a feature on a telephone through which incoming calls are answered by a recorded message and the incoming message is recorded   The same concept of functioning without a human operator also can be set up with a telephone facsimile machine, word processor, or other machine.

automatic assembly   in videotape editing, the putting together of a program automatically from instructions   In *linear assembly* (Mode A), the edit list is followed in sequential order. In *reel sequential assembly* (Mode B), the edit list is not followed in sequence, but instead is scanned for pickups from the reel(s) currently on the videotape recorders, and the other reels are put on the VTRs. The ultimate automation is performed in *look-ahead assembly*, in which the VTR finds the next edit-point and readies itself.

automatic brightness control (ABC)   a device on a TV set that maintains the luminance of the picture

automatic call distributor (ACD)   telephone equipment that handles incoming calls for an organization or business, holding the calls (if necessary) and routing them to the next available sales clerk or other representative, a process called *automatic call distribution*

automatic data processing (ADP)   [computers] the systematic handling of information and other data, without human intervention, with data-processing equipment

automatic dialer recorded message player (ADRMP)   a device used in computerized telephone marketing in which a phone call is made and a recorded message is transmitted to the recipient, all automatically

automatic dialogue replacement (ADR)   [film] a technique for recording a REPLACEMENT DIALOGUE TRACK in which the performer is cued by electronic beeps and other techniques   The *ADR editor* supervises the POST-PRODUCTION alterations of the dialogue tracks.

automatic fine tuning (AFT)   the use of a circuit that locks a TV receiver to the station frequency

automatic frequency control   a device in a radio or TV transmitter or receiver that reduces unwanted frequency changes

automatic gain control (AGC)   **1** [broadcasting] a device that maintains a consistent level of sound; also called *automatic level control* (*ALC*)   **2** [television] a system that minimizes picture differences resulting from changes in strength of incoming signals

automatic identification of outward-dialed calls (AIOD)   a system of recording the individual or station making a telephone call, the date, time, length, and other details; also called *station message detail recording* (*SMDR*) or *automatic message accounting* (*AMA*)

automatic merchandising   sales through vending machines

automatic message accounting   See AUTOMATIC IDENTIFICATION OF OUTWARD-DIALED CALLS.

automatic number identification (ANI)   a feature of telephone equipment that automatically records the number *initiating* the call, for billing and other purposes

automatic route selection   [telephone] a switching system that chooses the lowest-priced path from among several available owned or leased circuits; also called *least cost routing*

automatic typewriter   a simple form of WORD PROCESSOR, developed in the 1960s, used for repetitive output with little text editing

automatic volume control (AVC)   a system that maintains the sound level of a radio set despite differences in strength of the incoming signals

automation   the ability of systems to operate independently, with minimal human assistance, generally by computer control   For instance, on an automated radio station most or all of the programming and commercials are on tape, operated by computer, and there is little or no live talent.

autopositive   a type of photographic reproduction in which the black and white values of the original are duplicated in the copy (black remains black; white remains white)   Because there is no reversal of tones, no intermediate negative is required. Photocopying is an example.

auto-widow-adjust   a feature of a typesetting system that prevents blank spaces (widows) at the end of justified lines (aligned at the right margin)

aux   auxiliary; an abbreviation used by engineers to refer to a supplementary device, such as an input connection in an amplifier

auxiliary display   in a store, a unit, such as a basket, bin, checkout display, counter display, floor display, or rack, that provides selling space in addition to the section in which a product is regularly stocked

AV or **A.V.**   audiovisual; authorized version

A/V   AUDIO/VIDEO; AUDIO/VISUAL

availability   **1** [broadcasting] the time period available for purchase by advertisers; often called *avails* or *availability list*   **2** [public relations] the times and places that a spokesperson can be booked for an interview by a station or other communications medium

available a show-business word for a person who is at liberty and willing to be hired

available light existing illumination, without lights or flash

available sampling a survey of individuals selected for convenience, such as because they are in the classroom or other place in which the survey is being conducted, instead of a systematic selection of representatives of a group

avant a command for a ballet dancer to move forward; from the French word for "advance"

avant-garde referring to ideas, writing, art, or forms or techniques that are innovative, ahead of the times; the specific innovators; from the French term for "advance guard" or "vanguard"

Avant Garde a popularly used SANS SERIF typeface, such as *Avant Garde Book* or *Avant Garde Gothic*

AVC AUTOMATIC VOLUME CONTROL

average audience (AA) the number of households tuned to a radio or TV program during a minute or other period, as expressed in an *AA rating*

average daily traffic (ADT) a measurement of the audience for outdoor advertising The figure is generally expressed on an annual basis (ANNUAL AVERAGE DAILY TRAFFIC).

average net paid circulation the arithmetic mean of the number of copies of a periodical that were actually sold (not just printed or distributed) during the preceding six months

average page exposure (apx) the average number of times a reader is exposed to a page of advertising copy The measure is used with magazines by Alfred Politz Media Studies, New York.

average quarter hour (AQH) the audience during a typical (average) 15-minute period of a radio or TV program, the smallest unit of time used by rating services *AQH Persons* are the estimated number of individuals who listened to a station during an average quarter-hour. *AQH Ratings* are AQH Persons expressed as a share of the universe. *AQH Share* represents the AQH Persons of a station expressed as a percent of the total persons listening to radio or TV during that time period.

average quarter-hour audience (AQH) [radio] an average of the number of people listening to a specific station or network for at least five minutes in each quarter-hour over a specified period of time, such as a day or week *AQH persons* is a measure of total time spent listening. The *AQH rating* is the AQH persons divided by the population in the listening area.

average quarter-hour rating (AQR) [radio, television] a key statistic of the ARBITRON RATINGS COMPANY and other broadcast rating services, indicating the number of individuals listening to a station during the average quarter-hour of a day, expressed as a percentage of the total audience

Avery a trademarked white adhesive paper, with a removable backing paper, commonly used by commercial artists, made by the Avery Label Company, of Monrovia, CA; often called *sticky back*

A/W ALTERNATE WEEKS; ARTWORK

awareness [marketing] consciousness or knowledge of the name or attributes of a person, product, or other entity

AWRT AMERICAN WOMEN IN RADIO AND TELEVISION

a vista [theater] in view of the audience; in particular, an instruction that a scene change is to be made with the curtain up; from the Italian *cambiamento a vista*, "change within sight"

A-wind a film reel with the emulsion or dull side on the inside It is not the same as A-ROLL.

A wire the national circuit of a wire service, greater than the limited distribution within a metropolitan area, state, or region; the main or major wire

ax a selfish aim An *ax-grinder* is a news source who is subjective and may have an ax to grind, or an opinionated news story to circulate.

axiom a self-evident principle; an established rule, truism, or maxim

axis of orientation an imaginary vertical line at the left of a block of text, to which the eye automatically returns to begin successive lines; a *mental margin*

axonometric projection a drafting method in which a three-dimensional object is represented as a drawing (an *axonometric drawing*) with all the lines drawn to exact scale The technique is used in maps, guidebooks, and other materials.

Ayer Directory of Publications the former title of the oldest and most comprehensive directory of print media It is no longer published by the Ayer advertising agency and is now called the *Gale Directory of Publications*, after its publisher, the Gale Research Company of Detroit.

Ayer's No. 1 a classic layout of an advertisement, developed by N. W. Ayer (one of the first advertising agencies, now based in New York) It consists of a picture, a headline, a copy block, and the name of the advertiser, in that order.

AZ/EL mount [telecommunications] a pedestal commonly used as a base for TV SATELLITE terminals, as at TV stations It has a fixed position, to enable the parabolic antenna to receive signals from a specific satellite, and two angular settings, the *az*imuth (rotating path) and the *el*evation (tilt).

azimuth 1 a path; a term in astronomy and surveying 2 [recording] In audio and videotape editing and reproducing systems, the heads must be at a specific angle in relation to the tape and must follow the same angle or path (azimuth) as in the original recording.

azimuth angle [telecommunications] the angle of horizontal rotation that a ground-based parabolic antenna is moved to point it to a specific satellite in orbit; see AZ/EL MOUNT

azo dye a dye, containing nitrogen, that is moderately transparent and light-sensitive and is used in film and copying machine paper *Diazo paper* (containing two nitrogen atoms) is sensitive to ultraviolet light.

B

b or **B** book; born (as in a biography, followed by a period and date of birth); black, as in B/W (black-and-white); Bible

ba, b.a., BA, or **B.A.** BASTARD AMBER

baby a nickname for various small devices, such as a small spotlight (a BABY SPOT, or simply a *baby*); a hinged covering (a *baby door*) on a small spotlight; a metal plate (a *baby plate*) on a vertical pole that attaches to a wall or flat surface and supports a baby spot or a small LUMINAIRE; or a camera tripod with low legs (a *baby tripod* or *baby legs*) A *baby billboard* is a small poster, such as a CAR CARD.

babykicker British slang for a small spotlight (a *baby* spotlight)

baby N connector See BNC.

baby spotlight a small theatrical spotlight, generally 750 watts or less, smaller than a JUNIOR, with a PLANO-CONVEX lens; also called *baby spot, inkie, inky, inky dink, dinkie inkie,* or *inkie dinkie* (no kidding, as sung by Jimmy Durante) *To kill the baby* is to turn off the spotlight.

back **1** to endorse or provide funding, as by a supporter or *backer* **2** short for the BACKSTAGE area of a theater, sometimes called *in back,* or the back wall of a stage (*at back* means against the back wall) **3** In film, TV, and theater, *to back* is to bring in background music or sound effects. **4** part of a book, actually called a BACK STRIP, where the sections (SIGNATURES) are glued or sewn together and covered by the SPINE The spine itself sometimes is called the back. The process of affixing the *back strip* is called *backing;* a book that has undergone this process is *backed.* **5** [printing] the reverse side of a sheet of paper or the negative or plate from which the reverse or second side is to be printed

back and fill **1** to vacillate in action or decision; to go back and forth **2** [graphic arts] to zigzag

back-and-forth printing [film] the printing of a series of frames, such as a scene, in the conventional manner and then in reverse to achieve reverse motion, generally for comic effect

back announce [radio] a RECAP or summary by a disc jockey or announcer of the records, tapes, or discs broadcast during the preceding period

backbone [book production] the portion of a bound book joining the covers; also called the SPINE or SHELFBACK

back card [marketing] a POINT-OF-PURCHASE advertising message attached to the back of a MERCHANDISER or other display unit and projecting up

backcloth star British slang for a secondary performer who attracts attention away from the star

back coat a coating on the nonrecording side (the *back side*) of recording tape The back coat is electrically conductive and prevents static electricity from collecting on the tape.

back copy [journalism] an issue of a publication prior to the current issue; also called BACK ISSUE or BACK NUMBER

back cover the outer covering of a book or other item; the lower or bottom cover as compared to the front side, or upper, which covers the beginning of the book, magazine, record, or other item

back date to PREDATE; to date before the actual date, as with a purchase order written today but dated as if it had been written a month ago

backdrop [theater] a painted curtain at the rear of a stage set; also called a DROP and, in the United Kingdom, a *backcloth* More generally, it is the setting or background.

back edge [book production] the binding side of a page, the left edge of a right-hand page or the right edge of a left-hand page

backend **1** secondary or ancillary rights to a film or other production **2** [direct marketing] the cost after a primary production, such as for a follow-up telephone call or mailing after an initial solicitation

back-end promotion [sales promotion] a promotional tie-in that commences after something occurs (*the back end*); for example, the placing of a product in a movie that its manufacturer then promotes

backer a supporter who endorses (*backs*) a person or project by providing approval and aid

backer card an advertisement on a card on the back of a display of merchandise in a supermarket or other store

back file a collection of prior issues of a periodical

back flat [theater] a piece of scenery—a FLAT—that is UPSTAGE (in the rear of the stage area)

back-formation in linguistics, a common process by which a word is formed from another word that it appears to have preceded and been based upon *Edit*, for example, is a back-formation of *editor*; *editor* came first and *edit* evolved from it.

background 1 *background action:* a part of a picture or scene that appears in the distance or rear, a position of relative inconspicuousness or less importance than the foreground A *background plate* is a rear projection slide or film against which foreground action is photographed. 2 *background music:* subdued music or other sound faded to a lower or BACKGROUND LEVEL To *background the sound* is to reduce or fade it, as with a music background for a voice-over. 3 In computers, *background processes* have a lower priority and are conducted when the machine is not handling high-priority FOREGROUND PROCESSES.

background communication [computers] communication with an ELECTRONIC MAILBOX or the handling of other functions on a personal computer without interrupting the word processing or other primary (FOREGROUND) function

backgrounder [journalism, public relations] a briefing session or document As used by government agencies and others, the backgrounder may not be for direct or immediate attribution. In another context, a backgrounder may be a fact sheet or other document providing more extensive information than generally included in a news release or feature article; see BACKGROUND STORY.

background story [journalism] an article with the history of the circumstances or events preceding the current story, or an interpretative article to supplement current news; sometimes called a THINK PIECE or DOPE STORY (as in "what's the dope?")

backing something placed in back for support or strength; an endorsement or support for a person, such as a political candidate, or a group or cause, provided by *backers* A *backing track* provides musical accompaniment to enable a singer or other performers to record over it. On a theatrical set, backing or *backing flat* often refers to a piece of scenery (a FLAT) placed behind an opening such as a door (*door backing*) or window (*window backing*).

backing activities in retailing, use of sales personnel for unpacking, storing, setting up displays or merchandise, and other nonselling functions An INTRINSICALLY BACKED store has this policy; an EXTRINSICALLY BACKED store uses sales personnel only for selling.

backing and lining [book production] affixing the BACK STRIP, HEADBANDS, and LINING (material pasted down on the SPINE) to a book before the covers are applied; also called *lining up*

backing light [theater] illumination behind the main set, such as lighting in a hallway or through a window; the lights used to produce this illumination

backing strip a row about three feet long of low-wattage lamps, generally four to six, used to light a hallway or other off-stage scenery (*backing*) on a theatrical SET; also called *backing striplight*

back issue [journalism] a copy of a periodical prior to the current edition; also called a *back copy* or *back number* A *back-issue department* of a publication sells recent issues. At most newspapers, only the last edition of each issue can be purchased, as that is the *edition of record.*

back light [photography] lighting behind the subject or focused on the background; also called *edge light, hair light,* or *rim light* It is not the same as *backing light* or *backing striplight.* Backlighting adds a three-dimensional effect by forming a rim of light around the subject, particularly around the head or hair.

back lighted [photography] illuminated from behind, as in a shadow box or display, such as a backlighted transparency The process is called *backlighting.*

backlighting [photography] illumination from behind, directed toward the camera It tends to increase contrast, as opposed to FRONT LIGHTING. In film animation, back lighting (two words) illuminates the artwork from under the animation table; it is also called *bottom-lighting* or *under-lighting.*

back lining [book production] a sturdy paper or fabric strip adhering to the backbone, or SPINE, of a hardcover book

backlist previously published works (not part of the current season) of a publisher that are kept in print

back lit describing an outdoor advertising structure, display, or other translucent item with illumination behind it

back load the spending of a budget late in the fiscal period

backlog unfinished or unprocessed work

back lot an area of a movie studio or TV station where exterior scenes are shot It is no longer as common as in the Golden Era of Hollywood; today, exterior scenes generally are made in actual locations rather than on studio property.

back margins inner margins of facing pages in a publication; left and right together comprise the gutter These margins are eliminated when the page BLEEDS or is printed to its end.

back matter the appendix, bibliography, glossary, index, notes, and other material following the main text of a book

back number 1 slang for someone or something out of date 2 [journalism] any issue of a periodical prior to the current issue; also called BACK ISSUE or BACK COPY

back-of-book material at the end of a magazine, such as classified ads, or after the main part of a book, such as the appendix, bibliography, index, and notes

back order an order not yet filled, being held for future delivery

back porch [television] a portion of a composite video signal between the trailing edge of the horizontal synchronizing pulse and the leading edge of the video portion of the signal

back printing printed on the reverse side of a sheet of paper

back projection rear projection, a process in which the projector is behind the screen (instead of FRONT PROJECTION) or in which a background scene is projected onto a screen behind the performers

back room the stock room; a supply or production area

back shop the production department, such as the printing area of a newspaper

backslant or **back slant** [typography] a typeface that leans backward (to the left), as opposed to conventional ITALIC characters that slope to the right from the BASE LINE

backspace to move a typewriter carriage, word processor cursor, or other printing mechanism back along the line one character position at a time The backspace mechanism, such as a special key on the typewriter, is called a backspace.

backstage [theater] an area behind the performing area, or any part of a theater not visible to the public

backstamp a postal term for a postmark on the non-address side of an envelope or mailing piece indicating that it was received, dispatched, or missent

backstory [broadcasting, film, theater] the events in the characters' lives that preceded the story, as in earlier episodes of a series, a production before a sequel, or simply earlier action not shown to the audience

back strip [book production] paper, cloth, or other material to which the folded sheets (SIGNATURES) are pasted

backtiming or **back timing** [broadcasting] a technique in live news, variety, or other programs in which the last segment is rehearsed and timed Thus, in the actual broadcast, as the time to begin this segment approaches, the director is prepared to stretch it, speed it up, or replace it. In TV news programs, backtime is the clock time (the actual time) at which the last segment should begin if the program is to end on time. Thus, if the last segment is 40 seconds long and the newscast must end at 11:28:55 (55 seconds after 11:28), the last segment must begin at its backtime, 11:28:15. Each of the preceding segments also can be backtimed from the end of the program working toward the beginning.

back-to-back 1 adjacent, as with pages, advertisements, broadcasts, and commercials; also, printing on both sides of a sheet 2 [broadcasting] describing two tapes broadcast without narration between them

back up to print the reverse side of a sheet already printed on one side, called *backing up*

backup a replacement, reinforcement, reserve (a *backup machine*), substitute, or support (as with validation of expenses) In film, a *backup schedule* lists scenes to be shot if the scheduled locations or personnel are unavailable.

backup space or **back-up space** an advertisement that must be purchased in a magazine or newspaper in order to run an insert It is usually equivalent to one black-and-white page, called a BACK-UP PAGE.

Bacon's *Bacon's Publicity Checkers*, major directories of media, published annually for public relations people by Bacon's Clippings Bureau in Chicago

bad break [typography] an irregular interruption, such as a sentence split between two pages, a page that starts with a hyphenated word or has a first line with a WIDOW, or incorrect hyphenation

bad laugh audience laughter at a point in a play or other production that was not intended to be funny

bad letter [typography] a character that generates, positions, or reproduces improperly

baffle a partition that prevents interference between sound waves, as in a speaker, or a partition or other material for sound absorption, as in a concert hall or studio; also, a partition to control sound, light, air, or the flow of anything, including people

bagasse a residue of sugar cane and other plants used in papermaking, particularly paperboard

baggage man [theater] in the United Kingdom, a person in charge of luggage in a touring company who also helps onstage with the PROPERTIES, called a PROPERTY MAN or *property person* in the United States

baggy paper a roll of paper (a WEB) that unwinds and travels unevenly through the printing press A *baggy roll* may have variations in thickness (CALIPER) or weight; the *baggy area* can be determined by striking with a baton and listening for sound variations.

bailment the delivering of goods, such as artwork or a manuscript, to a recipient who is legally bound to take care of the items and return them

bait-and-switch advertising [marketing] a sales tactic in which an attractive or bargain-priced item is used as a lure (*bait*) to attract customers who then are encouraged to buy another, higher-priced item

balance the arrangement or proportionate relationship of elements of a layout, design, recording, film, or program A harmonious, satisfying, or "proper" relationship is balanced, or *in balance*. In film, a *balanced print* usually has had color corrections.

balance stripe a narrow band of magnetic coating on magnetic sound film, situated on the opposite edge of the magnetic soundtrack stripe to balance it so that it lies flat as it passes over the magnetic heads of the projector and rolls evenly on the reel Stereophonic sound film has sound-tracks on both edges, so that a balance stripe, also called *balancing stripe*, is unnecessary. The balance stripe also can be used for cueing or other audio processes.

balcony an upper floor in a theater or auditorium If there is more than one floor, the first upper floor often is called the MEZZANINE, the second is the *first balcony*, and the third is the *second balcony*. In British theaters and American opera houses and concert halls, the first upper floor is called the DRESS CIRCLE, the next tier of seats is the *upper circle*, the next tier is the balcony, and the top tier is the *gallery*. The *balcony box* is an enclosure for spotlights (*balcony front spots* or *balcony lights*) in front of the balcony that provide *balcony front lighting*, or *balcony lighting*, on the stage, operated electrically from a central board or manually by a *balcony operator*.

baldheaded row the first row of orchestra seats in a theater The origin is from the 19th and early 20th centuries, when older men sat in the front row at burlesque and vaudeville shows that featured chorus girls.

ballast a weight to provide stability In film lighting, a ballast is a device to control and stabilize the amount of electricity flowing through the cable.

ballgame a set of circumstances or situations involving competition, as in *to win or lose the ball game, a whole new ballgame*, or *the only ballgame in town*, common expressions among advertising and other communications people

balloon 1 a circular, oblong, or other space indicated as emerging from the mouth of a speaker and conventionally used in cartoons and comics to illustrate speech A smooth-bordered balloon usually indicates speech, while a jagged or broken line (a *scalloped balloon*) means thoughts. A line called a POINTER generally runs from the character to the balloon. 2 any circle that encloses text 3 a show-business verb for forgetting lines

ballpark figure a rough approximation; a common expression among advertising, media, and other communications people

ballyhoo loud talk, or exaggerated advertising or promotion; to promote extensively or in an exaggerated manner A *ballyhooer* is a person who promotes by sensational methods. The apocryphal origin is the town of Ballyhooly in County Cork, Ireland.

balop Balopticon, an OPAQUE PROJECTOR made by Bausch and Lomb (hence the name) that casts positive images by reflection for a TV camera The images generally are artwork on a large slide (a *balop*) used as background for a TV or film scene or as part of a sequence, such as a card or slide of a book jacket, product, name and address of a sponsor, or other identification.

banana slang for a comic, particularly in burlesque or vaudeville The *top banana* was the number-one performer in this category; next was the *second banana*.

banana plug an electrical connector commonly used to join audio wires or as jacks (*banana jacks*) in oscilloscopes and other equipment, often in pairs

bananas on bananas British slang for excessive or glitzy, commonly used in advertising and graphic arts

band 1 a thin strip; grooves on a record or disk with an entire song, movement, or other section 2 horizontal CORDS across the back of a book to which the sheets are attached 3 a group of people, particularly musicians 4 a range of radio-spectrum frequencies (*broadcast band*), including AM, FM, UHF, VHF, VLF, ham, police, commercial, and CB

band call [theater] a rehearsal of the musicians

banderole a pennant or banner, with an advertisement or inscription

banding a video defect in TV transmission in which strips of the picture differ from adjacent areas, often due to a videotape player

band space space between words and sentences; also called SPACEBAND

bandstand a platform for a band or orchestra An outdoor bandstand with a concave rear wall and roof is a *bandshell.*

B&W, B/W, or b/w black and white The term generally refers to a photograph or artwork to be reproduced in black ink on white paper.

bandwagon the winning side, as in *on the bandwagon Bandwagon effect* generally refers to a campaign in which the candidate or issue is presented as irresistible and thus leading to an inevitable victory.

bandwidth 1 the range of a frequency from its lower to upper limit 2 [broadcasting] the section of the frequency spectrum necessary to transmit audio and/or video The bandwidth of a TV channel is about 6 million cycles per second (6 MHZ). 3 [computers] the range in the number of data units that can be transferred per second along a channel Channel bandwidth is also called *bit rate,* which is usually expressed as the maximum number of data units. In facsimile transmission, bandwidth is the difference in cycles per second, or hertz, between the high and low frequencies of the band.

banger slang for an exclamation point

bangtail [direct marketing] a remittance envelope with a merchandise offer or other advertising printed on the non-address side

banjo a lightweight cloth used for backdrops in exhibits (and, of course, a musical instrument)

bank 1 a set of items; a storage area (*computer bank, data bank, memory bank*) 2 [journalism] the part of a headline below the main line; also, the personnel in a specific department (*news bank, rewrite bank, sports bank*), the type already set, and the materials in a department Magazines collect advertising in a *banked section,* often the front or back of the editorial section. 3 [film, TV] rows of lighting 4 [broadcasting] a pool or collection of commercials (*commercial bank*)

bankable likely to attract investment; having a reputation that insures success, such as a *bankable performer*

bank envelope an envelope with a pointed deep flap

bank letter a bulletin or newsletter issued by a bank or financial institution

Bank Marketing Association based in Chicago, the largest organization (4,500 members) of marketing people in a specific field (banking)

Bank Script [typography] an ornate typeface with flourishes in the capital and lowercase letters that almost are connected, as in handwriting

banner a flag; a display poster, or cloth or other material suspended or hung like a flag and printed on both sides In computer terminology, a *banner word* is the first word in a FILE.

banner line a large headline across an entire page or other large area; also called RIBBON, STREAMER, or SCREAMER

Banshees A New York social club of newspaper writers and artists, sponsored by King Features

bantam store a convenience store, small supermarket, vest-pocket supermarket, or superette

bar 1 [music] a vertical line across a STAFF, dividing it into measures, or a measure (the notes between the vertical lines) In 3/4 time, a bar line occurs every three quarter-notes; in 4/4 time, a bar occurs every four quarter-notes. 2 [typography] the horizontal crossing stroke, as in the letters T (the *T-bar*), A, or H

BAR BROADCAST ADVERTISERS REPORTS

bar chart a table or graph (*bar graph*) with quantities indicated by varying lengths or widths of vertical or horizontal bars

bar code 1 [marketing] variable-width stripes, generally black, on packages and other products that identify the item and provide other data when "read" by an OPTICAL SCANNER 2 [typography] in PHOTOTYPESETTING, small lines or bars that appear below characters for reading by an OPTICAL CHARACTER RECOGNITION (OCR) device (a bar code reader) and conversion into MACHINE CODES

bard a poet The word originally referred to an ancient Celtic (Ireland and nearby area) poet and singer of epic poems. William Shakespeare sometimes is called the Bard of Avon, or simply the Bard. Bard College, Annandale-on-Hudson, NY, specializes in the arts.

bargain books books sold considerably below their list prices, such as REMAINDERS

bargain square in a mass merchandiser or other store, the configuration of tables in units of four that form a square on which sale merchandise is offered

bar gamma a measure of the contrast in duplicating film and paper

barge out device a telephone answering machine that gives a recorded announcement to all callers

baritone the range of a voice, generally male, or an instrument, such as saxophone, that is deep-toned, between bass and tenor

barker a person in front of a store, theater, or showplace who tries to attract customers by loud talking (*barking*)

barn a large building, such as a theater that is too large for the size of the audience or cast

barn doors hinged flaps or blinders on the front of a spotlight to control the beam of light; also called FLIPPERS, SHUTTERS, or, in the United Kingdom, *barn-door shutters* A unit consists of two or four rectangular metal DOORS that can be moved separately. To *barn door* is to adjust the flaps.

barney [film] sound-deadening "housing" (a *barn*) around a movie camera A barney is a flexible waterproof covering or bag that covers the entire camera except for holes for the lens on one side and the eyepiece on the opposite side; a *heater barney* has electrically heated padding for use in cold-weather filming. It differs from a BLIMP, which is made of metal. An origin more colorful than a barn is an old comic strip, "Barney Google," in which a racehorse named Sparkplug wore a tattered blanket. Another possibility is that the two humps on the camera magazine resembled Barney Google's eyes.

barnstorm to travel about the country, particularly to small towns, for baseball exhibitions, speeches, plays, and other performances The word comes from the days when barns or barn-like buildings called *barn theaters* were used by *barnstormers* for their *barnstorming*.

Barnum a typeface with heavy horizontal strokes that simulate old-time circus posters; named after P.T. Barnum (1810–91), U.S. circus operator

barnyard a warehouse or other area where empty crates are stored, such as during an exhibition

baronial envelope a formal envelope, generally more nearly square than rectangular

baroque a style of art and architecture characterized by considerable ornamentation and curved rather than straight lines; a style of music characterized by highly embellished melodies, primarily produced in the 17th and 18th centuries (the Baroque period) Today, writing or any art form that is gaudily ornate may be called baroque. The term is from the Portuguese *barocco*, for "imperfect pearl." This type of pearl still is called baroque.

barracuda British TV and film slang for a telescopic light support, made from lengths of metal pole

barrel distortion [photography] a camera lens defect that results in the sides of a square image appearing to curve outward (*barrel-shaped*)

barrel mount [photography] a cylindrical device, generally detachable, that holds one or more lenses

barrel printer a high-speed automatic typewriter (PRINTER) with all print characters on the surface of a rotating cylinder (barrel)

barrel shutter [photography] a cylindrical revolving device on a film projector, with openings on opposite sides, to control the light passing through the film

Barrow process a method of repairing and restoring paper, such as old, deteriorating documents, named after William J. Barrow (1904–67), an American restorer of documents

bar sheet [film] a chart indicating the dialogue and number of film frames for each sound, syllable, and pause Used primarily in animation and for editing special effects and music scoring, it is also called a LEAD SHEET.

barter the exchange of advertising time and/or product mentions for merchandise or services supplied by advertisers A *modified barter* is product plus cash or a program supplied to a station with some commercial time slots kept by the supplier.

baryta paper stock coated with barium oxide (baryta) for use as a REPRODUCTION PROOF

base alignment [typography] the arrangement of all characters to "sit" on the same BASELINE (an imaginary straight line)

base artwork artwork, or nontext material, without halftones or other elements that may be added before printing; also called *black art*

base band [television] a low-frequency audio signal (6 MHZ) emanating from a TV camera, videotape recorder, satellite receiver, or other source It is lower than the frequency of TV stations and is not received on a conventional TV set, though TV stations have modulators to convert this signal.

base color [printing] the first color used as a background over which other colors are printed

base light [photography] one or more lights for uniform, shadowless, basic illumination; also called *base illumination, foundation light*, or *set light* The KEY LIGHTS or MODELING LIGHTS are added after the base light. It is different from BASIC LIGHT, which is simply one main light that does create shadows.

baseline [typography] an imaginary horizontal line on which the standard letters sit BASELINE DEFLECTION is the setting of a character above or below the baseline; it is also called JUMP.

basement the lower half of a full-size newspaper page

base-point pricing [marketing] a pricing system in which transportation is billed from a single point of origin without regard for the actual production site, a common procedure in the heavy-manufacturing industries A buyer located near a shipping point may be assessed "phantom freight charges," which are higher than actual transportation costs.

BASES [market research] a predictive modeling system for new product testing and forecasting developed by Burke, a Cincinnati market research company

base side [film] the dull underside of film stock, the opposite of the emulsion side A *base-to-base splice* is film or tape editing in which the base side of one piece is overlapped onto that of another. *Base-to-emulsion* is a reversal of the standard winding of film on a reel, from the A-WIND (base side upward) to the B-WIND (base side down).

base stock the supporting material for a photographic emulsion, such as film or paper; also, a paper that can be coated or further processed

basher 1 slang for an exclusive story; a SCOOP 2 a small portable lamp with a shovel or scoop-shaped reflector

basic [marketing] an item, color, or style that persists over a long period

BASIC the acronym for *b*eginner's *a*ll-purpose *s*ymbolic *i*nstructions *c*ode, a high-level computer programming language that uses English-like syntax

basic bus in transit advertising, use of all car cards in the vehicle by one advertiser; also called *total bus*

basic cable service a cable TV company's package of channels, including the broadcast channels, which excludes certain "premium" or pay channels

basic rate [advertising] a one-time or standard rate

basic reproduction page [printing] a sheet with CAMERA-READY material

basic set a film, TV, or stage set with furniture and scenery but without props

basis weight the weight in pounds of a ream (500 sheets) of paper cut to a given standard size For example, paper commonly called 70 pound (written *70#*) is determined by weighing 500 sheets cut to 25" × 38". The *actual basis weight* or *actual weight* is the true weight, which varies slightly with each manufacturer.

Baskerville [printing] a SERIF typeface available in several ITALIC and ROMAN forms, designed by John Baskerville, (1706–75), an English printer

bas-relief low relief, pronounced BAH-ree-leef, from the Italian *basso*, or "low" In photography, it is a process in which a negative and positive are pressed together slightly off-register. The print then made has less tonal gradation but may have a low-level three-dimensional effect.

bass the low end of the audible frequency range (15 to 256 hertz, or middle C on the piano), as with a male voice below baritone or a musical instrument like a bass fiddle or violin

bastard describing nonstandard or uncommon size (*bastard size*), form (*bastard copy*), or typeface (*bastard face*) A *bastard measure* is a line of type whose width cannot be measured in exact pica or half-pica lengths. A *bastard title* or *half-title* stands alone on a page, in the front of a book, without an author's name or COLOPHON.

bastarda [printing] informal gothic typefaces used in the early days of printing (15th and 16th centuries), including the types of William Caxton, the first English printer (1422–91) The French types were called *lettre batǎrde*; the German types were called *Schwabacher*.

bastard amber [theater] a pinkish amber (brownish-yellow) gelatin or other filter commonly used on stage lights; abbreviated as *B.A.*, *BA*, *b.a.*, or *ba*

bastard progs progressive color proofs showing in sequence every color combination possible in the four-color process; also called HOLLYWOOD PROGS

bat blacks [television] to fade out; to turn a picture to darkness or superimpose over a picture

batch the quantity made in one operation, such as a group of computer records or programs *Batch delivery*, *batch processing*, or *batching* is the assembling of similar items to be handled as a group. In photography, a *batch processor* is a photographic processing device in which the chemical solution is replaced rather than strengthened.

BATF BUREAU OF ALCOHOL, TOBACCO & FIRE-ARMS

bath a liquid or a liquid and its container in which a photographic negative or other item is dipped for processing A *stop bath* is an acetic acid or other solution that terminates one process, such as neutralizing the photo developer and preparing the photographic material for the acidity of the FIXER.

bathos an abrupt change in writing, a descent from the lofty to the ordinary; neither the same as an intentional anticlimax nor pathos PATHOS evokes sympathy, whereas bathos is false or exaggerated to the point of sentimentality or absurdity.

bathymetric map a relief map of the floor of an ocean or other body of water

batten a narrow strip of wood or metal used to fasten or make secure (to batten, as in *batten down the hatches* of a ship) scenery or other items in film and other productions In a theater, the battens from which lighting or scenery are hung are numbered, from DOWNSTAGE to UPSTAGE, as in *first batten* or *number-one batten* and *second batten* or *number-two batten*. A metal batten often is called a PIPE. A batten that holds lights is called a *light batten*. Scenery or lights are fastened to a batten with a *batten clamp*, which also fastens adjacent battens.

batter a damaged area on a typeface or printing plate *Battered type* is worn or broken type.

batters [printing] British slang for damaged letters

battledore a flat paddle In the late 18th century, this oval shape was used for the covers of a type of primer or textbook, called a BARNBOOK. The term is also used for a children's book consisting of a series of connected cards.

baud a unit of speed in data transmission, equal to the number of discrete conditions or signal events per second, such as one bit per second in a computer or $1/2$ dot per second in Morse code; named after the French inventor J. M. Baudot (1845–1903)

Baudit code [telecommunications] the five-bit code used when communicating with Telex and other telegraphy-based machines

bay mortise [photography] a rectangle cut out of a HALFTONE so that the picture surrounds three sides of the INSET

bayonet mount in film cameras, a type of mount into which a camera lens is snapped into place the way a bayonet blade is affixed to a rifle

bazooka 1 slang for a large item 2 [film] a device on the CATWALK of a studio to support lighting units In the Second World War, bazookas were weapons for launching armor-piercing rockets, named after a comic horn popularized by comedian Bob Burns (1896–1956), who, in turn, named it after the slang word *bazoo* ("mouth" or "nose"), which is probably from *bazuin*, the Dutch word for "trumpet."

B-B business-to-business

BBC BRITISH BROADCASTING CORPORATION

BBDO a major advertising agency, headquartered in New York, part of the Omnicom Group The full name, rarely used, is Batten, Barton, Durstine & Osborn.

BBnd BIG BAND

BC back cover

bcc or **b.c.c.** BLIND CARBON COPY

B copy [journalism] the bottom section of a story written ahead of an event that will occur too close to deadline for the entire story to be processed, usually consisting of background material

BCU a big closeup of a picture in photography, film, or television; ECU is an extreme closeup

bd. board; bound; bundle

B.D. BENDAY

BDI BRAND DEVELOPMENT INDEX

bds. [book production] bound in boards

BEA BROADCAST EDUCATION ASSOCIATION

beak [typography] the little strokes at the ends of ARMS and SERIFS, such as in the letters E, F, G, T, and Z

beam a slender shaft or stream of light or other radiation, such as a radio signal *Beamy* is radiant or bright. A *beam-combiner* is a two-way mirror or other device that transmits and reflects light. When used in photography, it enables the simultaneous photographing of direct and reflected views. A *beam-combiner* sometimes is called a *beam-splitter*, though the latter is a prism, mirror, or other device that directs the light gathered in two or more directions, such as on to different film. A *multibeam* is a compact variable-beam lighting unit.

beam projector [theater] a lensless spotlight commonly used to produce a narrow intense beam, such as of sunlight or moonlight

beard 1 a performer with whiskers 2 [printing] a projection, such as the portion of metal type that extends from the face to the shoulder (the surface on which the face rests) The beard depth varies considerably on different typefaces and letterpress printers used to trim the beards of large type sizes to obtain closer line spacing. 3 [television] *Bearding* is a video distortion appearing as short black lines to the right of bright objects. Sometimes called OVERDEVIATION or TEARING, it's caused by interruptions in the horizontal SYNC of the videotape.

bearers [printing] type-high strips of metal on the outside borders of letterpress plates or steel rings attached to the ends of lithographic cylinders; also called DEAD METAL

bearoff [typography] a process of adjusting spacing between characters or words

bear trap slang for a clamp used to attach lights; also called an *alligator grip*, a *gator grip*, or, more properly, a *gaffer grip* (after GAFFER, a chief electrician)

beat 1 [journalism] a geographical area or subject category assigned to one or more reporters, such as the *City Hall beat* or *police beat*, according to the *beat system*; also, an exclusive story, a SCOOP published before other media obtain it To *get a beat* is to conquer a rival by obtaining an exclusive story or other advantage. **2** [music] a regular and rhythmical unit of time, or the conductor's gesture or the symbol representing this unit of time; a supportive rhythm system **3** in acting, a brief pause; a count of one

beautiful music [radio] a format that features mostly instrumental popular music, often described as EASY LISTENING

Beautiful Music/Easy Listening (B/EZ) a radio station format featuring relaxing instrumental and vocal music that is middle-of-the-road and not jazz, rock, or experimental

beauty shot a photo closeup of a product

beaver shot a vulgarity for a photograph of female genitalia, showing pubic hair

be-bop See BOP.

Beck Awards annual awards (Frederic A. Beck Awards) for outstanding corporate speaking programs, presented by The National Association for Corporate Speaker Activities (generally called NACSA), Dayton, OH

bed a bottom or base In letterpress printing, the surface of a press on which type is changed is a *bed plate*, as on a flatbed press. To *go to bed* is to go to press, or start printing. The flat metal surface or table of a paper cutter (GUILLOTINE) on which the cutting is done is called a bed; the knife in the frame of a rotary cutting unit (a SHEETER) that cuts paper is a *bed knife*. In radio, *bed music* is the music behind a voice in a commercial, the platform on which the voice is set. To *bed a commercial* is to add background music, sometimes from a syndicator or company that sells a *canned bed music library*. In exhibits, *bed hooks* are metal hardware (in pairs, a male and a female) used to couple adjacent panels.

bedroom farce a broad comedy in which much of the action takes place in one or more bedrooms

beefcake a photograph or display of a nude muscular man, the masculine counterpart of CHEESECAKE

beep an audio signal used for alerting or warning, as on the soundtrack of a videotape for editing or notice of the forthcoming beginning of a scene, program, or commercial

beeper **1** [radio] a telephone interview Radio stations used to be required to insert a beep (audio signal) on recorded interviews to indicate that they were not live. Though this is no longer necessary, the term still is used to describe an interview conducted over the telephone rather than in the studio. It is also used to describe any long-distance interview. With the use of satellites, it is now possible to conduct long-distance interviews over television. A *beeper line* is a phone line connected to a tape recorder. **2** a small portable electronic device that emits a signal when the person carrying it is paged

Before Columbus Foundation a foundation that promotes American writing, based at the University of Washington in Seattle It presents the American Book Awards to authors.

begin even an instruction to a printer not to indent the first line of copy; to set FLUSH LEFT

beginner [theater] a performer in the opening scene of a play The stage manager's cue for beginners to take their places is, "Beginners, please!"

BehaviorScan [market research] a marketing service based on store SCANNER data and other information, conducted by Information Resources Inc. of Chicago

Belasco tendency a propensity in a play or other work to exact realism, a philosophy of David Belasco (1853–1931), American theatrical producer and director

bell [theater] a bell, buzzer, chime, or other sound to signal the audience that an act is about to begin Generally called an *intermission bell* in the United States and *bar bell* in the United Kingdom (because it rings in the bar or lounge), it is also called an *act call bell*, *lobby bell*, or *lounge bell*.

Bell and Howell [photography] a manufacturer of film cameras and projectors located in Skokie, IL *Bell and Howell perforation* (abbreviated as BH) is a type of sprocket hole (rectangular, with rounded corners) commonly used in 35mm negatives.

bell character a control character for computer users to call for help, such as by ringing a bell or blinking a light; abbreviated BEL It is also a code (BELL CODE) to distinguish special commands, such as those not in the conventional alphabet.

bell cow [marketing] a high-profit retail product

belles-lettres poetry, fiction, and other literature, as distinguished from scientific and technical writings From the French for "beautiful letters" or "fine literature," the term generally refers to creative writing that is elegant and in good taste.

Bell Operating Company (BOC) the telephone companies that before 1984 were part of the Bell System (AT&T), including NYNEX, Bell South, Southwestern Bell, and others

bellows **1** [music] an apparatus with an air chamber and flexible sides for directing a current of air, as in a pipe organ or an accordion **2** [photography] in older cameras, a collapsible part connecting the front area (shutter and lens) and the rear area (the film). The *bellows factor*, or DRAW, is the extra exposure needed to compensate for the loss of light that occurs when the camera lens is extended for close-ups.

Bell Ringer Awards the annual awards of the Publicity Club of Boston

bells and whistles special effects, flashy graphics, and other extras added to films, TV programs, or any audiovisual presentation

belly band a paper strip with promotional text that wraps around the outside of a magazine or product

belly board a flat mount on which a camera can be placed for low-angle shots

below [theater] the front of the stage; opposite *above* (the rear)

below minimum standards (BMS) a symbol used by the A.C. NIELSEN CO. to indicate an audience too small to be rated, such as a rating below 0.5

below the fold the bottom half of a standard-size newspaper, considered to be less important than *above the fold*, particularly on page one

below-the-line [film and television] referring to technical labor and production, as opposed to CREATIVE expenses These costs include salaries of the assistant director, crew, script clerk, unit manager, and technicians, and the cost of equipment rental, film, insurance, locations, makeup, music, set construction, special effects, taxes, and transportation.

belt to sing loudly and lustily with a driving rhythm, generally by using the chest (called *chest voice*) to produce a HEAD SOUND, akin to shouting Singers such as Ethel Merman, who "belt out" a song, are called *belters*.

belt press a rotary-web LETTERPRESS with variable-length endless bands for high-speed printing, as of an entire book in one operation The belts carry flexible plastic printing plates instead of rigid plate cylinders.

ben [theater] slang for a BENEFIT performance

benchmark a standard, yardstick, or point of reference in measuring or judging quality, as in a *benchmark study* in communication research

Benday or **benday** a process to produce shading variations by the application or laying on of tints, such as dots, lines, or other textures, on illustrations, negatives, or plates Benday also refers to the tinted screens, tint sheets, or plates, generally copper or zinc, applied to the section to be tinted or shaded. They were named after New York printer Benjamin Day (1838–1916) and sometimes spelled Ben Day, as the maker was the Ben Day Company, Inc. Benday is used by producers of low-budget publications and advertising as a means of creating a color or shading effect without adding a sec-

ond-color ink. An instruction to add tones to photographic negatives in offset lithography may be written as B.D., even though screens are used rather than Benday sheets. For example, 30% B.D. written over an area indicates that a screen of dots is to be placed over the area in order to produce a tint that is 30 percent of the solid color.

benefit a performance, ball, or other event that charges admission, with some of the income contributed to an individual or organization, usually a charity

Benguiat a widely used classical serif typeface named for its designer, Edward Benguiat (b. 1925), of New York; pronounced beng-get

benshi Japanese, a speaker or explainer In the early 20th century, a benshi was a performer who spoke the dialogue and explained the action during a silent film. The word is occasionally used to refer to a narrator in a play or other work and is sometimes capitalized.

Bern or **Berne** the capital of Switzerland The Berne Convention for the Protection of Literary and Artistic Works (commonly called the Berne Union) establishes international copyright standards. The United States joined the Berne Union in 1989. Previously, it adhered to a similar agreement, the Universal Copyright Convention.

best boy [film] the principal or first assistant to the chief electrician, a GAFFER or JUICER, on a motion-picture production The principal assistant to the GRIP (stagehand) is the *best boy grip*. The term may have originated in the days when young laborers assembled for possible work in theaters and the gaffer called, "Give me your best boy."

best food day the day on which newspapers feature a large amount of supermarket and food advertising, generally Wednesday or Thursday; more commonly called *food day*

Best in the West annual awards to advertisers, agencies, and others presented by the Western region of the American Advertising Federation, based in San Francisco Established in 1950, they are major awards encompassing 13 states.

bestseller or **best seller** a book or other product that is among those sold in the largest numbers Bestseller lists appear weekly in the *The New York Times Book Review* and *Publishers Weekly*.

best time available (BTA) an instruction with a purchase order for a television or radio station to broadcast a commercial at the most favorable time available

BET Black Entertainment Television, a Washington, DC, cable network

Beta a type of ½-inch videocassette recorder made by Sony and others primarily for home use

Beta test the second phase, in the field under actual conditions or at a *Beta test site*, after the initial laboratory test (ALPHA TEST) This type of testing generally is used for computer systems and programs, but the jargon also is used by market researchers and others in marketing.

Beton a typeface with square SERIFS

Better Business Bureau a nonprofit organization, headquartered in Washington, DC, that promotes ethical business practices (including advertising); called the 3 Bs or Three Bees

between set perforations [printing] the cross-perforations in a continuous FORM that define the end of one form and the beginning of the next

bevel 1 the sloping part of a surface 2 [printing] the edge around a *plate* that provides a surface for clamping it In book production, *beveled boards* have a slanted edge. The boards of deluxe heavy books often are beveled before leather or other covering material is applied.

B/EZ BEAUTIFUL MUSIC/EASY LISTENING

bf BOLDFACE

BFI brute force and ignorance, a computer-industry slang term for forging ahead without sensitivity

BFWS BIG FAT WIDE SHOT

bg. or **b/g** background

BH BELL AND HOWELL

B house a movie theater that shows second-rate, or B, movies

The Burbank Studios the production headquarters of Warner Brothers, located in Burbank, CA, a suburb of Los Angeles; also used by Columbia Pictures and other companies

biannual semiannual, referring to a publication issued twice a year, as opposed to biennial (every two years)

bias 1 a line diagonally across the grain 2 fixed voltage applied to an electrode 3 [broadcasting] a signal (*bias current*) added during recording to avoid distortion

bias light [television] internal illumination of a television camera tube that reduces or removes the halo (reflected light that extends beyond the desired boundaries)

bibelot a beautiful, often rare, object or trinket; a very small book

bible or **Bible** 1 a collection or book of writings sacred to a religion; an authoritative periodical or publication in a specific industry 2 [television] In the production of a series, the bible is the general outline of plots and character devel-

opment prepared before the first program of the season. Some producers refuse to *bible the show*, in order to maintain the flexibility to make plot and cast changes during the season.

Bible paper [book production] a thin, lightweight, bright, opaque, durable paper for Bibles, reference books, and portable books requiring many pages; developed in England and called *India Bible paper, India Oxford Bible paper*, or *India paper* It originally was made from vegetable fiber in China and Japan and incorrectly called India.

Bible style [book production] a flexible, round-cornered leather binding *Biblia pauperum* (Bible of the Poor) was a type of medieval picture book.

biblio prefix for book *Bibliofilm* is a type of microfilm used to photograph book pages. *Bibliotheca* is a catalog, library, or collection of books. *Bibliotics* is the examination of written matter, such as for authenticity.

bibliography a list of references, sources, or cited material The two major types are *analytic bibliography* (with comments) and *enumerative bibliography* (essential data). A DESCRIPTIVE BIBLIOGRAPHY, a type of analytic bibliography, includes publishing details. An enumerative or *systematic bibliography* is a listing of books or other references with some data but not description. A *bibliographer* writes about books. A *bibliographical ghost* is a book or other work listed in a bibliography or otherwise mentioned but whose actual existence is questionable. A *bibliographical note* is a statement set apart from the main text, either within the document, such as a footnote, or in an appendix, with a reference to one or more sources.

bibliophile a book lover or collector A *bibliopole* is a rare-book dealer.

bicycle theory an advertising concept holding that the media schedule of a CAMPAIGN should be changed periodically—*bicycling*—to eliminate the "I've seen this before" reaction

bicycling distribution of tapes or other materials from one recipient to another, such as station-to-station or school-to-school, as differentiated from simultaneous mass distribution The term comes from the days when couriers traveled by bicycle.

bidirectional printout a time-saving process in which a *line printer* alternately prints one line left to right and the next line right to left

biennial every two years, such as a periodical issued in alternate years (*not* twice a year, which is biannual or semiannual)

big very successful or involving a large production cost, such as a *big book* or *big movie* Other slang uses include *big lie* (a major untruth, generally political), *bigmouth* (a person who talks constantly or can't keep a secret), *big name* (a prominent person or reputation), *big noise* (important news or an influential person), *big picture* (the overall situation and not the details), *big production* (excessive planning or execution), *big shot* or *bigshot* (an important person), *big talk* (boastful claims), *big ticket* (high-priced), and *big time* (upper levels of a field, originally a description of important VAUDEVILLE circuits).

Big Apple Awards   annual awards of the New York chapter of the Public Relations Society of America; established in 1988

Big Band (BBnd)   a radio-station format featuring swing and popular music bands, particularly in recordings made before 1960

Big Blue   the nickname of IBM, the computer company headquartered in Armonk, NY   The company's official color, used on its printed materials, is blue, which is derived from the blue color of their mainframe computers in the early 1960s.

big eye   an extremely powerful light, specifically, a 100,000-watt floodlight

big fat wide shot (BFWS)   an instruction to a photographer or camera operator for a wide angle

big head   a close-up shot of a performer's head

big name   a celebrity or other prominent person, such as a *big name author*

big on the slug   describing a typeface with a large *x-height* and minimal ASCENDERS and DESCENDERS

big picture   the overall view or perspective of an event or situation

big time   a high level of success, as in the expression *the big time*   The term originated in the days of vaudeville, when theaters with mass appeal had three performances a day and were called *small time*, while elite theaters with only two daily performances were called *big time* and featured *big-time performers*.

big top   the main tent of a circus; also, the life or work of circus performers

bilateral soundtrack   [film] an optical soundtrack or film stock in which the sound modulations are on both sides of a longitudinal axis and run lengthwise down the track; also called *bilateral variable-area soundtrack*, because the area of the track varies in accordance with the different sound waves that are converted to electronic impulses

bilingual dictionary   a dictionary of words in one language, the SOURCE LANGUAGE, with their definitions in another language, the TARGET LANGUAGE   A bilingual dictionary may be *monodirectional* or *unidirectional*, such as French-English, or *bidirectional*, such as French-English and English-French.

bill   **1** a statement of charges; a list   **2** [theater] a printed program, such as *Playbill*, or the program itself (a list of performing acts, such as a vaudeville bill)   A *mixed bill* is a program with a variety of acts. A *handbill*, or paper poster, is used in outdoor advertising, stored in a *billroom* and affixed by a *bill poster*. See BILLS.

billback   a cooperative advertising technique in which the retailer bills back the manufacturer for the cost of the ad or other promotional allowance

billboard   **1** [advertising] an outdoor advertising sign, originally called a *show-board* and the source of the name of the show-business trade publication BILLBOARD; now preferably called *poster panel* or *advertising poster panel*   A *baby billboard* is a CAR CARD. Three-dimensional billboards have facsimiles of packages, figures, and other shapes added to a two-dimensional advertisement.   **2** [broadcasting] the opening or closing credits or an announcement of a forthcoming program or segment, as on a news or interview program; an announcement related to a sponsor or advertiser, perhaps not paid for, such as "this portion of the program is brought to you by...."   **3** a headline surrounded by a large amount of white space   A *laser billboard* has moving images that are generated by laser on a large surface, usually 9x6 feet, in airport terminals and other window and outdoor locations.

Billboard   a weekly publication (New York) of the entertainment industry

billboard pass   a free ticket to a show given to a retailer or other person who permits a poster to be displayed in a store or other place

billhead   a printed form used for bills or statements

billing   **1** a listing of performers and others on a program, marquee, sign, or advertisement, with position and size of type as indications of importance   *Top billing* is the number-one position; *bottom billing* is the lowest.   **2** the amount of business a company does during a specific period or the amount charged to a specific customer   In advertising and other agencies, the plural, *billings*, generally is used. *Gross billings* is the total dollar volume; *net billings* is the fee and commission part of the gross billings.

billing block   a portion of an advertisement for a motion picture or other attraction in which the names of performers and other credits are listed   The *billing block title* follows the artwork title and precedes the credits; it is also called the *regular title* or *follow title*. Types of billing-block credits include *first billing* or *first position, 100 percent of the title* (same size), or a portion of the title (called an *artwork floor* or *minimum*), *likeness billing* (with a photo or artwork), *equal likeness billing* (same size photo as of another performer), *top billing, solitary billing,* and *staggered billing* (one name on the left and the other on the right, but slightly higher).

bill-me order   an order that requires billing, rather than payment using cash or a credit card

bill pass   a free ticket to a theatrical performance given to a retailer in return for displaying a poster (a BILL) for the show; also called a *billboard pass*

bills   short for HANDBILLS, most commonly seen as *Post No Bills,* the warning stenciled on walls and signs that handbills should not be affixed

bill-sticker   a message affixed to an invoice, such as "second request, payment overdue"

bill-to-third-number call   an operator-assisted telephone call charged to a number other than the calling or called numbers

bimo   [journalism] bimodular, such as a headline with two different elements

bimonthly   a publication issued every two months, not twice a month, which is SEMI-MONTHLY

binary   [computers] composed of two parts, such as a numbering system made up of two digits   In binary computers, these digits are 0 and 1; the absence of an electrical pulse represents 0, and the presence of a pulse represents 1. A binary digit is called a BIT.

binaural   two-eared; stereophonic, such as a *binaural headset* with two earphones

bind   to join pages of a publication with adhesive, thread, staples, or other means   The *bind margin* is the gutter or inner side, from the binding to the beginning of the printed area.

binder   1 a person who joins together the pages of a publication, such as a *bookbinder*   2 a detachable cover for holding paper   3 a substance that helps produce bonding, solidification, or cohesion   4 In newspapers and other publications, a binder or *binder line* is a headline over a long article, the text of a speech or document, or several related articles, tying them together.

binder's board   stiff, heavy paperboard that is covered with cloth and used as book covers

binder's die   a design or lettering etched in metal used in *debossing* or *stamping* book covers; also called *binder's stamps* or *book-stamps*   A binder's die may be made of copper, brass (*binder's brass*), magnesium, zinc, or other materials.

bindery   a facility at which publications are bound   Most printers do not have their own

binderies and subcontract such work. Specialized binderies include those devoted exclusively to books, magazines, catalogs, or booklets.

binding   the fastening of pages of a publication, such as with wire staples, plastic, stitches, or glue   The edge where the fastening occurs is the *stub edge* or *binding edge.* In addition to the process itself, a binding is the textile, leather, paper, wood, or other covers and materials (including thread or glue) that hold a book together. *Full* or *whole binding* uses only one material, whereas *fractional bindings* (*three-quarter binding, half-binding,* and *quarter-binding*) use two or more, such as leather or vellum covering the spine and part of each side and cloth or another material covering the balance. *Limp binding* does not have stiffening boards. If a *binding order* specifies two or more types of bindings on the same job, such as *perfect binding* and *case-bound binding,* this is called a *split bind order,* with each binding called a *bind leg.* The *bind margin* is the *gutter,* or inner margin, from the binding edge to the beginning of the printed area.

bingo card   a card inserted in a magazine or other publication with many numbers on it (from the game bingo), enabling one to order products, brochures, or other materials from a number of advertisers or participants   The card is sent by the respondent to the publication; because it's usually postage-paid, it saves money for the consumer, though obviously it is not as strong an expression of interest as cards sent directly to each advertiser.

bio   a BIOGRAPHY   Academics frequently refer to a professional bio as a *cv* (CURRICULUM VITAE, Latin for "course of life"). It may be a single sheet of background information about an individual or a more fully written description, sometimes called a *profile,* or a book or other work.

biography   an account of a person's life, as written by a *biographer*   An *autobiography* is one's own biography. An *authorized biography* is written with the cooperation of the subject (if alive), or the subject's family, as opposed to an *unauthorized biography,* in which there is no such cooperation or permission. A *biographical novel* is a life story with the characteristics of a biography but that changes names and settings and includes composite characters and other fictional devices.

bionote   a brief identification or biographical information about an author, generally appearing at the bottom of the first or last page of an article or on the contributor's page; also called *bio block*

biopic   a filmed biography; contraction of biography and picture

Bioskup a silent film camera and projector developed in Germany in the late 19th century by Max and Emil Skladanowsky

bipack or **bi-pack** two loads of film, loaded together and simultaneously exposed in a *bipack camera*

bipack printing [film] a system of combining two series of images on TV on a single film The process, called *bipacking*, is done within the camera or with a printer; it is also called *bipack contact matte printing*, because the process involves two bipack films and mattes. The technique is used to combine live action with animation or titles (*bipack double print titles*) and to combine two films with live action.

Birch Radio Research a radio audience research company in Coral Springs, FL that measures local audiences on a monthly basis through telephone interviews The parent company, Birch/Scarborough Research, conducts market research.

bird 1 [broadcasting] a communications satellite *Birding* is slang for radio and TV transmission via satellite. The news value of a potential story for satellite transmission, especially overseas, is called its *birdability*. To *lose the bird* is to suffer an interruption of transmission. 2 [theater] slang for an unfavorable reception by an audience, as in *getting* or *giving the bird*; from the birdlike whistle of the spectators, particularly those in the balcony or bleachers

birdie a tweeting noise due to malfunctioning sound equipment

birdseye [film and television] a spotlight with a reflector back invented by Clarence Birdseye (1886–1956), who is better known for developing methods for quick-freezing foods

birdyback an invoicing term for container shipments that travel by air and ground transportation

birthday plan a program in which employees, customers, or others receive a gift or acknowledgment on their birthdays

bisynchronous [telecommunications] transmission of bursts of characters at the same time; faster than *asynchronous*

bit 1 a minor portion of a program, called a *bit part* or *bit role*, which may be performed by a *bit player*; a performance, act, or *shtick*, as in doing a ''Humphrey Bogart bit'' 2 [computers] contraction of binary digit, a single character of a system that has only two characters, 0 and 1, representing two absolute conditions: on or off, yes or no, true or false, one-hole or no-hole, pulse or no pulse A bit is the smallest piece of information in the binary system of notation used in all computers. The size of a computer memory bank is indicated by the number of bits it is capable of storing. A group of bits, generally eight, comprise a BYTE. The *bit rate* is the speed at which bits are transmitted, usually expressed as bits per second (BPS) or BAUD.

bite 1 an acceptance, as by a media person of an offering by a publicist A tentative acceptance is a *nibble*. 2 [broadcasting] a short segment, or a *take*, such as a 15-second SOUND BITE that is repeated on network radio and TV news programs. The major excerpt from an interview, a very quotable sentence or two, is called the *news bite* or *bite-of-the day*. A *strong bite*, the opposite of a *weak bite*, is dramatic. To *pull a bite* is to find a usable short section in a longer tape. 3 [printing] the corrosive etching action of acid on an engraving or a metal plate; also, a surface characteristic of paper that enables it to accept ink or other impressions

bite off 1 copy deleted at the end of an article for space or to conform to a layout 2 [broadcasting] the premature cutoff of a commercial, record, or program

bit map [computers] a digital representation of an image in which the *bit-mapped characters*, composed of dots or PIXELS, are readable on a screen

bit pad [computers] a small, flat surface (a drawing board) that corresponds to the graphics field on the video monitor An electric stylus or pen is moved over the bit pad, which is linked to a computer, to form a signal to create the desired images.

bit stream [computers] the total flow of digitalized information through a network

biz business, as in *show biz*

B.J. Bachelor of Journalism degree

bk. block; book

bl black; also blue, depending on the context, so when in doubt, spell out

BL BODY LINE

blab-off switch British slang for a remote-control device to mute the sound of a TV program, such as during the commercials

black very dark *Pitch black* or *pure black* means totally without light. *Television black* reflects a very small amount of light from the screen, about 3-percent reflectance. In British theaters, the forestage or apron is painted black and is called the *black*.

black and white (B&W) [printing] generally referring to a photograph or artwork to be reproduced in one color—black ink on a white page

black art BASE ARTWORK

blackboard a smooth surface, usually dark (but also green or another color) and generally slate, on which material can be written (if written in chalk, also called a CHALKBOARD) An *electronic blackboard*, also called a WHITEBOARD, is a device that electronically picks up written material and reproduces and transmits it.

black book a list of the names and addresses of contacts, such as media people Several directories, particularly of photographers, models, and related resources, have Black Book in their titles.

black box a device, particularly used with computers, with specified performance characteristics but with components or modes of operation unknown to the typical lay user You don't need to know what's inside as long as you know what it does.

black clipping a video control circuit that regulates, or clips, the bottom, or BLACK LEVEL, of the picture signal so that it does not appear on the transmitted picture

black comedy humor that is morbid, macabre, and cynical

blackface BOLDFACE; heavy-faced type

black hat a villain or a symbol of a villain, from the Western movies in which the bad guys wore black hats

black humor funny writing or other material that also is grim or grotesque; also called BLACK COMEDY It is different from GALLOWS HUMOR.

black letter a heavy, ornate boldface type with angular SERIFS, commonly used in medieval books and scrolls Black-letter typefaces are derived from 13th-century German writing and were commonly used in Germany until the 1930s. Some German newspapers still use them for their nameplates. Black letter (or blackletter) sometimes is called GOTHIC, but modern black letter lacks serifs; it is sometimes also called TEXTURA, because its ornateness appears to weave a texture on the page. Examples of this type classification are TEXT and OLD ENGLISH.

black level [television] the bottom part of the picture signal, containing control signals and other material that is suppressed from appearing on the video screen

black light invisible ultraviolet or infrared rays, used for photographing in the dark or for special effects

blackline a copy with black lines, similar to a *blueline,* made with DIAZO-treated paper by the WHITEPRINT process

blackout **1** suppression or concealment, as in a news blackout; to darken or suppress, often as two words, *black out* **2** [theater] a sudden, complete darkening to indicate the passage of time or the end of a scene or the play In vaudeville, a comic sketch often ended with a blackout. A *blackout switch* is a master switch that controls all lights on a stage or set. **3** [televi-

sion] a suppression or stoppage, such as a *news blackout* In sports TV, a blackout is the suppression of coverage in a particular area because of contractual agreements with the home team or the league. **4** [printing] a black masking patch Red or orange tape produces the same effect.

black patch in offset printing, black masking tape pasted into position in the exact size of a photograph to be reproduced; also called BLACKOUT or *window*

black printer negative [photography] a color-separation negative made with a yellow filter or a combination of filters The printing plate made from this negative then can be run on the press in black ink and therefore is called a *black plate* or *key plate.*

Black Rock the black-granite headquarters building of CBS in New York

blacks [film] fabric placed over windows or other openings to block out light

blacksmith [journalism] an inferior reporter, one who "pounds out" stories in the manner of blacksmiths making horseshoes

black space scheduled broadcast time not aired; also called *dead space* or *dead spot*

blacksploitation films depicting black stereotypes; also *blackploitation* or *blaxploitation* Though the characters may be heroes, these movies, popular in the 1970s, exploited blacks or pandered to black audiences.

Black Tower the administration building of Universal Studios (MCA Inc.) at Universal City in the Los Angeles area

black track print [film] a print without sound

black week [broadcasting] one of four weeks in the year, in April, June, August, and December, when the A.C. NIELSEN CO. does not issue weekly network rating reports In the 1960s, the networks scheduled reruns and documentaries during these weeks. However, in recent years Nielsen developed *overnight* reports that are issued throughout the year, including black weeks.

blad a flyer or other promotional material The word probably is a combination of *blurb* and *ad.*

blade the cutting part of a tool or machine In papermaking, a *blade coater* is a device that applies an excess coating to paper and levels and smooths it with a steel blade. A *blade scratch* is a hairline mark in the coated surface; a *blade cut* is a deep scratch, and a *blade streak* is a broad scratch.

blah boring, dull The *blahs* is a state of weariness or boredom. Idle, meaningless talk is called *blah, blah-blah,* or *blah-blah-blah.*

B-lamp a low-wattage incandescent lamp with a vacuum, as compared to an A-LAMP, a low-wattage lamp that contains one or more gases

blanc fixe white material, such as barium sulfate, used for coating paper and other graphic arts uses; a French term that means "permanent white"

blank 1 bearing no writing or marking of any kind In financial prospectuses or other documents, an otherwise blank page sometimes bears the notation, "This page left intentionally blank." A rule or other symbol, such as brackets, sometimes is placed in a manuscript, coupon, or questionnaire to indicate a blank space to be filled in with a page number, an answer to a question, or other information. 2 [photography] a transparent negative caused by underexposure or no exposure 3 [recording] a blank or dead groove lacking sound 4 [advertising] a sheet of heavy paper used for posters and displays *Blank ply* is an indication of its thickness. 5 [computers] A *blank character* represents a space or blank; it is also called a *space character*, because it's the visual representation of the space character on typewriters and used in printing. In computer graphics, *blanking* is the suppression of one or more display elements. To UNBLANK is to turn on the electron beam.

blanket 1 to cover, suppress, hinder, or obscure A powerful radio station blankets a weaker station on the same frequency; *blanketing* is one form of interference caused by a broadcast signal. 2 [printing] a rubber-surfaced fabric that is clamped around the cylinder and transfers the image from plate to paper *Blanket contamination* is foreign matter that adheres to the blanket and interferes with print quality. *Blanket creep* is a slight forward movement of part of the blanket. *Blanket pull* is the cohesion between blanket and paper. *Blanket wash streaks* are smears on the paper, perhaps from a blanket that was washed and remained damp. Intentional distortion of a solid or screened printed area, giving the impression of high and low sections, can be created with a technique of varying the blanket pressure, called *blanket embossing*. A *blanket-to-blanket press* or *unit perfecting press* simultaneously prints both sides of the paper as the paper roll (WEB) runs between two blanket cylinders, each acting as the impression cylinder for the other.

blanket brand [marketing] use of the same name for several products, also called FAMILY BRAND, as for Heinz soups, beans, and other foods

blanket contract [advertising] a contract with a publisher, station, or network that covers advertising placed for all products or services of an advertiser, whether handled by one or several agencies, generally over a specified period of time and/or for a specified amount of money; also called a MASTER CONTRACT

blanket head a large newspaper headline covering several articles or a department, perhaps extending over an entire page or two pages

blanket order a purchasing requisition for several items, such as all the publications of a publisher Librarians sometimes call this type of purchase a GATHERING PLAN.

blanket sheet a newspaper with pages wider and/or longer than the standard size

blanking 1 suppression, as of a video signal *Line blanking*, or *horizontal blanking*, is a standard procedure in television transmission in which the video signal is suppressed during the brief interval while the electron beam, or scanning spot, is retracing its path, that is, returning from the end of one line to begin another line. *Field blanking* or *vertical blanking* is the suppression of the video signal during the brief interval when the beam finishes scanning one area, or field, and returns to the top to begin scanning the next area. The interval during which the signal is suppressed is the *blanking period*. The pulses added to the video signal to suppress it are the *blanking signals*. 2 [television] the interval between picture frames The standard TV signal transmits 30 frames per second, with intervals so brief that the eye merges them to produce an illusion of motion; the same concept applies to film (moving pictures). Teletext or other material can be transmitted during the blanking interval. 3 in computer graphics, the suppression of one or more display elements; also called RETRACE

blanking area a white margin around the copy and/or illustration area of a poster, particularly a 24-sheet poster; also called *blanking*

blank verse unrhymed poetry, particularly in *iambic pentameter*

blast a sudden rush or explosion In broadcasting, *blasting* is excessive sound through a microphone.

blat a newspaper; from the word *blab*

bleed 1 [advertising and journalism] the part of an illustration or text, generally an advertisement, that overlaps the standard dimension of a publication's page, such as to the edge of the paper with no margin Advertisements produced in this manner, called *bleed ads*, often are assessed an additional *bleed charge*. The technique also is used in journalism and public relations to produce more dramatic effects in magazines, brochures, and other printed matter by trimming or eliminating the margin or white space. *Bleed pages* can be *full bleed* or *partial* *bleed*. Bleed also can refer to unintentional running or spreading of ink, as in to *bleed a page*. **2** [recording] original sound remaining after rerecording over tape so old it cannot be properly erased **3** [television] a small amount of space at the edges of a shot to compensate for any loss between the picture as it appears on the studio monitor and on the home screen

bleed-face [advertising] a poster or bulletin with no frame molding or margin, so the design area extends to its edges

bleed tab [printing] a marker, such as a solid ink square at the edge of a page, that serves as a guide for the location of specific printing; sometimes called a *bleed*

bleed through a page or sheet on which underlying printed material can be seen, such as a wet outdoor advertising poster on which an underlying poster is visible

bleep **1** [journalism] a euphemism for a vulgar or taboo word or phrase **2** [recording] a brief, high-pitched sound usually used as a cue **3** to record over a brief segment of a soundtrack, such as to cover an expletive It differs from a BLIP, which is a deletion simply silencing or erasing the section.

blend to combine, mix, or merge, as with colors or sounds A *blend word* is formed by combining parts of more than one word, as in SITCOM from SITUATION COMEDY; also called a PORTMANTEAU WORD.

blend-line [film] the line in a composite image that separates the components that are matted together or the area that is matted out; also called *matte-line* The goal is to blur the line so that the components blend.

blend word See PORTMANTEAU WORD.

B-level title in home video, a secondary movie that is not carried by all retail video outlets

blimp a soundproof housing for a movie camera or projector, more efficient than a BARNEY; often built-in (*blimped*) *Blimping* is the soundproof material.

blind [printing] without ink, such as a part of a plate intentionally designed not to accept ink A *blind typographic machine* has a *blind keyboard* that does not provide a visual record unless attached to a printer. A *blind perforator* does not provide a visual record of the punched characters. The *blind side* of something, such as a printing press, is away from the side receiving attention or has an obstructed view.

blind ad an unsigned advertisement, such as a personal ad with a box number

blind bidding a process of offering to purchase—*bidding* on—a film, book manuscript, or other work without seeing it

blind carbon copy (bcc or **b.c.c.)** a notation at the bottom of a copy of a letter or other written material, followed by a colon and the names of the recipients of the copies Because the notation does not appear on the original, the recipient is not informed that copies have been made. Though carbon paper has been replaced by photocopies in most offices, the *bcc* and *cc* notations still are used.

blind embossing a design that is stamped without ink, giving a BAS-RELIEF effect; also called *blind stamping*

blind folio a page number counted but not actually expressed in the makeup of a book, such as a blank page or an intentionally unnumbered page

blind interview a broadcast or article in which the identity of the subject (interviewee) is not revealed

blind mail illegibly or incompletely addressed mail, such as a *blind letter*

blind offer [advertising] an inconspicuously placed offer, often to measure reader attention to an advertisement; also called *buried offer* or *hidden offer*

blind P a reversed P with the counter, or inside area, filled ¶, used to indicate a new paragraph

blind seat [theater] a seat in which the spectator can see only part of the stage due to a column or other obstruction; more commonly called an *obstructed view*

blind test [marketing] a test in which a subject indicates a preference between identified and unidentified products

blink **1** to flash A *blinker* is a light that flashes to convey a message or warning, such as a signal to people in a studio. The off-and-on speed is the *blink rate*. **2** [advertising] In broadcasting, *blinking* is a type of FLIGHTING in which short periods of advertising rapidly alternate with short periods without advertising.

blinkering [advertising] the scheduling of media in the form of many TOTAL IN, TOTAL-OUT periods, each lasting no more than one or two weeks throughout the year The term generally refers to commercials on radio or TV. See also FLIGHTING.

blip [broadcasting] a brief interruption of sound on a program or tape; to interrupt or delete sound, as in *blipping* an expletive from a TV program

blister pack [marketing] a transparent plastic covering of a product affixed to a card to aid in stacking and display, provide protection, and prevent pilferage, commonly used with small items such as razor blades; also called BUBBLE PACK or *bubble card*

blitz [marketing] an intensive, aggressive, short-term campaign, such as an *ad blitz* or *media blitz*; from the German for "lightning"

blob a small lump of viscous substance, such as ink or paint; a small spot of color of vague or undistinguished shape

block 1 a piece or section In show business, *blocking* is indicating areas or movement for cameras or performers. A script with such directions is *blocked*. 2 [publishing] A clearly defined section of text in which the lines remain together as a unit is a *copy block*. In a *block paragraph*, the first line is flush with the left margin. A *block quotation* is an extract or other matter indented or set separately or in a different manner from the balance of the text. 3 [printing] a type-high printing surface mounted on a wood or metal base A *block letter* is in a SANS SERIF typeface (no serifs, and strokes of the same width). A *block print* is made from a wood, linoleum, or metal surface cut in relief. A *block book*, or xylographic book, is printed from wooden blocks cut in relief with an entire page on each block. To *block out* is to cover, as with masking tape, a negative or plate. The sticking together of paper or film sometimes is called *blocking*. 4 [computers] a set, string, or group of bits, characters, or other entities handled as a unit *Blocking* is the process of combining items into one block. *Block length* or *block size* is the number of bytes, characters, or words in a block. To *block copy* is to copy a file en masse. A *block-cancel character* deletes the preceding unit. A *block-check character (BCC)* is a character added to the end of a block to verify it. 5 [broadcasting] a group of consecutive time periods *Block programming* is the scheduling of programs with similar audience appeal. Air time set aside for special programming or deliberately not sold is *blocked out*. A *news block* is a segment devoted to news, such as a one-minute segment in a TV program.

blockbuster something extraordinarily effective or notable The origin is from the military—a bomb capable of destroying a city block—and, in the movie business, a film so attractive that it was booked individually and not as part of a block (group) of films, which was the practice in the early Hollywood era.

block diagram a chart or other graphic representation with geometric shapes

blocked call [telephone] a call that is not connected, usually due to a busy signal

blocked up [photography] describing overexposed or overdeveloped negatives, resulting in loss of detail

blocker [marketing] a receptionist or other person who prevents access (blocks) to the potential buyer

block face [direct marketing] one side of a street from one intersection to the next

blocking service a service of local telephone companies to restrict access to specific numbers so that children and/or others cannot call certain recordings and interactive numbers The *blocking option* can be limited to specific exchanges.

blocking tape on film, stage, and TV sets, tape affixed to places on the floor to indicate where a performer should stand

block move the transfer of a group of words—a BLOCK—from one location to another in a manuscript, accomplished in some word processors by using special characters called *block markers* at the beginning and end of the section

block-out [printing] a pattern used to prevent ink from touching specific areas Block-out designs include dots, jumbled numbers, and Chinese characters.

block printing reproduction of designs or other material on engraved blocks of wood, the earliest form of printing, originated in China and still used in Asia LINOLEUM-BLOCK PRINTING uses linoleum blocks that are carved.

block quotation a long quotation separated from the adjacent text by smaller type, less space between the lines, or narrower column or line width; also called an EXTRACT

blonde a medium-size (2,000-watt) quartz iodine lamp used in film and TV

bloom 1 a delicate coating, as on some plants and fruits, that sometimes forms on the rubber blankets of offset printing presses 2 [television] a halo or flare on the screen caused by reflection from a shiny object such as jewelry or lights, or a whitening in an overbright area; also called *blooming* or *puddling*

bloop a noise, such as the clicking sound of a poorly spliced film as it passes through reproduction or projection equipment An unwanted sound can be removed from a magnetic soundtrack with a magnet or by using *blooping tape* (a *blooping patch*) to cover the bloop; a *blooping machine* can apply quick-drying *blooping ink* to cover and silence the splice. These processes are called *deblooping*. The patch itself sometimes is incorrectly called a bloop.

blooper a mistake, particularly a clumsy or foolish error in filming, broadcasting, or other performances; a special-effects pneumatic device used in filmmaking to simulate a water explosion In broadcasting and film, a blooper may be the poor splicing that causes a BLOOP.

Bloopie awards tongue-in-cheek "awards" for notable errors in grammar and other misuse of language presented in *The New York Times*

Magazine column "On Language" by William Safire (b. 1929), a journalist and former public relations counselor

blotter 1 soft absorbent paper, usually used to absorb ink 2 a book or log for recording events, such as a *police blotter* listing arrests and charges at a precinct

blow slang for the punchline of a joke, also called a *button*; theatrical slang meaning to bungle or forget lines, as in *to blow a scene*

blowback [photography] an enlargement; a blowup blown back from a reduced size, as on microfilm, to its original size or larger

blower a microphone; a slang word used in the telephone industry for an amplifier

blow in [publishing] a card inserted, but not affixed, within a publication, generally used to promote its own subscriptions

blown quote [journalism] a phrase or sentence extracted from an article and used as a headline, subhead, insert, or other graphic device; also called a LIFTOUT

blow out 1 [journalism] to open up a layout, such as by adding photos and graphics to text 2 slang for a celebration, spelled *blowout*

blowup or **blow-up** [photography] an enlargement of a photograph or other visual material

blue 1 indecent, off-color A *blue movie* is obscene or pornographic. 2 [printing] *Blues* refer to BLUEPRINTS.

blue book a special type of book with a blue cover, such as for college examinations; a directory of socially prominent people; a directory or an official government report For example, the *Printing Trades Blue Book* is a directory of the graphic arts industry. The Social List of Washington possibly should have a blue cover, since it's a directory of *bluebloods*, but it has a green cover and is generally called *The Green Book*. The *Little Blue Book*, a series of small books (3⅓" × 5") with semi-stiff blue covers, was established in 1919 by E. Haldeman-Julius in Girard, KS. The precursor of today's paperbacks, these popular books were sold directly to the public via newspaper advertising; more than 300 million copies were sold before his death in 1951. On each business day Standard and Poor's publishes data about municipal bonds called the *Blue List* or *Blue Book*. The AUDIT BUREAU OF CIRCULATIONS publishes a semiannual *Blue Book of Publisher's Statements* of circulation. The weekly production schedule of a TV program production company often is called *the blue book*.

blue box [telephone] a small device that duplicates touch tones, used to bypass toll billing equipment It is illegal and probably no longer operable. The first such device was housed in a

blue box; not the same as a BLACK BOX, it is similar to a RED BOX.

blue coating a magnesium fluorite deposit on the surface of a camera lens that prevents reflected and scattered light from flaring an image

blue copy [publishing] off-color or obscene text

bluegrass a type of jazz country music featuring string instruments (banjo, fiddle, guitar, and mandolin), associated with the South *Bluegrass country* is a region in Kentucky where bluegrass is grown.

blue law [marketing] a law prohibiting the sale of products, such as alcoholic beverages, or other activities, particularly on Sunday or Sunday morning

blueline a BLUEPRINT

blue note a flattened note, generally the third, fifth, sixth, or seventh note of the scale typical of the blues (jazz music), which is played with a harmony to produce a melancholy sound

blue pages [film] pages of a script that have been revised The sheets may be any color, though they usually are blue.

blue pencil [publishing] to edit, correct, or delete A *blue pencil*, or *blue nonreproducing pencil*, often is used because its color is invisible to the camera when the text is reproduced.

blue plate a PLATE used for blue tones in color printing

blueprint a paper negative, exposed to light and developed to produce white lines against a blue background, sometimes referred to as *blue*, *blues*, or *blueline* Also, a photoprint of a MECHANICAL that serves as a *proof* of a publication prior to printing, printed in blue ink. At this point, additions or alterations, referred to by printers as AAs or author's alterations, are more expensive than when made at earlier stages of production. When printed in brown ink, the photoprint is called a BROWNPRINT or *brownline*.

blue-screen process [film] a technique of photographing action against a bright blue background; also called *blue-backing* or *blue-screen traveling-matte process*

blue sky describing worthless, extreme, far-out thinking

blue streak a line of blue ink on the front page of a daily newspaper to indicate a specific edition, such as an edition with the latest sports scores, called the *blue-streak edition*

blunting [broadcasting] scheduling a program at the same time as a similar one on a competing station or network

blurb a summary or excerpt of an article used before or within the article; any promotional copy, such as on a book jacket or record cover

Journalists sometimes refer to inconsequential material, such as a promotional quotation, as a blurb. The word was coined by humorist Gelett Burgess in his 1907 novel *Are You a Bromide*, in which a character was given the name Miss Belinda Blurb "to sound like a publisher."

blurp [recording] an undesirable sound on an audio track The origin of the word may be a hybrid of BLOOP (an error) and burp.

BMI BOOK MANUFACTURERS' INSTITUTE; BROADCAST MUSIC, INC.

B movie [film] a secondary theatrical motion picture of lesser budget and/or quality than a "major film"

BMS BELOW MINIMUM STANDARDS

BNC baby N connector, a twist-lock device to connect coaxial cable, commonly used in the TV industry and called by its initials

b.o. box office

board a flat surface Because a board often is used to display a schedule, *across the board* refers to a daily program or other item that appears in every column or section of the chart. A board may be small, such as the PASTEBOARD used for book covers, or it may be large, such as a poster or sign used for display. *Board art* is artwork (clippings, photographs, original art, and other materials) affixed to a heavy board that may be mounted on an easel or otherwise displayed. *Boards* is an old word for a theater stage and short for switchboard or control board, such as a device for controlling stage lighting (a *light control board*). In film, the *boards* or *production boards* are prepared prior to production with a scene-by-scene itemization of personnel and other details.

board fade lowering of the intensity of music or other sounds, the board being the audio or video console or control panel It is also called a PRODUCTION FADE but is different from a *studio fade*, in which the sound is reduced in the studio.

boat truck a British theatrical term for a low-wheeled platform that carries a set onto a stage during a production

bobbinet mesh, gauze, or other loosely woven material When used as a curtain on a stage, it's generally called a SCRIM.

BOC BELL OPERATING COMPANY

bock [book production] a sheepskin leather used in bookbinding

bodice-buster an erotic romantic novel, often with a historical plot; also called bodice-ripper

bodkin [printing] in typesetting, a sharp tool used to lift or pick out metal type from type already set

Bodoni one of the first modern typefaces, designed by the Italian printer Giambattista Bodoni (1740–1813), notable for its sharp SERIFS and strongly contrasting thin and thick strokes It is still commonly used (especially Bodoni Bold).

Bodoni dash [printing] a tapered dash, thicker in the middle than at the ends

body 1 the main part of an article or publication 2 [printing] the viscosity or consistency of ink; the opacity, density, and consistency of paper or ink—its *substance*, which is extremely important in terms of stiffness or softness; also, the shank portion of a piece of type The total vertical dimension of a type character, its *body size*, is measured in points. A 7-point typeface set on an 8-point body is expressed as 7 on 8, or $^7/_8$. 3 [advertising] the main COPY BLOCK of an advertisement, which is called *body copy* or *body text*, not including headlines, subheads, captions, coupons, or SIGNATURE

body brace [film and television] a camera support that attaches to the shoulders and waist of a camera operator

body fade a gradual decrease in sound intensity caused by physically turning away from the microphone The technique is sometimes used for transitions.

body line (BL) [typography] the length of a line of body type, used in making a layout

body size [printing] the length of a typeface measured from the top of the highest ascender to the bottom of the lowest descender

body stock [publishing] paper for the main part (*body*) of a publication For example, *Arizona Highways*, the beautiful monthly magazine of the Arizona Department of Transportation, is printed on 60-lb. body stock and 110-lb. cover stock.

body type [publishing] the major portion of the text or printed matter as differentiated from the headlines (DISPLAY TYPE) The text is sometimes referred to as *body copy* or *body matter*.

boff a gimmick; a device in a plot to move along the action; also called a *plot plant* or *weenie* A boff or *boffola* is also a loud laugh or a joke that provokes laughter.

boffo [theater] a box-office hit The word was coined by VARIETY, the entertainment trade newspaper, probably from *boff*, a joke or big laugh, although possibly from *box office* (BO).

bogart to behave truculently or to obtain by intimidation; from the tough-guy movie roles played by American actor Humphrey Bogart (1899–1957)

bogus type typesetting, generally at a daily newspaper, by union compositors of material already in existence or suitable for reproduction in accordance with the labor union contract

boil [journalism] to reduce the length of text, as in *boil it down*

boilerplate [journalism] a block of copy that may be picked up and reused, such as a sentence or paragraph describing a company and its products that often is the standard last section of a news release   The term is sometimes used for any type of clichéd material in journalism and advertising; also called FILL or abbreviated by journalists as *A.O.T.* (any old time). Boilerplate also refers to newspaper MATS and other *canned material* (in fact, this is the origin of the word). Many newspaper syndicates started in Chicago, including the American Press Association, which was founded in 1882 in the same building as a sheet-iron factory. Chicago printers dubbed the noisy American Press offices as a boilerplate factory. The term boilerplate was used derogatorily to describe the mechanical STEREOTYPE plates generally provided as single columns by syndicates; editors were criticized for filling their papers with plate matter cut into FILLERS and SHORTS, often on the basis of space rather than content, a process known as "editing with a saw."

boldface (bf) [typography] a type style that is heavier in appearance than its regular format; sometimes called FULLFACE   A wiggly line below characters indicates that they are to be set boldface.

Bolex a commonly used professional 16mm film camera made by Bolex/Paillard in Switzerland

bolt [publishing] in books, an uncut fold of paper at the top or other edge; the folded edges of a SIGNATURE, which then are cut

BOM 1 Book-of-the-Month Club, the largest company (New York) selling books by mail, offered monthly to subscribers (club members)   A *BOM proof* is a pre-publication copy of a book submitted by a publisher to the Book-of-the-Month Club and other book clubs.   2 Beginning-of-the-Month   BOM inventory is counted at the beginning of the month instead of the end (EOM).   3 BUSINESS OFFICE MUST

bomb a major failure, as of a film, play, or other work   In the United Kingdom, however, a bomb is a big success, so it all depends on where you bomb.

bomb crater [theater] a nickname for a depressed area or hole in a stage set

bon-bon [theater] a 2,000-watt spotlight, generally directed onto the face of a performer

bond border an ornamental rule or design on the periphery of a bond or other financial document, used as a design element on cents-off coupons or other items

bond paper a grade of paper used for correspondence, having strength, durability, and permanence   Its content can range from low-grade SULPHITE to 100% RAG.

bone a flat piece of ivory bone, or plastic, generally about 8 inches long and 1 inch wide and with rounded sides, used for hand folding of paper; also called a *bone folder*

bones flat sticks used as clappers in minstrel shows; an end man in a minstrel show (often called Mr. Bones)

bonus circulation [publishing] the printing and distribution of copies of a publication, such as a magazine, in excess of the minimum guaranteed to advertisers

bonus pack [marketing] a package with two items attached or one inside the other, both the same or one a smaller size or a PREMIUM, sold at or close to the regular price of one of the items

bonus print an extra film print or tape given to a customer as part of a larger or special purchase

bonus spot [broadcasting] a free announcement added to a schedule, most often to compensate for scheduling problems or to increase total volume of a package

boob tube an unfavorable description of a TV set   A boob is a stupid or foolish person.

boogaloo or **bugaloo** a shuffling dance; as a verb, to dance in this manner (to *boogie*) or to fool around

boogie-woogie a style of jazz piano music with a recurring left-hand pattern, popularized by Count Basie, Fats Domino, Jerry Lee Lewis, and Hazel Scott   It is also called *boogie*, though this word recently has taken a broader connotation of rock music and is used as a verb.

book 1 a set of written or printed pages; a bound volume; a talent contract; a libretto or text (without the music) of a play or other work; a portfolio of a person's work   2 [advertising] an audience ratings book   3 [journalism] a collection of articles from various sources, such as different reporters and wire services, about the same event   The term often refers to a magazine; a *woman's book* is a magazine with primary appeal to women.   4 [theater] short for *promptbook,* the text of a play or other work held by a *prompter,* who is *on the book* (follows the script); two pieces of scenery (FLATS) hinged so they can be folded for storage; instructions or summary of past performances, as in the book on a performer   5 To *book* means to hire, often an entertainer; in publicity, to set up an interview; or to make arrangements (*book a trip*). To *book a seat* in the United Kingdom is to buy a theater ticket (a *booked-up* show is sold out).

The person who books guests on a radio or TV program is called a *booker* (not a *bookie*). *For the books* means extraordinary, as in a book of record achievements.

Book Awards annual awards to authors of books published in the United States presented by the National Book Awards Inc., New York; formerly called the American Book Awards Currently the American Book Awards are presented by the Before Columbus Foundation, Seattle, WA.

bookbinding a process of attaching or holding together the pages in books, booklets, periodicals, and other publications The process often is done by a specialist, a *bookbinder*, at a BINDERY, using various types of *binders* and *binding machines*.

book block a bound assembly of a book's pages without the covers; also called *text block*

book card a page opposite the title page of a book on which appears a list of books by the same author or publisher; also called a CARD PAGE

book ceiling two pieces of scenery, hinged together to form the top, or ceiling, of a stage setting; also called a *two-leaf ceiling*

book cloth material used for the covers of a book or other publication, generally cotton of various weights and weaves finished (fitted or coated) with starch, pyroxylin, or plastic; also called *binding cloth* The quality or grade of the cloth is determined by the number of threads per inch and their tensile strength.

book club [publishing] an organization that sells books to members, generally at reduced prices, such as the Book-of-the-Month Club and the Literary Guild A *book club selection* is a book offered to members, either as the main recommendation of the month or as an *alternate selection*. The term also refers to a group of people who meet to discuss books, such as the Great Books Club.

bookend [advertising and broadcasting] a radio or TV commercial with an open area in the middle for insertion of a local dealer tie-in or other material; also called a *doughnut* (it has a hole in the middle) A *bookend ad* is an advertisement that is split, with half on one side of a page or facing pages in a publication, the other half on the other side, and editorial matter between the two. In the United Kingdom, bookend also is slang for the first and last episodes in a TV drama series.

book flat British for two pieces of scenery, hinged together; called a TWO-FOLD in the United States

booking an engagement, such as a lecture or performance, put in the *schedule book*, often by

a *booking agent* At some magazines, such as *Lear's*, the associate editor/bookings arranges for models to be *booked*, or hired, for photography. Advance sales, particularly of theatrical productions, are also called bookings. A *booking office* or *booking agency* makes arrangements for engaging (booking) performers.

booking board [radio, television] a calendar posted on a wall or bulletin board on which is written the names of interview guests and other information about forthcoming programs

book jacket a detachable protective paper covering placed around a book, attached by flaps folded over the edges of the cover; also called *dust cover, dust jacket, dust wrapper, jacket,* or *jacket cover*

book label a small BOOKPLATE with the name of the owner but with no motto or other extraneous material

booklet a small book or pamphlet, generally with paper covers

Booklist a semimonthly magazine of reviews, mostly of books, published by the American Library Association, Chicago

Book Manufacturers' Institute an organization in Stamford, CT of manufacturers and suppliers of book materials *BMI Specifications* is a system of textbook manufacturing standards that has been replaced by *NASTA Specifications*.

bookmark a piece of paper or other material placed between the leaves of a book or other publication to indicate a place for the reader, or a piece of thin ribbon attached to the top of the spine of a desk diary A *book mark*, more commonly called a *book number*, is a librarian's term for the combination of symbols that identify a publication in a collection.

book number [theater] a dance or musical selection (a *number*) that relates to the plot (*book*) of a musical comedy or other production

book paper [book production] a general term for coated and uncoated papers used in books and other types of printed material usually in 25" × 38" sheets

bookplate a label, often specially designed, pasted to one of the front endpapers of a book with the name of the owner and often with the words *ex libris* ("from the library of") and a decorative border

book pocket an envelope pasted inside the front or back cover of a book to hold a library card, microfiche, or other items

book post a mail classification for books that is at a lower rate than first-class mail The term is used outside the United States.

book producer a person or company that creates or helps create a manuscript and arranges for its publication; also called a *book packager*

bookragger a book reviewer who usually is very negative

book rate a fourth-class postal rate; a special rate for mailing books

books down a theatrical directive for performers in a rehearsal to work without their scripts (*books*)

book show [theater] a musical with a plot (a *book*)

book typography the conventional arrangement of the type elements in a book, often called the book's *layout*, usually in the following sequence:

    FRONT MATTER

    HALF TITLE

    FACT TITLE (verso, or left-hand page)

    TITLE PAGE (recto, or right-hand page)

    COPYRIGHT (verso)

    DEDICATION

    PREFACE

    ACKNOWLEDGMENTS

    TABLE OF CONTENTS (recto)

    LIST OF ILLUSTRATIONS

    LIST OF FIGURES

    INTRODUCTION (recto)

    BACK MATTER

    APPENDIXES

    INDEX

    COLOPHON

book wing a piece of scenery consisting of several (usually four) sections attached to a spindle so that each section, or flat, can show a different scene when the device is turned It is akin to the pages of a book and is used particularly in the United Kingdom.

boom 1 to increase in size or importance; to promote vigorously 2 a deep sound with low resonance *Boomy*, also called *tubby*, is sound with low-frequency resonance. 3 [film, broadcasting] a long movable stand, crane, arm, or pole for mounting and moving a microphone (*boom microphone*) or camera The *boom arm* is the circular arm on a camera platform that controls the vertical position of the camera. Thus, to *boom up* is to raise the DOLLY boom arm and camera in order to obtain a *tilt down*, or downward shot. The opposite is a *boom down*, or *tilt up*, shot, in which the dolly boom arm is lowered. A *boom shot* is a continuous single shot involving various movements of the camera boom. These shots also are called *crane shots*. The *boom operator* (formerly called

boom man) handles the microphone boom and associated equipment. 4 [telephone] a tubelike apparatus that extends from the headset and places the speaker close to the mouth so that no hands are required for operation

boom channel a path reserved for low frequencies, such as bass music, explosions, or other deep sounds In the Dolby speaker system, the two boom channels play on *boom tracks*; this bass-extension is called the *baby boom system*.

boomerang 1 [theater] a platform on casters with two or more levels, used to paint scenery or mount lights 2 [film] a receptacle in front of a light that holds a filter

booster a device for increasing power or effectiveness, such as an amplifier or a *booster light*; also, a person who increases effectiveness, a promoter *Booster solutions* are commonly used in film development.

booster light a light used to increase brightness, particularly an ARC or QUARTZ lamp used to increase daylight

boot 1 a protective covering (from the footgear), such as a small cover placed over the head of a camera tripod (a *boot* above the head!) or a small receptacle through which film moves during processing 2 [computers] A preliminary program called a *bootstrap* or *bootstrap loader* is used to locate and activate the main program in the memory. To *boot* is to start this initial program loader.

booth a small enclosed compartment, such as an announcer's booth or telephone booth; a small sales or display area, as in an exhibition

boothmanship communications skills of the personnel at a booth, as at an exhibition

bootjacking newspaper jargon for the selling of single copies, generally by boys on the streets The practice has been revived, as with the sale of newspapers at toll-booth entrances.

bop a style of jazz, particularly as played by trumpet players and other musicians in the period after the second World War, characterized by complex rhythms, experimental harmonic structures, and instrumental virtuosity *Bopping* also is a style of easy walking or strutting.

borax inferior, though attractive or impressive, goods The word's origin is not from the chemical but rather from the German *borgen*, "to borrow." Furniture stores were among the first to sell on credit to borrowers; credit stores that promote flimsy, flashy merchandise are called *borax houses*. However, *Borax premiums*, often cheap furniture, were provided in the early 20th century by the manufacturer of Borax alkaline soap.

border 1 a margin, rim, or edge; a line or strip that forms a box around a headline, article, or advertisement   A *border chaser* is blinking lights or other pre-programmed lighting around the edges of a sign.   2 [theater] a piece of scenery, generally a painted cloth called a *cloth border*, that represents a ceiling (*ceiling border*), foliage (*foliage border*), the sky (*sky border*), or some other view. A narrow border of canvas, muslin, or velour sometimes is hung above the stage to cover the ceiling area (the *flies*). The *first border*, or *number-one border*, is downstage; other numbers are successively upstage.

border blaster   a high-power clear-channel AM radio station with a transmitter in Mexico near the U.S. border and English-language programming beamed to the United States   These stations, with call letters starting with X, were very popular in the 1930s to 1960s, particularly for their evangelical and country-music programs.

border light   a strip of lights, often containing five 1,000-watt bulbs, generally in a metal trough above the stage; sometimes called a *light border*   The *first border* (or *number-one, X-ray, concert,* or *teaser border*) is downstage, closest to the audience; the *second* or *number-two border* is upstage.

borscht circuit or **borsch circuit**   a group of resort hotels in the Catskill Mountains (north of New York City) at which entertainment is provided for the guests   In the 1930s and 1940s, the hotels catered to Jewish guests and the menu included borscht (Russian beet soup). Jerry Lewis and other prominent comedians and singers started their careers at these hotels. The borscht circuit is also called the *borscht belt.*

Boston version   a theatrical show that has been sanitized to conform to the puritanism of audiences in Boston, a practice common in the first half of the 20th century

bottle collar   [advertising] a message printed to fit around the neck of a bottle; also called a *bottle topper*

bottle glorifier   a retail display that holds a bottle

bottle topper   BOTTLE COLLAR

bottom   the end, as in *bottom of the script*

bottom lighting   in film animation, illumination of artwork from under an animation table; also called *back lighting* or *under-lighting*

bottom line   the total cost; the ultimate result, such as the net profit or loss; the main or essential point

bottom out   [publishing] text at the bottom of a page   In the proper layout of a book or another publication, a paragraph should not bottom out, or begin on the last line. This can be rectified by editing or adding space between the lines.

bottom-up planning   a business planning system in which lower-level employees prepare their goals and plans for submission to top management; different from TOP-DOWN PLANNING and GOALS DOWN–PLANS UP PLANNING

boulevard drama   a sophisticated comedy, such as one by the English playwright Noel Coward (1899–1973)   It originated in the melodramas performed in the 19th century on the Boulevard du Crime in Paris.

bounce   1 [broadcasting] signals bounced off the ionosphere, satellites, or other *bounce points*   2 [photography] light bounced or reflected   A *bounce light* is a FLASH attached to a camera and pointed at the ceiling or wall to reflect light back onto the subject. Other types of auxiliary lights and devices, such as a common umbrella, also are used for bounce.   3 [printing] an alternating or up-down-up style sometimes used in headlines   If letters are unintentionally misaligned, the bounce is a defect.   4 [television] a sudden, unanticipated brightness in the picture

bounceback   [marketing] a card or enclosure to order merchandise or make a request, inserted within a direct-response mailing, in a publication, or with fulfillment of an offer

bourgeois   middle-class; and from this, the name for 9-point type, a common size

Bourges sheet   a tinted acetate sheet used as an overlay, such as to lighten photographs; pronounced "burr-gess"

boustrophedon printing   a process in which a LINE PRINTER first prints a line in the conventional manner, from left to right, and then, to save the time of the carriage return, prints the next line from right to left   This timesaver is no product of the computer age—the process goes back to ancient writing, and the Greek word *boustrophedon* means "turning like oxen in plowing"; it is also called BIDIRECTIONAL PRINTOUT.

boutique   [advertising] a studio or small agency, not full-service, specializing in creative work

bow   1 [photography] the tendency of film or paper to bend into a curve across its width; rhymes with wow   It is different from *curl*, which is a lengthwise rolling up.   2 In show business, to bow is to open, as with the debut of a film or play. And, of course, a performer who *takes a bow* is acknowledging applause.

bowdlerize   to expurgate; to remove offensive passages, as from a book   The expurgated word or words is a *bowdlerism*; the process performed by a *bowdlerist* is *bowdlerizing* or *bowdlerization.* Thomas Bowdler (1754–1825) was an English editor whose most famous book was *The Family Shakespeare*, an expurgated edition published in 1807.

bowl [typography] the circular part of letters such as *b*, *d*, and *p* that consists of the curved main stroke surrounding a closed space

bow-wow show-business slang for a failure or something unattractive

box **1** slang for a TV set, camera, guitar, or other stringed instrument, or an accordion **2** an item in an article, advertisement, or publication enclosed within BORDERS; a SIDEBAR To *box in* is to place type or art within a rectangular frame of ruled lines. A full box has a four-sided border; a three-sided border is called a HOOD. To *box-all* is to put the headline, story, and possibly also a photo within a box. **3** [film] a SET with four walls, instead of the conventional three **4** in theaters and elsewhere, a small enclosed group of seats or a designated section, such as the PRESS BOX at stadiums

boxed paper typewriter or other paper that has been cut and either wrapped or put in boxes The standard size of boxed paper is 8½"×11", except for paper purchased by the U.S. government, which is 8"×10½". (The one-inch saving has not appreciably reduced the national debt.)

box-fold cover [printing] an unattached cover with two creases (folds), such as a BINDER

boxhead headings in tabular matter, across the top, down the sides, and above the columns

box holder a person renting a post-office box, or a person in a rural area whose mail is delivered to an address known as RFD (Rural Free Delivery) with a box number

box office a small booth or other place where tickets are sold, as at a theater; the power of a performer or show to attract an audience, as an actor who has *box office* The adjective *box-office* pertains to film or theatrical gross sales, as in *box-office draw*.

box set **1** a film or TV setting in which a complete room or area is realistically reproduced except for one wall and the ceiling, to allow for the camera to enter **2** [theater] a three-walled room with the audience viewing through what would have been the fourth wall

box-top offer [marketing] a premium or other offer that requires the return of the package top, or part of it, as proof of purchase

boylesk a burlesque show featuring male performers

Bozo box audio equipment linked to a TV camera, so simple that even Bozo the Clown could operate it

B-page See A-PAGE.

bpi BITS or BYTES per inch

brace [printing] a typographic symbol used in pairs, { }, to connect or enclose words, lines, or staves of music or to show the relationship of text blocks, also called BRACKETS or squared parentheses; a layout with multicolumn headlines adjacent to a photograph A *stage brace* is an extendible piece of wood with metal fittings inserted behind flat scenery for support.

bracket **1** an L-shaped rigid structure; a symbol to enclose written material (a squared parenthesis); a classification or grouping; **2** [photography] to take the same shot with varying exposures as "insurance" or for an effect, a technique called *bracketing*

brady a theater seat set aside by the management for a friend, a practice of William A. Brady (1863–1950), a theatrical manager

Braille [printing] a system of embossed printing and writing in which characters are formed by patterns of raised dots, in combinations of six, so that blind people can read the characters by feeling them with their fingers, developed by Louis Braille (1809–52), a blind French teacher A *Braillewriter* is a machine with six keys corresponding to the six dots of the *Braille cell*. A *Braille slate* or *Braille tablet* is a device containing a metal blade with rows of Braille cells.

brainstorming a technique of generating ideas or creative solutions to a problem, generally in a relaxed atmosphere

Brand Development Index (BDI) [marketing] a measure of the popularity of a product; actually, the ratio of a product's percentage of sales to its percentage of the population A market where sales are above average would show a BDI greater than 100; a BDI lower than 100 would indicate a weak market.

brand name [marketing] the distinctive name of a product, the word part of a trademark; sometimes the name of the manufacturer The brand name may be used to identify several related products of the same manufacturer; this class of products is called the brand. For example, Kellogg's Special K is the brand name of one of the cold cereals made by the Kellogg Company, Battle Creek, MI.

brand rating [marketing] a measure of consumer awareness of the name of a product *Brand image* is the total perception of a brand by a consumer, reflecting his or her opinions and attitudes.

brandstand [sales promotion] an intensive short-term promotion of a product or brand

B-rate [radio] the lowest rate for commercial time, generally nights and Sunday morning The higher rates are AAA (peak time), AA, and A.

brayer [printing] a small hand roller to spread ink over type

BRC BUSINESS REPLY CARD

BRE business reply envelope

break 1 [broadcasting] intermission; a time segment—a few seconds or minutes—before, during, or after a radio or TV program or other activity; an interruption, as in a *station break* 2 [printing] a place for dividing or ending a line of type; to separate areas to be printed in various stages or colors (to *break for color*) 3 [journalism] a scoop or exclusive and the time when news is available for release; to make news available, as in to *break a story* or to *break* (violate or preempt) *a release time* 4 [theater] An *act break* is the time at which an act ends or the time between acts. To dismantle scenery is to *break a set. Break a leg* is a traditional good luck wish to a performer. 5 [exhibitions] The *show break* is the end of the exhibition. 6 [film, television] to move or relocate a camera

break a leg a wish of good luck, generally said to a performer—except, of course, to a dancer The expression means to give a maximum effort.

breakaway [theater] a prop designed to fall apart easily, as when struck by a performer *Breaking glass* is thin plastic.

breakaway scenery [theater] props that break in a predetermined manner

break-box [journalism] a RULE (line) around three or four sides of a headline with a gap in the center of the top rule into which a narrower headline is set

breakdown a separation into parts, such as a listing of the separate scenes or takes in a film or other production The separation process is called *breaking down.*

breaker head [typography] a subhead or divider set in type larger than the text

breaker page the first page of any section of a newspaper other than the first section

breaker rule [publishing] a short line (RULE), such as to separate a footnote from the main text when the footnote is run over from the previous page

breakers records that are currently being broadcast heavily on a majority of radio stations in a specific category of music, such as adult contemporary, rock, and other formats

break for color [printing] to separate the parts to be printed in different colors or to separate the elements, copy and art, by color, with each on a separate sheet

break-in a testing or training period; a rehearsal or tryout, as when a performer tests a new act

breaking news [journalism] currently happening or impending news; also called a *breaking story* Late-breaking news is even more "of the moment."

break it up an instruction to film a scene from several angles and distances, such as close-ups

break line [printing] a line of type that is shorter than the full measure

breakoff [printing] a kind of thin rule used in newspapers and other publications to separate unrelated text

breakover [journalism] a JUMP, or continued text, carried over from one page to another A *breakover page* is a page, generally at the end of a magazine or other publication, with several breakovers.

break the book to apportion space for editorial and advertising matter in a magazine or other publication

break to an instruction to move a camera

breakup 1 separation; dispersal A *breakup point* is a warehouse or other distribution point where shipments are subdivided. 2 [television] an image dispersal or distortion; any other video or audio interference, such as static

breathing a fluctuation, such as the fluttering of a film as it defectively passes through the camera GATE; also called *in-and-out-of-focus effect*

breathing space [graphic arts] the addition of white space or open area in a layout; also called *breathing room*

B-reel the second or pickup (receiving) reel in a two-reel film or tape system; also called B-wind The first reel is the A-REEL or A-WIND.

breve a mark, ˅, placed over a short or unstressed vowel or syllable; a musical note with the combined time value of two notes The source is the Latin *brevis*, "brief."

brevier [typography] the name for 8-point type Four-line brevier is 32 points.

bribe [marketing] an incentive, such as a premium, deal, or special offer

bricklayer [graphic arts] a layout in which the paragraphs are set narrower than the column width and then set with the white space alternately to the left and right

bridge a few words tying one element of news to another; a proofreader's mark indicating that two letters or words should be connected; a musical, visual, or other type of transition, particularly between scenes (a *bridging shot*) Also, a narrow platform on which stage lights (*bridge lights*) are mounted, usually called a *light bridge* in the United States or *lighting bridge* in the United Kingdom. A *bridge spot* (a spotlight on a bridge) is controlled by a *bridge operator*.

briefing book   a collection, often in a loose-leaf binder, of background material provided to a government official, executive, or other person prior to a news conference, annual meeting, or other event, consisting of potential questions plus suggested answers provided by a *briefer* (usually a public relations person)

briefing session   a type of press conference or other meeting at which general information, rather than hard news, is presented, though the objective—to inform or influence—is the same

bright   **1** shining; vivid; cheerful; smart   A *brightener* is both an amusing or cheerful feature and a chemical to intensify whiteness. *Brightness* is the dimension of a color in comparison to a series of neutral colors ranging from dark to dazzlingly bright.   **2** [photography] *Brightness range* is the variation of light intensities on a subject.

Brightype   [printing] a method of converting metal type or other letterpress material into a photographic image

brilliant   **1** full of light   **2** a color with high lightness and strong saturation   **3** describing sound that is sharp and clear   The relationship between the bass and treble frequencies can be regulated (*brilliance control*) to achieve a more brilliant quality.   **4** the name of an extremely small typeface, about 4 points

bring   to cause to be, as in to *bring down* (reduce) or *bring up* (increase) the audio or visual level of a recording, photograph, or other work

bring down the house   to evoke an enthusiastic response from an audience in a theater (a *house*)

Bristol   a stiff, moderately heavy paper used for ink drawings, postcards, index cards, and mailing pieces; generally called *Bristol board*, named after the city in England   *Bristol paper* usually is produced in 22½″ × 28½″ sheets. *Index Bristol* is a commonly used lightweight cardboard. *Drawing Bristols*, which are popular among artists, are available in smooth and matte surfaces in several weights ranging from single-ply (similar to bond paper) to three-ply Bristol board. Bristol often is not capitalized, though it should be.

brite or **bright**   a light-hearted or humorous story

British Film Institute   a nonprofit organization in London that operates the National Film Theater, maintains the National Film Archive, and publishes the quarterly magazine *Sight and Sound*

British Telecom   the major telecommunications carrier in the United Kingdom

broad   [photography] A *broad light*, or *broadside*, is a large floodlight.   *Broadlighting* is full illumination, such as a broad expanse of HIGH-LIGHT on the subject; its opposite is SHORT LIGHTING. A *single broad* has one lamp, such as a 500- or 750-watt lamp. A *double broad* links two lamps, such as two 1,000-watt lamps. A *multibroad* can be adjusted in its focus by using one knob.

broadband   [computers] in data transmission, describing facilities capable of transmitting data at faster speeds and in greater quantity and frequency ranges than the standard facilities used for the voice or NARROWBAND channels used for slow (under 200 bits per second) transmission of data

broad-brush   general, nondetailed description

broadcast   **1** a single radio or TV program; the transmission or duration of a program   Any message that is transmitted over a large area, not necessarily by a broadcast station, is said to be broadcast. For example, facsimile transmission of a document to more than one fax machine is called broadcasting.   **2** [advertising] A *broadcast calendar*, in which each month is planned starting on a Monday, is used to standardize program periods.

Broadcast Advertiser Reports (BAR)   a New York company that monitors and reports on network and selected spot TV and network radio commercial activity, useful in determining competitive spending and scheduling patterns

broadcast day   the period of time between the sign-on and sign-off of a radio or TV station

Broadcast Education Association   an organization in Washington, DC of universities and colleges that provides broadcasting education and radio and TV stations

broadcast home   a household with one or more radio or TV sets

Broadcasting   a weekly magazine in Washington, DC covering the broadcasting industry and publishing an annual directory

Broadcasting Rating Council   a New York organization that measures audiences of syndicated programs

Broadcast Music, Inc. (BMI)   a nonprofit organization of music publishers, composers, and songwriters based in New York   Originally named Broadcast Music, Inc., BMI collects royalty fees from radio and TV stations, film producers, nightclubs, and others for the broadcast or performance of music by its licensees. For example, a major radio station pays BMI 12 cents each time it broadcasts a record, tape, or cassette of popular music, and a TV station pays $1.50. ASCAP is its older competitor.

Broadcast TV Recording Engineers a local union in Hollywood, CA of the INTERNATIONAL BROTHERHOOD OF ELECTRICAL WORKERS (IBEW)

broad fold a printed sheet folded to make pages wider or of greater width than depth

broadsheet a full-size newspaper, not a TABLOID; sometimes mistakenly called a BROADSIDE

broadside a large sheet of paper, generally printed on one side and folded to a smaller size, often used as a direct-mail piece or for door-to-door distribution A broadside often is greater in width than height; in fact, a *broadside page* is a page in a publication designed to be read sideways, usually to accommodate wide tables or illustrations. A broadside is also a lighting unit used to illuminate a large area; see BROAD.

broad tape financial news services (particularly Dow Jones and Reuters) that transmit onto wide sheets of paper, as compared to the price-transmission wires of the New York Stock Exchange and other markets that use narrow ticker tape Surprisingly, the broad tape is not available on the trading floor of the New York Stock Exchange; in fact, it's banned, insofar as immediate news could give floor traders an unfair advantage over others.

brochure [publishing] a pamphlet or booklet, generally stapled or stitched; from the French *brocher*, "to stitch"

broken split; cracked; not in working order A *broken book* falls open at a place where the binding has been strained. A plate (a photo or illustrative insert) is *broken over*, or hinged, when it is not properly placed in the publication and does not lie exactly flat.

broken rule [publishing] a BORDER composed of small parallel lines; also called a COIN-EDGE

broker an agent A *printing broker* sells printing but does not own or operate a printing plant. A *prize broker* obtains prizes for contests, quiz shows, and other purposes.

B-roll [television] supplementary or backup material With video news releases, the B-roll generally follows the primary material on the same cassette. In film and tape editing, alternate scenes are arranged on two reels, an A-roll and a B-roll, and then assembled.

bromide 1 a platitude; a trite or commonplace statement The origin is potassium bromide, which was commonly used as a sedative and headache remedy and is still an ingredient in Bromo-Seltzer. 2 a chemical compound containing the element bromine Bromides are commonly used in photography; the term also refers to a photographic print that has been treated with silver and bromine.

bronzing a printing process of applying bronze powder or providing a bronze metallic appearance, as with prestigious covers of publications

Brownie camera a simple-to-operate camera that was extremely popular in the first half of the 20th century; designed in 1900 by Frank Brownell (hence the name) and manufactured by Eastman Kodak (Rochester, NY) For many years, its price was one dollar and a roll of its six-exposure film cost 10 cents.

brownprint a facsimile or checking copy, printed in faded brown from the offset film negative prior to final printing; also called *brownline* The more common blue-ink version is known as a BLUEPRINT.

browse mode a feature that enables many electronic slides or other items to be shown simultaneously on a video screen; useful for library browsers, TV editors, and others

Brute [film] the trade name of a high-intensity arc spotlight manufactured by Lee-Colortron, Inc., formerly Berkey-Colortron, of Burbank, CA A *minibrute* or *lightweight brute* is smaller and generally has a 650-watt lamp, such as for fill light. A *maxibrute* is a really big brute, usually with nine 1000-watt PAR lights.

B section the second section of a newspaper

B series sizes of stock paper, a system used in Europe in which the basic rectangular sheets are called the *A series* and sizes between the A sizes are called B sizes

BT BRITISH TELECOM

BTA BEST TIME AVAILABLE

BTV business television

bubblegum slang for banal, particularly used to describe pop music for pre-teens and teenagers

bubble memory a computer data storage system in which information can be retained even if the system is disconnected from its power source

bubble-pack a tamper-resistant package in which the product is enclosed in a plastic "bubble" attached to the backing; also called *blister-packer*, *blister pack*, or *bubble card*

buck 1 to move A BUCK SLIP is a message sheet or memo with routing instructions or brief comments 2 [broadcasting] a program in the same time period as another with which it competes (or bucks)

buck a book [publishing] a rough budget, often one dollar per copy, for the promotion of a hardcover book, so that a TRADE BOOK with a first printing of 10,000 copies may have a promotional budget of $10,000

bucket [graphic arts] a layout in which the second headline is centered under the top headline

buckeye 1 unsophisticated or vulgar advertising The word is not related to the Ohio buckeye tree. 2 poor-quality paintings, particularly landscapes, produced for the mass market

buckle 1 to bend, warp, crumple, or collapse Film jammed in the film transport system of a motion picture projector buckles due to improper threading, excessive dryness, or a defect. A *buckle-trip*, or *buckle switch*, is a circuit breaker in the film path of a camera that acts as a safety device if the film jams. 2 [book production] wrinkles that sometimes form in SIGNATURES when they are folded at right angles; also called GUSSETS

buckle trip a safety device on a camera, projector, or other equipment that stops the equipment if it jams up; also called a *buckle switch*

buckram a coarse, stiff cotton fabric used for book covers When tightly woven with heavy threads, it resembles canvas.

buck slip 1 a memo sheet passed (*bucked*) from one person to another within an office; also called a *buck tag* 2 a small sheet, perhaps 6 inches wide and 2½ inches high, enclosed in a mailing

buddy movie or **buddy picture** a type of film that features the friendship between two males

buddy system [graphic arts] a conventional layout without ORPHANS (isolated elements)

budget a summary of expenses; a list of articles, such as the daily summary of upcoming stories prepared by a wire service; a list of all articles in an issue An *adjusted budget* is a revised estimate, generally subsequent to an *estimate budget* (a rough approximation) and a preliminary or *prelim budget* (more detailed than an estimate budget). A *production budget* is fully detailed, such as that for a film production.

buff a devotee or enthusiast, such as a film buff, jazz buff, or media buff The word's origin may be traced to 19th-century volunteer firemen in New York, who wore buff-colored (brownish yellow, as from buffalo) uniforms.

buffer 1 something that lessens shock, protects, separates, or neutralizes, such as a buffer used in photographic developing 2 [computers] a device or area that temporarily stores data and then transfers or delivers it, generally at a different speed; also, the part of a computer that compensates for differences in operating speeds of various components

bug 1 [printing] the little oval, usually at the bottom of the page, indicating that a booklet or other printed matter was produced by a union printer (International Typographical or another union); the union insignia in the credits of a motion picture; more generally, a small, frequently used piece of art The insignia of the International Typographical Union appears on the dateline at the top of page one of many newspapers. 2 a malfunction, defect, error, or difficulty, as in a computer or other system To DEBUG is to remove the error or device. Computer programmers sometimes refer to a bug as an *undocumented feature*. The first computer bug allegedly was an actual moth that produced a computer hardware failure in the 1950s. 3 an enthusiast, devotee, or buff 4 a hidden microphone or eavesdropping device 5 a telegrapher's key

bug-eye [photography] an extreme wide-angle lens, more commonly called a FISHEYE

build to increase or intensify, as with an increase in business, the quickening of tempo of a performance, or the additional intensity of light

build day the day scheduled to erect a set in a film or TV studio; also called *set day* or *setup day*

building-in [book production] the process of drying the paste used to attach the CASE to a bound volume

build/strike to construct and/or disassemble a set for a film, play, broadcast, or show

buildup a process of amassing or increasing, such as buildup of a substance; a favorable publicity or advertising campaign or other praise

built piece [theater] scenery, such as stairs, doors, and windows, that is constructed as a unit; also called SOLID PIECE, RIGID UNIT, or SET PIECE

built-up fraction a fraction with large-size numerals akin to capital letters, such as 1/2, as compared to a small or SHILLING FRACTION, such as ¹/₂

bulk 1 [publishing] thickness of paper, not necessarily related to weight For example, coated paper generally has more bulk than uncoated paper. Added bulk can increase stiffness and thickness and thus make a book or other publication feel heavier or more important. To *bulk a book* is to use this *bulking* process, as by using thick, heavy paper instead of thin, lightweight paper. The *bulking index* (inches of thickness per pound of BASIS WEIGHT of the paper) is determined with a *bulking stick* or ruler. 2 [mail] *Bulk distribution* is loose or unpackaged, whereas BULK MAIL is packaged and organized by zip codes, so that identical pieces can be sent at a lower rate called a *bulk rate*. A *bulk record* is an itemized list of copies of a publication sent to an area.

bulk eraser [recording] a large electromagnet that demagnetizes and wipes—erases—an entire tape without running the tape through the recorder; a *degausser*

bulkhead a partition or wall, such as behind the driver in a bus An advertising message displayed on a bulkhead is a *bulkhead card.*

bulking dummy [publishing] a mock-up, dummy, or prototype of a book or other publication with blank pages, used to determine its thickness so that a cover, a mailing container, and other items can be prepared before the pages are printed

bulk mail third- and fourth-class mail delivered to post offices in bundles organized by destination The Postal Service provides bundle and sack labels, trays, rubber bands, sacks, and other free items for use by bulk mailers.

bull. BULLETIN

bullcrit a euphemism for bullshit; nonsensical, pretentious, deceitful

bulldog the earliest edition of a morning newspaper, published the preceding night A *bullpup* is the first edition of a Sunday newspaper, generally published at an earlier hour than during the week and sometimes printed in full or part before Sunday. *Bulldog Reporter* is a media and public relations newsletter published in Berkeley, CA. The words probably originated in the 1890s, when the *New York World* and other morning newspapers published early editions to catch the mail trains and the newspapers fought like bulldogs to make their deadlines. Another alleged origin holds that in 1905, William Randolph Hearst urged the editors of his *New York American* to write headlines that would bite the public like a bulldog.

bullet 1 [publishing] a dot or other decorative device to highlight or set off phrases or other copy, such as a centered dot used to call attention to one or more paragraphed items A *density bullet* is a solid symbol, round like an EN dot or square like an EM square, placed at the beginning or end of paper or film GALLEYS to aid in processing. 2 [recording] a notation on a chart of hit recordings that a specific record, tape, CD, or cassette is doing well and climbing up the chart A *super-bullet* is moving very fast.

bulletin 1 a statement, periodical (particularly of an organization), or news item (particularly an up-to-the-minute report) At the wire services, a bulletin is the first news about a major event or a new development in a continuing story; it is important but not as significant as a FLASH. 2 [advertising] a very large outdoor area, generally 14 feet high and 48 feet long, with extensions *Paint bulletins,* or *painted bulletins,* are painted, and *posted bulletins* use paper. A *high-spot bulletin* is a large advertising structure with high exposure.

bulletin board a wall panel or area on which notices are posted A *bulletin spectacular* is an outdoor advertising panel that usually is painted rather than papered.

bullhorn a portable electronic amplifier, commonly used by speakers at rallies, on film sets, and at other locations

bullpen a large room or enclosure for several people; an art studio or a section of an advertising agency or other organization with a staff of layout technicians, letterers, and other artists, generally on a junior or mechanical level and quartered in compartments rather than separate offices

bummer slang in show business and other fields for a failure or disappointment; bad news

bump 1 a blow, collision, jolt, or rapid or forceful change To *bump up* is to increase, promote, or move up, as with a person or a layout. The reverse is to *bump down,* whereas to *bump out* or *bump off* is to remove, as in replacing one article or element in a layout with another; bump off, of course, also implies the ultimate removal: murder. To *bump on* is to switch on, as with a stage light. 2 [broadcasting] to cancel a guest or segment 3 [television] a photo or brief segment to announce or tease a forthcoming segment of a program, usually with the words "coming up next" 4 [film] a *sound bump* is a blip or other irregularity, perhaps due to poor recording or editing Bumping up means to transfer from a narrow tape, such as $1/2''$, to a wider one, such as $3/4''$.

bumped head [journalism] headlines of the same or very similar structure (typeface, size, and width) placed side by side

bumper [television] a transitional device, such as fadeout music or "We'll return after these messages," between story action and a commercial; also called a *program separator*

bumper list [broadcasting] a list of musical selections to be played before a break, such as to lead into (bump) commercials

bumper sticker a narrow sticker displayed on the bumper of a car or other vehicle, often used for advertising; also called *bumper strip*

bump exposure an exposure in HALFTONE photography, especially with CONTACT SCREENS, in which the screen is removed for a short time, increasing highlight contrast and dropping out the dots in the whites The origin is *to bump up,* or increase.

bun wire service jargon for BULLETIN

buncombe or **buncom** insincere or nonsensical talk; from Buncombe County in North Carolina, which was represented in Congress from 1819–1821 by Felix Walker, who made long-winded speeches that he said were "for Buncombe"

bundle 1 [printing] two reams of paper (1,000 sheets) or 50 pounds of paperboard *Bundling* is tying together the sections of a book or other items. 2 The Postal Service defines a bundle as several packages of mail banded or tied together and handled as a single piece.

bunk or **bunkum** nonsense; see *buncom*

BUPPIE [marketing] black urban professional, a black YUPPIE

bur. BUREAU

bureau an agency, department, or subdepartment, such as a *government bureau, clipping bureau, lecture bureau,* or *speakers bureau;* also, a branch office of a news-gathering organization covering a specific geographical territory and providing material to the headquarters office The head of a bureau is called a *bureau chief.*

Bureau of Advertising the promotional division of the American Newspaper Publishers Association The exact name is the NEWSPAPER ADVERTISING BUREAU, and it's in New York, though the Association is in Reston, VA.

Bureau of Alcohol, Tobacco & Firearms (BATF) a U.S. agency, based in Washington, DC, that regulates the alcoholic beverage, tobacco, and firearms industries It includes a Product Compliance Branch, which issues advertising guidelines and regulations.

Burgoyne Inc. a major market research firm established in Cincinnati in 1940 that conducts telephone surveys, store checks, and other data collection, particularly in the food field

buried ad a print advertisement that is not adjacent to any editorial matter

buried offer a solicitation that is inconspicuous, hidden within the text of an advertisement, or not stated explicitly, such as something that seems to be free but isn't or that has restrictions, perhaps as a test; also called a HIDDEN OFFER

burin a short, pointed cutting tool with a round handle, used by engravers

Burke Marketing a market research firm headquartered in Cincinnati, particularly active in test markets Its AdTel division provides data in these markets from scanner purchase panels, scanner store audits, TV industry rating data, split cable cut-in capability, telephone tracking services, controlled store services, and coupon collection systems. A commercial that *Burked high* is one with a favorable rating. In 1986, Burke was acquired by SAMI, a subsidiary of Time, Inc.; the merged company was SAMI/Burke. In 1989, the company became independent and was named Burke Marketing Research.

burlesque any broadly comic or satirical imitation, such as a play or other writing or art that is a caricature; used as a noun, adjective, or verb It originates from the French, which is derived from the Italian *burlesco,* a jest. The slang spelling is *burlesk.* In the United States in the first half of the 20th century, variety shows, called burlesque, featured low comedy by a *burlesque comedian* and women dancers who undressed, primarily at *burlesque theaters.* A *burlesque queen* is a leading stripper, renowned for her *striptease* act.

burn or **burnish** to expose a photo negative or sensitized printing plate to light, a process used in photo-retouching and plate-making; to make smooth or glossy, creating a luster, as with a burnishing or polishing tool *Burnished edges* are gilt or colored edges of paper sheets that have been smoothed and brightened with a polishing tool. *Burnishing,* or rubbing, a halftone plate will lighten it and result in a darker print. To *burn out* is to overexpose or remove totally. To *burn in* is simply to give added exposure to specific areas of a photographic print.

In printing, to *burn twice* is to put the same image on opposite halves of the same plate. In television, a *burn-in* is a retention of an image by the camera tube. To *burn-in* is to superimpose titles or other text. To burn-in a new machine or piece of equipment is to let it run awhile. A new slang use of burn is the rate of sales or movement.

Burnett a major advertising agency (Leo Burnett Company Inc.) headquartered in Chicago

burn out [photography] to overexpose a REVERSAL FILM or paper, resulting in a loss of image when developed

burr a rough edge or ridge

Burson-Marsteller the world's largest public relations firm, headquartered in New York, owned by Young & Rubicam Inc. The name is often improperly spelled; there is no *t* in Harold Burson's name.

burst a graphic element like a circle, star, or other shape with the words "New! Improved" interrupting or inserted in a layout In typing, a burst is a series of keystrokes or signals, such as common words, that are entered or transmitted more rapidly than the standard speed; in data communications, it is a sequence of signals counted as a single entity; in broadcast advertising, it is a concentrated campaign over a brief period, more commonly called a FLIGHT. A burst is also a rapid, intense sequence of words, as by a speaker cramming material into a 15-second or other brief TV sequence. *Burst transmission* is the extremely rapid electronic transfer of voice or data, so rapid and compressed that it may be indecipherable to spies or other outsiders.

burst binding in adhesive binding of books, the puncturing of the SIGNATURE folds so that additional glue can be inserted in the cuts or holes

burster [printing] a device to detach CONTINUOUS FORMS at the CROSS PERFORATION

bursting strength in papermaking and printing, the resistance of paper to rupturing under pressure

burst signal [television] a reference mark, consisting of high-frequency pulses, placed at the beginning of each scanning line to ensure that the color signal remains in phase and in proper combinations of hues; also called a COLOR BURST or BURST FLAG

bury to conceal; to abandon A *buried story* or *buried advertising* is hidden in an obscure position where it is surrounded by larger or more important material and is unlikely to be noticed

bury the show [theater] to put away all scenery, costumes, and other items after the final performance

bus 1 an electrical conductor or group of conductors serving as a common connection for several circuits in the form of a bar—a *bus bar* 2 [broadcasting] a central connection for several audio sources or a row of buttons on a video switching panel 3 [computers] a network or circuit connecting several work stations or used in common by several components of a computer system, sometimes called a *highway* because of its considerable traffic; also, a main power lead or conductors to transmit signals, such as a telephone cable or a group of lines A *bus driver* or LINE DRIVER amplifies or controls—drives—the signals, and a *bus controller* generates the bus commands.

bus and truck tour a theatrical road show via bus for performers and truck for scenery and equipment

busback advertising on the back of a bus

bush lines [theater] slang for the strings attached to a puppet

business occupation, work, or trade A *business publication* or *business paper* is directed to a specific class of business, such as an industry (*vertical business publication*) or to businesspersons in various industries (*horizontal business publication*). In theater, business is an incidental action performed to fill a pause or provide special interest (a *piece of business*).

The *business department* of a publication is the commercial or non-editorial side. Sometimes this department is responsible for the preparation of special sections or supplements that are primarily advertising vehicles or sends material on behalf of advertisers to the editorial

department with a BOM (business office must) notation. This decree is not welcomed by the editorial department.

business communication the planned and measured management process to help organizations achieve their goals using the written and spoken word

business gift merchandise given by a business for promotional goodwill to its customers, employees, and others Unlike ADVERTISING SPECIALTIES, it often is not imprinted with the advertiser's identification.

business office must (BOM) an instruction to the editorial side from the business office of a medium to take a specific action, such as to insert a news item

business portfolio a set of business entities, such as product lines, categorized by growth potential or other criteria For example, the Boston Consulting Group, a management consulting firm, categorizes one type of business portfolio as consisting of STARS (high growth rate), CASH COWS (high profit but lower growth rate), QUESTION MARKS (high profit but lower growth rate), and DOGS (low profit and low growth rate).

Business Professional Advertising Association (BPAA) a group of industrial advertisers and others who do not advertise consumer products; based in Edison, NJ and formerly called the Association of Industrial Advertisers (AIA)

Business Publications Audit of Circulation (BPA) a New York organization of publishers and advertisers that audits and certifies the circulation of over 850 business and professional publications (paid and controlled) Commonly misspelled, the second word is plural, the last word is not. BPA was founded in 1931 as Controlled Circulation Audit.

business reply mail postcards (*business reply cards*) and envelopes (*business reply envelopes*) mailed free, bearing printed notice indicating that postage will be paid by the recipient The recipient, who must pay an annual *business reply fee*, pays the regular first-class rate plus the fee. Business reply mail can be used only within the country.

business television (BTV) videos and TV programs sponsored by companies, generally about their business and transmitted free via closed circuit or other distribution

business-to-business advertising advertising of a business product or service by a business to a business audience; sometimes called INDUSTRIAL ADVERTISING as opposed to consumer advertising

busker a street performer, particularly on the streets of London

buskin a laced boot, generally reaching the calf (called a half-boot, as compared to higher ones), worn by actors in ancient Greek and Roman tragedies Comic actors, in contrast, wore low shoes or went barefoot. A buskin thus became a synonym for a tragic drama. To *put on buskins* means to act or write tragedy.

busorama an illuminated advertising panel along the length of the top of a bus

bust to smash, break, or cancel; used as a command in journalism, as in *bust it* (stop broadcasting, cease writing); also, a sculpture of the head, shoulders, and chest A *bust shot* is a photograph of this area—not just of the bosom. A bust sculpture often is sculpted on a *bust peg*, a heavy flat board with a vertical post in its center.

busted head [journalism] a headline too wide for the available space

busy 1 cluttered with detail, as in a distracting, complicated design that's "too busy" 2 [telephone] in use or in an off-hook condition; abbreviated as BY A *busy lamp* is a light on a telephone instrument indicating that the associated line is in use. *Fast busy* is a signal that sounds at twice the regular rate of a busy signal (generally one interruption per second).

busy hour the 60-minute period within a 24-hour period in which the communication traffic load or other service is at its maximum; also called *peak busy hour* *Network busy hour* is the busy hour for a telephone or other network.

butt to join end to end without overlapping In journalism, *butted lines* are joined, as with two single-column sections pushed together to form a two-column text. *Butting heads* are adjacent headlines that are too close and may be read as one.

butterfly a large piece of cloth or mesh that is stretched on a frame to diffuse strong light on a scene being photographed

buttinsky slang for a person who butts in or interrupts; also for the one-piece telephone used by technicians to butt into calls

button 1 To *button up* a layout or other work is to complete it, as in fastening with a button. To end *on the button* is to end at the exact time planned. 2 [radio] a strong music or sound effect, such as the end of a commercial; also called a *stinger* 3 show-business slang for the end or climax, such as the punchline of a joke; also called a CAPPER or SNAPPER

butt registration [printing] the seamless alignment of color separations

butt roll [printing] a paper roll with most of the paper already used, leaving a butt; also called a *stub roll*

buy a purchase, such as of time or space in the media; approval or acceptance of a proposal To buy is also to accept as true or valid ("*I'll buy that*"). Upon completing a take, British film directors sometimes say, "*It's a buy,*" the equivalent of the American "That's a wrap."

buying service an organization specializing in the purchase of advertising time and space

buy off the page [theater] to purchase a script on its own merits, before it has been cast

buy-or-die message a statement on an envelope, enclosure, or other item that warns the recipient that failure to reply will result in elimination from the mailing list or other dire consequences

buyout in films and other businesses, a one-time payment, such as the purchase of a script or other work, instead of royalties or residual payments

buzz a sound like a bee's hum, a crowd, or a noisy activity; a signal or telephone call; a subject of talk or gossip *A big buzz* is a loud or prominent rumor. To buzz is to call on the telephone or to talk.

buzz to telephone; to signal (perhaps with a buzzer or device that makes a beelike hum); to agitate To *buzz about* or *buzz around* is to scurry; to *buzz off* is to leave hurriedly; to *have a buzz* on a person or thing is to be excited about the object of the buzz. Buzz is also short for *buzzword*.

buzz group a collection of people who discuss a topic, as at a conference or other meeting that breaks up into smaller groups

buzzword technical terminology, jargon, or another word or phrase that is used frequently within a group, perhaps to impress outsiders; a word or phrase that has "caught on" and is "in," though it may have little meaning or be a cliché

B-wind [film] with the base side (the dull side, rather than the emulsion side) up; the opposite of A-WIND It is not the same as B-ROLL.

B wire a regional circuit of a wire service, not as extensive as the A, or national, wire

BY busy, as in a busy signal on a telephone

byline identification of an author, generally below the title or headline in a magazine or newspaper; the line that starts with "By"

bylined article an article written by an individual whose name appears beneath the title or headline The writer is referred to as the *byliner*; the identification is the BYLINE.

byline strike [journalism] a technique in which newspaper reporters and other writers request that their names not be used in articles they have written, as a form of protest against their publishers

byte [computers] a sequence of adjacent binary digits (generally 8) considered as a single unit by a computer and operated on as the smallest unit of processing, thus generally synonymous with a single character The word stems from BIT and bite. As any computer programmer knows, a byte is a group of 8 bits used to encode a single letter, number, or symbol; and, of course, a bit is a binary digit—zero or one—used to encode computer data.

byword a proverb; a familiar saying, thing, or person

C

c or C CANCEL; CARTON; CASE; CELSIUS; CENTER; CENTERLINE; CENTURY; CHAPTER; CLOCK; COPY; COPYRIGHT; COUNTRY MUSIC; CYAN On invoices, particularly for books, *C* indicates that an order is cancelled.

C/A change of address

ca. CIRCA

CAB *C*abletelevision *A*dvertising *B*ureau; *Ca*nadian *A*ssociation of *B*roadcasters

cabbages printer's marks

cable 1 short form of CABLEGRAM or CABLE TELEVISION 2 an insulated bundle of wires, through which an electric current can be passed, such as from a TV camera 3 a rope, such as one attached to a camera shutter for remote or long-distance exposure; also called a *cable release*

Types of cables used to connect TV cameras to video equipment include *coaxial cable* (a central core and an outer conductor), *triaxial cable* (coaxial with an outer screen), *multiconductor/multicore* cable, and *fiber-optic cable* (using lightweight optical fiber). Wireless linkages can be radio (*radio mini-link*), laser (*laser link*), or infra-red (*infra-red link*). An *AC cable* connects equipment to a source of alternating current. A *cable man* or *sound assistant* assists the microphone boom operator, puts wires on the performers, and moves cable from the set to the sound mixer.

In a *cable television system*, the *trunk cable* (the major coaxial cable) branches out into *feeder cables* that connect to homes via *drop line cables*.

cablecasting 1 programming carried on cable television, as opposed to over-the-air broadcasting; also called *cable origination* 2 the transmission of such programming

cable control See CABLE TELEVISION.

cablegram a telegram sent via a cable laid underwater (such as a telegram to or from outside the United States)

Cable News Network (CNN) a national cable television news network, with headquarters in Atlanta

cable penetration the percentage of homes that subscribe to cable television, generally within a specified area

cable puller [film, television] a person responsible for setting up and handling power, sound, and picture cables Generally one cable puller is allocated to each camera. The cable puller follows the camera during moving shots and makes sure that the cables do not become tangled.

cable ready referring to a TV set with built-in circuitry to receive and translate cable TV signals without a separate converter Cable-ready sets generally cannot decode pay-TV signals and require a converter for these channels.

cable relay station a microwave facility for interconnection of cable systems or for expansion of the delivery area of a cable system

CABLESE condensed and special language used in telegrams, particularly by journalists It is usually capitalized, because telegrams are transmitted only with capital letters.

cable television (cable TV or **CATV)** a television distribution system whereby TV signals are transmitted via cable (insulated wire), rather than through the air, to TV sets of subscribers in a community or locality; originally called Community Antenna Television The mechanical connections or electrical conductors are operated by *cable control*. The multiple broadcast and/or nonbroadcast signals may be received over the air, by satellite or microwave relay, or from the system's studio or remote facilities. Cable television systems are generally called *cable systems*; the companies that own and operate them are known as *cable system operators*.

Cabletelevision Advertising Bureau a New York-based association whose purpose is to provide information about cable TV as an advertising medium

cabletext TELETEXT transmitted by cable or satellite to cable TV systems

cachet 1 a seal or stamp on an official letter or document 2 a mark or sign of official approval or showing something is genuine, authentic, or of superior quality 3 a commemorative design on an envelope to mark an historic or political event **4** distinction, prestige; pronounced kah-SHAY, from the French *cacher*, "to conceal." It is, however, not the same as *cache* (pronounced cash), a hiding place or anything hidden or stored in it.

cacophony harsh, jarring sound, dissonance; the opposite of euphony; pronounced ca-KOFF-uh-nee

CAD computer-*a*ided *d*esign

cadaster a public record of property ownership A *cadastral map*, or property map, shows the boundaries of individual tracts or other land areas.

caddy a small box or container, such as the plastic container for a videodisk

Caddy Awards annual awards for creative advertising by Detroit-area advertisers and agencies, presented since 1975 by the Creative Advertising Club of Detroit

cadence **1** the fall of the voice in speaking **2** inflection in tone **3** a rhythmic flow of sound **4** measured movement or the beat of dancing, marching, or other movement **5** a series of notes or chords indicating a partial or complete conclusion of part or all of a musical composition **6** the natural rhythm of speech and language, indicated by the alternation of stressed and unstressed syllables or other patterns It is commonly used as an element of poetry.

cadenza an elaborate passage for a solo musical instrument, usually occurring near the end of the first or last movement of a concerto or other composition, sometimes improvised

C.A.E. CERTIFIED ASSOCIATION EXECUTIVE

caesura a break or pause within a line of verse, indicated by the symbol ||; a rhythmical pause, such as a scene in a film or other work that breaks up the action.

caging [sales promotion] a service in which envelopes containing payments are opened (as in bank tellers' cages) and the monies credited to the account of the advertiser or other client

CAI COMPUTER-AIDED INSTRUCTION

cake a flat mass, such as a pancake; see CAKING

cakes British theatrical slang for a performer's supplementary allowance for hotel, meals, or other expenses, usually listed as a budgetary item: *and cakes*

caking [printing] a buildup of ink pigment on the press

cal CALENDAR

calendar (cal.) **1** a schedule of forthcoming events **2** a system of the beginning and end of a year and the divisions within it The new-style or Gregorian *calendar year* (named after

Pope Gregory XIII, 1502–85; abbreviated *CY*) is January 1 to December 31. Other calendars may start on dates other than January 1; the Hebrew and Moslem calendars have different months and start at different times.

calendered paper paper that has been made smooth or glossy, generally by being pressed between smooth rollers (*calender rolls*) with a machine called a *calender* A minimum of calendering produces *antique paper*; *machine-finish paper* has had more calendering. *English finish* is highly calendered, and a *super-calendered paper* is a high-gloss paper. In places where paper has adhered to the calender roll there may defects, called *calender spots*.

calf (cf) calfskin, leather from the hide of a young cow or bull, used in bookbinding

calibration **1** a determination of the caliber (diameter) of a tube **2** the adjustment or standardization of the gradations of a dial, quantitative measuring instrument, or other device

calico a printed cotton cloth; slang for a banner, pennant, or streamer

California [printing] a MODERN typeface, with serifs

California job case a shallow wooden box with compartments for each of the characters in a font, commonly used in letterpress foundries and printing plants Each case is a drawer that is stored in a cabinet with many such drawers.

caliper **1** a measure of the thickness of paper A *point* (or point of caliper) is $1/1000$ inch. PAPERBOARD thickness (called *board caliper*) is expressed in points. A paperboard that is 0.080-inch thick is called *80-point board*. **2** an instrument, with one fixed and one movable arm, for measuring dimensions **3** [printing] a device to prevent more than one sheet at a time from feeding into a press It is not the same as a *caliber* (the diameter of the inside of a tube or gun, or a degree of worth or distinction). **4** a three-sided box (for a caption) protruding from the side of a photograph

call **1** an actual or attempted communication via telephone **2** to initiate such a communication **3** a code or message transmitted to identify the sender or receiver **4** [computers] the action of bringing a program or routine into effect The *call control signal* establishes, maintains, or releases a call. The *call control procedure* is the set of protocols that establish or release a call. **5** [film, television, theater] the stipulated time to report for work on any given day **6** an offer of employment to a performer **7** an audition notice

call-back **1** an in-person or telephone call by an interviewer, researcher, or salesperson to a previously unavailable respondent or to a person who has not completed the interview or the purchase **2** an audition or job interview to which the applicant is invited after having auditioned or interviewed previously for the same position

callboard a bulletin board backstage in a theater for notices to cast and crew

call book a record of prospective customers and other data, used by a salesperson

callboy a person who tells performers when it is time to go on stage

Call Director a trademarked multiple-button telephone set, made by AT&T, New York

call duration the time elapsed between the establishment of a telephone connection and its termination

caller service a postal service provided, for a fee, to customers using a post office box number who are authorized to pick up their mail at the post office window whenever the post office is open, though they do not have an actual post office box

call forcing a feature that automatically directs a waiting telephone call to the first available recipient, such as an agent or other individual, usually with a headset

call forwarding a feature that automatically sends a telephone call to a number other than the one dialed This can be preprogrammed by the user when the user is not at his or her regular telephone.

calligraphy elegant or fine penmanship; from the Greek *kalus* (beautiful) and *grapho* (write) *Calligraphic type* resembles handwriting.

call-in referring to a radio or TV program that broadcasts telephone conversations with listeners

calling number the telephone number initiating a call, as opposed to the number being called (the *recipient*)

Calliope **1** the Muse of eloquence and epic poetry, from Greek mythology **2** an organlike keyboard instrument with steam whistles The Greek word *kalliope* means "beautiful-voiced."

call letters the name of a radio or TV station Most stations east of the Mississippi River have call letters beginning with *W*; west of the Mississippi, call letters usually begin with *K*. Canadian stations begin with *C*; Mexican stations, with *X*. All U.S. radio stations except a few of the oldest ones have four letters.

call number the set of symbols (letters and numbers) identifying an item in a library collection, including an indication of its location and,

generally, its *class number* and book number; also called *call mark* or *shelf mark*

callout **1** a word or words used to identify an element depicted in an illustration, usually linked to the element by a straight line or arrow **2** [theater] continuing applause by an audience, requesting, for example, a *curtain speech* or the reappearance of performers

call report a record (generally a memo) of a meeting, especially one between an advertising agency, or other firm, and its client; also called *conference report*, *contact report*, or *meeting report* The format generally lists date, place, name of individuals present, and subjects discussed, particularly decisions or assignments.

call sheet a list of dates and times the cast and crew must report for a TV, film, theatrical, or other production In film, the call sheet is generally prepared by the assistant director.

call slip [library science] a form filled out by a borrower to request an item from the closed collection of a library

call to quarters (CQ) a signal sent by shortwave radio operators as an invitation to begin communication

call waiting (CW) a telephone feature that emits a beep tone, light flash, or other signal to inform the party using a phone that there is another incoming call The incoming call is held.

calumny slander; a false and vicious statement, or the uttering of such a statement

cam a moving piece of machinery, such as a wheel or a projection on a wheel *Cam* by itself is not short for *camera*, but denotes the revolving mechanism that moves film frames in a camera or projector. The syllable can serve as a short form of camera, however, as in *Betacam* and *mini-cam*.

CAM classified *a*dvertising *m*anager; computer-assisted *m*akeup terminal

camcorder a combination TV camera and videotape recorder in one portable unit

cameo **1** a brief appearance by a prominent person in a film or other production **2** a camera shot consisting of a close-up with a plain (usually black) background or none

cameo binding a style of bookbinding that has the center of the boards stamped in relief, generally in imitation of an antique gem or medal; also called *plaquette binding*

camera an apparatus for taking photographs, generally consisting of a lightproof chamber in which the image of an exterior object is projected through an aperture onto a sensitized plate or film by a lens In printing, large cameras are used to photograph art and text to produce *negatives*. In television, the camera receives the image on a light-sensitive cathode-ray tube and transforms it into electrical impulses. A *movie camera* (moving-picture camera) produces a continuous succession of images on film.

camera angle   the position of a camera with regard to a subject   A *low camera angle* is one in which the camera is below the eye level of the subject. Other camera angles are *high* (camera above the subject), *up, down, wide, tight, oblique* (tilted to the left or right), *dutch* (tilted up or down), and *reverse* (opposite of the preceding shot).

camera axis   an imaginary straight line from the center of the lens to the subject, used in the posing of the subject and placement of lights

camera body   the main part of a camera, exclusive of the lens and other detachable components

camera car   a vehicle that carries cameras and crew and is in motion while they are filming; sometimes called an *insert car*, as the camera generally is installed on a platform within the flatbed truck or other vehicle

camera card or **cameracard**   a piece of cardboard bearing a name of a TV program, credits, or other visuals, generally on an easel and focused on by a camera   Camera cards are no longer common, having been superseded by computer-generated graphics.

camera chain   [television] the TV camera, cables, controls, and power supply

camera control unit (CCU)   [television] the apparatus in the control or engineering area that controls a TV camera   There is one CCU for each camera.

camera copy   material to be photographed; camera-ready material for offset reproduction

camera cue   a red light or buzzer indicating that a TV camera is shooting a scene for transmission, live or taped; also called *cue light, tally light,* or *warning light*

camera head   the basic camera unit, exclusive of tripod and accessories

camera identification mark   a trademark or other symbol of a specific camera model   It is photographed at the beginning of a film, so that any camera flaws or other problems on the film can be traced to their source.

camera jack   a receptacle on the camera for connection to a power source, or to sound or other equipment

camera left (or **camera right**)   the left (or right) as seen from the camera operator's or viewer's position, as opposed to that of the performer; hence, the left (or right) of the image when viewed

camera log   a record of filming (on a printed form) including data about personnel and equipment and a description of each *take* (uninterrupted shot); also called *camera report* or *shooting log*

camera lucida   an optical device (consisting of a prism or lenses) for projecting an image, to a desired size or scale, on a sheet of paper so that it may be copied; also called *lucy*

cameraman   [film] 1 the director of photography 2 the person (of either gender) operating the camera, also called first *cameraman*   In a large crew, the *second cameraman* is the actual operator of the camera, assisted by a *first assistant cameraman* or *first camera assistant* (the *focus puller*) and a *second assistant cameraman* or *second camera assistant* (the *clapper/loader*).

camera mixing   a selection of successive shots for transmission from TV cameras continuously operating in various positions; also called *camera switching*

camera noise   the sound of an operating camera   In an attempt to reduce this sound or prevent it from being recorded, the exterior of a film camera generally is covered or padded with a *barney, blimp,* or other device.

camera obscura   a darkened chamber in which the image of an object is projected in natural color through an opening or lens onto a surface for viewing, tracing, or photographing   It is the earliest form of a camera, developed by Leonardo da Vinci (1452–1519), Italian artist and scientist.

camera operator   [film] the person responsible for the actual operation of the camera during shooting   The camera operator reports to the director of photography and is assisted by the *first assistant camera operator* and *second assistant camera operator*. The operator is also called *operating cameraman* or *operator*, but not *cameraman* (who is the director of photography). In TV, the camera operator reports to the *associate director* or *technical director*, sometimes to the *director* (generally via headsets), or, on remote locations, to the producer.

camera opticals   special effects, such as *iris in* or *iris out*, that are generated using only the camera itself

camera original   film exposed in a camera, as different from film exposed outside of a camera, as in an optical printer

camera-ready   referring to the final form of an advertisement, a brochure, or other matter; that is, to be photographed for making into a plate for printing

camera rehearsal   [film, television] a *full-dress* rehearsal, one with costumes, at which the movements of the camera are blocked; more advanced than a *reading* or *script rehearsal*

camera report   CAMERA LOG

camera right   See CAMERA LEFT.

camera riser   a platform or device that raises a film or tape camera

camera shot   that part of the subject matter that is viewed and photographed by the camera

camera speed   the rate at which a movie camera operates, expressed in frames of film per second   The standard speed for conventional motion picture photography is 24 frames per second.

camera switching   CAMERA MIXING

camera talk   a film or tape situation in which a performer looks directly into the lens to deliver a message to the audience

camera wedge   [film] a flat piece of wood used by the assistant cameraman or head grip to shore up a camera mounting or lock a camera position

CAMIS   Computer-Assisted Makeup and Imaging System

camp   the action of an incoming call in waiting mode; also called *camp-on*   The call *camps* on the occupied line until the line becomes free, at which time the call goes through to the recipient, either via an operator or automatically.

campaign   the entire body of efforts in support of a product or service to achieve a marketing, public relations, sales, or related objective

campaign Bristol   a coated paper used for postcards; also called *coated Bristol*

Campaign Communications Institute (CCI)   a major telemarketing company, located in New York

campaign plan   1 a program to conduct a project   2 [direct marketing] a series of mailings intended to develop interest, such as a *teaser campaign*

Campbell's Soup position   the placement of an advertisement on a righthand page in the front part of a magazine, adjacent to editorial copy, a position preferred by the Campbell Soup Company of Camden, NJ

camp-on   a telephone feature that holds an incoming call until the recipient's line is free   The recipient hears a tone indicating that a caller is waiting, while the caller remains on the line (called *camp-on-busy*).

can   a metal container   A completed film is *in the can* both literally and figuratively, since to *can* means to preserve, conserve (as in a can), or make a recording, and film is stored in cans.

can.   cancel, canceled

Canada Post   the Canadian government agency (headquartered in Ottawa, Ontario) that operates the postal service in Canada   The Canadian Postal Code is the equivalent of the U.S. ZIP Code, except that it includes letters as well as numbers, totaling six characters. The first character is the province identification, starting with *A* in the East (Saint John); *L* and *M* are for Toronto.

Canadian Association of Broadcasters (CAB)   a broadcasting trade group, based in Ottawa, Ontario

Canadian Broadcasting Corporation (CBC)   the nationally owned radio and television broadcasting network of Canada, based in Ottawa, Ontario

Canadian Cable Television Association (CCTA)   the group representing the cable TV industry in Canada, based in Ottawa, Ontario

Canadian Film Board   SEE FILM BOARD OF CANADA.

Canadian Newspaper Unit (CNU)   a standardized measure of the size of advertisements, used by most Canadian daily newspapers, akin to the STANDARD ADVERTISING UNIT (SAU) of the United States

canalize   to channel into a particular direction   The process, called canalization, is used in selling that follows from a specific opinion or orientation of a prospect so as to foster a specific reaction leading to a sale.

canary   in show business, slang for an unidentified noise

cancel   1 an omission or deletion of typed or printed matter   Printed matter that is deleted and that which replaces it are both called *cancel* or *cancels*, though technically the excised portion is a *cancelland* or *cancellandum* and the replacement matter is *cancellans*.   2 [marketing] A *completed cancel* or *paid cancel* is an individual who has fulfilled a commitment to buy products or services (such as four books from a book club) or gone beyond it with additional purchases, before cancelling the agreement.

cancellation date   the latest possible date for deciding to omit a scheduled media appearance; generally, the last date for canceling a scheduled advertisement

cancellation period   the period of time within which a contract may be canceled

candela   a unit of light intensity, from the Latin word for candle

candlepower   light intensity, expressed in CANDELAS

candler   [marketing] a light-sensitive device used to detect material in an envelope   The origin is *candling* (originally, done with candles), the examination of eggs to detect fertilization.

C&P press a Chandler and Price letterpress printing press Such presses are still used for stamping and embossing.

c & sc CAPITAL and small capital

C and W country and western; see COUNTRY MUSIC

candy-apple a computer graphics design style that makes lines on a computer screen look coated or thickened like neon, akin to a candy-coated apple

can go over (c.g.o.) [journalism, publishing] a designation for material that need not be used immediately but is to be held for later use

canned pre-recorded, not live or original *Canned material* is a stock or existing item that is mass-distributed rather than original and exclusive. A *canned presentation* is a sales pitch or other talk or demonstration that is prepared for use on more than one occasion. In computers, a *canned format* is a series of commands used frequently for a standard layout, with specifications for typography, indentation, spacing, and other details.

canned spot a piece of advertising or publicity material prepared and supplied by a manufacturer or other sponsor to a distributor or retailer, or directly to a radio or TV station Such material is generally a tape, record, or film inserted in a can, though the phrase can also refer to a typescript or other printed matter.

Cannes a small city in southeastern France, on the Mediterranean coast (the Riviera), the location of an important film festival that takes place in May

cannibalize to draw sales away from another product of the same manufacturer The process is *cannibalization*.

canning a story writing an article about a forthcoming event in the past tense as though it had already happened The story is put *in the can*, to be published just after the event—a dangerous practice, unless the canned material is checked and updated.

canon 1 a law, rule, or criterion 2 the books of the Bible officially accepted by a church or religious body as divinely inspired 3 the complete works of an author, particularly those accepted as genuine (such as the Shakespeare canon); in general, a body of writings established as authentic 4 a list of recognized saints, individuals who have been canonized, such as by the Roman Catholic Church Thus, a revered person is said to be *canonized*. 5 [music] a contrapuntal device or a composition in which a melody introduced in one voice is restated by

one or more other voices 6 48-point type, an extremely large size

canopy head a headline with the first, main section, or *deck*, three or more columns wide and subordinate decks indented from the extreme left or right It is sometimes used as a *combination head* across two or more related stories or a story and horizontally adjacent photograph, called a canopy because it covers them.

CanP CANADIAN PRESS & BROADCAST NEWS

cans slang for HEADPHONES

cant 1 a whining, singsong speech (as used by beggars) 2 the secret slang of beggars, thieves, sects, or other groups 3 insincere talk 4 a chant (often meaningless) 5 argot; jargon 6 to tilt or slant A *canted shot* is tilted. For example, a camera shoots above an actor climbing along a floor and then the scene is tilted to make it appear that the action is that of climbing up.

canto a major section of a long poem, the equivalent of a prose chapter The word is Italian, from the Latin *cantus*, a song. *The Divine Comedy* of Dante (1265–1321) is divided into cantos.

canton flannel a cotton cloth fleeced (flecked) on only one side, sometimes used as backlining of a book cover

canvas a painting made on a heavy, coarse fabric; also, the fabric itself

canvass 1 to make a round of calls or visits, as by a salesperson in a territory 2 to determine degree of interest prior to a campaign, as in an *audience canvass* *Cold canvassing* is calling on prospects who have not requested it and without prior notice, as by telephone or door to door.

cap short form of CAPITAL

capacitance electronic disk (CED) a type of videodisk made by RCA, Camden, NJ

capacitor a device that stores an electrical charge

capacity the ability to accommodate, hold, receive, or store; the potential maximum quantity *Capacity utilization rate* is the ratio of actual output, production, or other quantity compared to the maximum potential quantity (*full capacity*), the proportion of capacity in actual use.

Cape morocco a goatskin leather used in bookbinding, made from goats from the Cape of Good Hope province of South Africa

caper film a movie, generally playful in spirit, whose plot revolves around a robbery or other illegal action

capeskin [book production] fine leather made from goatskin or sheepskin, such as Cape morocco leather, used in fine-quality book covers

capital (C, C., cap) uppercase letter   *C and lc, c. and l.c.*, CLC, C&LC, *u and lc, u/lc*, and *cap and down* are commonly used short forms of *capitals and lowercase* typesetting, in which appropriate initial letters are capitalized and the remaining type is set lowercase (as in a headline that has initial capitals omitted only for prepositions and articles). *Capitals and small capitals* (or C & SC, *C. and s.c., caps and small caps*) similarly indicates that type is to be set with appropriate initial capitals and the balance in small capitals; this style is often used for subheadings and for authors' names in bibliographies. In TV scripts, visual directions are written in *all-caps* in the lefthand column. The *cap line* is the top or uppermost limit of a capital letter; *cap size* is the height (in *points*) of a capital letter.

Capital Cities/ABC   one of the world's largest media companies, headquartered in New York   It owns American Broadcasting Company and major radio and TV stations, has a majority ownership of the ESPN cable TV service, and publishes newspapers (the Kansas City *Star*, Fort Worth *Star-Telegram*, and others) and magazines (the Fairchild Publications and many others).

capper   the end or climax, such as the *punch line* of a joke

capping shutter   a device that covers a camera lens between exposures, sometimes used on an animation camera

CAPRA   *Community Agency PR Association*

caps and smalls   type in which the first letter of a word is a full-size capital letter and the remaining letters are small-size capitals, as in AMERICAN; as opposed to all caps, which refers to all full-size capital letters, or *even small*, all small-size capitals

cap sheet   short form of CAPTION SHEET

capstan   a pulley or shaft that regulates the speed of the magnetic tape in a tape recorder

captain agency   the one of two or more advertising agencies that is responsible for a master contract, covering all advertising placed within one of the media for multiple products of one advertiser

caption   a description of the content or subject of a photograph or artwork that appears adjacent to it; also called a *cutline* (A photograph or piece of artwork is a *cut*.)   The caption generally is typed on a sheet of paper 8½ × 11 inches or smaller and pasted or otherwise affixed to the photo. Originally, the caption was copy that appeared above the photo or artwork, and a

description placed below was called a *legend*. However, caption is now commonly used to refer to both, as the word *legend* is rarely used.   **2** a descriptive phrase above an article, generally not followed by a period   **3** [television] a title superimposed at the bottom of the screen for hearing-impaired viewers or dual-language programs   *Open captions* are visible to all viewers; *closed captions* can be seen only with special decoding devices   **4** [film] a subtitle, generally at the bottom of the screen but sometimes placed elsewhere (at the top or middle) to identify a scene (as to time, place, or other circumstance)

captioned drawing   a cartoon in a newspaper, magazine, or other publication   The phrase was used in the early 20th century.

captioning   the process of affixing descriptive text (a caption) to a photograph, or of superimposing subtitles at the bottom of a TV screen

caption sheet (cap sheet)   **1** [television] a list of scenes; also called *dope sheet*   **2** [book publishing] a list of captions for a series of illustrations

caption title   the main or "head title" of a book   It appears at the beginning of the first page.

captive   imprisoned, confined, restrained, or controlled

captive audience   a group that is obliged to be present or to be exposed to something

captive market   customers who are obliged to buy a certain product or service, such as when there is only one source of supply or only one source that is convenient   Examples are shops in an airport terminal or resort hotel.

captive products   items made by a vertically integrated company, such as a company that owns or controls its suppliers and retail outlets

captive rotary   a set of outdoor advertising locations used by one advertiser

capture ratio   the ability of a radio or TV receiver to select the stronger of two signals at or near the same frequency

CAR   *computer-assisted retrieval*

carbon   **1** a nonmetallic chemical element in all organic (living) substances and in many nonorganic substances, particularly coal and charcoal   **2** a copy made with carbon paper

carbon arc   a high-intensity light, used in motion-picture photography and projection; also called *arc*

carbon black   an ink pigment consisting mainly of carbon

carbon copy (cc or c.c.)   a notation at the bottom of a letter (or other written material) indicating that one or more copies (perhaps made using carbon paper) have been circulated, generally followed by a colon and the name(s) of the recipient(s) of the copies

carbon microphone   one of the earliest microphones, invented by Thomas Alva Edison (1847–1931) It consists of a conductive diaphragm that moves in response to sound pressure and then makes contact with small carbon granules in a metal cup. Carbon microphones are still used in telephones.

carbon paper   a sheet of thin paper with carbon or other material (black, navy blue, or another dark color) on one side, for writing or typing copies along with the original Carbon paper produces an exact copy on paper underneath it of anything impressed on it. Nowadays, *carbonless* paper is frequently used for this purpose.

carbon tetrachloride   a colorless liquid used as a solvent for printing ink

carbro   a continuous-type photographic color print made from separate negatives: magenta, yellow, and cyan

car card   an advertisement mounted inside or outside a bus, train, or other public transportation vehicle Inside cards generally are 11 inches high and come in standard lengths, such as 28, 42, and 56 inches.

card   **1** [advertising] a small advertisement (similar to a business card) **2** a piece of cardboard or other small, flat, relatively stiff paper, such as a business card, calling card, display card, greeting card, identification card, or postcard **3** a program such as one of a sports event, especially boxing **4** to list on a card or insert in a program or catalog (such as a card catalog in a library) **5** [computers] a rectangular piece of stiff paper, generally 7 × 3 inches, that contains information It can be a punched card with a pattern of holes in a BINARY FORMAT. The holes represent data encoded according to a *punched card code*. Nowadays FLOPPY DISKS have generally replaced punched cards, whose use requires punch machines, card readers, and other equipment.

cardboard engineer   [graphic arts] slang for a person who designs display and packaging materials (which generally are made of cardboard)

card catalog   [library science] a collection of cards arranged alphabetically in boxes or drawers, each containing information about one item in the library's collection, including the location of the item in the library

card deck   [direct marketing] a collection of advertisements, usually printed as business reply postcards, sent as a package to potential customers

card font   the smallest complete set of a typeface in one size

cardinal number   a number, such as one, two, or three, used in counting or to indicate quantity; not the same as an *ordinal number* (first, second, third), which is used to indicate order

carding   the insertion of small amounts of additional space between lines of type In metal typesetting, carding, or *carding out*, was sometimes accomplished by inserting strips of cardboard between the lines and was often done to align adjacent columns or pages.

cardioid   referring to a heart-shaped pickup pattern of a microphone A *cardioid microphone* is more responsive to dialogue and other foreground sound than to background noise.

card jacket   [library science] a clear cover slipped over a catalog card to indicate such information is not available, on order, or closed reserve; that is, information about the book's status in the library rather than about the book itself

card page or **card plate**   [publishing] a page opposite the title page of a book on which is a list of books by the same author or from the same publisher; also called *book card*

card pocket   [library science] a flat pouch or envelope affixed inside the front or back cover of a book or other item to hold the *charge card* (the card identifying the item); not the same as *card jacket*

card rate   the official, stated cost of advertising, as printed on a *rate card*; the full charge, without any special discounts

card service   a publication that provides catalog cards, such as for periodicals, for use by libraries and updates them

card-stacking   the contriving or prearrangement of circumstances, usually covert and improper, such as the selective omission of details in an advertising or other campaign; also called *stacking the cards* or *stacking the deck*

care of (c.o. or **c/o)**   an expression used in addresses if mail is to be received on behalf of another person or organization

caret   a sign ($\wedge$) placed below a line indicating an omission or the position where something is to be inserted; from the Latin *carero*, meaning "there is wanting or lacking" An inverted caret ($\vee$) is used to insert an apostrophe, quotation, or superscript letter or figure, with the mark, letter, or number written within the caret.

caricature   **1** a drawing or other illustration in which features or characteristics of a person, style, etc. are deliberately exaggerated or satirized to humorous effect Prominent *caricaturists* include Honoré Daumier (1809–79), a French artist, and Al Hirschfeld (b. 1903), whose theatrical drawings have appeared for several decades in *The New York Times*. **2** a written humorous exaggeration or imitation

carload lot [printing] the minimum amount of paper required for railroad freight-car shipment at the *carload rate* (generally 36,000 or 40,000 pounds), a reduced price

carnival **1** a traveling commercial entertainment with sideshows, amusement rides, and games, performed and operated by *carnival people*. **2** an organized program of festivities and contests, such as a winter sports carnival **3** a period of revelry, such as that before Lent

carny, carney, or **carnie** slang for *carnival* or a person who works in a carnival

Carolingian pertaining to the area of Europe now known as France *Carolingian characters*, particularly representations of hands and other reference and index signs, were used in French manuscripts from the 8th to the 11th centuries.

carp [theater] slang for a carpenter

car pass a windshield sticker or other identification for a vehicle giving it access to a film studio or other restricted area; also called a *drive-on pass*

carpenter [film, television] a person who builds sets, flats, furniture, props, camera tracks, and other items (generally wooden) The supervisor is called a *chief carpenter* or *master carpenter*. In a film studio, carpenters work in a *carpenter shop* or *carpenter workshop*.

carpenter's scene [theater] a short scene performed in front of the curtain while the main area of the stage behind the curtain is being readied by the stagehands (carpenters) for the next scene; also called *in one*

carpet cut a slot in a stage in which a carpet or other floor covering is secured

carriage return (CR) an operation, key, device, or code that produces the end of a typewritten line and the start of the next line, such as one in a typewriter with a movable carriage; also called *carriage reset*.

carriage trade affluent or upscale customers The origin is from the days of horse-drawn carriages.

carrier a mechanism by which something is conveyed or conducted A broadcasting station is a carrier of electromagnetic waves (carrier signals or waves) operating on an assigned *carrier frequency*.

carry forward [printing] an instruction to the printer to transfer material to the next column or page

carry-out a customer who takes a purchase instead of having it sent, in a *take-transaction* as opposed to a *send transaction*

carryover a portion of an article or other text carried over from one column or page to another (the *breakover*) or from one day to another (*overset*) A *carry-over line* is any line except the first.

cart short form of CARTRIDGE, a case containing magnetic tape A *cart machine* is a tape-cartridge playback machine, used with a stack of perhaps a dozen cartridges, mostly to store and broadcast commercials and public service announcements on radio stations. In radio, a *cart directory* is a listing of cartridges in a rack or other storage, containing information about the cartridge number, title, artist, and running time.

carte French for *card* English terms include *carte blanche* ("white card"), or full authority; *carte du jour* (a menu), and *a la carte* (referring to items separately priced on a menu). Public relations firms and others sometimes ask clients to choose a la carte, that is, to select from among several suggested projects.

carte de visite a small-sized photograph of a person, printed on a card (about $2\frac{1}{2} \times 3\frac{1}{2}$ inches) and commonly used in the late 19th and early 20th centuries as a calling card; from the French, meaning "card of a visit" The plural is *cartes de visite*.

Carterfone decision a major ruling given in 1968 by the Federal Communications Commission that permits the connection of non-telephone company equipment to the public telephone network This decision, which spawned the telephone interconnect business, concerned an acoustically coupled device that connected a two-way mobile system to the telephone network. The device was invented by Thomas Carter (b. 1923) of Dallas, and called the Carterfone (though many people assume the decision was named after former U.S. President Jimmy Carter).

cartography the art or technique of making maps or charts A *cartogram* is a map with statistical or other data arranged geographically. A *cartographer* is a mapmaker.

cartoon **1** a humorous or satirical drawing, usually published alone or with a brief caption, as on an editorial page of a newspaper (an *editorial cartoon*) or in newspaper comic strips These are generally one panel (a series of drawings in one line) but can be two or more panels. **2** (less common) a preliminary sketch, not necessarily humorous **3** See CARTOON SHORT. The word was originally derived from the Italian *cartone*, the heavy paper on which drawings were made in preparation for murals, tapestries, or other works of art.

cartoonist an artist who draws cartoons

cartoon short a motion picture consisting of animated drawings of a humorous nature, generally around 10 minutes in length; also called *animated cartoon* or *cartoon*

cartouch or **cartouche** an ornamental border, scroll-like flourish, or other decorative element, generally an oval used on a package to draw attention to a sovereign's name or some other historical allusion, such as the name of a firm's founder; pronounced car-TOOSH

cartridge 1 a small unit of equipment or a case inserted into a larger unit, such as a case containing photographic film (used for easy loading in a *cartridge camera*) or reeled magnetic tape (in a *cartridge* or *cassette recorder*/player) 2 a replaceable unit in the pickup of an electric phonograph, containing the stylus or needle 3 [radio] a prerecorded magnetic tape containing commercials and public service announcements for broadcasts, also called *broadcast cartridge* or *commercial cartridge*, for use at radio stations After one item is broadcast, the cartridge usually moves automatically to the beginning of the next item on the tape. When the entire tape has been played, it recycles to the beginning.

cartridge paper an inexpensive, coarse drawing paper used in England It was originally used in the making of gun cartridges.

cart wrap a printed advertising message, generally on paper, affixed to a shopping cart

carve out to excerpt

cascade 1 to fall or drop in a cascade 2 to circulate, as to distribute informational materials

case (c.) 1 [book production] the covers of a hardbound book; *casing in*, the final process in bookbinding, is putting the covers on 2 [printing] a tray with compartments for a font of type 3 an example (as described in a *case history*) 4 any container (*shipping case, display case*) A manufacturer may provide a *case allowance* or discount related to the number of cases purchased. Merchandise priced by the case, rather than by the individual items within the case, is sold by the *case lot*. The number of units in the case is the *case pack*. A retailer may accept delivery by the *case-count method*, which refers to the number of cases on the invoice instead of an actual count of the cases delivered. 5 [mail] a piece of equipment containing separations (*pigeonholes*), used in post offices to sort mail 6 the syntactic relationship of a word in relation to other words in a sentence 7 a legal action or suit 8 a set of arguments or circumstances; a situation

CASE Council for the Advancement and Support of Education

casebook a publication used for reference (such as a law casebook) or teaching

case-bound [book publishing] referring to a book with a stiff cover that has been made separately The bound pages are inserted and affixed to the case.

case divider a strip of cardboard or other material that fits in a food freezer or another type of retail case to separate items It may contain product information or an advertising message.

case fraction a common fraction, such as $\frac{1}{2}$, that exists as a single character in a printing case; also called a *piece fraction*, differentiated from a *shilling fraction*, which has to be set specially

case history a report about an individual, event, company, or organization, used as an article or report, as in an advertising or public relations campaign; also called *case study*

casein a white protein found in milk and cheese It is used in printing ink and other substances, and sometimes in the making of printing plates (*casein process*).

case strip an identification or promotional message on a small piece of paper or other material that fits into the molding or price rail of a retail shelf, as in a supermarket; more commonly called a *shelf strip*

case wraparound a banner or other promotional material affixed to the sides of a case of merchandise, as in a supermarket

cash before delivery (CBD or **c.b.d.)** prepayment

cash discount a price reduction for prompt payment, generally 2 percent if paid within 10 days of invoicing Many newspapers provide this discount to advertisers; it is less common in other media.

cash on receipt (COR) payment for merchandise when it is delivered

cash option CASH RIDER

cash register display a unit with merchandise mounted on or near the cash register in a supermarket or other store, used for cigarettes and other items in order to stimulate impulse buying

cash rider [direct marketing] a technique used in direct-response marketing, in which an order form provides for delayed payment but a postscript, or rider, on the order form offers the option of sending full cash payment with order, usually with some saving over the credit price as an incentive; also called *cash option* or *cash up*

cash-send a retail purchase that is paid for in cash and delivered to the customer, as distinguished from a *cash-take* or *cash-and-carry* transaction, in which the customer carries out the purchase

cash up   CASH RIDER

cash with order (CWO)   payment in advance of a delivery

casing in   putting covers around a book, the final process in bookbinding

Caslon   a classic roman typeface, characterized by light, open strokes, designed by William Caslon (1692–1766) of England in the early 18th century

CASRO   COUNCIL OF AMERICAN SURVEY RESEARCH ORGANIZATIONS

Cassandra   a computerized system of analyzing TV programs, part of the A.C. NIELSEN CO. since 1980   The data includes demographics for specific programs and comparison with lead-in (preceding) and lead-out (subsequent) programs and with other programs.

cassette   1 a small box, a CARTRIDGE   In phototypesetting, a *supply cassette* holds unexposed material and a *takeup cassette* receives the exposed material.   2 specifically, a case containing unlooped magnetic tape for use in an audio- or videocassette recorder or player   A *movie cassette* has a tape that is the equivalent of a 12-inch single record.

Cassingle   a prerecorded audiocassette containing only one musical selection   The word is a trademark of IRS Records (International Records Syndicate, Inc. of Hollywood, CA) and is a combination of *cassette* and *single*.

cast   1 [film, television, theater] the entire group of performers in a production   2 to hold auditions to fill roles in a production   3 to appoint a performer to play a role   4 [printing] to calculate the amount of space that a given amount of manuscript copy will occupy when printed, or, conversely, the amount of manuscript copy required to fill a specific area of printed matter; also called *casting off*, *castoff*, *cast off*, or *fit*   To *cast up* is to measure a body of type so as to determine the space required to accommodate it and the typesetting charge; this is also called *character casting*. In *casting up*, spaces and punctuation are counted as one character each.

cast-coated paper   any high-gloss enamel-finish paper, dried under pressure against a polished cylinder   An example is KromeKote, made by Champion International Corp. of Stamford, CT.

cast commercial   a broadcast advertisement featuring the performers in the show

caster   short form of *broadcaster*, used to form compounds such as *newscaster*

casting couch   a couch or similar piece of furniture in the office of an agent, producer, or other man in a position to boost an actor's or actress's career   In the era of the big studios in Hollywood, before about 1955, starlets who granted horizontal favors on or near such couches were sometimes cast in parts that launched their careers vertically.

casting director   the person who selects the performers in a film or TV production   It is a staff position at a studio, production company, or casting agency, reporting to the producer and/or director.

casting file   a record of performers, generally cross-indexed with regard to talent, characteristics, and experience

castoff or **cast off**   a calculation of the amount of space a given body of manuscript copy will occupy when printed; see also CAST

casual publication   a periodical published irregularly or occasionally

cat.   CATALOG

CATA   Community Antenna Television Association

catachresis   an incorrect use of a word or words, particularly a strained metaphor or figure of speech

catalog or **catalogue (cat.)**   1 a list arranged systematically, often with descriptions of the items listed (such as a *card catalog* in a library)   2 a publication containing such a list (as of as the products of a manufacturer)   A company that sells its products from a catalog is a *catalog company*, *cataloger*, or *catalog house*. The catalog can be sent by mail (a *direct mail catalog*), by itself, or in a *catalog envelope* at a *catalog rate* (a special fourth-class mailing rate), or it can be purchased by customers in a retail store (a *catalog showroom* or *catalog warehouse*). A *catalog saver* is a scaled-down version (perhaps four to eight pages) of a full catalog, often used as a supplement or insert in a publication. A *deep catalog store* is a retailer of records, books, or other goods that stocks most of the items in the catalogs of major manufacturers. A *library catalog card* in a filing cabinet (*card catalog case*) has been prepared by a *cataloger* or *catalog librarian* to include the *catalog code* describing the cataloged materials.   3 to record or compile a complete, extensive list

catalog agency   a company, particularly a magazine subscription agency, that sells via a catalog

Cataloging in Publication (CIP)   a procedure by which the Library of Congress (LC) in Washington, DC, issues a reference number to a publisher for a book prior to its actual printing   This is the number by which the book will be found in the Library of Congress catalog. If it were not for this procedure, the first printing of a book would lack an LC catalog card number.

catalog price [advertising, marketing] the price to the supplier, not the customer

catch flies [theater] to distract attention from the primary performer by facial or body movement, as with pretending to catch a fly

catching up [printing] a condition of excessive ink in the mixture of ink and water, with the result that the non-image area takes on ink; also called *dry-up* or *scumming*

catch letters a CATCHWORD, or part of a word, placed at the top of a page or column

catchlight [photography] a tiny area that reflects light, such as a section of an eyeglass or the white part of the eyeball; also called a *glint* or *kick* A lamp placed near a camera to produce a similar glint also is called a *catchlight* or *eye light.*

catch line a ruled line between a photo (a *cut*) and its caption (*cutline*), commonly used in newspapers

catchline an identifying mark, guide, or label on an article or other written matter, generally a word or phrase that appears atop each page of typed copy; also called *guideline, slug,* or *slugline* It is not retained in the final printing.

catch-penny article a lure, such as a product sold as a LOSS LEADER or a story in a newspaper with a headline or beginning that attracts attention; from the 19th-century days of the PENNY PRESS

catch phrase a slogan, or often-repeated word or words, originally used to *catch* or attract attention

catch stitch [book production] a stitch used in binding a book to secure each section of pages to the preceding one at the top and bottom; also called *chain stitch* or *kettle stitch*

catchword 1 an often-repeated word 2 a key word; the first word of a page or column, or another word, used as a guide to indicate the contents of that section Catchwords were used for the first time about 1469 in a book about ancient Rome published in Venice, Italy; they were also called *custodes.* 3 [newspapers] the first word of a page printed at the bottom of the preceding page, used for articles that jump or are continued

catchword entry a title in a bibliography, catalog, index, or other listing, listed under its key word; also called *catch title* or *catchword title*

catchy attractive or easily remembered It's a *catchy* word, though, because it also means tricky or deceptive.

category [marketing] a class of products or services that are directed to fill the same consumer need

category development index (CDI) [marketing] the ratio of the percentage of sales of a category of product in a specific market to its percentage of sales in the general population A market where sales are above average would show a CDI greater than 100; a CDI lower than 100 would indicate a weak market.

category publishing the production of books of specific types, such as self-help, sports, romance, or mystery; also called *genre publishing*

caterer [film, television] a person responsible for food service to cast and crews, particularly at remote locations Generally it is an outside company (*catering company*) and operates *catering trucks* and other equipment.

cathedral style a type of 19th-century bookbinding with Gothic architectural motifs on the cloth or leather covers

cathode 1 in an electrolytic cell, the negative electrode from which current flows 2 in a vacuum tube, the negatively charged electron emitter *Cathode rays* are streams of emitted electrons that produce visible fluorescence when they strike certain chemical salts, as in a *cathode ray tube.*

cathode ray tube (CRT) a vacuum tube in which a hot cathode (negatively charged electrode) emits electron rays that are accelerated and focused on a fluorescent screen, such as the display screen of a word processor

cat's-eye a reflector glass, as on a road sign; also called a *reflector button*

cattle [printing] slang for an ink smudge on a printed page

cattle call an audition for minor roles, for which a large number of applicants is likely

CATV Community Antenna Television System; see CABLE TELEVISION

catwalk a narrow, elevated walkway or platform, also called *rigging* or *scaffolding* In theaters and studios, the *catwalk* is suspended overhead to provide access to lighting and other equipment. To see a catwalk in action, see the movie or play *The Phantom of the Opera.*

cause 1 anything producing an effect or result 2 an objective or movement that an individual or group is interested in and supports A *cause group* is an organization with a common interest or goal. *Cause marketing* is a promotional technique in which a company is linked with a nonprofit organization, a public service, or another *cause.*

caveat a caution or warning *Caveat emptor* is an axiom from the Latin meaning "let the buyer beware." Less common is *caveat venditor,* "let the seller beware."

cb coated back; see COATED-BACK PAPER

CB   CHAIN BREAK; CITIZENS' BAND

C-band   the range of audio frequencies from 3.5 to 6 gigahertz   C-band frequencies are assigned by the Federal Communications Commission to most domestic and international communications satellites and are used by most U.S. radio and TV stations. (Many stations also use the Ku-band.) *C-band* is not the same as CITIZENS' BAND (CB).

CBC   CANADIAN BROADCASTING CORPORATION

CBD   CASH BEFORE DELIVERY

CBN   CHRISTIAN BROADCASTING NETWORK

CBO   CONFIRMATION OF BROADCAST ORDER

CB print   a copy, or print, made by a process developed by the Charles Bruning Company, now the Browning Division of AM International, Inc., Itasca, IL

CBS   COLUMBIA BROADCASTING SYSTEM

cc   CARBON COPY; CHANGE COLUMN MEASURE; CHAPTERS; CHARACTER COUNT; collect call; cubic centimeter

c.c.   CARBON COPY

CC   CLOSED CAPTIONING; CONCLUSION; CONTEMPORARY CHRISTIAN

CCA   CONTROLLED CIRCULATION audit

CCC   one hundred call seconds, a unit of telephone call measurement   One *erlang* is 36 CCC, or one circuit occupied for one hour.

CCD   CHARGE-COUPLED DEVICE

CC filters   color-compensating devices (for red, blue, green, yellow, magenta, or cyan) used to modify color film during filming or processing

CCI   CAMPAIGN COMMUNICATIONS INSTITUTE

CCITT   COMITÉ CONSULTATIF INTERNATIONAL TÉLÉGRAPHE ET TÉLÉPHONE

CCS   COMMON CHANNEL SIGNALING

CCTA   CANADIAN CABLE TELEVISION ASSOCIATION

CCTV   CLOSED CIRCUIT TELEVISION

CCU   CAMERA CONTROL UNIT

c.d.   CASH DISCOUNT

CD   COMPACT DISK

CDA   COMPARATIVE DISTRIBUTION ANALYSIS

CDI   CATEGORY DEVELOPMENT INDEX

CDT   central daylight time

CDV   COMPACT DISC VIDEO

c.e.   COPY EDITOR

CEBA   *Communications Excellence to Black Audiences*

CED   CAPACITANCE ELECTRONIC DISK

CEDE   *Central Depository*

cedilla   a hooklike accent mark put under a *c* in some French words to indicate that it should be pronounced as an *s*, as *façade*

cel   a transparent plastic sheet on which a figure in an animation is drawn or painted, usually made of cellulose acetate   The term is derived from *celluloid* and is sometimes spelled *cell*. A *cel sandwich* is two or more *cels* layered together so that captions or other material can be superimposed.

celebrity   wide recognition, fame, renown; a famous or well-publicized person   The origin is the Latin *celeber* ("frequented"), which also is the origin of the verb *celebrate*.

cell   [market research] a small, homogeneous group within a larger sample; also called *sample cell*   **2** a group of linked individuals, several of which comprise a total sample   **3** a single image in a film or unit on a storyboard

cellar   [theater] the area under the stage, used for storage and access by performers to the stage via openings called TRAPS

cellosheen   cellophane   To cellosheen is to apply or affix cellophane.

cellular   **1** referring to an area or object like a cell   **2** referring to an item powered by a dry-cell battery or other cell   The *cellular* mobile radio telecommunications system uses *cellular telephones* in automobiles and elsewhere that are low-power transmitters in limited areas, or cells. *Cellular geographic franchises* (delimited by the Federal Communications Commission) are of two types: *wireline* (generally the local telephone company) and *non-wireline*. The Cellular Communications Industry Association and the Cellular Radio Communications Association are professional organizations based in Washington, DC.

celluloid   a flexible, transparent, flammable material (like cellulose), made from pyroxylin and camphor, used for various products, especially motion-picture film; originally *cellulose nitrate*, replaced by *cellulose acetate*   The term is sometimes used to refer to movies or the film industry. The original product was made and trademarked by Eastman Kodak, but the term is now used generically.

Celsius (C)   a scale of temperature, according to which the freezing point of water is 0°C and the boiling point is 100°C   It was invented by Anders Celsius (1701–44), a Swedish astronomer.

CEM   Certified Exposition Manager

cement splice   [film] in editing, the welding together of two pieces of film using a film adhesive that has been heated on a *splicing block*   The pieces are slightly overlapped and bonded together on the splicing block.

cen. or cent.   CENTER; central; century

census   a count of a population

center (C, cen., or cent.)   **1** middle, as in *stage center*   **2** a place of heavy population or interest (a metropolitan *civic, cultural,* or *financial center*) **3** to place in the middle, as with a word or headline **4** to concentrate or focus on

center dot or **centered dot**   a *bullet* or heavy full point used as an ornament or to set off items in a list   The dot is centered above the BASELINE.   **2** such a dot used as a multiplication sign; also called *center point*   This may not be heavier than other characters.

centered (C)   [publishing] indented equally from the left and right   A *centered head* is a headline with an equal amount of space on each side.

centering   a process in layout or typesetting of putting material in the middle (as of a page), with equal space on either side   A *centering rule* is a rule marked with measurements from the center to both edges. *Centering on display lines* is a typographic format in which the middle portion of a line is set in a different type size from the balance on either side. An example is a retail advertisement in which the price is set in a larger type than the product name and placed in the center.

centerline (C or **CL)**   **1** a ruled line on a sheet or negative to indicate the center of the trim margin, or for use in printing registration; also called *center mark*   **2** [printing] a line with alternating short and long dashes, especially one on technical drawings   **3** [theater] a real or imaginary line running through the center from front to back of a stage

center mark   CENTER LINE

center point   a *center dot* used as a multiplication sign

center spread   two facing pages in the exact middle of a publication, whose content generally omits the usual space (*gutter*) between the pages for added impact; also called *centerfold* or *natural spread*   Actually, the center spread can be in the middle of any *signature* (folded section of pages). The center-page spread in a newspaper or magazine also is called a *center truck*. In outdoor advertising, a center spread is two adjacent panels of an outdoor advertisement with coordinated copy or design.

center track   the narrow strip that is the audio band in the middle of double-perforation magnetic film

center up   an instruction to place an image in the middle of an area, such as a TV screen

cent mark   ¢, abbreviation for pennies, as in 69¢

Central Casting Corporation   an organization set up in 1926, operated by the Association of Motion Picture and Television Producers, to provide *extras* and *bit players*   The term *Central Casting* has become so well known that people refer to someone who is of a definite

character type, or *looks a part* (such as that of a cowboy), as *straight out of Central Casting.* The clearinghouse and payroll service now is operated by IDC Service of Burbank, CA.

Central Depository (CEDE)   a short form of *Depository Trust Company* (New York), a stock custody facility for stock-brokerage firms   The terms CEDE and *Non-CEDE* are used in financial relations.

central processing unit (CPU)   a part of a computer system consisting of the memory core and other main areas that interpret and execute instructions, as opposed to peripheral devices (printers, terminals) that transport the program and data into and out of the *CPU*   The *CPU* is also called the *host* or *brains* of the system.

Centrex   a telephone switching system that makes a customer's telephone system part of the central office of the telephone company   The equipment may be located on the customer's premises or at the central office. It provides direct dialing without going through a central switchboard.

Century   a commonly used serif typeface

Century lights   a line of theatrical lights used for a century in the theater and commonly used in film and TV   The Century Lighting Company was taken over and its products (no longer called *Century*) now are made by Strand Lighting of Compton (Los Angeles County), CA. Thousands of spotlights bearing the name *Century* are still used, and many people think that it's a generic name or that the company still exists.

Century stand   a three-legged portable metal stand that holds light reflectors or other devices, now made by Strand Lighting, Compton, CA, but originally made by the Century Lighting Company; also called *C-stand* or *C stand*

CEO   chief executive officer

CEO letter   a statement by the chief executive officer (*CEO*) to shareholders, at the beginning of a publicly owned company's annual or other report

ceremonial opening   [publishing] a large initial letter, generally ornate or with a flourish, at the beginning or within an article or chapter

Certificate of Mail   a postal-service receipt prepared by the mailer or window clerk to show evidence of mailing

Certified Association Executive (C.A.E.)   a designation of certification by the American Society of Association Executives, Washington, DC

Certified Exhibit Specialist (CES)   a professional in the exhibit industry   This is a designation of the International Exhibitors Association (Annandale, VA). A *Certified Exposition Manager*

(CEM) is a designation of the International Association of Exposition Managers (Alliance, OH).

certified mail first-class mail for which the sender is additionally provided with a receipt and a record of delivery Insurance coverage is provided for an additional charge.

CES CERTIFIED EXHIBIT SPECIALIST

cf CALF; CHANGE FONT; COATED front PAPER; COMPARE, an abbreviation used in dictionaries and reference books to indicate a cross-reference, from the Latin word *confer,* "to compare"

CF CUSTOMER FURNISHED

CFM or **cfm** confirm (international telex and wire-service abbreviation)

CG character-generated; CHARACTER GENERATOR

cgns bulletin (wire-service jargon)

c.g.o., CGO, or **C.G.O.** CAN GO OVER

ch, ch., CH, or **CH.** CHAIN; CHANNEL; CHAPTER; chief

CH CHANNEL

chad small dots or pieces of paper produced by punching holes in paper, tape, or data cards *Chadded* paper or tape has its chad, or punched-out dots of material, completely removed; *chadless* paper or tape is punched so that the chad is not entirely severed.

chafe to wear away by rubbing A *chafed book* has a worn cover.

chain 1 a connected series or group (three or more) of broadcasting stations, publications, stores, or other businesses under common ownership or otherwise linked *Chain authorization* is approval by the chain's headquarters for its individual managers to purchase an item, participate in a promotion, or undertake some other action. *Chain broadcasting* is the simultaneous airing of a program by the stations of the chain or network. 2 [computers] a set of operations performed in sequence or a set of data items linked in sequence A *chaining search* locates the next item in the sequence. A *chain list,* or *chained list,* has identifying pointers to locate the next item in the set.

chain break or **chainbreak (CB)** [broadcasting] a brief interruption within a program or between programs to identify the local station that is part of a chain or network *Chain breaks* can include one or more local commercials, often 20 seconds long. (These are sometimes called *CB* or *chain-break commercials.*) A *chain break* is more generally called a *station break.*

chain discount a series of discounts, each deducted from the previous amount For example, a chain discount of 10 percent, 5 percent, 5 percent is a discount of 40 percent off the manu-

facturer's list price plus 5 percent off of the discounted amount and 5 percent off that amount, so that the end discount is 45.85 percent off the list price.

chained book a publication attached to a shelf or table, such as a directory in a post office

chain letter a letter requesting the recipient to make and mail copies to others and sometimes to follow other instructions, such as to enclose money It is not the same as a letter sent by or to a *chain store,* nor is it *chain mail* (flexible armor). Chain letters have been banned by the postal authorities as a form of lottery. Some illegal chain letters are disguised as a pyramid plan, or a MULTILEVEL MARKETING PLAN. *Prayer chain letters* that promise good fortune are legal if they do not request an investment.

chain lines or **chain marks** thick *watermark* lines, usually about an inch apart, that run with the *grain* of LAID PAPER, produced by the *chain wires* twisted around *laid wires* in the DANDY ROLL of the papermaking machine

chain list or **chained list** [computers] a set of data with each item coded to locate the next item in the set

chain printer a computer-operated typewriter or impact printer that types at high speeds on continuous sheets of paper The type characters are joined to form a chain and then are printed when they are at the appropriate position in the print line, whereas in a BARREL PRINTER all of the characters are located on the surface of a rotating barrel.

chain procedure the standard method for constructing an alphabetical index, in which a complex or general subject is listed and then specific related terms are entered as subentries below it

chain stitch CATCH STITCH

chair easel a vertical display in a retail establishment that is held in place and stabilized by a protruding chairlike element

chair warmers [theater] an unresponsive audience

chalcography [printing] the art of engraving, as on copper or brass

chalk soft, compact limestone (calcium carbonate) or a piece of it It may be combined with silicon or other ingredients and is used for marking, drawing, or writing (on a *blackboard* or *chalkboard*); it can easily be erased. A *chalk talk* is a lecture supplemented with diagrams or other material chalked on a surface. In printing and painting, *chalking* is the powdering or rubbing off of ink or paint that results from too heavy a concentration of pigment and insufficient liquid.

chalk off [film, television, theater] to mark (with chalk, or more generally, tape) positions on the stage floor for use as reference by the performers *Chalking off* a scene is generally called *blocking* a scene.

challenge   a notation, by a copy editor or another reader, questioning the accuracy of a passage of text

chamois   a soft, yellowish-brown leather (made from the skin of a chamois, a small goatlike antelope), commonly used by artists as a cloth to wipe and clean pens and drawing instruments; pronounced SHAM-my   To *chamois down* is to dry a face, as in removing sweat from a performer.

chan.   CHANNEL

chance customer   a person who makes an unplanned visit to a store or other place of business

chancery italic   a 13th-century style of handwriting on which italic type designs were based   A chancery is a court or office of public records, such as the Roman Catholic diocesan office that writes and retains documents.

change bar   [publishing] a vertical rule in the margin adjacent to a passage of text, indicating that the passage has been revised; used in editions of textbooks subsequent to the first edition

change column measure (cc)   a typesetting command to alter the width of a column of type

change font (cf)   a typesetting instruction to change from one typeface to another

change leading (cl)   an instruction to alter the amount of space between typeset lines or characters

change order   a form to convey instructions about a printing job or other project in process

changeover or **change-over**   a transfer, conversion, or switch from one system or piece of equipment to another; in a movie theater, a transfer from one projector to another at the end of a reel   An imminent *changeover* is indicated by *cue marks* or *changeover cues* (circles in the upper right corner of the last frames of a reel).

change point size (cp)   a command instructing a typesetter to alter the dimensions of type, usually to a specified point measure, but not to alter the typeface

changes   [film, theater] the screenplay or script as it is revised during the rehearsal or actual production   The *change pages* often are color-coded and marked with the date they were composed. Generally the first set of *changes* is on yellow paper, the second is on pink, the third on blue, the fourth on green, and the fifth on yellow. Subsequent revisions may be accompanied by aspirin! The changed pages are also called *rewrites*.

changing bag   a lightproof black bag with sleeves, for the loading and unloading of 35mm film magazines in daylight   This procedure is sometimes necessary when a camera jams.

channel (CH, ch, or **Ch.)**   **1** a means of passage   **2** the path followed by signals, a unit running the entire length of a record, reel, or film   **3** [broadcasting] a frequency band assigned to a radio or TV station   Radio *channel* names generally are referred to with the word *station* followed by the call letters, particularly with AM stations. FM stations typically use the frequency number as identification. TV stations are mostly referred to by their channel numbers.   **4** [marketing] the route or passage through which items move from producer to consumer   *Channel control* is the process by which a product is moved from source to user (*distributed*) efficiently, through *distribution channels* or *trade channels*. *Channel fit* is the degree to which a product can be distributed efficiently.   **5** [music] a contrasting section of a song, a term used by jazz musicians; more commonly called BRIDGE or RELEASE   **6** to direct into or through a channel

Channel America   a programming service, based in New York, to low-power TV stations   The company's full name is Channel America Lptv Network Inc.

channel capacity   the number of channels available to subscribers of a cable TV service

channel letters   [advertising] any metal letters with recessed surfaces to accommodate bulbs or luminous tubing, for use in outdoor advertising

channel 1   the 44–50-megacycle spectrum, which the Federal Communications Commission assigned to land-mobile and two-way radio service in 1948   Hence VHF TV station channels start with channel 2.

channel shift   [printing] the crossing from one row to another in a micrographic or other reproduction system; also called *traverse*

channel strip   a piece of extruded molding covering the front edge of a retail display shelf, for indicating price, unit cost, or other information

chap.   CHAPTER

chapbook   a cheap, popular book sold through the early 20th century by *chapmen* (peddlers)   *Chapbooks* were the precursors of today's paperbacks.

chapel   a local branch of a printers' union

chapter (c.)   **1** a main division of a book; plural abbreviated *cc*   **2** a division within a larger group

chapter display   the type above the beginning of the text of a chapter in a publication

character 1 any one of the individual letters, numerals, punctuation marks, or symbols that together constitute the complete *font* (assortment) of a type style A *regular character* is a standard typeface set in the conventional manner; an *alternative character* is a modified typeface (perhaps with an added serif or other adaptation) or a character set in an unconventional manner, such as above or below the baseline. A *base character* is the character itself, under, over, or adjacent to which an accent mark may be placed. An *additional character* is a punctuation mark or other character not in the regular alphabet. A *quaint character* is a ligature (two or three consecutive characters designated as a single character). In OPTICAL CHARACTER RECOGNITION and computerized character placement, a character is placed within a rectangle called a *character box* (outlined by a *character boundary*). 2 the qualities or features that distinguish a person or group 3 a person as portrayed in a play, film, novel, or other work of art A *character actor* or *character actress* can play many roles, or characters, with varying traits, as distinguished from a *character part*, which calls for dialects or other distinguishing features. A *round character* is a fully developed, major character, as distinguished from a *flat character*, which is a minor one. 4 a reputation An unusual or eccentric person often is called a *character*.

character casting the process of counting characters and spaces to determine size and typesetting charge; also called *casting off* It is generally done by line average rather than by counting every character.

character code [computers] a method of representing a letter, number, or other character by a unique value, the system according to which such values are determined, or the value itself Examples are the ASCII and EBCDIC codes.

character count (cc or **c.c.)** 1 a method of estimating type sizes and space by counting the number of characters in the text 2 the average number of characters per *pica* (12 *points* of type) *Characters per line* can be calculated by multiplying the number of characters per pica by the number of picas per line (the *line measure*). *Characters per page* is the number of characters per line multiplied by the number of lines per page.

character delete (char del) a computer command causing a character to be omitted

character generated referring to electronically produced text that appears on a video screen; also called *key*, *chroma key*, *title*, or *font*

character generation [computers] the production of characters through a series of dots and line strokes, as on the face of a CATHODE RAY TUBE, instead of mechanically by means of metal type

character generator (CG) [computers] a unit that converts the coded representation of a letter, number, or other character into its actual shape

character key the control to process one character at a time

character master an original from which a typeset character is produced

character matrix an array of dots that forms a character

character memory an electronic or mechanical *buffer* area; a memory in which characters are stored, for example, while previously generated characters are being printed or otherwise processed

character pitch the number of characters per inch on a fixed-space or standard typewriter A *pica typewriter* types 10 characters per inch (abbreviated *cpi*), or *10 pitch*; an *elite typewriter* composes 12 *cpi*, or *12 pitch*.

character printer or **serial printer** a word processor or typewriter that prints one character at a time, as distinguished from a *line printer*, which prints a whole line of type at a time

character set the collection of characters available in a specific font or type style; also called *character repertoire* or *repertoire*

character-spacing reference line a vertical line that evaluates the spacing between characters, such as by equally dividing the distance between the sides of adjacent characters

characters per minute (c.p.m.) a measure of typing or typesetting speed Speed can also be expressed as *c.p.h.* (characters per hour) and *c.p.s.* (characters per second).

character style the distinguishing characteristics of a typeface

character type a classification of personality or traits Some *character types* are *tradition-directed* (conformist), *inner-directed* (reflecting parental and other early influences), and *other-directed* (influenced by contemporaries and media).

charcoal 1 a porous, amorphous form of carbon 2 a pencil made of this substance; also called *charcoal stick* 3 a drawing made with a black (carbon) porous wood material 4 a very dark gray or brown

char del short form of CHARACTER DELETE

charge [library science] a record of the loan of an item It is indicated on a *charge card*, which is either kept inside the book (a *book card*) or other item or filled out by the borrower. The complete record of charged items is maintained in the *charging file* (also called *circulation file*, *circulation record*, or *loan record*) by means of a *charging system* or *loan system*, using a mechanical or electric *charging machine*.

charge-coupled device (CCD)   a solid-state image sensor, very small, with a small silicon chip; also called *charge couple device* or *image sensor*   It is used in video cameras and in computer memories in which an image is converted into a sequence of electrical impulses that are then registered on a magnetic disk. In facsimile equipment, a charged-couple device is an array of sensors used in the scanning process to measure the black and white images of a document.

chargehand   a supervisor, such as a *chargehand painter*, the British term for a person in charge of the scenery-painting crew in a film or other production

charging desk   See CIRCULATION DEPARTMENT.

charity overlay   [advertising] a promotion such as a cents-off coupon, for which the advertiser makes a contribution (an *overlay*) to a charity or public-service organization

Charlie   an actor with a mustache, named after Charlie Chaplin (1889–1977)

Charlotte Street   nickname of Saatchi & Saatchi Advertising International, located at 80 Charlotte Street, London

chart   **1** a group of facts about something   Forms of charts include *bar*, *column*, *curve*, *pie*, and *surface chart*.   **2** a list that ranks best-selling books, movies, or records, computed regularly by a trade publication (such as *Billboard*); also used as a verb, as in a record that *charts*   In the trade, the term is usually used in the plural, as in *number one on the charts*, *moving up on the charts*, or *a bullet* (special indication) *on the chart*. A *two-scale chart* is a column chart in which two values are compared. Musicians sometimes refer to sheets of arrangements (of musical compositions) as charts.

charter issue   the first issue of a periodical, with its declaration of intent   A *charter subscriber* or *charter advertiser*, who starts with the first issue, generally is given a special discount.

charting   the process of making a chart, map, plan, or schedule   In outdoor advertising, *charting the showing* is the process of selecting poster-panel locations in a market.

chartist   an artist who produces charts

Chartpak   a trademarked line of pre-printed, pressure-sensitive adhesive-back tapes, made by Chartpak, of Leeds, MA

chart tape   an adhesive-backed plastic tape commonly used by artists on charts, signs, and displays   It is available in various widths, patterns, and colors, on a dispenser (similar to a cellophane-tape dispenser).

chase   **1** a pursuit   A *chase film* has a continuing pursuit, such as of a criminal, as the major plot. A *chase sequence* is the portion of a film or show in which a chase takes place.   **2** a rectangular frame (iron or steel) in which type or other printing matter is *locked up* (literally, closed), for use in making plates or for direct printing on a printing press   The term is probably derived from the French *chas*, "enclosure." A complete page of type locked in a chase is a *form*.

chased edges   the decorated edges of leaves of a book; also called *gauffered* or *goffered* edges

chaser   **1** a sequentially wired row of lamps that provides the illusion of movement (*chaser lights*)   **2** music accompanying the exit of a performer from a scene (*chaser music*), or after a performance as an audience leaves a theater   **3** an extra edition of a newspaper

chatting   [computers] communicating (*talking*) back and forth by electronic means, via telex, electronic mail, or other devices

cheap   inexpensive or of poor quality   A *cheap shot* is an unwarranted or unjust action.

cheat   the positioning of models or performers, not for the most realistic or dramatic effect, but to achieve an illusion or a better picture   The instruction to the performer may be *cheat it*, *cheat it out*, *cheat the look*, *cheat left* (or *right*, *up*, *down*, or *front*). A *cheat shot* is a picture or scene that simulates, such as one of a performer who is feigning riding in a car, jumping out a window, or some other action.

cheater   [typography] a typeface that is an imitation of a copyrighted typeface   A *cheater typeface* is generally different in several respects from a *true typeface*, though it often is used as an equivalent.

check (chk. or ck.)   an annotation in the margin of a passage of text, indicating that the content of the passage must be verified

check bit   [computers] a binary bit (*digit*) added to the data stream during verification to detect an error; also called *check digit*

checkbook journalism   the use of payment in order to obtain information from a source   This rarely used technique is quite controversial in that it raises questions of journalism ethics and impartiality. For example, the paid source may be inaccurate and motivated by the payment.

check copy   [printing] an unbound copy of a publication, to be inspected and approved by the printer and the customer prior to binding; also called *checking copy*

check digit   CHECK BIT

checker 1 [publishing] a researcher, as at a magazine, who checks to verify the accuracy of text; also called *factchecker* 2 a reference book, such as *Bacon's Publicity Checkers*, published by Bacon's Clipping Bureau, Chicago

checkerboard 1 a magazine layout in which quarter- or half-page advertisements are placed diagonally (such as one lower left, one upper right) on the same or facing pages with editorial material between them, so as to achieve maximum impact for the ads 2 a layout consisting of alternating squares, such as a group of equal-sized photos and captions or other boxes

checkerboard editing [film] a method of editing tape and assembling film whereby odd-numbered shots are placed on one machine (on the *A roll* or *A reel*) and even-numbered shots (on the *B roll* or *B reel*) on another machine; also called *checkerboarding* The assembled shots are joined on a printer, with invisible splices.

checkerboard programming [broadcasting] scheduling different programs in the same daily time period, as distinguished from *strip* or *across-the-board programming*, in which the same program is broadcast five, six, or seven days a week in the same time period

checking copy 1 [advertising] a publication or part of a publication sent to an advertiser to confirm that an advertisement did appear in it 2 [broadcasting] a verification that a commercial was aired 3 [publishing] CHECK COPY

check mark ✔, an expression of approval, of the presence of something, or signifying that someone has seen and registered the item checked

check-out chart a graphic representation, or chart, of the sequential steps in a process or system; also called a SPECIFICATION TREE

check-payment ordering system a procedure in which two copies of a signed blank check are sent accompanying an order The seller fills in the amount, deposits the original check, and sends the copy to the customer. This *cash-with-order* method is used to buy low-priced items for which the discount or exact price is not known by the customer. A statement limiting the estimated amount, such as *Not in excess of $100*, is generally written by the customer on the check.

checksum [computers] a summation check; the total (*sum*) of a group of data items (such as numerals) It is used to verify (check) that no digits have been changed since the previous summation, which would suggest that no errors have occurred.

cheesecake a photograph or work of art predicated on sexual appeal, originally of a woman showing her legs above the knee; also called *leg art* or *bust art* When using male models, it's called *jock art*. The originator of the word probably was a *New York Journal* photographer, James Kane, who in 1912 photographed an actress on the rail of an incoming steamship and compared her to a favorite New York sweet, cheesecake. *Cheesecakes* were formerly staples of press agents, particularly in Miami Beach, Las Vegas, and Hollywood.

Cheltenham a roman typeface characterized by upright strokes

chemical pulp [printing] in papermaking, wood or other fibers that are broken down with chemicals rather than mechanically

cherry picker [film, television] a mobile crane or wheel and ladder, with a long boom and work platform that holds an operator with camera and other equipment *Cherry picking* refers to various selection techniques, such as plucking signals from a satellite, or to taking the best items from a group, such as the best programs from a package or the best sales prospects.

cherry pie overtime pay

Cheshire a machine for affixing printed address labels The labels, called *Cheshire labels*, are printed in groups and then cut and applied with glue. Cheshire labels, which are cheaper than individual labels, perforated labels, and pressure-sensitive labels, are commonly used by mass mailers. They are made of *Cheshire paper*, which is generally 15- to 20-lb. white *offset paper*.

chestnut an old joke or phrase; a very familiar story, piece of music, or other work that is repeated too often

chest voice use of the diaphragm to push air over the vocal chords to produce loud sounds, a technique used by opera singers and BELTERS

chevron a type of cloth used for backdrops of exhibits

chew the scenery [theater] to overact An overly dramatic performer is called a *scenery chewer*.

chiaroscuro a technique of using light and dark areas, particularly to create a three-dimensional effect, called *modeling*; pronounced kee-AHR-a-SKOOR-o This Italian word, from the Latin *clarus* ("clear") and *obscurus* ("dark"), also refers to the print itself.

chiasmus a figure of speech in which the grammatical order of a phrase is reversed or inverted in the succeeding, related, clause or sentence An example is *She went to Paris; to New York went he.* Some of the memorable quotations of Churchill, Roosevelt, and Kennedy are *chiasmi*.

chicken coop [film] a rectangular light fixture covered by wire mesh, akin to a cage for chickens The most common contains six 1,000-watt lights and is used as an overhead light.

chilled type smudged or indistinct print The term originates from the Linotype machines that sometimes produced lead type at less than 680° Fahrenheit, which resulted in characters that did not retain their sharp edges. Too much wax on a negative or other errors sometimes produces the same smudging in typesetting that does not use metal type, and printers still call this chilled type.

chiller a shocking film or other work

Chilton a major publisher and market research company, located in Radnor, PA, owned by Capital Cities/ABC

chimes musical sounds produced by striking metal tubes with a hammer, used for radio-station identification (ID) preceding the call letters of the station or the name of the network, particularly the National Broadcasting Company (NBC), whose engineers referred to the ID as *the chimes* Ironically, the three musical notes used by NBC were GEC, the initials of General Electric Company, which acquired NBC in 1986.

chimney [publishing] a layout with headlines and/or photos of the same width stacked (hence the word *chimney*) so as to fill the page

china egg an individual who appears to be a good prospect but who does not become a customer

china girl [film] a model shown in a series of film frames, used as a color standard in film laboratories The woman may be Asian (hence the name) or American.

China paper a soft, thin paper made from bamboo bark, with a light-yellow or brownish tint, used for art reproductions

China pencil a grease pencil (thick pigment) commonly used to write instructions on film; also called *China marker* and *China-marking crayon* China pencils are bound with paper and the paper is unwound to expose the core.

Chinese referring to horizontal flaps on TV, film, or other lamps

Chinese blue a blue pigment, a high-quality variety of *Prussian blue*, commonly used in oil paintings

Chinese dolly [film] a backward movement of a camera on tracks that move to the side *Chinese* refers to this angle or slant.

Chinese ink a black ink commonly used for drawing, similar to India ink It is prepared in small sticks or cakes, which are mixed with a little water.

Chinese mirror a specially coated mirror that is reflective (as is a conventional mirror) when front-lighted and transparent when back-lighted; sometimes used in exhibits

Chinese red a red pigment, more commonly called *chrome red*

Chinese-style book an art or other special book, with doubly thick leaves intentionally left uncut and unprinted on the interior sides; also called *Japanese-style book*

Chinese white an intense opaque white pigment used for silhouetting photographs and in paintings

chip **1** a small piece **2** [computers] a thin square wafer or rectangular piece of silicon or other semiconducting material, an important constituent of a computer; also called *microchip* A chip contains thousands of units, or *memory cells*, each of which is capable of storing one bit. A *customer chip* is a chip designed for a specific function.

chipboard a coarse grade of cardboard, generally used as a stiffener in envelopes containing photos

chipchart a standard test chart consisting of two sets of horizontal gray scales, used to adjust a TV camera for black-and-white degrees of gray; also called *crossed gray scale* or *chip chart*

chisel-point pencil a holder with a piece of lead that has a flat, wedge-shaped point (like a chisel) that can be used to quickly draw wide or narrow lines over a large area, commonly used in rough layouts

chi-square a statistical method of comparing two or more variables, commonly used to determine whether a set of data is due to chance or not, for example, whether one group is significantly different from another group for reasons other than chance; also called *chi-square test* Chi is a Greek letter resembling an X, and chi-square is written X^2.

chk. CHECK

choke **1** [printing] a cutoff device, such as a two-sheet detector on a sheet-fed printing press that turns off the press when more than one sheet at a time is fed through the press **2** the reduction of thickness of the printing detail, the opposite of a *spread negative*, in which the image is thickened **3** to block up, clog, hinder, obstruct, or suppress

choke negative a photographic negative with the thickness of detail reduced

choker [film] a tight closeup, cutting off at the neck

chop to cut, such as to reduce the length of an article; *chop* generally refers to an abrupt, swift, or major reduction *Choppy prose* is rough, irregular, and jerky, with abrupt transitions.

chop-and-nest [printing] a technique in which one sheet is printed and then folded and cut to produce two items

chopper a right-angle (half a square) board laid over a photograph or artwork to cover (*mask*) the portion to be *cropped* (chopped off) Choppers are generally used as a pair and are extended so that they cover the opposite ends of the picture.

chopper fold a *cross-fold*, or right-angle fold, made after the first parallel fold and at right angles to it The *second chopper fold*, or *mail fold*, follows and is parallel to the *first chopper fold*.

chopsocky slang for a martial-arts movie

choral of, for, sung by, or recited by a choir or chorus, such as a *choral work* performed by a *choral group*

chorale 1 a hymn tune, or a choral or instrumental composition based on a hymn tune 2 a group of singers (a choir or chorus)

choreography 1 dancing, especially ballet; the arrangement or written notation of the movements of a dance; the art of creating dances A *choreographer choreographs* (creates or arranges) a work, generally a dance but sometimes a fight scene or other planned series of movements. Informally, to *choreograph* is to arrange a program, event, or other work artistically.

chorus 1 a group of dancers and/or singers, as in ancient Greek dramas, Elizabethan dramas, or modern musical shows 2 the part of a musical composition scored for such a group; the refrain (following the verse) of a song, the main tune, or, in jazz, a solo based on the main tune A *chorus boy* and *chorus girl* are members of the chorus in a musical

CHR CONTEMPORARY HIT RADIO

chrestomathy a collection of literary passages by one or more authors, used to study literature or a language

Christian Broadcasting Network (CBN) a television network, based in Virginia Beach, VA; a major source of *family programming*, transmitted via satellite to many cable systems

Christmas tree 1 [graphic arts] a layout with vertical elements aligned to the left or right of an actual or imaginary center line 2 a stand to which lighting fixtures are attached (sticking out and lit up like a Christmas tree), or a small vehicle on which lighting equipment is stacked

chroma 1 the composition of a color, its degree of intensity, the amount of black or white it contains, or more technically, that aspect by which a sample appears to differ from a gray of the same brightness or lightness 2 a boxed photo, art, or graphics, relevant to a news item, that appear on a TV screen next to the newscaster Sometimes the photo or art is shown behind the newscaster, projected by means of a rear projection or CHROMAKEY system.

Chromakey, Chroma-key, or **chroma key** an electronic process that alters the background scene without affecting the foreground, also called *color-separation overlay* (abbreviated CSO) In the *Chromakey system*, a saturated color (usually blue) forms a hole in the background picture so that a second video source (such as a camera) can fill this area.

chromatic 1 using or progressing by semitones, or using tones not in the key of a work 2 pertaining to color *Chromatic aberration* is color distortion produced because of the property of lenses that causes the various color in a beam of light to be focused at different points. *Chromatics* is the study of color.

chrome 1 slang for COLOR TRANSPARENCY 2 short for *chromium*, a metal used in printing It can be applied to a printing plate for protection and to use less ink. Bright-colored *chrome compounds* are used as ink pigments, particularly in order to apply a metallic finish, a process called *chroming*. Chrome pigments (lead chromate) include *chrome green, chrome orange, chrome yellow* (also called *Leipzig yellow* and *Paris yellow*), and *chrome red* (also called *Chinese red* and *Derby red*).

chrominance 1 an attribute of light 2 the portion of a TV signal that produces the sensation of color or hue, as distinguished from *luminance* (brightness) 3 the color of an object as measured quantitatively in terms of a reference color

chromo short for *chromolithograph* and a prefix meaning "color"; sometimes used as slang for a CHROME

chromolithograph a color lithograph, with each impression from the stone or metal plate a different color The *chromolithography* process was used in the 19th century and the prints were generally of poor quality. Accordingly, the abbreviation *chromo* became a slang word among artists for a cheap or gaudy picture.

chronogram a motto or inscription in which the capital letters express a date in Roman numerals

chrysography the art of writing in gold letters, as in medieval manuscripts *Chryso* means "golden" or "yellow."

chunk [market research] a portion of a population or area

chunk makeup [printing] a preliminary layout prepared by the typesetter

church paper stock used in bibles or other religious publications, usually called BIBLE PAPER

churn the turnover of subscribers to book or record clubs, cable TV, or other subscription operations

Chyron Corporation a major manufacturer (based in Melville, NY) of electronic image and character generators and TV graphics systems, particularly those commonly used by many TV stations and producers for lettering and graphics The systems are so common that the company name sometimes is used generically or as a verb (to *chyron* an identification). Popular Chyron systems include the *Scribe, Scribe Jr.,* and *Super Scribe.*

CIA cash in advance

Cibachrome a color print made directly from a color transparency, trademarked by the Swiss Ciba-Geigy Corporation, headquartered in the United States in Ardsley, NY

cicero [printing] a unit of horizontal measurement used in Europe; an alternative to the *point* system used in the United States A *cicero* is about 0.1776 inches, slightly larger than a *pica.*

CID COMPACT INDIUM DISCHARGE

CIF carriage, insurance and freight, a term on a printing price quotation or other document indicating that the price includes delivery

cigarette card a card packed with cigarettes in the United Kingdom, with photos of sports figures, ships, scenes, and other subjects, collected in a manner akin to U.S. baseball cards in bubble-gum packs

cinch a tight grip *Cinch marks* are scratches on the edges of a film resulting from too much tension on a tightly wound reel.

cinching the folding or buckling of tape, such as arises from the sudden stopping of a reel

cine or **ciné** the cinema A *cine camera* is a motion picture film camera. *Cine 8* film is motion-picture film that is 8mm wide.

CINE Council on International Nontheatrical Events

cinéaste 1 a person involved in motion-picture production, particularly a director or other creative person 2 a film enthusiast or devotee The original French word is a combination of *cinéma* and *enthusiaste.*

cinema 1 a movie theater 2 the movie industry; from the Greek *kinema*, "motion"

CinemaScope a trademarked wide-screen film system that employs a special lens in filming and projection (an *anamorphic lens system*); shortened to *Scope*; introduced in 1953 by the Twentieth Century-Fox Film Corporation of Hollywood, CA

cinema novo new cinema, a type of film that stresses social and political issues It was originated by Brazilian and other South American filmmakers in the 1960s.

cinema pur pure cinema, a type of film produced in France and Germany in the 1920s that used fast and slow motion, trick shots, and other cinematography techniques to create non-narrative visual effects; subsequently called *abstract film* or ABSOLUTE FILM

cinémathéque 1 a film archive 2 a film club or *art theater* The most famous archive is at the *Cinématheque Françqise* in Paris.

Cinématographe one of the first motion-picture cameras, developed in the 19th century by two French brothers, Auguste Lumiére (1862–1954) and Louis Lumiére (1864–1948) Louis Lumiére is sometimes called the father of the cinema.

cinematographer a motion-picture photographer, the head of the camera crew; also called *Director of Photography* (*D.P.*)

cinematography the art, science, and work of motion-picture photography

cinema verité a form of documentary film that stresses realism, from the French *verité*, "truth" A small, hand-held camera and unobtrusive techniques are used so as to record scenes under the most natural conditions possible.

cinemobile a very large, buslike vehicle for filming on location, containing dressing rooms and other facilities

cine orientation in microfilm, the positioning of the images perpendicular to the edge of the film, as they are on motion-picture film; as distinguished from *comic orientation*, in which the images are parallel to the edge of the film, as they are in a horizontal comic strip

cineplex a cinema complex, a building with several movie theaters

Cinerama a trademarked motion-picture process that produces a realistic effect via three-dimensional illusion developed by Fred Waller (1886–1954), chief of the special-effects department of Paramount Pictures Corporation, Hollywood, CA, and first shown at the New York World's Fair in 1939 In 1952, an improved system, using three projectors and three adjacent curved screens, was introduced.

CIP CATALOGING IN PUBLICATION

cipher 1 the symbol 0, zero 2 a system of secret writing based on a key or set of predetermined rules or symbols

cir. or **circ.** CIRCLE; CIRCULAR; CIRCULATION; circumference

circa (ca.) around (from the Latin), about; used before dates or other numerals to indicate approximation

circle 1 [theater] a tier of seats, such as the *dress circle* (encircling the orchestra; patrons of this section used to dress formally) 2 a group of people with common interests 3 a ring around a notation In photography and film, a circle often designates a selection. Circled numbers on a *contact sheet* or a *camera report* (a list of *takes*) indicate those that are to be printed. These are called *circled takes* or *OK takes*. In broadcasting, portions of a script that should not be read, such as cues and times, are circled. In copyediting, instructions to a typesetter and other matter not to be printed are encircled.

circled corrections [printing] corrections in a printer's proof that are charged to the author or customer

circle-in [film, television] an optical effect in which a picture diminishes and disappears as it is replaced by a second picture that grows in a circle from the center; the opposite of a *circle-out* It is also called *iris in* (whose opposite is *iris out*).

circle of illumination the area of an image that is seen through a camera lens Within this circle, the area that is the clearest is called the *circle of best definition*.

circle wipe [film, television] an optical effect in which an image first appears as a dot in the center and then grows to full size while covering (wiping out) the preceding scene

circline a circular fluorescent fixture, used in exhibits

circuit 1 a closed curve; the area enclosed by such a curve; the route of the curve, or the process of following such a route, such as a sales *circuit* 2 an association of theaters or teams 3 a closed path for electrical current 4 a configuration of connected components 5 a link between points

circuit board an insulated base on which *chips* and other components are mounted or printed to provide *circuitry* An *integrated circuit* contains many interconnected amplifying devices and circuit elements on a single chip of semiconductor material.

circuit edges [book production] flexible cover ends that bend over the body of a book; also called *divinity circuit*, since this type of binding is sometimes used for Bibles

circuit-switched digital capability (CSDC) [telecommunications] a technique that enables both a voice call and transmission of high-speed data to take place using the same connection

circular an advertising piece, circulated by mail (generally third class) or by hand; sometimes called *flyer*, *circ*, or *leaflet* (in the United Kingdom) *Circulars* are generally used for door-to-door distribution, in direct mail, or in sales pro-

motion. To *circularize* is to send a circular or to canvass for opinions or support.

circular file euphemism for a wastebasket A news release or other item sent to the circular file is thrown away.

circular screen [printing] a photographic screen, consisting of round pieces of optical glass that can be rotated to various angles (called the screen angle) to prevent the elements of a color halftone from appearing as dots

circulation 1 the distribution of a publication 2 the number of copies sold of a single edition of a publication, at a given time or as averaged over a period of time The word is generally used for periodicals. *Free circulation* refers to copies distributed free, as distinguished from *paid circulation*. 3 [broadcasting] the number of households tuned to a station a certain number of times within a specific period of time 4 in transit advertising, the number of riders (passengers) who observe a CARD during a specific period 5 in outdoor advertising, the number of potential viewers daily, generally computed at 1.75 persons per vehicle

Circulation Council a branch of the DIRECT MARKETING ASSOCIATION concerned primarily with the circulation of magazines

circulation department 1 the division of a newspaper or other publishing organization responsible for the distribution of individual copies, including *newsstand circulation* and *subscription* (mail) *circulation* 2 [library science] the loan department of a library, responsible for lending items to users, generally for use outside the premises Loans are processed at the *circulation desk* (also called *charging desk* or *discharging desk*).

circulation rate base the minimum number of copies guaranteed sold by a publication, the basis for determining the rate to advertisers

circulation waste those in an audience whom advertisers have paid to reach but who are not prospects because of demographics, unavailability of the product in the area, or other circumstances; more commonly called *waste circulation*

circumflex an accent mark used over vowels to indicate a specific sound, generally an inverted v (ˆ), but also – or ~.

circus makeup an unorthodox layout of a page or publication, containing irregular shapes, bold or heavy type, or other attention-getting effects, as if to emulate the frenzy of a circus

cit. CITATION; cited

citation (cit) a quotation, source, or confirmation To *cite* is to provide examples, to quote an authority or other source. A *citation index* or *citation file* is a list of sources or works that have been cited or from which the citations have been excerpted, a list of related sources cited in other works, or a list of works that were cited in later works and thus used to identify subsequent works that are related.

citizens' band (CB) frequencies assigned by the Federal Communications Commission for use by individuals such as those driving trucks or *ham* (amateur) radio operators (*CBers*), on dedicated *CB radio* equipment

citronella circuit a group of summer theaters, from the days when insect repellents, containing citronella, were used in tent theaters

city desk the local news department of a newspaper, also called *metropolitan desk* It is supervised by the *city editor* or *metropolitan editor*, a key position, and operates in a large area called the *city room*.

city edition originally, the edition of a daily newspaper circulated within the area in which it was published, as distinguished from the *national edition, mail edition*, and *state edition* Now, the circulation patterns have changed and the first edition—generally called the *city edition*—may be the edition mailed or sent by truck or plane to distant points, at the same time that it is sold locally. The subsequent edition is the *late city edition*.

city editor See CITY DESK.

City Grade Service the area closest to a TV transmitter, one of three areas of a TV station's coverage The middle area, which is further away from the transmitter, is called *A contour* and the peripheral area is called *B contour*.

city magazine a consumer publication whose subject matter revolves around its area, such as *New York, Washingtonian*, or *Los Angeles*; also called *citymag* or *regional magazine*

city zone circulation the circulation of a newspaper within the limits of the city in which it is published

CJR COLUMBIA JOURNALISM REVIEW

ck. CHECK

cl. carload; CHANGE LEADING; CLASS; classification; clause; CLEARANCE

c.l. carload

CL center left; CENTER LINE; left center; see AREA

cladding a layer of metal or alloy that is bonded to another metal; the welding or bonding process In fiber optics, the *cladding* is generally a glass material surrounding a glass core. The core is the center part that conducts light and the cladding prevents signal loss by reflecting light back into the core.

claim an assertion of the characteristics or benefits of a product or service

clambake **1** a party **2** a poor rehearsal, or an ineffective performance or program

clamper [television] an electronic circuit that sets the video level of a picture signal before the electron beam scans each line of the target area and also removes any hum or other low-frequency noise The process is called *clamping*.

clapboard [film] a slate board on which is written information about a scene to be filmed, such as the name of the director, the title of the film, the date, and the number of the *take* (shot); also called *clapper, clapper board, clapstick board, slate board*, or *take board* The *clapboard* is photographed at the beginning of each take. An *automatic clapper* or *automatic slate* automatically aligns the picture (with a flashing light) and sound (with a beep). The *clapper boy* operates the *clapboard*.

clapper CLAPBOARD

clapstick or **clap stick** [film] a device used at the start of a shot (*take*) to synchronize the audio to the picture by means of a clapping sound It is composed of two boards hinged together at one end and connected to the top or bottom of the *clapboard*. The clapper/loader operates the clapstick and loads the film. This position is also called *second assistant cameraman, second camera assistant, clapper and loader, clapper loader*, or *slateman*.

claptrap showy, insincere, empty talk or writing, intended to evoke, or trap, clapping or applause, or notice

claque a group of people paid by or on behalf of a performer to go to an opera or other performance and applaud that performer; a group of fawning followers or adulating admirers

Clarendon a class of typeface with bracketed serifs of the same weight as the main stroke It is named after Edward, first Earl of Clarendon (1609–74), an English historian and statesman.

Clarion Awards annual awards to women, presented by Women in Communications (located in Austin, TX)

Clarke orbit the circular orbit (22,000 miles above the earth's equator) in which *geosynchronous* satellites are placed; sometimes called the Clarke belt The satellites, sometimes called *Clarke-orbit satellites*, are used extensively for communications by radio and TV stations, telephone companies, and others. The concept was proposed in 1945 by the science-fiction writer Arthur C. Clarke (b. 1917), the author of the short story on which the movie *2001: A Space Odyssey* is based. (He also helped to write its screenplay.)

Clarke process [film] a system, developed in the 1950s by Charles G. Clarke (1899–1983), a director of photography at 20th Century-Fox, for filming live action through a *diapositive plate* This is a plate that has an image on part of it (such as clouds at the top) with the balance transparent so that the image on the plate and the live action appear together on the film.

claro obscuro 1 clear-obscure; also called CHIA-ROSCURO 2 a printing technique that uses several *blocks*, or engraving plates, successively to produce a balance between light and shade; also, the print made by this process

Clas CLASSICAL MUSIC

class (cl.) 1 a category, group, or division 2 a group of students studying together (in a class-room) or graduating together (as in *the class of 1989*) 3 excellence (as of style or appearance) 4 a division of broadcast time *Class A* time is the prime time period, or the period of maximum audience, such as 8:00–11:00 P.M. on TV. Advertising during *Class A* time is charged at the highest rate, followed by *B, C,* and *D.* In some cases, *Class A* time is further segmented, with the best as *AAA,* followed by *AA* and then *A.* (That's prime time, not shoe sizes.) 5 all items in a category of merchandise; also called *classification*

class. classic; classical; classification; classified; classify

Class A station an international classification of AM radio stations, corresponding to U.S. Class I

class book a book by or about members of an academic class, such as a high-school or college yearbook

Class B station an international classification of AM radio stations, corresponding to U.S. Classes II and III

Class C station an international classification of AM radio stations, corresponding to U.S. Class IV

classical traditional, as in classical music, which includes symphonic and other orchestral compositions, opera, and other music that is not folk, jazz, or popular music Radio stations with this format are called *classical stations.*

classification schedule [library science] a list of names or terms, symbolized by *class letters,* that identify the categories according to which a collection's holdings are grouped

classified advertisement (classified or **classified ad)** a brief, small-size advertisement in news-papers or periodicals, consisting wholly or mainly of text, set in single columns, and ar-ranged by product or service in a specific section (generally the back portion) of the publica-tion A *national classified ad* appears in the national edition of a newspaper (such as *The New York Times* or *The Wall Street Journal*),

which may also sell local *classified* space whose contents will appear only in local editions.

classified advertising manager (CAM) at a newspaper or other publication, a person in charge of selling classified advertising space

class magazine a publication for upscale read-ers, as opposed to a mass magazine, which has broader, or *mass,* audience appeal

class 1 office [telecommunications] a regional telephone toll center A *class 5 office* is a local central office.

Class I station a dominant AM radio station, operating on a CLEAR CHANNEL and generally with maximum power (50,000 watts) A *Class II station* is a secondary station on a clear chan-nel.

Class I time [television] preemptible time, as opposed to *Class II*

Class of Service a phrase used in the telephone industry and other fields to categorize the types and degrees of service features and facilities available

Class III station an AM radio station that oper-ates on a *regional channel* (not a *clear channel*), generally with a maximum power less than 5 kW A *Class IV station* operates on a local channel with a maximum power of 1 kW.

clay coating a layer of clay (firm, fine-grained earth) affixed to one or both sides of paper to improve the quality of the printing surface

Claymation a trademarked animation process using clay puppetlike characters, such as the dancing raisins in the California Raisin Adviso-ry Board television commercials, originated and produced by Will Vinton Productions Inc., a film producer in Portland, OR

clc or **c & lc** CAPITAL and lower case

clean 1 tidy, referring to something containing few errors, such as *clean copy* or a manuscript or printer's proof with few or no errors; not ob-scene (a *clean joke*); not ornate (*clean lines*); blank (a *clean sheet*) 2 [direct marketing] to re-move names or data no longer of value or out-dated, such as from a mailing list, to produce a *clean list* 3 [film] to remove unwanted noise from a soundtrack *Cleaning* a soundtrack can be done by wiping it between two pieces of soft cloth, a technique called *velveting sound* or *gloving sound.* 4 describing a theater or audi-torium with all seats sold, as in "the house went clean"

clean entrance 1 [film and theater] the move-ment of a performer from off-stage or off-camera into the action area during the action, as op-posed to the camera moving to the subject 2 a direction to a performer to enter a scene silently and without a shadow

clean exit the movement of a performer from the action area to the off-stage or off-camera area during a scene

clean up to make revisions, improve quality, or remove

clear 1 transparent 2 free from flaws 3 the release of a circuit, such as a telephone circuit, to return it to its idle position 4 in film developing, to remove unexposed and underdeveloped silver salts from a negative; the action performed by the *fixing bath* to remove milkiness 5 to erase, as with computer data for storage 6 [film] an instruction to a performer to move to a clear space, to appear unobstructed, as in *Clear yourself!* To *clear the frame* or *clear the set* is to vacate the set. A stage manager's or director's command for nonperformers to leave the area is *clear the stage, clear the set*, or simply *clear*. 7 to obtain permission (*clearance*) or to obtain time for a program, commercial, or event

clearance 1 the acquisition of a period of time to broadcast a commercial or a program on a station 2 the ability of a station to air an advertising or program schedule as ordered; also called *clearance time* A 75 *clearance* means that 75 percent of the stations that were offered a commercial or program accepted it. 3 the granting of permission, such as for use of a picture or other copyright material; or the notification that such permission has been given To *clear a number* is to obtain permission to present a musical performance of a copyright selection.

clear area a portion of text free of printing or other markings

clear-base film a colorless film coated with a photographic emulsion

clear-channel station an AM radio station authorized by the Federal Communications Commission (FCC) to dominate its frequency Such a station generally has the maximum power (50 kW) and is *protected* (has no other stations at its frequency) for a distance of up to 750 miles. Many clear-channel stations can be heard at greater distances on clear nights. *Clear channels* are specific frequencies to which the FCC has assigned a limited number of stations.

clear data any immediately readable material, not coded; also called *plaintext*

clear display the action of deleting all material from a visual monitor of a computer

cleat a piece of wood or metal, usually wedge-shaped, fastened to a surface to strengthen or stabilize it, or for attachment or other purposes Cleats are commonly used in the construction of scenery; a *brace cleat* braces or supports scenery and a *lash cleat* secures the

cord that ties or lashes together two pieces of scenery.

cleat sewing [book production] a mechanized version of hand-sewing in which *cleats*, or notches, are cut in the spine of a book and adhesive-coated thread is inserted in the notches; also called *cleat binding* or *cleat lacing*

cliché a trite idea or expression *Clicher* is French for "to stereotype," and a *cliché* was a STEREOTYPE printing plate.

click [film, recording] a measurement of musical tempo, akin to a metronome's beat; the number of frames for each musical beat, indicated by a series of clicking sounds on a *click track*

clicka an accent mark over a consonant, such as č; also called a *haček*

clicker a free admission pass to a theater or other place, from the use of a mechanical device to click off the number of admissions

client a customer; the company, organization, or person that employs an advertising, public relations, or other agency; the *account* or *sponsor*

client rough a layout presented to a client for preliminary comments and approval

cliffhanger a tight contest or tense situation of which the outcome is uncertain until the end The term originated in the era of movie serials in which each suspenseful episode or chapter ended with the hero or heroine dangling over a cliff or enmeshed in some other precarious situation.

climate the prevailing conditions or set of opinions

climate study a survey that measures opinions or attitudes

clinching tape slippage on a loosely wound spool; also called *windowing*; not the same as *embracing*

clinker an error, such as a misplaced musical note

Clio an advertising award, initially limited to radio and TV advertising but now broadened to include other categories (print, packaging, and specialty) The *Clio* statuettes are presented at an annual event by Clio Awards, Inc., a New York-based company, which conducts the project. Clio, the Greek muse of history, is associated with fame and glory.

clip 1 a segment of a film or tape A *news clip* (of about one minute) may be prepared by a publicist or other source for distribution to TV news stations. 2 short for CLIPPING 3 to cut, cut off, cut out, or trim

clip a cue [theater] to cut in on another performer's line before it is completed; also called *step on a line*

clip art previously existing drawings or other art that is cut out (from a *clip-art book*) and used in an article, advertisement, booklet, or other publication, as opposed to art especially commissioned for the purpose for which it is being used

clipboard a small board with a spring clip for clasping a writing pad or paper, designed to give a firm writing surface

clipped word a shortened word, such as *ad* for *advertisement* or *mike* for *microphone*

clipping **1** an article or item from a newspaper or other publication that is *clipped*, or cut out; the act of cutting such an item Often, this task is conducted by a group of professional readers, called *clippers*, at a *clipping bureau* or *clipping service*, and the item (a *clip*) is inserted in a *clipping book* or *clipping file*. In the United Kingdom and elsewhere, a clipping is referred to as a *cutting*. An electronic clipping service, such as NEXIS and other database research services, provides articles via computer. **2** [telecommunications] loss of a bit of information or speech at the beginning or end of a transmission **3** [computers] the removal of the parts of a display image that are outside of the display screen **4** a distortion of sound that occurs when a waveform reaches the limit of what the system can handle **5** [television] a technique of cutting off, or clipping, or an electronic circuit that removes the bottom level (*black clipping*) or top level (*white clipping*) of a video signal to eliminate control signals and other material

clip sheet **1** a collection of *clippings*, generally reproduced in quantity for promotional purposes **2** a collection of news releases and other items provided to newspaper editors, printed on one side to facilitate *clipping* or reprinting

clm. COLUMN

clock (c.) [radio] a wheel, divided into quarters, containing all the sequences to be broadcast in a 60-minute period A *global clock* is the overall format of the hour: the number of minutes of music, talk, news, commercials, and other sequences. A *hot clock* is the clock currently in use.

close conclusion, completion, end, as in the *closing shot*; to come or bring to a stop or conclusion It is better to *close* a sale (make or complete it) than to *close* a publication (terminate it).

closed assortment a collection of products packaged or stored such that they cannot be touched, sampled, or tried on by prospective customers

closed captioning (CC) a method of superimposing typed text (as of an audio track) over a television image, generally transmitted as a *crawl* across the bottom of the TV screen This is invisible on ordinary TV sets but is made visible by means of a decoder. It is extremely useful for the hearing-impaired and in dual-language programming. It is transmitted on line 21 of the VERTICAL BLANKING INTERVAL.

closed circuit referring to audio and/or video transmission for controlled reception, such as to theaters, hotels, meeting places for sports events, conventions, and other one-time transmissions Closed-circuit transmissions are also regularly sent to stations for their own personnel or for reviewers. Closed-circuit television (CCTV) is transmitted over cables to specific sites or broadcast in a scrambled format to sites that are provided with unscramblers.

closed display an assortment of merchandise in a locked or inaccessible display, as opposed, for example, to the open shelves of a supermarket

closed-door membership store a retail operation that requires customers to qualify on the basis of membership in a labor union, as a government employee, or as a member of a military family or other special group It may also require an initial or annual fee.

closed-end question a multiple-choice question, that is, one with a predetermined selection of possible answers, as opposed to *open-ended question*, such as an essay question Similarly, a *closed-end diary* limits the respondent to the printed questions or categories, whereas an *open-end diary* is not limited.

closed h an italic letter in which the shorter stroke curves inward toward the longer stroke

closed head [printing] the top of the SIGNATURE (section of folded pages), produced by a fold, so that when opened at the center the signature comprises one solid surface

closed joint [book production] a type of inside strip or hinge (*joint*) on which the cover boards are laced on tight against the spine; also called *tight joint* It is different from a free-swinging *open joint* or *French joint*.

close down [photography] to reduce the lens diaphragm opening by increasing the depth of field, giving a higher *f-stop number*

closed rehearsal a rehearsal to which visitors are not admitted, the opposite of an *open rehearsal* or *public rehearsal*

closed reserve [library science] a collection within a *closed stack* from which patrons may request items to be brought to them by staff members

closed set a studio stage to which visitors are not admitted

closed stack [library science] an area in a library not open to the general public; also called *closed access* or *closed shelves*   Its opposite is an *open stack*.

closed turn   a performer's movement away from the audience, the opposite of an *open turn*

Closed User Group (CUG)   a service on a database, videotex, or other electronic information system available only to preassigned users, such as lawyers, physicians, or other professional or affinity groups

close shot (CS)   a picture or scene taken with the camera near the subject; more commonly called *close-up* (CU)   A medium-close shot (MCS) is in between a close shot and a medium shot.

close space   1 [printing] a small, tight, or thin space   2 to reduce (tighten) or omit a space

closet drama   a play to be read rather than performed, perhaps written with that intention or, as with some ancient plays, because it is more effective or suitable as a text than staged

close up   to reduce space, as between words or characters, or to reduce leading between lines of type   In copyediting, a *close-up mark* (⌢) between characters indicates that they should be linked.

close-up (CU)   a tight photograph or shot, generally of the face and shoulders; a close shot

close-up lens   a camera lens for a *near focus* or *tight shot*; also called a *diopter lens* or *plus lens*

closing   the final step of a sales presentation, in which the customer is asked to make the purchase

closing date   the last possible time, or deadline, by which material must be received by one of the media in order for it to appear in a specific issue or broadcast

closure   1 conclusion   2 [direct marketing] a customer order placed as a result of direct-mail advertising

cloth   1 one of several possible bindings of a book, such as cotton or synthetic fibers   A cloth binding may be with or without boards, but the book is fully covered with a fabric. *Clothbound books* are fully bound in cloth over stiff boards, so technically *clothbound* is not the same as *cloth*. A *cloth joint* is a fold of *endpapers* reinforced with a cloth strip. *Cloth sides* denotes a book bound with a cloth front and back but a noncloth spine.   2 [theater] in the United Kingdom, a piece of canvas or other material that is hung from above a stage and used as scenery (called a *drop* in the United States)   A *sky cloth* is a blue cloth used to represent the sky.

clothes light   a *kicker light* (to the side or rear of a subject) or other light that enhances the texture or another aspect of apparel

cloud wheel   a theatrical device that projects a sky effect on a large white background

clout nail   a soft iron nail, commonly used in stage scenery construction   The nail can be driven through a piece of scenery and then bent (*clenched*) so as to hold it in place.

clubbing   [advertising] the sale of advertising space in a group of publications, at a combined rate that is less than the aggregate rates if purchased individually

club line   a short line at the end of a paragraph, longer than a WIDOW but not a full line

cluster   1 a small group   2 [journalism] a format in which related items are grouped together under one departmental heading

cluster box   a collection of mailboxes, such as those found in suburban communities   The unit consists of a minimum of eight individual locked compartments for the delivery and collection of mail.

cluster sampling   a survey research method in which successively smaller groups within a large population are randomly selected until a valid sample of manageable size is obtained

clutter   a multitude of commercial messages within a short space or period of time

cm   centimeter

CMA   CONSOLIDATED METROPOLITAN AREA

cml. or cmml.   commercial

C-mount   a single-thread screw device attached to a camera that functions as an adaptor for lenses, for example, to allow a 35mm lens from a still camera to be used on a video camera   C-mounts are commonly used to attach lenses to 16mm cameras.

CMSA   CONSOLIDATED METROPOLITAN STATISTICAL AREA

CMT   COUNTRY MUSIC TELEVISION

CMX   a trademarked, computer-interfaced video editing system, now made by Chyron Corporation, of Melville, NY, developed by a joint venture of CBS and Memorex

CNBC   Consumer News and Business Channel, a cable network based in Fort Lee, NJ, started in 1989 and owned by the National Broadcasting Company (NBC) and Cablevision Systems Corp.

CNN   CABLE NEWS NETWORK

CNS   COPLEY NEWS SERVICE

CNU   CANADIAN NEWSPAPER UNIT

co.   central office; company

c.o.   CARE OF; cash order

c/o   CARE OF COUNTY

coast   a shore   *The Coast* is show-business slang for the Los Angeles area of the West Coast, unless the term is being used in California, in which case *the Coast* could be New

York. *Coast-to-coast* means the entire continental United States, the 48 contiguous states.

coat or **coating** 1 a cover or covering layer for protection or decoration 2 to add, or the process of adding surfacing material to items 3 surfacing material *Coated book paper* is often used in letterpress printing; *coated offset* is used in offset printing.

coated-back (cb) paper a carbonless paper that transfers any impression made on it to a sheet underneath; a successor to *carbon paper*

coated blank a cardboard with a smooth (coated) surface on one or both sides, to be printed and used as a sign, display, or ticket

coated Bristol CAMPAIGN BRISTOL

coated paper a smooth paper, ranging from *dull-coated* to *enamel* (glossy) to *cast-coated* (very high gloss) *Machine-coated paper* has its coating applied in the papermaking machine, whereas *brush-coated* paper has a separate coating process. *Coated paper* is usually glossy but can be dull. It is surfaced with white clay or an other substance to provide a smooth finish, usually on both sides. *Coated-front* paper (abbreviated *cf*) is paper coated on the front only. Paper *coated one side* (abbreviated *c1s*) is cover or text paper that has been surfaced on one side, as for a cover.

coat out [advertising] the process of covering a painted bulletin with white or gray paint before a new advertisement is painted; also called *paint out* or *blankout*

coat weight a measure of the amount of coating applied to a stock

co-author one of two or more collaborators in writing a book or other work; to collaborate on a writing project

coaxial of two or more items having the same axis

coaxial cable 1 an electrical transmission cable capable of carrying complex signal information, such as multiple telephone conversations or TV signals; also called *coax* (pronounced CO-ax), or *co-ax*. 2 the cable hookup between stations in a network The wire consists of an outer conductor surrounding a central *core*.

coaxial magazine a film-reel container (*magazine*) with two chambers on the same axis (coaxial) that holds two reels, a *feed reel* and a *take-up* reel; also called CONCENTRIC MAGAZINE

cobalt a hard, metallic chemical, commonly used in inks, including *cobalt black* (black oxide of cobalt), *cobalt blue* (the most common of the cobalt compounds, a mixture of cobalt and aluminum oxides, a dark blue), *cobalt green* (cobalt zincate, a bluish green), *cobalt violet* (cobalt phosphate), and *cobalt yellow* (cobalt-potassium nitrate, a golden yellow)

COBOL [computers] *C*ommon *B*usiness *O*riented *L*anguage, a programming language based on English words and phrases, used in programming digital computers

cobweb spinner a device used in film to simulate a flimsy, gauzy web (akin to a web spun by a spider), using long strings of rubber cement that are extruded on the floors or walls of the set

cockamamie slang for something of poor quality, inferior, second-rate, or ludicrous The origin is from the French *decalcomanie*, a 19th-century fad for wearing decals. Cockamamie also was the name of a cheap molasses candy sold in the United States.

cock-and-bull story an absurd or improbable tale The origin may be from an old story about two barnyard animals carrying on a wildly improbable conversation, or it may be from the French *coq en l'âne*, "(to jump from) the cock to the donkey."

cockle 1 a wrinkle or pucker on paper, usually produced (unintentionally) in the drying process 2 a type of bivalve mollusk with radiating ribs (wrinkles) on its rounded shell (cockle-shell) *Cockle-finish paper* has a rough surface.

cockpit trouble slang for technical problems due to personnel (such as a sound engineer), as opposed to those caused by equipment trouble

cock-up a SUPERIOR letter, a character placed above the type line

COCOT customer-owned coin operated telephone

C.O.D. COLLECT ON DELIVERY

coda a more-or-less independent passage at the end of a musical composition or other work, added to reinforce the sense of conclusion; sometimes called a tag by popular musicians In a book, an *afterward* or *addendum* sometimes is called a coda.

code a system of signals, characters, words, and rules intended to convey information or define regulations *Machine code*, or computer instruction code, is machine language that a computer or other machine can recognize. *The Code* referred to the *Production Code Administration*, or *Hays Office*, a self-regulatory list of standards about what could and could not be shown in U.S.-made films. The Production Code was in effect at the Motion Picture Producers and Distributors of America from 1934 to 1968, when it was replaced by a rating system.

CODEC [telecommunications] *co*der plus *de*coder, a device that combines an encoder and decoder to convert DIGITAL signals to ANALOG signals and vice versa for transmission over voice-grade analog telephone lines

code dating the numbers, letters, or symbols printed on a package to indicate date of manufacture, time of shipment, the last date the item is to be sold, or other similar information

code number 1 a department reference symbol or other indication that appears in an advertisement (and sometimes in publicity or editorial matter); also called *code letter* Its purpose is to identify reader, audience, customer, or other source of response; the respondent quotes the code as a reference. 2 [film] *Code numbers* are numbers printed sequentially at one-foot intervals (by a *coding machine*) on the edges of a positive print and the same numbers printed on its soundtrack; they are not the same as *edge numbers*.

code price the price for a product or service paid by a retailer or others, not generally known to the consumer

code set a symbolic representation of a group (*set*) of characters

codex 1 originally, a code or body of laws 2 a manuscript volume; plural, *codices* Early books consisted of sheets of writing material fastened at one side and enclosed in a binder; one of them was the *Codex Theodosianus*, a collection of Roman laws. The *Codex Juris Canonici* is the official body of laws governing the Roman Catholic Church since 1918. The earliest *codices* were tablets of wood or ivory bound together (called a *tablet book*). Later versions consisted of sheets of papyrus, vellum, parchment, or paper.

coffee-table book a large-size art book or other highly visual, decorative publication that is intended for display on a coffee table or another prominent place in a home, rather than on a bookshelf

coffin case a food-store freezer cabinet with merchandise in a horizontal position The opposite is a DECKER WELL, which has horizontal shelves with merchandise stacked vertically.

COG customer's own goods

cognate related by family or having the same ancestor, such as a word related to one in another language

cognition the process of knowing, including awareness, memory, and judgment; the result of such a process *Cognition* is not the same as *perception*, although the term is often used in that sense.

cognitive consonance the agreement, consistency, or harmony between the beliefs of an individual and his or her actions The opposite is *cognitive dissonance*.

cognitive dissonance the conflict resulting from inconsistency between an individual's beliefs and his or her actions An example is a

person who consumes a product he or she considers to be harmful or from a distasteful source. The opposite condition is *cognitive consonance*, but that term is less frequently used.

cognitive judgment [marketing] a decision by a buyer based on a perception of how others evaluate the product or service CONATIVE, NORMATIVE, or VALUE JUDGMENTS are based on other considerations.

cognizance 1 a distinguishing mark or notice 2 observance; perception; conscious knowledge; recognition; awareness 3 official observation of or authority over something

cognoscente a connoisseur, a person with specialized knowledge or good taste; plural, *cognoscenti*

cohort a subgroup sharing a common factor in a statistical survey, such as age or income level

coil binding [book production] a technique of drawing a wire or plastic spiral (coil) through holes punched in the edges of the leaves; also called *spiral binding*

coincidental survey a technique for measuring or interviewing broadcast audiences by means of a telephone call while the radio or TV program in question is on the air

coined referring to a made-up, devised, or invented word or phrase, one not in standard vocabulary A word can be *coined* as a brand name or for some other special purpose.

coin-edge [graphic arts] a border composed of small parallel lines; also called a *broken rule*

col collect; college; COLOR; COLUMN

COL COLLATION; collect (international telex abbreviation)

COLA cost-of-living adjustment

cold 1 referring to something of low temperature or without warmth, such as a *cold color* (pale, often with a blue or green tint; the opposite of a vibrant, *warm color*) or *cold light* (fluorescent or other non-incandescent light producing little or no heat and with a different color effect from natural light) Cold colors are often calming. 2 referring to a show or program that begins either without an overture or introduction or without any (or sufficient) rehearsal, or to material without rehearsal To *go on cold* is to perform without rehearsal or preparation (*warm-up*). 3 [broadcasting, theater] referring to a lowering of the sound level, such as a FADE of background music during the last line of the announcer's voice-over (also called a *cool out*) Sound heard alone (without picture) is sometimes called *cold sound* (or *in clear*). A *cold audience* (also called a *cold house*) is unresponsive and provides a *cold hand* (little or no applause) and a *cold curtain* at the end of an act. 4 [marketing] unprepared or unused A *cold list* is one not previously used by the mailer. A *cold mail promotion* is directed to people who are not current customers. *Cold calling* is unsolicited telephoning or visiting of sales prospects.

cold press [printing] in papermaking, a manufacturing technique in which the paper is pressed to produce a smooth surface, but one with some texture (*tooth*) The paper, called *cold-pressed paper*, is commonly used for watercolor paintings. It is midway between rough paper and *hot-pressed paper*, which is very smooth.

cold type a photographic process of typesetting using film or sensitized paper; also called *photocomposition* No physical type is involved in this process. The older method of typesetting involved *hot type*, literally; the type was cast from molten metal. The most common hot-type machine, called a linotype, cast entire lines of type. In photocomposition, or phototypesetting, the *cold-type* letterforms are reproduced by means of a beam of light that is flashed through a film negative containing the characters. The images are then projected onto photosensitive film or paper. **2** any type that is not generated using hot metal This can include *strike-on, manual,* or *transfer lettering* methods of type production that are not typesetting.

Cole Publications a publisher (based in New York) of reverse telephone directories, in which the arrangement is by street address and telephone number instead of alphabetically by name Cole Directories are published for more than 2,000 U.S. cities.

coll. COLLATERAL; collect; college; COLLOQUIAL

collage an artistic composition consisting of materials pasted over a surface (from the French *coller*, "to glue")

collate **1** to arrange sheets or other items in order, as to assemble components of a press kit or gather signatures of a book into proper sequence **2** to produce a *master proof* by transcribing corrections from author's proofs and other sources onto one complete corrected proof A *collator* is a machine that organizes, gathers, and assembles sheets in proper sequence. Some giant machines can handle many thousands of sheets an hour.

collateral (coll.) any auxiliary or supplementary items, such as brochures, developed by advertising and public relations professionals for parallel, or collateral, use with advertising or other campaigns

collating mark [book production] a symbol, dot, or short line on the inner edge of the first sheet of each signature of a book that serves as a guide

to the proper order of the signatures If the symbol is a number or letter, the signatures should be gathered according to its place in the sequence. When lines are used (which is more common), the line on each signature appears a bit lower than the one on the preceding signature, starting near the top of the first signature. The collating mark often is a $1/8'' \times 1/4''$ black rectangle.

collation [library science] a description of the physical makeup of a book or other item, including size, number of pages, and number and type of illustrations

collect call a telephone call in which the caller requests that the called party pay the charge

collected edition a partial or complete collection of the works of an author, published in one volume or multiple volumes in a uniform format

collection box the term used by U.S. Mail for mail deposited in boxes on streets A mailbox inside a building or other internal location is called a *building box.*

collective mark an emblem, trademark, or other symbol identifying members of a trade association, labor union, or other group

collect on delivery (C.O.D.) a service of U.S. Mail, various alternative delivery companies, and other shippers whereby the shipping company collects payment from the recipient both for the item shipped and for the shipping costs, at the time the item is delivered

college traveler a publisher's sales representative who sells to the college market by making sales calls to faculty and others at colleges

collodion process a photographic process, invented in 1851 by English photographer Frederick Scott Archer (1813–57), in which a sensitized glass plate was dipped into a silver nitrate bath and exposed while still wet; also called *wet collodion process* It was used until the introduction of dry plates about 25 years later.

collograph an intaglio print (one whose printing areas are recessed) reproduced from a block onto which the original art is affixed, much like a COLLAGE (hence the name); also called INTAGLIO PRINT

colloquial (coll.) referring to conversational or informal speech or writing, not necessarily slang or jargon

colloquium a scholarly seminar or conference

colloquy **1** a formal conversation **2** a conference

collotype [printing] a process using a glass plate and a gelatin surface that carries the image to be reproduced, also called a *gelatin process* or *photogelatin process*; a print made by this process

colophon an inscription at the beginning or end of a book, perhaps containing information about its production; from the Greek *kolophon*, "finishing touch" The term is more generally used to designate the imprint of a publisher, though this usage is incorrect.

color 1 the sensation resulting from the stimulation of the retina of the eye by light waves of certain lengths 2 the property of reflecting light of a particular wavelength Related words include *shade* (degree of darkness), *hue* (modification of a basic color), *tint* (degree of whiteness, delicacy), and *tinge* (a small amount of diffused color). 3 any coloring matter: dye, pigment, or paint The Inter-Society Color Council–National Bureau of Standards (ISCC-NBS) system of *colorimetry* (color measurement using a *colorimeter*) defines 267 colors, according to degree of lightness, hue, and *saturation* (purity). *Primary colors* are red, yellow, and blue; they can be mixed to produce *secondary colors*. 4 to give color to 5 to alter or influence to some degree, as by distortion or exaggeration 6 [printing] the visual effect of the density of black type on a white sheet; also called *color spacing* 7 [journalism] human-interest, incidental, descriptive material used as background to HARD NEWS

Colorama a line of colored papers, commonly used for displays and other purposes, made by The Pervo Paint Company of Los Angeles

coloration 1 the condition of being colored; the manner in which something is colored 2 [recording] a deviation from the natural, live balance of musical sounds, such as a heavy bass

color bar [printing, television] a strip of gradation of primary colors and black, used for TV testing and for color standardization and accuracy, such as the Graphic Arts Technical Foundation Color Bar, or the color transmission standards of the Society of Motion Picture and Television Engineers, also called *colorburst* The standard TV color bars are vertical strips of white, yellow, cyan, green, magenta, red, blue, and black.

colorblind film a type of film with black-and-white emulsion that is sensitive to only one part of the color spectrum, usually blue

color break [printing] a demarcation (between areas inked or times of applications) between onc color and another In letterpress printing, a metal form was literally broken into separate forms, one for each color.

colorburst a COLOR BAR

color card a chart (*card*) with a spectrum of colors (a *color scale*); also called a *color chart* The

card is photographed on a piece of film and this film then is matched with the actual card to determine the color accuracy of the film and facilitate any color correction.

color cast an overall tint of a film It may be unintentional (as with a blue or pink tint resulting from faulty film or faulty processing) or intentional (as with a sepia tint).

colorcast a TV program broadcast in color

color circle a circular card or sheet on which the colors of the spectrum are printed In terms of a clock, red is at about 12 o'clock, blue is at 4 o'clock, and yellow is at 8 o'clock. In between are the hues (red-violet, violet, and blue-violet between red and blue; green-blue, green, and yellow-green between blue and yellow; orange-yellow, orange, and red-orange between yellow and red). COMPLEMENTARY COLORS appear opposite each other, so the chart has many uses.

color code a system of colors for purposes of identification, such as is used for sections of a publication or within a binder, or for wires or circuit components

color correction the improvement of color rendition, by such methods as *masking, dot-etching, re-etching,* or *scanning*

colored story a slanted or biased piece of writing

colorer [film] a person who fills in the colors on the animation *cels*; also called *opaquer*

color filter [photography] an optical device to increase contrasts or take photographs through haze; also called *color-balancing filter, color-compensating filter,* or *color-correction filter* It is not the same as a *color-conversion filter,* which adjusts the light to the color balance of the film, so that, for example, daylight (outdoor) film can be used indoors with tungsten lights.

color frame a square border (*frame*), generally metal, that holds the color gelatins attached to the front of theatrical lights

coloring tube a cathode-ray tube that is part of a television camera; also called *chrominance tube* or *color dissector tube* It is used to separate the red, blue, and green components of the chroma, or color, part of the video signal.

colorization the process of coloring, such as the addition of color to prints of movies originally produced in black-and-white

Color Key a proofing material made of a light-sensitive film It is made by 3M (a St. Paul, MN company) and supplied in various colors.

color match [film] the overall consistency of colors, balance, and harmony, from shot to shot and reel to reel, of an entire film

color overlay a clear sheet placed over artwork to indicate where color should appear on the printed version

colorplexer [television] an electronic device that processes three separate color signals, red, blue and green, coming from the cathode-ray tube into one composite signal

color process work [printing] the use of photographic SEPARATIONS; also called *process color* or *four-color* Four negatives are printed, one each using cyan, magenta, yellow, and black ink. These are then combined to produce a full-color print.

color proof [printing] a copy, or proof, of each color of multicolor process work

color reversal intermediate (CRI) a color duplicate film made from the original negative Since the CRI is a negative, and not a positive, RELEASE PRINTS can be made from it.

color separation [printing] a negative made from color art from which a color print is produced The negatives are made in the three primary colors, red, yellow, and blue, plus black; they are sometimes called *seps*. A *color-separation artist*, or specialist, can *pre separate* by using individual, or separate, OVERLAYS for each color.

color sequencing [computers] a process of changing the color of one or more PIXELS in a graphics display

color subcarrier [television] the wavelength on which is impressed information about the color signal In the United States, it is 3.58 MHz.

color temperature a measure of the color of a light source in terms of relative red or blue content, expressed in Kelvin degrees of temperature Noon in Venice, Italy, looks (and photographs) different from noon in Venice, California, as indicated by their different color temperatures.

color toning the shading of a black-and-white photograph with bleach, dye, or colors

color transparency a positive film or slide produced in color on transparent film

color-under a system used in some videotape recorders to record luminance (brightness) and chrominance (color) simultaneously

color wedge [printing] an exposure test to view the same image from zero to 100-percent color saturation

color wheel [theater] a metal disc that holds several circles of colored gel, attached to the front of a spotlight so that it can be rotated, with each gel producing a differently colored beam

colour British spelling of *color*

colporteur a peddler of devotional literature, such as a traveling sales representative of a religious group *Colporteurs* are seen on street corners. There is no connection with the song composer!

Columbia Broadcasting System (CBS) one of the major commercial radio and TV networks in the United States, formed in 1927 CBS owns radio and TV stations and provides programming to affiliated stations, and up until 1987, was in other communication fields, including records and publishing (these divisions were sold).

Columbia Journalism Review (CJR) a bimonthly magazine published by the Columbia University Graduate School of Journalism, New York

Columbian the name for 16-point type

Columbia Pictures Entertainment Inc. a major motion-picture company headquartered in New York It owns one of the renowned film studios (Columbia Pictures in Burbank, CA) and other film and TV properties. It is a subsidiary of Tri-Star Pictures, Inc. (based in New York).

Columbia Scholastic Press Association an organization at Columbia University (New York) to promote student writing through student publications (mostly in secondary schools, also at colleges)

column (col.) **1** one of multiple vertical divisions of a page of type Many reference books are printed two or three columns to a page (*two-* or *three-column format*). **2** a standard vertical unit of space in a periodical A magazine may have a two- or three-column format; a newspaper page may range from four to nine columns. The editorial or advertising space may be measured in *column inches*, the number of columns in width multiplied by the number of inches in depth. Advertisers (primarily) and publicists (sometimes) use *agate lines* instead of inches to measure column depth; there are 14 agate lines to a column inch. The width of a column is generally measured in *picas*. **3** a series of features or articles appearing regularly in a newspaper or magazine, by a particular writer (a *columnist*) or a certain subject

Column Five the fifth column on the front page of *The Wall Street Journal*, devoted each day to a specific department

columnist a bylined writer of a regular feature or other article (a *column*) that appears in a newspaper or other periodical

column rule a vertical line between rows of type, used in some magazines and newspapers

com COMMA

com. COMEDY; COMMENTARY; committee; COMMERCIAL

COM customer's own merchandise

coma an aberration of a camera lens that produces circular patches of light at the edges of the lens field

combat camera a hand-held camera used to film or tape warfare or other action

combat organ a military publication issued in a warfare, or combat, area

comber [printing] a device to fan out (*comb*) sheets so that they can pass through a press or folder one at a time *Comber marks* occur when the *comber wheels* of a folder pass over the printed matter, causing wet ink to smear.

combination camera a TV camera and recorder in one unit

combination rate a special rate for multiple advertisements placed in two or more publications of the same or affiliated companies; also called a *combination buy* Such rates are generally available only if the ads appear at the same time or within a specified time period.

combined move [film, television] the simultaneous movement of a camera and performer in the same direction; also called *compound move*

combo short form of *combination* At a small radio station, a *combo announcer* also works as an engineer. *Combo art* or a *combo plate* is a line drawing and photo; a *combo print* has more than one negative on a single sheet.

combo pack a combination package of two or more items, perhaps joined by a band or on a card, common in the food, health, and beauty-aids industries

come? a question as to whether additional copy or other material is forthcoming (*to come*), notated on copy and directed to an author or other source

comeback **1** a return to a previous state or an active career (such as one by a performer who had retired or was out of sight) **2** a retort (such as by a comedian to a heckler) **3** a ground for action or complaint; a recourse (such as a *comeback position*) prepared as part of a public relations strategy

Come back Tuesday [theater] a polite rejection to an applicant, particularly a performer

comedian a performer who plays comic parts; a humorous entertainer (Some theater observers distinguish between a *comedian*, who tells jokes and performs comedy, and a *comic*, who is inherently funny by virtue of a character or physical manner.) A *comedienne* is a female comedian.

come down **1** a direction to a performer to move toward the audience **2** an instruction to reduce intensity, particularly of light or sound

comedy (com.) a play or other work that is humorous Early comedies were nontragic dramas or narratives with happy endings, such as *The Divine Comedy* of Dante (1265–1321) or Shakespearean comedies. To *cut the comedy* is to stop joking or fooling around. *High comedy*, such as the plays of Noel Coward (1899–1973), appeals to and reflects the life of the upper social classes. *Low comedy* is COMMEDIA DELL'ARTE, slapstick, farce, or other humorous action and situations, as opposed to the sophisticated dialogue of high comedy. A *comedy club* is a nightclub specializing in presenting comedians.

comedy of manners a play or other work that depicts and satirizes the behavior (manners) of fashionable society Comedies of manners were popular in England and Europe up to the 18th century.

come in [film, television] an instruction by a director for the camera to move closer to the subject

come on [theater] to make an entrance

cometing **1** tiny spots of light on a film, generally caused by metallic pollution in the processing bath **2** streaking (*comet tails*) of a TV picture

comet tail [television] a streak, generally caused by an overloaded camera tube They can be prevented or minimized by means of an *anti-comet tail* (ACT) gun in the tube.

comic **1** having to do with comedy **2** a funny performer **3** [plural] a section of comic strips in a newspaper, such as the *Sunday comics*

comic book a magazine with a series of captioned drawings, often of an adventure story and not necessarily humorous

comic opera an opera with humorous situations, or a happy ending

comic orientation the positioning of images on microfilm parallel to the edge of the film, as in a newspaper comic strip, as distinguished from *cine orientation*, in which the images are perpendicular to the film edge, as in a motion picture

comic relief an amusing scene in a serious drama, or a character used for this purpose

comic strip a series of drawings, generally captioned with the conversation of the characters, most frequently in a horizontal sequence of several panels (a *strip*) and printed in daily newspapers

coming attractions a short film or tape about a forthcoming film or program; also called a *trailer*

coming of age transitional years, as depicted by a film or other work about adolescence

coming up following; referring to a program following the one being broadcast

Comité Consultatif International Télégraphie et Téléphonie (CCITT) a group that sets standards for telecommunications, including telephones and facsimile Called the International Telegraph and Telephone Consultative Committee, the group is part of the International Telecommunications Union located in Geneva, Switzerland.

comm. committee

comma chaser slang for COPY EDITOR

command a code to instruct a typesetter, word processor, or other computer device to perform a certain task

command performance a performance of a concert, play, or other work, presented at the request of the royal family or a ruler of a country; by extension, any presentation or meeting set up at the request of an employer or other person in authority

comma splice a run-on or fused sentence, consisting of two or more sentences written as one, spliced by a comma instead of a period

commedia dell'arte a type of Italian comedy developed in the 16th through 18th centuries, employing a stereotyped plot, improvised dialogue, and stock characters such as Pantaloon, Harlequin, and Columbine; from the Italian for "comedy of art" The term is also used to denote professional comedy.

comment 1 a remark, particularly an opinion 2 a marginal note to the editor or printer 3 an instructional statement in a computer program

commentary (com.) 1 explanatory notes, remarks, or observations, such as a personal memoir or an off-screen voice in a film or TV program, providing an explanation or opinion 2 written notes, accompanying a text being commented on or published separately

commentative sound 1 a commentary on action 2 any sound or soundtrack that is not the primary action sound; also called *extradiegetic sound* (*diegetic sound* being the primary or indigenous sound)

commentator a person who writes or delivers a commentary, which may include personal opinions, observations, and analysis, such as a *broadcast commentator* on a radio or TV program

commercial (cml., com., or comml.) a message paid for by a company or other sponsor for broadcast on radio and TV stations 2 that part of publicity that contains a brand name or other message, akin to the paid broadcast commercial of the sponsor 3 of or connected with commerce or trade 4 made, done, or operating pri-

marily for profit *Commercial radio* and *commercial television* are supported by advertising revenues, as opposed to public broadcasting and pay TV, which are paid for by government and corporate, foundation, and listener contributions (public) or subscription fees (pay TV). Commercials are described by length (as in a 15-, 30-, or 60-second commercial), format (live or recorded), content, the terms (local or network), and other categories.

commercial a the letter *a* with a circle around it (@), meaning *at*

commercial art drawings, paintings, layouts, and all types of graphics used in advertising, education, entertainment, media, or other areas of communication and business; art executed for an external purpose, rather than for its own sake (as is *fine art*)

commercial break an interruption in radio or TV programming for broadcast of one or more advertisements (*commercials*)

commercial cartridge See CARTRIDGE.

commercial code number a series of four letters followed by four numbers identifying a TV commercial by sponsor, content, and advertising agency, in accordance with a system standard throughout the industry

commercial impressions the total audience, including duplication (one person counts more than once), for all commercials in an advertiser's schedule; also called *impressions*

commercial lead-in a prelude or introduction by a program cast member about an upcoming commercial

commercial load the maximum amount of advertising time available during a broadcast time period, such as eight national minutes and four local minutes per hour; the total time of commercials actually broadcast during an hour or other specific time

commercial minute 60 seconds of actual television or radio commercial time

commercial pool a selection of television or radio commercials that an advertiser has available for airing at any one time

commercial protection a broadcast medium's guarantee to an advertiser that its commercial will be separated by a specified amount of air time from commercials for competitive products

commercial sign a structure on a roof, wall, or other outdoor surface to identify the occupant or provide information; not one on a leased advertising structure

commission a fee or percentage paid to a sales agent *Commissions* may range from 1 percent or less to as much as 30 percent or more paid to

commissionable media 104 compact disc

literary agents, lecture bureaus, or others who perform management or other functions in addition to sales. The standard commission, discount, or rebate paid by media to advertising agencies is 15 percent. Advertising and other agencies generally add a surcharge (usually 17.65 percent, but sometimes 20 percent) to printing, art, and other creative or collateral production expenses that they incur outside of their own agencies.

commissionable media newspapers, magazines, broadcast stations, outdoor advertising, transit advertising, and other media that pay a standard commission (generally 15 percent of the gross charge) to advertising agencies

commission circular a direct-mail piece purchased from a manufacturer or other source by an independent salesperson, who mails or distributes it to prospects (with the name of the sales agent rubber-stamped or overprinted) in order to receive a commission on any sales

comml. COMMERCIAL

common carrier a telecommunications company, such as a telephone company or Western Union, that provides communications transmission services to the general public

common channel signaling (CCS) [telecommunications] a digital system that transmits all signaling information for calls over a special network, a signal channel separate from the talking path *CCS systems* are used by telephone companies as rapid pathfinders.

common pages original copy used for two or more different publications, without change or with minor changes

common supplement a section inserted in several newspapers; also called a *common section*

communication 1 the transmission or exchange of information, signals, messages, or data by any means, such as talk (*verbal communication*), writing (*written communication*), person-to-person (*personal communication*), or via telephone, telegraph, radio, or other channels, within a group or directed to specific individuals or groups The term is often used in the plural. A *communicator* may send and receive such messages by talking, writing, or gesturing. 2 the conveying of thought from one party or group to another 3 the planned and measured management process to help organizations achieve their goals using the written and spoken word Communication skills involve the art of transmitting information, signals, or messages from one medium (person, device, or point) to another.

communication audit a professional review and evaluation of the history, policies, practices,

needs, problems, and other aspects of the communication behavior of an organization

Communications Excellence to Black Audiences (CEBA) annual awards in advertising, sales promotion, and packaging, started in 1978 by the World Institute for Black Communications (New York)

communications officer in the military, a person responsible for radio or other communication technology; not a public information officer

Communications Satellite Corporation (COMSAT) the first U.S. company in the communications satellite field, based in Washington, DC, formed as a result of the Communications Satellite Act of 1962 It provides satellite services between the United States and other countries. COMSAT, a corporation subject to government regulation, is owned by common carriers and shareholders.

communication theory a mathematical discipline dealing with the transmission of messages

Communication World a monthly magazine published by the International Association of Business Communicators, based in San Francisco

communicologist an expert or researcher in communications The word is sometimes used derisively.

community the people in an area, or the area itself In a broader sense, community refers to a group of people or nations with common interests, or society in general. *Community relations* is the aspect of public relations that involves dealing and communicating with the people within an organization's area.

Community Agency PR Association (CAPRA) an organization of nonprofit groups in the New York City area, which conducts the annual Effective Communications Contest

Community Antenna Television (CATV) the original term for CABLE TELEVISION

Community Antenna Television Association (CATA) an association of cable TV operators and owners, based in Fairfax, VA

community bulletin board a computerized system for exchanging messages

comp accompaniment (in music); COMPARATIVE; compilation; complete; COMPLIMENTARY; COMPOSE; composer; COMPOSITE; COMPOSITION; COMPOSITOR Jazz musicians refer to improvising as *comping*.

compact disc (CD) a small-size recording, 4–7 inches in diameter, made primarily of clear plastic and aluminum A CD plays on one side only but allows about 80 minutes of playing time. CDs are extremely long-lasting and relatively damage-proof. The recording system is *digital*, as opposed to the conventional *analog* system. Playback does not use a stylus; instead, a low-power laser beam reads the disc as it revolves at variable speeds, starting at about 500 revolutions per minute for the inside tracks and slowing to about 200 rpm as the laser moves to the outer tracks. The use of light instead of a needle reduces or eliminates distortions, surface noises, and disc wear and offers other advantages. Playback requires a digital *compact disc player*. Variations of compact discs (CDs, pronounced see-DEEZ) include *CD-ROM* (CD-Read Only Memory), for computer data and *CD-I* (CD-Interactive) for data, visuals, and sound.

compact disc video (CDV) a compact disc that contains both video and digital audio information Formats include *CDV single* (about 20 minutes of audio and 5 minutes of video), *CDV EP* (Extended Play, about 40 minutes), and *CDV LP* (Long Play, about 120 minutes).

compact indium discharge (CID) a type of enclosed arc discharge lamp that provides considerable illumination for its relatively small size; also called *compact iodide daylight*

compact source iodide (CSI) an iodide gas-discharge mercury arc lamp that is small-size and produces near-daylight illumination, used in film and TV

company a group of people associated for a business or other purposes, such as a group of performers (an *acting company, dance company, theatrical company*) The word is commonly used in the theater, as in *company call* (a gathering or rehearsal of the entire cast, including the orchestra), *company crew* (backstage and other nonperforming workers), and *company manager* (the business and administrative supervisor).

company culture the style and identity of a company; an amalgam of its beliefs, mythology, values, and rituals that characterizes the general way a company appears and acts In their book *Corporate Cultures* (1982), Allan A. Kennedy and Terrence E. Deal described such corporate cultures as *Macho/Tough Guy* (Bloomingdale's), *Work Hard/Play Hard* (Xerox, Mary Kay Cosmetics), *High Stakes, Slow-Feedback* (Exxon, Boeing) and *Low-Risk, Slow-Feedback* (Price Waterhouse).

comparative advertising any advertising in which an advertiser compares itself with its competitors, either by name or not (such as *Brand A* vs. *Brand B*) This type of advertising is considered aggressive and is sometimes perceived as negative.

comparative distribution analysis (CDA) the study of marketing channels and types of di-

rect and indirect distributors, sales agents, and dealers

comparison advertising the practice of overtly comparing a product or other advertised item with a competitor that is explicitly identified (not *Brand X*)

compatible color a system that produces a color signal that can be received by a color or monochrome (black-and-white) TV set

Compatible Quadrature Amplitude Modulation (C-Quam) a system enabling AM radio stations to transmit in stereo, made by Motorola Inc., based in Schaumburg, IL

compendium 1 a concise treatise; an abstract, generally longer than a summary 2 a digest, epitome, or synopsis

compensatory media weight any free commercial time or space or a cash credit given for improperly aired or placed advertisements or for vehicles that do not achieve audience guarantees

competitive check an analysis of rival advertising levels and patterns, usually conducted on the basis of syndicated data supplied by monitoring organizations, such as BROADCAST ADVERTISERS REPORTS and LEADING NATIONAL ADVERTISERS

compilation (comp) a collection of previously published or existing materials arranged in such a way that the publication is considered an original work and thus is eligible to be copyrighted

compilation film a collection of existing footage, such as in a news documentary or an assemblage of comedy clips

compiler 1 a person who assembles material from multiple sources and arranges it in an orderly manner, or a machine that composes or gathers together material from various areas or sources 2 [computers] a program that translates from a *language program* into a *machine-code program*

complementary color one of a pair of colors that, when combined at the proper intensity, produce white (or close to it) *Complementary colors* are in extreme contrast to each other: red and green are complementary colors (*complementaries*), as are yellow and violet, and blue and orange. The *complementary* of a *primary color* (red, yellow, or blue) is obtained by mixing the other two; mixing yellow and blue produces green, which is the complementary of red.

completed call a telephone call that has been switched (connected) to its destination, not one that has ended

completion bond an insurance policy that pays a specified amount if a motion picture or other project is not completed

completion services   film processing, special effects, sound mixing, graphics, and other services performed after the basic production; also called *postproduction services*

complimentary (comp)   referring to a free subscription, ticket, or other item, one for which the spectator has not paid   A *comp list* is the list of those designated to receive free items, called *comps* for short.

compose (comp)   [printing] to set type, as by a COMPOSITOR

composer   a person who creates (composes) a work, particularly a writer of music (but not the lyrics or words of a song)   In film, the *composer* works with the *music editor* and is often also the *conductor.*

composite (comp)   **1** a combination of elements, such as a *sound composite* (two or more recordings) or a *composite print*   **2** referring to something formed of distinct parts   A *composite work* is an original work consisting of separate and distinct parts by different people. A *composite volume* is made up of two or more separately published works, such as several pamphlets bound together as one item.

composite master   the completed original film or tape from which copies are made   In film, the composite master is a *positive* (a *print*) or a *negative*; in TV, it is videotape, neither a positive nor a negative.

composite print   **1** a positive print of a film with both audio and video; also called a *married print, wedded print,* or *single-system print*   **2** a photographic print produced by stripping together two or more negatives

compositing   combining elements, such as film and video, into one image

composition   **1** the setting of type, or the type itself   The *compositor* generally works in a *composing room,* from a *composition order* or *specification sheet*   A *composition house* specializes in typesetting and produces *composition-set type,* as compared to type set by a publication itself, which is *publication-set type* or *pub-set.* A *composing stick* is a metal tray in which lines of type are set. In computerized typesetting, *composition formatting* is the insertion into text of codes or symbols that will arrange a text in lines, blocks, paragraphs, pages, or other forms in a prescribed format or system. *Composition software* is the program that produces the typesetting, including routines for justification, hyphenation, editing, and other procedures.   **2** the arrangement of the elements of a paragraph, picture, photograph, design, or advertisement

composition order   a written specification of type to be set; also called SPECIFICATION SHEET

compositor   a typesetter

composograph   a composite photograph

compound   a word composed of two or more base units, hyphenated or not, such as *antifreeze, blackbird,* or *grandfather*; also called a *compound word*   A *compound sentence* has two or more independent clauses of equal importance, generally separated by *and, but,* or *or.*

compound move   [film, television] the simultaneous movement of a camera and performer in the same direction, as in a TRACKING SHOT

comprehensive   **1** a complete layout, prepared prior to final production of a *mechanical,* which will be reproduced; also called *comp* (plural, *comps*)   **2** a *cutline* (photo caption) with sufficient detail (sufficiently *comprehensive*) that no accompanying article is required   The plural is *comprees,* pronounced COM-preez.

compression   a process of automatic adjustment of variations in audio volume

Compugraphic Corporation   a major manufacturer of photographic typesetters including CompuWriter, EditWriter, and Unisetter; based in Wilmington, MA

compulsory subscription   a subscription to a publication that is obligatory, as part of the membership in an organization

computer   an electronic device that accepts information, applies processes, and supplies the results of the processes   It consists of *input* and *output* facilities, *storage, arithmetic,* and *logical* units, all under the supervision of a *control.* Computer associations include the Computer & Business Equipment Manufacturers Association (Washington, DC), Computer & Communications Industry Association (Arlington, VA), and Electronic Industries Association (Washington, DC).

computer-aided design (CAD)   a graphics system in which a computer is used to produce the design of a proposed product so that it can be manipulated, or revised, quickly on a computer screen

computer-aided instruction (CAI)   an educational process that uses study manuals, worksheets, and other learning materials in computer format; also called *computer-assisted instruction*

computer animation   use of a computer to create the image of moving pictures

computer-assisted makeup terminal (CAM)   a cathode-ray tube that shows type sizes and positions, so that text layouts can be obtained electronically

computer-assisted retrieval (CAR)   the obtaining, or retrieval, of data, using a computer; the retrieval of information on library microfilm using a computer index

computer composition   typesetting that is computerized and uses an optical system of character storage for reproduction on light-sensitive paper in which no lead or other physical type is involved; also called *computerized composition*

computer-enhancement   the use of a computer to bring out details of an image and make it sharper, such as applied to photos taken in a spacecraft; also called *digital enhancement*

computer film   an animated film, usually with abstract art generated by a computer, that originated in the 1960s

computer-generated   referring to imagery created by a computer

computer graphics   any diagrams, drawings, and other nontextual material that is computer-generated and displayed on a video screen

computer imaging   the use of a computer to create drawings or other images that then can be printed on paper, film, or videotape

computer letter   a letter generated by a computer with the recipient's name or other *fill-ins* (variables) in one or more places, commonly used for direct mail

computer personalization   the use of a computer to mass-produce individualized items, ranging from letters to publications, with the name of the recipient and other individual *fill-ins*

computer processing unit (CPU)   the central processing part of a computer system, not the printers, terminals, or other *peripheral* parts; more commonly called CENTRAL PROCESSING UNIT

computer resource unit (CRU)   a measure of the resources used in a computer system, such as central processing time, input/output, reports, or memory; not the same as COMPUTER PROCESSING UNIT

computer virus   a software program that uses a code to enter other programs and alter or destroy them; a deadly "disease" conceived by an unscrupulous computer expert

computer word   a set of characters in a single storage location of the computer memory and handled as a unit

COMSAT   *Communications Satellite* Corporation

con.   CONCERTO; CONCLUSION; connection; continued

conative judgment   [marketing] an evaluation or decision based on impulse

concealed joint   [book production] a cloth strip covered by the paste-down *endpaper*, not a visible *exposed joint*

concentric groove   a cut-off groove, the final groove on a phonograph record that starts the automatic change mechanism of the player

concentric magazine   a film- or tape-reel container (*magazine*) with the film or tape reels (supply and take-up) on the same axis, opposite and parallel (concentric) to each other; also called a COAXIAL MAGAZINE

concept   **1** a brief basic idea for a campaign, product, show, or other work   Research undertaken to assess reaction is called a *concept test*.   **2** [film] a brief summary preceding a full- or *outline* or *treatment*   A *high concept* is a plot that can be described easily; a *high-concept work* is one on a high aesthetic level.

concept video   a short TV program with a story or theme (a concept) and featuring a musical performer

concertina fold   a method of folding paper so that adjacent folds are in opposite directions, in a pleated manner   The term is used in the United Kingdom; in the United States, it's called an ACCORDION FOLD.

concerto   a musical composition for one or more solo instruments

concession   a department leased out by a retailer and operated by a *concessionaire*

conclusion (CC)   [broadcasting] the scheduled end of a program of indefinite duration   For example, a sports event whose length cannot be determined in advance may be listed in a schedule as 8:00 P.M.–CC.

concordance   an alphabetical list of all important words in a book (or by a writer), with references to the passages in which they occur; different from an *index*

concurrent processing   the ability of a computer to work on more than one task at the same time; also called *multiprocessing*

condensed type   a narrow or slender typeface, the opposite of *extended type*   Many typefaces are available in condensed form and are useful in saving space. A few faces also are available as *extra condensed*, or very thin.

condenser   a *capacitor*, a device that stores an electrical charge (has *capacitance*)   A *condenser microphone* (one of the earliest types of microphone) has a diaphragm that moves in response to sound waves and then comes in contact with a metal disc.

conductor   **1** a leader or director   **2** the director of an orchestra or other group of musicians   In TV, film, and theater, the *orchestra conductor* or *band leader* may report to a *music* (or *musical*) director.   **3** a substance that conducts heat, sound, electricity, or something else

cone   **1** a wedgelike shape with a circular base and curved sides that taper to an apex   **2** in a loudspeaker, a component used as a vibrator

cone lights [film] cone-shaped floodlights They come in three sizes: *senior cone, junior cone,* and *baby cone.*

conf. conference; confidential

confab [film] slang for an informal meeting, from *confabulate*

confabulate (confab) to chat or gossip A *confabulation* is a meeting or convention.

conference call a telephone call in which more than two individuals participate, generally from different geographical locations In a *meet-me conference call*, the operator notifies each person (*conferee*) of the number he or she should call at a specific time. In a *progressive conference call*, the operator places each person on the *conference circuit.*

conference report   CALL REPORT

confidence level [market research] a measure of assurance that samples or test results are accurate, expressed as a percentage, such as a 95-percent confidence level The optimum is 100 percent, so a 95-percent confidence level indicates a high degree of probability.

confidence playback [broadcasting, recording] the playing back of an audio or video track to make sure that it was not erased or damaged during editing

confirmation verification, such as an agreement from a station to an advertiser or its agency that clearance has been obtained for a specifically ordered schedule of commercials

confirmation of broadcast order (CBO) a written purchase affirmation by a station to an advertiser

confirming proof [printing] a copy sent to a customer, with no approval required or expected

conforming [film] the portion of the editing process in which the original film is cut and matched to the WORKPRINT, frame by frame The laboratory technician, called a *conformer* (or *negative cutter* or *negative matcher*), generally matches the *edge numbers* on both films. Conforming also is a part of CHECKERBOARD CUTTING, in which the original film is separated into *A* and *B* rolls.

confrontainment confrontational entertainment, a radio or TV talk show or other performance that features obscenities, insults, and other aggressive or confrontational behavior, generally toward the interviewees

Congressional Quarterly Service (CQ) a publisher of editorials and other materials, sent to newspapers and other subscribers, located in Washington, DC

congruent in agreement, corresponding, harmonious *Congruent communications* was defined by Don Hill (*Public Relations Journal,*

October 1982) as a process by which a message, which is understood by its sender, is transmitted through a medium to a receiver, and thence to an audience, which responds to it, all within a system whose elements are congruent with each other and with the total environment in which these six elements are operating.

congruity agreement, harmony The *theory of congruity* is that members of special-interest groups generally support themes and issues reflecting their own beliefs and interests.

conjugate 1 to give the various inflected forms of a verb or other word 2 to join together 3 [printing] a leaf that is half of a four-page sheet In a 16-page signature, pages 1 and 2 comprise leaf 1, which is the *conjugate* of (joined with) pages 15 and 16 (leaf 8). Thus, *conjugate leaves* are parts of a single sheet of paper.

connect time time during which a terminal is working with a computer It is the time between *sign-on* and *sign-off* and is longer than *compute time* (the portion of connect time in which an operator is actually utilizing a computer's resources).

connotation an idea or thought suggested by or associated with a word or words in addition to its or their explicit meaning, or *denotation* Communicators are aware that many words suggest or convey associations, overtones, or attributes, sometimes positive and sometimes negative, beyond their specific definitions.

connotative head a *teaser* headliner, such as a headline in a newspaper or other publication that is not descriptive of the contents of the article; common in tabloids, as in "Ollie Up" instead of "Oliver North Trial Starts Today"

consecutive action [film, television] action in the order in which it is actually filmed or taped, not necessarily in the sequence of the script

consecutive weeks discount a reduction of price to an advertiser who buys space or time continuously over a specific period, such as 26 weeks

consignment a body of merchandise sold to retailers which, if the retailer cannot sell it, may be returned to the manufacturer for full or partial refund *Consignment sales* are common in book publishing (from publishing houses to stores). The originator is the *consignor;* the recipient is the *consignee,* and the sale is agreed upon on *consignment terms.*

consistency 1 the condition or degree or holding together (thickness) 2 agreement, harmony, logical connection 3 [film] the continuity of lighting balance from scene to scene

console 1 an instrument panel, such as the table containing or supporting a visual display and other components of a word processing system **2** [broadcasting] a desk-type structure equipped with monitoring and other electronic devices; the control unit

Consolidated Metropolitan Area (CMA) an old designation by the U.S. Office of Management and Budget for an area of a million or more people plus contiguous high-population areas The newer designation is CONSOLIDATED METROPOLITAN STATISTICAL AREA (CMSA).

Consolidated Metropolitan Statistical Area (CMSA) the U.S. Census Bureau description for a major urban region, such as the greater New York City area Within each CMSA are one or more Primary Metropolitan Statistical Areas (PMSAs), such as Nassau and Suffolk counties on Long Island. A Metropolitan Statistical Area (MSA) is a single urban area, such as Syracuse, NY. These categories replaced the long-time description, SMSA (Standard Metropolitan Statistical Area), a county or counties of more than 50,000 population. There are over 300 SMSAs in the United States.

consonance 1 the harmony or agreement of elements or parts **2** a partial rhyme formed by a repeated consonant or pattern of consonants (but without repeating vowels); see ASSONANCE

constants [publishing] the elements in a periodical that remain the same from issue to issue, such as the *masthead* and *nameplate*

construction [film, television] the building of sets, flats, furniture, and other items The supervisor of the *construction area* is the *construction manager* or *construction foreman*, who reports to the *construction coordinator* (who reports to the *production designer* or *art director*).

construction board cardboard or other material commonly used by artists in constructing layouts, mechanicals, displays, or other items Types of construction board include *corrugated board, foamcore, line-up board*, and *mounting board*.

construction paper a type of inexpensive colored paper used for drawings, particularly in elementary school

consumer a buyer or acquirer of goods or services, generally a member of the *general public* as opposed to a specialist *Consumer goods* are food, clothing, and other items in general demand for personal use, as distinguished from *industrial goods. Consumer markets* are groups of consumers reached through advertising in *consumer media*, such as radio, TV, newspapers, and mass magazines.

consumer deal a price reduction or special offer to a consumer

consumerism the protection of the general public (consumers) through safeguards relating to proper labeling, warranties, safety standards, and other regulation of goods and services sold

consumer-perceived risks any potentially negative factors considered by a consumer when making a buying decision, including *functional risk* (will it work?), *physical risk* (is it harmful?), *financial risk* (is it affordable?), and *social risk* (is it embarrassing?)

consumer profile an overall picture of the buying habits and demographic characteristics of a user of products or services

cont. containing; CONTENTS; continue(d); CONTRACT; contraction; control

contact 1 the act of touching or meeting; a state of coming together or being in communication **2** a person who is a connection or link A representative of one of the media to whom a publicist conveys material, whether known to the publicist or not, is referred to as the *contact*. Several media directories and services are known as *contact services*. In a broader sense, a contact is any person with whom one deals or communicates and who represents an organization. Thus, to a media person, a publicist is a contact, and to a publicist, a media person is a contact. As with all of life, it's a matter of perspective. **3** to get in touch with; to communicate with

contact control guide [printing] a reference scale or guide, for exposure and other adjustments in making reproductions, or contact prints, of negatives or positives, such as the Kodak Contact Control Guide series by the Eastman Kodak Company, Rochester, NY

contact imaging material [graphic arts] a clear polyester film with an ink-pigmented coating that is sensitive to ultraviolet light An example is COLOR-KEY.

contact paper [photography] a slow-speed paper for printing a negative placed in contact with (against) it

contact print [photography] a print made from a negative or positive placed in contact with sensitized paper (called *contact paper*), film, or a printing plate The contact print, also called *contact copy*, is the same size as the negative. A *contact sheet* (generally 8½ × 11") is a group of contact prints on one sheet.

contact report a CALL REPORT

Contacts a weekly newsletter for publicists published by Larimi Communications in New York

contact screen [printing] a halftone screen (with degrees of varying density) photographically made on a film base, used in direct contact with a film or plate to produce a halftone negative of superior definition to one produced from a conventional glass screen

contact size [photography] a print the same size as the original, made with a *contact printer*

containerization the combining of separate lots of cargo in a single, standard large container, which is then shipped by rail (*piggyback*) or on *sea trains*, ships (*fishyback*), or other carriers

contd. continued

contemporary modern, current *Contemporary radio* stations have a format that appeals to youthful audiences

Contemporary Christian (CC) a radio-station format featuring nonchurch religious music, often in a country, jazz, or other contemporary mode

contemporary hit radio (CHR) a format designation for radio stations that broadcast current popular music and other best-selling records

content or **contents (cont.)** 1 a volume, area, or amount 2 the substance (not the form) or essential meaning (such as the *content* of a poem) 3 an outline of what something contains (generally plural, as in a *table of contents*) In a book, the *table of contents* generally starts on a *recto* (a right-hand page). 4 [computers] a display or printout of the accessible stored information

content analysis a research technique of studying media or other materials in order to systematically and objectively identify the characteristics of the messages For example, public relations researchers often analyze clippings and broadcast transcripts, for references to an organization or other client, and then analyze the content to determine trends and perceptions relevant to the client, such as the degree of favorability.

content curve [film] a table indicating the amount of time the average viewer will require to comprehend a shot The more complex it is, the longer the time needed to assimilate it.

contention 1 a statement or point that one argues for as valid 2 in data communications, a situation in which two or more communications devices attempt to transmit at the same instant over the same channel

contest a competition Participants or entrants are *contestants*, and the winners are selected on performance, not by chance. It is not the same as a *lottery* or *sweepstakes*, which are based on chance.

context the parts of a sentence or text next to a word or passage that help to determine its exact meaning A remark can be improperly quoted *out of context* by excluding its surrounding words. Context also refers to the entire situa-

tion, background, or environment relevant to a specific action. *Contextual* is the adjective.

contiguity programs or advertisements that follow, or are contiguous (*back-to-back*) Sponsors may receive a *contiguity rate*, a reduced price for such time purchased within one broadcast day (*vertical contiguity*) or across the board for a week (*horizontal contiguity*).

contiguous referring to something adjoining *Contiguous graphics* have no gaps between adjacent cells, in contrast to *separated graphics*.

continental seating an arrangement of seats in a theater or other place without a center aisle, common in continental Europe but not the United States

contingency plan a preconceived backup program, to be executed in the event of an unforeseen or accidental alteration of circumstances

continuation 1 the act of continuing 2 something that keeps up or goes on, such as a further chapter, supplement, or sequel in a series

continuation line a line of text indicating that copy follows from a previous page

continuation page [videotex] a page that cannot be addressed directly by number because it is part of a larger page (the *main page*)

continuity 1 a regular flow of messages over a period of time, such as that generated by advertisers or public relations practitioners 2 [broadcasting] a quality of a script, giving the broadcaster a continuous flow of spoken words A *continuity acceptance department* (or *continuity clearance department*) reviews programming and advertising to eliminate unsubstantiated claims and illegal or objectionable material. 3 [film, broadcasting] the impression that events, scenes, and shots flow smoothly and naturally in proper sequence, without any inconsistent transitions (*continuity flaws*) A *continuity link* is an audio or visual device that helps in the transition from one scene to the next. 4 [direct marketing] a series of sales made over a period of time; see CONTINUITY PLAN

continuity advertising the continuous consistent use of the same advertising campaign and media over a period of time

continuity breakdown [film] a listing, drawn up prior to a day of shooting, of the technical information for each scene to be shot, including cast, equipment, and props required

continuity clerk [film] a person who assists the director, particularly in preparing copies of the script and keeping tracks of sequences to ensure continuity from one shot to the next; also called *continuity person, script clerk,* or *script super-*

visor; formerly called *continuity girl* or *script girl*

continuity cutting the editing of a film to ensure continuity; also called *continuity editing*

continuity discount a price reduction given to advertisers who have purchased a regular schedule of advertising over a stated period of time

continuity editing CONTINUITY CUTTING

continuity notes [film] a log or record of information about each TAKE, including its number and duration, a list of its props, and a description of its action; also called *continuity sheets* or *take sheets* The notes are maintained by a CONTINUITY CLERK.

continuity plan [direct marketing] a series of mailings (also called *continuous plan*) or a type of sale that consists of a series of items delivered over a period of time (also called CONTINUITY PROGRAM)

continuity program 1 an offer of products over a period of time, as by a supermarket 2 [publishing] an arrangement whereby a customer agrees to accept regular shipments of books, commemorative plates, or other mail-order products in a series A *closed-end continuity* has a fixed number of items, such as volumes of an encyclopedia; an *open-end continuity* (such as a magazine subscription) continues until it is canceled.

continuity sheets CONTINUITY NOTES

continuity sketches [film] rough drawings of each shot that assist the art director in creating the sets and the director in the actual shooting

continuity strip an advertisement or editorial feature in the horizontal format of a comic strip

continuous action [film] uninterrupted action within a scene, including more than one shot filmed by different cameras or from different views

continuous drive [film] a mechanism in a camera that moves a film from the magazine, or film container, to the camera body and then back to the magazine

continuous innovation the alteration or modification of an existing product, as distinguished from introducing a totally new product (*discontinuous innovation*) Dynamic continuous innovation fills needs that are brought about by new or changing lifestyles.

continuous plan [direct marketing] a series of mailings, generally at regularly scheduled intervals; more properly called CONTINUITY PLAN

continuous printer [film] a machine in which the film negative and positive print move without interruption In a *continuous contact printer,* the emulsions of the negative and positive are in continuous contact as they pass the

aperture. In a *continuous optical printer,* each frame of the negative or positive is projected through a lens onto unexposed film in a camera, a common procedure in changing a film format, as from 35mm to 16mm.

continuous printing [photography] a method of making prints rapidly, in which the exposed and unexposed film are in direct contact as they move synchronously past a lens aperture during exposure in a rotary camera

continuous processing a system that automatically transports photographs or other items through the various stages of duplicating and printing

continuous revision [publishing] the revising of portions of a work with each printing, rather than only at the time of a new edition

continuous roll insert a color insert for newspapers, preprinted on a continuous roll and later fed into the newspaper press; also called HI-FI insert

continuous tone a type of photographic reproduction in which the tonal values vary continuously, in contrast to a *halftone,* whose tonal values are broken up into black dots of varying size, shape, and proximity to one another Conventional photographs are *continuous-tone* and must be converted to *halftone* for printing, using a *halftone screen,* for example.

continuous wave an electromagnetic wave of constant amplitude and frequency, such as Morse code

contour 1 the outline of a figure; also called a *run-around* or *wrap-around* 2 a surface, especially of a curving form, as indicated on a *contour map* (on which *contour lines* connect points of equal elevation) There are three concentric ring areas of TV signal transmission: *City Grade Service,* which is the area closest to the station; *A contour,* the middle area; and *B contour,* the outermost area. 3 to outline

contouring the setting of type in an irregular shape to wrap around (*contour*) a photograph or other artwork; type set in this way

contract (cont.) 1 a legal agreement, particularly one dealing with terms of purchase or employment; to undertake by agreement 2 to acquire 3 to hire

contract feature a sales or promotion item for which a distributor or retailer receives special compensation from the manufacturer

contract film a motion picture with all of the costs paid by a specified party, such as a production company

contract player a performer who is employed for a specific project or period of time

contract year the year commencing when a contract takes effect It need not correspond to the *calendar year.*

contrapuntal referring to something containing counterpoint *Contrapuntal sound* is sound whose effect is contrary to or in contrast to the action, such as laughter or light music during a somber scene.

contrast 1 a difference, especially a striking difference 2 [photography] the degree of difference between the lightest (*highlights*) and darkest areas of a photograph, film, or scene *High contrast* indicates sharp differences, with less-than-average gray or middle values. *Contrasty* refers to something of high contrast.

contrast glass [film] an eyepiece used by a director of photography to determine lighting contrast

contrast ratio the range of gray between the darkest and brightest values in a TV picture, expressed by comparing dark to light, as in 20:1; also called *contrast range*

contre jour to photograph with the camera lens facing a light source, from the French for "against day"

contrib. CONTRIBUTION; CONTRIBUTOR

contributing editor [publishing] a writer who is not on the staff of a periodical or book publisher

contribution [publishing] an article or other material from a source outside the staff, such as a *freelancer, contributing editor,* or *publicist*

contributor [publishing] a writer (generally paid) of an article or a portion of a publication

contributor's page(s) one or more pages in a magazine or other publication, generally at the beginning, containing information about the authors of works in the publication

control [market research] a group or area not exposed to sampling, publicity, advertising, or other components of a test situation This group is evaluated in the same manner as and compared to the *test group* or *test area.* In research, the *control base* is the characteristic or characteristics common to an entire population. It can be the basis for analysis in terms of deviations of a population sample from the control base.

control area an area from which recording audio or video functions are monitored, selected, altered, and transmitted The control area houses the engineer and producer (in radio and recording), director, and other creative and technical staff. Outside a studio, a mobile *control booth* or van is used.

control ball [computers] a movable ball used as a locator device to control and make changes on a video screen; also called a *track ball*

control character [computers] a character that begins, changes, or stops the carrying out of a particular action Control characters are not printed. They include the CARRIAGE RETURN character, space character, and paragraph indentation character.

controlled circulation referring to publications sent to subscribers who do not pay directly; also called *qualified circulation* The publication may receive all or most of its income from advertisers, or it may be subsidized in other ways, such as by membership dues in the case of publications for members of organizations.

control room [broadcasting, recording] the room in which the director, engineer, and others adjust sound and/or video

control track a series of evenly spaced electronic blips or spikes (called sync pulses) on videotape that function like the *sprocket holes* of film The control track is essential in editing videotape.

Conus a TV news company, based in Minneapolis, MN, that provides global news coverage to local TV stations that are members on an exclusive market basis The name is short for Continental U.S.

convenience sample a survey of individuals selected quickly, such as because they are available (for the convenience of the interviewer) An example is the *man-on-the-street interview.*

convenience store (c-store) a type of supermarket with limited selection and long opening hours, such as a 7-11 store (originally open from 7:00 A.M. to 11:00 P.M.)

conversational mode a form of communication between a computer and a terminal that allows for continuous, immediate responses

conversion 1 a shift or change, as from an inquiry to a sale The incidence of *conversions* is the *conversion ratio* or *conversion rate.* 2 a change of purchase orientation, opinion, or vote; a switch from one product, service, issue, or candidate to another

converter 1 a device for changing or transforming something from one form to another 2 [radio] the part of a receiver that changes or modulates high frequencies to low frequencies 3 [television] the device that adapts a TV set built to receive only VHF channels to receive UHF channels also 4 the box or hardware that converts a cable signal into individual channels on a TV set An *addressable converter* can be attached to a TV set so that the cable-system operator can turn on a channel specifically for pay-for-view events.

cooked referring to an overdeveloped negative, produced (sometimes intentionally to compensate for insufficient light) by increasing the temperatures of the film-developing solution

cookie CUKALORIS

cool referring to a classification of color that is relaxed and not vibrant *Cool* colors include blue, green, and violet.

cool out [radio] to gradually lower the sound of the background music at the end of a commercial with a voice-over

co-op COOPERATIVE ADVERTISING, COOPERATIVE PROGRAM, or any other service or facility that is shared or is owned and operated for the benefit of its members, such as a *co-op store* (pronounced KOH-op)

Cooper a heavy typeface, with serifs

cooperative advertising 1 the sharing of cost of an advertising campaign between a manufacturer and its retailer 2 advertising whose costs are so shared An advertisement paid for in this way is called a *co-op ad* or simply a *co-op*

cooperative mailing the inclusion of enclosures from several advertisers in one envelope; also called *group mailing*

cooperative program a network or syndicated program designed for local sponsorships on the stations over which it is carried; sometimes called *co-op*

cooperative publisher a company that produces books subsidized in full or part by its authors; also called *vanity publisher, subsidy publisher*, or *vanity press*

coordinate of the same or equal order or importance, as in *coordinate clauses* in a compound sentence, in which each clause generally is linked by *and, but,* or *or*

coorientation measurement an analysis of the views of two individuals or groups in relation to each other, demonstrating how, for example, two individuals view a situation and also how each perceives the views of the other

co-owned station a radio or TV station that has the same ownership as another station, such as a co-owned AM station (an AM radio station that has the same ownership as an FM station, with the same or different *call letters*)

cop., copr., or **copy** COPYRIGHT

Copley News Service (CNS) a news service for newspapers and radio stations, owned by Copley Newspapers, San Diego, CA

copperplate an engraved plate for printing or an impression printed from it, often used for elegant letterheads, particularly of cursive hand-

writing or script Hence, *copperplate writing* connotes fine handwriting.

Copperplate a sans-serif typeface, available only in uppercase

coppers short form of *copper engravings*, now rarely used

copter mount a support (mount) that attaches a camera to a helicopter, used in aerial photography

copublication the publication of a book or other work by two or more publishers, simultaneously or in the same period, with shared editorial and production costs (perhaps involving *coproduction*) Examples are a hardcover book published by one company and a paperback version published by another company or organization, or a book produced by two or more publishers in different countries.

copy (cop.) 1 the text of an article, news release, advertisement, booklet, or other written work 2 [printing] any material (whether text or art) used in production, though it's generally an *original* (to be copied) 3 to duplicate 4 (abbreviated *c.*) a duplicate, such as of a publication, or a *photocopy* 5 to receive a message or to understand a transmitted message, as in the radio transmission, "Do you copy me?"

copy approach a basic theme of an advertisement or campaign, not the opening part of an advertisement; also called *copy outline, copy plan, copy platform,* or *copy policy* It serves as a guide for copywriters and others to the major points and objectives.

copy block 1 a section of text or copy 2 [broadcasting] the portion of the script to be read In TV, this is written on the right half or two-thirds of the page, with cues and technical details written on the left. In radio, it's generally written across most of the page, with technical information in the upper left or lower right margins, in parentheses, circled, or otherwise identified so as not to be read on the air. The copy block is generally typed in all capital letters.

Copy Block an adhesive-back material, made by Craftint Manufacturing Company of Cleveland, OH, consisting of preprinted blocks of copy in various type sizes to indicate the area such copy will occupy in a layout

copyboard 1 a board or frame that holds an original while it is photographed for offset printing The original is taped or affixed to the surface of an open-faced glass cover or inserted in a glass-faced frame. 2 the flat level platform of a copying or duplicating machine, held in place by a *copyholder*

copybook a pamphlet or book with models of handwriting, formerly used to teach penmanship

copy boy [newspapers] an employee who carries copy and runs errands; if female, *copy girl*

copy caster a scale or chart that helps to determine the amount of space a block of text (in a specific typeface and type size) will occupy, a process called *copy casting*

copy check COPY EDIT

copy count COPYFIT

copy cutter an individual in a *composing room* who divides copy into *takes*, portions to be assigned to each typesetter so as to maintain a steady work flow The copy cutter also reassembles the typeset material in proper order.

copy desk a section of a publication responsible for editing material turned in by reporters and other writers; sometimes incorrectly called *rewrite desk* The headlines are generally written here. The supervisor of the copy desk is the COPY EDITOR and its staff are COPYREADERS or COPY READERS.

copy dot [printing] to photograph dot for dot, so as to exactly match the original (as of a screen)

copy edit 1 a process of proofreading or checking text (copy) for accuracy and consistency in form (such as footnotes, references, and other details); also called *mechanical edit* To copy edit is to carry out this process. Copy editing is the boot camp of journalism; many top *New York Times* editors and reporters started as copy editors, including Arthur Gelb and Peter Millones.

copy editor (c.e.) 1 one who performs copy editing 2 [newspaper] a person in charge of the COPY DESK

copyfit to edit text (copy) to fit a specific space The process is *copyfitting*, also called a *copy count.*

copyguard signals or other material inserted in computer tapes and videotapes to prevent duplication of the contents; also called *copy protection* Viewers of rented videotapes sometimes notice lines, jagged edges, darkening, or shifts in color and other manifestation of copyguard.

copyholder 1 one who reads manuscript, proofs or other material to the proofreader 2 a device that holds copy in place, as for a typist or typesetter

copyist a transcriber, a person who makes written copies A *music copyist* copies original sheet music to make parts for each performer.

copy line a slogan or primary phrase or message in an advertisement

copy negative an intermediate negative from which photographic prints (*copy prints*) can be produced mechanically in quantity, at a lower price than if produced individually by hand

copy outline COPY APPROACH

copy paper 1 paper, generally white, used in a duplicating machine 2 low-cost typing paper, generally yellow, used by newspaper reporters and others

copy plan COPY APPROACH

copy platform COPY APPROACH

copy policy COPY APPROACH

copy preparation the mechanical assembly of art and text prior to printing

copy protection COPYGUARD

copy reader or **copyreader** [newspaper] someone who works at a *copy desk* Copy readers are generally experienced veterans, skilled at rapid rewriting. Rarely identified in print, they are the unsung heroes of journalism.

copyright (c.,©, cop., Cop. R.) the exclusive legal rights of artists, authors, composers, publishers, and others to the contents of a publication, broadcast, or other piece of work, so that it is protected from plagiarism or imitation In the United States, copyright is granted to the *copyright holder* (owner) by the Copyright Office of the Library of Congress. In books, the *copyright notice* generally appears on the *copyright page,* the reverse of the title page. The *copyright symbol* is ©, followed by the year (*copyright data*) and the name of the author or copyright holder. The word also can be used as a verb.

Copyright Clearance Center an organization based in Salem, MA, that collects payments for use of material photocopied by companies and libraries and distributes these royalties to publishers, particularly of scientific and technical books and journals

copy schedule a listing of stories assigned for a forthcoming issue of a newspaper or other publication

copy slant [advertising] the way that the points in the theme (*copy platform*) are presented The platform can remain the same while the slant changes, to appeal to different audiences.

copywrite to write advertising or publicity text (*copy*) One who performs this task is a *copywriter.*

coquille board a heavy paper with a pebbled surface on which an artist can produce a sketch, with shaded effects, by quickly drawing with a crayon or pencil A *coquille,* pronounced cohKEEL, is a cockle shell or scallop shell with a pebbled surface.

cor. CORNER; CORRECTION; correspondence; CORRESPONDENT

c.o.r. CASH ON RECEIPT

coranto 1 an early 17th-century newssheet, the earliest form of a newspaper Corantos were published in Holland, Germany, and England and were devoted primarily to foreign news.

cordless sync [film] a technique in DOUBLE-SYSTEM sound recording in which the camera and tape recorder are synchronized without a *sync-pulse cable* or other cable (cord), as via a CRYSTAL SYNC system; also called *cableless sync*

cords [book production] the cotton or other strings or bands to which sections of a book are sewn in binding Instead of these thin cords, the sections may be sewn to *strips* (tapes).

core 1 the center, such as the central portion of a spindle or reel on which paper, film, or tape is wound 2 the shaft on which rollers of a printing press are mounted 3 the main memory area of a computer

corn something trite or mawkish The adjective form is *corny*.

corner (cor.) [book production] the place where the turn-in of one edge of a book cover meets that of another Types include *Dutch corner* or *library corner* (in which the covering material is not cut and an excess is taken up in two diagonal folds, one under each turn-in), *mitered corner* (in which a triangular piece of the covering material is cut off so that the turn-ins meet without overlapping), *round corner* or *rounded corner* (in which the board is rounded at the corner before the covering material, which is generally leather, is added), and *square corner* (in which a piece of the covering material is cut at the corner so that one turn-in overlaps the other, without additional folding).

corner bullet a small dot in each corner of an advertisement, or other printed matter, that serves as a guide to its positioning

corner card the text or art on an outer envelope to attract the recipient, as on direct mail

corner marks [printing] open parts of squares ($\_^|$ or $^|\_$) placed on original copy as a positioning guide

corporate art a collection of paintings, sculpture, or other works of art displayed by a company or commercial organization

corporate graphics any annual reports, manuals, or other materials designed and produced for commercial use by companies and organizations

corporate identity the individuality or personality of a company, expressed in the *house style*, that is, the set of conventions, such as the logotype (company signature) by which an organization presents (identifies) itself

Corporation for Public Broadcasting (CPB) a nonprofit, nongovernmental agency whose purpose is to promote and assist noncommercial radio and television stations within the United States It is funded by the U.S. Government and private sources and is based in Washington, DC.

corpse [theater] to frighten another performer onstage, usually to provoke laughter, as in a prank in which a corpse is replaced with a live actor or actress

corr. CORRECTION; correspondence; CORRESPONDENT

Corrasable the name of a trademarked typewriter paper that is erasable, manufactured by the Eaton Corporation of Pittsfield, MA

correct (CQ or CX) [publishing] an instruction to a typesetter to leave incorrectly spelled copy as is

correction (cor. or corr.) a removal of an error; a revision Occasionally, a publicist sends out a news release with an error and is required to follow up with a correction. To err is human, and the proof of this is that many publications now acknowledge their own errors with departments frequently called *Corrections*. A *correction sheet* is a small piece of coated paper placed over a typewritten error; when the erroneous key is struck again, the coating is transferred to cover the mistake. The major manufacturer is the Eaton Allen Corporation (based in Brooklyn, NY), whose product is called *Ko-Rec-Type*.

corrective a remedial or compensatory correction A newspaper may publish a *corrective* that discusses an error and is more extensive than a mere *correction*. In addition to an editor's note, the newspaper may even publish a *corrective article*.

corrective advertising any advertising ordered by the Federal Trade Commission or instituted voluntarily by an advertiser, the purpose of which is to correct an error or deception in a previous advertisement

corres. correspondence; CORRESPONDENT

correspondent (cor., corr., or corres.) a reporter who is a full-time or part-time employee of one of the media (not a *stringer* or *freelancer*) and who is based elsewhere than the headquarters of the employer

corridor panel a billboard or poster on the wall of a passageway, as in a railroad station or airline terminal

corrigendum a printer's error or other error to be corrected *Corrigenda* is a heading for a list of errors in a book with their corrections; it is also called *errata*.

corrugate to shape into parallel grooves or ridges

corrugation 1 a process that produces corrugated paper or cardboard, with a wrinkled surface, that is resilient and hence used for packing 2 a paper defect, consisting of small parallel ridges

corrupt referring to something that has been changed or contaminated, such as a text or a language that has been altered improperly or contains alterations, errors, or mixtures of foreignisms, as in a *corrupt text*

corx an instruction to a printer to correct the text

cost a price or charge In marketing, the *average cost* is the total cost of production and distribution divided by the number of units produced; the *average fixed cost* (*AFC*) is the *total fixed cost* (*TFC*) divided by the quantity; and the *average variable cost* (*AVC*) is the total variable cost (*TVC*) divided by the number of units.

cost-benefit the usefulness to the party paying for a product, process, or service in relation to its cost, expressed as a *cost-benefit ratio* The reverse, *benefit-cost ratio*, can also indicate the relative utility or economic efficiency. Benefit exceeding expenditure is termed *cost-effective* and *cost-efficient*, or *cost-effectiveness* and *cost-efficiency*.

cost center the department of an organization to which production and/or other direct actual costs are allocated If revenue is allocated to the same division, the *cost center* can also become a *profit center*.

cost efficiency the effectiveness of something in relation to its cost *Cost per order* (sales divided by advertising or promotional cost), *cost per thousand* (circulation or audience), and *cost per page per thousand* circulation are measures of cost efficiency.

cost-of-living adjustment (COLA) a change in rent, wage, price, or other fee related to the cost-of-living-index or otherwise linked to the overall cost of living

cost out to determine the cost

cost per impression a calculation of the cost of an advertisement or a message to reach an individual reader, viewer, or other audience member

cost per inquiry (CPI) [direct marketing] the cost of a mailing or other campaign divided by the number of responses, such as coupons, calls, or other inquiries

cost per interview (CPI) the total cost to the sponsor of market research of each interview completed in a project, including personnel, telephone, tabulation, and other expenses

cost per order (CPO) the cost of all advertising and sales expenses divided by the actual number of items sold or orders received, a measure of promotional efficiency In periodical sales, the ratio is expressed as *cost per subscription* or *cost per copy.*

cost per point (CPP) [broadcasting] the cost of purchasing or delivering one GROSS RATING POINT (GRP) It is a measure of media efficiency and is determined by dividing the cost of the advertising by the gross audience rating points. For any given spot announcement, unit cost ÷ audience rating = cost per point. Costs per point vary according to time of day and geographical area.

cost per thousand (CPM) the cost of advertising for each 1,000 homes reached by radio or TV, for each 1,000 copies circulated of a publication, or for each 1,000 potential viewers of an outdoor advertisement

cost-plus pricing a method of setting a price by adding a fixed or variable amount (generally a percentage of the cost) to the cost; also called *cost-oriented pricing Market-based pricing*, such as *market-minus* and *market-plus* pricing, is based on what others are charging.

cost ratio a comparison of advertisements within one issue of a publication, arrived at by assessing the readership of each advertisement and dividing each of those figures by the cost of the individual advertisement

costume the clothing and accessories worn by a performer, generally designed or selected by a *costume designer* A *costume maker* constructs costumes, generally in a *costume shop* that is part of a film studio or an outside company (a *costume company*). The sewing is done by *seamsters* (men) or *seamstresses* (women). The *costume designer* can also select from items in a *wardrobe department* and supervises the *wardrobe supervisor.*

Costume Designers Guild a Los Angeles branch of the International Alliance of Theatrical Stage Employees (IATSE)

costume plot a list (plot) of all characters in a play or other work and their costumes, generally arranged scene by scene; also called *dress plot*

costumer [film] an assistant wardrobe technician who works on a set to store and maintain costumes

cottage [book production] referring to a style (*cottage style*) of binding (*cottage binding*) in which the top and bottom of the center panel have a triangular or gable-like design (akin to a cottage), a characteristic of late 17th-century English bindings

couch potato a person who stays at home (sits on a couch) and vegetates (is sedentary, like a potato), especially by watching TV for long periods

couch roll a part of a paper-making machine that removes water from paper *Couch marks* are spots on paper from uneven or improper drying.

cough and a spit [theater] slang for a brief part

cough button a switch used by a radio announcer to cut off the microphone during a cough

Council for the Advancement and Support of Education (CASE) the major U.S. organization (based in Washington, DC) in the field of college fundraising and public relations, with over 10,000 members

Council of American Survey Research Organizations (CASRO) a professional organization (based in Port Jefferson, NY) of private survey research companies, with about 130 members

Council on International Nontheatrical Events (CINE) an organization of directors and others in short subjects, documentaries, and other nontheatrical films and tapes Based in Washington, DC, it presents annual CINE awards, including the Golden Eagle and Eagle Certificates.

count the total quantity of items in a collection, sample, or shipment, such as a *case count* or *word count* For outdoor advertising, traffic is counted in the morning (*AM count*) and the afternoon (*PM count*).

countdown or **count down** a numbered lead-in segment of a film or tape (with progressively lower numbers) to cue the projectionist

counter 1 a person or device that counts 2 a coin, token, or small piece (as in a game to keep score) 3 a long table (as in a store) 4 opposite or contrary 5 [printing] the white space within a type character The fully enclosed portion of a lowercase *e* is called a *full counter* and the partly enclosed portion below it is called a *partial counter.* 6 [computers] a storage location or other device that represents a number 7 [theater] for a performer, the act of moving in the opposite direction to another performer This is also called *countercross* or *countering.*

counteract to oppose

counter advertising any advertising against a company or group, as by a labor union urging consumers not to purchase a product

counter card an advertising card or point-of-sale display on a store counter

counter focus [theater] a technique in which some performers face toward (focus on) secondary characters instead of the principal character, so that all of the performers are not looking at the principal performer, as they do in *actual line focus* and *visual line focus*

countermark a secondary watermark on handmade paper, such as marks on paper made in the 19th century that show the initials of the maker, place, or date, often near the edge of the sheet

counterplot a subplot that contrasts with the main plot of a work, either reinforcing or controverting it

counter prepack a display unit with a small amount of merchandise, such as candies or paperback books, generally placed near the cash register of a retail outlet

counterprogramming the scheduling of a program (on a station or network) that appeals to one type of audience, to air at the same time as a program on another station or network appealing to a different type of audience

countersunk [book production] a book cover with a depression pressed or stamped on it to receive an inlay, label, or decoration

counter word a commonly used, trite word, such as *great* or *fine.*

counting in a system or process of assigning one or more units to each character and space in order to calculate the total area they will occupy, a process necessary for a headline

counting keyboard a typesetting or typing keyboard that subtracts the width of each character it has typed from the overall line measure, so that the line can be ended and *justified* at the proper margin

counting station a place where vehicles and/or pedestrians are counted, as by a government agency or an outdoor advertising auditor

count retention the ability of word processing equipment to retain and display the current and previous block, batch, and item counts

country referring to someone or something rural or small-town *Country copy* is news or feature material from correspondents and stringers in nonurban areas for a big-city publication.

country-club billing a practicing of enclosing copies of all sales checks with a monthly statement, as is done by social clubs and other organizations

country edition an edition of a newspaper distributed regionally or nationally For many years, the *New York Sunday News* published a country edition, containing features but no late-breaking news, that was distributed several days prior to its Sunday date

country music (C) a format designation for radio stations that play only or primarily popular music of the country style It was formerly called *country and western* (abbreviated *C and W*).

Country Music Television (CMT) a cable-television network that programs country music, based in Hendersonville, TN

county an administrative district, ranging from a city or part of a city to very large rural areas where the county government is located (in a town or city called the *county seat*) A. C. NIELSEN has designated all U.S. counties as *A, B, C,* or *D counties,* and this designation is commonly used by many marketers and others. An *A county,* any county in the 25 largest U.S. cities or their *consolidated statistical urban areas,* has the largest population. A *B county* is a major urban or suburban area and *C* and *D counties* are rural areas. There are five counties in New York City: New York (the borough of Manhattan), Kings (Brooklyn), Queens, Bronx, and Richmond (Staten Island).

coup de théâtre a successful play; a showy or sensational segment of stagecraft

couplet two successive lines of poetry, generally rhymed and having the same length and meter A stanza may consist of a pair of couplets, totaling four lines, in which the first two lines rhyme and the third and fourth lines rhyme.

coupon 1 a certificate or ticket entitling the holder to a specified right, such as redemption for cash or gifts or a reduced purchase price 2 a part of a printed advertisement for use in ordering goods, samples, or literature

coupon clipper [direct marketing] a person who responds to advertising by sending in free- or special-offer coupons without any intent to purchase the product being advertised

couponing the use of coupons in a product sales campaign

coupon pad a batch of cents-off certificates or other coupons attached to a CAR CARD or point-of-sale display

coupon page a sheet containing coupons, generally ones that offer *cents off* or other discounts or premiums related to food, drugs, or other consumer products, often preprinted on one or both sides and supplied for insertion in newspapers or other publications

coupon plan a program in which free goods, premiums, or other incentives can be obtained by sending in proof-of-purchase coupons

courtesy bias a tendency of people being surveyed to give an answer they consider socially correct or desirable

courtesy copy a copy of an original letter or other document sent with the original so that the recipient can route the copy and retain the original

courtesy line a credit line appearing immediately below an illustration or other item, indicating the source of the item, such as *Photo courtesy of U.S. Army*

courtesy of the profession [theater] slang for free admissions to a theater with professional identification, such as an Actors' Equity card In the United Kingdom, it's also called *on your card.*

courtesy pass a reduced-price or free admission ticket

courtesy reply envelope a preaddressed return envelope on which the sender must affix postage; not the same as a *business reply envelope,* which does not require postage by the sender Courtesy reply envelopes are used by banks, utilities, and others to expedite payment, though they are becoming superseded by *window envelopes.* They are also used in direct marketing.

cove 1 a recess 2 [film] a background-scenery baseboard that generally contains a row of lights; also called a *ground row* or *coving* This plain curved background can be used in photography to give the impression of infinity.

cover 1 an overlay, for protection or concealment 2 an envelope or mailing or other protective wrapper 3 the front or back of a book or other publication *Cover 1* is the outside front cover, *cover 2* is the inside front cover, *cover 3* is the inside back cover, and *cover 4* is the outside back cover; they are also known as *first cover, second cover,* and so on. If a publication's cover paper is the same type and weight as the inside, it is a *self-cover.* 4 an envelope with postal markings or cancellations, such as a *first day cover* (cancelled on the first day of issue of a new stamp) or a *first flight cover* (a souvenir envelope postmarked on the first day of service on an air route) *Mail cover* is a record of information on the outside cover of mail, made by the U.S. Postal Service for special purposes, such as to locate a criminal. 5 a new version of a previously recorded song or musical composition 6 [theater] an understudy; a backup performer; a performer who blocks another performer from the audience's view; to act as an understudy 7 to be responsible for executing or reporting, as to *cover* an event 8 to protect or insure

coverage (cvg) 1 [journalism] the media treatment, the extent to which an event is reported 2 [broadcasting] the geographical area (usually counties) in which a station is received by viewers or listeners, as indicated on a *coverage map* 3 [film, television] the photographing of a scene from various views and using various exposures 4 the circulation area, demographics, or other data pertaining to the sales of a publication

cover art art (an illustration and/or lettering) that appears on the cover of a publication

cover date a date appearing on the cover of a magazine or other periodical; not necessarily the date of publication, and generally a date in the week, month, or other period following the date of issue

covering the blocking or concealing of a performer from the audience or camera by another performer

covering power [film, television] the capacity of a camera lens to pick up (cover) a clear image over the entire frame

cover ink heavy ink, such as that used to print covers

cover letter a brief letter accompanying and presenting a manuscript or other item; not the same as a *query letter*, which is unaccompanied

cover model a model whose photograph appears on the cover of a publication A young female cover model is sometimes called a *cover girl*.

cover photograph a photograph appearing on the cover of a publication

cover position a cover of a magazine or other publication that is available to an advertiser, usually at a price higher than that for an inside page

cover price the retail price of a publication, as indicated on the outside or inside cover; also called *street price* or *newsstand price* This is different from the *home-delivered price* for newspapers.

covers bound in [library science] an indication that the original covers of a book or other volume are included, or to be included, in a later binding

cover scene a brief scene in a play that allows time for such backstage activities as a costume or scenery change

cover shot 1 [television] a wide or long-distance view, such as generally begins a sequence, to establish the location 2 a photograph or film to be used as a backup in case additional or replacement material is needed later

cover stock a paper used to cover a publication that is heavier than the pages inside

cover story an article featured on the cover of a magazine or other publication, generally the major article in the issue With the development of magazine-style TV programs, many print terms have come into use by broadcasters; thus *cover story* also denotes a major feature or sequence on a TV program.

cow catcher 1 a series of comments made before the introduction of a show or broadcast to capture attention 2 a commercial preceding or at the beginning of a program

cowlick slang for a hasty or cheap process, particularly a poorly varnished book jacket

Cox Enterprises one of the country's largest media companies, headquartered in Atlanta It publishes the *Atlanta Journal* and other newspapers and owns major radio and TV stations and cable TV systems.

CP CANADIAN PRESS & BROADCAST NEWS

CPB CORPORATION FOR PUBLIC BROADCASTING

cph characters per hour

CPI characters per inch (see CHARACTER PITCH); cost per inquiry; cost per interview

cpl characters per line

c.p.m. CHARACTERS PER MINUTE; cycles per minute

CPM COST PER THOUSAND

CPP characters per pica; COST PER POINT

C print a color print made from EKTACOLOR or another negative, less expensive than (and not of as high quality as) a *dye transfer print*; also called *type C print*

CPRS CANADIAN PUBLIC RELATIONS SOCIETY

c.p.s. characters per second

CPS CYCLES PER SECOND

CPU CENTRAL PROCESSING UNIT; computer processing unit

cq wire-service jargon for *correction*; its derivation is from CALL TO QUARTERS

CQ CALL TO QUARTERS; CONGRESSIONAL QUARTERLY SERVICE; CORRECT

C-Quam *Compatible Quadrature Amplitude Modulation*

CR CAMERA-READY; carriage reset; CARRIAGE RETURN; CENTER right; right CENTER

crab a method of moving a TV or film camera on a pedestal, on which all wheels are steered simultaneously; the mobile unit used in *crabbing* The method is used for lateral movements (*crab shots*), particularly in small areas. The instructions are *crab left* (or *truck left*) and *crab right* (or *truck right*).

cradle a mount to attach a large lens to a camera; also called a *lens support* or *support mount*

cradle book a publication using movable metal type, printed during the last half of the 15th century, the period known as the *cradle of printing*; also called *incunabulum* (Latin for "in the cradle")

Craftint Manufacturing Co. [graphic arts] a major manufacturer, based in Cleveland, OH, of commonly used supplies, including *Craft-Color* (acetate sheets), *Craf-Tech* (preprinted patterns), *Craf-Type* (wax-backed acetate sheets of type in many sizes and faces), and *Craftint* (acetate sheets commonly used in the BENDAY process)

craft service [film] people who provide snacks and run miscellaneous errands These are important functions on location, and those responsible are sometimes listed in the credits.

crane [film, television] a vehicle with a movable arm or *boom* (generally hydraulic) that moves a platform on which are a camera and a crew; sometimes called *whirly* A crane typically has three seats, for the director, camera operator, and camera assistant or *focus puller*. The base of the vehicle is called a *trolley*. Cranes are ubiquitous on movie sets. A *crane shot* or *boom shot* is a shot taken from a crane.

crane operator a person who operates the camera trolley; also called a *crane grip* The *crane operator* reports to the *key grip*.

craning the movement of film or TV camera cranes (*booms*) and platforms; also called *booming*

crank 1 a handle, such as one at the side of a movie camera whose function is to advance or rewind the film 2 to operate a camera, including a motorized model without a handle *Overcranking* is filming at a high speed, to produce a slow-motion effect when the film is projected at the regular speed.

cranks [advertising] the initial or preliminary plans, particularly a list of proposed media for an advertising campaign

crash 1 [book production] a coarse, gauzelike fabric glued to the backbone of a book as reinforcement; also called *gauze, mull,* or *super* 2 [computers] a blocked or misdirected action due to a hardware or software malfunction

crash finish a rough surface of some kinds of paper, akin to coarse linen

crash printing any method of duplicating without ink using pressure, as with carbon paper

crawl a body of typed information, such as a news bulletin, promotional message, telephone number, or cast credits, that is transmitted in a continuous flow across all or part of a TV screen (often the bottom); also called *crawl roll* The effect is produced by mounting the text on a drumlike mechanism, the *crawl roll*. The crawl can be horizontal (across the top or bottom of the screen) or vertical (from the bottom, moving up). It is positioned in the *crawl space*.

crayon a small stick of chalk, charcoal, or (most commonly) colored wax used for drawing or similar purposes A *lithographic crayon* is a hard black wax stick in a paper wrapper; it is used for *line art*.

crayon engraving a method of etching in which the drawing lines are imitated through the use of wheels, disks, or other tools

cream 1 to select the best parts of something *Creaming a list* is selecting its most desirable names, such as those of previous customers or the most likely prospects. The derivation is from the separation of cream from the rest of milk. 2 to defeat decisively or beat vigorously

crease 1 a wrinkle or fold 2 to make a partial fold in paper or board, such as in displays, cartons, and other items that are shipped flat and then assembled

creative 1 referring to something having, showing, or demanding artistic or imaginative effort 2 [advertising, public relations] referring to those people who are involved in developing the concepts and executing a campaign, as distinguished from the *production, accounting,* and other so-called *noncreative* people Publicists (and others) often meet to develop ideas in what may be called a *creative meeting* or *creative session*. In some agencies, media specialists, writers, and others may be grouped into a *creative department*, headed by a *creative director*.

creative strategy a general outline of a campaign, including its objective, audience, premise, and theme

credit 1 acknowledgment of work done, as in a film, play, or broadcast *Credits* may come at the beginning of a film (*opening* or *head credits*) or the end (*closing* or *tail credits*), or in a printed program or other publication (often in the publisher's letter or in a separate section of a magazine). In advertisements for motion pictures and other attractions, and in the opening title of a movie, poster, theatrical program, or other material, the order of names in the credits, size of type, and other visual aspects are extremely important to the individuals acknowledged; hence they are often specified in advance by their contracts. In a movie advertisement, the *presentation credit* precedes the title and may be in the form of a possessory *credit*, such as *Cecil B. DeMille's,* or a *special credit*, such as *Samuel Goldwyn Presents. Head credits* are at the beginning of a film and always end with the name of the director. When the principal credits are at the end of the film, the director's name appears first. The *tail credits* are at the end of a film and include the entire cast and other personnel. 2 an explicit reference to a product, company, or other source or sponsor; also called *plug*

credit line 1 the name of an artist, photographer, or other source or originator of a published text or illustration It generally appears immediately below and to the right of a photograph or art, sometimes as part of the *title* or *byline*. Though sources of wire-service stories are identified with the initials of the wire service in the *dateline* at the beginning of the story, sometimes the wire service is identified in a *credit line*, such as *By The Associated Press*, that is centered below the headline.

credit subscription an order to purchase future issues of a publication that is not accompanied by full payment A credit subscriber is not as committed to purchase as one with a prepaid subscription.

creep 1 a slow, gradual movement 2 a slip out of place 3 [printing] a movement or slippage of the blanket of a press, resulting in *misregistering*

creeper 1 a performer who is too close to the microphone 2 a *dolly* for a small camera

creeping title an optical effect in which text moves from the bottom to the top of a screen; see also CRAWL

creepy peepy a portable TV camera, or MINI-CAM; also spelled *creepy-peepy, creepie peepie*, or *creepie-peepie*

crew a group of workers on a site or production, as distinguished from performers (*cast*) A production crew includes a *lighting crew, prop crew, stage crew*, and other crews; a *house crew* is the staff of the box office and all areas except the stage.

crew call [film] a posted notice (*call sheet*) for production personnel, such as the *camera crew*, indicating the time and place of the upcoming shooting

CRI COLOR REVERSAL INTERMEDIATE

crib an instance or result of cheating or plagiarism

crib card [film] a *shot sheet*; a sequential list of dialogue, scenes, or sequences

crimping a process of pinching together or folding the edge of one part tightly over another, used in making packages and other paper products In broadcasting, a jack is attached to a cable by squeezing the sleeve of the jack around the end of the cable.

crit. critic; critical; criticism

critical focus [film, television] precision-sharp clarity of image; an instruction to a camera operator of this requirement for a specific scene Areas in front of and behind the subject may be blurred or imperfect.

critical hours [radio] the two-hour period following sunrise and the two-hour period preceding sunset A few AM radio stations are required by the Federal Communications Commission to operate only between the sunrise and sunset in their areas.

crix critics (a word coined by *Variety*)

crocus cloth a heavy cloth, commonly used as a gentle abrasive by commercial artists to polish the metal surfaces of pens and other tools It has a surface of *jeweler's rouge* (commonly called *crocus*), a reddish powder (mainly ferric oxide) used to polish metal jewelry.

Cromalin proof a full-color copy, created chemically; a trademarked product of Du Pont, of Wilmington, DE

Cronar a trademarked polyester photographic film base, made by Du Pont (based in Wilmington, DE) and commonly used for many printing products

crop to trim off or edit out one or more portions of a piece of artwork, or a photograph; an essential part of the editing process

cropmark a mark or line indicating a portion of a photograph or artwork to be eliminated

cropper's L a piece of cardboard or metal shaped like an L Two cropper's Ls are placed over a photo to form a rectangle, which helps to determine what portions should be cropped.

croquis a rough sketch, especially one by a fashion designer; from the French verb *croquer*, "to sketch" An alternative anglicized spelling is *croque* and the plural is *croques*, pronounced crow-KEY and crow-KEYS.

cross 1 [film, television, theater] a movement of a performer across a stage or set Types include *direct cross* (movement in a straight line) and *curved cross* (one or more curves in moving from one place to another). The starting and ending points of the movement are sometimes shown on the stage or stage plan with an *X* (cross). 2 a figure made by two or more intersecting bars or lines Among the most common crosses used in printing and art are: +, the Greek cross (a plus sign); †, Latin cross (a dagger); and X, St. Andrew's cross.

crossbar a horizontal stroke of a typed or typeset character that crosses the character's stem, as in a *t*

cross-couponing a technique whereby a cents-off certificate or other *coupon* promotes price reductions or special offers for more than one item

crosscut [film] to edit the shots of two or more scenes together so that bits of each scene are presented; also called *intercut parallel cut*

cross direction the direction across the grain of paper

cross dissolve 1 [film] an effect or technique in which one sound or picture fades out while the next fades in over it; also called *cross fade, dissolve*, or *cross lap* 2 the dimming of one light as another is brought in; also called *cross-dim*

crossed gray scale   CHIPCHART

cross-fold   a right-angle fold

cross front   a camera movement in which a lens is moved laterally

cross grain   [printing] a fold at a right angle to the direction of the grain of paper or to the binding edge of a book

crosshatch or **cross hatch**   1 a pair of parallel horizontal lines with a pair of intersecting parallel vertical lines (#)   One or more *crosshatches* are often used to indicate the end of a news release, article, or other text, centered on an otherwise blank line, such as # # #.   2 crossed lines that produce an OPTICAL GRID or matrix effect, used for shading in certain areas of a drawing

cross-head   a numeral or other identification of a subsection, as at the beginning of a subdivision of a chapter

crossing the line   [film, television] the movement of a camera across an imaginary line between two performers, so that the camera takes on a different perspective and the view is in a different direction from the preceding shot   This usually confuses the viewer and generally is the result of an unintentional error. It is also called *crossing the imaginary line* and *crossing the proscenium* (moving from one side to the other).

cross light   a sidelight directed across a subject that emphasizes texture; to light a subject from the side; to angle spotlights or other lights so that their beams meet at a right angle

crosslighting   illumination from the side of the subject, between *front lighting* and *backlighting*

crossline   a one-line headline, centered on a full line and part of a headline of several sections, or *decks*, such as those used in *The Wall Street Journal*

crossmarks   small hairline crosses that aid in alignment and registration in multi-stage printing

cross media ownership   ownership of two or more types of media, as of a newspaper and a broadcasting station; also called *cross-ownership*

crossover   1 a shift from one medium or style of artistic output to another, as with a country-music singer who performs rock music   2 referring to a work not in the style with which an artist is normally identified, as in a *crossover recording*   3 [photography] a condition in which the shadows and highlights of a color negative are not harmonious   4 [theater] a lateral passage, such as one behind the stage or from one aisle to another

cross-ownership or **crossownership**   ownership by one organization of interests in more than one type of medium   The term generally refers to ownership of print media (newspapers and/or magazines) and broadcast stations or networks.

cross-plot   [film] a one-page summary of a shooting schedule; an abridged *breakdown*

cross plug   a commercial for an ALTERNATE SPONSOR of a program

cross-question   to question closely; to cross-examine

cross-reader   [advertising] a bulletin or poster that is visible in the lanes on the opposite side of the roadway from where it is placed   It is not the same as an irritable reader!

cross-reference   a notation in a publication directing the reader to another part of the same publication

crossruff   an advertisement or other promotion involving two or more companies   The origin is from bridge and other card games, meaning alternate plays by partners.

cross-stemmed W   a styled letter, W, in which the central strokes cross

cross-stroke   a part of a typographic character that cuts horizontally across the stem   There are three cross-strokes in an *E*.

cross-talk   1 live conversation between broadcasters, as between an anchorperson and an on-site reporter   2 a voice, sounds, or noise heard on a telephone or other electronic receiver that has been picked up from another channel or circuit

crotch   the part of a typographic character that is inside an apex, such as the top part of *A*, or a vortex, such as two areas of *W*

crowd   1 to press, push, or cram   A *crowded* layout is too *busy* and has too many elements or elements too close together.   2 [printing] to intentionally heavily ink in order to print darker

crow foot   the metal brace on which a camera tripod is mounted

crow quill   a type of sharp pen point, akin to the stem (quill) of a crow's feather, used by artists for line drawings   A CROQUIS is sometimes made with a crow-quill pen.

crow's feet   metal brackets that fit into slots to form the support or feet of a point-of-sale display

CRT   CATHODE-RAY TUBE

CRU   COMPUTER RESOURCE UNIT

crutch tip   a rubber cap to cover the bottom of a leg of a metal stand or other pole, such as a lighting stand

CRV   How do you receive? (international telex abbreviation)

crystallization 1 the solidification of ink when it dries, preventing succeeding colors from adhering properly 2 the assumption of a definite form 3 [public relations] the art of raising consciousness or bringing to the fore previously dormant or subconsciously held opinions

crystal set an early radio receiver using a clear quartz (*crystal*) instead of an electron tube as a *detector*

crystal sync [film] a technique for simultaneously recording the image on film and the sound on magnetic tape, both in synchronization (*double system sound recording*) though without connecting cables (therefore *cableless sync* or *cordless sync*); also called *crystal cordless sync*, *crystal control*, or *crystal drive* The system uses oscillating crystals of the same frequency in the camera drive and in the sync pulse generator that is attached to the magnetic tape recorder.

crystal synchronization [film] a technique in double-system sound recording in which the camera and tape recorder are not synchronized by a cable but each has an oscillating crystal of identical frequency; also called *crystal control*, *crystal-controlled motor*, *crystal-controlled sync*, *crystal cordless sync*, *crystal sound*, or *crystal signal*

c1s coated one side; see COATED PAPER

cs. CASE

CS CLOSE SHOT

CSA CANADIAN STANDARDS ASSOCIATION

csc or **C & sc** large and small CAPITAL letters

CSDC CIRCUIT SWITCHED DIGITAL CAPABILITY

C section the third section of a newspaper

CSI COMPACT SOURCE IODINE

CSO See CHROMA KEY.

C-Span Cable-Satellite Public Affairs Network, a nonprofit corporation based in Washington, DC and formed in 1979 It broadcasts congressional hearings and other public affairs programming.

C-stand CENTURY STAND

c-store CONVENIENCE STORE

C/T color TRANSPARENCY

C-2-S referring to paper that is coated on both sides

ctn. carton

ctr CENTER; COUNTER

cu or **CU** CLOSE-UP

cub a novice, such as an inexperienced reporter

cubook [library science] the volume of space required to shelve the average-size book, pronounced CUB-book

cue 1 a signal in words or signs that initiates action, dialogue, effects, or other aspects of a production, such as an indication from a director for a performer or interview subject to begin or end Cues may be given with a *cue light*, such as an *On The Air* sign or a *warning light*. A *return cue* is a verbal or other signal to return to the studio from a remote broadcast, such as a sports event. 2 a perforation, beep, or signal in a film or tape to indicate something imminent, such as a commercial break or the end of a reel 3 to give a cue

cue burn any distortion at the beginning of a record cut, resulting from heavy use on a radio station

cue card a large card containing lines to be spoken by a performer, often used off-camera on TV; also called *flip card, idiot card,* or *idiot sheet*

cue channel a track or channel on a tape for audio information related to the production and other signals that are not to be part of the soundtrack they accompany

cue in to begin or initiate action, music, dialogue, or effects

cue light See CAMERA CUE.

cue line 1 a word or phrase delivered by a performer as a signal to the next performer 2 a telephone line between a broadcasting studio and a remote broadcast location, for cuing and other off-the-air conversation; also called *control circuit* or *ring-down line*

cue sheet an outline of all elements of a play or program, containing timings and cues A cue sheet is often used by a *sound mixer* in *dubbing* or *mixing* and is sometimes called a *dubbing cue sheet* or *mixing sheet*.

cue track 1 [television] one of the audio tracks on videotape, or a separate track for recording with cuing information to be used in editing; also called *address track* 2 [film] a soundtrack with dialogue that is replaced in postproduction

cue up to prepare and set in position a record or tape for immediate recording or playback

cuffo any work without payment, on credit or speculation; on the cuff

CUG CLOSED USER GROUP

cukaloris, cucaloris, or **cucalorous** a piece of netting or cardboard with shapes cut out of it, used to cast patterns of light on a FLAT, behind an actor; also called *cookie, cuke, kookie,* or *template*

culture development or improvement of the intellect, emotions, interests, manners, and taste, or the result of this, such as refined ways of thinking, talking, and acting; development or improvement of physical qualities by special training, such as body culture or voice culture; the ideas, customs, and other qualities of a specific period   *Culture shock* is the confusion or other feelings experienced by a person encountering the unfamiliar surroundings of a strange culture. A *culture vulture* is a person who professes great interest in the arts and other aspects of culture. A *culturist* advocates or is devoted to the advancement of the arts and other *cultural* advancements.

cum.   cumulative

cumdach   a metal or wooden box, often elaborately decorated, for holding a medieval manuscript; also called *book box* or *book shrine*

cume   **1** the total accumulated or cumulative audience (*not* total combined audiences, which would be duplicated repeatedly) of a radio or TV station during a broadcast day or time period, such as 6 A.M. to midnight, Monday to Friday   **2** the net, unduplicated number of individuals or households reached by an advertising campaign; sometimes called *cumes*

cum licentia   Latin for "with permission"; notice in a publication that it is published with the permission of the ecclesiastical or other relevant authorities

cum privilegio   a notice in a publication indicating that a religious or other authority has granted permission to print (CUM LICENTIA), exclusive for that publication or class of publications

cumulative index   a listing of articles that have appeared in earlier issues of a periodical, combining previously published interim indexes

cuneiform   wedge-shaped, such as the style of writing of Babylonian, Persian, and other ancient inscriptions

cup   a layout in which the second headline is centered under the top headline; also called *bucket*

curiosa   any curiosities, such as books with unusual subject matter   The term is often used as a synonym for *erotica.*

curl   a distortion or spiral wrinkle in phototypesetting or other photographic paper   The *curl side* is the concave side of the sheet. A *stovepipe curl*, along the length of the sheet, or a *windowshade curl*, across its width (causing the pages to roll up like a windowshade), may be caused by prolonged drying or excessive temperature. If wrapped around a spool for a long time, microfilm is likely to retain a curl.

curling   [printing] a condition of paper (generally covers) that does not remain flat after drying

curriculum vitae (cv, CV, or C.V.)   a listing of a person's education, positions, published works, and other professional background information   CVs are generally submitted by job applicants, particularly for academic positions.

cursive   **1** referring to something flowing or connected, or to handwriting with connected letters   **2** of type that resembles handwriting but with unconnected letters   Writing unconnected letters is called *printing.*

cursor   a movable indicator light on a computer video screen that marks the current position at which a character may be entered; equivalent to an electronic pencil point

curtain   **1** a large drape or other expanse of material, used to conceal a stage from an audience, to indicate the end of an act, or scene, or painted or otherwise adorned so as to provide a scenic effect   Theater curtains include an *act curtain* (opened at the beginning and closed at the end of each act), an *asbestos curtain* (also called *safety curtain*; a flameproof curtain at the front of a proscenium stage, now made of materials other than asbestos), and a *scrim* (a gauze curtain used to create various lighting effects, either at the front of the stage at the beginning of a scene or in other places at other times). The stage manager's warning that an act is about to begin is *Curtain going up!*; the command to lower the curtain is *Curtain down!* A *fast*, or *quick*, curtain is lowered or closed quickly.   **2** CURTAIN CALL   **3** [broadcasting] a cue to indicate the end of a program and that music should be brought up to full level

curtain call   applause or other reaction from an audience that summons performers to return for acknowledgment at the end of the performance, generally to appear in front of the curtain; the return of performers to receive such applause

curtain line   the last line of dialogue before the curtain falls   A dramatic curtain line is a *strong curtain*; an ineffective one is a *weak curtain.*

curtainraiser   *Wall Street Journal* jargon for an article that is published before an anticipated event; also called a WALKUP

curtain raiser   a short play or other performance presented before a principal production   In the late 19th and early 20th centuries, *curtain raisers* were presented while latecomers arrived, before the curtain was raised on the major attraction.

curtain speech   a speech that is not part of a performance, given by a performer or other individual associated with the production

curtain time   the time that a performance begins

curve chart   a graphical representation, or chart, with curved lines to indicate changes, as distinguished from a bar chart, pie chart, or other ways of representing data changes and comparisons

cushion 1 a device to reduce running time (such as a portion of a script that can be eliminated), deaden impact, or otherwise impart flexibility 2 a portion of a live broadcast or other program that can be lengthened or shortened so that the full program fits correctly into the allotted time; also called a *stretch*

customer furnished (CF) referring to material needed to do a job that is provided by the customer, such as paper or labels

customer-owned coin-operated telephone (COCOT) a pay telephone owned by a private company instead of the local telephone company

cut 1 an opening 2 the omission of a part of something, or the part omitted; to reduce, omit, or eliminate 3 a decrease 4 a passage or channel 5 a block or plate engraved for printing, or the impression made from it 6 an illustration (derived from *woodcut*) 7 [journalism] a photograph or artwork used in printing 8 [printing] an engraving (zinc, plate, or halftone) or *electrotype* used to reproduce a photograph 9 [film] a total film, generally in an interim state, that is, in the process of being *cut* or edited A *rough cut* is an early state of editing, in which the shots are assembled in proper sequence. A *fine cut* is a finished workprint, ready for final approval, prior to reproduction. An *answer print*, or *first proof print*, is between these two stages. A *director's cut* or *director's fine cut* is the last edited version of a film, as approved by the director. A *director's cut clause* in the director's contract guarantees the right of this approval. 10 [recording] the reproduction of sounds on a record 11 a single section (a *band*), such as one song on a record containing several different selections 12 a transition (or transition point) from one scene to another (a *visual cut*) or one soundtrack to another (a *sound cut*) A *late cut* is made (generally unintentionally) slightly after the indicated moment, whereas a *delayed cut* is intentionally withheld so as to create suspense or for other effects. 13 an instruction to end a scene or to shift from one scene to another The symbol for this command is an index finger drawn across the throat. 14 [telecommunications] to open or disconnect a circuit

cut and hold [film] a director's instruction to stop filming but for the performers to remain in position

cut-and-paste 1 to clip and affix existing pieces of previously printed or existing work in a different order; sometimes used pejoratively to describe a hastily assembled job 2 to rearrange

cutaway 1 [film, television] a *reaction shot* or a shot of an action, object, or person not part of the principal scene 2 an insert, such as between two scenes of an interview subject, usually a brief sequence that shows the interviewer

cutback or **cut-back** [film] a return to a principal or earlier scene following a reaction shot or other *cutaway*; also called a *cutback shot*

cut bite a portion of dialog spoken prematurely by a performer, before another performer has finished

cut-case display a shipping carton (as for canned foods) that can be opened by slicing off the top so that the carton remains usable as a display case

cut dummy any proofs of artwork pasted on (generally green) paper

cut film a flat sheet of negative film, used by professional photographers, cut to required size in a *cut-film holder* Using it is analogous to rolling one's own cigarettes. See SHEET FILM.

cut flush the trimming of a book (such as a paperback) with the cover and pages the same size, distinguished from a book trimmed with a cover larger than the pages

cut-in 1 the insertion of a headline (a *cut-in head*), blurb, or other material (such as a quotation or excerpt) within the text of an article; also called *insert, cut-in-note, cut-in side note, let-in note*, or *incut note* 2 the insertion of a local commercial or announcement in a broadcast

cut-in notes any material set in a margin adjacent to the main text

cutline 1 CAPTION 2 a small box or ruled area at the bottom of a column (generally the first or last column) of text, with the identification of the author 3 a series of dashes in wire-service copy sent to radio stations, to indicate that the announcer may *cut away* (*break away*) or interrupt at that point, such as for a commercial

cut list a term in use at *The Wall Street Journal* to describe paragraphs and sentences that may be omitted to suit editing and space requirements

cut off 1 the maximum dimensions of paper, as limited by the size of a printing press 2 printed matter completely or partly missing from a printed sheet 3 an interrupted telephone call, usually spelled *cut-off*

cutoff rule a line separating two advertisements or other adjacent items in a newspaper or magazine

cut-offs specific times (usually for late-night broadcasts) after which a spot cannot be aired

cutout 1 a visual device affixed to the molding or surface of a billboard; also called *embellishment* It either is three-dimensional or provides a three-dimensional effect. 2 an opening, such as one cut through masking paper in photographing a specific area **3** a piece of scenery cut out of a board to represent the silhouette of a building or other object

cut-out an album or recording deleted from a record company's catalog and then sold at a lowered price; the equivalent of a *remainder* in the book-publishing industry

cut-out drop [theater] a cloth, or drop, suspended from above the stage, with an opening so that scenery behind it is partially revealed; called a *cut-cloth* in the United Kingdom

cutover **1** a change or transfer **2** [telecommunications] the switching from one telephone system to another It can be instantaneous (a *flash cut*) or can involve an old and a new system operating together during the transition period (a *parallel cut*).

cutscore a sharp-edged knife used to make a partial cut in paper or board, to facilitate folding The knife is located slightly lower than the cutting rules in a DIE.

cut-size paper cut to a specified size for printing or other uses

cuts out any intermittent interruptions of a telephone conversation or other communication

cutter **1** a film editor or other person in a film-editing department **2** a long, narrow, large flag (also called a *finger*) that cuts off light, generally placed on a stand in front of a light

cut time hurriedly played music, particularly music with four beats to a bar played so quickly that there are only two beats to a bar, called playing *double time* In concert music, this type of playing is called ALLA BREVE.

cutting **1** a CLIPPING **2** [film] the editing or splicing of parts of a film, as done by a *cutter* or editor in a *cutting room* *Cutting negative* is the process of cutting a negative to match the final WORKPRINT, producing a *cut negative*. **3** [television] the ending or stopping of a scene *Cutting on the action* is a technique in which the camera switches, or cuts, from one event or scene to another. *Cutting on the reaction* is an orderly sequence in which an event or scene is followed by its results, impact, or reaction.

cutting continuity [film] a list detailing the *final cut* or *finished print*, containing information about camera setups, dialogue, and other aspects of each shot

cutting outline a guide sometimes used by a film editor, such as in preparing a documentary or other compilation of cuts from existing films

cutting room a facility where motion pictures are edited

cut to the chase slang for *speed it up, get to the point,* or *move to the action* Used in various fields, it is based on a film instruction to cut out slow passages and move directly to the chase scene.

cv, c.v., or **CV** CURRICULUM VITAE

cvg COVERAGE

CW CALL WAITING; CONTINUOUS WAVE; country and western (COUNTRY MUSIC)

CWO CASH WITH ORDER

CX CORRECT

CY calendar year

cyan **1** [printing] a greenish-blue color **2** ink of that color

cyc CYCLORAMA

cycle **1** a single complete execution of a periodically repeated phenomenon; a period of time within which a round of regularly recurring events or phenomena is completed At The Associated Press, United Press International, and other 24-hour wire services, each day is divided into two *cycles*, one from noon to midnight (originally oriented to morning newspapers) and the other from midnight to noon (for afternoon newspapers). At all-news radio stations, a cycle is about 22 minutes, with each cycle including some revisions, updates, and replacements. **2** [broadcasting] a period (generally 13 weeks) of broadcast programming, or for purchase of broadcast commercials or payment of performers A *cycle discount* may be provided for commercials broadcast during one or more cycles.

cycle animation the repeated use of graphics or animation cels to convey such continuing actions as a person walking, water flowing, and other repetitive movement

cycle billing a system of sending out statements throughout the month, on the same day each month to an individual customer It is used by banks and other organizations with very large numbers of customers.

cycles per second (cps) a measure of the frequency of an electromagnetic wave; hence, an indication of the broadcasting frequency of a transmitter (such as a radio station or a radio microphone)

cyclorama a curved seamless backdrop on a stage to give the illusion of sky or space; also used in film and TV A *cyclorama strip*, or *cyc strip*, is a bank of lights in the bottom of a cyclorama. In the theater, cyclorama is generally shortened to *cyc* (pronounced sike), as in *cyc borders* (cyclorama border lights, used to light a cyclorama), *cyc foots* (cyclorama footlights), and *cyc lights*. It is also shortened to *cyke* and *cyclo*.

A *hard cyc* is a wall; a *soft cyc* is a stretched fabric or other material.

cylinder a rotating chamber of a printing press that carries the paper or the curved printing plate or receives the ink or impression A *cylinder press* has a flat bed for the type and a revolving cylinder with the paper against which the impression is made.

Cyrillic a Slavic alphabet, used in the Soviet Union and other Slavic countries

D

d. data; day

D density of a film *D-max* is the maximum density that an exposed film can achieve; *D-min* is the minimum density of an unexposed film. D also is an abbreviation for *downstage.*

d.a. **1** desk assistant, generally in broadcast news **2** directional antenna **3** director's assistant **4** [telephone] doesn't answer (no answer to a telephone call), a term in telephone marketing to indicate a telephone number that is dialed but not answered

DAA DATA ACCESS ARRANGEMENT

dabber a small pad or flat-bottomed bag, generally leather or flannel, used to ink type or engravings by hand; common in the 18th century and then replaced by BRAYERS (rollers)

dactyl a poetic form consisting of three syllables, the first accented, or stressed, and the next two unaccented, or unstressed A *dactylic* verse is composed of dactyls.

Dada a nihilistic artistic and literary movement that originated in Zurich, Switzerland (1916–1922), characterized by abstract or incongruous creations and the rejection of conventions American artist Man Ray (1890–1976) used collages and surrealistic techniques in Dadaist films made in France in the 1920s.

dagger a typographic symbol shaped like a dagger, a weapon with a short pointed blade, used as a reference mark; sometimes called *obelisk* or *long cross* A *double dagger*, or DIESIS, has two cross marks and also indicates a footnote or other reference, usually with a dagger preceding it on the same page.

DAGMAR *d*efining *a*dvertising *g*oals, *m*easuring *a*dvertising *r*esults, acronym for a concept originated by Russell Colley in a 1961 publication of the Association of National Advertisers

daguerreotype an early type of photograph, developed in France by artist Louis Daguerre (1789–1851), in which an image was created on a light-sensitive silver-coated metal plate

daily **1** [newspapers] a daily newspaper, published five, six, or seven days per week There are about 1,700 dailies in the United States and about 100 in Canada. **2** [film] *Dailies* refers to

an unedited print—a RUSH—filmed the previous day. The *sound dailies* are called *track dailies;* the picture ROLLS are called rushes or *daily rolls.* An *assembly daily* is a selection of the best TAKES edited and put in sequence for daily review. The assembly dailies often are called *the dailies* or *rushes.*

daily effective circulation (D.E.C.) a measure of the potential number of people exposed to an outdoor sign over a one-day period, generally gauged as half of all individuals passing it during 12 hours (unilluminated) or 18 hours (illuminated)

daily electronic feed (DEF) a news service from a network (specifically ABC) to affiliated stations for possible subsequent broadcast Also called DELAYED ELECTRONIC FEED, it may be a morning and/or afternoon transmission.

Daily Report translations of broadcast and print news from thousands of foreign media, compiled and printed five days a week (Monday–Friday) by the Foreign Broadcast Information Service (FBIS) of the Central Intelligence Agency (CIA), Langley, VA The general public may subscribe.

dais a raised platform, such as one at a banquet, on which honored guests sit; pronounced DAY-is

daisy wheel a flat disk with characters around the rim (resembling the rays of a daisy), available in different typefaces and changeable on a typewriter without a fixed typebar

dakota a lead-in line of dialogue preceding a song in a musical comedy or other show

dance **1** rhythmic movement, generally to music, as executed by a dancer A *dance director,* who directs the dancers in a production, may also be a CHOREOGRAPHER (creator) and *dance arranger.* A *filmed dance* is a film of a dance, whereas a *film dance* is a dance created and performed in a film. The *dance count* is the tempo, counted out emphatically—one, two, three, FOUR, etc. A *dance-drama* is a story told via dance and other techniques, such as dialogue, singing, or mime (*dance-pantomime*). **2** [printing] the action of metal type that falls out of a form as it is lifted

dancer roll a weighted roller that rides on the paper roll of a printing press to maintain uniform tension; also called *rider roller*

dandy roll a roller or cylinder of wire gauze pressed on moist pulp to produce a watermark or other effects on paper The appearance is elegant; the name derives from the word for a meticulously well-dressed man.

dangler British slang for a decoration or sign that is hung, as from the ceiling of a store

dark [theater] referring to no performance, as in a *dark house*; also called *dark night*

darkcloth a piece of dark material placed over the top and back of a large-format camera to facilitate viewing by the photographer of images on a ground-glass screen, commonly used by studio portrait photographers in the early 20th century

dark-print process a technique to make blueprints by exposure to light and development in an aqueous solution so that black on the original becomes white on the copy and vice versa; the opposite of the WHITEPRINT process, in which black remains black and white remains white In the dark-print process, copies are made on iron-sensitized paper, called blueprint paper; in the whiteprint process, copies are made on diazo-coated paper.

darkroom a closet, room, or area without light (or with a SAFELIGHT) in which film is developed A *darkroom camera* can be used in a darkroom.

dash a short horizontal line used as a punctuation mark; the long signal used in combination with dots or short signals in Morse telegraphic code A *dash leader* is a series of closely and equally spaced dashes, as on a contents page linking the text with the page number. A *dot leader* serves the same function with a series of dots.

DAT DIGITAL audio tape

data information A *databank* or *database* is a collection of data transported by a medium, a *data carrier* such as magnetic tape, and stored and processed in an electronic device such as a computer.

data access arrangement (DAA) equipment that enables privately owned equipment, such as a facsimile machine, to be attached to a telephone system, computer network, or other equipment not owned by the user

database publishing facts in a computer's databank or database that are published as a print book or used in another form, such as video; a form of electronic publishing

data communications movement or transmission of encoded information via electronic or electrical communications channels A *data entry terminal* is a device, such as a keyboard, for entering data into the system. A *data file* is the output of a program in the form of raw data. A *data network* is a telecommunications system for transmission of data, as with a *dataphone*, rather than voice transmission via a conventional telephone.

data conversion the translation of information or coding from one computer language to another, from one alphabet code to another, from one code structure to another, or from one storage medium to another Data conversion may be done ON-LINE or through a telecommunications or DATA COMMUNICATIONS device.

Data Development Corp. a New York market research company that operates conference centers in New York and Chicago; established in 1960

datagram a message transmitted via a *packet switching network*, a packet of data transmitted computer to computer Commonly used in financial relations, it is akin to a telegram.

Datanews the high-speed news service of United Press International

data point a symbol used on charts, consisting of a variety of lines and shapes that are identified in a legend or key

data processing the preparation and storage of information by a computer The *database* (collection of data) may be stored in a data or information bank, or the organization itself that maintains the database may be called a *databank*. When used as part of a phrase, such as *database management system* or *database producer*, the words *data* and *base* are joined. Data processing and *data system* also are called *information processing* and *information system*.

data rings the guides around a camera lens that indicate the F-STOPS and other focusing information

Datastream the high-speed news service of The Associated Press

data tablet [computer graphics] a flat electronic surface on which drawings can be made, as with an electronic pen, and then transmitted into a computer and displayed

date citation information, as in movie listings, about when a movie was completed and when it was released for theatrical distribution, such as "1986, rel. 1988"

dated material material bearing a time or date Though dated also means old-fashioned or out of-date, in communications the meaning generally is the opposite. Envelopes from printers or producers of advertising and other deadline or rush materials often are stamped "Attention: time-dated material."

date file [journalism] a record of anniversaries, historic events, and other past and forthcoming newsworthy occasions In libraries, a date file lists the items borrowed from the collection, arranged by date due.

date format the arrangement of characters to indicate a date, such as May 10, 1927, which also can be written as 10 May 1927 (European format), 5/10/27, or 1927-5-10, sometimes followed by the hour, minute, and second; also called *dating format*

dateline a common journalistic term referring to the insertion, generally in the first line of a news story or release, of the city from which the news emanates and the date of issue The *page dateline* is the complete date that appears at the top of each page of a daily newspaper or the publication date at the top or bottom of each page, or alternate pages, of other periodicals.

date week in weekly publications, a reference in an article in relation to the publication date For example, if the publication date is Friday, as it is with many weeklies, the date week focuses on Friday. Thus, a news event that occurred during the preceding six days is referred to by the day, such as "a fire on Wednesday," whereas an event seven or more days before the publication date would be referred to by the actual date.

dating a line on a bill indicating when payment is due; also, the practice of extending credit or payment terms for a longer period than stated on the invoice

datum a point, line, or surface used as a reference; plural, *datums* A *datum line* or *phantom line*, consisting of a series of one long dash and two short dashes, is used in technical drawings to indicate an alternate position. A datum is also a fact; with this meaning, the plural is *data*.

dawn patrol an early-morning broadcast

day daylight or artifical light to simulate daylight, often used as a notation on a shooting schedule or other forms provided to a camera crew *Day exteriors* is outside daylight or light simulating it.

day and dating booking a film for simultaneous showing at several theaters, as indicated by the day of the week and date; also called *day and date release*

daybook a list of news events, usually for that day or the following day, issued by wire services in major cities for the use of their subscribing publications and stations; a book with a page or section devoted to each day of the month, such as is used by advertising copywriters for retailers and others whose ads change frequently

day file periodicals and other materials arranged in chronological order American libraries call this a *reading file*; in Canadian libraries it's a *continuity file*.

day-for-night (D/N) filming or taping in daylight with the intention of creating the illusion of night, achieved through special exposures or filters or subsequent processing

Day-Glo the trademarked name for colored inks or paints with a fluorescent or luminous quality, made by the Day-Glo Corporation, Cleveland, OH, used on displays and billboards *Day-Glo paper* contains fluorescent ink.

day letter a telegram sent during the day

daylight the light of day, not necessarily sunlight *Daylight film* is used outdoors during the day to produce *daylight pictures*, or indoors, as in a *daylight studio* with *simulated daylight lighting*. A *daylight tank* is a light-tight container in which film is inserted, or loaded, in the dark and then processed in normal light. A *daylight conversion filter* or *daylight filter* is a filter for a camera lens that enables color film for indoor artificial light to be used for outdoor natural light. A *daylight loading spool* is a reel that is protected by light-tight flanges or dark sides for loading or unloading in daylight.

day-out-of-days schedule [film] a schedule for major performers indicating when they will be expected to appear ("of-days") and when they will be off ("day-out")

daypart a programming segment of a broadcast schedule, such as morning and afternoon DRIVE-TIME and *night watch* for radio and morning, afternoon, early and late fringe, and prime time for television *Dayparting* is the scheduling of programs at specific parts of the day, targeted to specific audiences that are predominant during those times.

day picture a photo of a scene depicting the weather, used by newspaper and TV assignment editors

day player a performer hired on a per diem basis

dayside the daytime staff of a newspaper or other medium

daytime station an AM radio station restricted by its FCC license to broadcasting between 15 minutes before sunrise and 15 minutes after sunset; also called *daytimer*

dB or **db** decibel, a measure of sound intensity

DB or **D.B.** DAYBOOK, datebook; DELAYED BROADCAST

d.b.a. DOING BUSINESS AS

DBI *dull but important*, a description, used at *The Wall Street Journal*, of boring articles that contain vital information

dbl.   double

DBS   DIRECT BROADCAST SATELLITE

DC   down center, a portion of a stage; see AREAS

D county   an A.C. NIELSEN CO. designation of a county with fewer than 35,000 people

dd.   delivered

DDB Needham   a major advertising agency headquartered in New York; part of the Omnicom Group, representing a merger of Doyle Dane Bernbach and Needham Harper Worldwide

dead   no longer alive; lifeless; inanimate; quiet; without resonance; out of operation; lacking electrical charge or connection to an electrical source   To *deaden* is to make soundproof, less colorful, or less intense. News is dead if it's old, been killed (thrown out or cancelled), or used. Material already used may be filed in a *dead book* or *dead file*. A *dead copy* or *dead manuscript* is copy from which type has been set. *Dead matter* is type (*dead type*), engraving, or other material used and no longer needed, which is different from *dead metal*, a blank area of an engraving or type form. The *dead bank* is the area in the composing room where dead type is collected and reassembled. Dead also can mean exact or precise, as in *dead synch*, which is exact synchronization of audio and video.

dead air   a broadcasting term for silence, perhaps resulting from a *dead mike* (inoperative microphone)

dead and live copy   old and new versions of text

dead letter   an unclaimed or undeliverable letter, sent to the *dead letter office* (*DLO*) at a branch of the Post Office and destroyed if it cannot be returned to the sender

deadline   the latest time by which something must be done or completed; a common word in communications fields   Ironically, it originally meant a line around a prison area that prisoners were forbidden to cross lest they be shot. The first prison so equipped was in Andersonville, GA, for captured Northern soldiers during the Civil War.

Deadline Club   the popular name of the New York chapter of the Society of Professional Journalists/Sigma Delta Chi   The club does not have an office; its address is P.O. Box 2503, NY 10017.

deadly embrace   [computers] a rare condition that occurs when all processes active at the exact same moment become suspended while competing for the same resources

dead pack   scenery removed from the stage during a performance to be returned to the set for the next performance   *Live pack* is the scenery on stage or to be placed on stage.

deadpan   a blank, expressionless face

dead roll   [television] a technique of starting a taped program or a film at its scheduled time on a station but not broadcasting it, so that the preceding program, specifically a live sports or news event, is continued   When the live program ends, the dead rolling tape or film is telecast at the point it has rolled to, usually with the announcement, "We now join the program already in progress."

dead spot   an area where broadcast reception is weak; also called *dead space*   A dead spot is also a broadcast commercial or program not aired, sometimes called a *black space*.

dead stock   a product for which there is little or no demand   In retailing, it is also called a *sticker*.

deaerate   [printing] to remove air between sheets of paper in order to align them, usually with a device called a JOGGER

deaf aid   a small earpiece used by TV reporters, anchors, and others

deal   **1** a business agreement or transaction   In the film business and other fields, the *front end* of a deal is the money paid when the agreement is signed; the *back end* is when the deal is completed, as when the script is turned in.   **2** [marketing] a temporary offer, generally by a manufacturer to its distributors and retailers (DEALERS) for special considerations in their purchases, such as an extra free case, a price reduction (called an *allowance, temporary allowance,* or *buying allowance*), a premium or loader (called a *dealer loader* or *buying loader*), or a *display loader*, as an incentive to display the product   Price reductions for products sold on a deal basis may or may not be passed on to consumers. In some cases, the deal products may be specially packaged, as in a *deal pack* or *premium pack* (with a premium attached) or a *bonus pack*, which could be three bars of soap for the price of two. A product that is being promoted in any of these ways is *on deal*. A *deal sheet* describes the offer or promotion.   **3** [newspapers] to distribute, as by the head of a copy desk, who passes out copy to the copy editors

dealer   a retailer   A *dealership* is a franchise or appointment to sell an item, such as an automobile. The *dealer category* refers to the type of store or retail outlet, such as discount, drug, or supermarket. The *dealer coverage* is the number of retailers selling a product in a specific area. The *dealer price* is the price paid by the dealer to the wholesaler or other supplier.

dealer imprint   retailer information added to a manufacturer's ad, mailing piece, or other materials, usually at the bottom   If the ad is in the form of a MATRIX (MAT), it's called a *dealer mat* or *dealer ad*.

dealer listing   an advertisement, news release, booklet, or other item that lists retailers or dealers who sell a product or service, sometimes used as an inducement for the SELL-IN; also called *dealer tie-in*   It is generally part of an ad, typically at the bottom, or is an adjacent ad, such as a full-page magazine ad on the right-hand page and a one-column dealer listing in the adjacent column on the left.

dealer loader   a display rack, often located near a cash register in a retail outlet, that generally is maintained by the seller or seller's representative

deal letter   a written statement of intentions, a confirmation of a business arrangement prior to a more detailed contract; also called a *deal memo*

death   a failure, as with a show that dies or is death at the box office

death notice   a paid classified announcement of a person's death

debossing   a process in which an image is pressed down into a paper or other surface; a style of *embossing*, though the latter refers to a *raised* image

dec.   deceased; decrease

D.E.C.   DAILY EFFECTIVE CIRCULATION

decal   short for *decalcomania*, an adhesive paper with a design or advertising message affixed to store windows or other surfaces

decay rate   [marketing] the number of customers lost in a year or another specific period

decile   a unit in statistics: any of ten equal parts of a population sample

decimal   a numbering system with a base of 10, consisting of ten digits, 0 through 9   A *decimal fraction* is indicated by a *decimal point* before the numerator, as in .1 (to indicate one-tenth). To avoid confusion, a zero often is set before the decimal point, as in 0.1. A *decimal digit* is one of the 0 to 9 characters. The *decimal classification system* is used in many libraries to classify and identify books and other materials.

decision-making unit (DMU)   an individual or individuals who make the decision affecting a purchase or other action

Decision Research Corp.   a market research company in Lexington, MA, founded in 1971 It was acquired in 1987 by Research International, headquartered in London.

Decisions Center   a market research company established in 1965 and based in New York

deck   1 [printing] a secondary line or group of lines in a multiline headline, commonly used by *The Wall Street Journal*   Though each deck can be in the same size type, most journalists use the word for lines subsequent to the primary headline.   2 [television] *On deck* is to be ready; an *on-deck camera* is a TV camera whose picture is currently not being transmitted despite its readiness to become an *on-air camera*. A deck is also a component in an audio or video system, such as a *tape deck* (heads and tape transport mechanism).   3 [theater] slang for the stage   A *deckhand* is a stagehand.

decker   1 [journalism] having a specified number of DECKS—headline units—or layers   A *double-decker* has two lines or groups of lines, and a *triple-decker* or *three-decker* is a headline with three lines or groups of lines   2 [publishing] a 19th-century term for a three-volume set of novels

decker well   a food-store freezer cabinet with packages stored vertically   A *four-decker well*, for example, has four tiers or shelves. A *coffin case* displays the merchandise horizontally and often is on the floor, whereas the decker well usually is higher.

deck head   a heading having two or more groups of type

deckle   the untrimmed, rough natural edge of a sheet of paper, sometimes feathery (feather edge), used decoratively in books and other publications; also called *deckle edge*

deck panel   in outdoor advertising, a panel erected as part of a tier of two or more panels

decoder   an electronic device that translates signals transmitted in digital form or in another code back into the form of the original message

decor or **décor**   the decorative scheme of an area, such as a stage or film or TV set   With or without the accent, it's pronounced DAY-core. Show-business decor includes the furnishings—*decorative properties*—but not *action props*.

decorated cover   a book with a decoration or special letter, usually on the front cover; also called *illustrated cover*

decorative typeface   a novelty typeface used for aesthetic or attention-getting purposes

decoupage   a technique of decorating a surface with cutouts; cutting up, as in the division of a scene into shots   From the French *couper*, "to cut," it is pronounced as in French, day-koo-PAZH. In French films, decoupage is "ordinary" (not DYNAMIC) continuity editing, in which each shot simply follows the other.

decoy   in direct marketing, a name inserted in a list to monitor the usage of the list; also called a *summary name*

dedication   a commitment for special use or purpose; an inscription in a literary work as acknowledgment of special regard   A *dedicated line* is a line set aside for special use, such as a telephone line reserved for a MODEM or an electric line solely for a copying machine or computer. A *dedicated device* is designed to work in a specific system, such as a *dedicated flash unit* for a specific camera that automatically sets the shutter to the correct speed, whereas a *nondedicated flash unit* requires the shutter speed to be set manually.

dedication copy   a book personally inscribed and dated by the author and presented to the person to whom it is dedicated

dedication page   a page in a publication with an inscription of appreciation and acknowledgment to a person or group

dee jay   *disc jockey*

deep-etch   [printing] in offset lithography, a positive plate used for long runs, with the inked areas slightly recessed below the surface

deep focus   a film style with everything—foreground, middle ground, and background—in sharp focus to produce considerable depth of field, the opposite of *shallow focus*; also called *deep-field cinematography* Deep focus thus presents the entire set, as in *Citizen Kane* (1941) and *Tucker* (1988). The effect generally is obtained with small F-STOP and/or short-focal-length lenses.

deep throat   an anonymous source who is a tipster, particularly to the media, notably the person or persons who informed reporters Robert Woodward and Carl Bernstein of *The Washington Post* about the Watergate break-in in 1972

def.   defective; deferred; define; definite; definition

DEF   DAILY or DELAYED ELECTRONIC FEED

defeat   [broadcasting] to turn off or nullify

definition   a statement of what a thing is or its meaning; clarity, as in the sharpness, distinctness, or absence of fuzziness of a broadcast signal, a photograph, or printed material

definitive   decisive, conclusive, most nearly complete, and authoritative, as in a definitive edition or definitive biography A *definitive head* is a summary headline relating the major facts.

defocus   a film technique that suddenly switches from one plane of action to another, usually with a long-focal-length lens that reduces the depth of field and focuses on the foreground instead of the background; to change the focal length of a camera lens so that the resulting image is *out of focus* (indistinct). A defocus transition is a blurred effect, often used to introduce a dream or fantasy sequence.

defocusing dissolve   a TV technique in which one camera slowly goes out of focus while another camera slowly brings its image into focus

degauss or **degaus**   to neutralize the magnetic field, as in the erasure of an audio- or videotape for reuse; pronounced dee-GOUS A *degausser* is a device for erasing a tape.

degressive   gradually decreasing A *degressive bibliography* varies the length of entries, with more space devoted to more important items.

DEL   international telex abbreviation: delivered

delamination   a separation into layers, as of a coating from the base of a paper

delay card   a postcard sent to inform a customer of a delay in shipment of merchandise that was ordered, in conformance with the 30-Day Delayed Delivery Rule of the Federal Trade Commission

delayed broadcast (D.B.)   the broadcast of a radio or TV program at a time later than its original transmission, a common procedure in the Pacific time zone

delayed electronic feed (DEF)   a news service from a network, specifically the AMERICAN BROADCASTING COMPANY (*ABC*), to affiliated stations for possible subsequent broadcast; also called DAILY ELECTRONIC FEED

delayed fulfillment   a tactic employed in promotions whereby only a section of an AD SPECIALTY or other item is initially given to the recipient The component that makes the article useful or operative isn't delivered until the recipient responds as the advertiser desires.

delayed recall   an interviewing technique to determine what an individual remembers For example, TV viewers are called the day after they have watched television for at least half an hour and questioned about the programs and commercials regarding their opinions and the degree of idea communication and name registration.

delay time   **1** [broadcasting] a period of about seven seconds that can be inserted between actual broadcast and its transmission, during which the program can be interrupted for the deletion of objectionable material, as on a telephone call-in show **2** [photography] the period during which a flash unit recharges and becomes ready for use

delete (dele)   **1** [publishing] to cancel, omit, or take out The proofreader's mark for deletion is a line through the material to be deleted; such a line, called a delete, often is extended to the margin, where it ends in a circle or oval.   The delete (or *delete mark*), which looks like a small loop, (*ℓ*), is from the Greek letter delta, δ. A deletion also can be indicated by a horizontal line drawn through the unwanted letters or a vertical line through a single line of text. This vertical line should have a hook at its top, *ℓ* or *ℓ*. In deleting letters within a word, the delete and close-up signs should be used together, *ℓ* .

2 [computers] When an item is deleted, a record of it remains in storage, whereas to erase is to remove it totally.

delimiter [computers] a special character or word that indicates the beginning or end of a portion of a program or a segment of data

delivery the art, style, or manner of presenting something, such as delivery of a speech An inept performance may be due to *poor delivery* rather than poor material.

delphi method a forecasting system based on a consensus of expert opinions The procedure (in the tradition of the Oracles at Delphi, a city in ancient Greece) is to solicit opinions from a group of experts and then repeatedly review the opinions until a consensus is reached.

delta the fourth letter of the Greek alphabet, shaped like a triangle: Δ In typesetting, the delta symbol means to insert a space or blank character; so does a caret, which is an abbreviated delta: ×. In differential calculus, the delta symbol refers to the proportional change between two quantities; delta therefore has become a general term for change.

Delta Kappa Alpha an honorary organization of students (mostly) and others in film, headquartered at the University of Southern California, Los Angeles

demand creation sales promotion

demand-oriented pricing a strategy in which estimates are made of the number of units of a product or service that could be sold at varying prices The estimate of the amount of demand helps to establish the quantity to be produced; this identification of the *demand segment* prior to production and marketing is a marketing management concept.

demand stimulation sales promotion

demarketing the process of discouraging consumption of products or services, as in campaigns conducted by oil companies during times of fuel shortage or utilities during times of peak consumption Demarketing is the opposite of marketing.

demassified media channels of communications, or media, that reach small or selective audiences, as opposed to MASS MEDIA

demo demonstration, as in a *demo record*, or reel of a record or tape produced for an audition Demo or *demos* also refers to DEMOGRAPHICS.

demo art artwork added by hand to a photograph to point out certain details, such as an X or numbers to mark the spot of an accident; also called *marker art*

demographic edition a special edition of a magazine targeted for a specific demographic group, such as educators, executives, or students

demographics the external characteristics of a population, such as magazine readers, TV viewers, or purchasers of a product, as related to age, sex, income, education, marital status, and other quantifiable descriptions *Psychographic characteristics* pertain to personality, attitude, and lifestyle.

demos DEMOGRAPHICS

demy a size of paper, usually 17½″ × 22½″ The word is from *demi*, or half.

denotation the exact, explicit meaning of a word or words *Connotation* means what is suggested.

denouement the outcome, solution, or final revelation of the plot of a film, play, novel, or other work, or the point at which this occurs, usually following the *climax*; also called the *resolution* From the French *dénouer*, "to untie," it is often written with the accent mark (*dénouement*) and is pronounced day-noo-MON.

dense crowded, thick, slow, or opaque, such as a picture with good contrast between light and dark areas

densimeter [photography] a photoelectric instrument for measuring the optical density of a photographic negative by determining the reflection of light from, or the transmission of light through, the image on the negative; also called *densitometer* In printing, a densitometer "reads" such key qualities as the amount of ink on material.

density **1** thickness, dullness, heaviness; the degree of optical opacity as measured by a DENSITOMETER; relative lightness and darkness, such as of a photo negative Film density is the ability of a film to stop light. In terms of weight, density can be measured in pounds per cubic foot. **2** [computers] a measurement of the amount of information that can be stored in a medium A *double-density disk* has the capability of storing twice as much data as a *single-density disk* of the same size.

dentelle [book production] a style of toothlike or lacelike ornamentation on the borders of the binding of a book; used in 18th-century leather bindings

Dentsu a major global advertising agency headquartered in Tokyo

dep. DEPARTMENT (also *dept.*, *dpt.*); deposit; deputy

department a division, category, or entity within an organization, such as the news, features, sports, or other editorial department in a newspaper

depolarization the process of counteracting the movement (polarization) of light rays so that, for example, a camera can film through a window or other glass without glare or other light reflection

deposit copy a free copy of a newly published book sent by the publisher to the Copyright Office for the collection of the Library of Congress, Washington, DC

depth top-to-bottom length, as in a publication *In-depth* means extensive or detailed, as an in-depth BACKGROUNDER

depth clueing [computer graphics] changing an object's sharpness or brightness to create the illusion of viewing it closer (clearer) or farther away (less clear)

depth interview a technique of questioning individuals to obtain full information or elicit indepth answers rather than superficial or casual replies

depth of assortment the number of different products in a product category, such as in a retail store

depth of focus the distance from a camera lens within which the subject is in sharp focus; thus, the distance the camera may be moved toward or away from the subject *Depth of field* is the distance between the nearest and farthest points of a scene that are in sharp focus. A *depth-of-field scale* measures depth of field for a specific lens; a *depth-of-field table* lists the depth of field at various aperture settings.

DER international telex abbreviation: out of order

Derby red a red pigment, more commonly called *chrome red*

derivative taken from another source, not original, as with an article with material that is lifted—a *pickup*—or adapted, as a derivative literary style *Derivation* is the original form or source from which something is derived. A *derivative work* is an abridgment, musical arrangement, reproduction, translation, or other form that is adapted from an earlier version. *Derived sound* is the combination of two soundtracks.

desaturation the decrease or removal of color from a film stock Often unintentional, due to faulty film or faulty processing, it can be used intentionally to create a washed-out effect by such techniques as *preflashing* and *prefogging*.

descender the stroke below the main portion of lowercase letters, such as g, j, p, q, and y, which are called *descender letters* Specifically, the descender is that portion of the letter below the BASE LINE to the *decender line* (a line across the bottom of the letter). ASCENDER letters are b, d, f, h, k, l, and t.

descriptive bibliography a listing of books or other publications that includes publishing de-

tails; not just an enumeration of the title, author, and date

descriptive survey a study that collects data to describe a public or condition, as compared to an ANALYTICAL SURVEY, which attempts to explain the condition

descriptor [indexing] a term designating the subject and not a specific title or other work

descryption a process of decoding or unscrambling TV signals, as with pay-TV services

desensitize 1 to render inoperative or insensitive, such as to heat or light 2 to make the non-image area of a printing plate insensitive or nonreceptive to ink by etching or chemically treating the plate

desiderata a list of desires sent by a prospective buyer, a term used in the book business; also called a *want list Desideratum* is something needed or wanted.

design a plan or system, as in research or data processing; a visual plan or the visual elements A book or other work may be designed by a *designer*, who is concerned with the planning of all visual or artistic aspects of a work.

Designated Market Area an A.C. NIELSEN CO. term for a group of counties in which a TV station obtains the greatest portion of its audience Each U.S. county is part of only one such *DMA* (or *D.M.A.*). The *Designated Market Area Rating* is the percentage of TV homes within the area viewing an individual station during a particular time period. The concept is similar to ARBITRON'S AREA OF DOMINANT INTEREST (ADI).

desk 1 a department, particularly in the editorial or copy operation of a newspaper, that includes the *city desk* for local news, foreign desk, and national desk headed by a *desk chief* and staffed by a *desk editor* and *deskmen* and *deskwomen* A *universal desk* handles local and wire copy. 2 a music stand in an orchestra and, in the United Kingdom, a recording console (a *mixing desk*), also called a *board*

desk copy a complimentary copy of a book provided to a teacher for classroom use, generally when the book is provided or recommended to the students

desktop presentation a display of graphics created by a computer and shown at a meeting or other presentation

desktop publishing the use of a personal computer and printer to produce newsletters and other publications

desktop video a system that displays video games or other televisionlike video on the screen of a personal computer, sometimes also using audio; also called MULTIMEDIA COMPUTING

detail an individual part or item A *detailed article* in a publication has many informational items. The definition or resolution of a photograph is characterized by the clarity of the minute elements, so that a *detail exposure* is a clear, sharp picture.

detailing calling on physicians, retailers, or others to develop interest in a product or assist the customer, but not to make an actual sale The caller is a DETAIL MAN or, preferably, a *detailer* or *detail person*.

detail man a pharmaceutical sales representative who calls on physicians and others to provide details about drugs, or a representative of a manufacturer or distributor who calls on retailers to check on displays, inventory, and other sales details, but not necessarily to obtain orders; also called a *detailer*, a *missionary sales person*, or a retail, field, or marketing representative, terms that are preferable and more contemporary

detail paper semitranslucent thin paper used by artists; also called *layout paper*

detail scenery small items of stage scenery

detail set a part of a set used for closeups in film and TV; also called an *insert set*

detail sheet information provided by a lecture bureau, public relations agency, or other source to a speaker, performer, interviewee, or other person, generally arranged by city or day with the name of the person who will be at the airport, hotel arrangements, times, places and other data

detail shot an extreme close-up showing a part of a subject in detail

detective story a work of fiction in which a mystery, often a murder, is solved by a professional investigator (a detective)

detent a part that stops or releases a movement A *detent tuner* is a click-type TV tuner that rotates to each channel position.

deterioration index [direct marketing] the annual rate, expressed as a percentage of the initial response at which a mailing list becomes less effective with continuing usage

deuce two; slang for a floodlight with a 2,000-watt lamp, also called a *junior* A *light deuce* or *one-and-a-half* has a 1,500-watt bulb. A *gutless deuce* or *one-key* has a 1,000-watt bulb.

deus ex machina an unconvincing, forced, improbable, or contrived character or event brought into the plot of a play or other literary form to extricate a hero in trouble or provide a trick resolution; pronounced DAY-us ex MAK-ee-na The Latin phrase means "god from a machine" and is based on ancient Greek and Roman plays in which a deity was lowered onto the stage in a machine. A deus ex machina can be a CLICHÉ denouement.

develop 1 to bring forth or strengthen, as in *brand development* or *market development* 2 [photography] to immerse a film or other item in a chemical solution or *developer*; to make visible photographic images

development 1 a significant event or occurrence, such as a new development in a news story 2 [photography] the act or process of developing film In *tray development*, as opposed to machine processing, the chemicals are in metal or plastic trays.

developmental editor an editor who works with an author from the conception of the book or other project to the completion of the manuscript

device 1 a plan, scheme, mechanical contrivance, or design used to gain an artistic or other effect, such as a *rhetorical device* 2 [theater] a piece of scenery (a flat) two feet wide In vaudeville or a variety show, the *device act* or *device spot* is the position after the opening act, generally not filled by a top attraction.

Dewey Decimal System a classification procedure used in libraries that uses three-digit numbers preceding a *decimal point* and followed by one or more numbers It was developed by Melvil Dewey (1851–1931), one of the founders of the American Library Association, in 1876, when he was 25 years old. The decimal classification system, referred to by librarians as *D.C.*, contains 10 main categories: general works (numbers up to 99); philosophy (100 to 199); religion (200 to 299); social sciences (300 to 399); language (400 to 499); pure science (500 to 599); technology (600 to 699); the arts (700 to 799); literature (800 to 899); and history (900 to 999).

Dex the trademark name of a telephone facsimile machine distributed by Fujitsu Imaging Systems of America, based in Danbury, CT

dft. DRAFT

DGA DIRECTORS GUILD OF AMERICA

DGA Trainee an apprentice assistant director, a participant in the training program of the Directors Guild of America The title often appears in film credits.

diachronic of or concerned with changes over a period of time, as in language; different from *synchronic*, which is concerned with a specific moment in time without regard to the past

diacritic a mark, such as a cedilla, grave accent, macron, or umlaut, added to a letter or symbol for purposes of pronunciation or to indicate distinguishing characteristics It is a useful word for editors and typographers.

diag. diagonal; diagram

diagiography the art or process of converting actual images of characters into *digital* characters; also called *digitized typesetting*

diagnostics 1 distinguishing signs, characteristics 2 [computers] self-checking routines by which a machine can indicate malfunctions

diagonal cut the editing of a film or magnetic tape by splicing—cutting—it on a slant, such as a 45-degree angle

diagonal dissolve a merging of pictures in opposite corners of a TV screen, such as the lower left and upper right

dial 1 a graduated face, usually circular, on which a measurement is indicated; a panel on a radio or TV receiver on which the frequencies are indicated 2 [telephone] a rotatable disk on a telephone The *dial tone* is the sound in a telephone receiver indicating that the phone is operative and ready to be *dialed* (even without a dial, as with a phone with push buttons). *Dialing* also is used to describe the linkage of two computer terminals or other communication devices. The use of a telephone to establish the circuit is called *dial-up*. 3 [film] To *dial out* a sound is to cut out or eliminate an unwanted sound during filming; to *dial in* is to add a sound. The process of handling the sound dials—*dialing*—results in *dialed-out* or *dialed-in* sounds.

dial. dialect; dialogue

dial-a-porn a service of telephone companies enabling callers, generally using a special 970 exchange, to hear adult programming—a recorded pornographic message—for a fee

dialect local characteristics of speech A *dialect actor* or *dialect actress* specializes in the speech patterns of a specific area or group. *Dialecticians*, specialists in dialects, belong to the prestigious American Dialect Society, which is headquartered in the English Department of MacMurray College in Jacksonville, IL.

dialectic 1 logical argumentation, often in a series of questions and answers or a *thesis* that generates an opposing view (*antithesis*) 2 [film] *Dialectical montage* or *intellectual montage* is a type of editing in which shots collide or are in conflict.

dial-it telephone service a service of telephone companies enabling users of push-button telephones to call 976 and other exchanges to obtain data and services, including sports scores, prayers, jokes, and pornographic and other messages as well as interactive programs

Dialog one of the world's largest database research services, established by the Lockheed Corporation and acquired in 1988 by Knight-Ridder Inc. of Miami, FL The company name is Dialog Information Services Inc., based in Palo Alto, CA.

dialogue 1 words in a play or other program, or the lines in a script 2 [film] *Dialogue replacement* or *replacement dialogue*, also called LOOPING, consists of replacing dialogue after its original production. A *minus-dialogue mix*, also called an *M-E mix*, is a film track with music and effects but without the dialogue. When the dialogue is added, it's a *D-M-E mix*. A credit sometimes seen on movies or TV shows is *additional dialogue*, which is dialogue added to a script during or after the basic production or, occasionally, just before the start of production.

dialogue director [film] the person who coaches the actors and informs the script supervisor about any script changes made during the production

dialogue splitting [film] the isolating of the dialogue of different actors on separate tracks for modification or editing

dialup or **dial-up** the use of a telephone, *dial* or push-button, to initiate a station-to-station call A *dialup terminal* incorporates a MODEM to dial a number to reach, via telephone lines, a computer.

diamond an extremely small type size, about 4½ POINTS

diaper in bookbinding, a small diamond shape repeated in a design, as on the front cover

diaphragm a membranous or thin disk, as in a telephone, microphone, or loudspeaker, that moves or vibrates and converts sound waves to electric waves or vice versa In a camera, the diaphragm has a fixed or variable opening to restrict the amount of light going through the lens or optical system to the film or other light receptor.

diary a record A *desk diary* is a book with the dates of each day, with blank areas for writing in appointments or keeping records. Since the pages are not numbered, this is not an easy book for a bookbinder to assemble.

diary method a market research method to record listening, viewing, purchasing, and other habits and acts of consumers Well-known diaries are those distributed and analyzed by A.C. NIELSEN CO. and ARBITRON CO. The diary is the record of TV shows seen, purchases made, products consumed, or other data kept by an individual—a *diarist*—who is part of a *diary panel* that is a representative sample of the population. An Arbitron diary page has ruled lines to designate each quarter-hour of the day, such as 6:00–6:14 and 6:15–6:29, and columns for the viewer to check off or write in responses regarding TV set on/off, call letters and channel number of station tuned to, and name of program and specific viewers (male head of house, female head of house, other family members, and visitors).

diazo the combination of an organic chemical, a coal-tar derivative, with nitrogen (*di* means "two," so two nitrogen atoms), used as a coating for printing plates or paper; pronounced dye-AZ-oh *Diazo paper* is light-sensitive and is used in offset reproduction. Diazo supplies minimize *ghosting*, or shadows, during *diazo reproduction*.

dibit [computers] two BITS The four types of dibits are 0–0, 0–1, 1–0, and 1–1.

diced in bookbinding, a cover with a pattern of small diamond squares *Diced Russia* was a cowhide binding used in many 18th-century books.

dichroic having two colors A *dichroic filter* is placed over a light to change its *color temperature* so that it exhibits a different color. A *dichroic mirror* is a mirrorlike color filter used in TV to separate blue, red, and green light and direct each to the proper *pickup tube*. *Dichroic fog* is the visible deposit on film negatives, seen as red by transmitted light and green by reflected light.

dichroisms the property possessed by crystals and other substances to transmit light of different colors For example, a *dichroic* substance could appear to be one color when reflecting light and another color when transmitting light.

Dick strip a roll of mailing labels produced by a label-printing machine made by A.B. Dick of Chicago; commonly used to refer to any roll of single labels (*one-across* or *1-up*)

dict. dictation; dictionary

diction manner of expression in words, speaking, or singing; enunciation· To most people, diction means enunciation, speaking clearly and distinctly, as with a speaker who has good diction. However, diction also describes the choice and arrangement of words in writing, as in hurried or slow diction, or elaborate or simple diction.

dictionary a book of alphabetically listed words with definitions or other information A *descriptive dictionary* is traditional in its descriptions or definitions but offers no comments, whereas a *prescriptive dictionary* includes comments and labels, such as "slang" or "vulgar." An *abridged dictionary* has fewer words than an *unabridged* one. Main dictionary types are *general*, *subject-field* (limited to law, medicine, or other areas), and *special-purpose* (limited to an aspect of language, such as dialect or etymology). Specialized dictionaries include a *pronouncing dictionary*, a *slang dictionary*, a *spelling dictionary*, the *Dictionary of American*

Regional English (*DARE*), and dictionaries in specialized fields, such as this one. *Dictionary look-up* is machine-hyphenation done automatically by a computer or other machine. An *exception-word dictionary* or *hyphenation dictionary* is a special list of hyphenations provided by the user. In computers, a dictionary is a list of names generated by a COMPILER. An *internal dictionary* is used in electronic typewriters and computers to verify spelling, hyphenation, and other elements of typesetting.

DID DIRECT INWARD DIALING

didactic used or intended for teaching or instruction *Didactics* is the science of teaching. A *didactic work* may be fiction or nonfiction and generally is designed to be morally instructive.

Didot a narrow typeface developed by François Didot (1730–1804), a French printer The *Didot point system* is a European system of type measurement based on a unit of .0148 inches. Six didot points equal one *cicero*, called a *didot pica*.

die theatrical slang meaning to do poorly, as with a show that dies on the road or a performer who dies standing up

die cut a hole intentionally cut from a printed page as part of a design The cutting press that creates the shape or pattern uses a *die* to indicate the exact area of the opening. The term is sometimes hyphenated.

diegesis a narrative, or a statement of the case, as in a speech; the actual events of a work, its denotation and not its connotation See DIEGETIC.

diegetic referring to events and conditions that are recounted or told A *diegetic sound* or *active sound* in a film is a sound related to events, whereas *extradiegetic sound* or *commentative sound* comes from outside, as through imaginary voices or an off-screen narrator.

dieresis or **diaeresis** the separation of two consecutive vowels into two syllables The *dieresis mark*, two dots above the second vowel, generally has been replaced by a hyphen or is omitted.

diesis a *double dagger*, a reference mark consisting of a vertical line and two cross lines: ‡

die-stamping *intaglio* printing using lettering or other designs engraved into copper or steel; to emboss or to create a raised or recessed design

differential pertaining to a difference A *differential rate* pertains to the difference between higher national and lower local advertising rates at some media, or other distinctions, such as a difference in wages paid for the same work under different conditions, like night or rush work.

differentiated marketing an advertising or other sales promotion campaign designed to sell the same product or service to different segments of the same market or to different markets

diffuse spread out; not concentrated *Diffused writing* is long-winded or wordy. *Diffused lighting* is soft, indirect light on a photographic subject or scene.

diffuser a piece of cloth or mesh, or a translucent screen to soften shadows or diffuse lights; a device to blur the focus of a camera image; a panel to intensify or decrease sound in a studio or other place DIFFUSED light or sound is thrown back or reflected in different directions.

diffusion-transfer process a technique for producing an image by the intermingling—*diffusion*—of chemicals, commonly used in photocopying machines

digest a compact collection of summaries or condensed articles, generally more comprehensive than a synopsis; also, an abridgment itself

digest-size 5" × 7", the page size of *The Reader's Digest* An ad may be prepared in this size for insertion in publications the same size as *The Digest* or to appear on a larger page.

digit a finger; any one of the ten Arabic number symbols, 0 through 9, so called because they were originally counted on the fingers

digital 1 [computers] the primary method of data storage and transmission, in which each code is given a unique combination of BITS and each BIT generally indicates the presence or absence of a condition (on or off, yes or no, true or false, open or closed) A *digital computer* handles data in DISCRETE units, as compared to an analog or continuous computer. A *digital typesetter* produces its characters from codes stored in its computer. 2 [recording] referring to a recording technique in which sounds or images are converted into groups of electronic bits and stored on a magnetic medium, such as a *digital audio tape* The groups of bits are read electronically, as by a laser beam, so that the sound that is recorded and played back is virtually free of distortion.

digital animation COMPUTER ANIMATION

digital flashes small bursts of light on a computer screen

digital photography electronic still video, a technique of storing images on magnetic disks that can be played back on a TV screen by a combination of photography, computers, and video technology

digital plotter a computer-output device controlled by digital signals that produce graphic images

Digital Video Effects a system that produces electronic optical effects, commonly used in TV

digitize or **digitalize** [computer graphics] feeding a design into the computer by transmitting POINTS, the coordinates of the positions *Digitizing* is done with a drawing on a *digitizing table.*

digitized typesetting the formation of characters by a series of minute dots or lines

digitizer a device that translates analog data (nonreadable by a machine) into numerical or digital form (countable and readable) An example is a digitizer that breaks up a continuous-tone photograph into an array of electronic bits that are stored and later can be recalled to reconstruct a reproduction of the original image.

digitizer tablet [computer graphics] a device, resembling a small drafting board, on which a user can create images that simultaneously appear on a video screen; also called a *graphic tablet*

digraph a pair of letters, separate or bound together in a LIGATURE, pronounced as a single sound, such as *ea* in *head, heat,* and *read,* or *ch* and *ew* in *chew;* not the same as a DIPHTHONG

dim not bright; unclear In film, TV, and theater, to dim or *dim down* is to reduce the light intensity; to *dim up* or *dim in* is to increase the light gradually, and to *dim out* is to reduce the light to BLACKOUT. To *dim the house* is to turn off the main lights in the theater, generally immediately prior to the performance.

dim. dimension; diminished

dime novel a paper-covered fiction book that sold for ten cents in the late 19th century In England, a dime novel was called a *penny dreadful.*

dimension drawing a graphic representation that shows a cross-section of an object with the diameters or other dimensions of the parts

dimension line a thin solid line on a drawing, map, or other work that indicates the distance or other dimension between two points, except when it is interrupted by numerals or other descriptions of the dimensions

dimmer 1 a device to change light intensity 2 [television] an electrician who controls *dimming* by using magnetic amplifiers, *reactance dimmers,* resistances, transformers, and other devices, particularly silicon-controlled *rectifiers* and *dimmer/thyristor* devices, which are operated on consoles called *dimmer boards*

DIN a rating of film speed, as indicated by the light-sensitivity of the film emulsion DIN is from *Deutsche Industrie Normen,* the German counterpart of the American National Standards Institute. DIN ratings are commonly used in Europe.

dingadinga   a low-power spotlight; also called a DINKY

dingbat   a typographic decoration   No kidding. That's what they're called, except when they're called *flubdub*.

ding letter   a rejection

dink   a connecting element, such as between the two loops of the letter *g*

DINKS   a couple with *d*ual *i*ncome, *no k*ids

dinky, dinkey   a small locomotive; anything small or compact, particularly a low-power spotlight   A small incandescent spotlight is called a *dinky inky* or *inky dinky*. The origin may be from *dink*, which is Scottish for "neat," or from baseball slang—a slow curve, called a *dipsy-doo*, once was called a *dinky-doo*. A dinky dash is a very short line or dash, such as one *em*. In newspaper printing, a dinky is a half-roll (half WEB) of paper, measured along the width.

dinner theater   a facility that combines a restaurant with a theater, so that theatrical performances are shown to diners

diode   an electron tube with a cold anode and a heated cathode, a two-element receiving tube or semiconductor device

diopter   a unit of measurement of a lens, equal to the power of a lens with a focal distance of one meter, commonly used in eyeglasses   A lens with a plus (+) number of diopters is converging; a minus (−) number of diopters is diverging. A *diopter lens* is used as a supplementary lens to cover a TV or other camera lens and thus alter its focal length. A *plus diopter* is used for close-ups.

diorama   a display, usually three-dimensional or with that effect, generally specially lighted and sometimes moving or with lighting to produce animation or special effects, used in advertising and museums   In photography, particularly for motion pictures and TV, a diorama is a scene, set, or backdrop with a three-dimensional foreground blending into a two-dimensional background or created to give the illusion of an actual complete scene. The standard BACKLIT diorama in terminals and sports arenas is 62 inches wide and 43 inches high.

Dior do   a lavish costume, a theatrical slang term named after Christian Dior (1905–57), French couturier   A *do* is a party or party apparel.

diphthong   a gliding speech sound, as in the union of two vowels or semi-vowels in one sound or syllable (examples are the *oi* sound of

boil and the *oy* sound of toy); also, a *ligature*, such as æ or œ, pronounced as a single vowel

dipole   [broadcasting] a radio or TV antenna fed from the center, such as a rabbit-ear antenna

dir.   director

direct broadcast satellite (DBS)   a high-powered satellite authorized in 1982 for broadcasting directly to homes

direct buyer   a retailer or other customer who purchases directly from a manufacturer without a broker, wholesaler, distributor, warehouse, or other intermediary   Such a sale is called a *direct sale*, based on a *direct order* for *direct store delivery* or to the retailer's own warehouse.

direct cinema   a type of realistic documentary film, usually with long scenes, wide-angle views, and no narration   It is similar to CINEMA VERITÉ, although in the latter, the filmmaker usually is more involved and less objective

direct cut   [film] an instantaneous change of shots, without any optical transition device

direct distance dialing (DDD)   a long-distance telephone call without operator assistance

direct-entry typesetting   typographic composition produced by a self-contained automated device with input and output components; also called *direct-input phototypesetting*

direct halftone   a negative made by direct exposure to the original, rather than from a negative or copy print or by contact through a HALFTONE (picture) screen (a *direct screen halftone*)

direct house   a manufacturer, as of advertising specialties, that sells directly to customers and not via distributors or representatives

direct-image typesetting   typographic composition produced by a typewriter; also called *direct-impression typesetting*

direct inward dialing (DID)   an incoming telephone system in which calls are directed automatically to an individual's extension without an operator

direction   management, guidance, instruction, indication; relationship of positions; a line leading to a place   A *directional antenna* sends or receives signals in a specific direction rather than generally. A *directional station* transmits in a specific direction in order to concentrate on a specific area or to reduce interference with a station on the same frequency. A *directional screen* is a projection surface with a lens, beaded glass, or other material or device to concentrate reflected light in one direction. On a script, *general direction* notations in the left margin describe entrances, exits, and other movements; *personal direction* notations (generally in parentheses within the text) describe facial and body gestures and other such actions.

directional 1 [journalism] an abbreviation, word, or term in a caption or article that directs the reader to part of a photo, such as left, right, or center 2 [market research] a difference or conclusion that is not statistically significant but from which an inference, tendency, or direction can be suggested

directive interview a structured interview, such as specific multiple-choice answers, rather than a discursive nondirective interview

direct mail advertising or promotion matter mailed directly to potential customers, contributors, or other audiences The most common types are for mail-order products such as catalogs and book clubs, services, fund-raising, and political campaigns.

direct marketing distribution, promotion, and selling via one or more media linking the seller and buyer and designed to elicit a direct response, as differentiated from advertising by a manufacturer designed to motivate a consumer to make a purchase through an intermediary, such as a retailer A direct marketer can be a cataloguer, book club, or other manufacturer or supplier, including a retailer. Direct marketing generally makes use of customer files and lists, and includes a variety of selling techniques, such as door-to-door selling, media inserts, mail order, take-one cards, telemarketing, and videotex. It usually is more personal—directed to specific target audiences or individuals—than general marketing or media advertising. Direct marketing has expanded and diversified in recent years. These days, many department stores and other retailers sell via catalogs and other direct marketing techniques in which the customer *buys direct* without visiting a retail outlet.

Direct Marketing Association a major association headquartered in New York With over 5,000 members, it represents marketers in print, broadcast, telephone, mail, and other media that directly reach consumers and other customers. Prior to 1983, it was called the Direct Mail/Advertising Association (DMMA); originally, it was called the Direct Mail Advertising Association.

director a supervisor, such as an art director or research director When used alone, director generally refers to the person responsible for all audience-visible components of a program, film, or show, whereas the producer is responsible for the financial and other behind-the-scenes aspects. The *production director* selects and manages the suppliers. A *craftsman director* concentrates on film production and closely follows the script, whereas a *personal director* is more active in the script development or other artistic elements.

director of photography (DP) [film] the individual in charge of the camera operation, including lighting; also called *cinematographer* The director of photography sometimes also actually operates the camera and is called *cameraman, camera operator,* or *first cameraman.*

director's crew [film] the team reporting to the director, including the *first assistant director (A-D), second assistant director (second A-D),* script supervisor, dialogue director, cuer, stunt coordinator, and trainee

director's finder a viewfinder, commonly used by film directors and cinematographers to view a scene in different sizes and thus select a specific lens You've seen this device hanging on a cord or chain around the director's neck.

Directors Guild of America (DGA) an independent union of film directors and others, including broadcast directors, based in Hollywood, CA

director's notes comments about the script, rehearsal, or performance, written by the director

directory 1 a publication with listings, such as a classified telephone directory Advertising in a publication such as the Yellow Pages and Standard Rate & Data is called *directory advertising.* 2 [computers] a list of files in storage, as indicated on an index or table of identifiers on the display screen 3 [film] The *Directory* is the Academy Players Directory published by the Academy of Motion Picture Arts and Sciences in Hollywood, CA, with photos and information about actors and actresses.

directory assistance a service of a telephone company, popularly known as Information, that provides telephone numbers

direct outward dialing (DOD) a feature of a telephone system that permits a user to gain access to the exchange network without operator assistance, such as by dialing 9

direct pickup live, not recorded, broadcast

direct positive a copy, similar to a Photostat, produced photographically without an intermediate negative; abbreviated as DP

direct process a direct HALFTONE process used in color printing to produce halftone separation negatives for each color

direct recording a photographic recording made at a live performance or the production of an audio track simultaneously with filming

direct response advertising a direct mail, newspaper, or other advertisement with a coupon or other response device offering products or services directly to consumers, generally without an intermediary

dirge a funeral hymn; a slow, sad song, poem, or other composition It is shorter and less formal than an elegy.

dirty soiled; muddy, as a *dirty color*; obscene, as a *dirty joke*; unfair or unkind, as a *dirty look*; rough in tone, as a *dirty trumpet*; erroneous, as a *dirty mailing list*

dirty dupe a photograph or film print made from a print (instead of from an original negative) and thus possibly imperfect

dirty proof a printer's proof with a multitude of errors

DIS Defense Information School, an installation at Fort Benjamin Harrison, IN, operated by the U.S. Army to train military journalists and public affairs officers; DISSOLVE, a film term

DISA *d*irect *i*nward *s*ystem *a*ccess, a telephone feature that enables an individual to call a number (such as of the individual's office) and then access an outside line, such as a WATS line

disc a record or *platter*, such as a phonograph record The flat, circular plate (or platter) with magnetic surfaces for storage and retrieval of computer data is more commonly spelled *disk*.

disc. discount

disc jockey (D.J.) a radio or TV performer whose program consists mainly of records (DISCS); also called *jock* or *dee jay*

disclaimer a repudiation or denial of responsibility or connection, such as an announcement disassociating the station or sponsor from the editorial views presented on a program A *disclaimer title* commonly appears at the end of a film indicating that "the characters in the film are not based on actual persons living or dead, and any resemblances are purely coincidental."

disco a nightclub with recorded music on discs or tapes for dancing; a *discotheque*

disconnect in cable TV, telephone, and other fields, a subscriber whose service has been terminated, usually for nonpayment

discontinued list products no longer available or no longer approved for purchase by a local manager of a retail chain Such a list is prepared by the national headquarters of the chain.

discontinuity [film] a poor or abrupt transition from one scene to the next; a break in action called a *jump cut*; consecutive shots that do not match in costume, decor, lighting, or other details

discontinuous innovation the creation of a totally new product or type of usage, not a modification of an existing product

discount a reduction from the full or regular price, such as the difference between the price paid by the consumer and the cost to the retailer (*retail discount*) or the concession given to a customer for prompt payment (*cash discount*) or volume purchases (*volume discount, frequency discount*)

discount and dating a sales program of a record manufacturer or distributor that allows discounts and delayed billing to retailers

discount price a reduced price, lower than the regular or list price A retail store or other company that regularly sells in this manner is a *discount house, discount store,* or *discounter.*

discovery a revelation A *discovery dolly shot, pan discovery shot, discovery pan, discovery tilt,* or *discovery zoom* reveals or exposes something to the viewer that was not previously visible.

Discovery Channel a cable network headquartered in Landover, MD

discrepancy inconsistency; material in a broadcast that deviates from the script In a live announcement of a commercial script, a discrepancy or error may be rectified by a subsequent free commercial. Discrepancies are supposed to be noted in a station's log.

discrete separate, distinct (not the same as discreet, or prudent, though it's pronounced identically)

discrete media unconnected media; separate films, tapes, dictation belts, or other recording or playing units, handled manually and not automatic or continuous operation, as are continuous or endless loops

discrete stereo broadcasting [radio] a technique of transmitting on two separate (discrete) frequencies for stereophonic reception in the left and right channels

discrete word a separate word In dictionaries, the word being defined—the *main entry* word—sometimes is called a discrete or *primary* word.

discretionary hyphen [typography] a computer code inserted in a word so that the word can be hyphenated if necessary but not hyphenated if it does not fall at the end of a line

discretionary income the portion of income that remains after fixed payments and expenditures for necessities

dish a microwave transmitter or receiver with a concave (*dishlike*) reflector to concentrate and focus signals Dishes come in many sizes. A small dish can be attached to a microphone to pick up from a large area; a large dish can be set atop a tower or roof to transmit or pick up from a satellite. A communications satellite sometimes is called a *skydish* or *big dish* (in the sky).

dish development a method of developing film in which single sheets of film or prints are immersed in a shallow container, or dish, of developing fluid that is agitated by moving the container

dished not flat; concave, as in *dished* papers that curl at the edges

dishing [film] the unintentional dropping out of the center portion of film on a CORE, so that it becomes concave like a dish

dish night a promotion in U.S. movie theaters in the 1930s and 1940s in which all patrons on specific weekday nights were given free plates as part of the admission price

disk a round flat plate about the size of an LP record, coated with a magnetic substance on which data may be stored; also called *magnetic* or *computer disk* A *disk recording* or *hard disk* is magnetic information on a *platter*, not a tape. A *diskette* is a small floppy disk, a flexible sheet of oxide-treated mylar mounted and/or stored in a paper or plastic envelope. A *dual-density disk* is a floppy disk with twice the storage capacity of a standard disk. A symbol for a disk is

disk drive a peripheral unit in a computer system, consisting of a mechanism, a moving head, to house and move a disk

disk erase a function of a computer to eradicate the data on a disk or diskette and write over with other data, as is done with an audio or video tape recorder

diskery a record company that makes disks; a word coined by VARIETY

disk operating system (DOS) [computers] a program that controls the transfer of data to and from peripheral devices such as a hard or floppy disk

disk pack a removable group of computer disks connected to a spindle

dispatch a department at some daily newspapers that assists in various advertising functions, such as scheduling, processing, and delivery of proofs

display 1 [sales promotion] posters, cards, boards, bins, and other items used for sales promotion A *display allowance* may be given by a manufacturer to a retailer in return for setting up a display. When the display is removed, the retailer receives a *display loader*, which may consist of merchandise or a premium instead of actual cash payment. The product being sold may be all or part of the display. 2 [computers] visual information on the *display screen* or *video monitor* of a computer system *Display highlighting* is the brightening or blinking of characters or symbols on a *video display terminal* (*VDT*).

display advertising advertising in a publication other than classified advertising; sometimes referred to simply as *display* It can be illustrated, as compared to classified ads, which are all

text. A variation, *display classified*, permits illustrations and various typefaces.

display blank paper used for posters, show cards, and other displays, excluding DISPLAY BOARDS except for those that are thin (about 14-ply)

display board heavy paper used for point-of-sale and other store displays The standard size is 40″ × 60″ in varying thicknesses (expressed in *ply*, such as 28-ply, which is about one-tenth of an inch).

display carton a cardboard box that opens or folds out into a POINT-OF-PURCHASE display of merchandise; also called DISPLAY CASE

display case 1 a cabinet, open or with glass panels so that merchandise within is visible, as in a department store or a refrigerated cabinet in a food store 2 a cardboard carton with merchandise that is shipped to a retail outlet and opened to serve as a POINT-OF-PURCHASE display; also called DISPLAY CARTON

display store a showroom for display of items that can be ordered from a catalog; also called *catalog store* or *catalog showroom*

display type large-size characters, such as 14-point or larger (there are 72 points to an inch), used in headlines or titles; also called *display faces*

display typewriter an automated keyboard that composes characters on a lighted display screen rather than on paper; not a typewriter that composes display type

dissolve an optical technique to produce a gradual change in scenes in television or film The progressive blending of the end of one shot into the beginning of the next is produced by the superimposition of a FADE-OUT into a FADE-IN or by putting the camera gradually out of or into focus (a *cross-dissolve*). When the images are both at half-strength, they overlap; the effect is called a *lap*, *lap-dissolve*, *mix*, or *cross-lap*. An *out-of-focus dissolve* is a transition in which one shot is faded out of focus while another shot is faded in. *Dissolve in* is to fade in; *dissolve out*, to fade out. *Dissolve-lapse* is a series of brief shots filmed at different times and linked with fast transitions, similar to *time lapse*. *Dissolve animation* is a series of dissolves to suggest progressive stages in a process. In a *ripple dissolve*, the first scene is blurred or undulates, as in a FLASHBACK. The script notation for a dissolve is *X*.

dissonance discord or disharmony, as in the juxtaposition of jarring sounds, also called CACOPHONY; the juxtaposition of closely related vowel sounds, a poetic or literary device

dist. distance; distant; district

distance a gap or interval between two points in space or time To distance is to cause a physical or psychological separation, such as with another person, a reader, or an audience. *Aesthetic distance* or *psychical distance* is the separation between a work of art, such as a film, play, or book, and the spectator or reader.

distance shot a view in which the subject is a long distance from the camera or appears to be far away; also called a *long shot*

distant signal in cable TV, a station "imported" from a market other than the one in which the cable system is located

distortion misrepresentation; perversion; inaccuracy; poor reception of an audio or video signal An advertisement may be intentionally *distorted* to fit the space of a publication, as in reducing the width to accommodate the set columns. A photo may be deliberately distorted for a special effect.

distress to alter clothing to make it appear worn or old or otherwise changed in accordance with a film, TV, or other script

distress communications equipment and techniques used to convey information about emergency situations Common *distress calls* are SOS (Morse code) and MAYDAY (voice), which are transmitted on frequencies reserved for emergencies, called *distress frequency*.

distribution 1 [marketing] a process by which products move from origin to consumer; also, frequency or extent of occurrence, such as the number of copies of a publication or the area in which a publication or product is sold *Frequency distribution* is a statistical term indicating a grouping of data into classifications based on the quantity of repetitions of an item within a specific interval. A *distribution class* is a group of words or items with common features. A *distributor* is a wholesaler, broker, agent, or other person or firm involved in storing, selling, shipping, or otherwise moving a commodity from its origin to the consumer. The *Variety* abbreviation of distribution is *distrib*; a *distrib* or *distribbery* is a distribution company that works by *distribbing* records, films, or other *distribbed* (distributed) items. 2 [typography] the manual return of type to its case or the automatic return of a MATRIX to its channel in the MAGAZINE of a LINOTYPE or other machine

distribution flow the manner in which a medium is distributed, with independent units such as books, films, and records; continuous or linked units such as radio and TV programs; mosaic units like sections of newspapers and other media that are available separately Distribution flow also can be categorized as uni-directional or two-directional (interactive, such as VIDEOTEX).

district an area A *district reporter*, formerly called a *district man*, is a newspaper or other reporter assigned to a specific area or neighborhood.

dithering [satellite broadcasting] a process of rapidly shifting a signal up and down over a wide band of frequencies in order to minimize interference at any single frequency

ditto to repeat or duplicate; the trademarked term (*Ditto*) for a *spirit duplicator*—a direct-image duplicating machine, made by Ditto, Wiltinville, MA, that uses a carbon stencil

dittogram a repeated letter caused by a typesetting error, as in *rrepeat*

ditto mark a symbol (") used under a word to indicate that it is to be repeated

ditty bag a small container, originally used by sailors to carry toilet articles; also called *ditty box* The ditty bag used by camera crews is a cloth or canvas bag containing small items, sometimes attached to a tripod.

diva a female leading singer, particularly in opera; from the Italian for "goddess" Opera singers, particularly in Italy, are revered.

diversionary pricing a retailing practice of promoting a few sale-priced items to create, perhaps deceptively, the image that all items are low-priced

divider 1 a line or material used to separate sections, such as tabbed sheets of heavy stock in a loose-leaf book 2 [typography] a large subhead, generally at least 14 points; also called a *breaker*

divinity circuit a type of bookbinding with extended flexible cover ends that bend over the body of the book, also called *divinity edges* or *circuit edges*, and often used for Bibles and prayer books It was invented by William Yapp, a 19th-century London bookseller, and is called *yap-binding* in England. *Divinity calf* is a dark binding made of calfskin and used in the 19th century for the inside cover lining of prayerbooks.

divisionary title in a book, a leaf preceding a section or division, with its title or number on the right side and the reverse side generally blank

division label in newspapers and other publications, a letter indicating the start of a section of a stock-market table or other alphabetical tabular material, including classified Each section is called a *division*.

DIY DO-IT-YOURSELF

dj disc jockey; dust jacket

D.J. DISC JOCKEY

DJ copy a record with a recording on only one side, for use by a radio disc jockey

DJIA Dow Jones Industrial Average

dk. dark; deck

DK or **D.K.** don't know In financial relations, it refers to not knowing the address of a shareholder or the location of an item; the term is also used for respondents to market research or other surveys who do not know or have no opinion.

DL down left, a part of a stage; see also AREAS

DLO dead-letter office, the final repository for nondeliverable mail

DMA DESIGNATED MARKET AREA

D-M-E [film] the dialogue, music, and effects tracks, which are combined on one track via the process of *D-M-E mix* Before the dialogue is added, it is called an *M-E mix*, a *music-effects mix*, or a *minus-dialogue mix*.

DMU DECISION-MAKING UNIT

dn. down

D/N DAY-FOR-NIGHT

DNR a daily trade publication, the bible of the men's-wear industry, published by Fairchild Publications, New York; formerly called *Daily News Record*

do or **do.** DITTO; to duplicate or repeat, as indicated by *ditto marks* (") or the abbreviation *do*; pronounced "dough"

DOB date of birth

doc. document

dock a storage area, such as a *scene dock*, an area for storing scenery, often under the stage

doctor to repair, change, falsify, alter, or modify

doctor blade a straight-edge, metal, plastic, or rubber, used to remove ink, paint, or other substances; also called a *doctor*

docudrama a combination of documentary and drama, such as *Roots* and other TV shows that are semifictionalized versions of history

document a written or printed statement of evidence or information In word processing, a document is a portion of text treated as a single unit. *Document assembly* is the function of a word processor that enables files to be assembled and combined to form a new document. *Document filing* is the accessing and storage of text in the archives of a word-processing system. The text is identified by a number or code (*document ID*) and listed in a *document index* with identification information—a *document summary*—and document marking that indicates specific pages and lines. A symbol for a document is ⌐┘.

documentary a nonfiction film or program, generally about actual events or "real life" but often treated selectively or creatively

DOD DIRECT OUTWARD DIALING

dodge to reduce the intensity of a photo by shading during printing, as with a cardboard or the lab technician's hand to block the light The process is called *dodging*.

dodger a small sheet of advertising matter for enclosure with letters or for hand distribution; also called *handbill*

dog **1** an unattractive person; an inferior product or performance **2** [theater] a small town "To try it out on the dog" is to preview a play in a small city—to perform a *dog show* at a *dog house* in a *dog town*.

dog-and-pony show a presentation or description of results, perhaps involving several individuals plus audiovisual and show-business techniques; sometimes referred to as *show-and-tell* The term originates from vaudeville, where a trained dog and pony was a common act.

dogear a turned-down corner of a leaf of paper, folded back in such a way that it will not trim

doggerel trivial, poorly constructed verse, generally humorous

dogleg a line that is bent intentionally to point to an object The line begins horizontally, then curves—*doglegs*—toward the item, perhaps terminating in an arrowhead.

dog watch the time at a newspaper or other medium after the last edition or program, when a reduced or skeleton staff remains on duty

doing business as (d.b.a.) a term sometimes used by unincorporated businesses after an individual's name, as in (name of individual), d.b.a. (name of business)

do-it-yourself (DIY) [marketing] individuals who do their own car and home repairs or other activities of importance to marketers of relevant goods and services; the practice of undertaking what could be left to professionals

Dolby a trademarked system of Dolby Laboratories, Los Angeles, invented by Ray Dolby, that reduces or eliminates "noise" or hiss from recorded sound and improves the signal The *Dolby noise reduction process* is abbreviated as *NR*, as in the NR-encoded soundtrack used in the Dolby Stereo system.

dolly a mobile platform with three or four wheels for carrying a microphone, camera, or other items A *dolly shot* (the process is called *dollying*, *tracking*, or *trucking*) shifts the viewpoint of the camera, often by a crew member called a *dolly pusher* or *dolly grip*, and is taken while the dolly is in motion. To *dolly-in*, *dolly-up*, or *camera up* is to move the camera platform closer toward the subject; to *dolly-out* is to move it away and is also called *camera back*, *dolly-back*, *truck back*, or *pull back*. In a camera on three wheels, the most common type in TV, the *dolly mode* is a movement in which two wheels are fixed and one is used for steering.

The movement and appearance of certain dollies is the basis for their animal names. A *crab dolly* has four wheels and can move like a crab in any direction and into very small areas. A *cricket dolly*, made by Elemack in Italy, has a collapsible central column that can rise about four feet. A *spyder dolly*, also made by Elemack, has a hydraulic column. A *doorway dolly* is a narrow dolly that can move through a doorway. *Dolly tracks* or *camera tracks* are rails or boards on which a dolly moves. A *western dolly* has heavy wheels and can move over rough terrain, as in a Western movie.

domestics a classification of products that includes bed and bath linens, curtains, and related items

dominant station a clear-channel AM radio station, technically classified by the FCC as a Class I station

Domsat a domestic satellite, regulated by the FCC

donee a person who receives a gift or donation; pronounced dough-NEE The word is used by some marketers for when a *donor* sends a magazine subscription or other gift to a *donee*, as indicated on the enclosed *donor card*.

donkey roll a roll, or WEB, of paper half as wide as a standard roll, used at some newspapers

don't wants C.O.D. items refused by customers

donut a commercial distributed to stations with a blank central section to be "filled" with a local advertiser's message, which generally is live; see DOUGHNUT COMMERCIAL

door a branch store A chain may have many doors in a market, and a product sometimes is available only at specific ones, such as suburban doors.

door count the actual attendance at a theatrical performance as indicated by the number of ticket stubs, clicks of a counter, or another mechanism at the entrance

doorflat a flat piece of scenery—a *flat*—that functions as a door

door knockers salespeople who sell *door-to-door* to people at home

door list names of people to be admitted free to a theater, nightclub, or other site provided to the doorman or box-office clerk; also called *house list*

door opener an inexpensive gift offered by a salesperson to gain access (open the door)—literally, as in DOOR-TO-DOOR SALES, or figuratively, as with a premium enclosed or offered in DIRECT MAIL

doorstepping [journalism] waiting at a person's home or office in order to conduct an interview; also called *ambushing* or, in Australia, *intrusions*

door-to-door sales a distribution system in which salespeople call directly on customers at their homes or offices The largest company in this field is Avon Products Inc, New York.

doo-wop a group singing style popular in the 1950s involving a lead singer and a chorus usually standing in a straight line Their appearance and rhythm is called *doo-wop style*.

dope 1 [outdoor advertising] a thick, pasty substance used to affix posters To dope is to add a substance, as in to affix a poster. 2 [printing] *Doping* is adding substances to thin or change ink characteristics. 3 information, particularly advance information, as in "What's the dope?" A *dope-sheet*, also called a *poop sheet*, is a paper on which a photographer (or other person) jots down a story, film idea, or other information. The word is also used to describe a publication with private advance information—*dope*—and predictions, as in horse racing, by a *dopester*. A *dope story* is a background interpretive article. 4 [photography] a developer

Doppler effect the change in frequency of light and sound waves in relation to a moving source or observer, a phenomenon first observed by *Christian Doppler* (1803–53), a Russian mathematician and physician The concept—when the source and observer come closer, the observed frequency is higher than the emitted frequency—is used in audio enhancement and other aspects of film and broadcasting production.

DOS DISK OPERATING SYSTEM; pronounced doss

dos-a-dos back-to-back; from the French, pronounced dough-za-DOUGH In publishing, *Dos-a-dos binding* is two books bound back-to-back with a common back cover, so that the open side (the *fore-edges*) of one is next to the closed side (SPINE) of the other.

dossier a collection of documents about a person or subject The name is from the early custom of labeling a dossier file on the back (*dos* is French for "back").

dot 1 a tiny round mark, spot, or symbol with various meanings: period, or end of a sentence; decimal point; multiplication (used in middle of line instead of an X); short signal in Morse code In music, a dot after a note indicates that the note is to be prolonged by a half, and a double dot indicates prolongation by ³⁄₄. In printing a picture, the image is converted via a screen into a pattern of dots of varying sizes. The same concept is used in a *dot matrix printer* or *dot printer*, which has an element (*dot matrix*) that forms characters by printing a series of dots; this is different from a *character printer*, which produces solid characters. Dot matrix characters are the simplest form of digital type. The greater the dot density (*dots per inch* or *dpi*), the higher the character resolution. About 1,000 dpi is a minimum for optimum reproduction. A *hard dot* has a sharp, clean edge, while a *soft dot* has a halation or fringe around its edge. **2** [film] slang for a small disk put in front of a light to diffuse it

dot and tickle slang for use of the STIPPLE technique

dot *i*'s and cross *t*'s to be very careful and correct, as in completing a document or in any written or spoken material

dotless i a lowercase *i* without a dot, for use with accents in the space otherwise occupied by the dot

dot spread [printing] a defect in which dots print larger than they should, resulting in darker tones or colors

double a counterpart; a person resembling another; a performer's understudy; as a verb, to make twice, to duplicate, to fold in two, or to reverse or repeat (*double back*)

double bar two parallel vertical lines, the second thicker than the first, which signify the end of a musical section or composition

double bill a theater program—BILL—with two plays or other works

double broad a box-shaped 4,000-watt light, generally used as a fill light in film production

double-carding in transit advertising, the placement of two different CAR CARDS from the same advertiser in each vehicle

double cast to assign two performers to the same role so that they alternate or with one as an UNDERSTUDY

double chain [television] the simultaneous running of two projectors, each with different film or tape, in order to intercut from one to the other, such as for cutaway or reaction shots in an interview

double-coated stock paper coated twice on the same side

double column two vertical columns of type rather than type extending across the entire page

double dagger a reference mark (‡) used as a third order of reference; also called *double obe-*

lisk The first mark is an *asterisk*; the second is a DAGGER.

double-deck or **double-decker** **1** a headline with two units, a main DECK and a secondary deck **2** an outdoor advertisement with one panel atop another

double-decker lead an introduction to an article, generally one or more highlights or a quotation, written as a two-paragraph unit

double-deckle stock paper with parallel DECKLE (irregular) edges

double disk a two-disk audio or video album

double text inadvertently printed twice in the same publication, as in two sections of the same edition of a newspaper, or printed matter set twice; also called *doublet* A *photodouble* is a stand-in who resembles a performer.

double-duty envelope a self-addressed return envelope with a sales message or other additional portion that can be torn off

double exposure a photograph of two different images on the same negative It can be a composite or blended image.

double feature two theatrical motion pictures on the same program, generally a major (*A picture*) and a minor (*B picture*)

double flat a symbol, ♭♭, placed before a musical note to indicate that it is to be lowered two semitones (doubly lowered pitch); the opposite of DOUBLE SHARP

double frame to print each frame of a movie twice, thus slowing the speed of action

double image an effect of imperfect registration in printing or TV reception in which all or part of the picture appears twice

double keyboarding a computer-processing verification procedure in which identical input from two keyboard operators is compared, with discrepancies flagged by the computer

double letter two letters joined together, a LIGATURE, also called a *tied letter*

double numeration [publishing] a system of numbering with the chapter number (books) or volume number (periodicals, particularly journals), followed by the page number within the chapter or volume In textbooks, illustrations or tables often are identified with the chapter number followed by the number of the illustration within the chapter, such as Figure 5.3, the third item in the fifth chapter.

double-page spread an advertisement or article on two adjacent pages; also called DOUBLE TRUCK

double postcard two attached postcards, usually folded and perforated, one addressed to the recipient (customer) and the other arranged to be removed and mailed to the sender (seller)

double print 1 a sheet made by superimposing two different negatives; a composite shot; double exposure; a *subprint* 2 [printing] type *overprinting* another area, such as a photo

double printing [photography] a process of superimposing two or more images on one frame or film negative It is done with a printer, not in the camera.

double rule a RULE consisting of one thick stroke and one thin stroke; also called *oxford rule* or *scotch rule* It is not the same as *parallel rule*, which has strokes of the same weight.

double sharp a symbol, x or ⚌, placed before a musical note to indicate that it is to be raised two semitones (doubly raised pitch)

double-sided diskette a FLOPPY DISK with read/write capabilities on both sides; also called *flippy disk*

double-space typing with a full space between the lines of text (not two full spaces)

doublespeak obscure or ambiguous language, usually meant to be deceptive; coined in 1949 by George Orwell (1903–50), British author, in his novel *1984*

double spotting broadcasting of commercials—spots—consecutively or back-to-back without anything between

double spread or **double-spread** an advertisement or article on two adjacent pages

double system [film, television] recording audio and video separately, perhaps at different times, for subsequent combination

double-system sound a film technique in which a separate camera and microphone are used The picture and sound then are combined in the editing.

doublet a word or words unintentionally repeated in the same issue of a newspaper or other publication

double take a delayed reaction to a remark or situation, such as startled surprise, often used as a comic device

double talk ambiguous and deceptive talk, usually deliberately confusing

double title page in books, two title pages facing each other, such as in two different languages It differs from a *double-spread title page*, which is one title (and other information) spread across two facing pages.

Doubletone drawing paper on a board stock with two latent (invisible) SCREENS, one a light tone and the other a dark tone, that produces

shading with the application of a developer to either tone; trademarked by Craftint Manufacturing Co. of Cleveland, OH

double truck adjacent or facing pages in a publication, such as a single two-page advertisement or editorial layout It is also called DOUBLE SPREAD or DOUBLE-PAGE SPREAD, which generally refer to magazines, whereas *double truck* refers to newspapers.

double-up [film] the practice of showing two films in a theater for only one day—a *double-up day*—to promote a new film that is a forthcoming attraction This generally is done on the last day or close to the end of the *current attraction.*

double weight a photograph printed on heavy paper

doubling 1 performing more than one part in a play or other production 2 a procedure in printing, TV, or other transmission that produces a DOUBLE IMAGE or *doubled impression*

doubling day [direct marketing] the point at which half of the expected returns or results of a mailing are received, such as 30 days after the mailing

doublure an ornamental lining of leather, silk, or other material on the inside of a book cover; from the French *doubler*, "to line"

doughnut commercial a radio or TV commercial with a blank in the middle—the "hole"—into which is inserted a current price, the name of a local dealer, or other material; also called a *donut* The middle part often is instrumental music over which copy is read, preceded and followed by a jingle.

douser 1 a device that cuts off a light, such as on a film projector to block the beam during a changeover from one projector to another; sometimes spelled *dowser*

DOV data over voice, a process using the same wires for telephone (voice) and computer terminals (data) for simultaneous voice and data communications

Dowcom the internal communications system at Dow Jones, connecting all its bureaus and printing plants

dowel a pin that fits in a hole to fasten or align two adjacent pieces, such as a metal or plastic pin attached to a printing film support or plate to position it

Dow Jones & Co. one of the country's largest media companies, headquartered in New York It publishes *The Wall Street Journal*, Ottaway Newspapers, and *Barron's* and owns DOW JONES NEWS SERVICE and other companies. Note that the Dow Jones name is not hyphenated—the company was formed in 1882 by Charles Dow, Edward Jones, and Charles Bergstresser.

Dow-Joneser an article based on an interview of a company executive, transmitted by the Dow Jones News Service

Dow Jones Industrial Average (DJIA) an index of stock prices based on changes in a group of representative major stocks

Dow Jones News Service the *broad tape* or *news ticker* supplied by DOW JONES & CO., INC. to many thousands of subscribers

down not operational *Down time* is the period of non-operation. *Down in the mud* is poor lighting or sound.

down-and-under an instruction to decrease the volume of music or sound effects as the sound of dialogue begins and becomes more audible; opposite of *up-and-over*

downbeat 1 a downward stroke of a music conductor's hand or baton indicating the first beat of each measure 2 depressing, unhappy, or grimly realistic

downer a negative, pessimistic, or DOWNBEAT work; opposite of UPBEAT

downgrade list a term at *The Wall Street Journal* to indicate pending stories that are recategorized from high to medium or low priority, generally as a result of space limitations

downhold an old-time telegrapher's expression that means hold down, keep it short, or control expenses Because Western Union charged by the word, editors would use one word instead of two whenever words could be combined. Today, the organization of current and former staffers of United Press International is called the *Downhold Club*. (That's appropriate—UPI is known for its frugality.)

downlight a light beamed from above the subject or scene

downlink [telecommunications] the portion of a signal from the satellite down to the receiving point

download to transmit from a central computer to a terminal or other device; also called *down-line-load*

down market relating to a lower socioeconomic group, as in to move or position a product *down market*

downmarket downscale; individuals with lower incomes and other characteristics that are lower (down) than the median

down on the bill theatrical slang for a position toward the end of a variety program, more desirable than the acts at the beginning of the BILL, or program

downplay to minimize, reducing the size or significance, as of a newspaper story

downscale the low end of a demographic range, such as those with limited education or income; opposite of UPSCALE

downshift [typography] to move from uppercase to lowercase, or the code that signals such a change

down shot a high-angle shot in which a camera is focused on a subject below

downstage toward the audience or camera, the front of the stage; opposite of UPSTAGE

downstairs the lower half of a standard-size newspaper page; also called BASEMENT

downstream in interactive or two-way TV, the programming to the subscribers

down style a typographic system with a minimum of capital letters Most newspapers prefer this style.

downtown publication a bohemian, funky, or offbeat lifestyle magazine or newspaper published in lower Manhattan (as in the SoHo district) or the lower-rent areas of other cities

downtracking wire-service jargon for attempting to get a requested story

DP DIRECTOR OF PHOTOGRAPHY; DIRECT POSITIVE

dpi or **DPI** dots per inch, a measure of printing resolution, using an ink-jet printer The higher the DPI number is, the darker or heavier the printing is.

DR down right, a portion of a stage; see also AREAS

draft an interim or preliminary version of a news release, article, speech, or other material

drag 1 to lag behind or to be prolonged tediously, as in writing that drags; also, a dull person or situation 2 [printing] blurring due to register trouble so that the dots become enlarged toward the back or *non*-GRIPPER edge

dragon's blood a red resinous substance obtained from various tropical plants, particularly a Malaysian palm called *Daemonorups draco* Dragon originates from the Latin *draco*. Dragon's-blood powder is used in photoengraving to protect the plate from acid damage.

drama a literary composition that tells a story, generally of human conflict, through dialogue In its broadest sense, drama is the art or profession of writing, producing, or performing plays, or plays collectively, as taught in a *drama department* and reviewed by a *drama critic*. Most playgoers today consider a drama to be serious work, not a comedy. Drama also refers to any events that are so vivid—

dramatic—that they resemble a drama, such as *real-life drama.*

Drama Desk an organization of drama critics and other media people who cover the New York theater It presents the annual Drama Desk Awards.

dramatic time the period of time during which the action takes place in a film or other work; also called *script time*; not the same as the actual time of the performance

dramatis personae the characters in a play or a list of the characters, usually printed at the beginning of the text with their relationships or other identification; from the Latin for drama persons

Dramatists Guild a New York organization of playwrights, lyricists, and composers; a member of the Authors League of America, Inc. and located at the same address Dramatists Guild contracts, which cover various types of plays, provide for royalties to playwrights based on box-office sales.

dramaturgy the art of writing and/or producing plays Some theatrical professors call themselves *dramaturges* or *dramaturgists*, and some theatrical writers also like this classy word in such forms as *dramaturgic, dramaturgical*, and *dramaturgically.*

drape 1 to cover, hang, or decorate; cloth hanging, perhaps in folds, as in drapery or drapes, often used as a backdrop on a TV set 2 [film] The person in charge of carpets, drapes, and other coverings is called a *drape* or *supervising drape.*

drapery setting [theater] a stage set made of draperies, or curtains; called a *curtain set* in the United Kingdom

draughtsman a British word for draftsman, an artist who does drawings; a designation used in British films, particularly those with animation

draw 1 to pull, drag, select, sketch, or depict To *draw out* is to extend; to *draw up* is to arrange or draft. 2 [computers] an acronym for *Direct Read After Write*, a laser method of recording data on a videodisc 3 [printing] the gathered sections of a publication; in bookbinding, also the gathered sections Each batch is a draw; a *double draw* is two batches assembled, and a *triple draw* is three. 4 [photography] extra exposure to compensate for the light loss that occurs when a lens is extended for a close-up; also called the *bellows factor* 5 [marketing] an advance to a salesperson from anticipated commissions, as from a *drawing account* 6 [theater] an act, or anything that attracts interest; also called a *drawing card*

drawing the act of representing something by lines or strokes, made on a surface, generally with a pen or pencil; a sketch or other work of art produced in this manner, perhaps using drawing paper (often an opaque bond board) on a *drawing board* (a smooth board on which paper or other material is fastened) A project in the planning stage is *on the drawing board.* A lottery is a *drawing* in which the entries or winning numbers are *drawn* or picked from a container. *Drawing power* is the ability of a performer or other entity to *draw* or attract audiences.

drawing ink black ink, carbon pigment in a solution, used by artists for pen or brush drawing and writing; more permanent than *writing ink* Drawing ink usually is called *India ink*, particularly in the United States.

drawing pin British term for a thumbtack

drawing-room play a play that takes place in a living room or other room where guests are entertained This type of play was popular in the 18th and 19th centuries, particularly *drawing-room comedy*, and occasionally is performed today as a satire or a recreation of a *comedy of manners.*

drawn-on covers a common technique in libraries, in which covers are glued to the backs of periodicals and paperbacks When the endpapers also are pasted down, it's called *drawn-on solid.*

dream an imagined thought or story A *dream balloon* is a circular or oval area above a character in a comic strip, animated film, or other work in which the imagined sequence is visualized. Sometimes the *dream mode* or section occupies the entire panel or frame.

dress to arrange the furnishings and other components or properties (PROPS) in a set, display, or window; to ready a scene for a performance The final, full-costume rehearsal is the *dress rehearsal* or *dress.*

dresser 1 an assistant to the WARDROBE CHIEF or a personal wardrobe assistant to a performer 2 [film] a FITTER

dress extra a nonspeaking performer (an EXTRA) who receives an additional fee for providing his or her own special costume, such as formal attire

dressing room a backstage room in which a performer prepares by putting on a costume—*dressing*—and makeup A star performer has a private dressing room, as opposed to the *chorus dressing room* used by members of the chorus or minor performers. The assignment of rooms is indicated on a *dress-room list* posted backstage.

dress off a direction to a performer to take a position in relation to a person or object, such as *dress off the chair*, which means "sit on it"

dress plot a list of all characters in a play or other work and their costumes, generally arranged by scenes; also called *costume plot*

dress stage a direction to a performer to move slightly, perhaps to *balance the stage*; not common, and not to be confused with *dress a stage*, which is to arrange the furnishings and props

drift a slow change in the frequency or power of a signal

driography a printing process similar to lithography The *dri* means "without water."

drive a mechanism that transports or controls movement, such as in computers and tape recorders

drive-in theater an outdoor movie theater in which viewers remain in their cars

drive-on pass See CAR PASS.

drive out extra-wide spacing between words, to fill a line and force a syllable or word to the next line

drive period the time in which a promotion is presented by a manufacturer to retailers to push forward—*drive*—the sale

driver [film] a person who drives trucks and cars that carry equipment and personnel and reports to the *transportation captain* or *transportation coordinator* The *driver captain* is in charge of the vehicles and the drivers, including a *rig driver*, who drives trucks; *mobile studio operator*, who drives a production trailer; and *stunt driver*, who drives vehicles used in stunts.

drive time morning and afternoon hours when many radio listeners drive to and from work The hours vary depending on the area and time of year—generally 6 to 10 A.M. and 4 to 7 P.M. on weekdays.

drop 1 [theater] an unframed curtain that is part of a stage set or any theater curtain that can be lowered—*dropped*—or raised The first groove is at the front of the stage nearest the footlights. A drop in this groove is "in one," the closest that a curtain can get to the front of the stage. 2 [typography] a commonly used word, as in DROP CAP, DROP HEAD, or DROP INITIALS Though the type of drop sometimes is not specified, a headline writer, for example, knows that drop refers to a DROP-HEAD. 3 [mail] Drop is a common word with mailers. It's an opening in a mailbox for the deposit of mail; also called a *drop box, relay box,* or *storage box.* It's also short for various words indicating that items have been *dropped* (mailed), such as a *drop date,* when a mailing is sched-

uled to enter the postal system, and *drop letters,* which are collected by addressees, as at rural post offices. 4 [television] the hookup between a cable system and the subscriber's set; also, a synonym for *insert* Drops are sound effects inserted on an audio- or videotape after the initial recording.

drop-back a container that opens from the back

drop cap a single capital letter, larger than the standard type size, set into a block of text with one or more lines indented to accommodate it The top of the cap generally aligns with the top of the first line of text.

drop-dead date slang for the last day that a writer, artist, or other person can deliver a manuscript or other material to be produced—if you don't deliver, you're dead; also called *freeze date*

drop folio a page number printed at the bottom of the page; also called *foot folio*

drop-front a container that opens from the front

drophead or **drop-head** a subordinate bank or DECK of a headline; a smaller headline under a primary headline

drop-in ad a local commercial inserted into a national program, or, more generally, an advertising message inserted into a larger advertisement, as for a local dealer or retailer, or a phrase, such as a public service slogan, or symbol; also called *hitch-hike ad*

drop initial an enlarged capitalized first letter of a text section The top is aligned with the letters that follow, but the bottom extends into a space created by indenting the following line or lines.

drop-in [television] a channel that can be added to existing allocations without causing interference to stations located elsewhere but on the same channel

drop letter a letter mailed to and delivered from the same post office

dropline a line in a headline of two or more lines that is indented from the line above it

drop-line head a headline of two or more lines with the lines below the top line indented in an alternating or staggered manner

drop-out or **dropout** 1 portions of original artwork that do not reproduce, especially colored lines or background areas 2 in television, a defect in a tape resulting in a black flash, color loss, or other gap This signal loss can be concealed by a *drop-out compensator.*

dropout halftone a HALFTONE plate in which the screen is dropped out in the very light areas;

also called *high-light halftone*   The removal of the dots produces greater contrast.

drop scene   the front curtain on a theater stage; also, a short scene after a high point to drop or reduce the tension

drop shadow   a dark area adjacent to (generally below) lettering or an object

drop ship   distribution of merchandise from the manufacturer to the consumer, the order for which is placed with an intermediary who does not physically handle the item   A *drop shipment* is an item sent by the shipper to an area, such as the city in which the recipient is located, and then mailed or delivered locally, so that it's *dropped off* prior to delivery.

drop slot   an opening in the top or side of a container, such as a display or exhibit, in which to drop calling cards, entry forms, or other items

drug envelope   an envelope with a rounded flap

drum   1 a cylindrical percussion instrument   2 [photography] a large metal roller that is heated to dry photo prints   3 [printing] a large metal roller used for inking; a *disk* or *photomatrix* containing an assortment of typefaces   A *drum printer* has a revolving metal cylinder as the printing element.

drumbeater   a person, such as a press agent, who calls attention to someone or something

drummer   an old-fashioned word for a traveling salesperson

drum titler   [film, television] a device for adding credits, titles, or other printed copy by photographing the text as it revolves around a cylinder—*drum*—so that the titles move upward on the screen

dry   alcoholic beverages prohibited, as in a *dry county*; not sweet, as a *dry wine*; in drug retailing, an apothecary without food or beverage service; in food retailing, nonperishable products such as paper goods; in graphics, not wet or slightly moist

dry block   [film, television] a rehearsal without cameras

drybrush   a technique of drawing or painting with a brush slightly moistened with ink or watercolor paint on textured paper, so that the texture is visible

dry edit   preliminary editing of a film or tape in which notations are made but actual cutting is not done; also called *paper edit*

dry goods   apparel, curtains, towels, and other textiles and *soft goods*   Retail stores that handle these items and do not sell furniture, appliances, or other hard goods are called *dry goods stores*, ranging from mom-and-pop operations to major department stores.

dry mount   a process of bonding two paper surfaces with a paraffin-treated sheet between them and heat and pressure applied   The sheet—*dry-mount tissue*—is commonly used to bond a photograph or other art to a surface using a *dry-mount press*.

dry offset   a form of offset printing with a relief plate in which the areas to be inked are raised by etching around them and that thus does not require a water dampening system as in PLANOGRAPHY; also called *letterset* (not *letterpress*)

drypoint   an *intaglio* (recessed) printing process in which the metal plate is inscribed with a pointed needle, not with acid, producing a print called a drypoint, which generally has a softness in its lines

dry run   a rehearsal, generally at an early stage, with camera (in the case of film or television); a *walkthrough*; a test

dry sound   a sound or a recording with minimum reverberation   If too little, it's called *dead*.

dry up   to become parched or to wither; to make or become unproductive; to stop talking   A performer who forgets a line is said to dry up.

DS   drugstore

D section   the fourth section of a newspaper

DSS   digital scene simulation, the use of computer graphics—*digitizing*—in films

DST or **D.S.T.**   daylight savings time, a common abbreviation in broadcast schedules

dt.   date

DT   disc turntable, a record player

DTC   direct-to-consumer   An example is DTC materials sent by pharmaceutical companies directly to consumers rather than to physicians or pharmacists.

DTMT   dual-tone multifrequency, as in push-button or touch-tone telephones

DTP   DESKTOP PUBLISHING

dual address   an envelope or other item with two addresses, a street address and a post office box number   This should be avoided. The U.S. Postal Service delivers to whatever is on the line above the city and state.   *Alternate delivery companies*, such as Federal Express, deliver to street addresses, not to post office boxes, which can be reached only via postal mail.

dual audience   two segments of readers, listeners, or viewers, such as men and women

dual kickers   two small, short headlines above the main headline, one flush left and the other flush right

dual track two BANDS, as with dictation or recording equipment with two recording media

duarc a double-arc lamp

dub a dupe or duplicate; an insert in an audiovisual medium; also used as a verb, as in *to dub* something into the body of a radio or TV program or motion picture Material to be dubbed may consist of a different language soundtrack, new or updated material, or other editing. Simply combining different components of a motion picture, such as dialogue, music, and sound effects, into the finished film also constitutes DUBBING. When a duplicate tape is made at a different speed or width from the original, the process is called *dubbing down* if the dub is slower or narrower than the original or *dubbing up* if the dub is faster or wider. An editor may use a *dubbing sheet*—a chart or list of sources—for the *dubbing* MIXER. To *sub-dub* is to *mix-down* or reduce the number of tracks by mixing them.

dubber a person who duplicates a film or tape (makes a DUB); a machine such as an audio playback machine used to make a copy of a tape; a performer who LIP-SYNCHS or inserts dialogue into an existing film or tape, such as a translation (a *dubbed version*)

dubbing the process of recording, such as making a duplicate of a film or tape or replacing dialogue or a soundtrack with new material, as in a different language The process may require a *dubbing cue sheet* with the existing and new versions and be recorded at a *dubbing session* in a *dubbing studio* or a *looping stage.*

dubbing sheet paper used by a SOUND MIXER to mix in (dub) different soundtracks—music, voice, and sound effects—each listed in a separate column, with the footage number and other cueing information; also called a *cue sheet*

Dubner CBG a character background generator, a device that creates and manipulates characters and graphic images on TV, named after Harvey Dubner of Fort Lee, NJ

dub off to record from another recording

ducat an admission ticket to a show

duchess folded note paper and matching envelope

duck *Wall Street Journal* jargon for a straightforward article or item, originated by a Detroit bureau reporter who complained that writing routine news "is like being nibbled to death by ducks"

ducker [broadcasting] a circuit that automatically fades or reduces the volume of music or other background to enable a voice to be heard; also called a *voice-over ducker*

duckfoot quotes quotation marks used in England consisting of straight lines instead of curves; called *guillemets* in France: ` '

due bill an agreement for barter of goods or services, such as a hotel room in exchange for advertising or other services

dull nonglossy, as in dull-coated paper; to remove or tone down shininess, bright light, or unwanted reflections

dummy a preliminary layout, mock-up, or set of blank pages made up in advance to show the size, shape, form, and general style of a piece of artwork or printing; also, an empty package used for display

dump-bin display a container with an assortment of loose items, seemingly casually stacked or *dumped in*, available for sale in a retail store; also called *dump-bin* or *dump bin* On a dump table, merchandise is scattered rather than stacked; this procedure is common in mass merchandising A *dump bin* generally contains only one product, whereas a *jumble display* offers several.

Dun & Bradstreet the world's largest information resources company It owns A.C. NIELSEN, Donnelley directories, Moody's financial publications, and other companies, including the renowned D&B credit reports, and is based in New York.

duodecimo the page size of a book in which each FOLIO, or section, is made from a sheet folded into 12 leaves (24 pages), each about 5" × 7½"; also called *twelvemo* and written as 12mo or 12°

duologue a conversation between two people; a dramatic performance with two performers who speak, usually of brief duration, such as one scene

duopoly a market situation controlled by two sellers; a monopoly extended to two participants In broadcasting, the duopoly rule of the Federal Communications Commission prohibits a licensee from acquiring a second station in the same area. This one-to-a-customer policy has various exceptions, including AM-FM radio combinations.

duotone a photograph printed in two colors; also may be called HALFTONE Two plates, called HALFTONE PLATES, are made from the same black-and-white photographs; each then is printed in a different color, so that a black-and-white photograph can be reproduced in more than one color or shade.

dup. duplicate

dupe short for duplicate, a copy of a radio or TV tape or other audiovisual material; also called a DUB *Duping* is duplicating. A word or words, perhaps even an entire item, unintentionally repeated in the same issue of a newspaper or other publication is called a dupe or DOUBLET.

dupe negative   a negative made from a positive print of a film or any negative other than the original

duplex   twofold, as in machinery with two independent units on a single frame or equipment able to transmit messages in two directions   If the transmission of the two messages is simultaneous, it's *full duplex*; if alternating, it's *half duplex*. *Duplex paper* has a different color or texture on each side.

duplex envelope   a double envelope consisting of a letter-size envelope affixed to the face of a larger one

duplexing   the simultaneous use of more than one computer, file, or circuit as a backup in case of malfunction

duplicate plate   a printing plate made from an original, as for multiple distribution to print media

duplication   the number of homes, viewers, listeners, or readers that are exposed to the same message, through various media or in the same medium, two or more times   The *duplicated audience* is the total number of people reached by this media duplication. Duplication also is copying or reproduction. The duplicating process often is called DUPING.

duplicator   a machine that reproduces material   The term generally refers to a small machine, such as a *mimeograph* or small *offset press*.

du Pont   a major manufacturer of printing film, recording tape, and other products, headquartered in Wilmington, DE   The company was founded by Eleuthère Irénée du Pont (1771–1834), a U.S. industrialist who was born in France. Its full name is E.I. du Pont de Nemours & Company.

DuPont Awards   annual awards to the broadcasting industry for journalistic achievement   The formal name is the Alfred I. DuPont Award, presented by the Graduate School of Journalism of Columbia University in New York.

durable goods   products with long or extended life or usage, relatively imperishable and generally valuable, such as automobiles and major appliances (*hard goods*) and clothing (*soft goods*), as compared to food and other perishables

duratrans   a photographic process to produce a large *transparency*, such as those used as advertisements at bus shelters

dusting   [printing] an accumulation of very small particles of pigment or other material on the ink roller or elsewhere

dust jacket   a paper cover placed over book or magazine covers; also called *book jacket*, *wrapper*, *dust wrapper*, or *dust cover*   Dust wrapper (abbreviated as *d.w.*) generally refers to a protective wrapping on a rare book.

dutch angle or **dutch tilt angle**   a tilted position of a camera, other than vertical or horizontal

Dutch door   a magazine advertising space involving half-page *gatefolds*   A Dutch door is a door divided in half horizontally, as in a supply closet where the upper and lower parts open separately.

dutchman   a device to conceal a defect, gap, or poor workmanship   Remember the Dutch boy with his finger in the hole in the dike? In a theater, a dutchman is a strip of muslin, or other cloth about 5 inches wide, glued or affixed to link two pieces of scenery to cover the juncture.

Dutch shot   [film] the tilting of the camera to the side; also called a *Dutch tilt shot*, DUTCH ANGLE, or *off-angle shot*

Dutch wrap   [journalism] a layout in which the text is continued to the column at the right with no headline above the continued column   For example, a two-column article usually has a two-column headline, but a Dutch wrap format merely has a one-column headline above the first column.

duvetyne   a soft fabric used in exhibits; sometimes spelled *duvetyn* or, erroneously, duventyne

DVE   DIGITAL VIDEO EFFECTS

d.w.   DUST WRAPPER

dwell   a period of time during which paper is pressed by the type of a printing press; a programmed time delay in a computer   A *delayed dwell*, or time delay, is necessary for some printing processes, such as embossing, in which time must be allowed for heat to soften the stock prior to the embossing, or *dwell-on impressions*, or FOIL-STAMPING, in which time must be allowed to obtain proper adhesion.

dwg.   drawing

dyad   two units; a pair

DYANA   *Dyn*namic *Ana*lysis System, a weekly survey of households conducted by Market Research Corporation of America (Stamford, CT)

dye transfer print   an opaque color photographic print made from a transparency

Dylux   a trademarked light-sensitive proof paper made by du Pont that reproduces without chemicals or heat

dynamic   energetic, forceful   *Dynamics* deals with the motions of bodies or forces, such as a moving coil of wire in a magnetic field, as in a *dynamic microphone* (a diaphragm with an attached coil of wire that moves in a magnetic field), *dynamic headphone,* or *dynamic loudspeaker*

dynamic range [broadcasting] the audio volume limits or range, regulated by *dynamic range control* devices and circuits; the ratio of the strongest or loudest part of a sound to its weakest or softest part as measured in decibels

dystopia a hypothetical place, society, or situation in which conditions are dreadful, the opposite of utopia; a novel or other work depicting such a place, such as a dystopian society; ugly or fantastic shapes, as in science fiction or other works

E

e or **E**   east

E   EFFECTS; ENTRANCE

EA   EDITORIAL ALTERATION

Eagle Award   CINE Eagle and Golden Eagle certificates, presented annually by the COUNCIL ON INTERNATIONAL NONTHEATRICAL EVENTS, for amateur (CINE) and professional (Golden) motion pictures

E&L   ELRICK & LAVIDGE, INC.

E & M Leads   a pair of wires that carry signals The *Ear lead* receives and the *Mouth lead* transmits, as in a headpiece unit used by telephone operators and broadcasters.

E&P   EDITOR & PUBLISHER

E&S   EVANS AND SUTHERLAND

ear   **1** [journalism] boxes in the upper left and right top corners of a publication (generally a newspaper), flanking the title, which is called the *flag*, not the MASTHEAD   Ears are used for weather reports or other messages, including advertising, particularly in newspapers outside the United States. The weather report atop page 1 is appropriately called the *weather ear.*   **2** [music] the ability to recognize slight differences in sound, especially the pitch, rhythm, and other characteristics of musical tones   To have a *good ear* is to be proficient in this ability; to have a *tin ear* is to be "tone deaf." To *play by ear* is to play a musical instrument without sheet music or, in general, to improvise.   **3** [typography] an appendage or corner, such as the corner of a STEREOTYPE plate; a short stroke, such as is sometimes found extending from the letter *g*   (Anatomical parts are commonly used as journalism and printing jargon; others include EYEBROW, FACE, FOOT, HAIRLINE, and HEAD.)

earplug   [newspapers] an EAR

early fringe   a time period in TV broadcasting, preceding prime time, usually 5 to 8 P.M. on weekdays

earned rate   the actual rate for advertising space or time, taking into account any discounts for volume and frequency

earnest money   a token or partial payment, given by a publisher or other employer as a demon-

stration of good faith to a writer or other recipient

earn-out   in publishing and other fields in which advance royalties (author's fees or commissions paid before the work is completed) are issued, the point at which the actual earnings equal the advance payment   *To earn out* is to reach this exalted point. The expression *earning out* sometimes is used in other fields involving royalty or licensing payments.

EAROM   ELECTRICALLY ALTERABLE READ-ONLY MEMORY

earphones   a device, akin to a miniature loudspeaker, that reproduces sound and is worn over the ears; more commonly called HEADPHONES or HEADSET

ear prompter   a tiny ear plug connected to a small audio recorder, enabling a performer to hear a recorded script while on stage or on camera

earth station   equipment for transmitting or receiving SATELLITE COMMUNICATIONS, such as a parabolic or dish antenna that sends or receives TV signals over the air directly from satellites or other sources   Owners of earth stations include cable systems and individuals, who thus bypass cable systems.

EAS   EXTENDED AREA SERVICE

east   the right side, as of a drawing

Eastmancolor   a process, trademarked by Eastman Kodak, of Rochester, NY, of producing full color on one strip of film, instead of on three separate strips of film   The film, called *monopack*, is coated with three EMULSIONS, one for each primary color—red, yellow, and blue.

Eastman Kodak Company   a major manufacturer of cameras, film, and other products, headquartered in Rochester, NY, founded by George Eastman (1854–1932)

east/west labels   mailing label sheets arranged to read horizontally from left to right   (They should, more accurately, be called *west/east.*)

easy book   book publishing jargon for a children's book or preschool book

easy listening station (EZ)   a radio station that has a format of quality popular music, including instrumentals and music from films and musical comedies; formerly called *good music station*

eat slang for *absorb*, as in *eat the cost* or *eat papers* (pay for unsold newspapers)

eau-forte French for ETCHING

EBCDIC EXTENDED BINARY CODED DECIMAL INTERCHANGE CODE

EBI EFFECTIVE BUYING INCOME

EBS EMERGENCY BROADCAST SYSTEM

EC ELECTRONIC CINEMATOGRAPHY

ECG ELECTRONIC CHARACTER GENERATOR

Echo Awards the annual awards of the DIRECT MARKETING ASSOCIATION

echo chamber an environment or a piece of equipment that produces a reverberation effect, such as a room with specially designed walls or a device in a recording system Musicians use a *reverb* on instruments, especially electric guitars, to produce the effect of an echo.

echo effect the result of two or more forms of sales promotion, such as print and TV advertising and DIRECT MAIL, each supporting and enhancing the others

echo phrase a phrase similar to a well-known expression and used as an allusion (a literary or other reference) or as whimsy—for example, *milk over the dam* instead of *water over the dam*

ECLIPSE trademarked acronym for ELECTRONIC CLIPPING SERVICE

eclogue a short pastoral poem—one with a rural setting—such as the dialogues between shepherds written by ancient Greek poets

E-Com ELECTRONIC COMPUTER-ORIGINATED MAIL SERVICES

economic editor a term used outside the United States for a business or financial editor

economic shopper a customer who makes comparisons with other stores and buys on the basis of price, quality, and other factors This is the largest category of retail customer; the others are APATHETIC SHOPPER, ETHICAL SHOPPER, and PERSONALIZING SHOPPER.

ECPS EFFECTIVE CANDLEPOWER SECONDS

ecru light tan, the color of unbleached linen, as in *ecru paper*

ECU EXTREME CLOSE-UP

ed. education; edited by

ed. or edit. EDITION; EDITOR

E.D. EVERY DAY

Eddie Awards the annual awards for film editing presented by AMERICAN CINEMA EDITORS

Edelman, Daniel one of the world's largest public relations firms, headquartered in Chicago

Edgar Awards the annual prizes presented by the MYSTERY WRITERS OF AMERICA The full name is the Edgar Allan Poe Awards.

edge [book production] one of the three outer borders of the leaves, or pages—the *head* (top), the *fore-edge* or *front edge* (or thumb edge), and the *foot* or *tail* (bottom) The fourth edge (opposite side of the fore-edge) is bound.

edge enhancement [computer graphics] the electronic delineation of the boundaries, or edges, of one part of a picture from another part

edge fog the clouding of a side of film—the result of light leakage in loading, the loosening of the film roll, or other malfunctions

edge number one of the sequential guide numbers along the edge of film, one number per 35mm foot; also called *key number* In *edge coding* or *keying*, the edge numbers are inked onto the matching rolls of picture and sound.

edge printing letters, numbers, or other symbols on film outside the image area, identifying the manufacturer, type of film, or other information that will remain on the developed film

edge-staining [printing] the technique of coloring the trimmed EDGE of a finished book or other publication It may include the top only (*top-staining*), the thumb edge, or the top, thumb, and bottom edges.

edit to alter, correct, or revise a manuscript, film (to *cut*), or other work In film and tape editing, the *edit point* is the location of a splice, or the joining of two pieces. *Edit-in* is the process in which one video signal replaces another, or the exact point in the electronic editing at which this occurs, so that the signal is edited into the tape. *Edit-out* is the process in which a video signal that had been inserted is stopped or deleted, or the exact point in electronic editing of this process. In facsimile transmission, to edit is to exclude from transmission the margins, space between lines, or other nontext areas, thus reducing transmission time.

editing program computer hardware and/or software that allows revising to be done on a screen, or terminal (*editing terminal*), by an operator (*editor*) The editing program controls the performance of the video screen, editing keys, CURSOR movement, and sometimes the placement of line numbers and other notations.

editing room the room in which a film is edited or cut; generally called *cutting room*

edition the copies of a publication printed from a single typesetting, such as all the copies of a single PRESS RUN of a newspaper However, during the printing of an edition, the presses may be stopped for revisions and late news. A new edition starts when the type is changed in a major way. A daily newspaper may have a *mail* edition, *city edition, state edition, national edition, late city edition, final edition,* or *market final edition* (stock market prices). The last edition is the *edition of record,* the edition that is filed and also sold in the back-issue department. Similarly, a new edition of a book is published when there are major changes or when a different form of reproduction is used, such as a FACSIMILE EDITION or LIBRARY EDITION. Thus, an edition of a book may have several printings, or *impressions.* The term *edition* also may refer to the format of a book, such as a *one-volume edition* of the works of an author or the (*name of editor, publisher,* or *special feature*) *edition.*

edition binding   a process of binding books in hard covers; also called *case binding, publisher's binding,* or *trade binding*

editio princeps   the first printed edition of an ancient work

editor   1 the person responsible for the editorial or nonadvertising control of a publishing operation, such as the head of a department of a newspaper or of the entire editorial staff (sometimes called *editor-in-chief*)   The editor generally oversees the preparation of editorials, although sometimes there is a separate editor, or *deputy editor,* in charge of this department. At a newspaper, the *executive editor* (*ex. ed.*) often combines business and editorial responsibilities, whereas the *managing editor* (*m.e., mng. ed.*) supervises the departments, which are headed by the ASSIGNMENT EDITOR, *foreign editor, metropolitan editor* or *city editor* (*c.e.*), *national editor, news editor, picture editor, state editor, suburban editor,* and editors of specific beats or sections. Similar terms are used in broadcasting, such as *news editor, assignment editor,* and *managing editor.*

In book publishing, specialized editors include the *acquisitions editor* (recommends new works), *manuscript editor* (works with the author), *copy editor* (revises grammar and style), *managing editor* (coordinates resources), *production editor* (sometimes called *managing editor*), *content editor* (also called *developmental editor* or *substantive editor,* a general editor who acts as liaison between author and publisher), and *assistant editor.* In general, an editor does not do the original writing and instead supervises the writers and modifies their output. The editor, or compiler, of an anthology may be listed as the author of the work.   2 a device for revising film, tape, or other materials, including the actual cutting and splicing, or joining, which is done mechanically or electronically under the supervision of a person also called *editor* (or *film editor, sound editor,* or *tape editor*)   Under the film editor is the *assistant film editor,* who in turn is aided by an *apprentice*

film editor.   3 a computer software program or ROUTINE that is used in modifying programs or files or in processing data; also called *edit routine*

Editor & Publisher (E&P)   a weekly magazine, published in New York, of the daily newspaper field and the publisher of annual directories

editorial   1 referring to the nonadvertising portion of a publication; collectively, the editorial pages and editorial content   The editorial classifications are the subject areas or departments, such as financial, food, news, and sports. The *editorial environment* is the overall appearance, content, tone, and philosophy of a publication. For instance, *The New Yorker, Forbes,* and *Playboy* are three successful magazines with different editorial environments.   2 an opinion piece written by the *editorial page editor* or members of the *editorial board,* generally appearing on the *editorial page* in a newspaper or magazine   A station also may broadcast an editorial, reflecting the opinion of its management or a commentator, such as a staff member or outsider (*guest editorial*). The editorial authority of a publication or broadcast medium results from its integrity, objectivity, and accuracy. (An advertisement is biased in behalf of the advertiser and rarely is viewed with the same attention or respect as the editorial matter. An advertisement may be set in all text to convey an "editorial look.")

editorial alteration (EA)   a change made by the publisher or customer, at the author's or editor's request (AUTHOR'S ALTERATION), not because of a printer's error

editorial association   the concept that print advertising has a higher readership and respect if it appears within or adjacent to editorial material (news, features, or opinion pieces)

editorial authority   the concept that a publication represents the judgments of impartial experts, so that advertising in the publication is thereby enhanced

editorial copy   a book or other publication distributed within a publishing organization and not for sale

editorial department   1 [film] the group that edits (*cuts*) a film and maintains files of all unused shots, under the direction of an editor   2 [journalism] the group in charge of editorials (opinion pieces) or, more generally, of all news and nonadvertising material

editorial hall   British for the newsroom of a newspaper or other medium

editorializing   the insertion of an opinion   When editorializing occurs in a news article that is supposed to be unbiased, readers may be skeptical of the publication's objectivity.

editorial spine the main contents section of a publication

editorial synchronization [film] the technique of having picture and sound occur at the same time so that, for instance, appropriate words coincide with corresponding lip movements The process is done by the EDITORIAL DEPARTMENT; hence the name. It is also called *editorial sync.*, *editing sync.*, *edit-synch*, *dead sync.*, *level sync.*, or *parallel sync.*

editorial well the part of a publication devoted to news and other nonadvertising material The term sometimes refers only to the main section or to the section that contains longer articles, such as the central section of a magazine, and would thus not include departments in the front and/or back.

EDP ELECTRONIC DATA PROCESSING

Eds. editions; editors

EDT or **E.D.T.** Eastern Daylight Time

educational television an older term for PUBLIC BROADCASTING or noncommercial TELEVISION Some public stations accept modified forms of commercial announcements, but they are not totally dependent on advertiser support.

EEE international telex abbreviation: error

E.F. ENGLISH FINISH

effect a technique or device for producing a visual or auditory illusion, such as SOUND EFFECTS, SPECIAL EFFECTS, or OPTICAL EFFECTS

effect filter an attachment to a camera lens that produces a special visual effect, such as fog or haze

effective buying income (EBI) net (after-tax) income that is available for the purchase of goods and services EBI generally is expressed in relation to the households in a geographical market and thus reflects consumer purchasing power or disposable personal income in that market. The abbreviation *EBI* is used by *Sales & Marketing Management*, a New York publication, in its survey reports.

effective candlepower seconds [photography] the unit of measurement of the light output of an electronic flash

effective circulation the estimated potential number of people capable of seeing an outdoor or transit advertisement, calculated as one-quarter of the transit passengers or one-half of the drivers, passengers, and pedestrians who pass an outdoor advertisement

effective distribution the merchandise available for purchase, which is a net amount or lesser quantity than the total merchandise in the warehouse or other distribution channels

effective frequency the number of advertising exposures that are judged necessary to produce a positive change in awareness, attitude, or purchasing action

effective isotropic radiated power (EIRP) [telecommunications] a measurement of the strength of a satellite by an EARTH STATION

effective radiated power (ERP) a measurement of the signal strength transmitted by a broadcasting station from its antenna

effective rating point (ERP) a measurement of total AUDIENCE that has been adjusted to indicate the percentage of the TARGET AUDIENCE

effective reach 1 the number of unduplicated individuals or households that receive an advertising message 2 in RESPONSE ANALYSIS, the number of individuals the advertising sponsor seeks to attract The FREQUENCY level of the advertising campaign is set up and then adjusted to obtain the desired figure.

effect machine a slide or film projector that projects moving backgrounds or images on a backdrop or translucent screen; also called *effects projector*

effects property, impression *Special effects* are optics (*optical effects*) or visual effects to produce illusions. *Sound effects* are audio devices for simulation of a specific sound. The abbreviation is FX or sometimes, as with video effects, E.

effect shot [film] a shot designed to produce an emotional or other effect, such as ocean waves; not the same as EFFECTS However, effect shots are produced by MATTING or other SPECIAL EFFECTS.

Effie Awards the annual awards of the New York chapter of the AMERICAN MARKETING ASSOCIATION

efforting wire-service jargon for the attempt to obtain a requested story

EFP ELECTRONIC FIELD PRODUCTION

e.g. for example, from the Latin *exempli gratia*; sometimes confused with *i.e.*—Latin, "that is"

egg theatrical slang for a failure, such as a show that *lays an egg*

eggshell-finish paper a common type of pale yellow paper with a soft, nonglossy finish

ego the self or sense of self; a person's self-concept of personality; the seat of consciousness The concept of ego is essential in understanding behavioral goals and PSYCHOGRAPHICS, particularly in advertising campaigns related to vanity (excessive admiration of self). A *small ego* suggests a low self-image, whereas a *large ego* may indicate self-confidence or perhaps an overly developed sense of importance. Some contemporary therapists and philosophers use the term *ego* negatively to refer to selfishness and attachment to worldly achievements, as compared to a more fully evolved, spiritual consciousness. This usage predates New Age therapists and even Freud, as *egoism* is the ethical theory that places the supreme end of human conduct in self, as opposed to altruism. *Ego ideal* is a person's idealized self-concept; *ego involvement* is an individual's behavior as determined by the relationship between self-concept and the perceived characteristics of the outside world.

Egyptian a typeface with heavy straight SERIFS— or small decorative lines on letters, as in T—of the same weight as the main strokes Examples are Memphis and Lubalin Graph Book.

Ehrhart-Babic Group a market research firm in Englewood Cliffs, NJ, that specializes in new-product tests A field force of hundreds of auditors covers retail stores. The National Retail Tracking Index (NRTI) is a syndicated service of Ehrhart-Babic that analyzes distribution, out-of-stock, retail pricing, facing and stocking locations, and promotional activities of products sold in stores in STANDARD METROPOLITAN STATISTICAL AREAS.

EI EMULSION IN; EXPOSURE INDEX

EIAJ Electronic Industries Association of Japan, a trade group that has established various standards for Japanese television and other products sold in the United States and other countries, including EIAJ Type #1 Standard for half-inch videotape recorders

E-I-C engineer-in-charge, as of a TV production

eight ball a nondirectional, small round microphone

18-percent gray a cardboard commonly used by professional photographers It is a gray color of about 18-percent reflectance and serves as a substitute for the subject when the photographer takes a reflected-light-exposure meter reading.

800 number in long-distance telephone service, a toll-free number for incoming calls to airlines, hotels, and many other companies and organizations, which pay for incoming WIDE AREA TELEPHONE SERVICE lines The *800* precedes a seven-digit phone number.

8-sheet an outdoor advertising poster panel, about 5 feet high and 11 feet wide, smaller than a full-size, 24-SHEET panel An 8-sheet is a popular junior size, promoted by the Eight-Sheet Outdoor Association, of Independence, MO.

8vo short for *octavo*, a 16-page book (with 8 leaves)

84 Charlie military slang for *combat photographer* Charlie refers to the letter *c* (for *combat*).

80-20 principle the concept that 80 percent of total sales is obtained from 20 percent of customers

EIRP EFFECTIVE ISOTROPIC RADIATED POWER

EJ ELECTRONIC JOURNALISM

EK print [film] a release print made from the original negative (the standard procedure is to make a RELEASE PRINT from an INTERNEGATIVE) An EK print is of slightly better quality and is used for special screenings, such as an event at the White House. *EK* refers to Eastman Kodak, of Rochester, NY, though the film can be from other manufacturers.

Ektachrome a trademark of Eastman Kodak, of Rochester, NY, for transparent color film or color photographs made with Ektachrome film *Ektacolor* is Kodak professional-grade, high-speed color film and also the process by which full-color negatives or transparencies are made and then positive prints are processed by printing on color-sensitive paper (or, in the case of filmstrips and motion pictures, on film).

EL See ENTRANCE.

elasticity [marketing] the degree of potential change in demand for a product or service—that is, sales—if the price, advertising, or other factors are varied The price may be too high if the demand is elastic (changeable) or too low if the demand is inelastic (fixed, regardless of price). A *price elasticity* of 1 means that sales rise or fall by the same percentage as the price rises or falls, so that total revenue remains the same. A price elasticity greater than 1 means that sales rise or fall at a greater rate than the price rises or falls, so that total revenue increases.

electret microphone an ELECTROSTATIC microphone, such as a small lapel mike

electrical eye a photoelectric cell, an electronic device that operates in response to changes in light

electrically alterable read-only memory (EAROM) a type of erasable computer chip that can be reprogrammed easily, without removing it from the circuit board

electrical transcription (ET or E.T.) a recording process for producing commercials or programs on disks, commonly used in the early days of radio

electrical truck a vehicle that carries lights and other electrical equipment, generally for use in filming and sometimes equipped with a generator

electric department [film] the group in charge of lighting and other electrical equipment The chief electrician is commonly called a *gaffer*.

electrician [film, television, theater] a person who works with the lights and their power sources, commonly called a *gaffer*; not the same as a *licensed electrician*, who installs the electricity lines An *electrician's knot* is a knot that ties together cables at the connector joint.

electronic pertaining to *electrons*, which are subatomic particles with a negative electric charge *Electronics* is the science and technology involving free electrons and differs from electricity transmitted in wires. The *electronic media* are radio and TV.

electronic billboard [computers] an electronic sign to display messages or other information in airline terminals and other public places

electronic carbon copy transmitted electronically, rather than on paper (*hard copy*), as, for example, the transference of copy from a word processor to a computer bank The electronic carbon system is used by member newspapers of The Associated Press to send copies of their stories from their word processors directly to the AP computer system, instead of sending carbon copies of typewritten stories, as was done before 1977.

electronic character generator (ECG) [television] a typewriterlike machine that produces weather reports, sports scores, identifications, and other lettering as part of a TV picture

electronic character mix in photocomposition, the layout of data in the computer MEMORY that is used to create the type

electronic cinematography (EC) the use of video cameras to produce the picture quality of 35mm film cameras

electronic clapper a camera device that simultaneously flashes equal lengths of film and sound, so that visuals and sound can be synchronized

Electronic Clipping Service (ECLIPSE) a part of the LEXIS database research service of MEAD to locate references to specific names, events, and other data in articles and other material that appeared in newspapers and other media

Electronic Computer-Originated Mail Services (E-Com) a system, operated by the U.S. Postal Service and now discontinued, to provide delivery of computer-originated messages

electronic cue [broadcasting] an audio or video signal indicating the end of a tape or other instruction

electronic data processing (EDP) the handling of information, primarily by electronic means

electronic editing the use of a computer or control board, rather than manual splicing, for the editing, or cutting, of tape *Electronic cuing* is a signal, generally audible, to indicate the place for an insertion or other editing; it is also used in the transcription of typing.

electronic field production (EFP) the use of equipment (generally portable, such as a MINICAM, or electronic camera) outside a TV studio to produce nonnews material, such as programming or commercials See also ELECTRONIC NEWS GATHERING.

electronic flash a strobe light, a high-intensity source of short-duration illumination used by professional photographers for still pictures

electronic journalism (EJ) live transmission or videotaping from a location away from the television studio, by an *EJ camera crew*

electronic line replacement (ELR) a film process in which dialogue is rerecorded in synchronization with the movements of the performer's lips In TV, this process is called *automatic dialogue replacement* (ADR).

electronic mail messages sent by electrical impulses, such as via computer, to be read from a video display screen or printed on paper; also, the message storage area of a computer-based message system The *Electronic Mail Association* is a trade organization in Washington, DC. Electronic mail is also called ELECTRONIC MESSAGING.

electronic marketing the process of selling via computers, telecommunications, video display, and other electronic techniques instead of—or in addition to—retail outlets or conventional print and broadcast media

electronic matte the process of combining images from two TV cameras; see also MATTE

electronic mechanical the electronic merging of text and graphic elements to produce a finished form suitable for reproduction (A *mechanical*, in conventional printing, is a board with text—and illustrations, if used—pasted on it, to be photographed and made into a printing plate.) Color correction, photo retouching, and other design processes can be done electronically, using a terminal, video-display screen, and other components of a computerized system.

Electronic Media Rating Council a New York organization of broadcasting companies involved in audience analysis and other ratings

electronic messaging an electronic system of originating, transmitting, storing, and receiving messages without the intervention of an operator, postal clerk, or other third party; also called ELECTRONIC MAIL

electronic music the use of a tape recorder or other electronic device, but not an actual musical instrument, to produce musical sounds artificially

electronic news gathering (ENG) the use of an electronic, portable TV camera (MINICAM) to videotape or broadcast news from outside the studio By eliminating film, ENG has produced considerable savings in time and personnel and added a mobility to the news operations of almost all TV stations.

electronic pen [computers] an input device on which freehand drawing is translated into DIGITIZED form so that the image can be displayed and stored; also called *digitizing pad*

electronic press kit a package of publicity materials for broadcast media, including such items as interviews on audiotape and/or videotape

Electronic Program Guide (EPG) a schedule of forthcoming programs, shown on the TV screen for the viewer, generally by a cable system

electronic publishing the production of text (and illustrations, if used) on media other than paper, including cable TV, computer, TELETEXT, VIDEOCASSETTE, VIDEODISC, and VIDEOTEX Actually, electronic publishing is simply the use of computerized technologies in various aspects of publishing, including editing, typesetting, preparation of graphics or illustrations, page make-up, and pagination; the result may be linked to a printer that produces paper copies.

electronic setup (ESU) the prebroadcast time during which equipment is set up and tested

electronic shopping an interactive VIDEOTEX system that enables a consumer to obtain information and to purchase and pay for items ordered

electronic sports gathering (ESG) the use of cameras, mobile units, and other equipment to produce a telecast of a sports event

electronic still store (ESS) [television] an electronic still-frame storage device, with a storage area of photographic slides, titles, and other stills that can be selected instantly

electronic stylus a penlike device (stylus) commonly used on the screen of a cathode-ray tube to signal the computer with an electronic pulse

electronic transcription (ET or E.T.) a recording disk, including the 16-inch size used in the early days of radio

electronic typewriter a typewriter with limited word processing facilities, including correction features not found on an electric typewriter

electronic viewfinder (EVF) a small screen for monitoring while operating a video camera It may be built in or separate.

electroplate to coat or cover (to plate) with a thin layer of metal that is deposited electrically The metallic substance is suspended in a chemical solution, and an electrode emits an electric charge in the solution.

electroprint [film] an electronic process of transferring sound directly from the MAGNETIC TRACK to the OPTICAL TRACK of a RELEASE PRINT

electrostatic printing a reproduction process, used in copying machines, in which electrostatic or stationary electric charges form the image

of the material being copied in powder or ink on the paper or surface being printed

electrostatics the branch of physics dealing with static electricity In an *electrostatic speaker* or other electrostatic audio device, electricity applied to metal plates causes a diaphragm suspended between the plates to vibrate.

electrotype a metal duplicate of original print matter, generally an advertisement Used in LETTERPRESS printing, the electrotype is made by electroplating a lead, wax, or plastic mold of the original plate (see ELECTROPLATE). The process is cheaper than making duplicate ENGRAVING. It is frequently called *electro*; the plural is *electros*.

elegiac referring to a type of verse, used by ancient Greek and Roman poets, in which the second line of each couplet, or two-line rhyme, has an accented syllable only in the third and sixth feet (groups of syllables) This type of mostly unaccented rhythm was used for mournful laments (see ELEGY); *elegiac* refers to something sad or plaintive.

elegy a poem or song of lament and praise for the dead Elegies were originally composed in a special meter with accented syllables in specific places, resulting in a mournful tone. An elegy is not the same as a *eulogy*, which is a formal speech or statement in praise of a person, usually one who recently died.

element a fundamental part of an entity, such as the typing element (a DAISY WHEEL or other device) of a typewriter

elephant doors large doors to a TV studio or other place

elevation an improvement, such as the shift in the meaning of a word that assures a more favorable connotation; more commonly called MELIORATION or amelioration

elevator shot [film] a shot taken from a *camera elevator*—an elevator device on the floor or on a dolly—in which the camera is moved vertically It differs from a *crane shot*, in which the camera is moved horizontally.

11 o'clock number a rousing finale in a musical show, from the days when Broadway shows started at 8:30 P.M. and ended at about 11 P.M. Curtain time now is usually 8 P.M., but the phrase still is used.

ELF extremely low frequency

el-hi in textbook publishing, referring to the elementary and high school levels

e-line EXPO LINE

elision the omission, assimilation, or slurring over of a letter or letters, particularly in poetry, sometimes indicated by an apostrophe or asterisk, as in *th'* instead of *the* before a vowel sound In a broader sense, elision is the omission of a part, such as minor editing to remove unnecessary punctuation and redundant words.

elite a typewriter typeface, smaller than pica typewriter type. *Pica* type is any 12-point type (with 10 characters—letters or numbers—to the inch). On the pica scale, which is the standard measure in printing, elite type is 10-point, with 12 characters to the inch. It may be confusing, but, simply put, elite type is smaller than pica type.

ellipsis the omission of a few letters, a word or phrase, or a sentence or more; a pause; sometimes called *suspension points* The omission or pause is indicated by a mark or series of marks, such as three dots or asterisks. Here's a rule about *ellipsis points:* three dots refer to an omission within a sentence; if the omission is at the end of the sentence, use four dots (the fourth dot is the period at the end of the sentence). Ellipsis sometimes is used by columnists to separate brief items. The best-known *elliptic,* or user of ellipses, was Walter Winchell (1897–1972) in his newspaper column.

ellipsoid curved An *ellipsoidal spot* is an elliptical or circular-shaped spotlight.

Elmendorf a test of the tearing strength of a paper, expressed as percent Elmendorf

elocution a style or manner of speaking, especially a highly refined, stilted manner of public speaking The word is often incorrectly spelled with two *l*s.

ELR ELECTRONIC LINE REPLACEMENT

Elrick & Lavidge, Inc. a market research company in Chicago, owner of Quick Test Opinion Centers, a Philadelphia organization that conducts surveys at shopping centers Formed in 1951, E&L is a subsidiary of Equifax Inc., Atlanta.

Elrod a machine that produces metal LEADS and RULES of varying sizes for use in LETTERPRESS printing

ELS EXTREME LONG SHOT

em a unit of measure in typesetting to indicate the square, or space, occupied by a type character, usually the letter *M* Half the width of an em is called an EN. A 10-point em generally is 10 points high and 10 points wide, though it can vary somewhat, depending on the proportions of the typeface (there are 12 points to a pica, and 6 picas to an inch). A type specification of $10/11 \times 18$ indicates a 10-point type set in an area with an 11-point height and a line length of 18 ems. Since in this example an em is 12/72, or $1/6$ of an inch, 18 ems equals 3 inches. The term dates from the early days of typesetting, when an *M* was cast on a square body. Indentations and dashes are measured in ems: an *em dash*

(—) is one em in width. A *2-em dash* is used to indicate missing letters. A *3-em dash* indicates a missing word, with space on each side, or, in a bibliography, the repetition of the author in the preceding entry. A *30-em dash* is a dash used at the end of a newspaper story or other text, indicated as - 30 -, usually centered on a line by itself. An *em leader* consists of two dots or periods, spaced evenly within one em space and commonly used with an *en leader,* a dot centered in a one-en space, to create an ELLIPSIS of three dots. An *em quad,* or *mutt,* is a square space as wide as the point size of the type body. For example, a *pica em quad* is 12×12 points. The typesetter's designation for an em dash is 1/m. *Emage* is an area of text measured in ems.

In the days of metal type, printers sometimes played a game called *jeff,* in which the em quads were thrown like dice. The greater the number that fell with the nick side up, the higher the score (the *nick side* is perpendicular to the type side).

embargo a prohibition A *news embargo* forbids the use of news material by a publication or broadcast medium; generally a time is specified, after which the embargo is released.

embellishment in outdoor advertising, a cutout, extension, or decoration added to a painted bulletin or other structure, such as an arm extending above a sign

emblem book a written work, especially common in the 17th century, featuring designs or pictures (known as *emblems*), with proverbs or sayings on a familiar theme or moral idea

embossing the process of impressing an inked image in relief to produce a raised surface If the image is uninked, the technique is called *blind embossing.*

emcee master of ceremonies, the host of a broadcast or other program; the moderator of a seminar or other event; also called *M.C.*

emendation a correction made in a text, as in an attempt to restore the original version

emerald the name for $6^{1}/_{2}$-point type; also called *minionette*

Emergency Broadcast System a system, regulated by the Federal Communications Commission, by which designated radio stations participate in an emergency notification procedure during a major emergency Virtually every radio listener has heard an attention signal indicating that the radio station is participating in a test of the Emergency Broadcast System.

emergency lights lights that are operated by batteries or by a power source other than the primary power source in a building, such as a theater, and can be turned on during a power loss; sometimes called *panic lights*

emily slang for a *broad*, or floodlight, with one lamp; also called *single broad* Electricians (*gaffers*) are considered to have a way with words. In this case, the term probably was first used by a gaffer who had a friend named Emily.

Emmy Awards local and national awards to TV stations and broadcasters, presented since 1949 by the ACADEMY OF TELEVISION ARTS AND SCIENCES, in Hollywood The original name was *Immy*, after the image-orthicon tube used in television, but the name changed as a result of a typographical error. The award is a small statue of a woman with wings, representing one of the Muses.

empire *Wall Street Journal* jargon for its worldwide operations

empty useless *Empty dialogue* is meaningless or not essential to the plot.

empty sweep the path the eye takes between lines in columns when it is not reading

ems per hour the unit of measurement of the productivity of a word processing or other keyboard operator An EM represents about two characters.

emulsion 1 The suspension of globules of one liquid in another 2 a light-sensitive coating (generally grains of silver halide in a thin gelatin layer) on film or another surface

emulsion in (EI) describing film in which the EMULSION, or coated, side faces inward, the conventional method of placing film on cores or spools

emulsion number a three-digit number, written on a film container, following a four-digit number to indicate the film code The three-digit number identifies the emulsion (coating) of the film stock, to insure that all of the reels are the same

emulsion out (EO) referring to film in which the EMULSION, or coated, side faces outward The standard method of placing film on cores or spools is EMULSION IN.

en a unit of horizontal type measurement, equal to half an EM or half the point size An en in 16-point type is 8 points in width. An *en dash* or *one on long*, which is slightly longer than a hyphen, is used between numbers to indicate range, as in 18–35 age group. When specified on a manuscript, an en dash is written as 1/en. An *en leader* is a dot or period centered within the space of one en. An *en space* (also called *en quad* or *nut*) is a space one en wide, the space of an *N*.

enamel glassy, usually opaque protective or decorative coating *Enamel stock*, paper coated with enamel, has a smooth surface, which can be dull or glossy.

enc. or **encl.** enclosed; enclosure

enclosure anything mailed in an envelope or enclosed in a carton or container More specifically, the term refers to an item, called an *insert*, in addition to the principal item, such as a reply card enclosed with a letter.

encoding the process of translating or converting data—for example, in computers, the conversion of a character (letter or number) into BITS

encomium EULOGY

encore an additional performance, presented by popular demand; from the French word for "again" *Encore performance*, a term used in television for a repeat broadcast, is a redundancy.

encryption the process of encoding, as in the scrambling of TV signals Pay-TV transmission often is encrypted, and subscribers have devices that *decrypt*, or unscramble.

end aisle display a permanent display unit at the end of an aisle in a supermarket or other retail store Additional merchandise or an assortment of colors or sizes of displayed items generally is stored beneath the shelf.

end cap a capital letter at the end of a word

endcue [broadcasting] the last few words—generally four—of a taped report or interview, an important guide to the engineer, producer, director, and newscaster; also called *outcue*

end display a nonpermanent display unit at the end of an aisle in a supermarket or other retail store, generally for featured items or items on sale

end/end a notation at the end of a broadcast script or other item, similar to # # # and other notations; see also END MARK

end even a typesetting instruction to end a paragraph with a full line, rather than a WIDOW or a CLUB LINE

endleaf paper at the beginning and end of a book, half of which is pasted to the cover and the other half, called a *flyleaf*, to the inside of the book, to hold the cover to the first or last page Sometimes used for decoration, it is also called *endpaper* or *book endpaper*.

endless chain word-of-mouth advertising—that is, by informal communication among customers

endless loop film or tape joined at its ends for continuous recording or playing Endless-loop media are different from DISCRETE MEDIA, whose ends are unconnected and which do not automatically start over when they have run through.

endless tape printing or other tape for a machine without END-OF-LINE codes on the tape; also called *idiot tape, running tape,* or *unjustified tape*

end mark   a symbol to indicate the end of a news release or article, such as *# # #, 30,* or another notation

end matter   material printed at the end of a book, after the text proper, such as an appendix, bibliography, glossary, or index; also called *back matter* or *reference matter*

endnotes   comments or addenda (notes) at the back of a book or other publication or the end of an article or chapter   Also called *backnotes,* they are akin to footnotes and usually are labeled *notes.*

end of line (EOL)   a point at the end of a typed line or a code signaling the end of a line or of a command sequence

end-of-line decision   a determination by a computer or by a keyboard operator that a line of type is filled and that a new line should be started   A critical area—called a *hot zone*—often exists near the end of a line when a decision must be made to enlarge or decrease the spaces between the preceding words and also whether to hyphenate.

end of message (EOM)   a control character used in data communication indicating the condition of the transmission; also called *end of text*

end-of-page pressure   the psychological tension that increases as a typist or computer keyboard operator approaches the end of a page

end of text (ETX)   in data communication, a transmission control character indicating that the previous character was the last in the message; also called *end of message*

endorsement   a signature, as written on the back of a check; an approval or sanction, as of a candidate or product   An *advertising endorsement* is a statement of recommendation in advertising by a celebrity or other person, generally in return for a fee. A *product endorsement* is a recommendation for a product, in advertising or via other techniques, such as public relations. A *postal endorsement* is handwriting, cancellation, or stamping by the Postal Service on a letter or other mailing piece.

end papers   paper used for covering the inside of book covers, to fasten the case, or cover, to the book and for decoration; also called *endpapers, end leaves, end sheets, endsheets, lining papers,* or *paste-downs*

end rate   the lowest advertising charge for a radio or TV commercial, after frequency discounts and other reductions have been made

end sizes   the smallest and the largest sizes in an assortment of an item for sale

end stop   a punctuation mark at the end of a sentence, such as a period, question mark, or exclamation mark

end test   the development of the end of a roll of exposed film for evaluation before the roll is processed

end user   a consumer, the person or organization that uses a product or service

enfolding   a process of covering, as with an envelope or other folded cover

ENG   ELECTRONIC NEWS GATHERING

engineering of consent   the development of support for an issue or an institution by providing information in a persuasive manner   The basis of public relations, the term was popularized in a 1955 book of this title by Edward L. Bernays (1891–), published by University of Oklahoma Press.

engineering setup (ESU)   a TV technique to freeze an image on the screen   It is most frequently used, by an *ESU operator,* to project an image over the shoulder of the anchor, or news broadcaster, during the lead-in of a news item.

Engle-Kollat-Blackwell model   a system that characterizes consumer behavior as a sequence of *go/halt* or *go/no/go* cycles, developed by James F. Engel, David T. Kollat, and Roger D. Blackwell and described in their 1968 book *Consumer Behavior* (Holt, Rinehart and Winston)

English   **1** [film, television] vertical flaps on lamps, as opposed to Chinese (horizontal) flaps   **2** the name for 14-point type   *Double English* is about 24 points.

English as a Second Language (ESL)   education for individuals whose primary language is not English

English finish (E.F.)   a smooth, nonglossy coating for paper   *English finish stock* is high-bulk paper with a hard, even appearance, used frequently in books with photographs.

engr.   engraved, engraver, ENGRAVING

engraving   a printing plate made by cutting into the surface; the process of making such a plate; a print made from such a plate; additionally, the printing process in which the paper is pressed into recessed areas on the plate containing ink   The process of making an engraving adds to the time and cost of production. It is done by a specialist, an *engraver,* who uses a cutting tool, called a *burin* or *graver;* thus an engraving sometimes is called a *cut.* An *engraver's color proof* is made from color engravings, with color bars for checking ink density. An *engraver's spread* is the final layout prior to the making of the engraving. An *engraved letterhead* is stationery with a luxurious, three-dimensional feeling.

engrossing decorative hand lettering

enhanced service [telecommunications] the transmission of data signals in addition to voice signals

enhanced underwriting message on public TV and radio programs, a type of advertisement for "sponsors" in which announcements are made about the company; also called *enhancements*

enjambment the use of run-on lines; the running on of a sentence from one line of a poem or other literary form to the next with little or no pause The older spelling is *enjambement.*

enl. enlarged

enlargement a reproduction, especially of a photograph, that is larger than the original or the negative from which it is made An *enlarger* is a projector that holds the photo negative or transparency, for projection of the image on a light-sensitive paper. Varying the distance changes the size of the projected image. This process is called *projection printing.*

enlarging paper a paper used for printing an enlarged image projected from a negative

ensemble a group of items, such as clothes in a coordinated outfit or performers who work as a unit, as in an *ensemble scene*

ent ENTRANCE, a stage direction

enter [computers] to input a message, as on a computer keyboard for transmission to the computer

enterprise the willingness to initiate, particularly bold or risky projects, as in *enterprise journalism* or *enterprise coverage* An *enterprise shot* is an unsolicited photograph, perhaps submitted by a freelancer.

Entertainment & Sports Programming Network (ESPN) a major cable network, based in Bristol, CT, whose primary programming is sports

entr'acte entertainment performed during an INTERMISSION; from the French for "between acts"

entrance (E or Ent) [theater] a stage direction in a script indicating the point at which a performer first appears or the place from which the performer enters *EL* is *entrance left,* and *ER* is *entrance right. Entrance cue* is the dialogue line or action that signals a performer to enter (come on stage). The position sometimes is illuminated by an *entrance light.* The performer's first words are an *entrance line,* sometimes greeted by an *entrance round,* or applause. The opposite stage direction is EXIT.

entry a word or item, such as a main topic or listing in a dictionary; a place of entrance, such as an entry point in a computer In a bibliography, card catalog, or index, the *main entry* is the listing (such as an *author entry* in a card cat-

alog) under which full information is given. An *added entry* or *secondary entry* lists the names of the editor or translator or other information supplemental to the main entry.

enumerative bibliography a listing of books or other works, shorter and less detailed than an ANALYTIC BIBLIOGRAPHY

enumerative study research in which generalities are based on data from a sample of the population (the entire group being assessed), as differentiated from an ANALYTIC SURVEY

envelope a wrapper, covering, or folded paper used for mailing Common envelopes include *pointed flap, square flap, V-flap, wallet flap, air mail, window,* and *self-seal.* Sizes range considerably: *coupon, souvenir,* and *return envelopes* are small; *clasp envelopes* often are large. In business, the two most common sizes are *monarch* ($3^7/8'' \times 7^1/2''$) and *#10* ($4^1/8'' \times 9^1/2''$). A *bond envelope* is made of BOND paper, generally the same as the bond-paper letterhead, or stationery, that it carries. A *wove envelope* is a bit softer, and a *Manila envelope,* made of sturdy tan paper, is stronger.

envelope stuffer advertising or promotional material enclosed in an envelope with a letter, invoice, or other primary item

environmental graphics signs and outdoor displays, created by designers or other professionals and intended to blend into or enhance the surrounding area

environmental monitoring a study of outside influences on a public, such as for a business to "assess its corporate climate," including changes in social values, opinion trends, and events in the sociopolitical environment

environmental sound natural sound, such as from birds or vehicles, from a location being filmed or taped

EO EMULSION OUT

E.O.D. EVERY OTHER DAY

EOL END OF LINE

e.o.m. end of month On a bill, *e.o.m. terms* means that the cash discount and full payment begin on the first day of the following month instead of on the invoice date. For example, an invoice delivered on January 2 and marked *2/10, e.o.m.* indicates that a 2-percent cash discount may be taken up to February 10 and the full amount must be paid before the end of February.

EOM END OF MESSAGE

EOP end of paragraph

E.O.W. EVERY OTHER WEEK

ep end paragraph, a typesetting command

epenthesis a change in the pronunciation of a word, in which a sound or syllable is accidentally or incorrectly inserted—for example, *athlete*, often mispronounced as ath-a-lete

EPG ELECTRONIC PROGRAM GUIDE

ephemera short-lived or transitory material, such as clippings Librarians and collectors refer to miscellaneous printed matter, such as clippings, greeting cards, postcards, and programs, as ephemera. The plural is *ephemera*, *ephemeras*, or *ephemerae*.

epic a poem or other work narrating the adventures and deeds of a heroic character, often written in an exalted style A *mock epic* is a work in which a trivial subject is satirized, or ridiculed, by being treated solemnly.

epidiascope an optical device for projecting on a screen a magnified image of an opaque or transparent object, not necessarily a transparency

epigram a short, witty poem or clever statement

epigraph a quotation at the beginning of a chapter, especially at the top of the page, and sometimes on a PART-TITLE page

epilogue or **epilog** a closing section added to a novel, play, or other work, providing further information or interpretation; a short speech at the end of a play; the final section of a speech (a *peroration*) In TV, an epilogue sometimes is called a *tag.*

epiphany a moment of sudden intuitive understanding or insight, or a scene in a play or other work that occasions such a moment; pronounced eh-PIF-uh-nee

episode an incident; one of a series of related events, scenes, or sequences Episode sometimes refers to individual programs on a TV station; thus a station's audience may be measured by episodes per 100 TV homes. An *episodic* film or other work is composed of a series of incidents and relatively little continuity or transitions.

epistle a letter, particularly a long, formal, instructive letter, sometimes in verse; pronounced eh-PIS-ull

epistolary of or suitable to letters or letter writing; written in the form of a series of letters, such as an *epistolary novel* (common in the 18th century)

epitaph an inscription on a tomb or gravestone in memory of the person buried there; a short composition, such as a tribute to a dead person, sometimes humorous

epithet a word or phrase, sometimes added to a name or title, used to characterize a person or thing, such as *America the Beautiful* Epithets can also be disparaging—for instance, *Jack the Ripper.*

epitome a short statement expressing the main points; also, a person or thing that is representative of the essence of a group; pronounced eh-PIT-oh-me

eponym a real or fictional person from whom the name of a city, company, or other entity is derived

eq an abbreviation for *equal* used in copyediting, as in *eq#*, an indication to make the space (#) between words or lines equal; see EQUALIZER, EQUALIZATION

EQ EQUALIZATION

equalization (EQ) the process of altering the frequency response of an audio signal, as with a tone control or other device (an *equalizer*)

equalizer a system that normalizes an audio or video signal, such as a tone-control system that compensates for frequency distortion of an audio signal An *equalizing amp* is an amplifier that automatically adjusts the signal. The process of adjusting the audio or video signal is called *equalizing, equalization,* or *filtering.* To *add eq in audio* is to reshape a frequency response to emphasize some frequency ranges and eliminate others.

equal time a Federal Communications Commission provision that radio and TV stations must provide time impartially to all political candidates in a race and must sell or give time on an equal basis, exclusive of news coverage This policy, also called the *fairness doctrine,* was abolished in 1987.

Equifax See ELRICK & LAVIDGE.

Equity short for ACTORS' EQUITY ASSOCIATION An *Equity theater* abides by Actors' Equity Association contracts. An *Equity-waiver theater,* such as a community theater, does not pay the Equity scale rate.

ER See ENTRANCE.

Eras a sans-serif typeface—that is, one that does not have small decorative lines on the letters

erase to remove by rubbing, wiping, scraping, or other mechanical or electronic means, as from an audio or videotape In computers, *erasing,* the removal of data, can be accomplished with an *erase character* (more commonly called *delete character*) in which BINARY data are replaced with zeros or other *null codes.* In audio- or videotapes, an *erase head* is a device on a magnetic tape drive that removes previously recorded material.

eraser a device or an item for removing material, such as pencil or ink lines on paper, chalkmarks on a blackboard, or materials on a magnetic tape A *kneaded eraser,* which is commonly used by commercial artists, is very soft and can be formed into various shapes (kneaded) so that it can fit in small areas, to make fine corrections and pick up specks. An *art gum eraser*, also used by artists, leaves a crumbly residue that picks up dirt and smudges. A *fiberglass eraser* is a bundle of glass fibers resembling a pencil, used to gently scratch and remove ink from paper. A *bulk eraser* demagnetizes an entire magnetic tape.

erasing shield   a small piece of metal with holes of various shapes and sizes, through which an artist erases material in a specific area, while the surrounding area is protected

erect image   a vertical image, such as seen through a lens, with the correct side on top   An *erecting system* is a set of lenses or prisms in a camera that reverses the image so that it is not seen upside down in the viewfinder, but, rather, is seen correct side up.

erlang   an international unit of telephone traffic, named after the Danish mathematician A. K. Erlang (1878–1929)   One erlang is one circuit occupied for one hour.

erotica   literature or other matter intended to be sexually arousing

ERP   EFFECTIVE RADIATED POWER; EFFECTIVE RATING POINT

errata   errors discovered after the printing of a publication and called to the attention of readers on a separate printed piece, inserted or bound in   A single mistake is an *erratum*.

error line   a line with an error; not the same as CORRECTION LINE

error message   a statement flashed on a computer screen indicating that the user has done something wrong

error rate   in typing and typesetting, the ratio of *error words* (or *erroneous words*) to total words, or the ratio of lines with errors to total lines

ESC   EVEN SMALL CAPS

escalator   a clause or provision in a contract providing for changes—upward or downward—in wages, prices, royalties (authors' fees), or other items in relation to such factors as a change in the cost-of-living index or the number of copies sold

E-scale   [typography] a scale with the letter *E* in various sizes, used to calculate type size

escape   [computers] the change from one code or language to another, a common procedure in computerized typesetting and other processes   An *escape key* on a keyboard generates an *escape character*, which changes the subsequent character or characters. An *escape sequence* is a series of control characters, frequently used in computer graphics.

escapement   the mechanism that controls the lateral or horizontal movement of a typewriter carriage or typesetter and is responsible for the

spacing before or between characters   Some typesetters print a character (letter or number), then allow for (escape) the width of that character; other typesetters provide for (escape) the width of the next character, then print it. *Escapement value*, which is a concept from mechanical typesetting, is the width of the character just set or the next character, generally in relative units, that the typesetter must escape so that the characters do not overlap. On most standard typewriters, the escapement value of all the characters is identical, whereas in computerized typesetting, each character has its own escapement value; for instance, *i* and *l* have very small escapement values, while *m* and *w* have high values. The escapement value is determined by three components, the leading and trailing SIDEBEARINGS (white space) and the body width of the character. A LASER TYPESETTER does not use escapement but creates a line at a time instead of one character at a time.

escutcheon   a shield on which a coat of arms is displayed, used as an ornament on publications

ESG   ELECTRONIC SPORTS GATHERING

ESL   ENGLISH AS A SECOND LANGUAGE

esp.   especially, an abbreviation commonly used in dictionaries

esparto   a long, coarse grass from Spain and North Africa, used to make ESPARTO PAPER, a book paper with a fine texture

ESPN   ENTERTAINMENT & SPORTS PROGRAMMING NETWORK

esquisse   a small, rough sketch or layout; pronounced es-KEES and sometimes called a *thumbnail*

ESS   ELECTRONIC STILL STORE

essay   a short literary nonfiction composition, generally interpretive and subjective; from the Old French *essai*, meaning "to attempt"   An *essayist* is a person who writes essays. *Essayistic* refers to a work that has the reflective style of an essay.

essence   oil paint drained of its excess oil and diluted with turpentine or another solvent, used by artists, particularly in the 19th century, to make thin WASHES of opaque pigment

essential area   the part of the TV picture actually seen on the set   It is the central part of the picture, exclusive of the outer borders of the SCANNING area.

est   estimate

EST or **E.S.T.**   Eastern Standard Time

establishing shot   [film, television] an opening comprehensive view, a long shot to set the scene or acquaint the audience with the setting, characters, or plot, followed by details and closer action; also called *orientation shot*

estimate a statement of proposed or anticipated cost or budget; to compute or prepare such a statement A person who computes advertising, production, or other costs is an *estimator*. A *low estimate* is an amount smaller than anticipated by the purchaser or lower than competitors' estimates or, worst of all, lower than the actual costs.

estrangement effect the result in a film, play, or other work in which the audience is intellectually detached from the action; also called *alienation effect* This concept of drama was described, and utilized, by the German playwright Bertolt Brecht (1898–1956).

ESU ELECTRONIC SETUP; ENGINEERING SETUP

ET or **E.T.** ELECTRICAL TRANSCRIPTION; ELECTRONIC TRANSCRIPTION

et al. and others; from Latin *et alii*; sometimes incorrectly written *et alia* The abbreviation is commonly used in listings.

etaoin shrdlu words used by operators of LINOTYPE equipment to test their hot-lead typecasting machines The words, which include the five vowels and seven common consonants, are formed by running the fingers down the first two vertical rows on the left side of the keyboard.

etc. and so forth; from Latin *et cetera*, meaning "and others" The term is sometimes used by writers or speakers when they cannot think of any others in a list of examples. The *t* is pronounced in both words.

etch in OFFSET LITHOGRAPHY—a printing technique based on the principle that oil (ink) and water do not mix—an acidified solution to keep nonprinting areas from accepting ink

etching **1** a technique of drawing or printing using corrosive chemicals or electrolysis to produce areas that will be inked; the proof or print made from the etched plate An etching differs from an ENGRAVING, which is incised or cut with a tool. **2** to *etch*: to create an etching

etch stick an abrasive stick, made of pumice powder and flint, used to remove dirt or other unwanted specks on an OFFSET LITHOGRAPHY printing plate; also called *snake slip*

ethical drugs pharmaceuticals that require a physician's prescription, as compared to proprietary or over-the-counter medication *Ethical advertising* promotes prescription drugs.

ethical shopper a customer who feels obligated to buy in a specific store, perhaps because of a personal relationship with the owner or staff This is the smallest category of retail customer; the others are APATHETIC SHOPPER, ECONOMIC SHOPPER, and PERSONALIZING SHOPPER.

ethics morality; conformity to a code of fair and honest action Various professions have *codes of ethics*, which specify accepted or required standards of behavior.

ethnic media magazines and newspapers, radio, and TV stations, or other media that appeal primarily to specific races, nationalities, or other ethnic groups

ethos the primary attitudes, beliefs, or characteristics of an individual or group

E-to-E electronics-to-electronics, as in the monitoring of the output signal of a videocassette recorder (VCR) while the VCR is recording

et seq. and the following: a notation used in footnotes, indexes, and other lists; from the Latin *et sequens* The abbreviation *ff* is the English-language equivalent.

ETX END OF TEXT

etymology the origin and development of a word; the branch of linguistics that deals with word origins

etymon the original form of a word, in the same or a different language

eulogy a formal speech or statement in praise of a person, generally one who recently died An ELEGY is a poem or song of lament or praise for the dead. *Encomium* is another word for eulogy.

euphemism the use of a word or phrase that is less offensive than the one for which it substitutes—for example, *to go to one's reward* for *die*

euphony the quality of a word or phrase that gives it a pleasant or agreeable sound Such words are *euphonious*.

euphuism an elaborate, self-conscious, artificial prose style, named after *Euphues*, a romance written in 1579 by John Lyly It is not the same as EUPHEMISM.

European envelope an envelope that is about 5 inches wide, wider than an AMERICAN ENVELOPE

EV EXPOSURE VALUE

Evans and Sutherland (E&S) a company that produces a VECTOR GRAPHICS COMPUTER

even page the left-hand page of a publication; also called *verso* Even pages carry the numbers 2, 4, 6, and so on.

even small caps (ESC) the typesetting instruction (generally indicated by a double underline) to set all capital letters (caps) in a size smaller than regular caps, THIS WAY

even smalls type in which all letters are small capital letters, as in A.M.

event a happening, contest, or attraction *Event marketing* is a sales promotion related to a sports competition or other event, either an existing project or one created by or for the marketer. Marketers often refer to a special promotion as an event, such as an *inpack event* (a premium or gift inside a package) or an *onpack event* (a premium attached to a package).

even working [printing] a book or other printed work in which each section, or SIGNATURE, is of the same length

evergreen a timeless newspaper or magazine article, such as a feature that can be published at any time

every day (E.D.) an instruction used in scheduling advertising, such as at newspapers or broadcast stations The addition of the initials *T.F.* indicates that the schedule is to be followed *till forbid.*

Everyman a person or character representing the common person or all people; sometimes not capitalized *Everyman*, a well-known morality play originally performed in the early 16th century, was an allegorical drama with the characters of God, Death, Good Deeds, Good Fellowship, and others concerned with the future of Everyman's soul.

every other day (E.O.D.) a term used in ordering or scheduling advertising, such as newspapers, radio, or TV stations The addition of the abbreviation *T.F.* indicates that the schedule is to be continued *till forbid.*

every other week (E.O.W.) an instruction used in ordering or scheduling print or broadcast advertising The addition of the abbreviation *T.F.* indicates that the schedule is to be continued *till forbid.*

EVF ELECTRONIC VIEWFINDER

evg. evening

ex a Latin preposition, with various meanings: without, exclusive of, out of, free of, from, former Examples include *ex dividend* (without dividend, after the stock dividend has been declared) and *ex cathedra* (from the chair, with the authority that comes from high rank or office). The letter *x* sometimes is written as "ex" (the plural is "exes").

ex, Ex, or **ex.** examined; example; except; excepted; EXCHANGE; express; EXTRA

examination copy a book provided free or on approval to a teacher or other prospective buyer; also called *inspection copy*

EXCEL Award an annual award to an individual for excellence in communication leadership, presented by the INTERNATIONAL ASSOCIATION OF BUSINESS COMMUNICATORS

excelsior 1 wood shavings, used in packing 2 the name for the smallest-size typeface, about 3 points 3 [journalism] editorial matter (news and features) to fill space around advertising

exception dictionary special instructions for computerized hyphenation, spelling, punctuation, and other deviations from standard procedure; also called *exception word dictionary*

excerpt a part of a text

exchange 1 an indication that a book publisher or other manufacturer will accept books or other items returned from retailers for full credit 2 a system in which complimentary subscriptions are traded, generally with other publishers The practice is common at newspapers, where the traded copies are called *exchanges* and are sometimes under the supervision of an *exchange editor.* 3 companies, called *film exchanges*, that distribute motion pictures on a regional basis, from film producers to distributors or theater chains

exciter lamp in film projectors, a small bulb that beams a light on the optical soundtrack onto a photocell (on the other side of the film), which converts the voltage into sound The lamp thus excites or stimulates a reaction.

excl. exclamation; EXCLUSIVE

exclusive an interview, news release, or other material that is offered or provided to a newspaper or broadcast medium and not simultaneously offered to other media Sometimes the item may be a *partial exclusive*, which is offered exclusively within a media category or within a market area—for example, the item may be provided to a number of newspapers or other media in different parts of the country. Exclusivity also may apply to a product or service that receives limited distribution, such as to a single retailer in an area. An advertiser may obtain an exclusive in a magazine, television program, or other medium by purchasing sufficient space or time to contractually exclude competitors. In international advertising, the *exclusivity rule* is a tacit or contractual understanding that a client owns and can use any material created for it by any of its advertising or other agencies.

exegesis an explanation, analysis, or interpretation of a word or a text, particularly the Bible An *exegetic dictionary* is a listing of words in a text with a discussion of each.

exemplum an example or illustration, particularly a story with a moral point (the plural is *exempla*) Exempla were common in medieval sermons.

exhaustion [photography] the depletion or aging of processing solutions The term should not be confused with *exhaustive*, which means comprehensive.

exhibitor 1 an individual or organization that presents a display, of products or other items (an *exhibit*) The term *exhibition*, as generally used, refers to a collection of exhibits, as at a trade show or convention. *Exhibiting* is a communications medium, such as advertising, that involves conveying a message at a display on a site. **2** [film] a person, company, or theater that shows films (abbreviated by the trade publication *Variety* as *exhib*)

exit [theater] a stage direction in a script indicating the point at which a performer leaves *Exit cue* is the dialogue line or action that signals a performer to begin the *exit line* or *exit action* or to *exit without lines*. The opposite stage direction is ENTER.

exit light a light over an exit door in a theater or other building It must be lit during a performance, in case of emergency.

exit poll a survey of voters, taken as they leave their voting places, that asks about the choices they made

exit routine [computers] a procedure that permits a change, such as an error correction or the insertion of new text

ex libris Latin for "from the books of" The term is used on a bookplate or nameplate pasted in a book, with the name of the owner written or printed on it, and sometimes refers to a bookplate.

expanded typeface characters (letters or numbers) that are stretched or extended so that their width is greater than their height

expanding circle an optical effect in which an image starts as a small circle in the center of the screen and gradually expands The same effect can be achieved with an expanding square, diamond, or other shape.

expansion of time a technique in which the time of an action on film or tape is longer than the real or actual time of the events portrayed Generally, film and TV directors utilize *compressed time* (the dramatic action takes less time than actual events), but sometimes suspense can be attained by showing one character and then another (*cutaways*) and/or close-ups and various angles, so that the elapsed time is greater than in reality.

experimental period the time between midnight and sunrise, used by non-full-time radio stations for testing

expiration a subscription that is not renewed The *expiration date* is the date on which a subscription ends or a date after which a product, such as film, may no longer function at optimum usefulness. In the United Kingdom, the film expiration date is called the *expiry date*. An *expire* is a former subscriber.

expletive an obscene word or phrase Actually, the Latin *expletivus* is from *explere,* meaning "to fill out," and *expletive* also refers to a word or phrase added to a sentence merely to fill it out, such as *Well!*

explode [computers] to separate out elements of data and rearrange them—for instance, to rearrange a bibliography in which each listing appears as *author, title, publisher,* and *subject* and to change the order of the components or create new lists

exploded view a sketch or photograph in which the components of a machine or other item are spread out so that they can be identified, as in a user's manual or training manual

exploitation film a movie that is made for a quick profit, with little or no regard for quality or artistic merit It is generally sensational or hastily put together, to take advantage of a topical event or personality, and often relies heavily on advertising and other promotional techniques. *Exploitation books* or other works are similarly produced.

explosion wipe [television] the rapid replacement of one scene by another, with the second scene emerging from the center or moving in from the periphery

explosive [broadcasting] a sharp sound produced by a letter such as *p,* particularly when it is overstressed or when the microphone is too close to the speaker; sometimes called *plosive*

expo art a chart, diagram, or other expository or illustrative art

expo line short for *expository line:* a brief description under a photograph, perhaps just a name or a name and a title; also called *e-line*

export an item that is sent to a foreign country An *export edition* of a book generally is sold—perhaps by an *export representative*—at a lower wholesale discount and provides a lower royalty, or fee, to the author than the domestic edition.

expose **1** to reveal, make visible **2** [photography, printing] the admission of light

exposé the revelation of facts, often as the result of investigative reporting; from the French, pronounced ek-spo-ZAY

exposition a setting forth of facts or other material; a detailed explanation; writing or speaking that sets forth or explains; a large public exhibition or show (sometimes called an *expo*); part of a play or other work that reveals background information about the plot or character *Expository* material, such as an expository scene in a play, is explanatory.

exposure **1** a person's audio or visual contact with a MEDIUM, message, or other entity; the presentation of an advertisement, message, display, or other medium or entity, as measured by the number of people able to perceive it **2** [photography] the act or rate of allowing light to reach film, as calculated by an *exposure meter* or *light meter* An *incident meter* is hand-operated and measures the light falling on a subject; a *reflected light meter*, generally built into the camera, measures the light reflected from the subject. In a *multiple exposure*, two images (*double exposure*) or several images are superimposed in the camera (not by multiple printing).

exposure index (EI) a rating of the light-sensitivity of a film, generally one number (ASA or other standards) for daylight and another number for tungsten lighting; also called *exposure rating*

exposure sheet in film animation, a printed form with written instructions from the artist, or animator, to the camera operator specifying the necessary exposure to light and other details about each cel (frame)

exposure value (EV) a number to indicate the light sensitivity of a light meter The lower the EV number, the more sensitive the meter is to low light; the higher the number, the more sensitive the meter is to bright light. A 35mm camera with a through-the-lens meter often has an EV range of EV3 to EV18.

Express Mail the overnight delivery service of the U.S. Postal Service Letters and packages can be placed in special collection boxes or brought to post offices. *A-label service* provides delivery to a post office, not the addressee, before 10 A.M. of the next day; *B-label service* ensures delivery to the addressee before 3 P.M. of the next day; *C-label service* provides same-day delivery to major airport mail facilities. Express Mail Military Service and Express Mail International Service are also available.

expurgated referring to erroneous or objectionable material removed from a book, magazine, or other work prior to publication

ext or **EXT** EXTERIOR

ext. EXTENSION; EXTERIOR; external; extinct; EXTRA; extract

extended area service (EAS) a telephone-company service that provides a special reduced charge for calls near the local area

Extended Binary Coded Decimal Interchange Code (EBCDIC) a system, used in IBM computer equipment, that has 256 code combinations for all characters

extended cell ascription [market research] a procedure that transfers data from one study to another *Ascription* is the assignment of a quality or other item.

extended cover the cover of a publication, such as a brochure, that extends beyond the trim, or edge, of the pages; also called *overhang* or *overlap*

extended retail price a form of estimating a merchant's total sales volume of food or other packaged goods The figure, generally expressed on a daily basis, is computed by multiplying the retail price of an item by the number of cases shipped from the warehouse to the store.

extended terms an arrangement that provides an additional period in which to pay, as for purchased items

extended typeface characters (letters and numbers) whose width is greater than standard; sometimes called *expanded type*

extension **1** an additional period of time that prolongs an agreement or extends a deadline or delivery date **2** [direct marketing] the mailing of additional names after a portion of a mailing list has been tested **3** [magazine publishing] the continuance of a subscription beyond its original expiration date **4** an additional telephone converted to a line, either an internal line (an INTERCOM) or an external line **5** [advertising] an EMBELLISHMENT, a display, or an outdoor advertisement

exterior (ext or **EXT)** an outdoor scene or a set built to simulate an outdoor scene

exterior lighting [film] natural and artificial lighting used in the filming of an EXTERIOR

external publication a magazine, newsletter, or other matter directed to customers or others outside a company or organization The older designation was *external house organ* (*house* is the company or organization; *organ* is an instrument of communication).

external storage a diskette, cassette, or other medium that can be removed from a system and is not a physical part of the unit, as *internal storage* is

extn. EXTENSION

extra **1** a nonspeaking actor, as in a crowd scene Extras usually are hired by the *extra casting director*, who generally is employed by a casting company and works with the first assistant director or second assistant director. **2** a special EDITION of a newspaper, for late-breaking or very important news The first American newspapers to publish extras were in the mid-19th century; the practice is less common in the television era.

extrabold (XBLD) referring to a very heavy typeface

extract **1** a publishing and printing term for *block quotation*, a long quotation marked off from the text by being set in smaller type or on a narrower measure, or width, than the main copy **2** less commonly, a synonym for flashback in a film

extra dating an arrangement that provides extended payment terms For example, *2/10-30 extra* indicates that a 2-percent cash discount may be taken within 40 days of the invoice date, 30 days beyond the standard 10. Extra dating is the opposite of *immediate dating*, which is payment on delivery.

extravaganza a literary or other fantasy characterized by a loose structure and farce; a spectacular, elaborate theatrical production, particularly a musical, characterized by extravagance

Extravision the first national VIDEOTEX service in the United States, started in 1983 by the Columbia Broadcasting System It was an over-the-air electronic information service requiring decoders attached to or built into TV sets. See also PRODIGY.

extreme 1 [film] in animation, a key drawing—the beginning and the end of a movement, made by a *key animator* 2 [photography] a term, abbreviated *E* or *X*, often used as a modifier, as in EXTREME CLOSE-UP (*ECU, XCU*), *extreme high-angle shot* (also called *bird's-eye shot*), EXTREME LONG SHOT (*ELS, XLS*), *extreme low-angle shot*, or *extreme wide-angle lens* (also called *fish-eye lens*)

extreme close-up (ECU or XCU) a tight camera shot, close in and limited to one part of the subject

extreme long shot (ELS or XLS) a comprehensive or panoramic view, as photographed or filmed with an extreme TELEPHOTO lens

extremely low frequency (ELF) a radio band at a lower frequency than the band reserved by the Federal Communications Commission for commercial radio stations

extrospective research a study that examines the relationship of outside influences on a group, as opposed to *introspective research*, which compares factors within a group

eyeball to examine a layout or other work visually, instead of mechanically or electronically

eye bounce a technique, recommended to speakers on TV programs, in which the eyes do not move horizontally Instead, to achieve a side-to-side movement, the speaker looks down and then to the side. Eye bounce avoids a glaze or an appearance of being shifty-eyed.

eyebrow slang for a brief overline above a newspaper headline, photograph, or art; also called *kicker*

eye camera a camera for recording eye movements It is used in advertising research to measure relative amounts of visual stimulation.

eye contact the practice of looking a person in the eyes In film and TV, eye contact is achieved by looking directly into the camera.

eye-level the position of a camera for a straight shot of a standing person The exact height varies but is generally about 5½ feet from the floor to the camera lens opening.

eye light a small light or special illumination on a person to produce extra reflection from the eyes, teeth, or other features; also called *kicker* or *catchlight* An eye light is definitely not the same as *big eyes*, which is slang for a powerful light.

eyeline the direction the eyes are looking in In TV, a *cheated eyeline* occurs when a performer does not look directly at a subject, such as another performer, but turns somewhat toward the camera.

eyepiece the lens nearest the viewer's eye, such as the lens of a camera viewfinder The eyepiece used in film production by a director of photography often is a *contrast glass* to determine lighting contrasts.

eyes only confidential, not to be reproduced

eyewitness news a TV news format featuring on-the-scene reporters (eyewitnesses), generally with a MINICAM, a portable electronic camera

F

f focal length: the relative aperture of a lens, written as *f/* followed by a number; also, following (see FF); folio

F FAHRENHEIT; FOLIO

fable a brief story with a moral principle or lesson, generally about a legendary person or employing animals or inanimate objects as talking characters; also, a foolish or improbable story

F.A.C. fast as you can; rush!

facade the front part, as of a building On film and stage sets, a facade is made to resemble the front of a real building, but there often is little or nothing behind it.

face 1 [typography] the surface of a piece of type, as well as the style of type—hence, typeface 2 appearance or look, such as the look of a publication 3 a surface, particularly the front surface, as of an outdoor advertising structure to which an advertisement is affixed

faced mail envelopes and other mailing pieces arranged with all addresses and stamps facing the same way *Facer-cancelers* are machines that automatically *face*—arrange in order with all addresses and stamps facing the same way—letter-size mail and then cancel the stamps. A *facing table* or *pickup table* is a long table on which letters are gathered and arranged in the same direction before going through a canceling machine.

face margin in the printing of a publication, the end of the open side, opposite the *bind*; also called *outside margin*, *thumb margin*, or *trim margin*

face-out display a book on a shelf or in a display unit with its front cover, or face, visible, as opposed to a SPINE-OUT DISPLAY

facetiae coarsely witty sayings or books

face time the amount of time that the head of a TV newscaster or other person is shown on the screen

facia a board over a storefront with the name of the proprietor; also the British spelling of FASCIA

facing See FACINGS.

facing editorial page an instruction by an advertiser to a publication to publish its advertisement adjacent to a non-advertising, or editorial, page; also called *facing editorial matter* or *facing text Facing first editorial page* refers to the page before the first editorial page of the magazine or other publication; *facing last editorial page* refers to the page after the last editorial page.

Facing Identification Mark (FIM) a series of vertical parallel lines that appear on BUSINESS REPLY cards and envelopes as required by postal regulations These bars, used by the Postal Service for machine identification of the mailer, appear in the upper middle area and are different from the horizontal bars along the right side.

facings the number of units of a product visible on a shelf in a supermarket or other store A *four-facing* placement has more visibility and probably will sell more units than *two-facings*. To *face up* is to arrange products on the shelf or in a display in an orderly manner—that is, with the *face* or front toward the customer. This often is one of the responsibilities of a DETAIL MAN, *rack jobber*, or sales representative and is particularly important with books, whose covers can be obscured by a competitor.

In outdoor advertising, a BILLBOARD is called a *facing*, characterized by the direction it faces, as in a *south facing*, or as part of a group of adjacent billboards, as in a *double* or *triple facing*.

facing text matter placement of an advertisement opposite editorial matter

facs complete studio facilities, such as for a rehearsal or broadcast *No facs*, or *no fax*, is a rehearsal without facilities—no sets, lights, or cameras.

facsimile an exact or nearly exact reproduction, as in various graphics processes A *facsimile signature* often is used in printed letters and direct mail. A *facsimile edition* is an accurate reproduction of a book or manuscript, such as a fine-quality printing of a hand-illuminated medieval manuscript. See also FAX.

facsimile transmission a process of SCANNING graphic images to convert them into electric signals that are transmitted, generally via telephone lines or radio waves, to produce a likeness of the original; also called FAX and commonly used as a verb, as to *fax a docu-*

ment *Digital facsimile equipment* transmits and receives digital signals; blank areas of a document are passed over, thereby increasing the scanning speed considerably. *Telefacsimile*, which originated in the early 1950s, is the system of sending written material via telephone lines. The word was shortened to *telefax* and then to *fax*.

faction a coined word combining fact and fiction, as in a book or other work with imagined conversations or events involving real people, generally with their names changed and perhaps with other modifications; different from a NON FICTION NOVEL

factoid a printed statement, often incorrect or fictional, that is accepted as a fact The word was coined in 1973 by Norman Mailer (b. 1923), American writer, about statements in his book about actress Marilyn Monroe (1926–62).

factory art low-priced paintings, generally poor renditions of landscapes and other art, though individually painted Sometimes called *schlock art*, they are painted by the *factory school*, a group of workers who manufacture paintings in a mechanical, assembly-line style.

factory-owned outlet a retail outlet owned by the manufacturer or producer of the merchandise

factory pack a premium attached (*on-pack*) or inside (*in-pack*) a package

fact sheet a summary of data, generally presented in tabular or other non-narrative form, whereas a BACKGROUNDER tends to be written in a more conventional narrative form A fact sheet is common in sales (new-product information sent to a sales force and customers); advertising (used by an announcer to *ad lib* a live commercial); publicity (accompanying a news release or as part of a PRESS KIT); journalism (a list of essential facts); and broadcasting (a checklist or schedule of things to be done in a broadcast, also called a *run-down sheet*).

fact tag an informative label or item affixed to a product

fade to vary in intensity, as a gradual change of audio or video, as in *fade to white* (an instruction to change from dark to white), *fade to black*, or *fade to red* A *crossfade* is the *fading out* of one element while *fading in* another, as in radio, TV, or film. A *chemical fade* is produced by putting negative or positive film in a chemical solution to darken the image.

fadeback a drawing, photograph, or other image with one part reproduced distinctly and other parts less so, in order, for example, to emphasize a key object or an advertised item The technique is called GHOSTING.

fade-in a shot that begins in darkness and gradually lightens up to full brightness; also called *fade-up* The opposite is *fade-out* or *fade to black*. In relation to sound, fade-in can mean the gradual heightening of volume.

fade-out blue a very light blue color that is not reproduced by an offset camera Penciled instructions can be written in this color.

fader a device that reduces a signal level, such as a volume control or a lighting DIMMER

fader bar a video switch-control device to dissolve and fade the picture

fade under a direction, such as to reduce music or sound effects sufficiently that they're heard only in the background

Fahrenheit (F) a thermometer or a unit of temperature On the *Fahrenheit scale*, the freezing point of water is 32°F and the boiling point, 212°F. Named after Gabriel Fahrenheit (1686–1736), the German physicist who devised the scale, the term is important in film processing and other communication fields.

fail softly [computers] a malfunction in which the system falls back to a degraded mode of operation, rather than a CRASH, which has no response

fair a market, exhibition, or entertainment event, such as a *book fair*, *church fair*, *county fair*, *state fair*, or *world's fair*

fairing [film] a procedure in which a PAN—horizontal movement of a camera—starts quickly and then slows The origin is from engineering, in which fairing is a part added, such as to an aircraft, to reduce drag or resisting forces.

fair use the amount of copyrighted material that may be quoted without permission or payment The amount varies, depending on its proportion of the total work and other factors.

fairy tale a story about fairies or other imaginary beings; an unbelievable story; a lie

fake to pretend or perform falsely, such as for a performer to improvise or to simulate a motion—to *fake it*—or a set designer to create an illusion A musician who plays without reading music—*by ear*—is described as *faking*. In music, a FAKE BOOK contains the basic melodies and chord symbols of hundreds of popular songs. In printing, *fake color process work* or *fake process* is the reproduction in color of a black-and-white photo by using SCREENS at different angles. For example, a fake *Duotone* is a two-color reproduction made from a single HALFTONE negative (usually black) and a halftone screen tint for the background (usually color).

fake book a collection of music used by musicians, compiled illegally (no copyright fees paid) and generally inserted in a folder or binder

falloff the act of becoming less In photography, falloff (or *fall-off*) is the diminishing of the amount of light as the distance increases from the light source, through the use of *flaps* or other light-reduction techniques

fallow corners [newspapers] the top right and lower left corners of a page, called *fallow* because they are not as well read or well utilized as the upper left and lower right corners

false caps capitalizing the first letter of each word, for emphasis rather than because it is a proper name or other word requiring capitalization

false code [computers] a code that produces an invalid, or illegal, character, such as a letter that is not part of a specific alphabet

false color [printing] a color applied to a black-and-white image in order to differentiate its features

false reverse [film] a reverse-angle shot, the opposite or reverse of the direction or point of view of the preceding shot, in which the camera is moved too much or the transition is too rigid, so that the performer appears to be looking in the wrong direction; also called *false reverse-angle shot*

family a group of *typefaces* visually related to one another A family generally includes regular, BOLD, ITALIC, CONDENSED, and variations and combinations of these, such as *bold italic* and *bold condensed.* The same or similar members of a family sometimes are known by different names, depending on the manufacturer of the type.

family publication a newspaper (*family paper*) or other publication that appeals to families, including young people

family viewing time a TV time period before 9 P.M. suitable for viewing by all age groups

fan an ardent devotee, short for fanatic A *fan magazine* appeals to enthusiasts—*fans*—of celebrities. *Fan mail* or *fan letters* are sent to prominent people or organizations by admirers. In the sense of a fan shape, a *fan camera arrangement* is two or more cameras positioned so that their image areas overlap, as with a panoramic view shot by aerial cameras. FANFOLD is paper or other material pressed in a zigzag pattern like a fan or accordion, also called *accordion fold* and used in computer printers.

fanciful unreal; imaginative A fanciful word is a *coined* word, made up or invented.

f & g's folded and gathered sheets: printed signatures of a book loosely collated in sequence but unbound; also called F & G and, sometimes, a *check copy* F & g's are sometimes sent for pre-publication review or comments.

fanfare introductory music in a broadcast or show; more generally, a flourish, in music, as of trumpets

fanfold a business form made from paper folded like a FAN, lengthwise and crosswise Commonly used for computers and other machines and 9½" wide or wider, it is usually perforated and folded on the perforations in alternating directions so that the paper can be fed continuously into a printer.

far a considerable distance; advanced; extensive In photography, the *far point* is the farthest place from the camera that is in acceptable focus. At each F-STOP, the camera has a near and far point that determine its DEPTH OF FIELD at that setting. A *far shot* is more commonly called a *long shot.* The *far side* of a printing press is its nonoperating side.

farce an exaggerated comedy based on broadly humorous, unlikely situations; broad humor or something absurd—*farcical* The origin is the French word *farce*, which means "stuffing," as in a fowl, and early farces filled interludes between acts in the theater.

farm out to allocate a partial or entire job to a subcontractor

fascia a flat strip, such as the panel atop an exhibit, generally with the name of the exhibitor; also spelled FACIA

fascicle [publishing] a section of a book published in installments, a practice common in the United Kingdom in the 19th century

fast rapid; firm; resistant to fading A *fast film* is highly sensitive to light and is designed for or compatible with a short exposure time. A *fast lens* transmits more light than a slow lens. *Fast motion* is rapid action on motion-picture film that is achieved by shooting the film at a slower speed than the standard projection rate. *Fast-breaking* means rapidly developing, as with a story that is unfolding. *Fast talk* may be rapid chatter but is more likely to be deceptive or manipulative, as by a *fast talker.*

fast forward movement of a tape forward faster than the speed for regular viewing or listening The term has become so well understood that it now is used as a verb to describe any accelerated action.

Fast Weekly Household Audiences Report an A.C. NIELSEN COMPANY weekly report on network household audiences issued in advance of more comprehensive reports; no longer issued

fat soft; plump; desirable; lucrative A *fat part* in a play is desirable and does not require heaviness in weight or character. *Fat* or *phat type* is wide or extended, the opposite of *thin* or *lean type.* A *fat negative,* however, is underdeveloped. A *fat line, fat headline,* or *fat head* has too many letters for its space, the opposite of a *thin line*. In newspapers, a *fat table* or *fat page* has less text than usual, and the white space makes it appear fat, although another explanation for the term is that the printer does not have to work hard and can get fat.

fat-faced or **fatface** in typography, type that is heavy or massive

fat negative a photographic negative with a thickened image; also called a *fatty negative* or *spread negative*

faux accord *false accord*, a French film expression to describe a very smooth transition or a CUT that does not appear to be a *jump cut* and thus gives a false impression of continuity It is one of many French expressions in cinematography, indicative of the influence of French filmmakers. Others are AUTEUR, CINEMA VÉRITÉ, and FILM NOIR.

favor an instruction to a television camera operator to focus on a specific person or object, as in "favor (name of performer)"

fax FACSIMILE, particularly *facsimile transmission* of printed matter over telephone lines Facsimile transmission became so common in the 1980s that it is now used as a noun, verb (to *fax a document*), and adjective (a *fax number*, the telephone number attached to the fax machine). The plural of fax is *faxes*. *Fax* is also an alternate spelling for the abbreviation for *facilities* (see FACS).

FAY light a 650-watt bulb used in spotlights for even illumination, particularly in outdoor daytime filming, generally in a module or series of two, four, six, or nine lights called a *Molefay* light.

FBIS Foreign *Broadcast Information Service*

f.c. FOLLOW COPY; FONT change

FCB Foote, Cone and Belding Communications, Inc., a major advertising and communications company headquartered in Chicago

FCB Grid a market-research device to determine whether a product or service commands a high or low involvement of the consumer and whether the purchasing decision is based primarily on thinking or feeling Developed in 1978 by Richard Vaughn of FOOTE, CONE & BELDING (FCB), an advertising agency, it is also called the *Vaughn Grid*.

FCC or **F.C.C.** FEDERAL COMMUNICATIONS COMMISSION

FDA or **F.D.A.** FOOD AND DRUG ADMINISTRATION

feather to give a feather-edge A *feather-edge* paper has a thin, fragile edge or ruffle. In photography, *feathering* is using the peripheral area of the light beam, rather than the central area, to create a soft effect. In printing, feathering is the spreading of ink at the edges of the printed type.

featherweight paper lightweight stock that is thick in bulk

feature an article or broadcast that is lighter or more general, about *human interest* or lifestyles, than the *hard news* resulting from current events Similarly, a *feature photo* is of human interest; its features include columns, comics, and other material that is not hard news. In merchandising, a feature is an important characteristic of a product or service or an item receiving special promotion or pricing. To feature is to give prominent display or promotion or to emphasize a specific aspect of a story.

featured the technical designation of a key performer—*featured player*—whose name appears in a printed program or advertising directly below the title, often preceded by the word "with"

feature film a full-length motion picture, generally 60 minutes or more

feature player a secondary or supporting performer, subordinate to a star

featurette a short film or tape, such as a 10-minute promotional trailer for a forthcoming program or movie or a 5-to-30-minute *short subject*, perhaps with a public relations sponsor

Federal Communications Commission (FCC or **F.C.C.)** the U.S. agency that licenses and regulates broadcasters The *F.C.C. coverage area* is the region within which a specific percentage of radio or TV sets can be expected to receive the signal of a particular station. Formed in 1934, the F.C.C. licenses individual stations, not networks.

Federal Trade Commission (FTC or **F.T.C.)** the U.S. agency that maintains free enterprise and competitive trade by such activities as monitoring the accuracy of advertising It is a commission, not a committee. Formed in 1915, the F.T.C. is a federal agency and therefore is involved with interstate and foreign commerce, not intrastate.

Fedex Federal Express (Memphis, TN) This air shipment company has become so well known, particularly in the communication fields, that its nickname is used as a noun and verb, as in "to send a Fedex" or "to Fedex a letter." It is often written in all caps, FEDEX.

fee basis a method of compensation based on a predetermined sum instead of a *commission*, which is a percentage of advertising or other monies spent, or an hourly wage The fee arrangement can be a *fixed fee*, a *variable fee*, or a combination, such as a basic fee plus additional compensation for time in excess of an agreed-upon number of hours.

feed broadcasts sent by radio and TV networks to local stations or by a local station or medium to the headquarters office or other media Similarly, a publicist or other source may call in or feed news and other material directly to the medium. The origination point is called the *feed point.*

Generally, feed refers to material supplied to a machine, the apparatus that supplies the material, or the material itself. In computerized printing, *advance feed* is paper tape or film with a *feed hole* slightly forward in each frame, in order to move the tape. *Center feed* has the feed hole in the horizontal section of the frame. *Film feed* is the device that moves the photosensitive paper on film. When a printer adds an extra length of paper to a galley that is slightly longer than standard size, the process is called *film feed.*

feedback 1 individual or group response to an advertising, public relations, or other campaign or, more simply, opinion, information, or other data from employees, consumers, viewers, or other audiences Feedback can be positive (complimentary) or negative (critical). 2 a loud noise, squeal, or howl from a microphone or speaker, caused by improper placement, circuit noise, accidental closing of the circuit, or another error or problem

feeder a person or thing that supplies material In show business, the feeder is the STRAIGHT MAN who supplies the questions or opening lines—the *feeder lines*—to a comedian. A *feeder line* is a connecting link, such as a coaxial cable between amplifiers in a cable-TV system.

feedhorn in satellite broadcasting, a part of a receiving antenna—a DISH—that collects the signal reflected from the main surface reflector and channels it into an amplifier called a *low-noise amplifier*

feedline [broadcasting] a transmission line, such as a coaxial cable

feed reel the *A-reel* in a *reel-to-reel* tape or film system Also called the *supply reel* or *storage reel,* it is the FEED or *first reel* from which the unrecorded or unplayed material moves or *feeds* to the second or *pickup reel.* The pickup reel is the *B-reel.*

feed through unintentional transfer from a magnetic tape to an adjacent section, as on a reel; also called *print through*

feel-bad article an article about a death or other tragedy Feel-bad magazine articles, particularly by or about celebrities, often are promoted on *feel-bad covers.*

feet the base on which a piece of metal type stands, divided by a groove

feevee PAY TELEVISION, *pay cable, subscription TV,* or any other *fee-for-viewing* service The word was coined by *Variety.*

feltboard a display panel—*board*—covered with a fuzzy, springy fabric—*felt*—used to display messages or other items; also called *cloth board, flannel board,* or *hook and loop board*

felt side the top side of a sheet of paper, which comes in contact with the *felt blanket* of a papermaking machine and does not bear any indentations, as opposed to the *wire side,* which rests on the wire mesh or screen In the early days of papermaking, handmade paper was molded between *felts.* Now, the felt is the fabric belt that conveys the roll of paper through the machine. Woven wool and synthetic felts with distinctive patterns create a texture in the paper called a *felt finish, felt-marked finish, felt mark,* or *genuine felt finish.*

feminine rhyme rhyme in which the accent is on the next-to-last syllable of each of the rhyming words, such as *candy* and *dandy, tango* and *mango;* also called *penultimate rhyme* or *two-rhyme*

femtosecond a millionth of a billionth of a second, a unit used in FIBER OPTICS to characterize the transmission of information over glass fibers A femtosecond written numerically has 15 zeros.

fence a bracket, parenthesis, or other enclosure symbol

FEP Fast Evening Persons Report; also called F-14

fere-humanistica early gothic or BLACK-LETTER *sans-serif* typefaces used by Italian humanistic scholars; also called *gotico-antiqua*

ferric oxide tape a magnetic audiotape or videotape with a coating of ferric oxide (Fe_2O_3), a reddish-brown oxide of iron Since this chemical occurs naturally as rust (*oxidized iron*), tapes and tapeheads must be cleaned regularly.

ferrotype a photograph made by rubbing—*burnishing*—on a thin plate of iron coated with a sensitized film; also made on enameled tin and called a *tintype*

Festschrift or **festschrift** a collection of articles, particularly by colleagues and former students, about or in honor of a noted scholar; from the German *Fest* (festival) and *Schrift* (a writing) The plural is *Festschriften* or *Festschrifts.*

feuilleton a part of a French newspaper that contains reviews, fiction, and features; an article in this section or any light, popular piece of writing, including an advertisement in this style

ff following, such as a reference to the following lines or pages, sometimes abbreviated as *fol.*

and usually printed with the two letters tied together; FULLFACE type, FOLIOS

F-14 *Fast Evening Persons Report (FEP)*: a service of the A.C. NIELSEN COMPANY that provides network TV audience data from major markets within a few days of broadcast

FG FINE GRAIN; FOREGROUND

FI fade-in

fiber optics the technology that uses light as a communications medium transmitted in hair-thin glass fibers—*optical fibers*—often bundled into *fiber-optic cables* that are used in the telephone industry and elsewhere to carry DIGITAL information via light pulses or for other purposes, including *fiber-optic displays*, which are lighted signs with letters or art that usually is curved

fiche a *microfiche* or sheet of microfilm with text in reduced size; pronounced FEESH The plural is *fiches.*

fiddle [journalism] a term indicating that some editing is needed, though not as extensive as a rewrite

fidelity accuracy; the degree to which a broadcast or other system accurately reproduces the signal it receives

field **1** [marketing] A *field test* is the selling of a product or service or the examination of a concept under actual conditions—that is, *in the field*, as compared to laboratory or conceptual conditions. A promotion initiated by a sales representative or retailer, rather than at headquarters, is a *field-activated promotion (F.A.P.).* The sales rep often is called a *field man* or *field representative*, supervised by a *field* or *regional manager.* **2** [broadcasting] The strength of a station's radio or TV signal within its coverage area is its *field strength*, as shown by its *field-intensity measurement* on a *field-intensity map*, a contour map. In TV and film, the field is the part of a scene—called *field of view, field of action*, or *action field*—that's visible at any given moment or the area of a video screen on which identification titles or other text or art may be inserted. A *field pickup* is a remote transmission, not from the studio. In TV transmission in the United States, 60 fields are transmitted per second, each one containing either the odd or even *scanning lines* of the picture (odd or even fields), so that one field equals half of a picture FRAME. **3** [photography] the area covered by a viewfinder or lens; also called *field size Depth of field* is the amount of image area that is in focus in front of and behind the subject. **4** [graphic arts] the background area **5** [computers] a region, such as the area on a screen on which text may be entered; a section of text or data, such as the part of one TAB, or

beginning point, to the next tab; a group of related items handled as a unit In some word processing systems, a field is a subject of text or data and may be ranked by the order in which it will be put in sequence. The lowest-valued *key field* is sorted as the first RECORD; the highest-valued key field is sorted as the last record. A *fixed field* has a specific number of characters, whereas a *variable field* has beginning and end codes and is flexible in the number of characters.

field angle [film] an angle of 90 degrees from a *spotlight*

field camera a relatively small camera used to film or tape exterior scenes

field label an identification of an area of work In this book, field labels appear in brackets at the beginning of and within many definitions.

field producer [television] a person who works outside the headquarters studio—*in the field*—to supervise the production of programs or segments, as of a news program

FIFO or **F.I.F.O.** FIRST-IN-FIRST-OUT

fifteen and two the discount structure for advertising agencies by some media, notably newspapers, consisting of 15 percent of the gross rate plus a 2-percent discount for prompt payment

fifteen minutes! a warning call to performers shouted fifteen minutes before the performance In the United Kingdom, the call is "Quarter of an hour!" The first call generally comes 30 minutes before the performance and is called *half.*

Fifth Estate the broadcasting medium See FOURTH ESTATE.

fifty-fifty [film, television] a shot of two people, each occupying half of the field of view; more commonly called a *two shot*

fifty-fifty mirror [film] a special-effects mirror used to superimpose two images, the action in front of the camera and the action reflected by the mirror

fifty-fifty plan the standard arrangement in CO-OPERATIVE ADVERTISING in which the manufacturer and retailer each pay 50 percent of the advertising cost; generally written as *50-50 plan*

fig. figurative; figure

figurative representing by means of a figure or symbol; not in its original, usual, literal, exact sense Figurative language makes use of *figures of speech* and is not literal.

figure a single digit; an illustration or other display material accompanying a text In typesetting, *lining figures* are base-aligned with the accompanying text, whereas *old-style figures* are stylized, are not base-aligned, and appear above and/or below the BASE LINE. In computerized typesetting, *figure space* is a uniform width assigned to all figures in a FONT, a useful adaptation to align columns of figures.

figure eight a directional microphone that is more sensitive to sounds in front of or behind it than those on the side   A *cardioid microphone* is more sensitive to sounds in front of it, and a figure eight is a *double cardioid.*

figure of speech an expression that creates an effect, such as ANALOGY, HYPERBOLE, METAPHOR, PERSONIFICATION, or SIMILE

file   **1** a container for keeping papers in order or a collection of stored items; to arrange for reference   **2** [journalism] to dispatch a news story to a medium; also, one day's output by a wire service or other press association   **3** [computers] a set of related records treated as a unit, such as a *text file, program file,* or *data file*   *File gap* is the area on the TAPE that indicates the end of a file. *File maintenance* is the process of adding, removing, or revising material. *File conversion* is the transfer of all or part of records in a file from one medium to another, as in *non-machine-readable* to *machine-readable. File key* is a character used to identify a record in a file; it is not the same as a *search key.*

file film stock footage from the library or file of a TV station or other source   When used as background material in a TV newscast, file film generally is identified by a line at the top or bottom of the screen with the date on which it was originally taken.

file label an identification on a filing cabinet, computer file, or other storage medium   In a computer, an *external label* is attached to the outside of a disk or file holder and is not machine readable, whereas an *internal label* is part of a file (the first or last record) and is machine readable. In a computer file label, also called a *header label,* the first record, or block, in the file is a set of characters unique to the file.

file 13 the wastepaper basket; the *circular file,* as in "put this in file 13"

filigree lacelike ornamentation   A *filigree initial* is a capital letter with fine ornate lines.

fill or **filler** timeless text, called *time copy,* or a short item used in a publication to *fill space,* generally at the bottom of a column; padding or innocuous material to *fill in* or expand an article or other item, material that can be worked on by a printer or others as time permits, when there is no work of greater urgency   A publicist or other source may compile and send a sheet or collection of fillers for publication over a period of time. In broadcasting, fill can be biographical and significant background material, as well as

anecdotes and trivia, used to fill and kill time and as a *cushion* during lulls or dead spots, as in live coverage of a game, parade, or other event; also called *fill program* or *fill programming.*

fillet an ornamental line or band impressed on the sides of a book cover; pronounced FILL-it   A *French fillet* has three lines, unevenly spaced.

fill-in the insertion of a name or other personalized or localized words in a letter or news release; an UNDERSTUDY or SUBSTITUTE; in typing or printing, a condition in which ink partially or completely occupies open areas, such as within the letter *O*   A *fill-in act* replaces a performer or performers on a variety program when the originally booked act is unavailable. A *fill-in date* is a performance that takes up the slack or *fills in* the schedule, as on a tour.

filling in papermaking, the addition of calcium carbonate or another filler to improve appearance and receptivity to ink

fill leader a strip of film, generally colored white or yellow for easy identification, inserted in a *workprint* to indicate audio and/or video sections to be added or edited

fill light supplementary illumination—one or more lights—to lighten shadows or reduce contrast, common in portrait photography; also called *fill, filler light, filler,* or *fill-in light*

film a thin coating; a chemically coated material used to record still photographs or other visual material; a motion picture, as a category, the entire production or just the photographic material; the action recorded on film, as opposed to live action   In phototypesetting, film is photosensitive paper or other material, not necessarily transparent.

A *film advance* is the apparatus that positions the film for exposure or projection. A *film clip* is a sequence or short film distributed by media or publicists and used for insertion within a program. A *film library* stores films, particularly stock footage. *Film speed* is the rate at which a type of film reacts to light, generally expressed as an ASA (AMERICAN STANDARDS ASSOCIATION) number. A *film chain* is the complete system of cameras, power-supply controls, monitors, and projectors. A *film positive* is a positive print on film instead of paper. A *film slide* is a transparency on film instead of glass. *Film backing* is the coating on the nonemulsion side of a film. *Film base* is the material or layer on which the light-sensitive substance is coated. *Film-base density* is a measure of the degree of opacity of a film base. *Film cement* is a substance that joins strips of motion-picture film (actually, it's a welding solvent). A *film chamber* is the light-proof box, magazine, or other container in a camera that houses exposed or unexposed film, which is inserted by a *film loader*. *Film gauge* is the width of film as measured in millimeters, such as 8mm, 16mm, 35mm, and 70mm. *Film capacity* is the amount of film that can be held by a camera or projector. The *film gate* is the pressure plate and aperture plate in a camera or projector. A *film checker* inspects film for defects. A *film phonograph* reproduces sound from the audio track of a film. A *film pack* is a container with sheets of film for use as a unit within a camera. *Film perforations* are the holes in the edges of film that permit movement along the sprocket teeth of a camera or projector. A *film processor* is a machine for automatic development and fixing of film. A *film roll* is film on a spool. *Film tension* is the pull applied to film as it moves through a camera, projector, or processing device. A *film advance* is the apparatus that positions the film for exposure or projection. A *film island* is a slide and film projector group, as in a TV studio. *Film transfer* is copying onto film, as from tape to film. *Film transmission* is the transmission of a motion picture, as in TV. The *film plane* is the line along which a film moves through the GATE of the camera. A *film editor* or *picture editor* edits the workprint and dialogue tracks but not the tracks for music and effects, which are edited by the sound editor. *Filmstock* or *stock* is raw (unexposed) film. A motion-picture or TV program that is taped often is incorrectly called a film.

film card   MICROFICHE

film chain   a device that converts film into a format suitable for TV transmission It consists of a TV camera focused on the lens of a film projector. Film chains and other devices with the same purpose are called *telecine* machines.

filmdom   the motion-picture industry A *film critic* is a motion-picture reviewer. A *filmgoer* is a person who sees motion pictures. *Filmography*, writings about motion pictures, is not the same as *cinematography*.

filmic   of or having to do with motion pictures As used in the film industry, filmic refers to something in a film or on the screen, as opposed to *cinematic*, which describes anything connected with filmmaking or the film industry. For example, *filmic space* refers to editing that puts two scenes together, either on the same screen or with fast intercutting. *Filmic time* is the condensation or omission of time passages, ranging from a few minutes to years in the script that are condensed to a few seconds on the screen. Filmic techniques also are used in TV.

film jacket   a transparent plastic sleeve that holds *microfilm*, which then is called *jacketed film* The jacket may be notched to facilitate

the insertion of the microfilm frames or strips and may have ribs so that the jackets can be connected to form multiple sleeves.

film laminate   a clear plastic substance affixed to a book, record, or other cover or jacket to protect it

film loop   motion-picture film spliced end to end for continuous projection; also called a *loop*

filmmaker   a person involved in the production of motion pictures

film noir   a movie with a cynical mood, often characterized by violence or crime *Noir* is the French word for black.

filmograph   a film composed of a series of still photos

filmography   a list of films of a performer, director, or other individual, akin to a bibliography

film pickup   transmission of film to a TV station; now commonly replaced by videotape

film rundown   a list of films, such as a log of films shown on a TV news program

filmsetter   a *photographic typesetter* or *photocomposing* machine, a machine that "sets type" on film or photographic paper In fact, no actual metal type is cast.

filmsetting   composition of type onto film, an electronic process that does not use lead or actual type PHOTOTYPESETTING includes filmsetting and also type composition on sensitized paper. The process is also called *filmset*.

filmstrip or **film strip**   a series of photos, drawings, or text reproduced sequentially on frames of 35mm film (sometimes 16mm or smaller) for projection with or without sound on a filmstrip projector, used in schools and businesses; also called *stripfilm*

film transfer   a film copy of a TV program, segment, or commercial called a KINESCOPE, *kine*, television recording, *TVR*, or transfer Rarely used now, it has been replaced by videotape.

filmy   hazy, as if covered by gauze or a thin film

filter   a porous substance or device; an acoustic, electric, electronic, optical, or other device to selectively reject signals Filters, including cheesecloth or gauze, glass, and screens, are commonly used in photography, broadcasting, and printing. In photography, the *filter factor* is the amount an exposure must be increased to compensate for the light lost by the *color correction filter*, *haze control filter*, or other filter. *Color-compensating filters* are graduated hues of color on gelatin or glass used in front of or behind the lens of an *enlarger* to control color balance. *Color-conversion filters* are used in front of a camera lens to alter the light, such as from daylight to tungsten light. *Color-printing filters* are acetate sheets placed between the light source and the negative to control color balance. A *black-and-white filter* is used with black-and-white film to intensify the dark and light areas. A *color filter* is used with color film. A *daylight filter* is used for daylight photography. A *diffusion filter* is used to soften the hard edge-lines of a subject, or for special effects, as with a *fog filter* to evoke a fog effect. A *neutral density* (ND) filter is a gray filter that reduces the light without changing the color balance. A *polarizing filter* reduces light reflection. A *protection filter* is a clear glass that protects the camera lens, as from dust or rain.

filter mike a microphone modified to produce sound effects, such as an echo or the simulated sound of a voice on a telephone

FIM FACING IDENTIFICATION MARK

fin. financial; finish

final mile in satellite communications, the electronic facilities that connect the DOWNLINK to the receiving site; also called *last mile*

financial relations the planning and execution of communications programs of publicly owned companies with their shareholders and other business publics Financial relations include annual reports, meetings with financial analysts, and publicity in business media.

Financial World Annual Report Competition annual awards to companies for outstanding annual reports to shareholders, presented by *Financial World* magazine, New York

Findex an annual directory of market-research reports, published by FIND/SVP, an information and research company in New York

fine superior; pure; refined; thin; sharp

fine art or **fine arts** music, painting, and other forms of creative expression meant to be appreciated and not necessarily for commercial use Thus, *graphic art* or *graphics* are not generally considered fine art.

fine cut a version or stage of a motion picture after the *rough cut*, when the editing or cutting has been refined

fine-grain free of textural effects, as with a fine-grained print, film, or paper

fine print text that is difficult to read or comprehend due to its small size or the complexity or ambiguity of the language, as in a contract

fines in papermaking, blemishes formed of clumps of fibers

fine type small type

fine writing pretentious writing Thus, to call someone a *fine writer* may not be a compliment, depending on the context, and may refer to the excessive use of strained or artificial language.

finger a long, narrow, large flag or mask, like a very big finger, generally placed on a stand in front of a light to block or *cut off* light or to produce a shadow; also called a *cutter*

fingering the mail jargon for the action of a mail carrier who thumbs through envelopes and other mail in order to select pieces for delivery

fingernails printer's slang for parentheses

finial a decorative terminal part, such as the top of a lampshade support; a specially designed letter used at the end of a word or line, such as a *swash*, an italic letter with an elaborate extension

finish conclusion; completeness; refinement; the last treatment, coating, or polish of a surface, such as paper; to terminate, use up, or give a coating or texture *Felt-finish* paper resembles felt; *leatherette finish* resembles leather; *marble finish* resembles marble. *Medieval laid finish* is made with CHAIN LINES to create a shading effect. *Metallic finish* has a metallic luster. *Mother-of-pearl finish* is lustrous and pearl-like.

finished art material ready to be reproduced

finished insert an advertisement prepared in entirety by an advertiser for insertion in a newspaper or other publication

finishing line a thin border around a HALFTONE

fire flicker a cinematic technique that emulates firelight, such as by waving a stick with rag strips in front of a light

firm secure, definite, steady; a commercial partnership Though a firm may not be a corporation, the word generally is used to describe service businesses in which the emphasis is on individuals, including partners, such as a *legal firm* or *public relations firm*. A *firm order* is a commitment to purchase advertising or other services or materials that is noncancellable after a specific date. The *firm order date* is the time after which the purchase cannot be canceled.

firmware [computers] software that has been built into hardware, such as programs that are permanently in storage

first bound copy a periodical or other publication that is handbound or the first batch from the bindery, not necessarily representative of final quality; often sent to staff and advertisers

first-choice hyphenation the preferable manner of hyphenating a word, as compared to the alternative version also available

first-class mail letters and postcards that are handled individually and given the fastest nonpremium transportation service available within the country *First-Class Mail* is a trademarked term of the U.S. Postal Service.

first color down in color printing, the sheet printed with the first color

first cover   the front outside cover of a magazine or other publication

first-day story   the first article in a series; an article published immediately after an event, as compared to a *follow-up story* or a *second-day story*

First Folio   the earliest publication of the collected plays of William Shakespeare, published in 1623, about seven years after his death, in FOLIO size (about 12″ × 15″)   A *first folio* (not capitalized) is the first section of four pages in a book or other publication.

first generation   film, tape, photos, or other material copied from the original (the *master*)   It is not of quite as good quality as the original but is superior to a *second-generation* copy or to subsequent generations.

first-in-first-out (FIFO or F.I.F.O.)   an inventory-management system in which older stock is disposed of before newer stock, as opposed to LAST-IN-LAST-OUT   At the close of an accounting period, all of the inventory is valued at the price established at the beginning of the period.

first-line index   an index of poetry or other text with only the first line listed in the index

first man through the door   [film, theater] the villain from 19th-century melodramas, when the first character to enter was the villain

first mile   in satellite communications, the electronic facilities that connect the point of origin to the UPLINK

first-money guarantee   a promise that the first monies received by a theatrical producer or other business will be paid to the theater owner or other specific creditor

first night   the official opening performance of a production   The *first-night list* is a record of the critics, backers, and others invited to attend the *opening night*, as opposed to the *second-night list.*

first-proof print   the first composite print of a film with audio and video; also called *answer print*

First Quarto   the earliest publication of the plays of William Shakespeare, published in 1620 in QUARTO size, about 9″ × 12″; referred to by bibliophiles and Shakespearean scholars as Q1

first refusal   an option or right to accept or reject an offer prior to its being offered to other parties   In most book publishing contracts, a clause—the *right of first refusal*—requires the author to submit a subsequent work for consideration by the same publisher before submitting it to another. The publisher thus has the right of first refusal.

first run   the showing of a movie or other program or attraction preceding subsequent showings, as at a first-run theater   Theaters that show films afterward are *second-run* houses.

firsts   in books, first editions

first-string   the number-one violinist in a symphony orchestra   The term (originally not hyphenated) connotes excellence and sometimes is used as a synonym for the *A-team,* or first team.

first trial print   a master composite of audio and video of a film for screening by the director and others prior to the *release print*; more commonly called *answer print* and also called *first trial composite print* or *trial composite print*

fishbowl   a booth in a television studio for observers, such as sponsors and VIPs

fisheye   a wide-angle lens that covers an angle of view of about 180 degrees, producing a distorted circular image

fishpole   a pole, generally aluminum or bamboo, with a microphone attached at the end; also called a *fishing rod* or *fishpole boom*

fishyback   [marketing] slang for a shipment of cargo containers on a ship

fist   an old word for the *index mark* consisting of a hand with a pointed finger

fitted one   the numeral 1 set on a smaller body than other type in the same FONT to minimize spacing

fitter   [film] a person who adjusts garments to fit; also is called a DRESSER   A performer being *fitted* is paid a *fitting fee* for the *fitting time.*

fitting   an adjustment   A *TV fitting* is a type of rehearsal, generally of a forthcoming live news event such as a political convention, in which stand-ins are used to test camera angles and other technical details.

fit-up halftones   in letterpress printing, separately made halftone plates that are placed together

five and under   a TV role in which a performer has a maximum of five lines   A larger number requires a higher payment.

five-by-five   a slang expression of radio operators to indicate that everything is O.K., transmission is satisfactory in both directions

550 exchange   an exchange maintained by some telephone companies enabling callers to join in conversation with other callers; called the *gab line*   The per-minute cost that is billed to each caller is more than that for a local call.

540 number   an interactive program service of telephone companies enabling users of push-button telephones to respond to questions and elicit information

5K   a 5,000-watt lamp, also called a SENIOR

five minutes, please the traditional call to performers indicating that it is five minutes until the start of the performance; also termed an *act call*, sometimes specifying which act, or worded as "five minutes to curtain"

525-line the number—525—of horizontal scanning *sweeps* per frame, currently the standard for U.S. television transmission Its picture resolution is inferior to the newer *625-line*.

five W's who, what, where, when, and why—the five questions to be considered by journalists and publicists in the writing of a news story In addition to the five W's, there's an H—how.

fix to correct, set, arrest, and complete the development of a photographic image by use of a suitable chemical solution; to determine audio or video level A *fix* is a correction.

fixative a solution sprayed on art to provide a protective coating

fixed directory a telephone directory in which the number assigned to each subscriber remains the same, even if the subscriber's location is changed Such directories are common within a company or other organization.

fixed disk a computer platter with software to run the system; it cannot be removed from the computer

fixed focus a nonadjustable lens The camera lens is focused on a fixed, or set, point, as in a *box camera*.

fixed position the guaranteed location of an ad in a particular medium, such as opposite the table of contents in a magazine; the guaranteed location of a commercial at a specific time on a specific day; also called *fixed location*

fixed rate [broadcasting] a premium-priced commercial that is guaranteed not to be preempted

fixed spacing a typesetting system in which each character occupies the same space regardless of its width; also called *unit spacing*, as opposed to *differential* or *proportional spacing*

fixer a chemical solution—*hypo* or *fixing bath*—to complete and stop the development of photographic images on film or paper *Hardening fixer* is a solution that hardens and protects a film emulsion. A person who is a fixer can do many things, from *fix-it* repairs to guaranteeing the outcome of an election, contest, or event.

FK 5,000, as in a 5,000-watt lamp, used in film The *F* is for five, and the *K* is a symbol for 1,000.

flack a publicist The word probably was used first by *Variety*, the show-business publication, as a term for press agents, stemming from the

World War II term for anti-aircraft, which in turn emanated from the German *Flak*, an abbreviation of *Fliegerabwehrkanone*, an anti-aircraft cannon. Thus, a publicist is a *flak-catcher*.

flag **1** [journalism] the title or name of a newspaper or other publication—its NAMEPLATE or LOGOTYPE—that usually appears at the top of page one or the front cover in a distinctive typeface The flag is not the MASTHEAD, though the words are sometimes used as synonyms. A *floating flag* is a nameplate set narrower than the full width of the page and placed anywhere but the top. **2** [advertising] any item or indicator used to *flag*—call attention to—something, such as the word "New!" on a package or display *Flagging an account* is to pull it out for a specific reason, such as delinquency in payment. In outdoor advertising, *flagging* is the peeling or tearing of the edges of a poster so that it flaps in the wind. **3** [printing] a slug, or sometimes simply a piece of paper, inserted within the type to indicate that an insert or correction is to be made in that place In computerized typesetting, a *flag code* or *precedence code* is a symbol that changes the meaning of the subsequent character. **4** a piece of metal, cloth, or other material used to mask light; also called a *French flag*, GOBO, or *mask*

flagship station the principal or showpiece station of a broadcast network or group

flag waver a performance, particularly the last chorus of a song or a musical number, that arouses the audience, akin to the patriotic stir created by waving a flag

flak See FLACK.

flam a slang word used by jazz musicians for a drumbeat made by striking both drumsticks almost simultaneously on a drum

flange a ridge or shoulder, such as the projection along the edges of the back of a bound book

flanging in audio, mixing a delayed version of a signal with the original signal, creating a swooshing sound, originally produced by pressing, as with a thumb, against the *flange* of a tape recorder to slightly slow down the tape while another tape recorder simultaneously feeds the same soundtrack into a mixer The effect now is achieved by *electronic flangers* that produce a tape delay.

flanker brand a product launched by a company as an extension of an existing major product, designed to protect the basic BRAND by creating increased visibility of the name, increased shelf space, or other assets The word originates from the military, not football, as in a *category leader* covering or protecting its *flank*.

flannelboard a display panel—*board*—covered with a soft, loosely woven cloth, generally wool but also cotton flannel, used to display messages or other items

flap a projecting or hanging piece, such as an envelope flap, sometimes attached to the back of artwork or printed matter and folded over to protect or cover   A *book flap* is the portion of the DUST JACKET folded inside the book on which appears biographical information about the author or promotional material—*flap copy.*

flap-over an optical effect in a film that gives the impression that the picture has been turned over; more commonly called a FLIPOVER

flap paper wrapping paper commonly used in advertising and commercial art to wrap MECHANICALS, art, or other items, akin to a large envelope sized to the item with a flap that often bears the printed or embossed name of an agency or studio

flapping the process of folding over and affixing an end piece (the *flap*), as in mounting a display or art on a *board*

flare a sudden, intense flame; expansion (as with a *flared* material, such as a costume, that opens or spreads outward); a device that produces a bright light; a camera-lens reflection or film *fogging*, such as excess light on the film resulting from pointing the camera at the sun or another intense light source

flash 1 [film, television] a brief disruption of the picture   2 [journalism] a brief sequence or announcement, such as a news bulletin   3 [marketing] an item or fashion look that is attention-getting   4 [photography] a picture taken quickly with a *flashbulb* or other source of high-intensity light   An *open flash* is an exposure made by a *flash unit* during a time exposure. *Painting with flash* is a technique in which a very large area is divided into sections that are small enough to be covered by one flash, after which each section is photographed. 5 [printing] a device that controls light as it is directed through character images; the printing of an image via direction of a light beam   6 [recording] excess vinyl trimmed from the edges of a record after it is pressed   7 [telephone] to quickly depress and release the plunger or switch hook of a phone to signal an operator, or to use a button (a *flash button*) for this purpose   8 [theater] a sudden exposure of nudity   In German, the word for flash is *blitz.*

flash approach an outdoor advertising panel that is close to traffic and is so visible that it can be seen quickly, in a flash

flashback a repeat of something from an earlier scene or event in a narrative, such as a film, either as a reminder to the audience or as a memory on the part of one of the characters; also called *cutback*   An *automated flashback* is a

brief return to past events using only the sound; the visual or video remains the same, as when a character reminisces aloud. *Flash forward* is a similar dramatic or literary device that injects a future event. In film and TV, an *auditory flashback* is the use of sound, such as dialogue or music, to recall a previous event.

flash bulb a small lamp fitted with shredded aluminum or magnesium foil that is ignited by electricity from a battery or other source to produce an intense light of very brief duration for use in still photography   A *flash cube* contains four flash bulbs, each used only once. A *flash lamp* is reusable, whereas a flash bulb generally is not. A *flash unit* is the complete compact system, consisting of the *flash gun* (the holder with the battery), *flash tube* (gas-discharge device) or flash bulb, and perhaps also a reflector.

flashbulb memory instant recall of an event, such as remembering exactly where and when a person heard the news about the assassination of John F. Kennedy on November 22, 1963

flash card [market research] lists, statements, or other material on a card or sheet shown by the interviewer to the respondent

flashcaster a device for superimposing news bulletins or other text over the television picture, generally as a horizontal strip moving across the bottom of the screen

flash cutting [film, television] the use of a series of very brief shots

flasher an electrical advertising sign that turns on and off in rapid sequence   A *chaser flasher* is programmed for the lights to turn off and on in a ripple effect, as if one light is chasing another and turning it off. A *thermal flasher* button reacts to the heat of the electrical flow by breaking the current. A *random flasher* consists of several flashers acting in a nonprogrammed manner.

flash frame [film] a fogged or overexposed frame, a common occurrence at the start of filming when the camera is running below its full speed   A flash frame also can be intentional, such as one or more frames inserted within a shot for an effect or as a FLASHBACK or *flash forward.*

flash-in a double exposure of negative film

flashing a technique in which a film is intentionally exposed to a brief light flash under controlled conditions in the lab in order to increase the *emulsion speed* so that it can be used in low-light photography

flashline a brief one-line headline above the main headline, generally underlined and FLUSH LEFT

flash pan a very fast PAN shot—horizontal movement of the camera—to create a blur   Related to a *flash in the pan* in that the after-effect, too, is blurred, it is also called *flick pan*, *swish pan*, or *zip pan*.

flash panel an outdoor advertising poster that can be seen only at a distance of less than 100 feet If it can be seen only at a distance of less than 25 feet, it is given a zero evaluation in terms of effectiveness.

flash pot or **flashpot** a container with *flash powder* that is ignited to produce smoke, fire, or other theatrical effects

Flash Report a monthly study of advertising expenditures in newspapers compiled for *Advertising Age* by Media Records Inc., New York In retailing, a *flash report* is the total daily gross sales prepared at the end of each day by each department.

flash synchronization the simultaneous opening of a camera shutter and the firing of a FLASH BULB or other light source

flat 1 a photograph, *halftone*, or anything that is dull and lacking in contrast or level, straight, or thin, such as a *stage flat* or *set flat*, a smooth, upright piece of painted scenery with a two-dimensional appearance A *package flat* is a collapsed carton or display. A *flat display* is one in which magazines, books, or packages are displayed face up, with the front toward the viewer or customer. 2 [printing] in offset lithography, the assembled composite of negatives or positives, mostly on GOLDENROD PAPER, ready for plates A *lithographic flat* corresponds to a letterpress typographic form and sometimes is called a *form*. 3 [film] thin, as in a *flat film*, the regular-size screen version of a wide-screen picture or the two-dimensional version of a 3-D picture 4 [mail] oversize first- or third-class mail, including the commonly used 9" × 12" clasp envelopes, called *flat mail* The Postal Service, which handles *flats* separately from standard-size envelopes, considers a flat to be any wrapped or unwrapped mail under 15 inches long, 12 inches high, and ¾ inch thick 5 [writing] one-dimensional, or thin, as in a *flat story* (opposite of a *full story*) or a *flat character* (opposite of a *rounded character*) in a novel or other work

flat art a layout, photograph, or other material to be copied *flat* on a copying surface

flat back [bookbinding] a back or bound edge of a book that has not been rounded and thus is at right angles to the front and back covers; also called *square back*

flatbed a platform, such as a *flatbed truck* with a rear platform for loading A *flatbed film viewer* has a horizontal table over which film is run for viewing and editing. The word is sometimes hyphenated, as in *flat-bed editing machine* or *flat-bed editor*, also called *editing machine, editing table, horizontal editor*, and *table editing machine.*

flat-bed camera a camera used to *microfilm* large documents or other items in which the item is placed on a horizontal plane—FLAT-BED—with the film and document stationary during the exposure Since the process is not continuous, it is also called a *stepwise-operated camera.*

flat-bed press a printing press, sometimes called *flat-bed cylinder press*, in which a moving flat, horizontal surface holds the printing plates while an impression cylinder applies the pressure, as differentiated from a *vertical press* in which the bed is in a vertical position

flat colors colors that are dull, basic, without sparkle In printing, *flat color printing* simply means color printing without blending the colors with shades, tints, or other complexities of such techniques as *process color*.

flat-out a layout in which one column of type is set adjacent to a blank column or is floating in two columns; also called *1-up*

flat proof a reproduction made from type or before *make-ready* rather than from the printing press, used for *proofreading* rather than *quality check*; also called *stone proof*

flat rate a method of pricing for a service; particularly a per-line fixed or set charge, such as a telephone flat rate that provides unlimited service for a specified monthly charge, or the charge for advertising in a medium that does not offer a quantity or other discount

flat stitch the stapling or sewing of pages along the edge or side, also called *side stitch*; not the same as SADDLE STITCH, which is binding along the center fold

flat ticket an individual ticket to a performance with a specific assigned seat; also called a *hard ticket* Tickets for unreserved seats, as in a movie theater, usually are connected on a roll.

Fleet Street an old street in London, England, on which were located several newspaper and press offices; the general name for the London press

fleur-de-lis a heraldic device consisting of a stylized version of a three-petaled iris with the center petal flanked by two curved petals turned outward, used as the emblem of French kings The literal meaning is "flower of the lily."

fleuron a FLEUR-DE-LIS or other stylized flower used in decoration, such as borders or ornamental type

flex to bend In printing, a *flexing system* is a photomechanical arrangement to squeeze or reduce an advertisement or other material to fit a space. The *resizing* process involves movement of the film positive or negative and the *receiving sheet* at different speeds past a light source. See also PLEXOGRAPHIC PRINTING.

flex-form a style of DISPLAY advertising with an irregular, flexible form that seems to float alongside adjacent editorial matter

Flexichrome a process for converting a black-and-white photograph into a color photograph, such as with hand coloring

flexographic printing printing with rubber plates with the image set in relief and using a liquid ink (instead of the paste ink used in letterpress) on foil, cellophane, and waxed and other papers; also called *flexography* or *flex*.

flick a movie or a movie theater Movies used to be called flicks or *flickers* because of the flickering of the light from the projector.

flicker pen a type of lettering pen in which the point flicks open for cleaning, such as a model of SPEEDBALL pen made by Hunt Manufacturing Co., Philadelphia

flier or **flyer** a leaflet, circular, or other printed piece, usually one sheet, used as a HANDBILL or mailing piece; pronounced FLY-er

flies the area directly over a stage containing the overhead lights and other equipment, housed or operated on a *fly floor, fly gallery,* or *fly platform* The fly floor is above the stage.

flight an advertising campaign, generally for radio or TV, that runs for a specific period, such as four weeks The timetable may call for *pre-flight* activity. The period between flights is called a *hiatus,* and the flight itself may be called a *burst. Flight saturation* is the maximum or utmost concentration of advertising within a short period.

flighting [advertising] scheduling patterns characterized by periods of activity—FLIGHTS—separated by periods of inactivity *Blinking* (brief intermittent periods) and *pulsing* (a period of advertising activity of the same duration as the hiatus) are two forms of flighting.

flimsy a duplicate copy, a term used frequently at newspapers

flink [telephone] a signal that is a combination of a FLASH and a *wink*

flint paper a thin paper coated on one side with a shiny, sparkling, flinty color, used by artists to produce a glossy varnished appearance

flip to throw, reverse, or overturn quickly, as to flip a card among several cards on an easel; to change from one side to another, as to flip a record to the flip, or reverse, side; to flip a camera lens (move from one lens to another)

flip card a board or card with a title, name, or message, used on TV or in a show or presentation; also called CUE CARD

flipchart or **flip chart** a series of sheets, sometimes part of a tablet or pad and mounted on an easel, with each sheet connected at the top so that it can be turned—flipped—easily, as in a presentation

flip lens an attachment on an optical printer (or camera and projector linked) used to create a FLIPOVER in film editing

flipover or **flip-over** [film, television] a transitional optical effect, akin to turning over a page; also called *flip, flip frame, flip wipe, flipover wipe, flopover, optical flop,* or *turnaround*

flippers flaps or binders on a *spotlight;* commonly called BARN DOORS

flippy disk a double-sided DISKETTE

flip wipe [film, television] an optical effect in which the picture is turned over to reveal a new scene; also called *flipwipe* or FLIPOVER

float 1 British term for FOOTLIGHT 2 [film] the wavering of an image, such as due to faulty projection A *floating print* is a film print distributed for various showings; it floats from one theater to another, akin to *bicycling.* A *floating release* is a film that is widely distributed and not limited to selective FIRST-RUN theaters. A *floating wall* is part of a wall that can be removed, such as to allow for a camera DOLLY to move in or out of the set.

floater a drifter; a loose piece, such as portable scenery

flocculation [printing] a defective condition in which ink-pigment particles bunch together in *flocks;* also called *livering*

flocking a process of applying tiny fibers or particles of wood, cloth, or other material to form a velvetlike surface, as on wallpaper

flong [printing] a piece of thick, soft cardboard that is pressed onto type or another three-dimensional material so that an impression is made in the cardboard, which then is called a *mat*

flood a FLOODLIGHT *To flood* or *flood out* is to enlarge a beam. The maximum flood, as close to the lens as the lamp can be moved, is called *flood focus.*

floodcoating in papermaking, a process in which a paper is completely covered—*coated*—with a color surface

floodlight a high-intensity light, generally with a reflector, and also the beam of light from such a *luminaire;* commonly called *flood* and, sometimes, *floodlamp*

floor the sales display area of a store; the performance area of a studio In retailing, the *floor* *manager* is in charge of all departments on the floor. In TV, the *floor manager* (*FM*) is the director's assistant, akin to a stage manager in terms of responsibility for all actors, stagehands, and everything on the studio floor. A *floor man* is a GRIP or stagehand reporting to the *stage manager* or *floor director*.

A *floor stand* or *floor dump* is a self-contained standing display. A *floor pyramid* is a merchandise display on the floor, as in a supermarket. *Floor stock protection* is an assurance from the manufacturer to the retailer, such as guaranteeing a rebate if the manufacturer subsequently lowers a price. A floor also is a minimum price for a manuscript or other work.

floor pocket a metal box that contains electrical outlets recessed in the floor of a stage

flop a failure; to fail; to fall or turn, as in turning a photo negative or artwork so that the left and right sides are transposed The mirror image can be obtained without actually turning—*flopping*—the negative or other item; it simply can be exposed from the other or "wrong" side.

flopper a person in an audience who seeks a better seat than the one for which he holds a ticket, such as someone who moves from the balcony to the orchestra

floppy slang for a FLOPPY DISK or disk drive

floppy disk a thin, flexible, removable magnetic storage medium used in computers; also called DISKETTE

floret a small flower; a flowerlike typographic ornament

flow chart a diagram of a sequence of operations, events, or elements in a campaign

flower [printing] a type ornament shaped like a leaf or flower and used for decoration on a page or binding, or, sometimes, any small ornament without a border or frame; also called FLEURON, FLORET, or *printer's flower*

flow-of-life film a narrative film that realistically follows its characters over a period of time

flub an error; to bungle

flubdub a decorative type element; also called DINGBAT

fluff **1** an error, particularly in speech; to make an error **2** to make light and puffy **3** lint, down, or dust particles, as sometimes collect in record grooves or cause problems in printing and photography **4** something light, trivial, without substance. *Hard fluff* is entertainment that is informational.

fluid head a camera mount that has liquid between its moving parts to facilitate smooth movement of the camera on the *tripod* A common type is the *O'Connor fluid head*. Other

types are *geared heads*, such as the *Mini-Worrall* and *friction heads*.

fluorescent lamp an electric lamp that produces light by ionization of the gas within its glass tube *Fluorescence* is a neutral or cold light, as compared to *incandescence*, or warm light. *Fluorite* is a light-colored or colorless mineral.

flush [typography] to make an even or unbroken line or surface; to align with

flush and indent a printing instruction: the first line extended to the margin and the following lines indented, used in listings, as in dictionaries; the opposite of the conventional procedure in which the first line is indented and the following lines are extended to the margin

flush cover a cover that has been trimmed to the same size as the inside text pages

flush left (or right) [typography] type set to line up at the left (or right) margin; abbreviated as *fl* and *fr* in copyediting or proofreading In computerized typesetting, a flush left (also called *left aligned* or *left justified*) can be obtained with a *quad left* code. Flush right (also called *right aligned* or *right justified*) requires a *quad right* code.

flush paragraphs paragraphs without indentation

fluting **1** a decoration consisting of grooves that are long and narrow, like a musical flute; the grooves themselves, or the process of making the grooves **2** [film] the swelling and bending of a film edge due to humidity or improper (too tight) winding; also called *edgewaving*

flutter to wave; to flap; erratic vibration or distortion, such as from frequency deviations resulting from faulty recording or reproduction *Picture flutter* is irregular bouncing or flapping of the picture on a TV screen. In recording, flutter may be due to uneven turntable speed or uneven motion of a film or tape machine.

fly to suspend or move scenery or other items above the visible performance area, or stage This high area is called the FLIES or *fly loft*. A *fly plot* is a diagram of the lighting and other equipment attached to the flies; it is also called *grid plan* or *plot*, *rigging plan* or *plot*, *hanging plot*, or *line plot*.

flyback [television] to retrace, specifically the movement of a SCANNING SPOT, or electronic beam, from the end of a line of the target area or FIELD to the beginning of the next line or field

fly bill a pamphlet; see also FLY SHEET

flyboy a person who works in the upper area of a machine, such as one who drops inserts into a newspaper The origin is the slang word for an aviator. The flyboy is not the electrician or stagehand who works in the space above the stage called the FLIES.

flyer a small advertising circular; also spelled FLIER

fly-floor or **fly floor** a narrow platform in a theater midway above the stage floor or higher; also called *fly* The lines or ropes to the scenery are attached to the PIN-RAIL on the fly-floor. In theaters with more than one fly gallery, the lower or lowest one is called the fly-floor.

fly gallery a narrow platform on a side wall of a stage where the lines to the scenery are attached; also called *fly-floor* or operating gallery In modern theaters, the scenery usually is controlled from the stage.

flying head [recording] a device that erases—a *flying erase head*—or reproduces—a *flying reproduce head*—only one track of a tape instead of the entire tape

flying paster an automatic device that splices a new roll of paper onto one being used without stopping the press, common in high-speed newspaper WEB presses; also called *automatic paster*

flying spot a device that converts film into a format suitable for TV transmission It consists of a cathode-ray tube that sends a light—a flying spot—through each film frame onto a photocell. Flying spots and other devices with the same purpose are called TELECINE machines.

flying spot scanner a machine that transfers an image from film to videotape A white light is projected through each film frame and scans, or flies over, each line onto color photocell-receptors behind the film that react to changes in color and density encountered by the scanning light.

flyleaf a page that is free from printing but is part of a printed SIGNATURE, such as front or back pages in a book The *front flyleaf* sometimes is used for an inscription or autograph by the author.

fly sheet a pamphlet, such as a CIRCULAR that is distributed free; also called *fly bill* The origin is *flying sheet*.

fly title A HALF-TITLE of a book, printed on the right side of the leaf preceding the page with the full title; also called BASTARD TITLE

flywalk a narrow rim on the upper part of a stage wall near the ceiling lights

FM FREQUENCY MODULATION; FLOOR manager

fn. FOOTNOTE

FNN Financial News Network, a cable network and broadcast programming service based in New York

f-number a ratio of *focal length* to the effective diameter in the aperture of a camera lens system

FO fade-out; see FADE-IN

foamcore a board consisting of two sheets of shiny paper with Styrofoam (polystyrene, a lightweight plastic) between them It is commonly used for presentations and displays.

F.O.B. FREE ON BOARD

focal pertaining to focus The *focal length* of a camera lens is the distance between an *optical point*, called the *nodal point*, in the lens and the film when the lens is focused at infinity. It's the principal characteristic of a camera lens and also is called *angle of view*, *angular field*, or *covering power*. Shorter focal-length lenses cover wider *fields of view*. A 24mm lens, for example, has a field of view of 82°, as compared to a 200mm lens, which has a field of view of about 12°. The most common lens is 50mm, with a field of view of about 46°, comparable to that of the human eye. The *focal plane* is the position at the back of the camera where the image is focused on the film. A camera may have a *focal plane shutter*, a curtain next to the film with speeds faster than those of the standard lens shutter. The *focal point* is the place at which light rays converge, or are concentrated, after passing through a lens or being reflected from a mirror.

focus the position in which a camera image appears clearly To *focus in* or *focus up* is to move a camera lens so that the image appears clearly, as from a blur to sharpness; used as a direction to a photographer or camera operator, it is also called *iris in*. To *focus out*, or *iris out*, is to deliberately move the camera out of focus (*lose the focus*), as in moving from one scene to another. *Deep focus* has great *depth of field*, whereas *shallow focus* or *selective focus* emphasizes only one plane, such as the FOREGROUND.

focus group a market-research technique consisting of a discussion about a topic or product by several people, conducted by a *focus group leader*, to determine attitudes and opinions The cost of a typical session is about $2,500; an average study uses five sessions. The term often is misspelled as *focused group*, its original name. When used with another noun it can be hyphenated, as in focus-group research, in which the interviewer focuses the discussion on one or more specific subjects.

focus layout an arrangement, as of a newspaper or magazine page, in which there is a single prominent point of attention—the *focal point*—such as the major article on the upper right, a headline across the page, or a large photo or other element

focus puller [film] the first assistant cameraman, the person who adjusts the focus and changes the film magazines; primarily a British term A more common title is *first camera assistant.*

fog a blur or clouding, as on a photo negative, resulting from chemicals during development—*chemical fog*—or stray light during the picture-taking or development—*light fog*

Fog Index a method of evaluating the readability of sentences, based on average length and percentage of difficult, or foggy, words The system was developed by Robert Gunning and described in his 1968 book, *The Technique of Clear Writing.* For example, text with an average sentence length of 20 words, of which about 10 percent are three syllables or more, has a Fog Index of 12 (20 plus 10 is 30, multiplied by 0.4, which is 12), indicating that it's on the 12th-grade level.

foil **1** a thin sheet or leaf of metal, such as gold foil or silver foil, that is used for decorative packaging *Foil stamping* is a method of printing on foil. **2** a person or thing that sets off or enhances another by contrast, such as a meek or villainous *foil character* in a play or other work.

fold the space or crease at the junction of two folded parts or a part that has been folded over another Styles of folds include *upright* (vertical), *oblong* (horizontal), *parallel, accordion, right angle,* and *square.* The *second chopper fold* or *mail fold* is made after the first fold and is parallel to it. A *foldin* is a large sheet folded to fit into a publication; it is also called FOLDOUT or GATEFOLD. A *long fold* refers to paper with grain along its long dimension; its opposite, *broad fold,* is folded with its grain along the short dimension. *Above the fold* is the top half of a BROADSHEET.

foldback a type of small loudspeaker commonly used in a TV studio or on a stage so that performers can hear music or other sound; also called PLAYBACK

folded book a volume consisting of a strip of paper creased (folded) accordion-fashion and attached at one or both ends to stiff covers, used in the Orient and elsewhere, generally for scenic pictures; also called *folding book*

folded plate an oversize sheet (plate) bound into a book by one edge and folded to fit the book; also called *folding plate* It differs from a *double plate,* a double-size leaf folded in the center and attached in the center—at the FOLD.

folder a printed piece with one or more *folds* in which, when *folded,* each panel constitutes a separate page; also, a machine that folds paper

folding dummy [book production] blank sheets *folded* to resemble the finished product; also called IMPOSITION CHART

foldout a sheet or insert wider than the page width of a publication, folded one or more times to fit into or occupy the same width as the pages of the publication; also called GATEFOLD

fold symbol a letter or other symbol indicating the number of leaves of a book, such as *F* for FOLIO (a sheet folded once to make two leaves, or four pages)

Foley a replacement sound effect, performed by a *Foley artist* (a sound-effects specialist) or *Foley editor* using a *Foley mixer,* to add footsteps or other sounds to action already recorded on *Foley tracks* *Foley work* is done on a *Foley stage.* A *Foley walker* follows a performer and adds appropriate sound effects. Foley also is used as a verb to indicate the addition of sound to film, as in *Foleying in.* The *Foley crew* credits often appear at the end of movies, particularly those with extensive sound effects, though many viewers familiar with various photography and other credits are not familiar with the Foley credit. The inventor was Jack Foley (1891–1967) of Universal Studios.

foliation numbering of the leaves of a book

folio **1** a page number In book publishing, a folio is usually set in the upper right-hand corner of a *recto,* or right-hand page, and in the upper left-hand corner of a *verso.* **2** a sheet of paper 17″ × 22″, a standard size that when printed and folded results in two 8½″ × 11″ pages **3** a book with large pages, such as 15″ high. Other page sizes include *elephant folio* (about 23″), *atlas folio* (about 25″), and *double elephant folio* (about 50″). British book sizes include *Foolscap Folio* (about 13½″ × 10″), *Crown Folio* (about 15″ × 10″), and *Royal Folio* (about 20″ × 12½″).

In newspapers, the folio is the box or line, generally across the top of page one below the NAMEPLATE, with volume number, date, and edition; the page number appears at the top of each page on the *folio line.* In books and magazines, the page number sometimes appears at the bottom of the page and is called a *drop folio.* An *expressed folio* is a printed page number. *Folio publishing* is printing on paper, as opposed to electronic publishing.

folk of, originating among, or having to do with the common people, who transmit their general culture through succeeding generations in *folk art* and *folk music* A *folk dance* is a traditional dance of the common people of a country or region. *Folk songs* generally are anonymous, as is a *folk story* or *folk tale.* A *folk singer* specializes in singing folk songs. *Folk rock* is rock-and-roll music with words in a folk-song style.

folklore all of the unwritten traditional beliefs, legends, sayings, and customs of a culture; the myths, proverbs, songs, and stories of a people or FOLK

follow the second part of an article in a daily newspaper or other publication, appearing in the same issue as a SIDEBAR or update or subsequently as a *follow-up* or *second-day story*

follow copy an instruction to the typesetter to set the type exactly like the copy in every detail; sometimes spelled *folo copy* and also *follow style*

follow focus a movie-camera control to enable the lens to change focus as it or the subject moves, such as from close-up to long shot The member of the camera crew who does this is called a FOCUS PULLER. In British films and TV productions, the terms *follow focus* and *focus puller* often appear in the credits. In the United States, the term *first assistant cameraman* is used.

follow f-stop to change a camera lens setting from one F-STOP to another

following reading matter an instruction for an advertisement to appear next to or on a page subsequent to editorial material This preferred position, also called FULL POSITION, sometimes commands an extra charge.

follow shot a movement of a camera to follow the action; also called *following shot, action shot, moving shot, running shot,* or *tracking shot*

follow spot a spotlight that focuses on and follows a performer; usually located in the rear of the balcony of the theater, in a projection booth or sometimes on the sides of the balcony or mezzanine

follow-up a call, visit, advertisement, mailing, or other action subsequent to initial action A *follow-up question* is related to a previous one, as at a press conference. Some newspapers publish a column titled *Follow-up* with reports on what has happened regarding people or events previously in the news.

folo copy See FOLLOW COPY.

font a complete assortment of type of one size and style; originally spelled *fount* All of the sizes comprise a typeface. The *font number* identifies each font, so a typeface includes several font numbers. In typewriters or word processors, the font is the device that produces the characters, such as the *ball* or *daisy wheel* of a typewriter or the *dot matrix array* or *print chain* element of a word processor. The *font change character (FC)* is the control in these machines that changes the typeface, size, or shape of the set of characters or *graphemes*. Font also refers to the container used to

store the characters in a font, such as a *film strip*, DISK, *grid*, or *case*. It's also a TV instruction to superimpose text, such as titles, on the screen; this is more commonly called *key* (CHROMA-KEY) or *CG (character generated)*.

Food and Drug Administration (FDA or **F.D.A.)** the U.S. agency that regulates food and drugs sold in interstate commerce The F.D.A. was created in 1938 in accordance with the Food, Drug and Cosmetic Act.

food days days on which there is the greatest amount of supermarket and other food advertising, generally Wednesday and Thursday Many newspapers issue special sections on these days, which can be particularly important for food and other publicity.

foolscap a sheet of paper about 13″ × 16″; pronounced FOOLS-cap Originally, this large writing paper had a *watermark* of a gaily decorated cap with bells, as worn by royal court jesters.

foot the bottom edge of a printed piece; in literary composition, a combination of stressed and unstressed syllables that determine the rhythm, a unit of meter Types of feet include *anapestic, dactylic, iambic, spondaic,* and *trochaic*. The number of feet in a verse are *monometer* (one foot), *dimeter* (two feet), *trimeter* (3), *tetrameter* (4), *pentameter* (5), *hexameter* (6), and *heptameter* (7).

footage length A portion of a film is called footage, such as *daily footage* or *news footage*. The *footage counter* indicates the amount of film or tape already used or remaining in a camera, recorder, or projector.

footcandle a standard unit of illumination—the amount of light thrown onto a surface 12 inches from one candle or its equivalent

footer text at the bottom of a page, such as a page number or FOOTNOTE

foot irons metallic hardware used to weight scenery so that it falls to the floor and stays in place

footlights a row of lights along the front of a stage; also called *foots* The word often refers to the theatrical field in general. *Footlighters* are performers. A *footlight spot* is a small *spotlight* in the *footlight trough*, a recess or well at the front of the stage.

footnote (fn.) a reference, explanation, or comment at the bottom of a page or end of a chapter or article Material at the end of a book chapter also can be called *chapter notes*. The *footnote callout* is the number or symbol, usually an asterisk or dagger, within the text that directs the reader's attention from the footnoted material to the appropriate footnote. In an annual report or legal document, the footnotes may occupy a full page or more. *Footnote capability* is the ability of a computer system to identify footnote callouts and footnotes and handle the process of *footnoting*. An *automatic footnote tie-in* is a word-processing device that links a footnote to a specific text, so that if the text segment is moved, the footnote moves with it.

footnote reference system a method of citing references numerically at the bottom of the page

footprint [telecommunications] the area on earth in which the signal of a specific satellite can be received A *footprint map* shows *contour data* of satellites with various signal strengths.

force a group, such as a *sales force* In photography, *forcing* is *pushing* or overdeveloping film or paper, typically to compensate for *underexposure*.

forced distribution a marketing technique involving the purchase of a product by a retailer due to pressure or a special inducement from the supplier, such as in anticipation of considerable promotion

forced scale in multiple-choice questionnaires, omission of a "no opinion" choice

fore forward; front A *forecast* is a prediction. *Forefront* is the foremost or most prominent position. FOREGROUND is the part of a picture or scene closest to the viewer. *Forehand* means done earlier or in advance. *Forepart* is the first portion. To FORESHADOW is to suggest in advance, such as by revealing clues or tips in a script prior to the anticipated event or disclosure. *Foreshorten* is to curtail or compress, as with a wide-angle or telephoto lens that enlarges objects and brings the image closer but tends to distort or compress it. A FOREWORD is the preface or introduction to a book, often written by someone other than the author of the main body.

fore-edge the front edge of a book, the opposite of the SPINE The *fore-edge margin* is the outer margin of a page.

fore-edge painting a picture painted on the FORE-EDGES of a book that can be seen when the leaves are opened obliquely and fanned This technique was common in the 18th century.

foreground a part of a scene nearest, or represented as nearest, to the viewer; the most noticeable position *Foreground treatment* is the arrangement of props or other items in the foreground of a shot or scene. In computers, *foreground processes* have a higher priority than *background processes*.

foreground music indigenous or source music, originating from musicians, a radio, a record

player, or some other source shown in a film, play, or other work, as opposed to music added to the soundtrack

foreign advertising advertising in countries other than the headquarters of the advertiser In classified telephone directories, foreign advertising is in directories outside the city in which the advertiser is located A *foreign directory* is a telephone directory other than the local one.

Foreign Broadcast Information Service a unit of the Central Intelligence Agency (CIA) in Langley, VA that translates and publishes a DAILY REPORT of news items from foreign broadcast and print media; abbreviated as *FBIS*, pronounced FIH-bis

forelengthening a photographic or film effect that produces an exaggerated increase of depth in an image when using a *wide-angle lens*

foreshadowing an indication of something to come, such as a character in a play or other work, introduced in a seemingly incidental manner but really a sign or presage

foreshortening a photographic or film effect that produces an exaggerated decrease of depth in an image when using a *long-focus* or TELEPHOTO LENS In photography and art, some parts of an object or figure are represented as shorter than they are to give the illusion of their proper relationship. The technique is particularly important in depicting reclining figures or in other situations in which the dimensions otherwise would appear out of their correct proportion.

forestage the front part of a PROSCENIUM stage, the part that extends out into the audience area; more commonly called an APRON

foreword in a book or other work, a preliminary part before the main part, generally beginning on a *recto*—right-hand—page It is sometimes called a PREFACE or INTRODUCTION, though technically there are differences. In a preface, the author provides background information, such as how the project started, and also may list acknowledgments. The introduction, which follows the preface, may be written by someone other than the author of the book and sets the scene, perhaps with a summary.

forgetting rate a measure of the degree to which the recall or memory of an advertisement is retained, such as between appearances of the ad

form an assemblage of type and other printing materials *locked up* in a rectangular metal frame—a *chase*; also, several pages printed on one side of one large sheet that is folded to place the pages in proper sequence The standard number of pages to a form is eight, or multiples of eight, so that a large form for a large press can hold 16, 24, or more pages. The British spelling is *forme*.

formalism emphasis on form, structure, or technique, as opposed to content or subject   It was practiced by Russian and other formalist filmmakers in the 1920s.

format **1** general arrangement or plan   **2** [printing] the shape, size, binding, typeface, paper, and overall makeup of a job   **3** [broadcasting] the general character of the programs, such as all-news, classical, or country-and-western music   **4** [computers] the arrangement or layout of data   *Formatting a disk* is the procedure for making the disk compatible with the system. *Format codes* are called or called up to activate a specific size, shape, typeface, or other format. *Free format* permits spacing that is different from the system's. In word processing, format is the appearance of a page or document regarding spacing, style, layout, and other components. The *format tape* carries the layout or makeup instructions, particularly on the *format line*, the first line with instructions.

formative research a study conducted before or during a public relations or other campaign to help in its development by establishing goals or other criteria that can be executed

format 30 a style at *The New York Times* and other media that designates the end of a story with —30—

formatting the establishment of a format or procedure; in typesetting, the insertion of typographic instructions to direct the machine   *Galley formatting* produces text in continuous columns. *Page formatting* positions the text within a specific page area.

former a device on a *web-fed* printing press that makes a longitudinal FOLD   Full-size newspapers have such a fold, called a *former fold* or *newspaper fold*. A *double former fold* makes two folds, as with a large sheet. The former, or *former folder*, folds the web—roll of paper—in half in the direction of *web travel*.

form letter a standardized format for communication to several or many recipients; also called *guide letter*, *repetitive letter*, or *standard letter*   Form letters may be individualized or personalized with a *salutation* or other FILL-INS. A *form paragraph* is standardized text for convenient drop-in or other use in letters or other material; it is also called BOILERPLATE or a *canned* or *guide* paragraph.

forms close in print media, the *closing date* or last day on which an advertisement may be delivered for publication in a specific issue

forms flash a printing technique in which a *laser printer* prints part of a letter, ranging from just the *letterhead* to most of the message, with room for individualized FILL-IN; also called *forms overlay*   It is commonly used for invoices and other forms.

form-sided trim [printing] the cutting of all four sides of a sheet to remove any reference or registration marks and give a clear edge

formula a fixed form of words; a rule or method for doing something unoriginal, such as a formula for a sitcom (*formula writing*)

formula novel a fictional work produced in accordance with a specific format or guidelines, such as mysteries, romances, and Westerns

formula story a script or other work that follows a familiar plot

formulistic talk conventional (according to a formula) conversation that is relatively meaningless

Fortran a computer programming language for scientific problems and other subjects that can be expressed algebraically; from *Formula Translation*, and sometimes written in all caps

48mo *fortyeightmo*, a 96-page — 48 leaves — book

forwarding [book production] the process after the sewing or leaf affixing, including ROUNDING and BACKING, before the finishing

for your information (FYI) a notation, generally abbreviated, used frequently on memos or BUCK SLIPS   It is also the name of the Time, Inc. employee publication.

foto photo   A *fotog* is a photographer.

fotonovela a photonovel, a combination of photos with captions and conversation in balloons, akin to comic books, often with advertising   Fotonovelas are popular in Latin America. The types of themes include *fotonovela rosa* (featuring a virtuous heroine and her rich suitor), *fotonovela suave* (with middle-class characters), and *fotonovela roja* (with working-class characters).

foul referring to dirty copy, with many errors or hard to read   *Foul matter* or a *foul proof* is DEAD, no longer alive or needed, already corrected, or used.

foundation light a base light, for basic illumination, to which BACK LIGHTS, FILL-IN LIGHTS, and other lights may be added

foundry type type in which individual characters are set by hand, not necessarily in a *foundry*, which is a shop in which *electrotypes* and *stereotypes* are made   Foundry type is used repeatedly and is not remelted after a single use, as is LINOTYPE or other machine type.

fountain the reservoir on a printing press that holds and dispenses ink or another liquid, such as *fountain solution* (water and chemicals) used in the dampening system and to keep nonprinting areas from accepting ink *Split-fountain printing* is a multicolor process in which a divider separates the ink colors on the inking roller or the roller is actually cut so that the colors do not mix.

4-across-5 a layout in which four columns of set type are set in a five-column area

four A's American Association of Advertising Agencies, a trade association of major advertising agencies headquartered in New York

four-color process reproduction of artwork with a variety of printing plates, sometimes called *four-color process plates*; abbreviated *4/C* Four plates—yellow, red, blue, and black—are combined to create a complete range of colors. Technically, the blue plate is *cyan*.

Fourdrinier a papermaking machine that produces a continuous strip or roll, developed by Sealy and Henry Fourdrinier, 19th-century English papermakers

four-hour call the minimum work period for which some union workers may be paid, as at an exhibition

four-letter word an expletive or short word having to do with sex or excrement, generally four letters (though the term is also used generically for words of other lengths)

four P's product, price, promotion, and place—the four elements in the marketing of products and services The marketing strategy is a selected combination of the four *P's*.

fourth-class mail the mail category that includes domestic *parcel post*, bound printed matter, and special-rate items such as books, sound recordings, manuscripts, and *library-rate* materials

fourth cover the outside back cover of a magazine or other publication

fourth estate the press, as it became known when the statesman Edmund Burke (1729–97) referred to the *reporter's gallery* in Parliament as the fourth estate The three estates represented in Parliament were the clergy or church, the nobility or peerage, and the common people, or, as they are called in the English Constitution, the Lords Spiritual, the Lords Personal, and the Commons. The phrase often is capitalized.

fourth generation a device or system that is significantly more advanced than the preceding (third-) generation models, such as fourth-generation computers introduced in the 1980s that utilize microprocessors and memory chips

4to quarto, an eight-page (four leaves) book

four-up labels labels produced in four columns on a sheet with horizontal sequences; also called *four-up East-West* labels (though since it's horizontal from left to right, it really should be called *West-East*)

four wall an indoor theater A *four-wall booking* is a rental of a theater by a film distributor, with all costs borne by the distributor rather than the theater owner or exhibitor.

Fox Broadcasting Company (FBC) a major producer of programs for its own stations and affiliated independent stations, headquartered in Los Angeles, with the same ownership as 20th Century-Fox Television, a major producer of motion pictures and TV programs

foxing brown discoloration of paper produced by chemical or metal impurities *Foxed paper* often is found in old books.

fox message a standardized text, used as a test, that includes all the letters and numbers and some of the punctuation marks on a keyboard, such as "The quick brown fox jumped over the lazy dog's back, 1234567890."

foyer [theater] the outer lobby, the area with the ticket windows

FPF frames per foot of film

FPO Fleet Post Office, for the U.S. Navy

F.P.O. for position only: a notation on a layout indicating where artwork or photos will be located

fps or **f.p.s.** feet per second; FRAMES PER SECOND

fr. FRAME; from

f.r. FOLIO recto: right-hand page

FR or **fr** from, as on the *from line* of a memo, FR: (name of sender)

fraction a *quotient* of two quantities, consisting of a *numerator* on top or to the left, a *denominator* on the bottom or the right, and a line separating the two A *solid fraction* already exists in a FONT, such as ½ and other common fractions, whereas *piece fractions* or *built-up fractions* are created by the typesetter. A *split* or *horizontal fraction* consists of a numerator centered directly over the denominator, separated by a horizontal line, whereas the more common version uses a diagonal or SLASH line to separate the numerator and denominator and is called an *adaptable fraction* or *solidus*. An *em fraction* has a diagonal divider and is one EM in width. An *en fraction* has a horizontal divider and is narrower—one EN in width.

fractur German *black-letter* or *blackface* type, a Roman typeface with angular broken lines; also spelled *fractur* *Fraktur writing*, common among the Pennsylvania Dutch in the 18th century, generally was illuminated and ornamented and used for certificates as well as art (*fraktur painting*).

frame 1 each picture in a film or single unit on a storyboard; the *field of view* of a camera; to mount a photo or illustration or place it within a border or frame; to adjust a camera or projector using a *framing control* or other controls to adjust height, width, and centering so that a full frame appears on the screen 2 [television] a complete *scanning* of an image (525 lines in the U.S. system), requiring $1/60$ of a second each for the odd- and even-numbered lines for a total of $1/30$ of a second A *half-picture*, consisting of either the odd- or even-numbered lines, is called a *field*. In motion pictures, a frame runs $1/24$ of a second. The *frame frequency* is the number of times per second the picture area is covered or scanned. In TV, it is 30 *cycles per second (cps)*. A *frame store* is a video device to retain single frames for recall. A *frame enlargement*, often used in publicity, is a blowup of an individual frame. A *frame synchronizer* aligns or synchronizes pictures from different sources, such as inside and outside the studio. 3 [computers] a portion of a tape, sequence of bits, or other segment, such as a rectangular area in a facsimile system In computer graphics, a frame is a common term for whatever is on the screen. A *frame buffer* is a memory device that stores the contents of an image by handling one *pixel* at a time. The *depth* of the frame buffer, which determines the colors, is the number of BITS per pixel. A *frame grabber* is a device that captures a frame for storage or display. A *frame store* or *page store* is a memory unit for storage of frames. 4 [videotex] the basic unit of information storage and display, a discrete amount of material that can be accommodated at one time within the viewing area of a user terminal; also called a *page* or *screen Frame* or *page creation* is the process of assembling the elements of a single frame. A *frame set* is a group of frames in sequential order identified by a number. 5 [newspapers] a layout in which a single article fills the entire column on the left side and another article fills the entire column on the right, so that the two form a frame for the page

frame buffer in computer graphics, a memory device that stores the PIXELS The "depth" of the frame buffer is the number of BITS per pixel, which determines the colors.

frame counter a device in a film camera or projector (part of a *film counter* or *footage counter*) that counts the number of frames of each foot of film that passes through it

frame-grabber a device on a TV set to select still pictures—FRAMES—or blocks of text from a bank of such materials for cable-TV subscribers

frame line a narrow unexposed area between adjacent pictures on a film Actually, there are two horizontal frame lines, the bottom line on the frame and the top line on the frame below it.

frame margin the space within a film frame between the image area and the FRAME LINE, sometimes used as a code area to identify the item

frame pitch the distance between corresponding points in adjacent frames of a film

frame puller a control in a film projector enabling the projectionist to align the frames so that the FRAME LINES don't show; also called FRAMER

framer a control in a film projector ensuring that each frame is aligned and the FRAME LINES are not shown; also called FRAME PULLER

frame rate the speed at which film passes the lens of a camera (also called *camera speed*) or projector (also called *projector speed*)

frames per foot the number of frames in each foot of film; abbreviated as *FPF* 8mm film has 80 FPF; Super 8 has 72 FPF; 16mm has 40 FPF; Super 16 has 40 FPF; 35mm has 16 FPF, and 70mm has $12^4/5$ FPF.

frames per second the number of frames of a film that pass through a camera or projector each second; abbreviated as *FPS* Silent films were about 16 FPS; 35mm sound film is 24 FPS, or 90 feet per minute.

frame-stopping terminal a device that isolates a single photo or frame of a film for viewing as a *still* picture on a TV screen; also called *frame grabber* and *single-frame terminal*

frame story a narrative that connects a series of incidents or stories

framework structure; arrangement; system

franchise a contractual agreement between a manufacturer, service organization (such as McDonald's), or other *franchisers* and independent businesspersons—*franchisees*—who purchase the right to own and operate a retail unit and/or to sell the franchised products or services A *franchise label* is a brand sold exclusively in an area by a retailer. A company with an extremely dominant position in an area or market is said to have a franchise.

franchise position a specific position in a newspaper or magazine reserved for an advertiser through an agreement with the publisher

frank the privilege of sending mail free, as by members of Congress; a mark or signature indicating this privilege, such as on an envelope; any letter sent this way *Franked mail* must have the sender's signature printed on the envelope or wrapper.

Franklin Gothic   a *sans-serif* typeface designed by Benjamin Franklin, the 18th-century diplomat who also was a printer

freak   [journalism] a story about an odd or extremely unusual occurrence, event, or experience

free   in a layout, loose or open   A *free page* has an unconventional layout.

free association   the joining of two words, symbols, or ideas, as when a person spontaneously reacts to a stimulus, such as a word, sound, or image, with another word or phrase   This *nondirective* interview technique is used to encourage uninhibited reactions.

freebie   jargon for anything of value that is presented free, such as a press junket or trip

free cinema   a realistic nonfiction film, a British term for CINEMA VERITÉ

free circulation   a publication provided at no charge to readers

free frame   the effect of frozen or suspended motion by repetition of a single frame of a film; to hold a frame, or stop action

free goods   merchandise provided at no cost to a wholesaler or retailer as an incentive in a deal or other promotion

freehand   1 drawn by hand without the aid of a tracing, DRAFTING, or other device, such as a *freehand sketch*, which generally is a loose, open, or informal rendition   2 an omnidirectional camera support   Freehand is not the same as *freestyle*, which is a competitive event, as in swimming, in which the contestant has a choice of styles

freehand signature   a handwritten signature that is similar to the original, sometimes used in form letters

freelance or **freelancer**   an independent artist, photographer, writer, or other person who is self-employed; used as a noun and verb   Both words are commonly hyphenated (*free-lance*), and *freelance* is occasionally spelled as two words (*free lance*).

free matter   postal material for the blind and military mail transmitted free of postage, bearing the *postage and fees paid* indicia

free on board (F.O.B.)   no charge for shipping, generally followed by the location of the shipping point at which charges begin   For example, *F.O.B. Detroit* means that a customer pays for shipping charges from Detroit to the receiving point.

free publication   a publication distributed without cost to the recipient, via controlled or QUALIFIED CIRCULATION

free sheet   paper made of chemical pulp without any ground wood (mechanical pulp)

free-standing newspaper insert (fsi)   a printed section or supplement, generally advertising, inserted or *stuffed* in a newspaper or other publication   The largest producer is *Valessis Inserts*, Livonia, MI.

free-standing store   a retail outlet that is independent and occupies a separate area not connected with a shopping center or other stores

free verse   poetry without regular meter, rhyme, line length, or stanza form, generally using the natural speech rhythms of the language

freeze   to pass from liquid to solid by heat loss; to become rigid, fixed, or set; to maintain or hold a condition, as in a *salary* or *budget freeze*, or, in a performance, to remain completely still and in place   *Freeze frame* is a film technique in which a single frame is repeated or reprinted in sequence to give the effect of frozen, suspended, or stopped motion. Also called *hold frame* or *stop frame*, the technique often is used at the end of a theatrical or TV film as a final scene that remains motionless for a short period.

freeze date   the last day that copy or other material for a publication or other work can be changed, as the work then goes on press or is produced   To a writer, artist, or other creator, this day sometimes is called the *drop dead date.*

French curve   a prepared curve, made of plastic, in a variety of common irregular shapes, used by artists as guides

French doors   a type of GATEFOLD—an extended-size page folded over—that opens from side to side   This is more common than *Dutch doors*, which open at the top and/or bottom.

French flag   a small cloth attached to a pole or arm to block light; a type of GOBO

French-fold   a type of FOLD for pieces printed on only one side, usually an eight-page mailing piece, only four pages of which are printed; a common format for greeting cards

French guard   the back edge of an INSERT, turned over and folded around a SIGNATURE

French joint   [book production] the *free-swinging* inside strip—*joint*—produced by inserting the cover material into the space between the edge of the cover boards and the ridge of the back   It is also called an *open joint*, whereas a *closed joint* or *tight joint* has the boards laced on tight against the *spine.*

French letter   a narrow typeface, such as the DIDOT typeface developed in France by François Didot (1730–1804)

French rule a tapered *rule*, or dash, called a BO-DONI DASH, that is thicker in the middle than at the ends

French scene [theater] a part of a scene; a sequence

French's edition the authorized performance edition of a play, published by Samuel French of New York and London

French spacing the insertion of additional space after a punctuation symbol, equal to the regular space between words

freq. FREQUENCY; frequently

frequency (freq.) the number of advertisements, broadcasts, or "exposures" during a time period A *frequency discount*, also called *quantity* or *time discount*, is provided to advertisers for quantity purchases. Frequency and REACH are two primary measurements that often are linked. In outdoor advertising, frequency is the number of times in a month that an individual has the opportunity to see a particular advertisement.

frequency modulation (FM) the encoding of a *carrier wave*, such as the sound waves or audio signals of a radio or TV station, by the variation—*modulating*—of its frequency, resulting in little or no static and high fidelity in reception FM radio stations, from 88 to 108 *megahertz*, produce reception superior to that of *AM* or *amplitude modulation* stations, particularly of music in the high-frequency range. The early FM stations were devoted mostly to classical music and required special FM sets. Today, most radio sets have AM and FM bands, and over half of the American radio audience listens to FM programs. There are about 4,000 commercial and 1,300 noncommercial FM radio stations in the United States.

fresh air [graphic arts] white space, as in a layout

Fresnel reflected light devices, named after Augustin Jean Fresnel (1788–1827), a French physicist; pronounced fray-NELL or fruh-NELL *Fresnel mirrors* are two linked mirrors almost in the same plane from which light is reflected in slightly different directions. A *Fresnel light* has an adjustable lens, the *Fresnel lens*, which has concentric convex rings and is placed in front of the bulb as a *condenser lens* to concentrate the light. Because it is easy to handle, it is widely used in the theater, TV, and film—so commonly that Fresnel sometimes is not capitalized.

friar an archaic expression for a light ink blot A *monk* was a heavier smudge. The *Friars Club* is a theatrical club in New York.

friction head a camera mount in which the moving metal parts are in direct contact; not a

fluid head or *geared head* and therefore not used for slow, careful movements of the camera

friend-of-a-friend [direct marketing] a technique of offering an incentive to customers who refer new customers; also called *third-party referral*

frill a ruffle; wrinkling along the edge, particularly of a film *Frilling* of a film, plate, or print may occur in processing that is too hot, too long, or overly agitated so that the emulsion around the edges separates.

fringe area the outermost or weakest area of a broadcast signal or a publication's distribution

fringe publication a publication of secondary importance to a particular advertiser or audience

fringe time a transitional period of a broadcast schedule, immediately before or after the peak period—*prime time*

frisket a mask made of *frisket paper* or another material—*frisket solution*—placed over areas of a photo not to be retouched or used to cover other areas, such as *dead areas* not to be printed A *frisket knife* is a small knife commonly used in graphic arts, also called an *art knife* (though there are other types of art knives). It has a permanent blade and is disposable. In the *frisket technique*, which can be used on any surface, lettering or art is traced on translucent paper that is affixed, as with rubber cement, to the surface; the paper within the lettering or art then is cut away, and this area is sprayed or colored.

frisky furniture *Wall Street Journal* jargon for a dull article that was made a bit more sprightly with anecdotes and pithy quotations

Friz Quadrata a *sans-serif* typeface with incomplete *closures*, used for the entry words in this book

from line the line on a memo indicating the sender, usually below the recipient line:

> To: (recipient)
>
> Fr: (originator)

from the top from the beginning, a show-business expression The opposite is *from the bottom*. The term originates from the days when each scene in a script started at the top of a page.

front [retailing] the selling area of a store The *front end* is the checkout and cash-register area. In a theater, the audience area is the front or *front of the house*.

front. FRONTISPIECE; also, the first page, such as the front of a newspaper The *second front* is the first page of the second section of a newspaper.

front end [computers] the pre-processing of data before the production and output, as handled by a *front-end computer* or *front-end processor* In word processing and computerized typesetting, the *front-end system* includes input, editing, and specifications.

front-end display an advertisement on the front of a bus or other vehicle; also called *headlight display*

front-end load [advertising] placement of most of the advertisements in the front half of a publication, particularly a magazine

front-end system word processors and other equipment that originate material and are linked to printers, typesetters, and other communications components

frontispiece (front.) an illustration, often a *tip-in plate*, facing the title page of a book

front lighting or **front-lighting** illumination toward the camera or viewer, coming from the camera area or in front of the set or subject Front lighting tends to make the subject appear flat, with low contrast, as opposed to *back lighting.*

frontline [recording] a new release—an album or other recording—in the top price category; also called a *frontline product*

front list [publishing] new books and other works published during the past year; different from BACKLIST

frontload the scheduling of the bulk of a budget or sales during the first part of a campaign; also called *front-end load*

front lot [film] the interior studios and offices, as opposed to the *back lot,* or exterior areas

front matter material, such as the FRONTISPIECE, introduction, preface, and title page, preceding the main text The *preliminaries, preliminary matter,* or *fore matter* generally are not numbered or are numbered with Roman numerals.

front of book the first pages of a periodical, generally preceding the main editorial section, such as the letters-to-the-editor page; usually considered a desirable position for advertisers and often requested on insertion orders At some publications, the *front of the book* also includes the main news and feature sections and simply excludes service material or other sections in the *back of the book.* A *front-of-the-book meeting* may be held to plan the upfront and/or main sections.

front of the house (FOH) the lobby, box office, and manager's office of a theater, sometimes including the entire theater in front of the stage, illuminated by *front-of-house lighting;* the lobby and registration desk—*front desk*—of a hotel A desk clerk summons a bellboy by ringing a bell and/or calling "front."

front projection or **front screen projection** the reproduction of images onto the front of an opaque screen or other viewing surface in the conventional manner, as compared to *back* or *rear projection,* in which the images are projected onto the back of a translucent screen and viewed from the front Front projection or *front-axial projection* also is a method of filming in which a still or moving background is projected onto a screen behind the performers. The projection is from in front of the background, instead of behind it as in rear projection.

frost [graphic arts] to cover with a roughened surface, generally silvery white, resembling icy frost

fry 1 to cook over direct heat *Frying* is the hissing sound, as of food in a frying pan, emanating from a defective transmission line. 2 a scratch on a record; groove noise

FS full shot: camera coverage of an entire person or subject, full-length

FSAPO direction to FADE sound and picture out

FSI FREE-STANDING INSERT

f-stop a camera-lens aperture setting The *f* refers to *focal length.* The *f-number* is calibrated to change the amount of entering light by a factor of two with each succeeding number. The higher the f-stop number, the smaller the amount of light. Common f-numbers are 1.8, 3.5, 5.6, 8, 11, and 16. F16, for example, lets in half the light of the preceding number, F11. F numbers often are written with a capital *F;* the number is adjacent to the letter. The words f-stop or f-number are hyphenated or written with a slash—f/stop.

ft. foot

FTC or **F.T.C.** FEDERAL TRADE COMMISSION

FTP abbreviation used by a BINDER to designate folded, trimmed, and packed printed pieces

FTS Federal Telecommunications System, the network used by U.S. government agencies

fudge to falsify; to evade; to dodge A *fudge box* or *fudge jigger* is a detachable part of a page plate, generally two columns, that may be replaced with last-minute news, as at a newspaper.

fugitive fleeing, ephemeral; describing ink that fades *Fugitive material* is printed matter of fleeting interest, such as a program or journal for an event.

fulfillment completion, such as the processing and servicing of mail orders A *fulfillment executive* is responsible for fulfilling orders from customers. A *fulfillment house* is a company that ships products and handles other business, such as magazine and book orders. The subscription address on a magazine MASTHEAD usually is that of a fulfillment house, which is separate from the publisher and the editorial offices.

full aperture   the maximum opening of the lens diaphragm of a camera at the lowest F-STOP

full coat   magnetic film stock that has been coated with ferric oxide across its entire width, so that several soundtracks can be recorded on it

full-color printing   a method of reproducing an infinite range of colors by regulating the OVERPRINTING of the three basic colors of process ink (yellow, magenta, and cyan)   When restricted to these colors, the technique is called *three-color process*; with black or another color added, it's *four-color process*. In *multicolor printing*, each color is instead printed separately.

full-cover display   [retailing] a display of books showing the front covers instead of the *spines*; also called *flat display* or *face out*

full-dress   complete, as in a *full-dress inquiry* or a *full-dress rehearsal*, in which the performers are fully costumed or *dressed*

fullface   the "regular" typeface, not BOLDFACE, CONDENSED, or other deviations from the norm; sometimes erroneously called *lightface*, a typeface that is set lighter than regular

fullface envelope   an envelope without a window; also called a *closed-face envelope*

full house   a theater or other place that is sold out, filled to capacity   In the United Kingdom, it's called *house full.*

full line   a line of type that is tightly set, FLUSH LEFT and FLUSH RIGHT, and has no room for spacing

full mark   100-percent *markup* by a retailer, so that the customer pays exactly twice what the retailer paid

full measure   setting type to a full line without indentation

full out   an instruction to a printer to start lines at the margin rather than indented

full position   an instruction for an advertisement to appear immediately before, adjacent to, or following editorial matter   This preferred position sometimes commands an extra charge.

full run   [advertising] the insertion of an advertisement in every edition of a publication   The equivalent in transit advertising is a *full showing*, in which a *car card* is placed in every vehicle of the transit system.

full shot (FS)   camera coverage of the entire person or subject, full-length

full showing   the number of outdoor advertising BOARDS needed to obtain complete coverage in an area

fulltimer   a radio station broadcasting or permitted to broadcast 24 hours a day, as compared to a *daytimer* operating only during part of the day

fully scripted   a performance text with all of the dialogue lines, no *ad libbing* permitted

function   a quantity whose value is dependent on another quantity   A *function word* is a preposition, conjunction, or other type of word that indicates a grammatical relationship; it has a function within the sentence. A *functional shift* is a change in the syntactic function of a word, such as a noun serving as a verb. A *function room* is a place in a hotel or other facility in which a meeting or other event—a *function*—is held. In word processing and other computers, a *function code* is an indicator—flag—that the next code has a special meaning, such as to change FORMAT. In videotex and other computer systems, a function is a predictable procedure that is invoked by an uninterrupted series of keystrokes.

funeral notice   a classified advertisement or text (paid) about a death

funny papers   newspaper comics; also called *the funnies*

furn.   furnished

furnish   1 to provide or supply, such as to send material to a medium or production facility   A *layout* may bear a notation that a missing component, such as a photo, will be *furnished*, with an indication of the source or time.   2 in papermaking, the mixture of pulp, filler, dyes, and other additives from which the paper is made

furniture   [printing] blank strips of metal or wood used for margins or white space and to hold type and CUTS in place

fused sentence   a run-on sentence; two or more sentences with no period or other end mark separating them

future   a record of a forthcoming event, maintained in a log called a *future book, futures,* or *future file*

futures editor   a person in a news department of a network or major TV station who arranges for coverage of events the next day or thereafter, not for today's programs, and reports to the *managing editor*; sometimes called the *planning editor* or *features editor*

fuzz   a mass of fine particles, fluff, such as on a paper surface; to blur   *Fuzzy* is audio or video that is unclear or indistinct.

f.v.   FOLIO verso: left-hand page or on the back of the page

F wire   the financial wire of *The Associated Press* or other wire services

F/X or FX   special effects, a motion-picture term for animation, objects, and other techniques

and devices that are not real; also, an abbreviation for sound effects

FY   fiscal year

FYI   for your information

G

g or **G** gauge; good; gram; gravity

GA international telex abbreviation for go ahead, you may transmit

gab line a service of some telephone companies enabling callers to speak—*gab*—with other callers as part of a group of strangers

gadget letter direct mail containing an item fastened to or enclosed with the letter Such items, called *gadgets*, may be coins or toys.

gaff a hoax or trick It is not the same as *gaffe*, which is a faux pas or clumsy social error.

gaffer the foreman of a stage crew In film or TV, the gaffer is the head electrician. The word originated in the 16th century, when gaffer was used as an altered form of godfather or grandfather. In the 19th century, a foreman or overseer was called a gaffer, particularly in the United Kingdom, and was a master glassblower.

gaffoon an old colloquialism for the person who produces sound effects in a broadcast

gag an obstacle to speech; a joke A *gagline* is the punchline of a joke or the caption of a cartoon or humorous greeting card. A *gag rule* is a legislative or judicial restriction of discussion or news coverage.

gain progress, advancement, attainment, increase; increase of signal power, particularly sound volume The control that regulates the volume or another level is called the *gain*; hence, *turn up the gain*. To *ride the gain* is to monitor the control indicator.

gala festive occasion

Gale Directory of Publications and Broadcast Media an annual directory of media published by the Gale Research Company of Detroit

Gallagher *The Gallagher Report*, a weekly newsletter about marketing Started in 1952, the New York publication was ended in 1989 by Bernard P. Gallagher (1910–89).

gallery an elevated floor within a theater or other building (to *play to the gallery* is to cater to the general public, such as the audience in the balcony); a corridor or narrow place, as for displaying works of art; a series of pictures with little or no text in a section or insert of a magazine or other publication A *gallery hit* is a the-atrical production that is well received by the masses but not necessarily by the critics. In the United Kingdom, the production control room overlooking a TV studio is called a gallery.

galley a long, shallow tray, usually metal, with three sides to hold type, generally about 20 inches long and 7 inches wide An *unlocked galley* is a PROOF of the galleys before they have been locked up or closed.

galley proof a typeset copy of a manuscript prior to assembly into page position as *page proofs*; also called GALLEY or galleys Originally, galley proofs were made directly on a *galley press* or *proof press* from the *galley tray* in which the type is assembled. Because galleys are of text only and run the length of the galley tray, they are not the same as page proofs. A *bound galley* is a roughly bound set of galley proofs used in editing and sent to reviewers or others for prepublication reading.

gallows humor amused cynicism, as by a person facing execution or some other disaster or jesting about death under macabre circumstances

gallows mike a GOOSENECK microphone hung from a support base and used on a broadcasting table

Gallup & Robinson, Inc. an advertising impact and market research company formed in 1948 and headquartered in Princeton, NJ Surveys are conducted in about 150 cities, including inserts of a test advertisement into a program or magazine and telephone interviews soliciting reactions of viewers or readers. Because of its location near Philadelphia, Gallup & Robinson has developed several well-known services in the Philadelphia area. The company was formed by George Gallup, the country's most famous opinion analyst, and Claude Robinson, formerly of Opinion Research Corporation. Its best-known reports are the *Blue Book Report* on quantitative performance and the *Red Book Report* on qualitative performance of client and competitive commercials and advertisements.

Gallup Organization a pioneering opinion research company founded in 1935 by George Gallup (1901–84) and headquartered in

Princeton, NJ Best known for its *Gallup Poll*, it was acquired in 1988 by Selection Research Inc., Lincoln, NE.

galvanic skin response a physiological reaction to psychological stimuli, such as fear or arousal, whose intensity is measurable by the degree of skin conductivity created by varying perspiration rates; also called *psychogalvanic skin response* or *arousal method* Used to determine respondents' reactions to advertising, it is measured with a *galvanometer* or *psychogalvanometer*.

game show a radio or TV program in which contestants are asked questions or participate in contests to win prizes

gamma the third letter of the Greek alphabet; the third in a series, such as a *gamma test*, a FIELD TEST of a computer program or other new product following the *beta* or second test Gamma also refers to the degree of contrast between the darkest and lightest parts of a photographic image. A *gamma number* is a trigonometric unit. *High gamma* indicates high contrast; *low gamma* indicates low contrast. The Greek capital gamma is written as Γ and often is anglicized as a right angle: ⌐.

gammadion a figure consisting of four capital GAMMA letters radiating from a center An example is the *swastika*: 卍.

gang box a container with a variety of tools and supplies commonly used by exhibitors, including such diverse items as tape, scissors, and a screwdriver; also called a *trouble box*

gang run the printing of several different items simultaneously that then are cut apart A *gang* is a sheet printed from such an assemblage. *Gang separations* are several color prints or transparencies produced at the same time.

gang synchronizer a mechanism with two or more sprocket wheels, used in film editing to match (synchronize) a print to the original film, soundtracks to the workprint, or other parts A *three-gang synchronizer* can handle three strips of film.

Gannett Company, Inc. a major multimedia company, formerly of Rochester, NY, now of Roslyn, VA, that owns *USA Today*; *USA Weekend*; Gannett New Service, the nation's largest chain of newspapers; and radio, TV, outdoor advertising, and other media companies The Gannett Center for Media Studies, funded by the Gannett Foundation, is at Columbia University in New York.

gap 1 an opening, lag, or disparity; an interruption in continuity, such as a blank area on a recorded tape 2 [recording] a small space in an audio or video head across which the magnetic field is produced when recording and induced when playing back

gap character [computers] a character that is included in a fixed-length word that does not transmit any information and simply fills the space For example, if 15 characters are allocated for a person's last name and the name is only eight characters, then seven gap characters are inserted to fill the character count.

Garamond a typeface with *serifs* at the top and/or bottom of the letters, designed by Claude Garamond (1510–61) in France

garbage worthless, unnecessary, or offensive matter, such as meaningless data (also called *hash*); gibberish or anything of very poor quality, such as literary garbage When an attempt is made to dress up a shabby product, it may be pronounced, sarcastically, in a French manner, as gar-BAR-j instead of GAR-bij.

garbage matte a piece of black paper or other MATTE used to block out unwanted areas—*garbage*—as in preparing composite images in film animation work

garble table a chart or other aid that helps to correct incorrect, indecipherable, or garbled text, such as transposed or omitted letters

garzone an artist's apprentice; from the Italian for a "studio boy"

gas bells [photography] bubbles formed during processing that force the emulsion to separate from the base of the film

gate 1 a moveable structure in a passageway that controls entrance, exit, or flow, such as a gate in a spotlight or, in a camera or projector, the film aperture unit that positions film for exposure or projection *Gate float* (unsteadiness of the image during projection) and *hair in the gate* (a hair or other extraneous blemish) are annoying to movie-theater patrons; when seen on TV, they indicate that the image originates from a film camera. *Liquid gate* is a wet printing system in which a scratched or damaged film is passed through a liquid at the point of exposure in order to reduce or remove blemishes. 2 the total admission receipts or number of people at a show or event A *gate-crasher* gained admission without being invited or paying. *Gate cut* is a percentage of the admission receipts.

gatefold a page in a magazine or other publication larger than the other pages; folded over so that the page is the same size as the other pages and the extension can be opened or swung out like a gate

gatekeeper purchasing agents, association executives, switchboard operators, opinion leaders, professional communicators, media people, and others who control the flow of information and influence opinions and buying decisions

gate pass a ticket or identification that permits entrance to a film studio, stadium, or other place; also called *walk-on pass*

gateway 1 an entrance or access point 2 [computers, telephone] equipment to interface different networks, such as two VIDEOTEX or other systems, that enables a user of one system to communicate with a second system In 1988, a federal judge ruled that the Bell regional telephone companies can create audiotex or videotex gateways, including electronic bulletin boards that organize information from several sources, such as newspapers.

gateway city [telephone] a city through which international calls pass, such as Miami, New Orleans, New York, San Francisco, or Washington, DC

gather to convene or assemble; to collate or arrange items in sequence, such as the SIGNATURES in a book *Gathering* is the process of assembling, as of folded signatures in proper sequence.

gathering plan the acquisition of a group of publications, such as one copy of all the books or periodicals of a publisher; a BLANKET ORDER, as by a library, to purchase one copy of each title issued by a publisher

gauffer See GOFFER.

gauge a measure of thickness, width, or other dimensions *Narrow-gauge film* is smaller than 35mm.

Gaussian curve a normal distribution pattern illustrated by a symmetrical bell-shaped curve with a convex center and concave ends reflecting the typical distribution of items in a sample

gauze a thin transparent material, such as a mesh or cheesecloth, commonly used as a curtain on a stage; generally called SCRIM

gazebo in a retail store, a display fixture, generally free-standing and open, like a gazebo structure, holding several types of products

gaze motion the movement of a viewer's or reader's eyes as recorded and measured by an EYE CAMERA and used in media studies and other research

gazette 1 a newspaper The origin is from the *gazetta*, an Italian coin worth the price of a newspaper. Several newspapers, such as the *Phoenix Gazette*, use the word in their names. 2 an official publication, particularly the British journals with public notices

gazetteer a dictionary or index of geographical names

GCR gray component replacement, a color printing technique

g.e. GILT-EDGE

Geegee nickname of Greta Garbo (1905–), Swedish-born U.S. film actress who was renowned in the '30s and '40s Her enigmatic, solitary mystique evoked such expressions as "pulling a Garbo" (or Geegee).

gel GELATIN Colored gels are placed in front of stage lights to produce colored lighting. Gelling is placing a gelatin or any color medium in a theatrical lighting instrument. *Regelling* is replacing a color medium; it is also called to *gel-up*. Formerly made of gelatin, gel color filters are now made of plastic. Gel is also called *jelly* or, particularly in the United Kingdom, *gelly* or *jellie*.

gelatin a hard, transparent protein In theatrical lighting, a gelatin, or *gelatine*, is a type of thin membrane put over a light to provide color. The *gelatin process* is a direct-image duplicating system in which type or other matter is impressed onto a master paper; this image is pressed into a gelatin mass and then transferred to duplicator paper to produce a *gelatin print* or *jelly print*.

gem a small-size type, about four POINTS

gen to generate or produce, as in the generation or production of a newspaper story

genealogy [film, television] a numerical history of duplicates made from the master film or original videotape—the first GENERATION The first print or duplicate tape is the *second generation* in the genealogy; the next set of copies is the GAMMA or third generation.

general delivery mail to be picked up at post offices The service is intended primarily for transients and customers who are not permanently located or who prefer not to use post office boxes. Customers must present identification.

General Electric Co. one of the world's largest media companies, headquartered in Fairfield, CT GE owns the NBC network and major radio and TV stations and is a major company in electronics and other fields.

General Post Office (GPO) the main post office in a city with several branch post offices, commonly used by companies for postal boxes

general rate an advertising charge by a newspaper or other medium to a national advertiser; higher than the local rate

general store a retail outlet with many types of merchandise, but not a large store with different departments Formerly common in small towns, most general stores have been replaced by *general merchandise stores*, which are department and variety stores.

generation a class of objects derived from a preceding class In films and tapes, the master, or original, is the *first generation*. Any copy made from the master is *second generation*, called a *copy*, DUPE, or DUB, and a copy of a second-generation dupe is of the *third generation*. In computers, word processing, and other fields, each new major level of technology is called a generation, so that first-generation typesetters evolve into succeeding generations. Current laser typesetters are called *fourth-generation typesetters*.

generator   a machine that produces electricity or other products   In film and TV, a portable generator, which provides electricity for lights, cameras, and other equipment, is handled by a *generator operator*, who reports to the GAFFER or chief electrician.

generic advertising   the promotion of a category instead of a specific item

generic brand   a class of products that are sold with emphasis on the content rather than the BRAND NAME, packaging, or advertising

Genie Award   annual awards presented to Canadians by the film division of the Academy of Cinema and Television in Toronto; the Canadian version of Hollywood's OSCARS

genlock   [television] circuitry, separate or part of a SWITCHER or SYNC GENERATOR, that locks or coordinates a live camera signal with signals from a videotape recorder

genny   an electricity generator, particularly a portable generator on a film or TV set

genre   kind or type   *Genre painting* is realistic. *Genre publishing* treats specific subjects, generally fiction, such as romance and westerns; it is also called *category publishing*.

geostationary orbit   a path 22,300 miles above the equator where satellites circle the earth at the speed that the earth rotates   They maintain a constant position relative to the equator and thus are called geostationary.

gerund   a noun ending in *-ing* that has some of the characteristics of a verb

gesso   a plasterlike substance made of chalk, white pigment, and a binder, used in sculptures and also applied to flat surfaces   *Acrylic gesso*, which has a plastic binder, is used as a surface for acrylic paints. The Italian word, pronounced JESS-o, is from *gypsum*.

gest   a gesture; pronounced jest   In German theater, as popularized by Bertolt Brecht (1898–1956), a gest—pronounced guest—is the basic, meaningful part of a gesture.

gestalt   perception of the whole rather than the component parts, so that the effectiveness of the entire package, advertisement, or other item is greater than the sum of its parts; based on the German word for "whole"

get   to receive or acquire   Among theatrical "get" terms are *get a light* (turn on or project a beam); *get across* or *get over* (project across or over the FOOTLIGHTS to an audience); *get the needle* (to get stage fright); *get the show on the road* (to start, not necessarily to travel); and *get the spot* (to be the center of attention or get the SPOTLIGHT). To *get a city* or other location is to establish telephone or other communication, as in the command, "Get me New York!"

getaway column   a newspaper or magazine column written by a columnist before leaving on vacation—*getaway*—and scheduled to run during his or her absence, generally of timeless material

get in character   a direction to a performer to assume the stance and other attributes of the role—the *character*   The command is given by the director or an assistant shortly before the performance.

G.G.   See GEEGEE.

ghetto   a slum area or section inhabited by minority groups   In broadcasting, a ghetto is a period of the week for special-interest programming, notably the Saturday-morning *children's ghetto* on TV; *religious* and *public affairs ghettos* on Sunday morning on radio and TV and Sunday night on radio; and, formerly, the *education ghetto* early mornings on weekday TV.

ghost   **1** an anonymous writer who creates speeches, articles, and other material for attribution to others   **2** a secondary or double image on a TV screen or the improper reappearance of an image on a printed sheet   The *TV ghost* generally is caused by signal reflection, such as from tall buildings, or poor transmission conditions. The *printing ghost* may be due to improper ink or dampener roller setting.   **3** [theater] the manager of a theater company, particularly in the United Kingdom, when on payday (Friday) performers ask, "Has the ghost walked?" (a reference to Hamlet)

ghosting   **1** [computer graphics] a procedure in which two images are combined to create a shadow—ghost—effect   **2** [graphic arts] a technique to emphasize one part of a drawing, photograph, or other image and to show other parts less distinctly

ghost word   a spurious word, usually resulting from a typographical or other error and then repeated   The term was originated by Walter William Skeat (1835–1925), an English lexicographer.

ghostwriter   a person who writes speeches or other work anonymously for another person; also called a GHOST

GHz GIGAHERTZ; one-billion *hertz*, a unit of sound intensity

gibberish rapid, incoherent talk; unintelligible communication In computers, a *gibberish total*, also called *control total* or *hash total*, is accumulated for checking or control purposes and has no particular meaning.

giftbook an elaborately printed book or annual publication, popular in the early 19th century

gig a job, particularly for musicians

giga one billion; pronounced GIG-a A *gigahertz (GHz)* is one-billion *hertz*, a unit of sound frequency used in broadcasting. A *gigawatt (GW)*, a unit of light intensity, is one billion watts.

GIGO garbage *in*, garbage *out* The quality of the *input* into a computer or any system determines the quality of the *output* or result.

gilt-edge the edges of leaves of a book that are covered with a thin layer of gold or coated with a gold color The process is *gilding*, and the pages also are called *gild-edged* or *gilt-edged*. The term also refers to items of high quality, such as *gilt-edged securities*, which are abbreviated as *g.e. G.T.* is *gilt top*; *t.e.g.* is *top-edge gilt*. *Gilt extra* is additional gilding, such as on a book binding.

gimbal [film] a very large scaffolding—a *rig*—on which a set can be rotated This device enabled Fred Astaire to dance across the ceiling and walls of his hotel room in *Royal Wedding*. The origin is *gimbals*, a pair of rings pivoted on axes so that one is free to swing within the other, as used in a ship's compass that remains horizontal when suspended on gimbals. A *gimbal head* is a camera support that permits smooth horizontal movements of a camera on a tripod; it is also called *gimbal mount*, *gimbal head tripod*, or *gimbal tripod*. A gyroscopically gimballed mirror is used as part of an *image stabilizer* in front of a camera lens.

gimbel in computer graphics, perspective effects created by tilting the artwork

gimcrack a showy but useless thing, such as a typographic ornament

gimmick a tricky or deceptive device, trivial innovation, or clever idea to increase attention or enhance appeal; also called *boff*, *plant*, or *weenie*

giveaway prizes products awarded to contestants or audience members on TV game shows—*giveaway programs*—or other radio or TV programs

gizmo a gadget; a mechanical contrivance; a GIMMICK; a novelty item Gizmo is used as slang to refer to many items, such as the *limbo*, or neutral color or blank area, in printing and TV.

gl. gloss; glossy

glacé having a smooth or glossy surface, as in *glacéed paper*, or *glazed paper*

glance a brief look A *glancer* is a story or list summing up or giving highlights of a series of related stories.

glassine nearly transparent paper, heavier than tissue paper A common use is to print type on it for placement over existing art or other matter for evaluation or layout positioning. Glassine is also used for protection, to cover art or a publication.

glass shot [film] a special-effects technique in which a scene is painted on or a photograph is affixed to a sheet of glass

glaze a smooth, shiny coating, as applied to high-gloss or polished-finished *glazed paper*

gliss slang for *glissando* A *gliss sting* is a musical punctuation, as in a radio drama.

glissé a gliding step, one of the basic movements in ballet; also called *glissade* From the French, glissé is pronounced gliss-AY.

glitch a mishap, error, or malfunction, as in mechanical, electrical, or electronic equipment

glitterati slang for celebrities in media, publishing, and other literary fields

glittering generalities statements so closely associated with commonly accepted ideas or beliefs that they are accepted without backup or actual support

glitz glitter; ostentation

global complete In word processing, a *global search and replace* or *global find and replace* command is an instruction to replace every occurrence of a word with a different one.

global beam in satellite broadcasting, transmission from a satellite that covers about one-third of the earth INTELSAT satellites are aimed at the center of the Atlantic, Pacific, or Indian Ocean in order to reach the bordering land areas. U.S. domestic satellites, or DOMSAT, are aimed at the continental United States and can be received with a smaller DISH than the enormous ones, 30 to 100 feet in diameter, used to receive global beams.

global village the concept of modern telecommunications linking people all over the world and thus homogenizing their values and desires, first described in 1964 by Marshall McLuhan (1911–80), Canadian educator

glop a messy mixture, sometimes referring to poor writing The word originates from *glue* and *slop* and originally was slang for any soft, gluey substance.

gloss 1 surface shininess or luster; to give a bright sheen; to make superficially attractive *Glossy* means smooth, shiny, and showy. **2** explanatory words inserted in the margin or between the lines of a text The verb *to gloss* refers to such annotations, or *glosses*, as done by a *glossator* or *glosser.* A collection of explanations or synonyms is called a gloss or, more commonly, a GLOSSARY. A deliberately misleading interpretation sometimes is called a gloss. *Judicial gloss* is the accumulation of legal decisions and opinions on a statute, constitutional amendment, or other specific point.

glossary a list of difficult or specialized words with definitions

glossy print a photo with a smooth finish, as compared to a MATTE or non-glossy finish Most publicity photos are glossy prints, called *glossies.*

gloving sound a process of cleaning a soundtrack with soft cloth akin to gloves; also called *velveting sound*

Glue Stic a cylinder of paste, commonly used in cut-and-paste editing, made by the Dennison Manufacturing Company, Framingham, MA

gluing the process of applying an adhesive, sometimes called *gluing off,* as in applying glue to the SPINE of a book

glyph a PICTOGRAPH; a symbolic character, sign, or mark, often cut into a surface or carved in relief to pictorialize the service or product of a company or organization

GMA "Good Morning America," a morning news program of ABC-TV

G.N.H. GROSS NIGHT HOUR

GNS Gannett News Service; see GANNETT CO.

go **1** [broadcasting] a command to execute, such as *go theme,* an instruction from the director to the audio-control operator or sound engineer to start the theme music **2** a signal to perform To *go back* means to repeat, such as to rehearse again. In the United Kingdom, it's *go behind, go round,* or *go round again.* To *go on* is to enter or to appear in place of another performer, as when an understudy goes on.

go-ahead an expression of interest by an editor, producer, or other person with regard to the development of an article or other proposed work It may not be an assignment and may not include any guarantee of payment.

goals down-plans up planning a business planning system in which top management sets goals and lower levels of management develop plans to achieve the goals, common among large companies It is different from TOP-DOWN PLANNING and BOTTOM-UP PLANNING.

goatskin leather made from the skin of goats that is used in bookbinding It is commonly called Morocco after the goatskins tanned there, though goatskins for bookbinding also come from South Africa (Cape Morocco leather), Nigeria (Niger leather), and other countries.

go back [theater] to visit a performer backstage; also called *go behind,* and, in the United Kingdom, *go round*

gobbledygook unclear, confusing language, often redundant and pseudotechnical The word was coined in the 1930s by Maury Maverick, a Texas congressman, who was quoted in *The New York Times Magazine* on May 21, 1944: "Perhaps I was thinking of the old bearded turkey gobbler back in Texas who was always gobbledy-gobbling and strutting with ludicrous pomposity. At the end of this gobble there was a sort of gook." The word *maverick*—an unbranded stray animal or independent person—precedes Congressman Maverick and probably comes from Samuel A. Maverick, a 19th-century cattle rancher.

gobo a black flag, screen, piece of cardboard, or other material, generally mounted on a tripod, used to block light or cast shadows; a hole cut out of a FLAT or other scenery through which a camera shoots the scene In the theater, a shape or pattern, called a *gobo pattern,* sometimes is inserted in the GATE of a spotlight to project an image of the pattern on a curtain, wall, or other surface on the stage. A small rectangular gobo sometimes is called a FLAG; a long, narrow gobo is a *cutter* or *finger;* a round gobo is a *dot* or *target.* One or more gobos are mounted on a three-legged stand called a *gobo stand, century stand,* or *C stand.* Gobos also are used as movable panels or baffles in recording studios. These *sound gobos* are wood with fiberglass or all plastic, such as polyurethane, and are three or four feet high. The alleged origins are vaudeville slang for playing a scene in the dark or from "go-between." The plural is gobos or goboes, and it is sometimes misspelled as gobbo.

gods British slang for the uppermost seats in a theater or other auditorium

gofer a person who runs errands, such as to *go for coffee;* also spelled *gopher*

goffer a process of CRIMPING or PLEATING, as with paper or cloth *Goffered edges* are paper leaves with an indented pattern, commonly used in dictionaries and reference books to identify each letter or section. As a verb, goffer means to crimp or FLUTE; it also refers to a type of iron used in the process. The word originates from the French *gaufrer* ("to crimp"), and the older spelling is *gauffer.*

go-go of dancing to rock music, as in discotheques; of a dancer, often semi-nude, performing erotic movements, generally to rock music, as in a bar (a go-go dancer in a go-go bar) This slang word, popular in the 1960s and 1970s, is from the French _à_ (to) _gogo_ (abundance or galore) and also describes a rapid and dizzying tempo, as in the _a-go-go pace of life._

go hunting an instruction to a camera operator to move around and find a good shot, as in a game or other spontaneous event

going off speaking while moving off-stage, off-camera, or off-mike

going up! short for _curtain going up_, a warning to performers that the stage curtain is about to rise

going year 12 consecutive months, not necessarily a calendar year, used in a budget, broadcast schedule, or sales campaign

Gold Anvil annual award to a top public relations practitioner and a top educator, presented by the Public Relations Society of America, New York

Gold Circle annual awards to associations in various communication categories, presented by the American Society of Association Executives, Washington, DC

Golden Bell Awards annual awards for outstanding public relations and promotion by lodging establishments and associations, presented by Hotel Sales and Marketing Association International, Margate, NJ

Golden Globe Awards annual awards in film and television categories, presented by the HOLLYWOOD FOREIGN PRESS ASSOCIATION in Beverly Hills, CA

Golden Heart the annual awards of the ROMANCE WRITERS OF AMERICA of Houston, TX

golden mean the proportion or ratio of art to text in a publication; also called _golden division_, _golden section_, or _golden proportion_ The most pleasing proportion is generally considered to be 3/8 art to 5/8 text.

golden oldie a record, film, or other entertainment form that was once popular

goldenrod paper yellow or orange coated MASKING PAPER, called a _goldenrod flat_ or FLAT, on which negatives are taped in position prior to offset printing The paper itself is cut away around the image areas by a person called a STRIPPER, so that it is used to help in the assembling of the layout components prior to photographing of the BLUEPRINT. _Golden plast_ or _orange plast_ is a similar paper sheet used as a base, called _base sheeting._

Golden Trumpets annual awards for public relations campaigns, presented by the PUBLICITY CLUB OF CHICAGO

Gold Key Awards annual awards to public relations executives by PUBLIC RELATIONS NEWS, a newsletter published by Mrs. Denny Griswold in New York. Gold Key PR Awards are presented to individuals and companies by the American Hotel & Motel Association, Washington, DC.

Gold Quills annual awards honoring excellence in communications and public relations, sponsored by the INTERNATIONAL ASSOCIATION OF BUSINESS COMMUNICATORS of San Francisco

Gold Radio a radio-station format featuring popular music of earlier years, the _oldies_

gold record a record, cassette, or CD disk with over $1 million in sales or over 500,000 _units_ sold, as certified by the RECORDING INDUSTRY ASSOCIATION OF AMERICA in Washington, DC Prior to 1989, the number of singles or units needed for a _gold_ was one million. The highest category of record awards is a PLATINUM RECORD.

gold stamping the process of stamping or impressing a printing surface with a design in gold

Goldwynism a verbal _gaffe,_ such as those allegedly made by Samuel Goldwyn (1882–1974), the early Hollywood producer who became the G of _MGM_ (_Metro-Goldwyn-Mayer_)

golf ball in typewriters, the spherical typing head that produces characters

Golin/Harris Communications a major public relations firm, based in Chicago, acquired in 1989 from Foote, Cone & Belding Communications by Shandwick PLC, London

gondola a bank of shelving, open on both sides, in a retail store

gone to bed ready to be printed

gonzo journalism reporting filled with bizarre or extremely subjective ideas or commentary; a term originated in the early 1970s by journalist Hunter Thompson, who wrote for _Rolling Stone_

goo a sticky substance; sentimental drivel

good music station an older designation for a radio station with a FORMAT of high-quality popular music, such as from musical comedies, films, and light classics, now generally called an _easy listening station_

good night a salutation before leaving for the day BEAT reporters on newspapers check in with the DESK and are given a "good night," which means there are no more assignments for that day.

goof an incompetent person; a careless mistake; a FLUFF

goon stand a large three-legged stand, also called a _century stand_, that holds GOBOS or other devices Two legs are short and one leg is longer; the gobos are of various shapes; and the combined appearance is awkward, like a _goon._

gooseberry season [journalism] British slang for the dead months or silly season, as in July and August, when pranks are newsworthy

gooseneck a slender curved object, such as a lamp or desk microphone

Gorizont the Soviet Union telecommunications satellite

go-see an audition

Gothic a SANS-SERIF typeface with all strokes of uniform width, generally heavy, vertical strokes as in block letters It originated with late medieval calligraphers around the 16th century; hence, novels whose plots are in this period are called Gothic novels. Gothic letters also are called *black letters* and are still used today, particularly in BOLDFACE (or blackface). *Modeled Gothic* has some thinning of strokes, such as where the BOWL meets the stem, as in *b* and *d*.

gotico-antigua early Gothic or BLACK-LETTER SANS-SERIF typefaces; also called *fere-humanista*, used by Italian humanistic scholars

go to black to let the image FADE out entirely; a direction in film and television

go to Cain's [theater] to close a show, from the period of the late 1880s to the 1930s, when many theatrical costumes and sets were picked up by Cain's Transfer Company of New York and stored in its warehouse

go to table an informal reading of a script by performers; an early rehearsal sometimes done seated around a table

gouache opaque (not transparent) watercolor paint or a painting made with this type of paint; pronounced gwash

Goudy a typeface with varying thickness of lines designed by Frederic W. Goudy (1865–1947), an American printer *Goudy Text* is a descendant of old GOTHIC and has heavy strokes. Among the many other typefaces designed by Goudy are *Forum, Goudy Open, Hadriano,* and *Kennerley*. In this book, the opening initials for A–Z are in *Goudy Handtooled*.

gouge a groove A *gouge index* has a series of rounded notches cut out—*gouged*—along the fore-edge of a book, more commonly called a *thumb index*.

go up **1** to increase, such as move to a higher level of sound or intensity, or in a newspaper or other publication, to set material in a larger area, such as in an additional column **2** [theater] to forget one's lines of a script

government relations the aspect of public relations that involves working with government agencies and officials on behalf of an organization; the relationship of an organization with the government, not the relations of government with its publics

goyu a Japanese tissue paper used as hinges to mount stamps or other items

GPO GENERAL POST OFFICE

gr. grade; GRAIN; GROSS; GROUP

grabber [journalism] humorous, startling, provocative, or human-interest material used in a *lead* sentence or beginning as a means of developing interest in what follows

grace a period of time granted beyond the due date In magazine subscriptions, a *grace period* often is extended beyond the expiration date, so that a subscriber is *graced* with continued delivery.

gradation progression, such as successive steps of tones or tints

grader a technician in a film laboratory who examines negatives to determine improper exposure or timing and then makes corrections The term is used in the United Kingdom. In the United States, the technician is called a *timer*; the process is called *grading* or *timing*.

graduated filter [photography] an optical filter with both a color and a transitional area (or a graduated bleed line) between the clear and colored parts

graf paragraph Though the number of lines in a paragraph varies, newspaper editors often assign stories with a specific number of grafs. The FEATURE that appears in the bottom left corner of the second front page of *The Wall Street Journal* generally is eight grafs.

graffiti scribbled writing or drawing on walls, trains, and other public surfaces The word is the plural of *graffito*, Italian for a scribbling. The Italian verb *graffiare* means to scratch.

grain the degree of coarseness of a surface, such as a film, photo, record, or paper In paper, the grain is the direction in which the fibers run. Paper, particularly heavy *stock*, folds more easily and smoothly *with the grain* (or *grain right*) than *against the grain* (*grain wrong*). *Sheet-fed* book papers are classified as *grain long*, referring to the position of the fibers—*grain direction*—parallel to the longest dimension, the opposite of *grain-short*. In photos, a *grainy print* has a spotty or coarse effect, perhaps due to excessive enlargement. *Graininess* is the clumping of silver particles in film, producing a mottled effect. In printing, *graining* is the roughening of the surface of a metal *offset* plate to increase its capacity for holding moisture. A plate may be grained chemically—*chemical graining*—or mechanically, as with rotating brushes. *Grainy printing* is uneven, particularly in HALFTONES. A poor recording with a rough, gritty sound is called *grainy*.

grain of wheat jargon for a miniature lamp, such as the 4-volt snap-in lights used in exhibits

gram a metric unit of mass and weight; a record, such as a telegram; MAILGRAM

gram. GRAMMAR If written as *gram?*, the reader or editor is questioning the grammar of the author.

grammage in papermaking, a method of specifying the weight of a paper, used in European and other countries on the metric system, based on the number of grams per square meter of the paper, abbreviated as gsm or g/m^2

grammalogue British for a BOOKMARK

grammar the part of the study of language that deals with the forms and structure of words (*morphology*) and their customary arrangement in phrases and sentences (*syntax*), as opposed to the study of word meanings (*semantics*) A *grammarian* is a grammar expert. A *grammar hotline* is a telephone service, generally operated by a college or university, that answers questions about grammar and related subjects.

Grammies annual awards for recordings presented by the NATIONAL ACADEMY OF RECORDING ARTS AND SCIENCES in Burbank, CA The origin of Grammy is GRAMOPHONE.

Gramophone an early version of a record player invented in the United States by Emile Berliner (1851–1928), who replaced Thomas Edison's cylinders with flat, reproducible records—*Berliner discs* For many years, the British referred to a phonograph as a gramophone.

grangerizing a process of illustrating a book with illustrations or art from other sources, such as by cutting them out from other books and pasting onto blank sheets; also called *grangerization* The term was named after James Granger, whose 1769 book, *Biographical History of England*, included blank pages on which additional matter could be added in an act called *extra-illustrating*.

granite finish paper that has been mottled by the addition of fibers of a different color and resembles the hard crystalline texture of plutonic rock, or granite

granular granulated; having a grainy surface The degree of graininess is called *granularity*.

grapevine personal communication via a network of individuals spread out and connected like the vines that bear grapes, such as an *employee grapevine* Grapevine news via the *grapevine telegraph* may be authentic or unfounded gossip, rumor, or hearsay. *Grapevine copy* is timeless; it can be set in type and used at any time.

graph 1 journalism term for *paragraph*; also spelled GRAF 2 a curve, chart, or grid A *line graph* depicts the relationship of the variables by a curve of distribution; a *bar graph* or *histo-*gram shows it by columns that rise or descend from the X or horizontal axis (a *vertical bar graph*) or out horizontally from the Y or vertical axis (a *horizontal bar graph*).

grapheme an alphabet letter or letters that represent a single *phoneme*, or sound; also, a single element in graphics, such as x for *cross* (x-section) or *trans* (x-mission)

graphic a visual device that is drawn, handwritten, or printed on a material, structure, or surface; the product of GRAPHIC ARTS *Graphics* refers to all types of prints, including *etchings*, *lithographs*, and *serigraphs*.

graphic album a collection of comics, such as *Archie* and *Superman*, in book form instead of as a magazine

graphic arts a comprehensive term that includes printing, engraving, painting, drawing, lettering, writing, and all other arts using lines or marks on a surface

Graphic Communications International Union a labor union headquartered in Washington, DC, with about 200,000 members, representing the 1983 merger of two unions, Graphic Arts International Union and Lithographers and Photoengravers International Union

graphic designer a person who assembles various elements to communicate a message visually through the use of lettering, illustration, and other techniques *Graphic design* is the visual message, the end product of a graphic designer's work, including a *logo*, poster, brochure, letterhead, and other *graphics*.

graphic docudrama an adult comic book; a story, generally in the magazine format of a comic book, that is conveyed primarily with drawings

graphic novel a work of fiction that is mostly drawings; an expanded COMIC BOOK

graphite a soft, black, lustrous form of carbon used as lead in pencils

graphite paper a thin TRANSFER paper coated on one side with *graphite* It is similar in use to CARBON PAPER.

GRAS *Generally Recognized As Safe*, a designation of the FOOD AND DRUG ADMINISTRATION for food additives, chemicals, drugs, and other substances

grass roots the dispersed membership or constituency of an organization; the anonymous, scattered holders of opinions or attitudes

graticulation a technique for transferring a drawing from one surface to a larger surface by drawing corresponding squares on each and then copying the art within each square; also called *squaring*

graticule a linear grid placed over an image to identify locations on the image, such as latitude and longitude lines on a map

grave a nickname for a depressed area or hole in a stage set

grave accent from the French, pronounced grahv, a mark (`) downward from left to right above a letter to indicate stress or pronunciation; opposite of *acute accent*, which is diagonal from right to left

graver a BURIN or cutting tool used by engravers and sculptors

graveyard shift a late-night–early-morning work period, such as midnight to 8 A.M.

gravure a printing process in which the printing surface is depressed, the opposite of LETTERPRESS, in which the surface is raised; also called *intaglio*, which means cut or incised Gravure printing is used mainly for large quantities, as with Sunday supplements and preprinted advertisements in which the preparation cost of the fine-line screens is amortized by the large run.

gray card gray cardboard of about 18-percent reflectance that serves as a substitute for the subject when taking a reflected-light-exposure meter reading; also called *18% gray*

gray-collar workers postal workers, firefighters, and similar middle-class professionals

gray component replacement (GCR) a color printing technique involving replacing some of the colored ink with black ink; also called *achromatic color* or *integrated color removal*

gray goods See GREIGE GOODS.

gray out a dull appearance, as of a text page with type all of the same size

gray scale a strip of paper with tones ranging from pure white to black, used for contrast control in printing In television, the gray scale includes seven to ten shades, from *television white* to *television black*. *No. 5 gray* has about 18-percent reflectance and is commonly used as a standard for light readings. In facsimile transmission, *gray-scale capability* (also called *halftone capability*) translates pictures into shades of gray (generally 8 or 16 shades) instead of black dots.

grease paint theatrical makeup

grease pencil a thick pencil with a soft, waxy core for writing on photo prints, films, or other slick surfaces without damaging them

Great American Novel a significant work of fiction, a phrase sometimes used by neophytes and others who are writing or plan to write their MAGNUM OPUS

great primer a relatively large type size, about 18 points, formerly used in Bibles

grecque Greek In bookbinding, *à la Grecque* is a binding with boards cut flush with the cut edges of the pages and HEADBANDS protruding above and below in the style of 16th-century Greek books.

Greek type garbled type used to show location, size, and other aspects of a layout Similarly, meaningless shapes, called *Greek art* or *Greek*, can be used to indicate layout, text, package, concept, name, or some other feature. To *Greek it* is to produce such bogus lettering. In the United Kingdom, it is called *Latin type*.

green new; fresh; immature; unprocessed; inexperienced; naive A *green film* or *green print* is sticky, possibly from lack of coating or insufficient drying after washing. A *green proof* is uncorrected.

Green Book an annual directory of about 7,000 prominent individuals, primarily in the District of Columbia, titled *The Social List of Washington* and known as *The Green Book* because of its cover; published in Kensington, MD

greenery department in film studios, an area devoted to growing plants, trees, and other greenery and DRESSING sets with them A *greensman* works in such a department, which sometimes is part of the construction department.

green eyeshade a visor formerly worn by COPYDESK personnel and proofreaders

greenlighting the process of approval; a GOAHEAD

green out to take out descriptive phrases or other text; to edit tightly The term originates from the use of a green pencil for writing that does not reproduce; editors now usually use blue pencils and to blue pencil something has the same meaning.

green paper a printed document issued by the British government to stimulate discussion of a proposed policy

green river ordinances local laws that prohibit or control door-to-door selling; named after a 1931 ordinance in Green River, WY

greenroom in theaters, a room near the stage for performers and guests; in television, a room or waiting area for guests The origin is sometimes attributed to the wall color of rooms adjacent to studios at the National Broadcasting Company in New York and Los Angeles. Actually, the term predates television. The earliest such room probably was in the 17th century in Elizabethan theaters, where they were called *tiring rooms*. The green color is non-glaring and helps occupants to relax, though many of these rooms are not colored green. In the United Kingdom in the 19th century, *green-room gossip* was theatrical shoptalk.

green sheet a SHOPPER, a FREE-CIRCULATION newspaper that is all or mostly advertisements

greige goods unfinished cloth, sometimes called *gray goods* to reflect its pronunciation, that is actually grayish-beige, prior to bleaching, drying, finishing, printing, and other processes of a converter

grey variant of *gray*, particularly in the United Kingdom A *grey card* is a piece of cardboard with a specific tone of gray—*middle gray*—used as a standard in photography.

Grey Advertising, Inc. a major advertising and communications company headquartered in New York

grid 1 a *gridiron* or platform; a framework, pattern, or system 2 [typography] a device in a PHOTOTYPESETTING machine on which the characters are etched 3 [theater] the framework above the stage from which ropes or cables are strung to the scenery and lights A *grid plan* or *grid plot* is a diagram of the lighting and other equipment attached to the grid; it is also called a *fly plot, hanging plot, line plot, rigging plot,* or *rigging plan.*

grid card a tabulated rate card of a radio or TV station with rates for various time periods

Gridiron Club of Washington a social organization of about 140 daily newspaper reporters, cartoonists, and editors, renowned for satirical activities at its annual March dinner in Washington, DC

grid log a schedule, as of TV programs, printed in a set format, such as the charts now used by many newspapers instead of or in addition to a *running log*, or sequential list of programs In a grid log, the TV channels appear vertically in the first column, while their programs are listed horizontally in the time-period columns.

grille or **grill** a grating A *grille cloth* is a loosely woven material stretched over a loudspeaker to conceal the diaphragm and keep out dust.

grin and grip a traditional photograph of two people smiling and shaking hands on the occasion of receiving an award or at another newsworthy event

grip a general assistant in a stage, broadcast, or film production Originally, the person had to have a firm grip to carry or push equipment, though the job is made easier by a *grip chain* and a *grip truck.*

gripper a mechanical device that grasps and holds, such as the metal fingers of a printing press that hold a sheet of paper on its *gripper margin* and take it through the press during the printing process The *gripper edge* is the *leading edge* or first part of the paper as it passes through a press or folding machine.

Grolier a style of ornamental bookbinding, as with gilt geometrical figures, named after Jean Grolier (1479–1565), French bibliophile and patron of the arts

groove a narrow channel, such as the track cut on a record or the depression between the SPINE of a book and its covers

gross the entire amount of a bill, without advertising agency commission or other deductions; hence, greater than *net* Similarly, *gross sales* is the total income before deductions for costs, as in *gross* vs. *net income* or the *gross billings* of an advertising agency vs. its commissions and other net income. *Gross less* is jargon for the actual or *net cost* of an advertisement after advertising agency or other discounts from the *gross rate.*

gross audience [broadcasting] the total audience, including duplications, expressed in numbers of viewers or households, as distinguished from *net audience* or *unduplicated audience*

gross impressions the total number of individuals or households exposed to an advertisement or campaign, including replications, as differentiated from *net impressions*

gross margin the difference between the *net cost* to the manufacturer or marketer and the selling price paid by the buyer; sometimes called simply *margin* and expressed as a percentage of cost or selling price or a specific amount

gross message weight the total GROSS RATING POINTS of an advertising campaign

gross night hour (G.N.H.) the CARD RATE, or STANDARD CHARGE, for sponsorship of one hour of television or radio-station PRIME TIME, which is used as a basis for determining other commercial rates

gross rating point (GRP) a unit of measurement of broadcast or outdoor-advertising audience size, equal to one percent of the total potential audience UNIVERSE; used to measure the exposure of one or more programs or commercials without regard to multiple exposure of the same advertising to individuals A GRP is the product of media REACH times exposure FREQUENCY. A *gross-rating-point buy* is the number of advertisements necessary to obtain the desired percentage of exposure of the message. In outdoor advertising, GRPs, often used as a synonym for SHOWING, generally refer to the daily effective circulation generated by poster panels divided by the market population. The *cost per gross rating point* (*CPGRP*) is a measure of broadcast media efficiency comparable to the *cost per thousand* (*CPM*) measure of print media.

grotesque displaying a bizarre or incongruous style SANS-SERIF letters were called grotesques in the 19th and early 20th centuries.

ground plan the layout of a stage set with notations about scenery and PROP placement

ground row [theater] a container or trough along the floor of a stage to hold and somewhat conceal lights A *ground-row strip* is a striplight that illuminates a scenic ground row from below. A ground row is also a long, narrow piece of scenery with an irregular edge that gives the illusion of a landscape, city skyline, or other silhouettes, such as a *sea row* or *water row*.

ground wave a low-frequency radio wave that travels along the earth's surface and bends around the earth's curvature, not transmitted toward the sky like a *sky wave* A radio-station signal is transmitted farther over water or flat terrain than over dry rocky ground.

groundwood pulp [papermaking] mechanically mixed fibrous material—*pulp*—that is not chemically processed *Groundwood-pulp paper* is often used in newspapers and does not last as long as chemically processed paper. *Groundwood book papers* also are low in cost but are higher in bulk, softness, and smoothness.

group 1 several stations or other media, generally under common ownership, such as by GROUP W, the Westinghouse radio and TV stations, or affiliated for shared programming or to provide quantity or *group discounts* 2 independent retailers, members of a voluntary chain, or others who join together to purchase *group advertising* 3 a number of persons or things gathered together as a unit A *statistical group* has the same characteristics, such as age, sex, income, and other DEMOGRAPHIC statistics, whereas a *functional group* has the same or similar attitudes and *psychographics*.

grouped ads advertisements set together on a newspaper page or in other media, generally for the same industry or with a common theme

group mailing the inclusion of enclosures from several advertisers in one envelope; also called cooperative mailing or co-op mailing

group quarters college dormitories, military barracks, institutions, and other residences of unrelated individuals ARBITRON and other broadcast rating services generally do not include people who do not live in individual households.

Group III the third generation of telephone FACSIMILE machines, with faster speed and lower prices than those of earlier models (the second generation, or Group II)

Group W a broadcasting company, based in New York, that owns radio and TV stations and other broadcasting properties It is a subsidiary of Westinghouse Electric Company.

GRP GROSS RATING POINT

Grundyism a statement or act that is prudish and conforms excessively to conventional morality In Thomas Morton's play *Speed the Plough* (1798), *Mrs. Grundy* was a character never seen but repeatedly referred to with the question, "What will Mrs. Grundy say?"

grusical British slang for a horror film

g.t. gilt top; see GILT-EDGE

GTE General Telephone and Electronics of Stamford, CT, a major telecommunications company that operates the GTE Sprint long-distance service, the *Telenet* public data network, and telephone companies and manufactures telephones and other products

guarantee a commitment from a medium assuring an advertiser of a specific position—a *guaranteed position*, schedule, time period, circulation, rate, and other agreed-upon conditions

guaranteed circulation minimum circulation as warranted by a publisher to advertisers

guard band or **guardband** a buffer zone of unused FREQUENCIES on either side of the channel of a broadcasting station

guards [printing] the protective metal rules around type to be ELECTROTYPED; also called *bearers* In bookbinding, guards, or hinges, are strips of paper or cloth to which major individual leaves, such as illustrations, are attached. Guards sometimes are used to reinforce the first and last SIGNATURES, particularly in a large book. A *guard leaf* is an unattached or free END-PAPER faced with silk or another material that protects or complements the doublure, or ornamental lining on the inner face of the cover of a book. A *guard sheet* is paper, usually thin, inserted in a book to protect a place or illustration and often with descriptive text or art.

guidebook a handbook of information

guide edge the edge of a printed sheet at right angles to the GRIPPER or *leading edge* Sometimes called the *bottom edge*, this end of the paper travels along a *guide* on the printing press or folding machine.

guideline 1 a statement of policy or procedure 2 [journalism] part or all of a headline or identification that is repeated so that subsequent pages are identified 3 [printing] a SLUG to identify different GALLEYS or components; also called GUIDE WORD 4 [radio] a brief identification of a news story or feature

guide lines nonreproducing blue lines drawn on a board to aid in the assembly of illustrations and copy for the paste-up operation

guide marks [printing] CROSSLINES on the OFF-SET press plate to indicate the center of the sheet or plate or where the paper should be trimmed; also called REGISTER MARKS

guide number a numerical rating for the strength of a photographic FLASH lamp

guide side [printing] the end of the sheet toward the operator; also called *control side* or *operator side*

guide word a word or term at the top of a page of a telephone book, dictionary, or other publication with the first and/or last entry; also called *page-content heading*

Guignol a French puppet character created in Lyons, France, in the late 18th century, renowned as witty and audacious A 19th-century Paris theater, the *Grand Guignol*, was named after this character and featured live shows that were gruesome and horrifying. Macabre plays and other works now are called Grand Guignol.

guillemets quotation marks used in French printing, consisting of straight lines instead of curved ones (" "); called *duckfoot quotes* in England

guillotine a cutting instrument with a heavy blade used in paper cutting, such as for trimming the edges of the leaves of a book in what is called a *guillotine cut*

Gulf and Western Inc. the former name of one of the world's largest media and communications companies, headquartered in New York The company, which owns Paramount Pictures, Paramount Television, and Simon & Schuster, changed its name in 1989 to Paramount Communications Inc.

gum arabic a sticky substance exuded by African trees and tropical plants used as an adhesive, preservative, or spray in photography and printing

gumming up a process in LITHOGRAPHY in which a solution of GUM ARABIC and water is brushed over the nonprinting areas to make them repel ink

gurney a wheeled canvas hamper, commonly used to transport mail

gusset a piece of cloth or metal inserted or affixed to make a printing form sturdier or roomier In bookbinding, gussets or *buckles* are wrinkles that sometimes form on folded SIGNATURES.

gussie or **gussy** to decorate in a showy way, used derogatorily as *gussied up*; named after a woman, Augusta

gutter a blank space or margins between facing pages in a publication The gutter is filled when the page BLEEDS. *Gutter bleed* is printing all the way to the inner margin. *Gutter position* is next to the inside margin, which is considered less desirable for an advertisement than an outside position in the outermost column. Gutter also refers to *white space* between columns. When it is between the margin and the end of a page, it is called a *gutter margin*. If it is space toward the inside or centerside of the publication, which is the most common position, it is called *back margin* or *blind margin*.

gutter records an old expression for crime news

guy a rope, cable, or wire—*guy wire*—to hold or steady something, such as to support a TV antenna tower

GW GIGAWATT

g-w-p gift with purchase, a promotional technique to sell cosmetics and other items in department stores; also called *gift-with-purchase-offer*

gypsographic print a 15th-century woodcut with blind embossing; also called *seal print*

gypsy [theater] a dancer in a musical show who is prepared to move quickly to a new show or city, like a Gypsy wanderer

gyro a spiral; spinning, as with a *gyroscope* In photography, the *gyro head* atop the tripod has a heavy flywheel for smooth movement of the camera.

H

h or **hr.** hour The plural is *hrs.*

h. or **ht.** height

HAAT [broadcasting] height of antenna above average terrain

haček an accent or diacritical mark, as in č, in Czech and Lithuanian; pronounced HAH-check

hachure one of a series of parallel lines on a map to represent elevations Sometimes hachures are short, wedge-shaped marks instead of short parallel lines.

hack **1** a rough, irregular cut; to cut irregularly **2** a taxicab **3** a writer hired to do commercial or routine work; a person who undertakes boring, sometimes unpleasant assignments, mainly for payment A *hack writer* (the phrase is a redundancy) is a literary drudge who produces banal, routine work. *Hack journalism* is uninspired (*hackneyed*) work; the term sometimes refers to commercial assignments and generally is used derogatorily for mediocre work.

hacker [computers] an enthusiast, sometimes one who experiments with systems, perhaps seeking unauthorized or illegal access

hagiography the writing about or the study of the lives of the saints or, more generally, of an idolized subject A *hagiographer* is an author of a *hagiographic* book or other work. *Hagios* is Greek for "holy."

hairline [printing] a fine rule or line—specifically .003 inch thick; also, an unwanted line, which sometimes appears between characters—letters or numbers—or elsewhere A *hairspace* is a thin piece of metal, between ⅙ and ¹⁄₁₂ of an EM, used for spacing. *Hairspacing* is very thin spacing between lines. Though metal type has largely been replaced by more modern methods of typesetting, terms such as hairline still are used.

hairline register dot-for-dot or line-for-line accuracy in printing, SCORING, perforating, and numbering

hair space [printing] a thin space, abbreviated in copyediting as *hr#* See also HAIRLINE.

hairstylist a person who styles the hair of performers and others

halation the blurring, dispersal, or spreading of light around bright areas, such as the sun, on a photographic image; a ring of light, resembling a halo, around a bright object on a TV screen *Antihalation backing* is provided on films to absorb light after it has passed through the emulsion and to prevent the light from reflecting.

half-binding a type of bookbinding in which the spine and a portion of the boards, or sides, are covered in one material and the remainder of the boards are covered in another material A *half-cloth* or *half-linen* book has a spine covered in cloth and sides covered in noncloth material, such as paper. A *half-leather* book has a leather spine and nonleather sides.

half-diamond [printing] a style of double indent in which each successive line is shortened equally at both ends, resembling a half-diamond or *inverted pyramid* (another term for the process)

half-duplex transmission data communication over a channel that both transmits and receives, but in only one direction at a time; also called *two-way alternate transmission* It is not the same as *duplex* (or *full-duplex*) *transmission*, in which communication takes place simultaneously in both directions.

half hour a warning call to performers 30 minutes before the beginning of a performance; sometimes shortened to "Half!" Generally this is the first call.

half-lap [film, television] a split screen in which two images appear simultaneously on the screen—a side-by-side shot

half-life the time it takes for half the ultimate total of responses to a direct marketing campaign to be received The *half-life time*, or *first-half period*, as it is also called, generally is about two weeks after the advertisement appeared or the mailing went out; the second half, including stragglers that arrive many weeks later, usually takes much longer. The *half-life formula* provides an estimate, shortly after the first responses are received, of the total responses to be expected and thus makes it possible to decide—based on statistically valid partial data—whether to continue the campaign.

half-page spread an arrangement of editorial or advertising matter on the upper or lower half of each of two facing pages of a newspaper, magazine, or other publication

half run in transit advertising, the placement of advertisements (called *car cards*) in every other train, subway car, or bus; also called *half service* In outdoor advertising, the same concept is on alternate PANELS and is called *half showing*. Other fractions may be used as well.

half-shot a camera position in which the framing of the subject is between that of a CLOSE-UP and that of a LONG SHOT, for example, a photograph of a person from the head to the waist; more commonly called *medium shot*

half-title the title of a book appearing on a page preceding the first page of text, or a brief title on a page preceding the title page; sometimes called *bastard title* or *pretitle*

halftone a photograph or artwork with continuous or varying tones of gray, as reproduced from an engraving called a *halftone plate* A halftone is a print made from a *relief plate* whose negative is obtained by photographing the original photo or art through a finely ruled glass screen called a *halftone screen*. Halftones consist of light areas and shadows that, when printed, appear as a series of dots. The groupings and densities of the dots determine the intensity of color or darkness. Various densities of screen can be used to vary the tones or shadings. The term halftone is also used to refer to the photoengraving itself and sometimes to this technique of reproduction. The ingenuity of the halftone process is that it produces an optical illusion, in that the eye does not see the dots when they are properly reproduced. Thus a halftone—sometimes called *middletone*—is a tone or value halfway between HIGHLIGHT and a dark shadow. In actual practice, *halftone* refers to the conventionally reproduced picture or photograph in which light gradations are obtained by the relative darkness and density of tiny dots produced by photographing through a fine screen. A *ghosted halftone* is faded, as for a background.

half-up a layout, in a newspaper, magazine, or other publication with a half-column of white space; artwork that is 1½ times the size at which it will be reproduced

halide a chemical compound of a HALOGEN and an electropositive element (such as silver) Silver halides, or silver salts, are commonly used on light-sensitive film and paper.

halogen any of five chemically related nonmetallic elements, specifically astatine, bromine, chlorine, fluorine, and iodine A *tungsten-halo-gen lamp* has a filament of tungsten and a halogen and is smaller and more color-consistent than a standard *halogen lamp*. Halogen lamps are commonly used in film and other fields.

ham a performer who overacts or exaggerates; an amateur radio operator The word may come from the inept actors who desired to play Hamlet, or it may come from the ham fat formerly used by actors to remove makeup. Inept, overdone, or old-fashioned acting is called *hammy* or *ham acting*.

hammerhead a headline larger than the main headline, set flush left and not extending beyond the middle of the line, thus somewhat resembling the head of a hammer; also called *hammer*, used in newspapers and other media

hammers workers who assist the GRIP in handling film cameras and other equipment, except lighting They are not carpenters.

hammocking the practice of scheduling a weak TV program between two strong programs—suspended the way a canvas hammock hangs between two supports The popular programs are in the tent-pole positions and the weak one is settled in the saddle position.

hand 1 pertaining to the hand or its functions, such as *handwriting* (penmanship), as distinct from typewriting or typesetting 2 an actual object, such as handwritten, typed, or printed text, rather than a representation of it, such as the same text on a screen or in PHOTOTYPESET form 3 a round of applause An audience, when asked to give a performer a *big hand*, responds with resounding applause. 4 a manual worker; a participant 5 a mark consisting of a hand with a pointed finger, to call attention to a particular section; also called *index* 6 qualities of involvement A *heavy hand* is clumsy; a *fine hand* is deft; a *high hand* is overbearing. *Hands-on* suggests direct participation, as at a museum exhibition in which the displays may be touched. *Hand delivery* is personal delivery, as by messenger; *hand-carry* is an instruction to deliver an item, such as a confidential memo, personally. 7 [printing] *All in hand* is the stage at which all copy has been received, or handed in, and is being processed.

handbasher [film, television] a hand-held lamp, usually about 800 watts

handbill a single sheet—a circular or a flier—distributed by hand on streets or to homes and offices

handbook a concise manual with instructions or reference material It is often small enough to be carried in the hand.

hand composition the setting of type by hand rather than by machine; also called *hand set-*

ting Hand type was called *foundry type* in the early days of LETTERPRESS printing.

hand-holders in theaters, particularly movie theaters, very young members of the audience—from the idea that children hold hands with each other

hand-holding personal relations, including frequent communication, between an advertising agency, public relations firm, or other vendor and its client

handicapper a predictor of horse-race results The predictions appear in a newspaper column or a special publication devoted to handicapping.

H&J HYPHENATION AND JUSTIFICATION

handle 1 an opportunity or a means of achieving a purpose; an ANGLE, PEG, or theme 2 slang for a person's name, and also for the total amount of money bet on an event or in a place 3 an unscripted word or phrase used by a performer as a transition, such as *Well . . .* 4 to operate with the hands, manipulate, deal with, or have responsibility for

handler an operative or manager in charge of communications, such as a manager of a political candidate or of an athlete

handling allowance an allowance from a manufacturer to a distributor or retailer for handling merchandise requiring special attention, such as coupon redemption A charge made to a manufacturer by a distributor in lieu of a handling allowance is called a *handling charge.*

handmade made manually, as with paper made by hand as single sheets, often with a deckle-edge, or irregular, finish

handoff a transfer; in telecommunications, the shifting of responsibility from one ground station to another, a common procedure in aircraft control

handout a news release or other item distributed, or handed out, by a publicist or other source

handset a portable telephone mouthpiece or transmitter and receiver in a single unit, for holding in one hand; also called *transceiver* The receiver is on the upper end, to be held next to the user's ear, and the mouthpiece is on the lower end.

handsetting See HAND COMPOSITION.

handshaking a protocol in which a transmitting device, such as a TELETYPEWRITER, sends a signal, after which the receiving device sends a "ready" signal before transmission continues

hand tooling the technique of engraving a person's name on a book cover, or other hand-finishing of printed and other materials

hand type characters, usually lead, set by hand, as by selecting from a case, instead of from a typesetting machine

handwired referring to wiring that is inserted manually The term is generally applied to permanently wired electronic components, such as a *handwired computer*, in which the program LOGIC cannot be altered except by replacing the circuit boards or memories, or to any device that is built to perform a specific task and is not programmable

hand-worked house a theater in which the ropes to suspend scenery are adjusted manually; formerly called a *rope house*

hang a show theatrical slang: to set up the scenery for a play or other show

hanger-card a pennant or other hanging card on a display or shelf in a store

hanger marks edge marks on film, produced by the hooks on which film is hung during development, generally the result of insufficient AGITATION of the film

hang for ten a typesetting specification indicating that figures in a column are to be aligned by ones, tens, and hundreds

hanging figures old-style numerals with varying length, ascenders, and descenders (upward and downward strokes) Modern, or lining, figures are aligned on a base line and are all the same height.

hanging indent text, though not necessarily full sentences, that is indented In newspaper stories with a list of names, such as award recipients or accident victims, the style may be *hanging indent, names caps*, in which the names are set in all caps, flush left, and the information about each person is set indented under the name. A *hanging-indent headline* has the first line full width and the following lines indented. In a *hanging paragraph*, the first line is set flush at the left margin and the following lines are indented; an uncommon format, it is the reverse of the ordinary paragraph, in which the first line is indented and the subsequent lines are flush left.

hanging plan scale drawings of the rigging system (ropes, pipes, and other equipment for lights, scenery, and curtains) of a play or other show

hanging plot a diagram of the lighting and other items attached to the battens (pipes) in a play or other show; the duties of the *fly crew* (the staff that operates this equipment); also called *fly plot, grid plan, grid plot, line plan, rigging plan*, or *rigging plot*

hanging punctuation See HUNG PUNCTUATION.

hangover something remaining from a previous time or state, such as a sound that continues in a loudspeaker after the signal input has stopped

happening 1 an event—either spontaneous and improvised or planned—set up to create news and obtain attention 2 an art form often involving audience participation and/or staged on a street or public area other than a theater. Called *manifestation* or *realization* in England, this type of audio and/or visual event was developed in the 1960s; the more current term is *performance art.*

happy talk a format of TV news programs, featuring light banter among an ensemble of newscasters

hard containing or displaying excess contrast, as in HARD PAPER or HARD LIGHT

hard copy permanent, printed text, as produced by a computer printer, distinguished from the temporary visual display on a video screen

hard core extremely graphic or explicit, especially in reference to pornography

hard cover a hardback or hardbound book, bound in cloth, cardboard, or leather; not paperback

hard edge 1 a form of abstract painting with clearly defined geometric shapes 2 the distinct edges of a vignette (an unbordered design or portrait that shades off at its edges)

hard-edge wipe [film, television] a wipe (an optical effect between two succeeding shots) in which the border between the two images is sharply defined; the opposite of SOFT-EDGE WIPE

hardener a substance added to film or other surfaces to make it tougher and scratch-resistant; the opposite of softener

hard-front camera a camera with a single mount, or one hole for the attachment of a lens, instead of the movable turret on most modern professional cameras, which holds three or four lenses

hard goods merchandise that lasts and is used repeatedly over a long period, such as cars, refrigerators, and other appliances

hard light a narrow-beamed light, such as from a spotlight, that produces strong illumination, sharp outlines, and shadows, akin to sunlight It differs from *soft light*, which diffuses the illumination.

hard news reports of events of timeliness and/or importance *Hard-hard news* is an objective, behind-the-scenes article (not a commentary) about a news event—how and why it happened, who made it happen, and other reportorial details. A hard-news-show set generally has the newspersons, or anchors, at a desk; a SOFT-NEWS-show set such as the magazine-style

daytime programs—often has a couch or other furniture suggesting a living room.

hard paper photographic paper used to print negatives with considerable—that is, hard—contrast

hard proof a proof on paper, not displayed on a computer screen

hard return in computerized typesetting, a code that requires an action such as paragraphing In *soft return*, in contrast, the carriage return is variable and handled by the operator.

Hard Rock the nickname for the New York headquarters of Capital Cities–ABC Inc. (the American Broadcasting Companies), so called because the nearby black granite building of the Columbia Broadcasting System is called *Black Rock*

hard sell the overt, forceful effort to persuade; the opposite of *soft sell*, a more indirect, subtle approach

hard ticket a ticket of admission to a show with a specific number of reserved seats, such as a specially priced movie or a road-show attraction A scarce, hard-to-find, ticket for a hit show sometimes is called a *hard ticket.*

hardtop an indoor theater

hardware [computers] the physical equipment, such as the frame, printer, central processing unit, and disk drive, as compared to the programs and other software

hardwired [telephone] referring to equipment that is permanently connected into a wall, in contrast to portable equipment attached to a jack

harlequin 1 a clown 2 a pattern of brightly colored diamonds 3 [printing] heavy-set, decorative type elements

Louis Harris and Associates a major survey research firm in New York, headed by Louis Harris (b. 1921), who is well known for his syndicated newspaper column, based on the ABC News–Harris survey Founded in 1956 and acquired in 1975 by the Gannett Company, the Harris firm operates the National Research Center of the Arts, the National Center for Telephone Research, and other divisions.

Harris-Intertype Corporation a major manufacturer of offset printing presses, located in Cleveland

Harris shutter a device on a camera with a strip of three color filters and an opaque card at each end, so that three exposures are made of a subject, each through a different-colored filter that passes in rapid succession in front of the lens, thus producing a tricolor effect The shutter was designed by Robert Harris of the Eastman Kodak Company, Rochester, NY.

Harry system [film, television] a digital animating machine that stacks computerized graphics and other images on top of each other to create the illusion of three-dimensionality

Harte-Hanks Communications a publisher of newspapers and owner of radio and TV stations and other companies, headquartered in San Antonio, TX

Harvard comma a comma placed before the conjunction (generally *and*) in a series of items; more commonly called SERIAL COMMA

Harvard system a method of citing references at the end of an article, chapter, or book, instead of on each page (footnote reference system)

hash 1 a jumble; a hodgepodge 2 an electromagnetic interference 3 to mangle 4 to discuss carefully A *hash session* is an informal meeting to review (*hash over*) details.

hatch to mark an area of a drawing, photo, or other piece of art to indicate shading with fine, closely set parallel lines, a process called *hatching* Cross-hatching uses intersecting or crisscrossed lines. Parallel lines sometimes are used to indicate an area seen in cross-section.

hatch mark a character or symbol (#) indicating space or the word *number*; also called *hatcher*

Hathaway touch an unexpected, extra element in an advertisement, a reference to the eyepatch worn by the model in the advertisements created by the Ogilvy & Mather advertising agency for the Hathaway Shirt Company

having had a slang direction to a film or tape cast and crew to report back to work at a specific time, after having had lunch or another meal

hazard pay an extra fee to a stuntperson or other performer or technician for risky work

haze 1 a partially opaque atmospheric condition 2 [photography] a type of filter used for *haze penetration*, to diminish the effect of ultraviolet radiation or other haze, particularly in distant scenes; also called *skylight filter*

Hazeltine [film] a widely used, trademarked, electronic device that analyzes colors and displays them on a monitor, originated by the Hazeltine Corporation, Greenlawn, NY, and now made by the Hollywood Film Company, Los Angeles

HBA health and beauty aids: a category of products that makes extensive use of advertising and public relations services

HBO HOME BOX OFFICE

hd. HEAD

hdbk. HANDBOOK

HDTV HIGH-DEFINITION TELEVISION

head 1 a HEADLINE; a heading A *standing head* is one that is used again and again, often to identify a department or regular feature. A *read-ing head* is a column title in a table under which reading matter, rather than numbers, appears. 2 the beginning 3 the uppermost part, such as the top of a book, page, or printing form 4 the main part; the working end; the operative part 5 the projecting part—for instance, the head of a tape recorder, which records and plays back the magnetic signals 6 the designation of parts of a TV camera The camera consists of the *camera head* (the lens, tubes, viewfinder, and cable), *panning head* or *pan head* (platform and handle, for turning), and mounting. A *fluid panning head* uses silicon fluid to smooth the movement, whereas a *friction head* uses surface friction between the parts. A *cradle head* supports the camera, a *cam head* has cameras on two sides of the head, and *geared heads* have gears to control the movements.

headband in bookbinding, a small ornamental fabric strip, generally cotton or silk, sewn or glued at the head, or top, and/or foot, or bottom, of a book to fill the gap between the spine and the cover and add a decorative touch

headbox in papermaking, a storage tank at the front of the paper machine, for collection of the pulp mixture

headcap [bookbinding] a piece of leather or other material placed over the HEADBAND of a book SPINE

headend electronic equipment located at the start of a transmission system, usually including antennas, preamplifiers, frequency converters, demodulators, modulators, and related equipment The headend of a cable system includes the antenna, downlink, and subordinate transmission points within the community. A large system may have a *master headend* and *subheadends*.

header a marker or designation that indicates the beginning of a section of a publication or a computer FILE, or its location; a sign or other identification structure across the top of a display or exhibit Sections of articles and publications are identified by headers, usually with a number and title, with a *first-level header* identifying sections, *second-level header* for subsections, *third-level header* for sub-subsections, and *fourth-level header* for sub-sub-subsections. First- and second-level headers usually are in all capital letters, and third- and fourth-level headers usually have the first letter capitalized.

headline the title or description at the top of a page in a book or atop a news release or article, as a synopsis or to attract attention; sometimes called *head, heading,* or *hed* Subheads may be inserted within the text. A *headline schedule, head schedule,* or *hed sked* is a catalog or listing of all headlines regularly used by a publication, including typefaces, character counts (numbers of letters), and other details or, less frequently, a record of all headlines in an issue, sometimes including the size (unit count of characters and spaces). A *head slug* is a ruled line (generally 6 points in thickness) below the headline. *Head to come* (*HTK*) is a notation on copy that the headline will be written and set later. A *split head* is a headline of more than one line with a bad break between lines, such as a line ending in a preposition or a line with only part of a compound verb. Words are never hyphenated in headlines. The present tense often is used in newspaper headlines, even when referring to events that have already occurred, to enhance the sense of immediacy and because present tense verbs are a bit shorter than past tense. A *blind headline* is a headline with no obvious meaning, such as a *teaser headline* on a magazine cover or in a tabloid newspaper. Headlines are used in broadcast and other media, in addition to newspapers. For example, the lead item or indication of a forthcoming item on a broadcast may be referred to as a *headline*. The preliminary indication sometimes is called a *billboard*. See also HEADLINE SCHEDULE.

headline budget   a general budget, without specific details

Headline News   an all-news cable network, owned by the Turner Broadcasting System, in Atlanta   It operates in 30-minute cycles.

headliner   1 the featured performer   The leading attraction is called the *headliner act*. The process of providing top billing, major publicity, or prominent position on the program is called *headlining*. In vaudeville, the *headliner act* was presented before the closing act; it was not—as sometimes stated—the closing act, which was performed as some of the audience exited. In the United Kingdom, a headliner is called a *topliner*.   2 a machine to set type in large sizes, usually one character (letter or number) at a time

Headliner Awards   annual national awards presented by the Press Club of Atlantic City, NJ, to people working in broadcast and print news

headline schedule   a chart of types of headlines, designated by letter or number, regularly used at a publication   The largest single-column head is called an *A head* or *Number 1 head*. The letter system is more common, as the letter then is preceded by a number indicating the column width. A *2B head*, for example, is a large-size head (second to A) set in two-column width. A *J head* is a very small headline, as sometimes used above fillers.

headlinese   writing that has some of the characteristics of a newspaper headline but in an exaggerated way   It may be too staccato or overly compressed, have too many nouns (including the use of nouns as adjectives), or include ambiguous words or clichés.

head margin   the white space above the first line on a page of a publication

headnote   a brief introduction beneath a title or a headline with information about the author or the story, essay, or other work that follows

head of household   a person responsible for the management of a household or a family

head-on location   an outdoor advertising location facing oncoming traffic

headphone   a radio or telephone receiver held to the ear or ears by a band over the head

headpiece   a drawing or piece of art to decorate or accompany a headline or heading, often used at the beginning of a chapter or section of a book   The ornament at the end is the TAILPIECE.

headquarters call   a sales call made at the central buying office of a chain of retail stores

head rhyme   the alliteration of words or repetition of initial sounds in words, particularly in poetry

headroom   1 [film, television] the field of vision between the top of a performer in a film or TV program and the top of the motion picture or TV screen   In a close-up, the headroom is diminished.   2 [marketing] the potential for additional sales   3 [recording] the difference between the highest level of a signal and the maximum level that can be handled, without noticeable distortion, by the recorder or other audio device

head rule   a horizontal line across the top of the page of a newspaper or other publication   The page number and date appear above this line.

headset   an earphone, generally with an attached mouthpiece transmitter, used by telephone operators, rewrite personnel in newspaper offices, and others   Types of headsets include *dynamic, planar dynamic, electrostatic, circumaural* (fits over the ear), *open air,* or *supra-aural* (not as close on the ear as circumaural).

head shot   a still photograph of a person's head and shoulders; also called *mug shot*

head sound   singing in which sopranos and other opera singers and BELTERS and other popular singers push air from the diaphragm to vibrate the vocal chords, instead of contracting the chest and neck muscles; also called *headtone*

heads out   1 a tape or film in which the beginning is on the outside and is thus ready to be used; the opposite of *tails out*   the end is on the outside, as in the unrewound state   2 a method of folding circulars, newspapers, or other printed material with the printed side or the beginning on the outside

head spot a spotlight, or a beam of light, focused on the head of a performer

heads up a reel of film or tape with the first frame, or leader, outermost and ready for projection; also called HEADS OUT Heads up is obviously preferable to the opposite position of *tails up* or *tails out.*

head time the blank space at the top of a printed sheet, to be cut, or trimmed, usually by ⅛ inch.

head title the name or title of a written work, as stated at the beginning of the first page of the text; also called *caption title*

head-to-head [printing] the conventional layout of copy, with the top of both sides of a sheet of paper placed at the same end The opposite is *head-to-foot* or *head-to-tail*, a position in which the sheet is flipped over, from top to bottom as well as from back to front, to read the reverse side.

headword 1 a heading, of one or more words 2 a word modified by another word, generally a noun modified by an adjective, a verb modified by an adverb, or an adverb modified by a qualifier

Hearst/ABC-Viacom Entertainment Services a cable programming company in New York, owned by THE HEARST CORPORATION, THE AMERICAN BROADCASTING COMPANY, and VIACOM INTERNATIONAL

Hearst Corporation one of the country's largest media companies, headquartered in New York. Founded by William Randolph Hearst (1863–1951), the firm publishes newspapers and magazines (*Cosmopolitan, Esquire, Good Housekeeping*, and others); it also owns major radio and TV stations, cable-TV systems, and North American Syndicate (including KING FEATURES).

heart courage; the central part, or essence, as of a novel or other work

heat-developing film an exposed film, such as dry silver film, made visible—that is, developed—thermally (by heat) and not with chemical fluids The technique is used in dry-process copying.

heat up a light to turn on a spotlight or other light

Heaviside layer a region of ionized air about 60 miles above the earth's surface that reflects AM broadcast signals back to earth at night, named after Oliver Heaviside (1850–1925), an English physicist It is also called *Kennelly-Heaviside layer*, after Arthur Edwin Kennelly (1861–1935), an American electrical engineer.

heavy a serious dramatic role, particularly that of the villain (called the *heavy*) Actors playing such roles, like Sydney Greenstreet (1879–1954) and Charles Laughton (1899–1962), indeed used to be heavy.

heavy-up to intensify, as used in budgeting or scheduling For example, *heavying up* is the increased use of a medium, such as a radio station, by an advertiser.

heavy user a user of a product or a service whose rate of consumption is significantly above average *Heavy-half users* account for half (or more) of total consumption, but number less than half of the total user population.

hecto a combining form meaning 100 A *hectohertz* is 100 HERTZ.

hectograph a duplicating machine that uses a gelatin surface on which the image is transferred, on paper called *hectograph paper*; see also HECTOGRAPHY

hectography a printing process; also called *spirit duplicating* or *ditto* Hecto means 100, and the word *hectography* is based on the most commonly printed quantity of each job (100 copies).

hed HEADLINE

hedonic having to do with pleasure *Hedonic goods* are products purchased to provide pleasure and are generally not *utility items*, or necessary goods.

height-to-paper [printing] a length of type, standardized in the United States at .9186 inches from face to feet

helical scan a method of recording video on tape in which the signal is recorded in parallel diagonal strips, akin to a cylindrical helix; also called *slant-track* The first videotape recorders were longitudinal scan in which the signals were recorded in horizontal strips.

helical spiral [television] the standard method of scanning videotape (helical scanning), in which the tape moves from the supply reel in a helical, or spiral, path around one or more recording or replay heads In helical videotape recording systems, the heads are angled and the tape has a slanting path, so HELICAL SCANNING also is called slant-track scanning.

heliogravure PHOTOGRAVURE printing

Helios 1 the nickname for HELVETICA typeface 2 a trademarked line of papers and other materials used in dry DIAZO reproduction, made by the Keuffel and Esser Company, Morristown, NJ

heliotype See COLLOTYPE.

hell box a container into which discarded metal type is thrown before being remelted

helmer a director: a nickname coined by the trade publication *Variety*, from the helmsman who steers a ship

Help-Wanted-Advertising Index a monthly report of employment classified advertising linage The number of lines of such advertising is compared to the figure for a base year and expressed in points. The statistics are compiled and issued by The Conference Board, a management organization based in New York, as an indication of employment trends.

Helvetica a SANS-SERIF typeface, one of the most commonly used *Helvetia* is the Latin name for Switzerland.

hen-and-chicks a type of layout in which a large photograph or other large element is surrounded by smaller ones

herder [film] slang for *second assistant director*, who "herds" the extras, performers hired by the day, often for crowd scenes

herd instinct the tendency of people to follow the crowd and mindlessly do what everyone—or almost everyone—else is doing

hermeneutics the science of interpretation, particularly of the Bible and other sacred texts In its modern form as related to communication, hermeneutics is the study and interpretation of texts.

heroic of or characterized by heroes (of godlike strength and courage), as with a *heroic poem* or *heroic verse*, the form in which EPIC poetry generally was written A *heroic couplet* is a pair of rhymed IAMBIC pentameter lines first used extensively in English in the verse of Chaucer (1340–1400) and later by Alexander Pope (1688–1744). A *heroic quatrain* or *heroic stanza* is a poem or part of a poem (a stanza) consisting of two heroic couplets. A *heroic drama*, usually written in heroic couplets, was a type of play popular in England in the 17th century, in which the virtuous hero resolved a conflict, such as between honor or duty and love.

hertz (Hz) a unit of frequency of vibrations (sound intensity), equal to one cycle per second It is named after the German physicist Heinrich Hertz (1857–94). Radio signals are measured in hertz or Hertzian waves.

heuristic describing a technique for helping to discover or to learn, generally by trial and error An individual or a computer assesses each attempted solution in order to proceed with subsequent efforts to arrive at a solution. A *heuristic program*, as in market research, uses this empirical approach as a guide but is incapable of exact proof. A *heuristic ideation technique* (*HIT*) is a procedure for generating ideas or solutions to a problem by analyzing a series of generalizations.

hexastich a poem or stanza of six lines

hf HIGH FREQUENCY

hf. half

HFD a trade publication: the bible of the furniture, appliance, and home furnishings fields, published by Fairchild Publications, of New York; formerly called *Home Furnishings Daily*

HFR HOLD FOR RELEASE

H.H.I. HEAD-OF-HOUSEHOLD INCOME

HI a high-intensity lamp, such as a *high-intensity arc* (*HI arc*), *high-intensity carbon arc*, *high arc light*, or *high-intensity discharger* (*HID*)

H.I. HUMAN INTEREST

hiatus 1 [advertising] the period during a campaign when an advertiser's schedule is suspended for a short period of time, after which it resumes 2 [broadcasting] a period of inactivity or interruption of a program schedule, such as during the summer

hickey a spot or imperfection on a photograph or artwork or in printing, the result of dirt or other foreign matter; the plural is *hickies* A *doughnut hickey* is a printing defect consisting of a solid printed area surrounded by an unprinted area.

hi-con [photography] high contrast

hidden line a series of short, evenly spaced dashes designating a concealed or hidden component of a diagram or drawing

hidden offer a special offer presented inconspicuously in an advertisement, perhaps as a test; also called *buried offer*

hierarchical structure [computers] an arrangement of data items with several levels in a tree-like format so that one item leads to another

hieroglyphic a system of pictorial writing used by the ancient Egyptians Illegible or hard-to-read writing may be called *hieroglyphics*.

hi-fi 1 HIGH FIDELITY 2 [printing] a FULL-COLOR PROCESS produced as a continuous roll, usually by an advertiser at an outside printing plant, so that the sheet can feed into a newspaper printing press and be cut to fit the specific page size Usually, the advertisement is on one side of the sheet only; the other side is printed locally by the individual newspaper. SPECTACOLOR is a similar full-color process in which the pages are produced with REGISTRATION marks, to fit a newspaper page.

high angle the placement of the camera above the subject, pointed downward to produce a *high-angle shot*

highball to proceed at great speed; from the ball hung above railroad tracks, which was a signal to go ahead

high band tape videotape with superior resolution, or pictorial clarity, and of better quality than *low band tape*

high comedy humor resulting from witty dialogue, often reflecting the upper social classes, in contrast to LOW COMEDY

high-contrast a style of lighting or photographic development in which there is an absence of gray or middle tones; also called *high negative* The emphasis is on dark gray or black or extremes of white and black.

high-definition television (HDTV) a system with higher resolution, or pictorial clarity, and other qualities that are superior to techniques currently used by U.S. television stations In HDTV, more lines per picture frame are transmitted than is standard (525 lines per frame in the United States), resulting in sharper, more vivid images.

high end the upper-frequency portion of an audio or video signal *High-end noise* is any spurious, or unwanted, signal in the high frequencies of a signal.

high-end strategy [marketing] a prestige orientation emphasizing nonprice features

high fidelity (hi-fi) the electronic reproduction of sound in a broad range of frequencies with minimum distortion

high finish referring to paper with a smooth, hard surface

high frequency a radio frequency between 3 and 30 megaherz

high hat or **hi-hat** 1 a top hat 2 a snob 3 a light fixture placed within the ceiling 4 a short tripod or mounting for low-angle camera shots

high-key lighting lighting of a photographic subject or a motion-picture or television scene in which the KEY LIGHT is strongly emphasized The result is a brilliance, with the orientation to white. It is not exactly the same as HIGH-CONTRAST lighting.

high-key picture a CONTINUOUS-TONE photograph consisting mostly of white (HIGHLIGHT) areas

highlight 1 a major point, as in a speech or an article, or a major area, as in a photograph; to give emphasis 2 [photography] the brightest part of a picture—not the shadows To highlight is to emphasize, as with special lighting. 3 in word processing, to intensify the illumination of characters on the cathode-ray tube, in order to emphasize graphically the *highlighted text* 4 to use cosmetics to emphasize a specific facial feature, such as the cheeks

highlight halftone a PHOTOENGRAVING or print from which some of the screened dots have

been removed, so that these areas reproduce as white; also called *dropout halftone*

highlighting a process of emphasizing, as with a pen or marker that is used to draw a colored line through portions of a script or other work In computer graphics, highlighting is the process of emphasizing a part of a display field in relation to other parts—for instance, to intensify, BLINK, or create a REVERSE IMAGE.

high sign a signal, often by prearrangement, given secretly, such as a warning or a nonverbal expression of approval like a circle formed with the thumb and index finger

high spot in outdoor advertising, a heavy-traffic location, not necessarily on top of a hill

highway contract route a contract for carrying mail over a highway between designated points; formerly called *star route*

hilites [radio] highlights, a summary of the top news stories, totaling about 60 seconds

Hill & Knowlton Inc. one of the world's largest public relations firms, owned by the WPP Group of London

hinge 1 a thin, folded piece of paper, generally gummed, used to attach a postage stamp or other item onto a sheet 2 in bookbinding, a paper or muslin stub affixed to the BINDING EDGE as an inside strip to which is attached a map or other leaf

hinged in bookbinding, referring to plates that are folded or turned over a short distance from the back edge before being placed in the book, so that they will lie flat and be easily turned; also called *broken over*

hip-hop the culture of RAP language, style, and music, originated among young blacks, mostly in New York, in the 1970s Hip-hop words include *def* (meaning *the best*), *stupid* (*terrific*), *word* (*truth*), *homes* (*friends*), and *wack* (*awful*).

hi-spotting the practice of calling on selected customers who are the most likely to buy a product or service

histogram a bar chart

historic present the literary technique of describing past events in the present tense

hit 1 a success; successful, as with a *hit book* or *hit movie* 2 [printing] an impression 3 to postmark mail with a hand stamp 4 [direct marketing] a name that appears on two different mailing lists, which are then MERGED 5 [television] the loss of a portion of the video signal from a videotape, usually resulting from dirt, grease, or insufficient iron oxide on that part of the tape; also called *dropout* 6 a term used in a number of theatrical slang expressions, including:

hit the boards to appear on stage

hit the ceiling	to forget one's lines
hit the lights	to turn on the lights
hit the juice	to turn on the electricity
hit the mark	to move to a predetermined place
hit the nut	to cover expenses
hit the stand	to arrive at an engagement
hit the tanks	to tour small towns

HIT heuristic ideation technique; see HEURISTIC

hitchhike a free ride; a secondary offer, item, or commercial by the same or a different sponsor, accompanying the primary item Examples include a small insert in a mailing and a commercial accompanying a syndicated radio or TV program.

hit it to play loudly and suddenly; an order to musicians to start to play or to play livelier

Hit radio a radio-station format featuring current hit music records; also called *contemporary hit radio (CHR)*

hld. HOLD

HMI HYDRAGYRUM MERCURY MEDIUM ARC LENGTH AND IODIDE

Hobbesian relating to Hobbism, the philosophy of Thomas Hobbes (1588–1679), an English philosopher who believed in a strong government A *Hobbesian model* of behavior describes industrial buyers and others who are concerned with their relationship to their group or to the government.

hold (hld.) **1** an instruction to retain for future use **2** the repeated printing of a single frame or the freezing of an image on film; to keep in place, or *hold frame* **3** to temporarily leave a phone call, without disconnecting the call A call or caller is put *on hold* by pressing a *hold key* or using a *holding jack*. In *exclusive hold* or *i-hold* (*instrument hold*), only the telephone instrument that put the call on hold can retrieve it, whereas in *line hold*, others can retrieve the call. *Holding time* is the length of time a call is kept waiting or, in international telephone, the total time the circuit is used, from the time the telephone instrument is picked up to the time it is returned to its cradle. **4** a term used in a variety of theatrical slang expressions, including:

hold the curtain	to delay raising the curtain and thus delay the start of the performance
hold the picture	to stay in position
hold the stage	to remain popular
hold up the scenery	to have a small part

hold back [photography] to vary the density of selected areas on a print by temporarily shielding them during exposure; same as to *dodge*

hold cel a transparent sheet used in film animation (called a CEL) that contains scenery or other art that remains the same in several frames, so that it does not have to be redrawn

hold file [journalism] a folder or a part of a computer storage that holds copy indefinitely; used for features, advances, and background information

hold for release or **hold-for-release (HFR)** instructions or requests to retain material for use at a subsequent time, such as for a postdated news release or advertisement

holdings property; a collection, such as all of the issues of a periodical or other serial or all of the items in a library collection (called *library holdings*)

hold it down an instruction to reduce the sound volume

hold order an instruction to retain or *keep standing*—to retain type or other material for future use

holdout in papermaking, the degree of ink on the surface, in relation to the ink absorbed into the fibers *High holdout*—a high degree of ink on the surface—is desirable, so that the ink can dry by oxidation instead of absorption, unless the amount is excessive. COATED PAPER has low ink absorption and allows ink to set on the surface. Ink on paper with too much holdout can rub off onto the next sheet.

holdover an entertainer or a production that is retained for a longer period than originally planned

holdover audience that portion of a television or radio audience for one program who were tuned to the previous program on the same station; also called *inherited audience*

hold takes film scenes (takes) retained for potential use in the completed film; also called *keep takes*

hole **1** [graphic arts] space, such as an area in a layout **2** [journalism] the amount of column inches or area allocated for a department, such as the *news hole* **3** [recording] a segment of a soundtrack without sound

hollow in bookbinding, the open space between the spine and the back of an *open-back*, or *loose-back*, book (a book in which the binding material is not glued to the back) This type of book sometimes is called a *hollow book* or *hollow-back book*, though more generally it is called a *loose-back*. A hollow-back book curves outward when opened.

hollow lumber square cardboard tubes used in retail displays, particularly in contemporary-style boutiques and stores with a high-tech look

Hollywood a section of Los Angeles Many motion-picture studios were once located in or near Hollywood; the name now connotes the

West Coast motion-picture industry or the theatrical motion-picture industry in general.

Hollywood Foreign Press Association an organization in Beverly Hills, CA, of about 100 foreign correspondents who cover the entertainment industry It presents annual Golden Globe Awards.

Hollywood progs [printing] progressive color proofs—that is, proofs showing in sequence every possible color combination in the four-color printing process The proofs are very colorful, hence the name *Hollywood*, though they are more generally called *bastard progs*.

Hollywood Radio and Television Society an organization in North Hollywood, CA, of about 1,000 people in broadcasting and advertising The group presents annual International Broadcasting Awards.

Hollywood Ten a group of ten individuals in the motion-picture industry who refused to testify at Congressional hearings conducted in 1947 by the House Committee on Un-American Activities

holography a technique of producing three-dimensional images by using lasers on a fine-grain photographic plate The resulting picture is called a *hologram*. A *holograph* is a handwritten, signed document, such as an original manuscript written by the author.

home a household unit, a concept used as the basic unit of population in audience measurement surveys

Home Box Office (HBO) the largest pay-cable network Based in New York and owned by Time Warner, HBO transmits movies and other programs to several thousand cable systems.

Home Furnishings Daily See HFD.

home key 1 [computers] a key on a personal computer keyboard that, when depressed, moves the cursor or pointer to the beginning of the line, the top left side of the screen, or another specific place 2 [music] the basic KEY in which a work is composed

home print sheets printed at the local newspaper to accompany supplements or other preprinted material obtained from outside sources

home row the second row from the bottom of a standard typewriter keyboard, starting with *a s d f*, to which the fingers return *Nonhome keys* are on the rows above and below the home row.

Home Service a radio channel of the British Broadcasting Corporation (BBC), renowned worldwide for its news, plays, and other programs; now called simply *Radio 4*

homes passed in cable TV, residences not linked to a cable system, though they are in its territory

homes using television (HUT) the A. C. NIELSEN COMPANY term for the households, located in a specific area, that use one or more TV sets during a specific time period

Home Testing Institute (HTI) a market research firm in Port Washington, NY, that provides telephone and mail surveys It is a division of NPD GROUP.

hometown newspaper a weekly or daily newspaper serving a small geographical area and concentrating on local news

hometown story an article about a person who now lives or once lived in the area of the local media

home video (H.V.) forms of electronic entertainment or instruction played rather than broadcast through a television set, including videotapes, videodiscs, and video games. The term refers also to the medium, the video recorders, and other equipment and the programs. Over half of all TV households in the United States now have VIDEOCASSETTE RECORDERS.

homily a sermon; a solemn, moralizing talk or written work, generally long and/or dull

homonym a word pronounced in the same way as another word, but with a different meaning and often with a slightly different spelling (such as *bare* and *bear*); either of two people with the same name; also called HOMOPHONE

homophone a word or part of a word with the same sound as one with a different spelling; also called *homonym* Common examples are *foul* and *fowl*, *peak* and *peek*, *pedal* and *peddle*, *pore* and *pour*, *principal* and *principle*, and *sight* and *site*.

honey wagon a trailer or enclosure that has toilets and dressing rooms, for use when filming on location

honorific conferring honor, showing respect, as with an *honorific title*, such as *Dr.* Though there are other honorifics, such as *honorific word*, the phrase *honorific title* is so common that *honorific* often is used by itself to mean any title preceding a name, including *Mr.*, *Mrs.*, *Ms.*, and *Madam*.

hood [printing] a three-sided box, as around a newspaper headline

hoofer a dancer

hook 1 [advertising, journalism] an element in a news release, article, advertisement, or other vehicle that attracts attention by virtue of newsworthiness, pithiness, or some other quality In a song, the hook is the portion of the lyrics or snatch of music the audience tends to remember 2 [marketing] an inducement or offer, used to attract attention 3 [printing] a spindle to hold copy or proofs Operators of LINOTYPE presses used to work *from the hook*, taking the copy that was placed on the hook. **4** [telephone] the hookswitch or switch in a telephone instrument, on which the receiver, or handset, rests A phone is *on hook* when the receiver is resting on the switch. An *on-hook signal* indicates an unanswered or disconnected call. A phone is *off the hook* when the receiver is removed from its switch. An *off-hook signal* indicates that the phone is in use or that the receiver has been left off the hook. *Hookswitch dialing* is obtained by depressing the hookswitch. **5** [theater] In 19th-century vaudeville, a hook on a pole was used to pull a failing performer—generally an amateur—off the stage, and the expression *getting the hook* comes from that practice.

hook and bullet press   slang for publications, and their writers, devoted to the outdoors, hunting, and similar topics

hook and loop board   a display panel, covered with felt, flannel, or other soft cloth Small loops with hooks, to which items can be attached and displayed, are on the board.

hooker   **1** a surprise ending to an article **2** an announcement to arouse curiosity; also called *teaser* **3** a prize, a premium, or a trade-in offer to capture interest or make a sale

hookswitch   See HOOK.

Hooper   a radio-audience measurement organization, founded by C. E. Hooper and now part of STARCH INRA HOOPER, INC. of Mamaroneck, NY In the 1940s, C. E. Hooper, Inc. and its Hooperatings were as well known in the broadcasting and advertising fields as ARBITRON is today.

Hooven   a process for automatic typing of "robot letters" Developed in the 1930s, the Hooven machine recorded keystrokes on a paper roll similar to a player piano and was the forerunner of today's word processors.

hop   **1** a jump, skip, or bounce **2** [film] a vertical skip in film frames during projection

hor.   horizontal

horizontal arrangement   a shelf arrangement in a retail store in which all similar or related items (or all the items from one company) are placed adjacent to one another on the same shelf or shelves In a *vertical arrangement*, the items are placed from top to bottom in a separate section of the store. The typical arrangement in supermarkets is the horizontal one.

horizontal bars   [mail] a series of uniform, wide bars, parallel to the length of a mail piece, printed immediately below the *no postage necessary* endorsement on business reply mail Horizontal bars allow automated sorting equipment to recognize this type of mail.

horizontal buy   the purchase of advertising in a variety of media for maximum REACH; also called *horizontal saturation*

horizontal discount   a discount to an advertiser who buys television or radio time over an extended period, usually a year

horizontal layout   a magazine-style arrangement, with wide columns and broad headlines, in contrast to the conventional vertical layout of newspapers, with their long, narrow columns

horizontal music   the successive sounds that form the melodies, called the *horizontals*, as opposed to the simultaneous sounds that form the harmonies, called the *verticals*

horizontal publication   a business publication that has a broad orientation, encompassing several or all industries It differs from a *vertical publication*, which is slanted to a specific industry or field of interest.

horizontal spacing   [printing] the spacing between characters (letters and numbers) or between words; called ESCAPEMENT in typesetting

horn   **1** a microwave antenna **2** slang for *telephone*, as in *get on the horn*

hornbook   a book used as an elementary text, or a primer, popular in England before the 19th century It consisted of a sheet, generally parchment or vellum, mounted on a small board with a handle and protected by a thin, transparent plate of horn. The text usually was the alphabet, a table of numbers, and a prayer.

hors concours (H.C.)   outside or beyond competition The term or its abbreviation sometimes is written on an entry in a competition to indicate that it is not eligible to compete for a prize. The expression, from the French, is pronounced ore-cone-COOR.

horse   a device on a film-editing table that dispenses film, particularly LEADER

horse opera   a film or program about the American West or, more generally, a plot with emphasis on fighting and chases

horseshoe   a horseshoe-shaped area of a theater, usually encircling part of the area above the orchestra; also called DRESS CIRCLE

horseshoe staging   a performance on a stage that projects out into the audience so that part of the audience sits on each side of the front of the stage The audience configuration thus is shaped like a *U* or a horseshoe.

horsey   [graphic arts] describing artwork or type that is too large or poorly proportioned for the layout

horsing   the technique in which one person reads proof without the assistance of a copyholder (another proofreader)

host 1 the master of ceremonies of a broadcast or show 2 [computers] the system that performs the actual operations, such as a *host computer* (located at a *host site*) that is part of a NETWORK

hostess gift a product given as a present to a consumer who hosts a demonstration or other party in his or her home The product is given by Tupperware or another party-plan organization.

hot live, energized, or excessively bright (as in stage or film lighting); also, extremely successful or popular, as with a *hot director* or a *hot ticket* (hard-to-get ticket to a hit show) A *hot background* is too bright. A *hot camera* (film or TV) is warmed up and ready for use. A *hot frame* (or *flash frame*) is intentionally overexposed so that it becomes a marker or identification for editing, as at the beginning and end of a shot (a common technique) in filming. A *hot lens* on a LUMINAIRE narrows the beam of a high-intensity light. A *hot microphone* is turned on. A *hot set* is fully prepared and ready to be filmed. A HOT SPLICER has a built-in heating unit. A *hot switch* is a fast change, as from one TV show to another. A *hot wire* is not grounded.

hot box 1 a box in which lighting cables are plugged; also called *junction box* Hot refers to electricity. 2 a portable dark room (also called *loading closet*) on a movie set In this case, *hot* refers to the heat inside the room.

hot button anything that triggers a fast response or action Marketers often attempt to determine the sales message that is most likely to produce a favorable reaction, or pressing the consumer's *hot button*.

hot line a direct communications link, such as a telephone connection between heads of state; a telephone facility for individuals to talk about personal problems or obtain advice from experts, such as a *crisis hot line* Police departments, public transportation systems, and other organizations sometimes use a special telephone connection, called a *hot line*, to report news to media and other callers and also to receive information.

hot-metal composition the setting of cast metal type (HOT TYPE) by hand or machine

hot press a paper-manufacturing technique in which paper is pressed to produce a very smooth surface, as with *illustration paper* Paper produced from *cold press*, in contrast, is smooth but with some texture (called *tooth*).

hot shoe the holder for a flash unit of a camera

hot splicer in film editing, a block with a heating element to soften the cement that bonds two pieces of film The splicer usually has a built-in device to scrape off the EMULSION from the film before gluing it together, as the adhesive generally does not bond to the emulsion.

hot spot a burning spotlight; an area in a scene with too much light or reflection; an excessively bright area on a TV or movie screen

hot start the restarting of a system, such as a computer, after a *crash*, or unplanned interruption

hot type type made from hot, molten metal, cast by a machine, such as the classic Mergenthaler LINOTYPE

hot zone in word processing and computerized typesetting, an area, or zone, immediately before the right margin at which the machine will automatically hyphenate (if appropriate) and start a new line (or request intervention by the operator); also called *line-ending zone* The amount of the space in the hot zone can be predetermined.

house a building, such as a theater, or the audience itself *House equipment* belongs to the establishment, such as the theater owner, rather than to the troupe or customer. *House lights* illuminate the audience section; lighting cues include *house to half* (dim lighting halfway) and *house out* (darkness). The command to the operator of the house lights sometimes is simply "House!", indicating a change, such as *house up* (turn on the lights) or *house down* (turn off the lights). The staff includes a *house electrician*, *house carpenter*, and *house doctor*. A *full house* means that all seats are occupied—preferably as a *sold-out house* (all tickets to a performance were sold), rather than a *papered house* (free tickets, called *paper*, were given out). *House count* is the attendance figures for a specific performance. Related terms include *good house*, *poor house*, and *next house* (the next performance). A book publishing company commonly is called a *publishing house* or *house*. Its style of copy preparation (grammar, punctuation, and other rules) is called HOUSE STYLE.

house account a client or customer of the company management or owners, rather than of a specific account executive or salesperson

house ad an advertisement by a medium, such as a newspaper or a radio station, for itself in its own publication or on its own station

house agency an advertising agency owned or controlled by an advertiser; also called *in-house agency*

house brand a brand owned and sold only by a retailer or chain

household one or more individuals who live together in an apartment, house, or other dwelling unit, a common unit for classifying population data Income, demographics, and other data often are reported, particularly by government agencies, in terms of households—for instance, average household income in a market. Market research firms and other companies often compile statistics on individuals—that is, per person. The average number of persons per household currently is under two for the over-64-year-old group and between two and three for other age groups, except for the 35-to-54 year-old groups, which are over three persons per household. A TV HOUSEHOLD is a dwelling unit with one or more TV sets.

households using television (HUT or H.U.T.) an A. C. NIELSEN COMPANY term for the number of households in an area that have one or more TV sets in use during a specific time period, as expressed in a *HUT rating*

household tracking report a report by the A. C. NIELSEN COMPANY that provides a record, over a period of time, of individual TV-network program ratings

house line an identifying line at the bottom of manuscripts, proofs, and other items showing source, number, size, name of publication, insertion date, and other data; a similar identifying line on a commercial or other film or tape

house list 1 a mailing list owned by a company or an organization 2 the names of the people to be admitted free to a theater, nightclub, or other *house*; also called *door list*

house manager [theater] the person responsible for the front-of-the-house, or business, operations, as distinct from *stage manager* or *company manager*

house mark a symbol used to identify a company, organization, or facility, such as a banner or flag with a LOGO The term originates from 17th-century innkeepers who identified their "houses."

house order an order prepared by one department of a company requesting or authorizing work to be done by another department and to be charged to the issuing department

house organ an older term for a controlled-circulation publication, such as one published by a company for its employees, in which case it is an *internal organ* A publication for dealers or other outside audiences, in contrast, is an *external organ*.

house phone a telephone in a hotel, theater, or other place for internal calls

house rough a preliminary layout to be used only for discussions within internal departments (in-house)

house seats theater tickets reserved at each performance, for sale or free distribution to the producer or those associated with the producer The general procedure is that the house

seats are held until 6 P.M. of the day preceding the performance. If the holder of the house seats does not call for them by that time, the tickets then are released and sold.

house style writing, production, and other guidelines issued by an organization for the use of its employees, contributors, authors, and agencies

Howard-Sheth model a description of the behavior of buyers, developed by John Howard and Jagdish Sheth and described in their 1969 book, *A Theory of Buyer Behavior* (John Wiley & Sons)

howl [recording] a loud sound resulting from FEEDBACK in an amplifying system

howler a device at the exchange end that sends a signal (*howler tone*) to indicate that a telephone handset is off the hook but not in use

hpf or HPF highest possible frequency

hr. hairspace (see HAIRLINE); hour (plural, *hrs.*)

ht HALFTONE

HTK head to come; see HEADLINE

hubbing a book spine, generally leather, with one or more horizontal ridges The raised spine is an elegant characteristic of quality bookbinding.

huckster a hawker, peddler, or producer of advertising (generally used derogatorily); from Middle English *hukster*, meaning "to haggle"

Hudson Street the nickname of Saatchi & Saatchi Advertising, located in lower Manhattan at 375 Hudson Street

hue a shade of color, exclusive of white, black, and gray There are many hues and color is determined by the *quality* of hue.

hum a low droning sound, such as the background noise in a faulty sound station

human interest (H.I.) a feature about a personality, a story with colorful details and emotional appeal; any work that is not strictly HARD NEWS

hundred showing saturation, or 100-percent coverage, in outdoor advertising; also written *100 showing* Actually, it is the number of advertisements necessary to reach 90 percent of the population in an area in one day.

hung punctuation a typographic style that allows punctuation characters to *hang*, or extend beyond the left and/or right margins; also called *hanging punctuation*

hung up theatrical slang describing a performer left stranded without a cue

hunk show-business slang for a routine or series of jokes by a comedian, generally on one theme; also called *chunk*

hunt the method by which a telephone call is connected via a group of lines The most common method is the *top down hunt,* in which the incoming call is routed to the first line of a group. If the line is busy, the call is routed to the second line or to the next nonbusy line. In a *round robin hunt* the incoming call is routed to a line after the last one on which there was a connection, so that usage is equalized among all lines, a technique used with incoming sales calls.

hunt and peck   a method of typing in which the person looks for—hunts for—the proper key and then presses it—pecks—generally using only one or two fingers

HUT or **H.U.T.**   HOUSEHOLDS, or homes, using TELEVISION

H.V.   HOME VIDEO

hydragyrum mercury medium arc length and io-dide (HMI)   an enclosed ARC LAMP that provides high illumination with relatively low wattage, compared to INCANDESCENT LAMPS

hymn   a song of praise or glorification, generally of God   A *hymnist* is a composer of hymns, which are published in a *hymnal* (hymn book). A TV or other script sometimes is called a *hymnbook.*

hype   intentional excess to create attention, such as by a political candidate, entertainer, or other person, organization, company, or group; to use excessive promotion or other techniques (to *hype a product*)   The origin may be the Greek *hyper,* meaning "over" or "above." Some lexicographers attribute the origin to *hypodermic,* signifying "injection," though *hypo* means "under." The term probably is from HYPOSUL-FITE, a boosting or developing chemical used in photographic processing; to perform the process is commonly called *to hype.*

hyperbole   a figure of speech in which emphasis is achieved by exaggeration, designed for effect and not meant to be taken literally; from the Greek *hyperbole,* meaning "throwing beyond" or "excess"   It is pronounced high-PURR-bow-lee.

hyperfocal distance   the distance from a photographic lens to a point beyond which all objects are acceptably sharp and in focus   The *hyperfocal point* is the nearest point to the camera that appears sharp when the lens is focused on infinity.

hypermarket   an extremely large supermarket that sells food and nonfood items, including ap-

parel; also called *hyperstore*   The concept originated in France.

hypertext   electronic indexes to text matter, with cross-references

hyphen   a mark (-) to separate the parts of a compound word or the syllables of a divided word, such as a word carried over from the end of one line to the next line   A *discretionary hyphen,* or *soft hyphen,* is inserted by the operator of an automated typesetting system to avert an improper hyphenation (called a *bad break*) by the machine. If the word does not need to be hyphenated, the discretionary hyphen is not typeset. An *obligatory hyphen,* or *hard hyphen,* always is set, as in a compound word. A *computer hyphen* is automatically generated, according to the programming.

hyphenate   [film] slang for a person with more than one role, such as actor-director   The writer-actor-director Woody Allen (b. 1935) is an example of a *triple hyphenate.*

hyphenation and justification (H&J)   a system of adjusting blocks of type so that they are aligned both at the left and at the right (*justified*), with end-of-line hyphenation occurring as appropriate   Spaces between words (*word spaces*) are adjusted for good fit and overall appearance. Though hyphenation and justification are separate processes, they are often used together, so that hyphenation may enhance the neatness of justification. Justification that occurs without hyphenation is called *hyphenless justification.* See also JUSTIFICATION.

hyping   [broadcasting] promotional or programming support to increase a station's audience during the SWEEP periods, when the national rating services are studying the market; pronounced hipe-ing and also called *hypoing*

hypo   hyposulfite (solium thiosulphate), a white, translucent, crystalline compound used in the FIXING of photographs and as a bleach

hypocorism   a pet name or term of endearment, often a diminutive, such as *Jack* for *John* or *Jackie* for *Jack* or *Jacqueline*

hypsography   the science of measuring the configuration of land or underwater surfaces, or the configuration of these surfaces or their representation   A *hypsographic map* or *hypsometric map* is a relief map indicating the surface elevations.

Hz   HERTZ

I

I ILLUMINATED

IABC INTERNATIONAL ASSOCIATION OF BUSINESS COMMUNICATORS

iamb a rhythmic form consisting of two syllables, the first unaccented, or unstressed, and the second accented *Iambic pentameter* is a line of verse with five such pairs of syllables.

iambic of or made up of IAMBS, as in *iambic verse*; also, satirical verse written in iambs

I&e IDENTIFICATION AND EXPOSITION

I-and-I programming information and interview programs on radio and TV stations, particularly news and talk shows and magazine-style programs, such as "60 Minutes"

I&R INFORMATION AND REFERRAL

IAPA INTER AMERICAN PRESS ASSOCIATION

IATSE INTERNATIONAL ALLIANCE OF THEATRICAL STAGE EMPLOYEES AND MOVING PICTURE MACHINE OPERATORS OF THE U.S. AND CANADA

ib INDENT BOTH

ib. or **ibid.** IBIDEM

IB IMBIBITION PRINTING

IBC INSIDE BACK COVER

IBEW INTERNATIONAL BROTHERHOOD OF ELECTRICAL WORKERS

ibidem (ib. or **ibid.)** Latin for "in the same place" The term is used in footnotes and other citations to refer to the previous note or item.

IBM the world's largest computer company, headquartered in Armonk, NY IBM also is known as International Big Mother, as BIG BLUE, and by other affectionate and not-so-affectionate names; the actual name is IBM Corporation, which originally was International Business Machines.

IBS INTERCOLLEGIATE BROADCASTING SYSTEM; IOTA BETA SIGMA

IC or **I.C.** INCUE

ICA International Communications Association

ice theatrical slang for a premium price paid for a theater ticket

icebreaker the opening number in a musical comedy or a variety show

ices an ice show, a theatrical production with ice skaters

ICM INTERNATIONAL CREATIVE MANAGEMENT

icon 1 an image, such as of a religious figure 2 a pictorial element, such as a small symbol displayed on a microcomputer screen that represents a computer function or resource In some computers, a program is started or a file is displayed by pointing the CURSOR—generally an arrow—at the appropriate icon, perhaps using a MOUSE to move the cursor.

iconic relating to an ICON (an image or figure, particularly a sacred representation), statue, or other work, done in a conventional or representational style An *iconic model* is a replica, such as a model plane.

iconography a book or other collection of illustrations and other representations of a subject; from the Greek *eikon*, meaning "image"

iconoscope a TV camera tube that rapidly scans It is not as sensitive as the more modern IMAGE ORTHICON.

ID or **I.D.** IDENTIFICATION; INDEPENDENT DISTRIBUTOR; INTRODUCTION

IDD International Direct Dialing

idem Latin for "the same," from *id*, meaning "it" The term indicates a previously mentioned footnote reference, not necessarily the one immediately before (which is referred to as IBIDEM, abbreviated *ib.* or *ibid.*).

ident-and-expo IDENTIFICATION AND EXPOSITION

identification (ID or **I.D.)** 1 the establishment of the name or distinguishing characteristics of a person or an item; the name and affiliation of an individual shown in a photograph or referred to in an article or other medium 2 [broadcasting] the establishment of the name of the sponsor, such as in a 10-second commercial announcement, or of the station—*station identification*—composed of the call letters or a slogan

identification and exposition (I&e or **ident-and-expo)** a brief caption in which the first line (*ident line* or *identification line*) gives the name of the subject and the second line (*expo line* or *exposition line*) gives a brief explanation

identity an individual's awareness of his or her own personality; the manner in which individuals perceive a company or other organization (*corporate identity*)

ideogram a character or a graphic symbol representing an idea—for instance, a Chinese character or a symbol such as an ampersand (&) or a dollar sign; also called *ideograph*

idiom the use of words peculiar to a particular language, speech, or jargon; an expression that cannot be translated, word for word, into another language—for instance, *by and large*, meaning generally

idiot box derogatory slang for television

idiot card a cardboard sheet on which is written key words or a complete script to aid a speaker or performer; also called CUE CARD, *idiot board*, or *idiot sheet*

idiot tape [typography] raw, unhyphenated, unjustified paper or magnetic tape used in some forms of computerized phototypesetting

idle character in automated typesetting, a character that intentionally does not print out after transmission, so as to provide a blank space

idler rollers a set of cylinders, or rollers, in a WEB printing press, which supports and controls the paper and prevents it from wrinkling as it unrolls from the web

idle time the time that a computer, printing press, or other machine is available for use but is not in operation

i.e. that is; from Latin *id est* The expression, which is generally followed by a comma and then an explanation, is sometimes confused with *e.g.* (*for example*).

IEA INTERNATIONAL EXHIBITORS ASSOCIATION

IECA INDEPENDENT ELECTION CORPORATION OF AMERICA

IFB INTERRUPTIBLE FEEDBACK LINE

il INDENT LEFT

Ilford Test Chart a card, or chart, used to test the colors on a processed film It consists of various shades of grays (for black-and-white film) on one side that are equated to a color spectrum on the other side.

i-line an identification line, such as the name of a person under a photo

ill. ILLUMINATED; illustrated; ILLUSTRATION; ILLUSTRATOR

illegal character a character or combination of BITS that is invalid or unacceptable in a specific computer program or system, such as a character that is not part of a specific alphabet or set

illuminaire a light source; a lamp or any equipment that provides illumination The word is used in the film field, particularly outside the United States.

illuminated (I or ill.) brightened or decorated with lights, as an *illuminated billboard* A medieval *illuminated manuscript*, or book, was decorated in brilliant colors or precious metals, such as gold leaf.

illus. illustrated; ILLUSTRATION; ILLUSTRATOR

illusion mirror a special type of mirror that reflects when confronted with a light source and is transparent when illuminated from the rear; also called *Chinese mirror* or *one-way mirror* It is used at exhibits or to observe participants in a FOCUS GROUP.

illustrated cover a book with a decoration or special lettering, usually on the front cover; also called *decorated cover*

illustration (ill. or illus.) a picture, design, diagram, or any art used to decorate or explain A printed illustration, particularly a book illustration printed on different stock from the rest of the book, is called a *plate*.

illustration board heavy paper, or cardboard, commonly used by artists for mounting layouts and MECHANICALS *Hot-press illustration board* is smooth (with a *plate finish*); *cold-press illustration board*, which has a slightly rough finish, often is used for the painting of artwork. A *two-faced illustration board* has cardboard between two sheets of BRISTOL paper.

illustrator (il. or illus.) a person who uses nonphotographic means, such as ink or paint, to create art (illustrations) for advertising or text The heavy board or paper, finished on one side, used for wash and tempera drawings, is called ILLUSTRATION BOARD, *illustrator's board*, or ARTIST'S BOARD.

image 1 a body of impressions, feelings, or opinions regarding a company (*corporate image*) or other entity as held by its public 2 a visual composition (commonly called a *photograph*) as rendered by a camera 3 the area of a printing plate that is reproduced 4 in phototypesetting, the representation of a character (letter, number, or symbol), called the *master image*, on a font MATRIX, from which the typeset character is reproduced or generated 5 [public relations] an imitation or representation of a person or thing, or the concept of a person, product, or organization, held by the general public or specific public An *image consultant* helps modify or create this concept, perhaps by counseling an individual about speech, wardrobe, and appearance. 6 a figure of speech, such as a METAPHOR or SIMILE

image area [graphic arts] the area within a sheet or film frame actually occupied by the image

image card   a card with one or more holes, or apertures, to hold frames of microfilm; also called *aperture card*

image edge   [photography] the outline of the subject, which is clearly defined in a sharp-focus picture and fuzzy or blurred in an out-of-focus picture

image grabber   in computer graphics, a video camera that records an image   The image is recorded in an analog code that is converted by a computer to a digital code. An image grabber is not an essential part of a computer graphics system.

image liner   a brief, paid, INSTITUTIONAL announcement on a radio or TV station; also called POP-IN

image master   [printing] in PHOTOTYPESETTING, the negative that carries a type FONT

image modifier   a cameralike device that enlarges or reduces images from artwork by projecting them onto a translucent plate and then tracing or copying the images, using light-sensitive materials; also called *enlarging-reducing machine*, *enlarger-reducer*, or *Lacey Luci* (a specific model)   An image modifier is not the same as a *photographic enlarger*, which projects onto photosensitive paper or other photosensitive material.

Image 'N Transfer (INT)   a process, trademarked by the 3M Company, of Minneapolis, that produces PRESSURE GRAPHICS, by means of special sheets and chemicals

Image Orthicon (IO)   a TV camera pickup tube, trademarked by RCA, that is very sensitive to light; also called *Orthicon tube* or *orthicon*   The term also is used to describe photoemissive television pickup tubes made by other companies. As used generically, an image orthicon receives light from a scene upon its photoelectric surface to form an electron image; the photoelectrons are then forced from this surface toward a target surface, where there is a secondary emission of electrons, resulting ultimately in a video signal.

image processing   a technique of changing a video image, such as is done with computer graphics or other processes in which a picture is altered or combined with another picture or artwork; also called *video alteration* or *video manipulation*

image program   advertising and other techniques to enhance good will or achieve other objectives, not directly to promote or sell; also called *image advertising* or *institutional advertising*

image reversing film   a duplicating film that produces a negative from a positive or a positive from a negative   It differs from a direct-image film, which is nonreversing.

imagery   mental images, descriptions (generally visual), and figures of speech

imaging   [printing] the process of producing a photographic image, by electrostatic photographic or other means, on paper or some other *imaging surface*

imagism   a movement in poetry, from about 1909–17, characterized by precise images and free verse rather than complete statements   Imagist films used a series of images to create a mood or an abstract effect.

Imax   a movie camera that uses 65mm film for wide-screen projection—for example, on a curved screen or overhead dome, as at exhibitions and fairs

imbibition printing (IB)   a film process, perfected by TECHNICOLOR, in which color dyes are applied directly onto the print; also called *dye transfer process*   The result is an *imbibition print*. Imbibition is the absorption or adsorption of water.

immediacy cue   [broadcasting] a word or phrase that adds a sense of urgency, importance, or immediacy, such as *flash*, *this just in*, *stand by*, *we switch now*, or *at this moment*

imp.   imperative; imperfect; import; important; IMPRIMATUR

impact   effectiveness, impression, attention-getting ability; the net effect of a media message on the recipient

impact method   a readership recall service of GALLUP AND ROBINSON   It measures the depth of the impression an advertisement makes on a reader by reporting *proven name registration* (the percentage of readers who can recall the ad), *idea penetration* (the percentage who can describe details of the ad), and *conviction* (the percent who desire to see or purchase the advertised product).

impact printing   a method of reproduction in which the image is struck directly onto the paper or other surface, as with a typewriter, MATRIX, or DRUM PRINTER   In *nonimpact printing*, such as with INKJET, ELECTROSTATIC, or PHOTOELECTROSTATIC (laser) printers, no pressure is applied.

impact scheduling   the broadcasting of two or more of the same or similar advertisements within a short time period

impasto   unthinned paint that is laid thick on a canvas or other surface; also, a painting with such paint

impedance   [broadcasting] the resistance of an electronic component to the flow of a signal toward it, expressed as high impedance (hi-Z) or low impedance (low-Z)

imposition the process of arranging pages in a FORM so that, when printed and folded, they will fall in proper numerical order The table (generally steel- or marble-top) or slab on which the pages are made up is an *imposing stone*, usually called a *stone*. The master plan or arrangement is often done with the aid of an *imposition chart*, consisting of sheets—or *folding dummy*—folded to resemble the finished product. To *impose* is to arrange the sheets according to the plan.

impost 1 a tax or duty that is levied or imposed 2 [printing] an extra-charge item, such as a BIND-IN, BLEED, additional color, or TIP-IN

impresario an organizer-manager of a performing-arts event, series, or troupe The Italian origin, *impresa*, meaning "enterprise," is apt, since an impresario generally combines entrepreneurial and artistic skills.

impression 1 the intellectual or emotional effect made by a person or an organization 2 a printed copy or all the copies printed in a single operation from a set of unaltered type or other printing materials In books, the *impression line* is printed on the copyright page—generally on the last line, below the name of the country in which the book was printed—to indicate the current printing. Each time the book goes back on press for additional copies with few or no changes, a new printing or impression takes place. Among the types of impression lines is a row of descending numbers, 9 8 7 6 5 4 3 2 1. When a new printing is made, one number is removed, starting from the right. 3 the degree of impression between the printing plate and the paper When both sides of a sheet are printed, the first side to be printed, called the *first impression*, may become smudged when the reverse side is subsequently printed. A *kiss impression* is the ideal contact (in printing, that is).

impression control on a typewriter, the device that regulates the striking force of the keys

impression cylinder on a ROTARY PRINTING PRESS, the device that presses the paper against the plate

impression opportunity the potential, or opportunity, for an outdoor advertisement to be seen by individuals The term is sometimes used incorrectly as a synonym for *circulation*.

impression paper any stock that receives an image, such as paper used in printing or in photocopying

impressions [market research] the total audience, including duplications (those who have seen or heard a commercial message more than once)

Impression Studies research by STARCH INRA HOOPER Inc., of Mamaroneck, NY, on the impact of print and TV advertising on the audiences to whom the advertising is aimed

imprimatur (imp.) sanction, approval, endorsement; from Latin for "let it be printed" Bibles and books representing the authentic teaching of the Roman Catholic Church have the word *imprimatur* (generally printed on the back of the title page), indicating official approval. Note the spelling; there is no *e* at the end.

imprint anything printed or marked The word generally refers to the name, logo, or symbol of an advertiser. Sales promotion materials sometimes have a space for a local retailer or distributor to print or affix its name and other information. A printer, designer, or other producer may add its name, symbol, or other identification, as an imprint to a brochure or other item, generally at the bottom of the last page. In outdoor advertising, an imprint is a small sign at the base of a billboard or advertising structure showing the name of the owner, such as Gannett Advertising. In publishing, the publisher's name and other data (address, date) is its imprint. The imprint appears at the bottom of a book's title page. The *imprint date* is the year of publication of a work, including manufacture and distribution, as it appears in a bibliography or catalog.

imprinter a device, such as a printing press, typewriter, pen, or cash register, to stamp, impress, or produce a mark or impression; also, pressure devices such as those used with credit cards and address plates It is also called *imprint unit*, particularly when it is part of a printing press.

improvisation the act of extemporizing The *s* is pronounced as a *z*. A comedy club in Los Angeles, Improvisation, is nicknamed The Improv.

impulse buying the act of purchasing an item or items impetuously or on the spur of the moment, such as at the point of sale—for example, at the cash register

IMRAD the formula for the organization of a scientific or academic article: *i*ntroduction, *m*ethodology, *r*esults, *a*nd *d*iscussion

IMS International Inc. a global research firm, specializing in the pharmaceutical industry and headquartered in London (the main office in the United States is in New York) The initials stand for *International Medical Statistics*; the company's major services are the ongoing audits, in about 50 countries, of the monetary value and unit volume of ethical (prescription) and proprietary (nonprescription) pharmaceutical sales to retail outlets. Other services include audits and indices of hospitals and physicians and the publication of directories (including *Hospital Purchasing Guide*) and journals in many languages. IMS was acquired in 1988 by DUN & BRADSTREET.

in 1 to move toward, as with a performer moving toward the camera, a camera moving closer to a performer, or equipment moving in to a position 2 toward the center of the stage 3 currently popular, as with an *in-joke* or an *in-list*; currently in power or in a favored position, as with an *in-group*

in or **in.** inch

IN INTERNEGATIVE

in-ad coupon a coupon in a retail advertisement, redeemable only at that particular store or chain of stores

in-betweens in film animation, the intermediate drawings, produced by artists called *in-betweeners*, that occur between key changes in position of the animated characters

in boards an obsolete, inexpensive style of bookbinding in which the pages of the book were trimmed, or cut to size, after the board sides had been laced on, rather than before

inc. income; incorporated (generally capitalized)

inc. or **incompl.** incomplete

inc. or **incr.** increase

INCA INFORMATION COUNCIL OF AMERICA

in camera privately, as with a hearing held by a judge with the public and press excluded; from the Latin words meaning "in the chambers"

incan incandescent

incandescent lamp an electric lamp that produces light by the heating of a filament It differs from a FLUORESCENT (or *cold*) *lamp*, in which light is produced by the fluorescence of phosphors. *Incandescence* is a warm glow.

inches per second (ips or **i.p.s.)** [recording] a measurement that generally refers to the speed of an audio tape, such as $7^1/2$ *inches per second* (for reel to reel), $3^3/4$, or $1^7/8$ *inches per second* (for extended playback cassette)

inching the process of moving a film slowly—inch by inch—through a camera or projector, by hand-turning an *inching knob* or *incher*

incidental music music played before, during, or after a scene as background, to create a mood or other effect *Incidental sound* is music or sound effects for background atmosphere.

incidentals minor items or expenses

incident light light striking a subject or surface

incipit from the Latin meaning "here begins," a word sometimes placed at the beginning of medieval manuscripts and early printed books

incl. including; inclusive

in clear [film] referring to sound heard alone, without an accompanying picture; also called *cold* or *cold sound*

inclusive edition an edition of all of an author's works, written or published up to the time of publication of the current volume or volumes It differs from an *author's edition*, which is the complete or nearly complete works of an author.

incognito (incog.) with true identity unrevealed or disguised; under an assumed name The source is the Latin *incognitus*, meaning "unknown."

incr. increase

increment an increase, generally one of a series, such as the *minimum*-LEADING *increment* in typesetting

incue (IC or **I.C.)** 1 [broadcasting] the first few words—generally four—of a taped report or interview, written on a script to help the engineer identify the tape and use it 2 [film] a signal to begin action; usually hypenated (*in-cue*)

incunabulum a book printed before the 16th century, before the development of movable type by Johann Gutenberg in the mid-15th century The plural is *incunabula*. The word has a delightful origin: it is from the Latin for "in cradle," or infancy. Antiquarian book collectors sometimes call such works *incunables* or *cradle books*. About eight million incunabula were printed, and many have survived!

incut note a subheading set in a rectangular space surrounded on three sides by text; also called *cut-in note* and, more properly, *cut-in side note*

ind. independent; INDEX; indigo; industrial

indent to cut or notch; to set in from the margin *Indentation* or *indention* is the process of indenting, or the blank space itself, between the margin and the beginning of the line. Indentation generally is inward from the left margin (*left indent*), but it can be inward from the right margin (*right indent*) or from both margins (*centered indent*). Typesetting commands include *ib* (indent both margins), *il* (indent left margin), and *ir* (indent right margin). A *delayed indent* takes place only after a minimum number of lines have been set. A *hanging indent* occurs on every line of the text block except the first. A *text indent* (or *variable hanging indent*) has a specific point on the first line, below which the subsequent margins are aligned. A *nested indent* is measured from the margin of the previous indentation, rather than from the absolute margin. A *paragraph indent* is the traditional indentation at the beginning of the first line of a paragraph. A *runaround indent* or *margin field* varies the width of a specified number of lines, generally adjacent to an illustration. A *skewed indent* varies with each line, generally to give a slanted appearance.

Independent Association of Publishers' Employees the organization, akin to a labor union, of employees of DOW JONES & COMPANY and *The Wall Street Journal* and other Dow Jones employees who do not belong to the NEWSPAPER GUILD

independent contractor an individual or organization, such as a printer, whose work is purchased on a specific assignment basis, rather than on a continuing retainer basis

independent distributor (ID or **I.D.)** a wholesaler who distributes magazines and paperback books to newsstands and retail outlets other than bookstores

Independent Election Corporation of America (IECA) a clearinghouse for stockbrokers Located in Lake Success, NY, it distributes proxies and other materials to shareholders.

independent station a radio or TV station not owned by a national network (American Broadcasting Companies, Columbia Broadcasting System, or National Broadcasting Company) It may be part of a group. It is also called *independent* or, in *Variety* jargon, *indie* or *indy*.

independent store an individually owned retail outlet or a small chain (with no more than three outlets)

independent television market a geographical area in which local television stations have a larger combined share of viewing than that of stations from outside the region

independent writer a freelance writer, a person who writes for a publication or other medium but is not on its staff

in-depth comprehensive, as with an *in-depth study*

index (ind.) 1 an alphabetized listing following a printed work, indicating the page numbers on which specific items can be found The references may be to pages within the text itself or to pages in another work (such as an index, published in book format, that provides date and page location of items in a newspaper). The plural is *indexes* or *indices*. A *thumb index* is a series of notches cut into the edges of a book, as in a dictionary, for easy access to chapters or other divisions. A book also may be indexed with protruding tabs. 2 the type character used in printing to call attention to a particular section It consists of a hand with a pointing index finger, or second finger, next to the thumb. 3 a

list, called a *list index* or *condensed index*, such as a list on page 1 of a newspaper, indicating the page numbers on which the various departments appear 4 a computer command to find a story by the key word or words An *automatic index* is prepared by computer selection of key words. If the automatic index is checked or augmented by an individual, it is called an *augmented keyword index*, *enriched keyword index*, or *machine-aided index*.

Index the list of books that Roman Catholics were forbidden to read or retain without permission from Church authorities The full name was *Index Librorum Prohibitorum;* it ceased publication in 1966. It was also called *Roman Text*.

indexer a person who produces an index Professional indexers belong to the *American Society of Indexers*, in New York.

index letter a letter—generally upper case—to identify or key a text item or part of an illustration The explanation is in the legend, or caption describing the illustration, or in the accompanying text. See also INDEX NUMBER.

index map a single map showing the total geographical coverage of a series of maps It is not the same as a *map index*, which is an alphabetical list of names or features portrayed on a map or maps.

index number a number to identify a key or text item or part of an illustration

index page in VIDEOTEX and other computer systems, a FRAME containing entries for routing the user farther down the HIERARCHICAL STRUCTURE of the database

index word (IW) a listing in an alphabetical list

India ink heavy, black, waterproof ink, made from carbon and used in drawings The term is used mostly in the United States; in Europe, it is often called *drawing ink*.

India paper strong, thin, opaque paper, used in Bibles and reference books *Oxford India paper*, or India Oxford Bible paper, is soft, sturdy paper, originally made and used by Oxford University Press in England and now used by other publishers of books requiring many pages in compact form.

India proof paper a soft, absorbent paper used to soak up ink from an engraved plate during the printing process

indicia a notice, or information; characteristic marks, particularly identifying marks to denote payment of postage, such as a postal permit number or other imprint on an envelope or mailing piece, which is mailed without a postage stamp or postage-meter imprint; pronounced in-DISH-ee-a

indie theatrical slang for *independent*, a term used to describe a small producer in contrast to a major film studio

indigenous existing, inherent *Indigenous sound* is the actual or live sound in a scene, as distinct from indirect, off-screen, voiceover, or other *nonindigenous sound*

indirects [film, television] the rent, equipment, staff, and other basic costs not directly related to a specific production

individual brand a distinctive identification for a single product, as compared to a *family brand,* in which the same brand name is attached to all the products distributed under that name

individual location in outdoor advertising, a single bulletin or poster at one location, as distinguished from several at one location

indoor panel an advertising sign inside a stadium, terminal, or other building It is not the same as an INSIDE PANEL.

industrial a sponsored film, show, or other audiovisual presentation produced in behalf of a company or organization in any type of industry On their résumés, performers and producers make a distinction between industrials and theatrical films and broadcast programs.

industrial advertising the promotion of machinery and other producer goods and services to manufacturers and other purchasers who are not the end users of the products made with these machines and services

inf. inferior; infinitive; INFORMATION

inferior character in typography, a small character (letter, number, or symbol) set below the base line, such as $_2$ in H_2O; also called *subscript* A character set above the line is a *superscript* or *superior character.*

infill [television] to change tone or color, a common procedure done electronically

infinity an indefinitely large number or an unbounded space In photography, objects at a few hundred feet are considered to be at infinity; in television, the camera setting for infinity may be at 75 feet.

inflight or **in-flight** referring to a service or product aboard an airplane, such as *inflight movies* (shown to passengers) or *inflight publications*

infographics informational graphics, such as the graphs and charts increasingly used in newspapers

infomercial an audio or video segment that combines advertising with information, sold as a commercial and available on some cable networks and other broadcast media

informatics the study of the structure and properties of information

information 1 knowledge acquired in any manner; ideas and facts that have been communicated in any format In general, *information* refers to news or factual intelligence, though the data can be inaccurate, perhaps provided by an informer. An *information agency* is an organization, such as a government department, whose primary function is to provide news and other information to the public. An *information center* or *information clearinghouse* is an organization or a unit of an organization that collects and disseminates documents, bulletins, and other materials and data. An *information manager, information officer,* or *information specialist* answers queries, as in an *information department, information service, information staff* or other reference operation or at an *information desk* (in a library, museum, or transportation terminal) and also may have public relations responsibilities, particularly if he or she is a *public information officer. Disinformation* is the release of dishonest or inaccurate information. 2 [computers] any data that can be stored and retrieved in machine-readable form

Information telephone directory assistance service, as provided by an *Information Operator*

information and referral (I&R) a type of service that provides information, such as a reference service maintained by a library or via telephone

information broker a researcher, particularly one with access to database services

Information Council of America (ICA) an organization in New Orleans, LA, whose goal is to promote "truth through the media"

information nut [journalism] a READOUT (transitional headline) with a fact or highlight of an article

Information Please the name of a long-time radio program on which a panel of experts answered difficult questions submitted by listeners It is now the title of an almanac and reference book.

information processing the searching, gathering, recording, and providing of data—all the operations involved in the handling of data; also called *data processing*

information provider (ip) 1 a company or organization that provides sports scores, stock prices, and other recorded messages to callers of special premium-charge numbers and receives part of the telephone company's revenue from these calls 2 the provider of news, sports, weather, or other information to a VIDEOTEX system, generally for a fee

Information Resources Inc. a market research firm in Chicago that operates consumer panels and such services as *BehaviorScan* (which stores SCANNER data collection) in test markets Other services include *InfoScan* (the tracking of consumer purchases of items with a Universal Product Code) and publication of the *Marketing Fact Book.*

information service   the study of the creation, use, and management of all forms of information, though the term generally refers to computer data, as in an INFORMATION SYSTEM *Information storage and retrieval (ISR)* involves the processes of data INPUT and OUTPUT.

information system   a method for the systematic storage and retrieval of data, the network of all computerized functions within an organization; also called *data system*

information technology (IT)   the acquisition, processing, storage, and dissemination of data by a combination of computer and telecommunications techniques

infotainment   a combination of information and entertainment, such as that provided by some of the VIDEOTEX and cable-television services

in frame   referring to an image that accidentally appears on camera during filming; often called *in shot*

infrared   referring to electromagnetic radiation whose wavelengths are greater than visible light and shorter than MICROWAVES (*infra* means "below") *Infrared rays* or *invisible light* is used in photography with infrared-sensitive film. Infrared motion-picture film is sometimes used to penetrate haze or for special color effects.

ingenue   an innocent, inexperienced young woman; the role of such a character, or the actress portraying such a role   From the French, it is pronounced on-geh-NOO.

inherited audience   the segment of the audience of a radio or TV program that stays tuned and is carried over to the next program; also called HOLDOVER AUDIENCE   The inheriting program thus benefits from the preceding program.

in-house   referring to a division or unit that is part of or within a company or organization, as differentiated from a vendor or an outside agency

initial   as used in typography, a large single capital letter, sometimes ornamented (*ornamental initial*) at the beginning of a chapter or portion of an article or elsewhere, for design purposes; also called *initial letter*   The base of a *stickup initial* or *rising initial* is on the same line as the text that follows, whereas a *cut-in initial*, or *drop initial*, extends below the first line. A *two-line initial* is two lines high; a *three-line initial* is three lines high.

initial caps   initial capital letters: a direction to a typist or typesetter to capitalize each word, as in a headline or title

initial public offering (IPO)   the first shares of a company to be offered for sale to the public, as described in a prospectus by the Securities and Exchange Commission

ink   **1** a pigmented, viscous liquid used in writing and printing   *Ink mileage* is the amount of ink consumed on a job. *Printing ink* is ink that is made especially for printing. The term *printer's ink* refers to the graphic arts; *Printer's Ink* was also the name of a long-time advertising trade publication, which was terminated in the early 1960s. *India ink*, commonly used in drawing, is black, opaque, and waterproof. *Acetate ink*, which has good adhesive qualities, is used on acetate plastic. *Drawing ink* is a thin, waterproof liquid, akin to watercolor paint.   **2** slang for print publicity, as in *Get me some ink!*   **3** To *ink* is to sign, as in to *ink a contract*; a signed contract is known as an *inked contract.*

inkjet printing   a nonimpact computerized printing process in which a coded tape controls tiny laser-activated nozzles that spray ink onto paper to create type and other images   The device is called an *inkjet printer.* In nonimpact printing, there is no pressure or contact from a printing press. As a noun, ink jet is two words.

ink trap   an area between the strokes of a character that collects ink, such as in *E* or *M*

The Inky   the nickname of *The Philadelphia Inquirer,* a daily newspaper

inky dink   a small (hence, dinky) INCANDESCENT LAMP (hence, inky), generally with an enclosed 100-watt bulb or an unenclosed 200-watt bulb; also called *dinky ink, inky,* or *dinky*

inlaid   set in pieces into a surface of another material   In *inlaid paper,* a portion is cut out and a piece of graphic material, such as an illustration, is pasted into the inset; it is not the same as *laid paper,* a type of paper with a pattern of lines within it. An *inlaid book* has a piece of another leather or other material, or another color set in to the cover. The inserted piece is called an *inlay.*

inlay   **1** in bookbinding, the paper strip used to stiffen the SPINE   The process is not the same as *book lining,* in which a piece of fabric or paper is glued to the spine of a book.   **2** See INLAID.   **3** an insert in a television picture, such as titles or other characters or material that is keyed in (also called a *keyed insert*)

in-line   [computers] a system in operation and under the control of the CENTRAL PROCESSING UNIT; the same as ON-LINE

inline type   a kind of ornamental display typeface with a thin white line (the *inline*) inside each stroke (the *outline*)

in medias res   in the middle of the action, a literary device in which a film or other work begins with a death, a battle, or another dramatic event   The Latin phrase literally means "into the midst of things." It is not a common term and, when used, is often incorrectly pronounced or spelled; the correct pronunciation is in-MAY-dee-ahs-RACE.

inner circle   a small group of people who control or influence many areas of society, especially economic and political

Inner Circle   an organization of about 100 reporters who cover New York City government and local politics   The organization, located in the Press Room (Room 9) of City Hall in Manhattan, holds an annual dinner lampooning politicians and other newsmakers.

inning   a period of time; a baseball and cricket word used by VARIETY, as in *this inning*, meaning currently

in one   the front area of the stage (*downstage*), such as in front of the curtain   Script notations include *act in one*, *scene in one*, and *work in one*. A scene performed *in one* is sometimes called a *carpenter's scene*, as the area behind the curtain is being readied by the stagehands. The stage areas behind *in one* are consecutively numbered: IN TWO, *in three*, *in four*.

in-pack coupon   a store-redeemable coupon enclosed in a product package, for potential later use by the buyer   The coupon, which is generally promoted on the exterior of the package, may be redeemed on a subsequent purchase either of the same product or of a different product (*cross-coupon*).

in-pack premium   a premium item, or gift, enclosed in a product's package   It is usually offered with the product at no extra charge, as in boxes of cereal and snacks (such as Cracker Jacks).

in press   in the process of being printed

in print   referring to a book that is available from the publisher; the opposite of *out of print*

in pro   in proportion, an instruction to enlarge or reduce the size of a photo or other item and retain the same relationship of height to width

input   incoming material, such as data entered into a computer system or a signal fed into an audio or visual service; the opposite of *output*   The source of the entering material may be an *input device*, such as a CATHODE terminal.

input/output (I/O)   the entry and retrieval of data, as compared to its processing   *Input/output control system* (*IOCS*) is a set of routines, or instructions, for managing the entry and retrieval operations of a computer.

inq.   INQUIRY; question; query

in quires   referring to an unbound book in which the printed sheets are folded but not cut   The term has the same meaning as *in signatures* but not the same as IN SHEETS (cut signatures). A QUIRE also is a quantity of paper, but in this sense a quire is a SIGNATURE.

inquiry (inq.)   **1** a request from a potential customer, made in response to advertising or publicity   **2** a question or request, as of a computer

inquiry publication   a business publication that features, totally or primarily, new products and other items designed to elicit reader inquiries, usually on a BINGO CARD or other multiple-order form   Generally, these publications—such as *Potentials for Marketing*—have controlled circulations.

inquiry test   **1** a research technique involving random calls, or inquiries, to respondents   **2** an evaluation of the effectiveness of an advertisement based on the number of inquiries that were received about a promoted item

in-reading   linked, uninterrupted   *In-reading cutlines* are two or more captions placed together; *in-reading headlines* are two or more headlines about different articles, placed together. For example, a photo can appear below another photo, and instead of a caption below each photo, the two captions appear below the bottom photo.

in-room video   a TV service in hotel guest rooms, including both pay-per-view movies and free programming

inscription   a message engraved (as on a monument), printed (as with a dedication in a book), or handwritten (as in a book or on a gift card)   An *inscribed book* has a presentation inscription, written by the author or donor.

insert   **1** a printed sheet or section—generally advertising—inserted in a publication, as with a magazine   The insert may be bound in, as by stapling, or loose (not bound in, called a *free-standing insert*). In books, insert pages, such as illustrations, maps, and other specially printed items, are generally not included in the regular page numbering and may have separate numbering—for instance, Roman numerals. If the inserted sheets are not an integral part of the publication, they are called a *loose insert* or *throw-in*. An *outsert*, in contrast, is a WRAP AROUND placed on the outside of a publication or a signature (a sheet on which a book is printed).   **2** an enclosure, as in a mailing   **3** a word or section to be added to material already typed or set in type, or spliced into a tape or film   The first insert is marked *Insert A* or *Insert 1*, and subsequent inserts are lettered or numbered sequentially.   **4** a secondary signal introduced into a television picture, such as titles or other material that is *keyed in*; also called a *keyed insert*, CROSS-FADE, or WIPE

insert car a flatbed truck or other vehicle with film or tape camera equipment installed (inserted) on a platform within the vehicle, usually called a *camera car*

insert edit in videotape editing, the independent editing of the audio and video tracks, separately or together, without affecting the CONTROL TRACK The procedure is more common than the ASSEMBLE EDIT process.

insertion order a printed form or other authorization from an advertiser or advertising agency to the media to publish advertising material; a purchase order

insert set a part of a set used for close-ups in film and TV; also called *detail set*

inset an INSERT, such as a smaller picture or other artwork or text set within a larger picture or other larger area

in sheets referring to an unbound book, with the printed sheets folded and cut

in shot referring to an image that accidentally appears on camera during filming; often called *in frame*

inside back cover (IBC) the inside of the back cover of a publication, called the *third cover* in a magazine

inside delivery the transfer of cartons or other shipment to the interior of a building It is often more expensive than *outside delivery*, to the sidewalk or loading platform. Inside delivery does not necessarily include delivery directly to the floor, unless it is specified. In ordering printing or other items that are delivered on skids (wooden platforms) or in heavy containers, it is essential to specify the delivery instructions.

inside-out in periodical publishing, the collection of demographic and other data about readers of a publication and the later use of the data to promote the publication to advertisers

inside pages the contents of a magazine other than the covers; the contents of a newspaper other than page 1; also called *inside*

inside panel an outdoor advertisement that is not closest to major traffic An *outside panel* is closest.

inspection copy a book provided free or on approval for examination by a teacher or other prospective purchaser; often called *examination copy*

installation art sculptures and other art set up, or installed, on streets or other sites

instant book a book—generally paperback—produced in considerably less time than conventionally, such as a few days after a major event

instant coupon a cents-off or other discount or promotional coupon affixed to or inserted in a

package The *instant* refers to the coupon being acquired at the time of purchase, though it is usually not redeemed at that time.

Institute of Outdoor Advertising (IOA) the marketing, research, and promotional arm, located in New York, of the Washington-based OUTDOOR ADVERTISING ASSOCIATION OF AMERICA The IOA presents annual Obie Awards.

Institute of Public Relations (IPR) an organization, in London, of over 2,000 public relations practitioners, primarily in the United Kingdom and Europe

institution [marketing] an establishment (not an individual consumer), such as a restaurant, hotel, hospital, factory, or college Large or special packages (*institutional size*) often are sold to these establishments, sometimes by a separate sales force (*institutional sales*).

institutional advertising advertising intended to create good will for a company or organization, rather than to advertise goods or services overtly; also called *image advertising* or *image program*

institutions advertising advertising by colleges, hospitals, hotels, restaurants, and other institutions It is not necessarily the same as INSTITUTIONAL ADVERTISING.

instructional materials books or other items for students and teachers Children's books are sometimes classified as instructional materials.

instructional television programs for students in the classroom or at home

Instructional Television Fixed Service (ITFS) a 28-channel system using microwave signals in the 2-GHz band to transmit programming Use is restricted by the Federal Communications Commission to nonprofit groups.

insurance 1 [photography] the practice of taking additional pictures, particularly at different camera settings 2 [television] the technique of framing a scene wider than needed, to allow for movement

insured mail a postal service that provides loss or damage insurance The insurance was formerly available only on third- and fourth-class mail but can now be purchased for first-class mail.

in sync displaying exact synchronization, as of the audio and video elements of a film

int. interest; INTERIOR; internal; interval; international

INT IMAGE 'N TRANSFER; INTERIOR

intaglio 1 a figure or design incised, or cut, beneath the surface of hard metal or stone, or the process of carving such a design 2 [printing] a process in which the image to be printed is depressed below the plate surface, as in an EN-

GRAVING or GRAVURE The word, from Italian *intagliare,* meaning "to engrave," is pronounced in-TAL-yo.

integral reflex viewfinder a viewfinder system built into a film camera that displays the F-STOP, filter indicator, and other information

integrated circuit a combination of interconnected elements inseparably attached to a base, as on a computer chip

integrated commercial **1** an advertisement often delivered by one or more members of the cast of a radio or TV program and woven into the program Such commercials were common in the golden age of radio but are less so now, particularly because of multisponsorship, spot advertisements, and reruns. **2** a commercial promoted more than one product made by the same company

Integrated Services Digital Network (ISDN) a system in which voice and data services are provided over the same transmission and switching facilities, started in 1985 by global telephone companies

integrating [photography] the practice of obtaining an exposure setting by averaging several readings of a light meter

integration the process of creating a whole or harmonious entity by bringing parts together An *integrated format* is a radio or TV program with several sponsors.

INTELPOST INTERNATIONAL ELECTRONIC POST

Intelsat INTERNATIONAL TELECOMMUNICATIONS SATELLITE ORGANIZATION

intensity **1** degree of brightness or strength **2** the amount and kind of outdoor advertising space, based on a mix of illuminated and nonilluminated poster panels In outdoor advertising, full coverage is described as *100-intensity.*

intentional fallacy the error, or fallacy, of judging a work by the alleged intentions of the author, artist, or other creator

inter. intermediate

interactive combining INPUT and output; the ability of a device or procedure to allow an operator to make decisions that influence the outcome of a procedure in process In *interactive cable-TV systems,* or *two-way TV,* a viewer can respond to a question, order merchandise, pay bills, or perform other functions. In computers, the *interactive mode* (or *conversational mode*) is a sequence of alternating entries and responses between the user and the machine, akin to a dialogue.

Inter American Press Association (IAPA) an organization in Miami, FL, of about 1,400 members in the print media and other fields, whose goal is "to protect freedom of the press in the Americas."

intercept interview [market research] the questioning of a person picked at random, such as a person *intercepted* from among a crowd in a shopping mall or on a street

Intercollegiate Broadcasting System (IBS) an association in Vails Gate, NY, of radio stations at schools and colleges

intercom a radio or telephone intercommunication system linking one or more offices or other areas

interconnect **1** a supplier of telephone equipment other than the company providing local service **2** the joining together of two or more cable-TV systems, for programming or advertising A *hard interconnect,* or *true interconnect,* consists of two or more cable systems linked by cable or microwave relays so that the signal for advertising or programming is fed to the combined cable system by one HEADEND. A *soft interconnect,* or *simulated* (or *paper*) *interconnect,* has no direct electronic connection between the participating systems. In this case, a commercial can be inserted at the same time by each system operator, so that an advertiser can purchase time as if the system were a network.

intercutting [film, television] a rapid series of shots, generally of the same scene, taken from different angles A shot, called an *intercut,* of part of the scene may be inserted between two shots of the entire scene.

interface the point or surface at which two machines, people, or organizations are in contact, generally with some amount of communication; a surface that is the common or shared boundary between two components, such as hardware that links two devices or converts from one type of INPUT to another format; a device that connects two other devices and translates the signals of one into signals understandable to the other An interface can be one-way or two-way.

interference [broadcasting] the inhibition or prevention of the clear reception of a signal, or the distorted portion itself, such as static from power lines

interim copyright a temporary or short-term copyright issued in the United States before 1982, when this type of copyright was eliminated; also called *ad interim copyright*

interim statement a sworn, unaudited statement by a periodical publisher presenting circulation figures

interior (INT or **int.)** a notation on a script

interior monologue a monologue—heard by the audience of a play or other dramatic work—that is supposed to be taking place only in the character's thoughts

interlace in television transmission and reception, the scanning of alternate lines of an image An electric gun scans, or reads, first the odd-numbered lines in sequence and then the even-numbered lines in sequence. This double scanning fills in the spaces and reduces flicker. The process is *interlacing*. Interlacing is a similar type of scanning in computer graphics and VIDEOTEX to reduce *image flickers*.

interleaf a blank leaf, or two-sided sheet, between two leaves of a book To *interleave*, or *slipsheet*, is to insert blank pages or special sheets, such as *interleaving paper* (tissue or other nonopaque paper placed over illustrations, which then are called *interleaved plates*).

interline 1 in typesetting, the space between lines; also called LEADING 2 to insert text between written or printed lines, such as lines in one language and alternate lines of translation, a process called *interlining* or *interlineation*

interlock 1 a stage in the production of a TV commercial or other audiovisual in which the edited WORKPRINT and soundtrack are played together 2 [computers] a procedure to prevent a machine or device from commencing further operations, until the current operation is completed; also, a protective feature to prevent unauthorized or accidental access 3 [film] an electrical or mechanical link between two or more motors so that they operate synchronously In DOUBLE SYSTEM SOUND (sound on one STOCK and picture on another), an interlock mechanically links the two in sync. Movies generally are edited by this system; the *interlock phase*, in which the sound and picture are joined, is very important. 4 [printing] the joining of type characters, such as a ligature (æ) *Interlocking lines* are set so closely that the *descenders* of the letters of one line, as in the letter *g*, project into the *ascenders* of the line below, as in the letter *h*.

interlude an intervening episode; entertainment between acts; a short musical composition used as a BRIDGE between parts of a song, play, or other work

intermedia a combination of art forms, such as audiotape and print matter, or film and live performance; also called *mixed media* or *multimedia*

intermediate copy a photographic copy, such as a negative, from which other copies are made

intermission an interval of time between periods of activity, such as between acts of a play or other work; in the United Kingdom, called *interval act wait* The warning to the audience that the intermission is about to end is the *in-*

termission bell. A curtain dropped during the intermission is called the *intermission drop* or *act drop*.

intermission crasher a person who enters a theater, without an admission ticket, during the intermission of a play or other work

intermission dropout a member of the audience who does not return after the between-the-acts intermission of a show

intermittent movement the stop-and-go action of the film transport mechanism in a camera or projector, which keeps each frame stationary during the instant of exposure or projection *Intermittent pressure* is applied to the film while it is stationary, or in the stop position, in the *intermittent-movement cycle*.

internal publication a magazine, newsletter, or other periodical directed at employees or members of an organization; formerly called a *house organ* or *internal organ*

International Advertising Awards Film Festival an annual competition, held in June, in Cannes, France Awards include Lion statuettes (gold, silver, and bronze), Grand Prix, and Palme d'Or. The U.S. representative is Screenvision Cinema Network, of New York.

International Alliance of Theatrical Stage Employees and Moving Picture Machine Operators of the U.S. and Canada (IATSE) an AFL-CIO union, in New York, of about 60,000 theatrical and film technicians The acronym is pronounced YAT-see.

International Association of Business Communicators (IABC) a professional association for editors of INTERNAL PUBLICATIONS, public relations professionals, and other communicators The publisher of *Communication World*, it is located in San Francisco.

International Brotherhood of Electrical Workers (IBEW) an AFL-CIO union, in Washington, DC, of about one million members, including broadcast engineers A rival union is the NATIONAL ASSOCIATION OF BROADCAST ENGINEERS AND TECHNICIANS.

International Computer Animation Competition annual awards to individuals and organizations, presented by the National Computer Graphics Association, Fairfax, VA

International Creative Management (ICM) a major talent agency in New York It is a subsidiary of Josephson International, Inc., headed by Marvin Josephson.

International Electronic Post (INTELPOST) an international electronic mail facility of the U.S. Postal Service that provides FACSIMILE transmission of printed material

International Exhibitors Association (IEA) a trade association, in Annandale, VA, of companies and organizations that exhibit at conventions and similar functions

International Federation of Phonogram and Videogram Producers an organization, in London, of producers and distributors of audio and video recordings

International Film & TV Festival of New York an annual event, held in November in New York, at which awards in over 100 advertising and audiovisual categories are presented It is operated by Gerald Goldberg (b.1929).

International Medical Statistics See IMS INTERNATIONAL INC.

International Morse code a communications system in which letters and numerals are represented by dots (short pulses) and dashes (long pulses) It was named after Samuel F. B. Morse (1791–1872), American inventor of the system, and is commonly used in telegraphy.

International Paper Company (IPCO) a major manufacturer of paper products, founded in 1898 and headquartered in Memphis, TN Its printing papers include the Springhill, IPCO, and Hudson lines, and it publishes POCKET PAL, a graphic arts production handbook.

International Public Relations Association (IPRA) an organization in Geneva of "senior" public relations practitioners

International Reply Coupon a certificate that can be purchased at U.S. post offices (the fee in 1989 was 95 cents) and sent to foreign countries where it is exchangeable for a postage stamp of that country, to be used for international postage on a surface-mailed letter The coupons, which are relatively unknown, are used by, among others, freelance writers who send a manuscript with a self-addressed envelope to a foreign publisher. Obviously, U.S. stamps are not valid for return mail from a foreign country; the International Reply Coupon serves as a prepayment for the foreign stamp.

International Standard Bibliographic Description (ISBD) a set of rules for preparing the descriptive part of bibliographies, established in 1971 by the International Federation of Library Associations and Institutions, of The Hague, Netherlands

International Standard Book Number (ISBN) a system of 10-digit numbers maintained in the United States by R. R. Bowker Company, of New York, for identifying books and their publishers Publishers are identified by their assigned prefix. A similar system, called the INTERNATIONAL STANDARD SERIAL NUMBER, is used to identify periodicals. Over 40 countries participate in the ISBN and ISSN systems. Each country administers its own system; the inter-

national coordinator is the International ISBN agency in Berlin, West Germany.

International Standard Serial Number (ISSN) a system for identifying periodicals and their publishers The assigned identification number generally appears in the upper right corner of the cover or on one of the front pages. A similar system, the INTERNATIONAL STANDARD BOOK NUMBER, is used to identify books. In the United States, the system is maintained by the National Serials Data Program at the Library of Congress in Washington, DC. The international coordinator is the International Serials Data System in Paris.

International Standards Organization (ISO) an organization, in Paris, that sets standards in many fields, including definitions of data communications and information processing vocabulary The U.S. affiliate is ANSI. In film, ISO numbers provide information about film speed and other factors, as the *ISO exposure index.* U.S. dictionaries of computer terms are based on ISO definitions and also those of the American National Dictionary for Information Processing Systems (ANDIPS).

International Telecommunications Satellite Organization (Intelsat) an organization in Washington, DC, that owns and operates the international satellite system that provides the majority of telecommunications services outside the United States to over 100 member countries. It was formed in 1974 and includes COMSAT.

International Telecommunications Union (ITU) an organization, in Geneva, Switzerland, of over 160 countries that sets standards in radio, telegraph, telephone, and other communications fields

International Travel and Talk slang for ITT, a telecommunications company headquartered in New York

International Typeface Corporation (ITC) a company, in New York, that develops and licenses new typeface designs, promotes artistic typography, and publishes a tabloid newspaper, U&LC

International Typographical Union (ITU) an AFL-CIO union in Colorado Springs, CO, with over 500 locals Its membership consists of about 100,000 typesetters and others in printing and publishing, including mailers of periodicals.

internegative (IN) a negative made from a color transparency, a color or black-and-white print, or an INTERPOSITIVE, to produce additional prints, a process commonly used by publicists and others to mass-produce MACHINE PRINTS

interpositive (IP) 1 an intermediate photographic or photostatic positive produced to enlarge or reduce the original image size **2** [film] a positive prepared for use in optical effects, while permitting the original negative to be preserved unchanged *Interpositive/internegative* (IP/IN) is the standard process for making a RELEASE PRINT. A *master positive*—the first IP—is made from the original negative; then an INTERNEGATIVE, or *master negative*, is produced, from which the prints are made.

interpreter 1 one who translates orally from one language to another All interpreters are translators, but the reverse may not be true, as a translator may provide a written translation. **2** a computer program that translates and executes one instruction before proceeding to the next

interpretive journalism writing, in newspapers and magazines, that analyzes the background and implications of an event or situation, without taking sides or editorializing

Interpublic Group of Companies one of the world's largest advertising companies, based in New York The firm includes Lintas, Lowe Marschalk, McCann-Erickson, and other advertising agencies.

interrobang a punctuation mark, combining an exclamation point and a question mark, used to convey incredulity or strong disbelief Created in 1962 by the advertising executive Martin K. Speckter (1915–1988), the interrobang looks like this: ‽

interruptible feedback line (IFB) a telephone line for a producer or a director to talk to a newscaster or an interviewer during a broadcast

Intersearch Corp. a market research firm, headquartered in Horsham, PA

Intersputnik the international network of satellites operated by the Soviet Union

interstitial programming [television] the placement of short programs between full-length programs For example, Home Box Office (HBO) and other movie channels schedule programs of about 2 to 25 minutes between the full-length movies.

intertitle [film] any TITLE CARD, such as an identification of time or place, or SUBTITLE that appears between the head credits (at the beginning of the film) and the tail credits (at the end)

interval a British word for a theatrical INTERMISSION

interval scaling [market research] a system of ranking with identifiable intervals between the units

interview a colloquy or dialogue, with the *interviewer* asking questions and the *interviewee* providing responses The same type of conversation, with variations, can be held with a group, for journalism, research, or other purposes. Types of research interviews include *behavior sample interviews, directive interviews, focus group interviews, free association interviews, individual interviews, nondirective interviews,* and *phone interviews.*

interword spacing word spacing, or spacing between words

intl. international

into frame a filmscript notation indicating that a performer moves into a shot that is focused on another subject It differs from INTO VIEW.

into view a filmscript notation indicating that the camera moves during a shot to focus on, or bring into view, a new subject It differs from INTO FRAME.

in-transit media publications and audio and video programs for the use of passengers on airlines, trains, and other transportation, including *inflight movies* and *inflight magazines* aboard airplanes

intro or **Intro.** INTRODUCTION; introductory

introduction the beginning, such as the opening portion of a news release, program, or other work; anything introduced, brought into place or into use, such as the preliminary section of a book or other work or the opening section of a musical composition or speech An introduction to a book generally is an essay that states the author's intentions and prepares the reader for the work. It is similar to a *preface* and is a preliminary section that is part of the front matter. Technically, an introduction is different from a preface, in which the author briefly lists background details and sometimes includes acknowledgments. The introduction, which follows and may be longer, provides the background of the subject and perhaps a summary of the book. The introduction may be written by someone other than the author of the book.

introspective research a study within a group, self-inspection; as opposed to *extrospective research*, which examines the relationship of a group with one or more other groups or outside influences

intrusions slang in Australia for AMBUSH JOURNALISM

INTV ASSOCIATION OF INDEPENDENT TELEVISION STATIONS, INC.

in two the front area of the stage, behind the curtain It is not the most forward area—which is in front of the curtain and called IN ONE—but is in front of the middle (*in three*) and rear (*in four*) areas.

inventory 1 in broadcast advertising, the number of commercial positions In actual use, *inventory* refers to the *unsold* time that a station or network has available for advertisers

2 available merchandise at a manufacturer, warehouse, distributor, retailer, or other level of distribution

inverted comma British for a *quotation mark* (')

inverted heading a heading with the words transposed from the ordinary sequence, to bring a key, or major, word to the first position, followed by a comma, such as for a keyword index—for instance, *wild animal* becomes *animal, wild*

inverted letter a character, or letter, that is upside down or opposite its standard position To invert a letter is to reverse it or turn it upside down.

inverted page an upside-down page

inverted pages the contents of a volume with one text that starts at the front and another text, such as a translation, that starts at the back; also called *tête-bêche*

inverted pyramid 1 a heading in which each successive line is shorter than the one above it **2** one of the most common styles of journalistic writing, in which the most important news elements are presented first, in the *lead*, with successive increments of detail added in the body, or main part The structural image of a pyramid resting on its point is misleading, as the beginning, or *top*, of a news story should be sharp and pointed, rather than the end, or bottom. The image is apt only in that the traditional style of editing is to slash from the bottom. **3** a style of double INDENT in which each successive line is shortened equally at both ends, resembling an inverted pyramid or *half-diamond*

investigative journalism reporting that systematically researches or inquires in order to search out and uncover the facts

Investigative Reporters and Editors (IRE) an organization, in Columbia, MO, of investigative reporters at newspapers and other media

investor relations (IR) communication activities by a public company with its current and potential shareholders; see FINANCIAL RELATIONS

invisible cut [film] a switch, or cut, from one shot to another, done unobtrusively (invisibly), such as by overlapping the action or by using two cameras simultaneously or consecutively; also called *invisible editing*

invocation the act of calling on God or some other source of help or inspiration; a formal prayer asking for such support, particularly at the beginning of a religious service or an event; a formal plea for aid, such as from a Muse, at the beginning of an epic or other work The Muse of epic poetry was Calliope.

invoice allowance a discount given by a manufacturer or supplier to a retailer or distributor

for advertising or other promotion The amount often is a percent of the price of the order and is deducted by the retailer when payment is made.

involvement device [direct marketing] an item designed to motivate the consumer to take some action, such as to check off answers, punch holes, or paste on stamps; also called *action device*

involvement study a method of measuring the degree of thought, planning, or effort made by individuals prior to making a decision, such as a purchase A *low-involvement decision* is akin to impulse, or spur-of-the-moment, buying, whereas a *high-involvement decision* involves considerable research, as when buying a house.

inward wide area telephone service (INWATS) a service that allows individuals to make toll calls free of charge (the cost is paid by the organization receiving the call); also called *800 service*

INWATS INWARD WIDE AREA TELEPHONE SERVICE

IO IMAGE ORTHICON

I/O INPUT/OUTPUT

IOA INSTITUTE OF OUTDOOR ADVERTISING

ionosphere a region of the earth's atmosphere about 30 to 250 miles above its surface, consisting of several ionized layers (an *ion* is an electrically charged atom or group of atoms) The ionosphere varies in its density. A high, or heavy, density reflects radio signals back to earth more efficiently than a low, or light, density; thus the ionosphere can affect radio, television, and other signal transmission.

Iota Beta Sigma (IBS) an organization, in Vails Gate, NY, of student broadcasters and others in academic broadcasting

IP INFORMATION PROVIDER; INTERPOSITIVE

IPCO INTERNATIONAL PAPER COMPANY

IP/IN INTERPOSITIVE/INTERNEGATIVE

IPO INITIAL PUBLIC OFFERING

IPR INSTITUTE OF PUBLIC RELATIONS

IPRA INTERNATIONAL PUBLIC RELATIONS ASSOCIATION

ips or **i.p.s.** INCHES PER SECOND

ir INDENT RIGHT

IR INVESTOR RELATIONS

IRE INVESTIGATIVE REPORTERS AND EDITORS

iris the round pigmented membrane surrounding the pupil (opening) of the eye, to regulate the amount of light entering the eye The counterpart in a camera is called *iris diaphragm*, which has overlapping blades to regulate the amount of light passing through the lens aperture, or opening.

Iris Awards annual awards presented by the National Association of Television Program Executives (NATPE), in New York, to TV stations for outstanding locally produced programs

Irish funny papers journalism slang for *obituary page*

iris in to begin a scene in a film or television program by opening the camera from a completely closed position, so that the scene appears within an expanding circle The opposite is *iris out*. The terms are also called *circle in* and *circle out*.

irony a method of humorous or subtly sarcastic expression in which the thoughts or words are incongruous, different from their usual sense, or in contradiction to the stated or ostensible meaning, action, or truth Irony in a literary or other work can be *comic irony, dramatic irony* (or *tragic irony*), or *verbal irony* (or *rhetorical irony*).

irony journalism reporting that ignores or treats lightly any negative news about a colleague or those related to a colleague

irreg. irregular, irregularly; see IRREGULAR PUBLICATION

IR setting a mark, generally indicated by a red dot on the camera lens mount, for use in photography with INFRARED (IR) light

is back story an article about a person who *is back* in the news, perhaps after being inactive or away

ISBD INTERNATIONAL STANDARD BIBLIOGRAPHIC DESCRIPTION

ISBN INTERNATIONAL STANDARD BOOK NUMBER

ISDN INTEGRATED SERVICES DIGITAL NETWORK

island a display or exhibit in a store, exhibition, or elsewhere, accessible on all sides Since the *island display, island exhibit,* or *island unit* has aisles on all four sides, it sometimes is called an *aisle display,* which coincidentally is pronounced the same as *isle display.*

island positioning an advertisement on a page surrounded by editorial matter; sometimes called *island* An extra price is paid for this advertising space. Though the advertising does not necessarily occupy half a page, it sometimes is called an *island-half position.*

iso slang for *isolated* For example, a film or TV camera may be isolated (*iso'd*) from others being used in a production (an *iso camera*) so that its film or tape can be used as a backup or replacement.

ISO INTERNATIONAL STANDARDS ORGANIZATION

isolated commercial a radio or TV commercial with no advertising before or after it An *isolated 30* or *isolated 60* is such a 30- or 60-second commercial.

isolated market a geographical area that is distinctly separate from other areas, with minimum overlap (SPILL-IN and SPILL-OUT of advertising and distribution) or contamination

ISSN INTERNATIONAL STANDARD SERIAL NUMBER

issue 1 a subject, generally controversial, often reported on or discussed in an *issue paper* produced by a government agency, association, or other source 2 all copies of a periodical published on a given date, including the various EDITIONS

issue life a period during which a specific issue of a periodical is assumed to be read by the average reader of that periodical—typically five weeks for a weekly and three months for a monthly

issues analysis the process of studying a controversial subject and then projecting its likely impact on an organization

issues management the process of identifying problems and subjects relevant to an organization and then developing and executing a program to resolve the problems This systematic identification and action generally involves public policy matters of concern to the organization.

IT INFORMATION TECHNOLOGY

ital. ITALIC

Italian rehearsal [film, television] a speedy reading of a script to help the performers learn the lines

italic (ital, ital., italx, itlx, or x) a style of printing type in which the letters are slanted to the right and often have rounded corners and serifs Patterned after Italian Renaissance script, italics provide emphasis. *True italic* resembles handwriting. Typefaces whose original designs are slanted (such as Era) are not italic. In computerized typesetting, it is possible to produce a *pseudoitalic,* or oblique, version of a ROMAN typeface by skewing the DIGITIZED character. The typesetter's direction to italicize is to draw one line under the desired characters or words and/or write *ital* in the margin.

I-team a team of investigative reporters, working to ferret out facts

item 1 [journalism] a relatively brief news article, which may be part of a large article; a sentence, paragraph, or other brief text written by a columnist, in which case it is often referred to as a *column item* Sometimes the item appears by itself and is referred to as a *filler item*—that is, something that editors use to fill a small space on the page. The broadcast equivalent, which also can be referred to as a *filler item,* generally is on the lighter or feature side of the news and often is the last part of a radio or TV broadcast.   **2** [marketing] a unit of a product or service, such as one size and one form of a product

iterate   to repeat, as in an *iterative computer process*, which is repeated continuously The process, called *iteration*, may be controlled by instructions on an *iterative loop*.

ITFS   INSTRUCTIONAL TELEVISION FIXED SERVICE

itlx   ITALIC

ITU   INTERNATIONAL TELECOMMUNICATIONS UNION, INTERNATIONAL TYPOGRAPHICAL UNION

ITV   INSTRUCTIONAL TELEVISION

IW   INDEX WORD

J

jabberwocky gibberish, meaningless syllables that seem to make sense The term is from Lewis Carroll (1832–98), the English mathematician who wrote *Through the Looking Glass*, in which Alice discovers a poem called "Jabberwocky" printed backward and reads its nonsense words in a mirror, or looking glass.

jacket a protective and decorative cover on a book; also called *book jacket* or *dust jacket* *Jacket copy* is material about the book and the author that appears on the front and back of a jacket. A *jacket band* is a removable strip around a book jacket, generally with a promotional message.

Jacob's ladder a type of display with horizontal panels that can be flipped to expose the opposite side Jacob's ladder displays are in airport terminals and other places where the ripple movement of the panels, showing one message on one side and then another message on the other side, is attention-getting. The term originates from the Book of Genesis in the Bible and refers to the seemingly endless ladder from earth to heaven that Jacob saw in a dream.

jaggy a jagged or notched line or edge, as sometimes occurs in computer graphics The undesirable occurrence of jaggies is called *aliasing*.

jam a pileup, such as the wedging of film or tape in a camera, printer, or projector; also called *salad*

jammed lead in a newspaper or other article or broadcast report, a first sentence (called a *lead*) that contains so much information that it is confusing

Japan colors thick, fast-drying, waterproof paints in an oil-free solution Commonly used for metal, plastic, and wood signs and displays, the paint is then covered with a protective varnish.

Japanese-style book an art book or other decorative volume with double leaves, or pages, intentionally uncut and unprinted on the interior sides; also called *Chinese-style book*

Japan paper a strong mottled paper, used for the interior pages and the binding in art books and other high-quality publications Imitations include *French Japon* (note the o) and *Japan vellum*.

jargon the specialized or technical language of a group or profession

Javelle water a water solution of potassium or sodium hypochlorite, used as a paper bleaching agent Named after Javel, a town in France, it is sometimes spelled Javel.

jaw folder a cylindrical device attached to a web-fed printing press used to fold paper The paper is held by the part of the device called the *jaws*, and the folds that are made are called *jaw folds* or *parallel folds*.

JCL JOB control language

jellies gelatins, or transparent gelatin filters, used to diffuse light or change its color to the color of the gel

jelly print a copy made by a gelatin duplicating process, as on a HECTOGRAPH

jenny a portable electric generator, as used in film and TV

jet printing a high-speed (over 1,000 words a minute!) process in which charged ink droplets are emitted from a nozzle onto paper

J-hook a device attached to a shelf, to hold a small amount of merchandise; also called *spindle*

JIC JUST IN CASE

Jiffy bag the brand name for a puffed mailing bag, padded with shredded paper, commonly used to mail books Jiffy bags are made by the Sealed Air Corporation, Holyoke, MA.

jigger 1 a device that operates with a jerking, or jiggly, motion 2 [printing] a detachable part of a plate that may be replaced; also called *fudge* 3 [theater] a wooden strip that hinges scenery together; more commonly called *dutchman*

jim dash a short centered line, generally about 3 EMS wide, used to separate sections of a heading or of the text of an article in a newspaper or other publication

jingle a musical commercial, usually sung

JIP JOIN IN PROGRESS

jitter 1 [television] the jumping of a picture 2 [computers] undesired rapid or jumpy movement of elements on a display

jive jazz music, a slang word used in the 1930s and 1940s; talk that is exaggerated or flippant The word is also used as a verb (to speak in a misleading way) and an adjective (insincere).

JOA JOINT OPERATING AGREEMENT

job 1 a specific piece of work, a term commonly used in computers, printing, and other fields 2 [computers] a set of data or related programs *Job control language* (JCL) identifies a job or its requirements.

jobber a wholesaler, a marketing intermediary between the original supplier and the retailer or buyer-user; also called *distributor*

job control language (JCL) [computers] a set of problem-oriented rules that identify a unit of work and describe its requirements to a computer operating system

job lot an incomplete assortment of products, generally offered at a reduced price, in a factory outlet, discount store, or other retail facility specializing in *odd-lot* merchandise

job press a small printing press using paper fed by hand

job shop a firm, such as a small, local commercial printing plant (a JOB PRINTER), that produces made-to-order or specialty items for its customers

job ticket a document, usually an envelope (*job jacket*), to transmit manufacturing instructions It accompanies the job through various stages and places of production. The terms are most often used in printing.

jock a *disk jockey*, a broadcaster who announces musical records or tapes

jog 1 to move or nudge 2 [printing] to align paper in a stack A *jogger* is a vibrating device that aligns the paper. 3 [television] to make position adjustments in the layout of the picture *Jogging* is the process of moving a videotape forward or backward, one frame at a time. 4 [theater] a small piece of scenery that protrudes or is at right angles to other scenery

John Hancock slang for a person's signature, a reference to the bold, easily legible signature of John Hancock (1737–93) on the Declaration of Independence

Johnson box a rectangular outline, in the shape of a box, made up of a series of asterisks, within which is a short message The box is commonly used in direct mail letters.

join in progress (JIP) an instruction to a station to cut in and start broadcasting a program already started, such as live coverage of a news event

joint in bookbinding, the inside strip or HINGE, either of the two portions of the covering material that bend at the groove and along the ridge where the covers are opened or closed

joint author a collaborator, a person who writes with one or more others; a co-author

joint operating agreement (JOA) an arrangement, authorized by the Newspaper Preservation Act of 1970, that permits two competing newspapers to share facilities and publish together, while keeping their editorial staffs separate

Jones plug a multiprong electrical outlet used in the theater and in exhibitions

journal a diary or a daily record—hence sometimes used as a synonym for a newspaper; a printed record of proceedings—hence used to describe a publication issued by a legal, medical, or other professional organization *Journal advertising* refers to promotion placed in journals and other professional publications. The origin is the Old French word *jornel*, meaning "daily."

journalism the profession of gathering, writing, editing, and publishing news, as for a newspaper and other print and broadcast media *Electronic journalism* refers to the broadcast media. *Journalese* refers to the jargon, or special language, of journalism and also to a writing style characteristic of mass media that emphasizes brevity and popular appeal. A *journalist* writes for the news media. The origin is from the Latin *diurnalis*, or "daily."

journeyman a person who has served an apprenticeship and is an experienced, competent worker The word sometimes refers to an individual who has achieved an acceptable level of competence but lacks creativity.

joystick a rod for manual control requiring the use of one hand, such as the control level that moves the CURSOR on a computer display screen

Jr or **Jr.** junior, referring to the son of a father with the same name Current style is to omit the period.

J school or **J-school** short for *journalism school*, such as the Columbia University Graduate School of Journalism, the University of Missouri School of Journalism, or the Medill School of Journalism at Northwestern University

JTC joke to come: a script notation in optimistic anticipation that a writer will be developing a joke or funny bit

judder 1 a vibration or jump, as in the poor projection of a film 2 in facsimile transmission, the overlapping of the elements of a picture, caused by a lack of uniformity in scanning

judicial gloss the accumulation of legal decisions and opinions concerning a statute, constitutional amendment, or other specific point

juice slang for *electricity* A *juicer* is an electrician.

jukebox or **juke box** a coin-operated, push-button machine that plays records in restaurants and other places The word is from the Gullah dialect of blacks in the coastal area of South Carolina and Georgia, who use the word *juke* to mean wicked or disorderly, as in *juke-house*, a brothel, and *juke joint* or *jook*, a cheap roadhouse, where these machines—typically in a gaudy, illuminated cabinet—were played.

jumble basket a bin or display unit in a store with several different products in a scrambled stack It is not the same as a *dump bin*, in which all the jumbled items are the same product.

jumbo roll [printing] a paper roll larger than 25 inches wide

jumbo stat a large photostat, which may be as large as 5' × 12½'

jump 1 a break in continuity, such as the skipping of a phonograph needle while playing or of a film during projection 2 [journalism] to continue an article from one page to another (usually not the immediately following page) A *jump line*—sometimes set in parentheses—appears at the end of the first portion and indicates where the article is continued; a *jump head* identifies the beginning of the continued portion. The article is said to be *jumped*. The continued part is the *jump, jump page, breakover, break-over page,* or *carryover*, and the entire article is a *jump story*. 3 [typography] the setting of a character—letter, number, or symbol—above or below the line; also called *base line deflection* 4 To *jump the gutter* is to tie the facing pages of a newspaper or magazine together with a headline or other material across the gutter, the margin between the pages. 5 [computers] a departure from the regular order—for example, an instruction, called a *jump instruction*, to go to a new sequence or use a new routine 6 [theater] a one-night stand; also, the gap between two or more such performances 7 a notation in a script indicating physical movement 8 To *jump a cue* is to begin dialogue before another performer has completed the cue.

jump cut a transition in a film or TV program that breaks continuous time by skipping forward from one part of an action to another, obviously separated from the first by a space of time

jumper in electronics, a short wire to close a break in, or cut out part of, a circuit or to make a temporary connection, as with a *jumper cable*

jumping out the process of removing individual frames from a film or a tape

jumpover a layout in which type is interrupted by a photograph or other inserts, so that the reader's eyes must jump over them to follow the text

junction box a unit that connects several electrical sources

junior page an advertisement, 7" × 10" (or smaller) for insertion as a full page in a digest-size magazine or as a partial page in a larger publication; also called *junior unit*

junior panel a transit or outdoor advertising poster smaller than standard size (12' × 25'), such as 6 feet high and 12 feet wide

junior spot [film] a medium-intensity spotlight, generally 1,000 to 2,000 watts Commonly used in film studies, it is also called a *junior*.

junket a free trip, such as a publicity trip, common in the motion-picture and travel industries; also, a trip paid for by public funds, such as one made by members of Congress

junk line codes, instructions, or other text with information for an editor or typesetter but not to be set in type, published, or broadcast

junk mail direct mail advertising and other unsolicited material, generally sent third class: a derogatory term used by some consumers, but not by the mailers, who abhor the usage

jury [theater] the first-night audience and/or the critics

justification the process of typing and typesetting so that margins are aligned *Justification range* is the space remaining at the end of a line of type; the range determines whether the last word is to be hyphenated or whether *justification space* is to be added between the words on the line to fill out the line. *Photographic justification* is the uniform expansion of all space between characters and between words (*word space*). *Internal justification* is the insertion or deletion of space within a line or body of text. In the days before justification devices, the process was done by hand, often by retyping. One novel invention (which now seems amusing) was typing paper crinkled in such a way that each line could be pulled out to the desired measure, or width. The result then was reproduced by offset lithography. *Serial justification* is double typing—that is, the text is typed first and then retyped to align the right margins.

Justification generally involves the adjustment of the spaces between words, but it also can involve the spacing between characters. In *vertical justification*, the spaces between lines are adjusted so as to produce columns or pages to a predetermined depth or length. A *justification routine* is a computer program method to produce justification. The *justification zone* is the area within which justification can be produced. In *horizontal justification*—from one margin to the other—the left margin may be justified (*justified left*), the right margin may be justified (*justified right*), or both may be. When the right margin is not aligned to its full width, it is called *ragged right* or *rag right.*

justified composition typesetting in which the lines are FLUSH (same starting or ending point or edge) on the left and right margins   In specifying typography, the initial *J* means justification or flush left and right.

just in case (JIC) a notation in a manuscript alerting the printer to be prepared for a possible change

Justowriter a cold-type composing machine, with automatic JUSTIFICATION

juveniles children's books, as found in the juvenile department   A *juvenile biography* is a narrative account of a person's life (generally not a juvenile or young person), written for young people.

K

k KILO

K **1** a symbol for 1,000 **2** KELVIN **3** [computers] 1,024 bytes, or units of data (slightly more than 1,000) *10K* is about 10,000—more exactly, 10,240 bytes. **4** the first letter in the call letters of U.S. radio stations west of the Mississippi, as well as a few eastern stations, such as KDKA in Pittsburgh **5** an abbreviation for kilowatt (more commonly *kw*) **6** abbreviation for black

Kabel a heavy sans-serif typeface—that is, one with small decorative lines on the letters

kabuki a form of Japanese drama that is well known in the United States and elsewhere for its formalized pantomime, dance, and song, performed by all-male troupes

Kahn a system, made by Kahn Communications, Westbury, NY, that allows AM radio stations to transmit in stereo

kalogram a monogramlike design that contains all the letters of a company or other name

Kalvar the trademarked name of a film used in printing, made by Kalvar Corporation, Minneapolis, MN

kanji the characters on which Oriental writing (Chinese, Japanese, Korean, and other languages) is based

kaolin a fine white clay (hydrous aluminum silicate) used as a filler or a coating in paper and other material (It is also used in the treatment of diarrhea.)

Kappa Tau Alpha an honorary coeducational fraternity for journalism students, headquartered at the University of Missouri School of Journalism, Columbia

Kb or kb KILOBIT

K band an audio frequency, assigned by the Federal Communications Commission, in the 11 to 36 gigahertz range The frequency is used by radio and TV stations for satellite transmission.

KBI KEY BUYING INFLUENCE

KBN KILL BAD NAME

kc KILOCYCLE

KD or kd KNOCKED DOWN

keep to retain or use, a common instruction to typesetters, as in *keep down* (use lowercase type), *keep in* (use narrow spaces between words), *keep out* (use wide spaces between words), and *keep up* (use uppercase type) In film, *keep takes* are retained, to be used in the completed version.

keeper **1** [direct marketing] a premium, or gift item, that can be kept by the consumer even if payment is not made for a purchase—for example, a book or other item offered with a magazine subscription **2** [film, television] a segment of film or tape that is to be retained and is likely to be used, or kept, in the final *cut* (edited version) **3** [journalism] a story held for possible broadcast or publication

keep in [typography] an instruction to use narrow spaces between words—that is, to keep the words fairly close together

keep out [typography] an instruction to use wide spaces between words—that is, to keep the words relatively far apart

keep-out price a very low price, perhaps on a loss leader (an item priced to attract customers) The purpose is to discourage or keep out competition.

keepsake in the 19th century, an elaborately printed book, often presented as a gift; also called *giftbook*

keep standing an order to a typesetter or a printer to retain type or print matter, for possible subsequent use

keep takes film scenes (takes) retained for potential use in the completed film; also called *hold takes*

keg light a spotlight shaped like a cylinder or a keg, generally about 500 watts

Kelly Award an annual award for the outstanding advertising campaign in a magazine, presented by the MAGAZINE PUBLISHERS ASSOCIATION (MPA). The $25,000 prize is named for the late Steven E. Kelly, who was publisher of *Sports Illustrated* and president of the MPA.

Kelvin (K) a unit of thermodynamic temperature, used in photographic processing and other fields On the Kelvin scale, the zero point, at −273°C, is considerably lower than on the Celsius scale. It is named after William Thompson, Baron of Kelvin, a British physicist (1824–1907). In film and television, *Kelvin temperature* is the amount of red, yellow, and blue quality in light coming from spotlights and other lamps; it is referred to as *color temperature* and is expressed in degrees Kelvin (°K). It should not be confused with *foot candles*, which measure the intensity of light.

kenaf a tropical plant grown for its fiber, which is similar to jute Kenaf is being used experimentally to make newsprint, as a substitute for wood pulp.

Kennelly-Heaviside layer a region of ionized air about 60 miles above the earth's surface that reflects AM broadcast signals back to earth at night; named after Arthur Edwin Kennelly (1861–1935), American electrical engineer, and Oliver Heaviside (1850–1925), English physicist It's also called *Heaviside layer.*

kerning [typography] the technique of adjusting the spacing between two characters to bring them closer, so that part of their letter shapes overhang The opposite, LETTER SPACE, is the placement or retention of space between letters. The *kern* is the projecting portion of a letter that overlaps with the adjacent letter. It is not the same as *ligature,* which is a stroke linking two letters or two or more letters printed together as a single character. Some characters, such as, *i, l,* and *t,* have adjacent white space as part of their standard width; when these characters are set together, they appear too widely spaced. Kerning actually causes them to be set with a slight overlap, so that they look properly set. In a computerized typesetting system, specific pairs of characters may be defined with specific kerning values. When type is set, kerning automatically takes place between those pairs. Kerning often is necessary with italic letters, such as with the letters *f, v,* and *w,* because the forward slope results in excessive space on the base line.

key 1 an identification of the positions of text or art in a layout, by the use of letters, numbers, or symbols; also called *legend* 2 an indication, by means of letters, numbers, or codes, of the source of a response to an advertisement or other promotion For instance, the code *Department T* may be included in the return address in a coupon to identify the publication in which the coupon appeared, so that the advertiser can measure the responses elicited in various media. 3 to place a key, or code, in an advertisement; also called *keycode* 4 the relative lightness (*high key*) or darkness (*low key*) of a photograph, painting, or theatrical set A

high-key picture has few or no dark tones. 5 to light a set 6 [television] an instruction to superimpose text on the screen; short for *chromakey* 7 [computers] one or more data items that identify the type or location of a record or the ordering of data; see KEYWORD 8 a marked lever or button on a KEYBOARD; a switch on a computer console 9 to set copy from a KEYBOARD; the same as to *keyboard*

keyboard 1 to set copy with a keyed typesetting machine (a machine with a keyboard); to *key* 2 a set of levers or buttons—keys, as on a computer, piano, or typewriter A typist or typesetter is called a *keyboarder.* A *keystroke* is the stroke of a key on the keyboard processor. *Key-to-disk* is the transfer of data from a keyboard to a magnetic disk or diskette. A *blind keyboard* (or *idiot keyboard*) has no display unit, nor does it justify—that is, it does not align type at the margins. A *noncounting keyboard,* as on a standard typewriter, cannot count character unit widths and cannot justify. *Split keyboarding* is the use of one keyboard for input and another for output.

key buying influence (KBI) an individual in a family or group who is the decision maker for purchases, particularly major purchases

Keyfax a teletext magazine—relayed by satellite and broadcast on television—produced by Keycom Electronic Publishing Company, of Schaumburg, IL

keyhole journalism investigative reporting based on spying and peeping into the private lives of individuals

keyless inking an OFFSET printing system that requires no keys or levers, to adjust the ink flow A keyless offset press that automatically combines ink and water in the proper balance was introduced in 1988 by Tokyo Kikai Seisakusho, a Japanese company known as *TKS.*

key light a spotlight or other main source of light in a scene The *key-light level* is the intensity of illumination of the main light, a primary factor in adjusting the other lights. *High-key lighting* has a large proportion of the total illumination from the main light, so that there is relatively little lighting contrast, a common situation in color photography. *Low-key lighting* has a lower proportion of the total illumination from the main light, so there is more contrast, as in black-and-white photography. "Don't block the key" is an instruction to one performer not to cast a shadow over another.

keyline 1 the explanation of symbols that appears at the bottom of dictionaries and other reference books 2 [graphic arts] an outline drawing (a *keyline drawing*) on finished art or on a mechanical (a board with type and/or art affixed to it, to be reproduced), to indicate the exact shape, position, and size for such elements as photographs and line sketches; also called *type mechanical, keyline,* or *key* Instructions about the keylined areas are included on an instruction overlay attached to the art or mechanical and coded, or keyed. Colors in the key have specific meanings—for instance, black generally indicates the retention of a line or area; red generally indicates removal; blue generally refers to a tint. *Keylining* is the process by which the outline areas are indicated.

keynote the lowest, most basic note or tone of a musical scale; the basic idea of a speech or other work A *keynote speech,* as delivered at a political or other convention, presents the key points of a policy. The *keynote speaker* at a convention or other meeting is called a *keynoter.* In publishing, a *keynote* is a brief description (25 words or less) of a book.

Key Number System an indexing system of West Publishing Company, of St. Paul, MN, publisher of legal opinions and court decisions Each of the many sections of legal text is identified by a number and a drawing of a key used as an arrow.

keypad a limited KEYBOARD with one or a few buttons or keys, used, for instance, to make selections from a VIDEOTEX system

key page a page without advertising, such as the editorial page of a newspaper, or with minimum advertising

key plate in color printing, the plate used as a guide for the register, or accurate positioning, of other colors The key plate—generally the black-ink plate or the plate with the most detail—is printed first.

keypunch a device for punching holes in data processing cards The holes enable the cards to be sorted according to the information they contain.

key shot the major photograph in a sequence or layout

key station the station from which a program in a network or group broadcast originates; also called *master station*

keystoning distortion of a screen image In overhead projection, as the height of the image increases, the image becomes wider at the top than at the bottom; the fault can be corrected by tilting the top of the screen forward. The same kind of distorted image—wider at the top, like the *keystone* at the top of an arch—can occur in films when a camera or projector lens is not at a right angle to a surface.

keyword or **key word** [computers] **1** one or more characters—letters, numbers, symbols—that contain information about a set of data; also called *key* or *control word* **2** a word or

words used in indexing or to help in the retrieval, or calling up, of data on a terminal; also called *descriptor* A *keyword index* uses a significant word in a title as the identifying word in an index.

keyword in context (KWIC) an indication that the identifying word in an index listing is within the listing and not the first word

keyword index an index, or systematic guide to the contents of a document or text, in which a significant or informative word is selected to begin or identify each entry In automatic indexing, a computer is used to prepare a keyword index by excluding specific insignificant words (*indexing by exclusion*) or by selecting specified significant words (*indexing by inclusion*).

kickback an improper gift, rebate, or commission provided by a vendor

kicker **1** an attractive item, article, or photograph used to brighten a page, sometimes in the left column to *kick off,* or start, the page **2** a short line of text above a main heading or headline, as in a newspaper or magazine; also called *teaser, eyebrow,* or *highline* **3** on a TV or radio broadcast, an inconsequential, humorous, or even zany final item; also called *zipper* **4** a light to the side or rear of a subject; also called *kicker light, kick light, stringer light, rim light, cross backlight,* or *side backlight*

kideo home video for children

kidvid a television program or home video for children

kill **1** to eliminate—for instance, to turn off lights or remove scenery; to cancel, such as to void an order A performer who *kills a laugh* delivers a line so ineptly that the audience responds with little or no laughter. To *kill a hand* is to cut off applause prematurely. A newspaper story is killed by being *spiked*—put on the spindle on an editor's desk—or, in the days of hot-metal typesetting, having the type thrown into the HELL BOX. To *kill a widow* is not morbid; it entails eliminating a short line (especially at the top of a page or a column) by editing or adjusting the preceding lines. **2** to succeed tremendously, as with a performer who *kills an audience* (wows them, knocks them dead) The opposite is to *bomb* (be an intense failure). **3** a removal or cancellation A *mandatory kill* is an order absolutely, positively to eliminate or not use something.

kill bad name (KBN) [direct marketing] an instruction to eliminate, or kill, an invalid name—called a NIXIE—on a list

kill copy a proof or other copy with *kill notations,* indicating the items to be canceled or removed

kill date the time after which a news announcement, such as about an event, is outdated and should not be used

killer bars the wavy parallel lines that cancel stamps in the mailing process so that they cannot be reused, sometimes incorrectly called *postmarks* Actually, the cancellation marks appear to the right of the circular postmark, which bears the postal information, originating city, and date of cancellation.

kill fee the payment to a freelance writer by a magazine or other medium when an article or other submission has been voided, or killed, prior to publication or other usage

kill order an instruction to cancel something

kill report a wire-service bulletin indicating that a previous transmission should be voided—that is, killed—or revised

kilo (k) a prefix for 1,000, used in such words as *kilocycle* (*kc*), *kilogram* (*kg*), *kilohertz* (*kHz* or *khz*), *kilometer* (*km*), *kilovolt* (*kv*), and *kilowatt* (*kW* or *kw*) *Kilocycles per second* is abbreviated *kcs* or *kcss*; *kilometers per hour* or *per second* is abbreviated *kmph* or *kmps*.

In computer terminology, however, *K* refers to the number 1,024 (2 to the tenth power) and specifies the amount of storage available on a disk or in memory. A *kilobyte* is 1,024 bytes, and a system with 10K of memory has 10,240 bytes of storage capacity.

kilobit (Kb or **kb)** a computer term for 2,000 binary digits, or bits

kilocycle (kc) 1,000 cycles per second, or 1,000 alterations of current or sound waves per second; also called *kilohertz* (*kHz* or *khz*) The number of kilocycles determines a radio station's frequency, and thus its position on the dial.

kilroy the defective framing of a TV picture in which the lower portion of the heads of performers or others is cut off The origin is a cartoon character in the Second World War made famous by the motto scrawled on thousands of walls, "Kilroy was here."

kinescope a film made of a transmitted television picture; also called *kine*, pronounced KIN-ney Kinescopes, which have been replaced by videotape, are no longer common. Originally, kinescope was a synonym for *picture tube*.

kinestasis [film] a process of photographing a still photo, one frame at a time, so that when projected, the rapid cuts (24 frames in one second) evoke staccato movement; also called *filmograph, kinestatis, phonokinesis,* or *photokinestasis* The word is from the Greek *kine,* "movement," and *stasis,* "standing still."

kineto a prefix meaning "moving" The *kinetograph,* which was developed in the late 19th century in the laboratory of Thomas Alva Edison (1847–1931), was a camera that produced short strips of film for viewing in a *Kinetoscope* (also called a *peephole machine*).

king's English standard or correct usage of the English language, as sanctioned by the British monarchy; also called *queen's English* and sometimes capitalized, as in the King's English Both terms usually begin with *the*.

king-size poster a large poster, perhaps 2' × 12', mounted on the outside of a bus

kino-pravda film truth: the Russian version of CINEMA VÉRITÉ, or a type of documentary film

kinship name a word indicating relationship to a person When used before or as a substitute for a proper name, the kinship name is capitalized, as in "Happy birthday, Mother" (*but* "My mother lives in. . . .").

kiosk a small structure open at one or more sides, such as a newsstand Kiosks in banks and elsewhere are generally 3 to 6 feet high and contain a screen and a KEYPAD or KEYBOARD (or maybe a TOUCH SCREEN) connected to a microcomputer or a phone linked to a computer. The unit, which also may contain a printer and a telephone, is commonly used as an automatic teller machine and often is called simply a *terminal*.

kiss pressure [printing] the minimum pressure at which proper ink transfer can be achieved

kitchen play a type of play, or drama, in which performers sit around a kitchen or dining-room table

kitsch pretentious poor taste, especially in decoration and the arts The origin is the German word *kitschen,* meaning "to smear."

kleen a typesetter's instruction to clean a smudge or other imperfection It is deliberately spelled incorrectly so that the typesetter will spot it as an instruction and not as a word to be set.

Klieg light a powerful, wide-angle carbon arc lamp used in motion-picture, theatrical, and TV production; pronounced kleeg and sometimes misspelled *Kleig* The lamp was invented by John Kliegl (1869–1959) and Anton Kliegl (1872–1927); actually, then, the correct name should be *Kliegl*. The German-American Kliegl brothers were theatrical-lighting designers whose inventions included the *Kliegl stage plug system,* containing an array of plugs and sockets for a variety of lamps.

klinker a mistake, particularly an obviously wrong note played by a musician

kludge slang for makeshift, a term used to describe an improvised part in computer hardware or software

knee a bend; a gradual rather than sharp change It is used to describe a feature of an electronic device, such as the knee or bend at the upper end of the exposure curve (as compared to the lower end, or toe) of a TV camera.

knee shot a camera view that covers about three-quarters of the length of an individual ending just below the knees

Knight-Ridder one of the country's largest media companies, headquartered in Miami It publishes the *Detroit Free Press, Journal of Commerce, Miami Herald, Philadelphia Inquirer*, and other periodicals and owns major TV stations.

knocked down (KD or **kd)** an item, such as a display or exhibit, shipped flat and unassembled, and requiring on-site assembly; also called *knockdown*

knocking on the grass [journalism] slang for what happens when a reporter, assigned to interview a bereaved person in a tragic situation, is reluctant to do so and knocks on the front lawn instead of on the door

knockoff an unauthorized copy

knockout 1 [printing] a black, red, or orange patch pasted onto a layout sheet to create a window on the negative, into which separately photographed material can be inserted; also called *blackout* **2** [typography] reverse or dropout type, appearing in white on a black or dark background; also called *knock-out, liftout, reverse*, or *dropout*

KNT News Wire a major news service, combining the Knight-Ridder Newspapers, New York News, and Chicago Tribune Press Service It is located in Washington, DC.

Kodachrome 35mm color film (or color transparency made from this multilayer film), manufactured by the EASTMAN KODAK COMPANY, of Rochester, NY, for still and motion-picture photography *Kodacolor* is another type of color film made by Kodak. A *Kodamontage* is a transparent photograph consisting of an assemblage of Kodachromes.

Kodak See EASTMAN KODAK COMPANY.

Kodalith a brand of heavy, opaque, high-contrast film, manufactured by the Eastman Kodak Company, of Rochester, NY, and used in printing

Koh-I-Noor a brand of technical pens made by Koh-I-Noor, Inc., of Bloomsbury, NJ

Ko-Rec-Type a typing correction sheet made by the Eaton Allen Corporation, of Brooklyn, NY

Korinna a serif typeface—that is, one in which the letters have small, decorative, projecting lines

kraft a strong, durable brown paper used for large envelopes, bags, and wrapping paper The same material—unbleached sulphite wood pulp—is used as a cardboard called *kraft board*, often as an envelope stiffener. The word, which is not capitalized, is from the German word *kraft*, or "strength"; the products are not made by the food company Kraft, Inc.

Kray a stock custodial facility for members of the Midwest Stock Exchange in Chicago

KromeKote the trademarked name of a heavy, high-quality, coated paper made by Champion Paper Company, of New York, and used for displays

Kroy a trademarked lettering system—made by Kroy, Inc., of St. Paul, MN—that uses *Kroytype* in various type styles and sizes

Krylon the trademarked name for a clear spray used as a fixative or protection on artwork, made by Krylon, Inc., of Norristown, PA

Ku band an audio frequency in the 12-to-14-gigahertz range Part of the K BAND, it is assigned by the Federal Communications Commission and used by radio and TV stations for satellite transmission. The communications satellite that operates in the Ku band is the *Ku satellite*; its relays can be received with a relatively small dish, or microwave transmitter, such as those next to small homes. The dishes are also seen atop TV news trucks—*Ku trucks*—which are mobile units for satellite transmission. The vehicle is sometimes called a *12-14 truck* or *12-14 unit*, after the gigahertz range.

kW or **kw** kilowatt (1,000 watts)

KWIC KEYWORD IN CONTEXT

KWOC *keyword out of context*, the use of an incorrect word—not the most significant word—within the context of a title or other text to identify the text, as in a KEYWORD INDEX

Kyoto News Service a major international news wire, in Tokyo

L

l or L large; late; LEFT; LENGTH; line, as in a line of type When followed by a number, the abbreviation indicates the line number, as in *L2* (second line). The plural, lines, is *ll*.

L when written next to or under a letter or word, an indentation instruction or paragraph mark

lab short for *laboratory*, where photographs, films, tapes, and other items are processed and duplicated

label **1** a slip affixed to an item describing its contents—for instance, a *package label*—or indicating its destination—*mailing label*—or providing other information Types of labels include *gummed label* (requiring moisture, and commonly used by consumers), CHESHIRE *label* (generally used by mass mailers), *pressure-sensitive label* (it requires no moisture, since the label is pulled off a backing sheet and then pressed on the envelope or other item), *heat-activated* or *heat-seal label* (no longer much used, it requires heat to activate the adhesive), and *heat-transfer label* (the label has a reverse carbon image of the name and address printed on the back and thus can be used as a printing master to transfer the image onto an envelope by the application of heat; it is no longer commonly used by mass mailers). **2** the identifying feature (as printed on the wrapper) of a package or other item; a descriptive word or phrase characterizing a person or a group **3** the name of a recording or other company, as indicated on its records, tapes, discs, or other products **4** to affix a label **5** [book production] a piece of paper or other material, with the name of the author and the title, affixed to the spine or to the front cover **6** [computers] a name or other identifier of an instruction in a program or of the contents of a data file

label head [journalism] a descriptive headline that identifies, or labels, a story but usually lacks a verb and often is dull and limited It generally consists of one or two words. Label heads are seen frequently in weekly newspapers and small-circulation magazines, or in periodicals to identify a department or a regular feature.

labeling the use of key phrases, or labels, such as in a speech or an interview

label set a group of names and addresses separated out from a list for printing on labels; also called *label panel* or *label split*

label string a segment of a LABEL SET, arranged in ZIP Code or other sequence for presorted mailing in accordance with postal requirements

laboratory effects the special audio or visual elements of a film that can be produced during the processing of the film, rather than during the shooting

LAC LIVE action camera

lace **1** a delicate fabric with an open, weblike pattern; a cord or string for tying together (such as a shoe lace) **2** to fasten (with a lace or laces); to trim (with lace or lacelike fabric); to streak (with fine lines) **3** [computers] to punch extra holes in a punch card The process, *lacing*, usually is done to indicate the end of a run. A *laced card* has extra holes, intentionally or unintentionally punched, in addition to the original identifying holes. **4** to thread film into a projector, a process called *lacing*

Lacey Luci the trademarked name of an enlarging–reducing machine, a cameralike device that is used to enlarge or reduce images The name is from *camera lucida*; see also LUCI.

lacing in [book production] a method of inserting cords through holes in the cover boards (*laced boards* or *laced-on boards*) and then adding a covering material

lacquer a clear or colored glossy coating, used on printed materials, cans, and packages, to protect the item and provide a lustrous appearance *Lacquering* or varnishing—for example, spraying a fixative on reproduction copy—is the application process.

lacuna a gap or space where something has been omitted, such as a missing part of a manuscript

ladder **1** a set of symbols or a name used to identify or describe an item, record, message, file, or storage address **2** [typography] three or more consecutive lines that end in hyphenations, a sequence considered to be undesirable

LADT LOCAL AREA DATA TRANSPORT

lady of the house (loh) an old-fashioned term, used in telephone marketing, for the woman who is the head of the household

lag **1** an interval or a delay between events; a condition of slowness or retardation **2** the blurring or smearing of an image caused by camera movement

laid-in music track background music or sound that was part of a scene during the shooting of a film, not music or sound that is edited in afterward

laid paper a type of uncoated paper that has a pattern embedded, or laid, into it, with equidistant light parallel lines (*laid lines*) running across the grain The *laid marks* are produced by wires in the DANDY ROLL (a *laid dandy roll*) of the papermaking machine. Laid paper sometimes also has chain lines, which are thicker lines that intersect, or cross, the wire marks. Laid paper also can be handmade. *Laid antique paper* has a pattern of vertical and horizontal lines. *Wove paper*, in contrast to laid paper, lacks the ridged pattern and does not show distinct wire marks.

LA lock the most common type of lock for mailbags and parcel post sacks The initials stand for *lock Andrus*; the lock was developed by a mail-equipment official named Burton Andrus.

lam. laminated

Lambs a theatrical club in New York The actual name is *The Lambs*; the group is often called *The Lambs Club*. The executive director is known as *The Shepherd*.

Lamda Iota Tau an honorary society in literature, based at the Department of English, Ball State University, Muncie, IN

lamination a process of uniting or pressing together two or more layers of thin sheets—for instance, plastic adhered to paper *Laminated* book or record jackets have an outer film of clear plastic for protection and enhanced appearance. *Liquid laminate* is a liquid coating affixed to book and record jackets and other covers.

lamp a bulb, tube, or other device for producing light; also called *luminant* It differs from a *luminaire*, which is a floodlight fixture, including the lamp, reflector, support, housing, and cable. To *lamp down* is to replace a lamp with one of lower wattage.

lampblack a gray or black pigment made from soot, used in printing

lamp house the portion of a projector containing the light

lampoon **1** a piece of satirical writing or other work generally ridiculing a person The *Harvard Lampoon* is a publication, renowned for its satire, put out by students at Harvard University, in Cambridge, MA. **2** to attack or ridicule, generally humorously, as by a *lampooner* or *lampoonist*

lamp schedule a list of lamps, with data about them, to be used in production

lamp sing the humming sound made by a light filament that is improperly vibrating

LAN LOCAL AREA NETWORK

land the part of a grooved surface that is not indented, such as the surface between the grooves of a record

landline a circuit connecting two ground locations, such as a telephone line

L&M LAYOUT and manuscript

landscape format a layout in which the larger dimension is horizontal—that is, the width is greater than the height The more common arrangement is the *portrait format*, in which the height is greater than the width. A sign, display, or other item whose width is greater than its height is called a *landscape*.

language a body of words, symbols, signs, and systems for communicating among people of the same group or nation *Machine language* or *computer language*, such as Fortran or COBOL, is understood by computers and/or by humans. *Natural language*, or human speech, is more flexible than artificial language and has variations in meaning and usage, whereas machine language is rigid and highly precise. Types of computer language include *application-oriented, assembly, command, control, high-level, linear, low-level, object, problem-oriented, procedure-oriented, programming, source, symbolic*, and *target*. "To break the language" is to alter a typeface style or visual harmony with something incongruous.

language simplification a process of editing text and design to enhance the readers' comprehension of the material Techniques for making a text easier to read and to motivate readers have been developed by Rudolf Flesch, Wilson Tucker (cloze procedure), Alan Siegel (of Siegel & Gale, New York), and others (Dale-Chall formula, Gunning formula). For example, the Flesch formula measures average sentence length and average syllables per word (Reading Ease Score) and the percentage of *personal* words and sentences (Human Interest Score), as compared to impersonal words. Other procedures measure the number or proportion of long, uncommon, abstract, or redundant words.

lantern a transparent case for holding a light; an old-fashioned term for a slide projector (*lan-*

tern slide projector or *magic lantern*) that holds transparent glass slides (*lantern slides*) In the United Kingdom, *lantern* often is used as a synonym for a theatrical light source, such as a spotlight or other lamp.

lap **1** a term for various portable devices that are small enough to be held in a person's lap, whether or not they are actually used in that position—for instance, *lap computer* or *lap reader* (a microfilm magnifier) **2** a part that extends over another part (an *overlap*); to fold (*to lap edges* under or over) The *lap* of a printing press or other machine is a part extending over another part, or the slightly extended area or margin of a printing surface, such as a color plate, to permit easier registration (alignment). **3** in papermaking, a layering of the fibers

lap dissolve **1** [film, television] an optical effect or type of transition in which one scene is gradually replaced by a new image; also called *lap, cross lap, cross-dissolve,* or *mix* **2** [theater] a crossfade, or fading out of one light while another light is faded in

lapel mike a small microphone clipped to a lapel, necktie, shirt, or elsewhere, or worn hanging around the neck; also called LAVALIERE

large-paper edition (l.p.) a book printed from a standard-size edition on larger paper with wider margins, often with better-quality paper and binding; also called *large-paper copy*

large print an imprecise term that generally refers to any type size over 16 points (there are 72 points to an inch) A *large-print edition* is a newspaper or other work printed in big letters, for the benefit of those who have difficulty reading standard-size type.

large-size page a standard-size page, not a tabloid or junior-size page

Larimi Communications a company in New York that publishes *Contacts*, a newsletter for publicists In 1988, Billboard Publications in New York acquired the media directories formerly published by Larimi.

laryngophone a throat microphone, attached more closely to the neck than a LAPEL MIKE; pronounced la-RING-guh-fone

LAS LIMITED ASSORTMENT STORE

laser acronym for *light amplification by stimulated emission of radiation*, the source of a single-color, very narrow, coherent (focused) beam of light Unlike most light, laser light may be focused very precisely with little dispersion. Lasers are used in phototypesetting and imaging devices. In photocomposition, laser beams traverse the area to be reproduced in a series of scan lines, similar to the way a TV picture is formed. *Laser typesetters* create one line at a time, rather than one character (letter or number) at a

time. *Laser printers* are commonly used to produce multiple correspondence and other items very quickly. LaserWriter is a laser printer made by Apple Computer. The laser technology of converting images into electric impulses has other printing applications; it is used in color separation and in platemaking.

LaserVision (LV) an optical videodisk, made by Phillips, of Holland

last-chance method a sales technique in which the potential buyer is warned that the quantity, time of sale, or other elements are limited; also called *standing room only (SRO)*

last color down in sequential color printing (the procedure in which each color is printed separately), the last color printed

last frame of action (LFOA) the final frame of film that has been shot It is followed by the *tail leader*, a blank strip of film at the end of a reel.

last telecast (LTC) a term used at a TV station to indicate the last program of the broadcast day

last watch the staff at a newspaper that produces the final edition It is not the same as the LATE WATCH.

LAT Los Angeles Times *LATS* is the Los Angeles Times Syndicate, and *LAT–WPNS* is the Los Angeles Times–Washington Post News Service.

LATA LOCAL ACCESS AND TRANSPORT AREA

latchkey children children at home alone, before or after school, who constitute an important TV audience of several million boys and girls The origin dates from the Second World War, when working mothers put house keys around the necks of their school children; the term may apply today in families where both parents work or where there is only one parent, who works outside the home.

late fringe [television] the time period following prime time, usually from 11 P.M. to sign-off

latency [computers] the time required for a device to begin physical output of data once processing is complete

latensification a process to increase the density—that is, increase the shadow area of a latent, or invisible, image on film (generally underexposed)—by exposing the film to low-level illumination over a long period

latent image **1** the invisible image on undeveloped film, made visible by developing **2** the process in OFFSET PRINTING in which the image is photographed and remains invisible until developed

lateral reversal the technique of producing a change of image from left to right or from right to left—that is, the creation of a mirror image For example, when metal type is printed, it is laterally reversed from its original form; contact prints, or photographic proofs, have laterally reversed images. The perception of a laterally reversed image is called *lateral orientation.*

late watch   the staff at a daily newspaper that begins work after the last edition, or at a station after the last newscast; also called *dog watch, graveyard shift,* LOBSTER TRICK, *lobster watch,* or *night side*   It is not the same as the LAST WATCH.

Latin   [graphic arts] British slang for garbled letters used in a layout to indicate size or position; called GREEK TYPE in the United States

Latin alphabet   a 21-letter alphabet (without *j, u, w, y,* or *z*) used in ancient Latium and Rome, the predecessor of the "Latin languages" (Spanish, French, and Italian) and different from such other alphabets as Greek and Cyrillic   To *latinize* is to transliterate into the Latin alphabet, or to *romanize.*

latitude   [photography] the extent to which a negative may be underexposed or overexposed without significant loss of quality

laugh track   the audio component of a TV situation comedy or other program on which audience laughter is inserted, from tape cassettes with various types of actual or artificial laughter

launch   an introduction, generally of a new product or service

Laurel Leaf Awards   annual awards given by the American Composers Alliance, an organization in New York, to individuals and groups for fostering concert music

lavaliere (lav)   **1** a pendant worn on a chain around the neck; pronounced lav-a-LEER   **2** [broadcasting] a microphone worn like a necklace

law binding   buckram or other durable material for the covers of law and other books   The cloth resembles calfskin (called *law calf*) or sheepskin (*law sheep*) coverings that previously were used, generally decorated with gold titles.

lawn finish   paper with a linenlike finish, made with a fine sieve or mesh, called a *lawn*

law super   a type of bookbinding reinforced with heavy cross threads

lawyered   *Wall Street Journal* jargon to describe material scrutinized by one of its libel or other lawyers, as in "This article has been lawyered and can move"

lay   **1** the state of the bed on which paper rests before the paper enters a flatbed printing press   The *lay sheet* is the first of several sheets run through the press to check LINEUP, REGISTER, and other factors.   **2** short for LAY-

OUT   **3** to *lay the paper:* to produce a layout; to *lay the ads:* to show the placement of display advertisement on a page   **4** the process of splicing a soundtrack to match the images; also called *lay-in*   The editing of the soundtracks to align them for the mixing—the blending of audio and video—is called *laying tracks.*   **5** to *lay down:* to record, as in *lay down a track*   **6** to *lay it on thick:* to apply heavily (such as ink or paint); to exaggerate or to flatter effusively

layback   the nonprintable area of a printing plate, from the edge to, and including, the gripper margin (where grippers, or clamps, hold the plate on the press)

laydown sequence   in sequential color printing, the order in which colors are printed

laydown speed   in photosetting, the rate at which characters (letters, numbers, and symbols) are exposed onto the film or other photographic material

layercake   a newspaper layout with two or more across-the-page headlines, so that the upper ones are separated from their articles

layout   a drawing, sketch, or plan of a proposed advertisement, brochure, or other material   At its early or preliminary stage, it is a *rough layout* or a *rough.* When more carefully done, it is called a *comprehensive layout* (*comp*) and then, in its final stage, a *finished layout.* The artist (*layout person*) often works with translucent paper (*layout paper*), on which instructions can be written. A *layout and manuscript* (L&M) is a layout accompanied by the text.

Lazy Susan display   a point-of-purchase unit, such as a case for jewelry or watches, that revolves manually or with a motor on a turntable base

LC or **L.C.**   LIBRARY OF CONGRESS

lc   LOWERCASE

LC   left center (of a stage)

lca   LOWERCASE-ALPHABET LENGTH

LCD   LIQUID CRYSTAL DIODE

LCE   left center entrance (by a performer)

ld   LEAD

lead (ld.)   (pronounced leed)   **1** the first; the most important   **2** [journalism] the beginning of a story   The most common type of lead is the *direct lead,* the workhorse of journalism. It may be a traditional, factual exposition, or it may be an anecdote, a quotation, a question, or perhaps a clause, phrase, or single word. The other basic type is the *delayed lead,* a more leisurely approach more often used for soft news and features, or by the newsweekly magazines, to set the scene or establish a mood. A *new lead* (also called *new top*) is an updated or fresh beginning. A *lead-all* is a brief beginning of a new story; it may be part of an existing lead, such as an updated revision preceding a story. In broadcasting, a story may begin with a *perspective lead* (one that relates the report to previous events), a *quote lead* (a quotation), a *new story lead* (for the first time an event is reported), a *folo lead* (a follow-up to an earlier story), or a *segue lead* (a transition, generally to a related story; pronounced seg-way). The *lead sentence*—sometimes simply called *lead*—is the first sentence of a news release or news article. In a full-size daily newspaper, the *lead story* on page one is the most important article, generally on the upper right side, and the *off-lead* is the second most important, generally on the upper left side. **3** a tip about a possible news story or idea, as when a reporter says, "I have a *lead* on a story." **4** [marketing] a tip or clue to a prospective customer *Leadflow* is the volume of leads over a period of time. *Lead generation* is the stimulation of leads, as through advertising. *Lead shortfall* is an insufficient number of leads, generally in comparison to a predetermined goal. **5** [film, television, theater] the principal performer or the principal role in a work **6** a cable or wire that serves as a connector **7** [film] a space left in front of a moving subject, so that the audience does not have the sensation that the subject is moving off the screen In thrill scenes, the *lead space*, as it is also called, is reduced or omitted, to heighten the tension. See also LEDE.

lead (pronounced led) **1** a metal **2** [typography] a thin strip of metal (1–4 points thick) used for inserting space between lines of type *Leaded matter* has extra space between lines. In phototypesetting, lead is the distance, in points, between BASE LINES of typeset copy. **3** to add space between lines of type, a process called LEADING

leader **1** a length of film joined to the beginning of a reel for threading through the camera or projector; any blank framed film used to link other film *Academy leader* contains numerals and is used at the start of the reel to establish focus. Other commonly used leaders include the AMERICAN NATIONAL STANDARD leader (ANS) and the SOCIETY OF MOTION PICTURE AND TELEVISION ENGINEERS universal leader (SMPTE). A *tail leader* is one inserted at the end of a film. **2** a deal or a special offer to a customer who purchases a specific amount of merchandise **3** [typography] a series of dots, dashes, or other characters that lead horizontally across a page or column, from one item of text to another Leaders are sometimes used in lists or in tables of contents, where a series of dots links chapter titles and page numbers.

leader record [computers] a record that contains information about subsequent records

lead-in **1** an introduction, such as by a newscaster preceding a report **2** a connecting wire—for instance, from an aerial to a receiver or from an antenna to a transmitter

leading (pronounced ledding) [typography] the insertion of space between lines of type *Negative leading* uses a *leading value* smaller than the point size of the type, so that the descenders of one line (for instance, the tail of the letter g) may overlap the ascenders of the subsequent line (as in the letter h). *Double leading* refers to the use of twice as much space between lines as usual—as on page 1 and the editorial page of newspapers. *Leading out* is the insertion of extra spacing between lines. *Extra leading* is an instruction to a typesetter to add white space, such as between two blocks of type or at certain locations throughout a manuscript. *Primary leading* is the line spacing used in the general body of a text, whereas *secondary leading* entails a different amount of spacing—for instance, between paragraphs or in a specific section of the work.

leading (pronounced leeding) principal, as with a *leading article* or *leading actor*, or guiding, as with a *leading decimal point* preceding a number

lead line a line that leads to and points out an item, as in a diagram; also called *leader line* It may end in an arrowhead.

lead pencil a pencil with a core of graphite, generally mixed with clay or other materials, but not lead The origin of this misnomer is that graphite once was called *black lead*. Writing pencils—lead pencils commonly used for writing—are graded by degrees of hardness: 1 (softest), 2 (most common), 2½, 3, and 4. Drawing pencils—lead pencils used by artists—are made in many grades, including 6B (softest) and 9H (hardest).

lead sheet (pronounced leed) **1** a musical accompaniment score, for use by the conductor A *song lead sheet* includes the music and lyrics and the names of the composer, lyricist, and publisher, and copyright data. **2** a chart used in film with the dialogue on one side and next to it the exact number of frames for each syllable, sound, or pause; generally called a *bar sheet* The lead sheet is used in animation, special effects, and music scoring.

lead time or **leadtime** (pronounced leed) **1** the time before the actual start of a project; the preparatory period **2** [journalism] the period of production; the time between the completion of a manuscript and its publication or, more generally, the interval between the medium's deadline for receipt of advertising or editorial material and the time of its appearance in the publication Some publications promote themselves as having a short lead time, perhaps a few days or a few weeks. Monthly magazines require three to six months of lead time for receipt of proposed editorial material prior to actual publication.

lead title (pronounced leed) the most important book or a publisher's list of books of volumes

lead to come (LTC) (pronounced leed) a notation on copy, often made on a developing story sent to an editor or to the composing room, that the beginning section of the article will follow

leaf a folded sheet, each side of which is a page *Leaf affixing* or *page affixing* is the fastening together of the leaves of a book. A *leaf book* contains an account of an earlier book and includes an original leaf or leaves from that book (such as a rare defective book). *Leaf* also is short for *gold leaf*, the sheets of metallic foil used in the design of book covers or other items.

leaflet a small, thin pamphlet, such as a four-page publication printed on one sheet that then is folded

League of Resident Theatres (LORT) an organization of about 80 local theaters, headquartered at the Milwaukee Repertory Theatre in Wisconsin Performers work in accordance with a *LORT contract*, an Actors' Equity contract that provides for lower salaries than at Broadway theaters. LORT-A, LORT-B, LORT-C, and LORT-D are descriptions of theater size, with LORT-A the largest.

leak a disclosure, as by a government official or company employee A leak may appear to occur by accident, but the intent of the leaker may be to convey information that would otherwise not have been made public. Information can be *leaked* to the media and then can be called a *news leak*, or it can be revealed to individuals.

lean-faced referring to type that is thin or delicate

leapfrogging the technique of bringing in distant signals on a cable-TV system

learned journal a scholarly periodical More than 100,000 learned journals are published throughout the world.

The Learning Channel an educational cable network in Washington, DC

leased department a concession or section in a multiline store, such as a discount store or a department store, that is rented to an outside company The lessee or concessionaire may sell jewelry, cameras, and other products or provide travel, optometric, and other services. *Leased inventory* is merchandise provided by a manufacturer or wholesaler to a retailer on credit, such as the first inventory of a new store.

A *leased line* is a telephone or other communications channel rented by a telephone company for the exclusive use of a company or other customer.

leatherette imitation leather Paper with a leatherette finish is made by embossing the wrinkled pattern.

leave-behind a brochure, proposal, or other item provided to a prospect, or potential customer, at the conclusion of a sales presentation

lectern a reading desk with a slanted top, often used by public speakers It differs from a podium (elevated platform).

LED LIGHT-EMITTING DIODE

ledd the phonetic spelling of LEAD, to add space between lines of type The process is called *ledding* or LEADING (the current spelling).

lede the correct, original spelling (though it is rarely used) for LEAD, as used in journalism It may refer to the first sentence or the first part of an article, or to the primary piece, or *lead article*, in a publication. Generally, the lead article appears on the first page of a magazine, though many magazines now contain a variety of letters to the editor and service columns preceding the first or primary article. The lead article in a magazine sometimes is featured on the cover, in which case it is referred to as a *cover article*. The lead article in a newspaper generally is determined by its prominent position, often at the top right corner of page 1. Within a newspaper, there can be several lead articles, including the primary articles on various pages or sections.

leder (pronounced leeder) a major article, as in columns 1 and 6 on page 1 of *The Wall Street Journal* The British origin of the term refers to stories that *led* a newspaper—that is, were prominently featured.

ledger paper a strong, smooth paper with qualities for writing, such as strength and erasability, used as drawing paper, as photographic paper, for accounting records (ledgers), and for other purposes; also called *ledger-weight paper* or *record paper*

leerics slang for song lyrics that are sexually suggestive, from *leer*, a sly look

left (l or L) 1 [typography] an indication to set lines flush left and ragged right—that is, aligned at the left margin but not at the right 2 [theater] stage left, from the viewpoint of the performer (abbreviated *L*) *L1* or *L1E*, or *left first entrance*, refers to the first entrance of a performer, on the left side of the stage; *L2E* is *left second entrance*.

left-hand art a photograph or other art in which the viewer's eye is directed from left to right, the conventional manner for readers of European languages The opposite is *right-hand art*.

leftover matter [typography] material that is typeset but not used, or OVERSET

leg **1** a vertical subdivision of a mass of type—for instance, one column or part of one column in a multicolumn layout **2** [theater] a long drape or cloth, usually on each side of a stage A pair of legs connected by a horizontal border can be used to mask the wings of a stage. A leg is also called a *leg drop, leg piece,* or, in the United Kingdom, a *leg cloth* or *tail.*

legal cap legal size (8½″ × 13″ or 14″) writing paper used by lawyers for documents, usually folded at the top and with a ruled left margin The *cap* is from *foolscap,* a long sheet of paper.

legal notices advertisements by government bodies about forthcoming meetings, elections, and other matters, generally required by law to appear publicly (as in a newspaper); also called *legals*

legal paper paper that is longer than letter paper (8½″ × 11″), such as 13 or 14 inches long It is usually white, lined, and padded (a *legal pad*).

leg drop a cloth, or a drop, cut out in the center and used as a stage curtain

legend **1** a title or a description, other than the caption, below or beside a photograph When it appears as a lead-in to a caption, a legend often is set in all capital letters (sometimes SMALL CAPITALS). When it appears above or to the side of a caption, a legend often is set in headline type, with the first letter of each word capitalized. **2** an explanation of symbols, as on a map or chart **3** titles or information keyed, or superimposed, on a TV picture

legitimate theater drama or standard plays, excluding burlesque, melodrama, vaudeville, and some forms of musical comedy; informally called *legit*

leg lady theatrical slang for a *chorus girl*

leg man a reporter who gathers news and relays it to the writing and editing staff; also called *legman, legger,* or *leg person* (less common, though nonsexist) The term also is used to describe a public relations practitioner, researcher, or anyone else—including, of course, a woman—who assists in operations, or functions of the job; *leg* refers to running "on the street" or in the field.

legs the ability of a movie or other work to obtain sizable audiences on a continuing basis A movie that opens to strong box office, but fizzles a few weeks later, has *wobbly legs,* whereas a movie that continues to be profitable many weeks after its opening has *strong legs.* A book with legs is so successful that it "walks out of the store."

leg show a revue or other theatrical entertainment featuring scantily clad chorus girls, or *leg ladies;* also called *leg piece*

Leipzig yellow a yellow pigment, more commonly called *chrome yellow*

leisure unemployment *At leisure* refers in particular to an unemployed performer.

leitmotif a dominant or recurring theme, particularly a musical theme associated with a specific character in a film or other work; from the German *leitmotiv* (also the alternate spelling in English), which is from *leiten,* meaning "to lead," and *motiv,* or "motive"

Lekolite an ellipsoidal spotlight with individual push-shutters for focusing the light, used in television to create background effects and also used in film and theater Commonly called *leko,* it is made by Strand Lighting, Compton, CA.

length (l or L) **1** [printing] the ability of ink to flow and form filaments A *long ink* has good flow but may *fly* or *spatter* on a high-speed press; a *short ink* is preferable. **2** in 18th-century British theater, a page of a performer's lines, consisting of 42 lines; now called *side* or *page*

lens a curved piece of glass or other transparent substance that changes the convergence of light rays, used to magnify or to form a sharp image, as in the eye or in a camera A *lens shade,* or hood, may be fastened to the lens of a camera to minimize the effect of direct rays of light. Several lenses may be attached to a *lens turret,* or revolving mount. The *lens speed* is the measure of the light-gathering ability of a lens. A *fast lens* has a large opening and a high efficiency for transmitting light, such as a 1.5 f-stop. A *slow lens* has a smaller opening and a low efficiency for transmitting light, such as a maximum f-stop of 2.8. The *lens diameter* is expressed in millimeters; a 50mm lens is the most common. A lens 25mm or less is a *wide-angle,* or *short, lens;* a lens with a focal length over 50mm, such as a 100mm lens, is a *telephoto,* or *long-focus,* lens. A *normal lens* reproduces an image as seen by the human eye, so its field of view is between that of a wide-angle lens and a *long-focus* or *telephoto lens*—for instance, a 35mm lens with a focal length between 25mm and 50mm. A *prime lens* has a standard fixed focal length for a specific camera. The *lens aperture* is the opening, controlled by the diaphragm (sometimes called the *lens stop*). Standard f-stop numbers are 1.4, 2, 2.8, 4, 5, 6, 8, 11, 16, and 22. A *lens system* has two or more lenses arranged to work together. A *lens adapter* is attached to the front of a camera to facilitate the changing of lenses. A *lens barrel* is a cylindrical mounting for the lens. A *lens cap* is a cover placed over the lens to protect it when not in use. A *lens coating* is a solution applied to a lens to minimize unwanted reflection. *Lens makings* are calibration numbers and reference marks imprinted on a lens to indicate f-stop numbers and other data. A *lens mount* is a device for attaching a lens to a camera. A *lens support* is a brace at the front end of a camera to hold a long lens. *Lens tissue* is soft paper used to clean a lens. A *lens turret* is a rotating mounting plate for two or more lenses. A spherical lens is called a *flat lens*, because it is nonanamorphic. An *anamorphic lens*, used in wide-screen filming, can produce two different magnifications. To *lens a film* is to photograph or shoot a movie.

lenser a photographer or cinematographer

lensless copying a direct contact process that does not use a lens to form images on the photosensitive material; also called *direct copying*

lens line a TELEPROMPTING system that shows one line at a time at the center of the TV camera lens, visible to the performer but not televised

lens louse a pushy or overly aggressive performer; a person who pushes in front of a camera

lenticular referring to a lens A *lenticular screen* has small cylindrical lenses on its surface and is used as a projection screen that is very bright or for other photography purposes. It also is used in some light meters, to gather light.

Leroy trademarked mechanical lettering equipment, made by the Keuffel & Esser Company of Morristown, NJ

let-in note a subheading set in a rectangular space surrounded on three sides by text; also called *cut-in note, cut-in heading, cut-in side note,* or *incut note*

Letraset a trademarked line of *transfer type* (sometimes called *instant type*), made by Letraset USA Inc of Paramus, NJ *Letrasign* letters are trademarked self-adhesive vinyl letters, commonly used in making displays.

letter **1** a written symbol or character that is part of an alphabet and represents a sound, from the French word *lettre* Letters refers to literary culture (a *person of letters*). *Letterform* is the design or development of alphabet characters. The first forms of gothic type used in the 15th century were *lettre de bâtarde* (cursive or joined together); an informal style, *lettre de forme* (pointed, formal), and *lettre de somme* (round, less formal). **2** a written or printed communication Types of letters written by authors to publishers include *query letter* (inquiring about a proposal), *confirmation of assignment* (also called a *go-ahead letter*, confirming that an arti-

cle or other work is being written), *deadline postponement letter* (asking for more time beyond the due date), *jog letter* (inquiring about the status of previously submitted material), *demand letter* (a stronger inquiry about status, such as time of publication and payment), *granting rights letter* (a contractual agreement with regard to reprinting or other rights), and, most important, *fan letter* (also called a *thank-you letter* or *bread-and-butter letter*). *Day letters* and *night letters* are types of telegrams, named according to when they are sent. **3** to draw letters by hand, as distinguished from typesetting, for reproduction **4** short for NEWSLETTER

letter banner two long parallel ropes between which are affixed rectangular pieces of cloth with letters, so that, when suspended across a street or other area, the ropes are a banner with a message

letterbox format the ratio of width to height (the *aspect ratio*) used in showing a film on TV so that the film has the same relative dimensions as it did when shown in a widescreen movie theater Films shown on a TV screen generally do not have their original aspect ratio. Occasionally, as with the film *The Color Purple*, the producer insists on aspect ratio, and the notation *letterbox format* appears on the home videotape. In such cases, an unused horizontal band on the top and bottom of the TV screen is used, so that the picture has a horizontal format akin to that of a theatrical screen.

letter carrier a Postal Service employee who delivers and collects mail on foot or by vehicle

lettered proof an impression, or proof, of an ENGRAVING, with the title and name of the artist or printer engraved in the margin

letterfit the quality of the spacing between letters and other characters

letter gadget an item enclosed with a letter, such as a pencil, miniature toy, or other item It is frequently used in direct mail.

letterhead a printed heading at the top of stationery; sheets of paper printed with a name and/or other information at the top or elsewhere

lettering the process of applying letters and other characters on a book cover, poster, or other surface, perhaps by using precut letters or transfer letters or by tracing the shapes with a stencil or mechanical tracing guide

lettering brush a long, flat brush in a holder, used by artists for lettering; also called *show card brush*

letter paper correspondence paper, stationery; also called *boxed paper* Letter-size paper usually is 8½" × 11".

letter-perfect   **1** completely correct   **2** referring to a person who has mastered a text, such as that of a role

letterpress   a method of printing in which the area to be printed—the printing surface—is raised, inked, and then pressed against the paper   An ordinary rubber stamp works in this manner. The use of raised metal letters once was the most common form of printing. It is sometimes called *relief printing*, in the sense of *relief* as an elevation or unevenness. Letterpress is distinguished from INTAGLIO (recessed surfaces carry the ink) and *planography* (printing and nonprinting surfaces are flush, or on the same level). Planography (which includes LITHOGRAPHY) now is the most common type of printing. *Flexography* is a type of letterpress printing that is commonly used for paperbacks.

letter-quality   referring to a document, produced by the printer of a word processor computer, that looks similar to the output of a typewriter, especially in the sharpness and solidity of the letters

letterset   a form of OFFSET (*not* letterpress) printing, although the word is from *letter*press and off*set*   Letterset is relief offset printing that does not use a water-dampening system; therefore it is also called *dry offset*.

lettershop   a mailing house or facility that offers printing (not necessarily LETTERPRESS) and other related services

letter space   the allowance for more space between letters, in typing or typesetting, than is standard; also called *letterspacing*

letter symbol   the designation, by letters, of the size of a book—for example, *F* stands for FOLIO and *Q* for QUARTO

lettre bâtarde   an informal gothic typeface used in the 15th and 16th centuries; also called *bastarda*

lettre de forme   a formal gothic letter, used for early religious books; also called *texture*

lettre de somme   a round, informal letter

lettre grise   a large ornamental capital letter first used in the 16th century   *Gris* is French for "gray."

Levant   a thick goatskin leather, used in quality bookbinding, made from the skin of the Angora goat, particularly from the Levant area in the eastern Mediterranean

level   **1** the degree of sound volume   A radio engineer or recording studio technician may ask for a *level*—that is, request that the performers speak in order to determine a general setting of the volume controls.   **2** the intensity of a video source, the channel, or the track   **3** [computers] the degree of subordination of an item in a list

levelness   the evenness of a paper's thickness, as determined by the distribution of its fibers

lexicon   a dictionary; the special vocabulary of an author or a field   A *lexicographer* is the compiler of a dictionary; *lexicography* is the process of compiling a dictionary.

Lexis   a computerized legal research service of Mead Data Central, Inc. of Franklin, OH

lf   LIGHTFACE TYPE; LOW FREQUENCY

LFOA   LAST FRAME OF ACTION

lhp   left-hand page, VERSO

libel   written, printed, or broadcast defamation; a statement or a picture that is malicious or damaging to a reputation   Spoken defamation—other than on a broadcast—is called *slander*.

liberty   unemployment   *At liberty* refers in particular to an unemployed performer.

library   a collection, such as all the typefaces available in one type shop, or the reference files of a publication, called a *morgue*   Specialized libraries include a *photo library* (containing still or motion pictures), a *stock photo library* (stock or library shots or scenes—those on hand and not made on order), and a music library. A library service rents out stock films, music, or other existing audio and/or visual materials. The term also refers to a collection of files, including computer files or data banks. Individuals who maintain specialized libraries include *music, photo, computer, tape, videotape,* and *research librarians*. A *library binding* is any type of specially reinforced binding for library use. A *library edition* or *special edition* is a book with an especially strong binding.

Library of Congress (LC or **L.C.)**   the federal facility in Washington, DC, with the country's largest collection of books   The *L.C. system* is the Library of Congress's classification system for its books. Publishers send a copy of every book to the Library of Congress, which issues an *L.C. catalog number* on an *L.C. catalog card*.

library rate   a special postal rate for books and other fourth-class mail sent by libraries, schools, and a variety of nonprofit organizations

libretto   the text of a musical work, as written by a *librettist*   *Libretto* is Italian for "small book."

license   legal or official permission, granted by a *licensor* to a *licensee*   A name, product, program, or other item may be licensed or sold for a specific period or under specific conditions. In broadcasting, a license from the Federal Communications Commission is required for a station to broadcast, initially by a *license application* and subsequently by *license renewal*. A license may be challenged (opposed or contested) and transferred from one owner to another.

lieder German songs, particularly a popular type with lyrical words Singers who specialize in this type of music are called *lieder singers.* The singular is *lied,* which means "song."

life the length of time that responses to a specific advertisement or advertising campaign are received

life cycle the stages in the life of a person or other entity Individuals often are categorized in these age groups: *preschool* (up to 5 years old), *grade school* (6–12 years), *adolescence* (13–18), *young adult* (19–24), *acquisitive years* or *full nest* (25–44), *empty nest* (45–64), and *golden age* or *solitary survivor* (65 and over). The life cycle of a product includes introduction, development, decline, and extinction.

life letter in direct mail, a small memo or other communication accompanying the primary sales letter, usually carrying an attention-getting line such as "Read this if . . ."

lifestyle, life style, or **life-style** the way in which a person lives, including purchasing habits, manner of dress, and other expressions of personality and values The section of a newspaper or periodical that deals with food, fashion, relationships, and other personal subjects is called the *lifestyle page* or *style page* (or section). It includes what formerly was called the *women's* (or *family*) *department.*

Lifetime a cable network headquartered in New York

lift **1** [journalism] to use previously published material, with permission or from a previous edition, or to plagiarize **2** [printing] the number of sheets that can be handled—for instance, the maximum number of sheets that can be cut at one time **3** [broadcasting] a portion of a radio or TV commercial for use as a shorter, separate commercial For example, to save on production costs, a 30-second commercial can be produced with a 10-second lift within it, for use as a separate 10-second identification. **4** the increase in basic cable penetration caused by the introduction of a new programming service **5** in the United Kingdom and elsewhere, an elevator or a section of a stage that can be raised or lowered, such as an *orchestra lift* (a platform that elevates the musicians)

liftout light letters on a dark background; also called *dropout, knockout,* or *reverse*

ligature **1** two or more letters joined together and cast on the same body of type, like æ, fi, ff, or ffl **2** the letters designating a wire service or other source, such as *AP* or *UPI* The ligature appears in parenthesis as part of the dateline of a newspaper article after the date.

light degree or source of brightness The lights or lamps used in film and other media include the *key light,* or principal light, which tends to produce strong contrasts (*hard light*), and *fill light* (*soft light*), for less contrast. *Low-key lighting* is dimly lit and has strong contrast; *high-key lighting* has lower contrast. *Flat lighting* produces a minimum of shadows and very little contrast. Supplementary lights include a *back light* (to illuminate the subject from behind), *accent light,* and *effects lights* (for specific areas of the subject), *base light* (diffuse or soft illumination of a larger area), and many sizes of LUMINARIES (lighting instruments, ranging from small bulbs to *spotlights, floodlights,* and *arc lights*). Film, stage, and TV electricians have dozens of colorful names for lights, including BABY, BROAD, BRUTE, KICKER, POLECAT, PUP, and SCOOP. To have one's name *up in lights,* as on a Broadway theater marquee, is to receive an electrifying acknowledgment of success.

light box a device with a translucent screen, lighted from behind, for viewing photographic transparencies; also called *light board*

light bridge a narrow platform above the front area of a stage, on which are mounted lights and other equipment

light curtain a bank of lights, on or in front of a stage, that are directed toward the audience or that are high-intensity so that they serve as a curtain or wall

light-emitting diode (LED) a type of semiconductor that lights up when electrically activated, used in television and video display terminals

lightface type (lf) type in which the characters (letters) have thin strokes, or lines The typeface prints in a light tone, in contrast to bold, or black-faced, type.

lighting illumination; the distribution of light and shade In film, theater, and other fields, it is the art, practice, or manner of using and arranging lights, under the supervision of a *lighting director* or *lighting engineer,* who is in charge of a *lighting crew.* The lighting director works with a *lighting plan,* generally with a *lighting switchboard* that controls the lights on a set. Lighting also refers to the lights themselves (see also LIGHT). A *lighting instrument, luminaire,* or *luminary* is a lighting instrument, including the lamp, or bulb, and other parts, such as a reflector, stand, or cable.

light meter a device that measures the amount of illumination on a subject, for determining the settings on a camera; also called *exposure meter*

light pen a small photosensitive device, shaped like a writing instrument, attached to a video display terminal by a wire and used to point to a spot on the display screen   A *cursor*, or *light spot*, on the video display screen is more commonly used.

light piping   leakage of light through the edges of a film base, which results in fogging   It generally is unintentional but can be deliberate to create an effect—in which case it is called *piping in the light.*

light rehearsal   a rehearsal of lighting changes and cues, not a superficial, or light, run-through

lights   [theater] slang for an electrician

light stand   a support for lights; also called *pipe* or *pipe stand*   If it has one or more horizontal arms, it is called a *tree* or *light tree.*

light stealer   an unlighted point-of-purchase display that reflects light from overhead fixtures or other sources

light-struck   referring to undeveloped film that was exposed to light, generally unintentionally   A *light-struck* LEADER is intentionally exposed.

light table   a box-shaped glass with light from below, used in matching two or more photographic, printing, or other sheets so that lines or other material on them are aligned   It is also used to compare old and new versions of copy or art to make sure that revisions have been made.

light tower   a vertical pipe or structure to which spotlights or other lighting equipment is attached   It can be a LIGHT STAND or a *light tree.*

light trap   a technique or material that keeps extraneous light from striking unexposed film, a system of entry to a photographic darkroom to prevent unwanted light from entering

lignin   a celluloselike substance, in trees and other plants, that acts as a binder for the cellulose fibers   When paper is made from wood pulp, the lignin interferes with the process of bonding the cellulose fibers, so quality paper requires a high cellulose content with as much lignin removed as possible. Because lignin changes color when exposed to heat and light, old newspapers or other publications sometimes turn yellow or become discolored.

Likert scale   [market research] an attitude measurement technique in which respondents are asked to indicate their agreement or disagreement with a statement (in a series of statements) by checking one of several categories (generally five), such as strongly agree, agree, uncertain, disagree, or strongly disagree   It differs from the THURSTONE SCALE.

lilliput edition   a tiny book; also called *miniature edition*   In Jonathan Swift's *Gulliver's Travels, Lilliput* was a land inhabited by people about 6 inches tall.

lily   the standard colors at the beginning or end of a movie film roll, for checking accuracy during the developing

limbo   **1** a neutral background—generally white—or the absence of a background, in a scene   A *limbo background* or *limbo set* also can be black.   **2** [photography] a background that contains no detail and that appears to stretch into infinity

limelight   a brilliant light; the focus of public attention   The origin is a stage light in which lime (calcium oxide) is heated to incandescence.

limen   the threshold of a physiological or psychological response   Liminal awareness is conscious recognition of stimuli, whereas subliminal awareness is below the threshold.

limited assortment store (LAS)   a low-overhead store with a relatively small selection of items and few services

limited edition   a publication or other work issued in a specific number of copies, generally fewer than for a regular edition   The copies often are consecutively numbered and are made of fine-quality paper, binding, or other materials.

limp binding   a style of bookbinding with thin, flexible cloth on leather, without boards

limpet mount   a camera stand that can be attached to a platform or other base by suction cups, akin to a marine limpet such as a lamprey

linage or **lineage**   the total number of advertising lines in a publication, in one issue or over a period of time   The term also can refer to editorial space (that is, news, features, and opinion pieces) or advertising and editorial space, but it generally indicates advertising.

Lindley Rule   [journalism] a rule for material that is not for attribution, by which such phrases as "according to official sources" are used instead of a specific person being quoted   The policy, formed in the 1940s by Ernest K. Lindley, Washington reporter for *The New York Herald Tribune,* is now called *deep background.*

line   **1** a row of type characters—letters, numbers, and symbols—set as text (abbreviated *l*)   A line gauge is a printer's ruler marked off in *picas* (there are 6 picas in an inch, and 12 points in a pica) and *nonpareils* (6 points), and sometimes also in centimeters and inches. *Line measure* is the width, from left to right, of a line, expressed in picas (the length of a line is called its *width* or *measure*). *Line weight* is the thickness of a line. A *loose line* contains too much space between characters or between words; a *tight line* is crammed in its measure. The speed of a typesetting machine is expressed in LINES PER MINUTE (*lpm*), *lines per hour* (*lph*), or *lines per page* (*lpp*).   **2** short for *agate line,* one-fourteenth of an inch of a column The *line rate* is the advertising charge per agate line, especially in newspapers. **3** an assortment of merchandise for sale at a store or manufactured by a company, usually consisting of a variety of items A *product line* is the collection of forms and variations of a manufacturer's item sold under the same name, brand, or label. A LINE EXTENSION or *brand extension* is a new product related to an existing product and marketed under the same name, brand, or label. **4** dialogue, as in a script A *line rehearsal* is practice of dialogue, not of a chorus line. **5** short for HEADLINE, though the full word or *head* is the more common usage **6** in television transmission, a single track from the scanning beam Distortion caused by wavy lines is called *linebeat* or *moiré*. **7** a particular phone or one extension of a phone **8** a wire, such as a *coaxial line* A *line feed* connects a remote location to a broadcasting facility. **9** [theater] a rope that supports scenery Each hanging piece of rope, called a *drop*, has a *short line*, *center line*, and *long line*. **10** [film, television] the area on a set within which action occurs; also called *action line*, *imaginary line*, or *axis of action* The camera generally is supposed to focus on the action and not *cross the line*. To *down the line* is to transmit a radio or TV program to a station for internal use prior to broadcast. **11** an indication—represented by a vertical line in the margin—that a correction has been made

line and Ben Day a line drawing that includes some shading and tone, produced by the BEN DAY process

linear perspective the view from which objects are portrayed as they are actually seen, as converging lines that indicate spatial relationships A rectangular solid can be shown in three types of linear perspective: *angular perspective* (two surfaces of the object are shown, both receding at angles from the front), *oblique perspective* (three faces shown), and *parallel perspective* (one surface shown in full, parallel to the viewer).

line art a drawing or other artwork with solid lines or areas that have no gray tonal values; a piece of art that can be reproduced without the use of a HALFTONE screen A *line drawing*—sometimes also called *line copy*, particularly when it consists of text and art, as long as no halftone screen is used—prints solid, without shadings or tonal values. A *linecut* (also called *line cut*, *line block*, or *line plate*) is an ENGRAVING that is similarly solid, without shadings, and is produced from a line drawing. A *line negative*, or *line shot*, is made from line art without use of a screen.

line-busy tone an audible telephone signal sent to a calling party to indicate that the called party is on another call or that the receiver is off the hook

linecasting the technique of setting a whole line of type at one time; also called *slugcasting* See also LINOTYPE.

line conversion a photographic process that converts a photograph or other piece of art so that it can be reproduced with no middle tones to increase contrast, emphasize part of it, or create some other special effect It is the transformation of continuous-tone (photographic) art into LINE ART, using screens through which the artwork is photographed.

line density a measure of the opacity of photographic images; also called *image density*

line division mark a vertical or slanting line or other mark to indicate the end of a line in a bibliography, poem, or other text

line editor a person at a book publishing company who goes over a manuscript closely for accuracy, style, and other details, before it is typeset A proofreader, in contrast, reads the typeset copy against manuscript to catch errors.

line extension a new product that is a variation, such as a new flavor, of an existing product sold by a company

line-fall the manner in which a line of type ends For example, a *free line-fall* or *English line-fall* is ragged right (not aligned at the right margin) and has no hyphens at the end of the line.

line film a high-contrast film that produces negatives of black and white without grays

line for line (L/L) an instruction to a typesetter to set each line as a separate unit, so that a manuscript line is the same as a typeset line, rather than to set the text as a continuous passage

line hit an irregular electrical current surge; also called *spike*

line-in a jack through which a video signal is fed into a TV set or other receiver; also called *line-in jack* or *video-in*

line microphone a directional microphone with an acoustical transmission line in front of the transducer, often with a pole at least 2 feet long Commonly used in film and TV studios, it sometimes is called a *shotgun microphone*.

linen a grayish-yellow thread or cloth made from the flax plant; paper (called *linen paper*) that is made from flax fibers or that has a lustrous, woven finish resembling linen (called *linen finish*)

linen tester a magnifying glass or *loupe*, commonly used to examine photographs and other graphics and also to analyze linen and other cloth

line-out a jack from which a video signal is fed from, or out of, a TV set or other equipment

line plot a diagram of the scenery, lighting, and other equipment that is attached by ropes, or lines, to the grid on the theater ceiling or elsewhere; more commonly called *fly plan, fly plot, hanging plot, rigging plan,* or *rigging plot*

line printer a high-speed system that prints a whole line of characters (letters, numbers, and symbols) almost simultaneously, as distinguished from a *character printer,* such as a typewriter, which prints only a single character at a time   Line printers are often used in computer typesetting. *Line-printer proof* is text printed in typewriter type on computer paper. This is a quick, inexpensive way to reproduce text originating on the keyboard of a word processing system, together with code symbols indicating typesetting specifications, to be typeset in final form after the proof is reviewed and corrected.

line producer a film producer who supervises a specific production, generally under the direction of the executive producer

liner 1 an inside wrapper, or LINING, of a package, book, or other item   2 a salesperson who *lines up* prospective customers and then turns them over to another salesperson—a *closer*—to complete the sale   3 a cosmetic applied in a fine line, such as *eyeliner* to accentuate the eyes

liner cards large index cards with typed copy, for use by radio announcers and disk jockeys   The cards contain slogans, information about current promotions and upcoming programs, and other on-air remarks, messages, and chatter.

liner notes text giving information about a record or cassette, printed on the cover or inside sleeve or as an insert

line shot See LINE ART.

line spacing or **linespacing** the insertion of space between lines of print; also called LEADING (pronounced ledding)

lines per minute (lpm) a standard measurement of typesetting speed, in which it is assumed that the text being set is in 9-point type on an 11-pica line, with about 30 characters, or letters, to the line (there are 12 points in a pica, and 6 picas in an inch)

line spread in photocopying, an undesirable thickening of lines, generally the result of excessive exposure or development; also called *bleed line*

lineup 1 the arrangement of items in a newscast   2 a group of stations broadcasting a specific program

lineup board [graphic arts] a large card (BRISTOL BOARD) with a pale blue grid, used for making layouts   The blue is invisible when the board is photographed for printing.

lineup table a surface used in printing to align the components of a LAYOUT

line-up tone a steady single-frequency tone that is recorded at the beginning of a soundtrack of a film in order to adjust the sound volume before adding the dialogue, music, and other sound to the balance of the track

lingo dialect; jargon; the special vocabulary of a particular field of interest

lingua franca a hybrid language, from the Italian words for Frankish language, particularly as formerly spoken in Mediterranean ports and now used to describe any type of common language between peoples, such as PIDGIN ENGLISH

linguistics the study of the nature and structure of speech

lining 1 the inside covering or coating of a package or other item; also called *liner*   2 the process of applying the liner or lining   3 in bookbinding, the paper or cloth material pasted on the spine to reinforce the glue and hold the folded signatures, or sheets, together   Lining made of paper is not the same as LINING PAPER. *Lining-up* is the addition of lining material before the covers are applied.

lining figures numerals that align at the base of a line, the numbers in a typeface that do not have ASCENDERS or DESCENDERS extending beyond the body of type; also called *modern figures*   The opposite is *old-style figures.* These are lining figures: 1, 2, 3, 4.

lining paper an *endsheet* or *endpaper,* a folded sheet of paper placed at the front or back of a book, with one part pasted to the coverboard and the other remaining free, as a decorative sheet

lining up [film] the process in which the location of the camera is selected, by the director and/or cinematographer, generally using a DIRECTOR'S FINDER or camera VIEWFINDER; also called *lining up a shot*

linkage a series or system of connecting rods or other links   In film, *linkage editing,* or *constructive editing,* involves connecting a series of short shots.

linked books separately bound books that are related

Linkrule a flexible ruler that can be stretched across a photograph or other item to scale it—that is, to determine the exact units of measurement for enlarging or reducing it   The ruler is manufactured by the Linkrule Company of Los Angeles.

Linnebach lantern a box in which a slide is inserted for projection on a rear wall or other surface of a stage set Though this simple device has no lens, its light can be moved various distances behind the slide to change the size of the projected image.

linoleum cut a piece of linoleum mounted on a wooden block, with a design hand-carved in relief on the surface, or the print made from this type of block; also called *linocut*

Linotron a trademarked high-speed electronic typesetting machine, made by the Mergenthaler Linotype Company of Plainview, NY

Linotype the trademarked name for a keyboard-operated machine for setting LETTERPRESS type, in which a complete line of type is produced as a single slug, or strip of metal, rather than one letter at a time, as in handsetting or MONOTYPE; pronounced LINE-oh-type The machine was invented in the United States about 1880 by Ottmar Mergenthaler. Until about the 1960s, Linotype operators, sometimes wearing green caps or eyeshades, sat at rows of Linotype machines, and the clanging sound of the slug falling into place permeated newspaper and other printing plants. Today, Linotype machines are still in use, particularly at weekly newspapers and at some older plants, but they are becoming an extinct species and no longer are manufactured. (For many years, a popular column in *The Chicago Tribune* was titled "A Line a Type or Two.") One of the pioneers in manufacturing typesetting equipment (Linotype) and printing presses (under the *Mergenthaler* name), the Mergenthaler Linotype Company now is headquartered in Plainview, NY. This book was set using Mergenthaler's Linotron 202.

linter a short, fuzzy fiber Cotton linters, the short fibers that remain stuck to cotton seeds after ginning, are used in cotton-content paper, though such soft paper is not as strong as paper made from rag fiber.

Lion Awards annual awards, in the form of gold, silver, and bronze lions, for TV commercials They are presented in June at the International Advertising Awards Film Festival in Cannes, France.

lip **1** in printing, the edge, rim, or margin **2** in bookbinding, the allowance for overlap of part of the open-side edge of a folded section of a publication; also called *lap*

lip flap an unintentional absence of sound, resulting from the improper synchronization of audio and video tracks, as when a performer's lips move, or flap, and no sound emerges

lip sync or **lipsynch** short for *lip synchronization*, the technique by which the sounds of words are timed to match the corresponding lip movements, either by direct recording or by dubbing; also, pantomime in which a performer mimics the sound being heard, such as by synchronizing movements to a recorded song

liquid crystal a low-viscosity material that does not emit light but has good visibility, commonly used to make the digits visible on a display panel, such as a liquid crystal diode (LCD) screen of a computer

Liquid Paper a trademarked chemical solution, an opaquing fluid, applied to paper to cover—"erase"—typed material; also called *white-out* or *correction fluid*, made by the Liquid Paper Corporation of Boston

list **1** a group of items, such as names and addresses An *exchange list* is one that is traded in return for another list—for instance, between two noncompeting direct mail advertisers or publishers who provide each other with complimentary subscriptions. **2** the titles of all the books issued by a publisher, including the *backlist* (previously published books) and *frontlist* (current titles) Books generally are published either in the spring or in the fall as part of what are called *seasonal lists*, though romance novels and other mass-market paperback titles are issued more frequently, such as monthly.

list ad an advertisement containing a list of items, such as books

list broker a business organization that arranges, on behalf of mailers, the rental of mailing lists compiled by others; also called *list house*

list compiler a business organization that puts together special mailing lists for sale or rental to advertisers and others who use direct mail techniques

listener a person in the audience of a radio program The *listening area* is the geographical span of a station's coverage (the term applies specifically to radio, but sometimes is used to refer also to TV). A *listener diary* is the record, or log, of programs heard by a respondent in an audience-rating survey. *Listener characteristics* are the demographics of a typical listener of a program or station.

listening shot a film or TV shot of an interviewer or performer listening, usually called a *reaction shot* or *cutaway shot*

list manager a business organization—representing magazine publishers, direct mail cataloguers, and other owners of mailing lists—that arranges for rentals of the lists It is not the same as a LIST BROKER, who represents the mailers.

list price the suggested retail price, which is higher than the reduced or discount price; sometimes simply called *list*

list source a source from which names are obtained for a mailing list

lit LITERATURE

literal letter for letter or word for word; actual, not figurative; accurate Typesetters sometimes use the term *literal* to indicate a grammatical or typographical error. *Literals* are type characters; to *proofread for literals* is to check each letter.

literary related to literature or books A *literary agent* is an author's representative who obtains a commission (10 percent or more) for selling a manuscript to a publisher or other buyer. *Literary Market Place*, the annual reference directory of the publishing industry, is issued by R. R. Bowker of New York.

literary magazine a periodical devoted primarily to fiction, poetry, and the arts

literati the literary intelligentsia, a plural noun referring to people of letters, scholarly or learned people

literatim letter for letter; literally The word derives from the Latin *littera*, meaning "letter."

literature the profession of an author; writings in prose or verse, particularly fiction or other imaginative or critical writing, as distinct from journalism or other transitory writing; the writings of a specific time, country, region, or subject, such as English literature or medical literature

lith., litho, or **lithog.** lithograph; lithographic; LITHOGRAPHY

lith film a very high-contrast film with a thin ORTHO emulsion, processed in a special developer called a *lith developer* It produces a negative with dense blacks and clear whites.

lithography the technique of printing from a flat, or planographic, surface that contains no ridges (as there are in LETTERPRESS) or depressions (as there are in GRAVURE), so that the image and nonprinting surfaces are on the same even plane The lithographic printing press was invented in Germany about 1796 by Alois Senefelder. A smooth plate is attached to a revolving, or rotary, cylinder on the press. In *direct lithography*, the plate prints directly on the paper (the method used for displays, labels, and posters). In indirect lithography, or *offset lithography*, a more frequently used technique, the plate imprints its design onto an intermediate rubber roller that becomes the printing surface. A *lithograph* is a print or work of art made by the lithographic method—especially by the original (preindustrial) form of the process, in which the image was drawn on a smooth stone (*lithos* is Greek for "stone").

litholine any photographic material or chemical that produces black or white, but not the in-between grays

Little America method [advertising] the adaptation of a national campaign to the local media

Little Annie the nickname for the STANTON-LAZARSFELD *Program Analyzer*, a system used by a network or a producer to test program popularity among randomly selected audiences

little magazine a noncommercial publication of relatively small circulation, with fiction, poetry, essays, and other literary material, often academic or avant-garde; also called *literary magazine*

little merchant plan in newspapers and other fields, the arrangement in which the delivery person is considered to be an independent contractor and not an employee; sometimes capitalized

little theater a small theater or theater group, particularly a noncommercial repertory or an academic-based group with amateur performers

liturgy prescribed forms of ritual for public worship in various religions A *liturgical drama* was a play performed as part of the ritual of the medieval Catholic Church, and, by extension, a *liturgical play* is a play with a religious theme.

lit week a week in which a theater has a show or other performances so that the house lights are turned on Facilities are categorized by the number of lit weeks over a period of time.

live referring to a real or actual performance that is simultaneously transmitted, as by a *live action camera* (LAC), as distinct from a taped or delayed broadcast *Live animation* is the imparting of motion to photographed objects, as in STOP-ACTION or stop-motion film. *Live action* refers to a film featuring people instead of animated characters. *Live music* comes from an actual performance instead of a recording. Sound emanating from the stage or the set rather than from a recording is known as *live sound*; *live fade* refers to a reduction in the live sound, in contrast to (control) *board fade*. A *live stage* is a stage containing scenery. *Live pack* is a stack of scenery to be used during a theatrical performance; *dead pack*, on the other hand, is scenery that has already been used and set aside. A *live tag* (or *local tag*) is a short message added by an announcer to a recorded commercial—informing the audience, for instance, of the name of the local retailer or the current price. A *live title* is photographed by a studio camera instead of inserting a slide or film. *Live matter* is copy that is ready to be printed, though it may be held for future use. *Live* also may refer to type to be used again; *dead type* is to be discarded. The *live area* is the portion to be printed. *Live* *postage* refers to stamps, as opposed to metered mail.

live-er a LIVE report without accompanying tape or other material

live on tape referring to a TV or radio program of an actual performance, recorded and broadcast subsequently and therefore not really LIVE

livering 1 an accumulation of ink spots on a printed sheet, resembling liver spots on a person's skin; also called *flocculation* 2 a solidification of oil paint on an artwork, caused by impurities in the pigment

living newspaper a type of play about contemporary social issues, sometimes with quotations from actual newspapers, performed in the United States in the 1930s

ll lines

L/L LINE FOR LINE

LM LOWER MAGAZINE

LO LOCAL ORIGINATION

load 1 to increase an order by offering the retailer or purchaser a premium or other incentive, which is called a *dealer loader, buying loader, loader,* or *loading deal* 2 to put into a device—for instance, to enter data into a computer or to insert a film or tape into a camera 3 [broadcasting] to place a termination across an audio or video line, such as a resistor to prevent a signal from bouncing back along the line

loaded full, as with a detailed script or a camera with a supply of film

loaded words weighted or biased text, generally to be avoided in objective journalism

loader merchandise, gifts, or other incentive provided to a dealer or other trade customer, to spark interest in a purchase; also called *dealer loader, buying loader,* or *loading deal*

loader boy a movie crew member who inserts film into the camera

load factor the average number of passengers per automobile, used in estimating exposure to outdoor advertising

loading 1 the insertion of impedance into an electronic circuit to change its characteristics For example, *load coils* or *loading coils* (inductors) may be put into a telephone line (a *loaded line*) to minimize distortion and improve voice quality. 2 the addition of costs or items, especially excessive ones, such as the practice of selling a customer add-on items to accompany an appliance 3 in papermaking, the treatment, usually with clay but sometimes with other materials, such as zinc sulfide, to smooth the paper, increase opacity, or brighten color

load-up a technique used in mail order when the original order has been made for a *series*

purchase—with items to be bought over a period of time—and the customer is offered the opportunity to buy the entire series at one time

loanword a word taken from another language, intact or modified, such as *cinema*

lobby a hall or waiting room of a building, such as a hotel or theater The area adjacent to the assembly hall of a legislature is called a *lobby*; it is open to nonlegislators, including individuals who congregate there to meet and influence the lawmakers. *Lobbyists,* as they are called, act (*lobby*) on behalf of special-interest groups (sometimes called *lobbies*)—that is, formal or informal organizations seeking to influence public policy—by urging the legislators to vote for or against bills or other matters. The same process of *lobbyism* may also be used in an effort to influence government agencies and other bodies.

lobster trick early-morning working hours; also called *lobster shift* or *lobster watch* The term frequently is used to describe the dawn shift at a newspaper. One supposed origin is attributed to the publisher William Randolph Hearst (1863–1951), who frequently visited the printers during the 2–9 A.M. shift at the *New York American* and observed that their noses were red (like a lobster), probably from visits to neighborhood bars. There are many other colorful origins of this term.

Local Access and Transport Area (LATA) a geographic area served by a local telephone or communications company

local angle the aspect of an article or a publicity release that has a geographical interest to the audience or to the medium in which it appears

Local Area Data Transport (LADT) an electronic network for data delivery among VIDEOTEX systems

Local Area Network (LAN) a privately owned communications system that interconnects telephones, computers, and other communications equipment within a building or limited geographical area

local channel an AM radio channel assigned by the Federal Communications Commission for use by a low-power station There are six local channels, each occupied by 150 or more CLASS IV stations (under 1000 watts).

local color 1 the normal or true color of an object, in ordinary daylight 2 vividness, as in a literary work, resulting from the presentation of authentic qualities of a specific place

local origination (LO) a TV channel or other communications medium that originates programming

local rate a reduced rate offered by a medium, such as a newspaper, to advertisers in its locality The rate is lower than the general rate paid by national advertisers.

locals short news items about local residents, common in weekly newspapers

local supplement a section in a newspaper, generally on Sundays, prepared by the newspaper, as distinct from national supplements, such as *Parade*, that are published by an outside organization and are included with newspapers in various parts of the country

local time (LT or **L.T.)** an indication that the time of a broadcast or other activity is that of the area in which it is taking place, instead of, for example, at different times in different time zones

location 1 an actual setting, as distinct from a studio, used for a film or TV show To film or tape *on location* is to shoot a motion picture or to tape in such a setting. The *location manager* is the person who finds sites for shooting outside the studio, with the assistance of *location scouts*, and who then makes arrangements for the use of these sites. 2 the site of a performance, such as a theater 3 the site of an outdoor advertisement A single outdoor ad is called an *individual location*. 4 [computers] the storage area of data

location codes in outdoor advertising, an indication of the location of an advertising structure on a roadway, commonly abbreviated:

E/S—east side	E/O—east of
F/E—facing east	
W/S—west side	W/O—west of
F/W—facing west	
N/S—north side	N/O—north of
F/N—facing north	
S/S—south side	S/O—south of
F/S—facing south	
C/—city limits	

The *location list* is a listing of the sites of all panels in a specific showing.

location manager a member of a film or TV production staff in charge of the logistics of a shooting outside the studio The location manager sometimes also serves as a LOCATION SCOUT.

location scout [film, television] a member of the production staff who finds off-studio sites and arranges for accommodations, permits, and other arrangements prior to the shooting

location symbol a letter, abbreviation, word, or other indication in a bibliography or a catalog to indicate where a book or other item may be found; also called *location mark*

loc. cit. abbreviation for Latin *loco citato*, meaning "in the place cited," a term used in footnotes or other references to indicate that information about a source is included in a previous citation; pronounced lock sit It sometimes is followed by a page number. *Loc. cit.* is similar to *op. cit. (opere citato)*, which means "in the work cited." Both terms sometimes are written without periods; since they are abbreviations, however, the periods should be used.

lockbox a locked container, such as a *post office box*

locking up [television] the brief period when a videocassette wobbles as it starts to play, before it is stabilized and runs smoothly

lockout or **lock-out** [telephone] to disconnect or make inoperative; the inability of one or both subscribers to get through because of excessive noise or other factors It is a common problem with SPEAKERPHONES and MOBILE COMMUNICATIONS, where there is continuous transmission from one party and the other party is *locked out*. A *lockout system* or *echo suppressor* is a device that blocks simultaneous transmission in both directions.

lock step a mode of marching, in which the marchers closely follow each other *Lock-step journalism* refers to the practice in which a newspaper or other medium closely follows and emulates its competition—for example, by picking up on a continuing story.

lockup 1 the closing of the forms, or devices for holding type in place during printing, in LETTERPRESS printing In general, the term refers to the process of readying material for printing. At *The Wall Street Journal*, for example, the first-edition lockup is about 7 P.M., and the second-edition lockup is about 10 P.M. 2 *to lock up:* slang for completing arrangements

locution a particular style of speaking or a particular way of expressing an idea; a word or phrase characteristic of a group or region (*Elocution* is a style or manner of speaking, especially formal public speaking.)

Loewy panel a type of outdoor advertising poster (with metal or plastic molding) designed by U.S. designer Raymond Loewy (1893–1986)

log 1 a diary, listing, or record, such as the listing of a station's programs, commercials, and everything else actually broadcast A *running log* is a sequential listing, such as the listing of TV programs by time period 2 to enter To *log on*, LOG IN, or *logo* is to sign into or start, as with a computer system. To terminate work is to *log off*.

logbook a record of occurrences

loge a box in a theater or the forward section of the mezzanine or balcony; pronounced lowzh

logic 1 the study of the principles of reasoning; from Latin *logica* and Greek *logos*, which mean "speech" or "reason" 2 [computers] the systematic scheme of interaction of signals, the circuitry or the graphic representation of the circuitry A *logic circuit* or *logical circuit* is a switching circuit that performs an arithmetic logic function. Professor George Boole (1815–64), an English mathematician, devised a system of symbols (*Boolean logic*) for logic or logical operation, with synonyms for *and* (logical multiples), *or, not,* and other terms. Boolean algebra, in which all variables have the value of either zero or 1, is the basis for most digital computers.

logic diagram a graphic representation of the interconnected elements of a system, such as a *flowchart*, which displays a sequence of operations, as in an organization or campaign

logic tree an indexing system for the information stored in a database

log-in to access, or enter, a computer system, generally by providing a code, or *log-on* identification The process is called *logging-on;* the termination procedure is called *logging off.*

logo LOGOTYPE

log-off [computers] to end a period of usage

log-on [computers] to begin a period of usage The user logs-on by turning on the machine and entering an access code or other start procedure.

logo programming [computers] a simplified programming language, sometimes with symbols (logos or LOGOTYPES) representing words

logotype (logo) originally, a word set on a type body; now, a unique trademark, name, symbol, signature, or device to identify a company or other organization A publisher's logotype is its NAMEPLATE or FLAG.

loh LADY OF THE HOUSE

lollipop display a large, round outdoor advertisement mounted on a pole

long form [broadcasting] a special, or featured, single program that is exceptionally long, such as over two hours; a TV station with a format of mostly movies and other long programs, such as station WTBS in Atlanta This slang phrase, which is not commonly used, is adapted from the Internal Revenue Service term for a detailed tax return.

long grain describing paper made with the machine direction of fibers parallel to the longer dimension of the sheet

long ink an ink with good flow that can be drawn out in a long thread without breaking

longitudinal video recording (LVR) a system in which many audio and video tracks are recorded on one videotape, akin to a multitrack

long letter a character that ascends above the middle area of a line and descends below the BASE LINE The primary example is a scripted *f.*

long page a sheet with more printing (a line or two) on it than is customary for that size paper or in comparison with the other pages in the same publication, or with more type lines on it than was specified

long play a phonographic record, generally 33⅓ rpm, that plays at a slower speed and hence for a longer period of time than a 78-rpm record

long primer an obsolete type size, about 10 points

long s the *s* used in old forms of printed English, resembling an *f*

long shot (LS) a camera view that takes in the full vista, or breadth, of a scene or that is taken far away from the subject

long take a film or TV camera shot maintained for an extended period

look-see an audition, particularly of models

look-up table [computers] a collection of data organized for convenient reference—for instance, arranged in columns In computer graphics, a look-up table, which is commonly used, provides the values of PIXEL intensity so that color changes can be made quickly.

loop 1 tape or film whose ends have been spliced so that it plays repeatedly In *looping,* a performer records dialogue while watching a section of *looped* film, in order to synchronize precisely. 2 a short length of film that is left slack A *Latham loop* (also called *American loop*)—developed for the camera by Major Woodville Latham and for the projector by Thomas Armat—is commonly used to prevent tearing as a film starts and stops. 3 [broadcasting] the connection (called a *local loop*), via microwave or wire, of a station to the network transmission 4 [computers] a set of instructions that can be executed repeatedly *Loop body* is the primary part of a loop, as determined by *loop control. Loop initialization* refers to the parts of a loop that set its starting values. A *closed loop* is a system that uses feedback about the output, whereas an *open loop* does not have its output monitored. 5 a conference or a network To be *in the loop* is to be within a network or group of insiders, a position perhaps achieved by the skill known as *loopmanship.* 6 [typography] a bowl that serves as a flourish, as is sometimes found in the lower part of a *g*

loose informal, casual, or unstructured, as with sketchy artwork A *loose shot* is a photograph that allows room for improvement; a *tight shot* is less flexible. *Loose blues* are blueprints that are separate, particularly of art.

loose-back a type of binding in which the covering material is not glued to the back of the book; also called *hollow-back* or *open back*

loose in binding a book in which the case, or cover, has become separated, so that the leaves are loosened

loose-leaf referring to a notebook, catalog, or other item with removable pages (not the same as LOOSE IN BINDING) Examples of *loose-leaf binding* are *ring binding* (pages are held in place by large metal loops that open and close) and *post binding* (pages are inserted on vertical metal dowels). A *loose-leaf catalog* or *sheaf catalog* is made up of sheets fastened together in a loose-leaf binder. *Loose-leaf service* describes a serial publication, such as a reference book, that is revised by means of new or replacement pages inserted in a loose-leaf binder.

loosen up to increase the visible space, as in a layout or around a subject

loose sentence a sentence in which the essential element comes first, the opposite of a PERIODIC SENTENCE

Lorimar Telepictures Corporation a company in Culver City, CA, that produces TV programs and films and owns other companies

LORT LEAGUE OF RESIDENT THEATRES

lose the light to have insufficient light for filming; a TV direction indicating that the *tally light* on a camera has gone off, meaning that the camera no longer is on

loss leader a retail item whose price has been considerably reduced—it will make little or no profit for the merchant—in order to attract customers (*traffic*) for other purchases

lot a parcel of land, such as the area owned by a movie studio, called a *movie lot*

louder a broadcasting instruction, signaled by an upraised palm or a raised hand The cue directs a performer or other individual to speak more loudly or an engineer to increase the intensity of the sound.

loudspeaker a device (a TRANSDUCER) for converting electric current to sound waves and then amplifying the sound; also called *speaker*

Louma a crane, with a camera mounted on it, that can be controlled from a distance (with a TV camera and a monitor to enable the camera operator to see what the mounted camera is filming); also called *Louma crane* The device was developed in France in the 1970s by Jean-Marie Lavalou and Alain Masseron; the name comes from syllables in their last names, *lou* and *ma*.

low-angle shot a shot in which the camera points upward toward the subject

low-band tape videotape with inferior resolution to that of *high-band tape*

lowbrow a person who lacks cultivated interests, as in the arts

low comedy humor resulting from action and situation, such as farce or slapstick; the opposite of HIGH COMEDY, or witty dialogue In the 18th and 19th centuries, one of the standard performers in a stock company was called the *low comedian*, who worked with the tragedian and others in the repertory group.

low contrast describing photography in muted colors, or with a long gradation of tones from white to black A *low-contrast filter* is a camera lens that mutes colors.

low-end strategy a sales orientation that emphasizes inexpensive features, such as low rent and self-service, so that low prices are an important part of the promotion

lowercase (lc) referring to noncapitalized letters, sometimes called *small letters*—though, of course, the size can vary; also called *unshift* (*uppercase* is the shift position on a standard typewriter) In copyediting, proofreading, and typesetting, the instruction to change from uppercase to lowercase is indicated by putting a diagonal line through the capital letter:

E

If many letters are to be lowercased, the notation can be written as:

EEEEEE

To avoid confusion, *lc* should be written in the margin and/or the symbol / should be written at the place of correction. In the days of hand composition of metal type, the capital letters of a typeface were kept in the upper case (with receptacles in the box or case for each letter and number) and the noncapital letters were kept in the lower case. The stroke above the main portion of a lowercase letter, as in *d, f, h, k,* and *l,* is called the *ascender,* and the stroke below the main portion is called a *descender,* as in *g, j,* and *p.*

lowercase-alphabet length (lca) the length, expressed in points, of a line of all the small letters (minuscules) of a typeface (there are 12 points in a pica, and 6 picas in an inch)

lower magazine (LM) a storage compartment of a typesetting machine; see also MAGAZINE

lower third the bottom third of the TV screen, on which identifications and other captions generally are displayed

low finish describing nongloss paper or other material that has a tough, rough surface

low frequency (lf) a radio frequency in the range of 30 to 300 kilocycles per second

low key describing a performance conducted in a soft voice or tone, or an individual who is subdued

low-key light illumination of reduced intensity A scene lit by such illumination would have primarily dark tones.

low-level language a computer programming language that is closely related to the machine code language of a computer and is simpler to operate than *high-level language*

low-noise amplifier in satellite broadcasting, a microwave device attached to an outdoor receiving antenna to amplify the signals received, without adding interference (noise)

low-power television (LPTV) a type of TV station, authorized by the Federal Communications Commission in 1982, in an effort to allow several thousand stations with secondary status to provide limited-range service in a small area The call letters of LPTVs are not as simple as those for VERY HIGH FREQUENCY. An example of an LPTV is W13BE in Chicago.

lows the deeper sound tones, such as bass, or the less assertive colors, such as whitish-gray

loyalty index a measure of the frequency of listenership or viewing of a radio or TV station

l.p. LARGE-PAPER EDITION; long play

L.P. Limited Partnership, a designation for a type of business that sometimes appears after the name of the firm or other entity, akin to *Inc.* or *Ltd.*

lpm letters per minute; LINES PER MINUTE

LPTV LOW-POWER TELEVISION

LR lower, as in the lower position on a typecasting machine, the location for the most frequently used weight of typeface (not lightface, boldface, or italic)

l.s. letter signed (handwritten signature)

LS LONG SHOT

lt LIGHT

LT or **L.T.** local time

LTC LAST TELECAST

LTC or **LTK** LEAD TO COME

luci or **lucy** a large cameralike enlarger/reducer used in the graphic arts The generic slang word is from LACEY LUCI, the name of the original equipment of this type. To *luci* artwork is to use a camera lucida or a device like it for enlarging or reducing. A camera lucida is a prism or series of lenses that transfer the image of a three-dimensional object onto a two-dimensional plane, enabling the image to be copied by hand in a size larger or smaller than the original.

Ludlow the trademarked name of a LETTERPRESS printing press, frequently used in newspaper printing, and a hot-metal typesetting system, now rarely used, in which handset type is cast into single-piece lines of type (slugs) The type-setting equipment, called the *Ludlow Typograph*, was commonly used for large headlines and display advertising.

Lulu Awards annual awards given by Los Angeles Advertising Women to women in western states

lumen a unit of measurement of the flow of light, with one lumen related to the light emanating from one *candle* (actually one *candela*, since there are all sizes and types of candles) One lumen per square centimeter is a *lambert*, and one lumen per square foot is a *footcandle. Lumens per watt* is the number of lumens that are produced for each watt in a light source.

lumia a device that produces moving abstract patterns of light on a screen The art form, popularized by Thomas Wilfred in the 1950s, was called *lumia light sculpture* and was the predecessor of the lightshows that were part of rock music concerts in the 1960s.

luminaire a floodlight fixture, including the lamp, reflector, support, housing, and cable

luminance light; brightness A TV signal is made up of luminance (which carries the black-and-white portion of the image) and *chrominance* (which carries the hue).

luminant a light source

luminary a lighting source or instrument, including the bulb and other parts

luminosity the amount or degree of light or perceived brightness of a light source

luminous giving off light; glowing in the dark (as with a paint containing phosphorus)

Lund Award an annual award (Paul M. Lund Public Service Award) to one person for outstanding public service, presented by the Public Relations Society of America, New York

lux a unit of illumination, equal to one LUMEN per square meter (the plural is *luxes* or *luces*) In video cameras, light sensitivity is measured in lux. The lower the lux number of a camera, the less light is required to produce a viewable image. A light-sensitive camera can operate with as little as 10 lux.

luxe elegance, luxury; luxurious (short for *deluxe*)

LV LASERVISION

LVR LONGITUDINAL VIDEO RECORDING

Lyonnaise binding an ornamental bookbinding, with a prominent central design and large corner ornaments, named after a former province in France

lyric 1 suitable for singing *Lyric poetry* appeals primarily to the senses and the emotions, by presenting vivid images, or word pictures, whereas *narrative poetry* relates a story (it may also contain images). A *lyric role* is sung, as in a *lyric drama*—an opera—on a *lyric stage* or in a *lyric theater* (both terms refer to theatrical productions specializing in lyric or operatic works). A *lyric sheet* contains the words of a song, generally typed in all-capital letters, single-spaced, with two or more spaces between verses. *Lyrics* are the words to a popular song, written by a *lyricist*. *Lyrical* refers to poetry or other works suitable for singing or, more generally, a characterization of rapture or enthusiasm. *Lyricism* is an emotional or poetic expression of enthusiasm. A *lyre* is a small stringed instrument, akin to a harp, used by the ancient Greeks to accompany singers and reciters; the Latin word is *lyra*.

M

m or **M** EM (printing); magenta; meter; mile; month; morning

M Monday; Monsieur *M* is Latin for *merides*, or noon—not midnight. Avoid *M* as an abbreviation for noon, as it is likely to be confusing; see also MERIDIAN. *M* is a symbol for 1,000 and sometimes 1,000,000; see also MEGA. *M weight* is the weight in pounds of 1,000 sheets of a paper cut to a specific size. The M weight is important in buying paper for printing, since paper is priced by the pound. /M is an indication of *per thousand*, as in *$25/M*, or $25 per thousand items.

MAC MOTION ANALYSIS CAMERA

macaronic a literary composition, film, song, or other work in a mixture of two or more languages; from the Italian word *macaroni*

MacGuffin an inanimate object in a motion picture on which considerable action revolves, often in a suspenseful manner The term was originated by the director Alfred Hitchcock (1899–1980) and is spelled in various other ways, such as *McGouffin* or *Maguffin*. The concept is also referred to as a *weenie* or *wienie* (a small wiener, or hot dog, held in front to tantalize).

machine address [computers] a pattern of characters (letters, numbers, and symbols) that identifies the storage location of specific data; also called *absolute address*

machine binding bookbinding done by machine, such as library binding (a type of specially reinforced binding), rather than by hand

machine-coated paper an inexpensive grade of coated paper *Machine-glazed paper* (*MG*) or *machine-finish paper* (*MF* or *mf*) has a smooth, glossy finish, resulting from mechanical treatment—called CALENDERING on the paper-making machine, rather than coating.

machine composition the setting of type by machine rather than by hand

machine direction in papermaking, referring to the formation of paper parallel to its forward movement on the machine; also called *with the grain*

machine leader a strip of durable blank film, called a *leader*, that is attached to an undeveloped film in order to guide and pull it through a film processing machine

machine-readable pertaining to a document or other form of data—such as a computer card, paper tape, or a document typed for an optical character reader—that can be read directly by a machine The document is in *machine language, machine-oriented language*, or *computer-oriented language*, as distinct from artificial or symbolic language, which must be interpreted or converted to machine language. *Machine translation* is the automatic translation from one language to another, such as from French or another natural language to English, or from symbolic to machine language.

Machine Readable Cataloging (MARC) a magnetic-tape format of the Library of Congress, in Washington, DC, in which catalog numbers and other data are transmitted to libraries and other subscribers

machine-sewn book a book that is bound by means of sewing rather than adhesive

machine unit in computerized typesetting, the smallest distance that the typesetting mechanism can move, generally one unit in relation to the smallest point size (there are 12 points to a pica and 6 picas to an inch)

machine word a computer word

mackle or **macule** a spot, particularly a blurred or double impression on a printed sheet resulting from a wrinkle in the paper or other printing imperfection; from the Latin *macula*, meaning "spot"

macrocode (sometimes called simply *macro*) a coding system that simplifies by assembling sets of computer instructions, or a single instruction code that has a specific name and represents a set of computer instructions; from the Greek for "large" or "inclusive"

macro focus extremely close focus—for example, 4 millimeters from the front lens of a video camera A *macro lens* is used for extreme close-ups or the photographing of very small objects without a microscope, as in *macrocinematography*. A *macro-focusing tele-*

photo lens (also called *macro-telephoto lens* or *macro-telelens*) is a long-focus (telephoto) lens used to photograph small objects.

macroform a transparency—for instance, one used in an overhead projector—or other medium whose images are large enough to be read without magnification

macro lens a camera lens that provides considerable enlargement for extreme close-ups

made-for referring to a production created for a specific medium, such as a *made-for-television movie* or a *made-for-home-video movie*

made-up copy an incomplete or imperfect rare book that has been completed with leaves, or sheets, from another copy of the same edition

Madison Avenue a street in New York, between Fifth Avenue and Park Avenue Several advertising agencies are, or were, located on this street, and the name loosely refers to the advertising agency business. *Madison Avenue* is also the name of an advertising trade magazine.

Madison Square Garden Network a regional cable network, located in New York, that shows mostly sports programs

madrigal 1 a short poem, generally pastoral or romantic, that can be set to music 2 a musical composition, generally contrapuntal, with parts for several voices Madrigals, particularly Italian and English, were popular in the 15th–17th centuries.

mag 1 short for *magnetic*, referring specifically to cards, tapes, disks, or any recording and storage medium used in computers—for instance, *mag card* or *mag track* (MAGNETIC TRACK) 2 slang for MAGAZINE (publication)

magalog a mail-order catalog that contains editorial matter, such as brief features on celebrities, travel, or fashion, in addition to the product sales material

magazine 1 a periodical (generally published weekly, biweekly—once every two weeks—monthly, or bimonthly), 7" × 10" or other dimension smaller than a full-size newspaper, usually printed on coated, or shiny, paper, and sold on newsstands or by mail or distributed by controlled circulation (such as in-flight magazines); sometimes shortened to *mag* Types include newsmagazines (such as *Time* and *Newsweek*), business magazines (*Fortune*), and special-interest magazines (*Sports Illustrated*). The origin is the French word *magasin*, derived from the Italian *magazzino*; the original meaning was "storehouse," and, indeed, a magazine can be a storehouse of information. A *magazine layout*, as in a newspaper, has large areas of white space, wide columns, and other elements akin to the arrangement of material in a magazine. A *magazine-style* radio or TV program

presents interviews and feature segments instead of just a succession of news reports. 2 the part of a camera that holds the undeveloped film 3 the part of a typesetting machine that stores the matrices, or collections of typefaces Each typeface and point size is in a separate magazine, such as the *lower magazine (LM)* or the *upper magazine (UM)*, arranged in a systematic manner.

magazine concept in broadcast advertising, the scattered placement of commercials during a program on a participating or spot basis The opposite is *program sponsorship*, in which all the advertisements aired during a program are from the same sponsor.

magazine plan the concept of advertising in magazines that are distributed in a specific geographic region

Magazine Publishers Association Inc. (MPA) an organization in New York of publishers of consumer and other magazines Affiliated with the AMERICAN SOCIETY OF MAGAZINE EDITORS, it operates the Publishers Information Bureau. Its annual fall meeting is a key event in the magazine field.

magazine-style program a TV or radio show that contains a variety of interviews and features; also called *magazine format program* An example is "All Things Considered," on National Public Radio.

magazine supplement a section of a newspaper in the format of a magazine or tabloid newspaper (smaller than standard size), generally inserted in a Sunday edition and with a variety of articles and features.

magenta a purplish-red or blue-red color that absorbs green light Magenta is important in printing, where it is used as one of the primary-color inks (also called *process red*) in four-color printing.

Maggies the annual awards given to outstanding magazines, presented by the Western Publications Association, of Los Angeles

magic hour [photography] the brief period at dawn or dusk when the sunlight produces a special quality—magical, surrealistic, poetic

magic lantern See LANTERN.

Magic Marker the trademark for liquid color dyes that come in felt-nibbed dispensers and are used for making color layouts, signs, and other displays The manufacturer, Magic Marker Industries Inc., is in Trenton, NJ. The name also is used generically to refer to *markers*.

Magid Associates a market research company in Cedar Rapids, IA, specializing in advising TV stations, particularly on news formats The firm was started by Frank N. Magid, a social psychologist who helped bring the ACTION NEWS format to many stations.

magnetic bubble [computers] a device in which information is stored in magnetic film that holds its pattern even if power is lost; also called *bubble memory*

magnetic disk a flat circular plate with a magnetic surface, used in computers for data storage The data are accessible anywhere on the disk, rather than in sequence, as on a tape.

magnetic ink character recognition (MICR) a technique in which the images of characters (letters, numbers, and symbols) are recognized by the pattern of the magnetic ink in which they are printed, rather than by reflected light, as in OPTICAL CHARACTER RECOGNITION MICR is the system used to read the encoded numbers on business checks and was the first character recognition system in widespread use.

magnetic media [computers] magnetically coated tapes, disks, and other recording materials

magnetic stock a tape or film with a base that is coated with iron oxide; also called *mag stock* or *fullcoat* Magnetic filmstock is called *magnetic film* or *mag film*. MAGNETIC TAPE usually is referred to by its width, as in *quarter-inch tape.*

magnetic stripe a magnetic strip, for sound recordings, on the edge of a film; also called *mag stripe* or *mag strip*

magnetic tape (MT) a plastic tape coated with iron oxide for use in recording audio, video, or computer instructions or printed with metallic pigment or ink that can be magnetized so that the printed characters will be recognized electronically

magnetic-tape Selectric typewriter (MTST) a typewriter that records onto magnetic tape, printing what is typed onto a piece of paper inserted in the machine It is the forerunner of the mag card machine.

magnetic track a soundtrack recorded on a magnetic stripe on the border of a motion picture film; also called *mag track* or *magnetic soundtrack*

magnum opus a great work or masterpiece, particularly in art or literature; from the Latin phrase for "great work" Sometimes the expression is used ironically, as when a writer refers to "my magnum opus." The phrase suggests something akin to the *Great American Novel.*

magoptical a combination of MAGNETIC and OPTICAL A *magoptical track* is a soundtrack that has both magnetic stripe track and optical track. A *magoptical release print* (or *mag-opt print* or *mag-opt*) has both types of soundtracks on a film. It can be projected in conventional theaters, using the monaural optical track, or in theaters equipped to handle magnetic soundtracks with stereophonic speakers.

magpie effect the leaking of information, particularly to the media A *magpie* is a bird that chatters noisily and, from this, refers also to a person who talks too much.

magtab a magazine in the format of a tabloid newspaper (smaller than standard newspapers), but with a heavier cover, as on a magazine Special longer issues of the trade publication *Variety* are produced this way.

mahlstick a lightweight stick, about 3 or 4 feet long, used by painters to rest and steady the brush or hand; sometimes spelled *maulstick* The origin is Dutch: *malen,* meaning "to paint," and *stok,* or "stick." Traditional mahlsticks are wooden, with a soft leather ball at the end nearest to the canvas. Other mahlsticks have aluminum rods with rubber tips.

mail letters, packages, and other matter conveyed by a postal service, perhaps carried in a *mailbag* and delivered in a *mail truck* by a *mail carrier* or *letter carrier* (*mailman* or *mailwoman*) to a *mailbox* or *mail drop* The government system (Postal Service) itself is called the *mail,* though mail also is handled by FEDERAL EXPRESS and other private carriers. *Inter-office mail* is handled within a company or organization, usually within a building or other premises and not including postage or postal service. The word is from *mala,* Latin for "bag."

The U.S. Postal Service has a variety of mail classifications, including *first-class mail* (individual letters and cards), *second-class mail* (periodicals), *third-class mail* (printed materials and other bulk mail), and *fourth-class mail* (parcels).

mail art picture postcards

mailbag a sack or pouch for carrying MAIL

mail chute a glass-fronted enclosure with a slot on each floor of a tall building Letters are dropped through the chute into a box on the street floor for collection.

mailer 1 a DIRECT-RESPONSE advertiser or other mail user, or the advertising piece itself; a carton or wrapper enclosing the advertising piece or other contents 2 a mailing machine 3 a ship that carries mail

mail fold a crease, or fold, made on a web-fed printing press after the first CHOPPER fold and parallel to it, so called because the two folds reduce the size of the sheet so that it is suitable for mailings; also called the *second chopper fold*

Mailgram a Western Union telegram delivered by the U.S. Postal Service

mail-in a box top, label, proof of purchase, coin, or other item associated with a product, mailed by the consumer to obtain a premium, rebate, prize, or other offer

mailing a batch of mail or a single item sent by mail, or the postal distribution process itself

mailing list a list of names and addresses used in DIRECT MAIL advertising, fundraising, distribution of publicity releases, or other mailings

mailing-list profile the common characteristics of the individuals or organizations on a MAILING LIST

mail order (MO or **mo)** a method of generating sales—such as by a *mail order house* or company—through the distribution of catalogs, letters, or other printed materials or via broadcast advertising The appeal is made by the seller directly to the consumers, rather than through retailers or other intermediaries between the seller and the consumer. The direct marketing field has expanded and diversified in recent years, and many department stores and other retailers have mail order departments, which enable customers to order via mail or telephone.

mail order action line (MOAL) a service of the Direct Marketing Association, in New York, to assist consumers in resolving mail-order problems

mail panel [market research] a group of people whose opinions are solicited on a continuing basis by mail

mail preference service (MPS) a procedure provided by the Direct Marketing Association, in New York, for consumers who request that their names be removed from mailing lists

mail-response list a list of customers or others who have previously responded to a mailing offer

main [theater] short for *main switch*, as in *house main* (the switch that controls the lights for the audience areas) or *stage main* (controls all stage lights)

mainframe an older term for the central processing unit for a full-size computer system; also called *main frame*

main section the news section of a newspaper, as generated by the foreign, national, and local news staffs and differentiated from the sports, style, business, and other departments Sometimes, especially on Sunday, it is in more than one unit and the parts are called *Main One, Main Two, Main Three*, etc.

Main Stem old slang for the Broadway theater area

maintained mark-on the difference between net costs and gross sales, expressed as an amount; also called *maintained markup*, which is expressed as an amount or a percentage *Maintained mark-on* and *maintained markup*

generally refer to sales over a period of time, rather than to a single item or transaction.

maintenance crew [television] the people who maintain the cameras and equipment, a function so important that they sometimes are listed in the program credits

majors [film] the big Hollywood producers/distributors, specifically Columbia, Disney, MGM/UA, Paramount, 20th Century-Fox, and Warner Bros. The *mini-majors* are the next rung, such as Embassy, Orion, and Tri-Star.

majuscule a large letter, or writing that has large letters; the opposite of MINUSCULE The word derives from the Latin *majusculus*, meaning "somewhat great" (the diminutive of "major" or "greater"). In French, *majuscule* means "uppercase."

make a line [publishing] an instruction to a writer to add a few characters or words to fill out a space, the opposite of *lose a line* or *save a line*

make an entrance to come on stage or to appear, particularly with impact

make good (MG) advertising time or space provided free by a station or a publication to an advertiser whose commercials or advertisements were preempted or were broadcast (or published) improperly

make over [newspapers] to revise an entire page during the press run of an EDITION, or between editions; a *makeover* (one word) is a page that has been revised or rearranged

makeready all the preparation done prior to the final printing, including adjustments of the presses and other equipment; also called *start-up* The paper used to start the production run, called *makeready sheets*, usually is discarded. Formerly spelled *make-ready* or *make ready*, it is sometimes called *making ready*.

make the eagle scream to print in large bold headlines

make the rounds to go from one potential employer or purchaser, particularly theatrical producers, to another

makeup **1** a layout; an arrangement of type and art, as on a newspaper page or in an entire publication; also spelled *make-up* A *makeup restriction* may be imposed by a publisher on advertisers to prohibit specific sizes, such as irregular proportions. A *makeup rule* is a flat piece of steel used by printers in layout work. **2** cosmetics A *makeup artist* applies cosmetics and other materials for performers, on the face and other parts of the body. Special makeup, such as latex masks, hairpieces, and other transformational materials (for instance, those used by a young performer to play the role of an elderly person), is applied by a *prosthetic* *makeup artist.* The command "makeup!" on a TV set is a request to apply cosmetics, generally a touchup of powder by the *makeup department* (headed by the makeup artist). The *makeup call* is the time a performer reports to be made up. *Makeup Artists & Hair Stylists* is a local unit of IATSE in North Hollywood and New York.   **3** to wind several film reels onto a single roll; also spelled *make up*

making order a custom or special job

malapropism the ludicrous misuse of words The origin is *Mrs. Malaprop*, a character in *The Rivals*, a work by the English playwright Richard B. Sheridan (1751–1816). An example is *child progeny* (instead of *prodigy*).

mall an enclosed shopping center The term comes from *maul*. In the 17th century, a large, heavy mallet was used in the game *pall-mall*, which was played in a lane or an alley. Later, *mall* referred to a shaded walk or public promenade, and then to a street for pedestrians only, with stores on each side.

mall intercept a survey research method in which consumers are stopped, or intercepted, at random in a shopping MALL and interviewed

Maltese cross movement a mechanism in a film projector or camera that produces intermittent movement of the film in front of the aperture Each frame thus is projected (in a projector) or exposed (in a camera). The shaft has four slots, akin to the cross used by the medieval Knights of Malta. The device is also called a *Geneva movement*, since it is based on the Geneva movement of Swiss watches. It has no connection with the 1941 movie *The Maltese Falcon*, directed by John Huston (1906–87).

man in audience and market research, a male who is 18 years old or older

man. MANUAL

managed news information that is contrived or manipulated and not necessarily in the public interest

management by objective (MBO) an organizational approach involving a collaborative effort with measurable goals, against which performance is evaluated

management information system (MIS) data processing procedures to aid in management functions

mandatory carriage rule a Federal Communications Commission rule, declared illegal in 1985, that required cable TV systems to carry all local broadcast TV signals in their market The affected stations were called *must-carries.*

mandatory copy words legally required on labels and in the advertising of certain products, such as cigarettes, liquor, and drugs

M and E or M & E morning and evening newspapers; the music and sound effects portion of a movie soundtrack, exclusive of the dialogue

manet a direction to a performer to remain on the stage, common before the 20th century but no longer used; from the Latin word for "remain"

manière criblée a relief method of engraving, in which small holes are punched in a plate or black; they appear in the print as white dots on a black background The print is called a *dotted print. Criblée* is from the French word for "sieve."

manifold multiple *Manifold paper*, also called onionskin, is thin, translucent paper for making carbon copies.

Manila paper thick, smooth, sturdy paper, usually buff color, made from Manila hemp fiber (from a Philippine plant related to the banana) or wood fibers The paper is commonly used for large mailing envelopes.

manipulate in word processing, to rearrange sentences and other components of the text skillfully

Manning, Selvage & Lee one of the world's largest public relations firms Headquartered in New York, it is owned by D'Arcy Masius Benton & Bowles, a major advertising agency.

man on the street (MOS) an interviewing technique in which the opinions of the general public are sought

manual (man.) of or having to do with a hand or hands, from the Latin *manualis* Thus a *manual* is a handy book for reference, a handbook, or simply a compact guidebook or list of instructions. A *manual catalog* is a card catalog, as in a library, with the cards inserted by hand.

manufacturer's brand a brand or item sold by a manufacturer, in contrast to a *retailer's brand*—one distributed under the store's own label—or a generic item

manufacturer's representative a sales representative of a manufacturer The individual may be an independent agent, generally representing several manufacturers, a salaried employee, or a broker.

manufacturer's sales office a local unit of a manufacturer that sells the company's products or services; also called *manufacturer's store* The office generally handles only the products or services of the company—as distinct from a wholesaler or retailer, who deal with goods from many sources—and sometimes sells direct to consumers. Some companies sell exclusively in this manner; other companies operate with dual sales forces, in which some sell direct to consumers through the company's own offices and others sell to wholesalers and retailers.

manuscript (ms, ms., or MS.)   the text of an article, book, or other written work, as prepared by an author prior to publication; the plural is *mss, mss.,* or *MSS.* Originally, a manuscript was written by hand (manually); most manuscripts now are typed or prepared on a word processor, not necessarily by the author. A *manuscript book* is a handwritten volume, generally dating from before the introduction of printing in the 15th century.

manuscript cover   a heavy, durable paper, often light blue, used as the top sheet for legal documents and some manuscripts

map   a drawing or other representation of all or part of the earth's surface, though specialized maps, such as anatomical maps and sky maps, may represent other areas   To *map out* is to arrange or plan in detail, as in the development of a campaign. To *put on the map* is to make well-known; the opposite is to *wipe off the map.* A *map index* is an alphabetical list of names or features portrayed on a map, with a key to locating their precise position on the map.

map pins   small, straight pins with rounded colored heads, commonly used on maps and displays to indicate the location of, for instance, elements in a campaign

marble paper   cover stock, endleaf—the paper attached to the inside covers—or other sheets decorated with an irregular or mottled pattern like marble; also called *marbled paper*   Reference books sometimes have paper with marbled edges.

marbling   the process of staining or transferring designs, resembling the mottled appearance of marble, to paper or some other surface

MARC   MACHINE READABLE CATALOGING

M/A/R/C   a market research company in Irving, TX, that specializes in automated telephone interviews   Services include the National Neighborhood Panel, telephone, mail, or personal interviews of about 38,000 households, formed in 1965. M/A/R/C Inc. (the exact name of the company) is an abbreviation of Marketing and Research Counselors Inc.

marg.   MARGIN

margin (marg.)   **1** the difference between the net cost of producing an item and the price paid by the retailer or other buyer   Also called *gross margin,* it may be expressed as a percentage of the cost or price, or as an absolute amount.   **2** the space between the printed area and the edge of a sheet   A *margin line* may be printed on a manuscript typing page or layout sheet to indicate the outer limits of type or other matter. There are two vertical margins, the *left margin,*

or *inside margin,* and the *right margin,* or *outside margin,* and two horizontal margins, the *top margin,* or *head margin,* and the *bottom margin,* or *lower margin.* On a standard typewriter, left and right margins are set and released with specific keys that regulate the carriage. The space between two adjacent pages in a bound work is the *back margin* or *gutter.* A *margin field* (or *runaround indentation*) is a series of different indentations to set text around artwork or for special effects.

marginal analysis   the determination of the quantity of production that would be needed in order to produce income equal to the cost of manufacture   At a certain level in production, *marginal revenue* equals *marginal cost*—that is, the change in total cost that results from producing one additional unit, called the *marginal cost,* is the break-even point.

marginal cost   the change in total cost of a product that results from producing one additional unit

marginalia   notes (called *marginal notes*) or headings (called *marginal heads*) on the MARGIN of a page   *Side notes* are written or set in the side margin; *shoulder notes* appear in the top margin or in the corner; *footnotes* are placed in the bottom margin. *Marginal side heads* appear in the area of a page outside the text area.

marginal revenue   a change in total revenue derived from selling one additional unit of a product

Maritz Inc.   a market research company in St. Louis, MO, that owns Maritz Marketing Research, Quartra Marketing Research (in Minneapolis), Houlahan/Parker Marketing Research (in Los Angeles), and other subsidiaries   Maritz was formed in 1973.

mark (mk.)   a trademark, punctuation mark, spot, or other indication   A script is *marked* to indicate changes or cues to the performers; a stage is *marked* to indicate the positions of scenery or performers.

markdown   the process of reducing the price of goods for sale, or the amount of the reduction

marker   **1** a bookmark   **2** a milestone   **3** a sign or a person or object that indicates or points out—for instance, a symbol in an index or a computer program   **4** [graphic arts] a device for highlighting, lettering, or other types of marking, usually a plastic cylinder with a brush or point   Types include *art markers* and *studio markers* in a variety of colors.

market (mkt.)   the geographical area in which products or services are sold   Sometimes the term also refers to the sellers and/or buyers. A market can be categorized as *wholesale, retail, consumer,* or *industrial* and also may be identified by the types of consumers targeted or the types of products or services offered, such as *retired persons' market* or *automotive accessories market*. A *local market* can be defined in several ways—by its geographical location, its population (for instance, a STANDARD METROPOLITAN STATISTICAL AREA), the communications medium that advertises to it (such as *television coverage area*), or the sales territory of the specific company, product, or product category. A *major market* generally is considered to be one of the top 100 in population or one of the 50 largest television markets (based on number of TV households).

market-basket pricing a promotional concept in which *loss leaders*—that is, items that bring in little or no profit—are advertised or featured, to attract volume business and to enhance the potential for sales of items priced at regular MARKUP and also of high-profit merchandise

market-by-market (MBM) a system of appropriating local advertising expenditures in proportion to the actual or potential sales in each specific market

market demand the estimated total sales of a product or service that may be obtained, generally within a specific geographical area and time period

market development 1 the movement of a company into a new geographical area, or a strategy to increase sales by gaining new types of customers 2 the rate of usage of a product or service in its current markets or the quantitative number of units or sales of a product or service calculated as a percentage of population within an area during a specific period of time This can be expressed as the *market development index (MDI)* or *category development index*, or sometimes simply as *market index*.

marketer a person, company, or organization that offers a product or a service for sale

Marketest a research service in food and drug stores, conducted by MARKET FACTS INC.

Market Facts Inc. a market research firm in Chicago that conducts mail, telephone, FOCUS GROUP, and other interviews, including MARKETEST It was formed in 1946.

market index See MARKET DEVELOPMENT.

marketing the activities in the transfer of goods and services from producer to consumer, including advertising, public relations, distribution, pricing, sales, credit, warehousing, MARKET RESEARCH, and other functions The *marketing director* is responsible for some or all of these functions, which are mapped out in a *marketing plan* (or *concept*, *strategy*, or *program*).

Marketing and Research Counselors Inc. See M/A/R/C.

Marketing Intelligence Service a market research company in Naples, NY The publisher of several newsletters about new products, it tracks trends and other aspects of marketing.

marketing mix a combination of business activities and variables in the marketing of products or services, such as sales, advertising, packaging, public relations, distribution, pricing policies, and the product or service itself

market leader the top seller or dominant company within a specific product category or geographic area; also called *market maker*

market letter a report on investments (including the stock, commodity, and bond markets) issued by brokerage firms or other publishers

market maker See MARKET LEADER.

market-minus prices products or services priced lower than competitive items in the survey area or MARKET The opposite is MARKET-PLUS PRICES.

market-minus pricing a manufacturer's system of establishing the retail price of an item and then deducting all discounts and commissions in order to determine the maximum amount available to produce the item; also called *demand-backward pricing*

Market Opinion Research a market research company in Detroit that specializes in political campaigns and the health-care field It was formed in 1941.

market order an instruction to buy or sell an item at the current MARKET PRICE

market pattern the extent of concentration of purchases within a category, geographical area, or period of time, ranging from *thin market pattern* (meager) to *thick market pattern* (heavy)

market penetration the degree or rate of usage of a product, service, or category among current users

market persons in market research, the estimated number of individuals of a sex–age group in a geographic area; also called *population universe*

market-plus prices products or services priced higher than competitive items in the same area or MARKET; the opposite of MARKET-MINUS PRICES

market potential the maximum sales that can be obtained by all sellers within a particular geographical area, industry, or product category; also, the estimated sales volume at a given price for a particular product within a selected market Maximum sales may be expressed as *share of market*, *brand potential index*, or *sales potential*. The unexploited or remaining potential for additional sales is called *headroom*.

market price the selling price at the point of sale—that is, the actual sales price, which is not necessarily the price originally established or suggested by the manufacturer or retailer, and may result from supply, demand, competition, and other factors in the marketplace

market profile the characteristics of a group or an area, including data on buyers and sellers as well as on the economy, trends, and other items

market research the study of the demands or desires of consumers (or other publics) in relation to actual or potential products and services, conducted by *market researchers* or *market research firms*

market-ripe referring to fruits and vegetables shipped prior to maturity, timed to ripen at the destination

markets [journalism] the securities, commodities, and other investment markets; the newspaper section devoted to information about them At farm, fashion, real estate, and other specialized consumer and trade publications, the *market report* refers to the particular field covered by the publication.

market share the portion or percentage of sales (in dollars or in units) in a category of goods or services that a brand, product, line, or company holds

market skimming the establishment of the price of a product or service to produce maximum revenue The price is sometimes determined when a product is new and unique; it is lowered as competition is introduced or market saturation takes place. The policy of skimming is the opposite of *penetration pricing*, in which the price of a product or service is established at a lower level in order to discourage competition and develop sales more quickly and extensively.

market specialist [advertising] a buyer of advertising time and space who concentrates on just a few geographical areas (markets), thus developing expertise in consumer habits in media and advertising rate fluctuations in these markets

market temper the feeling among wholesale or professional buyers in a market about sales forecasts and other outlooks

market test a sales test in a geographical area A new product is *test-marketed* in selected regions to see how well it will sell and whether it should be introduced in other areas.

marking the placing of call numbers—codes indicating the location of books in the library—or other symbols on the outside of books and other items

marking up the first fitting of theatrical costumes The term refers to the chalk marks for alterations that are indicated on the garments.

mark it [film] an instruction by the director of photography to an assistant (the second assistant camera operator, or clapper/loader) to hit together the hinged boards on top of the clapboard and mark on the slides the details of the take, or shooting

mark-on or **markon** the difference between cost and price, expressed as an amount; sometimes called *initial markup*

mark sense to write on cards, paper, or other nonconductive surface with an electrographic or electric pencil The copy is to be read (*mark sensed*) by a recognition machine (a *mark-sensing machine*).

markup 1 the price spread—that is, the difference between total cost and selling price The term generally refers to the amount the retailer adds to its cost to establish the price to the customer. Also called *initial retail markup, retailer's discount,* or sometimes *mark-on,* it may be computed as an actual amount, or as a percentage of the retail price, or as a multiple of the cost, as in *100-percent markup.* In the jewelry business, a *keystone markup* is a 100-percent markup. The term *markup* also may refer to an increase in price. 2 written instructions to the typesetter, artist, retoucher, or others involved in production

marquee a rooflike structure that projects over an entrance to a theater or other building; pronounced mar-KEY It is also an indication of a star performer, as in *marquee billing* or *marquee value.*

marriage mail a type of direct mail, in which two or more items are combined in one package Such *shared mail* is more economical to advertisers than *solo mail.* Marriage Mail is a copyrighted product of Advo-System, in Windsor, CT, the largest company in the shared mail field. A typical Marriage Mail package contains three printed advertisements surrounded by a wrapper—instead of an envelope—which also is an advertisement. The wrapper has space on it for a label that bears the household address.

married referring to the synchronized picture and sound on a single film; locked in or fixed, as in being married to a specific script, budget, or plan

married print a composite print, with audio and video on one strip of film

Martini binder the trademarked name of a popular machine used in bookbinding, particularly paperbound books, to assemble the signatures, or sheets, and apply adhesive binding and covers (the *perfect binding* process)

mascara a cosmetic preparation for coloring hair, particularly eyelashes and eyebrows; from the Spanish *mascara,* or "mask" It is generally black, though theatrical mascara includes *white mascara* to whiten hair.

maser the acronym for *microwave amplification by stimulated emission of radiation* Just when you are getting used to lasers, here's a new word, with significant applications in communications. A *maser* is a device that amplifies electromagnetic radiation and makes it more coherent, or focused. It is used in ground stations to amplify the weak signals received from communications satellites and make them more discrete, or specific.

mask **1** any shield or screen to cover, conceal, or protect **2** [photography] an intermediate photographic negative or positive used in color correction *Contrast masking* is a photographic procedure to control contrast and hold the detail, as when a black-and-white film is made from a color negative. A *dropout mask* is a type of photographic mask to withhold exposure of the background or other undesired areas. **3** an opaque material used to protect open or selected areas of an OFFSET printing plate during exposure **4** an opaque rectangle with a cutout area the size of one line of copy, sometimes used by proofreaders to enable them to read one line at a time and not skip any lines **5** to cover an area so that it will not appear **6** to fit a shield to a camera lens to reduce or give a specific shape to the camera's field of vision

masked-identification test a test of advertising memorability Respondents attempt to identify sponsors in advertisements in which brand names and trademarks are covered.

masking paper a coated, or shiny, paper, generally orange or yellow (and thus commonly called *goldenrod paper*), used in assembling and positioning negatives, to be photographed and made into printing plates in OFFSET lithography

masking tape adhesive strips, commonly used in printing, photography, and design to cover, protect, or secure items in place

masque an elaborate form of entertainment that originally—in the 16th century—featured masked figures, called *masquers*

The Masquers a social organization of performers, located in Los Angeles The executive director is called the *Harlequin.*

massage **1** to revise and revitalize (as in a physical massage) an advertising campaign or specific advertising material **2** [computers] to process text, such as by adding line measures and instructions for the positioning of material

mass communications the delivery of information to large audiences via print and electronic media

mass display a display of products in a store, separate from the same products on a shelf, in an aisle or at another location The display is placed in a prominent location where it can be seen by the mass of customers.

mass magazine a periodical intended for the general audience, as distinct from a *class magazine,* aimed at a more elite audience—such as *Atlantic Monthly*—or a special-interest magazine, whose readers seek information in a particular subject area, such as a computing magazine

mass-market book a book with broad or popular appeal Mass-market books are distributed in a variety of retail outlets—including such locations as drugstores and airport shops—to a wide audience. Trade books or quality paperbacks, in contrast, appeal to a more selective readership and are sold in bookstores.

mass marketing the selling of a product or service to as many customers as possible, as compared to *selective marketing,* aimed at more specific, carefully chosen groups

mass media forms of communication that reach large audiences, such as newspapers, magazines, radio, and television, in contrast to newsletters or other media that are more specialized MEDIA is the plural of *medium.*

mass merchandiser a retail outlet or chain akin to a department store, with several or many categories of products and a discount price policy or the appearance of a discount store

mass storage [computers] a storage area with a large capacity, such as the *auxiliary memory* (sometimes called *bulk memory*) that supplements the main memory; see also MEMORY

master a metal matrix, or mold, used in printing or other reproduction, such as phonograph recording; also, the original film, tape, or other item from which copies are made

master agency the advertising agency responsible for a *master contract,* covering all the advertising placed with a medium (such as television) for a number of products and created by two or more advertising agencies; also known as *captain agency*

master antenna television (MATV) a system used in hotels and apartment houses for pay TV and other TV reception

master card a card, usually the first in a series of punched cards with data that identifies or controls the other cards in the group; also called *master data card* It has no relation to Master-Card credit cards.

master character the image of a letter or other type character that is reproduced in photographic typesetting

master copy [graphic arts] the mechanical, or board with type and/or art affixed to it, that is photographed for printing or reproduced in another way; also called *repro* or *original*

master file the storage area of a computer containing information relevant to other files or capable of generating new files

master galley the final copy of a proof, with all corrections, prior to printing In books, a later stage is the *page proof*.

master image in computerized typesetting, the DIGITAL representation or the character image on a FONT MATRIX from which the typeset character is generated or the art design from which a photographic or digital representation is produced

master of ceremonies (MC, mc, or emcee) the host of a TV or radio show, or a banquet or other function, who introduces the speaker or performers and often provides banter To *emcee* is to act as host of a show or a function.

masterpak a package containing several small packages—for instance, of cold cereals

master shot an overall scene, generally taken from a distance (a *long shot*), often filmed or taped for a long period so that it can be edited in a variety of ways

master size the size in which a print advertisement is originally prepared, usually the largest size to be used

masthead an area in a publication that indicates its name and other information, such as year founded, personnel, motto, and statement of policy Contrary to popular usage, the masthead is not merely the publication's name (which is the title, or flag, and appears on page 1). The masthead generally appears on the editorial page of newspapers and on the contents page of magazines. The origin is the top part of a ship's mast, which displays the flag of the country of origin. *The Masthead* is the name of the publication of the National Council of Editorial Writers.

mat 1 a die or mold—in particular, the impression of an article or an advertisement that has been set in type; also called *matrix* Matrix paper is a dry material that is moistened to make a wet paper-maché (or papier-mâché), called *flong*. Molten lead then is poured into this mold; the hardened metal is used in LETTERPRESS printing. In the early 1900s, several large companies developed services solely to enable public relations practitioners to have feature articles written and produced in mat form and sent to weekly newspapers. At the present time, most weekly newspapers print by OFFSET reproduction, rather than by letterpress; therefore, the "mat services" now provide them with glossy proofs, suitable for offset printing. However, many people still use the term *mat* to refer

to a feature article distributed to newspapers and other publications, whether for letterpress or offset. In printing, the duplicate of the original engraving or plate used to create a mat, and the subsequent replications of the mat, are called *stereotypes*. 2 a decorative border of cardboard or similar material placed around a picture as a frame or as a contrast between the picture and the outer frame; also called MATTE 3 loose sheets or corrugated material used as a filler, as in a carton

mat board a stiff cardboard used to make a MAT for framing pictures Whereas *illustration board* generally has a gray base, mat board usually has a white base to which is affixed thin paper on one side. Most mat is made of wood pulp, but high-quality mat board is made with rag. Mat board is cut with a *mat cutter* or *mat knife*.

match 1 the comparing or merging of two or more items, such as the typing of a number of names, addresses, and salutations onto copies of a letter with a preprinted body 2 [computers] a technique of comparing the KEYS of two or more records to select or reject items 3 [direct mail] the merging of identical items on two or more lists The identical items that are matched are called a *pair up* or *hit*.

matchbook cover a piece of cardboard that is used to cover a folder of matches and is often printed with advertising on the outside and/or inside Matchbook-cover advertising is a major medium; information about types of covers, sizes of advertising space (generally 51 AGATE lines on the outside cover and 45 agate lines on the inside cover), quantities (in the millions for national advertisers), rates, distribution, and other data is provided by matchbook manufacturers, brokers, and agencies.

match cut a quick transition, or cut, from one film or TV camera to another, or a smooth transition from one shot to another, with the action appearing to continue seamlessly

match dissolve (MD) a film and TV technique in which a shot fades, or dissolves, into another of similar form or action, perhaps to suggest the passage of time

matched negative in offset printing, the combination of two or more parts of a negative that is too large for a single exposure The negative parts are joined, or matched, by splicing and taping them together.

matched sample [market research] a pair of two individuals or groups that are identical in demographics or other identifiable variables

matching [film] harmonious blending, as in matching action (a smooth transition from one scene to another)

material bibliography a listing of books and related information in chronological sequence, also called *historical bibliography*

matinee an afternoon performance; pronounced mah-tin-AY A *matinee idol* is an old-fashioned term for a stage actor who is popular with women. The French word *matinée* derives from *matin*, meaning "morning."

matrix 1 an array of numbers arranged in rows and columns (the plural is *matrices*) 2 a metal plate for casting typefaces, or the mold from which the plates can be cast; see also MAT The word originates from the Latin *mater*, or "mother." 3 in photocomposition, the arrangement of type characters in a case or on a film or disk

Matrix Award an annual award to a woman in communications, presented by the New York chapter of Women in Communications Inc.

matrix film a *stripping film*, or special thin paper or film used to correct tones in photoprints

matrix paper a pâpier-maché material that is moistened to make a mold for use in typesetting; also called *dry mat paper*

matrix printer a high-speed line machine—a system that produces a whole line of copy rather than a single character (letter, number, or symbol) at a time—in which the characters are composed of dots rather than of continuous flowing lines; also called *dot printer, stylus printer,* or *wire printer* A *matrix proofer* electrostatically forms dot characters on proof sheets to be photographed and then printed.

mat shot [film] the imposition of a title, figure, or component of a scene over another, resulting in an integrated image; also called *traveling mat shot* or *matte shot* The process involves exclusion of the background and differs from a *superimposition* (in which the background is retained) and a *blend* (in which the background loses its identity as it is combined with the one imposed on it).

matte 1 a dull surface 2 a cardboard or other border placed around a picture (the process is called *matting*); also called *mat* A *camera matte* or camera *mask* (also called a *gobo*) is a surface to create visual effects. For example, a *foreground matte* (or *female matte*) is a cardboard with an opening, through which the camera shoots, producing a *matted shot* (akin to a matted picture, with a border). Other types of camera mattes include an *insertion matte* (the subject is inserted into an area within a foreground matte) and a *transparent matte* (often with lettering or graphics on it) through which the camera shoots. A *counter-matte* is the negative image of a matte, so it is opaque in areas in which the matte is transparent. In *self-matting,*

the effects are obtained electronically, without actual mattes or masks.

matte artist [film] a person in the special-effects department who designs and paints backgrounds on mattes for combination with live action in composite images; also called *matte painter*

matte bleed [film, graphic arts] an imperfect composite (matted) image, in which the border (*matte lines*) is visible

matte box a container mounted in front of a camera lens, to hold camera mattes and filters It also can serve as a lens shade.

matte finish a dull finish without luster, generally textured A *glossy finish*, in contrast, has a shiny surface.

matte line the border between the original background and the inserted material in a composite or matte shot (or painting) If poorly produced, the matte line is visible as an outline of the area that was matted in. See also MAT SHOT.

matte print a photoprint with a dull finish

matter 1 [typography] type, or material to be set in type *Printed matter* already is set in type. *Live matter* still may be used and is being held, whereas *dead matter* is no longer needed. *Open matter* has spaces, or leading, between the lines; *closed matter* is solid and without leading. *Fat matter* has WIDOWS or other undesirable open spaces; *lean matter*, in contrast, is compressed. 2 material sent through the mails

matting 1 in computer graphics, the technique of leaving a window or hole in an image that can be filled in with another image; the two are then composited, or combined 2 the process of affixing a cardboard or other border, called a MATTE, or producing a dull surface, a MATTE FINISH

mature audience [film, television] an audience for which sexual, violent, or other adult material is considered appropriate

MATV MASTER ANTENNA TELEVISION

max or **max.** maximum

maxibrute a BRUTE—a high-intensity arc spotlight—that is sealed and contains nine 1,000-watt PAR lights, in three vertical rows; also called *nine-light*

maxim a brief statement of a self-evident or fundamental truth or rule of conduct

maximil the MILLINE RATE—that is, the cost of an AGATE line of advertising space in a newspaper that reaches a circulation of one million—before any discounts; also called *maxiline* The opposite is MINIMIL, the milline rate after discounts for quantity and frequency.

maximum depth requirement in a newspaper or other publication, the maximum linage, or amount of advertising space, allowed per column that also contains nonadvertising (editorial) material Beyond the allotted amount, an advertiser must pay for a full column.

Mayday an international signal for help used by planes and ships in distress; probably from the French *venez m'aider*, "come help me"

MB megabyte See MEGA.

MBM MARKET BY MARKET ALLOCATION

MBO MANAGEMENT BY OBJECTIVES

MC or **mc** MASTER OF CEREMONIES; sometimes written *M.C.* or *m.c.*

MCA Inc. one of the world's largest entertainment companies The owner of Universal Pictures, Universal Television, MCA TV, and recording, publishing, and other firms, it was formed in 1924 by Dr. Jules Caesar Stein (1896–1981) as *Music Corporation of America*, a talent agency for dance bands that became a major power (nicknamed *The Octopus*) in show business. No longer in the talent agency business, MCA is headquartered at the Universal City Studios, Universal City, CA.

McCain sewing in bookbinding, side sewing with thread inserted by a machine named after its inventor

McCollum/Spielman International a market research company, headquartered in Great Neck, NY, that specializes in pretesting commercials and print advertisements It operates AC-T (Advertising Control for Television, a group of theaters in which commercials are tested). The firm was formed in 1968.

MCI a major company in the telecommunications field, originally called *Microwave Communications Inc.* The company, located in Washington, DC, broke the long-distance telephone monopoly of AT&T.

McKettrick's Directory a directory of advertisers and agencies, no longer published

McNugget a brief item in *USA Today*, the Gannett national newspaper, a "fast read" suggesting McDonald's or other fast-food restaurants

McPaper a nickname for *USA Today*, the Gannett national newspaper that is a "fast read," akin to McDonald's fast-food restaurants

MCS medium close shot See MEDIUM CLOSE-UP.

MCU MEDIUM CLOSE-UP

MD MATCH DISSOLVE; MUSIC DIRECTOR

M.D. Doctor of Medicine Some medical journal editors and others omit the period from the abbreviation (MD).

MDI See MARKET DEVELOPMENT.

MDS MULTIPOINT DISTRIBUTION SERVICE

MDS/PRA Group the country's largest media mailing company Located in New York, it is the product of a 1988 merger of Media Distribution Services and PRA Group (formerly PR Aids).

meal penalty a payment, made in accordance with union regulations, to a motion-picture performer or crew member who works during the specified time for a meal break

mean the arithmetic average; the sum of all items divided by the number of items

meanline in typography, the top of a lowercase letter that has no ascender, or upward stroke—for instance, *a, c, e,* or *g*; also called *waistline*

measure (meas.) 1 capacity, dimension, or extent, as determined by a standard 2 a rhythm in verse; a unit of verse 3 the notes between two vertical lines on a music staff; musical time or rhythm 4 [typography] the width of type, usually expressed in PICAS; the length of a single line of type; the width of a column or page

measurement a system of determining the extent or impact of a project or an event, such as the effectiveness of a communications campaign Communications measurement techniques include surveys, focus groups, telephone interviews, and other QUALITATIVE RESEARCH, as well as audience and circulation data and other quantification of results.

meat the essence or principal part, such as of an article A *meaty article* or other work is solid, substantial.

meat axe slang for a piece of wood or cardboard attached to a pole and used to block light It looks like a butcher's axe. The black sheets and other items that are also used to block light or create shadows come in many sizes and shapes, as indicated by their colorful names, such as CUTTER, DOT, FLAG, and GOBO.

mechanic a film technician who produces mechanical special effects, such as fire or rain The Motion Picture Studio Mechanics in New York is a local union of IATSE.

mechanical assembled type, artwork, and other material, usually affixed to a board, that is ready to be reproduced; also called *paste-up, keyline,* or *camera-ready artwork*

mechanical binding the joining of the leaves, or sheets, of a book through holes or slots made in their edges Types of mechanical binding include loose-leaf, plastic, spiral, and wire binding. It is not the same as MACHINE BINDING.

mechanical dictionary a listing of MACHINE-READABLE words; an "electronic dictionary"; also called *automatic dictionary*

mechanical drawing a cross section, diagram, or other technical plan, for use by a mechanical engineer or other expert The term relates to the T-square, French curve, and other mechanical devices used by technicians or others who draw such plans, and by designers.

mechanical edit   the process of reading or checking text (*copy*) for accuracy and consistency in form, particularly footnotes, references, and other details; also called *copy edit*

mechanical requirements   the layout and MAKE-UP specifications of a publication, to which prepared advertising material must conform

mechanicals   **1** the machines and gadgets used to produce mechanical special effects during the actual production of a film, as distinct from optical special effects and other post-production special effects   Mechanical animals, stunt equipment, and other mechanical effects are created and produced by a *mechanical effects* designer.   **2** royalties, or fees, paid by record companies to songwriters and music publishers for the right to reproduce their songs or other music on records   The actual term—*mechanical royalties*—refers to the automatic, or mechanical, payment, as mandated by the U.S. Congress in 1902 and regulated by the Copyright Royalty Tribunal. Current payment is about five cents per record that is sold. In other countries, mechanicals also are paid, usually as a percent of the price of the record. The term now includes tapes and discs, in addition to records.   **3** plural of MECHANICAL

mechanics' library   a type of private library that existed primarily in the 19th century for artisans, engineers, and apprentices; also called *apprentices' library*

media   categories of communication vehicles, such as newspapers, magazines, and radio and TV stations   As vehicles, media bridge the gap between the advertiser, journalist, public relations practitioner, and other communicators and their audiences. Technically, *media* is the plural of MEDIUM, though increasingly the popular usage is only of the collective noun. A *media person* is a journalist or other person; a *media buyer*, working in the *media department* of an advertiser, or for an agency or *media buying service*, purchases advertising space or time. The head of the media department is the *media director*. A *media center* is a department or area, as in a school, with a variety of audiovisual equipment and services. The coordinator of such a department, or *media specialist*, sometimes is called a *learning resources specialist* and is assisted by support personnel, including *media aides* or *media technicians*. In Canada and other countries outside of the United States, common terms include *media luncheon* and *media officer* (an executive or government official involved in press relations). As defined by Canadian writer Marshall McLuhan (1911–

80), *hot media* transmit high-definition data with minimum involvement of the recipient, such as radio and film, and *cold media* transmit low-definition data that require more of the recipient's participation, such as television and telephone.

media blitz   the intensive scheduling of all types of advertising and/or publicity targeted to a particular market, demographic audience, or type of media   Such a program is commonplace with new-product introductions, political campaigns, and other projects or events in which tight scheduling is particularly important.

media carriage   the part of a phototypesetter that contains the photographic material   The carriage moves vertically a line at a time.

media coverage   **1** the percentage of potential audience, the actual number of readers and/or viewers, or another measurement of the reach, or effectiveness, of an advertising or public relations campaign   **2** a listing of the publications and stations that print or broadcast relevant publicity

media ecology   the study of the relationship between, on the one hand, communication channels and materials—that is, the media—and our society, or environment, on the other

media event   an occasion usually conceived and set up by a public relations practitioner and designed to attract attention   The term frequently is applied to the *photo opportunities* (*photo ops*) and other events at which public officials, including the President of the United States, are captured on camera or on videotape in highly favorable settings.

mediagenic   attractive and appealing to TV viewers, newspaper readers, and other media audiences

Mediamark Research Inc.   a market research company in New York that publishes reports based on personal interviews about advertising

media mix   the combination of communication vehicles—MEDIA—chosen in order to achieve the goal of an advertising or other campaign

Media News Keys   a media service for public relations practitioners   Published in Queens, NY, it includes Radio-TV Contact Cards, which have information about radio and television programs.

media objectives   the goals of a public relations or other campaign, as stated in specific communication vehicles (MEDIA) that are desired

media option   the characteristics of an advertisement that determine the type of media, such as size of a print ad or length of a broadcast commercial, usually described in a MEDIA PLAN

media plan   specifications of media to be used in an advertising campaign, including reasons for their selection, cost, MEDIA OPTIONS, and MEDIA STRATEGY   A *media planner* is a person in the media department of an advertiser or advertising agency who selects the media that are appropriate to the plan and are likely to reach the target audiences and achieve the objectives of the campaign.

Media Records Inc. (MR) a research organization specializing in newspaper advertising data   Formed in 1927, it is located in New York.

media relations the connection, or relation, between an individual or group and the communication channels (MEDIA) it uses

media strategy the method used to select the types of media to be used in an advertising campaign

media tour an itinerary of cities or markets in which a spokesperson or other publicity representative is sent, generally for a day or two   For example, it is customary for an author, corporate spokesperson, or other interviewee to be sent on a tour of major localities in which a particular book, motion picture, or product is to be heavily publicized via an intensive schedule of interviews on TV and other media, perhaps starting in the morning and ending late at night.

media weight the total impact of an advertising campaign, in terms of REACH and FREQUENCY

medium   **1** an agency by which something is accomplished, conveyed, or transferred (*medium* is the Latin word for *means*)   **2** a means or vehicle of communication, including billboards, direct mail, radio, TV, magazines, newspapers, and other channels that appeal to large numbers of people (*mass media*), as well as journals, newsletters, trade publications, lectures, and other vehicles whose audiences generally are smaller (*specialized media*) (The plural of *medium* is MEDIA.)   **3** the method and/or tool used in executing a work of art, such as oil, watercolor, ink, or pencil

medium-close shot a picture or scene with the camera between a position close to the subject (*close shot*) and a middle position (*medium shot*); abbreviated as MCS

medium close-up (MCU) a camera position that is between a MEDIUM SHOT and a close-up, generally showing a person's head and shoulders and part of the chest; also called *medium close shot* (MCS) or *loose close-up*   A medium close-up generally does not show the hands or forearms.

medium-long shot (MLS) a camera position between a LONG SHOT and a MEDIUM SHOT; also called *full shot*

medium shot (MS) a camera position between a close-up and a long shot—for instance, the view

of a person from the head to the waist or lower; also called midshot or *half-shot*

mega (M) one million   A *megabit* is a million binary digits; a *megabyte* (*MB*) is about one million bytes (actually 1,048,576) or characters of data—thus a *megabyte disk* has the potential for recording 1,048,576 characters of data. *Megahertz* (*MHz*) is one million hertz, a measure of sound frequency.

megaphone a funnel-shaped device for increasing the volume of the user's voice and directing it toward the listener   Megaphones were commonly used by film directors in the days of silent films, and now have been replaced by electronic amplifiers, usually called *bullhorns*. See also MEGGER.

megger slang for a person who used a MEGAPHONE, such as a director in the early days of films, and also the assistant who held the megaphone   (Now that was a job!)   Rudy Vallee (1901–86) was a singer who often used a megaphone; he was called a *crooner* rather than a *megger*.

meiosis the use of understatement for the purpose of emphasis, such as in the British expression *Good show!*

melioration an improvement, such as a change in the meaning of a word in which the term takes on a more favorable or positive connotation   In linguistics, this semantic shift is called *elevation* or *amelioration*.

melodrama a play that displays an excess of theatricality, generally with suspense and a happy ending

mem member; MEMOIR; memorandum; memorial

member-get-a-member (MGM) [direct marketing] a technique of offering an incentive (such as reduced dues or a gift) to members of an organization who refer new members

memo MEMORANDUM

memoir (mem or **mem.)**   **1** an autobiography, particularly a very personal account, or a biography written by a relative or friend   **2** a report or record, more generally called *transactions*, of an event, a study, or proceedings   *Memoirs* refers to a collection—usually a book—of reminiscences by the author.

memorabilia a collection of anecdotes, mementos, or items about a subject

memorandum a short note, usually a reminder (the Latin verb *memorare* means "to remember"), a record, or confirmation of an agreement; a communication, usually informal, such as from an agency to a client or one department to another in an office   Memos are sometimes written on small *memo sheets* or letter-size *memo paper*.

memorandum purchase the buying of an item by a retailer or other intermediary in which payment is not made until the item is finally sold to the consumer; also called *memo purchase* or *memo buying* The buyer takes title upon receipt of the goods and thus cannot return unsold items, as is possible in consignment purchasing. The confirmation of the purchase is called a *memorandum bill* or *memo bill*.

memory the internal storage capacity of a computer system Memory is generally located on a magnetic device such as a disk, tapes, drum, or core. Data are stored in digitally encoded bytes—the basic unit of computer operations—and manipulated as needed during calculation processes. The amount of memory a computer has directly affects its ability to perform complex functions. *Main memory* is located in the central processor and accessed directly by the computer, as opposed to memory located on peripheral devices such as disks or drums. A *memory typewriter* (the predecessor of the word processor) is a typewriter with storage capacity, such as with a MAGNETIC TAPE cartridge, to record and type input. A *memory cell* is the basic storage unit in a chip.

Memphis a typeface with short square serifs, or decorative strokes, attached to lines of uniform thickness Memphis was the capital of ancient Egypt.

mention a brief reference, as to a person, product, or other subject within an article, broadcast, or other medium

menu a list of available functions on a computer system, generally displayed on a video terminal so that an operator may choose a function to initiate (*menu selection* or *menu-driven program*)

mercantile library a private library, primarily for retail clerks, popular in the 19th century Today, there still are a few commercial or business reference centers with the name, such as the Mercantile Library Association in New York.

merchandise mart a facility at which manufacturers or other producers have showrooms for trade customers It is not open to consumers. Well-known merchandise marts are in Chicago, Los Angeles, and Dallas. A mart may be limited to a specific industry, as with 200 Fifth Avenue, the toy industry building in New York. The building housing the showrooms may itself be called *Merchandise Mart*, as is the structure in Chicago.

merchandise mix the variety of stock offered by a distributor or retailer, or the various products and package sizes of a brand, category, or marketer

merchandise pack a retail package that offers a premium, or gift, usually enclosed

merchandising marketing functions related to the presenting and selling of products and services, including advertising, display, promotion, and public relations A *merchandiser* is a marketing expert or, more generally, a retailer or manager of a retail outlet. The *merchandising committee* is a group that determines the purchase of products and services and how to promote them. A *merchandising director* is the person at the manufacturer, agency, distributor, or retailer in charge of planning the sales effort; at department stores, this is a key position.

merchandising allowance an amount paid by a manufacturer or producer to a retailer as an incentive for promoting goods or services

merchandising bus a mobile showcase of products or services

merchandising service 1 a service, often free, offered by a newspaper, broadcast station, or other medium to help promote an advertiser's products 2 a company that sells promotional material to retailers

MERComm Inc. a company, based in New York, that sponsors the National Media Conference and presents the annual ARC awards for annual reports, both projects conducted prior to 1988 by Larimi Communications It also presents the annual MERCURY AWARDS.

Mercury Awards annual awards to individuals, companies, and organizations for public relations programs, presented by MERComm, New York

merge to combine two or more texts, sets of data, or other items, as in a *merged letter*, which is formed by bringing together portions of the text of two or more letters

merge and purge in direct mail, to combine two or more lists and eliminate duplications or unwanted names, such as deadbeats (delinquent payers) and NIXIES; also called *merge/purge*

Mergenthaler Linotype Company a pioneer in typesetting and printing equipment, particularly the Linotype machine invented in the 1880s by Ottmar Mergenthaler (1859–99), a U.S. engineer born in Germany The company is located in Plainview, NY.

meridian of or at noon A.M. is the abbreviation for *antemeridian*, or "before noon"; P.M. stands for *postmeridian*, or "after noon." Perhaps this is obvious, but its significance relates to the designation of noon. It is not 12 A.M., nor is it 12 P.M.—a common error in broadcast schedules. It's simply 12 noon. Actually, *meridian* refers to the highest apparent point attained by the sun or another celestial body in its daily course. And from this definition comes the name of one of the highest-point type sizes: 44 points, *Meridian type*, also called *four-line small pica*. (A *small pica* is 11 points instead of the usual 12, and there are 6 picas to the inch.)

mesh the series of open spaces in a network, or the material surrounding these spaces, or the entire network itself *Meshbeat* is a television distortion of wavy lines; it is also called *linebeat* or MOIRÉ. *Meshwork* is a group of meshes or a network.

message **1** a communication, a statement, a basic theme, or significance The Canadian educator Marshall McLuhan (1911–80) stated, "The medium is the message," meaning that the communications vehicle—such as television—itself can be so significant that the content it presents becomes relatively unimportant. **2** a group of characters (letters, numbers, and symbols) or a unit of information; a single transmission of data in one direction *Message routing* is the process of selecting a route (such as a telephone) or circuit path and destination, perhaps by means of intermediate points. The routing, or *message switching*, may be achieved via a message-switching center.

message band a group of musicians whose songs, usually rock music, convey an idea or theme, such as peace

message center a facility or service that takes down telephone-call messages and other information, often by a telephone operator or receptionist or electronically on a computer

message unit a method of charging for local telephone service, such as by counting a short-duration local call as one message unit and a longer or more distant call as several message units *Message Unit Detail (MUD)* is a report that itemizes each local call.

message waiting an indication, by a light on a phone or information on a video display, that a call or other message was received while the desired recipient was not available Information can be obtained from a MESSAGE CENTER.

message weight the gross number of impressions, or total audience, in an advertising campaign

meta a Greek prefix, meaning "changed in position or form"; equivalent to the Latin *trans* *Metamedia* refers to two or more media combined, as in a sound–light show. *Metamarketing* is "changed marketing" and includes such techniques as going beyond traditional practices to involve causes (*cause marketing*)—for instance, a supermarket offers to donate groceries to the homeless if consumers do the same (the items, of course, must be purchased in the store)

metallic paper a sheet coated or laminated with a fine-gauge metal, such as bronze or aluminum

metal oxide semiconducter (MOS) a solid-state sensing device used in a video camera that doesn't have a tube An MOS sensor has *bloom resistance*—that is, images are not distorted.

metaphor a figure of speech in which two objects or entities are linked or compared, even though they are not actually related, such as "the dawn of an era" or a "wave of opportunity" It differs from a *simile*, which links or compares the two objects by using *like* or *as*. A *mixed metaphor* consists of two or more metaphors that are incongruous or ludicrous.

metathesis transposition or interchange, such as the transposition of letters or sounds within a word The process often is initially unintentional, but as a result of repeated usage it becomes acceptable. Many Old and Middle English words have been altered as a result of a metathesis; for example, Old English *bridd* became *bird*.

meter in literary composition, a measured or regular rhythm, determined by the number and type of *feet* (group of stressed and unstressed syllables) The number of feet in a line of verse is identified as *monometer* (one), *dimeter* (two), *trimeter* (three), *tetrameter* (four), *pentameter* (five), *hexameter* (six), *heptameter* (seven), or *octometer* (eight).

metered mail any mail that has been processed by a postage meter, a machine approved by the Postal Service Metered mail is imprinted or bears a METER STRIP, akin to a postage stamp. *Meter postage* is the amount recorded by the postage meter for each piece of mail.

metered markets geographical areas in which TV ratings are drawn from a sample of homes with a meter attached to a television set New York, Los Angeles, and Chicago are metered by ARBITRON.

meter strip an adhesive label upon which a postage-meter imprint is stamped Produced in rolls that are cut for each label, the strip includes the postage amount, meter number, city of origin, type of mail, and sometimes an advertisement.

method acting an introspective, realistic style of performing in which the performer strives for close personal identification with the role Prominent proponents were Konstantin Stanislavsky (1863–1938), who taught the Stanislavsky System or Method in the Soviet Union, and The Actors Studio in New York; sometimes called *the Method*

metonymy a figure of speech in which one word or phrase is substituted for another that it suggests or with which it is closely associated, such as *White House* for *President* or *crown* for *monarch* or *royal power* A *metonym* differs from a *synonym*, which is a word whose meaning is similar to that of another, such as *president* and *leader* or *crown* and *tiara*.

metrical foot a unit (a *foot*, which is a group of stressed and unstressed syllables) that determines the rhythm, or METER, of a poem

Metro short for METRO-GOLDWYN-MAYER

metro area short for *metropolitan city area*—a major city and the surrounding urban and suburban area Such a region generally is smaller than the coverage area of a television station, Arbitron's ADI, or Nielsen's DMA.

Metrocolor a color film process of MGM Laboratories (METRO-GOLDWYN-MAYER)

Metro-Goldwyn-Mayer (MGM) one of the major U.S. film studios The company merged with United Artists and is now part of MGM/UA COMMUNICATIONS COMPANY. MGM was formed in 1924 in Culver City, CA, by Marcus Loew, who merged Metro Pictures Corporation, Goldwyn Picture Corporation (formed by Samuel Goldwyn), and the production company of Louis B. Mayer.

metropolitan editor at daily newspapers, the editor supervising the reporters who cover the area in and near the city where the publication is headquartered; also called *metro editor* Some newspapers publish a *metro section* featuring local news.

metropolitan statistical area (MSA) a U.S. Bureau of the Census term for an area of one or more counties that includes a central urban area An MSA has a minimum population of 50,000; there are over 300 MSAs in the United States, some of which cross state lines. Before 1983, an MSA was called an SMSA, a Standard Metropolitan Statistical Area. It sometimes is called a *metro survey area* or *metro statistical area*.

metteur-en-scène a director; from the French for "one who puts in place" The term is no longer common; today's French film director is called a *réalisteur* ("one who realizes") or *directeur*.

mezzotint an engraving method in which a copper or steel plate is scraped (roughened) and burnished to produce light areas—via the scraping—and dark areas—via the burnishing—with a velvety effect; also, a print or etching made from a plate engraved in this manner The word comes from the Italian *mezzotinto*, or "half tint."

mf medium FREQUENCY

mf or mtf more follows or more to follow, as marked on a manuscript with more copy to come

MF or mf machine-finish paper See MACHINE-COATED PAPER.

MGM METRO-GOLDWYN-MAYER (see also MGM/UA COMMUNICATIONS COMPANY); MEMBER-GET-A-MEMBER

MGM/UA Communications Company one of the country's largest entertainment companies, established through the merger of METRO-GOLDWYN-MAYER and UNITED ARTISTS In 1988 the firm was divided into two entities, MGM (film and TV production) and *United Artists Corporation* (film production and distribution), both in Los Angeles.

MI MOVE IN

mic or mic. MICROPHONE

mica a group of silicate minerals that crystallize in translucent or colored forms It is used on greeting cards and other coated paper, giving them a *mica finish.*

mickey [film] slang for a type of LUMINAIRE with a 1,000-watt light

mickeymousing playing around, perhaps deceptively In film, one type of mickeymousing is the use of a music score to overstimulate emotions. Of course, the word is from the cartoon character created by Walt Disney in 1928; it is sometimes written as two words, *mickey mousing*. Occasionally the expression simply means the close synchronization of sound, a technique often used in animated cartoons, such as a drum beat synchronized with footsteps. The technique generally is too obvious to be used with live action films.

MICR MAGNETIC INK CHARACTER RECOGNITION

microcomputer a very small computer, one that uses a MICROPROCESSOR; also called *personal computer*

microfiche a sheet—often file-card size, such as 4" × 6"—of film (MICROFILM) capable of accommodating and preserving a considerable amount of material, such as pages of a publication, in reduced form; pronounced my-crow-feesh and also called *fiche* A *microfiche duplicator* produces the microfiche; a *microfiche reader* is used to display the images magnified to their original size. A *microfiche catalog* is a listing of microfiche items, produced by microfilming or by a computer.

microfilm a negative, or sensitized film, on which printed materials are photographed in reduced size (called *microform images*) Microfilm equipment, such as a *microfilm camera* or *microfilm reader*, produces and/or projects the microform images. A *microfilm card*—for instance, an aperture card, camera card, or copy card—has a microfilm affixed to it. A *microfilm jacket* or *film jacket* is a transparent plastic sleeve into which a microfilm frame or strip is inserted.

microfont an uppercase typeface designed for use in MICROFILM, such as for easy-to-read titles

microform an arrangement of reduced-size images, as on MICROFILM or MICROFICHE; also called *microtransparency*

micrographics the science and technology of creating, storing, and retrieving MICROIMAGES, such as MICROFILM and MICROFICHE

microimage a reduced-size reproduction, such as a microphotograph (of a document or other item) that is too small to be read or viewed without magnification; also called *microcopy* or *microrecord*

micromarketing the technique of selling to segments of the total market Individuals or groups are identified as markets based on geography, demographics, psychographics, or other criteria.

microopaque or **micro-opaque** a reduced-size image photographed or printed on white paper, shown by enlarging with a reflection device rather than projection Since the sheet bearing one or more microimages is opaque, a microopaque sheet also is called an *opaque microcopy.*

microphone (mic.) a device for transforming sound waves into electrical impulses in an audio system; also called MIKE

microphone shadow [film, television] a shadow of a microphone visible to the camera; also called *mike shadow*

microphotograph a photograph requiring magnification for viewing, as on a MICROFILM

microprint a type of opaque sheet (6″ × 9″) with microimages arranged in rows and columns

microprocessor a single electronic unit (generally one chip) capable of processing information It generally does not have RANDOM ACCESS MEMORY or an input-output device. A microprocessor can serve as the central processing unit of a microcomputer. Memory generally is provided via linkage with an external memory chip.

micropublishing the publication of documents or other material in MICROFORM Microrepublishing involves previously published material.

microreproduction the reproduction of documents or other material in MICROFORM; also called *microimaging* or *microrecording* Unitized microreproduction is the conversion of one item at a time; collective microreproduction is the conversion of several or many items.

micro-sales analysis the examination of products, geographical areas, or other MARKETING

plan components that failed to achieve an expected share of sales

microstrip a filmstrip, which is a short sequence of MICROFILM images

microwave an electromagnetic wave of extremely high frequency, above 1,000 megahertz, used in communications and in a type of oven

Microwave Communications Inc. See MCI.

middle break a station identification in the middle of a radio or TV program

middle distance the area in a photograph, painting, or other work between the *foreground* and the *background*

middlemen wholesalers, distributors, jobbers, brokers, and other intermediaries between the manufacturer and the consumer

middle-of-month dating (MOM) a system of invoicing or billing Invoices dated between the first and the 15th day of the month are considered dated the 15th. The credit period for invoices dated after the 15th begins on the last day of the month.

middle of the road (MOR) 1 popular music of general appeal: the format of a radio station that plays a variety of popular music 2 describing a course of action between extremes

midget slang for a small item—for instance, a popular spotlight, also called a *mini,* consisting of a 200-watt light and a 4-inch FRESNEL lens

midline record an album or other recording that is in the middle price range, costing less than *frontline*

midlist or **mid-list** [publishing] the group of books that are neither best sellers nor poor sellers, but occupy a position in the middle of the publisher's list of titles, or those books that have less sales potential than the leaders (potential best sellers) on a publisher's list of new titles

mighty [film] slang for an open, variable-focus LUMINAIRE with a 2,000-watt light

mike microphone A *mike boom* is a crane or arm that holds a microphone. A *mike box* is a unit connecting one microphone with others, as on a lectern or table at a press conference. A *sitting mike* is a table microphone. A *rifle mike* is a long, narrow, directional microphone that can be aimed like a rifle. See also MIKING.

mike fright fear of performing, particularly with a microphone

mike mugger a speaker who is too close to the microphone

mike stew unwanted background sound picked up by a microphone

miking the setup and arrangement of microphones, such as their placement on a stage or on performers Performers are *miked* when their microphones are attached and are *overmiked* when the amplification is too loud or artificial-sounding. *Close miking* is the placement of a microphone very close to the sound source; the opposite is *loose miking.*

mil　1/1,000 inch　This unit is commonly used to measure the size of dots in printing screens (see HALFTONE) and also the thickness of recording tape (ranging from less than 1 mil to about 1½ mils).

mileage or milage　**1** the amount of actual or potential benefit, service, or use obtained from an undertaking or endeavor　**2** the surface area of paper　A ton of lightweight paper contains more paper for printing than a ton of heavier paper and therefore has more mileage.

milestone chart　a graphic representation of the stages in a process, event, or other production, usually with *milestone chart symbols,* such as arrows and diamonds that are blank or contain letters or numbers to indicate the time of projected or actual start or completion or other information

milk　to press out or squeeze　To *milk a scene* is to extract every ounce of drama from it—that is, to exaggerate the emotional qualities.

milky　subdued, opaque white, not clear, as in a *milky photo*

milky way　a theatrical district, such as the Times Square area of New York, ablaze with lights, suggesting the Milky Way or a luminous band of stars

mill　slang for a reporter's typewriter, a term from the days when typewriters, not word processors or computers, were used at newspapers to grind out material, as at a mill

millboard　a hard, flat pulpboard used for book covers; also called *binder's board*

mill brand　the trademarked name of a line of products made by a manufacturer, such as a paper mill

mill department　in a film studio, the place where lumber is cut for the construction of sets

Miller, Joe　an old joke, named after an English stage comedian, Josias Miller (1684–1738)　*Joe Miller's Jest-book,* a collection of jokes attributed to him, was published in 1739.

milli　a prefix meaning one-thousandth　A *millisecond* is one-thousandth of a second.

millimeter (mm)　a metric unit equal to one-thousandth of a meter, or .03937 inches　Standard-size films are 8mm (for home movies), 16mm (movies for schools, groups, TV), 35mm (theatrical feature films, films for TV), and 70mm (wide screen). In film, the abbreviation is mm, immediately following the number with no space between and no periods. Films are pro-

jected at different speeds; for instance, 8mm films are projected more slowly (14.5 feet per minute; 16 frames per second) than the other types, all of which are projected at 24 frames per second, though their speeds vary: 16mm at 36 feet per minute, 35mm at 90, and 70mm at 225.

milline rate　the cost of a line of advertising in a publication—such as an AGATE line in a newspaper—multiplied by one million and then divided by the circulation of the publication; pronounced MILL-line　The milline, or *tru-line rate,* thus can be used to compare advertising rates among different publications, since it is the cost per line for one million readers or one million units of circulation. A milline rate in a market also can be computed by multiplying the cost of an agate line by one million and then dividing by the population.

mime　the representation of an action without using words, as by a *mimic, mime,* or *pantomimist*　In film and TV post-production, *miming* is the synchronization of sound and action, as in lip-sync.

mimeograph　a duplicator that makes copies from a stencil (generally prepared, or cut, on a conventional typewriter without using a ribbon) fitted around an inked drum; also called *mimeo*　Originally a trademarked name of the A. B. Dick Company in Chicago, the word has become generic and also refers to the process (*mimeographing*) and the copy (a *mimeographed* publication) from the duplicator; *to mimeograph* is to make the copies. Though not as widespread as in the days before photocopying, mimeograph machines still are common in many schools and organizations. In film and TV studios, the *mimeo department* reproduces scripts, though no longer on a mimeograph machine. *Mimeograph paper* is letter-size (8½″ × 11″) or legal-size (8½″ × 14″) paper with good ink absorption.

mimesis　imitation or representation, such as the mimicry of human speech

min or min.　minimum; minute

mini　a prefix (from *miniature*) meaning lesser or smaller　It is sometimes used by itself (such as *mini* for *miniseries*) or as slang for a small item, such as a popular spotlight (also called a *midget*) consisting of a 200-watt light and a 4-inch FRESNEL lens.

miniature　**1** a small portrait, painting, or letter, or anything considerably less than standard size　A miniature camera takes pictures smaller than 35mm. A miniature book has a very small format (often an inch square). Popular in the 19th century, miniature editions included the Bible, almanacs, and other popular books.　**2** a small replica or model of a building, vehicle, or other object that is created and then filmed (a *miniature shot* or *model shot*) so that it appears full-size (or any desired size) A *hanging miniature* is inserted in front of the camera, to be incorporated in a live action scene or used as background. In *miniature rear projection*, live action is projected onto a screen behind a miniature so that the two are combined. A *moving miniature*, such as a model train or other vehicle, is filmed as it moves. A *miniature designer* in the special effects department creates and constructs the miniatures, assisted by *model makers*.

minibrute a high-intensity spotlight—a *brute*—with nine lamps, in three vertical rows; also called *nine-light* It is slightly different from a MAXIBRUTE in the type of light: a minibrute has FCX lights that are balanced for indoor filming, and a maxibrute has PAR lights.

minicable system a small cable-TV system, such as a satellite-fed master antenna television system (SMATV), a system within a building that receives its signal from a satellite; also spelled *mini-cable*

minicam a small, self-contained portable TV camera, for videotaping on-site news events When linked to a mobile transmission unit (*minicam van*), the minicam can provide live coverage at relatively low cost. It thus has tremendously changed TV news programs at all types of stations.

minicomputer a small computer, with more memory and other features than a microcomputer, or personal computer

minidoc short for *minidocumentary*, a segment, perhaps two to seven minutes long, on a TV program, particularly a newscast, that runs on one or more days; also called *segment report* The material generally is prepared in advance but often has a live lead-in.

minikin the British name for the smallest type size, 3-point; also called *excelsior*

minilite [film] a compact, high-intensity lighting unit (usually with a 650-watt lamp), equipped with metal flaps, called *barn doors*, and a reflector, generally used for *fill light* (supplementary)

minimarket a small submarket of a major selling area

minimicrowave [television] referring to the transmission of a video signal from a nonstudio site—such as a news event—to a mobile unit or a transmitter on a nearby roof The transmitter then sends the signal directly to the station or possibly to one or more intermediate points, such as atop a tall building or other high point.

minimil the MILLINE RATE—the cost of an AGATE line of advertising space in a newspaper that reaches one million in circulation—after dis-

counts for quantity and frequency; also called *miniline* The opposite is *maximil*, the milline rate before discounts.

minimum depth requirement the minimum length, such as one inch per column, of an advertisement in a newspaper or other publication Thus a newspaper generally will not accept a two-column ad that is less than two inches in depth.

minion 1 one who is esteemed or favored; also, a follower or subordinate (from the French *mignon*, or "darling") 2 [typography] formerly a popular type size, about 7 points A *minionette*, or *emerald*, was 6½ points.

miniseries [television] a short series or sequence of related programs, such as one every night for five consecutive nights rather than one a week over a 13-week or other extended period Miniseries are generally dramas or docudramas (fictionalized versions of real events). A *maxi miniseries* is a miniseries in which each program lasts two or more hours, perhaps totaling 12 hours.

minstrel a medieval entertainer In the 19th century, *minstrel shows* were popular in the United States, as variety programs consisting of white performers in blackface, with repartee between an interlocutor in the middle and men on the ends of the troupe.

mint undamaged, fresh A new book, coin, or postal stamp or other item is sometimes described as being in *mint condition*. Actually, a *mint* is a facility for making coins.

minuscule small cursive script developed about the eighth century and used in medieval manuscripts; originally called *Greek type* The term now refers to very small lowercase letters. It is from the French, which in turn is from the Latin *minusculus*, or "very small," the diminutive of *minor*.

minus leading typesetting in which the lines are crammed together, such as 10-point type on 9-point leading (pronounced *ledding*), or space, instead of 9 or 10 on 11

minus lens a lens attached to a camera lens that extends its range, so that the two together become a long-focus, or *telephoto*, lens

MIP-TV Marche International des Programmes de TV, an annual international convention and marketplace of television program producers, held in April in Cannes, France

miracle play a type of medieval drama, popular chiefly before the 16th century, about the lives of saints and divine events or actions (miracles) It was a predecessor of the MORALITY PLAY and the MYSTERY PLAY.

Mire a French word for the test charts used to standardize the legibility of MICROIMAGES A frequently used chart is *Mire #1*. These tests are approved by the International Standards Organization (ISO), and, for example, a $10\times$ ISO Mire #1 test chart requires $10\times$ magnification to restore the image to its original size. *Micromire* is a collection of these test charts.

mired a unit to classify a color filter or the color temperature of a light source Mired value is one million divided by the KELVIN value of a light source. The word *mired* is from microreciprocal degrees. A *decamired* is one-tenth of a mired.

mirror ball a sphere (ball) with many small mirrors attached to it Mirror balls may be hung from the ceilings of dance halls or discos and sometimes are used on theatrical sets, so that spotlights beamed at them as they revolve produce flashes of light.

mirror chalkboard a glass on which writing can be done, as with an art pen, used for displays in restaurants for menu specials

mirror lens a camera lens system with mirrors to reflect light rays up and down the lens tube so that focal lengths are increased

mirror shot [film] an image, or shot, of a performer as seen in a mirror; a method of increasing the sense of depth by shooting into a mirror; a shot made with a mirror to achieve a ghostly or transparent effect

MIS management information system

misbound describing a book or other work in which the pages are in improper order

misc. miscellaneous

miscast to assign a theatrical role that is unsuitable or inappropriate

mise en scène or **mise-en-scène** the staging or the overall composition or arrangement of a scene, including performers, scenery, and lighting; from the French *miser*, or "agreement"— hence the process of combining the elements of a scene Film critics use this term to describe a style of directing in which the camera (particularly by its positions) is actively involved in the image effect.

misprint a typographical error; to print incorrectly

misredemption the illegal redemption of coupons by individuals who have not purchased the product for which the coupons were issued

missal a prayer book Actually, the Missal is a book with all the services for celebrating Roman Catholic Mass throughout the year. *Missal caps* are decorative capital letters printed with blackletter, or gothic, type.

missionary salespeople individuals who provide assistance to retailers, sometimes actually working at the counter of a department store, as in cosmetics The individual represents the manufacturer, however.

mistracking improper movement of an audio or video tape past the head of a tape recorder, usually resulting in NOISE

Mitchell a 35mm film camera, manufactured by the C. H. Mitchell Company, of North Hollywood, CA The Mitchell has been used for several decades in the film industry, particularly the *NC* (a noiseless camera with four lenses) and *BNC* (one lens) models, which are very heavy, and the *Mitchell Mark II*, which is lighter in weight.

miter 1 to bring together two surfaces, usually at 45° angles, called *a miter joint* The angles can be measured with a *miter square*, or the pieces can be cut through a *miter box* to guide the saw. 2 [printing] to join lines or rules at angles less than 90° 3 in bookbinding, to join materials at an angle without overlapping

mix 1 to record separate soundtracks into a single track (*to subdub*), or to blend audio and visual components to produce a master (from which copies are made), an optical dissolve, a rerecording, or some other combination or mixture, called a mix

mixdown a combination of two or more audio sources, sometimes produced with a complex MIXER called an *automated mixdown* To *mix down* is to create such a combination.

mixer the unit that controls and blends audio and/or video signals; the technician who operates the unit (also called a *rerecording supervisor* or *chief recording mixer*) In a TV studio or on a film set, the work is done by a *floor mixer*. A *music mixer* edits recorded music. The *mixing console* (generally called simply a *mixer*) combines *premixed tracks* (as in the first phase of mixing) with signals from playback machines and other sources, including a *mixing panel* (a small mixer), based on instructions on a *mixing cue sheet*. An *active mixer* amplifies audio signals, usually with preamplifiers, thus compensating for loss of signal strength as the signals pass through the mixer. A *passive mixer* does not have its own electrical power or preamplifiers and the signal strength is reduced as it passes through it. The British call a video mixer a *vision mixer*.

mixing [typography] the setting of more than one typeface or point size in one word or one line

mix minus a feature that prevents a broadcaster from hearing his or her own voice echo back

mk. MARK

mkt. MARKET

mktg. MARKETING

mm MILLIMETER; million

MNA MULTINETWORK AREA

mnemonic a device or symbol to assist in remembering *Mnemonics* is a memory system using devices, such as pictures, famous names, common associations, or other cues to improve the storage and recall of tedious or complicated material. Note that the first *m* is silent.

MNS international telex abbreviation of *minutes*

mo. month (plural, *mos.*)

MO or **M.O.** MAIL ORDER

MO MOVE OUT

MOAL MAIL ORDER ACTION LINE

MOB mail order buyer

mobile communications cellular telephone, radio, and other signal-exchange equipment that is transportable

mobile unit a vehicle for originating broadcasts from on-the-spot locations, away from the studio, or for carrying equipment for on-location film or tape production; also called *mobile production unit*

Mobius annual awards given by the U.S. Television & Radio Commercials Festival, of Elmhurst, IL

mock interview a simulated interview, generally conducted by a professional communicator, to help develop the communications skills of the interviewee

mock-up or **mockup** a scale model or full-size three-dimensional replica

modality an arrangement, manner, or mode; the tendency to conform to a general pattern, type, or mode

mode 1 the particular condition or state under which a computer or other device may operate—for instance, *insert, delete,* or *merge mode, communications mode,* or *binary mode* Operations or commands may take on different meanings in different modes. 2 the typesetting style, such as justified (aligned at margin), ragged right (not aligned), or ragged left

model 1 an imitative representation of an entity, generally smaller, though it can be full size Set designers sometimes refer to a *model* as a part of a MINIATURE, such as a replica of a specific building in a set resembling a city. 2 a person who poses for a photographer or an artist (painter or sculptor), or to display clothing, as in a fashion show

modeling the three-dimensional appearance of a photograph or artwork created with lighting (in photography) or shading (in drawing); also called *chiaroscuro,* from the Italian *chiaro,* "light, clear," and *oscuro,* "dark"

model paper paper with various areas marked off to facilitate typing or paste-ups, with the area lines invisible to the camera when the work is photographed for printing For example, a printer may provide the customer with a special-size paper that serves as a convenience, since it is marked off in spacings equivalent to typewriter spacings. The type area has been marked according to the size of the finished book, finished type size, and camera setting.

model release a document signed by a photographic model allowing use of pictures of the individual

model sheet composite drawings of animated cartoon characters that are used as masters or guides by animation artists

model stock the amount of merchandise (inventory) and space in a retail store required for the full line or desired assortment of sizes, colors, and other variations of a product

modem acronym for *modulator/demodulator,* a device that converts a digital signal to an analog signal and vice versa, often used to communicate signals from a telephone line to a computer; also called a *data set*

modernism the style of artists, writers, and culture in general in the first half of the 20th century, featuring experimental techniques and other contemporary, or modern, practices *Postmodernism* (or *post-modernism*) refers to the period after modernism, roughly the second half of the 20th century.

modern style a kind of roman typeface, developed in the 18th and 19th centuries It is characterized by extreme contrast in the weight of the thin and thick strokes of the letters, sharp horizontal serifs, or small decorative lines, and a circular formation of the endings of several of the lowercase letters. A well-known example, still widely used, is Bodoni. Also called *modern type* or *modern-face roman,* it is more perpendicular than *old-face roman.*

modish in the current fashion or style

modular composed of standardized units, or *modules,* of flexible arrangement

modulate 1 to vary the tone, pitch, or volume of the voice 2 to change the frequency, phase, or amplitude of a carrier wave (as in radio transmission) A *modulator* is a device to change such a wave.

modulated stage the radio frequency stage to which the wave frequency adjuster (the modulator) is coupled and in which the continuous wave (carrier wave) is adjusted, or modulated, in accordance with the system (*AM* or *FM*) and the wave characteristics The modulator stage is the last part of the modulating wave. Thus the *amplitude modulator stage* is the last amplifier stage of the modulating wave that modulates a radio frequency stage.

module an interchangeable, self-contained component of a system

moiré **1** a fabric, such as silk, with a wavelike or watery appearance; a watered or wavy design produced on a fabric with engraved rollers or by superimposing one pattern over another; also spelled *moire* From the French *moirer*, meaning "to water," it is pronounced mwah-RAY. **2** [printing] a wavelike effect that sometimes results when photographing a halftone through a screen that is at an incorrect angle **3** [television] a wavelike distortion; also called *meshbeat, linebeat, herringbone,* or *crawling dot pattern*

mold **1** a hollow form; a matrix **2** [printing] a metal, plastic, or wax impression made from an original printing plate and used for making duplicate plates

mold-made paper a machine-made paper with a deckle (uneven or feather) edge and a texture resembling handmade paper

Molevator a type of mobile light stand, generally three-wheeled, that can be elevated

molly printer's slang for an *em*, a unit of linear measurement equal to the letter *M* in a typefont

MOM international telex abbreviation of *moment*, or wait or waiting; MIDDLE-OF-MONTH DATING

mom-and-pop store a small, family-operated shop In cable television and other fields, *mom-and-pop systems* are small, single-ownership local systems.

monarch a paper size, generally abut 7″ × 10″—smaller than standard 8½″ × 11″ letter-size—often used for personal stationery

monaural a monophonic or single-channel audio system, usually with one microphone and one speaker

Mondrian grid a traditional layout of vertical columns and rectangular boxes, named after the Dutch painter Piet Mondrian (1872–1944)

monitor **1** a device for checking or regulating performance—for instance, an instrument that receives TV signals by direct wire rather than over the air, as in a TV studio or closed circuit, sometimes without the sound **2** to record, verify, or check a radio or TV program, or to supervise, verify, or check any operation, such as an event, sales campaign, or computer program

monitoring service an organization that checks magazines, newspapers, and other publications for mention of a company or other client, or for other recording and evaluation purposes A *broadcast monitoring service* checks the electronic media.

monitor sheet a list of everything broadcast on one or more competing stations, used by pro-

grammers to determine the exact records or other items aired by the competition

monk an archaic expression for a heavy smudge or blotch of ink A *friar* was a lighter blot.

monochrome a painting, photograph, or other art in different shades of one color A *monochromatic* item has only one color, but a *monochrome combination*, with two tints of a color, may be considered a two-color printing process. *Monochromatic TV* is black-and-white.

monogram a design based on one or more letters, such as the interlaced initials of a name

monograph a learned or scholarly treatise

monologue or **monolog** a prolonged talk by a speaker; a dramatic soliloquy, as performed by a *monologuist* (also spelled *monologist*)

monopod having one leg A *monopod camera* is mounted on one pole or column, as compared to a *bipod* (two legs) or *tripod* (three legs).

monopole **1** an advertisement erected on a single steel pole or column, as in a shopping mall or a transportation terminal; also called *unipole* **2** a single-rod indoor antenna

monoseal a MONOGRAM forming a shape, especially suggesting the form of a seal or insignia

monospace a typeface in which each character has an identical ESCAPEMENT VALUE, as on a typewriter with a fixed-unit spacing system, as distinct from proportional spacing, in which the spaces vary In monospacing (as on typewriters and line printers), each character receives the same amount of horizontal space.

monotonal type a typeface with strokes of equal weight and no serifs (small decorative lines), such as gothic

monotype a one-of-a-kind print, made from a metal or glass plate on which a picture is painted or inked; also, the method itself of making such unique prints

Monotype a trademarked tape-driven, hot-metal typesetting machine that produces individual characters and sets each in a justified line (aligned at the margins), as with tabular data It was invented by Tolbert Lanston (1844–1913) about 1888 and originally made by Lanston Monotype Machine Company, in Philadelphia.

montage a combination of clippings, photographs, artwork, or other materials, which may overlap each other or be positioned irregularly, to create an overall effect In motion pictures, a montage is produced by dissolving into each other a series of different photos or scenes, often to indicate the passage of time. Among the various types of montage are *straight cuts* (abrupt transitions) and *soft cuts* (gradual changes, with bridges or other effects). In the *Hollywood mon-*

tage, the images overlap, often with rapid dissolves.

Monte Carlo method   any technique for estimating via sample observations   It's chancy; hence the reference to Monte Carlo gambling.

monthly   a monthly publication, such as a magazine or journal   A periodical may not be published during one or more months, such as during the summer, or it may be published twice during one or more months and still be called a *monthly.*

month preceding   the 30-day period immediately before the time of publication of a periodical, used to specify the closing date for receipt of material

mood   emotional state   *Mood music,* or background music, is designed to establish or create a state of mind, feeling, or impression.

mopic   military word for motion picture

MOR   MIDDLE OF THE ROAD; MARKET OPINION RESEARCH

morality play   a type of allegorical drama, popular in the 15th and 16th centuries, in which the characters personified moral qualities, including virtues and vices   The best-known morality play is *Everyman* (late 15th century).

moray   [television] a video disturbance caused by flashy jewelry, brightly colored apparel, or other sources, commonly called a *moray pattern,* named after a type of brightly colored eel called a moray

more   a direction written at the bottom of a page to indicate that it is not the last page and that more material is coming, immediately or at a later time   The expression generally is written as - *more* - and sometimes as *more/more.*

morgue   a library or reference department or collection, particularly in a newspaper   The word originates from the file of biographies prepared in advance of the death of prominent individuals.

morocco   leather made from goatskin, used for fine-quality books for many centuries but now rarely used   The leather was first made by the Moors in northern Africa. Types of *morocco binding* include *French morocco* and *Turkish morocco* (fine-grained), *Levant morocco* (coarse-grained leather from goats in the Levant area along the eastern Mediterranean), *Niger morocco* (leather tanned with the sumac plant on the banks of the Niger River), and *Persian morocco* (very fine-grained leather).

morpheme   the smallest meaningful unit in a language, an affix (such as *con, dis,* or *un*) or a base (such as *do* in *undo*); an element of language that indicates the relationship between words (SEMANTENES) or parts of words and has

no smaller meaningful part, such as *and, but, if, nor, not, or,* or *with*

Morris, William   a major talent agency   The full name is *William Morris Agency Inc.*   Formed in 1898 by William Morris, it is headquartered in New York.

mortise   **1** a cutout area for the insertion of art   **2** to kern hot-metal type by removing pieces of metal from the "white-space" areas of character molds so that two characters will fit together more closely (see also KERNING)   *Mortise copy* (also called *white inset*) generally is black type in a white box within the black background of a picture.

mos.   months

MOS   **1** MAN ON THE STREET   **2** METAL OXIDE SEMICONDUCTOR   **3** a direction that no sound is to be recorded during the filming of a scene, or an indication that the film is silent; loosely derived from the German *mit-out sprache* ("without sound").

mosaic or **mozaic**   **1** a picture or decoration made with small pieces, such as colored glass and stones or overlapping photographs (as with aerial photos patched together to form a continuous map or composite picture); pronounced moe-ZAY-ic   **2** [television] the photosensitive plate in the camera tube   It has about 367 microscopic dots; the picture is formed in a pattern of electrical charges on the mosaic.   **3** a type of bookbinding, called *mosaic binding,* composed of fine-quality leather into which other kinds of leather or other decorations are inserted

motif   a recurring or dominant subject theme, idea, or technique in an artistic, literary, musical, or other work

motion analysis camera (MAC)   a camera that operates at extremely high speed, so that several thousand frames can be photographed, as in films for scientific research or industrial use

motion-control photography   a technique, using a tape or computer, to control, record, and repeat the movements of a camera   It is used in animation and special effects.

motion picture   a moving picture, movie, or cinefilm: a sequence of individual still photography, with or without sound, projected at speeds ranging from 16 to 24 frames (single images) per second to give the appearance of continuous motion   A *motion-picture camera* exposes *motion-picture film,* to be run through a *motion-picture projector,* perhaps produced by a *motion-picture company* for showing in a *motion-picture,* or *movie, theater.* The term *motion pictures* refers to the medium (the motion-picture industry) and also to the product. Some people prefer the word *film.*

Motion Picture Association of America (MPAA) the largest organization, based in New York, of producers and distributors of motion pictures, television, and home video

motion-picture guilds groups of artists and technicians involved in film production Organizations include the *Motion Picture Costumers* (Hollywood), *Motion Picture Editors Guild* (Los Angeles), *Motion Picture Illustrators & Matte Artists* (Los Angeles), *Motion Picture Screen Cartoonists* (North Hollywood), *Motion Picture Studio Cinetechnicians* (Hollywood), and *Motion Picture Studio Grips* (Los Angeles), all of which are locals of IATSE.

motivational research study of the reasons that consumers make purchases or respond to products, advertising, and other stimuli The application of psychological and other probing techniques, as in focus groups and individual interviews, is an essential part of market research. A *motive*, or *drive*, is a desire, impulse, or stimulated need that is sufficiently pressing to direct the person toward the goal of satisfying that urge. Buying choices and other actions are influenced by four major psychological processes— motivation, perception, learning, and beliefs and attitudes.

motivation lighting theatrical lighting from an overhead light or stage light that mimics the light from a prop, such as a floor lamp or table lamp

MOTO Awards annual awards to journalists and public relations practitioners, presented by the National Automotive Journalism Association, Las Vegas, NV MOTO refers to automotive.

motorboating undesired audio-frequency oscillation in a low-frequency circuit, akin to the putt-putt sound of a motorboat

motor cue the first of two small circles shown in the upper right corner of a movie screen close to the end of a reel to alert the projectionist to start the motor of the projector with the next reel The second circle is the CHANGEOVER CUE.

mottle a spot or blotch; a variegated pattern (as in marble) In printing, *mottling* is a speckled appearance that results from dirty ink or other flaws. In bookbinding, *mottled calf* is a calfskin binding with a variegated pattern produced by acid or ink; it is called *tree calf* when the pattern resembles gnarled wood grain.

mount an object to which another is affixed or on which another is placed for accessibility, display, or other use—for instance, a board on which a photograph or artwork is posted; a camera platform; a base to support a printing plate or other item Types of satellite antenna mounts include *AZ/EL mount* (two angular set-

tings, the azimuth, or rotation, and elevation, or tilt), *horizon-to-horizon mount* (motorized for 180-degree rotation), *patio mount* (commonly used for small dish antennas mounted on home patios), and *polar mount* (motorized for rotation). In advertising displays, a *mounter* is an individual, studio, or firm that does *mounting*, generally on a *mounting board*. There is even a New York Mounters Association. An *optical mounter* is an apparatus that cuts, positions, and secures microfilm (miniaturized photography of documents) in APERTURE CARDS in a single step.

mouse 1 a small pad or sponge to pick up excess rubber cement from a paste-up; also called *pickup* 2 a hand-held controller of material on the video screen of a computer The mouse has a button on top and is connected by a cable to a computer; moving the mouse on a table activates an arrow or cursor, or indicator light, on the video screen to move correspondingly. The *Stanford mouse* is a type of activator that looks like a mouse on roller skates. *The Mouse* is a Wall Street nickname for the Disney Corporation.

mouse type [typography] slang for very small type

mousy or **mousey** pale in color, weak

movable type type that is cast as individual, single-character units, capable of being combined into words and then, after printing, redistributed and reused Movable type was developed by Johann Gutenberg, a German printer, in the 15th century.

move 1 to transmit text over a newswire or other communications medium, as in *to move a story* 2 an instruction to a typesetter to change the position of copy, often written in the margin of a proof to indicate that material should be repositioned

move in (MI) a direction to move a camera or microphone closer to the subject

move out (MO) a direction to move a camera or microphone away from the subject

move-out bulletin a memorandum sent to exhibitors, containing instruction about disassembling their displays at the end of a trade show or similar event

movie a film, a moving picture, shown in a *movie theater*, on television, or elsewhere Large, ornate movie theaters, built in the 1930s, were called *movie palaces. Home movies* are made by amateurs, generally featuring their families, for showing on their own projectors in their own homes. The word *movie* now is used as a synonym for a videotape production. A *made-for-television* movie is a motion picture made primarily for showing on TV.

movie of the week (MOW) a theatrical film or a made-for-television film shown weekly on television

Moviescope a small boxlike device for viewing and editing sound film

Movietone a trademarked sound-on-film process, one of the earliest sound systems, used by the Fox Film Corporation—the predecessor of 20th Century-Fox—originally in 1927 and for several decades following for its Fox Movietone newsreels The *Movietone frame* is the standard frame of sound film with an aspect ratio of 4:3 or 1.33:1, which was the width-to-height ratio in the early years of sound film.

moving off movement by a subject away from the camera or microphone; also called *fade off*

moving on movement by a subject closer to the camera or microphone; also called *fade on*

moving shot a filming or videotaping technique in which the camera follows the action; also called *follow shot, running shot,* or *action shot*

Moviola the trade name for an upright film-editing machine that reproduces film in miniature The generic spelling for this type of machine—which also reproduces sound—is *movieola.* Though once ubiquitous in film-editing rooms, the Moviola has been replaced by flatbed editing machines, or horizontal tables, and also by videotape editing processes.

MOW MOVIE OF THE WEEK

mozaic alternate spelling of MOSAIC

MPA MAGAZINE PUBLISHERS ASSOCIATION

MPAA MOTION PICTURE ASSOCIATION OF AMERICA

MPS MAIL PREFERENCE SERVICE

mr MOTIVATIONAL RESEARCH

MR MEDIA RECORDS INC.

MRB Group Inc. a market research company located in New York A subsidiary of the *WPP* Group, MRB includes SIMMONS Market Research Bureau and WINONA Market Research.

MS MEDIUM SHOT

ms, ms., or **MS.** MANUSCRIPT

MSA METROPOLITAN STATISTICAL AREA

MSI McCOLLUM/SPIELMAN INTERNATIONAL

MSO MULTIPLE SYSTEM OPERATOR

M.T. **1** MAGNETIC TAPE **2** Mountain Time, the area west of the *Central* and east of the *Pacific* time zones Its clock readings are one hour earlier than those in the Central Time Zone. The two types are *M.S.T. (Mountain Standard Time)* and *M.D.T. (Mountain Daylight Time).* The Mountain zone includes Denver and other large cities, but, because its total population is lower than in the other three time zones in the continental U.S. *(Eastern* is the third), many commu-

nicators—particularly Easterners—know little about M.T. markets.

MTST MAGNETIC-TAPE SELECTRIC TYPEWRITER

MTV MUSIC TELEVISION

muck [theater] slang for greasepaint, particularly clown white, an opaque white greasepaint used by clowns; see also MUCKRAKE

muckrake to search for and expose alleged or real corruption or wrongdoing, as by an investigative reporter (a *muckraker*) *Muck* is filth or manure.

muddy lacking clarity or contrast, as in a photograph; dull

mug a face A *mug shot* is a photograph of the face or of the head and shoulders. *Mugging* is the display of exaggerated facial expressions, as by a performer.

mull a coarse gauze or starched cotton used to reinforce the back of a book; also called *crash* or *super*

Mullen tester a machine for determining the bursting strength of a paper, expressed as a *percent Mullen*

muller a device to grind substances, such as printing pigments A *muller tester* usually is hand-operated, for small quantities; an automatic muller, used for large quantities, is power-driven.

mult box an electrical device that combines and regulates the flow of electricity and distributes a regulated or consistent audio feed It is used by radio and TV crews, particularly at events with considerable equipment tapping into the speaker's lectern or other site.

multicam the use of two or more cameras simultaneously to shoot a scene from more than one angle

multicasting the simultaneous transmission of two or more programs or signals on the same station frequency; also called *multiplex system* It is used by networks to provide greater flexibility to advertisers by targeting programs and commercials to specific audiences or areas. It also makes possible reception of radio signals in stereo.

multidimensional scaling a survey technique with paired comparisons that result in three-dimensional models to position a company, product, or other entity

Multigraph a trademarked machine for typesetting and rotary printing, in which the type is moved, by keys, from a typesetting drum to a printing drum The process formerly was popular for producing form letters, using a wide ribbon and type mounted on a drum or flatbed press. The Addressograph-Multigraph machines made by AM International, Inc., Chicago, and others like them still are used, for a variety of purposes; the term *multigraphed letter*, however, has come to refer to a printed form letter.

multilevel marketing plan a technique in which sellers—often door-to-door—are encouraged to recruit other sellers, so that they can receive commissions from the sales made by their recruits; also called *pyramid plan*

Multilith a trademarked press that prints from paper masters rather than metal plates It is manufactured by AM International, Chicago, formerly Addressograph-Multigraph.

multimedia the combination of two or more types of media, such as live performance and videotape, in the same show or presentation; the use of more than one medium, such as oil and watercolor, in the same painting, also called *mixed media* A *multimedia kit* is a collection of items, such as filmstrips, posters, and videotapes, in one package, used in schools and elsewhere.

multinetwork area (MNA) a compilation, prepared by the A. C. NIELSEN COMPANY, that provides estimates of TV audience size in areas served by the three major TV networks (American Broadcasting Companies, Columbia Broadcasting System, and National Broadcasting Company) *MNA ratings*, issued weekly, are conducted by Nielsen in the top TV markets—about 70—in which the three networks compete.

multiplane camera a film-animation device that mounts and lights the CELS to create the illusion of depth

multiple branding a marketing system in which each item within a line of products is identified separately—that is, each has its own brand name The technique differs from *family branding*, in which a company name or other easily recognized identity is associated with a group of products.

multiple pricing the practice of offering more than one retail unit for sale at a single unit price, such as three for 50 cents

multiple processing a procedure used by the A. C. NIELSEN COMPANY to clarify information about the TV viewing habits of various members of a household, so that data can be released about households rather than about individuals

multiple submission the practice of submitting manuscripts of a book or other work simultaneously to more than one potential publisher or producer

multiple system operator (MSO) a company that owns and operates more than one cable-TV system

multiple-unit sale a reduced price involving more than one item

multiple voice referring to a commercial on which more than one speaker is heard

multiplex referring to the simultaneous communication of two or more messages on the same wire or radio channel; the merging of audio and video signals onto a single transmission channel; the channeling of signals from several sources into one camera or system

multipoint distribution service (MDS) a system using omnidirectional microwave signals to carry data, text, and other video services to subscribers MSD is over-the-air (not cable), line-of-sight broadcasting to homes, offices, and other locations with specially equipped antennas.

multiscreen referring to a system in which several screens—generally three—and projectors are used The setup, sometimes used at exhibitions and fairs, enables several slides and/or films to be shown simultaneously on the combined screen.

multisystem radio a radio receiver that automatically adjusts to stereo signals

multitracking a technique of recording sound on sound If unintentional, it's called *overdubbing*.

multivision 1 referring to a MULTISCREEN presentation, using an assembly of screens for a multi-image 2 referring to the juxtaposition of several images on one frame

Multi-Vision an outdoor advertising device See also TRI-VISION.

multo ring a loose-leaf binder that has a number of rings one-half inch apart

mumbo jumbo gibberish, obscure or meaningless talk The word probably originates from an 18th-century African dialect in which *jumby* was a ghost or an evil spirit

mummer a person who wears a mask, disguise, or costume for fun In the Middle Ages, *mummers* were the actors who celebrated Christmas and festive occasions; the Philadelphia Mummers, a group of musicians in that city, has continued this tradition. By extension, a *mummer* is any actor or performer. *Mummery* is a performance by mummers and also a display or ceremony that is pretentious or hypocritical.

Munsell color scale a system of charts used in color television to verify HUE, brilliance, and CHROMA

mural a large painting, photograph, or other work of art affixed to a wall, ceiling, or other surface

MUS a script notation for MUSIC

muse the spirit that is believed to inspire a poet or other artist, the source of genius or imagination In Greek mythology, the Muses were nine goddesses who presided over the arts and sciences: *Calliope*—eloquence and epic poetry; *Clio*—history; *Erato*—erotic lyric poetry; *Euterpe*—music and lyric poetry; *Melpomene*—tragedy; *Polyhymnia* (also *Polymnia*)—songs to the gods (sacred poetry); *Terpsichore*—dance; *Thalia*—comedy and pastoral poetry; and *Urania*—astronomy.

mushy   maudlin, sentimental, and soft (from the thick cereal called *mush*), as in a *mushy script*

music   a combination of vocal or instrumental sounds or tones in varying harmony, melody, rhythm, and timbre   A *musical* is a stage, film, or other work featuring songs and music, and generally dance, such as a musical comedy. The individual who is in charge of hiring the players, or *musicians*, often is the *musician contractor*. A *music arranger* adapts existing music for specific performers or a specific production. In film and TV, the *music department* creates or acquires music and supervises its performance. A *music recording supervisor* is responsible for the recording of music on the soundtrack. A *music editor*, or *music mixer*, edits the music and coordinates it with the picture during the post-production, assisted by an *assistant music editor*.

musical   a film, theatrical, or other production in which the music is the major component, such as a musical comedy, in which the plot often is funny, seriocomic (partly serious), or completely serious (a *musical play* or *musical drama*)

musical contractor   a person who hires musical performers

musical director   a person in charge of music for a film, TV, theatrical, or other production, including arranging for the composer (if original music) and supervising the recording or scoring sessions   The musical director may also be the composer or orchestra conductor.

musicale   a party or social affair that features a musical program

Music Corporation of America   See MCA.

music cues   directions that indicate the volume, level, starting and stopping time, and other changes for music used in films or television   *Music down* is an instruction to reduce the volume; *music fade*, to reduce it slowly until inaudible; *music in*, to start; *music in and under*, to start and then reduce (also called *music up and under*); *music out*, to stop; and *music up and out*, to increase and then stop.

music director (MD)   a person at a radio station who selects records to be broadcast and usually reports to the program director

music hall   a movie theater that presents live entertainment and films, such as *Radio City Music Hall* in New York, or a theater for variety shows   It is not a concert hall, which presents live musical performances, especially of classical music.

music sweep   the practice, in radio, of broadcasting several records, tapes, or disks consecutively without interruption; also called *music segue* (pronounced SEG-way)

Music Television (MTV)   a cable network company, formerly owned by Warner Amex Satellite Entertainment and now owned by Viacom   It is headquartered in New York and provides several advertiser-supported music-video program services, including the MTV network, "Nickelodeon" (for children), and VH-1 (Video Hits One).

music track   [film] the component of the soundtrack devoted to music, as edited by a *music editor* or *music mixer*   The other two components are dialogue and sound effects.

must   an executive order to indicate that an article or other copy *must* be printed   It is sometimes called *business office must*, and the abbreviation *B. O. Must* appears at the top of the article. *Must story* is a term used at *The Wall Street Journal* and elsewhere to indicate a high-priority article.

must-carries   a former reference to the TV stations in a market, all of which had to be carried by the cable-TV system in that market in accordance with the Federal Communications Commission's *mandatory carriage rule*. In 1985, this requirement was ruled illegal.

mut-and-nut   a style of indenting type one EN (or *nut*) at the end of each line, used in newspapers to create white space between columns

mute   a device used to soften or muffle sound   Mutes are used on musical instruments—for instance, the cone placed in the bell of a trumpet or the piece set onto the bridge of a violin. Millions of TV viewers are familiar with the *mute button* on their remote-control devices. When the button is pressed, the sound is cut off, and, on some sets, the word MUTE is displayed on the screen.

mute negative   a movie negative without a soundtrack   A *mute print* also lacks a soundtrack.

mutt   an EM space; also called *mutton*   The word is used by printers so that the em quad is not confused with the EN, or *nut*, which is half the width of an em.

Mutual Broadcasting System   a radio network, headquartered in Alexandria, VA   Formed in 1934, Mutual was one of the pioneers in broadcasting. It does not own any stations and is still a radio programming service.

Muzak   recorded background music (called *functional music*) transmitted by wire to thousands of locations, including elevators, professional offices, and factories   The music is noted for its innocuous quality. The system is operated by Muzak, Inc., a division of Group W Cable, in New York.

Mylar   a trademarked polyester film, made by du Pont, of Wilmington, DE, used in recording tape and in the STRIPPING phase of printing

mystery play   a type of medieval drama, popular before the 16th century, about biblical events, particularly the life and death of Jesus, often presented by craft guilds in marketplaces   It is sometimes called a *miracle play*, though most of the miracle plays (about saints and divine events) were performed earlier; see also MORALITY PLAY.

mystery shopper   a person who poses as a customer in a store for quality testing, on behalf of the store owner, or for other purposes, on behalf of a supplier to the store

Mystery Writers of America   an organization in New York of writers of mystery stories   It presents an annual prize, appropriately called the *Edgar Allan Poe Award* (or "the Edgars").

myth   a traditional story of unknown authorship, frequently involving the exploits of gods, heroes, or imaginary persons; a fictitious story or unscientific account or belief   *Mythology* is the study of myths, a book of or about myths, or myths collectively.

N

n or N EN, a printing measurement; noon; note; noun; number An *N* following a page number in an index indicates that the indexed item is in a FOOTNOTE on that page.

N narrow An *N-format* in a newspaper uses narrow columns, such as eight columns on a page. *N-matter* is type or other material set in narrow columns.

NA international telex abbreviation: correspondence to this number is not permitted

N.A. NIGHT ANSWER; NO ANSWER; not applicable; not available

NAB NATIONAL ASSOCIATION OF BROADCASTERS; NEWSPAPER ADVERTISING BUREAU

N.A.B. code standards established by the NATIONAL ASSOCIATION OF BROADCASTERS for acceptance and content of commercials and other guidelines for stations Some independent stations did not adhere to the code and accepted advertisements for drugs or other items not advertised on *code stations*. The code was dropped in 1982 because of antitrust concerns of the Justice Department.

nabes local movie theaters, generally showing films after their initial run *Nabe* is short for neighborhood.

NABET NATIONAL ASSOCIATION OF BROADCAST EMPLOYEES AND TECHNICIANS

NABTS NORTH AMERICAN BASIC TELETEXT SPECIFICATION

N.A.D. NATIONAL ADVERTISING DIVISION

NAFB National Association of Farm Broadcasters, based in Topeka, KS

Nagra a line of audiotape recorders commonly used in the film industry, made by Nagra Magnetic Recorders, Inc., of Los Angeles

nailed down merchandise that a retailer makes every effort *not* to sell, such as low-priced advertised items used as *bait* to attract customers

nailhead a paperback book with a thick SPINE resembling the head of a nail

NAK negative acknowledgment, a Teletype or other communication code for *No!* or *message not received*

naked column text without a headline or art at its top

name well-known, as with a *name brand* or a *name performer* A *big name* is very well known.

name-and-date system a method of citing references within the text in parentheses rather than at the bottom of the page in FOOTNOTES

name index an index in which the entries are names of persons and organizations cited or referred to in the text; not precisely the same as an *author index*, which also may have entries of authors

nameplate the name of a periodical as it appears on the front page and at the top of other pages; also, a piece of metal or other material on which a name appears In the automotive industry, the name of a line of cars, such as Cadillac or Lincoln, is its nameplate.

name slug a LOGOTYPE

name-title reference a FOOTNOTE, BIBLIOGRAPHIC item, or other reference to an author and title, such as *refer from* or *refer to*

nano one billionth, from *nanus*, Latin for "dwarf" A *nanosecond* is one billionth of a second, or a *millimicrosecond*.

NAPL NATIONAL ASSOCIATION OF PRINTERS AND LITHOGRAPHERS

NAPLPS NORTH AMERICAN PRESENTATION LEVEL PROTOCOL SYNTAX

NAPTS National Association of Public Television Stations, based in Washington, DC

NAR script notation for NARRATION

NARAS NATIONAL ACADEMY OF RECORDING ARTS AND SCIENCES

narration the telling of a story or happenings, or the story or account itself *Narrative writing* or a *narrative* is an account as related by a *narrator*, perhaps as a *narrative passage* between scenes. A *narrative film* or play tells a story, generally dramatic, not comedic. In film and other media, an *unauthorized narration* is talking—narration—by a character who allegedly is unaware that the audience is listening, as when dreaming or talking to himself. A *narration script* is read by a narrator, as at a voice-over recording session. The *narrative present* is the time in which the primary action of a film or other work takes place.

narrowband a communication channel that transmits data at relatively slow speed, up to 200 BITS per second The reduced BANDWIDTH improves the signal-to-noise ratio. Stereo audio generally is *wideband;* monaural often is narrowband.

narrowcast a broadcast targeted to specific demographics or audience interest Narrowcasts are broadcast by financial, health, sports, and weather cable networks, among others, and are common in radio.

narrow lighting a type of illumination sometimes used in studios for portrait photography in which the lighting on the side of the face toward the camera is reduced, thus balancing the shadow area of the side away from the camera; also called *short lighting*

NASCA National Association for Corporate Speaker Activities, an organization based in Dayton, OH It presents the annual BECK AWARD.

NASDAQ *National Association of Securities Dealers automated quotations,* the system of reporting bid and asked prices for over-the-counter stocks

Nashville Network a cable-TV network oriented toward country music, owned by GROUP W Satellite Communications in Stamford, CT

NASTA National Association of State Textbook Administrators, Oklahoma City, OK *NASTA specifications* are the textbook manufacturing standards required of books sold to public schools.

NATAS NATIONAL ACADEMY OF TELEVISION ARTS AND SCIENCES

National Academy of Recording Arts and Sciences (NARAS) an association of the recording industry, based in Burbank, CA

National Academy of Television Arts and Sciences (NATAS) an organization of individuals in all areas of television, headquartered in New York, that presents the annual EMMY AWARDS

national account a chain of stores or a major customer of a manufacturer or other seller This customer may be served directly by the manufacturer, rather than through a broker or other intermediary, and may be given special services. The opposite is a *local account.*

National Advertising Division (N.A.D.) a component of the Council of Better Business Bureaus that reviews complaints about accuracy in advertising Supported by the American Advertising Federation, American Association of Advertising Agencies, Association of National Advertisers, and Council of Better Business Bu-

reaus, it was formed in 1972 and was originally called the *National Advertising Review Board.* It is based in Arlington, VA.

National Analysts a market research company in Philadelphia; a division of Booz, Allen & Hamilton, a New York management consulting company formed in 1943

National Association of Broadcast Employees and Technicians (NABET) an AFL-CIO union in Washington, DC, of about 9,000 technical workers in broadcasting, at over 50 locals, including many engineers at NBC The ones in New York are Locals 11 and 16. NABET is a rival of IBEW (*International Brotherhood of Electrical Workers*).

National Association of Broadcasters (NAB) a major organization of radio and TV stations and networks, based in Washington, DC Founded in 1922, it has a staff of over 100 and holds a prominent annual convention.

National Association of Printers and Lithographers (NAPL) a major association of the printing industry, based in Teaneck, NJ

National Association of Television Program Executives See NATPE INTERNATIONAL.

national audience composition an A.C. NIELSEN CO. term to describe audiences of TV programs as described in such reports as the National Audience Demographics Report, with information about individual viewers and households

national bibliography a list of books of or about a country

national biography a book or collection of biographies of people of a country

National Black Network a radio network headquartered in New York that provides programming to about 100 AM and FM stations in the United States

National Book Awards annual awards for literary excellence presented in November by National Book Awards, Inc., a nonprofit organization based in New York The awards were presented for many years by the Association of American Publishers. From 1950 to 1979, they were called the National Book Awards; the name then was changed to the *American Book Awards* but now is back to National. More importantly, they are no longer presented by the Association of American Publishers, though many people, even in the book industry, still don't know this. The American Book Awards are presented by the Before Columbus Foundation, based at the University of Washington at Seattle.

National Broadcasting Company (NBC) the oldest of the broadcasting networks, formed in 1926 as part of *Radio Corporation of America,* which owned radio stations Now owned by GENERAL ELECTRIC CO., NBC owns TV stations and provides programming to affiliated stations.

National Cable Television Association (NCTA) the Washington, DC-based association, founded in 1952, of operators, manufacturers, and others in the cable television industry

National Composition Association an Arlington, VA, organization representing the typesetting industry It is an affiliate of the PRINTING INDUSTRIES OF AMERICA.

National Council of Editorial Writers an organization in Rockville, MD, of editorial writers for major newspapers It publishes *The Masthead.*

National Family Opinion a market research company in Greenwich, CT, whose exact name is NFO RESEARCH

National Film Board (NFB) a Canadian government agency founded in 1939 and headquartered in Montreal, Quebec, that produces films, including world-renowned animated shorts and documentaries

National Investor Relations Institute (NIRI) a major organization of executives in investor relations based in Washington, DC The abbreviation is pronounced NEAR-ee.

National Magazine Awards annual awards of the AMERICAN SOCIETY OF MAGAZINE EDITORS in New York

National Media Conference and Public Relations Forum an annual conference in New York, started in 1979 by Larimi Communications and conducted since 1988 by MERComm Inc.

national newspaper a newspaper that is circulated throughout the country, such as the *Christian Science Monitor, The New York Times, USA Today,* or *The Wall Street Journal* Outside the United States, in countries with smaller areas such as those of the United Kingdom, national newspapers are more common.

National Newspaper Association a Washington, DC, organization of editors and publishers of about 6,000 newspapers, mostly weeklies and small dailies

National Postal Forum an annual meeting of business mailers and postal officials to discuss common problems and solutions, alternately held in Washington, DC, and at a regional site

National Press Club (NPC) an organization of newspeople, located in the National Press Building in Washington, DC

National Press Photographers Association an organization in Durham, NC, of print and TV news photographers

National Public Radio (NPR) an organization that produces and distributes programs to noncommercial radio stations Funded primarily by member stations, it is based in Washington, DC.

national rate an advertising rate charged by local media to national or regional advertisers, generally higher than the local advertising rate

National Research Group a market research company in Los Angeles that primarily conducts audience surveys in the film industry Founded in 1978, it was acquired in 1988 by Saatchi & Saatchi, the British advertising conglomerate.

National School Public Relations Association an organization in Arlington, VA, of public relations directors of school systems

national spot radio or TV time purchased by a national advertiser from a station rather than via a network It is commonly called a *spot,* though a spot is any commercial, including a local spot purchased by a local advertiser.

National Television System Committee (NTSC) a unit of the Federal Communications Commission, Washington, DC, that establishes television standards in the United States, such as *NTSC Color,* a standard for color that also can be received on black-and-white sets

national trading area a primary area of shopping, different from a *fringe trading area;* sometimes called *primary trade zone,* in contrast to *secondary trade zone*

National Yellow Pages Service Association (NYPSA) a promotion group, based in Troy, MI, for advertising in classified telephone directories

natl national

NATPE International an organization based in New York, formerly called the *National Association of Television Program Executives*

natsot natural sound or ambience

NAT sound NATURAL SOUND; more commonly called *ambient sound* and sometimes *wild sound, background, background sound,* or *BG sound*

natural finish [book production] a soft finish given to book cloth

natural fold a GATEFOLD or other printed piece with a text that flows and is not disjointed as the piece is unfolded

natural sound animal noises, weather conditions, and other actual sounds recorded for broadcast or other use, as contrasted with *artificial sound* or *sound effects*

navigation [videotex] the movement within a videotex system, such as from FRAME to frame, subject to subject, or DATABASE to database, based on *menu* choices

n.b. or N.B. *nota bene,* Latin for "note well," an instruction to take particular notice

NB NARROWBAND

NBC National Broadcasting Company

NBI Nielsen Broadcast Index, a measurement of Canadian TV audiences conducted by the A. C. Nielsen Co.

NC no charge; no circuits available, an international abbreviation; non-color-sensitized emulsion

NCEW National Council of Editorial Writers

NCH international telex abbreviation: subscriber's number has been changed

N connector a device to connect *coaxial* cable that is commonly used in the TV industry, including a large screw-in N connector and a smaller twist-lock type—a *baby N connector* or *BNC*

NCR No Carbon Required paper; no change in rate, a notice in a contract that the advertising charge may not be increased without notification and approval by the customer

NCT National College Television, a cable network operated by Campus Network of New York

NCTA National Cable Television Association, Inc.

ND neutral density filter; news director; nondirectional microphone

ND or **n.d.** no date

ND filter neutral density filter

NDM newspaper designated market, the geographical area that a newspaper considers to be the one it serves Newspaper publishers may report their circulation by city zone, retail trading zone, or *newspaper designated market*. Since these definitions are established with the approval of the Audit Bureau of Circulations (ABC), the markets sometimes are called *ABC-NDM*.

NDT no dial tone (of a telephone)

NE or **NEP** *new edition pending* of a book

NEA Newspaper Enterprise Association, a newspaper syndicate owned by United Features Syndicate, based in New York

Neal Awards annual awards for editorial excellence in business, trade, and professional periodicals, named for Jesse H. Neal and presented by the Association of Business Publishers, based in New York

near pack a product offered free or at a special price as a premium with the purchase of another product displayed adjacent to it or nearby, perhaps in a *near-pack display* The promotion of a near-pack premium is called a *near-pack event*.

near point [photography] a spot within an area that is closest to the camera and still sharply in focus

near-print typed copy, photographed and reproduced by *offset,* such as news releases Near-print means *nearly printed.*

near-print publication a work reproduced by a mimeograph or copying machine rather than on a printing press; also called *processed publication* As copying machines become more sophisticated, as in color copying machines, the term near-print becomes less precise.

Nebula Awards annual awards to science fiction authors, presented by the *Science Fiction Writers of America* of Wharton, NJ

neck the upright side between the shoulder and face of the projecting character on a piece of type

neck line the amount of space under a heading, particularly a running head at the top of each page

needle a pointed stylus that transmits vibrations from the grooves of a phonograph record; a pointer on a dial To *bend* or *peg the needle* is to increase the sound until the volume-indicator needle hits the top of the scale. *Needle chatter* or *needle talk* is noise created or picked up by the stylus on a phonograph record.

needle drop the use of a recording in a broadcast or other production Usage fees often are based on the number of needle drops in a program.

need to know a security policy that limits distribution of materials or access to information to trustworthy individuals whose duties require such access This label indicates less tight security than "Top Secret" but is generally more confidential than items marked "Confidential."

negative (neg. or **neg)** the reversed image of an original in which light areas appear dark and vice versa; as most commonly used, a film, plate, or other photographic material containing such an image, such as black-and-white or color still and motion-picture film stock A *negative photostat* is a photostat in reverse values. A *thin negative* is underexposed or underdeveloped and appears less dense.

A completed movie also is called a negative; the negative cost is all production expenses, including the final answer print made from the final negative. *Negative pickup* or *pickup* is an arrangement in which a movie studio buys and distributes an independently produced film. *Negative numbers* are a series of four- to six-digit numbers at intervals of 6 to 12 inches on the edge of negative film; they are more commonly called *edge numbers*.

negative acknowledge (NAK) a statement indicating that a message was received with errors, indicated by pressing an *NAK character key*, the opposite of the acknowledge (ACK) character

negative advertising a commercial or other advertising that deprecates and is downbeat, as by pointing out the terrible consequences of life without the sponsor's product or life with the competitive product that is attacked

negative cost [film] the cost of production of a film prior to its release, exclusive of distribution and promotion

negative cutter [film] a person who edits—cuts—an original NEGATIVE to match the final WORKPRINT; also called a *negative matcher* or *conformer* and supervised by a film editor The process, called *negative cutting*, generally is done in a *cutting room*.

negative option a technique used in direct response marketing whereby the recipient must notify the seller if he or she does not wish to order or purchase It is often used by book and record clubs.

negative pulling a motion picture process of cutting the original negative to match the EDGE NUMBERS on the work print

negative spacing [typography] the placement of letters with less than the standard space between them

negs abbreviation for film NEGATIVES

NEMO a remote pickup, a broadcast not originated by the station transmitting it; pronounced NEE-moe The acronym is for *not emanating from main office*.

neologism a new word or a new meaning for an existing word; the use of such coined words

nest a set of objects of graduated size that can be stacked together; a set of sequential data or related procedures, such as, in word processing, *nested indents Nesting* is placing one enclosure within another before insertion in an envelope.

nested phrase a phrase within a sentence, generally several words separating a subject and verb and/or disrupting the continuity of a sentence, a practice that is avoided in broadcasting

net NETWORK; also, the quantity remaining from a GROSS amount after deductions, such as *net rate*, which in advertising is the gross advertising cost minus the advertising agency commission The word *net* appearing alone on invoices *not* from media indicates that the full amount is to be paid. This frequently is confusing because, to many people, net implies a lower price. However, a discount is available only when terms are indicated, as in *net 2%/10,*

which means 2-percent cash discount when payment is made within ten days.

net audience the number of individuals or households reached by a medium over a specified period of time, such as those reading a single issue or tuned to a specific broadcast or broadcast period, such as a day Because each person or household is counted only once regardless of the number of exposures to the medium, this figure also is called *net unduplicated audience* or *unduplicated audience*, which indeed is logical. What is confusing, at least to the lay person, is that it's sometimes called *accumulated audience, cumulative audience*, or, simply, *cume*, even though it is unduplicated and *not* the *gross audience*.

net circulation in periodicals, the total number of copies actually sold; also called *net paid circulation* Some unsold newsstand copies are returned to the publisher, so that the total number of copies printed often is considerably higher than the *total net paid.* In outdoor advertising, net circulation, also called *net advertising circulation*, is the total number of individuals who pass an advertisement within a specific period.

net glossary a list of networks, such as all departments in fire, police, or other organizations

Net Net or **net-net** the bottom line; the end result; the actual total cost; the remainder; the final net figure (price, income, or other amount); the outcome

net plus the GROSS advertising rate minus frequency or other applicable discounts but including the advertising agency commission Thus, net plus is the *net cost* paid by the advertiser to the advertising agency, which then deducts its commission and pays a *net rate* (sometimes called NET-NET, no kidding) to the medium.

net profit the difference between total cost and sales price; also called *net income*

net rating a percentage of total potential audience to which a radio or TV commercial, program, station, or network is exposed, with duplications deducted or omitted Each percentage is a *net rating point (N.R.P.)*.

net weekly audience [broadcasting] the number of individuals or households tuned in at least once a week to a daily radio or TV program or to a program broadcast more than once a week The *net weekly circulation* is the number of individuals tuned to a radio or TV station for at least five consecutive minutes during a week.

network a group of radio or TV stations that broadcast the same programs The stations can be owned by a headquarters company—the network—that is the source of the programs or can be independent—an *affiliate* or *network affiliate*. Networks or groups of affiliated companies exist in many fields, such as a network of advertising or public relations agencies. *Network compensation* is the amount paid by a network to its affiliates for broadcasting its programs or commercials. A *computer network* is two or more computers linked together in order to share files, programs, and peripheral devices.

network feed the system of telephone lines, co-axial cables, microwave relays, satellites, and other means of transmitting a signal from a source to broadcasting stations A program or program service provided by the NETWORK to stations also is called a network feed, such as the *afternoon news feed* transmitted by ABC, CBS, and NBC to affiliated stations for subsequent broadcast.

network identification the name or identification of a radio or TV NETWORK, made at the beginning of each hour and/or the beginning and end of network programs

networking linking, as with stations or other members of a NETWORK On an individual basis, networking is contacting people, often for the exchange of information or in a job search. The concept is that one person leads to another, and at the end of the network is an employer or another goal.

Network Mail a type of direct mail in which two or more items are combined into one package This type of *shared mail* is a copyrighted product of *Advo-System* of Windsor, CT, the largest company in the field. A typical Network Mail package contains three preprinted advertisements with cents-off coupons surrounded by a similar sheet that serves as an outer wrapper instead of an envelope. Network Mail is the same as *Marriage Mail*, except that the former has a wrap with coupons.

network participation a network *spot* buy, such as the purchase of commercials on a network radio or TV program but not total sponsorship of the program

network promo an announcement broadcast by a NETWORK to promote a specific program or the network itself, generally at the end of a network program

network time a time period, such as PRIME TIME, during which a local radio or TV station agrees to broadcast NETWORK programs; also called *network option time*, since the network has the option to use it

neutral angle a camera angle with the action directly in front of the camera at about eye level

neutral color a color without hue, matching other colors well, as gray does A *neutral-density filter* is a gray filter that reduces exposure.

neutral-density filter (nd filter) a camera FILTER made of gelatin or glass in a gray—*neutral*—color to reduce the light intensity without changing its color Thus, in a scene with intense light, such as bright sunlight, it may not be necessary to reduce the lens *aperture*. Graduated neutral-density filters can reduce light from part of a scene.

neutral gray any level of gray with no color or hue

never leave an audience in the dark an admonition to the projectionist in a movie theater to start a film before turning off all the house lights and to slowly bring up the lights during the end credits, so that the theater is not pitch black

Newbery Medal an annual award for excellence in children's book publishing, presented by the *American Library Association* in Chicago; named after John Newbery (1713–67), a British publisher Note the unusual spelling, which has led to countless misspellings since the award was first presented in 1921. Newbery's most famous book was *Little Goody Two-Shoes* (1765).

Newhouse News Service (NNS) a newswire, based in Washington, DC, for Newhouse Newspapers and other subscribers

new journalism a form of writing with personal involvement and subjective interpretation, as contrasted with the objectivity of traditional journalism It sometimes includes a composite character, invented quotations, and other fiction techniques. The term was used in the 1960s to describe the works of Hunter Thompson, Tom Wolfe, Truman Capote, and others and no longer is apt.

new lead (NL) one or more paragraphs to be substituted for the beginning of an existing story or to precede (lead) it; generally an update; also called NULEAD

news fresh information *Hard news* refers to reporting of current events, whereas *soft news* is more likely to be human-interest features or less current or less urgent news. A *news feature* is an elaboration on a news report. The *news department* of a radio or TV station or network, headed by a *news director*, prepares and/or broadcasts news reports. At a newspaper, news is handled by several desks, or departments, such as business news, local news, and national news, that cumulatively may be called the *news department*, as differentiated from the advertising, circulation, and production departments. The news department often is located in a large open area called the newsroom. *Old news* or *stale news* may have originated a few hours or a few days ago, depending on subsequent events.

news advisory an announcement of a forthcoming event, such as one provided by a public relations source to the media

news agency an organization, such as a wire service, that provides news coverage to subscribers

newsbook a pamphlet about current events, generally published weekly; popular in the 16th and 17th centuries

newsbreak an event worthy of reporting, used in television to describe a brief segment, about one minute long, with a few news items; a late-breaking news item, generally appearing on page one of a newspaper or on the first news page of a magazine At *The New Yorker*, the fillers at the end of articles are called newsbreaks.

news butcher a vendor of newspapers

newscast a straight news program on radio or television with relatively few features

news conference a meeting, often arranged by a public relations source, to present information about a newsworthy event, action, or announcement to the news media; also called PRESS CONFERENCE

News Corporation Ltd. one of the world's largest media companies Headed by Rupert Murdoch and headquartered in Sydney, Australia, it publishes major newspapers in Australia and the United Kingdom. In the United States, it publishes the *Boston Herald* and *New York* and other magazines and owns several TV stations, Fox Broadcasting Company, and 20th Century-Fox. In late 1988, News Corporation acquired Triangle Publications, including *TV Guide.*

news dealer a person, particularly a retailer, who sells newspapers and periodicals; short for NEWSSTAND dealer

news doctor a consultant retained to study and revise the news operation of a broadcast station

new season [television] the *broadcast year* that is ushered in during the fall with new program introductions and new episodes of returning series

news editor a staff member who supervises the gathering of news and its rewriting and editing on radio or television or at a publication

news element the facts; straight or *hard* news

news envelope a brief news segment, such as a 60-second news *update* on a local, network, or syndicated program, with its own local or national sponsor

news gap the time between the actual occurrence of an event and when it is reported in the media

news hawk old-fashioned slang for a newspaper reporter, generally male A female reporter was called a *news hen.*

news hole the space in a newspaper allotted to news, illustrations, and other nonadvertising material

newsletter a bulletin or other informational publication, generally without advertising and for individual subscribers or members of a group

newsline a brief news item, a term used at VARIETY

newsmonger a person who gathers news; slang for a gossip columnist

newspaper a publication issued daily, weekly, or at frequent intervals, containing news and advertising; also called *paper* A *newspaper chain* is a group of newspapers under common ownership. (The largest in the United States is *Gannett.*) A *newspaper supplement* is a separate section prepared by the newspaper or an outside source. A *newspaper syndicate* prepares and sells BYLINED articles (columns), comics, and other news and features to newspapers. A *newspaperman* or *newspaperwoman* works for a newspaper.

Newspaper Advertising Bureau (NAB) an association for the promotion of advertising in daily newspapers, based in New York

The Newspaper Guild an AFL-CIO union in Washington, DC, of over 30,000 newspaper writers and others in the publishing industry Reporters at unionized newspapers are *Guild members.*

newspaper line a standard copy measurement of type 11 PICAS long with about 30 characters to the line, used as a standard of performance—lines per minute—for typesetters

newspaper rod a long stick used in libraries to hold one or more issues of a newspaper; also called *newspaper stick*

newspeak a style of saying something ambiguous or contradictory or in the guise of something different or the opposite, used by government officials It was coined by George Orwell (1903–50), the English author who invented this language in his novel *1984,* and is pronounced NEW-speak.

news peg an event or other *point* on which a news article or broadcast is based

newsprint paper on which newspapers are printed Newsprint ink smudges much more easily than ink in magazines or books; the ink on a newspaper reader's fingers often is called newsprint. Newsprint generally is 30-pound *basis* weight, which is lightweight compared to paper used in magazines and books.

newsreel a short film about recent news events Prior to television, theatrical newsreels were produced by *Fox Movietone*, *Pathé*, and other major companies and shown in thousands of movie theaters.

news release a news or FEATURE article written and prepared by a publicist and sent to newspapers, trade publications, and other media; generally called a *press release* or simply a *release* and referred to informally as a *handout*, since it is handed out or distributed free It is one of the most common forms of mass communication used by professional communicators.

newsroom an area of a newspaper or other medium in which news is prepared

newsstand a retail outlet at which magazines and newspapers are sold, including special shelves or sections in bookstores, drugstores, supermarkets, and other locations, as well as kiosks on streets and counters in lobbies; called *news stalls* in Britain The person who operates the newsstand is a *newsstand dealer*. *Newsstand sales* is abbreviated as *N/S*.

newsstand circulation the total number of copies of a publication that are sold at NEWSSTANDS, as distinguished from mailed subscription copies

newsstand draw the number of copies of a publication provided to a *newsstand dealer* Unsold copies, or merely their covers, are returned; these are called *N/S returns*.

news weekly a publication published weekly and devoted primarily to news National news weekly magazines include *Time*, *Newsweek*, and *U.S. News & World Report*. Local *news-weeklies* (generally written as one word), which are published in many major cities, usually are tabloid newspapers, such as the *Boston Phoenix* and *Chicago Reader*.

newswire a *wire service* or news agency, such as *The Associated Press*, *United Press International*, *Reuters*, and other services that provide news and other material to print and broadcast subscribers Private newswires (the two largest in the public relations field are *PR Newswire* and *Business Wire*) distribute material only from publicity sources free to media. Initially, newswires provided their material via Teletype machines and telegraph wires; now they operate with computer data banks and other means of distribution.

newsworthy an event or action that merits being reported by a newspaper or other medium; having the qualities of timely importance or interest

newsy containing considerable news

newszak a news format for a variety or entertainment TV program; a contraction of news

and *Muzak*, the musical service transmitted to public places

New York Times Company one of the country's largest media companies, headquartered in New York near Times Square It publishes *The New York Times* and other newspapers and *Family Circle* and other magazines and owns radio (*WQXR* in New York) and TV stations as well as other companies.

Nexis an on-line DATABASE research service providing published material in newspapers, magazines, and other publications, distributed by *Mead Data Central, Inc.*, in Franklin, Ohio Started in 1979 as a computer-based data service offering *The Associated Press* and other news material, it was expanded in 1983 to include *The New York Times Information Bank* and now includes many major media. The name is a variation of the word *nexus*, which is a link between individuals in a group. A companion service is the *Lexis* system, which is used for legal and accounting research.

next screen a word processing feature that displays the last part of one group of lines along with the succeeding text

next to reading matter (N.R.M.) the positioning of an advertisement adjacent to editorial or reading matter on a page within a publication; an instruction on a purchase or INSERTION ORDER in the ordering of ad space

next week, East Lynne theatrical slang in the early 20th century indicating that a touring show was not doing well The remedy was to follow it with *East Lynne*, a show that had been popular in the late 19th century.

n/f no funds *N.S.F.* means not sufficient funds.

n.f.a. news and feature assistant, generally an employee of a TV network

NFB or **N.F.B.** NATIONAL FILM BOARD

NFO Research a market research company in Greenwich, CT, founded in 1946 and acquired in 1982 by AGB Research (now Pergamon AGB), that operates a MAIL PANEL of over 400,000 households; formerly called National Family Opinion

NG no good

nibble a small quantity; a mild expression of interest A *bite* is fuller, such as acceptance of a proposal. In computers, a nibble is half of a BYTE.

niche market a special segment of the total group, such as a product aimed primarily at a specific DEMOGRAPHIC or geographic composition The process of selling to this segment is called *niche marketing*.

nick **1** a notch, cut, or indentation **2** [typography] the identification groove on the front of the body of a piece of type

Nickelodeon a cable network in New York that transmits children's and teen programs to many cable systems A nickelodeon was a movie and/or vaudeville theater to which admission cost a nickel. *Odeon* is a French word from the Greek *oideion;* an *odeum* was a Greek roofed theater. A nickelodeon also was a player piano or early jukebox operated by insertion of a nickel; in this case, the origin is a combination of nickel and *melodeon,* a small organ.

Nielsen Co. the world's largest market research company, whose full name is *A.C. Nielsen Co.* Nielsen's fame is such that millions of Americans know the name, particularly with regard to TV ratings. In addition to broadcast measurement, it functions in many areas in over 25 countries. Founded in Iowa in 1934 by Arthur C. Nielsen (1897–1980), the company now has over 20,000 employees and well over $700 million in annual sales and is headquartered near Chicago, in Northbrook, IL.

The largest of its seven groups is not media research—that's not even second! The largest group, market research, audits products in retail stores (mostly food and drug) and reports on retail inventories, brand distribution, prices, displays, and other aspects of sales performance and market share, categorized by region, store type, package sizes, and other classifications, and based on on-site observation, *ScanTrack* (data from scanning cash registers, called scanning-generated data), and other systems. The *Nielsen Drug Index (N.D.I.)* measures product inventory, sales, and share of market of clients' products in drug and mass-merchandising stores. The *Nielsen Food Index (N.F.I.)* provides the same local checking and national projections in food stores. The *Media Research Group* provides TV audience ratings based on a national sample of households with *Audimeters* attached to their TV sets for automatic recording of on/off information and channel selection, plus households that record their viewing in weekly diaries or via *people meters.* The *Nielsen Audience Demographic Report (N.A.D.)* is a publication with data on TV audiences by program and time period. *Nielsen Coverage Services (N.C.S.)* provides TV-station audience data on a county basis. *Nielsen Market Section Report* describes TV audience size in specific markets. Perhaps the best-known services are the Nielsen ratings of TV-program audience size, including the *Nielsen Station Index (N.S.I),* which covers local stations, and *Nielsen Television Index (N.T.I.),* which issues the famous biweekly reports of network audience size

based on the Audimeter records or people meters in *Nielsen homes.*

The service that involves almost all consumers is the *Clearing House Group,* headquartered in Clinton, IA, which redeems coupons. The *Neodata Services Group,* in Boulder, CO, maintains mailing lists, including magazine circulation lists. So whenever you send a cents-off coupon to Clinton or a magazine subscription renewal to Boulder, you're sending it to Nielsen! The *Petroleum Information Group,* headquartered in Littleton, CO, collects data on oil and gas exploration and production and produces maps and other reports. *Dataquest,* headquartered in San Jose, CA, provides information in technology and industrial fields, and *Custom Research Services* conducts other projects. The *Nielsen Homevideo Index (NHI)* measures cable, pay cable, home video, and related technologies. In 1984, Nielsen became a wholly owned subsidiary of the DUN & BRADSTREET CORP. of New York.

Nieman Fellowship a one-year grant by the *Nieman Foundation* in Cambridge, MA to journalists for study at Harvard University Alumni—*Nieman Fellows*—include many prominent journalists. Lucius William Nieman (1857–1935) was a newspaper reporter, editor, and publisher in Milwaukee.

niffnoff banter among TV newscasters, generally before or after a report, such as by ANCHORPERSONS with the weather or sports reporter

Niger a soft goatskin leather used in bookbinding, made from small goats in Nigeria and elsewhere in Africa

night answer (N.A.) a telephone-system feature common in large offices in which incoming calls during non-business hours (*night service*) are automatically rerouted and ring only at specific places (*night answer-assigned*), such as the security department (*night answer-offsite*) A common system called *night answer-universal* enables a person to answer an incoming call by pushing a specific key or keys, such as the numbers 1 and 4. In such systems, an *auxiliary ringer* (a *night chime*) often is located on walls throughout the office and is activated by placing the switchboard or console in the night position.

night-for-night [film] night sequences actually shot at night, in contrast to DAY-FOR-NIGHT

night letter a reduced-rate telegram sent at night

night side the late-night and early-morning shift at a newspaper or other medium; also called *dog watch, graveyard shift, late watch, lobster shift,* or *lobster trick*

night watch or **nightwatch** late night and early morning at a newspaper, radio station, or other medium, when one person or a small staff is on duty to monitor emergencies or major news

nihil obstat Latin for "nothing hinders," a statement of sanction for publication issued by a Roman Catholic book censor and generally found on the back of the title page

900 number a telephone toll service for a large quantity of calls to a single number Callers pay for the calls, as compared to 800 numbers, which are free. 900 numbers are used to provide information, such as sports results, and for opinion polling. The actual name is *Dial-It 900 Service* or *DIS*.

nine-light a LUMINAIRE with three vertical rows, or banks, each with three lamps A commonly used spotlight, it usually has side reflectors and also is called a MAXIBRUTE or MINIBRUTE, depending on the type of lights.

970 number a service of telephone companies enabling callers to hear adult programming, generally referred to as *dial-a-porn* The telephone numbers begin with the digits 970.

976 number a service of telephone companies enabling callers to hear a recorded message, such as a weather report The telephone number is 976 followed by four digits.

1900 box a metal box that houses several electrical receptacles, a type of JUNCTION BOX commonly used in exhibits and show business

90-day cancellation the standard period required in outdoor advertising for notification by an advertiser or its agency to cancel an order

95 wire-service jargon for an urgent message

ninja an old Japanese word for a being who can fly and perform superhuman feats Thus, *Superman* is a *ninja movie*.

nip 1 a small piece 2 [printing] a creaselike line, as at the joint of a hardbound book

nipping [book production] the compressing of folded sheets of paper to remove air The tightened sheets are called *nipped sheets*.

NIRI NATIONAL INVESTOR RELATIONS INSTITUTE

nit slang for a foot LAMBERT, a metric unit of surface brightness

nitrate film a film with a base of cellulose nitrate It is no longer used, as it was inflammable and deteriorated in storage. Nitrate film has been replaced by cellulose acetate, called *safety base*.

nitrogen-burst processing a film-developing system that uses automatically timed injections or bursts of inert nitrogen gas to agitate the developing solution

nixie mail that is undeliverable and returned, usually because it has an incorrect, illegible, or insufficient address A *nixie clerk* at major post offices specializes in handling this type of mail—among America's unsung heroes. The origin is *nix*, which means refusal.

n.l. new line

NL NEW LEAD

NNA NATIONAL NEWSPAPER ASSOCIATION

NNS NEWHOUSE NEWS SERVICE

no or **no.** number

no, No, or **noh** a classic form of Japanese drama, well known outside Japan because of its elaborately masked and costumed male performers and stylized acting Unlike *Kabuki*, *no* drama was for aristocratic audiences, who appreciated its subtlety.

no. abbreviation for *number*

no answer (N.A.) a term used by researchers to request the reason for the absence of data from a response to a question or questions

no carbon required (NCR) paper, such as bank deposit slips, that is chemically treated so that writing or any impression on one sheet is reproduced on the sheet below The name is clever, as the initials also are those of the manufacturer, NCR Corporation, of Dayton, OH.

nod [theater] a bow at the end of a performance

nodders [television] reaction shots of an interviewer, in which he or she usually is simply nodding

node a point, as in a computer network, or an interconnecting position

no fax a rehearsal without technical facilities

noise sound, especially loud, harsh, or unpleasant; electrical disturbance that interferes with a signal, static; in computers, irrelevant or meaningless data; a complaint or protest; rumor, talk; an impression, not necessarily aural, such as the stir created by a campaign or a medium or the effect of competing advertising NOISE IMMUNITY is the ability of a computer or other device to accept valid signals and reject invalid ones.

noise-canceling microphone a specially designed microphone that filters out background sounds

noises off sounds of crowds, thunder, and other effects made offstage

noisy describing an aberration in sound or light *Noisy black* is a break in uniformity, such as white spots, in the black area of television or other pictures. *Noisy white* is nonuniformity, such as black spots, in the white area.

nom de plume pseudonym, from the French for "pen name" *Nom de guerre*, French for "war name," is a military pseudonym.

nominal scaling [statistics] a system of identifying categories of a population with minimal measurements

nominative the subject of a verb, such as a noun or pronoun

non-bleed printed matter that does not BLEED, or extend to the outer edge of a page

nonbook 1 a book of little intrinsic literary merit 2 [library science] a file, audiovisual material, or some other item that is not a traditional publication

nonce word a coined word, or NEOLOGISM, sometimes used only once

non-color-sensitized emulsion (NC) a photographic coating sensitive only to blue, violet, and near-ultraviolet light; also called *color-blind emulsion* NC film is used for copying.

nondurable goods products consumed immediately or in a few usages, such as food, drugs, or gasoline

nonfiction novel a literary work in which real events and people are written about in narrative form, with actual names and other facts not camouflaged (as they are in a ROMAN À CLEF) but with conversations and other writing created by the author, as in *In Cold Blood* by Truman Capote (1924–84) and other works of NEW JOURNALISM

nonimpact printing a method, as in OFFSET printing or PHOTOCOPYING, in which the image is transferred without pressure

no-no something unacceptable, taboo; a *faux pas*

nonpareil 1 having no equal, peerless 2 a type of candy consisting of a flat piece of chocolate about the size of a nickel covered with white pellets of sugar 3 [typography] 6-point type 4 long colored strips of cloth used for festive decoration; bunting It is pronounced non-pa-REL.

non plus ultra a very small type size, about 2 points

nonprobability sampling a survey technique in which the respondents are selected by chance—accidentally—or by personal knowledge, but not mathematically

non-repro blue [printing] blue markings on camera-ready material that are not picked up—not reproduced—by the camera

non-response (N.R.) a missing response to a survey question or an entire questionnaire The *non-response rate* is the percentage of respondents who do not answer all or part of a questionnaire.

non sequitur a remark or statement with no bearing on what has just been said or written From the Latin for "it does not follow," it is abbreviated as *non seq.*

noodle to improvise, particularly music, as in *noodling* by jazz musicians To *noodle around* is to play around in a haphazard manner.

noodled 1 greatly detailed, for photographic realism 2 background music along with the titles and credits

nook light a small light; from *nook*, a corner or small area It is also called *nookie.*

NORC a social science research organization affiliated with the University of Chicago Founded in 1941 as the *National Opinion Research Center* and popularly known among market researchers by its initials, in 1983 its name was changed to NORC: A Social Service Research Center.

normative judgment an action or decision based on a standard, such as a moral obligation

North American Basic Teletext Specification (NABTS) a standard that specifies the coding system for *teletext* services It is based on the videotex standard developed by the AMERICAN NATIONAL STANDARDS INSTITUTE (*ANSI*) and CANADIAN STANDARDS ASSOCIATION (*CSA*).

North American Presentation Level Protocol Syntax (NAPLPS) an ALPHAMOSAIC presentation standard developed by the AMERICAN NATIONAL STANDARDS INSTITUTE (*ANSI*) and CANADIAN STANDARDS ASSOCIATION (*CSA*) for use by videotex systems in North America

northlight a LUMINAIRE used for diffused light; not the primary or key light

North/South labels mailing-label sheets that read from top to bottom, whereas *East/West labels* are arranged in horizontal rows

Norton split a payment schedule introduced by New York publisher *W.W. Norton & Co.,* in which authors were given more than the conventional half of royalties from paperback sales Introduced in the 1970s and greeted enthusiastically by authors, the Norton split was dropped in the early 1980s.

nos or **nos.** numbers

no-stretch paper a specially prepared type of paper that resists expansion due to stretching or water, used for photographic prints

NOT not our title, a notation written on a book order form indicating to the customer that the book is not available from the publisher or other recipient of the order

notation a system of figures or symbols; a brief note or annotation

notch an area cut out of a printing plate so that type may be inserted

notch binding [book production] the puncturing of the SIGNATURE folds to make v-shaped holes—notches for glue to pass through

note an instruction to a typist, printer, or computer operator, not meant to be printed; a statement or explanation appearing at the bottom of a page (footnote) or at the end of a publication (*end note*) or written to readers by a newspaper or other editor (*editor's note*); a progress report or research report in a journal, shorter and less formal than a full-length paper

notebook 1 a book, frequently spiralbound or loose-leaf, in which comments, explanations, or other notes are kept, as by a student or journalist 2 a small, thin, lightweight computer

noted famous, as in a *noted author*; in publication research, noticed or observed, as with the percentage of readers who remember an advertisement

notice a formal announcement or warning, such as a sign or legal notice published as an advertisement; a brief mention or review of a book, play, or other work of art *Mixed notices* are varying—favorable and unfavorable—reviews. To *give notice* is to terminate employment.

novel a work of fiction, generally book-length

novelette a short novel; also called a NOVELLA

novelization a fictional book based on a film, play, TV program, or other work, generally produced as a tie-in with the other medium

novella a short work of fiction, longer than a short story and shorter than a novel; sometimes called a novelette and from the Italian for "short novel" In television, a *novela* is a melodrama series produced in Spanish and shown on Hispanic stations.

np new paragraph

n.p. no place to fit an item in a layout

NP international telex abbreviation: no party with the name of the recipient of the message

NPA NUMBERING PLAN AREA

NPC NATIONAL PRESS CLUB

NPD Group a market research company, based in Port Washington, NY, and established in 1953, that operates consumer panels that keep diaries of purchases These diary panels provide extensive data, including brand share, volume, number of households buying, penetration, purchase frequency, average price, and source of purchase. The NPD Group includes the Home Testing Institute.

NPPA NATIONAL PRESS PHOTOGRAPHERS ASSOCIATION

NPR NATIONAL PUBLIC RADIO

NR DOLBY noise reduction

N.R. NON-RESPONSE

N.R.P. NET RATING point

NRM NEXT TO READING MATTER

n.s. not specified

n/s not sufficient; newsstand sales

NSI NIELSEN Station Index

nth name a method of selecting names from a list, such as every tenth name in the telephone directory

NTI NIELSEN Television Index

NTSC NATIONAL TELEVISION SYSTEM COMMITTEE

NTT Nippon Telephone and Telegraph Corporation, the major communications carrier in Japan

nudie a film or other work that features naked or near-naked performers

nulead (NL) See NEW LEAD.

null invalid; insignificant; nonexistent; zero; the absence of information In printing, a *null character* is blank and is used to fill space or time or to pad a format.

null hypothesis a statement to be tested on the assumption that it will be rejected For example, a proposition that there is no connection or difference between two *variables* will be examined, and a conclusion may be reached that the variables are related. Thus, in statistics, a null hypothesis is a proposition that is set up to produce an objective inquiry with regard to potential or chance effects.

number 1 a numeral 2 a musical piece 3 a brief act or performance 4 an item of apparel The word has many slang uses, such as to *do a number* (put on a performance); a *hot number* (a fast-selling item), to *make the numbers* (obtain high or desired ratings or sales projections), and other terms related to lotteries and anything numerical. For example, insiders refer to *21*, the restaurant at 21 West 52nd Street in Manhattan, as *Numbers*. In computers, a *binary number* is represented only by combinations of 0 and 1.

numbered copy a limited-edition book or other work with a number indicating that specific copy

Numbering Plan Area (NPA) [telephone] an area in the United States and some other countries within which each seven-digit telephone number is different, with each number preceded by its area's three-digit area code

number 100 showing a saturation buy, or purchase, in outdoor advertising: the number of panels needed for exposure to 90 percent (almost 100) of the local adult population every day of the month Outdoor BOARDS are rented by the month, so a *number 50 showing* is half the number of boards as the basic *full showing*, or *number 100 showing*.

number 10 the most common size of business envelope, $4\frac{1}{8}'' \times 9\frac{1}{2}''$

numeral a figure, letter, or word expressing a number *Arabic numerals* are 0, 1, 2, 3, etc.; *Roman numerals* are I, II, X (ten), L (fifty), etc. *Aligning numerals*—or modern numbers—are the same height and do not descend below the base line. *Nonaligning numerals* vary in height and may have descending elements.

numeral mark a symbol—#—indicating a number, a *pound* (also called a *pound mark*), or another reference Sometimes incorrectly called a DOUBLE DAGGER, which is ‡; it actually is a double-double dagger or a HATCH MARK.

numeric pertaining to numbers

nut the total cost of a project or program; an EN space, or half the width of an EM QUAD Various kinds of metal nuts are used to screw onto threaded bolts and other parts of communications devices. For example, an *acorn nut* or *cap nut* is a decorative piece of metal put on the end of a bolt in an exhibit.

nut paragraph the theme or core of a feature article A term used at *The Wall Street Journal* and other newspapers, it often is the third paragraph in a page-one feature, generally containing more of the facts or essential—nut or kernel—information than the first two paragraphs, it is also called the *nut graph*.

nut space [printing] an EN space, or half an EM space

nutting truck a wheeled platform commonly used in postal facilities and elsewhere, with two slatted ends for pushing by hand or pulling by tractor Named for its designer, Elijah Nutting, it also is called a *platform truck*, *platform trailer*, *float*, or *tram*.

NXX the first three digits of a seven-digit telephone number, indicating the telephone-company central office These codes previously did not use a 0 or 1 as the middle digit, but this now is permitted.

NYP New York Press, an abbreviation on New York license plates to identify accredited press people; not yet published, a term in book publishing to indicate a forthcoming publication

NYPO *New York Publicity Outlets*, an annual directory of media published for publicists by Harold Hansen in New Milford, CT; popularly called NIGH-poe

NYPSA NATIONAL YELLOW PAGES SERVICE ASSOCIATION

NYT The NEW YORK TIMES

O telephone operator

o/a on or about

OAAA OUTDOOR ADVERTISING ASSOCIATION OF AMERICA

Oakley, Annie See ANNIE OAKLEY.

oak tag a heavy semigloss paper that is buff colored (akin to an oak leaf)

O & M OGILVY & MATHER INC.

O&O owned and operated, as with the radio and TV stations in New York and other major cities that are owned and operated by the NET-WORKS

oater a Western movie, with oat-eating horses; also called a *sagebrusher* or *horse opera*

ob. or obl. OBLONG

OB outside broadcast: not in the studio, from a REMOTE location

OBC outside back cover of a magazine

Obie **1** annual awards to playwrights and others associated with OFF-BROADWAY theater, presented by *The Village Voice*, a New York weekly newspaper **2** annual awards for creative excellence presented by the Institute of Outdoor Advertising in Washington, DC **3** a small, rectangular, open-faced spotlight, commonly used near or mounted on a film camera

obit abbreviation for *obituary*, a death notice, as in a newspaper; sometimes further abbreviated as *ob*

object code a code or program understood by a machine or computer, rather than in the language of the operator; also called *object program* or *target program*, as compared to a *source program*

obligatory scene a scene in a play that is so expected by the audience that the playwright is obliged to write it; also called a *plot scene* or *scène à faire*

oblique **1** slanting; inclined; indirect; devious **2** [photography] a shot taken with a camera in a tilted position **3** [typography] a skewed typeface that slants to the right and looks ITALIC, called *pseudo-italic*

oblong (ob or obl.) elongated; a printed piece bound unconventionally along the short dimen-sion instead of the long dimension An *oblong book* is wider than it is high.

OBR optical bar recognition, a machine-reada-ble coding now commonly used on products sold in supermarkets See also OPTICAL CHAR-ACTER RECOGNITION.

OBS ORGANIZED BEHAVIORAL SYSTEM

observational method a research technique in which individuals' work habits or other activi-ties are studied (observed), as opposed to such *unobtrusive methods* as analyzing data about the individuals

obstructed view a seat in which the spectator can see only part of the stage due to a column or other obstruction; sometimes called a *blind seat* Tickets for such seats are marked "ob-structed view."

obtained score the percentage of respondents who prove their recall of a printed advertise-ment in a GALLUP AND ROBINSON readership test

obverse turned toward the observer; the side of an object, such as a coin, with the main design The other side is the *reverse*.

O.C. order cancelled, a customer's notation on an invoice, particularly for a book, indicating cancellation of a previously placed order

O.C. or O/C on camera: action in front of a TV camera, visible to the audience In a TV script, it's a direction indicating on which person or scene the camera is focused.

OCC or OC international telex abbreviation: subscriber is engaged, or occupied

occupant list a mailing list that contains only addresses without names An *occupant direc-tory* or *address directory* can be purchased from some telephone companies and other publish-ers, sometimes including names but arranged by streets.

OCR OPTICAL CHARACTER RECOGNITION

octal a numbering system based on eight digits, 0 through 7, used on some computers (though the most common is the BINARY system)

octavo folded into eight leaves; abbreviated as *8vo* or *eightvo*, which is 16 pages Most books are bound with SIGNATURES of 16 pages each. *Octavo paper* generally is 9³/₄" high. *Octavo* *books* range in size from *Post Octavo* (6¹/₄" high × 4" wide) to *Imperial Octavo* (11" × 7¹/₂") and include various intermediate sizes, such as *Foolscap Octavo, Medium Octavo, Royal Octavo*, and *Super Royal Octavo*. British book sizes include *Foolscap Octavo* (6³/₄" × 4¹/₂"), *Crown Octavo* (7¹/₂" × 5"), *Large Post Octavo* (8¹/₄" × 5¹/₄"), *Demy Octavo* (8³/₄" × 5⁵/₈"), *Medium Octavo* (9" × 5³/₄", and *Royal Octavo* (10" × 6¹/₄").

octopus cable a grouping of wires or cables with several jacks at one or both ends, used in television to attach equipment with dissimilar jacks

oddball pricing a policy in which an assortment of items is sold at the same price, as in "Every item on this table $1"

oddments the parts of a book that are not the main text, such as the FOREWORD and INDEX

odd page a right-hand page, carrying an odd-numbered FOLIO, such as 3, 5, or 7

odd pricing a policy in which the retail price is set below an exact dollar amount, such as $1.98; also called *odd-ending pricing, odd-number pricing*, or *odd-even pricing Odd prices* may be perceived as sales or special prices by consumers or may have other advantages, such as permitting tax to be added to total a rounded number like $1.

odd sorts [typography] nonstandard or special type characters

ode a lyric poem or other literary composition, generally addressed to a person or thing

odeon slang for a theater The actual word is ODEUM. A NICKELODEON was a movie and/or vaudeville theater to which admission cost a nickel.

odeum a concert hall, from the Greek *oideion*

O'Dwyer *Jack O'Dwyer's Newsletter*, a weekly New York newsletter about public relations The company also publishes annual directories of public relations personnel and agencies.

O.E. Old English type, characterized by heavy black strokes called BLACK LETTERS

off 1 distant; interrupted; removed; ended; wrong; marginal; skewed; opposite of ON In the United Kingdom, to *be off* is for a performer to miss a cue or entrance. 2 [broadcasting] OFF-CAMERA: outside the image field; *off-mike*: directed away from the microphone; OFF-SCREEN or *off-camera announcer*: an announcer heard but not seen; OFFSTAGE: not visible to the audience; *off the air*: not broadcast, program terminated 3 [marketing] *off invoice*: in retailing, a deduction or allowance to a retailer in exchange for promotion; *off label*: a sale price marked over the regular price, or an inferior grade or specially labeled brand

off air [broadcasting] a program received via conventional radio or television and not via cable *Off the air* refers to the ending of the transmission of a program or the termination of a program.

offbeat unconventional

off-Broadway or **Off Broadway** theatrical activity, often experimental and low-budget, in theaters other than the traditional commercial theaters in the Broadway–Times Square area of Manhattan *Off-off-Broadway* is farther removed from the mainstream, as with an *avant-garde* theatrical production

off-camera [film, television] not within the view of a shot, as with an *off-camera* sound coming from an *off-screen* source

off-card [advertising] a special rate, lower than that on the printed rate card

off-color improper, of doubtful propriety or taste; describing paper or ink that does not match a specified sample

offcut [printing] the portion of a sheet that has been cut off, folded separately, and inserted in the middle of the folded SIGNATURE, so that the leaves become consecutive

offer a proposal or presentation; the exact terminology to describe the product, price, and terms in a *mail order* or other proposed sale

offhand without preparation; extemporaneous; *off-the-cuff*

off-hook a condition in which a telephone receiver or handset is removed from its switch, resulting in a signal—an *off-hook signal*—that is a request for service by an operator or indicating a busy condition While off-hook, or off-the-hook, the telephone is inaccessible to incoming calls.

offhour a period other than the time of greatest activity

official envelope a number-10 envelope, the most common business size

Official Mail a Postal Service classification for mail without postage sent by Members of Congress The envelope must have a printed FACSIMILE signature or other required marking instead of a postage stamp. This FRANK also is used by the Vice President of the United States. The President usually uses regular stamps.

official newspaper a newspaper designated by a local government unit to receive OFFICIAL NOTICES

official notice advertising, generally a small block of text, by a government unit in a publication in its geographical area or area of interest, legally required to inform the public about proposed or new regulations and actions

off its feet describing metal type that does not stand up straight in the FORM holding it and therefore prints improperly

off-key deviating from the correct tone, pitch, or notes of music; irregular, abnormal, or inappropriate

off-line a condition in which a device or system is not connected to a central device, such as not connected with the CPU of a computer Transmission from an off-line device must be via telephone or manually carried material, such as a DISK or tape.

off-line edit a rough assembly of segments with abrupt transitions, followed by an *on-line edit* with smooth transitions and other improvements

offload to unload

off-mike a sound that is directed away from a microphone, intentionally or unintentionally, or that is not within the primary PICKUP ZONE of the microphone

off-network describing a program available for syndication after it has been broadcast on a NET-WORK

off-network series programs formerly broadcast on a NETWORK, such as ABC, CBS, or NBC, and now *syndicated* to individual stations

off-press proofing, or another printing process not conducted on the press itself; already printed and off the press

off-price reduced price

offprint an excerpt of an article or a reprint from a larger publication, such as a magazine; additional sheets of or part of a publication printed at the time of the full-run initial printing; to reprint separately

offscreen (OS) out of sight of the viewer, as in an *offscreen sound* originating outside the view of the camera

off-season a time of the year other than the busiest period

offset a printing technique in which the ink image is transferred—offset—from the printing plate to a soft covered rubber blanket or roller and then from the blanket to paper This method of printing, also called *offset lithography*, is now more common than LETTERPRESS printing. It is based on the fact that grease, as in ink, and water do not mix. An *offset plate* is paper or metal, such as aluminum, magnesium, or stainless steel, that holds moisture on one side and is coated with a light-sensitive solution. An *offset printing press* is a rotary press with the offset plate curved around the cylinder. An offset, or *setoff*, is a mark on a sheet caused by contact with wet ink. In satellite broadcasting, offset refers to a FEEDHORN that is set off below the center of the parabolic dish antenna for improved reception.

offset paper specially coated paper for OFFSET lithography that repels water more than uncoated paper does and results in superior reproduction of photographs, art, and colors

offsetting unintentional or faulty transfer of ink not yet dry from a printed sheet to a sheet or surface laid over it; *offset printing*

off-shelf display a point-of-purchase display elsewhere in a store from where the product is stocked

offstage a part of a stage not visible to the audience, such as the wings; in or from this area, as with an *offstage whisper*

off the cuff extemporaneous

off-the-rack ready-made; in stock; also called *off-the-shelf*

off-the-record describing material presented to the media either not for publication or in various other ways designed to be BACKGROUND information Generally, this is a technique to be avoided by spokespeople and prudent public relations practitioners, who should be aware of the importance of attribution *on the record*.

off-the-shelf research an existing published study, as compared to a customized original study

off to Buffalo [theater] a step used by a dancer to exit from the stage, as in the song lyric "Shuffle Off to Buffalo"

off-white grayish or yellowish white

off year a period of reduced activity

Ogilvy & Mather Inc. a major advertising and communications company headquartered in New York, part of the Ogilvy Group; acquired in 1989 by the WPP Group

Ogilvy Group a major advertising, public relations, and communications company, headquartered in New York City, acquired in 1989 by the WPP Group, London

ogize a correction marked on a printing DUMMY

oil can a slang term among artists to describe a common container for rubber cement thinner The shape, with its spout, resembles a motor-oil can, which some artists actually use.

oiled paper heavy paper treated with oil, such as wrapping paper

oilstone a whetstone, or abrasive, such as carborundum, used to sharpen art tools The stone generally is moistened with oil.

OK international telex abbreviation: do you agree; okay

OK takes film shots—*takes*—that are approved (*OK* written on the LEADER) for development and to be included in the WORKPRINT

O.K.W/C or **OKw.c.** a notation indicating that the proof or other item is okay except for (*with*) the indicated corrections

Old English (O.E.) the English language from about the 5th to 12th centuries; an angular BOLDFACE letter invented in the 17th century based on earlier handwriting, also called BLACK LETTER or *Elizabethan letter* The NAMEPLATES—logos—of *The New York Times* and *Los Angeles Times* are customized modifications of an Old English typeface.

old-face roman a style of ROMAN type characterized by relatively uniform strokes plus curved and slanted SERIFS These typefaces were used from the 15th to 18th centuries and include *Aldine*, developed in the 16th century in Italy, and *Baskerville*, developed in the 18th century in England.

oldie or **oldy** an old joke, movie, music, or other work *Golden oldies* are renowned, hit records of earlier years.

old man an old term for the boss, such as the *managing editor* These days, the boss may be neither old nor a man.

old style (OS) or **old-style** a ROMAN typeface classification characterized by uniform thick and thin strokes, a slanted upper SERIF in LOWERCASE letters, and a freedom of design that has kept it in use centuries after its creation, soon after the invention of printing from movable type by Johann Gutenberg in the 15th century *Caslon, Cheltenham, Elzevir,* and *Garamond* are old-style types. Old style and *modern* are subdivisions of roman type. Old-style and *old-face* roman generally are synonymous, though old style sometimes is delineated as a 19th-century adaptation of old-face roman.

old-timer [film] a flexible pole used in lighting to hold FLAGS or SCRIMS in front of light sources to shade or diffuse the light

oleo or **olio** a painted BACKDROP, sometimes used at the front of the stage for a brief scene while the scenery behind it is changed

olio a combination of musical numbers, a medley; also an alternate spelling of OLEO

olivette a floodlight consisting of a metal container with the inside painted white and a bulb, generally 1,000-watt, usually mounted on a telescopic pipe stand Since it does not have a *reflector*, as do the scoop floodlight and other floodlights, the olivette produces a wide, diffuse beam.

OM OPERATIONS MANAGER

OMB OUT-OF-HOME MEASUREMENT BUREAU

omni short for an OMNIDIRECTIONAL microphone

omnibus an anthology, or collection, of previously published works, as by a single author or on one theme

Omnicom Group a publicly owned communications company, headquartered in New York, that owns *BBDO, DDB/Needham, Doremus, Porter/Novelli,* and other advertising, public relations, and related firms

omnidirectional capable of transmitting or receiving signals, as with an *omnidirectional microphone* that picks up sound from all directions

omnies [broadcasting] crowd noises as picked up by an OMNIDIRECTIONAL microphone

omnifont [typography] all—*omni*—FONTS; the ability of optical, magnetic, or other recognition devices to process a variety of type styles

on in contact with; in operation, functioning, as with a mechanism that is *on* A performer who is on is functioning well, the opposite of being *off,* and, of course, is employed, whereas an unemployed performer is off. On also means through the use or through the medium of, as with a performer who appears *on stage, on radio,* or *on television* (but *in* film), or a musician who is *on guitar* or another instrument. On is short for *onstage* or toward the center of the stage, as in *move on.*

On-Air Lab a facility of Westgate Research Inc., a market research company in St. Louis that tests consumers' recall of TV commercials by inserting the ads in a situation comedy

once and a half 1½, or one-and-a-half Artwork that is *once and a half up* is one-and-one-half times the size it will appear when reproduced.

one-and-a-half heads principle [television] a system with a separate head that records the vertical information near the lower edge of the tape, used in TELETEXT and systems with special signals inserted outside the regular picture area The 1.5 heads system thus retains such special signals as vertical interval reference signals and vertical interval test signals.

one and one an instruction to musicians to play one verse and one chorus *One and two* refers to one verse and two choruses.

one-and-one-half spacing wider-than-standard spacing, with one-and-one-half space increments between letters, words, and lines, used in *headings*

one-cent sale two retail items, the same or different, sold together, with the second priced at one cent

one-hundred showing (100 showing) the saturation-coverage buy in outdoor advertising, providing the opportunity for exposure to approximately 90 percent of the local adult population in one day

one-key a FLOODLIGHT with a 1,000-watt bulb A *one-and-a-half* has a 1,500-watt bulb.

one-light dupe a DUPE, a film NEGATIVE made from an original negative, incorporating all lighting changes so that balanced prints made from it, called *one-light prints*, can be exposed at one light level Abbreviated as *1-lite dupe* or *1-lite*, it is also called a *color reversal intermediate*.

one-light print [film] a color print made on a CONTACT PRINTER with the same level of light—hence, one-light—for each of the primary colors One-light prints are commonly used during film production to produce the DAILIES quickly from a DUPE negative, called a *one-light dupe*.

one on a style of bookbinding in which thread is passed through the fold of each section and around each CORD or tape; also called *all along* and *one sheet on*

1p4c one-page four-color, generally referring to a magazine advertisement Other designations are *1p2c* (2-color) and *1pBW* (black-and-white).

one-price policy *nonvariable* pricing, not subject to reduction due to bargaining or sales

one-quarter position [film, television, theater] the position of a performer who is facing the audience at a 45-degree angle, midway between full front and profile, which is a 90-degree angle; also called *three-quarters front*

one-rhyme a rhyme (as in a poem or song) with the last word (if one syllable) or last syllable of the last word on a line; also called *ultimate rhyme* (as opposed to *penultimate rhyme* or next-to-last syllable) or *masculine rhyme* In Latin poetry, the masculine form of a noun generally has one syllable and its feminine form has two syllables, so *two-rhyme* (or *penultimate rhyme*) is also called *feminine rhyme.*

1S one side, as in a paper coated on one side as compared to 2S, which means on both sides

one-sheet a poster consisting of a single sheet, 28" × 42" or 30" × 46", commonly used in movie theaters and on subway and railroad platforms Larger sizes are *two-sheet, four-sheet,* and 24-sheet.

one sheet on a style of hand-sewn bookbinding; also called *one on*

one-shot a project produced only once

one-shot developer a chemical bath, or developer, used only once to process, or develop, a single film, or shot

One Show an annual awards event conducted by *The One Club for Art & Copy, Inc.,* for advertising agencies and others; based in New York

one-sided sheets paper printed on one side only, blank on the reverse side

one spot [theater] the first act on a variety program

one-stroke brush a type of paintbrush commonly used for lettering, sign writing, watercolor painting, and other artwork requiring very thin lines; generally called a *single-stroke brush*

one time only (O.T.O.) referring to an advertisement or other work to be broadcast, published, or used only once

one-time rate a charge for a nonrepeated advertisement; also called OPEN RATE or *transient rate*

one-to-one-shot a photo or art to be reproduced the same size as the original

one-two-threes [film] an instruction indicating the number of exposures for each animation drawing The printed sheet—exposure sheet—has three columns called ones, twos, and threes, indicating whether a drawing is to receive a single, double, or triple exposure.

1-up a layout in which one column of type is set adjacent to a blank column or floating in two columns; also called *flat-out*

one up/many down a television or teleconference format with a single origination site and many receiving sites

one-way mirror a glass partition commonly used with FOCUS-GROUP or other QUALITATIVE research A one-way mirror enables a researcher to observe or photograph individuals inside a room, whereas the individuals see the specially treated glass only as a mirror.

one-way set a set with a single flat background

onionskin a thin, hard-finished, translucent paper used for tracings, carbon copies, and a prestigious effect in books and brochures

onlaid a piece of paper or other material attached to a surface as a book cover, but not necessarily INLAID

onlay [book production] a leather binding into which leathers of other colors or kinds have been inserted for decorative purposes; also called *inlaid* or *mosaic* binding The onlay also is the decorative material that is glued to the cover.

online or **on-line** in progress, ongoing; under the control of or connected to a central computer, part of an automated system *Online processing* generally refers to data entered into a remote computer via telephone communications and ready to be utilized, rather than simply stored, in contrast to BATCH PROCESSING.

onomatopoeia a word or words that echo, imitate, or resemble the sounds they describe, such as bang, blast, buzz, chickadee, hiss, rustle, slush, spurt, tinkle, and whisper

on-pack a piece of merchandise, a premium, advertising matter, or a coupon attached to or part of the exterior of a product package

on-pack premium a premium affixed to the exterior of a product package

on-page coupon a coupon that is part of a printed advertisement

on-sale date the day on which a publication actually is available, which in the case of magazines generally is a few days or weeks prior to the date printed on the cover, or *cover date*

on space describing payment to a writer based on the number of words or column inches produced

onstage or **on stage** on a stage, before an audience, such as a performer who appears onstage To be *on the stage* is to be in the theatrical field.

on string a non-staff writer paid by the assignment; a freelance writer or STRINGER

on the air a broadcast in progress

on the beam on target; on the right track; operating correctly *On the radio beam* is within the effective range of the microphone.

on the button perfect or accurate; also called *on the money* or *on the nose*

on-the-clock jargon for a printer, postal clerk, or other worker who is on duty or at work with the *time clock* running When the worker punches out, as recorded on a time clock, he or she is *off-the-clock*.

on the head 1 on time; describing a film, photograph, or other work produced exactly, as at the correct exposure; also called *on the nose* 2 [broadcasting] slang for blunt, obvious, or heavy-handed

on the shelf completely produced and awaiting shipment or use

o-o theatrical slang for once-over, a quick check, as when a stage manager gives *the o-o* to the stage set

OOP OUT-OF-POCKET expenses

OOS out-of-stock, a retailing term for merchandise that is not on the shelves or available for sale; also abbreviated as *o.s.* and *o/s* Related abbreviations include *o.s.c.* (out of stock and therefore order is canceled), *o.s.f.* (out of stock but item will follow when available), *o.s.i.* (out of stock indefinitely), and *o.s.t.* (out of stock temporarily).

ooze [book production] an infusion of oak bark, sumac, or other vegetable matter used in tanning leather *Ooze calf* has a soft velvet or suede finish. Ooze leather binding without underlying stiff *boards* is called *limp ooze* and is used on Bibles and small reference books.

op opposite (also *oppos.*); OPUS; OVERPRINT

OP or **o.p.** out of print A book that is out of print and *canceled*—no longer on the publisher's list—is *o.p.c.*, whereas *o.p.p.* is out of print *at present*, and *o.p.s.* is out of print and someone is *searching* for a copy.

opacity the state, quality, or degree of being not transparent or translucent; a characteristic of paper related to the degree to which ink bleeds through so that it can be seen on the reverse side A paper stock that resists STRIKE THROUGH is highly *opaque*, such as *90-percent opaque*, as a result of such factors as the density of the reflective surface, its thickness, and the use of mineral or other fillers.

opal a translucent mineral *Opalescence* is an iridescent appearance. An *opal glass* is used to diffuse light. *Opaline* is a translucent, milky variety of glass, often silk-screened, that is used for advertisements on the sides of bus shelters.

opaline paper a glossy type of parchment paper

opaque impermeable to light; dull or dark; to cover up or paint out an area on a NEGATIVE so that it will not appear on the printing plate or print In film animation, artists—*opaquers*—fill in the colors on each CEL, a process called *opaquing*.

opaque projector a projector that casts an enlarged image of flat material, such as printed pages of an open book, by using a light source that shines directly on the object; also called a *balopticon* It is not the same as an *overhead projector*, which shines light through a *transparency* rather than an opaque object.

opaque screen a nontransparent—opaque—material on which an image is produced by reflected light from a projector in front of the screen (not *rear projection*)

opaque white paint a water-based paint commonly used by artists to cover dye, ink, paint, and other materials, particularly to silhouette photographs by outlining the subject, correct inked lines, and letter over a dark background Opaque white paints vary in their opacity.

op art *optical art*, abstract designs that create OPTICAL ILLUSIONS

OPC Overseas Press Club, a New York organization of journalists with foreign news experience

op. cit. *in the work cited*; from the Latin *opere citato*, a term used in a series of FOOTNOTES or other bibliographic references with the name of the author followed by *op cit.*, thus indicating that preceding information about the author or book applies; pronounced op-SIT and similar to *loc. cit.*, which means "in the place cited" (*loco citato*) Both terms sometimes are written without periods, which should be included because they are abbreviations.

op ed [newspapers] the page adjacent to—*opposite*—the *editorial page*, used for columns and opinion articles, including those by outsiders (non-staffers) In some cases, BYLINED op-ed articles and letters to the editor appear on the editorial page itself rather than opposite or near it.

open to begin To *open cold* is to start a program or show without an introduction or sometimes without a rehearsal, preview, or out-of-town tryout. A TV performer *opens left* by starting at the left side of the picture. To *open right* is to start at the right side of the picture. For a performer, to *open up* is to turn toward the audience. To open up a layout is to add space. An *opened book* is one in which the folded edge of one or more of the sheets were not cut during the binding and must be separated by hand, using a paper knife.

open account a shipment of merchandise without payment in advance

open ad a WANT AD or other advertisement with full information, such as the name of the employer; the opposite of a *blind ad*, which omits the name of the employer or advertiser

open back a *hollow-back* or *loose-back* binding in which the covering material is not glued to the back of the book

open-back pamphlet file a box enclosed at the top and bottom and on three sides, commonly used in libraries for holding brochures, magazines, or other materials

open call a general audition

open dating the marketing of products with a specified date beyond which they should not be sold because of deterioration or other factors Sometimes referred to as *dating*, the term is confusing in that one would assume open dating refers to sale over an unlimited period of time and is different from *closed dating*.

open distribution availability of a product to any dealer or retailer, as opposed to *exclusive* or *limited* distribution

open-end or **open-ended** [broadcasting] a recorded audio or video program, sequence, interview, or commercial in which a local announcer can participate to add a local or live dimension to the beginning or end, ask questions, or insert local information; a program with no specific conclusion time

open-end envelope an envelope that opens on the short side instead of the conventional long side; also called *open-side envelope*

open-end question a question that a respondent may answer in any manner, not confined to multiple-choice

open-face type a type designed with white space in the middle; also called *outline type*

open format [newspapers] a layout style with no lines between columns; not the same as OP FORMAT

open full [theater] to start a show with the entire cast ONSTAGE

open house an event to which a company or other organization invites employees, suppliers, customers, neighbors, alumni, members, shareholders, or others to visit its facility (*house*)

opening the first day of business (such as a store opening or *grand opening*); a first performance In show business, the *opening night* is the first performance seen by the critics. In the fashion business, an opening is the first showing to buyers of designers' collections, such as the *Paris openings* or *Rome openings*. In books, an opening is the two facing pages of an open book, as of a book on display.

opening billboard the introduction of a radio or TV program, which may include highlights or names of the cast or sponsors

open layout a liberal use of white space; not tight In typesetting, open refers to excessive spacing between letters or words.

open-letter an OUTLINE letter An *open-letter proof* of an engraving has an inscription with the name of the artist or printer engraved in OUTLINE TYPE.

open mike a live microphone; an instruction to turn on or activate a microphone; in nightclubs, an evening or other time when singers, comedians, and other performers can do their acts, without compensation, for the experience and audience reaction

open negative [photography] underexposed to produce a fuller or darker print

open publication in a loose condition, with room for more advertising or editorial material; opposite of *tight* A newspaper or other publication with a great deal of excess space (often *plugged up* with ads for the publication itself) is called *wide open*. However, an *open style* may be intentional with regard to a large amount of *white space* in the layouts. Open style also may refer to minimal use of punctuation marks.

open punctuation the minimum of necessary punctuation

open rate the basic charge to advertisers by a medium; also called *one-time rate* It is the highest rate, as compared to *contract rate* or other discounts for volume or frequency.

open reel a film or tape reel not enclosed in a cassette or cartridge, as used on a *reel-to-reel* recorder, player, or projector

open score   a sheet of music—*score*—for two or more voices in which each part is written or printed on a separate STAFF

open set   [theater] a set without walls, delineated by curtains or other DROPS; the opposite of a *box set*

open stage   a stage that is open to the audience on three sides   Also called a *thrust stage*, it has no PROSCENIUM or front curtain. *Open staging* is a stage designed in this manner, not necessarily in an open-stage theater. Perhaps the best-known open stage was the Globe Theatre in England in the 17th century, at which the plays of William Shakespeare were performed.

open style   See OPEN PUBLICATION.

open-to-buy (OTB)   the amount a buyer at a retail store or other business is permitted to buy during a specific period; also, uncommitted monies available for purchases, as in an advertising budget

open turn   a performer's movement toward the audience, the opposite of a *closed turn*; also called a *stage turn*

open up   1 [graphic arts] to enlarge and/or add white space, as to *open up a layout*   2 [photography] to close down a camera lens so that less light passes through its aperture; also called STOP DOWN

operations manager (OM)   the assistant manager at some radio stations   The operations manager, who supervises administrative staff and also may be the programming manager, reports to the general manager.

Operator 25 Service   a system of Western Union enabling consumers to call a local number and receive—from Operator Number 25—the names of local dealers or other information provided by national advertisers   Though still popular, the service is now used less because of the proliferation of toll-free calls to 800 numbers.

OPF   one-piece folder   In book production, a one-piece mailing carton is generally custom-made to fit a specific book size.

op format   the optimum or most desirable format, such as a full-size newspaper with six columns on each page

opiner   a person with an opinion; a newspaper columnist or broadcast commentator; pronounced oh-PINE-er

opinion   belief; judgment; evaluation; impression   *Public opinion* is the expression of an attitude on a subject, often a controversial one, by a group or by a majority of people in an area or category. *Public opinion research* is a systematic attempt to determine these beliefs.

opinion leader   a person who influences others   In the *trickle-across* or *trickle-down* concept of marketing, opinion leaders are encouraged to sample new items or services first, so that their usage and opinions influence others. If the influence affects the same social class, such as peers, it is called *horizontal opinion leadership*, whereas if the influence is trickle-down or *vertical opinion leadership*, snob appeal can be established. This two-step-flow theory of communications is an essential component of word-of-mouth advertising.

Opinion Research Corp.   a market-research subsidiary of Arthur D. Little, Inc., Cambridge, MA, a management consulting company, that specializes in periodic surveys such as Caravan, in which clients share the costs   Founded in 1938, it is known among market researchers as ORC and is based in Princeton, NJ.

opp.   opposite

opry house   slang for a run-down theater, generally specializing in country-and-western music, particularly the *Grand Old Opry House* in Nashville, TN   The origin is from the 19th-century opera houses built in Western towns for touring musicals.

optical   a type of special effect, such as FADE, DISSOLVE, or WIPE, used in films   An *optical answer print*, or *optical*, is a print in which optical effects have been incorporated and various color and other corrections have been made.

optical center   the subjective or perceived center of a page or scene, slightly above the true, objective center

optical character recognition (OCR)   a method of converting typed, printed, or other graphic material to electronic symbols by means of a reading device—an *optical character reader*—programmed to recognize character shapes, as contrasted with *magnetic ink character recognition*   *Optical bar recognition* (OBR) uses parallel lines instead of letters, as on product codes.

optical disc   a DIGITAL storage medium, also called an *optical memory disc* or *optical storage disc*, in which LASERS are used to "read" the data—text, graphics, images, or sound   *Compact discs* (CDs) are optical discs with sound, particularly music.

optical effects   artificially induced changes in a still or film photographic image, such as DISSOLVES, FADES, SUPERIMPOSITIONS, and WIPES; also called *opticals*

optical flare   a light that bounces around the glass surfaces of camera lenses, causing FOG or other effects

optical illusion   a visually perceived image that is deceptive or misleading

optical printer a film printer in which the original, generally a negative, and the printing stock are not in physical contact (as in a *contact printer*) during the exposure

optical scanner a device that uses light to read—*scan*—text, graphics, or other visual images and convert them into signals, generally digital, that can be processed by a computer

optical soundtrack an area on a film, one or more tracks and generally not in color, that lets varying amounts of light pass through to a PHOTOELECTRIC cell that converts it into electrical impulses The photocell "reads" the light variations and translates them into sound. The soundtrack area is on the outer edge of the film, between the frame and the sprocket holes.

optics [film, television] visual techniques to produce OPTICAL ILLUSIONS; also called *effects*

option a choice; an exclusive right, usually obtained for a fee or by contract In broadcasting, *option time* was the arrangement by which a local station agreed to give time priorities to network programming. In 1963, the Federal Communications Commission banned network *option clauses*. Option time also is the final period by which an agreement, such as to renew a contract or continue a program, must be executed.

opt out the moment during a network news transmission or other live feed when a local radio or TV station has the option of discontinuing and returning to its own programming

optrack an OPTICAL SOUNDTRACK on film, different from a MAGNETIC SOUNDTRACK (magtrack)

opus a work, particularly a musical work, numbered in order of composition or publication (the *opus numbers*)

Oracle a sans-serif typeface; also, a British TELETEXT system

oral history a record or biography of an individual, company, or organization compiled through interviews, generally tape-recorded, by a professional interviewer, an *oral historian* The technique was originated in 1948 by Allan Nevins (1890–1971), an American historian.

orange goods [marketing] broadly distributed products, such as clothing, that are moderate (between red and yellow) in the amount of required service, profits, and turnover

orange peel [recording] an irregularity (akin to the bumpiness of the skin of an orange) in the surface of a record, a defect in the manufacture from being pressed with PLATENS that are not perfectly smooth

oration a formal public speech, particularly in connection with a ceremony, as delivered by an *orator*, who generally is an eloquent speaker

orbit the path of a satellite (or other body) as it revolves around the earth (or other body) or one complete revolution of such a body Communications satellites orbit at 22,300 miles above—perpendicular to—the equator. Because this *synchronous orbit* is the same speed as the earth revolving on its axis, the satellites are in *stationary orbit*.

orbiter a telecommunications satellite that moves in orbit around the earth

ORC OPINION RESEARCH CORPORATION

orchestra the main floor of a theater; a large group of musicians, such as a *symphony orchestra* The *orchestra pit*, also called the *pit*, is the space in front of and below the stage where the orchestra musicians sit. The *orchestra leader* is the *conductor*. The *orchestra rail* separates the pit from the audience. To *orchestrate* is to arrange a musical SCORE or other project.

order a logical, methodical, or prescribed arrangement or instruction In typesetting, order refers to a system in which headlines or other text components are ranked. A *first-order headline* is larger than a *second-order headline*.

order-blank envelope an envelope with an *order form* attached, generally a SELF-MAILER or printed so that the order form can be detached and inserted in an envelope

order card a return card to be filled out, checked, or initialed by the inquirer or customer and mailed back to the advertiser Order cards are often SELF-MAILERS.

order cycle time the interval between placement of an order and its delivery

order getting a *dynamic* process of generating sales as opposed to the *static* process of order taking, which is merely filling orders as received

ordering [broadcasting] the process of deciding on the order of stories or segments in a news program; also called FORMATTING or STACKING (putting in order in a stack)

order of appearance in film or other credits, a listing of performers or characters in the order in which they appear for the first time in the work This chronological order, which is common in plays, is different from an alphabetical arrangement or a listing in order of importance.

order processing fulfillment of orders In broadcasting, the *order-process* department prepares cost estimates and contracts for advertisers.

ordinal number a number used to indicate order in a series, such as first, second, etc., as opposed to a *cardinal number* (one, two, etc.); sometimes called simply *ordinal*

ordinal scaling a statistical system of identifying categories of a population and ranking them in order

ordinary mail a Postal Service designation for all mail other than registered, insured, certified, COD, special delivery, special handling, or Express Mail

organization chart a diagram that shows the personnel or parts of a company or other organization and their reporting relationships, usually with rectangles connected by vertical and horizontal lines The standard layout for names, titles, or other information included in the rectangles is for the primary name or words to be set in all capital letters on the first line and other information to be centered below it in capitals and lower case.

organized behavioral system (OBS) the manner in which individuals and groups react, including physiological, psychological, and sociological components

original first; fresh; the initial source from which copies are made, not an *adaptation* or copy

original parts a publication issued in installments, such as the 19th-century novels of Charles Dickens, William Thackeray, and other popular authors whose works were printed serially on a weekly, monthly, or other regular basis, with each part generally appearing in a distinctive illustrated wrapper

originate to produce and transmit a program or other material In broadcasting, the *origination point* is called the *feed point.*

Orion a major producer of theatrical films, based in New York Millions of viewers have seen the Orion logo; the company's exact name is Orion Pictures Corp., and the pronunciation is similar to O'Ryan.

ornament [typography] a decorative device such as a border, special letter, or design

orphan 1 an isolated article At *The Wall Street Journal,* the daily orphan is the article at the bottom left corner of page one of the second section. These brief articles often are whimsical, personal, or offbeat, including unconventional *orphan headlines* that may have periods, parentheses, or other teasing stoppers. 2 an element of type, such as a word or a line, that leads into a larger block of type and is intentionally left by itself at the end of a page or column; sometimes erroneously called a *widow* A *no-orphan technique* is a layout without orphans; it is also called the *buddy system.*

orphan brand a product with a small sales volume; in the pharmaceutical field, a prescription drug with annual sales of under $5 million

orthicon a television-camera pickup tube that is very sensitive to light and uses a low-velocity electron beam; from ortho-iconoscope Developed by RCA, the original model is called *Image Orthicon.*

orthochromatic a film, plate, or emulsion that renders all colors except red in tones of gray approximating their relative brilliance *Orthochromatic film* is not sensitive to red light and therefore is used where reproduction of red is unimportant or not wanted.

orthogonal projection a representation of a single two-dimensional view of an object projected along lines perpendicular to the view and the drawing surface; also called *orthographic projection*

orthography a mode or system of spelling; the science or study of letters and spelling; the representation of the sounds of a language by written or printed symbols *Orthographic* and *orthographical* (adjectives) and *orthographically* (adverb) pertain to spelling, except in *orthographic projection,* which relates to perpendicular lines and is preferably called ORTHOGONAL PROJECTION.

ortho litho film an ORTHOCHROMATIC *lithography* negative, insensitive to red but sensitive to blue, green, yellow, and ultraviolet light

OS off-screen; OLD STYLE; OUT-OF-STOCK (also *o.s.* or *o/s*)

Oscar the nickname for the annual awards—golden statuettes—of the *Academy of Motion Picture Arts and Sciences* in Beverly Hills, CA One version of its origin is that the executive secretary of the Academy observed that the first figurines looked like his Uncle Oscar in Texas. Another story is that after Bette Davis (1908–89) won the award for best actress in 1935 (the movie was *Dangerous*), she named the figurine for her first husband, bandleader Harmon Oscar Nelson. Still another attribution is to Margaret Herrick, a librarian at the Academy, who said in 1931 that it looked like her uncle Oscar.

OSI out of stock indefinitely (really not available!)

Osmiroid a pen with interchangeable points (nibs), commonly used for drawing and calligraphy, made by the Hunt Manufacturing Company in Philadelphia

OSS OVER-THE-SHOULDER SHOT

OTB open-to-buy, the amount a buyer at a retail store or other business is permitted to buy during a specific period

OTF off-the-film, as with an *OTF flash meter,* in which the amount of light from the flash is measured by a photocell as the ambient light—the light from the subject that passes through the lens—hits the film

O.T.O. one time only, generally referring to an advertisement to be broadcast or published only once

out **1** the end; the conclusion; the shortened form of OUTTAKE In general, out means to remove, as in a script notation to remove a sound. The OUTCUE is a signal that a program, scene, film, or tape is about to end. **2** [broadcasting] a completed communication, as in *over and out* The *out time* is the time at which a program ends. **3** [typography] an instruction indicating the omission of a word or words **4** [theater] To *move out* is to move away from the center of the stage, the opposite of move in.

outcue [broadcasting] the last few words—generally four—of a recorded song or a taped report or interview, an extremely important guide to the engineer, producer, director, disk jockey, and newscaster; also called *endcue* The outcue of a commercial or other taped segment is scripted, so that the live announcer knows when to start. In broadcasting, film, and theater, an outcue is the last few words of a part, signaling the next performer.

outdoor outdoor advertising, such as roadside BILLBOARDS, produced at an *outdoor plant* by an *outdoor operator* or *outdoor service* and purchased by an *outdoor space buyer* All the outdoor structures in an operator's area are also called the *outdoor plant.*

Outdoor Advertising Association of America (OAAA) a national association of the standardized outdoor advertising industry, based in Washington, DC

Outer Critics Circle an organization of theater writers and critics of national and non-New York media (hence the word "Outer") that presents annual awards The Drama Desk is the organization of New York critics.

outgoing in outdoor advertising, panels or other outdoor advertisements that are seen by traffic leaving a central business district or other area

out in the alley beyond the range of the microphone

outlay expenditure

outline a silhouette or a photo—an *outline cut*—with the subject outlined, or clearly defined, and the background faded or removed

outline drawing a drawing in which the subject is shown only in its outline, with no shading or internal details

outline font a typeface that is displayed on a computer screen with the outer edge of each character The pixel squares that are located within the outline are highlighted to produce the letter and then the outline is modified, as by enlarging serifs, flattening curves, or thickening

sections, to use all of the pixels within the character and fit the character more fully over the grid. Thus a user of outline-font software can create new typefaces via this process, called *grid fitting.*

outline letter [typography] a character with each stroke represented by two lines instead of one and with white space between the lines, used as DISPLAY type or in other large sizes

outline type characters with white space within their borders; also called OPEN-FACE, OUTLINE LETTER, or *outline*

out of frame a subject or action that is OFF-CAMERA and not seen within the FRAME of the picture; a misalignment in a film projector so that parts of two frames appear on the screen, easily corrected by the projectionist turning the *framing knob*

out-of-home advertising BILLBOARDS, posters, and other advertising on streets, buildings, and other outdoor locations, as well as in terminals, bus shelters, and other places outside the home; a new, broader name for *outdoor advertising*

out-of-home audience a broadcast audience not at home, such as listening (or viewing) in cars or at the beach

Out-of-Home Measurement Bureau (OMB) an organization in New Canaan, CT, of plant operators, advertisers, and advertising agencies that provides circulation verification for EIGHT-SHEET POSTERS and bus-shelter advertising

out-of-pocket cash paid out, such as for meals and other expenses of someone traveling, or costs for phone, postage, printing, or other items or services purchased from a supplier outside the organization

out-of-print a publication no longer available from the publisher

out-of-stock (OOS, OS, o.s., or o/s) [marketing] merchandise that is not on the shelves or available for sale In publishing, an out-of-stock book (OS) is not currently available but probably will be available, unless it's out of stock indefinitely (*OSI*).

outpack a premium attached to the outside of a package

output the act of producing or the amount of production; information produced by a computer, resulting from and the opposite of *input* An *output device* is an electronic or mechanical machine, such as a printer, that produces solid, readable, reproducible copy (*hard copy*). An *output tube* is a video display (a cathode-ray tube) that displays the results of computer processing. When there is no hard copy, the display material sometimes is called *soft output.*

outrigger a horizontal *rule*, or line, such as is used above and below text to set it off from the rest of the page It is increasingly common in newspaper and magazine layouts.

outro the standard conclusion of a radio or TV program; an exit speech in a scene; a TAG at the end of a commercial Outro is the opposite of *intro* (introduction).

outs outtakes; rejected or unused film or tape

outsert an advertising or promotional card or wrapper that is on the outside of part or all of the front and back covers of a magazine or other publication; also called a *wraparound* It can be editorial text, such as a folded sheet (four pages, though generally printed only on the outer side) or sheets, wrapped around the outside of a publication or a folded SIGNATURE.

outside form a side of a sheet that when folded contains two outside pages of a SIGNATURE These are always the lowest and highest FOLIOS in the FORM.

outsizes the smallest and largest sizes in a line of products; also called *endsizes*

outspace at *Time* magazine, an idiomatic verb that means to drop or edit out an item or part of a text for lack of space

outtake, out-take, or **out take** unused film or tape; a section or scene that is filmed or taped but not used in the final version for editing or other reasons, often consisting of FLUBS; also called TRIMS or *outs*

outyear the final year or years of a budget cycle or program

over longer than expected or scheduled; also called *overboard*

over and next text matter an instruction for an advertisement to appear above and adjacent to non-advertising, or editorial, matter

over-banner a BANNER or large headline *above* the NAMEPLATE, such as atop page one of a newspaper; also called *skyline streamer*

overcasting [book production] a method of hand binding in which one section is sewn to another by passing the thread through the back edge and diagonally out through the back When done through holes prepunched by machine, this method is called *oversewing*.

overcoat a protective layer on film or paper

overcrank [film] to speed up a camera so that it films at more than 24 FRAMES per second; the opposite of *undercrank* The resulting film appears to be in *slow motion* when projected at the standard speed of 24 frames per second.

over-door display in transit advertising, a CAR CARD or advertisement above the vehicle door; also called *top-end display*

overflow type for which there is insufficient space in PAGE MAKEUP; sometimes called *overset*

It is placed outside the printing area and keyed to its proper position.

over frame an unseen narrator; also called *voice-over* The speaker or source of the sound does not appear in the FRAME of the picture.

overhang cover [publishing] a cover larger in size than the pages it encloses; opposite of a FLUSH COVER

overhead the cost of doing business not specifically associated with the basic production of goods or services, such as rent and telephone

overhead projector a type of projector that enlarges and projects a sheet of paper onto a screen and does not require the production of slides; so called because the sheet is laid flat horizontally and the lens system projects the image up and then forward onto a vertical screen

overlap 1 to extend over and partly cover; to have an area in common with another A performer who overlaps moves or speaks before the cue. 2 [film, television] the running of two projectors or tape machines in synchronization so that a changeover can be made from one to the other; a segment of a DISSOLVE in which the images are superimposed and the shooting of scenes longer than necessary to provide leeway in editing 3 [typography] characters that are linked or partially over each other, such as a LIGATURE

overlay 1 a superimposition or covering; to lay, cover, or spread over, as with a transparent flap, showing additional details or highlighting specific areas, placed over a map or other item 2 [advertising] a strip of copy added to an outdoor advertisement to provide a date, price, or other information; the overall theme of an advertising, public relations, or other campaign 3 [graphic arts] a superimposition, such as a composite picture, tissue, transparent paper, or acetate positioned over artwork or other material to indicate revisions, colors, or other printing instructions or changes A *separation overlay* is an acetate sheet placed over a mechanical, one sheet for each separate color to be printed. A *tinted acetate overlay*, which is coated with a colored ink, can be used in color separations. 4 [printing] the paper affixed to the impression surface of a press to help make a uniform impression

overline a caption above a picture or art; a line above a headline, usually FLUSH left and underlined; also called *eyebrow* or *teaser* Common in *The Wall Street Journal*, it is technically part of the headline.

overload [journalism] the cramming of too much material into one sentence or section

overnight or **overnite** 1 a story usually written late at night for the afternoon newspaper of the next day; also called *overniter* It is most often used by the press services. **2** The overnight staff at a newspaper is the *skeleton crew* during the late night or early morning hours. In broadcasting, the overnights are the TV rating estimates, available within a day of broadcast and drawn from households in markets with audience-metering devices.

overprinting printing of an advertisement above editorial matter, as in the advertisement called *Scoreboard* that appears above sports scores in some newspapers; printing over an area that already has been printed It is also called *overset* or leftover matter.

override a commission to a sales manager or other supervisor or agent based on the sales of the salespeople who report to him or her This commission to the manager, which is in addition to the commission received by the subordinates, thus *rides over* their commission. Though commonly used and acceptable, the word probably originated as a mispronunciation of *overwrite*; it is also used as a verb.

overrun the act of exceeding estimated costs or quantity or the amount in excess; overflow; copies printed in excess of the specified quantity The general practice permits delivery and charge for up to 10 percent in excess of the quantity ordered, as by a newsstand dealer.

overrunning a program that is behind schedule, running over, running late

overs the surplus left after the required number of printed pieces or other items have been used; also, short for OVERSET

overset typeset copy not used and retained for possible future use; leftover matter; overset matter; overmatter; type set in excess of available space The opposite is *underset*.

oversewn [book production] the individual sewing of each leaf of a book or other publication for extra strength, as with a LIBRARY BINDING or a rebinding The oversewing process sews together small groups of leaves with overlapping stitches across the spine. An *oversewn book* does not lie open flat.

oversize [printing] art or copy that is larger than the size it will be when reproduced An *oversize book* is too large for a regular-size library shelf.

overstock excessive inventory, usually sold at a discount or returned to the supplier

overstrike the substitution of one character for another; to imprint a character in the same position as one already on the page or video screen

over-the-roof a headline at the top of page one of a publication, above the NAMEPLATE

over-the-shoulder shot (OSS) a camera shot made from behind a performer, sometimes including all or part of the head and shoulders, with the camera focused on the spot at which the performer is looking; also called *XS*, for across shoulder

over the transom unsolicited material, such as manuscripts sent to a publisher; also called *slush* or *slush pile* The original is from the open panels above doors through which packages were tossed.

over-39 light slang for AMBIENT LIGHT or soft light that is flattering to performers over 39 years old

overture a musical introduction to a performance of a musical work The warning to the stage performer is "Overture!"

overwire hanger an advertising BANNER or pennant suspended from a cord or wire strung along the ceiling of a retail outlet

overwrite to write over other writing; to write too much or in a style that is too flowery or labored; to receive a commission based on the sales of representatives or employees The sales overwrite sometimes is called an OVERRIDE.

owned-and-operated station (O & O) a local radio or TV station owned and operated by a NETWORK

ownership mark a BOOKPLATE, stamp, label, or other identification of the owner of a book or other item A metal or rubber *ownership stamp* or embossing often is used by a library to mark its ownership of a book.

Oxberry a manufacturer of commonly used special-effects optical printers and other film equipment, particularly for animation; now a division of Cybernetics Products Inc., Carlstadt, NJ

Oxford comma a comma placed after the next-to-last item in a series (more commonly called a *serial comma*), a style favored by Oxford University Press of Oxford, England and the widely used style manual published by the University of Chicago

oxford corners border rules, or lines, that cross and project beyond each other and thus do not form a perfect rectangle (or other shape), used as a decorative effect on a title page of a book or a book cover

oxford rule a rule, or line, consisting of one thick stroke and one thin stroke; sometimes called a *Scotch rule* or *double rule* It is not the same as a *parallel rule*, which has strokes of the same weight. A *double oxford rule* has three strokes, consisting of one central thick stroke and two outer thin strokes.

oxymoron a figure of speech that combines contradictions, such as "thunderous silence" or "jumbo shrimp" The Greek word *oxymoron* means "acutely silly."

Ozalid a trademarked process for producing photo prints on DIAZO-coated paper, similar to a *blueprint* except that the lines are black on a white background; also called a *white print* Ozalids are made by Bruning, Itasca, IL.

ozoner a drive-in theater; coined by *Variety*, from ozone, or fresh air

P

p past; PER

p. or P. PAGE (*p-1* is *page 1*); PART; print: a mark made on a part of a film negative to indicate to the laboratory that it is to be printed

PA personal assistant (in the United Kingdom); PRESS AGENT; production assistant; PUBLIC ADDRESS SYSTEM; PUBLIC AFFAIRS; *per annum*, Latin for "by the year"

PABX PRIVATE AUTOMATIC BRANCH EXCHANGE

PAC political *a*ction *c*ommittee

pace [theater] the tempo, overall speed, intensity, and rhythm of a performance or a production; also called *pacing* Pace is a desirable quality; a show that lacks pace may seem labored or dull. To be *off the pace* is to be behind the leader, who *sets the pace.* A *change of pace* is a variation in tempo or mood.

pack a package, packet, or container; a collection or bundle of items; a set or group In retailing, an *inpack* is a premium or other giveaway item inside a package, such as a cereal box. An *onpack* is a premium affixed to the outside of the package. A *near pack* is an item, generally free with purchase, set up in a bin or other receptacle near where the product is for sale—for instance, a flag or other item too large to be an inpack or an onpack. In computers, a *disk pack* is a removable assembly of recording surfaces, or disks.

pack to fill In the computer field, to *pack* is to store data in a compact form in a storage medium. To *pack the house* is to fill a theater with an audience—to *pack 'em in*—resulting in a *packed house.*

package (pkg. or pkge.) 1 a container or wrapping; the exterior appearance of a single unit or product; a container and its contents, such as all the elements in a mailing 2 a plan or offer that includes several components, often called a *package deal* 3 [broadcasting] a radio or TV program or a combination of radio or TV programs or commercial spots offered to a sponsor as a unit, usually at a discount 4 a taped television report, generally :45 (45 seconds) to 2:30 (2½ minutes)—a *short package* A *long package* is a special report or a report to be edited and broadcast over a period of days (a *two-parter, three-parter, four-parter,* or *five-parter*).

package band a paper tape or other strip that attaches a gift item or premium to a product package The premium is called an *onpack premium* or *banded premium.*

packaged goods products wrapped or packaged by the manufacturer—particularly food, household supplies, liquor, tobacco, and other mass-consumed items The phrase—which also appears as *package goods*—refers to these product classifications, as distinct from appliances and hard goods (including automobiles), apparel, and nonpackaged soft goods. Actually, package goods are alcoholic beverages, as sold in *package stores,* retail stores licensed to sell them for drinking elsewhere.

package enclosure a premium or other item enclosed in a package; also called *inpack*

package flat a carton shipped collapsed for use as a point-of-sale display bin

package insert 1 a folder or other printed item included with the product in its carton or other package—for instance, a patient-information sheet accompanying a prescription drug 2 a sheet or other promotional material inserted into the overall package, as in a shopping bag at the grocery checkout counter

package outsert a booklet or other printed item attached to the outside of a package

package plan discount a discount offered to advertisers for the purchase of a quantity of commercials broadcast within a specified period, such as a week A special rate for five commercials in a week is called a *5-plan.*

packager a person or organization that produces a finished product, such as a book, TV program, or motion picture, for another company The role of packager in publishing and show business has increased considerably in recent years; the term generally refers to someone who provides a variety of services but does not necessarily produce a completely finished product or program.

package show a show that is provided in entirety at a theater or other site, including the whole cast If the cast includes well-known performers, the deal is called a *star package*.

packer a company that fills cans or other packages with a product, usually food

packer's label the brand name, or *label*, of a product owned by a packer or a manufacturer

packet 1 a small package or bundle 2 [computers] a sequence of signals arranged in a specific format and handled as a whole, as in *packet switching* or *packet sequencing*, via data-terminal equipment called a packet-mode terminal

packing 1 processing and packaging, particularly of food products (by a packer) 2 material used to prevent leakage or seepage 3 [printing] sheets used to build up or increase the height of the pile of sheets to be printed, to facilitate the flow of the paper 4 sheets (called *packing* and *underpacking*) inserted behind the blanket or plate used in OFFSET printing *Packing down* is the gradual decrease in the thickness of the blanket, which then requires insertion of sheets to maintain the same pressure and contact.

packing density [computers] the number of storage cells per unit area, length, or volume

packing slip a sheet or document accompanying a shipment, with a list of the items in the shipment

pack journalism reportage that is similar, by a group, or a pack, of journalists who are assigned to the same story, such as the press corps covering an event or a government official

pad 1 [graphic arts] sheets of paper glued together along one edge; also called *tablet* 2 an absorbent cushion soaked with ink for use with a rubber stamp; also called *ink pad* or *stamp pad* 3 to lengthen an article, program, or other matter with extraneous material or without adding anything substantive

pad copy news stories not scheduled but available if needed

padding 1 extraneous or unimportant material added to a speech, article, or other matter to make it longer; also called *filler* 2 [computers] a technique that incorporates fillers in data 3 blank leaves to fill out a SIGNATURE or for other reasons

paean a song or hymn of joy, triumph, or praise; sometimes spelled *pæan* In ancient Greece, it was a hymn of thanksgiving to the gods, particularly Apollo, the god of music, poetry, prophecy, and medicine. The origin probably is Paian, the physician of the Greek gods. The word is pronounced PEE-un.

page (p., P., or pg.; plural, pp., Pp., or pgs.) 1 one side of a leaf, or sheet, of paper in a publication, often with reference to its contents, as with the *sports page* of a newspaper, or location,

as with the *front page* The printed area of a page available for advertising is called a *full page*, though it may not actually occupy the entire sheet, unless it bleeds—covers the outside borders and extends to the edges. 2 [computers] a fixed-length block—generally a maximum of 52 single-spaced lines of 80 characters (letters or numbers) each, totaling 4,160 characters, and transferred as a unit *Paging* or *page swapping* is the exchange of pages between two areas, as between the main and the auxiliary storage of a word processor. *Paging* also is simply the display of segments of data on a terminal screen. To *page up* is to move up a full page (such as 26 lines of text) on a computer screen; to *page down* is to move in the opposite direction. 3 [videotex] a full screen, generally 24 lines of 40 characters each 4 a person, often in uniform, who carries messages, as in a hotel or legislature; to try to find by calling, as on a public address system or beeper (see also PAGING)

page a curtain to guide each half of a draw curtain to make sure the two halves meet at the center of the stage; also called *walk a curtain* The stagehand who guides the curtain is sometimes called a *page*.

pageant lantern British term for a PROJECTOR LAMP

page break an indication of the end of one page and the beginning of a new page An *enforced*, or *required*, *page break* may not be deleted, regardless of the amount of blank space remaining on a page—for instance, before a new chapter in a book.

page-content heading a word or words at the top of a page to identify its contents, as in telephone directories and reference books; also called *guide word* A common style in dictionaries is to list the first and last words on the page or on the two facing pages. The style generally is *flush left* (aligned at the margin) on left pages and *flush right* on right pages.

page frame a skeleton or layout page, providing information about the art or other matter that is to be inserted

page header 1 identifying information at the top of a sheet of paper 2 [computers] the top row or line, usually including the subject, date, and time, as in TELETEXT

page makeup the pasting of galleys, headings, and other components into final page form

page map a diagram or layout of a page as shown on a screen and used in computerized page makeup

Page One Awards the annual awards of the NEWSPAPER GUILD OF NEW YORK The awards were established in 1934.

page opening a print readership technique in which two adjacent pages are lightly glued together, so that a researcher can determine if the reader opened it

page previewing [computers] a process that shows on a screen what a page will look like when it is printed Some programs can show many pages on the screen at the same time.

page printer a device that prints one page at a time, such as a cathode-ray-tube printer, film printer, or xerographic printer, also called *page-at-a-time printer*; different from a LINE PRINTER

page proof the exact copy, or proof, of a page as it will look when printed Sometimes illustrations, especially photographs, do not appear in the proof but appropriate space is left for them.

page rate 1 the advertising cost of a full page 2 [publishing] payment to an author per printed page, rather than per word or on some other pricing schedule

page spread two adjacent pages with art or other material BLEEDING to the middle area so that the entire area functions as a single unit or page; also called *double-page spread* or *spread*

page swapping [computers] the exchange of pages between the main storage and the auxiliary storage

page turner 1 an arrow, a sketch of a hand or index finger, or some other notation at the bottom of a page of a magazine or other publication, indicating that the article is continued 2 someone who sits next to a solo pianist to turn the pages of the sheet music 3 a book, script, or other work that is so interesting that it encourages the reader to go to the next page

page turning [computers] the transfer of pages between the main and the auxiliary storage; also called PAGING

page view terminal (PVT) a video terminal, or screen, that displays a full page

pagination the assignment of numbers to pages, or the sequential arrangement of pages of a publication *To paginate* is to number pages. Pagination was first used by a German printer in 1471. A *pagination sheet* is a form on which all pages, including blanks, are numbered. The sheet is used in the arrangement of the pages for printing (they are printed on large sheets that are then folded and cut).

paging 1 [printing] the making up of pages or the numbering of pages; see also PAGE 2 [computers] the transfer of pages of instructions or data between storage media, such as from a magnetic tape or disk to the central processing unit computer 3 the process of calling—for instance, on a portable radio receiver (a *pager* or *beeper*) to alert the recipient to a phone call or

message The electronic device is called a *paging receiver*.

paid for a line, required by federal law, spoken at the end of a broadcast political commercial or inserted at the bottom of a printed advertisement, indicating the source of payment ("Paid for by the Jones for Congress Committee")

paint a mixture of pigment and oil, water, or other substances Commercial artists generally use *water-soluble* paints, which dry more rapidly and are easier to use than *oil-based paints*, called *sign writer's paints* (they are also used on posters and SHOWCARDS). *Animation paints*, which are used in film animation, are water-soluble and generally contain acetate or acrylic. Common types of water-soluble paints, besides acrylic, include casein, gouaches, and watercolors. A picture with excessive paint is called *painty*.

painted bulletin a billboard advertisement that is painted, instead of of a printed poster

painted display an outdoor advertisement—larger than a BULLETIN (about 14' × 48')—that is painted on a wall or bulletin structure and is usually illuminated A POSTER is purchased in monthly segments for as short a period as one month, whereas painted displays generally are contracted for a minimum of one year. The contract may specify repainting and copy changes within the year.

painted edges speckling, gold leafing (gilt edging), or other decoration applied to the front edges of the leaves of a book such as a dictionary or other deluxe volume

painter light a carefully controlled source of illumination in a machine that makes film prints

painterly characteristic of a painter, particularly in relation to high technical and aesthetic standards

paint out [advertising] to cover or paint over a PAINTED BULLETIN in preparation for a new message; also called *blankout* or *coat out*

paint program [computers] a software program that provides for the creation of visual images, including an array of colors; different from a *draw program*, which uses graphics stored in the system A *paint and draw* program uses original and stored images.

paint time [computers, videotex] the number of seconds required to display a frame with graphics, measured from when the frame begins to appear until it is completed

paired comparison questionnaire a series of questions from which the respondent chooses between alternatives

PAL PARCEL AIRLIFT MAIL; PHASE-ALTERNATION SYSTEM

paleography the study of ancient written documents, or the ancient writing itself

palette a board on which an artist mixes colors; the range of colors or other qualities (in music or other art forms) In computer graphics, a palette is the array of available colors. It is not the same as PALLET, though the words are pronounced the same and *pallet* is sometimes used as an alternate spelling.

palette knife **1** a small, flexible blade, generally steel, attached to a handle, generally wood, sometimes plastic, used to mix paint on a PALETTE **2** to scrape and clean a palette, and sometimes to apply paint to a painting

palimpsest **1** a document, generally on parchment or vellum that was written over one or more times, with the earlier written material partly or completely erased or covered A *double palimpsest* has had two rewritings and is prized by paleographers. **2** a painting that covers an earlier one; any canvas or other surface that has been reused

palindrome a word, phrase, sentence, or verse that reads the same backward or forward Examples are "Name no one man" and "Madam, I'm Adam."

pallet **1** a portable platform for storing or moving **2** a paddlelike tool used by an artist for mixing and shaping clay **3** a tool for applying gold leaf, as on books The word (in all meanings) is not the same as *palate* (roof of the mouth) or PALETTE, though the three words are pronounced the same and *pallet* is sometimes used as an alternate spelling for *palette*.

Palme d'Or an annual award for the production of a TV commercial, presented in June at the International Advertising Awards Film Festival in Cannes, France

pam. PAMPHLET

pam box a PAMPHLET file

pamphlet (pam. or pph.) an unbound booklet or nonperiodical printed work, usually with a paper cover (of the same stock as the text or heavier), generally 6 to 48 pages; a short essay or treatise, generally political (written by a *pamphleteer*) Technically, a *pamphlet* is unbound, whereas a *booklet* is bound. However, in general usage, a *pamphlet* may be a bound publication, often SADDLE-BOUND, and the process is called *pamphlet binding*. A library may bind pamphlets with *pamphlet boards*, usually a plain stiff cardboard with cloth hinges, and store them (bound or unbound) in a box or other container (*pamphlet box* or *pamphlet file*). A *pamphlet volume* has several pamphlets bound together, perhaps with a title or contents page.

pan **1** a negative review of a play or other work The reviewing is called *panning*. To *put on the*

pan is to criticize severely; the origin is the frying pan. **2** [film, television] a direction given to the person operating the camera, so that the camera eye moves slowly and evenly, vertically or horizontally, in a *panorama* (the source of the term) A *pan shot* also is called a *blue pan*, *swish*, *whipshot*, or *wiz pan*. The process of *laterally* moving the camera to photograph a wide view is called *panning*. In the *pan and scan* technique, a regular-size screen image (1.33:1) is selected from a wide-screen image by moving the camera from side to side—panning—across the original. **3** [photography] short for PANCHROMATIC, black-and-white film that registers color as gray values A *pan master* is a fine-grained panchromatic black-and-white film or slide made from a color original. **4** [theater] to move items such as spotlights, usually horizontally, as in to *pan left* or *pan right*, and sometimes vertically, as in to *pan down* or *pan up*

Panafax the trademarked name of a telephone facsimile machine distributed by Matsushita Graphic Communications Systems, of Melville, NY

pan and scan a technique for changing the ASPECT RATIO of the frame of a wide-screen film so that it can be transmitted for TV

Panavision a wide-screen, 35mm film system with a special anamorphic lens—one capable of different magnifications—developed by Panavision, Inc., of Los Angeles, that results in a width-to-height ratio of 2.35:1 *Super Panavision* and *Ultra Panavision* use 65mm film. A frequent screen credit is "Filmed in Panavision."

pancake **1** a disk **2** a small platform A *pancake box* generally is 2 inches high, about ¼ the height of a standard *apple box*. **3** heavy make-up used by performers Actually, *Pan-Cake Make-Up* is a trademarked face powder pressed into a flat cake, made by Max Factor & Co., Los Angeles. **4** slang for a large reel of audio tape, wound on an open hub (with no side supports) and purchased by recording studios so that it then can be spooled onto smaller conventional reels The pancake may be blank tape or it may have recorded material, such as consecutive copies of the same commercial or other work, that is then unspooled and cut into sections, with one commercial or other work on each tape.

panchromatic sensitive to light of all colors A *panchromatic film* is a silver-emulsion black-and-white film sensitive to the entire visible color spectrum, whereas *orthochromatic film* is not sensitive to red. A *panchromatic master positive* is a 35mm black-and-white print made from a color negative. *Panchromatic film* shows the colors in various shades of gray.

P&D PRESSING AND DISTRIBUTING

P & H postage and handling charge

P&L profit and loss

P&W PENSION AND WELFARE

pane a small block of stamps sold as a sheet or in a booklet (a *booklet pane*) The U.S. Postal Service considers a pane to be one-quarter of a full sheet, such as 50 stamps from a sheet of 200; consumers often refer to a pane as a *sheet*.

panegyric a formal speech or piece of writing, often elaborately laudatory, such as a eulogy

panel **1** a group of individuals, who are questioned on a continuing basis for their opinions and other research; a discussion group at a meeting In a *true panel*, the respondents are measured repeatedly on the same subject (such as TV viewing habits), whereas in an *omnibus panel*, the subjects may change. In broadcasting, a panel is a group on a discussion, quiz, or other program. To panel is to place a person on such a program. **2** an individual board used for outdoor or transit advertising A *blocked panel* has an obstructed view. *Stacked panels* or *deck panels* are built vertically. **3** a raised or depressed area, generally rectangular, on a letterhead or card (such as a formal announcement or invitation) **4** a square or rectangular space on the cover or spine of a book, enclosed by lines or impressed, as on a cover, between BANDS or lines, as on a spine **5** a rectangular picture, such as a comic strip, comprising one or more panels

panel pictures individual photographs of uniform size, pasted up as one unit, with the pictures touching one another It is reproduced in printing as a single HALFTONE.

panel quote a quotation extracted from a text and inserted within a square or rectangular border adjacent to or within the text; also called *blurb, pull quote,* or *readout*

panels per facing (PPF) the number of outdoor advertising panels—usually one, two, or three—on a structure that face the same direction

pan glass an eyepiece with a brownish-yellow or bluish-green filter, used by a film director or director of photography to evaluate lighting contrast and tone values It is commonly seen dangling from a cord around the director's neck and therefore familiar as the badge of identification of a film director. The name refers to the way the view will appear on PANCHROMATIC film.

panning lateral, or horizontal, movement of a camera, as in film, or of a video image, as in computers; see also PAN

panning gear [film] a mechanism that moves a camera so that each movement receives one exposure, used in animation

panorama a broad view, generally scenic

panpot [recording, theater] a panoramic potentiometer, an instrument that varies the position of a sound by changing the signal strengths to two or more speakers

panto British slang for PANTOMIME

pantograph **1** an instrument for copying a drawing or other art by tracing the lines with a stylus, on the same or a different scale **2** an accordionlike device, such as a movable, extensible arm for a telephone or lights

pantomime a dramatic presentation that contains no words, only actions and gestures, as performed by a *pantomimist* or *mime* The word is from the Greek *mimos,* "mimic." To pantomime or to mime is to use the face and body expressively.

Pantone Matching System (PMS) a series of ink-matching guides for the graphic arts, published by Pantone, Inc., of Moonachie, NJ The Pantone Color Specifier, for example, contains about 500 color swatches for coated, or shiny, and uncoated stock. An identifying number for each color is shown beneath a tear-out color swatch in the sample book. *Pantone* (also known as *PMS*) *267 C,* for example, is a deep purple, designed for coated stock. These swatches are widely used by graphics designers and printers.

pantry audit an examination and listing of the brands of drug, food, and other items in the kitchen and other areas of a household, conducted by a market research firm

pantsfolder *Wall Street Journal* jargon, usually derisive, for a how-to feature, such as "How to Fold Your Pants in Luggage"

PAO PUBLIC AFFAIRS OFFICER

paparazzi photographers, especially freelancers, who take candid photographs of celebrities and sell the photos to publications, often to the distress of the subjects The paparazzi are noted for their aggressiveness. The word is Italian, probably from the French *paperasse,* "waste paper." The singular is *paparazzo.*

paper **1** short for NEWSPAPER **2** a monograph, report, or publication, such as a position paper A *white paper* is an official government report or other in-depth study. **3** complimentary tickets or passes to a performance, often distributed to *paper the house* (*house* refers to the theater or arena) **4** a thin sheet of cellulose pulp Paper is prepared from the finely divided fibers of wood pulp, rags, cotton, or other fibrous material that is mixed and matted into sheets. The word is from the name of the plant—*papyrus*—that the Egyptians used over 4,000 years ago to make the material. Types of paper include sheet or roll, coated or uncoated, smooth or rough, glossy or dull, sized or unsized, handmade or machine-made, laid or wove, high-acid or acid-free, and bleached or unbleached. *Adhesive-coated paper* has glue or other adhesive on one side that is sticky or can be made sticky by moisture or heat. *Acid-free paper*, which has a pH above 6, and *alkaline paper*, which has a pH above 7, can last longer by withstanding our acidic environment. *Alkaline resistance* is the degree to which a paper resists discoloration when exposed to adhesives, soap, or other alkaline substances. The apparent density of a paper is a measure of the weight of a sheet. A *high-bulk paper*, such as many book papers, is thick; *low-bulk paper* is thin and smooth. A *high-finish paper* has a smooth, hard finish, such as by the calendering process. A *low-finish paper* is dull and is weak in light-reflective properties. Impregnated paper, or *pigmentized paper*, is coated with an invisible film. In *long-grain paper*, the fibers run parallel to the longer dimension of the sheet, whereas in *short-grain paper* the fibers run parallel to the shorter dimension. *Mould-made paper* is a deckle-edged sheet (with a rough, irregular edge) made on a roller or cylinder. *Surface-sized paper* is sized material added by applying a film to the surface. The *top side* of uncoated paper refers to the top of the roll of paper, called a WEB. The other side, the *wire side*, comes in contact with the wire ribbon or mesh on the paper machine. *Bleached paper* is chemically treated to whiten the pulp fiber; in contrast, *unbleached paper* has a light brown color. *Uncoated paper* or *unglazed paper* has no finishing or coating. *Uncut paper* or *machine-trimmed paper* is cut, with a rotary cutter, from the web, or roll of paper. Paper is packaged with its wire side down. Watermarks appear backward when viewed from the wire side. **5** to *put on paper*: to write or print something, as distinct from a spoken statement *On paper* refers to anything in written or printed form, or something in theory, not necessarily proven or not an *actuality*.

paperback a book bound in paper instead of cloth, plastic, or leather; also called *paperbound* or *soft cover* Paperbacks in conventional rack sizes are called *mass-market paperbacks*; *trade paperbacks* are generally larger and more expensive volumes. A *paperback original* is a work not previously published as a hardcover; a *paperback reprint*, on the other hand, is a book that has appeared previously in another format. *Paperback rights* constitute permission to publish a work in paperbound format.

paperboard a type of heavy paper or cardboard, such as is used in making boxes (*boxboard*), displays, or book covers See also PASTEBOARD.

paper cut [television] a detailed plan for editing, or cutting, a tape, keyed to time codes or cues, prepared prior to the actual editing

paper edit preliminary editing of a film or tape in which notations are made—on paper—but the actual cutting is not done; also called *dry edit*

papering 1[film] a process of using paper tape, tags, or other markers to indicate the start and end of sequences to be edited in a film lab, or to be projected or transferred (as from film to videotape) 2[theater] the distribution of free tickets to a performance, as in *papering the house* (filling a theater with free admissions)

paper jam in typewriters and printing devices, a condition in which the paper flow is inhibited, resulting in overprinting of lines

papermark See WATERMARK.

paper negative sensitized paper used as a photographic negative

paper of record a highly regarded, authoritative publication, such as *The New York Times*

paper rhyme written words that appear to rhyme but, when properly pronounced, do not, such as *bomb* and *tomb*

papers a collection of personal documents, often of a public figure—for instance, *presidential papers*

paper tape a medium that is used in computerized typesetting and other automatic machines, consisting of lengths of paper $7/8$ inch or 1 inch wide and perforated with holes representing computer bits; also called *papertape* A more current term is *punch tape*. A *paper tape system* includes a *paper tape sender* (*PTS*) and *paper tape reader* (*PTR*).

paper-tape punch (PTP) a device for producing holes in PAPER TAPE, used in a *paper tape sender* (*PTS*) and *paper tape reader* (*PTR*)

paper throw in printing devices, movement of the paper at excessive speed

paper-to-paper [film] use of paper tape, tags, or other markers to indicate the start and end of sequences to be edited in a film lab, or to be projected or transferred

papier-mâché pulped paper—that is, a mixture of wood and paper fibers—molded while moist into various forms It is used in advertising and printing to make matrices (MATS) or copies of stereotypes and other printing plates.

papyrus a tall water plant (it may reach 7 feet) in the Nile area of Egypt, used to make a writing material (which is also called *papyrus*) The word refers, moreover, to the ancient documents or manuscripts, written on this material, including those of the Greeks and Romans, as well as the Egyptians.

par.   PARAGRAPH; PARALLEL

par. or **paren.**   PARENTHESIS

PAR   PRODUCT ACCEPTANCE & RESEARCH

parable   a story illustrating a moral issue, usually shorter than an ALLEGORY

parabola   a two-dimensional curve formed by the intersection of a cone and a plane parallel to one of its sides   A *parabolic antenna* is a dish-shaped concave antenna for focusing a radiated signal as from a broadcast station transmitter or a satellite, into a tight beam.

paradigm   an example or model; the set of all inflected forms of a single word, as the conjugation of a verb (*I go, he goes,* and so on)

parados   the area on the sides of ancient Greek amphitheaters through which the chorus entered and exited

paragon   **1** a model of excellence or perfection   **2** [typography] a type size of about 20 points (there are 72 points to the inch)   A two-line paragon, or *double paragon,* is 40-point type.

paragraph (par.)   a distinct portion of text, usually beginning with an indentation   A *paragraph mark* or *paragraph starter* indicates the beginning of such a portion. Paragraphing instructions to a typesetter may be indicated by a paragraph mark (¶) or an indentation mark (⌐). In newspapers, the short form *graf* or *graph* is often used to refer to a paragraph. A brief item in a newspaper, perhaps totaling more than one paragraph, may be called a *paragraph.*

paragraph assembly   [computers] the technique of bringing together paragraphs or portions of text from the computer storage

para-journal   a periodical that summarizes the contents of other scholarly periodicals, particularly scientific and professional publications

parajournalism   tendentious or opinionated reporting

paraleipsis   a rhetorical device in which the speaker or writer (a *paraleiptic*) claims to deny or omit a point and in the process mentions it, such as "I won't call my opponent a liar, but ..." or "Far be it for me to mention the subject, but ..."

parallax   **1** the apparent movement of an object that occurs when it is observed from different points of view   **2** [photography] the difference between FIELDS as seen by the viewfinder and the lens

parallel (par)   **1** the platform or raised area on a stage; also called *rostrum* (the plural is *rostra*) The platform takes its name from the fact that it is constructed so that it folds up into parallel sections.   **2** a wheeled platform that can be elevated for high-angle camera shots

parallel cutting   [film] the technique of moving back and forth from one angle to another or one scene to another; also called *intercutting, crosscutting,* or *parallel action*

parallel folds   one or more folds made in the same direction, such as an ACCORDION FOLD   In a web-fed press, the first longitudinal fold made by the FORMER (a folding device) is the *former fold* or *newspaper fold,* the next fold is the *first parallel fold,* and the next is the *second parallel fold.* The parallel folds also are called *jaw folds,* because the paper is held by a device called jaws.

parallel imports   recordings legitimately manufactured abroad and imported into the United States, where they compete with the identical (parallel) but domestically produced versions

parallelism   **1** the use of elements of similar grammatical structure within a sentence or a brief passage—for instance, the two infinitive phrases in the sentence "I wanted *to wash the car* and *to buy gas*" Errors in parallelism, or *parallel structure,* as it is also called, are common among writers. In this example, faulty parallelism would be something like "I wanted *to wash the car,* and *gas was also needed*"—a confusing and awkward mixture.   **2** a rhetorical device in which similar or dissimilar ideas are expressed in grammatically similar form, to emphasize the points by repetition of structure or to heighten the contrast between similar form but quite different meaning or intention   **3** [marketing] the practice in which two competing companies set the same prices for competing products or engage in other identical activities   If the practice is *conscious parallelisms,* it may be illegal collusion.

parallel location   a billboard or outdoor advertisement parallel to the street, or very slightly angled, so that it is visible to traffic in both directions   A *parallel single* (*PS*) is a single panel with no other nearby panel, a highly desirable factor.

parallel rule   a rule, or line, consisting of two or more strokes of the same weight and set parallel to each other   It is sometimes called a *double rule* (or *Oxford rule* or *Scotch rule*), but actually a double rule has strokes of different weights (a thick stroke and a thin stroke).

parallel scene   in a play or other work, a segment in which there is no conflict and the characters progress along parallel paths

parallel sign   **1** a mark consisting of two short lines (‖) used in typesetting and proofreading to indicate that the adjacent texts should be aligned   **2** a similar mark placed near text indicating that the copy is referred to in a footnote or other citation

parallel transmission the transfer of data simultaneously over separate channels, rather than one after another (*serial transmission*)

parameter 1 [computers] a variable that is given a constant value for a specified application or instruction, such as a code that defines the type size, style, and other specifications in a written work A *parameter word* designates one or more parameters. A *program parameter* specifies a process to be performed and remains unchanged during the execution of the process. A *hardware parameter* is a permanent characteristic of a machine that functions by establishing the capabilities or limitations of the machine. 2 [market research] a variable constant, or factor, such as a standard deviation used in population sampling—that is, when groups among the population as a whole are selected to participate in a survey or other study In a *parametric sampling*, it is assumed that the samples are random (that the participants were chosen without bias toward achieving a specific result) and standard in deviation. In *nonparametric sampling*, such assumptions are not made.

Paramount Communications Inc. one of the world's largest media and communications companies, headquartered in New York Its subsidiaries include Paramount Pictures, Paramount Television, and Simon & Schuster. The company changed its name in 1989 from Gulf + Western Inc.

Paramount Pictures Corporation a film and TV producer that is a subsidiary of Paramount Communications Inc. (formerly Gulf + Western) It is headquartered in New York, but its renowned studio is in Hollywood. Paramount also owns Famous Music Publishing and other companies.

paranomasia the art or practice of punning The adjective, paranomastic, refers to a pun.

parapet a low wall or railing, such as along a balcony of a theater or in front of a stage

paraph a flourish below or at the end of a person's signature, as a personal identification (The term is not short for *paragraph*, though the two words are derived from the same Greek roots.)

paraphrase 1 a rewording of a written or spoken statement, to clarify or condense the meaning of the passage A paraphrase may accompany the original text (the paraphraser is saying, literally or figuratively, "in other words") or may replace the original version. Reporters may use paraphrase when they are not sure of the verbatim, or exact, quotation or if they prefer not to quote directly.

parasite [marketing] a small unit in a high-traffic area, such as a kiosk in a mall or a newsstand in the lobby of a building

Parcel Airlift Mail (PAL) a reduced-rate category of the U.S. Postal Service for military parcels sent by air to overseas destinations

parcel post fourth-class, nonletter mail The majority of parcel-post mail now is carried by alternate delivery companies, such as United Parcel Service (UPS).

parchment a translucent or opaque writing material, originally made from the inner side of sheepskin or goatskin Imitation parchment paper now is used for documents; the term *sheepskin* to mean a diploma is figurative.

parenthesis (par. or paren.) a word, phrase, or other text—usually brief—within a sentence or a passage, set off as an aside, comment, or explanation The *parenthetical copy* is marked off by curved lines called *parentheses* (plural), one at the beginning (*open parenthesis*) and the other at the end (*close parenthesis*). Dashes, commas, or other punctuation can also be used to set off explanatory or nonessential text. The abbreviation of the plural is *parens*.

parent store the main store, not a branch

pariaktos scenery mounted on rollers for easy movement The term is from the early Greek theater, where a *periaktos* was a three-sided revolving apparatus situated at each side of the stage and painted with scenery.

Paris yellow a yellow pigment, more commonly called *chrome yellow*

parity [computers] a method of verifying the accuracy of a transmitted pattern of BITS by examining the code (with a *parity bit* to determine whether its value is even or odd) Characters with an even number of bits (*even parity*) are separated from characters with an odd number of bits (*odd parity*).

parity product an item that has the same or similar characteristics and benefits as other brands in the same category The challenge to advertising and public relations practitioners is to develop a campaign designed to influence potential consumers to perceive the product or service as different—and preferable. A service similar to others in its category is a *parity service*.

park to store or hold a telephone call *Call park* is a feature that enables a call to be transferred to another phone—for instance, if a phone in an office is not answered after four or five rings, the call "jumps" to a phone in a reception area.

parlance a style of speaking or writing, particularly a style characteristic of a field or profession

PAR light   a commonly used sealed trademarked spotlight with a *parabolic aluminized reflector* (*PAR* is an acronym made up of these first three letters or short for *parabolic*.) Developed by Clarence Birdseye (1886–1956), who is better known for his development of quick-freezing foods, it is also (rarely) called *birdseye*. A *Molepar light*, made by Mole-Richardson, Hollywood, is a LUMINAIRE with several 1,000-watt PAR bulbs.

parody   a literary or musical work that imitates the characteristic style of another work or of a writer, composer, or other person in a satirical manner, as written or performed by a *parodist*

paronym   a word derived from the same root as another word; more commonly called *cognate* Two or more such words are *paronymous*.

parquet   the main floor of a theater, generally called the *orchestra*; also called *parquette* Sometimes, however, the *parquet* is that portion of the orchestra not overhung by balconies, and the separation between the parquet (the front of the orchestra, also called *parterre* or *orchestra circle*) and the *parquet circle* (the rear part, under the balconies) is marked by a *parquet rail*. Parquet is French for a small enclosed section; it is pronounced par-KAY. Parquette is pronounced par-KET.

parse   to describe and analyze a word or a sentence according to grammatical rules

part (p or P)   **1** a role in a program, musical work, or other performance   **2** a volume of monographs (long scholarly essays) or other bibliographic units bound into one volume   *Original parts* is a librarian's term for the first edition of an item published in installments, or parts.

partial dial tone   a high-pitched tone indicating that a telephone call has not been completed—for instance, insufficient digits have been dialed or punched

partial sponsorship   the sponsorship of a TV or radio program by several advertisers; also called CO-SPONSORSHIP

participating announcement   a commercial from one of several sponsors of a TV or radio program

participation   a contractual agreement in which a performer or other person shares in the profits of a film or other work, instead of or in addition to receiving a fee or a salary

participation program   a radio or TV program that has several sponsors   An *audience-participation program* involves the studio or home audience in the broadcast.

participle   a grammatical form that has the qualities of both verb and adjective   The present participle ends in *-ing*, and the past participle ends generally in *-ed* or *-en*. Some writers have problems with the *dangling participle*, in which the participle modifies the wrong noun or pronoun in a sentence: *Tying her sneaker, the shoelace broke* instead of *Tying her sneaker, she broke the shoelace.*

parting gifts   products or services announced or advertised during (generally at the end of) TV talk or game shows, in return for *promotional consideration* from the manufacturer or dealer—such as hotel accommodations and airline transportation for the guests on the program

part-issue   an installment of a publication, with the segments bound together when all of them have been published

part title   a leaf preceding the beginning of a major section or subdivision of a book, with the title or name and/or number of the section on the right page; also called *divisional title* or *section title*

party line   a telephone circuit shared by several subscribers; also called *shared line*   A *private line*, on the other hand, is for the exclusive use of one subscriber.

Partyline   a weekly newsletter for public relations practitioners, published in New York

party plan   a form of door-to-door, in-home, or direct selling, in which the hosts invite their friends for a demonstration of household or other products

par writer   British slang for a writer of paragraphs or brief items

pas de deux   a dance, particularly ballet, for two performers   The term is from the French for "step for two." A *pas de trois* is for three performers; a *pas de quatre* is for four performers.

pass   **1** the processing run through a computer or other system to accomplish a specific result, such as an *editing pass* or a *sorting pass*   More than one pass or cycle may be required for a final result.   **2** [film] a single take, exposure, or passage through a camera or a film printer   **3** [typesetting] a complete set of procedures to produce a GALLEY   In computerized typesetting, a job may take more than one pass, each pass consisting of input (the first pass) or editing, data assembly, typesetter output, proofreading, and possibly other stages.

pass-along deal   a special offer or reduced price provided to a retailer who is encouraged to relay or share it with the consumer

pass-along readership   the readers of a publication other than the original purchasers; also called *pass-on readership*   Some magazines provide a sizable bonus audience because of the large number of pass-along, or secondary, readers. Examples include *National Geographic* and periodicals in professional offices, barber shops, libraries, and other public reading places.

pass door [theater] a door linking the backstage area and the auditorium or front of a theater, for the use of the staff

passepartout or **passe-partout** a picture mounting or a method of framing in which the glass, picture, backing, and mat are bound together. The gummed paper or adhesive strips used to bind the parts together or the mat sometimes is called *passepartout*. The word is French and means "passes through."

passim frequently or throughout; from the Latin for "here and there." The term is used in footnotes to indicate a reference that appears in various parts of the work.

passing shot [film] a shot in which a subject moves past a stationary camera or the camera moves past a stationary subject

passion pit slang for DRIVE-IN MOVIE THEATER

passion play a play that depicts the life of a god, particularly the Passion (agony and sufferings) of Jesus. Passion plays were popular in Europe in the Middle Ages and a few still are performed, particularly the production given every 10 years in the town of Oberammergau, in Bavaria, West Germany.

passive typesetter an output device that provides a continuous readout or electronic representation but that cannot be changed or edited while in operation—it is not *interactive*; also called *soft typesetter*

pass-on-readership PASS-ALONG-READERSHIP

pass-out a member of an audience who leaves during a performance (with a *pass check* or *pass-out check*) and is expected to return

passport photo a photograph of an individual's face, affixed to his or her passport. Since 1914, passport photos have been required by the U.S. Passport Bureau.

password a secret word, phrase, series of numerals, sign, or other characters, used for identification, such as to gain access to a computer system. To preserve the secrecy, the password is generally not displayed on the terminal screen after it has been input.

pasteboard 1 stiff board, used for matchbook or other covers, made of pressed pulp or sheets of paper pasted together; also called *pasted board*, though, technically, *pasted board* is a PAPERBOARD (as used in book covers) made of two or more layers of board (called *pasted chipboard*) or board and paper, pasted together. 2 slang for ticket

pasted blanks unprinted stock or heavy paper, pasted together to increase thickness—for instance, 12-PLY

paste-down paper glued to the inside covers of a hardback book; also called *endpapers*, *end sheets*, *end leaves*, or *lining papers*. It is not the opposite of PASTE-UP.

paste drier [printing] a combination of lead and manganese compounds or other substances (particularly cobalt) added to inks to increase their drying speed

paste-in a revision or an addition, supplied after the printing of a work and pasted on or opposite the page to which it applies; also called *slip cancel*. It differs from *errata*, which is a list of corrections inserted (tipped in) or printed on an existing page.

pastel a type of crayon made of pigment, chalk, gum, and water; an artwork (frequently a sketch) made with this crayon, generally in soft, delicate hues, so that pastel also refers to any light tint or pale color. The term is from the Italian *pasta*, or "paste." Since a *pastel stick* breaks easily, it often is held in a *pastel holder*, a metal container akin to a mechanical pencil. *Pastel paper* is a textured paper used by artists working with pastel sticks and pencils. The name does not refer to the color of the paper. It is sometimes called *charcoal paper*, since it is suitable for charcoal as well as pastels.

pastepot a container that holds adhesive, or paste. Up until the early 20th century, pastepots were used in the offices of newspapers and other publications in making layouts of pasted-down text and graphics. A pastepot was on the copy desk and elsewhere in a newspaper, and the word came to be used as slang for *newsroom*. For example, the July 28, 1988, issue of *Winners & Sinners* (a newsletter of the editorial staff of *The New York Times*) contained the phrase *around the pastepot*.

paster an attachment on a folding machine or WEB-fed press for gluing or pasting edges of paper, as in a booklet

paste-up an assemblage of all the elements of a printed piece—such as an article or advertisement—ready for reproduction; also called *pasteup* or *camera-ready art* (since it will be photographed for printing) or *mechanical*. The elements, which may include type and line art (that is, not photographs), generally are affixed to PASTEBOARD. Paste rarely is used; paste-up artists use rubber cement or wax. To *paste up* is to prepare a mechanical.

pastiche a literary, artistic, musical, or other composition made up of bits from various sources; a potpourri or hodgepodge; a PARODY intended to imitate or caricature another artist's style

pasting in   the technique of inserting and adhering one or more sheets or other items into a publication; also called *tipping in*

pastoral   of shepherds or rural life   A *pastoral work* (or, simply, a *pastoral*) is a written or other work dealing, generally in an idealized way, with rural life. A *pastoral elegy* is a peaceful or joyful poem about shepherds or rural life; the form was used by ancient Greek and Roman poets and by such English poets as John Milton (1608–74) and Percy Shelley (1792–1822). A *pastoral idyll* is a short lyric poem about the beauty of the countryside and of simple living; examples include poems by William Wordsworth (1770–1850) and Alfred Tennyson (1809–92).

patch   a small piece of cloth or other matter used in repairing, correcting, or revising, as with a tape or film   The procedure of making small-scale repairs or changes may involve rough pasting or sewing (*patching*) as well as careful soldering or stripping into an original (as in printing or artwork). A *patch revision* is a new edition or printing of a book or other work with relatively few changes. The revisions have been *patched in* or inserted in the previous edition. **2** [broadcasting] a device that ties together several circuits or pieces of apparatus   *Patching in* is the process of connecting, by means of a *patch cord*; a *patch board, patch bay,* or *patch panel* has jacks from various circuits so that patch cords can link specific circuits.   **3** [computers] a machine-language instruction added to a program to alter it or correct an error

paten   a plate; a thin disk of metal

patent   an exclusive right or title   *Patent insides* is an old journalism term for preprinted newspaper pages (also called READY-PRINT).

patent register   the symbol ®, indicating that a product is registered with the U.S. Patent Office; also called *patent mark* or *trademark*

pathetic fallacy   the attribution of human feelings to inanimate things, such as *angry sea* or *stubborn door*   The term was first used in 1856 by the British writer John Ruskin (1819–1900), who criticized the use of pathos (feelings) as a literary device that was false to nature. The term differs from PERSONIFICATION, in which human qualities of various types—not just feelings—are attributed to nonhuman entities.

pathos   a quality in a real situation or a literary or other work that evokes compassion, pity, sorrow, or sympathy; the feeling itself

Patsy Award   the name of annual awards presented by the American Humane Association, of Denver, CO, for the best performing animals in films and TV   The name is an acronym for Picture Animal Top Star of the Year; the awards have been given since 1951.

patter   language peculiar to a group, or, more generally, rapid, glib speech or idle, meaningless chatter, as by a *patterer*; rapidly spoken or sung comic lines, as in a musical comedy   Such a song is called a *patter song*. Danny Kaye (1913–87) was a successful *patterer* (or *patterist*).

pattern   an exemplar or model worthy of being copied; a plan; a representative sample; a design; a composite of features   In television, the *test pattern* is a standardization diagram transmitted to determine picture quality. In printing, a *pattern plate* is the master electrotype from which other electrotypes and mats are made. *Pattern recognition* is the automatic identification of shapes, such as by the optical character recognition (OCR) process.

pattern speech   a basic speech that can be given by the same or different speakers

pause   [poetry, music] a moment of rest in the rhythm

pause control   a device on a machine, such as a tape recorder, that provides for a brief stop or interruption without the machine having to be turned off

PAV   PUBLIC ACCESS VIDEOTEX

pawl   a mechanical device that rotates only in one direction   In a camera or projector, the *pawl sprocket* is the mechanism that transports the film forward one frame at a time, by engaging the sprocket holes on the film.

PAX   private *a*utomatic exchange   See PRIVATE AUTOMATIC BRANCH EXCHANGE.

pay cable   PAY TELEVISION via cable   The largest company in this field is Home Box Office (HBO); the second largest is Showtime.

payment   remuneration   Types of payment to writers include *payment on acceptance* (prior to publication) and *payment on publication*.

payoff   **1** a settlement, such as the payment of money owed   **2** a bribe   **3** the punch line of an act

payola   money or favors given to public figures, broadcast producers, or others to improperly promote a record or other item

payout   the profit, or return, on an investment; also called *payback*   The *payout period* is the time of negative cash flow before the break-even point is attained.

pay-per-view TV   **(PPV)**   a system in which payment is made for a single showing of a program   Subscribers of the pay-television company can phone in their "orders" prior to a showing, activate the system—that is, clear the scrambled channel—or press a button to utilize two-way equipment that activates the system. PPV is often used in hotel rooms; popular shows include movies and sports events. The largest PPV distributor is SpecTradyne Inc., of Dallas.

pay television (pay TV) home television programming for which the viewer pays by the program or by the month; also called *pay-television, subscription television (STV)*, or *toll-TV* Pay television includes over-the-air transmission (with scrambled signals) and cable transmission (*pay cable*). Major over-the-air operations include National Subscription Television in the West and Wometco in the East. The biggest cable operation, Home Box Office (HBO), is considerably larger than any of the over-the-air companies. A *maxi-pay service* is a pay-TV service with programs that are available at least eight hours a day.

PBP PLAY-BY-PLAY

PBS PUBLIC BROADCASTING SERVICE

PBX PRIVATE BRANCH EXCHANGE

p/c petty cash; PLEDGES/COST

pc or **PC** PERSONAL COMPUTER; PICA, PROVISIONAL CUT

pc percent (also *pct.*); PERSONAL COMPUTER; petty cash (also *p/c*); POSTCARD; the *power cord* that connects a flash unit to a camera; prices current

PCM PULSE CODE MODULATION

PCR PROVEN COMMERCIAL REGISTRATION

pd. paid

p.d. PER DIEM

PD or **P.D.** PUBLIC DOMAIN; PROGRAM DIRECTOR

PDI PICTURE DESCRIPTION INSTRUCTION

PDT or **P.D.T.** Pacific Daylight Time; PUBLISHED DATA TAPES

PE or **p.e.** PRINTER'S ERROR

Peabody Award short for the George Foster Peabody Radio and Television Award, established in 1940 and presented annually by the University of Georgia School of Journalism, in Athens, for public service in radio and television The award is named after George Foster Peabody (1852–1930), a banker who graduated from the University of Georgia.

pea bulb a tiny bulb inside a film or TV camera, also called a pea lamp In a film camera, the bulb lights up at the start of a shot so that it fogs the first few frames. When developed, these frames are used to synchronize the picture and sound tracks.

peak referring to the highest or most important point, such as *peak audience* (highest rating) or *peak season* (highest retail sales) Peaked refers to the highest point, declining, or ending in a peak (pointed).

peak white [television] the brightest, or whitest, portion of a picture signal, corresponding to the signal's highest frequency

peanut fixture [film] a small luminaire, usually with a 75-watt bulb, attached to an object (but out of view) to make it appear that light is shining from the object

peanut gallery theatrical slang for the topmost seating area in a theater or hall The origin is not that the spectators looked, from the stage, as small as peanuts, but rather that the audience in the cheapest seats often ate peanuts.

pearl [printing] a very small type, about 5 points There are 12 points in a pica and 6 picas in an inch.

pebble board a coarse, heavy paper that produces a stipple, or dotted, effect when charcoal or other drawing materials are applied

peculiars [typography] seldom-used characters of a typeface, especially characters with accent marks, as in phonetics or foreign words

pedestal a support or foundation, such as a camera mount; a direction to move a mounted camera

peer group individuals who are close in age, economic status, interests, or other factors Members may identify with their peer group more readily than with other groups in the society, and appeals to such identification are often used in advertising.

peewee a very small person or thing, such as a small incandescent luminaire with a 50-watt bulb

peg a strong element or point that is relevant to a news story or other topic of interest; also called ANGLE, HOOK, or SLANT, though there are shades of difference

pegboard a board with holes into which pins (pegs) or hooks are placed An object that is *pegged off* is mounted away from its supporting surface, such as a pegboard. In printing, negatives with holes are positioned over pins in a pegboard and then taped together to make a single form.

peg count a tally of the number of telephone calls made or received during a specific time period

pegging 1 giving support, relevance, or perspective to an idea, news story, or other work by relating it to something else 2 the swing of the needle on a sound volume meter all the way to the right, in the red zone, indicating that the sound is too loud

peg registration [photography] the process by which pegs or pins are dropped into the sprocket holes along the edge of the film, to move the film within the camera *Pin-registered cam-*

per diem (p.d.) generally referring to individuals who receive compensation calculated by the day, or to a daily allowance for expenses; from Latin, "by the day"

perf PERFORATION

perfect [grammar] a grammatical term expressing a state of action completed at the time of speaking or at the time indicated   Verbs have three perfect tenses: *simple* (or *present*) *perfect*—*he has cooked; past perfect* (or *pluperfect*)—*he had cooked;* and *future perfect*—*he will have cooked.* A *perfect* PARTICIPLE is the same as a *past* participle.

perfect binding a technique of affixing the pages of a book or other publication to the spine (the section between the front and back covers) by using glue instead of stitches or staples   A book manufactured this way is *perfect bound.*

perfecting press a press that prints the two sides of a sheet at the same time; also called *perfector press*   *Perfecting* is the backing-up of a sheet already printed on one side of a double-end perfecting press.

perforated film a film with sprocket holes along one or both edges, to aid in transporting the film in a camera or projector   See also PAWL.

perforation (perf) a hole or series of holes produced by punching or boring, usually by a device (a *perforating machine*)   Sheets of postage stamps are perforated—as are checkbooks, coupons, and many other items—so that they may be separated more easily.

perforator an input device that provides holes in tape for use in typesetting or other automated functions   It is not the same as a perforating machine used in printing.

performance allowance a manufacturer's rebate to a retailer, paid upon acceptance of proof that a promotion has been performed

performance area the place on the studio set of a TV talk or variety show where singers or other entertainers perform, such as between the host's desk and the band

performance art entertainment, generally multimedia, by artist-performers

performance royalties payments by radio and TV stations, theaters, nightclubs, and other places of musical performance to songwriters and music publishers for the right to play their music   The collection and distribution of performance royalties is handled by ASCAP, BMI, and SESAC, organizations to which publishers and songwriters belong.

Pergamon/AGB PLC one of the world's largest market research companies, headquartered in London   AGB was founded in 1962 by Messrs. Audley, Gaber, and Brown and was acquired in 1988 by Pergamon Professional & Financial Services (owned by Robert Maxwell, British publishing and media tycoon). In 1982, AGB acquired NFO Research (Greenwich, CT). AGB people meters measure TV audiences in many countries. The company also has systems to measure purchases of consumer products.

perigee lowest or nearest point—in particular, the point at which the moon or an orbiting communications satellite is closest to the earth   The opposite is *apogee.*

perimeter booth an exhibit space located along an outside wall of an exhibition

per inquiry (p.i.) referring to a system in which an advertiser pays a TV station or other medium based on the number of inquiries or actual sales in response to a specific advertisement, rather than for the time or space used

period an interval, such as of time; an end, such as a dot at the end of a sentence; a unit of a song, generally eight bars

period bibliography a list containing all the items published during a specific period of time

periodical a regularly published work, such as weekly, monthly, quarterly; also called *serial*   Periodicals generally are published more frequently than once a year, though, for instance, a *biennial*—published every two years—is a periodical. Newspapers and other *daily* publications generally are not classified as periodicals.

periodic reordering an inventory control system in which a retailer reorders merchandise on a regular basis, such as on a specific day each month, though the quantity may vary; also called *P-system*   In the *Q-system,* the reorder period varies but the quantity remains the same.

periodic sentence a sentence in which the essential element is at the end   A periodic sentence must be read fully (to the period) in order to understand or appreciate it. It sometimes is called a *suspended sentence,* as it holds the reader in suspense, and is the opposite of a loose sentence, in which the essential element comes first.

period printing the production of a book in the style of the time, or period, when it was first published or reflecting the time with which it is concerned

peripeteia a sudden change of fortunes or reversal of circumstances, a word generally limited to its use in drama; also spelled *peripetia* or *peripety*   The term is from the Greek word meaning "reversal."

periphrasis circumlocution, or the use of excessive words, a literary technique that can be either pretentious or eloquent

periscope ending a play or other work in which a glimpse or hint is provided about the future of the characters

periscope shot a picture in which the camera is mounted at a low angle, perhaps on an *periscope stand* with angled mirrors

permastat a photostat on special paper that produces a soft tonal effect

permission formal consent or authorization, as for the right to reprint copyrighted material Permission may be free or may require a *permission fee.*

peroration 1 the concluding part of a speech, in which there is a summation and emphatic recapitulation; sometimes called *epilogue* 2 a bombastic speech

per person interview value (PPIV) [market research] the number of individuals in a sex–age group represented by each interview; what the SAMPLE represents

pers personal; persons

per se Latin, "in or by itself"; intrinsically

persistence of vision a psychological phenomenon in which the eye briefly retains an image after the object that produced it has been removed from view

persona 1 a character in a play or other work (plural, *personae*) 2 the role a person takes on, in displaying conscious intentions (the plural for this meaning is usually *personas*) Both terms are from the Latin word *persona*, meaning "actor's face MASK."

personal [journalism] an article about an individual *Personal classifieds* or *personals* are classified advertisements offering services, generally by an individual rather than a company. They are not the same as *commercial classifieds* or *commercials.*

personal author the individual (or two or more individuals) chiefly responsible for the creation of a work

personal computer (PC) a small, easy-to-operate, low-cost computer for home or business use, consisting of a single compact unit or system, including a keyboard, storage device, and video screen; sometimes called a *desktop computer* Based on microcomputer chips (a MICROCOMPUTER), a personal computer is smaller than a MINICOMPUTER and is personally controllable.

personal identification number (PIN) a code or password entered by a user into a computer terminal to transfer information or complete a transaction PINs frequently are used in conjunction with automatic teller machines to withdraw or deposit money.

personal income total income from all sources before the payment of taxes

personality 1 characteristics, traits, attitudes, and habits of a person 2 a person with exceptional qualities; a celebrity 3 the format or general character of a medium, such as the type of programs on a radio station 4 a radio or TV host or master of ceremonies

personality journalism reportage about the private lives of public figures—the focus on celebrities typified by *People* magazine

personalizing shopper a customer who favors stores or other businesses in which he or she feels comfortable, as with personnel who are known Small neighborhood stores may use the appeal of familiarity to attract customers. See also APATHETIC SHOPPER, ECONOMIC SHOPPER, ETHICAL SHOPPER.

personal papers the private documents accumulated by an individual; also called *private papers*

personal word processor (PWP) See SCREEN-BASED ELECTRONIC TYPEWRITER.

personification a figure of speech in which an inanimate object, animal, or abstract entity is represented by a human being or is described as having human qualities or characteristics

persons using radio (PUR) the percentage of the over-12-year-old population in an area listening to radio at a specific time

persons using television (PUT) the percentage of the over-12-year-old population in households with television that is watching TV at a specific time

perspective the illusion of depth *Free perspective* or *linear perspective*, in photography and painting, shows objects as they appear to the eye—that is, with reference to relative distance or depth.

perspective sound a sound that appears to originate at a distance from the camera or viewer

perspective story a type of newspaper or magazine account that differs from an analysis, in that it attempts to refrain from interpretation and conclusions; it also differs from a commentary, in its omission of opinions The perspective story relies on the reporter's expertise to bring an understanding, as of one event in relation to others.

PERT chart a diagram, usually with circles or rectangles connected by arrows, that shows the relationships of events in a program The system was developed by the U.S. Navy and is used by many companies. The acronym refers to *Program Evaluation and Review Technique.*

pg. PAGE

PG parental guidance for children under 17, a designation of the MOTION PICTURE ASSOCIA-

TION OF AMERICA for a film PG 13 applies to children under 13.

ph. phase

pH the measure of acidity or alkalinity of a solution based on the potential of hydrogen Neutral solutions have a pH of 7, acidic have less than 7, and alkaline have over 7. The concept is important in photography and printing. Acid-free paper has a pH of 6 or higher (called 6 +). The water or fountain solution used in OFFSET printing should be alkaline (7 +) to compensate for any residual acidity in the paper.

phantasmagoria a rapidly altering series of real or imagined figures, events, or scenes The term was originally used to describe a show of optical illusions, in which images change size and blend into one another. *Phantasmagorical* is the adjective describing the process.

phantom [photography] a ghost—that is, a transparent image superimposed over a subject

phantom post office box a post office box that does not actually exist but is used in direct marketing to key or identify mail by the box number For instance, a coupon sent to "P.O. Box FC3" would indicate that the item had appeared in the March issue (the third month) of *Family Circle.*

phantom section a drawing or rendering of the exterior of an object as if it were transparent, or in order to reveal interior detailing; also called *ghosted view*

phantom shopper a person who poses as a customer, to test retail personnel in behalf of a manufacturer, store management, or other employer or client

Pharmaceutical Data Services a market research company, based in Phoenix, AZ, specializing in the prescription drug market

phase-alternation system (PAL) a color TV format, with 625 lines per frame, that is used in Europe PAL provides a higher resolution (clearer picture) than the U.S. and Canadian systems. INTELSAT satellites often use the PAL system, which is incompatible with the U.S. system, though U.S. TV stations can view the images on a black-and-white monitor.

phasing [broadcasting, recording] the playing or transmission of the same sound at the same time from two different sources The resulting "whooshing" sound produces a dramatic effect, as in rock music. Phasing is not the same as echo, or reverb, which is the repetition of sounds one after the other.

phat to hold type (called *phatted type*) for possible repeated later use The term is from the days of metal type, and is not the same as *phat type* or *fat type,* which is wide or extended type.

phatic of or given to *formulistic talk* or meaningless sounds, such as *phatic noises,* used to establish social contact but not really communicate ideas

philippic a bitter verbal attack The word is derived from the oration in which the Athenian orator Demosthenes denounced Philip II (382–36 B.C.), king of Macedon (an ancient kingdom in southeastern Europe, now a part of Greece).

Phi phenomenon the illusion of motion and three-dimensionality produced by a film (which really is a series of two-dimensional still photographs); also called *Phi effect* This psychological, and not physical, phenomenon is based on the *persistence of vision,* in which the human retina continues to see an image for a brief "afterimage period."

phonathon a fundraising, sales, or other campaign conducted by telephone

phone EARPHONE; TELEPHONE The Greek *phone* means "sound." To *phonate* is to produce speech sounds.

phone it in [film] to write a script poorly, as by a writer who dictates a draft and telephones it to a secretary

phoneme a small unit of speech, such as a single letter or sound, that enables users of a language to distinguish units of meaning *Phonemics* is the study of those units; *phonetics* is the more general study of speech sounds. A *phonetic alphabet* is the representation of these sounds by *phonetic symbols* to aid in pronunciation (the sound of *ph* would be symbolized by *f,* for example). The *phonetic spelling* of a word indicates its pronunciation.

phoner an interview, as on a radio program, conducted via telephone

phonetic alphabet names or words used to avoid misunderstanding in spelling or pronouncing, a system commonly used by military, police, and other organizations; for example, Alpha, Bravo, Charlie, Delta, Echo, Fox, Golf, Hotel, India, Juliette, Kilo, Lima, Mike, November, Oscar, Papa, Quebec, Rodeo, Sierra, Tango, Uniform, Victor, Whiskey, X-Ray, Yankee, Zulu; or Adam, Boy, Clark, David, Edward, etc.

phonic relating to sound, especially speech sound *Phonics* is a method of teaching reading in which learners are taught to recognize the sound of each letter rather than to memorize whole words by sight. The two methods have created controversy among educators because of the unphonetic nature of English.

phonogram a sign, symbol, or character (such as a letter) representing a sound, word, or syllable

phonograph a machine that reproduces sound from a disk or record Invented in 1877 by Thomas Alva Edison (1847–1931), who called it a "talking machine," the early phonographs used cylinders that were individually recorded; subsequently, phonograph records were mass produced from original masters.

photo from the Greek word for "light" *Photography* is the process of forming and fixing an image by the chemical action of light on a surface (film) which is sensitive to light. A *photocopy* is made directly on paper, as with a Xerox machine or other photocopier, with no intermediate negative. A *photogram* is a positive photographic print of objects in silhouette form made by placing the objects on special paper and exposing it to light. A *photoprint* is a photographic print or positive. A *photomontage* is an assemblage of photos or parts of photos.

photoactive capable of responding to light

photoboard a set of still photographs, made from a film or videotape, or recorded off a TV screen, with accompanying script, usually produced on a $8\frac{1}{2}" \times 11"$ sheet of paper so that it is a transcript of a commercial or a segment of a TV program

photo call a request to photographers to cover an event, a term used in the United Kingdom; akin to PHOTO OPPORTUNITY

photocomposer a machine that positions and exposes multiple copies of an image on the plates or cylinders of a large lithographic or gravure press, so that several copies can be printed simultaneously and then cut and separated The term should be distinguished from *photocompositor*, which is a photographic typesetting machine for PHOTOCOMPOSITION.

photocomposition a method of setting type photographically, by using OPTICAL or DIGITAL masters of character images, light sources, magnifying lenses, and photosensitive paper

photocopy a reproduction, or copy, about the same size as the original, produced directly on film or paper by radiant energy (bright light), made by a photographic device called a *photocopier* The photocopying process also is called *photoduplication, photographic reproduction,* or *photoreproduction.* The best-known photocopying process is XEROGRAPHY.

photo dulling spray a varnish that is sprayed on glossy, or shiny, photographs and other materials to reduce glare and produce a matte, or dull, finish

photoelectric referring to electrical effects caused by illumination A *photoelectric cell* (also called *electric eye*) is an electronic device whose electrical output varies in response to light. A *photoelectric scanner* produces color separations, negatives, positives, or other photography, printing, and reproduction materials by scanning, or moving over the surface to be copied with an electric eye.

photoengraving a photographic process for making a metal relief block for LETTERPRESS printing; also called *process engraving* The term also refers to a print made by this process.

photo feature a story or article that features photographs or is composed entirely of photos

photoflash a flashbulb used in photography

photoflood reusable tungsten lamps used in photography A *photoflood bulb* has a low-voltage filament that is overloaded to produce an intense light of short duration.

photogelatin a photomechanical printing process that uses a gelatin-coated glass plate for the quality reproduction of art or photographs The print made by this process is called a *photogelatin,* or a *collotype*. In the photogelatin process, inked reproductions are transferred to paper directly from an image formed on a sheet of hardened gelatin. Photogelatins or collotypes frequently are used in advertising displays in shopping malls, terminals, and bus shelters.

photogram a photograph

photograph a picture produced by the action of light on a light-sensitive material (such as film) and then reproduced on photographic paper, which is coated with a light-sensitive emulsion on one side (*simplex paper*) or both sides (*duplex paper*) The activity (*photography*), as performed by a *photographer*, involves *photographing* (with a camera) and *photographic* processing and printing.

photographic tape an opaque black adhesive tape used on photograph negatives to block out light

photogravure a process by which photographs are reproduced on INTAGLIO, or etched, printing plates or cylinders; the plate or cylinder itself or a print made in this manner, usually with a satinlike finish; see also GRAVURE

photojournalism news reporting that emphasizes photography

photolettering the process of producing type photographically, using light-sensitive paper Photolettering usually is produced without computer assistance, whereas PHOTOCOMPOSITION or PHOTOTYPESETTING usually is computerized. A *photolettering machine* is used mostly for headlines and other display type.

photomacrography photography of small objects at a size greater than their actual size with the illusion that they are larger, obtained by means of a long bellows, microlenses, or other devices

photomatic a low-cost, preliminary version of a TV commercial made with still photographs (film transparencies), to show the stages in the STORYBOARD A photomatic is similar to an ANIMATIC, which uses drawings instead of photos.

photomatrix a disk, drum, grid, or form for the storage of phototypesetting master character sets from which copies are photographed The plural is *photomatrices.*

Photomechanical Transfer (PMT) a process, trademarked by Eastman Kodak, of Rochester, NY, for making black-on-white reproductions by DIFFUSION TRANSFER, so that artwork is reproduced without a negative

photometer a light-exposure meter, used to determine the amount of light a film must be exposed to (the brighter the day, for instance, the less exposure time is needed) It uses a PHOTOELECTRIC cell and sometimes is called a *photoelectric meter.* The stress is on the first syllable.

photomicrography photography through a microscope, producing a *photomicrograph*

photomural a very large photograph used as a mural, as on a wall of a lobby

photonics technology that uses pulses of light for information transmission and other uses A *photon* is a quantum—the smallest unit—of electromagnetic energy. *Photonic systems* are lightwave communication systems that use laser pulses transmitted through very thin glass fibers. These systems have greater capacity than the copper cable used in telephone transmission.

photo-offset a method of OFFSET PRINTING in which material is photographically transferred to a metal plate from which inked impressions are made on a roller

photo opportunity an event of visual appeal or special interest to still and motion picture photographers, sometimes shortened to *photo op;* a common technique used by government officials The term was first used during the administration (1969–74) of Richard M. Nixon, though the technique was used earlier.

photoplay a stage play adapted to a motion picture The term sometimes is used as a synonym for films in general.

photoset to photocompose, or set type by PHOTOCOMPOSITION A *Photosetter* is a trademarked photocomposition machine of the Harris Intertype Corporation, Melbourne, FL.

photostat a copy of original artwork or other material made on photographic paper by the trademarked device developed for the process; also called *stat* or *photomechanical transfer* (*PMT*) *Photostat machines* produce a negative or wrong-reading copy (with white and black re-

versed), from which a positive or right-reading photostat is made on opaque paper, using a bellows camera manufactured by the Photostat Corporation, now a part of the Itek Corporation, of Rochester, NY. The high-contrast copies are often used for major changes in size from the original items—for instance, a newspaper review of a play may be photostatically blown up, or enlarged, and framed as an eye-catching poster in a theater lobby. The word usually is not capitalized, though it can be, since it refers to a trademark. The development of photocopying machines has diminished the use of stats, though they still are common in advertising and publishing.

phototypesetting a method of setting type photographically; also called PHOTOCOMPOSITION or PHOTOTYPOGRAPHY

phrase a group of words that function as a syntactic unit; a short, distinct musical passage or unit of a song, generally four bars

phrase book a publication of common words, idioms, expressions, and sentences in a foreign language, with their translations

phrasemaker a person who coins catchy words or expressions, which may sometimes be cogent or at other times inane

physio British slang for physician The word sometimes appears in the credits of British films and TV shows that have a medical consultant.

pi PICA; the accidental mixing of printing type, also called *pie* The mixed unusable type is called *pied type.* A modern-day use of this venerable printer's word is to refer to type characters that are not letters or numbers, such as a bullet (•), dagger (†), or star (*). A *pie line* is a machine-set line of *x*'s or random letters just to fill the space. A *pi font* is a collection of nonstandard characters.

p.i. PER INQUIRY

PI PUBLIC INFORMATION

PIA paid in advance; PRINTING INDUSTRIES OF AMERICA

PIB PUBLISHERS INFORMATION BUREAU

pic slang for pictures; plural, *pix*

pica (pi or **pc)** a typographical unit of measure for the width and depth of characters (letters and numbers) and for the spacing between lines, expressed in points; pronounced PIE-ka The word originates from the medieval Latin for a table of rules used to select the correct church service. One pica is 12 points; 6 picas, or 72 points, equals 1 inch. Picas are used to measure text; art is generally measured in inches.

This typeface is 9 points high and is set on a 10-point line; the measurement is expressed as

9/10, or *9 on 10*. One point of space, or *leading* (pronounced *ledding*), is inserted between the lines of 9-point type.

Pica type is any 12-point type. Pica type on a typewriter has 10 characters to the horizontal inch and is larger than *elite type*, which has 12 characters to the inch. Since a pica has 12 points, 11-point type sometimes is called *small pica*; 22-point type is called *double small pica*; 24-point type is called *two-line pica* (or *double pica*); 60-point type is called *5-line pica*; and, finally, 72-point type is called *6-line pica*. Cardboard thickness also is measured in picas, with 1 pica equal to .001 inch. A cardboard display may be 4 picas, or 48 points.

pica gauge   a ruler marked in picas (also called a *line gauge*), used by printers

pica grid   a transparent sheet printed with horizontal lines one pica apart

picaresque   referring to a literary work in which the main character is a clever, generally amiable scoundrel—for instance, the novel and film *Tom Jones* A *picaresque narrative* is a type of fiction (originating in Spain in the 16th century) that describes, in episodes, the adventures of a rogue hero. The origin is the Spanish *picaro*, or "rascal."

pick back   the ink or other surface material that adheres to an adhesive tape when the tape is pulled off the surface

picket fencing   irregular reception (as if on a picket fence) of FM radio signals, modulated by AUTOMATIC FREQUENCY CONTROL (AFC)

picking   [printing] the raising of the paper surface or the lifting of particles of paper, as a result of the excessive pull of ink that is too sticky

pick it up   a cue or instruction to a performer or musician to speed up or to start from a specific point in the script or score

pickle   jargon for the remote-control device attached by a cable to a slide projector Buttons on the device activate forward or backward movement of slides.

pickle jar   a glass container used in the development of overhead transparencies and other DIAZO-treated paper A sponge in the bottom of the container absorbs the ammonia, and the lid prevents the escape of the ammonia fumes. The completed print is removed dry.

pickup (PU or **p/u)**   **1** [recording] a device that produces audio-frequency currents from the vibrations of a needle or stylus moving in a record groove, or the pivoted arm holding this device **2** [broadcasting] the reception of sound or light, or the apparatus used for the reception **3** a place (also called a *remote*), outside the studio where a program is broadcast or aired; also, the

electrical system connecting the remote to the station **4** the upbeat, or unaccented, musical note—in contrast to the downbeat **5** [public relations] the use of a news release or other publicity material **6** a transient group of musicians, rather than a permanent troupe or band In a *pickup orchestra*, for instance, the members perform together only for a particular project; the group then disbands. **7** [advertising, publishing] the insertion or inclusion of existing or previously used material—for instance, part of the text from a first edition is *picked up*, or used again, for the second edition *Pickup art* refers to previously used photographs and drawings that are to be included in a later edition or other work. **8** an existing movie or other work acquired for distribution **9** [typography] an instruction marked in text to indicate where the typesetting is to begin or resume **10** type that is unused or left standing since its first use **11** to *pick up a light:* to increase its intensity A *pickup light* adds illumination to a scene. **12** to *pick up a cue:* to speak in response to a cue **13** to *pick up a scene:* to enliven the action

pickup line   an instruction, abbreviated as *p.u.*, to a printer to start at a specific place in a text, usually indicating the first two words to be picked up, and the place in the text, such as "p.u. John Jones, 6th graf"

pickup recorder   a playback unit used in films to stop and roll back for rerecording

pickup rehearsal   a brush-up or touch-up rehearsal, such as after a vacation

pickup shot   a film shot taken from the point where the previous shot ended—the action is resumed, or picked up

pickup tube   in a video camera, the unit that receives and processes the image transmitted by the lens; also called *pickup device*

pico   one-trillionth, or 10^{-12} (10 to the minus 12th power) A *picosecond (ps)* is a trillionth of a second. If you can envision that, you are a computer. A *pico processor* is a high-speed computer unit for data transfer and other functions.

pictogram   a pictorial representation of data, such as a chart or a graph

pictograph   a picture, picturelike symbol, or simplified drawing; a SYMBOL representing a word or idea It is sometimes called *hieroglyph*.

pictorial   **1** pertaining to pictures or photographs **2** an illustrated periodical A *pictorialist* is a noncommercial photographer who takes pictures for aesthetic reasons.

picture   a visual representation, such as a drawing, painting, artwork, or photograph; the visual component of television; a motion picture The plural, *pictures*, refers to the motion-picture industry, as in "I want to be in pictures."

picture book a publication, generally a book for children, that is made up entirely or mostly of illustrations A *picture storybook* has text.

picture car [film] an automobile that is filmed, as distinct from a car used for transportation

picture description instruction (PDI) a set of coded instructions that "build," or create, graphic images by using geometric shapes, such as points, lines, arcs, rectangles, and polygons PDI is used in COMPUTER GRAPHICS and VIDEOTEX.

picture frequency the number of times per second that an image is scanned by the TV camera for transmission and by the cathode-ray tube (CRT) for receiving In the United States, the frequency is 30 frames per second. The CRT of a TV receiver is called the *picture tube.*

picture-in-picture (PIP or **P.I.P.)** a recently developed feature of television sets in which the viewer can see one videotape or program inside a small window on the screen while watching a videotape or another program on the same screen

Picturephone a trademarked device of AT&T, New York, that combines telephone and television communications Its predecessor, the Picture Telephone, was developed in 1927 (!) by Bell Laboratories. The system received sound and picture by wire and wireless between New York and Washington, DC.

PICTURE START the first frame of a film It is the beginning of the head leader, or series of frames before the actual motion picture, and is literally labeled *PICTURE START* and/or edge numbers 1A0000.

picture story a sequence of related photographs, as in a newspaper layout

picture-window envelope an envelope with an opening through which the recipient's name, address, or a portion of the contents can be seen before the envelope is opened

pidgin a mixed language or jargon, with a simplified grammar not generally the native or main language of the speaker The origin is not the pigeon, but probably a Chinese pronunciation of *business. Pidgin English* is a simplified form of English, originally used by Chinese and other Asian people.

piece 1 an article, essay, or other literary or artistic work—for instance, a *piece* about education in *The New York Times* 2 a scenic unit 3 a part ownership of a show or other property 4 a term used by the U.S. Postal Service for any article of mail

piece count 1 [mail] the total number of items in a specific mailing, as determined by meters that indicate quantity, actual count, weight, size, or other measures 2 in the marketing of packaged goods, the number of boxes, cases, or other containers within which are a quantity of the packages or items In the marketing of apparel and other nonpackaged goods, in contrast, the term refers to the actual number of items.

pie chart a circular chart with wedges resembling pieces of a pie The sizes of the "slices" usually represent the relative sizes of the segments of a whole—such as a budget.

pied type scattered, mixed type that is unusable; see also PI

pigeon a riser or portable platform to elevate a camera, other equipment, or a performer It is bigger than a pancake (a small platform) and smaller than an APPLE BOX.

pigeonhole 1 a small compartment or recessed area, as in an old-fashioned desk 2 [printing] excessive space between words 3 an advertisement that displays merchandise under various categories, as by a department store

piggyback 1 referring to the shipment of goods in containers, such as in trucks, ships, and planes 2 referring to the presentation of two commercials by the same sponsor in sequence, enabling the sponsor to purchase them as a single unit A commercial used in a piggyback configuration is called a *split commercial.*

piggyback coupon a pop-up coupon or card inserted in a publication

pig Latin phony Latin, English words to which Latin endings, such as *ere, i, o,* or *um,* have been added to make them appear erudite; also, a secret language game played by children, in which the first sound of a word is placed at the end and followed by *ay* (thus *pig Latin* becomes *igpay atinlay*)

pigskin strong, grained leather made from the skin of pigs, sometimes used to bind books

pigtail 1 in audio, the end of a cable with its bare wires and no jack or other connector 2 [theater] a short piece of electric cable or wire that hangs or protrudes from a lighting instrument or other source; also called a *lead* (pronounced leed) or, in the United Kingdom, a *tail*

pilcrow or **pilcrowe** a sign for a paragraph (¶)

piling the buildup or caking of ink on the blanket (the device that transfers the image), plate, or roller of a printing press

pilot a sample or prototype broadcast or other proposed project A *pilot study* or *pilot test* is a small-scale trial or research project conducted before a larger study is made. A *backdoor pilot* is a movie made for TV that could become a series. A *pilot issue* is a sample issue of a proposed publication.

pilot pins pins in the film GATE of a camera that move down into the perforations in the film frame during exposure and then move up to enable the film to move on; also called *register pins* or *registration pins*

pilot tone a videotape technique to monitor and correct color

pin [computers] a metal prong, lead, or wire on a unit that plugs into a socket and connects it to a system, such as an input, output, or ground pin A *nine-pin printer* uses nine tiny wires to produce the dots that form the letters, numbers, and other characters; a *24-pin printer* uses 24 pins and produces a superior quality image.

PIN [computers] *personal identity number*, an identification code used in cash machines, alarm systems, and other equipment

pinch roller [recording] a rubber wheel that presses the tape against the capstan (the shaft in the recorder that drives the tape); also called *capstan idler* or *puck*

pincushion distortion [photography] a distortion of an image resulting from a defective lens, in which a square image appears to curve inward, like a rounded cushion

PIN diode [computers] a semiconductor diode, which is a two-electrode tube, with a layer between the positive and negative junctions The PIN acronym (*positive, intrinsic, negative*) sometimes is not capitalized.

ping [theater] to speak softly and without emphasis, the opposite of PONG

ping-ponging 1 [recording] overdubbing, or adding sound on sound, as is done intentionally when a tape is copied and tracks are added 2 [television] the rapid switching from one person (such as an *anchor* or newscaster) to another

pinhole [photography] a tiny transparent spot on a negative or a black spot on a print A *pinhole camera* was an early model camera with a fixed aperture.

pink noise a static-like sound in various frequencies, used to test a sound system, particularly in a theater

Pink Pearl a soft pink rubber eraser, commonly used by artists and others, made by Eberhard Faber Inc., of Wilkes Barre, PA Sometimes used generically, *Pink Pearl* is actually a trademarked name.

pink sheet 1 quotations of bid and asked prices of over-the-counter stocks (shares sold directly to buyers and not through the stock exchanges) The National Quotation Bureau of the Commerce Clearing House publishes, in Jersey City, NJ, on each business day, a list of bid and offered prices of over-the-counter securities. The list of stocks is printed on long pink sheets of paper. 2 unaudited circulation figures provided by magazine and newspaper publishers to the Audit Bureau of Circulations The name,

again, comes from the color of the sheets. The actual figures, printed on *white sheets*, generally are lower than the publishers' estimates.

Pink Sheet a pharmaceutical newsletter published by F-D-C Reports, Inc., of Chevy Chase, MD The term derives from the color of the paper. The company also publishes the *Blue Sheet*, the *Rose Sheet*, the *Gray Sheet*, the *Gold Sheet*, and the *Green Sheet*, but pink is its best-known color.

Pinnacle Award the name of annual awards in broadcasting, public relations, and other communications fields, presented by the New York chapter of American Women in Radio and Television of Washington, DC

pin-rail a beam or rail on one side of a stage to which is anchored the ropes or lines from the ceiling that are used to move (fly) the scenery

pin seal soft, lustrous leather made from the hide of young seals, formerly used to bind fine-quality books

pin spot a spotlight that produces a narrow beam of light, generally narrower than a *head spot*, which illuminates a performer's head

pinup a picture, particularly of an attractive person or celebrity, that can be pinned or affixed to a wall

PIP or **P.I.P.** PICTURE-IN-PICTURE

pipe to play, transmit sound, or distribute a signal, as in *to pipe in* A recent slang use of *to pipe* is *to fake*, as with a rare journalist who *pipes a story* by making up characters or events.

pipe and drape a common instruction in exhibits: to put up the side rails, or pipes, of an exhibit and then hang fabric, or drapes, from it

pipe artist a journalist who makes up quotations

pipe batten a metal rod, or pipe, attached to the ends of several ropes (a set of lines) hanging from the ceiling of a stage, to facilitate the movement of scenery

pipe grid an arrangement of pipes and beams along a ceiling of a stage or studio, to which lights are attached

pipeline the amount of a product that a manufacturer has sold but that has not yet been purchased by consumers; hence wholesaler and retailer inventories are said to be *in the pipeline*

pipes theatrical slang for *vocal chords*, particularly of a singer

Pirandellian combining illusion and reality, a theatrical technique used by Luigi Pirandello (1867–1936), Italian playwright, novelist, and poet, who won the Nobel Prize for Literature in 1934

pirate to reproduce a work of art, a book, film, record, or other item illicitly, without permission of the copyright owner The bootlegging or counterfeiting process is called *pirating*. A *pirated edition* or *pirated reprint* is a publication issued without the authorization of the copyright holder.

pit the section, generally recessed, in front of a stage in which the musicians (making up a *pit orchestra* or a *pit band*) sit

pitch **1** the process of suggesting or proposing an article, interview, or other proposition; in general, a presentation to a prospect The proposition itself, including the name of the client, name of the product, description of the product, or other selling points, is also called the *pitch*, as is the high-pressure, colorful sales talk that is typical of such presentations. To *make a pitch* is to present a proposal, especially in a fast-talking manner **2** [music] the relative position of a tone in a scale; to set in a particular key **3** in typewriters without proportional spacing (different amount of space allotted for different letters, depending on width), the number of characters in one inch *Multiple pitch* is the feature that permits a choice of 10, 12, 15, or other number of characters per inch. *Dual pitch* provides two choices, generally 10 or 12 characters per inch. **4** [film] the distance between perforations on the edge of a film *Long pitch* or *standard pitch* is an extended distance between the perforations, used in the printing process in which the print stock is on the outside of the original negative and requires a bit more length (than the negative) to pass over the same sprockets in the printer. The original film has *short pitch*.

pitch black [graphic arts] extremely dark, as pitch (tar)

pitch letter a letter sent to an editor or other media person by a public relations practitioner outlining the proposed publicity; any sales or proposal letter

Pitney-Bowes, Inc. the largest manufacturer of mailing equipment and the originator of the postage meter and metered mail; headquartered in Stamford, CT

pivot a pin, short rod, or shaft on which something turns or swings; a key person or thing on which much depends

pivoting shot a movement of a film camera lens so that one edge of the frame remains in place while the balance changes

pix show-business jargon for *motion pictures* or pictures in general

pixel the smallest controllable element that can be illuminated on a display screen, usually seen as a dot The word is from *picture element* and also is called a *pel*. A *pixel array* is a

collection of pixels that cumulatively represent the color and form of an image.

pixie a fairylike creature, playfully mischievous, such as a puckish character in a play or other work

pixie tubes high-intensity lamps with filaments usually in the shape of numerals or other figures, used in exhibits

pixilation whimsical, unbalanced, intoxicated behavior; an animation technique involving a combination of STOP-MOTION photography and live talent

pkg. or pkge. PACKAGE

PL phone line, such as a telephone line that links a film or tape production unit with the control room or vehicle

placard a poster, small card, plaque, or other advertisement or notice put on display; pronounced PLACK-erd

placement **1** an arrangement, such as the placement of an item in a layout or of items in a display **2** an article or broadcast that is arranged, or placed, in full or in part, by a public relations practitioner or other source A practitioner who specializes in publicity may be called a *placement specialist*; one whose expertise is in a specific medium may be called, for instance, a *magazine placement specialist*.

places a command from a director or other person to alert performers and other personnel to be in their proper positions and ready to begin; sometimes expressed as *places please*

plagiarize to use the words or concepts of another, without permission or acknowledgment The person who unlawfully takes ideas from others is a *plagiarizer*; the process is *plagiarism*.

plaint a lament or *complaint*, particularly one in verse

plaintext [computers] readable, uncoded; also called *clear data*

plan a marketing strategy It may be referred to as *the plan*, and the attainment of the objectives or goods is called *on plan*. The creative strategy or proposed campaigns of a client may be reviewed by an agency's *plans board* or by a company's *plans committee*. **2** a combination of commercial spots, programs, or advertisements offered by a medium—such as a TV station—and referred to as a *package plan*, at a reduced or *plan rate*

planchette **1** a small device that writes out a message, as used with a Ouija board, on which it points to letters and words as it is moved **2** a colored disc that is inserted in specially made paper, such as stock certificates, the authenticity of which can be determined by security devices that sense the discs

plan costs nonrecurring expenses, such as manufacturing or art production *Above plan* refers to items that are not part of a planned budget.

planeography a process of printing from a plane, or flat surface; any printing technique, such as lithography, in which the printing surface is flush with the nonprinting surface Planographic printing differs from letterpress, in which the printing surface is raised, and intaglio printing, in which the printing image is below the surface. A *planograph* is an impression from a flat surface.

planer [printing] a smooth block of wood used to level metal type that has been set in a FORM; pronounced PLANE-er

planned obsolescence the strategy of manufacturing or producing an item that is designed to wear out (by *functional obsolescence*), or to become obsolete or out of date, such as when a more contemporary-looking style is introduced to replace an existing style

planning editor the person in the news department of a network or major TV station who arranges for coverage of features or events in the future, not for today's programs; sometimes called *feature editor* or *futures editor*

planogram a diagram of the ideal manner in which a product or product category should be stocked on retail shelves, typically prepared by a manufacturer for use by its sales force

plan sequence [film] a scene that is planned to last a minute or more (a *long take*), so that the entire scene is filmed, often with considerable movement of the camera, in one take; also called *sequence shot*

plant 1 land, building, and machinery for use in manufacturing or services, such as printing In typesetting, *plant costs* are one-time expenses, such as composition and art, as compared to *running costs*, such as paper, ink, press time, and binding, that depend on the quantity of work being produced. 2 a person placed, or planted, in an audience as part of a performance; a trick, a spy A *plot plant*, which is a trick planted in the plot, also is called a BOFF, GIMMICK, or WEENIE. 3 to arrange for publicity, to place items or other material in media A press agent who plants publicity is a *planter*. 4 all the outdoor advertising structures operated by a company, called a *plant operator Plant capacity* is the number of #100 showings (achieved by 100-percent exposure to all the people in the market) available in a plant. Capacity is computed by dividing the total number of panels operated by the company in the market by the number of panels needed to make a #100 showing. 5 in a novel or other work, a character that is introduced or information that is revealed and that is related to subsequent developments in the plot A *false plant* or *red herring* is a character or information that is irrelevant or misleading—an intentional device often used in mysteries. A *dangling plant* is a character or information that is introduced and not referred to again, but not necessarily designed to mislead.

plant lines dialogue in a play or other work that relates to subsequent developments, such as a clue planted early in the plot

plaquette binding a book cover with a design stamped in the center It is akin to a plaque, a thin piece of metal or other material used for identification or ornamentation.

plasma panel the part of a VIDEO DISPLAY TUBE or other display device that consists of a grid of electrodes in a flat, gas-filled area (a *panel*) in which the energizing of the electrodes causes the gas to be ionized (the ionized gaseous discharge is called *plasma*) and light to be emitted; also called *gas panel* or *gas tube*

plastic comb binding the mechanical process of binding the pages of a book with a spiral plastic fastener, called a *comb*; also called *plastic binding* or *comb binding*

plastic shrink wrap a packaging method in which a book or other item is inserted into a folded roll of polyethylene film and then sent through a heat tunnel, where the film shrinks tightly round the item

plate 1 an ENGRAVING, ELECTROTYPE, STEREOTYPE, or other flat sheet used in printing, photography, and other reproduction processes A *bimetal plate*, used in long-run printing, has the printing area in one metal (copper or brass) and the nonprinting area in another metal (aluminum, chromium, or stainless steel). 2 a book illustration, usually full-page or large-size

plate finish a polished hard surface, as on an illustrated page in a book

platemaking the conversion of photographs, text, and other material into reproducible printing form on metal, plastic, or other hard surface, which then is utilized in a printing press One such plate is a LETTERPRESS engraving.

platen 1 the part of a typewriter (the roller) or printing press on which the paper is supported to receive the impression, or that presses the paper against the printing surface; rhymes with *fatten* A *platen press* is a printing press that works with an open-and-shut motion in which the metal type is pressed against the device—the platen—carrying the paper. 2 in film animation, a flat sheet of glass that holds animation CELS over background as they are photographed

platform 1 a raised stage or flooring for performers, speakers, and others *Platform skills* are speaking abilities and other attributes of public speakers. **2** a statement of principles and policies, as in a political party platform or the *copy platform* of an advertising campaign

platforming the distribution of a motion picture to a relatively small number of theaters, a technique designed to establish word of mouth publicity for prestige or other purposes

platform play a performance that is mainly a reading, often by one person using a script on a lectern; also called *readers theater* It is akin to a speech presented on a platform, though sometimes with costumes and scenery.

platinum record the designation for a record, cassette, or compact disk that has sold one million units, as certified by the Recording Industry Association of America, in Washington, DC Prior to 1989, two million units had to be sold to qualify for this category, which is the highest honor in the industry. More common is a gold record, which requires 500,000 units.

platter slang for phonographic record

play **1** a dramatic composition; to perform a role or a musical piece; to operate a device **2** emphasis or display given to a news story or picture—such as its size, by location, typeface, or size of headline Play may be *light* (an event is *played down*, or de-emphasized) or *heavy* (*played up*, or trumpeted). Media attention sometimes is called *press play*. **3** to produce results or create an effect, as in "How did the story play?" or "How did it play in Peoria?" (that is, how did it strike mainstream Americans?)

playact or **play-act** to pretend, to perform, or to behave in an affected manner

play agent a specialized type of literary agent who represents playwrights Play agents work mostly in England.

playback **1** reproduction of sounds, images, or other material from a recording or other source; the control for such reproduction on a recorder or other device **2** reaction, opinion, answers **3** a recording that is reviewed immediately after it is produced During a recording session, several *playbacks* are reviewed by the performers, producers, and other personnel before selecting the final version to be retained and manufactured. A *playback operator* handles the playing of prerecorded music, dialogue, or other sound, under the supervision of a *production sound mixer*. A videotape player or other device that reproduces audio and/or video but does not record is called a *playback machine*. To *play back* (also to *playback*) is to run through a recording.

playbook a collection of scripts of theatrical plays; a booklet or other collection of the in-

structions and diagrams of the plays and procedures for members of a sports team

play-by-play referring to a description of each move or action in a game or other event, as by a *play-by-play announcer*

play doctor a person who revises a play or other work, particularly one that is ailing

player **1** an athlete; a musician or other performer **2** an apparatus that gives out sound, particularly music, such as a *record player* **3** a major participant in a business, particularly in film and related fields A *big player* is really important; a *gross player* is paid from the gross receipts (receipts before expenses and taxes are paid), receiving considerably more income than a *net player*, who gets a percentage of the net income or profits (after expenses and taxes are paid).

Player's Guide a directory of theatrical performers, published in New York

playgoer a person who goes to the theater regularly or frequently

playhouse a theater

playing acting A show that is currently being performed is said to be *playing. Playing position* is a performer's position on stage in relation to the audience, such as full front or left profile. *Playing space* or *playing area* is the part of a stage used for a specific scene. *Playing time* is the duration of a scene or of an entire show.

playing weeks a measurement of activity of a theatrical show or of an entire theatrical area For instance, there were 1,116 *playing weeks* of Broadway shows in the 1987–88 season, indicating that all the shows at all the Broadway theaters were playing for a total of 1,116 weeks that season.

playlist a schedule of recordings on a radio broadcast

play off to interact, as when two performers bounce off each other's lines with enhanced conflict or rhythm

playoff See PLAY ON.

play on **1** a brief musical passage to introduce a performer—usually music associated with the performer, as on a TV program or a variety show; sometimes hyphenated **2** music to begin a program or a performance *Playoff* is music to end the performance.

play on words a pun

playout **1** the PLAYBACK or review of previously recorded material, such as of a perforated tape or other encoded medium **2** the music played by an orchestra as the audience leaves a theater The orchestra is said to be *playing 'em out*, or playing *exit music*. **3** to complete a scene or other work

play to the balcony to overact or seek applause, by catering to the audience in the cheaper seats In the United Kingdom, the expression is *play to the gallery*.

play up to give prominence to, as when a performer emphasizes some of the dialogue

playwright a person who writes plays, a dramatist; sometimes misspelled as *playwrite*

PLC PROGRAM-LENGTH COMMERCIAL; PUBLIC LIMITED COMPANY

please use a request, as from an editor or publisher, to publish an article It is not as commanding as *must use*.

pledgathon an appeal for contributions or pledges conducted on a radio or TV station, a common fundraising technique on public stations

pledges/cost (p/c) an analysis used by fundraisers to compare the amount of money pledged with the cost of the fundraising procedures themselves

pleonasm a redundant word or words

plié a common movement in ballet in which the back is held straight and the knees bent outward; pronounced plee-AY

Plinge, Walter a fictitious name used in British programs to conceal the identity of the performer, perhaps because one actor plays more than one role. In the United States, the name *George Spelvin* is used for the same purpose.

plopping focus a hasty movement from one camera shot to another with the same camera; also called *throwing focus*

plosive 1 a speech sound requiring complete closure of the oral passage, as in a hard *d* 2 [broadcasting] an explosive sound in a microphone, as when letters such as *b* and *p* are overstressed

plot the outline of the action or story of a drama or narrative; a plan or series of events The *plot line* is the story line or summary. A *subplot* is a sequence or story thread that is less important than the main plot but that often sheds light on it by providing contrastor amplification. In a theater, electricians follow a lighting schedule or *lighting plot*; stage hands follow a *scene plot* for setting up scenery.

plot lines dialogue in a play or other work that relates to the story, as distinct from dialogue that is aesthetic, emotional, or not related to the plot

plot scene an obligatory scene, a scene in a play to advance the story, or plot, that is so expected by the audience that the playwright is obliged to include it

plotter [computers] an output, or producing, unit that presents data in a two-dimensional graphic representation—for instance, a *drum plotter* (the display surface is mounted on a rotating drum) or *flatbed plotter* (paper mounted on a flat surface with a *plotter pen* that moves over it) Thus a *plotter* is a type of printer.

plow folding the on-line folding feature of a web printing press (that is, a press that prints on a roll of paper rather than on separate sheets) The *plow fold*, made by a blade, or plow, is parallel to the direction of the roll of paper.

PLS international telex abbreviation: please

plu. plural

plug 1 a promotional announcement or mention; the part of a publicity article or other vehicle that contains the product name and/or description or other points that reflect the interest of the advertiser or other source, though not necessarily that of the editor or other media person Media people sometimes acknowledge (a) that the plug is an inherent part of the news or feature element of an article or broadcast, and/or (b) that, in a kind of quid quo pro arrangement, it is inserted in return for the services provided by the public relations practitioner, which may range from considerable research to simply suggesting the overall theme of an article or broadcast. 2 [journalism, printing] filler copy, text that can be fitted—plugged—into any open area (called a *hole*) 3 a jack; an electrical device with projecting prongs fitted into an outlet or to connect circuits A *phone plug* is a jack commonly used as a microphone connector, often with audio amplifiers. 4 [theater] a small piece of scenery that is inserted in a larger piece, such as a *window plug* that is inserted into a door to give the illusion that it is a window

PLUGE [television] an electronically generated pattern of bars to adjust picture monitors to standards established by the Institute of Electrical and Electronics Engineers

plugged a letterpress printing condition in which the DOTS in a halftone have become invisible; see also PLUGGING

plugger 1 a press agent or other person who seeks to promote a song or other item by boosterism techniques 2 [newspapers] a small promotional filler—generally two or three lines long—in behalf of the newspaper itself

plugging an offset printing condition of dirty or spotty sheets due to dot area that has become filled in or plugged; see also PLUGGED

plugola payoff or PAYOLA to obtain broadcast of a record, or other PLUGS or promotion

Plumbicon a camera tube made by Philips of the Netherlands that has a lead oxide target and is commonly used in color TV The camera using this tube is called a *Plumbicon camera*.

plusing the boards jargon for adding a creative element to a STORYBOARD, or illustrated script of a TV commercial, such as a change in the script made by the director during the production

ply a thin layer; a unit of thickness, as in paper, board, fabric, or other materials In paper, 12-ply is about 1 millimeter or .042 inch.

PM PUSH MONEY

PM or **P.M.** a newspaper published in the afternoon

PM, P.M., pm, or **p.m.** *post meridiem*, Latin for "afternoon" The abbreviation also may be written in small capitals: PM or P.M.

PMA PRIMARY MARKET AREA

PMS PANTONE MATCHING SYSTEM

PMSA PRIMARY METROPOLITAN STATISTICAL AREA

PMT PHOTOMECHANICAL TRANSFER See PHOTOSTAT.

P/N please note, a marginal notation in a manuscript or other item calling attention to something, as by an editor to a typesetter; also, Porter/Novelli, a public relations firm

PNR comparative proven name registration, a magazine survey technique, used by GALLUP & ROBINSON, to determine readers' ability to recall the names of magazine advertisers The information is obtained via telephone interviews conducted on the day after the issue is read.

PO, P.O., or **p.o.** Post Office

POB or **P.O.B.** POST OFFICE BOX

pocket a type of envelope or holder affixed to a book cover, to hold a library card, a supplement to the book (called a POCKET PART), or some other enclosure

pocket book a generic word for *paperbound book* The term derives from *Pocket Books*, a major publisher that now is a division of Simon & Schuster, New York. The term often is incorrectly written as one word.

Pocket Pal a graphic arts production handbook used by thousands of designers, advertisers, and others It was first published in 1934, and many editions have been published since. The publisher of the work, which provides information on printing and related topics, is International Paper Company, of Memphis, TN.

pocket part an update, revision, or other publication placed in a POCKET, or holder, inside a book; also called *annex*

pocketpiece a nickname for the *Nielsen National TV Ratings Report*, issued every two weeks by the A. C. NIELSEN CO. The document is small, to fit into an inside jacket pocket, and is used by network salespeople.

pod a container; a group A *commercial pod* is a group of TV advertisements, generally bunched together in a *two-minute pod.*

POD PROOF OF DELIVERY

podium an elevated platform, as used by an orchestra conductor It is not a *lectern*, which is a reading desk with a slanted top. A lectern often is set on a table or stand on a podium or dais.

poem an arrangement of words, often rhymed and rhythmic, expressing experiences, ideas, or emotions in a more concentrated and generally more artistic manner than in ordinary speech, or prose *Poetry* is the art, theory, or structure of poems; poetic works; or the rhythm, spirit, and meaning of poems. Types of poetry are *dramatic* (such as Shakespeare's plays), *narrative* (those that contain a narrative), and *lyric* (those that present an image or vivid emotional response). A *poet* is a person who writes poems or displays the imaginative thought that is characteristic of good poetry. A *poetaster* (pronounced PO-e-taste-er) is an aspiring poet or a mediocre poet. *Poetic prose* is elaborate writing that makes use of rhythm, figures of speech, or other aspects of poetry.

poetic license a disregard of facts or conventional rules A writer or other artist may claim the privilege accorded to poets to use incorrect grammar or other deviations.

poet laureate the official or most respected poet of a nation, such as the court poet of England, who is appointed by the monarch to write poems celebrating national events

point (pt.) 1 a unit of measurement, direction, designation, gist, purport, item mark, punctuation symbol, sharp edge, or scoring unit (as in games) 2 [broadcasting] a unit of measurement of audience size, usually 1 percent 3 [typography] a unit of measurement of the size of type, about $1/72$ of an inch in depth; thus, one point is about .0138 inch

The point system was developed by François Didot in 1770 (the *French didot system*) and by Pierre Simon Fournier in 1878, and also in 1886 by an American printer, Nelson C. Hawkes (the system used in English-speaking countries). Previously, type sizes were referred to by names, such as Brilliant, Diamond, or Pearl. Eight-point type is $1/9$ inch. Odd-numbered and even-numbered sizes are used below 12 points; above that, only even-numbered sizes usually are used. The *point size* is determined from the top of the *ascender* (such as the tall stroke in the letter *t*) to the bottom of the descender (the stroke in the letter *p*). A point is also a designation of paper thickness; one point is .001 inch. Each thousandth of an inch is called a *point of caliper* or *point*. Fifty-point board, used as paperback covers, is .05 inch thick.

point blank   close-range (as in photography); straightforward or blunt   The term originates from gunnery.

point-of-purchase advertising (p-o-p or POP) displays, signs, and other materials to identify and promote products at their point of sale, such as at a counter in a retail store   *Permanent p-o-p* are long-term displays, generally made of metal, plastic, wire, or wood. If the display includes merchandise, such as in a bin, it is designed to be restocked. *Temporary p-o-p* displays and signs are generally made of cardboard and paper and are designed to last for less than six months.

Point-of-Purchase Advertising Institute, Inc. (POPAI) a trade association in Englewood Cliffs, NJ that represents the producers and users of advertising signs and displays at retail counters and similar locations   The abbreviation is pronounced POP-eye.

point-of-purchase scanning (POS) the technique of electronically reading data imprinted on products—for instance, the optical character recognition code, called the Universal Product Code, a series of vertical bars on an item that identify the item   The encoded material may be price or other information. The abbreviation, *POS*, actually should be *POPS*.

point-of-sale (p-o-s or POS) a retail store or other place where a product or service is offered to prospective customers   The term usually refers to the display material accompanying the product on a counter or elsewhere in the store.

point of view (POV)   **1** an appraisal, attitude, perspective, standpoint, or position from which something is observed or considered   **2** [film, television] a camera shot seen from or obtained from the position of a performer so that a viewer sees what the performer is seeing; also called *subjective camera*

point service a news summary, generally provided by a press association, such as a wire service

Poisson distribution the probability or frequency distribution used to describe the occurrence of uncommon events, as when the probability of success is very low   It is named after Simeon Poisson, a 19th-century French mathematician.

polar diagram a sketch or diagram that shows the pickup capability or direction pattern of a microphone, drawn from a polar (head-on) point-of-view

polarity a property or characteristic of two opposite poles (as in a magnet) or other opposite qualities   In television, *polarity reversal* is the

electronic conversion of the shading of a picture from white to black and vice versa.

polarization the state in which rays of light exhibit different properties in different directions, a division or concentration within a group into opposing positions or views   *Polarized light* vibrates in only one plane. A *polarizing filter* produces polarized light from unpolarized light and thus reduces glare. One such trademarked transparent material is *Polaroid*, as used originally in sunglasses and then by the same inventor, Edwin Land (b. 1909), in the portable camera that originally was called the *Polaroid Land camera* (now generally called just *Polaroid*), made by the Polaroid Corporation, Cambridge, MA.

polecat a small support for lamps used in studio photography, named after the polecat, a small animal like a weasel   A polecat often has collapsible, or telescopic, sections of tubes that are extendible so that it can fit between two walls or between the floor and the ceiling.

pole display a point-of-purchase exhibit mounted on a pole extending above a bin, rack, or other grouping of products

polemic   **1** controversial   **2** argumentative; also spelled *polemical*   **3** a controversial discussion   A *polemicist* (or *polemist*) is a person skilled or inclined to participate in arguments. *Polemics* (plural noun) is the art or practice of controversial discussion. The word is from the Greek *polemos*, meaning "war."

policy the basic tenets of an organization that determine the pattern of its attitude and activities

policy bulletin a statement of a basic position or other announcement, frequently sent to employees or members of an organization prior to the general announcement

political action committee (PAC) a group of people, in business, labor, the professions, or other areas, organized by special interests to raise funds to be contributed to candidates, political parties, and others involved in government and PUBLIC AFFAIRS

political advertising rates the cost for TV time bought by candidates   A federal regulation requires broadcast time to be sold to political candidates at no higher rates than for commercial advertisers. During an election campaign (45 days before a primary election and 60 days before a general election), the political advertising rate cannot be more than the station's *lowest* rate for the time period, provided the candidate appears in the commercial.

Polk Award a name for annual awards given by Long Island University, in Brooklyn, NY, for journalistic achievement in various print and broadcast categories   Established in 1949, the award is named after George Polk, a CBS news correspondent who was slain in Greece.

poll 1 a survey of the attitudes, opinions, and/or desires of a group The plural noun *polls* refers to the place where votes are cast. 2 to cast, receive, or record votes

polybag a polyethylene bag, made of translucent, lightweight, tough plastic material, commonly used in packaging and mailing

polychrome a multicolored work of art, particularly ancient and medieval buildings and sculptures The term also is used to describe works done or decorated in several colors. *Polychromatic* refers to various or changing colors.

polyglot a person who reads, writes, or speaks several languages; a book, particularly a bible, with the same text in several languages

polymer colors pigments mixed with an acrylic polymer resin Polymer paints are harder and more brilliant than nonacrylic oil paints.

polymerization 1 a chemical process in which the molecules of a simple compound (a *monomer*) are rearranged into a new compound (a *polymer*) that is more complex and has different qualities 2 [printing] an ink-drying process in which the ink molecules bind together

polyphonic having or making many sounds—for instance, a piano or other musical instrument that can produce more than one tone at a time, or a letter (such as *c*) that can be pronounced in more than one way *Polyphonic prose* is writing that has the alliteration or other qualities of verse. *Polyphony* is a multiplicity of sounds, as in an echo, music, or language.

polyvision an image made up of several images, as produced by multiple exposures, multiple superimposition, multiple screens, or other motion-picture techniques The term was coined by Abel Gance (1889–1981), a pioneering French filmmaker whose extraordinary silent films included *Napoleon* (1927), which used a triple-screen projection system.

POM professional or managerial, a demographic category used in advertising and other fields Individuals generally are referred to as POMs.

pong [theater] to emphasize a line; to ad lib, or improvise (*ponging it*); the opposite of PING

pony 1 describing something of small or reduced size, such as *pony service* or *pony wire* (abridged or part-time newswire), *pony spread* (an advertisement or an article on part of each of two adjacent pages), or *pony unit* (the reduced-size version of an ad, a junior unit) 2 a translation or a condensed version of a literary work, often used surreptitiously in doing schoolwork

pool 1 an arrangement whereby a limited number of reporters and photographers are selected to represent all those assigned to an event, resulting in *pool coverage* 2 the full complement of radio or TV commercials—called the *commercial pool*—available for broadcast at any one time The development of commercials to be added to the pool is known as *pooling out* or *filling the pool*; each new commercial is a *pool partner*. 3 a collection of available stories, called a *story pool*, either as possibilities to be assigned for coverage or already existing, to be selected for possible broadcast or publication

pool-hall lighting a lighting technique that uses (or appears to use) a single light source suspended in the middle of a set, akin to a pool hall (a room in which the game of pool is played)

poop sheet a concise compilation of facts or a fact sheet, used by sports announcers or others responsible for ad-lib speaking

pop 1 the quality that provides sparkle and explosive excitement to a printed piece, such as a magazine article, or to an audio or video work—that makes the work *pop out* 2 the traditional name for the doorkeeper at a stage entrance 3 short for *popular*, as in POP ART or *pop* music

pop. POPULATION

p-o-p or **POP** POINT-OF-PURCHASE ADVERTISING

POPAI POINT-OF-PURCHASE ADVERTISING INSTITUTE, INC.

pop art an art form depicting everyday objects, such as soup cans; stylized adaptations of photography, commercial art, comic strips, or other art forms

pop filter a device, such as a sponge-rubber or plastic foam cap, placed over the end of a microphone to reduce such unwanted vocal sounds as popping *p*'s and sibilance

pop-in 1 a brief paid announcement on a radio or television program, such as "Best wishes for a very happy holiday season from your friends at the Mail-Rite Company"; also called *image liner* 2 a card or other item that is loosely inserted in a publication, not bound in or affixed; also called a pop-in card, or, more commonly, a BLOW-IN

pop-off a sudden move, such as the quick removal of an object or the departure of a performer from the scene A *pop-on* is the reverse: a sudden or quick entry.

pop-on See POP-OFF.

popping explosive sounds of microphones with high volume or speaker too close, particularly with a strong consonant such as *p*

pop'ra pop rock opera, such as *Jesus Christ Superstar*

pops 1 a symphony orchestra that plays popular music, such as the Boston Pops 2 [broadcasting] heavy crashes on a transmission line caused by outside disturbances

population (pop.) **1** all the people in an area In some industries, population refers to the number of customers or has other special meanings, such as the number of videocassette recorders in home use. **2** the whole group (also called the *universe*) from which a sample is obtained

pop-up a piece of paper or cardboard that is DIE CUT and folded or pasted so that part of it assumes a vertical position—that is, pops up—when opened or unfolded A *pop-up advertisement* (an advertisement with a pop-up) may not be inserted in a publication—as a *pop-up insert*—that has second-class mail privileges, because such publications are restricted to printed sheets and the U.S. Postal Service does not consider three-dimensional pop-ups to be printed sheets. Pop-up advertisements are used in direct mail and point-of-purchase displays. A *pop-up coupon* is a tear-off perforated card affixed in the binding of a periodical or other publication. A *pop-in* card or *blow-in* card is loosely inserted rather than bound in or affixed.

pop-up bin a holder that opens to form a self-contained display—for instance, a cardboard box with products in which the top cover has printing on its inside surface so that it can be pulled open to become a sign

pop zoom a very rapid change in the position of a camera

pork text held over from one edition to the next

porkchop a half-column photograph of a person in a newspaper or other publication, also called *thumbnail* The term originates from the jowly or piglike faces sometimes shown in these photos.

pornography sexually explicit writing or other work, perhaps obscene or licentious, depending on the times and standards; also called *porno* Hard-core pornography is more explicit than soft-core pornography.

porosity the state or degree of permeability or porousness, such as the amount of liquid absorbed by a particular kind of paper

port **1** [broadcasting, recording] an opening, such as an air duct, in a *ported microphone*, which usually has many ports to control its frequency response and pickup pattern **2** [computers] an entrance or exit for a data network, location on a computer where peripheral equipment can be connected **3** PORTRAIT

portapak a self-contained, portable, battery-operated videocassette recorder

porta-panel an outdoor advertising poster panel that is mobile—can either be wheeled or carried by hand

Porter/Novelli a major public relations firm, headquartered in New York, owned by OMNICOM

portfolio a portable case for holding drawings and other items; a collection of drawings, photographs, or other items (including such nonartistic entities as stocks and bonds)

portfolio test a trial run; a dummy or a specially created publication in which the advertisement or other item being tested appears

portmanteau word a word that is created by fusing two other words, such as *sitcom* (from *situation comedy*) or *smog* (from *smoke* and *fog*); also called a *blend word* A *portmanteau* is a suitcase that opens into two compartments. Lewis Carroll (1832–98) originally used portmanteau or blended words for their humorous effect in *Alice's Adventures in Wonderland. Variety*, the weekly newspaper, is renowned for its coinage of blends.

portolan chart an early type of map or chart for guiding mariners

portrait (port) a representation of a person, particularly of the face; a description (such as in an article) or a dramatic portrayal of an individual A *portrait layout* is an arrangement of text and pictures—as, for instance, in an advertisement—in which the height is greater than the width. A *portrait sign* has similar relative dimensions.

pos. POSITION; POSITIVE

p-o-s or **POS** POINT-OF-SALE

POS POINT-OF-PURCHASE SCANNING

poser [journalism] a baffling question or problem, as asked of an advice columnist or broadcaster

position (pos.) **1** the location of an article, advertisement, commercial, display, or other item An advertiser may request a *good position* or a *position next to reading matter*, or indicate a specific page or part of a page. A *position request* does not require an extra payment, whereas a *preferred position request*, or specific order, generally does. **2** the order of appearance *Top position* is first in a variety show or other program or the best place in a sequence. **3** one of the five basic stances in ballet: *first position* (feet outward, heels touching), *second position* (feet outward, heels about 12 inches apart), *third position* (heel of one foot touching the instep of the other foot), *fourth position* (one foot forward), and *fifth position* (heel of one foot touching toe of the other foot)

position bias in opinion research and multiple-choice tests, a systematic or recurring error resulting from the order of presentation of the choices

positioning the creation of a distinct identity, image, or concept for a product or service via advertising, public relations, or other techniques The arrangement of a product, service, or other entity in its marketplace or other arena in relation to the audience can determine how well it sells. A product is *positioned* to appeal to buyers with specific demographics, such as young people.

position media outdoor, transit, and point-of-purchase advertising

position paper a statement about a subject, generally by a political candidate or other source of views on a subject

Positions! a call to performers to take their place on stage in readiness for a performance *Positions for curtain!* is a call for the beginning of an act or a curtain call at the end of an act.

positive (pos.) a still photograph, motion-picture print, printing plate, or other item corresponding to or akin to the subject, with light and dark values in their natural relation corresponding to those seen by the eye A *negative* is the reverse.

positive correlation [market research] an agreement, link, or accord of variables in the same direction

poss. possessive; possible; possibly

possible 20 a show-business expression for the possibility of a 20-minute recess The director's command *take 10* means that the crew can take a break for 10 minutes. If a set is being prepared or if the director is not certain about how long the break may last, the command may be *possible 20,* indicating that the respite may stretch to 20 minutes.

POSSLQ *persons of the opposite sex sharing living quarters,* an acronym of the U.S. Bureau of the Census

post **1** to put up or display in a public place, such as a poster or PLACARD **2** to send by mail or postal system **3** to transfer an item, as putting, or posting, in a bookkeeping ledger or publishing a name on a list **4** to enter a unit of information on a computer record or in computer storage

postage-due mail mail on which additional postage is collectible on final delivery; also called *short-paid mail*

postage meter a machine that prints INDICIA on envelopes and other mail to indicate that postage has been paid by the mailer It was originated by Pitney-Bowes, Inc., Stamford, CT.

postage saver an unsealed envelope mailed at a lower postal rate For many years, Christmas

cards and a great deal of direct mail was sent in this manner. This mailing category no longer is available.

postal the mails, or referring to the mail service The term comes from *post horses;* the animals were used by sentries at their posts, or stations, and for rapid movement from post to post. *Postage* is the charge for mailing an item, sometimes computed on a *postal scale,* affixed by a *postage meter* (a machine that prints the correct amount of postage on mail) or represented by a *postage stamp* and delivered by the POSTAL SERVICE.

postal permit mail with indicia—a printed design showing that the sender has paid postage—instead of a stamp

Postal Service the U.S. Postal Service (USPS), established in 1971 as the successor to the Post Office Department An independent agency within the executive branch, the organization operates the post offices and delivers the mail; it is headed by the postmaster general and headquartered in Washington, DC.

postal stationery envelopes, postal cards, aerogrammes, and wrappers with stamps printed or embossed on them; formerly called *stamped paper*

post binding a mechanical technique using screw posts, as in a loose-leaf binder, to fasten a book

postcard (pc) an informal card, often with a photograph, painting, or other image, with space on the reverse side for a message and mailing address Hotels sometimes provide postcards with photographs of the building or grounds as a form of advertising, and tourist attractions frequently sell postcards featuring a scenic spot. Postcards are mailed at a lower rate than letters. A *postal card* is sold by the POSTAL SERVICE and has one side for the mailing address and the other side entirely for a message.

poster a printed announcement, an advertisement, or a work of art, affixed on a surface A poster may be framed (in a *poster frame*), tacked on a bulletin board, or pasted on a wall or panel (*poster panel*). Outdoor advertising posters may be prepared in a *poster plant* for *posting* on panels for a specific *posting period;* the space is generally sold by the month. Outdoor advertising structures are of two types, *poster panels* (about 12′ × 24′) and BULLETINS (usually about 14′ × 48′). The *posting date* is the first day of the posting period, though there is a POSTING LEEWAY of several days for all the posters to be put on display. A *rated poster* is one for which visibility, traffic, and other data are available.

poster bench a seat, as at a bus stop, on which advertising is painted

poster board a cardboard with thin paper mounted on it, commonly used as signs; also called *showcard* It is usually sold in 24" × 44" size, though it can be cut.

posterization a technique for adding posterlike qualities to a photograph by emphasizing and separating the tones

poster showing a package, or group, of outdoor advertisements, such as a *25-showing* (the minimum number of locations in an area), *50-showing* (adequate coverage in the area), *100-showing* (more intense coverage), or *200-showing* (the maximum impact)

post-flashing a technique in which the colors on a film are muted, to provide detail or other effects The process includes exposure to light—flashing—after shooting. See also PRE-FLASHING.

posting leeway a grace period (generally an extension of five working days) after the scheduled date, to permit an outdoor advertising company to complete the affixing of all posters without having to pay a penalty to the advertiser

posting paper the paper used on advertising bulletins (posted bulletins)

Post-it colored squares, often yellow, of paper with a light adhesive backing that does not permanently stick or mar Manufactured by 3M, of St. Paul, MN, the note pads are useful for writing memos affixed to correspondence or other matter.

postmark a cancellation imprint on letters and packages showing the time, date, and post office or origin

postmark advertising an advertising message printing by a postage meter

post office box (POB or **P.O.B.)** a locked box, located in a post office lobby or other authorized place, that customers may rent for delivery of their mail; formerly called *lock box*

post office statement the number of subscribers of a publication, as stated by the publisher annually on a post office form

postpaid (ppd.) postage paid in advance, such as by the buyer or seller in mail order

post-production referring to the stages after the principal photography of a film, including editing, dubbing, mixing, and printing A *post-production supervisor* is in charge of or coordinates the processes after the principal filming, working with a *film editor* and others.

postscript (P.S.) **1** a few words or more added at the end of a letter, below the signature, or at the end of an article, book, or other work, as an afterthought or to provide new or supplementary information **2** a correction or change made

during the press run of an edition of a newspaper A page made over between editions for corrections or updates is called a *postscript page* or a *replate.*

postsynchronize or **post-synchronize** the addition of sound to a film; also called *postsync* or *post-sync* The editing of a postsynchronized track during the POST-PRODUCTION period is commonly called *post.*

post-test a test conducted after an event, sales period, study, or project

posture position, view, orientation, mind-set, or general theme, as of a public relations campaign

pot POTENTIOMETER

pot. potential

POT Plain Old Telephone: a single-line telephone with no special features, such as redial memory

potboiler a book or other work, usually of inferior quality, produced quickly and primarily for the money The income keeps the writer's pot boiling (presumably with food in it).

potential audience the number of households that receive an issue of a publication, or the number of radio or TV set owners in an area The term is ambiguous because it also is used to indicate the number of radio or TV sets *in use* at a particular time. Furthermore, the term is vague if it does not indicate the specific time period.

potentiometer (pot) an instrument for measuring voltage and controlling electrical flow (or the *potential* or flow); also called *attenuator, fader, gain control,* or *mixer* It is most commonly used to control sound level in radio and TV receivers and audio systems. To *pot-up* is to increase the sound level; to *pot-down* is to decrease the sound level.

pothook a sharply curved end part of a letter, particularly common in italic letters, such as *w*

POTS Plain Old Telephone Service: the system that uses the conventional telephone instrument without data communications capability or other special features

pouch a small bag, such as a *mail pouch* to carry mail, identified by its leather-strap locking device A *mail sack,* on the other hand, is not locked but tied.

pounce pulverized charcoal or other fine powder sprinkled on a stencil or other surface to improve ink absorption It was formerly used to smooth or dry writing paper. A *pounce box* contained sand or other drying material and had a perforated top, much like a salt shaker. As a verb, the word means to sprinkle or smooth with pounce.

pounce pattern a technique used in painting outdoor advertising BULLETINS The design is projected onto large sheets of paper and traced in outline form. The entire outline is then perforated with an electric needle so that the outline or pattern—the pounce pattern—can be removed and held against the painting surface.

pounding brass telegrapher's jargon for the transmission of wireless (radio) telegraph

pound mark the symbol #, which designates pounds (16 ounces) of weight and other references, such as a space or a numeral It is sometimes incorrectly called a *double dagger*, which is ‡. Actually, the # mark is a double-double dagger or a *hatch mark*.

pound sign a symbol (£) for the pound, the basic monetary unit of the United Kingdom

POV POINT OF VIEW

powderman a film crew technician who designs and executes explosions and fires

Power, J. D. a market research firm in Agoura Hills, CA, founded in 1968 by J. David Power III and specializing in the automotive industry The Power surveys of customer satisfaction and auto buyer profiles are advertised by many car and truck companies and are well known among consumers.

power alley the front of a retail store, an area generally devoted to sale or promotional items

power belt a belt with rechargeable batteries, worn by a camera operator to provide power to a portable camera

power center a new (late 1980s) type of shopping center, smaller than a major mall and larger than a typical STRIP CENTER, with coordinated signage and bright colors

power pack a unit to supply voltages for video or other equipment The portable unit may be attached to a camera, worn by the camera operator as a belt (a *power belt*), or carried as a separate unit.

power typing the automatic typing of repetitive material

poz proofreader's slang for APOSTROPHE

pp. pages; past PARTICIPLE; privately printed (PRIVATE PRESS)

Pp. pages

PPB paper, printing, and binding

ppd. POSTPAID; prepaid

PPF PANELS PER FACING

pph (news)papers per hour, an indication of the printing speed

pph. PAMPHLET

ppi pages per inch: the number of pages in a one-inch stack of paper

PPIV PER PERSON INTERVIEW VALUE

PP of A PROFESSIONAL PHOTOGRAPHERS OF AMERICA

PPS a postscript following another; from the Latin, *post postscriptum*

PPV PAY-PER-VIEW TV

PR or P.R. PUBLIC RELATIONS In jargon, *PR* may refer to a practitioner or the process. Similarly, *PA* and *PI* (PUBLIC AFFAIRS and PUBLIC INFORMATION) identify the function, practitioner, and end result.

practical lighting the use of ordinary lighting fixtures, such as with household incandescent bulbs, on a stage or set

practicals stage props that are functional—that is, that actually work *Nonpracticals* are dummies or nonworking replicas.

practical set an actual film location or a set with real walls and fixtures, as opposed to a set with movable walls (*wild walls*) and façades

praeteritio or **preteritio** a rhetorical device in which a speaker or writer states, "I will not mention . . . ," while in fact not only mentioning but emphasizing the subject by the very assertion of bypassing the point; from the Latin *praeter*, "beyond" or "past"

PR Aids See PRA INFORMATION GROUP.

PRA Information Group a mailing service in New York, in the public relations field In 1987 the name was changed from PR Aids; the company was acquired in 1988 by Allied Lettercraft of New York, which owns Media Distribution Services.

praiser a public relations practitioner, a term used by *Variety*

pratfall a fall on the buttocks, generally intentional and for comic effect

prattle idle chatter, by a *prattler*

preamble a preliminary statement

preamplifier an electronic device that controls and selects signals for intensification (in an amplifier), as in a radio receiver; sometimes shortened to *preamp*

prebound referring to a new book with a cover imprinted, akin to the publisher's binding but intended for library use; also called *pre-library bound* A prebound book is not the same as a *library edition*, which is a book with *reinforced binding.*

precanceled stamps postal stamps canceled by an imprint across the face before they are sold to large mailers Such stamps need not go through the canceling machine at the time of mailing.

precede 1 [journalism] new developments in a story, placed before or at the beginning of an existing story The item may be marked *bulletin* *precede.* **2** an explanatory note before an article

precedence code in word processing and computerized composition, a symbol that changes the meaning of the character (letter or number) it precedes; also called *flag code*

pre-choice the broad reference or opinion of a respondent prior to exposure to an ad or other item being tested

precinct an election district or a neighborhood of a city A *precinct campaign* involves working with local officials and civic leaders, and is based on the *precinct principle* of the importance of *precinct leaders* who are particularly active in politics.

precipitation **1** the settling of chemical particles to the bottom **2** [printing] inks that contain solids that are nonsoluble in water

précis a concise summary; an abstract Often spelled *precis*, without the acute accent, it is pronounced pray-SEE. The North American Precis Syndicate is a New York-based company in the public relations field that originally provided article abstracts to editors and now provides preprinted articles and other materials to the media.

preclusive buying a competitive strategy in which an item is purchased by a company to prevent its use by a consumer or to inhibit, or *preclude,* competition, as in a market test situation It may sound incongruous, but if no one gets to try a new product, for example, there will be few reorders and the product will fail.

predate an edition of a newspaper bearing the date of the next day, such as a morning newspaper which starts its press run the preceding evening (also called the *bulldog edition*)

predatory pricing the strategy of pricing an item at a lower-than-regular price in order to inhibit competition The policy is sometimes established when a product is introduced or when a new store or other retail operation is opened in a market.

predesigned sample a group of respondents chosen before a study begins

preem slang for PREMIERE

preemie [publishing] slang for the premature return of a publication, prior to its expiration date, as with a magazine that is returned by a newsstand dealer to a wholesaler even though the cover date is current

preempt **1** to replace a regularly scheduled program or commercial A *preemptable* may be sold by a radio or TV station at a reduced rate (*preemptable rate*); the program or commercial is subject to cancellation prior to broadcast if another advertiser pays a higher rate or if a pending news event replaces, or *bumps,* it. **2**

to acquire or appropriate A *preemptive claim* is an advertiser's statement of a benefit or characteristic of a product, before a competitor makes a similar claim. Presumably it is then too late for the competitor to promote the claim, as it would appear imitative to do so. A *preemptive price* is set extremely low to keep out or deter competition.

pref. PREFACE; prefatory, preferred, prefix

preface (pref.) an introduction—for instance, a description by an author, before chapter 1, of the material in the book A preface generally starts on a recto, or right-hand page. A *foreword* differs from a preface in that it is usually written by someone other than the author.

prefade or **pre-fade** to start the final part of a radio or TV program (the *fade*)—for example, music—at a predetermined time in order to end on time

preferential mail mail that receives preferential handling; also called *hot mail* Types include EXPRESS MAIL, international mail, FIRST-CLASS MAIL, PRIORITY MAIL, SECOND-CLASS MAIL, and SPECIAL DELIVERY.

preferred position a premium or special page or place within a publication that is more desirable because it has a greater readership Advertisers can pay an extra price for such a location, and public relations practitioners seek to obtain publicity in such a position.

preferred postal rates postage rates maintained at low levels through congressional subsidies—for example, the third-class rate for nonprofit organizations and free mail for the blind

pre-flashing a technique in which the colors on a film are muted, to provide more realism or other effects The process involves exposure to light—flashing—before shooting, as opposed to POST-FLASHING, in which light flashes after shooting.

prefocus to adjust the camera setting prior to photography or videotaping

prefreeze station one of the 108 pioneer TV stations that were broadcasting (or granted a construction permit) prior to September 30, 1948, when the Federal Communications Commission established a freeze, or limitation, on new stations

preliminaries the front matter of a book, preceding the main text, including the TITLE PAGE, PREFACE, and DEDICATION; also called *prelims*

preliminary edition a copy of a book or other publication issued before final publication, for comment or criticism; also called *provisional edition* or *prelims*

prelude an introduction or preface, especially a musical composition preceding the main work, such as a short romantic piece of music

prem. PREMIERE; PREMIUM

premature returns the return of periodicals by retailers to publishers or wholesalers prior to the off-sale or expiration date; also called PREEMIES

premiere (prem.) the first public performance or broadcast of a dramatic, musical, or other work Note: *premier* means first in position, as with a *premier brand* in a category, and is spelled differently.

premise an assertion that serves as the basis for an argument, story, or other work; a maxim, postulate, or truth on which a concept and story line are based

premium an item of value offered free or at a reduced rate as an incentive to purchase a product or service A *premium container*, or *container premium* (such as a decorative glass jar or tin box), is reusable by the consumer and thus has an added value. A *premium pack* contains a gift (*inpack premium*) or has a gift affixed (*onpack premium*). A *referral premium* is a product or other incentive provided to someone who refers a new customer. An *advance premium* is given before a purchase is made, in the hope of inducing a purchase. A *bonded premium* is attached to a product by an adhesive, such as tape. A *continuity premium* is a succession of items offered over a period of time, such as one offer per week for six weeks. A *dealer premium* is offered by a manufacturer to its dealers or retailers. A *direct premium* is given to a customer at the time of purchase, and does not require a mail-in by the consumer. A *display premium* is used as part of a point-of-purchase display and then can be used by the dealer. A *premium rep* is a commissioned salesperson who represents one or more premium suppliers.

premium book paper a high-quality stock, such as that used in some art and reference books

premium channel a TV channel for which viewers pay an extra charge, such as Home Box Office

premium charge an extra fee charged for rush work or other special services or for a preferred advertising position; also called *premium rate* A *premium-priced* product has a higher price than others in the same category.

pre-mix [film] the initial dubbing or mixing of soundtracks; also called *predub* or *preliminary mix*

prep or **prep.** preparation; preparatory; prepare; preposition

prepack display a display case or bin shipped with products already in it, so that a retailer

merely opens and pulls up the top or other part; also called *prepack shipper*

prepricing the printing or affixing of the retail price on an item or its package by the manufacturer; also called *preticketing* A ticket attached to the item and indicating the price is a *price ticket.*

preprint 1 a brief publication, usually one or more pages, generally advertising, printed at a central plant before the publications into which it is inserted are printed An example is HI-FI COLOR, which is printed on newspaper rolls. 2 the reproduction of advertising material, a magazine article, or other copy, provided prior to publication for display or promotion

preprint order form a printed list of items for sale, used by food and other wholesalers to simplify ordering by retailers

pre-production the casting, scripting, and other activities prior to actual filming or production

prequel the reverse of SEQUEL (and rhymes with it); a film or other work about the lives of characters that begins earlier in their lives than a previous work about them

prerecord to record a TV or radio program prior to broadcast or to record sound or part of a scene to be inserted later

pre-roll [film, television] the wobbly warmup period from when a film or videotape camera starts until it is stabilized in the roll mode

prescore or **pre-score** to compose and/or record music or other sound before the dialogue and the visual portion of the film or tape have been produced

preseed explanatory matter or new material before an article, a slang word used primarily at newspapers and wire services

presence 1 proximity in time or space 2 [broadcasting] sound quality that gives the impression of being close to the source

presentation 1 exposition, description, or demonstration, generally of a proposed plan or project 2 the bestowing of a gift, award, or other item A *presentation copy* of a book is a gift from the author, with an inscription (a signature, and sometimes also a message and date).

Presentation Level Protocol a set of rules, or protocol, for the encoding of VIDEOTEX and TELETEXT

presenter a British term for a newscaster, the equivalent of an anchorperson

presort a form of mail preparation, increasingly being used by mass, or bulk, mailers; pronounced pre-sort Senders prepare *presorted mail* in which the pieces are arranged by ZIP Code or other specifications that enable it to bypass some postal operations. *Presort* is a U.S.

Postal Service trademark. It now is used in other countries, including Canada. Presort first-class mail, properly arranged and in minimum quantities of 500 pieces, is provided at a discount.

press 1 print journalists or the print media The term now loosely refers to all media. 2 publicity; news coverage An event or individual who receives *good press* is treated favorably by the news media, while *bad press* is negative reporting or an unflattering review. 3 a printing machine or printing establishment To *go to press* is to start the printing of a publication.

Press the name of many newspapers, such as *Pittsburgh Press* or *Detroit Free Press* More common names of newspapers, however, are *News* (most frequently occurring), *Times*, *Journal*, *Herald*, *Tribune*, or sometimes a combination of these, such as *Herald Tribune*.

press agent (PA) a publicist, a person who arranges for PUBLICITY The term sometimes is used pejoratively, though it need not be. Similarly, publicists sometimes are referred to as FLACKS, perhaps referring to their ability to shake things up.

press aide an assistant to a government official or an executive who deals with the media, or an assistant to a PRESS SECRETARY or PUBLIC INFORMATION officer

press alert a letter, newswire, telegram, telephone call, or other means of advising the media of a forthcoming event or other activity that may be of interest; also called *press advisory* The alert may sometimes be considered a press invitation—that is, a request that the media attend or cover a forthcoming event.

press association 1 a news agency or wire service, such as THE ASSOCIATED PRESS, UNITED PRESS INTERNATIONAL, or REUTERS 2 an organization of publishers, such as the AMERICAN NEWSPAPER PUBLISHERS ASSOCIATION or the regional and state associations of newspaper publishers

press availability an informal or unscheduled news conference, a term used by the White House

press badge an identification carried or worn by an accredited media person

pressboard a heavy glazed paper or PASTEBOARD, used to cover the cylinder of a printing press

press box a section in a stadium or other facility for newspaper and TV reporters, reviewers, and other media people

press card the identification, on a card, of a news representative from a print or broadcast organization, generally issued by a police de-

partment, legislative body, or other agency It is not the same as a PRESS PASS.

press club an organization of reporters and others The National Press Club is located in Washington, DC, the Overseas Press Club of America is in New York, and other press clubs are in Richmond, VA; Agana, Guam; and many other cities.

press conference a meeting to acquaint the media with news or other information Some organizations prefer the term *news conference*, partly because it suggests a more direct focus on news events and partly because *press* conceivably refers only to the print media and thus excludes the broadcast media. Nevertheless, broadcast, or electronic, journalists still seem to accept the term *press conference*.

press council an organization that monitors and maintains integrity and high performance in the media

press gallery an area in a legislature or other building for observation by reporters and other members of the media

pressing a copy of a phonograph record stamped, or pressed, from a master (the original); also, the process of stamping a record

pressing and distribution (P&D) two key operations of a record company *Pressing* refers to the manufacture of the disk; *distribution* includes marketing and sales.

press kit a collection of materials provided by an outside source—such as a public relations practitioner—to the media The kit, which contains information and sometimes promotional material (to enhance the image of the subject), is intended to provide print and electronic media with background details to be used in articles or programs. Press kits may be distributed by organizations—for instance, an environmental group seeking to publicize an issue—or by performers, political candidates, and other individuals, companies, and groups. Sometimes the kit is enclosed in a cover or portfolio, referred to as a *press kit cover*.

press list a list of print, radio, and TV media, such as that compiled by a public relations practitioner prior to a news event

pressman an operator of a printing machine (press) The form for women is *presswoman*

pressmark a notation in the margin of a printed sheet indicating the specific printing press on which it was printed

press pass a ticket or other identification for individuals representing accredited media, entitling them to free admission to a specific event It differs from a PRESS CARD.

press-paste a method of binding books and other publications with adhesive

press proof a copy taken from a printing press for final checking before the full run of the printing job begins It is sometimes reproduced on a special press, called a *proof press.*

press release a suggested article, the most commonly used means of communication between public relations practitioners and the media, generally consisting of a page or more, written in the form of a news or feature article; also called *news release* The copy is sometimes referred to by media people, perhaps deprecatingly, as a *hand-out,* reflecting the process of distributing the press release. The format of the press release may vary, but generally the source appears in the upper-left corner; various other conventions, such as double-spacing, have become useful to the media (editors or reporters can make revisions directly on the news release copy). Press releases sometimes may be used almost intact, perhaps with minor changes, as the basis of an article or feature, or some of the material in them may be incorporated in an article written by someone else.

pressroom or **press room** 1 the area in a newspaper office or other building in which the printing presses are located 2 a room or area for reporters and other media people, such as at a convention or other news event. It may be temporary or permanent, as in a government building in which several media people regularly cover the activities.

press run the total number of copies of a newspaper or other matter that is printed; also called *run*

press secretary a person in charge of publicity for a government official or other person

press show an event for the media, set up in order to obtain publicity, such as at the introduction of a product; also called *press showing*

press table a table set up for media people at an event, generally near the speakers

presstime [printing] the time that an item is on the printing press; the time the press or presses are running; the time the press or presses start

Presstime the name of the magazine of the American Newspaper Publishers Association, in Reston, VA

pressure group an organization or collection of people that advocates a viewpoint and attempts to influence government officials, legislators, and others by means of lobbying, letter writing, publicity, and other techniques

pressure-sensitive paper paper with an adhesive coating, which will stick without moistening and which is protected by a backing sheet until used; also called *pressure-stick* paper or *pressure stick* It is most often used for mailing labels.

pressure transfer lettering a manual lettering process in which the characters are printed on an acetate sheet that, when rubbed on the back, transfers to a sheet of paper

pressure-zone microphone (PZM) a type of small electrostatic microphone with a flat base plate, in which sound waves are in phase in its pressure zone PZM is commonly mounted on a wall or other surface near the sound source.

press view British term for a preview (as of an exhibition) for the press

presswork the operation of a printing press; printed matter produced by a press

Prestel a British VIDEOTEX or interactive information service, in which subscribers use a terminal linked to their TV sets

pretest a test conducted before an event or experiment

pre-ticketing See PREPRICING.

preview or **prevue (PV)** 1 a showing or performance prior to general availability, "public release," or actual opening 2 [film, television] the promotion of a forthcoming attraction; also called *trailer*

Preview House a theater in Hollywood, CA, operated by Audience Studies, Inc., in which participants use dials at their seats to rate TV programs

preview light the green warning light on a TV camera, which indicates that it is about to transmit

preview monitor (PV) a TV screen used by the director to monitor and select a picture to be used from among shots by various cameras and other sources

preview sheet a bulletin or other material sent by a manufacturer to distributors and retailers to announce the introduction of a new product or item, such as a film or home-video title

prevue See PREVIEW.

prewrap merchandise wrapped by the manufacturer or retailer before being placed on the shelf, such as boxes of candy at holiday or peak sales periods

prf. PROOF

price elasticity the extent to which the price of a product or service can be changed in relation to its sales A relatively small change in the price may result in a greater proportionate change in the potential or actual quantity to be sold.

price inflater the addition of features to increase the selling price of an item or a service

price leadership the practice in which the price of an item is established by one company and then other companies in the industry follow suit The price set may be more favorable to the companies than could be achieved independently, and this strategy is called *umbrella pricing.*

price lining the practice of setting prices for various lines (styles or categories) of products For instance, a store may group products into price categories, called PRICE POINTS.

price pack a retail package with a reduced price; also called *price-off pack* or *cents-off pack*

price point a retail price Retailers generally group items with slightly different wholesale costs at the same price point and establish that price at a level considered to be attractive to consumers, such as $9.95 instead of anything from $9.50 to $10.50.

price range variations in prices of a product or service, with a minimum and a maximum within which PRICE POINTS are set

price reducer the practice of providing cents-off coupons, manufacturer's rebates, or other reductions in the established price The price reducer may be passed on to the consumer or used as an additional source of profit by the retailer.

pricey high-priced

primacy the state of being first In public relations, the *principle of primacy* is that in any contest or competition (as between advertised products), the opinions that are stated first are more likely to be remembered and believed than contrary opinions stated subsequently.

prima donna the principal woman singer in an opera or concert, generally a soprano; from the Italian for "first lady" Because such singers traditionally had a reputation for being vain, arrogant, and temperamental, the expression is sometimes applied to individuals—other than singers—who display such characteristics.

Prim & Grim the nickname of *Procter & Gamble,* in Cincinnati, OH, one of the world's biggest advertisers

primary audience the readers in a household to which a publication is sent The term can be misleading or ambiguous, because the individuals within the household to whom the publication is mainly directed should be thought of as the primary audience, while "incidental" readers in the same household are actually secondary readers. The term also is used in broadcasting and advertising, where it is equally ambiguous, as it can refer to the potential audience for a single commercial or to the listeners/viewers who are the major prospects or targets. A *primary household* is one that includes a subscriber or purchaser; a *primary reader* is a person who has looked at a publication or advertisement; and a *primary viewer* has seen a program or commercial, or regularly watches the program or station. As with all terms of this type, it is essential to identify the source, context, and specific details.

primary color one of three groups of colors—red (magenta), yellow, and blue (cyan)—from which all other colors can be mixed

primary market area (PMA) the principal area of editorial and advertising coverage of a newspaper—such as the city zone of a daily—or other medium; the principal area of sales for a product; also called *heartland*

Primary Metropolitan Statistical Area (PMSA) a major urban market, as defined by the U.S. Census Bureau A cluster of PMSAs comprise a METROPOLITAN STATISTICAL AREA (MSA).

primary service area the major or central area reached by a broadcasting station, as compared to the outer or fringe area, where the signal is weaker or erratic

primary trading area the principal area in which a marketer or retailer has buying or selling dominance

prime 1 a slanted mark written above and to the right of a letter or number, to distinguish it from a character of the same kind, such as A and A', or to indicate such elements as number of feet, minutes, angle, as 12' 2 in phototypesetting, a button or switch to clear all previously entered instructions; also called *reset*

prime location the best possible site, as in outdoor advertising; sometimes called *100 percent location*

primer 1 an elementary textbook, or a book that covers the basic elements of a subject; pronounced PRIM-mer 2 [typography] several basic sizes of type: *long primer* is 10 points, *great primer* is 18 points, and *two-line great primer* or *double great primer* is 36 points (see POINT); pronounced PRIM-mer 3 an undercoat of paint, or a substance applied to a surface to prepare it for painting; pronounced PRIME-er

Prime Ticket Network a regional cable network, in Los Angeles, that features mostly sports

prime time the time period that has the greatest number of viewers or listeners, generally 8 to 11 P.M., Eastern Time

prime-time access the 7:30-to-8 P.M. segment available to local stations, prior to the beginning of the network PRIME-TIME program period The closeness to prime time provides local stations with access to a peak audience.

Prime Time Access Rule (PTAR) a former Federal Communications Commission mandate to local broadcasters to devote prime time, such as 7:30 P.M., to local programming, with network programming limited to three hours, 8 to 11 P.M. *PTAR I, PTAR II,* and *PTAR III* were the three phases of the regulations, but the second never went into effect, and the 1982 deregulation of the FCC eliminated PTAR altogether.

primitive element [computer graphics] a point or line that can be called up by the computer and combined with other points or lines to form circles, rectangles, and other shapes Primitive elements are commonly called *primitives*. An *input primitive* is a basic data item from a keyboard or other input device.

princeps the first edition, particularly of ancient authors; also called *editio princeps* or *princeps edition*

principal a performer who plays the leading role; also called *principal actor* or *principal actress*

print 1 a positive copy—that is, with light and dark values corresponding to those seen by the eye—of a photograph on paper or film 2 newspapers, magazines, and other media produced as impressions made with ink on paper on a printing press, as distinct from electronic or broadcast media; also called *print media* 3 type—that is, text or letters produced by typewriter or typesetting The expression *small print* or *fine print* refers to clauses in a contract—traditionally set in small type—that may be detrimental to one of the signers. 4 a reproduction on paper, by a printing press, of a work of art, such as an oil painting 5 an original work of art—for instance, a woodcut or a lithograph—intended for reproduction in limited quantities under the supervision of the artist A *signed print* bears the signature of the artist; a *numbered print* indicates the sequence in a series of printings of a work—for instance, *35/400* indicates that this print is the 35th printed in a limited edition of 400. 6 to carry out any of the preceding actions; to write in nonscript letters resembling printed ones

print. or ptg. PRINTING

printability the characteristic of a paper in terms of how well it receives ink to produce printed matter of acceptable quality

print and tumble the technique of printing one side of a sheet and then turning it; also called *work and tumble* To *print and turn* (also called WORK AND TURN) is to print one side and then turn the sheet over from left to right.

print bar a bar printer, or impact printer with a type bar, used in automated printing

print barrel a print drum, or rotating cylinder, with characters at more than one print position, used in automated printing

print block the area on the page occupied by printed matter; also called *print box*

print down [film] to make a print with less light to compensate for an overexposed film

printed bulletin an outdoor advertisement with printed material, as opposed to a *painted* bulletin

printer 1 a person or firm involved in printing, specifically on a printing press; technically, a typesetter, platemaker, or anyone else involved in the reproduction stage 2 a recording device that provides a readout Examples are an *automatic typewriter* (such as a *character printer*, which produces one character at a time), *electrostatic printer* (as in a copying machine), *impact printer* (characters are on a daisy wheel, metal band, ball, or other carrier that strikes a carbon or cloth ribbon against the paper), *ink jet printer* (very finely directed sprays of ink produce a character image), *laser printer* (a laser beam generates the character image), *line printer* (an entire line is reproduced at a time), *matrix printer* (character images consist of patterns of dots rather than lines), *thermal printer* (uses heat-sensitive paper), and *wire printer* (characters are pressed against a ribbon, as in a typewriter).

printer's devil an apprentice in a printing plant The term, and the job, now are rare. Prior to the 20th century, printer's devils frequently received board and lodging and little or no salary. The devils generally were boys or young men and often delivered newspapers to the homes of subscribers, as well as conducting other errands, while they were learning the printing craft.

printer's error (PE) a typographical or other error that is the fault of the typesetter or printer No extra charge for correction is imposed on customers, as it is in the case of an *author's alteration* (*AA*), when the writer or publisher makes a change or corrects an error.

printer's flower an ornament or decoration in the shape of a small flower or leaf; also called *floret* or *flower*

Printers' Ink a weekly advertising trade magazine founded in 1888 in New York and merged in 1969 into *Marketing/Communications*, a monthly magazine In 1911, at the request of *Printers' Ink*, a group of advertising people developed a model code on deceptive advertising. Called the *Printers' Ink Statute*, it has been adopted by most states and holds that the source of an advertisement that contains any assertion, representation, or statement of fact that is untrue, deceptive, or misleading shall be guilty of a criminal misdemeanor.

printing (print. or ptg.) 1 the process of producing copies, on film, paper, or other material, by using ink (*printing ink*) applied to type or other surface to transfer the image onto paper or other material fed into a machine (a *printing press*) Major types of printing are RELIEF PRINTING (LETTERPRESS, MULTIGRAPHING, FLEXOGRAPHY), PLA-

NOGRAPHIC PRINTING (LITHOGRAPHY or PHOTO OFFSET, SPIRIT DUPLICATING, HECTOGRAPHIC printing), INTAGLIO PRINTING (gravure), LETTERSET PRINTING, and STENCIL PRINTING (mimeographing, screen-process printing, electrostatic screen printing). In *double printing*, two images are superimposed in the printing process (the technique should not be confused with a photographic DOUBLE EXPOSURE). **2** a motion-picture effect—called MULTIPLE PRINTING—in which each successive frame is individually duplicated, resulting in a slow motion or FREEZE FRAME

printing broker an intermediary between client and printer Such a person can render a valuable service, by assisting in the preparation of printing specifications (directions for the preparation of the work) and locating the best possible source or sources. The broker may deal with trade printers or others who offer reduced prices and also may extend credit and provide other services. However, the customer should know if the person indeed is a broker and thus lacks some or all on-premise facilities.

printing depth the minimum depth to which a letterpress plate or cylinder must be etched or engraved to print properly

printing down the process of making a photographic print or printing plate from a negative

printing-image carrier any of various plates, screens, cylinders, and other forms to convey and convert images during the printing process

printing in the technique of adding exposure to specific areas of a photographic print; also called *burning in*

Printing Industries of America (PIA) an association, in Arlington, VA, of commercial printing firms Formed in 1887, it is a large group.

printing office a place where printed material is produced, especially a government facility

printing wind the direction in which a film print (generally 16mm) is turned so that the emulsions of the print and the original are facing each other (in an OPTICAL printer) or in contact (in a CONTACT printer) The printing film is in A-WIND (wind rhymes with *find*).

printout **1** HARD COPY; printed text from a computer **2** an enlarged copy made from a microfilm, microfiche, or other microform

print regardless an instruction to a photographic laboratory to process a negative, even though it may be of poor quality

print syn [film] the placement of the sound track so that it is not exactly aligned with its corresponding picture track, but rather slightly ahead This is necessary because the sound head in a projector is slightly ahead (in 16mm) or behind (in 35mm) the lens, so by adjusting the tracks, in the married, or combined, print,

the projection of both is in alignment. Print syn is also called *printing syn, printer sync, printer's sync,* or *projection sync.*

print-through the unintentional transfer from one layer of magnetic tape to other adjacent layers; also called *feed-through*

print up a blowup made from a smaller-gauge film to a larger-gauge film (such as 16mm to 35mm)

print wheel a type wheel, or rotating disk, with characters at a single print position, used in automated printing

priority a system within an automatic camera that has a built-in light meter Such cameras have one or both of two priority systems—the *shutter priority* (the user sets the shutter speed and the meter indicates the lens opening for optimum exposure) and the *aperture priority* (the user sets the lens opening and the meter indicates the proper shutter speed).

Priority Mail first-class mail weighing more than 12 ounces, principally FLATS (large envelopes) and parcels Priority Mail provides faster delivery for such items by the U.S. Postal Service than PARCEL POST.

prior restraint a restriction of the media by the government, prohibiting the publication, broadcast, or other dissemination of news considered to be detrimental to the national or public interest

private automatic branch exchange (PABX) a telephone system for an organization or company for internal and/or external use When limited to internal use, it is called a *private automatic exchange.*

private branch exchange (PBX) a small local telephone office, either automatic or manually operated, such as a telephone switchboard in a business office, that serves extensions within the office and provides access to an outside public network

private brand the brand name of a product produced by or for a wholesaler or retailer for distribution within the company's own outlets; also called *private label* It differs from a *generic*, which is not branded. An example of a private label is A&P's Ann Page.

private carrier a trucker or other hauler that provides services for a single company

private line a telephone circuit for the exclusive use of a single subscriber A party line, in contrast, is shared by several subscribers.

private-party ad advertising placed by an individual, generally a CLASSIFIED AD in a newspaper It is priced at a lower rate than that available to commercial advertisers.

private press an organization that prints limited editions of publications, generally quality books set or printed by hand or other special crafts processes Privately printed books may be sold or selectively distributed free.

private sector the nongovernmental segment of the community, such as companies, nonprofit organizations, or citizen groups The *public sector*, in contrast, generally refers to government.

privileged communication confidential information that a lawyer, doctor, reporter, or other person cannot be made to divulge and that is not subject to charges of libel or slander (written or spoken defamation of character)

privishing a legal term describing the practice of privately publishing, specifically, publishing a book without promoting it

prize broker an individual or company that arranges for products or services to be presented as prizes in contests or giveaways, such as on radio and TV programs The broker usually is paid by the advertiser or source of the prizes, particularly for low-priced items. The prize broker sometimes is paid by the medium. For example, with trips, cars, or other high-priced giveaways, the advertiser may provide only the prize, with no cash fee, or, in some cases, the TV or radio station or other medium may pay the broker or pay a less-than-the-cost price to the advertiser or other source.

PRIZM a qualitative audience measurement service provided by Claritas/PRIZM of New York, based on statistically homogeneous ZIP market clusters, each with a distinctive neighborhood life style The 40 clusters throughout the country are broken down by ZIP codes; these smallest groupings carry titles that identify the community: Young Suburbia, Young Homesteaders, Blueblood Estates, or Bunker's Neighbors (Archie, that is), for example.

PRO or **P.R.O.** PUBLIC RELATIONS officer

proactive public relations the process of anticipating a situation and being prepared to execute a planned communications program (such as an advertising campaign) It is generally an aggressive rather than a passive approach. An after-the-fact campaign, or *reactive public relations*, is conducted in response to events that have already occurred.

pro-am a sports competition of professionals and amateurs, sometimes sponsored

probability sampling a survey technique in which the respondents, or participants, are selected mathematically (not randomly) so that they accurately reflect the larger group they represent (their *population*) The types of probability sampling are *cluster sampling, sim-*

ple random sampling, stratified sampling, and *systematic sampling*. In a *probability sampling unit*, the number of individuals chosen is sufficiently large so that the results will be considered valid.

problem detection study market research conducted to determine problems or negative aspects of a product or service In *problem inventory analysis*, interviewees are provided with a description of problems and asked to suggest solutions, such as potential products.

problem play a drama about a social problem, generally with a solution

problem-solution an advertisement format in which a problem is stated and a solution (such as the advertised product) is provided

pro bono for the public good, as in public service advertising or other work that is donated on behalf of nonprofit organizations The full Latin phrase—not commonly used—is *pro bono publico.*

proc. proceedings

procedure word a communications word that has a commonly understood meaning, such as *out, over, Roger,* or other radio communication jargon; also called *proword* It is analogous to a PROSIGN.

process camera 1 [film] a camera—including Acme, Oxberry, and others—used for special effects: MATTE shots, BIPACK printing, and OPTICAL printing, in which two or more elements are combined for a composite picture 2 [printing] a copying camera

process color a method of printing that optically mixes the primary colors (red, yellow, and blue) with each other to create orange, green, purple, and other colors *Process four-color printing* is the use of yellow, red, blue, and black for reproducing almost any color.

process letter a letter that is printed to imitate typing, used in direct response advertising It is not the same as PROCESS LETTERING.

process lettering a PHOTOLETTERING method in which the characters are assembled by hand and then photographed

process photography a film technique combining front-action and rear-projection photography, using a *process camera* operated by a *process projectionist*; also called *process cinematography* The most common example consists of performers in a car or other vehicle, with scenes of the street or outdoors shown through the windows, to create the sensation that the vehicle is moving, when actually the performers are in a stationary vehicle.

process plates two or more color plates, used in combination with each other to produce other colors and shades *Process printing* usually refers to process four-color printing and involves the application of the primary pigments—yellow, magenta (red), and cyan (blue)—and black.

process printing See PROCESS COLOR and PROCESS PLATES.

process red magenta, one of the standard primary colors used in PROCESS COLOR printing

process shot 1 a shot, or scene, in which the moving background is photographically produced by a projector in synchronization with the camera, so that the foreground action can be photographed against this REAR PROJECTION 2 any shot using a PROCESS CAMERA; PROCESS PHOTOGRAPHY

proclamation an official announcement or statement, usually issued by a government

Pro-Comm International Award annual awards to advertisers and advertising agencies, presented by The Business/Professional Advertising Association, Edison, NJ

prod product; PRODUCTION

Prodigy a subscription videotex service, based in White Plains, NY and owned by IBM and Sears, that operates via personal computers

producer 1 the manager of an event, show, or other work, usually the individual in charge of finance, personnel, and other nonartistic aspects in the development of commercials, plays, movies, and other works In TV, the producer has more creative responsibilities and control than in the movie industry; it is the *associate producer* who is in charge of the business elements of production. In film, the associate producer usually is in charge of POST-PRODUCTION. In some fields, the functions of the producer may depend on the individual's inclinations and talents. In music, for example, the producer often initiates and coordinates the creation and production of a record. 2 a manufacturer or supplier (such as a farmer) who provides goods for industry or consumers 3 an individual who creates something A salesperson who is successful is called a *big producer.*

Product Acceptance & Research (PAR) a market research firm in Evansville, IN, that specializes in new products Services include controlled store testing, retail distribution studies, packaging and promotion research, focus groups, diary panels, and studies on awareness and trial and repeat purchase.

product differentiation characteristics that distinguish a company's products or services from those of its competitors

product disfeature a characteristic of a product that a customer (or a potential customer) does not like

production (prod) 1 the creation or making of an item, or the total number of items 2 a public performance, as of a play 3 the period of the major filming of a motion picture, preceded by *pre-production* (planning) and followed by *post-production* (editing), though the term *production* often refers to the entire process, as administered by a *production company* A *production board* or *breakdown board* is a chart with the shooting plan, or production schedule, indicated by a color-coded step for each scene. A *production camera* films the action and is used for special effects during the filming (it differs from a *process camera* for post-production special effects and other laboratory use). Similarly, *production sound* is recorded during the shooting, whereas *post-production sound* is added after the principal photography. The *production manager* handles the *production budget* (the payroll) and other costs, supervises the *unit production manager*, and reports to the line producer, who reports to the executive producer. The *production designer* is the art director who designs the film and coordinates the work of the set designer, costume designer, and others. The *production office coordinator* handles many administrative details of a film or TV production, including daily or weekly financial reports. The *production sound mixer* supervises the sound recording on a set or on location. A *production still* is a photograph taken during the filming, often used in publicity. *Production values* is a measure of the quality of a film and/or of the cost of the film. Thus *high production values* may be a compliment (referring to a well-made film) or a criticism (of the excessive costs of sets, costumes, and other BELOW-THE-LINE items).

production add-on a charge added by an advertising agency or other vendor to the cost of production work, such as art and printing, done on behalf of a client The charge may be 17.65 percent, which results in a 15-percent commission of the total price to the agency. For example, an agency buys for a client a noncommissionable item (no discount to the agency) for $100 and charges its client a production add-on of 17.65 percent, or $117.65. When you compute it, you will see that 15 percent of $117.65 is $17.65 ($17.6475, to be exact), so the agency has marked up the item in order to obtain for itself a 15-percent commission.

production assistant a person who aids a producer, director, assistant director, or others involved in film or TV production

production associate a script supervisor in a taped TV production The job includes timing each scene.

Production Code a self-regulatory code of ethics created in 1930 by the Motion Picture Producers and Distributors of America The MPPDA was headed for many years by Will H. Hays (1879–1954), and the code was called the *Hays Code* and administered by the *Hays office*, though the director of Code Administration was Joseph I. Breen. The Production Code Seal was essential for general distribution of a movie, and the Production Code was extremely influential in creating standards of morality. It was replaced in 1968 by a rating system administered by the Motion Picture Association of America.

production illustrator an artist who sketches scenes in a film in sequential order (called a *storyboard*); more commonly called *storyboard artist* or *sketch artist*

production manager the person in charge of production or manufacturing, as in a printing plant, publishing company, or advertising agency; also called *production director*

production number a large-scale routine, or act, in a variety show or musical comedy, with the entire chorus participating and generally with elaborate staging

production show a nightclub, theatrical, or other show that does not consist merely of a singer or other performer but also has props, scenery, and other aspects of an elaborate *production*

product item a distinct unit within a PRODUCT LINE that is distinguishable by size, price, package, or other attributes; sometimes called STOCK-KEEPING UNIT (*sku*), *product variant*, or *product subvariant* A company's PRODUCT MIX may consist of several product lines, each of which may have several sublines. The total number of items in the product mix may be considerable, sometimes numbering in the hundreds or thousands.

product life cycle the stages in a product's history: development, introduction, growth, maturity, and decline The phases may be charted to predict familiar patterns, including S-SHAPED (the most common), *cycle-recycle* (the result of a promotional push in the decline stage), *scalloped* (a succession of cycles), and *roller-coaster* (fast-up, fast-down, and out, as with a fad).

product line a group of products that are closely related and produced by the same seller

product manager the person in a company responsible for the marketing of an item, sometimes called *brand manager*, who may also be responsible for development, design, and other functions

product mix the set of all PRODUCT LINEs and items offered by a manufacturer or other seller; also called *product assortment*

product placement test market research in which an item is provided to a consumer for appraisal; sometimes called *home audit*

product proliferation a line of products in which individual units are similar or closely related, sometimes displaying only minor differences—as when the original product spawns variations

product protection a guarantee by a medium, such as a TV station, not to run competing advertisements adjacent to each other; also called *commercial protection, protection,* or *competitive separation*

product space the characteristics of a product Products with the same or very similar characteristics occupy the same product space.

product spotter in a retail market, a sign on or attached to a shelf to call attention to a product

product-with-purchase (p-w-p) a merchandising technique, commonly used in the marketing of health and beauty aids, in which a product is provided free, or at a lower-than-regular price, when another item is purchased

proem a brief introduction, preface, or preamble, such as before a speech

professional magazine a magazine for members of a professional group, such as *Medical Economics, Medical World News,* or *Diversion,* which are magazines (not scholarly or scientific journals) for physicians

Professional Photographers of America (PP of A) an organization of photographers, based in Des Plaines, IL

professor show-business slang for *orchestra conductor*

profile 1 a brief biography *The New Yorker* magazine uses this term to describe its articles about individuals. 2 the combination of characteristics that describe a person or a group; also called *audience composition* 3 extent of visibility of an individual, especially one in public life Taking a *high profile* is to be conspicuous or prominent; a person with a *low profile* avoids publicity.

profile piece a cutout or other two-dimensional (flat) scenery designed to resemble a window or other items or a view

profile spot British theatrical slang for a commonly used spotlight with an ellipsoidal reflector, also called a *profile*; similar to BIRDSEYE and PAR lights

pro forma invoice a mailing piece designed to look like an invoice but that is actually a selling piece It is sometimes used by phony solicitors of advertising, as for an unauthorized or nonexistent advertisement or listing in a directory. *Pro forma* means "as a matter of form"; a pro forma invoice may be issued with the understanding that the amount will not be paid in full. Thus, though it may be legitimate, it is issued *for the record* and sent to the customer prior to shipment to confirm the specifications.

program 1 a plan or description of an advertising or publicity campaign The word, in all uses, is spelled *programme* in the United Kingdom. 2 a show or broadcast 3 a set of instructions or a routine, such as for a computer To program is to develop these instructions; the process is called *programming*. 4 a sheet, folder, or brochure given to the audience of a theatrical, musical, or other performance It lists members of the cast, musical selections to be played, or other relevant information and sometimes special features. A *souvenir program* is more elaborately produced and is sold rather than given away.

program analyzer a machine for recording audience reactions to radio or television programs

program coverage the number of individuals or households, or the percentage of a population, that is able to receive a program from one or more stations

program delivery rating the percentage of households within an area estimated to be tuned in to a radio or TV program at a given moment

program director (PD or **P.D.)** a person in charge of programming at a radio or TV station

program effectiveness the degree to which a program meets expectations or achieves anticipated results

Program Evaluation and Review Technique (PERT) a management system in which various factors are diagrammed, a type of critical path method for planning and scheduling

program following a radio or TV program that follows another on the same station or network; also called *lead-out*

program-length commercial (PLC) a 30-minute (or other length) program that is devoted entirely to a commercial It resembles an entertainment or information program but is produced by a sponsor, who purchases the broadcast time.

programmable read-only memory (PROM) in a computer or other device, the memory, or storage and recall capacity, that is programmed for the user and cannot be altered by subsequent instructions

programmed instruction a teaching method in which information is presented in sequential units, with a correct response required before the student can proceed to the next unit

program notes information on a printed program—for instance, background and comments about a composer, performer, or other highlights of a concert

program opposite a TV or radio program that is broadcast on another network at the same time as a competing program

program package a series of commercials to be broadcast on several programs of a station or network, offered in combination to an advertiser

program preceding a radio or TV program that precedes another on the same station or network; also called *lead-in* The carryover of audience can be important to both, particularly the program following.

program profile 1 a chart or graphic summary of audience reaction to a program in terms of minute-by-minute viewing levels or other measures 2 the demographic or psychographic characteristics of a program's audience

program separator a brief announcement or other transition in a radio or TV program before the commercials; also called *bumper*

program station basis (P.S.B.) a key system of rating based on the percentage of radio or TV sets in a coverage area tuned to a program at a specific time In finance, a *basis point*—such as for mortgages or other debt instruments—is $1/100$ of 1 percent, or .0001, whereas in broadcasting, a point is 1 percent.

program type a classification of broadcast programs, as defined by the Federal Communications Commission, including the following:

A	agricultural
E	entertainment
EDIT	editorial
I	institutional
N	news
O	other
PA	public affairs
POL	political
R	religious
S	sports

progression proofs a series of proofs—or sheets of typeset copy—starting with a *first proof*, followed by *marked proof* or *corrected proof*, and ending with a clean or *final proof* The term should not be confused with PROGRESSIVE PROOFS.

progressive proofs a set of color photographic proofs; also called *progressive* or *prog* The first set consists of a separate proof of each color; the last set contains all (generally four—red, blue, yellow, and black) colors on one sheet. Progressive color proofs are provided to advertisers and other users of four-color printing

prog rock progressive rock music, a radio station format: an obsolete term, now called ALBUM-ORIENTED ROCK

projection 1 attribution or identification of one's feelings and attitudes to another   Motivational researchers use such *projective techniques* as picture interpretation, role playing, sentence completion, and word association in order to identify attitudes.   2 a forecast—called a *sales projection*—or the process of estimating on the basis of existing data   3 the process of displaying images on a surface   For instance, a slide, filmstrip, or movie is fed through a device—a *projector*—and the images are magnified on a screen, wall, or similar surface. At a movie theater, a *projectionist* operates the equipment, generally in a *projection booth* (a room in the rear of a theater), and also operates the lights.   4 a photographic method with a lens between the FONT (which is on a film negative) and the light-sensitive material   5 the ability to project or convey a forceful or charismatic personality

projection printing the process of enlarging photoprints by projecting the image through a lens system (called an *enlarger*)   A *projection print* is larger than a *contact print*, which is the same size as the negative.

projection sync.   [film] the displacement of the sound and picture tracks so that they are not in exact parallel alignment and thus are not synchronized; also called PRINT SYNC   This process is necessary because the sound and image are not in exact alignment in a projector.

projection television   a system of lenses and mirrors used to produce an enlarged TV picture on a screen, used in bars and other places

projector lamp   1 a lamp used in a projector   2 a lighting instrument that produces a narrow beam, used as a theatrical spotlight or footlight, sometimes called a *projector unit*   In the United Kingdom, it is called a *pageant lantern*, *projection lantern*, or *projector lantern*.

projectural   a slide or other transparent or opaque material from which an image is projected on a screen, as with an overhead projector; also, the image itself

prolegomenon   a preliminary remark   The term is generally used in the plural, *prolegomena*, to designate a series of preliminary statements at the beginning of a book.

prolepsis   a figure of speech in which a future event is described as if it had already happened, or in which a question is answered before it is asked

prolix   wordy; verbose; using more words than necessary

prologue   an introduction to a play or other work

PROM   PROGRAMMABLE READ-ONLY MEMORY

promise   the assurance or expectation of excellence or satisfaction in a product, service, or advertising campaign

promo   short for *promotion* (the short-form plural is *promos*)   The term refers to the overall activity conducted by a radio or TV station, or any organization, designed to help sell a particular product or service. More specifically, the word refers to the preliminary advertisement or announcement of a radio or TV program, broadcast earlier in the day of the program or on the preceding day or days.

promotional books   previously published books (generally those with expired copyrights or those that are out-of-print) that are reissued, usually in a larger, more attractive format   The covers, in particular, may be redesigned, and the title may sometimes be changed. Most importantly, the works are sold as bargain books. The company often is a *promotional publisher*, specializing in promoting bargain books.

promotion allowance   a subsidy provided by a producer to a seller, such as by a manufacturer to a retailer, to promote or advertise the sale of a product or service; also called *promotional allowance* or *merchandise allowance*   Thus the retailer would receive a discount on the cost of goods that it agreed to advertise.

promotional package   banners, displays, and other items sent to a retailer to help sell a product or service

promotional spot   [broadcasting] a commercial advertising a program, station, or network

Promotion Marketing Association of America an organization in New York, established in 1911, of promotion, sales incentive, and premium sellers and buyers   It was formerly called the *Premium Advertising Association of America*.

promotools   materials—including catalogues, contests, coupons, displays, and exhibits—used in the advertising or promotion of goods and services

prompt   a message on the computer screen that questions or prompts the user, as with a *prompt character* that requests further information or input

prompt corner   the position in a theater of the prompter, usually downstage right in the United States and downstage left in the United Kingdom   In opera houses and European theaters, the prompter usually is in a hooded area, called a *prompt box* or *prompter's box*, facing the front center of the stage.

prompter   1 in theatrical performances, a person who assists actors who have forgotten their lines   The individual uses a *promptbook* or *prompt copy* of the script and works in a *prompt* *box* or *prompter's box* in an alcove below the front center of the stage, facing the performers. During rehearsals, the stage manager often works at a *prompt desk* or *prompt table* on the side of the stage, left (U.S.) or right (U.K.), called the *prompt side* (PS), *prompt wing,* or *prompt corner.* **2** a device to enable speakers and performers to read a script while looking at the audience or at the camera In *video prompters,* the *prompter copy* is typed on ordinary 8½" × 11" sheets of paper that are taped to become continuous rolls, or is typed on rolls of paper called *computer video prompters.* In professional prompter systems, the prompter copy then is scanned by a vidicon camera and transmitted to one or more prompter/monitor readouts that are mounted on or off a TV camera. The *prompter script* can be superimposed over the *taking lens* of the TV camera so that it is visible to the speaker but not transmitted to the home viewer. The first video prompters were made by the Teleprompter Corporation, a New York company that now is defunct. Its TelePrompTer no longer is made. A commonly used TV prompter is the Videoprompter, made by Q-TV Inc., of New York.

pron.   PRONUNCIATION

pronouncer   [broadcasting] the phonetic spelling of a word, particularly important in helping announcers pronounce foreign names (see PHONEME)

pronunciation   the act or manner of speaking words, especially with reference to the production of sounds and the placing of syllable stress, intonation (voice modulation), and other factors The term more specifically refers to the correct, or conventional, pronunciation of words. Note the spelling; the word is not pronounciation.

proof (prf.)   an inked impression of material to be printed, made before printing to check accuracy and quality The process of taking the trial impression is called *pulling the proof.* Proofs sometimes are produced on a special, hand-operated press, or *proof press.* Individuals who read the proof and compare it with the original copy are called *proofreaders.*

Common proofreaders' abbreviations include *bf (boldface), cap (capitalize), ital (italic), lc (lowercase), lf (lightface), rom (roman), run in (no paragraph), sc (small capitals or see copy), sp (spell out), stet (let it stand), tr (transpose),* and *wf (wrong font).* The marks made on the type proof to provide instructions for corrections are *proofreaders' marks.* Common proofreaders' marks include:

align ‖
apostrophe ⩗
broken type ✗
capitalize C̲ or Caps̲

center ⏋ ⏌
close up space ⌒ or ℯ#
comma ⋏
delete ℯ
down (move down) ⊔
equalize space   eq.#
indent, move right ⏌‖
insert ∧ or ∨
italic   *ital.*
lowercase *l.c.*
paragraph ¶
parentheses (⁄)
period ⊙
push space down ⊔#
small capitals sc or SM. CAPS̲
space #
straighten ‖
up (move up) ⊓

Proofs are designated by their form: a *galley proof* is a long sheet of copy; on a *page proof,* the copy is separated into the pages of the book or other publication. Proofs are also designated by their destination or purpose (*artist's proof, author's proof, book club proof, engraver's proof, foundry proof, plate proof,* or *reproduction proof*). In offset printing, proofs are contact sheets made by the DIAZO process from photographic film, such as a *whiteprint* (a positive print from a positive film), *blueline* (blue color), *vandyke,* or *brownline* (brown color).

proof of delivery (POD)   a document that accompanies a shipment and is signed by the individual to whom the deliverer gives the package

proof of purchase (PROP)   evidence, such as a receipt, box top, or label, that a consumer has purchased an item A PROP may be sent to a manufacturer (or to a mailing house) to obtain a rebate or a premium.

proof print   a copy of an illustration; also called *proof impression* It differs from a proof sheet, which is a copy of text.

prop   a show-business term referring to objects, or PROPERTY, and other paraphernalia used during a performance A *hand prop* or *personal prop* is an item worn or used by a performer. A *set prop* is furniture or other items on the stage, excluding scenery.

PROP   proof of purchase

propaganda   communications—including written works, speeches, and other forms—intended to influence public opinion From its earliest use, in the 19th century, the word has had a nefarious connotation, particularly when the source of the propaganda is not disclosed The word suggests, as well, the use of distortions and manipulations rather than the dissemination of facts.

properties an itemization of all the objects not structurally part of a scene or set; also called *props list* or *properties plot*

properties truck a portable cabinet for storage of hand props (small objects)

property 1 a script 2 a performer under contract 3 any article except costumes and scenery used in a play or other production; often called *prop* or *props* The backstage crew in charge of props are called *property personnel*. *Production property personnel* are paid by the producer and are part of the show. *House property personnel* are paid by the owner of the theater or studio and are assigned to the facility. In the United Kingdom, property personnel sometimes are called baggage personnel, as they also are in charge of the luggage of a touring company. In film, the *property department* obtains and maintains the props, under the supervision of a *property master*. The *property handler* places the props in accordance with a *property sheet* and a *property plot* or *property plan* (a layout of the location of the props) and using a *property truck.*

proportion the comparative relationship between parts, such as the ratio of width to depth in a design or layout; to arrange the parts or elements of a whole, as in a layout, to be harmoniously or properly balanced (in *good proportion*)

proportional spacing (PS) the characteristic of a typeface in which each letter has its own *escapement value*—the amount of space it occupies; also called *differential letter spacing* Some typewriters and computer printers, known as *proportional spacing machines* (*PSMs*), provide type elements that use proportional spacing, so that, for instance, the letter *i* occupies less space than the letter *m*.

proportion rule a graphic arts device used to establish the amount of reduction, enlargement, ratio, and proportion for copy; also called *production scale* or *scale*

proration assessment (from *pro rata*, Latin for "proportionately")

proscenium in conventional theaters or other buildings, the apron of the stage—that is, the part of the stage between the front curtain and the orchestra; pronounced pro-SEEN-ee-um, *not* pros-SEN-ee-um It is the part that juts out into the audience area, sometimes including the curtain and its arch (the *proscenium arch*). A *proscenium theater* is different from THEATER-IN-THE-ROUND. The *inner proscenium* or *false proscenium* consists of vertical scenery on either side of the front of the stage and an overhead horizontal curtain or piece of scenery; these three *flats* are adjustable and create various sizes of openings.

prose the ordinary form of spoken or written language, not poetry; from the Latin *prosa*, "direct" Prose can be artistic, though the adjective *prosaic* means dull, unimaginative, or flat. A *prose poem* is a brief work not written in the form of poetry but with rhythm, vivid language, and other elements of poetry.

prosign one or more characters frequently used by radio, telegraphic, and other communicators to represent one or more words An example is SOS.

prosodic symbols accent marks and other symbols used in versification (prosody), including:
- ´ accented syllable
- ` lesser stress
- ˘ no accent or short vowel
- ¯ long vowel
- ‖ pause (a caesura)
- χ or / separation (a virgule)

prosody the science or art of versification or poetic composition, including meter, rhyme, and stanza forms

prospect a potential customer Thus *prospecting* is the searching for new customers.

protasis in Greek and Roman drama, the opening of a play in which the characters are introduced In contemporary drama, a *protatic character* appears briefly to provide information or to advance the plot.

protected rate the price of an item that a supplier agrees to maintain, for a specific period of time, to a purchaser, despite later increases in price to other customers

protection 1 a duplicate film or other item, held in case of loss or damage to the master or original—for instance, a *protection shell* or *safety shell*, which is a model made from a plate (generally a color plate) 2 in consignment selling, the policy in which the manufacturer (such as a book publisher) agrees to accept unsold merchandise returned by a retailer (such as a bookstore)

protection shot [film, television] a shot, or scene, that can be used if another shot proves to be poor or unusable, or if the continuity between two shots is erratic

protective flat scenery at the side or back of a set to prevent camera coverage of the walls or other areas

protocol 1 a procedure or plan, such as for an experiment or project, or a set of rules governing the exchange of data between two computers or other devices 2 the first copy of a treaty or other document prior to ratification; a preliminary draft or record

proud [printing] type that is placed separately, isolated from the rest of the text on a page

prove to pull a PROOF

provenance the place of origin, or the derivation, especially of a work of art In book publishing, the term refers to the record of ownership of a book or manuscript.

proven commercial registration (PCR) a measure of the effectiveness of a radio or TV commercial to compel attention It is an audience-survey technique, used by GALLUP & ROBINSON, to determine viewers' ability to recall the names of broadcast advertisers.

proverb a brief, pithy saying, or adage, expressing a common sense truth *Proverbs* is a book in the Old Testament, containing fundamental or profound truths.

provincial relating to the outside territories or rural areas, especially of the United Kingdom, Canada, and other countries in which the governmental districts are called provinces Rural or unsophisticated newspapers sometimes are called *provincial papers* or the *provincial press*.

provisional cut (PC) a portion of a film or production that can be omitted if necessary; also called *tentative cut*

provisional edition See PRELIMINARY EDITION.

proword PROCEDURE WORD

proximo terms a notation on an invoice indicating the time and other details of payment For example, *2%, 15 proximo, n/60* means that a 2-percent discount may be taken if payment is made before the 15th of the month following the purchase, with the full amount to be paid no later than 60 days after the first of the month following the purchase. *Proximo* means "of or in the following month"; *mo* is short for month.

proxy a document or authorization empowering a person to act for another, as in voting at a shareholders' meeting of a publicly owned corporation A *proxy fight* is the effort of a group to win the voting support of other shareholders. A *proxy solicitation* is the process of contacting shareholders, generally made by a document called a *proxy statement*. The stockholders indicate their choice for members of the board of directors and auditors and sometimes other issues by checking off boxes and signing the *proxy card* and returning it to the company.

Proxygram a shareholder vote (as in a PROXY fight) received by phone (an 800 number), electronically recorded and transmitted via electronic mail or other means It is a trademarked service of Churchill Communications Corporation, New York.

pr reporter a weekly newsletter, published by Otto Lerbinger and Patrick Jackson in Exeter, NH The *pr* stands for *public relations*. The name is not capitalized.

PRSA PUBLIC RELATIONS SOCIETY OF AMERICA

PS PROPORTIONAL SPACING

P.S. POSTSCRIPT An additional postscript is abbreviated *P.P.S.* (*postpostscriptum*).

PSA or **P.S.A.** PUBLIC SERVICE ANNOUNCEMENT

p's and q's manners, behavior To *mind your p's and q's* is to be careful about your words and actions. The expression probably originated in the days of metal type, when printers could easily mistake these two letters.

P.S.B. PROGRAM STATION BASIS

pseudo-event an event contrived to obtain publicity The word was originated by American historian Daniel Boorstin (b. 1914) and popularized by him in a 1961 book, *The Image: A Guide to Pseudo-Events in America*, and by other social historians who generally are critical of the orchestration of synthetic, staged events, particularly by politicians; also called *media event* or *staged news*

pseudonym a fictitious name; an assumed name A pseudonym used by a writer is also called *pen name* or *nom de plume*.

P.S.U. PROBABILITY SAMPLING unit

psychoacoustics the study of what is actually spoken as compared to what an individual perceives

psychographics the study of social class, lifestyle, and personality characteristics of individuals and groups, as compared to demographics (age, income, occupation, education, race, religion, and other more quantifiable data). Psychographics are measurable, however, and often are more accurate in predicting behavior.

P-system an inventory control plan in which a retailer reorders merchandise on a regular basis, such as on a specific day each month, though the quantity of the order may vary; also called *periodic reordering* In the *Q-system*, on the other hand, the same quantity is reordered at varying intervals.

pt. PART; PAYMENT; pint; POINT; PORT

PTAR PRIME-TIME ACCESS RULE

ptg. PRINTING

PTL a TV network operated by Heritage Village Church, in Charlotte, NC Supported by contributions, it transmits the *PTL Club* and other programs, via satellite, to cable systems. The initials stand for *Praise the Lord* or *People That Love*. The network was terminated in 1988.

pto, PTO, or **P.T.O.** please turn over (the page): an indication that something appears on the back of a page

PTP PAPER TAPE PUNCH

PU or **p/u** PICKUP; PERSONS USING TELEVISION

pub. PUBLIC; PUBLICATION, published; PUBLISHER

pubcaster a broadcaster on a public radio or TV station or network, or a broadcaster of publica-

tion or teletext   The word was coined by VARIE-
TY.

public (pub.)   a smaller group within the general
population, linked by common interests, such
as the *reading public* or the *voting public*   Ex-
ternal publics are those outside an organization—for instance, potential customers—
whereas *internal publics* are members, employees, and others within a group. A *public
company* (or *publicly held* or *publicly owned
company*) is owned by shareholders who purchase shares of stock on the open (public) market. In the United Kingdom, such companies
are called *publicly quoted companies,* a reference to the buy and sell stock prices that are
publicly stated (quoted). This may be confusing
to some Americans who think of "publicly
quoted" in reference to statements of executives quoted in the media. The expression *to go
public* is to make something known.

public access   the availability of broadcast facilities for use by community interest groups, a
key condition of most cable TV franchises

public access channel   a channel reserved by a
cable company for community or other public
service programs   It is generally available to
nonprofit organizations and others.

public access videotex (PAV)   an interactive
electronic service for information and transactions at user-controlled terminals in public locations, such as shopping malls and airline
terminals

public address system (PA)   an electronic amplification apparatus, consisting of one or more
microphones and loudspeakers (such as music),
used in theaters and elsewhere for disseminat-
ing announcements or other sounds to be conveyed to an audience   Audio professionals call
a PA system a *sound reinforcement system.*

public affairs   the aspect of public relations that
involves working with governments and groups
with regard to societal (public) policies, action,
and legislation; the relationship between an organization and the government, community, or
society in general   *Public affairs* sometimes is
used as a synonym for *public relations,* but
more often the term refers to activities that are
thought to be in the public interest. In a corporation, a *public affairs officer* or *public affairs
director* is involved with external publics and
not with employees or shareholders.

public affairs officer (PAO)   a person in the military who is in charge of PUBLIC RELATIONS, communications, and media   In the United States,
the designation previously was *public information officer* (PIO). See also PUBLIC AFFAIRS.

publication   the process of publishing; the
printed material itself   The *publication date* or

release date (also called *pub date*) of a book is
the date on which it is available for sale. Copies
issued in advance are called *pre-pubs.* The publication date of a monthly magazine is the
month during which it is sold, though copies
generally are available the preceding month.
The publication day or date of a weekly magazine or newspaper may be the first day of issue,
the last day of the week it is sold, or somewhere
in between.

public broadcasting   nonprofit radio and TV
stations that are supported by individual subscribers, foundations, government, and other
funding sources, including corporations   Program sources include the Public Broadcasting
Service (PBS), in Alexandria, VA. The intent of
the federal government in setting up PBS was to
create and encourage alternative stations to
broadcast quality or educational programming.
The original name for the TV stations was *ETV*
(educational TV); many of the stations are
owned and operated by colleges or universities.

Public Broadcasting Service (PBS)   an organization in Alexandria, VA, of noncommercial TV
stations that produces and distributes TV programs to its member stations

public domain (PD or P.D.)   the condition of being free from copyright or patent and thus open
to use by anyone   A book or other work whose
copyright has expired is *in the public domain.*

public information (PI)   the process of communicating, providing publicity and other data to
various groups, directly and via the media   In
government, a communicator is often called a
public information officer (PIO).   See also PUB-
LIC AFFAIRS OFFICER.

Publicists Guild   an organization in Sherman
Oaks, CA, of public relations practitioners, including many in show business   The full name
is *American Publicists Guild.*

publicity   a public relations technique in which
information from an outside source—usually a
public relations practitioner—is used by the media   A message is developed and distributed,
without specific payment to the media, through
selected outlets (magazines, TV, and so on) to
further the particular interests of the clients.

publicity chaser   a person eager to obtain publicity; also called *publicity hog* or *publicity
hound*

public limited company (PLC)   a British designation, written after the name of a company, indicating that it is publicly owned   Privately
owned companies have limited liability and are
designated as *Ltd.* In the United States, public
and private firms are designated as *Incorporated*
(*Inc.*).

public opinion the views of the general population A *public opinion study* attempts to determine and evaluate these views with regard to a specific issue.

public policy the position of an organization with regard to an issue

public radio noncommercial radio, supported primarily by grants and contributions from listeners and others, rather than advertising Programming includes news, humor, and classical and popular music.

public relations (PR or P.R.) the activities and attitudes intended to analyze, adjust to, influence, and direct the opinion of any group or groups of persons in the interest of any individual, group, or institution Though many people work in *public relations agencies* (companies or firms exclusively devoted to the development of public relations activities in behalf of clients), the largest number work in government agencies, companies, and organizations. In its broadest sense, *public relations* includes advertising and all forms of communication. In a narrower conception, however, the field generally excludes advertising except for institutional, or good-will, advertising or other targeted advertising. The field is categorized by the publics to which appeals are made to accept, support, or purchase certain public policy decisions, political candidates, or products and services, such as community relations, employee relations, financial relations, legislative relations, and "general-public" relations. Ideally and in its broadest sense, public relations helps an organization and its publics to adapt mutually and/or to achieve the cooperation of groups of people. Public relations practitioners conceive and execute programs designed to achieve objectives related to specific groups (publics), goals, and strategies, utilizing publicity and other communication techniques. An organization with *good public relations* has a favorable image or reputation, perhaps as a result of public relations activities.

Public Relations Journal the monthly magazine of the Public Relations Society of America, in New York

Public Relations News a weekly newsletter, published by Mrs. Denny Griswold in New York The newsletter presents annual Gold Key awards to outstanding public relations practitioners.

Public Relations Society of America (PRSA) a national organization, headquartered in New York, of public relations practitioners

public release the time that a film or other work is available to the general public, following the previews or private screenings

publics target audiences

public sector the segment of society that belongs to or represents the total community The term generally refers to government; the *private sector*, on the other hand, includes corporations, nonprofit groups, and citizens' organizations.

public service advertising time or space provided by a station or a publication at no charge to nonprofit organizations Such advertising is common in broadcasting and magazines, less so in daily newspapers.

public service announcement (PSA or P.S.A.) a message, usually broadcast free by radio and TV stations The announcements usually are provided by government agencies and nonprofit organizations and are considered to be in the public interest. In recent years, some public relations practitioners have developed creative techniques for distributing PSAs in behalf of commercial clients, such as by linking them with nonprofit organizations or public service issues.

public service corporation a private company that provides an educational or other beneficial service to the general population, usually with government support, sanction, or regulation

public television noncommercial television, supported primarily by grants and contributions rather than by advertising

published data tapes (PDT) a TV audience research report issued to subscribers by the A. C. NIELSEN CO. in computer tape and diskette form

publisher 1 a producer of written material, such as books, newspapers, and other print media, and nonprinted material, such as computer tapes and videotapes *Publisher's binding* is the regular binding (not custom or hand binding) of a book; it is also called *edition binding* or *trade binding*. A *publisher's representative* is a salesperson who is employed by (a *house representative*) or represents (a *commissioned sales rep*) the publisher; the terms *sales rep*, *traveler*, and *book traveler* are also used. 2 the chief executive at a newspaper or other publication, sometimes the owner or the representative of the owner At some periodicals, the publisher is in charge of advertising and perhaps other business functions, but not editorial functions; thus the editor does not report to the publisher and the two (editor and publisher) report to the owner, who may have the title of president or chairman (chairwoman).

Publishers Advertiser Reports a subsidiary, formed in 1983, of Interactive Marketing Systems in New York The reports provide data about magazine advertising, under a contract from the Publishers Information Bureau. From

1945 to 1983, the service was provided by Leading National Advertisers, a New York company.

publisher's audit a circulation report on a publication, issued by the publisher, usually called the PUBLISHER'S STATEMENT

Publishers Clearing House a subscription agency, in Port Washington, NY, that solicits subscriptions on behalf of publishers, primarily by mass mailings to households It is a private company and not an association.

Publishers Information Bureau (PIB) a component of the Magazine Publishers Association, in New York, that provides monthly reports on advertising pages and revenue in magazines and newspaper supplements There is no apostrophe in the name.

publisher's letter [direct marketing] a solicitation letter or note from a publisher of a magazine or other periodical, enclosed together with a longer letter; sometimes called a *why not* letter, as it asks, "why not take advantage of this offer?"

publisher's mark a symbol or logo used by a publisher; also called *publisher's device* It differs from a *colophon*, which provides information about printing specifications of a book—for instance, its typeface—generally on the last page, whereas the publisher's mark appears on the cover, title page, or one of the front pages.

Publishers Row originally, Park Avenue South in New York, a street on which many book publishers were located The term now refers to book publishers, collectively, wherever they are.

publisher's series reprinted books issued by a publisher in uniform style, generally under a common overall title, such as *Modern Library*; also called *trade series* (if the works are trade books, intended for the general public) or *reprint series*

publisher's statement a circulation report, on colored paper, about a publication, provided semiannually by the publisher to the AUDIT BUREAU OF CIRCULATIONS, which issues an official verified report, on white paper, called a WHITE AUDIT

Publishers Weekly (PW) a weekly magazine of the book publishing industry, founded in 1972 and issued by R. R. Bowker in New York No apostrophe!

publishing history a chronology of the editions and printings of a book, listed on the copyright page, starting with the earliest publication

pub set or **pubset** referring to an advertisement in a newspaper or other work in which the type is set by the publication The alternative is for the advertiser to provide pasted-up layout of the ad ready for printing.

puck 1 in a tape recorder, a rubber wheel (shaped somewhat like a hockey puck) that presses the tape against the capstan 2 a manually operated control device (also akin to a hockey puck) to direct the movements of an arrow or cursor on a computer screen It is similar to a MOUSE.

puffery exaggerated, perhaps unjustified, praise, often used in advertising, promotion, and publicity A *puff piece* is a laudatory article or broadcast.

Pulitzer Prize the name of annual awards in journalism, literature, and the arts, established in 1917 Named after newspaper publisher Joseph Pulitzer (1847–1911), the awards are presented through the Graduate School of Journalism of Columbia University, New York.

pull 1 degree of demand; to draw or attract *Pulling power* is the degree of effectiveness of a personality, product, medium, or other entity in attracting attention or action. A theatrical show that attracts an audience *pulls 'em in* or *pulls good*. 2 to *pull a proof*: to make a PROOF—that is, an inked impression of copy for inspection prior to printing The British word for *proofs* is *pulls*.

pull air [film] to find a portion of the soundtrack on which no one is speaking and the only sound is background tone (air) and then to take (pull) this and insert it into the edited version

pull back 1 to remove a product from a market or area 2 to move a camera or DOLLY away from the subject, resulting in a *pull-back shot*, in which the scene is enlarged

pull-case a protective box for a book or other publication; also called *pull-off box*, *pull-off case*, or *pull-off cover* The publication is placed in the lower part of the case; the upper section then is slipped over, covering the top of the book.

pull-down the portion of a film moved (by use of a film advance device) after exposure or projection

pull in to publish material without waiting for corrections, as when type is "pulled in" or "railroaded" (rushed without careful consideration)

pull-out a free-standing section, inserted within a publication, such as a weekly TV program guide or special supplement included in a Sunday newspaper

pull quote or **pullquote** a quotation that is taken, or pulled, from the text—generally of a newspaper or magazine article—and set off, or displayed as a blurb or insert, perhaps surrounded by ruled lines (a *pull quote box*)

pull strategy a marketing strategy in which monies are spent or a special effort is made with advertising, public relations, and other activities designed to intensify consumer demand, as opposed to a PUSH STRATEGY

pull-up **1** a loop of film in a projector that remains slack and is necessary for smooth continuous movement over the sound head **2** to rearrange a film shot so that it is tightened by removing unnecessary background, so called because of the pulling of the lens focus

pulp in papermaking, the mixture of wood or other cellulose material that is ground up, moistened, and then pressed into sheets *Mechanical pulp* is made by grinding, the process used for groundwood paper, whereas in *chemical pulp* the fiber is softened with sulfite or other chemicals. *Alpha pulp* is highly refined wood pulp, used in quality paper.

pulp magazine a magazine printed on groundwood pulp or other coarse, cheap paper, as contrasted with magazines printed on coated, glossy paper (called *slicks*) Regardless of the paper stock, the pulp magazines (also called *pulps* or *pulp sheets*) are designed to appeal to less sophisticated audiences than the slicks and include those devoted to romance (such as *True Confessions*), crime, and other mass-appeal subjects.

pulse the perceptible underlying feelings or opinions, particularly of a group

Pulse a defunct research organization in New York that reported audience estimates based on personal interviews and other market surveys Founded in 1941, the company was known for its radio ratings. It went out of business in 1976.

pulse code modulation (PCM) the conversion of voice signals into digital code

pulsing a FLIGHTING pattern consisting of alternating weeks (or two-week units) of advertising activity and inactivity The strategy is to sustain awareness levels over time.

pun a play on words, generally a witty use of a word in two incongruous senses Puns are punned by *punsters*, who enjoy punning punningly.

punch [film] a term that refers to several devices: a device to produce a *cue mark* in a film leader, a device to remove splicing sounds in a print, and a device to perforate the edge of an animation sheet so that it fits onto the pegs of the *animation stand*

punch-in a cue to indicate the start of a recording

punch line the climax of a joke or story

punch scene a fight

punch supervisor a person who perforates, or punches, the edges of film animation sheets so that they fit onto the pegs of the animation

stand The assistant, the *post-punch supervisor*, does the photocopying.

punch up to add vigor, such as to a design or a layout In radio, recording, and other fields, to *punch it up* is to press buttons in order to bring something to the fore, such as to cue a tape to be broadcast.

punctuation the use of points, marks, or symbols in written or printed material to separate text into sentences, clauses, and phrases and to clarify or emphasize meaning

PUNCTUATION AND OTHER SYMBOLS
acute accent ´
ampersand &
apostrophe '
arrow; indent →]
asterisk *
at sign @
braces { }
brackets [ ]
breve (vowel) ˘
bullet •
caret ˆ
cedilla ¸
cent sign ¢
circle ○
circumflex ˆ
colon; ratio :
comma ,
congruent ≡
copyright sign ©
dagger †
degree °
dieresis (above vowel) ¨
dissimilar ≠
division ÷
dollar sign $
double dagger ‡
nearly equal ≈
down; inferior to ↓
ellipsis . . .
1 EM dash —
1 EN dash –
equal sign =
exclamation point !
female ♀
grave accent `
greater than >
hyphen -
identical =
infinity ∞
less than <
line ___
macron (long vowel) ¯
male ♂
minus –
minus or plus ∓
multiplication dot ·
multiplication sign ×

number #
paragraph ¶
parallel ‖
parenthesis (open) (
parenthesis (close))
period .
percent sign %
plus +
plus or minus ∓
proportion; as to ∝
question mark ?
quotation mark (open) ''
quotation mark (close) ''
quotation mark (open, single) '
quotation mark (close, single) '
rectangle ▭
register mark ®
rule _____
second ''
section symbol §
semicolon ;
similar ~
therefore ∴
trademark ™
underline __
up; superior to ↑
virgule, slash /
vinculum (bar above two or more algebraic terms) $\overline{a+b}$

Many printers have characters for other signs, symbols, and designations, including dozens of astrological, foreign, mathematical, meteorological, and scientific words and notations.

punk [journalism] slang for news stories not of immediate interest or of marginal news value, usually marked CGO (can go over to a later edition or issue)

pup **1** a small item, such as a small light The pups used in films generally are 500 watts, so smallness is relative to the specific situation. **2** a section of a Sunday newspaper printed earlier in the week, generally delivered to wholesalers on Friday The term originates from the bulldog, the first night edition of a morning newspaper.

purchase cycle the frequency with which a product or service is purchased by a consumer, such as once a year or once a month

purchase household in periodicals, the primary readers within a household subscribing to a publication

pure program rating the estimated TV or radio audience size during a survey period, excluding the period during which any regularly scheduled programs are preempted

purple prose an ornate or elaborate literary style A *purple passage* is vivid, akin to the color purple. However, along with a *purple patch*,

it often is derogatory, suggesting overblown description.

purposive sampling a survey technique in which respondents, or participants, are selected by the researcher based on his or her knowledge of the population (large group) being studied and the purpose of the study

push [photography] the use of special developers and other techniques to force a film beyond its regular ASA emulsion rating

push-button telephone a telephone with keys, or buttons, instead of a rotary dial The use of such a telephone is called *push-button dialing*.

push in to move a TV or film camera toward the subject

pushing the process of compensating for a dimly lit action scene by overdeveloping the film

push money (PM) an incentive provided to salespeople for selling certain products, especially during special promotional periods; also called *push merchandise* or *spiff* The products may be new or laggards. PM is a common practice in shoe retailing.

push-off [film] an optical effect in which an image displaces, or pushes off, a previous one; also called *pushover* The shift is quick, as compared to a gradual WIPE, though it's sometimes called a *push-over wipe*.

pushover [film] a push-off, an optical effect in which an image appears to push the preceding image off the screen

pushpin a pin with a very large head, in a long cylindrical shape, instead of the flat head of a thumb tack The long head is easy to grasp, and pushpins are often used on maps and displays. The item is so common in the graphic arts that a prominent design studio in New York, founded by Milton Glaser and Seymour Chwast, is named *The Pushpin Group*.

push strategy a marketing strategy that provides for intensive activities by the sales force designed to move, or push, the product through the distribution channels, such as pricing policies or retailer allowances; see also PULL STRATEGY

put [typography] an instruction to change or do something, such as *put down* (change to lower case) or *put up* (change to upper case or capital letters)

put to bed to complete or to retire and take out of use, a term used by printers, as when the last press run at a newspaper is completed

PV PREVIEW; PREVIEW MONITOR

PVT PAGE VIEW TERMINAL

PW PUBLISHERS WEEKLY

p-w-p PRODUCT-WITH-PURCHASE

PWP personal word processor; see SCREEN-BASED ELECTRONIC TYPEWRITER

pylon a support for an outdoor advertising display or a tall outdoor sign

pyramid a common form of news writing in which the major elements (the five W's: *who, what, when, where,* and *why*) appear at the top or beginning of the story

pyramid makeup a layout, generally of a newspaper, in which larger advertisements are positioned at the bottom of the page so that the more important editorial matter is at the top A *double pyramid* is a layout with editorial matter in the middle of the page flanked by advertising on each side. *Pyramided advertisements* are a group of ads, with the largest on the bottom.

pyrotechnic specialist [film, television] an expert in smoke bombs, fireworks, explosive and fire effects, and other pyrotechnics Note that *pyrotechnic,* as an adjective, has no *s* and, as a noun, *pyrotechnics* takes a singular verb. *Pyrotechnics* also refers to a dazzling display, such as of eloquence, virtuosity, or wit.

pyroxylin or **pyroxyline** a nitrocellulose plastic material, used in paint or for coating or impregnating book cloth or paper (*pyroxylin-coated paper*) to make it water-repellant

PZM PRESSURE-ZONE MICROPHONE

Q

q quart; quarter; QUARTERLY; QUARTO; QUERY; question; QUIRE

Q a lighting cue, derived from QUARTZ lamp

QA or q.a. QUERY AUTHOR

Q and A QUESTION AND ANSWER

q.c. **1** QUAD column, a printer's instruction to insert space in the middle of a line, as between two columns **2** quality control

Q.E.D. *quod erat demonstrandum*, Latin for "which was to be demonstrated," a term used in mathematical equations

Q group [market research] people who tend to read the same articles in a publication

Q.I. QUALITY INDEX

q.l. insertion of QUAD space at the left margin

QI First Quarto, the earliest publication of the plays of William Shakespeare (1564–1616), issued in quarto size (at that time, about 9" × 7") Subsequent revised printings are called Q2 (*Second Quarto*), Q3, and so on.

qn. question; plural, *qq.*

qq. questions

qr. quarter; QUARTERLY; QUIRE

q.r. insertion of QUAD space at the right margin

Q-rating a qualitative evaluation of radio and TV programs, a technique developed by Marketing Evaluations, Inc., of Port Washington, NY Consumers are questioned by mail to determine how many are aware of a specific product, performer, or radio or TV program; that percentage is called the *familiarity rating*. The Q-rating is the number who regard the item as a favorite. The combination of scores is called the *TV-Q*. On a scale of 0 to 100, a Q-score of 22 is average and above 30 is good.

Qs cues

Q-system an inventory control plan in which a retailer reorders the same quantity of merchandise at varying intervals In the *P-system*, or *periodic reordering system*, in contrast, the reorder period always is the same and the quantity of merchandise varies.

qt. or qty. quantity

Q-TV [television] a trademarked cueing system of Q-TV Inc., New York, in which an electronic roll is reflected on a glass plate in front of the camera, beveled (angled) so that it can be read by a performer but not seen on camera

qu? proofreader's query for "is this correct?"

quad **1** a measure of indentation, equal to one EM (an *em quad* or *mut*) or to a half-em (an EN *quad* or *nut*) Actually, in LETTERPRESS printing, a quad, or *quadrat*, is a hollowcast metal blank, lower than the raised typeface, and used for spacing at the beginning or anywhere in a line. It is half the square of the type size, and one or more quads can be used for spacing or indentation. *Quadding* is the positioning of the type lines, to center the line or fill it out so that it is flush left (*quad left*) or right (*quad right*). In copyediting, a quad mark is a small square, □. Multiple quad spaces are indicated by the appropriate number of squares or by one square with a number written within, such as □□ or ②. A quad mark to the left of a typed line indicates an indentation of one EM from the left margin; to the right of a typed line, it indicates an indentation of one em from the right margin. A quad mark with a vertical line suspended from one of its sides indicates indentation of the number of lines alongside the vertical line. **2** 2-inch highband videotape; no longer used It was referred to as *quad* because four heads were required for running the tape. **3** QUADRAPHONIC

quad box a unit with four electrical outlets, commonly used in show business and exhibits

quadlite a LUMINAIRE unit with four floodlights, usually 500 watts each

quadraphonic (quad) sound recorded and reproduced through four separate sources, to achieve a natural sound-surround effect Monoaural has one channel, and stereophonic has two channels.

quadrille paper a bond paper with a grid of light blue lines, commonly used in paste-ups because the lines are not picked up by the camera when the work is photographed for printing It differs from graph paper, on which the lines generally vary in thickness. A *quadrille* is a small square with intersecting lines that form four squares within it.

quadruplex fourfold, as in a standardized videotape recording system with four magnetic recording heads mounted around a head wheel *Quad recorders* no longer are commonly used at TV stations, which now use helical-scan or slant-track videotape recorders. In telegraphy, a quadruplex was a former system in which two messages were sent simultaneously in each direction.

quadruplexing in computerized typesetting, the assignment of four type styles with the same width to a single disk or other image master

quad split a TV switching effect to produce four different images on the screen at the same time

qualified circulation referring to readership eligible to receive a controlled-circulation periodical—that is, a publication that is sent only to individuals who meet certain requirements; also called *qualified distribution*

qualified customer one who meets the creditworthiness or other attributes of a potential buyer Thus a qualified customer is a strong prospect.

qualitative ratings an assessment of an audience's impact, influence, and psychological and sociological characteristics, as compared to quantitative, or numerical, measures (statistics) Qualitative evaluation services include Nielsen Product Audience Reports (NPAR), W. R. Simmons Market Research Bureau (SMRB), Quantiplex (a TV service of John Blair), Qualidata (for radio), Mediamark Research Inc. (MRI), Scarborough (for radio and TV), and Marketing Evaluations (Q-RATINGS).

qualitative research a study based on differences of kind or condition It is subjective research, based on such techniques as focus-group interviews.

Quality Index (Q.I.) a measure of the per capita purchasing power of a geographical area, based on a scale of 100 for the entire country, as published annually by *Sales & Marketing Management*, a periodical in New York

quality paperbacks paperbound books that appeal to an educated, sophisticated readership They are larger and more expensive than mass-market paperbacks. Quality paperbacks also are called *trade paperbacks*, as a traditional bookstore (the *Trade*) is more likely to carry them and to stock them on conventional bookshelves instead of paperback racks.

Quantel Paintbox a computer device made by Quantel Inc. of New York, in which an artist draws with a stylus onto a bit pad (a plastic board with electronic sensors), enabling the graphics to be transmitted onto a TV screen

quantile [market research] one-fourth of a group, such as an audience that has been divided into four equal groups according to their amount of TV viewing or other common characteristics

quantitative research a study based on statistical differences of amount or degree It is objective research, using such methods as sampling and polling.

quantity prints multiple still or film prints, generally machine-made (rather than individually printed by hand) from a *copy negative* and commonly used for publicity mailings

quarterbacking controlling the circulation of a magazine or other periodical by paying for and/or supplying display racks in supermarkets and other retail outlets

quarter binding a quality bookbinding technique in which one material, such as leather, is used for the spine and another, such as cloth, is used for the covers

quarter-hour maintenance [radio] a programming format in which a top record or other item of high interest is played on the quarter-hour

quarter-hour persons individuals who have listened to a radio station for at least five minutes during a 15-minute period

quarterly (q or **qr)** a periodical published four times a year

quarter showing the placement of advertising—called *car cards*—in one-fourth of the available subway cars, buses, or trains; also called *quarter run* or *quarter service*

quarter spacing [printing] the use of one-fourth of the regular spacing between lines The special spacing is used to position subscripts (as in chemical formulas—H_2O), superscripts (as in mathematical exponents—3^{10}), or other symbols.

quarter tone in LETTERPRESS printing, particularly for newspaper advertisements, a print sometimes made from a halftone (photographic) negative The process entails making a print from the halftone negative, enlarging the print to the desired size, retouching the print, and then making an engraving, called a *quartertone engraving.*

quarto (q) a page size obtained by folding a whole sheet into four leaves, with eight pages The term also refers to a book of this type, generally about $9\frac{1}{2}'' \times 12''$. Pages of this size are called *quarto pages.* Quarto books range in size from Foolscap Quarto ($8\frac{1}{2}'' \times 6\frac{3}{4}''$) to Royal Quarto ($12\frac{1}{2}'' \times 10''$) and include such intermediate sizes as Crown, Large Post, Demy, and Medium. British book sizes include Foolscap Quarto, Crown Quarto ($10'' \times 7\frac{1}{2}''$), Large Post

Quarto (10½" × 8¼"), Medium Quarto (11½" × 9"), and Royal Quarto (12½" × 10").

quartz a common hard crystalline mineral consisting of silicon and oxygen (silicon dioxide) A *quartz crystal*, used in electronics, is a carefully cut slice of quartz that vibrates at a specific rate. A *quartz lamp* is a high-intensity incandescent lamp, containing mercury vapor and enclosed by quartz. It emits ultraviolet radiation when heated by a filament and is used in photography because it retains its COLOR TEMPERATURE and light output for a long time. *Quartz bulbs* commonly used in films and television include a halogen bulb, metal-halide bulb, metal-halogen bulb, quartz-iodine bulb, and tungsten-halogen bulb.

quatrain a stanza or poem of four lines, the most common stanza form in English verse

QUBE a two-way interactive cable-TV service, introduced in Columbus, OH in 1977 but no longer in operation Subscribers could respond or participate in broadcasts or perform other computerized functions.

que a newspaper term for a computerized file; short for *queue* (as in a line, or file, of individuals) In newspaper jargon, the *que* is the code that provides direct access to the computer terminal or the individual editor or reporter. The plural is *ques*.

queen's English standard or correct usage of the English language, from the idea that the use was sanctioned by the British monarch; also called *king's English* The term generally is preceded by *the*.

queen-size poster an advertising display on the side of a vehicle, such as a public bus Measuring about 96" × 30", it is smaller than the maximum, or king, size (about 144" × 30").

query (q or qy) 1 [journalism] a request by a public relations practitioner, freelancer, or other source to a media person, to determine interest—for instance, to find out whether a magazine is interested in publishing a proposed article 2 a request for information 3 a word written by a proofreader to call the author's attention to possible error In place of the word *query* itself, the proofreader may print a QUESTION MARK.

query author (QA or q.a.) a marginal notation on a manuscript made by an editor or a typesetter, indicating that there is a specific question for the author

ques. question

question and answer (Q and A) a format sometimes used in advertising, articles, brochures, and other written material in which commonly asked questions about the topic are printed, fol-

lowed by answers The format provides easier access to facts than an extended passage would.

question-and-answer machine a computerized telephone device that "talks" to callers by asking recorded questions, waiting for responses, and then recording the answers

question mark the symbol *?* used after a sentence in the form of a question The mark placed before or after a word means that it is being questioned. A question of spelling is sometimes indicated by *?SP.*; a question of fact, *?F.*; a question of grammar, *?G.*; and illegal or questionable copy, *?C.*

questionnaire a list of questions to gather information, such as a *mail questionnaire* (a survey sent by mail) or a *telephone questionnaire* The answers are tabulated and used, for instance, in market research.

queue 1 [computers] a sequence of stored documents, data, or programs awaiting processing The items will be processed sequentially by a printer or other device, in what is called *job queuing*, though most systems provide for special placement into and out of queue. 2 [journalism] an indication on a video terminal that shows the status of an output file: what is moving on a newswire and what is stacked up to go A newspaper also may have a queue, or a dedicated space, set aside in its computer for reporters to write their stories. Since the work is done prior to editing, such a queue is called a *scratchpad*.

quick change [theater] a rapid change of costume, makeup, or scenery A *quick-change artist* is a performer who specializes in such changes, sometimes done in a *quick-change room* near the stage.

quick cutting a rapid sequence of short scenes in a film

quickie something done or made hurriedly or in less time than usual or desirable, such as a quickie movie

quick printer a store or firm that provides photocopies, offset printing, and other printing while you wait

quick reference index a listing of major categories in a reference book An abbreviated index, it may appear in the front of the book (with the complete index at the end) or it may precede the complete index. A quick reference index commonly appears in the front of classified telephone directories.

quick study a performer who can quickly memorize a script; a person who can rapidly size up a situation, understand the circumstances, and be able to react

quidnunc an inquisitive, gossipy person; a busybody; from the Latin, meaning "what now?"

quid pro quo Latin for "something for something," or "one thing in return for another" A quid pro quo occurs when a public relations practitioner provides, for instance, a magazine article or a service to a publication or a TV station, in return for the publicity or "free" space or time.

Quidproquo a literary device involving a misunderstanding by two or more characters, so that one situation leads to another The term is derived from QUID PRO QUO.

The Quill the monthly magazine of the Society of Professional Journalists/Sigma Delta Chi, Chicago

Quill and Scroll Society an organization of high school editors and journalism students The society is headquartered at the University of Iowa School of Journalism, Iowa City, and publishes *Quill and Scroll*, a quarterly magazine.

quintile [market research] one part, or segment, of an audience that has been divided into five equal groups according to their amount of TV viewing or other common characteristics

quire (q or qr) a set of 24 sheets of paper of the same size and stock; one-twentieth of a ream; four double sheets (17" × 22") of paper Quire is a commonly used word in the paper trade. Fine-quality, less coarse paper is 25 sheets to a quire. In publishing, a quire is a SIGNATURE.

quiz show a radio or TV program in which panelists or contestants are asked questions, generally for prizes Among the pioneers were the *Quiz Kids* and *Information Please* (hosted by Clifton Fadiman).

quoin a wedge-shaped block of wood or metal, used to lock type in a LETTERPRESS form or chase A *quoin key* is a T-shaped device inserted between quoins and turned to tighten them.

quonking extraneous sounds picked up by a microphone

quota a sales assignment or goal

quota sampling a market research technique in which interviewers are provided with overall characteristics of potential respondents, such as age, sex, marital status, and geographical location, and also with a set number of interviewees or respondents In the quota-sampling survey technique, the respondents are selected based on characteristics directly related to the study.

quotation the repetition or restatement of the exact words of another The passage generally is set off with *quotation marks* at the beginning (*open quote*) and at the end (*close quote*). A person whose remarks or writings are worthy of being repeated is considered to be *quotable*. A *quote story* is an article or interview with a considerable amount of quoted material. A *partial quote* is a few words, generally less than a sentence. A *double quotation* mark (" ") is not available on some computer terminals, so *single quotation marks* or italics are often used.

quotation mark a symbol used in pairs to enclose a quoted term or statement, an *open quotation mark* placed at the beginning and a *close* or *closing quotation mark* at the end; also called *quote mark* A *double quotation mark* encloses a direct quotation and a *single quotation mark* encloses a quotation within another. The period and comma are placed within quotation marks; the colon and semicolon are placed outside. Question marks and exclamation points are inside quotation marks when they are part of the material quoted and outside when they are not.

quote **1** to repeat the words of another, generally with acknowledgment of the source **2** to state a price or requested price, as in securities services

q.v. or q.q.v. *quod vide*, Latin for "which see," used in some dictionaries and scholarly papers to indicate a cross-reference

R

R *repeat; remote source; registered trademark,* generally printed within a circle: ®; RIGHT

RAB RADIO ADVERTISING BUREAU

rabbit ears a two-pronged antenna attached to a TV set

rabbit-skin glue a water-soluble powder commonly used by artists as a binder to size—stiffen—a surface

race [typography] a primary division of a typeface, such as ROMAN or MONOTONAL This delineation rarely is used; all races are grouped together under the name of the typeface. For example, MODERN is a division of Roman and GOTHIC is a division of Monotonal, but generally they are called simply Modern or Gothic typefaces.

raceway a line or enclosure or channel for cables, wires, and other lines; also called WIREWAY

rack **1** a cabinet or its vertical support or frame; in photography, a frame used for film drying; in printing, an upright framework for holding type cases In television, the *lens turret* sometimes is called a rack. In retailing, a system of shallow shelves, hanger hooks, or hoppers for storage and display of small items, such as tobacco and magazines, often is set up, or *racked,* near the checkout counter in a store and perhaps maintained by a *rack jobber* or *rack merchandiser.* A standing *waterfall rack* holds garments; bars protruding from the main section allow shoppers to hang garments for inspection. Newspapers sometimes are sold from unattended open racks or boxes (a *rack sale*), generally coin-operated and occasionally with payment on the honor system (*honor racks*). Train timetables, recipe booklets, and other small printed pieces—*rack folders*—may be distributed in racks. About half of all records and tapes are racked, or sold in *record racks,* by rack jobbers to such *racked accounts* as K-Mart, J.C. Penney, and Sears. At hotels and other businesses, the *rack price* is the regular rate for a room or the LIST PRICE. **2** to set up on a rack or to set up generally, such as to place a film reel on a projector, or to *rack it up* To *rack a film* is to thread it on the reel. To *rack a tape* is to put it on the tape player. To *rack* or *rack over* a camera is to flip or move from one lens to another by rotating the turret. To *rack focus,* also called *pull focus, select focus,* or *shift focus,* is to change focus during a shot.

rack-and-pinion focusing a manual or nonautomatic system of changing the focus of a camera by turning a knob or wheel to move the lens, using a gear (a pinion) with teeth that fit into a bar (a rack)

rackover viewfinder an internal viewfinder system behind the lens of a movie camera Part of the Mitchell 35mm cameras, it is used when the main body of the camera is moved, or *racked,* to the side so that the camera operator can view the scene directly through the lens, right side up the way it will be filmed, with no PARALLAX.

radar *ra*dio *d*etecting *a*nd ranging, a method of reflecting high-frequency radio waves from objects and analyzing their location, speed, or other characteristics RADAR, an acronym for *Radio's All-Dimension Audience Research,* is also the name of the network radio audience measurement service conducted by Statistical Research of Westfield, NJ.

radio a mass communications medium (over 500 million radio sets in the United States!) consisting of audio signals transmitted in various bands of waves by stations (over 16,000 in the U.S.) classified by the type of signal AM (amplitude modulated) stations have a long, direct, more powerful signal that travels an average of several hundred miles, compared to FM (frequency modulated) stations, which transmit signals that do not follow the curvature of the earth and offer noise-free reception, unhampered by atmospheric interference, within about 50 miles.

Volume purchases of commercials—advertisements or sponsored messages—can be purchased in concentrated FLIGHTS, which in radio generally are 6 to 13 weeks during specific time periods or scattered throughout the broadcast schedule. *Spots* in standard durations of 10, 20, 30, and 60 seconds are considerably cheaper than at TV stations—generally less than $100 each. A minimum schedule might be five commercials a day. ARBITRON and other research services estimate the audience of a station so that advertisers can compute the cost per thousand (CPM) listeners to a commercial using the GROSS RATING POINT (GRP), which is based on the average number of listeners in a 15-minute period, or other units for measuring cost efficiency.

Radio Advertising Bureau (RAB) a promotion and research organization, in New York, to promote radio to advertisers on behalf of the radio industry

radio common carrier (RCC) an FCC designation for systems such as radio paging and mobile telephone services

Radio Expenditure Reports Inc. the publisher of *Spot Radio Report (SRR)*, which provides data about radio advertising expenditures by company, brand, and product category; located in Mamaroneck in Westchester County, NY

radio face an unattractive person

Radio Free Europe (RFE) a broadcasting service in Washington, DC, and Munich, Germany, that is beamed to the Soviet Union and other countries in several languages and also operates Radio Liberty (RL)

radio frequency any frequency, or number of cycles per second of a wave, between the audible sound-wave portion and the infrared light portion of the spectrum It is between about 10 kilohertz and a million megahertz. See also RADIO SPECTRUM.

radio microphone a wireless microphone that operates with a miniature transmitter and antenna, commonly used for broadcasts at special events and other REMOTES and on movie sets

Radio 1, 2, 3, 4 the four radio channels of the British Broadcasting Corporation (BBC) Radio 4 formerly was called the HOME SERVICE.

radio spectrum the range of electromagnetic FREQUENCIES used for radio, RADAR, and other communication, including television, from about 10 kilohertz (10,000 cycles per second) to about 300,000 megahertz (300,000 million cycles per second) AM radio operates in the middle of the spectrum—medium frequency—and FM radio and TV operate at higher frequencies.

radiotelephony transmission via radio, sometimes using a speaker and receiver akin to a telephone but not using telephone lines

Radio-Television News Directors Association an organization in Washington, DC, of over 2,000 heads of news departments of stations and networks

radiothon a lengthy broadcast or series of broadcasts to raise money

radio wire news reports, prepared in terse broadcast style, provided on teletype machines by wire services, such as the Associated Press to radio stations

rag a newspaper, a word often (though not always) used disparagingly

Ragan *The Ragan Report*, a weekly newsletter for communicators, published by Lawrence Ragan in Chicago

ragged an unjustified margin in which type is not flush with or extended to the full width of the line, so that a series of lines may have a ragged look This generally occurs only on the right margin—*ragged right*—but copy can also be *ragged left*. *Ragging* is the setting of irregular lines of type.

rag paper a high-quality, durable paper made from cotton or other textile fiber or rags The amount is indicated by a percentage, such as 50-percent *rag bond*. A *rag book* is made with *rag-pulp* paper.

rag trade slang for the apparel business; the garment industry

rail a device in a hot-metal typesetter that allows the setting of an alternate typeface, usually italic or bold, to match the main typeface, without replacing the MAGAZINE By going to the *upper rail*, the alternate typeface is accessed; going to the *lower rail* returns to the original typeface. A code used in some computer typesetting systems automatically accesses the next higher typeface number (upper rail) or the next lower (lower rail). A *rail line* is the setting of part or all of a line in an alternate FONT. A rail also is a horizontal bar or panel, such as the divider between exhibits or the top or bottom crosspiece of a piece of scenery.

railroad to rush or push through quickly, perhaps to prevent careful consideration In printing, *railroad copy* is set in type on an emergency basis with little or no editing or proofreading.

railroad showing an outdoor advertising poster at a railroad station or along the tracks; also called *station poster* or *transportation display poster*

rain lap a technique of pasting BILLBOARD sheets starting with the bottom row and covering the top edge of the bottom sheets with the sheet above, similar to the way shingles are laid on a roof, thus preventing rain from peeling the sheets This procedure of pasting overlapping horizontal sections also is called *rain lap posting*.

rain standard [film] a sprinkler attached to a high support—a stand or standard—to provide the effect of rain in a small area A *rain cluster*, a series of sprinklers suspended over a set, provides rainfall over a larger area.

raised represented in relief, as in a surface design; *embossed* Raised printing generally refers to THERMOGRAPHY, a process that produces a raised image without an ENGRAVING. *Raised bands*, which appear as protruding ridges on the spine of a book, can be real or false—imitative—bands.

raisonneur a character in a play who observes and comments on the other characters as the author's spokesperson or narrator This device was common before the 20th century and still is used in plays, such as Stephen Sondheim's *Into the Woods*. The word is from the French, meaning "reasoner."

rake a slanting or inclination, as of the walls or floor of a stage A *raked stage* slopes upward from the front to the rear. The *rake of a stage* is its angle of inclination. *Raking flats* are scenery set at an angle instead of parallel to the main curtain.

RAM random *a*ccess *m*emory, the most common type of computer memory, the contents of which can be altered Solid-state RAM uses semiconductor circuitry instead of *core* and differs from core memory in that it retains its program by using standby power while power is off. A measure of a computer's capacity, *RAM capacity*, which is the main memory for data storage, is measured in *K* (1,024 BYTES of memory). *D-RAM* is *d*ynamic random *a*ccess *m*emory.

ramping [computer graphics] the procedure of dividing a color into gradations—*ramps*—on a palette, so that different colors can be selected from a PALETTE MENU

R & B rhythm and blues

R and D or **R&D** RESEARCH AND DEVELOPMENT

R&F or **R/F** REACH AND FREQUENCY

rando *Wall Street Journal* jargon for one of its editorials, from its editorial page heading, *Review and Outlook*, though often pronounced *rambo*

random access a prearranged method to directly locate and retrieve data or other material from a computer tape, disk, or other medium, rather than doing a sequential search through other records; see also RAM

random-digit dialing (RDD or **R.D.D.)** [market research] the dialing of telephone numbers with a random set of digits after the exchange digits to obtain interview respondents This gives access to unlisted as well as listed numbers and assures that there is no specific pattern to the numbers called in surveys.

random error a mistake that occurs by chance, a term used in connection with survey data

random sampling [market research] a selection technique in which each unit in the population has an equal chance of being included The samples are called *simple random sample* or *unrestricted sample*, as compared to *quota sample*, in which DEMOGRAPHIC characteristics of respondents are predetermined, such as those based on census data.

range **1** limits or area of variation; the maximum distance that can be traversed by a broadcasting signal; the maximum operating distance of a microphone, camera, or other device A *range finder* is an acoustical, electronic, or optical instrument to determine the maximum or effective distance, such as for focusing the lens of a camera. A *range-finder camera* incorporates such a device, generally attached to the lens focusing rings. Using a range finder as a VIEW-FINDER is not exactly the same as looking directly through the lens; a problem of PARALLAX may occur—that is, a difference between FIELDS as seen by the viewfinder and the lens. Sophisticated range-finder cameras are used for long distances and have parallax corrections. **2** In typesetting, range refers to variations in point sizes and also is a British synonym for FLUSH, or the absence of indentations, as in *range left* or *right range*. **3** A singer's range or the range of a musical instrument is the full extent of pitch from the highest to lowest tones.

rank relative status In *ranking* or comparing entities, one (or first) is the highest or top rank, and two (or second) is lower. In *rank order correlations*, variables are scored by rank instead of quantity.

RAP international telex abbreviation: I will call you again

rap music contemporary pop music consisting of rhythmic chanting with a fast-paced, hard-boiled beat, originating in the fast-talking conversation—rap—of street-smart urban youth

rare uncommon A rare book is highly valued because relatively few copies exist. Degrees of rarity include *unique* and *extremely rare* (an antiquarian book specialist may see such a book once in a lifetime), *rare* (once in a decade), and *scarce* (perhaps once a year).

raster a single image field or single TV frame, the scanned illuminated area of a TV picture tube or *CRT* Actually, it's the set of parallel horizontal *scan lines* that are reproduced many times per second to form an image. *Raster scan* is the generation of a beam of light or electrodes in a predetermined rather than random pattern. *Raster scan*, or *raster scanning*, is a technique in which display elements are generated, displayed, or recorded by means of a line-by-line sweep across the display space. The *raster count* is the number of identifiable points (pixels) or scanning lines on the video screen or within a display area. In computer graphics, *rastering* is the use of little dots or pixels instead of vector lines to create images. *Raster graphics* thus results in light and color shading, akin to the screen in printing. A *raster image processor (RIP)* is a device that prepares data for output on a raster image device, such as a laser typewriter or printer.

ratchet a mechanism with a hinged catch—a PAWL—that engages the sloping teeth of a wheel or bar to produce movement in one direction only In a typewriter, the ratchet is the toothed wheel at the end of the platen that controls vertical spacing by moving the platen and paper.

rate an amount, such as the charge to advertisers for space or time The card or booklet issued by an advertising medium containing its advertising rates and requirements is called the *rate card* or *rate book*. The price paid by the advertiser sometimes is called the *card rate*, as differentiated from the *discounted rate* that may be obtained by negotiation (*rate cutting*), such as by a media buying service. In broadcasting, the *rate class* is the type of rate during a time period, such as *prime-time rate*. *Rate differential* is the difference in rates charged by local media to local and national advertisers. The *rate base* is the audience or circulation figure from which the advertising charge is determined.

In general, a rate is a quantity considered in relation to units of something else, a price, degree of speed, rank, or rating. A *rated aperture* is the maximum diameter of a camera lens diaphragm; it is also called *effective aperture* or *working aperture*. Telephone companies and others avoid the word "price," though that's what their rate is.

rated poster an outdoor advertising poster for which visibility, traffic, and other data is available

rateholder an advertisement placed primarily to fulfill a frequency, quantity, or other contractual requirement or to qualify for or earn a DISCOUNT For example, an advertiser may agree to purchase 5,000 agate lines of advertising over a 12-month period and by the eleventh month have used only 4,900 lines. By inserting a rateholder (in this case, at least 100 lines of advertising), the advertiser meets the terms of the contract and avoids having to pay a higher retroactive rate for all the preceding advertising. The contractual agreement to publish advertising in every issue within a period of time for a considerably reduced rate is common in newspaper classified ads, particularly for movie theaters, restaurants, auto dealers, employment agencies, and realtors.

rate protection a guarantee given to an advertiser by a medium against price increases for a specific period of time

rating 1 a position on a scale; an evaluation; a classification 2 [broadcasting] the popularity of a program The *AA rating* is for *Average Audience*, which the A.C. NIELSEN CO. expresses in four ways: (1) number of households tuned to a program in an average minute; (2) percentage of all TV households; (3) share of audience during an average minute of the program, expressed as a percentage of all TV households using TV at the time; and (4) average audience per quarter hour expressed as a percentage of all possible TV homes. The key figure is the percentage of all TV households. 3 [film] classification with regard to "taste"—sex, violence, and other standards—by an organization to guide the audience In the United States, the rating system before 1968, called the Production Code, was administered by the Code Administration of the Motion Picture Producers and Distributors of America. The system since then, administered by the Motion Picture Association of America, has these ratings: *G* (general audiences); *PG* (parental guidance); *PG-13* (parental guidance for children under 13); *R* (restricted, children under 17 not admitted without an accompanying adult); and *X* (under 17 not admitted).

rating point the size of a radio or TV audience expressed as a percentage of the total potential audience Advertising agencies frequently purchase commercial time by rating points (such as 100 rating points/week/market) and express it as *cost per point*. One rating point is 1 percent of the total potential audience—households or individuals. Rating points against the same base can be added to yield *Gross Rating Points (GRP)*. In 1988, there were about 88,800,000 TV households in 212 markets, categorized by Arbitron as *ADI markets*. One rating point, or one percent, was about 880,000 TV households. In the New York market, the nation's largest, one rating point equals about 70,000 TV households. In 1988, "Good Morning America" (GMA) had a five rating, which meant that it was seen in about 4,440,000 TV households, whereas the "Today Show" had a six rating, or 5,358,000 TV households. In late 1989, a rating point represented 921,000 households.

rating service an organization that conducts research about radio and TV audiences Major companies include ARBITRON, BIRCH, NIELSEN, and PULSE.

ratio the relationship between two things, such as the degree of enlargement or reduction of a photo in relation to the original A 2:1 ratio is a copy two times the size of the original.

ratio scaling [market research] a system of identifying categories and comparing them to one another

rave review high praise

raw copy a manuscript to be typeset

raw sound actual sound; in radio, the natural sound or background sound at the news site

raw stock unexposed or blank material, such as unused film or tape

raw tape a computerized typesetting tape with no hyphenation or justification information

R.C. right center part of a stage; also called *CR* or *center right* RCE is right center entrance.

RCC RADIO COMMON CARRIER

RCF REMOTE CALL FORWARDING

RC paper a photographic paper with a resin-coated base

RCVD international telex abbreviation: received

RDA RETAIL DISPLAY AGREEMENT

RDD RANDOM-DIGIT DIALING

RDX ready, as in *ready to transmit*

reach the range or scope of influence or effect; in broadcasting, the net unduplicated radio or TV audience—the number of different individuals or households—of programs or commercials as measured for a specific time period in quarter-hour units over a period of one to four weeks; also called *accumulated audience, cume, cumulative audience, net unduplicated audience,* or *unduplicated audience* For example, for a weekly TV program watched by 10 million people, it may be determined that 50 percent of the audience watches it twice during a four-week period and 50 percent watches it only once. Thus, its reach is computed by taking 10 million times 2, totaling 20 million, and then adding 10 million times one, so that the cumulative audience is 30 million.

reach and frequency (R&F or R/F) **1** [advertising] the total impressions (REACH) and how often they are published or broadcast (FREQUENCY) **2** [broadcasting] the unduplicated cumulative audience—individuals or homes—of a radio or TV program or commercial (REACH) and the average number of exposures (FREQUENCY) over a period of time, generally one to four weeks Gross rating points (GRP) are the product of *media reach* multiplied by *exposure frequency.*

reaction shot a shot of a person in a film or tape showing a response to action or words in the preceding shot

reactive public relations a process of responding—often defensively—to a situation after the fact

react piece a newspaper article or broadcast report about reaction to an event, generally interviews with experts or the "man in the street"

read to absorb the meaning of something, generally but not necessarily written, as in *lip reading;* to speak aloud from written material, as a performer *reads lines* of dialogue; to interpret, as with dreams or signals, or to interpret in a particular way, as in a *reading* of a musical composition by a conductor; to study; to record and show, as by an *instrument reading;* to obtain information, as by a computer or other device Read is also short for proofread. A *good read* is a book or other work that is enjoyable reading.

readability the capability of being read easily; the ability to accurately measure test results A *readable market* is an area in which accurate data can be obtained. *Readability formulas* are techniques for accessing the ease and degree of reader comprehension. See also LANGUAGE SIMPLIFICATION.

readability study an analysis of a message to determine whether it is written at the educational level of its audience

reader a person at a publishing company or studio who reads and evaluates manuscripts; an anthology; a person who checks printer's proofs; a person who reads a publication or advertisement A *first reader* screens incoming manuscripts at a publishing company. *Reader confidence* is the loyalty of those who regularly read a publication. A *reader impression study* is a survey to assess the significance of print advertisements to those who have read them. *Reader interest* is the level of interest in an article or a print advertiser's product or service, measured singly or in comparison to others in the same issue of the periodical. *Reader response* is actions taken by readers, as indicated by calls, letters, and sales. *Readership* is the total of readers, *primary* and *pass-along,* of a publication—the readers collectively, formerly called *readerage.* A *readership study* is a survey of the demographics of the readers of a publication, also called *reader characteristics* or *reader demo. Readers per copy* is the number of individuals in a household plus pass-along readers who read a single copy of a publication, generally expressed as an average, such as 2.8 readers per copy. *Reader traffic* is the pattern of attention shift from one part of a publication to another. (Some people read page one, then the index or contents page, and then move forward and/or backward to specific pages or sections.) *Reading days* or *issue exposure* is the total readership of a periodical multiplied by the average number of days an average reader is exposed to its contents. *Read most* is a category used by

STARCH, a market research firm, to indicate individuals who read more than half of a specific advertisement in a periodical. A *sound reader* (sometimes called a reader) is a film-editing machine in which the sound can be heard from a loudspeaker or via earphones.

A reader also is a device that senses, interprets, or reads the punched holes in the tape of a *typesetting* machine or other tape-activated automated machine. In broadcasting, a reader is a report without accompanying tape or other material; it is also called a *copy story*, a *live*, a *live-er*, or a *read*.

reader-printer a machine that magnifies a MICROFICHE or other MICROFORM on a viewing screen—a *reader screen*—and produces an enlarged PRINTOUT of the image

Reader's Digest a monthly magazine, one of the largest circulation periodicals in the world, published in Pleasantville, NY; often called The Digest

Readex a research firm in St. Paul, MN, that measures the interest claimed by readers in the editorial matter and advertising of publications The results of the questionnaires mailed to subscribers are described in a *Readex Report*.

read-in a cutline or caption in which the first word or words is in large or DISPLAY type and the following words in regular or body type

reading 1 a recitation, ranging from a preliminary rehearsal—a *read-through*—to a performance involving written material 2 the information indicated by a gauge or instrument, such as a light exposure meter commonly used in photography

reading copy a written or printed text, as of a speech The reading copy may be provided to the press and others and may differ from the speech actually given by the speaker.

reading file correspondence or other materials arranged in chronological order

reading level the average age or school grade at which students are able to comprehend specific written material Some publications or parts of publications are written for a junior high school reading level; others are written for lower or higher reading levels.

reading notice an all-text advertisement in a newspaper typeset to appear as editorial matter If it is paid for, it generally is labeled "advertisement" to prevent deception. In rare cases, it may be free, perhaps as a favor to an advertiser by the publisher. Sometimes called a *reader*, a reading notice may also be a brief text advertisement on page one or at the bottom of other editorial pages, often set in small type. Because of its prominence, however, the charge per line is higher than any other advertising space.

reading time the average number of minutes spent by an individual on a specific issue of a periodical; also, the amount of time necessary for an average reader to read a specific article

reading type body or text type, generally 8, 9, or 10 points

read only memory (ROM) memory programmed into the computer at the time of manufacture and not erasable or reprogrammable

readout 1 a visual presentation of computer data 2 a transitional headline, such as below a short title on the cover of a magazine. In newspapers, a large headline often is used across several columns or an entire page with a *readout headline* used above a column, or perhaps two columns, to identify one or more components of the story.

readout lines lines on light meters and other instruments that connect data, such as from one scale to another

read-through a cutline or caption in which the first word or words is set in boldface and all capital letters

ready a cue, as in movies and broadcasting, to indicate that performers should be prepared, such as *ready on the set, ready camera one*, or simply *ready*

readyprint preprinted material, commonly provided to newspapers in the late 19th and early 20th centuries as supplements, generally with some of the pages blank and available for advertising and editorial material to be printed by the local newspaper It is still used for Sunday color comics.

realia actual—real—objects and not models or representations, such as objects used in classrooms to relate to real life

reality-based TV program a program that combines news and other techniques such as discussion, dramatization, or entertainment

reality programming [broadcasting] programming that is based on current events, such as a documentary

real time 1 [broadcasting, theater] the actual time required for a performance according to the script 2 [computers] the actual time the computer is in use, exclusive of interruptions or delays by the operator Real or actual time is measured from the time a task is initiated, such as feeding data into a computer, until it is completed. A *real-time environment* pertains to the performance of a computer and its operator with no interruptions or delays. A *real-time program* continuously reacts to new *input* data. This *real-time procedure*, in which each entry elicits an immediate response, is called *interactive processing*, whereas *batch processing* accumulates input so that it can be processed at intervals.

real-world test research in a store or under other actual conditions, rather than simulated or hypothetical

ream 500 sheets of paper; also called a *printer's ream* Actually, a printer's ream is 516 sheets, called a *perfect ream. Ream weight* is the weight of one ream, also called *basis weight.* A ream originally was 20 QUIRES, or 480 sheets. Paper today generally is sold in quantities of 1,000 sheets. The origin is the Arabic *rizma,* a bale or packet.

rear-end display an advertisement on the outside rear of a bus or other vehicle; also called *tail-light display*

rear projection (RP or R.P.) the projection of images, generally from behind a screen, backstage or away from the audience or TV viewer, onto a translucent screen, to create a backdrop or background; also called *rear screen projection* or *process screen* A *rear projection slide* (also called a *background plate*) or *rear projection film* is prepared especially for this use.

reason-why arguments to support a claim in an advertisement *Reason-why advertising* states a specific reward or benefit and provides "objective facts" in their support to give consumers a reason why they should buy a product or service. Originally popularized by Claude Hopkins in the early part of the 20th century, this style of advertising was identified with David Ogilvy of OGILVY & MATHER.

reax reaction; a direction for a REACTION SHOT, a common abbreviation in TV news

rebate a legitimate refund or credit, such as to an advertiser from a medium for purchasing time or space beyond a specified minimum, thus resulting in a lower rate that is applied retroactively; a deduction from a bill or return of part of payment

rebind a book that has been *rebound,* often including rehabilitation and rebacking, putting on a new BACKSTRIP

rebroadcast a repeat of a previous broadcast shortly after the original broadcast, such as when delayed due to time zone differences or scheduling conflicts, or a rerun weeks, months, or years after the original broadcast

rebus a pictorial representation of a word or part of a word

rec. RECORD; RECORDING

recall the ability to remember information, such as the content of a broadcast or advertisement *Recall method* is listing one's recollection, such as *day-after-recall*—retention the day after viewing a program or reading an advertisement. A product recall is a manufacturer's request for return of a product, such as a defective item, by purchasers for replacement, repair, or refund.

recall testing a method of judging the effectiveness of advertising or other material by determining what is remembered 24 hours (or another time period) after it was read or viewed or heard In an *unaided recall test,* little or no aid or hints are given. In *aided recall,* the context or other assistance is provided to the respondent.

recan a small piece of unused film stock, such as at the end of a roll—a short end—or cut from a long piece

recap a recapitulation, summary, or concise review

recd. or **rec'd** received

receiver a device, such as part of a telephone; a radio or TV set that takes in—receives—electromagnetic signals and converts them into perceptible forms, such as audio or video It is commonly used to refer to the entire radio or TV set, though this is incorrect because the set also includes the player, speaker, and other parts.

recension a revision of a text based on critical examination of earlier versions and sources

reception a reaction; a welcome; a social function In broadcasting, reception is the manner in which the signal is received and reproduced, as in *good reception* or *bad reception.*

recipient line the line on a memo, usually the top line, indicating to whom the message is intended (*To: (recipient)*), usually with the *from line* below it, indicating the sender

reciprocal trading an agreement by a company to do something for, or to buy something from, a customer in return for its business

recognition awareness; acknowledgment *Advertising agency recognition* is acceptance by advertising media, entitling the agency to credit and discounts. *Recognition method* is a technique for assessing the impact of a product or advertisement, generally using aids or hints to assist the respondent, such as where the advertisement appeared or another context or frame of reference.

record 1 an account, register, or history *Off the record* means not for publication or direct attribution. *On record* is the taking of a specific stance, position, or view. 2 [computers] a line, paragraph, or segment of text treated as a unit A group of records comprise a FILE. 3 a sound disc Audio signals may be *recorded* in a specially equipped facility—a *recording studio.* A *recording* can be a disc or tape. The first recording discs were invented in 1888 by Emile Berliner (1851–1929), a German-born American who played the records on his Phonautograph, a successor to the phonograph invented in 1877 by Thomas Edison.

recorder a device that receives and retains or preserves audio or video signals A *tape recorder* is not a playback machine, though the two generally are combined.

record film a film that is an exact unedited representation—a record or account—such as by an amateur or experimental filmmaker

recordimeter a NIELSEN device that registers the amount of time that a TV set is in use, though not specific stations, in order to compute total audience at specific time periods It is no longer used.

recording something on which sound or visual images have been preserved The *recording area* of a microfilm or tape is the total area capable of being exposed or receiving a signal. The *recording head* is the part of the tape machine or other recorder that makes the recording, such as by magnetizing the tape; it is the opposite of the *erasing head.*

recording engineer a person who supervises the taping or recording of music and other sound at a *recording session* in a *recording studio* (not on the set, where it is handled by a *recording supervisor*)

recording supervisor [film, television] a person in charge of sound recording on a set or on location (but not in a recording studio, where it is handled by a *recording engineer*); also called a *floor mixer* or *recordist*

recordist [film] a technician in charge of sound on the set or on location but not in a recording studio, where it is done by a *recording engineer*; also called a *floor mixer* or *recording supervisor*

record paper smooth-finished stock used for recordkeeping, also called *ledger paper*

recruited interview [market research] the questioning of a person selected from a specific group, as opposed to someone randomly approached on the street or in a shopping mall

rectified corrected, as in *rectified prints*, on which errors have been removed or corrected

recto a right-hand page, generally odd-numbered To *start recto* is to begin on a recto page, as in most books. A *verso* page is a left-hand page.

recycle to use again *Recycled paper* is waste paper that has been reprocessed.

red. reduced; reduction

redaction a process of editing, revision, or arrangement of text for publication; the reissued or edited work itself To *redact* is to edit or put in order. A *redactory service* is an editing service.

red board or **redboard** [book production] a thin, tough paperboard used in flexible binding

Red Book a classified directory of listings generally, but not necessarily, with a red cover, such as telephone (the *Yellow Pages*); advertisers (*Standard Directory of Advertisers*); advertising agencies (*Standard Directory of Advertising Agencies*); and public relations products and services (*Professional's Guide to Public Relations Services*)

red box an illegal device to produce tones simulating that of coins being deposited in a pay phone The name is from the small size of the device, small enough to be placed inside a Marlboro cigarette box with its red logo.

redemption the fulfillment of an offer, such as providing prizes, premiums, or rebates; the turning in of coupons or trading stamps, as at a *redemption center* *Redemption rate* is the percentage turned in relative to the number issued.

red eye [photography] a reddish color in a print due to improper use of an electronic flashbulb

red goods quickly consumed products with a high turnover but low profit margin, such as food; the opposite of YELLOW GOODS, such as appliances

red, green, blue (RGB) the primary colors, from which other colors are derived The RGBs are the basic colors in TV transmissions.

red herring a preliminary prospectus of proposed financing for a company or government, so called because of a warning notice on the cover page, generally in red ink Some of the information may be changed before the final prospectus. A red herring also is a character or device in a fictional work, such as a mystery, designed to mislead or confuse; also called a *false plant.*

red light the warning light over a door of a studio indicating that it is in use; a light on a TV camera indicating that it is in use

red mail REGISTERED MAIL The term originated when registered mail was dispatched in red-striped pouches.

redo something done over; a revision

redox oxidation-reduction, a chemical reaction in which one reactant is oxidized (loses one or more electrons) and the other reactant is reduced (gains one or more electrons) A *redox blemish* on old or defective film is reddish or yellowish.

red patch [printing] a piece of red material placed on a photocopy or an original layout to be photographed as a clear window into which a halftone negative will be placed without the need for STRIPPING Sometimes a *black patch* is used.

redressing replacing decorations, props, and furniture on a set, either in exactly the same positions as in the previous shot or with some changes

red rope envelope a large envelope, ranging from 9" × 12" to 20" × 26", generally buff-colored with a red string stapled to the flap, commonly used in advertising, graphic arts, and other fields

red streak a red line along the margin of page one of some daily newspapers, indicating a specific edition

red tag publications newspapers identified with a red tag by the U.S. Postal Service to expedite mail delivery

reducer a substance that diminishes or changes another substance, such as by decreasing or removing oxygen Reducers are used in photography to decrease the contrast or density of a negative or positive. The reducing process thus can diminish or clear fogged or overly dense areas. Reducers also can remove nonmetallic components, as the reducing agents used in photography to change or convert silver salts to metallic silver. In printing, reducers are solvents or other chemicals to dilute or soften ink.

reducing glass a double-concave lens to reduce the size of artwork; opposite of a magnifying glass

reduction print a film print that is reduced or made narrower than the original, such as a 16mm print made from a 35mm negative The process is *reduction printing*; the smaller print is a *reduction duplicate*.

redundant keyboarding [typography] setting copy a second time, such as first to produce human-readable copy and then to convert it to machine-readable

red under gold a method of treating the edges, generally the top edges, of book leaves, usually of Bibles and deluxe reference books, with red staining that is then GILDED; also called *red under gold edges*

redux restored or returned, as a leader who has returned, from the Latin *reducere*, "to lead back"

red zone the flashing red lights outside a TV or film studio that indicate a production in progress

reefer a few words within an article that refer the reader to another article in the same publication

reel 1 a cylinder, frame, spool, or other device to wind up film, tape, thread, wire, or other flexible materials 2 [film] a spool that holds about 400 feet of 16mm film and 1,000 feet of 35mm film, which provides about 12 minutes of showing time A *one-reeler* is a film, such as a SHORT SUBJECT, about 10 minutes long. Feature-length films use many reels, which must be changed. For continuity, two projectors are used in movie theaters. *Reel to reel* refers to tape recorders or movie projectors with two reels so that the tape or film goes from one reel to the other, whereas a self-contained cassette has two spools in one unit. Generally, 35mm films are supplied to theaters as double reels (two reels of film, about 1,900 feet, on one 2,000-foot reel) and 16mm films in 3-reel (1,200 feet) and 4-reel (1,600 feet) lengths. The projectionist refers to anything on one reel as a reel.

reenactment [radio, television] a dramatic recreation of factual events using actors and/or original participants

refer an item directing a user's attention to another item, a *cross-reference*; a notation, sometimes called a BLURB, on page one or elsewhere in a publication referring the reader to an article; also called a REEFER

reference 1 the direction of attention to a person or thing 2 [journalism] *Second reference* generally means the second time that a name is used or a fact cited in an article. For example, *The New York Times* style for men's names is to use the full name for the first reference and Mr. preceding the last name in the second and subsequent references. 3 [publishing] a note in a publication referring to another passage or source, the passage or source itself, or the mark directing the reader *Reference matter* often appears at the end of a chapter, as in many textbooks, or at the end of a book as part of the end matter. When more than one REFERENCE MARK is used on a page, the first one is indicated with an ASTERISK, followed by a DAGGER, DOUBLE DAGGER, SECTION, PARALLEL, and PARAGRAPH MARK, or else small superscript numerals (superior figures) are used, starting with the number 1. Other common references are *see* and *see also* and, on the receiving end, *refer from*. A *reference book* is an information source, such as a directory, encyclopedia, or this book. 4 [printing] *Reference marks* are REGISTER MARKS or CROSS MARKS placed at the corners of sheets to aid in alignment.

reference group a population group with which an individual identifies; individuals or the type of individuals that a person considers in setting standards for behavior or values

reference mark a letter, number, or symbol directing the reader to a FOOTNOTE or listing elsewhere Symbols in order of use are * (asterisk), † (dagger), ‡ (double dagger), § (section mark), || (parallels), and ¶ (paragraph mark).

referral premium a product or other incentive provided to someone who refers a new customer

reflect to cast back from a surface, as with heat, light, or sound; to give back an image or likeness A *reflector* is something that throws back or reflects, such as a curved DISC attached to a light source to concentrate the light in a specific direction.

reflection throwing or bending back, as with heat, light, or sound An *antireflection coating* on a camera lens reduces reflection of light and thus minimizes flaring and GHOST images. *Reflected light* is reflected on an image and then directed back through a lens. A *reflection copy* is a photographic print or other original copy that is photographed by light reflected from its surface. In *reflection copying*, the negative or reflection copy is then used to produce positive copies. (The use of the DIFFUSION process can produce negative and positive copies in one operation.) Reflection often is abbreviated as *reflex*.

reflection button a small glass or plastic *reflector*, used in combination with others to form letters or designs in unlighted outdoor advertisements or displays

reflective art in PHOTO-OFFSET printing, artwork that is not transparent, such as on paper or board, photographed using light reflected from its surface

reflector a surface that throws back light, sound, or anything else that hits it Among light reflectors used in film and TV, a *hand reflector* is lightweight and portable, a *hard reflector* is highly polished (generally silver or aluminum foil) akin to a mirror, and a *soft reflector* (generally coated with a duller silver or gold) diffuses or softens the reflection.

reflector button a small piece of reflective glass or other material, as on a road sign; also called a *cat's-eye*

reflex short for REFLECTION, as in REFLEX CAMERA

reflex camera a camera in which the image is reflected by a mirror behind the lens to view and FOCUS In a *single-lens reflex camera* (*SLR*), the mirror retracts immediately after the shutter is released. In a *twin-lens reflex camera* (*TLR*), the mirror is fixed and immobile behind the viewing lens. In a single-lens reflex camera, the scene is viewed through the same lens as the one that transmits the light, whereas in a twin-lens reflex camera, a top lens is the viewfinder and the bottom lens takes the picture.

reflex exposure a process of making a copy, called a *reflex copy* or *reflex print*, by placing photosensitive material on an original and exposing the original to a light source

refraction the bending or deflection of a heat, light, or sound wave in passing from one medi-

um to another in which the transmission speed differs The refraction takes place at the boundary between the two media. In photography, the greater the light-bending power of an optical glass, the greater its *refraction index*.

refrain a phrase or verse repeated at intervals throughout a poem or song, such as at the end of each STANZA; in general, a repeated theme

refresh [computers] the process of repeatedly producing an image on the DISPLAY screen so that it remains visible and constant This regeneration is essential with a cathode-ray tube—the screen—because the phosphor in the tube will not hold an image for more than an instant.

refresh rate the speed at which the image on a cathode-ray tube is regenerated It is generally 30 to 60 times per second, which indeed is refreshing.

regelling replacing a GELATIN or other color medium in a theatrical lighting instrument; also called *gel-up*

regen to regenerate; REGENERATION

regeneration [computers] the sequence of events in the development or generation of a display image, as in computerized printing Printers call this process *generating* or *regenning*, akin to the setting of copy when type was handset.

Reggie the annual awards of the Promotion Marketing Association in New York for promotion campaigns

region a section, area, territory, unit, or zone

regional channel an AM radio channel shared by many stations, each operating in its own region There are 11 regional channels in the United States, and more than 2,000 stations, called Class II stations, operate on them.

regional edition an edition of a national periodical distributed to a specific area Advertisers can purchase space limited to an edition at a regional rate. The editorial content sometimes varies among the editions, such as a page or section with local news or articles used as fillers of unsold space on the *regional pages*.

regional feed programs that are broadcast to stations in an area; also called *sectional feed*

register 1 a record or list; a device for recording or metering; a division of the pitch of a voice or musical instrument; alignment To register an emotion or affect is to demonstrate it, as with a facial expression by a performer. 2 [computers] a storage area The *control register* or program counter is a waiting area that holds the identification or instruction word to be used after the current operation. The *program register* or *instruction register* holds the program instruction. 3 [film] An *off-register* effect may be intentional, such as vibrating the camera to simulate a rocking motion.   **4** [printing] the fitting of two or more colors or images on the same paper in exact alignment with each other *Registration* is the process of *registering* or obtaining a register, of being *in register* or *out of register*. A faulty register also is called *off register*. A *close register* or *tight register* requires considerable accuracy in the press printing position.

registered mail   an extra-fee postal service that provides a record that first-class mail has been sent and also that it was received, as well as indemnity in case of loss or damage; sometimes called RED MAIL, a reference to earlier days when registered mail was transported in easy-to-identify red-striped pouches

register marks   crosses, angles (angle marks), or other reference marks or devices applied to original copy prior to photography; used for positioning negatives in REGISTER or to register two or more colors in process printing Register marks, such as a dash or plus mark along the fold line of a newspaper sheet, are used as guides for folding. The common procedure is to print three register marks in the lower margins of a mechanical and the acetate overlays. Another common register mark is a + over a circle (⊕).

register paper   a thin BOND paper used in multiple-copy forms

register pins   pins in the film gate of a camera that hold the film in place during exposure by moving into the film perforations; also called *pilot pins*

registration   [printing] the process of combining images and exactly matching their position—to be *in register*; in color printing, the exact imposition of successive colors as they are printed over each other   *Registration marks* or REGISTER MARKS are reference patterns placed on the original artwork or copy to aid in the alignment.

registrum   a list—register—of the manner and order of collating or BINDING

reglet   [typography] a flat piece or strip of wood to separate lines of type (a process called blocking) in the CHASE, usually 6 to 12 POINTS thick

regular   orderly; symmetrical; customary; periodic; habitual   A *regular package* is the standard, most common size and shape. A *regular panel* is an unlighted BILLBOARD. A *regular audit* is a survey of circulation or other data conducted annually or periodically. In typography, *regular spacing* provides uniform spacing between sentences, with more spacing (such as a QUAD space) between sentences than between words, as compared to *French spacing*, in which the

space between sentences is the same as between words.

reinforced edition   a book with a BINDING that is heavier or stronger than the regular binding, commonly provided to libraries; also called *single binding*

reissue   a second or subsequent publication of a book or other work with minimum changes, such as a new title page and cover and changes in the front and back matter; not a new edition

rejection slip   a printed form or note from a publisher, editor, or other person indicating that a manuscript or other item has not been accepted

relamp   [theater] to replace a light

related-item display   a counter RACK, floor bin, or other unit, generally in a store, holding several products with a seasonal, functional, or other commonality

relational editing   [film, television] the placement of two scenes together or consecutively that are in opposition, contrast, or another special relationship; also called *associational editing*

relations   the connections or dealings between or among persons or groups   The types of relations generally are expressed in terms of the recipient, so that *financial relations* deals and communicates with the shareholders of an organization and the investment community; *industry relations* deals and communicates with companies and groups within an industry; and *minority relations* deals and communicates with individuals and groups within a minority.

relative unit (RU)   a measure of the width of a type character relative to the EM of its POINT size or to the widest character in its FONT   For example, in an 18-unit system, the narrowest character, *i*, generally is 5 units, and the widest character, *w*, is 18 units. The number of relative units is a measure of a system's ability to produce fine adjustments; the broader the range, the more variations are possible. Common relative unit bases are 18 units per em and multiples of 18, such as 36, 54, 72, and 108.

release   a deliverance or authoritative discharge; a legal agreement, such as a *model release*, which is written permission for the use of an individual's name, likeness, or words in advertising or another promotion; distribution of a record, film, or other production—a *wide release* is one that is widely distributed   The film or record itself also is called a release; when it's just issued—*released*—it's called a *new release*. Most commonly, release refers to distribution, as in a *press release, news release,* or *publicity release*, which is a news or feature article distributed free by a public relations or other source to media.   As a command, *release cam-*

era informs the camera operator that the shot has been completed. In film, *release crew* and *release studio* command the personnel to stand down or move on. Musicians sometimes call a contrasting or transitional section of a song a release, though a more common word is *bridge.*

release date 1 the time at which a NEWS RELEASE, article, or other item may be published, broadcast, or used 2 [film] the date that RELEASE PRINTS are sent to distributors; the date of the first showing in a theater In subsequent years, the release date usually lists only the year and not the month. 3 [public relations] either the day or time at which a news release was distributed—released—or the time when it may be used The release date thus is an essential part of a news release and generally appears at the top right side, though sometimes it appears at the end.

release 1.0 [computers] the first version of a software program Subsequent revisions are numbered 1.1, 1.2, etc. A computer industry newsletter is named *Release 1.0.*

release print a print of a film that has been screened and approved for showing

release sticker a form pasted on the back of a photo with information about the photo and reproduction rights It is used by many media people, photo archivists, and government agencies, but generally not by publicists.

reliability [market research] dependability The ability to produce consistent results in repeated trials is called *test-retest reliability.* The ability of one part of a test design to produce results compatible with those from the remainder is called *split-half reliability.*

relief 1 temporary release from a job or post (*relief shift*) 2 the projection of letters or art from a flat background or such an appearance A *relief map* depicts configuration and contours. *Relief printing* has inked surfaces raised from the base, as in letterpress printing. 3 a reduction of tension or the lightening of a burden, such as a *relief song* after a dramatic scene in a musical comedy or *comedy relief* in a drama

religious conflict [marketing] slang for strong or passionate opposition, as to a specific competitor

reload [film, television] to place a new film magazine in the camera or a tape in the recorder or TV camera; as a verb, a common instruction

remainder a book or other product that remains unsold and then is *remaindered*—sold at a reduced price—in a *remainder store,* in a regular store on a *remainder table,* or by a *remainder house,* a company that sells remainders by mail *Partial remaindering* is the selling by a publisher or other manufacturer of part of the

excess stock. Sale or promotional books, generally reprints of previously published hardcover books, are specially printed for distribution in *remainder outlets.*

remake a contemporary version of an old motion picture or other work

remarque a mark, such as a small design or sketch, made on the margin of an engraved plate—a *remarque plate*—or written, often in pencil, on the proof itself, to identify a particular production stage of the plate The proof bearing such a mark is called a *remarque, remarque proof,* or *artist's proof.* If the mark appears on a print, it is called a *remarque print.*

Rembrandt lighting [film] a type of dramatic lighting with highlights and shadows, akin to the paintings of the Dutch painter Rembrandt (1606–1669) The term was used first by Cecil B. de Mille (1881–1959) with regard to a silent film he directed in 1915.

reminder advertising repetitive, generally brief reminders of a familiar product name or slogan, designed to stimulate impulse sales and reinforce an ad campaign

reminder postcard in direct marketing and market research, a postcard sent following a mailing, requesting a response

reminiscence the narration of past experience

remnant space unsold magazine advertising space, usually in regional or geographic editions of national magazines, sold at a reduced price

remote a broadcast from a place other than the station's studio; also called *remote pickup, pickup, field pickup, outside broadcast,* or *remo*

remote call forwarding (RCF) a service of some telephone companies enabling calls to one number to be automatically transferred to a different number The number called can be a local number set up for this purpose, so that the caller's local call is forwarded to an operative number, such as a company's main business number. The business thus can have a local telephone number and pay for each forwarded call.

renaissance a new birth; from the French, *renaître,* "to be born anew" The Renaissance period in the 14th to 16th centuries in Italy and western Europe was characterized by a revival and flowering of learning and the arts based on classical sources and was a transition from the Middle Ages or medieval period to the modern age of enlightenment. A *Renaissance person* is skilled and well versed in the arts and sciences, akin to the intellectual and artistic scholars of the Renaissance.

rendering a drawing, as by an architect, or mockup, such as a COMP

renewal a periodical subscription that has been renewed or continued In broadcasting, a *renewal right*, or FIRST REFUSAL, is an option to continue sponsorship of a program. In outdoor advertising, renewals are extra posters to replace damaged ones.

rep repertory; repetition; report; reporter; reprint; *representative*, or agent, usually a sales agent, as in broadcasting and publishing, in which an independent firm serves as a rep for media to sell their time or space (generally at 10-to-20% commission on the net sales) Book publishing salespeople are called *house reps*, even though they work for only one company and often are salaried. A *commissioned rep* works on commission, representing one or more publishers. In photography and other creative fields, a rep also may function as manager. *Repping* is common in many fields, and thousands of manufacturer's reps call on retailers. To rep is to represent. Rep. is a member of a state or federal House of Representatives. Rep is also an abbreviation for REPEAT, as in a TV listing indicating that a program was broadcast previously.

rep. repetition; REPORT (also REPT.); REPORTER; REPRESENTATIVE; REPRINT

repeat rerun; REBROADCAST; repeated broadcast

repertoire a set of available characters in a FONT, commands in a program, or another group of functions; also, the stock or inventory of plays and other material that a person or troupe is prepared to perform A *repertory group* or *rep company* is a group that performs from its repertoire in its own facility—a *rep theater*—or elsewhere.

repertory a storehouse, repository, or collection, such as a group of plays or other works (a *rep show*) performed by a group (a *repertory company*) from its REPERTOIRE at a *repertory theater*

repetend a sound, word, or words that are repeated, as in a poem It sometimes is called a REFRAIN, but the two are not identical: a refrain appears in a poem or song at regular intervals, whereas a repetend often appears irregularly.

repetitive doing again, repeating A *repetitive key* continues to strike as long as pressure is applied, such as the space bar on a typewriter. A *repetitive typewriter* is an automatic typewriter, such as one with text storage that can be repeated. A *repetitive letter* is a standardized letter with an individual insert, such as the name, address, and salutation, as typed with a repetitive typewriter.

rep finish ribbed paper

replacement demand interest in the purchase of a product or service resulting from obsoles-

cence, depreciation, or elimination of existing items

replate to make or produce a new printing plate, called a makeover, as in a new edition of a newspaper or a revised page during the run of an edition At major daily newspapers, replates are common. Sometimes, a special page-one replate is heralded as an *Extra.*

replay to play again, as in an *instant replay* of a videotaped sports broadcast; a showing of a movie or broadcast subsequent to the original showing; printing text that is recorded and stored, as in word processing

replenish to fill or make complete again, as with an inventory of supplies In photography and printing, a *replenisher* is a solution added to a *working solution* to keep it at its effective composition or strength.

replica a copy or reproduction, particularly of a work of art To *replicate* is to reproduce, copy, repeat, or to fold over or bend back on itself. A *replication* is a fold or folding back, a copy or reproduction, the art or process of reproducing, or a reply, rejoinder, or response.

Reply-O Letter a trademarked mailing package with a pocket for a letter or reply card, made by Reply-O Letter, New York The card is addressed to the recipient and inserted in the pocket with the name and address visible through a WINDOW in the envelope.

report an account, such as a news report or reportage by a REPORTER *Reportorial* is an objective, factual writing style, rather than subjective, interpretive criticism or commentary. *Reportage* is anything that is reported or the overall body of reported material. One day's copy sent by a wire service to a subscriber is called a report.

reporter a person who gathers news and other journalistic material and writes or broadcasts it—the basic job in journalism A *cub reporter* is a novice, while a *veteran reporter* is very experienced. Reporters are categorized by the types of material on which they report, as indicated by their BEATS or the areas to which they are assigned, such as *financial reporter*, *general assignment reporter*, *police reporter*, or *sports reporter*. In broadcasting, a *street reporter* works outside the studio and an *on-air reporter* is shown on camera, either from outside the studio or within it, whereas an *anchor* is in the studio.

repositioning an adjustment of the characteristics, or perceived characteristics, of a product or service to differentiate it from competitors or simply to differentiate it from itself, as with a product that has been in the marketplace for a long period of time and is faced with a sales plateau or decline

representative an example that is typical of others in the same classification; a delegate or agent elected or authorized to act on behalf of others Examples of representatives, or REPS, include full- and part-time sales agents and agents who sell on behalf of artists, authors, photographers, and others.

reprint the reproduction of material after its original publication The copy may be made in small or large quantities and may be purchased from the medium or specially prepared, as by a publicist or advertiser. In daily newspapers, a review or late-breaking news report may appear only in the late editions and be reprinted in the early editions on the following day. In publishing, a reprint is a new publication made intact from an earlier work. A *reprint series* or *publisher's series* is a collection of reprinted books, not necessarily by the same author or on the same subject.

reprinter a publisher of non-original material, such as a paperback book publisher

reprise a repetition, such as all or part of a song performed earlier in a musical comedy or other work

repro a reproduction proof; a final copy ready to be REPRODUCED

reproduce to generate or make a copy, image, close imitation, or counterpart *Reproduction* is the copying process or the copy itself. *Reproduction flow* is the series of processes in reproducing an image. *Reproduction paper* or *repro paper* is coated on one side, the reproduction side, for a good-quality proof or copy. A *reproduction proof* or *repro proof*, also called an *etch proof*, is a final copy ready for OFFSET printing. *Reprography* is the art of reproducing documents, books, or graphic material, especially by electronic means, such as photocopying or offset printing. *Reproducibility* is the ability of a *halftone* or other matter to be reproduced accurately. The *reproducible area* is the area on a sheet that will be reproduced, excluding printer's marks and identifications. The *reproduction master* is the *repro proof* from which copies are made. *Repro typing* is suitable for reproduction.

reproduction See REPRODUCE.

reproduction copy text and/or art, called *copy*, that is ready to be replicated or reproduced; also called CAMERA-READY COPY Each page is called a *basic reproduction page*.

reprographic paper a sheet, generally uncoated, for use on a copying machine

reproportioning the process of changing one dimension of a photo or art so that its height is

increased or decreased while its width remains the same, or vice versa

reprostat a reproduction PHOTOSTAT, a glossy Photostat or a stat from which copies are made

request for proposal (RFP) a specifications document issued by an organization, generally a government agency, seeking bids or applications; not the same as a *request for quotation*, which simply is an inquiry about a price

rerecording the recording of a *soundtrack* or record from one or more sources, called DUBBING or SOUND MIXING The *rerecording supervisor*, or *dubbing mixer*, in the sound department or recording studio supervises the postproduction mixing of soundtracks.

rerelease to distribute—RELEASE—something again, particularly a motion picture, subsequent to the original distribution

rerun a repeat or repetition of a film, TV show, or other performance or process, such as a computer rerun, which is a repeat of a machine run

research scientific investigation or careful study conducted by a research firm or laboratory or a research department of a company, perhaps under the direction of a *research director*, *market research director*, *product research director*, or *consumer research director*

research and development (R and D, R&D) a study, followed by execution of its conclusions or recommendations, often conducted by an R&D department of a company or organization

Research International one of the world's largest survey research companies, headquartered in London, acquired in 1987 by the Ogilvy Group, which in 1989 became part of the WPP Group Units include Decision Center Inc., New York, and Cambridge Reports, Cambridge, MA.

reset to start again; to change the reading or format, such as to set in type again

reshipper [publishing] a wholesaler or distributor who mails stock to retailers, generally small or rural accounts, rather than offering direct delivery by truck

resident [theater] not touring, as with a *resident company* that performs at its own theater—a *resident theater*—headed by a *resident manager* or house manager

resident buyer a purchasing agent who represents other buyers, such as a buyer in New York who represents out-of-town retailers in connection with the fashion and other markets in New York

residual a payment to performers— talent—in broadcast programs or commercials for use beyond the original contract, according to a formula developed by AFTRA, S.A.G., or another union; also called *talent payment, re-use fee,* or *S.A.G. fee* In publishing, *residual rights* are publishing rights that remain with or revert to the author or other copyright holder. Residual also refers to remains, such as *residual dye-back* (blank particles or dark streaks remaining on microfilm after processing) and *residual hypo* or residual thiosulfate (hypo remaining on film or paper, as determined by a residual hypo test).

resist enamel or another coating that remains on a printing plate to protect the printing area

resize an advertisement adapted from a master size for a different, usually smaller, space The process is called *resizing.*

res-line resolution line, a line used to make up the image on a TV screen

resolution a formal expression of opinion, determination of action, explanation, or solution; the action or process of separating or reducing something into parts In photography, *resolution* or *resolving power* is the relative ability of an emulsion or lens to record fine detail, generally expressed as the maximum number of vertical black lines with equal intervening white spaces that can be distinguished per millimeter. The same determination of *resolvable* detail is made by viewing a test pattern on a TV screen. In general, resolution is the degree of detailed reproduction after printing or transmission. In computer graphics, the fineness of detail is expressed in lines or points per millimeter or inch. In VECTOR displays, resolution is measured in lines per inch. In RASTER displays, resolution is expressed as the number of vertical and horizontal PIXELS that can be displayed. Maximum or optimum resolution generally is expressed as *high resolution,* the opposite of *low resolution.* In a play or other literary work, the resolution is the DENOUEMENT, the unknotting of the plot as explained in the events following the climax.

resolve to break up into parts; to transform; to dissolve; to make visible the individual parts of an image In film, a *resolver* is used to resolve sound so that it plays at the same speed as it was recorded and is synchronized with the picture. The process is called *resolving.*

resolving power [photography] the ability of a lens or a film to determine detail, expressed in number of lines per millimeter that are distinctly recorded or visually separable

respi-screen [printing] a type of fine mesh contact screen that produces gradations of tones

respondent an individual who answers a questionnaire or is the subject of an interview

respondent set the body of attitudes of a RESPONDENT; also, the total number of respondents to a promotion

response rate the percentage of returns from a mailing; the percentage of individuals in a sample or group who participate in a survey or promotion

resting theatrical slang for unemployed; also termed at leisure or at liberty

Restoration the period in 17th-century England after the monarchy was restored in 1660 *Restoration comedy,* produced in England in the late 17th and early 18th centuries, featured graceful writing and elegant licentiousness.

restore list a term at *The Wall Street Journal* to indicate pending stories that previously were downgraded in priority and now are returned to active status

restrainer [photography] a chemical to control or slow the action of a DEVELOPER

restricted not to be sold in an area or to be sold under legal restrictions with regard to age, medical prescription, or other conditions The headquarters of a chain or national company may prepare a *restricted list,* also called a *selective list,* indicating the items that are authorized for purchase by branch or store managers.

restrike an impression, such as a print, made—struck—from a plate or other surface after the original edition; the artistic equivalent of going back to press

résumé a summary, particularly of a person's background and job experience; from the French, the past participle of *résumer,* "to summarize" In academe, a résumé (pronounced REZ-oo-may) is called *curriculum vitae* or *CV,* which is Latin for "course of life."

retail audit a checking of inventory in a retailing outlet; a term indicating the examination of elements in the retailing process

retail display agreement (RDA) a procedure, common in the paperback book and magazine field, in which the retailer agrees to display the publications in return for remuneration from the wholesaler or publisher

retail display allowance a payment by a manufacturer to a retailer who provides a premium or special location within the store for the display of the manufacturer's product In paperbacks and periodicals, the retailer signs a RETAIL DISPLAY AGREEMENT.

retailer a marketer or dealer who sells directly to the final consumer The act of selling is called *retailing.*

retailing the invoice listing suggested retail prices on an invoice to a retailer

retail rate an advertising rate for local retailers, lower than the national rate

retail trading zone an area whose residents patronize the retailers of the central urban area, as designated by the AUDIT BUREAU OF CIRCULATIONS

retake a scene that is rephotographed or done over

retarder a device on a sheet-fed printing press to stop and knock down a sheet of paper prior to its being fed into the press

retention the capacity to remember In marketing, the *retentive* stage of a product cycle is that period when the product name and attributes are generally known and recognized, so that sales are maintained with less promotional effort.

reticle a network of fine lines in a camera viewfinder You've seen this grid—now you know what it's called.

reticulation the formation of a network A *reticulum* is a netlike formation. In photography, reticulation is the cracking or other defects of the emulsion surface of a film, generally due to sudden temperature changes during processing.

retouch the altering of a photograph, positive or negative, done by hand by a *retoucher*

retrace [television] the interval between picture FRAMES; more commonly called BLANKING

retraction a withdrawal, particularly of an inaccurate or unjustified statement The recanting, disavowal, or drawback is not the same as a correction, though the two often are issued simultaneously, nor is it technically an apology.

retree a substandard batch of paper

retrieve [computers] recalling, regaining, or recovering stored data, such as bringing a document from the archive DISKETTE to the system DISK; also called *retrieval*

retrofit a change in design or construction; in video and other communications equipment, an add-on accessory

retronym a new name to update an old thing, a word coined by William Safire (b. 1929), American journalist, to describe such terms as *acoustic guitar, day baseball,* and *over-the-air network*

retrospect a review, survey, or contemplation of something from the past, such as a FLASHBACK or CUTBACK in a film, TV show, or performance

retrospective looking backward; an exhibition of the work of an artist or group over a period of time

return a response (which may be measured by *returns per thousand* circulation); a report, such as a tax return

return card a self-addressed postcard

return date a repeat performance; also called *return engagement*

return flat scenery set at an angle to the main FLAT It generally runs offstage and sometimes is used to narrow the stage opening or mask a backstage area.

return headings the top part, generally about two inches, of the cover of an unsold periodical, sent back by a retailer or wholesaler to establish that it was not sold without incurring the shipping costs of sending the full copy A *return credit,* one of the major frustrations of magazine publishers who sell on newsstands, is then issued.

return key a part of a keyboard that, when pressed, ends the line by bringing the left margin of the paper and the typing element into proper alignment to begin a new line

return monitor a TV screen linked to a TV camera, so that an interviewee or broadcaster in one studio, for example, can see the interviewer or anchor in another studio Ordinarily in such situations, the interviewee only can hear the interviewer.

return receipt the card signed by the addressee of an Express Mail, COD, REGISTERED, certified, or insured article and returned to the mailer as evidence of delivery The mailer pays a fee for this service.

returns merchandise sent back, as from customer to retailer or retailer to manufacturer; deposit bottles carried back to a store; results, as in an election The *returns level* or *rate of returns* is the rate at which a book or other item sold on consignment is returned. If 200 of 1,000 books are returned by booksellers to a publisher, the publisher's returns level is 20 percent.

re-use fee a RESIDUAL payment—a fee paid to performers and others for repeat broadcasts of a commercial or a program in accordance with AFTRA, S.A.G., and other union contracts

Reuters a major news agency and wire service, British-owned and headquartered in London with bureaus all over the world, founded in 1849 by Baron Paul Julius von Reuter (1816–99), who was born in Germany Note that his name did not end with an s, nor is there now an apostrophe in the name of the company. The news wire was called Reuters News Agency, abbreviated as RN.

rev. reverse; reversed; review; reviewed; revise; revision; revolution

reveal 1 to disclose; to bring to view 2 [film, television] a shot in which the camera is pulled away or the lens zoomed or focused outward to enlarge the scene In television, a reveal is a succession of computer-generated lines of text that give the impression of one line at a time being added to the screen, a common technique in newscasts such as weather, sports scores, and other lists.

reverb REVERBERATION

reverberation a reechoing or reflection of light or sound   *Artificial reverberation* can be produced in various ways. In audio enhancement, for example, a *reverb unit*, also called a *delay unit*, can produce an echo, a fast repetition of sound, or other audio effects.

reverberator an electronic or mechanical device to produce echo-like sounds (REVERBS); an echo chamber

reversal ending the end of a play or other work in which a major character has changed (for example, a villain has become a hero)

reversal film a film that produces positive transparencies when developed instead of the more common negatives; also called *direct-reversal film*   *Color-slide films* are reversal films. *Reversal processing* is the production of a positive from a positive (a *reversal print*) or a negative from a negative, instead of a positive from a negative or vice versa.

reversal process a photographic process by which a positive image, instead of the conventional negative image, is produced on film   *Reversal materials* are color print papers, called *reversal color print papers*, transparencies, and other materials designed to be processed to a positive.

reverse opposite values in printing in which white areas appear black and black areas appear white; also called *reverse combination*   The type used thus is called *reverse type*, generally referring to white type against a dark background, not necessarily black.

reverse action [film] movement in a direction opposite from the direction in the original filming   Also called *reverse motion*, it can be produced in several ways within the camera or optical printer, including back-and-forth printing (printing forward and then printing film in reverse).

reverse blueline a copy made from a photolithographic negative in which the white image appears on a dark blue or black background; also called a *white-on-black* or *whiteline print*

reverse indentation the opposite of usual paragraphing style, the first line is full width and the other lines are set in; also called *hanging indentation*

reverse instructions [printing] an order, such as *reverse B to W* (change the image from black to white) or *reverse L to R* (flop the image)

reverse kicker a word or phrase set above a headline in larger type than the headline; also called *barker* or *hammer* and sometimes underlined and followed by an exclamation point

reverse P a paragraph mark: ¶

reverse phone book a telephone directory with the listings arranged by address instead of alphabetically by subscriber   Reverse phone directories are also arranged by telephone number in numerical order. These publications are commonly used in direct mail and telemarketing. The largest publisher is Cole Publications in New York, whose reverse phone directories are called *Cole Directories.*

reverse pitch a sales approach (pitch) that is contrary (reverse) to the conventional method, such as negativeness about the product or service

reverse plate a printing plate in which a section is left unprinted, such as for subsequent imprinting by a dealer

reverse-reading [printing] copy that is read backward; also called *negative-reading* or *wrong-reading*, the opposite of *right-reading*

reverse shot (RevS) a *reverse-angle* shot, photographed or filmed from a direction opposite to the previous scene

reverse-6 the movement of the eye as it quickly scans a newspaper page in a pattern resembling a reverse 6 or a 9, swinging around the top and then going down the right side

reverse video a feature on a cathode-ray tube to ease reading by changing white characters on a dark background to dark characters on a white background

reversing film a duplicating film that produces a negative from a positive or a positive from a negative; also called *image-reversing film*

review a survey; a reexamination; an evaluation; an inspection; a critique by a *reviewer* or critic   Reviews are categorized by the medium in which they appear (such as a *newspaper review* or *magazine review*), the subject being reviewed (a *drama review, dance review, music review,* or *TV review*), and the nature of the reviewer (in professional journals, *peer review* consists of an evaluation of a proposed article by other experts or peers of the author). A periodical primarily devoted to articles of criticism is called a review, such as a *literary review*, and often has review in its title, such as the *Paris Review. Review copies,* also called *editorial copies,* of books are sent free to critics and others. Reviews range from RAVE REVIEWS (ecstasy for the author or performer) to *bum reviews.*

revise [publishing] a proof on which corrections have been made; a book or any item that has been corrected, edited, changed, or revised; also called *revision*   A *first revise* is the first proof after corrections have been made.

revised proof [publishing] a second or subsequent proof made after corrections have been made in the preceding proof—not a proof with corrections on it

revision history a page or part of a page in the front of a book or other publication with a list of the dates of previous versions or editions A *page-by-page revision history* is maintained by publishers of textbooks, technical manuals, and other often-revised publications.

revisionist a person who revises or favors a review of an accepted theory, doctrine, or work; not necessarily the same as a *revisor*, who updates or revises an existing work to produce a revised edition

revival a new presentation of an old play, film, or other work

revolutions per minute (rpm, RPM, or R.P.M.) speed of rotation, as a *33 rpm record*

RevS REVERSE SHOT

revue a type of musical show consisting of sketches, songs (often parodies), and other entertainment

rewrite something written again, usually revised In journalism, particularly at newspapers and wire services, the *rewrite desk* is staffed by writers (formerly called *rewrite men*) who receive copy from reporters, often by telephone, and write the actual stories. In *The Front Page*, "Lou Grant," and other fiction about journalism, reporters call in from telephones at a news site and snarl, "Get me rewrite!" or "Gimme rewrite." The rewrite personnel generally wear headphones and are fast typists. They do not receive BYLINES or other recognition, though their writing (not just typing) skills make them indispensable.

RF RADIO FREQUENCY

R factor characteristics of articles in a publication that tend to be read by the same people

RFD rural free delivery: a type of mail service that enables farmers and others to pick up mail at a post office in a small town; now called RURAL DELIVERY SERVICE

RFE Radio Free Europe

R-F-M basis a system of maintaining a mail order or direct response list by analyzing recency of last purchase, frequency of purchase, and money (amount of purchase)

RFP REQUEST-FOR-PROPOSAL

RGB red, green, and blue; see RGB RECORDS

RGB records separate black-and-white copies—POSITIVES—of the red, green, and blue values in a color negative; also called *master positive separations*, since a color NEGATIVE can be produced from them They are similar to *YCM separations*, except that RGBs are made from negatives and YCMs (yellow, cyan, and magenta) are made from INTERPOSITIVES.

RH running head, a headline that is repeated, such as at the top of each page of a book or magazine article

rhetoric the art, science, or skill of using words effectively in speaking or writing; artificially eloquent or elaborate language or literary style A *rhetorical figure* is an arrangement of words for greater effectiveness or emphasis. A *rhetorical question* is asked to achieve a stylistic effect; the writer or speaker, who knows the answer, uses this device to elicit it to make a point or in support of an argument.

rhp right-hand page, RECTO

rhubarb the background sounds of a crowd in a film or broadcast sequence, allegedly derived from the repetition of the word rhubarb by murmuring actors in early radio dramas; a heated discussion or argument

rhyme a piece of verse, as in a poem or song, in which there is a regular recurrence of corresponding sounds, particularly at the ends of lines; such verse or poetry in general; a word that corresponds with another in sound A *rhymer* is a person who composes rhymes. A *rhymester* is a maker of trivial or inferior rhyme. A *rhyme scheme* is the pattern of rhymes, particularly end rhymes, usually indicated by letters. For example, *ababbcc* is a seven-line stanza in which the end of the first line rhymes with the end of the third line; the second, fourth, and fifth lines rhyme, as do the last two lines. Such a stanza is called a *rhyme royal* or *Chaucerian stanza*, as written by Chaucer (1340–1400) and other English poets, including Shakespeare (1564–1616).

rhythm and blues (R&B) a form of American popular music, influenced by the *blues* and with a strong beat Radio stations with an R&B format are now more generally called *urban contemporary* and are often oriented to blacks.

Rialto a theater district, particularly the Broadway area in Manhattan

ribbon 1 a narrow strip, such as the inked band used in a typewriter or the perforated paper roll feeding or guiding printing and other equipment 2 [journalism] a headline smaller than and set below a big BANNER headline or across the top of an inside page of a newspaper or other publication 3 [television] the horizontal CRAWL superimposed at the bottom of the screen, such as for news bulletins or promotional announcements

ribbon copy text produced by a typewriter or other machine in which keys are struck against a paper or fabric ribbon to form an impression

ribbon microphone a microphone with a thin corrugated foil strip—a ribbon—that vibrates between the magnet poles to which it is attached; also called *pressure-gradient micro-phone*

ride to move, operate, or monitor, as in *ride the needle* (monitor the AUDIOMETER) or *ride the pot* (monitor the POTENTIOMETER)

ride-along an advertising enclosure or insert enclosed within a package containing a product; a technique used by mail-order companies and others to promote related products

ride focus [film] a technique of operating the FOCUS control on a camera lens while the camera is moving so that the action is kept in focus; also called *follow focus*

ride gain the continuous monitoring of sound level; also called *ride the gain*

rider roller a cylinder in a printing press that rotates with another cylinder In a WEB printing press, the rider roller, also called a *dancing roll*, rides or rolls along the paper to keep it under a uniform tension.

ride the showing to survey or inspect a group of outdoor advertisements (a showing), to see it as motorists and pedestrians do; also called *ride the boards*

riff a constantly repeated musical phrase, as in jazz music The process is *riffing*, in which a musician *riffs* or *plays a riff*. A new slang use of riffing is to jive or provoke, to pick up the energy level. It probably is an altered version of RE-FRAIN, though its origin may be *riffle*, as in leafing through a book.

rig equipment or special apparatus; to make in haste; to manipulate dishonestly In film, a *flying rig* is a special-effects device used to simulate a performer falling or flying. Stage scaffolding is called *rigs* or *rails*, and stagehands who construct it and handle equipment are called *riggers*, particularly when setting up lights, a process called *rigging*.

rigger a lettering brush that is half the width of a standard lettering brush of the same numbered size, used by artists for lettering and drawing lines The origin is from the sailing ships called *riggers*, with *rigging* or *tackle* to support the sails, which were popular subjects for artists before the 20th century.

right (R) [typography] lines set FLUSH right and RAGGED left

right-angle fold [printing] the second FOLD, made perpendicular—at a right angle—to the first fold, which is the *parallel fold* These folding procedures are routinely handled in a folding machine, which may be attached to a printing press.

right reading text that is *positive-reading* and can be read in the standard manner, the opposite of *negative-reading*, *reverse-reading*, or *wrong-reading* In photography, right reading refers to the way a picture is viewed. For example, negatives and transparencies should be viewed with the emulsion or dull side down and the base or glossy side facing the viewer.

rights a legal claim or title, such as the privilege of buying certain stock or the authorization to use copyrighted material In publishing, the copyright holder owns the material and the right to publish it. *All rights reserved* is a printed notice that any publication or other use requires the consent of the copyright owner. The *subsidiary rights director* at a publishing house controls REPRINT and other subsidiary rights, which refers to all uses other than the book itself, such as *dramatic rights* for dramatization as a play, film, or television show; *foreign rights*; and *syndication rights*. The term *serial rights* often refers to sales to periodicals, which themselves are called serials. Prepublication *serial rights* or *first serial rights* pertain to the serialization of sections of a book prior to its publication; *post-publication serial rights* or *second serial rights* are used after publication in another medium. Simultaneous rights are sold at the same time to two or more noncompeting media. *One-time rights* are for a specific use, the opposite of *all rights*, which means unlimited use. Other rights include U.S. serial rights, North American serial rights, and foreign serial rights, and rights for condensation and abridgment, translation, quotation, merchandising, and other ingenious means of producing income for the author and his or her entourage of agents, lawyers, and rights specialists.

rim an outer edge, often circular, such as the outer edge of a copy desk at a newspaper The copyreaders and REWRITE staff sit around the desk, or its rim, and the supervisor, such as the department editor, sits in the slot, or inside. The copy desk often is not round and is rectangular or horseshoe-shaped. The senior person on the rim is the *rim editor*. In photography, a *rim light* is used to illuminate the edge of a subject, and may be placed behind it to produce a halo effect.

rim shot a rapid roll of drum followed by a cymbal clash, used in vaudeville, burlesque, and nightclubs immediately after a comedian's punch line, to accent and call attention to it

ring a circular object or arrangement; an enclosed area, not necessarily circular; a sound, bell-like or continuous; the amount of a sale as recorded on a cash register (to *ring up* a sale); a telephone call; a circle around a copy correction In copy editing, a ring around an abbreviation indicates that it should be spelled out, which can be confusing because a ring around a full word indicates it should be abbreviated. A more precise procedure is to write *abbr.* (abbreviate) and spell out the abbreviation. A ring often is put around a period to make it more obvious to the typesetter. Linotype machines used for corrections once were called *ring machines*, operated by a *ring man*. In theater, to *ring down* is to drop the main curtain, the opposite of *ring up*. The origin is the ringing of a bell, called a *ring act bell*, to signal the end of an act.

ring binder   a loose-leaf notebook, generally with metal rings fixed on a metal spine that can be opened to put in or remove pages with prepunched holes to fit on the rings

ringdown   a method of signaling a telephone operator in which a ringing current is sent over the line, such as by depressing the cradle switch or using a signaling bell, buzzer, or lamp

ringer   a contestant entered dishonestly; a person who strikingly resembles another—a stand-in

ringing tone   a sound indicating that a telephone number is being called and is not busy

RIP   rest in proportion, a printing instruction that all elements are to be enlarged or reduced in the same proportion

rip and read   the tearing off of copy from a newswire machine at a radio station and reading it almost verbatim on the air, a practice at low-budget stations or to save time, as with a news bulletin

ripple dissolve   an optical effect in which the picture shimmers, ripples, or has wavy blurs as it dissolves from one scene to another, perhaps to set apart an imaginary sequence or FLASHBACK

ripple finish   paper with a wavy appearance

rise   to go up, as with a stage curtain   *At rise* is what the audience sees on stage when the curtain is lifted.

riser   the vertical part of a stair step; a small portable platform to elevate performers, equipment, or props

rising front   an adjustment on a press camera (and others) to permit the lens to be raised a bit without tilting the camera

rising initial   the first letter of a word set in larger type than the subsequent letters and/or in ornamental form   It aligns with the line of type and projects up, as compared to a *drop initial*, which projects down below the line.

Risley   the juggling of an acrobat by an acrobat who is lying on the floor and pedalling his (or her) feet in the air, a trick of Richard Risley Carlisle, a 19th-century U.S. circus performer

river   a ribbon of white space on a page, such as sometimes occurs with the accidental positioning of word spaces immediately below each other from line to line down a page

rl   ragged left, a typesetting command for a left margin that is not *justified* (aligned)

rm.   REAM; room

RN   Reuters News Agency

RO   1 receive only   2 [computers] terminals or other equipment that receive data but do not have a keyboard or other input device

road   a tour, such as a *road show* that travels *on the road*—on tour—to various cities   The origin is from *railroad*, though today it refers to travel on highways, such as by a *road company* (a troupe).

roadblock   [broadcasting] the purchase of advertising at the same time on most or all stations in an area, so that listeners or viewers will hear or see the same commercials, regardless of the station being watched

roan   [book production] a soft, flexible sheeplike leather that resembles morocco (goatskin) but is less expensive

ROB   RUN OF BOOK

robot letter   an automatically typed letter

Roche box   *Wall Street Journal* jargon for a boxed item within an article that refers the reader to one or more related articles; named after Kevin Roche, a *Journal* editor who devised the computer codes to set up the insert

rocker   a radio station featuring ROCK MUSIC

rocket   a critical inquiry from a newspaper editor to a correspondent or reporter

rocket head   a format sometimes used at the beginning of a major newspaper or magazine article, in which the first words are set in large type and serve as the headline   Subsequent lines decrease in size until the standard body size is reached.

rock music   popular music characterized by strong rhythm, evolved from *rock-and-roll* but definitely not designed to rock a baby to sleep and more likely to rock the house with vibrations   *Hard rock*, *punk rock*, and *heavy-metal rock* are harder, stronger, faster, and more pungent in their music and lyrics, often with sexual and violent themes. *Speed-metal rock* is the ultimate (at least, as of 1989).

R.O.G.   receipt-of-goods, an invoice notation that the discount period does not begin until the customer receives the merchandise; also called *R.O.G. dating* or *A.O.G.* (arrival of goods)

Roger   an affirmation, such as "Right!" or "Yes, I understand," commonly used in radio transmission by pilots and others   From the military system that designates a common name beginning with *R* for the word *received*, it was first used by the British Royal Air Force in the 1930s.

roi   return on investment

ROI relevant, original, impact—three criteria for advertising and other copy

role a character or part; characteristic social behavior of an individual A *role model* is an individual who serves as a prototype or model to be emulated. *Role-playing* is a technique in which individuals imagine a part or attitude and portray it.

roll a reel or spool of tape, film, paper, or other material; to move, revolve, or play a film or tape; the vertical movement of a film or TV picture A *rollback* is the reduction of prices or wages to an earlier lower level. A *roll-in* is the insertion—cut-in—of a commercial into a program, sometimes for an extra *roll-in charge*. In film, *roll*, *roll it*, or *roll 'em* is the director's order to begin operating the movie camera. A few seconds later, when the camera reaches operating speed, or is *rolling*, the command, "Action!" is given to the performers. In live TV, the *roll cue* applies simultaneously to the camera operator and performers. To *roll 'em in the aisles* is to delight an audience.

Early manuscripts, rolled on a rod, were called rolls or *scrolls*. A roll is also a REGISTER, a list of names of members, voters, or attendees; a cylindrical mass or shape; a swaying or rocking motion, as to *rock-and-roll* music; a rapid succession of sounds, as in a *drum roll*; and a revolving tool used in bookbinding.

roll-back mixing [film] a technique of RERECORDING sound in which the DUBBING device is stopped and rolled back for the addition of new sound; also called ROCK AND ROLL, though, of course, it can be used for any type of music or sound

roll call the reading aloud of a list of names; the time for the reading or the signal, as on a bugle for a military roll call

roll curtain [theater] a curtain that is rolled around a batten, or pipe; also called a *roll drop* or *roller drop*

rolled edges the edges of a book cover decorated with a finishing tool—a roller—that has a design

roller [printing] a revolving cylinder, usually made of hard rubber, to spread ink over the type before the paper is pressed over it The *cocking roller* is the guide roller that feeds the paper in a web-fed printing press.

roll-film camera a camera that uses rolls of film instead of cartridges

roll focus a direction to begin or end a scene out of FOCUS, simply by adjusting the lens while filming or taping

rolling billboard a panel truck that carries an electronic, painted, or printed BILLBOARD or other display The truck drives around or parks in specific locations, such as near a convention hall.

rolling title [film, television] credits that roll up from the bottom of the screen; also called *crawl title*, *creeping title*, or *running title*

roll off, roll-off, or **rolloff** a gradual loss of signal clarity of a radio or TV station at the edges of its transmission band, what you hear when the radio station is not exactly tuned in Generally, a roll off is a gradual weakening of sound. A *bass roll off* is a gradual reduction in the low frequencies (bass); a *treble roll off* is a reduction in the high frequencies (treble).

rollout a movement of a product into new markets, such as a regional or national rollout following test marketing; a mailing to a full list of names after a test mailing; to flatten into a sheet, as by rolling with a roller, or to spread out or unroll

rollover reinvestment or renewal, as of a bank certificate; the vertical movement, or roll, of a TV or film picture, the FLUTTER or lack of vertical synchronization

roll tickets tickets on a spindle, or *roll*, for films or events for which there are no reserved or assigned seats, though roll tickets often are serially numbered; also called *sequence tickets*

roll-up [printing] a check of the first impressions produced in a press run

roll-up titles [film] credits—*titles*—printed on a strip of background material and rolled on a revolving cylinder so that they appear to crawl up the screen

Rolodex a trademarked index-card unit with removable cards on a revolving cylinder, made by Rolodex Corp. of Secaucus, NJ

ROM READ ONLY MEMORY

Romaji Romanized version (transliteration) of Japanese words

roman à clef a novel in which actual persons, places, or events are disguised; French for "novel with a key"

Romance French, Italian, Spanish, and other languages derived from vulgar, or popular, Latin and also called the *Latin languages* A romance originally was an adventure verse or prose written in a Romance dialect and then evolved into fiction with an emphasis on love and adventure.

romance card a card, slip, or folder with information on the origin or history of the product it accompanies

Roman Index the list of books that Roman Catholics were prohibited from reading, published until 1966

Romanization the transliteration of non-roman characters of a language such as Greek, Hebrew, and Japanese into roman characters, as of the

English language; sometimes spelled with a lowercase *r* to differentiate it from the Roman Catholic Church

Roman numerals numbers represented by any of these letters: *I* (1), *V* (5), *X* (10), *L* (50), *C* (100), *D* (500), or *M* (1,000) Thus, 1990 is MCMXC (XC is 90, or 10 subtracted from 100).

roman type letters, partially derived from Roman designs, characterized by perpendicular or upright lines, not slanted as italic, and with serifs Originally, roman type was categorized into two subdivisions, Old Style and modern; examples are *Caslon* (Old Style) and *Bodoni* (modern). Roman is the primary typeface within a typeface family in that it is not light, bold, italic, condensed, expanded, or any other variation.

Rome Report a semiannual publication listing advertising expenditures in specific media of over 50,000 advertisers; published in New York by MMS/Rome Reports, which also publishes an international edition

rondeau a type of poem with a format of only two rhymes in its 15 lines or sometimes 10 lines A *rondel* is a type of rondeau that is 13 or 14 lines, with the first two lines repeated as the seventh and eighth lines and again at the end; sometimes only the first line is repeated at the end.

rondo a musical composition or movement (particularly the last movement of a *sonata*), with the principal theme stated three or more times in the same key; from the French RONDEAU and sometimes spelled that way, though rondeau also has other meanings

R.1 *stage right*, a direction to a performer to indicate the first entrance DOWNSTAGE as he or she faces the audience; also written *R1E* (right first entrance) *R.2* and *R.3* are the second and third entrances downstage on a large stage where there is more than one entrance point.

room tone the general noise in a room, ambient sound from water in the pipes, air conditioning, or other sources, an important consideration in recording and filming; also called *room noise* or *room sound*

ROP RUN-OF-PAPER

rope house a 19th-century term for a theater in which the ropes used to suspend scenery are adjusted by hand; also called *hemp house* Such a theater, which is now uncommon, is called a HAND-WORKED HOUSE.

r.o.r. run of reel, a broadcast term describing the scheduling of a public-service announcement or other item within one REEL containing several such items

ROS RUN-OF-SCHEDULE; RUN-OF-STATION

roser See ROSR.

ROSR radio on-scene report, which features a reporter's voice from a news scene, generally without background sound

Ross board a heavy paper, a type of BRISTOL board, with a textured surface so that a crayon or pencil drawing with shading effects can be made on it, commonly used for fashion sketches; also called *coquille board*

Ross Reports a monthly booklet with TV casting agent listings, published in Queens, NY

rostrum camera an adjustable camera commonly used in TV and film animation to shoot artwork or other graphics on a table or other horizontal surface

rotary a billboard that is moved to different locations

rotary plan [advertising] periodic movement of an outdoor panel to various locations to achieve balanced coverage of a market

rotary press a printing press with a rotating cylinder to which curved plates are attached, over which a continuous roll of paper then passes; commonly used for printing newspapers

rotation the random scheduling of commercials at unspecified times; in outdoor advertising, the movement of an outdoor advertising structure to various locations in an area; the movement of older retail items to the front of selling areas; the presentation of sales, announcements, advertisements, or programs in a scheduled order; the turning of a picture a specified number of degrees, as in a layout The process of moving an outdoor bulletin, often every two or three months, is called *rotating bulletin*.

rotogravure (roto) a type of printing on a rotary press; an INTAGLIO printing process in which the image is etched below the surface of the metal engraving *Gravure printing* often is used for Sunday newspaper supplements, which may be referred to as *roto sections*. A *roto comp* is an advertising COMPREHENSIVE, including a VELOX and REPRODUCTION PROOF, for rotogravure reproduction. Rotogravure paper is SUPERCALENDERED English-finish paper made for gravure printing.

rotoscope an attachment to a special-effects camera that projects individual frames of live action onto a matte board or an animation stand; made by several companies, including Oxberry, in Carlstadt, NJ It is a prism-and-lamphouse assembly that is set behind the lens of a bipack camera (a camera with a double load of film) to produce a TRAVELING MATTE and is used in film animation.

rotoscoping an animation and special-effects technique, using a *rotoscope*, in which, for example, newsreels or other live-action film are traced onto CELS If the original footage was black-and-white, color then can be added.

rough a preliminary sketch or informal layout; also called *visual*

rough cut an early stage in the film-editing process Selected takes are gathered in the order planned in the script, usually polished by more exact cutting and rearrangement, and finished with the addition of sound.

rough edge a paper not trimmed perfectly smooth The pages of books sometimes are trimmed *rough front and foot* with the front and foot edges somewhat ragged.

rough proof a copy of typesetting at an early stage; sometimes called *reader proof*

roundelay a short, simple song in which one or more phrases or lines are repeated, sometimes accompanied by a dance also called a roundelay

rounding a process of filling out and making round In bookbinding, rounding is the molding of the book spine into a convex shape. This generally is followed by the creation of a shoulder, or slit, in the spine for the covers to fit into, a process called *backing*; the two steps together are called *rounding and backing*, the end result of which is called a *round back.*

round robin a telephone conference call or network of stations with contributions from each during a call or program; a letter or petition sent among members of a group, often with each person adding comments and/or signing (sometimes in a circle to conceal the order of signing); a tournament, as in tennis, in which each contestant is matched against every other contestant

roundup a summary, such as a brief news program or a published list of items; an extended article or a radio or TV program bringing together a variety of sources

roundy round [film] to turn the camera 180 degrees

rout to expose to view, uncover; to dig up, hollow, scoop, or gouge out In *letterpress* printing, routing is to cut away or deepen the nonprinting area of a *cut* or plate so that it will not be inked. The cutting machine is called a *router.* Rout rhymes with out.

route a road; the means of reaching a goal; a fixed course or territory assigned to a sales or delivery person; to circulate or distribute to a list—a *routing memo*—or in accordance with a schedule

routine [computers] a part of a program or a set of instructions that is frequently used Types of routines include a *dump route*, instructions to transfer or dump data; *input routine* or *input section*, the storage area for the receiving of data; *library routine*, a proven, organized collection of programs; *output routine* to organize the outbound or output process; *subroutine*, which

is part of a routine; and *utility routine* or *service routine*, a routine in general use, such as an input or output routine.

rover [television] a portable camera, particularly the Sony Portapack

rowback [journalism] a story that attempts to correct a previous article that had been incorrect without indicating the error or taking responsibility for it

Rowland Company one of the world's largest public relations firms, headquartered in New York and owned by Saatchi & Saatchi

royal box a partly enclosed seating area near the stage—a box—for the king, queen, or members of the royal family

royal paper large-size paper, 19″ × 24″

royalty an agreed-upon portion of income from a work paid to the author, composer, or other creator or inventor, as indicated on a royalty statement In publishing, a royalty is generally issued semiannually.

RP or **R.P.** REAR PROJECTION

rpm, RPM, or **R.P.M.** revolutions per minute, a speed of rotation, as on a *33 rpm* record

RPO mail returned by the Post Office

R-print an inexpensive color print for use in a layout but not for high-quality reproduction

RPT international telex abbreviation: *repeat* or *I repeat*

rpt wire-service jargon for *repeat*; report

rr ragged right, a typesetting command for a right margin that is not justified (aligned)

RS right side

RS-232 Port [computers] the standard plug—an interface—that connects the computer with a MODEM, printer, and other peripheral input/output devices It has 25 pins and is commonly referred to as *RS-232* or *RS-232C.*

RSV the Bible, Revised Standard Version

RSVP international telex abbreviation: please call back

R.S.V.P. abbreviation for the French *répondez s'il vous plaît:* "respond if you please" or "please reply" It is commonly used on invitations, followed by a colon and the date for latest reply and name and phone number or address for the response.

rt. right

RTNDA RADIO-TELEVISION NEWS DIRECTORS ASSOCIATION

RTZ RETAIL TRADING ZONE

RU RELATIVE UNIT

RU or **R.U.** right upstage, the right rear part of a stage area

rub unevenness of a surface A *rubometer* or *rub tester*, also called a *scufftester*, measures the degree of rub or scuff (roughness). In printing, rub refers to ink that comes off. A *rub-proof ink* is dry and not likely to produce a *rub-off*. *Low-rub ink* has high *rub-resistance*.

rubaiyat a collection of four-line stanzas (quatrains), particularly the *Rubaiyat of Omar Khayyam*, the 12th-century Persian poet, which is a long poem translated into English by Edward FitzGerald (1809–83)

rubber-banding [computer graphics] a key procedure in the creation of images in which the ends of a set of straight lines are moved with a stylus while the other ends remain fixed, so that the outline of the shape, called a *rubber band*, stretches or contracts like a rubber band

rubber cement a transparent, smooth-flowing, quick-drying adhesive, generally made of latex, a rubber derivative; commonly used by artists to mount items on paper It is easy to clean off or remove.

rubber-chicken circuit slang for lectures or performances at lunch or dinner meetings at conventions or organizations, at which the main course often is chicken that tastes like rubber

rubber stamp a portable printing device with a raised print surface on a rubber block, used with an inking pad to quickly and economically imprint messages Though old-fashioned, rubber stamps still are widely used, such as on the backs of checks for deposit, on the outside of envelopes to indicate the type of mail, and on invoices to proclaim *PAID*. Many direct-marketing companies use a graphic device resembling the imprint of a rubber stamp, particularly on envelopes. *To rubber-stamp* means to approve routinely, with little attention.

rubbing an impression taken from a raised or indented surface, such as stone *Tombstone rubbings* are made by placing strong thin paper over the surface and rubbing with a lead pencil.

rubdown type letters on transparent plastic sheets that are transferred to layouts or other surfaces by rubbing; also called *rubdown graphics* or, more commonly, *transfer type*

rub-off ink on printed sheets after insufficient drying that transfers to other sheets, smears, or comes off on the fingers when handled; also called *scuffing* In bookbinding, an impression of the lettering or design, particularly on the spine, is a *rub-off*, *rub*, or RUBBING.

rub-on a clear acetate sheet with characters or art that is dry-transferred by BURNISHING or RUBBING

rub out to erase or delete material In computerized typesetting, a *rub-out character* nulls or deletes; it is also called *delete character* or *erase character*.

rub-proof an ink that has reached maximum dryness and does not smudge in normal use

rubric a chapter heading, initial letter, or title, as at the top of a page; the beginning of a magazine article or section of a publication, particularly if it is decorative or printed in red It is derived from the Latin for ruby or red. The verb *rubricate* means to illuminate, mark, print, or write in red. *Rubicated manuscripts* and early printed books had initials or words written or printed in red and sometimes in other colors.

ruby the name of $5\frac{1}{2}$-point type, commonly called *agate*

Rubylith a commonly used, separable two-layer acetate film of red or amber emulsion on a clear base, most often used for color separations by hand; made by Ulano, Brooklyn, NY Because the red or amber photographs as black, the rubylith thus serves as a mask to cover a specific area.

Ruder-Finn one of the world's largest public relations firms, headquartered in New York, founded by William Ruder and David Finn

rug [advertising] a musical theme used as background for a radio or TV commercial, under the audio and/or video, like a rug

rule a thin metal strip for borders, designs, column dividers, and other lines; to mark with straight lines, as with a *ruler*, a straight-edged strip, on *ruled* paper

ruled insert an item or story related to the main story and inserted between ruled lines within the story

ruling the number of lines per inch in a screen, such as a *halftone* screen

ruling pen a device that holds ink, paint, or other liquid, with a nib—point—that can be adjusted to produce lines—RULES—of varying width It is commonly used by artists.

rumble [broadcasting] a low-frequency vibration

rumble pot [film, theater] a container of boiling water into which dry ice is placed to produce a FOG effect

run 1 the total quantity of pieces required in a printing job (*press run*); the total number of presentations of a commercial or show (a *long run* is a hit, a *short run* probably is not); the complete execution of a job, edition, or program (*press run*, *computer run*, or *machine run*) 2 a scheduled or regular ROUTE, including the territory or BEAT of a reporter, particularly outside of major metropolitan areas 3 to publish or print *Run flat* is an instruction to print without changes. 4 to move In theater, to *run scenery* is to slide it across the stage floor instead of carrying it. See also RUN BACK and RUN IN.

run-around a type area set in measures that are adjusted to fit around a picture or another element of the design

runaway production films or other work produced outside the United States by American companies, generally to save money; no longer a common expression

run back (r.b.) to move material as a continuation of the preceding line; also called *run in* and the opposite of RUN DOWN (R.D.), to move material from the end of one line to the beginning of the next

rundown a summary; a schedule of scenes in a production or segments of a program; also called *rundown sheet* or *timing sheet* In typesetting, to *run down* is to move material from the end of one line to the beginning of the next.

rune a character in an early Germanic alphabet, circa A.D. 300; also, a mystical or obscure—*runic*—poem or other work *Runic type* consists of these characters.

run in to typeset as a continuation, without a new paragraph, or to incorporate more than one paragraph into one; also called *run on* A *run-in head* appears on the same line with subsequent text.

run lines in a theatrical or other rehearsal, to read lines of dialogue of a script

runnability [printing] the ability to operate smoothly, continuously, and efficiently on a press; the characteristic of a paper in terms of how well it performs on the press

runner 1 [marketing] an item, generally fashion, that sells better than anticipated and requires repeated reorders 2 [typography] letters or numbers set in the margin of a page, usually for reference

runners [film] scaffolding or overhead tracks from which lighting and other items are hung

running foot a title repeated at the bottom of each page or alternate pages, as in a periodical; also called a *footline*

running gag a funny line or situation used repeatedly in a play or other work

running head (RH) a headline or title repeated at the top of each page or alternate pages of a publication; also called *running title*

running lines the rehearsal of dialogue, as when a performer *runs lines* or *runs over lines*

running shot [film, television] a shot in which the camera moves to follow a moving subject

running story an article that continues over into several editions or several days of a news-

paper or other publication; a serialized broadcast

running tape [typography] continuous input tape with no end-of-line or justification information; also called *uneducated tape* or *idiot tape*

running text continuous text in the body of an article, not the headlines, captions, or BLURBS; also called *straight matter*

running time the time from the start to the end of a program, segment, or commercial, or the minutes it takes to show a movie Different versions of the same film often vary by several minutes.

run of book (ROB) an advertising position anywhere within a publication, rather than a preferred position specified by the advertiser The *ROB position* is charged at the regular rate, which is lower than the preferred-position rate.

run-of-paper (ROP) anywhere within a newspaper or other publication *ROP color* indicates a capacity to print color anywhere, rather than only in a specific section.

run-of-schedule (ROS) an instruction to maintain the same conditions throughout an advertising schedule

run-of-station (ROS) an instruction to broadcast a commercial anytime during a station's schedule, the broadcasting equivalent of RUN-OF-PAPER position

run out an instruction to set the first line of the first paragraph full measure, or not indented

run over a program or performance lasting longer than scheduled or planned; also, to review a script for evaluation or to rehearse a program or other performance, as in to *run over the lines*

runover type that must be continued—run over—from one line or column to another; also called *breakover* The page on which the material is continued is the *runover* or *breakover page*.

run-through a preliminary or partial rehearsal or a complete rapid rehearsal or review

Runyonesque in the style of Damon Runyon (1884–1946), U.S. writer renowned for his colorful characters, mostly in the Broadway area

rup wire-service jargon for ROUNDUP

rural delivery service a postal route operated primarily to deliver and collect mail from roadside boxes owned and maintained by residents of communities without convenient postal facilities; formerly called *rural free delivery*

rush a direction to speed up or expedite

rushes a rough, unedited print of film made the preceding day; also called the DAILIES

rush seat [theater] a seat made available at the BOX OFFICE at a reduced price shortly before a performance The practice no longer is in use in the United States, though similar versions are the TWO-FER and other reduced-price tickets sold at booths in Times Square and elsewhere. See also RUSH TICKETS.

rush ticket a general-admission ticket for a non-reserved seat, placed on sale on the day of the event The term is used in Canada, the United Kingdom, and elsewhere.

russia leather high-quality calfskin and other leather, generally colored red, used in bookbinding It was originally made in Russia.

rustic plain, rough, unsophisticated Rural *Rustic capitals* were informal letters used in early manuscripts or uppercase typefaces that suggest logs or other woodsy or folksy motifs.

S

s second; slides; small; SIGNATURE, or SECTION, of a book If preceded by a number such as *8s, 16s,* or *32s,* this indicates the number of pages in the signature.

S. and S.C. SIZED and SUPERCALENDERED paper, a high-quality paper that is water-repellent and highly polished

S.A. Société Anonyme (anonymous society), the French designation after a corporate name, akin to Inc.; semiannual; studio address

S.A.A.I. SPECIALTY ADVERTISING ASSOCIATION INTERNATIONAL

Saatchi & Saatchi PLC one of the world's largest communications companies Headquartered in London, it owns Backer Spielvogel Bates, Dorland, Campbell-Mithun, William Esty, Cadwell Davis, Siegel & Gale, Rowland, and other companies.

Sabatier effect an image reversal, as when a developed image is exposed and redeveloped The phenomenon was studied by Paul Sabatier (1854–1941), a French chemist.

sack a bag, such as a *postal sack* used to transport nonpreferential second-, third-, and fourth-class mail, air parcel post, and loose-pack mail It is closed with a draw cord and fastener and not locked, as is a *pouch.*

sacred cow a person immune from criticism; individuals or subjects favored by the media The term derives from the veneration of cows by Hindus.

saddle [broadcasting] the time slot or position of a weak program that is scheduled between two popular programs The positioning procedure is called HAMMOCKING, an attempt to increase the audience of the middle program, so that it will become as popular as the programs in the outside, or TENT-POLE, positions.

Saddleman Awards annual awards of the Western Writers of America in Sheridan, WY

saddle sewing in bookbinding, the fastening of folded sheets, such as SIGNATURES, by sewing with thread or wire through their center folds In saddle sewing, or *saddle stitching,* the section is laid on the saddle, or arched part, of the stitching machine.

saddle wire the binding of a publication by wiring it with staples or wire through the middle fold of the sheets; also called *saddle stitch, saddle-wire stitch,* or *saddleback stitch*

S.A.D.I. SELLING-AREAS DISTRIBUTION INDEX

safe-action area [television] the area—about 90 percent—of the TV screen that is not eliminated during transmission; also called *safe area* The outer or peripheral area—about 10 percent—often is not seen on the screen of a TV set.

safelight a low-level light used in a darkroom, with one or more color filters so that light-sensitive film and paper are not exposed

safety 1 [printing] the distance between the edge of a page, as in a magazine, and the printing area It is not to be trimmed off, as it is part of a full or partial BLEED, and is not the same as a GUTTER. 2 [television] the outer area, or *safety area,* of a television film or tape, often eliminated and not seen on the screen of a TV set Broadcasters therefore confine text and action to the centered area—about 90 percent—called the SAFE-ACTION AREA.

safety curtain a fireproof curtain in front of the main curtain of old PROSCENIUM theaters; also called *asbestos curtain*

safety film movie film with a cellulose acetate base that is less likely to ignite than regular film

safety paper STOCK that is difficult to alter or counterfeit, used for printing checks and documents

safety shell a mold or replica, often copper, of an original printing plate made for standby protection in case of damage or loss; also called *protection shell* or *safety mold*

safety shot an extra picture, taken by a photographer or camera operator for "insurance" in case the first one is unusable or lost

SAG SCREEN ACTORS GUILD

saga a long story of adventure and heroic deeds

SAI SALES ACTIVITY INDEX

salad a pileup, such as the wedging or jamming of film or tape in a camera, printer, or projector; also called *jam*

salamander a heater used on a stage

sale date a date on which an item, such as a magazine or other publication, is available to be sold

sales activities involved in selling products or services; gross receipts; the amount of goods or services involved in transactions in which they are exchanged for money or other remuneration; the salespeople who handle the selling process

Sales Activity Index (SAI) a measure of retail sales per capita in an area, as compared to the entire country, as compiled by *Sales & Marketing Management*, a publication in New York A high index number indicates heavy buying by nonresidents of the area, such as by business workers and tourists.

sales agent a manufacturer's representative who handles the entire output of a company that does not have its own SALES FORCE

sales aids items used to help a sales effort, including merchandising materials and point-of-sale advertising

sales analysis a measurement and evaluation of actual sales in relation to goals

Sales and Marketing Executives International (SMEI) an association, based in Cleveland, OH, of over 20,000 members in various areas of sales and marketing

sales area test a market area for a trial effort; a TEST MARKET

sales audit a periodic measurement of dollar and unit movement of a product through retail stores

sales budget a conservative estimate of expected sales volume used for making production decisions

sales call norm the estimated number and length of calls to be made by a sales representative based on an annual call schedule and time-and-duty analysis

sales contest an incentive program for sales representatives and/or customers

sales control the monitoring of sales results

sales department the department at a radio or TV station that solicits and accepts advertising The analogous department at print media is called the *advertising department*. The sales department at print media handles the selling of the publication to readers through subscription sales and circulation personnel.

sales effectiveness test an analysis of advertising or other promotion in relation to actual sales

sales estimation a forecast of projected sales

sales force all individuals involved in selling, including account executives, agents, clerks, consultants, field representatives, manufacturer's representatives, marketing representatives, sales representatives, service representatives, and others who work on salary and/or commission and who range from order-creators to order-takers

sales forecast expected sales based on previous experience, market tests, surveys such as the *purchase probability scale*, and other analytic methods

sales incentive a premium, gift, or other reward in excess of regular remuneration to encourage efforts by salespeople

sales letter a written communication to a prospective customer

sales life the period of viability of quality and customer interest level of an item; SHELF LIFE

sales management the planning and supervision of all sales operations, under the direction of one or more *sales managers*

sales meeting a gathering of salespeople for information, motivation, and training

sales performance the measurement or evaluation of results—who or what failed to meet the planned sales goal

sales portfolio a manual for use by a salesperson for reference and/or display to a potential customer; also called *sales kit*

sales potential the area for additional sales; sometimes called *headroom*

sales promotion tools and techniques to encourage sales, including sales-force promotion, such as bonuses, contests, and meetings; cooperative advertising; dealer contests; free goods; merchandise allowances; PUSH MONEY; and consumer promotion, such as contests, coupons, demonstrations, displays, games, money-refund offers, PREMIUMS, PRICE PACKS, prices-off, and trading stamps It is also called *merchandising* or *promotion*. These and other techniques are planned and executed by a *sales promotion department* or agency and may be supported by or be part of an advertising or public relations campaign.

sales quota an assigned volume or target for a marketing unit

sales response function a forecast of probable sales volume in a specific time period, associated with various possible levels of marketing elements The best-known sales response function is the *demand function*, which correlates price and sales.

sales service visits to retailers or customers by a manufacturer's salesperson to help in equipment maintenance, to provide other aids, and also to develop sales

sales terms the time and types of discounts and other aspects of payment

sales territory a designated geographical area assigned for selling

sales to thirds sales within a company, as from one division to another

sales variance analysis a determination of the relative contribution of different factors to a gap in sales performance

salt 1 to add humor or piquancy, as to salt a speech; to give false value; also called *salting* 2 [direct marketing] the insertion of decoy or *dummy* names (*salt names*) in a mailing list to confirm that the list is used; also called *salting* or *seeding*

salutary product an item that is wholesome or beneficial to the consumer, though sometimes not perceived that way and thus requiring information or other promotion

SAM SPACE AVAILABLE MAIL

same size (S.S.) an instruction to a photographer, platemaker, or stat house to reproduce a photo in art in the same size as the original A *same-size shot* is a photo or art reproduced in the same size as the original.

SAMI a market research company that provides product consumption information Founded in 1961 in New York as Selling Areas Marketing, Inc. and owned for many years by TIME INC., the firm merged with Burke in 1986, and in 1987, SAMI/Burke was acquired by Control Data Corp., which merged it with *Arbitron*. The combined company, Arbitron/SAMI/Burke, was the second-largest market research company in the United States. However, in 1989 Burke became independent, and SAMI is now a division of Arbitron/SAMI, New York.

The company produces monthly *SAMI reports* that show the warehouse movement of dry grocery and household supplies, frozen food, health and beauty aids, and refrigerated items for about 54 major markets, called *SAMI markets*. Reports are provided to retailers, who are paid for their cooperation in obtaining the data, and to manufacturers. Among its various reports are *AMSBT* (*All Market SAMI Brand Trend*) and SARDI (STANDARD RETAIL DISTRIBUTION INDEX). *SAMSCAN* scanner data tracks sales checkout counters with scanning devices in 48 major markets. SAMI Reports represent over 80 percent of national food sales; the SAMI markets therefore are used by manufacturers and their agencies for geographical and population guidance. For example, the markets in the Northeast include Albany-Schenectady-Troy; Baltimore-Washington; Boston-Providence; Buffalo-Rochester; New York; Philadelphia; and Syracuse.

samizdat a system by which manuscripts denied official publication in the Soviet Union are circulated secretly in typed or other form or are smuggled out for publication elsewhere; Russian for "self-published"

SAMMY an annual award for jingles and other music in radio and TV commercials, presented by the Society of Advertising Music Producers, Arrangers and Composers, in New York

sample a small quantity, single portion, reduced size, or other representation of a product or service, distributed free or at a reduced price, to introduce it and encourage its trial and subsequent purchase A *sampler* is a person who tests products for appraisal and quality control or who distributes samples; it is also a package with representative items, such as a candy sampler with different varieties. *Sampling* is the process of taking a sample, as in statistics, or distributing samples, as in a specific geographic area, or sample area. In market research, a sample is a representative set of people, or elements, drawn from a population in order to describe and estimate their characteristics that correspond to those of the entire market, audience, or population within acceptable limits of statistical error (the *sampling error* or *sampling variation*). *Sample adequate* is a sufficiently large and representative segment to provide accurate results.

sample copy a book or other publication provided free

sample design [market research] the basis on which a sample, or small group, is selected to be representative of a large group; the foundation on which rests the projectability of the small selected group It includes *sample size* (the number of participants), *sample frame* (where the segment is obtained, such as telephone households), and *sample selection* (how the individuals are selected).

sample rebate a procedure in which a distributor or retailer purchases SAMPLES of a product from the manufacturer and receives a refund when a specific amount of the product is sold

sample recovery [market research] obtaining a response to a survey from as high a percentage of the designated SAMPLE as possible

sample reel a composite selection of TV or radio commercials or other sequences, used for an audition or demonstration by a model, photographer, or other TALENT or agency; also called *sample tape*

sample tolerance [market research] confidence in the numerical accuracy of the information collected from a SAMPLE It statistically predicts the extent to which the findings could vary if identical surveys employing the same methodology were conducted.

sampling   **1** a statistical procedure for selecting a representative group of people for testing or other market research   **2** [advertising] the random selection of individuals; the free distribution of small sizes of products, such as by mail, door-to-door, or directly to consumers on the street or elsewhere

sampling error   in statistics, the difference between a sample and the entire population—the *universe*

sampling frame   in statistics, a list of all sampling units in the entire population—the *universe*

sampling precision   in statistics, the degree of variance a unit of data shows on repeated testing   The smaller the variance, the greater the reliability of the sample statistic.

S and D   song and dance, as in vaudeville days of an act consisting of two or more performers who sing and dance.

sandbag   a bag, generally canvas, filled with sand, used as a weight to anchor scenery and other theatrical items

sandwich   **1** [advertising] a recorded commercial with a middle portion that can be replaced with live copy; also called a DONUT, though either way it's not edible   **2** an interpolated notice within a text calling the reader's attention to a related article, generally enclosed (as in a sandwich) with decorative RULES above and below   **3** [photography] two or more slides bound together to create a montage   Producing a *sandwich commercial*, *sandwich slide*, or other sandwich is *sandwiching*.

sandwich board   two large wood or cardboard signs hinged at the top by straps for hanging over the shoulders of a person walking on the street, with one board suspended in front and the other in back, resembling a sandwich   It is used for advertising, such as for a nearby restaurant or store, or for picketing, and can be only one board.   A *sandwich man* (or woman) sometimes also distributes handbills.

sans serif   a typeface without (*sans* is French for "without") the fine lines or decorative crosslines—SERIFS—at the ends of the main strokes of a letter; also called *block letter*   Examples include *Futura*, *Kabel*, *Vogue*, and other modern gothics.

SAP or **S.A.P.**   SEPARATE AUDIO PROGRAM; soon as possible, a direction to do something quickly— as soon as possible (*ASAP*)   *Sappest* is a humorous superlative.

sapp   photographs, products, and other materials provided to an artist for guidance in preparing advertising artwork

Saral paper   a *transfer paper*, akin to carbon paper, used by artists; made by S.B. Albertis in New York

SARDI   STANDARD RETAIL DISTRIBUTION INDEX

SASE   self-addressed stamped envelope, a common term in classified advertisements to instruct a respondent to enclose a stamped envelope addressed to him- or herself; also called SSAE

SAT   a communications satellite system (SATCOM I, II, and III, and others)

satchel   a small bag, such as the pouch used by mail carriers   The large satchel used for collections from mailboxes is a *Saratoga bag*.

Satcom   a communications satellite owned by RCA   The first in this series, *Satcom I*, was launched in 1975 as the first television satellite.

satellite   a relay station for audio and video transmission, orbiting in space or terrestrial   A *satellite station* is a radio or TV station used as a relay, broadcasting on the same or a different wavelength as the originating station. Almost all communications satellites are SYNCHRONOUS satellites that hover in the same place in the sky, 22,300 miles above the earth, in *stationary orbit*.

satellite master antenna TV (SMATV)   a TV system in an apartment complex or other private property in which TV sets are wired to a private satellite master antenna that receives TV signals from a satellite instead of a cable

satellite media tour   several interviews, generally on TV but sometimes in other media, during a specific period, such as one hour, in which a celebrity or SPOKESPERSON in one location is interviewed via satellite by journalists elsewhere; also called *satellite tour* or *satellite press tour*

satellite store   a small store close to and competing with a large store, such as a store adjacent to or near a shopping center

Saticon   a sophisticated high-resolution TV camera tube with a target layer of selenium arsenic tellurium instead of lead oxide; made by Hitachi and RCA

satisficing   achieving adequate—satisfactory— gratification   Consumers *satisfice* when they obtain results that meet their requirements, though they are not necessarily fulfilled or totally gratified. Satisficing is not spelled the same as satisfying, though it may be equivalent.

saturation   sufficient coverage and/or frequency, via advertising or other techniques, to achieve maximum impact; an intense color or degree of purity of a color (its freedom from dilution by white or darkening by black); a solution or item at its full strength, such as the peak point in a circuit; the point of maximum magnetization of a tape; the state of being soaked with moisture

Saturday rate a lower advertising rate available at several big-city daily newspapers that have smaller circulations on Saturday

S.A.U. or SAU STANDARD ADVERTISING UNIT

save to stop or preserve a film process or other action; to turn off, as in *save the lights*

save it an instruction that a film is to be developed or a TAKE is to be printed

save out the British term for *reverse out*, to reproduce characters or put a white image on a color or black background

save the food [theater] an instruction to fake an action during a rehearsal, such as not to eat the food

save the lights [theater] an instruction to turn off the lights on a set; also called *save the arcs* or *kill the lights*

saw a familiar saying, generally worn out through repetition; also called *old saw*, which is a redundancy The origin is *sawe*, an English word for speech.

saw-kerf binding in bookbinding, a form of SIDE-STITCHING in which the thread is laid in slits cut into the back in a *dovetail* pattern (A kerf is a channel made by a saw.)

SBET SCREEN-BASED ELECTRONIC TYPEWRITER

SBN Standard Book Number; see INTERNATIONAL STANDARD BOOK NUMBER

SBU STRATEGIC BUSINESS UNIT

SC script notation for SCENE

SC or S.C. single column; small capitals (capital letters about the same size as lowercase letters of the same style); SUPERCALENDERED paper

SCA Storecast Carrier Authorization; SUBCARRIER STATION; subsidiary communications authorizations, granted by the FCC to FM broadcasters for the use of other communications subcarriers on their channels

scale 1 in advertising and show business, the standard union fee or other minimum standard for a model, actor, or other TALENT who is working for scale or *scale rate* 2 a system of notation in which the value of numbers is determined by their place relative to a fixed constant Thus, *scaling* in statistics is the arrangement of data in graduated series. 3 [graphic arts] to indicate the ratio or proportion by which photography or other art is increased or decreased to fit an indicated space In scaling, the enlargement or reduction in size of art or copy, the width (usually the controlling dimension) is stated first; it is also called *sizing* or *dimensioning*. In most fields, a work executed in a large size or grandiose manner is done on a *grand scale*, which generally is a compliment.

The opposite is on a *small scale*. 4 [photography] the range of tones of photographic film or paper; a device—*vernier scale*—to denote distance from a camera lens 5 [broadcasting] the audio SPECTRUM delineation by FREQUENCY ratios

scallop [television] a wavy picture

scamp a rough sketch, as an idea for an advertisement

scamped work [graphic arts] careless work

scan to look over quickly by eye or computer; to move a beam of light or electrons over a surface to reproduce an image, as in printing or television The TV system in the United States is based on a *scanning time* or *rate* of $\frac{1}{60}$ of a second for each *traverse*, or movement, of a beam across the TV screen. *Scanning frequency* is the *scan lines* per second scanned in a TV picture tube; in the United States, it's 525 lines × 30 frames, or 15,750. In *overscanning*, the TV picture is expanded and its edges are lost. In *underscanning*, the TV picture does not occupy the entire screen.

scanline or scan line one line of a TV picture

scanner an electronic or optical device that senses or records information for modification, storage, or transmission In color printing, a scanner electronically produces process-color film negatives or positives by separating a full-color master into the four process colors. A *police scanner* is a radio, usually in a car, that picks up police department transmissions.

scanning area [television] the part that the camera actually sees It is larger than the essential area, or SAFE-ACTION AREA, which is the central part of the picture received and seen on the TV set.

scansion the act of scanning or analyzing verse in terms of its rhythmic components, including the pattern of accented and unaccented syllables and the grouping of lines

s caps small capital letters

scarehead a big, bold, sensational headline that scares or alarms readers because of its content, commonly used on page one of TABLOIDS

scare picture a horror movie or other film designed to frighten the audience; also called *scare movie*

scat jazz singing in which meaningless syllables are improvised, such as by Ella Fitzgerald (b. 1918)

scatological relating to *scatology*, the study of or an obsession with excrement or excretory functions and, more generally, interest in or preoccupation with obscenity, as in literature

scatter the scheduling of commercials throughout a broadcast schedule rather than at specific times, such as rotating throughout the day or night or both; also called *scatter plan* or SCAT-TER BUYING

scatter buying pattern [television] the purchase of advertising time during the season or close to the broadcast date rather than in an early *up-front* contractual agreement *Scatter buys* generally are negotiated in an attempt to obtain bargain discounts.

scatter sales TV commercials sold during the broadcast season at different rates from the *up-front sales* made before the beginning of the fall season

scenario a synopsis or outline of a plot, literary work, show, film, or hypothetical projected series of events A *scenarist* is a screenwriter.

scene a picture, view, setting, or place in which action occurs; a subdivision of an act in a theatrical presentation; a SEQUENCE in a show or film occurring at one time in one place *Behind the scenes* is backstage or private. A *scene stealer* is a performer who draws the attention of the audience, not necessarily when the script calls for it. A *scene chewer* is a performer who overacts. A *scene plan* is a diagram of the stage settings; it is also called *floor plan* or *ground plan*. A *scene sheet* or *scene plot* is a list of sequences or shots.

scène à faire an obligatory scene The French phrase means "scene to be made." It is also called a *plot scene*, a scene generally late in a play that is expected by the audience, so that the playwright is obliged to write it.

scene in one a short scene played in the extreme front area (*one*) of the stage, in front of a curtain, generally while the scenery behind the curtain is being set; also called *carpenter's scene* A *scene in two* is played farther back on the stage.

scenery a landscape; painted or other BACK-DROPS on a stage or set; on location, the natural background In film, FLATS and other scenery are stored in a *scenery dock* or *scene dock*.

scenery chewer a performer who overacts or is overly dramatic; also called *scene chewer*

scenic in general, of the stage, dramatic, theatrical; more specifically, related to SCENERY, such as rendered by a *scenic artist*, who paints scenery In film, the scenic artist is a member of the art department supervised by a *chargeman scenic artist*.

Scenic & Title Artists a Los Angeles local union of *IATSE*, technicians who produce lettering and other graphics used in film

scenographer [theater] a scene designer often involved with all visual aspects of a production, a process called *scenography*

scented product an item with odor impregnated or added, such as stationery and toilet tissue Scented products are also used to demonstrate fragrances in direct mail, to provide a whiff of food as part of an advertisement, and for other product advertising.

schedule **1** a program, plan, or timetable **2** [advertising] a list of media in an advertising campaign **3** [broadcasting] a list of consecutive programs **4** [public relations] a timed plan of projects and procedures An advertising, public relations, or other schedule may be planned according to size of markets or other categories, such as an *A schedule* (largest) or a *B schedule* (smaller).

schema an outline, diagram, plan, or preliminary draft The plural is *schemata*.

schematic a structural or procedural diagram, such as a drawing of the layout of a system

schlieren regions in a translucent medium that have a different density and index of refraction than the rest of the medium A *schlieren lens* is used for video projection.

schlock inferior, shoddy, or vulgar, as in *schlock merchandise*; from the Yiddish, commonly used in the apparel industry and communications fields A *schlockbuster* is a successful *piece of schlock*, such as an exploitational film or video.

schmaltz or **schmalz** anything excessively sentimental or maudlin The original is the German word for lard and the Yiddish word for melted fat, so a broader connotation is advertising and other material that is too commercial, corny, or fat. The adjective is *schmaltzy.*

schoolgirl style an old term, no longer used, for highly emotional, sentimental writing

Schrotblatt a type of dotted print

schtik, shtick, or **schtick** a funny routine or piece of business used by a performer or, more generally, a special trait, talent, or attention-getting device; from the Yiddish for a prank or caprice

Schufftan process [film] a method of creating a composite shot, such as by combining a still photo, a miniature set, or a background with live action This SPECIAL EFFECT, which uses a mirror angled in front of the camera, was developed in 1923 by Eugen Schufftan, a German cinematographer.

schwa the neutral vowel sound of most unstressed syllables, such as the *a* in ago, the *e* in agent, and the *i* in insanity The schwa symbol is ě.

Schwabacher a gothic or BLACK-LETTER typeface used in early German books

science fiction creative writing in which scientific facts or potential scientific discoveries, such as interplanetary travel, are a part of the plot; not the same as *fantasy*, which is more imaginative and less scientific It is informally called *sci-fi*, pronounced sigh-figh.

sciopticon a device that projects slides

scissoring [computer graphics] a process of removing the parts of a display image that are outside the display screen area; also called *clipping*

scissors editing cutting out copy or other matters with a scissors, razor, or other instrument

sci-tech scientific and technical publishing

Scitexing a process of electronically altering a photograph or other image, using an electronic imaging machine made by the Scitex America Corporation, Bedford, MA, or a similar system

scoodling unauthorized duplication of recorded music, a slang word based on the pirate Scoodler in *The Wizard of Oz*

scoop 1 a light with a shovel-shaped reflector, generally a circular floodlamp of 500 watts or more, used in films and TV; sometimes called a *basher* Scoops are the most commonly used floodlights in TV, particularly those with an 18-inch-diameter reflector and a 1,000-watt lamp. 2 an exclusive news story To scoop is to top, beat, or outmaneuver a competitor by acquiring and publishing or broadcasting a major exclusive story, or to get a beat. The origin is the German *schoppe*, "shovel," and *schöpfen*, "to dip out" or "to create."

scope range, area; a viewing instrument, such as microscope or telescope In film, the *scope image* is an expanded screen area, such as produced with an *anamorphic* lens. Scope is also short for *CinemaScope*, as well as the generic word for any anamorphic format, lens, or process.

score 1 a tally; the results; a hit or success; to obtain successful results 2 the written form of a musical composition; music for a show 3 [printing] to impress a line on paper to facilitate folding *Dry scoring* is denting paper with the printing press without the ink rollers so it can be folded. Other scoring methods include *string-and-rule* (a piece of string and two thin strips of metal or RULES); *Collins rule* (a metal rule impressed by the printing press); *cut score* (a cutter or cutting rule that actual cuts partway into the paper); *hairline score* (a partial cut made with a fine rule); and *scoring wheel* (a wheel that runs over the paper). Since a score is a line, *scoring* is the making of lines. An *underscore* is a line under a character or characters.

scoring the process of composing and adding music—a *screen score* or *film score*—to a film,

sometimes done in a studio called a *scoring stage*, a sound stage with screening facilities

Scotchlite a trademark reflective material used on outdoor signs, made by the 3M Company in St. Paul, MN

scotch page an advertisement occupying most of a page, such as all except one column

Scotchprint a trademarked name for a copy made by the 3M Company of St. Paul, MN, on dull-finish, nonshrink STOCK from original engravings; used for reproduction

Scotch rule a double rule with one thick stroke and one thin stroke running parallel

scotch spread an advertisement across part of two facing pages of a publication; also called *scotch double truck* Generally, the ad is bordered with editorial matter on the top and on each side, so that it is also called an *island.*

scout a person who observes, such as a *talent scout* who searches out new talent A person who looks for specific items, such as old books, is called a scout or PICKER.

scrambled merchandising in retailing, the handling of items unrelated to the type of store; increasingly common, particularly in supermarkets and in drug- and hardware stores

scrap any visual materials used by an artist in the early stages of a graphics project

scrapbook a book or binder with pages or acetate sheets for mounting and preserving items, such as clippings and other publicity

scraperboard a British word for SCRATCHBOARD

scrap file a collection of items for reference, often literally clippings and scraps of paper

scratch a cut or mark; a hasty scribble, also called *scratchmark*; groove noise on a record *Scratchy* means bruised, irregular, or rough, as in a *scratchy record*. It can also mean to strike out, remove, or cancel, as by drawing a horizontal line through a word or a slanted vertical line through a SECTION.

Scratch-and-Sniff a microencapsulation process to convey a specific scent that is released by scratching the paper to break the microscopic plastic scent bubbles, thus releasing the aroma; trademarked by the 3M Company of St. Paul, MN

scratchboard or **scratch board** a piece of clay- or chalk-covered cardboard overlaid with a surface of paint or ink, usually a white surface painted black and scratched to let the white show through The scraping away of portions of the ink can create an engravinglike design. Scratchboard is called a *scraperboard* in the United Kingdom.

scratch comma [graphic arts, typography] a comma that is a straight line and not curved: ,

scratchpad **1** sheets used for notes or sketching **2** [computers] an internal register for temporary storage; also called *scratchpad memory*

scratch print a film with a deliberate scratch down the middle to prevent its use, done during the editing process; also called *scratched print* Scratch prints are sometimes provided for viewing by a potential customer. Similarly, a *scratch track* is a sound recording used during editing.

scratch wig [theater] a rough wig, as worn by comic performers

SCR dimmer a silicon-controlled rectifier used in lighting control in TV

screamer an exclamation point; a BANNER headline

screed a long, tiresome speech or piece of writing

screen **1** [film] a surface onto which a visual image is projected The projection of photographic images is called *screening*. A *screening room* is used for editing, previews, or special showings. The film industry is called the *screen industry*, or *screenland*; the script for a film is a *screenplay* written by a *screenwriter*, and a *screen test* is an audition film by a performer. The *screen ratio* is the ratio of screen width to height, as in a *wide-screen* movie. *Screen brightness* is the degree of luminance of a projection screen, measured with a projector lamp focused on it without film or slides in the projector. A *beaded screen*, generally made of minute glass beads, has a high reflective surface. *Screen direction* is the direction in which the action moves on the screen (toward or away from the audience, to the left or right of the screen). *Screen left* is the left side of the screen as seen by the audience, *screen right* is the right side, and in between is *screen center*. As a result of the proliferation of multiscreen theaters, movie attendance figures and other BOX-OFFICE data now are given in terms of individual screens, such as an average paid audience of 10,000 people/screen/week.

2 [printing] a grid pattern of lines crossing each other at right angles that reproduce various tones in a photo Screens are available in various sizes in accordance with the types of printing papers. The number of rows of dots, called lines, per inch gives the screen its number, such as a *100-line screen*. Screen also refers to the gradations of color tones, such as a 50-percent screen of black; the higher the number, the "finer" the screen—that is, the dots or tones are closer together. *Screen ruling* is the number of lines per inch on a screen. A *screened paper print* is a HALFTONE illustration on photographic paper. A *screened print* is a VELOX or other print made from continuous-tone material that is

screened during photographic exposure. A newspaper is printed with coarse screens, such as 55-line; books often are printed with 150-line screens, and gravure or other finer-quality printing use very fine screens, such as 300-line. *Screen process printing* is a form of *stencil* printing that uses a metal, nylon, or silk screen through which ink is forced to form an image on paper, fabric, or other material. *Screen angle* is the inclination at which the screen is turned to avoid a noticeable dot pattern, such as a 45-degree angle for black-and-white photos. *Screen tint* is film with uniform dot size that is rated by its approximate printing dot size value, such as 50%. For a screen that is 65 lines or coarser, the minimum-size square dot that is recommended is 3 *mil* ($^3/_{1000}$") for a highlight and 8 mil ($^8/_{1000}$") for a shadow.

Screen Actors Guild (SAG or S.A.G.) a national union of film performers, founded in 1933, including STUNTPERSONS but not EXTRAS, that sets minimum salaries (*SAG scale*) Former presidents of SAG include Edward Asner, Charlton Heston, and Ronald Reagan. The power of SAG also extends to television, since many films are shown on TV, and SAG developed the concept of RESIDUAL payments (*SAG fee*).

screen-based electronic typewriter (SBET) a typewriter with some word-processing and computer capabilities It includes a video screen.

screen determiner [printing] a device that indicates the *screen count* of a *halftone* print. The small plastic gauge that is slowly moved over the print also has *agate, pica,* and inch rules.

Screen Extras Guild (SEG or S.E.G.) a union of extras in motion pictures, based in Hollywood, CA

screenload [computers] the maximum number of characters or lines of text that can be displayed at one time on a video screen, not necessarily a page

screenplay a script written for a motion picture In anticipation of numerous revisions, the finished screenplay is called the *first draft, final draft,* or *temporary screenplay*. Subsequent revisions by the same or other writers result in a *second temporary screenplay, third temporary screenplay,* etc., leading to the *final screenplay*, which may be further revised (*first revised final screenplay, second revised final screenplay*), ending with the *revised final*. In Hollywood slang, to screenplay is to move forward with a project.

screentone [printing] a *halftone* film with dots of uniform size, rated by the dot size in relation to the total area, such as 20 percent; also called *screen tint*

Screen Writers Guild (SWG) a union of motion-picture writers

scribal copy a written manuscript, produced by a SCRIBE, not the same as an original manuscript produced by the author or from the author's dictation

scribe a writer; a professional copyist or penman who copied manuscripts before the invention of printing, not the same as a SCRIBER

scriber a sharply pointed tool, such as a technical pen or a lettering scriber, used to cut lines on film, metal, or another surface, such as a *scriber lettering template;* sometimes called *bug* or a *scribe* The process is called *scribing.*

scrim a transparent fabric used as a stage curtain; a net or mesh cloth to diffuse lighting in photography A scrim also may be glued to a surface, such as a sculpture, for reinforcement or as a base for plaster or other material.

script **1** the text of a speech, play, film, commercial, or program or simply a schedule or sequential account written by a *scriptwriter* The *script girl* or *continuity girl* is the director's assistant responsible for script preparation and distribution and other chores. Almost all individuals with this job are young women; the sexism is balanced by the term BEST BOY for an assistant to an electrician. A popular contemporary term is *script supervisor.* The various revisions of a film script or other work are called *script generations,* resulting in a final script or *shooting script.* **2** [typography] a typeface similar in appearance to handwriting

scroll a roll, especially for a document; a function on a CRT or video display screen in which the lines move up and down for viewing The process is called *scrolling.* To *scroll up* or down is to move the material up or down on the screen.

scrub to clean; to erase; to eliminate

scruto [theater] a sheet consisting of thin strips of wood attached to a piece of canvas, used as a small curtain to cover a TRAP or opening

SCSA STANDARD CONSOLIDATED STATISTICAL AREA

scuff a worn or rough spot on a surface

scuffing ink that comes off or smears; also called a *rub-off*

scufftester an instrument for the measurement of *scuff resistance,* or *rub,* of a printed surface; also called *rub tester* or *rubometer*

scum a filmy layer of extraneous or impure matter, such as an ink film on parts of a printing plate not intended to be printed; see also *scumming* Ink-dot scum is a type of oxidation on aluminum plates with scattered pits that print as dense dots.

scumble to soften the colors or outlines of a drawing, painting, or other art by rubbing, applying a thin coat, or covering with a film of *opaque* or nearly opaque color Scumbling is used to create an appearance of age, as on painted scenery; added color is *scumble.*

scumming [printing] a condition in which the nonprinting areas of a photographic printing plate attract ink and transfer it to paper The process is unintentional and undesirable.

S-curve a chart of occurrences shaped like an ∿, in which, for example, initial sales are at a low level, then increase considerably and taper off

scuttlebutt gossip; rumor

scut work routine or menial labor

sd. SOUND

SD SPECIAL DELIVERY mail

SDX SIGMA DELTA CHI

SE SOUND EFFECTS

seal an initial, design, or other device placed on an envelope, letter, document, or other item as a mark of authenticity; also, the stamp or other device used for making the impression Seals were originally used by nobility or government officials and now are used more popularly; common types include Christmas seals or other ornamental stamps. In graphic design, a seal is simply a name or several words rendered in a cohesive form.

seal of approval a symbol granted by a publication, such as *Good Housekeeping* magazine, for use in advertising, stating that the advertised product has been tested and found satisfactory

seal print a type of woodcut popular in the 15th century to which blind embossing—a SEAL—was added after the print was made; also called *gypsographic print*

sealskin in bookbinding, a leather made from seals, used for limp bindings

search an examination; a probe; the location of an item in a computer storage system Search mechanisms to locate a sequence or other point in a videotape include *index search,* which moves the tape to magnetic marks; *address search,* which numerically identifies each magnetic mark, or index stop, and stops at it; and *skip search,* which slows the tape at each index stop.

search and replace a computer function in which a character or word in a text is sought and then replaced with another character or word The process can occur for every appearance in the text of the item to be replaced.

search pan [film] a horizontal movement—a *pan*—of the camera seeking an object, person, or position

season [broadcasting] a period in the fall when new TV programs are introduced by the networks Originally 39 weeks (from the days of network radio programs), *the season* now refers to the fall season of 13 weeks. *Mid-season* is between the fall and spring seasons or any time after the beginning of the fall season when a show is replaced (a *mid-season replacement*). A full-season show generally contains only 24 episodes; the balance are reruns.

seasonal products or services purchased at certain times of the year, as measured by a *seasonality index* For example, cold remedies have a high winter seasonality index.

seasonal discount a reduction in costs to advertisers or other customers limited to a month or other specific period of time, generally the *slow season*

season average an A.C. NIELSEN CO. term to describe the average audiences of network TV programs from the season premiere to the current report, as published in the biweekly *NTI (Nielsen Television Index) Pocketpiece*

season dating a method of invoicing in which credit is extended to the customer by setting the payment in the future, such as the next season; also called *seasonal dating* or *advance dating*

second 1 substandard or defective merchandise sold at a discount, usually called *seconds* A company may have a first or quality line and a second or lower-priced line. 2 a unit of time A 60-second TV segment or commercial is written as :60, called a *sixty*.

secondary audience PASS-ALONG or secondary readers of a publication; an audience of a radio or TV station in an area—a *secondary service area*—in which the broadcasting signal is of secondary or inferior quality

secondary color a color derived by mixing two primary colors The primary colors are red, blue, and yellow; secondary colors include purple, green, and orange.

secondary document the item that is inserted in a fill-in letter or other word processing that involves a merging operation The basic letter is the standard or *primary document*; the fill-in that is selectively inserted is the secondary or *variable document*. A *document* is a text entity, a collection of one or more lines of text.

second assistant camera operator [film] a member of the camera crew who marks the SLATES, calls out the TAKE number, operates the CLAPPER BOARD, and maintains a record of all takes on CAMERA SHEETS; also called a *clapper/loader*

second assistant director [film] a person who assists the assistant director, who is the first assistant director Responsibilities include preparing and distributing the daily CALL SHEETS and supervising the DGA TRAINEE.

second cameraman [film] the person who actually operates the camera and reports to the *director of photography* He or she is more generally called a *camera operator*, *operating cameraman*, or *operator*.

second-class mail a category of mail consisting of newspapers and periodicals to which readers subscribe, available at a rate considerably lower than *first-class mail* provided it is packaged (sorted and sacked) and meets other Postal Service specifications Almost 10 percent of all U.S. mail volume is second-class mail.

second coming type enormous-size type, such as is used by newspapers for extraordinary events; also called *Victory type*

second company a touring TROUPE; a group on location, as in a film production outside of the studio

second cover (2C) the front inside cover of a periodical

second-day story a follow-up newspaper story; an article describing new developments

second feature the secondary or less important film in a *double feature*, a showing of two films

second front the first page of the second section of a newspaper

second generation a more advanced model than the original Second-generation computers were made with transistors, instead of vacuum tubes, in the 1950s and 1960s. A second-generation typesetter uses photomechanical technology instead of hot metal, with light flashed through the character images on disks or filmstrips to photosensitive film or paper. However, a second-generation *dupe*, or *duplicate*, is a copy of a film or other item made from an original.

second rights permission to print previously published material, such as a newspaper or magazine article excerpted from a book; also called *second serial rights*

second run a showing of a movie or other program or attraction after the first wave of showings, often at a *second-run theater*

second season a period after January when unsuccessful network television programs are replaced or rescheduled and new programs are aired In recent years, these schedule changes have been increasing to the point where as many are made prior to January as after, almost making the term obsolete.

second unit a secondary or backup group, such as a film or TV production crew on location

The filming or taping generally is supervised by a *second-unit director*.

secretarial shift   a keyboard key that, when depressed, moves or changes all characters, such as from lowercase to capital letters

section   **1** a component   **2** a district, such as a sales territory or part of the country   **3** [advertising] a piece of a BULLETIN that can be removed and moved to a new location   **4** [broadcasting] In SPOT TV, commercials are sold in three classifications; *section I* spots have the highest rates and are less likely to be preempted than *section II* or *III* spots. *Sectional announcements* are limited to a region. A *sectional feed* is a program, announcement, or commercial transmitted to one or more sections in a region. **5** [graphic arts] A *sectional view* is an illustration or drawing with a three-dimensional effect in which a part has been removed to show the interior. *Sectioning lines* or *section lines* are closely parallel diagonal lines that show a sectional view of the exposed surfaces.   **6** [typography] See SECTION MARK.   **7** [publishing] a distinct portion of a periodical, also called a *dedicated section*, such as the financial section, sports section, or *style section*, or an article, identified by a first-level header   A *subsection* is a separate portion within a section identified by a second-level header. Further subdivisions are called *sub-subsections* and *sub-sub-subsections* and are identified by third- and fourth-level headers. *Sectionalizing* is arranging a publication in sections. A section also may be separately published. A regional edition of a periodical or a publication appealing to readers in a specific area is a *sectional publication* targeted to the *sectional center*, or central area of its region. A *sectional story*, or running story, is an article that appears in segments or installments over several issues or within the same issue. In books, a section is a folded printed sheet—a SIGNATURE—together with any plates or inserts, or major subdivision, such as several chapters, generally preceded by a page with the *section title*; it is also called *divided title* or *part title*.

section mark   a mark used to indicate a REFERENCE or a SECTION, as in a publication, consisting of an uppercase *S* interlocked vertically with another uppercase *S*: §

sector   the smallest part of a magnetic recording disk before subdivision into bytes   A *hard-sectored disk* can receive and store only records exactly the size of a sector. A *soft-sectored disk* can receive records of varying lengths.

sector plan   in transit advertising, a purchase of coverage in a specific geographical area; also called *sector showing*

"see also" reference   a reference from a name or term used in a HEADING, as in a *bibliography* or *index*, to one or more *related* names or terms that also are used as headings; also called *"see also" cross-reference*   It is not the same as a "see" reference or "see" cross-reference, which is a reference to a name or term used as a heading from another form of the name or term that is not used as a heading. Librarians understand the difference; most writers indicate any cross-reference as "see," usually followed by the word or words in small capital letters.

see copy   a proofreader's mark instructing the printer to compare a proof with the original copy

seed   the source or origin   *Seeding* is the insertion of something tiny, like a seed. In direct marketing, seeding is the insertion of decoy or dummy names in a mailing list to confirm the use of the list; it is also called SALTING. *Real seeds* are actual names of people, generally employees or others associated with the *seeder*, instead of fictitious names.

seen/associate   the percentage of readers of a publication who, when interviewed, remember having seen a particular page or ad and are able to associate it with the subject, advertiser, or brand name; a term of the research firm of Starch INRA Hooper, Inc., of Mamaroneck, NY, originally used by Daniel Starch   It is also called *seen-associated*.

see-through   the visibility of printed matter from one side of a sheet to the other; also called *show-through*   Though the two terms are used synonymously, they are not identical. See-through actually is the degree to which printed matter on an underlying sheet can be seen through the sheet above it, whereas show-through is the degree to which printed matter on a reverse side can be seen through a sheet of paper.

see you   a customer who asks for a specific salesperson   The origin is from the receptionist or other person who greets the customer, then calls the salesperson by stating, "Someone is here to see you."

SEG   SCREEN EXTRAS GUILD; SPECIAL-EFFECTS GENERATOR

segment   a part; a component; a group of purchasers or other individuals who share a common characteristic—a market segment   A *segment sponsor* is one of several advertisers on a radio or TV program. In *market segmentation* or *subsegmentation*, consumers are divided into segments or *subsegments* in order to develop a strategy in which separate products and/or marketing mixes are directed to different groups.

segmented rate card an advertising *rate card* or, more likely, a *booklet*, usually for a newspaper, with varying rates for categories, such as retail, food, recruitment, financial, and classified

segment producer [television] a producer of a part, or segment, of a program or series, such as an interview or magazine-style program For example, a daily talk show (such as "Donahue" or "Oprah Winfrey") has several segment producers, each responsible for procuring guests and producing their sections in entirety.

segment report in TV news, a series, generally over a five-day period (a *five-parter*) and usually on a major topic or issue, such as an *investigative report*; also called *mini-documentary*

segue 1 to make a transition from one action, scene, or musical selection directly to another without interruption; pronounced SEG-way, from the Italian *seguire*, "to follow" 2 [radio] the continuous flow of recorded music 3 [film] a sound DISSOLVE or *cross-fade*

Selby, Harry a fictitious name occasionally printed in a theater program to conceal the identity of the performer, perhaps because the performer also plays another character, as an inside joke, or, according to theatrical lore, for good luck The name GEORGE SPELVIN is more commonly used for the same purpose.

selected chosen A *selected take* is the final, approved version of a filmed or taped shot.

selective binding a magazine with special advertising and/or editorial material for specific groups of readers (such as older or affluent people, students, etc.), bound into the regular edition

selective clubbing a reduced-rate offer to magazine subscribers from a company representing several publishers, such as Publishers Clearing House, Port Washington, NY

selective distortion the tendency to adapt information to a personal mind-set, so that different people perceive the same message differently *Selective retention* exhibits the same variability regarding what is remembered or retained. *Selective reinforcement* is the tendency to receive and retain messages that confirm preexisting attitudes.

selective distribution limited distribution, such as the selection of prestigious or other specific retail outlets in order to avoid saturation or distribution in all, or almost all, types of retail outlets

selective focus a photographic technique using narrow DEPTH OF FIELD to blur the background and foreground and emphasize a small distinct area

selective headline an advertising headline directed to a segment of the readership

selective key light a type of lighting in a film or other work in which the KEY LIGHT illuminates only part of the performer's face or body

selective sound a type of editing or mixing in film or other media that emphasizes specific sounds for dramatic or other effect

selective magazine a special-interest magazine

selective plan [advertising] the use of media to reach specific types of audiences

Selectronic a computerized system of R.R. Donnelley & Sons Co., of Chicago, in which a magazine subscriber's name appears as a personalized message within the publication

self-addressed stamped envelope (SASE) a stamped envelope addressed by and to the recipient, commonly requested in classified advertisements

self-blimped a movie camera that produces a low noise level during operation A *blimp* is a soundproofed camera case.

self-contained exhibit a display that is an integral part of its shipping or carrying case

self-contained picture a photo without an accompanying article

self-cover a booklet or publication with a cover of the same paper STOCK as the inside pages, though not necessarily the same size; not the same as SELF-WRAPPER

self-lining the first and last pages of text paper pasted to the cover of a book without endpapers

self-liquidator a premium with its cost covered by the purchase price for which it is offered; also called *purchase-privilege-premium*

self-mailer a direct-mail piece designed to incorporate its own envelope or produced so that no envelope or wrapper is required, such as a *double postcard*

self-publishing the production, or arrangement for production, of a book or other publication by the author The author-publisher publication may be by a VANITY PRESS, a small business set up by the author and often operated at home, or a one-time, limited, or specialized operation.

self-seal an envelope with adhesive that requires no moisture for sealing A *self-seal reply form*, commonly used by mass mailers, is a sheet that can be folded along the indicated lines and sealed like an envelope.

self-selection a retailing arrangement that enables a customer to choose merchandise and give it to a nearby salesclerk for payment and other services, such as delivery; different from SELF-SERVICE It is common in department stores.

self-service a retailing arrangement with a minimum of sales personnel A customer brings merchandise to the cash-register checkout, as in a supermarket.

self-wrapper a paper cover of a publication that is the same size and STOCK as its pages The cover is part of a SIGNATURE and not an addition by the BINDER.

sell a portion of an advertisement, speech, article, or other message that encourages the sale of a product, service, or concept *Hard sell* is overt, obvious, and perhaps crass. *Soft sell* is subtle, more subdued, and less "commercial."

sell down the process of moving through the channels of distribution before the ultimate sale to the consumer

sell-in a period in which a product is sold to wholesalers, distributors, dealers, or retailers prior to its availability to consumers

Selling-Areas Distribution Index (S.A.D.I.) a continuous retail distribution measurement system of products conducted by Audits & Surveys, a market research company headquartered in New York that provides in-store measurements, primarily of food and drug products

Selling Areas Marketing, Inc. See SAMI.

selling idea a slogan, basic concept, or selling proposition

sell-off a resale or unloading of contracted advertising space or time or otherwise unsalable products

sell sheet a promotional message, generally one or two pages about a product or service, used for advance selling or to support a sales campaign

sell through an effort to increase the rate at which a product is sold through retailers; not the same as SELL IN In videocassette stores and industries that rent products, a sell-through is an item that is sold rather than rented.

selsyn an electric motor that can be used to synchronize several mechanisms, such as in a movie projection system

selvage an edge of paper or fabric, generally to be trimmed off or covered The main area on a postage-stamp sheet is called selvage or *selvedge*. The word is from *self* and *edge*.

sem semicolon

semanteme an element of language that expresses a definite image or idea, such as a word or part of a word

semantic of, or pertaining to, meaning, especially in language Semantics is concerned with speech forms, contextual meaning, and the referential meaning of signs and symbols.

semaphore an apparatus for signaling, such as by an arrangement of lights or flags The *two-flag semaphore system* involves different positions of the flags to represent the letters of the alphabet. In computers and communications, the *semaphore method* ensures the synchronization of cooperating processes and prevents interference when two processes simultaneously seek to use a resource.

semi half; twice in a period of time A *semiannual* work is published twice a year; a *semimonthly* is published twice a month (not the same as a *bimonthly*, which is issued every two months); and a *semiweekly* is published twice a week (not the same as a *biweekly*, which is issued every two weeks).

semi-liquidator a premium offered with a retail item that is not fully a SELF-LIQUIDATOR—a *semi-self-liquidator* or *partial self-liquidator*

semiotics the analysis of signs and symbols, especially in language As used in advertising and public relations, semiotics deciphers hidden messages and the system of codes through which people communicate—verbally and nonverbally, consciously and unconsciously.

semis in bookbinding, a decoration of flowers, leaves, or other small figures repeated frequently to produce a powdered or sprinkled effect on the binding

semi-spectacular an embellished painted outdoor advertising BULLETIN with special lighting or other features but not as elaborate as a SPECTACULAR

semi-tuck a layout of a two-column article with a headline above each column, the first headline occupying a larger, deeper area

send down to transmit a story from the copy desk or editorial department to the composing or typesetting department; also called *send out*

send-off a start; a demonstration of good wishes, particularly to a person starting a new job or undertaking

send-up a satirical takeoff

senior spot a large, high-intensity spotlight with a FRESNEL lens and generally with a 5,000-watt lamp; also called *senior* It is common in films.

sensitivity responsiveness to stimuli, such as heat, light, and sound In photography, sensitivity is the degree to which a photographic emulsion reacts to light; a film with high sensitivity needs less exposure to light than a film with low sensitivity. In electronics, it is the minimum input signal required to produce a specific output signal, such as a measure of a camera's ability to produce an acceptable image in marginal light conditions.

sensor a sensing device that responds to light or other stimulation

sent del sentence delete, a computer command for a sentence to be deleted

sentence completion a research technique in which a respondent is asked to complete a series of sentences

sep or sep. SEPARATE; SEPARATION

separate [publishing] a separately issued article, chapter, or other portion of a larger work, generally printed at the same time as the original and thus not the same as a REPRINT; also called OFFPRINT

separate audio program (SAP) an audio channel that can be received by a stereo TV set and used in a multichannel stereo sound system

separate cover a cover of a brochure or other publication that is not the same stock as the inside pages; not a SELF-COVER

separation 1 [broadcasting] a time period between competing commercials; space between microphones 2 [printing] the isolation of the blue, red, yellow, and black negatives or plates Each *separation negative* is printed individually to produce a COLOR SEPARATION or isolated by means of camera filters.

separatrix a diagonal line; also called a VIRGULE, SLANT BAR, or SLASH

sepia a type of monotone film or photographic printing paper for a *sepia print* yielding brown tones instead of black; pronounced SEE-pee-a

seq. SEQUEL; SEQUENS, Latin for "following" If several items follow, the plural is *seqq.,* for *sequentia*

sequel a continuation, such as a literary work that is complete in itself (and therefore not a SUPPLEMENT) but continues an earlier work

sequence 1 the following of one item after another 2 [film] a series of single shots to form a unit or episode A *basic sequence* in film or TV is a series of related shots, such as a long shot as an opening, establishing shot and a medium shot as a close-up and reestablishing shot. To shoot in sequence is to film in the chronological order of the story or the order in which the production schedule is set up; the opposite is to shoot *out of sequence.* A *sequence shot* or *plan-sequence* is a single shot, generally a *long take* of a minute or more. 3 [computers] a series of items, usually arranged according to a specified set of rules, such as alphabetically, chronologically, or numerically *Sequential access* is a method of locating text or other data by searching from the beginning rather than going directly to the desired place (*random access*). *Sequential filing* is entering data in a fixed position.

sequence tickets tickets on a spindle that are serially numbered, as at movie theaters; also called *roll tickets*

sequential camera a camera, such as a microfilm camera, that produces a series of separate images according to a predetermined SEQUENCE; also called *step-and-repeat camera*

sequential numbering system a method of citing references in numerical SEQUENCE

ser. SERIAL; SERIES

serenade a vocal or instrumental performance of music outdoors at night, particularly by a man—a *serenader*—under the window of his loved one; a piece of music or a poem akin to a song

serial 1 a SERIES published or produced at regular intervals in installments, such as a periodical or soap opera Research papers, proceedings of societies, and other publications often are published on a continuing basis, as in a *numbered monographic series.* In the 1940s and earlier, adventure films (*serials*) were issued in installments, called *chapters,* shown weekly, primarily for young audiences. A *serial catalog* lists the periodicals and other serials in a library. The *serial number* identifies the order of publication, with each item assigned a specific serial number, such as an *International Standard Serial Number* (*ISSN*). The *serial record* is a file with information about each *serial title* on a *serial card,* perhaps administered by a *serial librarian* in a *serials department.* 2 [computers] the sequential treatment of digital information *Serial storage* is the recording of information in sequence as it is entered, so to locate a unit requires searching everything up to that point.

serial comma a comma placed between elements in a series An OXFORD COMMA, also called a *Harvard comma,* is placed before a conjunction, generally "and" or "or" Some *stylebooks,* such as *The New York Times Stylebook,* recommend omission of this comma except when needed for clarification or emphasis.

serial correlation a sales and market forecasting technique that uses past trends as the basis for future projections

serial distribution a promotion in which an advertiser presents a series of *ad specialties* at regular intervals; see also SPECIALTY ADVERTISING

serial number the number that identifies the order or sequence in which a publication in a series was published; see also SERIAL

serial rights permission to publish copyrighted material in a serial publication (a periodical) in one or more issues *First serial rights* are granted to the first publisher by the *copyright holder,* generally the author. Subsequent rights are *second serial rights* or *reprints.*

serial service a periodical that provides revisions and other new material in the form of new or replacement issues rather than replacement pages, which is provided by a *loose-leaf service*

seriatim   one after another in order; point by point; *serially*

series   **1** a group of items in succession, such as broadcasts or articles on successive days or weeks   **2** [typography] all sizes of a single typeface   **3** [publishing] separate books in the same category or on the same subject, generally in the same or similar format, issued by one publisher

serif   a short, thin line projecting above and/or below the main strokes of letters such as *a*, *h*, and *v* so that the letters do not have uniform thickness   Type styles with strokes of uniform thickness are called *sans serif*. A *square serif*, also called *black serif* or *stab serif*, has straight lines instead of curved ones. Square-serif typefaces include Beton, Cairo, Girder, Karnak, Memphis, and Stymie. American Square Serif is a typeface with the serifs heavier than the main strokes. Egyptian Square Serif is a typeface with the serifs the same weight as the main stroke. A *bracketed serif* joins the main stroke of the letter at its curve, as in Old Style Roman.

serigraph   a print made by a SILK-SCREEN process, or *serigraphy*, by a *serigrapher*

service article   an article in a newspaper or other publication about a product or activity with information designed to be useful—*of service*—to the reader

service button   an insignia pin indicating membership in a labor union, fraternal organization, or other group

service magazine   a periodical providing a service to its readers, such as a *women's service magazine* with recipes, patterns, and other services for homemakers

service mark   an identifying word, words, or emblem to identify services of a specific company or organization that can be registered, as with a product TRADEMARK, under the Trade-Mark Act

service provider (SP)   [videotex] a company that sells services to videotex subscribers   Types of service providers include advertising, information, and transaction providers.

service video   television programs produced about or on behalf of nonprofit groups for showing on cable-TV access channels, on commercial channels (as a public service, not purchased time), or to groups

SES   SOCIOECONOMIC STATUS

SESAC Inc.   an organization in Nashville, TN, of about 2,000 songwriters and music publishers that licenses and collects fees for broadcast or other use of the works of its members; pronounced SEE-sack   The original name was *Society of European Stage Authors and Com-*

posers. The other two U.S. organizations that collect performance royalties, *ASCAP* and *BMI*, are considerably larger.

session   a meeting or a period of time, such as the time during which a user of a terminal can communicate with an interactive system (the elapsed time between *log on* and *log off*)   In music, a *session musician* is hired to play for a specific *recording date* and may be paid a *session fee*.

set   **1** a collection or series of data; a series of music pieces, as when a band plays a 40-minute set; the decor of a stage play or the location of a film, TV, or other production   To set is to write or fit, as with words to music or music to words; to place a scene in a locale, or to arrange sceneries or properties on a stage. A *set designer* or *set decorator* creates the decor of a play, movie, or show; a *set dresser* constructs and decorates it with *set dressing*—props, furnishings, and related items. An *abstract set* has a neutral background, as on a TV news program. A *basic set* is empty and without props.   **2** [typography] to typeset, or arrange type for printing; to produce or reproduce printed matter   Set also refers to the overall appearance of type as determined by the relative widths of characters and the SPACING between them.   **3** a radio or TV receiver   **4** the disposition of a person to respond in a certain way to stimuli, as in *mind set* or *attitudinal set*

set and hold   an instruction to a typesetter to set type and hold it for future use

set-and-light   a director's instruction to a film or tape crew to prepare for shooting

setback   **1** the distance between an outdoor BILLBOARD and the road it faces, measured from the center of the panel to the beginning of the road   **2** [printing] the distance from the front edge of the press plate to the image area

set close   [typesetting] to reduce the spacing between characters and/or words

set day   the day scheduled to erect a set in a film or TV studio; also called *build day* or *setup day*

set dressings   furnishings on a stage or set, as placed by a *set dresser*

set light   separate illumination of a stage or studio set as a whole or in part other than that provided by the lights on the actors

set off   the transfer of ink from one printed sheet to another; also called *offset* (not the same as offset printing)   Set off is undesirable and is preventable, as by insertion of a SLIPSHEET between the printed sheets.

set open   in typesetting, to add space between characters and/or words

set piece a piece of stage scenery that suggests the environment, such as a *street set piece* or *garden set piece*

sets in use (SIU) a percentage of households with radio or TV receivers, or sets, turned on at a specific time, as expressed by *sets-in-use rating (SIU)* or *tune-in rating*

set size the width of a TYPEFACE; also called *set* or SET WIDTH Typefaces of the same *point* size vary in their set width, particularly old style compared to modern. Generally, the set size equals the point size, though the set size is the actual width of the widest character in a particular size and style. In condensed typefaces, the set size is less than the point size, and in extended typefaces the set size is greater than the point size.

set solid an instruction to set lines of type next to each other with no LEADING, or SPACING, between the lines

set the scene to provide an introduction or background, particularly to a play; also called *set the stage* Literally, it is to put scenery and properties on a stage.

setting the position, as on a radio receiver dial; the time, place, and other circumstances of an event, film, play, or other work, or, more specifically, simply the SCENERY; the music, or composing of music, for a set of words

setup a single camera and lighting position before which action takes place; a configuration for a presentation, photography, filming, or painting In show business, a setup is dialogue or a plot arranged in anticipation of a climax, such as a *setup situation* or a *setup line* that precedes the *punch line* of a joke. To *set up* is to assemble, as in the erection of a display. A *set-up drawing* is the assembly plan to be executed by *set-up personnel*. In film animation, a setup is a CEL placed on a background.

set-up sheet [printing] a master form for layout and positioning

set width in typesetting, the horizontal dimension or width of a character, generally expressed in machine width, or the width of a line of type, generally expressed in *picas* and *points*; also called *set size* Set with adjustment (also *white space adjustment* or *overall kerning*) is the reduction (sometimes called *reverse letterspacing*) or expansion (sometimes called *letterspacing*) of set width by changing the white space between characters.

setwise referring to the width of a typographic character

Seven Arts the seven areas of study in Europe in the Middle Ages: arithmetic, astronomy, geometry, Latin grammar, logic, music, and rhetoric

750 a small spotlight, 750 watts, called a seven-fifty

7-7-7 rule an FCC restriction that formerly limited ownership by one company to a maximum of seven AM, seven FM, and seven TV stations, of which only five could be VHF; now 12-12-12

Seven Sisters the seven big-circulation women's SERVICE MAGAZINES: *Better Homes & Gardens, Family Circle, Good Housekeeping, Ladies' Home Journal, McCall's, Redbook,* and *Woman's Day*

Seventh Avenue the New York fashion industry Though many apparel companies are located on Broadway or elsewhere in Manhattan, the term still is apt and is commonly used to describe the garment industry, particularly women's apparel.

73 wire-service jargon for "best regards"

sewing in bookbinding, the use of thread in the joining of the folded sheets, such as SIGNATURES; called *thread binding*, as compared to stitching with wire staples or adhesive binding Types of sewing include *cleat sewing, McCain sewing, oversewing, saddle sewing, side sewing, Singer sewing,* and *Smyth sewing. Sewing through the fold,* or *fold sewing,* involves passing the thread or wire through the center of the fold. Sewing is done by machine, by hand (*bench sewing*), or by a combination.

sewn book a type of bookbinding in which the SIGNATURES are gathered in sequence and then sewn individually, so that the threads are visible at the center of each signature

sexn a SECTION page; the first page of a newspaper section other than the first section

sexploitation a film or other work that is primarily pornographic and made for exploitation—a quick profit

sextodecimo a 32-page booklet; also called a *sixteenmo,* since 32 pages is 16 leaves Its standard page size is $4\frac{1}{2}'' \times 6\frac{1}{2}''$. The Latin origin is *sextus* (sixth) and *decimus* (tenth), or $\frac{1}{16}$.

sf or **SF** SCIENCE FICTION

SFX. or **S.F.X.** SOUND EFFECTS

sgd. signed

SGU STANDARD GEOGRAPHICAL UNIT

sh 1 a share of stock 2 a sheet of paper 3 a SHILLING BAR, which is a VIRGULE, or slanted line, used in fractions, to separate alternatives such as and/or, as a symbol of the word per as in miles/hour, or to indicate the ends of verse lines printed continuously

shade a part of a picture or scene depicting darkness; a gradation of darkness; the degree to which a color is deepened, darkened, or mixed with black To shade is to screen from light or represent degrees of darkness, or to add a shadow or repeat strokes of a typeface to create a three-dimensional effect.

shaded type a typeface with a shadow, or *drop outline*, designed to appear three-dimensional, generally used only for uppercase letters

shader a nickname for a video control engineer, who is in charge of video but not audio

shading lines or other marks to represent gradations of darkness in a picture A *shading medium* is a preprinted pressure-sensitive sheet used to add a pattern of shading to artwork. Shading may be produced in other ways, such as with a STYLUS, pen, or pencil on a stencil or other surface.

shadow box a frame around *copy* to give the illusion of a shadow; a boxlike frame for display, as in a store or studio

shadow face a class of typeface that appears to have a shadow, used for a newspaper LOGO or other display

shadow mask a perforated shield behind a color television screen that separates the electron beams producing red, green, and blue The electron beam is directed through a piece of perforated metal—the *mask*—to the desired phosphor color element. The perforations are round or vertical. A *slit mask* or *slot mask* has vertical slits or slots.

shadows the darkest parts of a picture or photograph

shaken referring to a book with weak or torn inner joints

shaky cam slang for a film or TV segment made by a hand-held (hence, shaky) camera such as a *minicam*

shammy the alternate spelling of CHAMOIS (reflecting its pronunciation), a commonly misspelled word

Shandwick one of the world's largest public relations firms Headquartered in London, it owns several U.S. firms, including Rogers & Cowan of Los Angeles and Golin/Harris of Chicago.

shank a leg, stem, or stalk In typesetting, the shank is the type body, a piece of type exclusive of the printing surface, as measured in POINTS.

share 1 [broadcasting] share-of-audience: the percentage of the total audience in a specific time period tuned to a program or station 2 [marketing] the percentage of purchases in a product category, called *share of market, share of retail sales*, or *brand share* A *share point* is one percent of the total. Share is a competitive evaluation, not a quantitative or absolute number of customers or products sold or of audience size.

shared identification a commercial spot with the name of the station or program superimposed on part of it; also called *shared I.D.*

shared line one telephone line with several subscribers; also called *party line*

shared-logic a system of several input and/or output devices linked to one host computer, as compared to a *stand-alone* or single-unit system

share of choice a consumer research technique in which one product or service is varied in its price and characteristics while others are kept constant and consumers are asked to choose which product they would purchase

share of mind a percentage of all brand awareness or brand-advertising awareness in a category of product or service, usually elicited on an unaided basis

Share of Voice (SOV) a brand's percentage of its advertising in relation to the total advertising in its category

sharp distinct; keen; fine; acute; clear in form and detail, as in sound or image *Sharpening* can be a decrease or increase in strength or other factors. For example, a *halftone* can be sharpened by decreasing the dots or making them smaller, the opposite of thickening them. *Sharpness* is a measure of precision, such as a sharp or clearly defined contrast, or intensity of a sharp or high-pitched sound. In music, a sharp is a note or tone one-half step above another, indicated by the symbol ♯.

shave [printing] excessive trimming of the top or bottom margins of the sheets so that the top or bottom lines of type are grazed However, to shave paper is to cut a slight trim.

Shavian of or characteristic of George Bernard Shaw (1856–1950), the British playwright, such as a *Shavian ensemble* that performs his plays A Shavian is an admirer of Shaw or his work; it is pronounced SHAVE-ee-un.

sheaf a bundle; a collection of papers or other items A *sheaf catalog* is composed of sets of sheets fastened together in a loose-leaf binder.

sheet 1 a cut or trimmed piece of paper; slang for newspaper, particularly a TABLOID 2 in outdoor advertising, a unit of billboard- or poster-size paper An *in-sheet book* is printed on paper cut into sheets, as compared to a *web book* printed on paper in a continuous roll, or *web*. The basic sheet size of most bond papers is 17" × 22", which is cut twice to make four 8½" × 11" sheets, a common size for stationery. A *square sheet*, not necessarily square-shaped, is equally strong and tear-resistant with and against the grain. An *Eight Sheet Outdoor Advertising Association* in Independence, MO, promotes 6" × 12" *junior panels*. 3 music printed on unbound paper—*sheet music Mu-*

sic Sheets, as they originally were called, featured decorative covers.

sheeter a device at the end of a *web-fed* printing press to cut the roll, or *web*, of paper into *sheets* The cutting process is *sheeting*.

sheet-fed printing on separate sheets of paper, in contrast to *web-fed*, such as *rotogravure*, which is done on a continuous web, or roll of paper A *web press* is faster than a sheet-fed press.

sheet film negative film that is cut into flat sheets, not wound on a roll or in a cartridge; also called *cut film* Standard sizes are 4" × 5" and 8" × 10".

sheetwise a method of printing in which each side of a sheet is printed on a separate press run with the forms changed for printing the front and back; also called *work-and-turn*

sheet-writer a salesperson who sells subscriptions to a periodical, generally door-to-door, often receiving as a commission most or all of the subscription price

shelf in retailing, a physical facility for displaying products, generally on horizontal tiers above the floor or on the wall The products are identified and promoted with a *shelf card*, *shelf display* (using the products themselves), *shelf extender* (a traylike extension to a shelf), *shelf marker* (placed in or hung from a channel strip on the front edge of a shelf), *shelf pack* (a container holding one or more items), *shelf strip* (attached to the front edge of a shelf), *shelf talker* (hung over the shelf edge), and *shelf tape* (adhesive tape affixed to the shelf edge). *On the shelf* is in a state of disuse, or out of circulation. To take something *off the shelf* is to use a standard item, something from stock or already in existence.

shelfback a SPINE or backbone of a book

shelf fill the amount of merchandise ordered by a retailer to fill the shelves of a store, a term used in the home video business

shelf life the SALES LIFE of a retail product: the period during which it retains its quality and may be sold

shelf miser a *point-of-purchase display* that fits on a shelf, holds products, and also has a promotional message; also called *space miser*

shelf movement an analysis of sales of a product in a supermarket or other store; the speed with which an item is purchased from a shelf and replaced by another unit of the same brand *Fast shelf movement* indicates a higher sales volume than *slow shelf movement*.

shelf space the amount of space occupied by an item in a retail store, measured in terms of linear or square feet or number of FACINGS

shelf warmer a slow-selling product that is dormant on store shelves

shelter magazine a periodical with focus on the home, such as *House Beautiful* or *Better Homes & Gardens*; also called *shelter book* or *home service book*

shf or SHF superhigh frequency

Shibata a STYLUS-tip configuration for playback of four-channel records

shield law a law that protects journalists from revealing sources of information It varies by state and is subject to judicial interpretation.

shift to move or transfer, as from small letters to capital letters, in a typewriter, by depressing the *shift* key on a keyboard A *segment shift* is a device to change modalities, such as the capital letter key on typewriters. The origin is from hot-metal typesetting, in which the font-matrix sorting mechanism is shifted to a position to access the uppercase characters. Shift also refers to other transfers or movements, such as moving characters in a table from a column to the adjacent column. In theater, to shift is to dismantle—STRIKE—the scenery of one set and replace it with another.

shilling bar (sh) a *virgule*, or slanted line, used in fractions, to separate alternatives such as *and/or*, as a symbol of the word *per* as in (miles/hour), or to indicate the ends of verse lines printed continuously; also called a SLASH or SOLIDUS

shilling fraction a fraction consisting of numerator, SHILLING BAR (diagonal line), and denominator, set in the same size as surrounding type, such as 3/4

shingle 1 a small rectangular signboard, as on the front of a building with the name of a physician or lawyer *To hang out a shingle* is to announce the opening of a new office; a shingle is also a rectangular piece of asbestos, wood, or other material laid in overlapping rows on the outside of buildings. 2 in bookbinding, an allowance in fractions of an inch per a specific quantity of sheets to adjust the bind margin to compensate for bulking

shingling 1 the creation of a layout from various components on which the border and other white space are overlapped, or shingled 2 [printing] partial overlapping, as with roofing shingles, of sheets or other items to separate SIGNATURES or other groups This stacking process often is used by laypersons in collating. In bookbinding by the SADDLE-STITCH method, shingling is sometimes used in books with many sheets of heavy STOCK, in which the inside margins are reduced on the leaves closer to the center so that the outside edges of all sheets are aligned.

The Shiny Sheet the nickname of a newspaper, *Palm Beach News* in Palm Beach, FL, issued daily during the season from October to May and semiweekly the rest of the year   This full-size newspaper is renowned for its society news and photos, which are published on high-gloss paper.

shirt-board advertising advertising printed on the cardboard stiffeners enclosed with laundered shirts—a novel idea, but uncommon

shirttail a short article related to a preceding longer article

shive a splinter, such as an imperfection—an uncooked wood particle—in paper

shmaltz See SCHMALTZ.

SHN Scripps-Howard News Service of Washington, DC

shock radio talk shows and other radio programs that feature aggressive hosts who often insult interviewees and listeners who call in

shoe a part forming a base   In cameras, the *accessory shoe* (also called *hot shoe*) attached to the side or top of a camera is the holder for the flash unit and other attachments.

shoehorn to squeeze in or add copy or visuals to an advertisement or other work

shoestring inexpensive, as with a *shoestring production* or *shoestringer*

S-hook a type of metal hardware in the shape of an *S*, used in displays to hang items or to hang stage scenery; also called *keeper*

shoot a session at which performances are filmed, especially on location instead of in a studio (to go *on a shoot* or *to a shoot*); to film, photograph, or record such a session or any scene; an instruction to start the camera   To *overshoot* is to shoot too much footage; to *undershoot* is to shoot too little.

shoot around [film] a technique of shooting a scene without one of the performers or objects, which will be filmed separately and inserted

shoot-'em-up a violent film or TV program, with considerable shootings

shooting all action by photographers, camera crews, performers, and others involved in a still or motion-picture photography session as it occurs

shooting call instructions to a photography or film crew about when and where to report

shooting date the day of commencement of photography or taping

shooting log a form on which a camera-crew member records data about a photography or filming session, including type of equipment used; also called *camera log* or *camera report*

shooting off the unintentional inclusion in a picture of the area beyond the set or standard position, such as more of the background than usually is shown in a portrait; also called *shooting over*

shooting ratio the amount of film or tape used to film or tape all scenes compared to the amount or length of the final film or tape   The higher the ratio, the more waste. A ratio of over 10:1—a *double digit shooting ratio*—is very costly, not because of the film stock but rather the time of the performers and other production costs. Ask Elaine May about *Ishtar*.

shooting schedule a list of shots in a film script put in order of what is most convenient to produce rather than of how they will appear in the finished film

shooting script a script for a film or TV production

shooting to playback a film technique in which performers are filmed as they *lip sync* to dialogue or music that has been prerecorded

shooting upside-down filming (shooting) with the camera turned upside down

shootout a competition, as among agencies competing for an account

shop a place where goods or services are offered for sale, such as a beauty shop; a specialized department or section in a large store; a place where a particular kind of work is done, such as a *print shop*

shop card a bulletin board or other display sign indicating that the employees are members of a labor union; also called *store card*

shopped a script or other property that has been offered to producers and other prospects and rejected

shopper a *pennysaver* or free-circulation *throwaway* newspaper   A shopper is generally TABLOID and all or mostly advertising.

shopping radius an area around a store from which it attracts customers

shop print a blueprint made on vellum or another durable surface for use in the shop or field, such as by architects and engineers

short a nonfeature film, generally less than three reels, or 30 minutes   Theatrical shorts shown in movie theaters no longer are common (anyone remember Pete Smith?), but shorts have made a comeback on pay TV, where they are shown after feature films to fill out time periods. A short is also a brief story or article, a short circuit or electrical malfunction, or an *underrun*, such as a print delivery of less than the ordered quantity.

short and an *ampersand:* &

short dash a line about three EMS long used between DECKS of a headline; also called *jim dash*

short discount less than the full discount For example, some academic books are sold at a 20-percent discount from the retail price, compared to TRADE or popular books sold to bookstores at discounts of 40 percent or more.

short end [film] unexposed blank film remaining in a camera *magazine* after shooting that is not long enough for another *take* The entire magazine is removed for processing.

shortfall the failure of a publication to meet its guaranteed minimum circulation, or *circulation base*, generally resulting in a proportionate credit or rebate to advertisers

short fold a method of folding a sheet with one or more pages shorter than the rest

short-grain paper STOCK with the machine direction of most of the fibers in the shortest sheet dimension

shorthand any system of speed writing using quickly made symbols to represent letters and words; also, to communicate a message without providing all details, the *shorthand version*

short-hour worker a part-time employee, particularly one who works at peak periods of activity

short ink thick, greasy ink that does not spread smoothly, the opposite of *long*, or thin, *ink*

short lighting a type of illumination sometimes used in studio photography for partial profiles (rather than full-face) in which lighting is decreased on the side of the face toward the camera and/or lighting is increased on the side of the face away from the camera; also called *narrow lighting*

short list in a competition, such as an agency selection, the narrowed-down list of finalists

short rate an additional cost incurred for print or broadcast advertising that has not earned a previously planned and billed discount rate

shorts items temporarily not in stock

short screen [computers] a display, as on most personal computers, that is not long enough to show a full letter-size page Most PC screens are 8 inches long, or less than the standard page length of 11 inches.

short spacing 1 [typography] the use of less-than-standard spaces between words 2 [television] the reduction of space between stations on the same channel so that new stations can be *dropped in* The original FCC allocations provided for a minimum of 170 miles between stations on the same channel in the northeast, 190 miles in the west, and 220 miles in the south.

short stop water or diluted acid used to curtail development of film or printing paper

short story a fictional work—a STORY—that is not as long as a novel or novelette and is generally restricted in characters and complexity A *short short story* is briefer, such as a sketch of a character or an incident.

short-story copy a commercial or other advertisement that tells a story, such as a SLICE-OF-LIFE narrative

short-term subscription a periodical SUBSCRIPTION of less than one year

short wave international broadcast transmission in the frequency range of 6 to 25 MHz The carrier waves are sent out so rapidly that the distance between them is short, only about 37 to 150 feet—shorter than the electromagnetic waves used in commercial broadcasting.

shorty the nickname for various small devices, such as a short-legged TRIPOD used with a movie camera

shot an exposure made on a camera; a scene, such as a single continuous filming; a STILL photo of a product (*product shot*); the head of a person (*head shot*); a person from the shoulder upward (*shoulder shot*); a photo taken in a photography studio (*studio shot*) In outdoor advertising, an advertising structure is colloquially called a shot; a well-placed, highly visible *bulletin* or poster is called a *good shot*.

shot box an instrument panel attached to or part of a TV camera with control push buttons for ZOOM and other lens changes

shot breakdown a list of SEQUENTIAL scenes with notations about equipment, positions of equipment and people, and other data

shotgun a *scattered* or dispersed campaign, as contrasted with the selective targeting of a rifle An example is a *scatter plan* of commercials that are broadcast throughout the day. A *shotgun microphone* is a long microphone capable of picking up sound over a great distance, often used in outdoor scenes or large sets.

shotgun head a single headline over two or more columns with two DECKS, each referring to a different article

shot list a sheet or card with a SEQUENTIAL summary of scenes, or shots; also called *shot sheet*

shot plot a drawing, or *plot*, of a photography, film, or taping session, with camera angles and other technical notations

shot/reverse-shot [film, television] the cross-cutting of alternate direct and reverse shots, as in conversations in which the camera shows one person and then the other

shot sheet a SEQUENTIAL list of scenes or other items in a production; also called *shot list*

shoulder an extended flat surface or platform on the body of type on which the raised image is set; the space between the bottom of the letter and the edge of the SLUG or SHANK on which it is cast

shoulder brace   a support for a film or TV camera to hold it on the shoulder of the operator; also called *shoulder pad*

shoulder head   a subheading on a separate line, FLUSH with the left margin of the text; not the same as a SHOULDER NOTE

shoulder note   a heading at the top of a page, generally at the outer corner, as in a text or reference book

shout   an exclamation point, or SCREAMER (not a common term)

show   a performance, program, display, or exhibition   *Show business* is the theater and all performing arts. Performers are *show folk* or *show people*. A *showgirl* is an elaborately costumed woman in the chorus of a musical or variety show. A *showman* is a producer, ideally possessed of a dramatic flair called *showmanship*. A *show-stopper* is part of a scene that receives so much applause that it interrupts the show. A *show town* is a locality where productions are presented; a *good show town* has a generally favorable audience, and a *bad show town* does not. A *show-wise* audience is sophisticated.

show business   a public exhibition or entertainment; all of the performing arts, including broadcasting, movies, concerts, stage, fairs, and circuses; also called *show biz*

showcard   cardboard covered with a thin matte or glossy paper, commonly used for posters and signs; also called *posterboard*   *Showcard lettering* is the single-stroke lettering done by hand by sign writers, generally with a brush or pen; it is also called *sign writing*.

showcard brush   a long, flat brush in a holder used by artists, particularly for lettering, such as on *showcards* and SIGNS; generally called *lettering brush*

showcase   a display case or cabinet; a setting to display a person or item to advantage   In show business, a showcase is a performance, perhaps in a small theater or nightclub, to demonstrate the talent of a performer, as at a solo performance or by a neophyte.

showing   a presentation of a film or tape   In outdoor and transit advertising, a showing indicates the number of advertisements that can be seen by the adult population in an area. A *50 showing* is the number of BILLBOARDS necessary to provide a daily exposure of 50 percent of the adult population in an area. Common showing sizes are 25, 50, 75, and 100.

show print   [film] a high-quality print made for special showings

show stopper   a performance, such as a song, that is so enthusiastically received by an audience that it stops the show during the applause

show-through   the visibility of printed matter on the reverse side of the paper or on the preceding sheet, which generally means that the paper is too light or the printing is too heavy

Showtime   a subscription cable-TV service owned by Viacom International in New York

show tune   a song in a musical comedy or other show

shriek   an exclamation point; a SCREAMER; a SHOUT; a BANNER headline (not a common term)

shrinkage   the loss of items or weight of items due to natural causes or pilfering; the reduction in size during molding and drying of a matrix from which printing plates are cast, which requires enlarging the original or allowance for shrinkage to retain the desired size

shrink lens   an *anamorphic* lens mounted in front of a camera lens to reduce length or width, used to make an advertisement fit into a smaller space

shrink-wrap   a tamper-resistant package with heat-sealed, transparent, tight-fitting plastic covering the entire product; also called *shrink package*

shrunk negative   [printing] a photographic negative or film with the image thinned by reducing the thickness detail to knock out color or background, generally so that a black screen or another color can be printed on that area; also called *choke negative* or *skinny negative*

shtick or **schtick**   a characteristic attribute; a talent or trait; an entertainment routine

Shubert Alley   a private street that runs between West 44th and West 45th streets in Manhattan, onto which the stage door of the Shubert Theatre opens   The Shubert Organization, a company of theater owners and theatrical producers, is renowned in the theatrical world, and Shubert Alley sometimes generically refers to the Broadway theatrical district.

shutter   **1** [photography] a device that opens and shuts the lens aperture of a camera to expose the film or plate   The speed of the shutter (*shutter speed*), size of the opening (*f-stop*), and type of film (*film speed*) are the three variables in determining film exposure.   **2** [theater] movable metal flaps attached to the front of SPOTLIGHTS; also called BARN DOORS

shuttle   an oscillating tooth arrangement that pulls motion-picture film through a projector; also called *claw*

S.I.   sponsor identification

SIA   STORAGE INSTANTANEOUS AUDIMETER

sibilance a hissing sound, such as with *s*, *sh*, or *z*

sic Latin for "thus" or "so"; pronounced sik It is often used within parentheses or brackets to show that an item is precisely reproduced, though it may be inaccurate, misspelled, or questionable.

S.I.C. STANDARD INDUSTRIAL CLASSIFICATION

side **1** [publishing] the front or back BOARD of a book cover **2** [theater] a page with the lines and cues for a performer

sideband [radio] the FREQUENCY or frequencies on either side of a carrier frequency that are generated during the modulation, or variation of frequency

sidebar **1** a news item or feature inserted within, adjacent to, or following a related article; also called *side story* or *with story* When the sidebar follows the main story, it is called a *follow*, is separated by a short dash, and may have its own small headline. **2** a secondary event, as at a convention or fair

sidebearing white space In typing and typesetting, a *leading* (pronounced leed-ing) *sidebearing* is the space before a character, word, or words; a *trailing sidebearing* is the space after it.

side-by-side shot a composite shot in which two images appear simultaneously on the screen side by side; also called *half-lap*

sidecar in cable TV, a small module attached to the converter terminal of the subscriber's TV set to enable the subscriber to order items such as pay-per-view films

side guide a device to align paper on one side, commonly used in photocopy machines and sheet-fed printing presses in which one side is permanent and the other side is flexible in accordance with the size of the sheet

sidehead or **side head** a headline placed in the margin instead of within the type body, used in magazines and books; in newspapers, a headline that starts at the extreme left—FLUSH LEFT—or ends at the extreme right—FLUSH RIGHT To be more precise, it should be called a *flush left head* or *flush right head*.

sidekick a display attached to the edge of a counter in a store

sidelight illumination from the side; incidental information, such as a SIDEBAR or secondary story with color, background, or other human-interest material

sideline a subsidiary category of merchandise; secondary activity; a line of large or DISPLAY type below a photo and preceding the CUTLINE or caption

sideline musician [film] a musician or performer who pretends to be playing an instrument during filming of a scene, with the actual music prerecorded or recorded in postproduction

sideman [music] a band member other than the leader, or *front man*, or a featured soloist

side note a heading in the margin of a page, as in a textbook

side position [advertising] a car-card position along the side—inside or outside—of a bus or other vehicle rather than on the front or rear

sides a partial script with the cues and lines of only one performer

sidesaddle headline a headline used on the side of an article instead of above it

sidesewing or **side sewing** in bookbinding, the passing of the thread through the side of the book along the binding edge, as opposed to SADDLE SEWING, which is threading through the middle of the center folds of each SIGNATURE A side-sewn book cannot be opened fully flat.

sideshow a small separate show in connection with the main show, such as a circus; also, a subordinate event

side sorts characters not in a standard FONT of type; also called *odd sorts*, *pi characters*, or *special characters*

side stage the side of the front area of a stage, used for a NARRATOR, transitory action while the main stage is being changed, or other purposes

sidestitch or **side stitch** the binding with thread (*side-thread stitch*), wire (*side-wire stitch*), or glue of sheets of a publication on the side near the SPINE; different from *saddle stitch*, which fastens the pages through the middle fold of the sheets In side stitching, the pages cannot be opened completely flat.

side title a title impressed into the front cover of a bound book

sidetone in a telephone conversation, the hearing of one's own voice, sometimes a problem in overseas calls

sig. signal; SIGNATURE

sight gag an action joke or bit of comic business fully or mostly visual, dependent on action instead of speech

sightline or **sight line** a line of unimpeded vision from a point in a theater to the stage or screen Some seats have obstructed viewing or are on the periphery or outside of the sightlines. The *horizontal sightlines* pertain to viewing along a horizontal axis, such as from the orchestra floor or main floor. The *vertical sightlines* pertain to viewing along a vertical axis, such as upward from the front row of the orchestra and downward from the balcony.

sight reading   the act or skill of performing from unfamiliar written music, or of translating from something written in a foreign language, readily on sight, without previous study   The verb is to *sight-read* or *sight read*.

Sigma Delta Chi   a professional society of journalists with about 30,000 members, headquartered in Chicago   It publishes *The Quill*, a monthly magazine, and presents annual awards to distinguished journalists and educators. The name has been changed to the *Society of Professional Journalists/Sigma Delta Chi*.

sign   a board; a poster; a placard; a symbol; an indicator, such as an action or gesture to convey an idea, information, or a command   *Sign paper*, specially made for printed signs, generally is a smooth white paper; it is also called *banner paper*. Colored sign paper sometimes is called *background paper*.

signage   a series of signs of varying content, generally with a common design system or other commonality

signal   an indicator; something that incites action; a device or sound that conveys a message; an electrical impulse representing sound, image, or a message transmitted or received in radar, radio, telegraphy, telephone, television, or other means, via wire or in the atmosphere   *Signal area* is the territory within which broadcast signals are received. *Signal strength* is its intensity.

Signal Corps   a branch of the U.S. Army in charge of technical aspects of communication and meteorological, photographic, and other services, but not public information

signals   bells on a wire-service machine to alert news personnel of a bulletin; see also INDEX letters

signal-to-noise ratio   a ratio of the power of a communications signal to unwanted noise; abbreviated as *S/N ratio*

signature   **1** a person's name or an identifying characteristic, such as an individual performer's way of walking, dancing, or talking; a theme song or other audio and/or visual identification of a person or program   **2** [advertising] the name of the advertiser, generally at the bottom or end of an advertising message, sometimes accompanied by the advertiser's symbol or LOGO-TYPE   **3** [music] a sign or signs at the beginning of a STAFF to show the key or time   **4** [book production] a large sheet of paper that has been printed, folded, and trimmed   The section of a book or other publication obtained in this manner may be 4, 8, 12, 16, or more pages and is also called a *gathering* or *quire*. When signatures were folded by hand, the folders initialed their work; hence the word *signature*. The first signa-

ture is not lettered or numbered, as it would be on the title or first page, and is unnecessary, so that signatures usually start with *B* or 2. *J* and *V* also often are omitted to avoid confusion with *I* and *U*. *W* sometimes is written as *UU* or *VV*.

signature cut   a cut or engraving of the LOGO-TYPE or name of a company, organization, or individual

signature mark   a dot, line, number, or other indication on the first page of a SIGNATURE to indicate the sequence of gathering

signature montage   a series of brief scenes at the beginning of a TV news program, SITCOM, or other TV show to introduce the program—its SIGNATURE

signature title   an abbreviated form of the author's name and/or title of a book printed toward the inner margin of the first page of each SIGNATURE   This identification generally is used only with lengthy books and appears on the same line as the SIGNATURE MARK.

signer   slang for a BY-LINED article; a *byliner* or *siner*

significance graf   *Wall Street Journal* jargon for the paragraph in an article with the vital information; usually called *nut graf* or *nut paragraph*

sign-in book   a register, which can range from a fancy leatherbound album to a ruled yellow pad, signed by media people and other guests at a news conference or other event

signing   a collection of signs, particularly display signs; also called SIGNAGE

sign off or **sign-off**   a slang term for the end or an ending; the end of a transmission, or of a station's broadcast day

sign on or **sign-on**   the beginning of a transmission or the day's programming on a broadcast station

signpost   a piece of wood or other material (a post) bearing a sign, particularly on a road to provide directions; a clear indication or clue

sign writing   lettering, generally one letter at a time, not connected writing, on signs, posters, and showcards with a brush or pen; also called *showcard lettering*   Sign painters on a ladder or scaffolding often use a *sign cloth*, a durable oilcloth made waterproof with coats of oil paint.

silent   no sound; abbreviated as *SIL*

silent auction   a fundraising technique, used by public TV stations and others, in which bids for prizes are entered in writing and the top bidder is selected without any interactive bidding

silent cue   [theater] a visual cue, not spoken

silent reading   the checking of a *proof* for grammar, continuity, and clarity but without the original copy; also called *cold reading*   To check against the original copy is *proofreading*.

silent speed in motion pictures, the exposure rate of the film, generally 18 frames per second, which is faster than nonsound, or silent, films, which were 16 frames per second

silhouette an outline; an illustration from which the background has been cut or etched away

silked in deluxe art books, describing a leaf covered with transparent silk

silking a process of repairing or preserving a precious sheet of paper by applying silk chiffon or other transparent material to one or both sides

silk-pajama journalism interviews of celebrities in their homes

silk-screen a method of producing a STENCIL in which a design is imposed on a stretched silk or fabric screen After the blank areas are coated with an impermeable substance, paint or ink is forced through the screen, as with a SQUEEGEE, onto the printing surface. A different silk or fine wire screen is used for each color.

sill iron a strip of metal (iron) at the bottom of a piece of theatrical scenery that functions as a door The metal gives rigidity to the scenery, which often is made of cloth.

silly season a period when news is slow, such as late summer, and news reporters use trivialities

Silurians a New York social organization of older reporters and other media people The membership criterion is employment for 15 or more years at a New York newspaper or other medium. The name is from the Silures, a Welsh tribe conquered about 80 A.D. by the Romans. Today's Silurians are not *that* old.

Silver Anvil an annual award of the Public Relations Society of America (PRSA) in New York, presented for outstanding public relations campaigns in various categories

silver bromide a pale yellow crystalline compound that turns black on exposure to light and is used as the light-sensitive component on photographic film and plates

silver chloride a white granular powder that darkens on exposure to light and is used in photography and optics

silver halides particles of light-sensitive material containing silver As used in photography, these silver salts are suspended in gelatin emulsion and applied to film or paper. A *halide* is a compound of a halogen with another element, in this case silver. A halogen is any of five nonmetallic chemical elements, and silver halides include silver bromide, silver chloride, and silver iodide.

silver iodide a pale yellow powder that darkens on exposure to light, used in photography and as an antiseptic

silver nitrate a corrosive, colorless crystalline powder that darkens on exposure to light and is used in photography, mirrors, and silver plating

silverprint a photocopy used as a printing proof It is a photographic reproduction with principal lines traced in ink that is then bleached to remove the photographic image and used to make accurate line-cut representations. Called a silverprint because the photographic emulsion is sensitized by silver salts, it sometimes is inaccurately referred to as a VAN DYKE or BLUEPRINT.

silver salts compounds containing silver that are light-sensitive, such as SILVER BROMIDE, SILVER CHLORIDE, SILVER IODIDE, or SILVER NITRATE Used in photography, they are also called SILVER HALIDES or HALIDES.

Silver Spur annual awards of the Texas Public Relations Association, Houston, TX

SILVTR silent videotape recording, a notation on the can or reel of a commercial or other videotape without sound, particularly where a live *voice-over* is to be added, so that the studio engineer does not go berserk searching for the soundtrack

sim SIMILE

simile 1 a figure of speech involving comparison or likeness, generally using *like, as, so,* or *such as* "He is strong as a rock" is a simile; "he is a rock" is a METAPHOR. 2 [music] a direction to continue in a similar pattern; abbreviated as *sim*

Simmons Market Research Bureau a New York subsidiary of *MRB* Group, owned by the WPP GROUP, which also owns the J. Walter Thompson advertising agency The *Simmons Study of Media & Markets* includes extensive data on media and consumer purchases. Simmons reports are widely used by media, particularly the *Simmons Study of Local Newspaper Ratings.*

Simon & Schuster a major publisher of books, based in New York, owned by Paramount Communications Inc., merged with Prentice Hall as Simon & Schuster/Prentice Hall

simplex a telegraphic system or other transmission circuit in which only one message may be sent at a time or in which transmission is in only one direction, whereas SIMULTANEOUS TRANSMISSION is transmission of data in two directions at the same time

simulation an imitation; a mock interview for coaching of an interviewee or another type of feigned or rehearsed test; a hypothetical situation or model

simulcast a broadcast of a program at the same time on a television station and a radio station or on two radio stations, generally one AM and one FM

simultaneous-scene setting a stage set that is a composite of two or more locales, formerly called a *multiple setting* and called a *composite setting* in the United Kingdom

simultaneous transmission two-way transmission, such as sending and receiving on the same device

SIN the Spanish Information Network, the name of which was changed to SIN National Spanish Television Network and now is Univision-Spanish International Network, a Spanish-language programming service to UHF and cable TV stations; founded in 1961 and based in New York

Sindlinger & Co. a market research company appropriately located in Media, PA, near Philadelphia Broadcasters, who tend to condense and simplify, often report on surveys conducted by research firms by using the company name as a verb, as an adjective, or by itself, such as the *Nielsens* or *Sindlingers.*

sine qua non an essential or indispensable condition or element; Latin for "without which not"

siner wire-service jargon for a BYLINED article; also called BYLINE or *signer*

sing. singular

singer a person who sings, such as a *background singer* (who sings as part of a chorus, or background, behind a lead singer), *Broadway singer* (who sings in theatrical shows), *cabaret singer* (who sings in nightclubs), *lead singer* (the principal singer in a group), or *lieder singer* (singer of German songs called *lieder*)

Singer sewing in bookbinding, the passing of thread, using a Singer sewing machine, through the middle (SADDLE SEWING) or sides of the sheets It was named after the American inventor *Isaac M. Singer* (1811–75).

singing an undesired continuing audio-frequency oscillation of electrical currents in a circuit, caused by excessive gain or feedback in radio transmission or other unbalances The resonance is akin to humming and is prevented by an *antisinging device.*

single solo, as with a performer working alone; a record with one song

single binding a book with a binding that is heavier or stronger than the regular binding; also called a *reinforced edition*, commonly provided to libraries

single-color press a printing press that can print only one color at a time, as compared to a multicolor press

single-copy sales the sales of publications, particularly magazines, at newsstands and other retail outlets, not to subscribers

single framing the use of a button or other mechanism on a movie camera, called a *single-frame release*, to expose only one frame, as in time-lapse cinematography; also called *single-frame shooting*

single-line store a retailer with a limited line of merchandise, as compared to a *multiline store* with a greater array of merchandise

single-perforation film film, particularly 16mm, with a soundtrack along one edge and perforations, or SPROCKET holes, along the other edge; also called *single sprocket* or *single perf*

single-price policy an offering of all items in a category at the same price, such as all items on a table or retail counter marked down to the same price regardless of the original cost; not the same as *one-price policy*

single printing a process of printing one side of a sheet and then the other side, as compared to *perfector printing*, in which both sides are printed at the same time WORK-AND-TURN and WORK-AND-TUMBLE are methods of single printing.

single-rate card an advertising card of a communications medium with no separate local and national rates

single-space typing without a blank line between the lines of text

single-stroke brush a flat brush commonly used for lettering, sign writing, and other artwork requiring thin lines; also called *one-stroke brush*

single system 1 a system for recording audio and visual components on the same film or tape at the same time 2 [film] a *single-system camera* that records visuals and sound simultaneously on the same film or separately with the sound on a separate magnetic or optical track to be combined on the same piece of film

single-system sound audio recorded directly onto film or tape using a microphone attached to the camera; different from *double-system sound*

singleton a one-line caption, usually in type a little larger than a multiline caption

Singletone a drawing paper with a latent—invisible—screen that produces a shadow on a drawing or other matter when a developer is applied; trademarked by the Craftint Manufacturing Company of Cleveland

single-unit media cassettes, belts, and other recording and storage media that are not endless loops and must be replaced or returned to starting position; also called *discrete media*

sink 1 the amount of blank space at the top of a page above the first line of type, generally an amount of white space greater than usual, such as at the beginning of a chapter of a book or an article in a publication; also called *sinkage* 2 [computers] the point of usage of data in a network, a receiving station of a data transmission—a *data sink* or *message sink*

sinking the placement of sheets behind the blanket of an offset press to maintain its thickness as it gradually wears down; also called *packing*

siphoning [broadcasting] the drawing off of programs by one medium from another, as when network television attracted the most popular programs on network radio or when cable TV transmitted programs previously available on broadcast TV

sister publications periodicals produced by the same publisher

sister station radio or TV stations owned by the same company

sit com situation comedy, a humorous TV show featuring the same characters on each program, generally once a week

site a place or location *At-site* or *on-site* means at the actual location, as of an event.

sit into the shot a direction for a performer to sit down as soon as SHOOTING starts

situationer an article about a continuing event that summarizes the background or history, the *situation*, and also includes analysis or interpretation; slightly different from a BACKGROUNDER, which may not include analysis

SIU SETS IN USE

six C's the factors involved in marketing strategy: commodity (the product), company, competitors, channel members (distribution), consumers, and community (area)

six-sheet poster a relatively small outdoor advertising poster, about 4 feet high and 10 feet wide

16mm film that is 16mm wide

16mo *sixteenmo*, a 32-page (16-leaf) book

625-line the number (625) of horizontal scanning SWEEPS per frame in the European TV transmission system, which produces better picture resolution than the 525-line system that is the standard in the United States

sixty a 60-second commercial, written as :60 Actually, a film generally has 60 seconds of video and 58 seconds of audio to allow for the brief

lag of sound at the start, whereas a tape has 60 seconds of video and audio.

64mo *sixtyfourmo*, a 128-page (64-leaf) book

size [graphic arts] to indicate proportions or dimensions The process is called *sizing*. Size also is a material added to paper to change its ink or water absorbency, such as a preparation made from glue or starch to fill the paper pores to give it a coated finish or a thin, pasty substance used as a stiffener or filler. The process of applying the substance is called sizing, too. *Tub sizing* is the immersion of paper in a tub of glue. Good grades of rag-content bond paper are tub-sized. *Surface sizing* is a process of spraying a sealant on a sheet while it is in the papermaking machine.

Size letters formerly were used to indicate the size of books, such as *F* (FOLIO) and *Q* (QUARTO). *Size rules* are used in various fields to indicate type sizes, photo proportions, and book measurements (a book size rule is 30 centimeters long, with size letters and corresponding SIGNATURE folding symbols).

sized describing paper that has been treated with resin or other substances to make its surface less receptive to water Blotting paper is *unsized*. Offset paper, writing paper, and other heavily sized paper with high degrees of moisture resistance are called *hard-sized*.

size water a mixture of glue and water used for binding (SIZING), such as in paints for theatrical scenery

skate to slide a FLAT—rigid scenery—across a stage floor

sked slang for schedule

skein a television-program series; pronounced skane The word was coined by *Variety* from a skein of yarn, a quantity wound around a coil.

skeleton an outline or sketch; a word with its basic consonants and without its vowels, used in spelling software programs in which vowels and consonants are added to skeletonized words to reconstruct correct spellings To *skeletonize* is to reduce drastically, such as to condense a lead sentence or paragraph into a headline or to eliminate articles and other words for telegraphic transmission. A *skeleton page* or *page frame* is a blank page on which a photo, art, or other material is to be inserted; see also SLIP-SHEET.

skene a long, low building behind the stage of ancient Greek amphitheaters The performers entered and exited through doors in the skene, which was akin to the *backstage* area of modern theaters.

sketch a quick drawing; a rough layout; an incompletely developed story; a short scene, generally humorous, also called a *skit* A *sketchbook* is a drawing pad. *Sketchy* refers to a sketch in that something is superficial or incomplete. A *sketch artist*, more commonly called a *production illustrator*, prepares preliminary plans for film or other sets. A *character sketch* is a short story, play, or other work about an interesting personality.

skew   an oblique or slanting course; to take such an oblique course, to turn at an angle, or to distort; asymmetric, distorted, biased, slanted, or misaligned line. In statistics, skewed data is not symmetrically distributed (as on a bell curve). In television, *skewing* is a slanted or zigzag pattern on the screen.

skid   a support or platform, generally wooden, often used for stacking paper before or after it is printed It can be on rollers to be moved. A skid sometimes is called a *pallet*, but its supporting cross-members are more likely to permit sliding (hence the name, skid) across a surface. A quantity of paper, about 3,000 pounds, often is called a skid. *Skid paper* is frequently used STOCK that a printer buys by the skid. A *skid tag* on a load of work, as in going through a printing plant or bindery, carries the job number and often is color coded for the department to which the skid is moved.

skin   an outer covering or layer; a set of drums; a tracing, perhaps using onionskin paper A *skin drawing* is a preliminary sketch or plan.

skin flick   a movie with emphasis on nudity and explicit sex

skinny   journalism jargon for inside information

skinny negative   a photographic negative or film with the thickness of detail reduced, such as an image thinned down to knock out color or background; also called *choke negative, shrink negative,* or *shrunk negative*

skin pack   a product on a card, tightly wrapped in a plastic film to prevent pilferage or tampering; also called *blister pack*

skip   **1** [marketing] a customer who fails to pay, causing a *skip loss* of the amount owed **2** [recording] a jump over a part of a recording, usually due to a defect

skip charge   [direct marketing] a special charge to a mailer or user of a mailing list for omitting specific names on a list

skip distance   [radio] the length of travel of a reflected or indirect SKYWAVE, the smallest separation between a transmitter and a receiver that permits radio signals to travel by reflection from the ionosphere

skip-frame printing   a motion-picture process of removing FRAMES, such as every second or third frame, to give the illusion of accelerated action or to reduce the length of the film; also called *skip printing*

skip-print   a film print in which the rate of action has been accelerated by deleting frames at regular intervals; also called *skip-frame*

skit   a short form of SKETCH; a short piece of satirical or humorous writing or a short comic play or scene

skiver   soft, thin sheepskin leather split with a cutting device called a *skiver* and used in bookbinding

SKU   stock keeping unit: every color and size of a product, style, or other item in a store

skull   [theater] an admission pass

skull shot   [film] slang for an extreme close-up shot

sky   [television] an overbright area Streaks in the sky are called *comet tails*.

Sky Awards   annual awards to outstanding individuals who have been in the communications field for less than 10 years, started in 1989 by the Chicago chapter of Women in Communications

sky box   promotional material within a border—a *box*—at the top of page one of a newspaper, above the FLAG

sky filter   a disk of colored glass, gelatin, or plastic, usually yellow, that absorbs or filters daylight; commonly used in landscape photography

skyline   a page-one BANNER headline above the NAMEPLATE of a newspaper, used by TABLOIDS and also called *skyline streamer* or *over-banner*

sky pan   a floodlight that produces a wide beam of light

skywave   a low-frequency radio wave reflected by the ionosphere and not radiated into space; also called *indirect* or *ionospheric wave* At night when there is no sun and the ionosphere is less ionized, skywaves are reflected toward the earth to a greater degree. Thus, radio stations are heard at more distant points at night. Radio waves passing along the ground and not emitted toward the sky are called *ground waves*.

skywriting   a process of producing advertising messages in the sky with trails or closely grouped puffs of smoke emitted by an airplane In *skytyping*, the puffs of smoke are closely spaced by two or more planes flying in formation.

sl.   slightly

SLA   SPECIAL LIBRARIES ASSOCIATION

slab off   a common procedure at newspapers in which the printers quickly cut and discard the outer dirty or damaged layers of the *web*, or roll of paper, on the press

slack   loose, slow, sluggish, inactive, or careless; a loose part or condition To *slacken* or *slack up* is to become less active. *Slack-sized paper* is lightly SIZED so that it absorbs water and thus has substandard water resistance.

slack fill an incompletely filled package, containing air instead of the product

slam a harsh criticism Contrary to its use in the card game of bridge, in which a slam is a winner, in show business a *slammer* is a brutal review.

slander oral defamation; not libel, which is in writing

slant **1** an angle; the emphasis or theme of an article or campaign A *slanted view* is subjective or biased. **2** the angle of a typeface *Slant type* (slanted to the right) is called *italic*.

slant bar a diagonal line; also called a *virgule*, SLASH, *slant line*, or *solidus* The origin is the long *s*—ʃ—used in England to separate shillings from pence. A common use today is in the term *and/or*.

slant track a videotape on which the signal is recorded diagonally—on a SLANT—in adjacent strips, as in a helix or spiral; also called *helical scan*

slap theatrical makeup

slapstick crude comedy The literal origin is a wooden implement called a slapstick used by a clown or vaudeville performer to whack the buttocks of another performer for comic effect.

slash a stroke A slash can be a diagonal mark called a *virgule* between letters or words or a horizontal line through a letter or word to designate deletion or editing or inserted for legal reasons. In broadcasting, a slash mark between words means a pause; double slash marks—//—indicate a longer pause. Computer terminals at many newspapers translate a slash into control symbols or other characters, so many wire-service editors use a hyphen instead of a slash.

slash head a headline with two elements, each two lines long, separated by a heavy diagonal line

slate a blackboard slate attached by a hinge to a thin board that is clapped down at the beginning of each TAKE or scene of a film production; also called *skateboard* On the slate is written the SCENE NUMBER and TAKE NUMBER of that scene. The clapping sound is to cue the action. Electronic markers now are used, but identification slates still are common and have a traditional importance in filmmaking. The instruction from the director to the *slateman*, or second assistant cameraman, to clap the sticks together is *slate it* or *stick it*. To slate it does not mean to write on the slate. In one type of automatic slate or slating device, a *slate light* flashes in synchronization with a beep on the soundtrack. The audio equivalent of the slate is called an *audio billboard*, an identification at the beginning of an audio tape, such as a brief designation of the news event, the reporter, the number of the TAKE, and a countdown, such as *three, two, one*. The audio billboard sometimes is called a *slate* or *audio slate*.

slave a device that has no intelligence of its own or acts as if it does not but is driven by the intelligence of another device A slave, or *slave unit*, operates under the control of a master. A *slave computer* is a backup system that is a replica of the master computer and takes over without interruption if the master computer fails or malfunctions. Many typesetters, even though they may have some computer capacity, are driven as slaves by *front-end* systems that make all the computational decisions and simply instruct the typesetter what mechanical activities are to take place. In recording, a *slave unit* is a device that produces copies from a master recording. In photography, a slave unit is a mechanism that activates other flash units linked to the primary flash, such as the one on the camera.

slave machine a computer, duplicator, or other machine controlled by a master unit

sled a bracket that attaches a lighting device to a wall

sleeper a book, movie, or other product that achieves unexpected success A sleeper product that becomes very popular may become a *runner* with repeated orders or reruns of production.

sleeve a protective casing, or jacket, for photographs, artwork, and phonograph records

slewing rapidly rotating an antenna, microphone, or other *transducer*; changing the tuning of a receiver, as in sweeping through all frequencies on a radio set

slice of life a realistically enacted dramatic simulation of a personal life situation, as in a commercial

slick a magazine printed on glossy coated paper, sometimes referring to a superficially attractive publication lacking depth or literary appeal; a proof carefully made on glossy or enamel paper suitable for reproduction, also called an *enamel proof* Co-op ads provided by manufacturers to retailers often are called *slicks*.

slide text, an illustration, or an image printed or reproduced on a transparent plate or film, generally 35mm, and mounted on glass or in a cardboard, plastic, or metal frame (a *slide mount*) for projection (via a slide projector) on a screen A *slide film* is composed of a sequence of slides, perhaps shown rapidly to give the effect of motion or in tandem with other projectors. A *slide commercial* consists of one or more slides. A *slide viewer* is a small device with a built-in viewing glass or translucent screen.

slide-chart a rectangular or circular card—a wheel—with a sliding section, die cut, or other device to combine two or more tables or sets of information, often used as an advertising specialty

slider [broadcasting] a potentiometer—a device for controlling electrical flow—that operates with a straight-line motion instead of a circular one

sliding rate a price for paper, photoprints, or other items, including advertising time and space, that diminishes per unit as the number of units purchased increases

slipcase a protective box for a book open on one side to expose the SPINE

slip cuing [broadcasting] a method of starting a record at its proper speed so that the first few seconds are not too slow The technique, also called *slip start*, is simply to let the turntable rotate at full speed while the record is held in place and released when needed on *cue*.

slippage the purchase of a product with the unfulfilled intention of claiming a promotion reward, such as a refund, coupon, or premium The ratio between such purchases and those by people who claim the reward is usually stated as a percentage of total purchases and is called the *slippage rate*. In continuous printing, slippage is a defect that occurs when one film surface slips while in direct contact with another, resulting in blurred images.

slip proof a *galley* proof; a proof taken of type before makeup, or layout It is different from a *page proof*.

slip-sheet or **slipsheet** a blank sheet of paper inserted between printed sheets to prevent transfer of ink, particularly when just printed The process is called *slip-sheeting* or *interleaving*, terms that also designate the insertion of *skeleton pages* in proper sequence. A skeleton page is a blank page on which an illustration or other item is to be inserted. It is akin to a slipsheet, except that each skeleton page has a marginal or other notation indicating what is to be inserted on it.

slip-tracing tracing an object whose position is shifted to obtain different configurations

slit-card a counter card, poster, or other display piece that is notched or *die-cut* to hold a book or other product

slit on press [printing] to cut printed sheets while on the press and before they are folded

slitting cutting lengthwise into strips or a smaller size In printing, the process is done with cutting wheels or disks on the printing press or on a *slitting machine*. Automated *slitters* and other slitting machines are used to open mail.

slogan a motto or other phrase that is an important part of the message or, in the case of advertisers, the commercial or advertisement

slop [printing] overset material, left after all pages of a newspaper or other publication are filled; also called *slopover*

slopover metal type crowded out of a FORM

slop print an unedited film print quickly developed to look for mechanical defects This quick development, often in portable equipment on the location of the filming, is called *slop-test processing.*

slot a section of the copy desk at a newspaper or other publication where an editor or chief copyreader sits, generally the inner edge of a U-shaped desk A man who works the slot is the *slot man.* A slot is also the location of a program, announcement, news item, interview, or commercial on a broadcast schedule. Communication satellites are positioned—parked—in orbit in slots two or more degrees apart.

slotting allowance a payment by a manufacturer of a food or other product for shelf space—a SLOT—in a supermarket or other store, sometimes required for a new product

slow 1 [photography] a film that is less sensitive to light than fast film or a lens that transmits less light than a fast lens 2 [marketing] poor sales, as in *slow business* or a *slow day* (or night, week, or any other period)

slow clap slow, rhythmic applause by an audience, such as to express impatience before a tardy performance

slow down a broadcasting and theatrical signal to slow down action or to talk more slowly It is conveyed by stretching one's hands, as in pulling taffy.

slow in/slow out [film] a type of *pan*—horizontal movement of the camera—or *traveling shot* in which the camera starts and ends slowly and smoothly

slow motion action shown slower than normal by shooting it on motion-picture film at a rate faster than the standard rate of projection or by slowing the speed of projection, as with a tape machine; also called *slo-mo*

slow news day a day with relatively little *hard news*, or news of consequence; also called a *light news day* The opposite is *heavy news day* (not *fast news day*).

SLR single-lens reflex camera

slug 1 [newspapers] a word that identifies a news story, which may be taken from the headline or the name of the reporter or writer; also

called *catchline, guide, guideline,* or *slugline*
2 [printing] a blank line for spacing   This use is
becoming archaic as its origin is from the HOT-
TYPE era of Linotype and Intertype machines,
when a metal line six POINTS high was called a
slug.   **3** [publishing] to compare the first words
of each line of a revised copy with the previous
versions   **4** [television] a section of blank film
or tape that separates news stories or sequences
Thus, as with many communications words,
the usage started in printing, became common
in newspaper journalism, and then was picked
up in television.   **5** [film] a piece of blank film
injected or *slugged* into a work print to temporarily replace missing footage or for other purposes during the editing   It sometimes is called
a *leader,* though a leader generally refers to the
blank film at the beginning or end of a reel.

slur   [printing] a smudged, smeared, or blurred
impression   A *slurred* sheet may be due to excessive pressure from the press.

slurry   in papermaking, a water suspension,
such as is used for coating paper

Slurvian   a type of spoken English in which a
word is used incorrectly as a result of lazy or
other poor pronunciation and articulation   The
word was coined by John Davenport in a 1949
article in *The New Yorker* magazine. Examples:
"I have a *dense* appointment"; "I'm tired of
pain all these bills"; "It's your turn to *pal* the
canoe."

slush   maudlin or silly sentimentality   In publishing, the *slush pile* (or *slushpile*) consists of
drivel, slop, or useless material or simply unsolicited or unwanted manuscripts.

slush pile   a stack of unsolicited manuscripts

SM   sales manager; STAGE MANAGER; supermarket

small caps (sc)   small-capital letters, uppercase
letters that are almost the same height as the
lowercase letters in the same type style   The
typesetter's direction to set in small caps is to
draw two lines under the desired characters and
write *sc* in the margin.

small format camera   a camera that uses film
2¼" × 2¼" or smaller

small hours   the early hours after midnight and
before dawn, as at media

small letters   letters without *ascenders* or *descenders,* specifically *a, c, e, i, m, n, o, r, s, u, v,
w, x,* and *z*

small-paper edition   a book printed in a smaller
size than a *large-paper edition* printed from the
same type

small press   an alternative, regional, specialized, or other publisher that is more limited
than a full-size publisher

smart   intelligent; possessing several capabilities, as with a *smart terminal* or *smart card,* a
plastic card with a processor and memory used
as a credit card

smarten   to improve in appearance or stylish-
ness; to quicken

smash   **1** in show business, a hit or big success
2 [printing] pressure exerted on printed sheets to
compress and push them together before they
are trimmed and bound   The process is called
smashing. A smash is also a damaged piece of
type. A *smashed* or weak blanket on a printing
press is not firm and can cause an area of excessively light printing.

smash cut   [film] a transition, or cut, from one
scene to another that is abrupt and obvious to
the viewer; also called DYNAMIC CUT

SMATV   SATELLITE MASTER ANTENNA TELEVISION

S.M.C.   selective market coverage: partial distribution to households in specific areas, as with
mailed circulars that are also inserted in newspapers

S-M-C-R-E model   a method of describing the
steps or elements in the communication process: source, message, channel, receiver, effects

SMDR   Station Message Detail Recording, a system of recording various details of telephone
calls

smear   **1** an oily, dirty, or sticky substance or a
stain from such a substance   In printing, too
much ink may cause smearing in which the impression is SLURRED or unclear.   **2** [television] a
video picture in which objects are blurred at
their edges, sometimes because of poor lighting
or a defective tube in the camera   In this bloat-
ed picture condition, the blur usually appears to
extend horizontally.   **3** a sullying, defamation,
or vilification, as in a *smear campaign* in which
a political candidate *smears* an opponent

SMEI   SALES AND MARKETING EXECUTIVES INTER-
NATIONAL

Smithee, Alan   a fictitious name used in film
credits as the name of the director, a procedure
mandated by the DIRECTORS GUILD OF AMERICA
for members who do not want to use their real
names   The counterpart in the theater is
GEORGE SPELVIN, a fictitious name used by performers.

SMSA   STANDARD METROPOLITAN STATISTICAL
AREA

smut   a soiled spot, such as an ink smut; pornographic or indecent talk or writing

Smyth sewing   bookbinding in which sheets are
sewn down the middle, in the *gutter,* before a
backing is affixed, so that even the pages of a
thick book open flat; pronounced smithe   The
continuous thread links each SIGNATURE, or SEC-

TION of pages, with the next. A Smyth-sewn book thus differs from a *side-sewn* or *perfect-bound* book. It was named after David M. Smyth (1833–1907), who invented the first thread sewing machine for books in 1856 and later formed the Smyth Manufacturing Company. Today, the process can be done on several types of machines, and the word sometimes is not capitalized.

SNA systems network architecture: a set of rules to enable communication through computer networks SNA is used by IBM and includes specifications of its products and their relationships—the *architecture.*

snake a cable that combines several cables, as on a stage or in a studio

snake slip an abrasive stick to remove specks or other matter from an *offset* printing plate; also called *etch stick*

snap a photo with high contrast Printing ink with snap has a tacky or adhesive quality and is not overly smooth; also called *snappy* In TV, the snap of the director's fingers is a signal to switch from one camera to another in a process called *snapping the shots.*

snap line [theater] a cord that is saturated with chalk and then snapped against flat scenery to mark the places to be painted

snapper a dramatic close or exit line in a show, speech, or sales presentation; an extra incentive or offer to stimulate purchase of a product

snapshot a photo (*shot*) taken (*snapped*) with a small camera, generally by an amateur A current use, particularly in newspapers and magazines, is to refer to a brief article, particularly about a personality, or a chart or other summary, as a *snapshot.*

snatch basket [theater] a basket used by a prop person to gather (snatch) small props from a stage set

snatch line [theater] a rope (line) that attaches a piece of scenery to a PIPE BATTEN or other holder

sneak 1 the slow fading in or out of sounds or images in a film 2 short for SNEAK PREVIEW

sneak preview a showing of a film prior to its formal opening to gauge audience reaction or to develop word-of-mouth promotion; also called *sneak*

sniffer in retailing, a point-of-purchase display or product with aroma

sniglet a coined word, generally a *portmanteau* word—that is, a combination of two words into one new one Sniglets are a feature of the HBO television program "Not Necessarily The News."

sniper a person who pastes up outdoor posters legitimately, as on BILLBOARD panels, or surrep-

titiously, as with countless posters affixed to walls and traffic poles A *snipe* is a sheet with a retailer's name or other information, affixed to the bottom of an outdoor poster.

snoop a person who pries into the personal affairs of others, a term sometimes used to describe a gossip columnist or investigative reporter; also called *snooper*

snoot [photography] a snout- or cone-shaped shield on a light to direct the beam over a small area

snorkel collection box a mail-collection box placed at curbside, fitted with a chute to receive mail deposited from a vehicle; also called *courtesy box* or *motorist mailchute*

snow 1 [television] fluctuating spots on a television screen resulting from a weak signal 2 a free pass to a theater

snow effects in a film, TV, or stage production, the illusion of snow, such as with white cornflakes blown by a fan

SN, SNR, or **S/R** signal-to-noise ratio

S.N.R. subject to nonrenewal, as with a contract

S.O. SPECIAL ORDER; STANDING ORDER

soak 1 to wet heavily or absorb; to charge heavily 2 [computers] to run a program under closely supervised operating conditions to uncover any problems in the software or hardware The origin is from the immersion or soaking process.

soap dish a plastic container for an audio cassette

soap opera a dramatic SERIAL TV program, originally sponsored on radio mainly by Procter & Gamble and other soap companies; also called *soap, soaps, soaper,* or *daytime drama* (because they originated during the day)

sobriquet a nickname or an assumed name; a fanciful or humorous name or title given by others

sob sister an old term for a news reporter who writes overly sentimental stories

SOC the society section of a newspaper; pronounced sock

social audit an analysis, or audit, of a company or organization in relation to public issues and concerns in its community or society in general

social class a group of people—a division of society—with similar behavior, interests, and values. The six generally accepted stratifications are upper uppers (the social elite and smallest group), lower uppers (nouveaux riches and other high-income achievers), upper middles (professionals), lower middles (white collar, gray collar, aristocratic blue collar), upper lowers (blue collar, the largest group), and lower lowers (unskilled laborers and the unemployed).

Social Register an annual directory of socially prominent people (*high society*), commonly called the *Blue Book* The publication has operated with a minimum of fanfare for a century. Most professional communicators (unless they are listed) are unaware of where it is published, as it is not listed in media directories. It is located at 40 Plimpton Street, Boston 02118. However, this low-key operation may change. As of 1989, companies can advertise in a New York-area local edition called *Local Listings.*

Société Radio Canada the French name of the Canadian Broadcasting Corporation, based in Ottawa, Ontario, which broadcasts in French and English

Society for Collegiate Journalists an organization based in Springfield, MO, with over 30,000 members in about 150 chapters, that evaluates journalism and media programs at colleges

society news announcements of engagements and weddings and reports of parties and other events, originally limited to the rich, fashionable, or influential social class but now including larger segments of the community Society news is reported on the *society page* of a newspaper (generally Sundays) under the direction of the *society editor.*

Society of Professional Journalists/Sigma Delta Chi a professional organization of journalists, headquartered in Chicago

Society of Stage Directors & Choreographers Inc. a labor union (located in New York, on Broadway, of course) of theatrical directors and choreographers

socioeconomic status (SES) the level in society of an individual or group resulting from education, wealth, and other demographic factors A *high-SES* person is more likely to be media rich (having a VCR and other media in the house) and more oriented to print media and informational programs than a *low-SES* person, who is more likely to be media poor and more oriented to broadcast media and entertainment programs.

sock theatrical slang for very successful, as with a *sock show*; also called *socker* or *socko* A *sock line* is a punch line or climax of a joke or scene.

sodium process a film method of combining foreground action with a background shot using a yellow screen lit by sodium vapor lamps and a moving (traveling) matte; also called *sodium light process* or *sodium vapor traveling matte process*

SOF or **S.O.F.** SOUND-ON-FILM; sound film

soft 1 deficient in hardness; subdued in sound; not glaring in color; mild, gentle, not difficult, not trying 2 [photography] A *soft focus* creates a diffused image deliberately through the use of special filters or lenses, gauze, or other materials, or unintentionally due to improper focusing or a dirty lens. A *soft negative* or *soft print* lacks contrast. 3 [marketing] A *soft season* is one in which sales are soft or less than anticipated. A *soft sell* is a subtle or low-pressure method of selling or persuasion.

soft copy 1 a manuscript or other copy that is transient, not final or hard copy; see also *soft news* 2 [computers] a visual representation on a video screen, as compared to *hard copy* on paper

softcover or **soft-cover** the outer STOCK of a publication that is not the same as the inside pages, as on a paperback book A softcover is not as rigid as the *board* or other stock of a *hardcover.*

soft-edge wipe [film, television] a WIPE (an optical effect between two succeeding shots) in which the border between the two images is blurred or softened, such as by shooting out of focus

soften to make soft; to subdue, as in photography; to deemphasize, as in writing or speaking

soft goods apparel, curtains, towels, and other DRY GOODS that are less durable than appliances and other *hard goods*

softly a broadcasting signal: with palm down, the hand is lowered to request that the voice be lowered

soft news feature articles and other journalistic material that are not urgent and not necessarily time-specific or related to a major event (*hard news*); also called *soft copy*, which also refers to a visual display or representation of text on a video display terminal—transient images as distinguished from the permanent printed text (*hard copy*) from a computer

soft out [broadcasting] an instruction to permit a broadcast to go past the scheduled end time

soft return in computerized typesetting, an instruction to remove the automatic line-feed or carriage return so that margination can be changed, as in *variable* WORD WRAP

soft-roll to move a typewriter platen by hand, as to reduce or enlarge the space between lines or to type in a SUBSCRIPT or SUPERSCRIPT

softshoe a nearly noiseless type of tap dancing without metal taps on the shoes

software instructions, programs, and other material used in the operation of computers, as distinguished from the *hardware* or computer machinery

solander a one-piece box for holding books or other items that generally opens from the back (*drop-back*), rather than the front (*drop-front*);

different from a *pull-case*, which has a lower part and an upper cover Invented by *Daniel Charles Solander*, an 18th-century botanist, it is also called a *Solander case*.

solarize to overexpose, as with a photographic film or plate The process, *solarization*, can be intentional, such as to produce a *bas-relief* effect. A *solarized photo* has been overexposed. Solarization can be chemical or electronic and changes colors in film. Blue becomes yellow; red becomes cyan, a mixture of green and blue; and green becomes magenta, a mixture of red and blue.

solecism nonstandard grammar; a language error or impropriety The origin is Soloi, a Greek city where a substandard dialect was spoken.

solid continuous, with no interrupting space Lines that are *set solid* have no *leading*, or interlinear spacing, added between lines and are called *solid matter*.

solid black all black Many publications have restrictions with regard to 100-percent black areas. For example, here are the specifications for advertising in *The New York Times:* Type exceeding 4-pica thickness must be screened to 75 percent of black, except for trademarks up to 1 to 2 inches (depending on length) and reverse areas up to ½ to 1½ inches (depending on length).

solid piece scenery, such as stairs, doors, and windows, that is constructed as a unit; also called *built piece* or *rigid unit* It is different from a *profile piece*, which is a cutout or other scenery designed to represent or emulate an item and is not as fully constructed as a solid piece.

solid state in electronics, utilizing transistors instead of vacuum tubes

solidus a diagonal line, also called a SHILLING BAR, SLASH, or VIRGULE

soliloquy the act of talking to oneself or, in theater, talking to the audience as if the character were thinking, a technique used by William Shakespeare

solo mail an advertisement for one company (rather than several companies, which is *shared mail*) mailed to prospective customers

solubility the amount of a substance that can be dissolved in a solvent; the degree to which a substance such as a solid will mix with a liquid or other solvent

SOM START OF MESSAGE

song a piece of music for voice, performed by a singer; the act or art of singing To *break into song* is to start singing. A song also can be a poem in a regular metrical pattern designed to be sung. *Song and dance* is slang for an explanation that is evasive or pointless, as in to give someone a song and dance. A *songbird* is a

woman singer. A *song cycle* is a series of songs by a composer that form a single work. A *song-fest* is an informal gathering of people for singing, particularly *folk songs*.

song-and-dance man a leading male performer in a musical comedy

song plugger a promoter of popular music

songwriter a person who writes the words (*lyrics*) or music, or both, for popular songs

The Songwriters Guild of America a New York organization of songwriters Originally called the *Songwriters Protective* Association and then *The Songwriters Guild*, it merged with the *American Guild of Authors and Composers* and was called *AGAC/The Songwriters Guild*. The AGAC then was dropped from the name, though the group still provides AGAC services, including the *AGAC Uniform Popular Songwriters Contract*.

sonnet a poem, generally 14 lines with a specific verse and rhyme format, often iambic pentameter (alternating accented syllables in a line of five segments) Well-known *sonneteers* include Dante and Shakespeare.

soon as possible (S.A.P.) an instruction to rush

SOP or **S.O.P.** standard operating procedure, an instruction that normal basic routine is to be followed

sore-thumb display a *counter card* or other retail display that is so conspicuous that it stands out like a sore thumb

sort 1 to arrange by class, kind, or size in alphabetical or other order 2 [typography] an individual character in a FONT of type; also, symbols, characters, and designs not in a regular font To be *out of sorts*—cross or ill-humored—originated in the days when a printer might run out of type.

S.O.T. sound-on-tape: sound and video recorded on the same machine, as distinguished from *sync-sound* recording with separate video and sound tape recorders

sotto a command, as in broadcasting, to speak softly The word derives from the Italian *sotto voce*, or "under the voice," for an undertone or a whisper.

soubrette the role of a pretty, flirtatious young woman, particularly a lady's maid or dance-hall singer, or the actress who plays this coquette

sound the sensation of hearing produced by vibratory waves The programming format or orientation of a radio station, such as rock or country, is called its sound. A *sound engineer* is responsible for the audio portion of a broadcast or film. The *sound-effects person*, generally called *sound man*, is responsible for the SOUND EFFECTS, or sounds other than music and human voices, abbreviated as *S.E.* or *S.F.X.* An interior area for filming motion pictures, a *sound stage,* is soundproof (not penetrable by outside sound), acoustically controlled, and suitable for simultaneous sound recording and filming; it originated in the early days when sound was added to silent movies. In film and TV, *direct sound* is from a source onscreen, as compared to *offscreen sound,* whose source is offscreen.

sound advance   the distance on a piece of film between a frame and the point in the soundtrack with its synchronized sound Optical sound is ahead—in advance—of its corresponding image, but magnetic sound is 28 frames behind its image on 35mm film.

soundbite   the audio track of a portion of a radio or TV interview A 15-second soundbite is common on radio newscasts.

sound box   a chamber in a violin or other musical instrument that intensifies the sound

sound crew   [film] the personnel in charge of recording sound, headed by a *sound mixer* and including a *sound recorder* or *sound camera operator, boom operator,* and others The sound crew is part of the *sound department,* which also includes the *sound editor* or *mixer* and *sound cutters.* A *sound cutter* or *track layer* places the soundtracks in proper relation to the picture.

sound dissolve   an overlapping of two sounds as one fades out while the other fades in; also called *cross-fade*

sound editor   [film] the person responsible for combining (*mixing*) the various soundtracks into a master soundtrack, more commonly called a *mixer* or *sound mixer,* as the sound editor sometimes is responsible only for some of the tracks, such as the SPECIAL EFFECTS tracks The other tracks are handled by the ADR EDITOR (dialogue), music editor, and others. The *supervising sound editor* supervises all these sound editors, assisted by an *assistant sound editor,* who is assisted by an *apprentice sound editor.*

sound effects (SE, S.E., SFX, or **S.F.X.)**   animal, traffic, weather, and other sounds other than dialogue and music, produced from an actual source or artificially, for use in broadcast, film, stage, or other production Sound-effects records, tapes, and tracks may be obtained from sound-effects libraries or produced by sound-effects consoles. See also FOLEY.

sounding board 1 a thin, resonant plate of wood in a musical instrument, such as a piano or violin, also called *sound board* 2 a person or group used for the testing of ideas, concepts, or proposed campaigns; a group or device to promulgate an idea

sound log   a sequential record of sound recordings made during a production; also called *sound report*

sound loop   a piece of audio tape or soundtrack film that is attached at both ends to form a loop This endless tape can be played continuously to repeat the sounds of rain, ocean waves, traffic, or other sound effects.

sound mixing   the recording of a soundtrack from one or more other soundtracks Actually, it is RERECORDING, also called DUBBING.

sound-on-film (SOF or **S.O.F.)**   a sound film; sound recorded on film

sound on sound   the DUBBING or adding of sound to an existing soundtrack

sound presence   the appearance or effect of the audio on a film or tape coming from the area in the scene where the speaker or sound source is located This matching of the sound presence with the specific area of the video is called *sound perspective.*

sound recordist   [film] a person in charge of recording sound during shooting; also called *floor mixer* or *sound mixer*

sound roll number   [film] a number on each roll of magnetic tape or film on which sound has been recorded

sound sheet   a flat magnetic piece of vinyl used for recording, such as dictation

sound speed   the rate of motion necessary to reproduce sound properly, such as 24 frames per second in a 16mm film projector

sound stage   a soundproof studio, a common term for the indoor stages used in film production At a major film company, such as Universal Studios, the many sound stages, which resemble warehouse buildings, are numbered. Some numbers, such as 7 and 13, are omitted for superstitious reasons.

sound synthesizer   an electronics device that produces music or speech from its constituent amplitude/frequency characteristics

soundtrack or **sound track**   the audio portion of a film or tape In a film, the track is a thin band along one side with an image (*variable area track*) or bars (*variable density track*) that modifies a beam of light to reproduce the recorded sound.

sound truck   a vehicle equipped with a loudspeaker, usually on top, used in electioneering and for other purposes

soup   film developer, a chemical solution that makes the exposed image visible *Soupy* means foggy or, in recording, describes sound that is mushy or not clear.

source   a person or point of origin, such as an individual or organization that provides information to a journalist A news source may be anonymous or, preferably, identified. The source of a news release generally is identified in the upper left corner of the first page. A *source book* or *source file* is a collection of individuals and organizations capable of providing information and also a primary document, such as a basic reference book.

source-control drawing an engineering diagram or design that shows the name of and other information about the manufacturer, contractor, or other source of the equipment or other item and is labeled such adjacent to the title

source language in a bilingual dictionary, the language that is defined In a French–English dictionary, the source language is represented by the entry words in French, the TARGET LANGUAGE being their English definitions.

source music music that is adapted, or *borrowed*, from earlier music, such as popular music with melodies the same or similar to classical music, a technique frequently used for background music in films

source program [computers] a data processing program written in the language of the *compiler* or *assembler*, such as BASIC or COBOL, and then converted into compatible computer or machine language (called an *object program*)

south the bottom part, such as on an animation chart; slang for failure, as in an idea or campaign that "goes south" (However, a successful campaign is not hailed as going north.)

Souvenir a SERIF typeface

SOV SHARE OF VOICE

soybean-oil ink ink made from soybean oil instead of petroleum, commonly used in color printing, particularly of newspapers

sp spell out, a proofreader's abbreviation

sp. special; specialist; spelling

space 1 an area; in music, an interval of silence or time; in telegraphic transmission, a blank interval

2 [advertising] the portion of print media, including outdoor and transit, available for advertising (The broadcasting equivalent is *time*; advertising buyers are called *space* and *time* buyers.) Advertising space may be purchased from a *space rep*, a sales representative of a publication, perhaps at a *space discount* for frequency, volume, or other factors from the regular *space charge* in accordance with a *space schedule*, a list of specified media, dates, sizes, position, and other requirements. A *space spot* is a small advertisement sold at a reduced price in specified quantities, such as 78 over a 13-week period, with no specific space designation. In outdoor advertising, *space position value*

(SPV) is a measurement of the value of a specific location regarding its size, angle to the roadway, and visibility, the number and speed of travelers, and the amount and distance of other advertising. Values range from 100 percent (best) to a *zero panel* (worst).

3 [journalism] an area in a publication A reporter sometimes is assigned to write for a specific space, such as a story that when set in type will fill 15 column inches. A story that's too long is *over space*; one that's too short is *under space*. Publicists refer to an area in a print medium devoted to publicity as space, sometimes called *free space* because it is not purchased as an advertisement. A *space grabber* is a publicity seeker, a term that may be used with a negative connotation.

4 [exhibitions] an exhibit area, an exact location that is indicated by a *space number* The *space rate* is the rental cost per square foot of the exhibit area.

5 [typography] the area between typographic elements *Spacing* is the arrangement of the elements, as in *letter spacing*, *word spacing*, or *line spacing*; sometimes the spaces themselves are called *spacings*. The space between lines is reserved for the *ascenders* and *descenders* of the letters. A *space band* is a thin wedge-shaped device used in typesetting to create spaces between words and to justify lines. Spaces or *space characters* are pieces of blank type metal of less than type height and of varying thickness used to create spaces. *Proportional spacing* is typing or typesetting in which each typed character occupies a space equivalent to its width. A *fixed* or *required space* is a special character that prints as a space and can be used within a word where, for example, a letter is intentionally deleted. The symbol for a space, called *leading* in typesetting, is #. A *space dot* is a center dot.

space allocation [marketing] the area on a floor or shelf of a store or other retail outlet allotted to a product

Space Available Mail (SAM) a reduced-rate category of the Postal Service for military parcels transported by land to an exit port and then flown on a space-available basis to an overseas destination

spaceband in typesetting, the space between words; also called WORDSPACE Originally, a *space band* was an actual thin wedge-shaped device used in hot-metal typesetting machines to expand the space equally between words in order to spread a line and obtain justification. Some modern typesetters also have *vertical spacebands* for line spacing to fill out a page or other depth.

space blanket [photography] a lightweight reflective sheet, usually plastic taped to a wall, to soften light bouncing off it

space code [computers] a command that instructs the typesetting or other machine to skip a determined space, indicated on a manuscript by a symbol, usually _ or #; also called *skip code*

space miser a *point-of-purchase* display that fits on a shelf, holds products, and also has a promotional message; also called SHELF MISER

space out in typesetting, an instruction to add space between characters, words, lines, paragraphs, or elsewhere in order to fill a particular width or depth The process is called *spacing out*. The condensation of space for the same purpose is called *spacing in*.

spacer a blank piece of film used to fill in spaces during editing A spacer may also be a round device placed between film reels to keep them aligned for feeding film into and taking it up from a SYNCHRONIZER, an editing device that uses two or more reels.

space segment [telecommunications] a scheduled time slot on a satellite; also called WINDOW

space spot special small advertising sizes, generally ranging from 25 to 100 AGATE lines, available at some newspapers at a reduced rate if ordered on a regular basis, such as a 30-percent discount for a minimum of six insertions per week for six consecutive weeks

spacing the arrangement of blank areas, such as between characters, words, or lines, or the space itself

spadea a newspaper term for a single sheet inserted in a comics or other section and folded over the front, often containing advertising

spaghetti Western a movie set in the American West, filmed in Italy with a mostly Italian cast, with English dubbed in; generally low budget Common in the 1960s, spaghetti Westerns sometimes featured American performers, notably Clint Eastwood, and also were made in Yugoslavia and Spain.

Spanish finish in bookbinding, a cloth cover coated with an antique finish of plastic

Spanish n the letter ñ The TILDE above the letter indicates a soft pronunciation—nya.

spanner heading a primary heading in the top, or *boxhead*, of a columnar table that encompasses two or more column headings, or *subspanner heads*

S paper *stabilization paper*, common in typesetting because it is quickly processed

sparklies a type of NOISE picked up by a TV receiver due to a weak signal, consisting of black-and-white dots that are sharper than the more common *snow*, or soft dots

sparks a studio electrician; a radio engineer or operator

Spartan a SANS-SERIF typeface

speakerphone a telephone with a speaker-microphone, thus permitting hands-free conversation by one or more individuals

spear a headline under a photo that is one column wider than the photo

spear bearer [theater] a walk-on performer, such as a soldier; also called *spear carrier* The origin is the battle scenes in opera and other works in which the soldiers carried spears.

spec 1 specification, the plural of which is *specs* or *spex*; to specify or indicate the requirement or instruction, such as to *spec type* **2** speculation, such as a proposal prepared without obligation of payment, *on spec* or on speculation that it will be accepted and paid for

special a single radio or television show that replaces regularly scheduled programming; a one-shot

special character [computers] a graphic character other than a letter, digit, or space, such as a punctuation mark, dollar sign, or other symbol

special delivery a system of the U.S. Postal Service, available for all classes of mail except Express Mail, that provides preferential handling in processing and delivery

special edition an edition of a book or other work that differs from the original with regard to one or more distinctive features, such as paper, binding, illustrations, or new material A library edition with a strong binding sometimes is called a special edition. A newspaper or periodical devoted to a special subject, such as an anniversary, may be called a *special edition*, *special issue*, or *special number*.

special effects (SFX, SPFX, SP-FX, or SP-EFX) visual effects produced optically, electronically, or by other artificial means, rather than direct recording of live action; also called *optical special effects, special optical effects, special photographic effects*, or *special effects cinematography* They can include sound effects but generally refer to visual illusions. Manipulative camera or laboratory tricks include such standard opticals as DISSOLVES, FADES, *freeze-frames, inserts, split-screens,* SUPER-IMPOSITIONS, and *wipes,* and also such constructions as mechanical beasts, miniatures, models, the appearance of bleeding and flying, and weather conditions like fog, rain, and snow. A *special-effects generator (SEG)*, which often is part of a SWITCHER, is a device that creates special effects. The special effects crew, managed by a *special-effects coordinator* or *visual-effects supervisor,* works in a *special-effects department* or at a separate, specialized *special-effects company.*

special event a project, program, action, or *happening* generally involving public participation, such as a performance or competition designed to obtain publicity or other exposure

special feature [broadcasting] weather, traffic, and stock-market reports or other broadcasts of particular interest that may be sold at a higher advertising rate than RUN-OF-STATION

special fraction (SF) [typography] a numerator, SLANT BAR, and denominator in which the numerator is slightly higher than the denominator, which is on the BASELINE, whereas a SHILLING FRACTION is all on the same line (Here's a special fraction: ³/₄.)

special-interest publication a periodical with a particular theme or appeal; not a general-interest publication, though it may have an enormous circulation *National Geographic* and *Modern Maturity* are among the world's biggest-circulation magazines, though (or perhaps because) they are of special interest.

Special Libraries Association (SLA) an international organization of professional librarians and information experts, based in Washington, DC

special number a special issue of a newspaper or other publication, such as one commemorating an anniversary (*anniversary issue* or *anniversary number*) or devoted to a special subject, with or without a special identifying or SERIAL number

special order (S.O.) a nonroutine purchase, such as in bookstores and other retail outlets when a customer orders an item not in stock

specialty advertising a medium of advertising, sales promotion, and motivational communication employing imprinted, useful, or decorative products called ADVERTISING SPECIALTIES A specialty-advertising supplier manufactures, imports, converts, imprints, or otherwise produces or processes ad specialties that are offered for sale through distributors.

Specialty Advertising Association International (SAA) a trade association in Irving, TX, of manufacturers and sellers of advertising specialties Total sales volume of the industry is estimated at over $3 billion per year.

specification-control drawing an engineering diagram that includes names and addresses of the suppliers of the components and other information about the item It is labeled *specification-control drawing* adjacent to the title.

specification cover board a type of paperboard, generally between .06″ and .12″ thick, used for book covers

specifications a detailed—specific—description of something to be produced; commonly called *specs*, or *spex* A *specifier* is a person who prepares the items in a set of specifications, such as a graphic-arts designer who specifies the type, paper, and other details of a printing or other graphic-arts project, sometimes writing the specs on the copy (*specified copy*, abbreviated as *spec'd*).

specification tree a chart of the sequential steps in a process or system, arranged like a tree with a trunk and branches; also called CHECK-OUT CHART

specimen page a sample page to show type and other features

specs SPECIFICATIONS

Spectacolor **1** a trademarked technique for printing four-color advertisements on rolls of paper with electronic scanning cues so the pages can be cut and inserted in a newspaper; developed in the 1960s, now generic for pre-printed gravure roll-fed newspaper inserts **2** a company, Spectacolor, Inc., that operates an electronic sign, at 1 Times Square in New York, with animated advertisements and messages

spectacular a large, elaborate outdoor advertising display with animation or other special effects; an elaborate show

spectrogram a diagram, graph, or photograph of a SPECTRUM, such as the relative sensitivity of a photographic material to different colors of light

spectrum a bank of colors produced when sunlight passes through a prism, consisting of red, orange, yellow, green, blue, indigo, and violet; a continuous series of colors or any broad sequence or range of related items

specular in stage, film, and other productions, the reflection from a performer's eyes or teeth A *speculum* is a mirror. *Specular light* or hard light is a narrow spotlight beam, generally used to produce sharp shadow edges. In television, it refers to a moving area of bright light on the picture.

speculation (spec) contemplation Writing, art, or other work may be submitted *on spec* in the hope that it will be accepted and paid for.

speculum a mirror or reflector in an optical instrument *Specular* refers to a mirrorlike substance or device or something produced by a mirror, such as reflected light waves.

speech the art or manner of speaking; a talk given to an audience; the language, dialect, or tongue of a group of people; the study of the theory and practice of oral expression A *speechmaker* is a person who makes a speech; a *speech writer* writes speeches. A speech or discourse can be prepared or impromptu. An *address* is a more formal, more carefully prepared speech. An *oration* may be more eloquent and a *talk* more informal. A *speech transcript* is a written record of a speech.

speech synthesis   the production of speechlike sound via an electronic device, a SPEECH SYNTHESIZER

speech synthesizer   an electronic device that produces sounds corresponding to spoken words according to stored text or command

speech tag   an attribution, such as "he said" or "she stated"

speed   the operating rate of a device, such as revolutions per minute   *Film speed* is the rate at which the film reacts to light, generally expressed as an *ASA number*, or the rate at which the film is projected in FRAMES per second. The speed of a lens is its widest possible F-STOP setting; the larger the f-stop (as indicated by smaller f-stop numbers), the faster the speed of the lens. With film, the sensitivity of the emulsion to light also is expressed as speed. A high-speed or fast-emulsion film is more photo-sensitive and is used in dim or low light; slow-speed film is used in bright light. Speed is also a cue indicating that a tape or movie camera or projector is turned on, has reached the proper speed, and is ready for action. To bring a performance or project *up to speed* is to operate in the optimum manner for success.

Speedball   a line of pen points commonly used by artists for lettering on posters, signs, and displays   *Speedball pens*, which are made in a variety of shapes with various nib, or point, sizes, produce a smooth, rapid stroke, a style of lettering called *Speedball writing*. The word is sometimes used generically. Speedball products are made by the Hunt Manufacturing Company in Philadelphia

speed calling   a technique of telephoning with a code, usually one, two, or three digits, instead of the entire telephone number, to selected programmed numbers, such as commonly called numbers; also called *abbreviated dialing*

speed lines   lines drawn behind figures in comics or animated films to indicate motion

speed table   a dump bin or display area in a bookstore or other retail outlet for items at a sale price or set up for fast movement

speed up   a signal to a performer to talk more rapidly   The nonverbal speed-up signal is both hands rotating in a circular motion.

spelling error detection   in word processing, a program with a dictionary of words in storage to detect incorrect spellings

spelling table   See SYLLABARY.

Spelvin, George   a name used on a theater program to conceal the performer's real name, perhaps because he or she is appearing in more

than one role   If the character in the play dies, *George X. Spelvin* sometimes is used. The female equivalent is Georgia or Georgiana Spelvin.

spex   SPECIFICATIONS

SPH   sheets per hour, the number of sheets of paper that pass through a printing press in one hour

spherical aberration   an optical defect, such as in a camera lens, in which light rays passing through the lens do not come to a common or sharp focus

spherical antenna   a large, round-surface (*not* parabolic or concave) antenna used to receive satellite TV transmission

spider   [film] a metal device to support the legs of a camera TRIPOD that opens to form a horizontal Y shape: >—   It is similar to another device called a *triangle*. Both are used when the tripod is on a slippery surface.

spider box   a small, portable receptacle for several electrical outlets, such as for lighting units; also called *junction box*   It is commonly used in film, theater, TV, and exhibitions.

spider dolly   a camera mount with projecting legs on wheels; also called *spyder*

spiff   [marketing] an incentive, such as an extra commission, to a salesperson to sell a specific item; also called *push money (P.M.)*, and sometimes referred to as *99*   The salesperson who sells a P.M. item, such as an unpopular model of shoes, or a *dog*, is *spiffing* the customer, so the word also refers to taking advantage, particularly of a gullible person. A salesperson eager for push money is a *spiffer* or *P.M. hound*.

spike   1 [newspapers] a six-inch-long nail or spindle on which stories are placed for later use or because they are rejected   *Spike it* means to kill a story or cancel a project. Stories put *on the hook* are rejected, or spiked.   2 [computers] a *line hit* or irregular current surge that can disrupt and damage a computer or other electrical system   3 [theater] to mark the positions of scenery or props on a stage, as with chalk, tape, or a peg called a spike, on the floor   *On the spike*, or *on spike*, refers to an item in its proper position.   4 [marketing] a unique quality of a product or service, a marketing niche

spill   to pour out or spread beyond limits   In broadcasting, a *spill-in* is the transmission of a radio or TV signal into a secondary market area from the original area; a *spill-out* is the transmission from the original area. *Spill-in circulation* or *coverage* measures the circulation of a newspaper outside the original market. *Spill light* is extraneous illumination from a light.

spill-in   the extent of exposure to media from outside an area

spill-out the degree to which a medium reaches outside its headquarters area

spin **1** [writing] a new angle or fresh approach, as in to *put a spin* on a story or project, in allusion to spinning or rotating An older meaning is to draw out a lengthy story, as in *spinning a yarn* on a spindle. **2** language used to slant, twist, or manipulate a position, concept, or event or an interpretation or modification designed to alter the public's perception of it—to *put spin* on a statement Spinnish, a play on the word Spanish, is the language of *spin control*. The origin of spin is the twist given to a billiard ball, tennis ball, or other ball. It is now a common word in politics and reported on by journalists.

spin control the management of communications; from tennis, in which the player controls the spin of the ball To put a SPIN on a story, speech, or other item is to give it a *twist*, a new *angle* or dimension. A *spin doctor* is an expert at spin control, primarily in politics, who might call a *spin moratorium*, or truce, with the opposition.

spindle a slender rod or pin, such as the shaft onto which film reels are mounted during viewing or rewinding In retailing, a spindle is a device attached to a shelf to hold a display or a small amount of product; it is also called a *J-hook*.

spine **1** [printing] the backbone of a publication connecting the front and back covers; in a book, the part of the binding that conceals the back or bound edge and usually bears the title—*spine title* or *back title* **2** [typography] the main curved arc section of the letter *S* **3** [television] the basic plot or story line of a dramatic series

spinner display a revolving floor stand with shelves for paperback books, drugs, or other retail items

spinoff a product, show, or other item derived from an existing or earlier work

spiral binding a coiled wire binding for a publication, such as a reference book or notebook

spirit duplicator a machine that reproduces copies that are pressed in direct contact with the master, akin to a MIMEOGRAPH machine The process is called *spirit duplicating* or *fluid duplicating*, because the paper is moistened with the vapor (*spirit*) of a duplicating fluid; a small amount of carbon from the master is dissolved to produce the image. A major manufacturer is the A.B. Dick Company of Chicago.

spirit gum a sticky substance, generally gum arabic dissolved in ether, used to attach a false beard, mustache, or other items to a performer's face

splash in English newspapers, the lead story

splayed M [typography] a letter, M, in which the outer strokes come outward

splice [broadcasting, film] to join together, electronically or mechanically, with glue, heat, or tape The connection itself is called a splice; a *splice failure* is a break in a splice. *Splicing* often is done on a device called a *splicing block* or *splicer*, a grooved platform also called a *splicing bar* or *edit bar* that links the end of one piece with the beginning of the next (a *butt splice*) or creates a transition (*lap splice*). A *butt splice* has the two joined ends abutting each other. A *lap splice*, which is more common, has the two narrow ends overlapping. A *negative splice* is a narrow piece of transparent negative film used as a lap splice. A *positive splice* is a wider piece of positive film, sometimes used to repair a print. A *hot splice* uses cement applied with heat and pressure by a *hot splicer*, whereas *tape splicing* is done with Scotch tape or other clear adhesive tape, to produce a *cold splice*. The former is more effective but results in a slight loss of tape due to the overlap of the joined pieces. A feature film involves thousands of negative splices. A television network or station may impose a *splicing charge* for inserting a film or tape commercial into a program.

spline a long, flat, flexible strip, generally plastic but also wood or metal, used by artists to create curves, particularly large curves It can be bent to any curve and kept in that position by hooking weights onto a groove in the strip. A FRENCH CURVE is a type of spline that often is used for smaller curves.

split 30 two 30-second commercials broadcast separately during the same program and charged as a single 60-second commercial, which is less than the charge for two 30s

split commercial two commercials for different products of the same sponsor, broadcast consecutively and sold as one unit; also called *piggyback*

split focus a technique to give the same clarity to two subjects at different distances from the camera

split frame two or more scenes shown simultaneously on different parts of the movie or TV screen; also called *split image* or *split screen*

split galley a *galley proof* cut to a shorter length, such as in half, to make it easier for reviewers to read

split head a headline of more than one line Headline writers try to avoid *bad splits* in which one line is incomplete, dangling, ambiguous, or disconnected.

split leather leather that has been divided into two or more thicknesses for use in bookbinding

split page the front page of an inside section of a newspaper; also called *break page* or *second front page*

split play a news article in which one side of an issue is presented prominently first and the other side receives less time and attention This unbalanced treatment may be due to an inability to obtain quotations or material from the second side.

split reel a type of film reel with a removable side, so that film can be inserted or removed without winding; used in film editing In silent film, a split reel was a short movie that did not fill an entire reel.

split run 1 [advertising] a method by which an advertisement appears in different forms in various copies of the same issue of a publication for purposes of testing 2 [direct marketing] a comparison of the pulling power of different advertisements mailed to equivalent audiences

splitscan a special-effects animation, such as the illusion of a tunnel obtained by photographing through a slit with a moving camera

split week in show business, a week *on the road* in which a touring performer or group works in more than one place

spoilage printed matter damaged or spoiled in printing or binding, generally anticipated by the printer

spoken-word publishing the production of recorded readings of books or other material

spokesperson an individual who speaks on behalf of a government agency, company, or other organization Although a spokesperson generally is employed by the sponsor, some organizations have found it useful to retain, on a full- or part-time basis, individuals who represent them by virtue of expertise or other interests that make them publicizable or influential.

spoking distortion of film on a reel due to excessive curl

spondee a metrical foot with two successive stressed syllables, such as the word "heartbreak"

sponsor a broadcast advertiser who pays for part or all of a program The word now is used loosely to indicate any broadcast advertiser, including a sponsor of an individual SPOT or commercial. *Sponsor identification (S.I.)* is the announcement at the beginning and/or end of a sponsored program or one with several *participating sponsors.* A single sponsor may own the program and seek sponsor identification with the program or performers on the program. In the financial community, *sponsorship* refers to the investment firm or other company that stands behind or recommends a stock or bond issue.

sponsored book a publication subsidized in full or part by a company or other sponsor with a vested interest, such as a book about or related to the company's history, personnel, or products

sponsoring editor a person at a large book publisher who has overall responsibility for a manuscript but does not necessarily do the actual editing

spoof a hoax, joke, or deception; light parody or satire; to deliberately induce a user of a communications, computer, or other system to act incorrectly in relation to the system, or to deliberately cause a component of the system to perform incorrectly In data communications, *spoofing* is a technique to enable several computers to be linked with different types of terminals.

spool a cylinder or roller on which tape, wire, or other material is wound

spooling 1 [recording] the movement of tape from one reel to another without being in the recording or playback mode 2 [computers] the process of temporarily storing data on a disk or tape for later processing

spoonerism an unintentional pronunciation error or *slip of the tongue,* particularly the interchange of the parts of two or more words The term was named after Rev. W.A. Spooner (1844–1930) of Oxford University, who was renowned for such slips.

SportsChannel an all-sports regional cable network based in New York

SportsVision an all-sports regional cable network based in Chicago

spot 1 a small mark; a spotlight; a location In photography and other fields, to spot is to remove white spots, as with a brush. *Spotting out* is the removal of spots or other defects with a scraping knife or the application of a transparent dye; it is also called *opaquing.* A *rifle spot* is a cylindrical spotlight that emits a narrow beam of light, generally over a long distance. A *hot spot* in a scene is excessively lighted. In outdoor advertising, a *spotted* or *spotting map* indicates the location of BILLBOARDS or other advertisements. In retailing, a *spot display* is created to be conspicuous. Print media use *spot news,* which is hard news, particularly late-breaking items, as opposed to *feature news.* 2 [printing] a decorative typographical unit, not a smudge A *spot correction* is made in a specific area without replacement of type or other elements. *Spot color* is a dab (or more) of color added to a black-and-white layout. A *spot drawing* is a small drawing, sometimes called a *vignette,* added to a text layout. 3 [broadcasting] advertising time purchased on an individual basis as compared to a multistation network or other national purchase The broadcast commercial itself is called a spot or *spot announcement.* News items, public service messages, and segments of a program also are called spots. The *first spot* opens a show; the *last spot* closes it. A *wild spot* is a spot announcement of a national or regional advertiser used on station breaks between programs on a local station. A *spot carrier* is a syndicated program available to several advertisers. *Spot programming*, or *spotting*, is the purchase of time by *spot buyers* from local stations as indicated on a *spot schedule*, or list of spots, which is so extensive that local station advertising in general is called spot or *spot sales* on *spot radio* or *spot TV.* Spots purchased on network programs are called network participation or *network spot buy.* A *spot program* is a local broadcast.

spot display a merchandise arrangement prominently displayed in a store, perhaps with an attention-getting sign or device

spot glue adhesive in a small area, such as for fastening a TIP-ON to a sheet of paper

spotlamp a bulb used in a SPOTLIGHT or, sometimes, the spotlight itself

spotlight 1 a light with a directed beam; a *spot* Most of the lights in film studios and theaters are spotlights, with considerable range in sizes and with many colorful names. An *open-faced spotlight* does not have a focusing lens in front of the bulbs. A common lens is the FRESNEL lens. *Spotlighting* is the illuminating of a person or area to produce a circle of light. In show business, to spotlight is to give favored treatment or a featured position on the program. 2 [marketing] the absence of inventory

spot meter a *reflected light meter* used on or with a camera; also called *spot brightness meter* or *spot exposure meter* This type of meter has a narrow angle of acceptance and is used to point toward a subject and measure light from small areas. An *incident light meter*, in contrast, measures light falling on a subject and is pointed toward the camera.

spot news coverage of a current event; *on-the-spot* hard news, as compared to features (soft news) or ENTERPRISE REPORTING A *spot news picture* is a photo of such an event.

spot set [broadcasting] a group or cluster of commercials In radio, this is also called a *stop set*; in television, it is a *commercial pod* or *pod.*

spotted map in outdoor advertising, a map of a market with dots—*spots*—to indicate the locations of panels or bulletins of a specific SHOWING

spotter a person who inserts or removes marks (*spots*) or who looks for something, such as an

assistant to an announcer, particularly a sports announcer, who helps to identify the participants in a game

spotting the process of marking with dots, or spots; looking for something (by a *spotter*); a variety of tasks related to the preceding definitions of SPOT, particularly in photography In the mixing of sound in film, spotting relates to specific places, such as finding and marking the locations of specific sound to be synchronized with the picture. Various people, such as a director, composer, and music editor, work together at a *spotting session* to link the music with the picture. Similarly, the locations for TITLES and SUBTITLES, as in a foreign-language film, are itemized at a spotting session.

spread 1 a large area, such as a large layout of an advertisement, article, or other printed matter, specifically a double-page advertisement or two-page spread *Spread discounts* sometimes are provided to advertisers. To *spread a story* or art is to give it widespread distribution or prominent display, frequently on two pages. 2 [broadcasting] the part of a program taken by unplanned material, such as audience laughter and applause To *spread a program* or sequence is to stretch it to consume more time.

spreader a person or thing that spreads, such as a knife, or keeps things apart, such as a bar It is also a common portable device, a circular disc from which three arms are extended in a Y or T configuration, used to provide support to TRIPODS and other items on slippery or angled surfaces. For obvious reasons, it is also called a SPIDER, TEE, or TRIANGLE.

spread head a multiple-deck headline with one or more decks three or more columns wide but less than the full width of the page

spreading the process of widening, as with an individual type character or an entire layout, or diffusing, as with a light beam

spread negative [photography] a negative with a thickened image, sometimes called a *fat negative*

spread sheet a computer business program, also called a WORK SHEET, in which horizontal lines and vertical columns of data are automatically calculated according to formulas that can be chosen and varied by the user A spreadsheet may have over 2,000 rows and 200 columns; the box where they intersect is called a *cell.* The Lotus 1-2-3 spreadsheet, the most widely used personal-computer worksheet, has 2,047 rows, each designated by a number, and 256 columns, each designated by a letter or a pair of letters. Material from a chart wider than the regular $8^1/_2$-inch page generally cannot be displayed in its entirety on a video screen and is broken into components or *windows.*

spring back   a type of strong binding, as used on accounting ledgers, with a clamping action so that the book snaps open and shut

sprinkled edges   in bookbinding, a reference or other book with the edges of its leaves spattered with color, generally with a brush

sprint   a brief period of intense activity, such as a brief promotion   SPRINT is a long-distance telephone service operated by United Telecom of Kansas City, MO, formed in 1976 by Southern Pacific.

sprite   in computer graphics and video games, a movable object and figure on a video screen

sprocket   a toothlike projection, as on a wheel rim; a series of pins, as on a typewriter platen to guide the paper or in a camera, printer, projector, or processor to move the film   The process is called *sprocket feed* or *pin feed.*

spud   a pipe support for a lighting device

spun   [photography] a light DIFFUSER made of gauze

Spur Awards   annual awards of the *Western Writers of America* in Sheridan, WY

square   to set type or other material in straight lines or to make corners perpendicular; also called *square off* or *square up*

square book   a book with its width in excess of three-fourths of its height but not greater than its height

square capitals   simple straight-line letters, all capitals, used in early Latin manuscripts and on tombstones and monuments

square end   in transit advertising, a large area near the doors of a train or bus that is square or almost square, in contrast to the rectangular units in the middle of the vehicle

square finish   an illustration with a square or rectangular edge, not irregular due to *silhouetting*   Most illustrations have a square finish.

squares   the edges of a book cover that project beyond and protect the pages of the book; the parts of the *turn-in* on a book cover not covered by the endpaper

square serif   a group of typefaces with uniform strokes and vertical or horizontal rather than curved SERIFS; also called *block serif* or *slab serif*   Examples include *Benton, Cairo, Girder, Karnak, Memphis,* and *Stymie. American squares* have serifs heavier than the main strokes, whereas *Egyptian squares* have serifs the same thickness as the main strokes.

squaring   a technique for transferring a drawing from one surface, such as drawing paper, to another, larger surface, such as a BILLBOARD or wall   The original drawing is ruled into squares, and the larger surface is ruled into the same number of squares. Each section is then copied more easily than if the work had not been sectioned, or squared off. The technique also is called *squaring off* or *graticulation.*

squawk box   a loudspeaker generally used within an office or other building, such as an intercom

squeegee   in printing and photography, a rubber roller used for wiping, smoothing, pressing, or squeezing; to remove excess or unwanted chemical or other matter, as from a film or plate   The word is pronounced skwee-jee. In film processing, an *air squeegee* is used to blow water from film before it is moved to the drying area.

squeeze   [television] slang for a visual inserted in a window or on the screen, generally to the right of a newscaster to identify the subject of a news report   It is more commonly called a *topic box.*

squeeze track   16mm film prepared from 35mm film

squib   **1** a brief news item   **2** [film] a gelatin capsule with a gunpowder charge that is used in battle scenes   The process, *squibbing,* involves putting the squib inside a *blood bag* (a *squibbed bag*), which is a small balloon containing imitation blood. The charge is set off by a SPECIAL EFFECTS technician to simulate a bullet wound. The explosion itself sometimes also is called a squib.

SRDS   STANDARD RATE & DATA SERVICE, INC.

SRI International   a research company, formed as the Stanford Research Institute and based in Menlo Park, CA, renowned for its VALS system

SRI Research Center   a market research company, based in Lincoln, NE, owned by Selection Research Inc

SRO   STANDING ROOM ONLY, a theatrical term for a sold-out house, tickets for all seats having been taken   In sales, the *SRO method* is a technique in which the prospect is warned that the quantity is limited and may soon be sold out; it is also called *Last Chance Method.*

S.R.P.   suggested retail price

SRR   Spot Radio Report: data about radio advertising expenditures published by *Radio Expenditure Reports Inc.* of Mamaroneck, NY

SS, S.S., or **S/S**   same size, an instruction to a photographer or printer; a sworn statement by a publisher of a periodical's circulation; stock shot

SSAE   stamped self-addressed envelope, a common notation in classified advertisements and other ads, as used by companies that provide free booklets and want to save mailing costs; also called SASE

SSO single-system operator, a cable-TV company with one system; not an *MSO*, or multi-station operator

st. or **St.** STANZA; start; state; statue; street

ST or **S.T.** standard time

sta. STATION

stabilene film tear-resistant film, opaque or translucent, used for engineering drawings and other purposes

stabilization the maintaining of equilibrium In photographic development, a *stabilization processor* is a machine for a two-solution process (*stabilization processing*) in which one solution activates, or develops, while another solution stabilizes, or halts, the image development.

stabilization processing a film-developing system that produces black-and-white prints faster than the standard develop-stop-fix-wash method *Stabilized prints* are not permanent, because they still contain light-sensitive silver halide.

stable all the writers, performers, or others who work for or report to an editor, manager, or other employer or agent

stab marks punctures made in folded sheets of a book or other publication before sewing, as in *cleat sewing*

stack 1 a pile or collection of items In a library, stacks are rows of freestanding shelving that hold the main part of the book collection. 2 [computers] a reserved memory area to accumulate (stack) data to be used later; also called a *push-down list* or *push-down stacks*, in which items are added and removed on a last-in, first-out basis 3 [typography] characters set atop those below with no space between A stack is also one column (or STICK or leg) of a multicolumn article. For example, a four-column article has four stacks of type.

stack ads an arrangement of small advertisements, often alphabetical or by neighborhood, for movie theaters, restaurants, and other categories, commonly found in newspapers The alphabetical listing of plays sometimes is called the *ABCs*. A chain of movie theaters often produces its own stack ad with a small space for each theater.

stacked antenna an antenna with elements vertically mounted instead of all on one plane, used to receive long-distance broadcast signals from different stations; also called *stacked array*

stacker a device that collects, compresses, and bundles publications or parts of publications, such as a *newspaper stacker*

stacking [broadcasting] formatting, the process of determining the order of stories or segments and timing them to fit the program, a key function of a producer and/or editor of a news program

staff a group of people or workers, such as the staff of a publication; the five horizontal lines and four spaces between the lines on which music is written

staff box a list of editorial personnel At newspapers, the staff box generally appears on the editorial page, sometimes as part of the masthead, and includes only the top editors and executives. At magazines, it is usually a longer list, sometimes including the entire staff, and appears in the front, on or near the contents page. A notable exception is *The New Yorker*, which does not print a staff box.

stage 1 a platform; a level (physically, as well as a step, phase, or period of time) 2 [printing] to protect an area of a plate from etching by applying a lacquer or shellac 3 [theater] a platform or any area, in which plays, speeches, or events are presented; to present, represent, or exhibit on a stage; to prepare a play or other work for presentation on a stage *The stage* refers to the theater, drama, or acting as a profession. *Stagecraft* is skill in, or the art of, writing or staging plays or theatrical works. A *stage effect* is an effect or impression, created on the stage, as by lighting, scenery, or sound. Many stage terms refer to the acting area of a theater, though they may have been adapted by film and TV. In film, the floor of a studio used for sound filming is called a SOUNDSTAGE or stage. *Stage directions*, generally phrases typed in parentheses, are script notations about movements of the performers. *Stage left* (SL) is to a performer's left facing the audience, and *stage right* (SR), to the performer's right, whereas *camera left* and *camera right* mean the opposite, from the viewpoint of the camera or audience. *Stage center* (C) is the center of the acting area. A *stagehand* works backstage to set up scenery and props; a performer conducts actions called *stage business*. A *staging plan* is a floor plan of sets and activities to be used in a performance. A *stage flat* is a flat piece of scenery. A *stage whisper* is intended to be heard by the audience but not by the other characters. *Stage fright* is nervousness experienced by a speaker or performer. To be *stage-struck* is to have an intense desire to be associated with the theater, particularly as a performer.

stage call a shout or warning that brings performers to their stage positions for the beginning of a scene; a meeting of the cast and director onstage

stage carpenter a person in charge of constructing scenery in a theatrical production; also called *master carpenter*

stage crew a group of workers in a theatrical production, including the stagehands, stage carpenter, and others involved in the construction of the set—the *building crew*

staged presented on a stage; contrived *Staged news* is created, such as an event set up solely to obtain publicity.

stage door a door on the outside of a theater or other building leading to the *backstage* area, used by the cast and crew A *stage-door Johnnie* is a man who waits outside the stage door to greet or court a female performer. The guardian of the stage door is often referred to as "Pop."

Stage Door Canteens facilities established in World War II by the AMERICAN THEATER WING for free performances and refreshments for armed-forces personnel One of the canteens still is open in the Times Square area of New York.

stage fall a performer's drop to the floor, done in such a way as to appear realistic but avoid injury

stagehand a person who sets up and removes scenery and props and operates the curtains in a theatrical production In film and TV, though the term sometimes is used, the worker is generally called a *grip*.

stage house the entire stage area of a theater, including the ceiling and walls

stage manager a principal assistant to the director of a play or other theatrical production who oversees the cast and production crews during rehearsals and all performances The *assistant stage manager* assists the stage manager and also may be the *prompter*. To *stage manage* is to make arrangements for any type of performance, particularly from behind the scenes.

stage money fake money

stage mother a woman whose child is a performer and who often is overly solicitous

stage plug an electric connector that can handle more power than a conventional plug, used in film, stage, and TV for distributing electricity to lighting equipment

stager an experienced performer

stage screw a large screw used to fasten a scenery support to the stage floor

stage-struck or **stagestruck** having an intense desire to be associated with the theater, such as by a neophyte performer

stage version an acting edition of a play; a play derived from a novel or other nontheatrical work

stage wait a period of time in which a performer is onstage and waiting to perform, as when scenery is being changed or there is a planned or unplanned delay

stag film a movie with explicit sex for showing to men (*stags*)

stagger in typesetting, characters set at alternating forward and backward slants; erratic character spacing or other deviations to produce a *bouncing baseline*

staggered schedule a plan or purchase order for advertisements in two or more publications or stations, with alternating or rotating dates of appearance

stagger head a *drop-line* headline with the lines below the top line indented and with the indentations alternating in a staggered fashion

stagger-through a first TV rehearsal with cameras

staging 1 planning and producing a play or event, or reenacting all or part of it in stages or steps The *staging area* of a parade or other event is the place where the participants assemble. 2 [printing] the protecting of parts of a plate with a varnish or other coating

stagy or **stagey** theatrical Often used in a negative sense, stagy refers to unreal or affected activity, such as *stagy diction*, or a performance that is affected or pretentious.

stain a spot, smudge, or discoloration; to color with stain or pigment, as with the stained leaf edges of a reference or other frequently used book A *stained label* is a colored panel printed or painted on the SPINE or front cover of a book as a background for lettering.

stakeholder an individual or group with a special interest—a *stake*—or ownership in an organization

stakeout the assignment of a reporter to a *news site* for a prolonged period

stamp to form or cut out with a DIE, mold, form, or other device; to imprint or impress with a design, mark, seal, or other item; to affix a postage or other adhesive stamp The item used in the imprinting process is called a stamp; the mark or other impression produced in the stamping process also is called a stamp. Types of stamping include *cold stamping*, as with a printing press; *hot stamping*, as in the affixing of gold leaf to a book cover with heat; and *blind* or *blank stamping*, without ink.

stamps-by-mail a mail-order retail service for purchasing stamps Customers use a SELF-MAILER order form and pay by check for stamps to be delivered with their regular mail.

stand a position (to *take a stand*); a location or structure (*newsstand, music stand, bandstand*);

the *stands* or seats in a stadium or other site or at a parade; a support, such as a lighting or luminaire stand; a stop on a performance tour, such as a *one-night stand*; a synonym for *epode*, a poem with long verses alternating with short ones   A *stand-in* is a substitute. A *stand-up* is a solo performance, as by a *stand-up comic*. A *standee* is a person who stands at a performance in the *standing-room* area behind the seats. In outdoor advertising, a *stand of paper* consists of the sheets of one *complete* poster.

stand-alone [computers] self-contained, as in a complete system, as compared to a system with several input and/or output devices linked to one host computer

stand-alone service   TV programming provided by individual videotapes rather than transmitted via satellite or cable

standard (std.)   a flag or banner, particularly of a nation but also of a person or company, as carried by a person called a *standard bearer*; a bannerlike sign identifying an advertiser, as on a package; an *upright* or vertical support of a sign; a criterion or acknowledged measure of comparison   In statistics, *standard deviation (S.D.)* measures the dispersion in a variation, the deviations from the norm. In general, standard refers to basic levels, as in *standard art* (low-cost, ready-made *stock art*), *standard colors* (not custom-prepared), and *standard sizes* (conventional, in STOCK). A *standard highway painted bulletin* is about 42 feet long and 13 feet high; a *standard streamliner bulletin* is a bit longer and higher. A *standard newspaper* is full-size, about 14 inches wide and 21 inches in depth, and bigger than a TABLOID. The *standard AM radio broadcast band* is the frequencies from 535 to 1,605 kilohertz. The *standard opening* of a program is its theme music or other beginning regularly used; it is also called its *intro* or *stock open*.   The *standard close*, the ending or conclusion of every program in a series, is also called its *lock out*, *outro*, or *stock close*.

Standard Advertising Unit (S.A.U. or SAU)   a system of standard sizes for newspaper advertisements, developed by *American Newspaper Publishers Association (ANPA)*, based on a page width of six columns, each $2^1/_{16}$ inches wide and 21 to $22^1/_2$ inches deep, for full-size newspapers

standard broadcast   the AM (amplitude modulation) radio band, as opposed to the FM (frequency modulation) band

standard broadcast billing month   the month beginning with the Monday on or immediately preceding the first day of the calendar month and continuing until the final Sunday of the calendar month

standard broadcast billing week   Monday through Sunday

standard broadcasting   AM radio, the earliest broadcast service

Standard Consolidated Statistical Area (SCSA)   a designation of the U.S. Office of Management and Budget of a STANDARD METROPOLITAN STATISTICAL AREA (SMSA) with a minimum population of a million plus one or more adjacent SMSAs

standard document   the primary document with text that remains constant while items from a secondary document, such as names and addresses, are merged into it

Standard Geographical Unit (SGU)   a county, ZIP Code, or other area for which specific boundaries, population, and other data are known

Standard Industrial Classification (S.I.C.)   a coding system defined by the U.S. Bureau of the Budget for classifying types of businesses

Standard Metropolitan Statistical Area (SMSA)   an older designation for a metropolitan market as defined by the U.S. Office of Management and Budget

standard operating procedure (SOP or S.O.P.)   a basic routine to be followed

Standard Rate & Data Service, Inc.   a publisher of reference books of advertising rates, with separate volumes for media and types of advertising, such as network SPOT   The company, referred to as *Standard Rate* or by its initials, SRDS, is based in Evanston, IL.

Standard Retail Distribution Index (SARDI)   a service of SAMI that provides reports to grocery manufacturers on retail availability of products in specific markets

Standards and Practices   a broadcasting network department that reviews programming and commercials for adherence to moral code and other self-regulation   At an individual station, this function generally is called *Continuity Acceptance* (see CONTINUITY).

stand by   a request for a person to be ready to go on the air or to remain quiet because the performance is about to begin and the microphone or camera may be operating momentarily

standby guest   a person who is available to be interviewed should there be a cancellation of a scheduled interviewee on a program

standby space   advertising space available at a substantial discount but with no commitment as to when or where it will appear   Major publications, such as *The New York Times*, offer standby space in specific sizes as a way to fill unsold space on a last-minute basis, as airlines do with standby passengers.

stand camera   a camera, usually large-format, mounted on a tripod or other stand

stand down [film] an instruction to personnel to terminate work, such as at the end of the day or upon completion of a scene or other activity

standee a person who stands, as in the rear of a theater; a cardboard cutout or other display that stands in a store or elsewhere

stand-in a substitute performer, such as a temporary replacement or a stuntperson

standing upright, as with a free-standing display; permanent and unchanging, as with a *standing form* that will be used repeatedly by a typist or printer; status or duration

standing ad an advertisement that runs in several consecutive issues

standing details [advertising] the LOGO and other elements that must appear in every advertisement for a product

standing order (S.O.) a purchase request to be filled automatically over a period of time, such as a request to purchase an annual directory without specifically reordering

Standing Room Only (SRO) a theatrical term for a sold-out house, tickets for all seats having been sold In sales, the *SRO method* is a technique in which the prospect is warned that the quantity is limited and may soon be sold out; it is also called *Last Chance Method.*

standing set a set that has been constructed and is ready to be used or is in place for continued use (left standing), as in a TV SOAP OPERA or a theatrical production

standing type type held for future use; also called *standing matter*

stand of paper in outdoor advertising, sheets of paper needed to compose a complete poster advertisement

stand-up an *on-site* TV report or interview, as compared to *in-studio*; a performer, particularly a comedian, who does an act standing alone on a stage with a microphone (a *stand-up act* by a *stand-up comedian*)

standup copy a TV script or text without visuals

standupper a report at the scene of an event with the TV camera focused on the reporter, who is standing up and not seated

Stanton-Lazarsfeld a program-analyzer system developed by Paul Lazarsfeld of Columbia University and Frank Stanton of the COLUMBIA BROADCASTING SYSTEM for testing the popularity of programs among randomly selected audiences Developed in 1937 for radio, the system (nicknamed *Little Annie*) still is used by CBS in New York and Los Angeles. Young men and women hired by CBS stand on street corners and invite passersby to a screening room with rating dials on the arms of the chairs.

stanza a group of lines in a poem or song, such as a *couplet* (two rhymed lines), *tercet* (three lines, generally with a single rhyme), or *quatrain* (four lines, the most common stanza in English poetry)

star a celestial body; a performer or individual with a leading role or popular appeal; an asterisk; a graphic design with four or more radiating points Stars are used to designate the various editions of a daily newspaper, starting with the first or *one-star edition* and ending with the third or *three-star*, fourth or *four-star*, and fifth or *five-star* editions; they are also often used for ratings, as in a four-star movie or five-star restaurant, both generally tops in their leagues. *Star billing* is large type (*star letters*) used atop an advertisement or playbill. A *star entrance* is the first appearance of a leading performer in a production. A *superstar* is an extremely prominent person, perhaps characterized by a *star complex*, an affectation of superiority. A *star maker* is a producer or other person who develops a *star performer*, such as a neophyte with extraordinary charisma or potential called *star quality*. The *star system*, as practiced by the film studios several decades ago, favors leading performers. A *star turn* is an act in a variety show by a top comedian or other popular performer.

Starch INRA Hooper, Inc. a market research firm When Daniel Starch died in 1980 at the age of 95, he left a legacy of consumer research techniques and words such as *Starch Reports* and *starched* that are in the basic vocabulary of print advertisers. His firm, Daniel Starch and Associates, no longer is a separate entity; one of its merger partners, C.E. Hooper, was a pioneer in radio-audience studies. The third component is International Research Associates, a network of researchers in 33 countries. Headquartered in Mamaroneck, NY (Westchester County), Starch INRA Hooper is best known for its *Starch Advertisement Readership Service*. It is a subsidiary of the Roper Organization, founded by the prominent pollster Elmo Roper, which publishes the Roper Reports and Roper Campus Reports.

Each year, Starch announces its magazine schedule, the specific issues of publications that will be studied via individual interviews with readers. Included are trade and business publications, consumer magazines, and newspaper supplements, whose publishers pay to be *starched*. Advertisers then may purchase the Starch Reports. A Starch Advertisement Readership Report consists of a labeled copy of the publication showing *As-a-Whole* and component-part (headline, illustration, copy) readership for all ads studied in the issue. Three basic degrees of readership are reported for each ad: *Noted*, the percentage of readers of the issue who remembered having seen the advertisement; *Associated*, the percentage of readers who had seen or read an indication of the brand or advertiser; and *Read Most*, the percentage who read 50 percent or more of the written material in the ad. Over two million Starch-studied labeled ads, starting in 1937, are available for several thousand advertisers in the *Starch Ad-Files*. A Starch ad rating could be "50 percent noted, 47 percent associated, and 15 percent read most."

stardom   the celebrity status of a performer or other prominent person; also, such STARS collectively

star filter   a sheet of glass (a filter or screen) engraved with lines; also called *star screen*   When placed in front of a camera lens, it produces star-shaped reflections.

starlet   a young actress who aspires to be famous (a STAR)   The word could refer to actors, but in the days of the big Hollywood stars, a starlet was female, and it is still used for a female performer who is being promoted as a possible future star.

star pagination   page numbers bracketed by asterisks—STARS—used to identify the pages of published court decisions and opinions   Developed by the English jurist William Blackstone (1723–80), the system is still used by legal publishers, though sometimes with symbols other than stars.

star-route box holder   a person living in a rural area to whom mail is delivered by a private carrier under contract to the Postal Service; not the same as a *rural-route* box holder, who is served by a government postal carrier   The term *star route* has been replaced by *highway contract route*.

star system   emphasis on the importance of major actors or actresses, or STARS, common at the movie studios in the early days of Hollywood

start   in bookbinding, a section of leaves that has not been properly secured and projects beyond the rest of the book; a break between the sections of a book, sometimes caused by forcing open a volume that has been bound too tightly

start of message (SOM)   a character or group of signals at the top of a story that tells a computer that this is the start of an item; also called *STX*, or START OF TEXT

start of text   in data communications, a transmission control character (abbreviated as *STX*) that ends the heading of a message and indicates that what follows is the beginning of the actual message

stat   a PHOTOSTAT   A *stat-type pasteup* is an assemblage of type photostats or proofs, perhaps

with art, or a rough layout. It is also used as a directive to indicate "rush" or "immediately," which derives from the Latin *statim*, "at once."

state editor   a person at a major daily newspaper, wire service, or other medium in charge of news coverage of the state   At a newspaper such as *The New York Times*, there is no state editor, as the state is covered by both the metropolitan editor, who is in charge of the metropolitan area, and the national editor. At other newspapers, such as the *Des Moines Register-Tribune*, the state editor supervises the bureaus, correspondents, and stringers throughout the state. A few newspapers publish a state edition, supervised by a *state editor* at the *state desk*, with considerable news from throughout the state.

static   stationary electrical charges; random noise or specks on a TV screen produced by atmospheric disturbance; in general, any interference with clear communications, such as electric interference on AM radio   In photography, *static marks* are treelike lines produced on film or other materials due to static electricity discharges in dry conditions.

station (sta. or STN)   **1** a post; a broadcasting facility; an *input* or *output* point of a communications system such as a telephone or of a multiuser computer   Broadcasting stations include original and relay, AM and FM radio, UHF and VHF television, commercial and public, and other types, supervised by a *station manager* and presenting a station FORMAT, the details of which are recorded in a *station log*. The station's *call letters* or number and location—its identification or I.D.—are broadcast at a *station break* between programs or sequences. A station's advertising time may be sold by a *station representative* or rep. A *station-produced* program is one prepared by the station and not by a network or other source. A *station lineup* is a group of stations that broadcasts a particular program or commercial campaign. A *station promo* is a promotional announcement made by a station on its own behalf or for an advertiser but at no cost. *Station time* is the period for local or non-network broadcasting. **2** a transit facility   A *station poster*, an advertising BILLBOARD on the station platform or nearby, is now also at airport facilities. The most common sizes are a vertical *one-sheet station poster*, 46 inches high by 30 inches wide, and a 46-inches-high by 60-inches-wide two-sheet.

statistical demand analysis   correlation analysis in which a dependent variable is assumed to be related to an independent variable, such as the correlation of age and income   Independent variables, called *X-values*, affect dependent variables, called *Y-variables* or *factors*, but not the reverse.

statistics   an analysis of numerical data, particularly of population characteristics—the *statistical universe*—by inference from sampling (thus introducing the *statistical error*) The degree of accuracy is determined by various tests of *statistical significance*, such as a *T-test* expressed as a percentage of 100, or total accuracy. A *statistical bank* is a collection of advanced statistical procedures for learning more about the relationships within a set of data and their statistical reliability, whereas a *model bank* is a collection of models representing real systems or processes.

status   a stage of progress; a position In word processing, the *status line* is the first line at the top of the screen with the identification number and other data about the page or section.

statutory   pertaining to a law decree or rule—a *statute* *Statutory copyright* is a right granted in accordance with federal law.

stave   a set of verses or lines of a poem or song Stave paper is music paper, a sheet with horizontal lines for the placement of musical notes. The paper also has a *staff*, a symbol to indicate the pitch, and sometimes is called *staff paper*.

stay in character   [theater] to remain in a role and not resume one's own personality, such as when onstage and interrupted by applause or other audience reaction

stay with the money   an expression meaning to concentrate on whatever has the greatest commercial appeal, such as a direction to focus on a STAR performer

std.   STANDARD

Steadicam   [film] a 35mm camera support worn by a *Steadicam operator* for hand-held operation, made by Cinema Products in Los Angeles The Steadicam system (there are several models) compensates for body movements and facilitates smooth movements of the camera.

steal   [theater] to attract attention, as to *steal a scene* or show To *steal the spotlight* is to attract attention unfairly, away from the star or other performers; to *steal a bow* is to take an undeserved bow. Steal also means to move imperceptibly, as in changing the intensity of light or sound.

sted   replace word or words, a printer's symbol that is the opposite of STET

steel-die engraving   a steel printing plate in which an image has been engraved to produce raised—engraved or INTAGLIO—printing

Steinbeck   a film-editing machine on a horizontal table (a *flatbed*) instead of reels vertically mounted Commonly used in the film indus-

try, it is made by W. Steinbeck and Company in Chatsworth, CA.

stem   the vertical STROKE or strokes of a letter

stencil   a sheet of celluloid or other material in which lettering or designs have been cut out so that ink or paint applied to the sheet will reproduce the pattern on the surface beneath *Stencil paper* is strong, thin paper waxed or treated for making stencils. A STYLUS or typewriter removes the wax in specific areas so that ink can pass through to a sheet of paper; the stencil thus can be used as a printing plate, as on a mimeograph machine. A *stencil knife* is used to cut stencil paper and other papers; a *stencil brush*, a round-headed brush with stiff bristles, is used to apply paint through openings in a stencil. A *lettering stencil* is a metal, plastic, or paper sheet into which letter forms have been cut.

step   a movement, such as a dance step; a short distance, such as the space between the units in lighting settings To *step up* is to increase, as the temperature of a photographic solution. To *step on a laugh* is to speak a line before the audience has finished laughing at the previous line or comic action. To *step on a line* is to speak a line before another performer has given the cue.

step and repeat   [printing] to repeat a character or image, as to produce a border or design

step-and-repeat camera   a SEQUENTIAL camera, such as a microfilm camera, that produces a series of separate images according to a predetermined sequence

step deal   an arrangement by which a proposed TV series or other project is developed and submitted in stages, subject to revocation at any stage

step it up   to increase, such as to increase the sound volume or speed of action

step line   a segment of a headline that is indented in comparison to the preceding line; also called *dropline*

step on   to begin to speak before another performer has finished his or her lines of dialogue

step outline   a summary or condensed treatment of a script, with the action indicated at each scene, or step

stepover   in LITHOGRAPHY, the repetition of an exposure by moving, or stepping, it along the gripper edge of the printing plate; also called *side-by-side exposure*

stepped head   a multiline headline with each line of about the same length but with different margination, such as the first FLUSH left, the second centered, and the third flush right

step printer   [film] an intermittent printer, contact printer (a *step-contact printer*), or projection printer (a *step-optical printer*) that exposes one FRAME at a time by means of an advance mechanism and shutter *Step printing* is the procedure of printing one frame at a time.

step up [direct marketing] the sending of PREMIUMS or other incentives to a mail-order customer to encourage an increased purchase

step up/step down [typography] to set adjacent characters increasingly larger or smaller to create an effect of movement or a three-dimensional effect In lithography, *step-up* is the repeated exposure of a negative by stepping it back from the gripper edge of the plate; it is also called *up-and-down exposure*.

stereo a three-dimensional effect A *stereophonic* sound reproduction system uses two or more separate channels to give a fuller, more natural three-dimensional distribution of sound. *Stereoscopic photography* or *3-D movies* impart a three-dimensional effect to two photographs (a *stereograph*) of the same scene taken at slightly different angles and viewed through special *3-D glasses* or the two eyepieces of a *stereoscope*, a 3-D optical instrument.

stereo broadcasting multichannel sound AM, FM, or TV stations that transmit sound from two or more separate sources that is received on matching, separate speakers are called stereo broadcasters.

stereograph a picture seen in three dimensions when viewed in a *stereoscope*, an instrument in many homes in the 19th century *Stereoscopic* views of an object were taken at slightly different angles so that two stereographs viewed side by side through the dual eyepiece appeared to have depth.

stereoscopy the science of three-dimensional, or *stereoscopic*, effects and techniques, such as the viewing of a STEREOGRAPH in a *stereoscope*.

stereotype a conventional concept or opinion; a person or group considered to typify or conform to a general pattern, lacking individuality The origin is from printing, in which a metal printing plate is cast from a *matrix*, or mold. *Stereotyping* is the printing process in which duplicates or copies are made, as of an advertisement, for use in a LETTERPRESS publication. The matrix, which is a reversed imprint of the original printing surface, is used to produce the molten metal casting, or *stereoplate*.

stet an instruction to a typist or printer to retain or keep matter in print regardless of crossing-out or other previous instructions The procedure is to underline the material in question with a row of dots called *stet marks* and write the word *stet* in the margin. In show business, stet means to retain dialogue, props, or other specified items while others are changed.

A radio or TV program with the same opening or closing or another constant format is said to have a *stet opening* or *closing*. Stet is from the Latin for "let it stand."

stick a metal tray that holds type, called a *composing stick*; also, the contents of a stick, called a *stickful*, about two column inches or about 100 to 150 words A *newspaper stick* is a rod, used in libraries to hold one or more issues of a newspaper.

sticker 1 a gummed or adhesive label 2 [marketing] an unsold item that has been taking up space for too long 3 [newspapers] a page that is not to be changed from one edition to the next, such as a page with advertising or FEATURE material

stick it an instruction from a film director to an assistant (generally the *second assistant cameraman* or *clapper*) to clap together the sticks on the *clapboard*, thus marking the beginning of a TAKE; also called *sticks*, *sticks in*, or *slate it* (After the tenth TAKE, some performers and crew members are ready to "stick it.")

sticky back paper affixed with an adhesive to a backing sheet The paper can be removed and applied by pressure on another surface An example is the line of self-adhesive labels made by the Avery Label Company of Monrovia, CA.

stiction surface friction, as between parts of a TV camera or other mechanisms

stiff rigid, firm, not fluid or loose A *stiff ink* has too much body. *Paper stiffness* is its degree of resistance to bending. Among the many colloquial meanings of stiff is excessive, as in a *stiff price*.

stile a vertical piece in a panel or frame, such as a door, a window, or a flat section of scenery

still a two-dimensional photo, which is motionless compared to a motion picture with action Each individual FRAME of a motion picture may be called a still. A *still photographer* uses a *still camera* to take *still photos*.

still imaging the processing of STILL photos or other graphics Still images can be created via computer graphics, captured and stored electronically in a *still store* or electronic storage, and retrieved and transmitted via telephone FACSIMILE.

stills [television] slang for the STILL photographers of the print media, as when TV crews shout, "Down stills!," a request to still photographers at a media event to stoop down so that the TV cameras, generally behind them, can "catch the action"

still store [television] an electronic memory unit—STORAGE or *store*—for retaining single "visuals," such as graphics and photos used in newscasts

sting a musical phrase or a sound to add emphasis or dramatic effect to a commercial, program, or production; also called *stinger* or *button*

stipple to draw, engrave, paint, or apply dots or points instead of lines or solid areas   The art or method of this process, and the end result, are called stipple or *stippling*. Stipple generally is the use of dots to achieve tonal effects in artwork or a speckled finish on printing paper. A *stippler* produces a stipple or *stippled work*. A *stipple engraving* has dots instead of lines.

stirrup a ring with a flat bottom used as a footrest by horseback riders or a support resembling this shape, such as a *stirrup hanger* used to hang luminaires on sets or in theaters

stitching bookbinding with wire staples in which a stitching machine or *stitcher* feeds a continuous roll of wire, rather than individual staples from a stapler   The two types of stitching are SADDLE STITCHING or *saddle-wire stitching*, in which the leaves of booklets, magazines, and other publications are stapled through the folded edges, and *side stitching* or *side-wire stitching*, in which the leaves of books and thick publications are stapled through the side along the binding edge. Stitching formerly referred to bookbinding with thread, but thread binding now is generally called *sewing*.

stitch line evenly spaced short dashes used in SPECIFICATION drawings to indicate sewing

STN STATION

stock unexposed film, paper, or other material used in printing and other reproduction; standard merchandise in inventory, such as retail stock, or in a *stock room*   From the latter meaning comes *stock art, stock cut, stock film, stock footage, stock music, stock photo, stock set, stock sheet, stock shot*, and other items already produced and in a library for repeated use.

stock character a familiar fictional role; sometimes also called a *type character* typical of a group or class of people

stock company a group of performers who regularly work together, as at one theater, on a tour, or in a continuing series

stock depth the number of units of an item necessary to maintain a complete assortment, such as different sizes, flavors, and types of packaging

stock open a standard opening (introduction) of a program   The closing (ending) is a *stock close*.

stockout out of STOCK, referring to an item not in *inventory*

stock part a familiar type of role, perhaps played by a performer who is identified with stereotypical, or conventional, roles; also called *stock role*

stock reel a feed, storage, or supply reel on a tape recorder from which the unrecorded or unplayed tape is taken

stock response a predictable reaction by a reader or audience, particularly to a stock character or situation

stock role a standard or STEREOTYPED part in a play or other work, such as the beautiful *ingenue*

stock setting a standard set, such as a street, used for a variety of plays, films, or other work

stock situation a frequently recurring or STEREOTYPED pattern or incident in a play or other work, such as the shootout between the hero and villain

stock solution the concentrated, undiluted solution of a processing chemical, such as a DEVELOPER used in photography

stock turn the relative speed or velocity with which a retail item is sold; also called TURNOVER

stock weights commonly available weights of paper   Since printers refer to paper as *stock*, this term could be *stock stock* or *stocking items* (stored in warehouses, not in stockings).

stomp a tube of rolled soft paper or cloth resembling a pencil with a sharp point, used by artists to apply chalk, charcoal, paint, pastel, or other media

stone a table or hard surface used in printing, art, and other production

stone proof an impression or *proof* of type in a form; not a press proof, which is produced at a later stage   The term refers to the early practice of assembling type on a table called a *stone*.

stooge a performer who feeds lines to a comedian or acts as a FOIL; an underling

stop 1 cessation; a punctuation mark, especially a period   In the early days of the telegraph, the word was commonly used to indicate the end of a sentence. Today, a *stop code* pertains to the end of an operation. *Stop press* is an order to stop the printing presses. Other *stop orders* include *stop check*, which is an instruction to a bank to withhold payment on a check. A *stopwatch* can be instantly started and stopped by pushing a button. It is used to measure the number of seconds of a commercial and other carefully timed sequences. To *stop the show* is for an audience to interrupt a performance with applause.   2 [music] a handle, key, or lever for halting or pausing, such as a *fret* for a guitar or stringed instrument; a hole on a wind instrument or a key to close it; a *rest* in a musical composition; a consonant such as *k*, *p*, or *t* that requires the air passage to close for enunciation **3** [photography] a perforated screen or diaphragm that limits the lens opening and thus improves definition of the subject

stop action an effect of suspended time and action produced by repeated printing of a single frame of a film (*freeze frame*) or electronically holding the tape; not the same as STOP MOTION

stop bath a chemical solution, usually a weak solution of acetic acid, used to end the development of a film, followed by the final process, called FIXING

stop code [computers] in automated typesetting, a machine-readable code on a perforated tape to indicate the end of the job; in word processing, a magnetic code to stop the system during a printout

stop down to reduce, as in to *close down* the diameter of a camera lens aperture, to decrease the f-stops and thus lower the amount of transmitted light A lens set at f2 that is adjusted to f4.5 is *stopped down* two steps. *Stopping down all the way* is setting a lens at its highest f-stop number.

stop motion a procedure often used in animation to produce an effect of motion by moving an object slightly between FRAMES or photographing a plant or other changing scene at intervals

stop out a liquid chemical used to delete unwanted areas of a printing plate The process is called *stopping out.*

stopper an attention-getting headline, work of art, or device

stop set [broadcasting] a period of time, generally two minutes, during which commercials are broadcast

storage a part of a computer that retains or stores information for subsequent use or retrieval Data is entered or stored in the *memory storage* or *memory. Storage capacity* of a word processor is expressed in characters. *Storage dump* is a printout of the contents of the computer storage area.

Storage Instantaneous Audimeter (SIA) an electronic information device installed by A.C. NIELSEN CO. to meter one or more TV sets in a household and thus provide overnight ratings (actually, two days after broadcast)

store a retail outlet A *storecast* is an announcement, such as of special items, "broadcast" on loudspeakers in a store. A *store-distributed magazine,* such as *Family Circle* or *Woman's Day,* is sold primarily in retail stores, particularly supermarkets. A *store panel* is a group of stores used for market research.

store and forward the collection of an input message in a computer for later transmission

store audit an analysis of sales of a product or other research conducted at the retail level

store book a periodical sold primarily in supermarkets and other stores, such as the *National Enquirer, Family Circle,* or *Woman's Day*

store-door delivery the distribution of perishables and other products directly to each store in contrast to warehouse delivery

Storer a major broadcasting company in Miami, FL, that primarily owns TV stations and cable systems; part of SCI Holdings

story **1** a narrative **2** [journalism] any nonfiction or news article or report, not just a prose work of fiction The *story line* is the plot of a prose or dramatic work. A *soft story* lacks HARD NEWS details or journalistic strengths. **3** [film] A *story analyst* or *reader* works in a *story department* to evaluate SCRIPTS, SYNOPSES, TREATMENTS, and other material and submit recommendations to a *story editor,* who functions like an editor at a publisher in recommending acceptance to a producer and then working with the writer and others at *story conferences* and other meetings to develop the *story script* (the dialogue and scene descriptions without the technical details, which are in the *shooting script).*

storyboard a series of illustrations (*storyboard sketches*) or layouts of scenes in a proposed TV commercial or other work, used as a guide prior to production A *storyboard artist* also is called a *production illustrator* or *sketch artist.*

story count the number of stories on one page, particularly page one of a newspaper

story line the plot of a film or other work

story within a story a narrative interspersed within another narrative

stow a direction to a printer to keep or store, as with a filler or timeless story; to place an article, such as a FEATURE, on a newspaper page early in the day

straddle head a heading typeset over two or more columns of tabular material (*straddling* it)

straight **1** extending continuously without curves; erect and upright; direct and candid To *be straight* is to be forthright, honest, and without eccentricities. **2** [broadcasting] In broadcast advertising, a *straight 60* is a 60-second commercial for one product. **3** [journalism] *Straight reporting* is factual, not subjective. **4** [photography] *Straight photos* are not retouched or altered; *straight processing solutions* are undiluted. **5** [typography] *Straight matter* is text all the same size, type, and column width; *straight text* is solid text with no art. **6** [theater] A *straight play* is a drama, not a comedy or a musical, featuring *straight roles* or parts. A *straight line* is a feeder line spoken by a STRAIGHT MAN (a foil) to a comedian.

straightedge a ruler

straight-grain morocco in bookbinding, goatskin leather with parallel crinkles produced by pressing *grained plates* with parallel lines on the leather

straight man a performer who *plays it straight*—direct, with no jokes or STUNTS—and serves as a foil for another performer, particularly a comedian

straight matter continuous text with no art, headlines, or other "interruptions"

straight up a broadcasting signal, such as to an announcer, to start when the clock's second hand is at 12; not the same as *stand-up*

strapping the bundling of newspapers and other publications with plastic or other bands (*straps*), generally done with *strapping machines*

strategic business unit (SBU) a component of a company that sells one product or a group of related products to a specific market

stratified sampling a survey technique in which the population is divided into small, homogeneous groups from which individuals are selected for random sampling for more accurate representation

stratified selection the separation of a target audience into various levels or strata, such as buyers by level of importance to the advertiser

strawboard a PAPERBOARD made from straw or stems of grain

straw hat a summer theater

straw man an unimportant person; a weak argument or a phony issue set up to be easily attacked and knocked down to produce an easy victory; a person or issue used as a *blind*, or concealment, to disguise the true intentions or activities

straw vote an unofficial vote or poll (a *straw poll*) to determine opinion on an issue or about a candidate, perhaps conducted by a newspaper or other media

streak 1 a long, narrow mark or band of a different color or texture than the surrounding area 2 [photography] a blemish, such as those caused by uneven immersion of the film negative in the developing solution

streaking [television] a distorted picture condition in which the picture or a part of it is expanded horizontally

stream flow [computers] a flow of data, such as an *input stream, output stream, format stream*, or *text stream*

streamer a very large headline, also called a BANNER; a vertical grease-pencil line on a film

workprint that marks a cue point for music and other recording

street jargon used in the record industry for consumers; the general public In the financial community, *The Street* refers to Wall Street in lower Manhattan, on which the New York Stock Exchange is located, or the entire U.S. securities market, as in "Heard on the Street," a column in *The Wall Street Journal.*

street-address directory a telephone directory with listings by street address instead of by name, useful in surveys, market research, and political and other campaigns

street column a newspaper column that covers all aspects of city life for "ordinary people" on the streets Jimmy Breslin is a street columnist for *New York Newsday.*

street sale copies of a newspaper or other periodical sold at newsstands or in racks in the street

street video innovative, artistic forms of TV productions, such as by students and other alternative television groups, often taped on street locations

stress in music and speech, an accent, such as a note, syllable, or word that is emphasized

stress marks black lines or streaks on a photo negative due to excess pressure, as in winding the roll, or friction

stretch a signal to slow down action or talk more slowly; also called *stretchout* The nonverbal signal for stretch is similar to pulling taffy. Stretch also refers to an extension, so performers call a role a stretch when it requires great effort.

stretch framing a technique of slowing down the action of a film shot by repeating each frame two or three times, resulting in a jerky movement, sometimes used for a comedic effect; also called *stretch-frame printing* or *stretch printing* When each frame is printed two times, the process is called *double framing* or *double-frame exposure.*

strike to dismantle a theatrical or studio set; to make a duplicate; to stop work

strike-on type a method of reproducing letterforms by striking the raised image of a character onto a carbon carrier; often called *typewriter type* The process is called *strike-on printing* or *impact printing.*

strikeover the typing of a correct character in place of an incorrect character

string 1 a cord, a thin line, a series of related items, or a set or group 2 [computers] a SEQUENCE or a set of data, such as a series of characters or codes processed as a group *String substitution* is the replacement of several characters with others. *Search string* is a computer command to locate a sequence of characters in a file.

string & button envelope an envelope with two reinforced paper buttons, one on the flap and the other on the back To close, a string locked under the flap button is wound alternately around both buttons.

stringer a correspondent, generally part-time, for a newspaper or other publication, who is not on staff The origin is from *on the string*—that is, being paid a variable amount depending on quantity and acceptance by the editor who keeps the freelancer on a string. Some editors paid a part-time reporter by keeping the reporter's clippings on a string and literally paid by the number of clippings or the number of column inches published, perhaps measured with a string. A *second stringer* is a journalist or anyone of a lower rank than the *first team*.

stringout [film] the first phase of editing, in which the film sequences are assembled in order; also called *assembly*

strip to remove, as in photography, printing, or other fields; a long, narrow piece (probably originating from STRIPE), such as a *comic strip*, a row of lights (*striplight*) on a movie or TV set, or a program broadcast serially (a *strip show*) the same time every day (from the daily appearance of newspaper comic strips); a piece, such as a two-to-four-foot section of perforated computer tape; see also STRIP IN and STRIPPING

strip center a group of stores on a strip of land along a street or highway, not enclosed and not as large as a shopping mall

stripe 1 a long, narrow band, mark, streak, or strip 2 [film] the magnetic coating (magnesium oxide) applied to one or both edges of a film for recording sound; also called SOUND STRIPE Film with only one track is called *single stripe*, *1-stripe*, or simply stripe, though such a film also has a second, narrower band, called a *balance stripe* or *balancing stripe*, on the edge opposite the sound stripe to balance the thickness of the stock so that it is smoothly wound. A common type of 35mm film is *3-stripe*.

stripfilm a series of STILL pictures printed on a single strip of film, usually 35mm; a FILMSTRIP

strip in [printing] to insert, as in offset lithography, in which negatives or positives are positioned in their correct locations on a flat (a *goldenrod*) prior to platemaking; to produce a combination of two or more negative *strip-ins* into one illustration, a composite; to insert a negative or other material into a photographic negative or positive; also called *strip up* A *stripper's blotter* is cardboard or other material used to remove moisture or air bubbles from

stripping film. *Stripping tweezers* are used to separate materials. See also STRIP and STRIPPING.

striping the process of applying a stripe, such as the *sound stripe* on a film

striplight a lighting unit with a row—a *strip*—of bulbs, generally 5, 10 (a *tenlight*), or 12 1,000-watt bulbs, commonly used on stages and sets along the floor, such as a *border light* or *cyclorama strip* on the bottom of a large rear *backdrop* The standard unit is open, does not have lenses, and provides even illumination over a wide area. A *horizon striplight* or *strip* is usually placed at the base of a *cyclorama* or scenery that resembles a sky.

stripped publication a paperback book or magazine with its cover removed The procedure in the publishing industry is to permit retailers to return to wholesalers or publishers only the covers of unsold copies for full refunds. The coverless or stripped publication then is supposed to be destroyed. The idea is to save shipping costs on the returns.

stripper 1 a person who removes something, such as blemishes or unwanted material in photography and printing; a performer who removes clothing as part of a performance 2 a narrow piece of canvas, more commonly called a *Dutchman*, used to cover the seam when two pieces of scenery are attached

stripping 1 [film] cleaning, as in the treatment of a soundtrack to eliminate extraneous noise 2 [printing] assembling two or more images to produce a composite for reproduction, also called *stripping up as one*; removal of excess detail, as with a *stripping film* 3 [television] preparing a series for reruns and syndication by reducing—*stripping*—or editing the programs, generally to permit more commercial time; see also STRIP and STRIP IN

stripping film a negative, or film, with a light-sensitive emulsion on a membrane that is bonded to a base In PHOTOLITHOGRAPHY, the film is developed and the base then can be removed, or stripped away, with the membrane retaining the photographic image.

strip-title [film] one or more horizontal lines of text anywhere on the screen, such as a SUBTITLE at the bottom

strobe light a *stroboscopic* light that produces high-intensity, short-direction light pulses used to create pulsating visual effects, as in a discotheque, or to create the illusion of movement (*strobing* or *strobe effect*) Strobe lights are also used as an electronic flash on still cameras to stop action or give multiple exposures in a fast exposure of rapidly moving objects, as in some phototypesetters.

stroke 1 [computers] a keystroke, a character image or command generated by the depression of a single key on a keyboard; a line, such as the generation of a character image on photosensitive material by means of a series of strokes created by a moving spot of light   2 [typography] a line, or part, of a typeface   A thin stroke often is used as a horizontal line, or *cross stroke*, and a thick stroke as a vertical line (the STEM).

stroker slang among salespeople for a person in a store or other sales area who pretends to be a potential customer but really is not interested in buying

strophe in the ancient Greek theater, the movement of the chorus from right to left on the stage or the part of the song performed by the chorus during this movement; a STANZA or group of lines in a poem   *Antistrophe* is the return movement, from left to right, or the stanza after the strophe.

struck-image direct-impression printing, as with a typewriter or computer printer

strut a swaggering walk; a brace, such as a support for scenery

stub 1 the short end remaining after something has been used, as of a theater ticket or check   2 [journalism] a short headline, or a *stubhead*, that identifies the left-hand column of a table or chart with the categories or guiding entries   The *stub column* is the column of listings under the stubhead.   3 [printing] a narrow strip of paper or fabric sewn between sections of a book for attaching a folded map or other bulky matter; a narrow strip of paper or fabric bound into the front or back of a volume for the addition of a pocket, as for a library card

studhorse type an extremely large type size, as in a BANNER headline

studio a room in which an artist or photographer works or with facilities for other types of artists, such as a recording studio, radio- or TV-station studio, or movie studio   A group of artists or photographers or film stages also may be called a studio, as well as the company itself (a *movie studio*). A *studio camera* is used in a studio, as compared to a *minicam* or other cameras used on location. A *studio exterior* is an outdoor set constructed and often photographed in a studio. A *studio manager*, like a plant manager, is in charge of operations but not of specific filming. A *studio picture* is a film made primarily in a studio and not on location. The studio era of Columbia, MGM, Warner, and the other big Hollywood studios popularized the *studio system* of performers and others on staff or under *studio contract*, which is different from the methods of today's packagers and independents.

studio address (S.A. or **SA)** a loudspeaker system in a recording or broadcasting studio for use by a director or other personnel in the control room

studio camera a full-size camera with sound insulation and other accessories used to film or tape in a SOUND STAGE or studio

studio card [television] a piece of cardboard, generally 11″ × 14″, on which is mounted a photo, lettering, or other graphics photographed by a *studio camera* during the production

studio finish a photo with a matte or non-glossy surface

studio session a sequence of photos taken in a studio, as compared to on-site or location photography

studio tank a large container, often 15 feet deep and 50 feet long, set up in a studio to shoot water scenes (*tank-shots*), including underwater scenes through portholes or windows and the simulation of ocean scenes using model boats

stuff theatrical slang for a dance routine or other specialty   *Do your stuff* is a request for a performance of a specialty.

stuffer an advertising enclosure placed in other media, such as newspapers, merchandise packages, or envelopes

stuffs items that are inserted   For example, an inserting machine at a newspaper can insert 20,000 supplements, or stuffs, per hour.

stump 1 a short roll of paper or other material, including leather or rubber, used for rubbing on a charcoal or pencil drawing to shade or soften it, more commonly called a STOMP by artists; to touch up a drawing by using this type of pencil-shaped implement   2 to travel extensively for political purposes   Such a campaign is called *on the stump*, from the days when tree stumps were used as speakers' platforms.

stunt a feat or trick; an event set up to attract media attention   The origins of publicity stunts go back to the early days of press agents who created something humorous, bizarre, or off-beat to attract media attention. Today, public relations professionals tend to abhor the word "stunt," although a euphemism such as "event" often is the same thing and is designed to achieve the same objective. A *stunt player*, *stunt actor*, *stunt performer*, or *stuntperson* (*stuntman* or *stuntwoman*) performs difficult or dangerous acts in movies or TV, sometimes as a STAND-IN for a performer, under the supervision of a *stunt coordinator*.

stunt box a device that controls specific operations, such as the nonprinting functions of a printer

stunting in publishing, film, show business, television, and other fields, the use of unusual techniques to develop audiences or customers, such as starting the TV season with a two-hour episode of a program that regularly lasts 30 or 60 minutes

STV SUBSCRIPTION TELEVISION

STX START OF TEXT

style 1 [journalism] standards of grammar and writing that are considered to be generally acceptable and desirable The most commonly used *stylebooks* are those published by *The New York Times*, The Associated Press, and the University of Chicago Press. A *style sheet* or *style page* is a guide to typography and other preferences issued by a publisher for its own staff or contributors. The *style page* or *section* of a newspaper, formerly labeled the *women's page* or *section*, features *lifestyle* articles, covering food, fashion, and other topics, and is produced by the *style* or *lifestyle department*. The term appears in various newspapers as lifestyle, *life/style*, and *life style*. 2 a fashion or design, such as a TYPESTYLE 3 a pointed instrument, such as a STYLUS

stylist a person who arranges food, apparel, hair, or other items used to prepare models or scenes in a photography or film studio or on location

stylus an instrument with a sharp point of steel or wood used for engraving, drawing, marking, and writing; a phonograph needle; a sharp pointed tool for cutting record grooves, sometimes called STYLE A *stylus printer* is a matrix or dot printer in which each character is represented by a pattern of dots.

Stymie a serif typeface

sub substitute, such as a direction to replace a piece of copy or art, or material to replace (substitute for) previous material; subordinate; subscriber; subscription In newspaper jargon, *subfire* means to substitute an update about a fire.

subbing [photography] a clear coating to facilitate adhesion between an emulsion and the film base; also called *subbing layer*

subcarrier station a radio station that operates in a limited area on the frequency of an FM station and is received only on special FM radios, called *subcarrier receivers* or *SCA receivers* The Storecast Carrier Authorization (SCA) concept was developed for broadcast to shoppers and now is also used at sports sites and other places.

subheading a secondary headline used below the primary or main headline or within the text of an advertisement or article; also called *subhead* or *subcaption* It generally is set in smaller type than the main head.

subject something or someone that is the basis of or key element in a story, program, photo, or other work; the part of a sentence that performs or receives the action of the verb In photography, *subject reflectivity* is the degree to which the person or subject reflects the light shining on it.

subjective 1 not objective; personal 2 [film] a SUBJECTIVE CAMERA shoots from the subject's point of view; *subjective sound* presents what the subject hears, remembers, or imagines hearing.

subjective camera a film technique in which the camera takes the position or point-of-view of the performer This camera perspective, such as looking down from a roof or looking up at an approaching car, is called a *subjective camera angle*.

subliminal perception stimuli that are perceived but are below the level of normal consciousness In the case of advertising, a split-second announcement on television, though not consciously perceived, could have an effect. Such advertising is unlawful, though the term sometimes is used to describe *soft sell* or indirect advertising. Actually, many factors influence the viewer of a TV commercial, such as the apparel, scenery, and ethnicity, all of which are part of the conscious and subconscious impression.

submission an offering, such as a manuscript sent to a publisher *Simultaneous submission* is the sending of several queries, outlines, or manuscripts to several potential publishers at the same time.

subordinate (sub) 1 inferior; secondary 2 [typography] a number or letter set smaller than, and at the bottom of, the character it appends, as in a chemical formula; also called SUBSCRIPT or *inferior character*

subplot a subordinate plot; a secondary narrative or arrangement of incidents in a play, novel, or other work

subscriber a person who has contracted (with a SUBSCRIPTION) for the purchase of delivered copies of, or programs from, a medium, such as a periodical or pay television

subscript a character below the BASELINE, such as a number in a chemical formula; also called *inferior character*, the opposite of SUPERSCRIPT

subscription a purchase for a specified period of time, such as for a periodical or a series of performances; abbreviated as *sub*

subscription circulation the total number of copies of each issue of a periodical paid for in advance

subscription television (STV) pay television, in which subscribers, or viewers, pay a monthly fee, as for HBO

subsidiary auxiliary; subordinate In publishing, *subsidiary rights* are those of the copyright owner after the original publication. In the case of a book, subsidiary rights, which can be more valuable than the original book itself, can include sales to book clubs, SERIALIZATION, SYNDICATION, excerpts in other media, broadcasts, motion pictures, records, foreign translation, adaptation, printing in other formats such as paperback, and even sales of components such as the title, character rights, or the general theme.

subsidiary communications authorizations (SCA) rights granted by the FEDERAL COMMUNICATIONS COMMISSION to FM broadcasters for the use of other communications subcarriers on their channels

subsidy publisher a company that publishes books for which the authors pay all or part of the costs; also called *subsidy house* or *vanity publisher*

subs previous a wire-service term for a major news bulletin or story that subordinates and replaces all previous material on an event

substance essence; basic matter; solid quality; consistency; body In papermaking, the *basis weights* are used to designate regular sizes of various kinds of papers. For a REAM, or 1,000 sheets, the *substance number* or *substance weight* may be 60 or 70 pounds.

substitute a replacement, such as copy or art that replaces previous material

substrate an underlying layer, such as paper or film on which light-sensitive or other material is affixed; also called *substratum*

subsurface illuminator a LIGHT BOX used in optical copying to eliminate shadows

subtext an underlying meaning; the "real meaning" of a script or other work

subtitle a secondary title of a book or other work; a translation of dialogue in a foreign movie shown at the bottom of the screen; a superimposed caption at the bottom of the TV screen

subtractive a photographic process that produces a positive image by superimposing or mixing substances that selectively absorb colored light Color photography is based on the subtractive principle in which the subtractive colors, or primaries, are cyan, magenta, and yellow. Each of these colors represents white light, which is a combination of the three additive primary colors, red, yellow, and blue, minus one (subtractive).

suburban newspaper a weekly, semiweekly, or daily newspaper serving an area near a city

succès de scandale notoriety gained from a scandal, from the French

succès d'estime a play or other work acclaimed by the critics but not a financial success; from the French for "success of esteem"

succès fou an extraordinary success, including financially; from the French for "mad success"

successive approximations statements about a problem that come closer, upon refinement, to a definitive result

suction feed a printing or other process in which paper or another item is picked up and fed through a printing press by air suction rather than hand feed or friction feed

suds SOAP OPERA

suffix coded field [computers] an identification signal at the end of a set of characters

suitcase [film] a flag about the size of a suitcase, two or three feet long, generally a black mesh rectangular SCRIM placed on a stand in front of a LUMINAIRE to soften or control light

suits slang, particularly in show business, for executives, who wear suits instead of casual clothes The word is generally disparaging. More disparaging is *three-piece suits*, who are vested executives.

sulfite or **sulphite** a salt or ester of sulfurous acid, commonly used in paper

summary a brief statement outlining a longer text that precedes or follows it, sometimes shorter than an abridgment, compendium, digest, or synopsis

summary lead the highlights of news, such as the first paragraph of a news story

summative research a study to evaluate whether the goals and objectives of a public relations or other campaign were achieved; a summing up of the results, as opposed to FORMATIVE RESEARCH

sunburst a decorative device with many pointed extensions

Sunday ghetto the daytime period on Sunday when relatively few radio and TV sets are in use, commonly used for religious and public affairs programming With network news programs now broadcast on Sunday morning and Sunday afternoon sports programs, the Sunday ghetto viewership has increased compared to the 1950s.

Sunday supplement a local or national magazine or special section, such as a TV guide or comics, included with a Sunday newspaper The largest-circulation Sunday supplements are *Parade* and *USA Weekend.*

sun gun a portable high-intensity lighting device

sunk bands in bookbinding, cords—bands—laid into grooves across the back of the sections to produce a smooth back or spine Sunk bands are different from *raised bands*, which protrude as ridges.

sunk up   film slang for sound that is synchronized with the picture

sunrise-watch   the shift at a newspaper after the last regular edition; also called *dog-watch*, *graveyard shift*, *lobster shift*, or *lobster-trick*

sunshade   [photography] a device attached to a camera that can be moved to shade the lens from sunlight or stray light; also called *lens hood*   A circular sunshade often is attached to the matte box of a motion-picture camera in front of the lens that holds filters or mattes; a rectangular sunshade is attached to the bellows attachment.

sunshine laws   laws that require government meetings and public records to be open to the press and the public

sup.   superior; super; supplement (also *supp.*, *suppl.*)

super   **1** [book production] a gauzelike fabric glued to the SPINE for added strength; also called *crash*   **2** [theater] a supernumerary person; an *extra*   At opera performances, many buffs and prominent people vie for the honor of working as supers in crowd scenes.

super band   a range of radio frequencies from 216 to 600 megahertz, used for *citizen's band (CB)* and cable television

supercalendered paper   highly smoothed and polished paper, glossy but not coated, produced by running it between rolls or *calenders*; also called *super paper*   An example is English Finish paper.

supercase   in phototypesetting, a set of characters that are neither upper- nor lowercase, usually special symbols designated supercase because they can be accessed by a special *super-shift* code without changing typefaces; also called *third case* or *supershift*

superfine paper   high-grade writing paper

superimposition (super)   placing one image on top of another, such as a slide superimposed on the image received from a television camera   A super may be used for a local station insert within a national telecast or the addition of a local retailer identification at the end of or within a commercial for a national sponsor. A *superboard* or *superslide* is a board or slide printed in reverse, with white or light-colored lettering on a dark surface, for superimposition on a televised scene, generally for explanation. A *super-imp* is a composite image created by the superimposition of one camera image over another. The camera command to achieve this is simply "super" or, more often, "super!" *Super in sync* is a superimposition, such as a slide, synchronized with sound. *Lower-third super* re-

fers to text superimposed on the lower third of the video screen, the most common place for titles.

super in sync   a direction to SUPERIMPOSE words or an image on a TV screen while an off-camera voice reads the text

superior (sup)   a letter or number smaller than the standard type size and set above the BASELINE to serve as a FOOTNOTE callout reference or for symbolic notation; also called SUPERSCRIPT or *superior character*   There are actually six possible correct positions for superior and inferior numbers relative to the baseline.

superscribe   to write, mark, or engrave a name or other text at the top or on the outer surface of an envelope or other surface   *Superscription* is the act of superscribing, as with a name and/or address.

superscript   a character above the BASELINE, such as a numerical exponent; also called a SUPERIOR CHARACTER

superstar   an extremely prominent celebrity

superstation   a local TV station transmitted via satellite to cable systems in many markets, such as WTBS-TV in Atlanta, WGN-TV in Chicago, or WWOR-TV in New York   The word was coined and copyrighted by WTBS-TV.

Super VHS (S-VHS)   a new type of videocassette recorder developed by the JVC Corporation of Japan   With about 1,430 lines instead of 240 lines, it has vastly superior picture quality and improved resolution.

supper club   an exclusive nightclub

supplement   a separate section such as *Parade*, *USA Weekend*, or other national and local Sunday newspaper supplements inserted into a periodical or bound into a publication, such as an addendum to a book   A *comic supplement* is a color section devoted to comic strips. A supplement or CONTINUATION also may be issued independently as an update to a previous publication.

supplier   an independent contractor who provides art, photography, printing, or other materials or services to an advertiser or other customer

supply reel   a feed or storage reel on a reel-to-reel tape recorder

sur.   surface

surface chart   a graphic representation with the plotted points in a sequence connected by lines   The area below these lines is shaded or cross-hatched to the horizontal line running across the bottom, thus providing contrast to the blank area above the connected lines and making the diagram easier to read.

surface plate a flat metal plate—a *planometer*—such as used in printing In *letterpress*, the images are raised above the surface of the plate; in *lithography*, the entire surface is on the same plane.

surprint to SUPERIMPOSE over a previously printed item, as in putting one negative over another, commonly used to add words such as "new," "sale," "void," "discontinued," and "sold out"; also called *overprint* (not the same as printing excessive numbers of copies)

surround [film] a channel (the *surround channel*) played from the rear and/or sides of a theater, so that the audience is surrounded by the sound A *split-surround* arrangement of speakers (*stereo surround*), combined with a stereo soundtrack, produces a *quadraphonic* effect.

survey a comprehensive view; a study; an examination; an analysis A *mini-survey* is a more modest survey. In a *disguised survey*, the respondents are not told the reason for the survey.

survey week [broadcasting] the week in which a station's audience is monitored and rated The *Arbitron Ratings Company* in New York surveys radio stations throughout the year and assigns *survey week numbers* to each week starting with January 1.

suspended-interest story a format in which the story is told in sequence, building up or leading to a climax; the opposite of the INVERTED PYRAMID, in which the key facts are given at the beginning

suspended sentence a sentence with a surprise or major point at the end, designed to hold the reader in suspense It is also called a *periodic sentence*, as it must be read to the final period.

sustaining program a nonsponsored broadcast, generally PUBLIC SERVICE In advertising, a *sustaining campaign* maintains demand without attempting to increase it.

Suzy the pseudonym of Aileen Mehle (b. 1918), a newspaper columnist, based in New York, who writes about society *Suzyesque* is an adjective referring to society, as with Suzyesque guests at an event.

S-video new high-resolution TV The *S* is for separate wires, one for *luminance* (brightness) and the other for *chrominance* (color), the two parts of the TV signal.

S-V-O rule a journalism rule about sentence structure: begin with the subject, and follow closely with an action verb that leads directly to the object

SVP international telex abbreviation: please, from the French, *s'il vous plaît*

SW SHORT WAVE; switcher (see SWITCH)

swan song the final creative work of a person such as a performer or writer before retirement or death The origin is the sweet song sung by a dying swan in ancient fables.

swapping [computers] interchanging, as in *page swapping*, in which a page is transferred from main storage to auxiliary storage and vice versa

swash letter an ornamental *italic* letter with elaborate flourishes

swastika a design in the form of a cross with four right angles This ornament has been used in many societies, including the following:

卐 American Indian swastika

卍 German Nazi swastika

swatch a small strip or square cut from cloth, paper, or other material used as a sample or specimen *Swatchbooks* are samples in a variety of colors and patterns, generally bound together with a pin or loop, commonly provided by manufacturers of inks, paper, and other materials to artists and other customers.

sweating mounting an engraving or electrotype on a metal base to provide added support during a long press run

sweep 1 [broadcasting] a period of the year in November, February, May, and July when rating services measure station audiences During sweeps, networks and stations employ more sensational programming and audience contests and promotions. A *sweeps report* is published by a research organization such as NIELSEN or ARBITRON for each *sweep month*. 2 [television] the repetitive movement of the cathode beam over the phosphor screen Of the two sweeps, one traces horizontal lines and the other moves vertically at a slower rate. 3 [theater] the curve of an arch in a stage FLAT

sweephand a large pointer (hand) on a watch or clock that indicates the seconds; also called *sweep hand* or *sweep second hand* The sweephand is important in timing commercials and programs.

sweep link in radio commercials, a transitional recorded jingle, such as between bits of copy read live by an announcer

sweeps broadcasting ratings (see SWEEP); also, short for SWEEPSTAKES

sweepstakes a lottery, a contest in which the winners are randomly selected from all entrants; also called *sweeps* To prevent infringement of lottery laws, commercial sweepstakes do not require entrants to purchase products or provide any monetary consideration.

sweetening enhancing; adding anything pleasant, as in *sweetening a plot* or *sweetening a deal* In the mixing of sound in films, sweetening is the addition of sound effects or other new sounds.

sweetening session [film] the concluding session of mixing—combining—the sound with the picture

sweet nothings murmured words of endearment, sometimes used as a script notation or direction to performers

swell an increase, as in sound volume; the thickness of a book at its binding edge

swell allowance a reduction from an invoice price to compensate for merchandise damaged in transit

SWG SCREEN WRITERS GUILD

swim [computers] undesired, slow movements of elements on a display, slower than JITTER

swing [theater] an understudy or STANDBY performer

swing gang a production crew that works on the night shift

swing shift a work period between the early and late shifts—in a 24-hour operation, from about 4 P.M. to midnight In news media, the swing shift is worked by employees who swing, or rotate, from one shift to another.

swipe to steal; to filch A *swipe file* is a collection of art or other material for *idea generation*, adaptation, or other use.

swish pan a rapid horizontal movement of a movie or TV camera resulting in a blur; also called *blur pan, flash pan, flick pan, whip pan,* or *zip pan* The transitional or blurred scene itself also is called a swish pan.

Swiss cheese [graphic arts] slang for a TEMPLATE, which has many holes

Swiss-cheese release a news release with blank spaces—holes—for localized fill-in, such as the name of a local dealer

switch 1 a device for changing an electrical connection or controlling the flow of electricity; transferring or shifting, as of an opinion or vote 2 [broadcasting] a direction to move or change, as from one camera or video source to another or to change camera angles The device (video mixer) or person (studio engineer) responsible for camera mixing or switching is called a switch or *switcher*. Switching is the selection process among the various audio and video sources in a production. 3 [computers] a device or programming technique for making a selection A *switch code* is a command to move from one storage location to another, such as to merge names, addresses, or other fill-ins onto a form letter.

switchboard a panel, or board, equipped with apparatus for controlling the operation of a system of electric circuits, as in broadcasting or a telephone exchange Manually operated switchboards, common in the first half of the 20th century, used pairs of cords and keys on a horizontal desk and strips of jacks in panels on a vertical face, operated by a *switchboard operator* at the telephone company or on the subscriber's premises.

SWOP Specifications for Web Offset Publications: recommendations for advertisers, publishers, and other big users of *web* printing presses; developed by the SWOP industry review committee and published in the SWOP manual, which is distributed by printers and by the American Association of Advertising Agencies, American Business Press, and the Magazine Publishers Association

swung dash a symbol, —, used to indicate a repeated word; akin to a ditto mark, also called a *similar*

syllabary a set or table of syllables or abbreviations, characters, and signs that represent syllables with their full spellings; also called *spelling table*

syllepsis a grammatical construction in which one word is used to modify or link two or more words, though it grammatically agrees with only one of them A *sylleptic* example is, "Either they or I am wrong." It may be grammatically correct but use different meanings of the same word. For example, as Groucho Marx said, "She left in a Cadillac and a huff."

symbol an object, emblem, mark, or other representation of something else, such as the cross as a symbol of Christianity, a dove as a symbol of peace, or such complex symbols as the white whale in *Moby-Dick* by Herman Melville (1819–91) The adjective *symbolic* refers to something expressed as a symbol; *symbolism* is the representation of things by symbols, as created or used by a *symbolist*. To *symbolize* is to represent by a symbol or to use a symbol or symbols. A list of punctuation symbols appears under PUNCTUATION. Following is a list of symbols commonly used in mathematics and other fields, many of which are available in computer and other FONTS:

Symbol	Meaning
≈	approximately
÷ or /	divided by
=	equal to
≧	equal to or greater than
≦	equal to or less than
>	greater than
<	less than
−	minus
× or •	multiplied by
/	not
≠	not equal to
Ω	ohm

symbolic quote a quotation that is a composite of remarks by more than one person A symbolic quote is not the same as a *paraphrased quote*, which is an adaptation of remarks by one person.

symmetrical public relations a system of relative equality of input and output in the two-way flow of communication between an organization and its publics

symmetry correspondence in size, form, and arrangement, such as a *symmetrical layout* in which text and art are placed in matching columns or areas

symphonic poem a musical composition for a symphony orchestra, usually in one movement and based on a literary, historical, or other nonmusical subject; sometimes called a *tone poem*

symposium a meeting, generally academic or professional, with several speakers; a collection of articles on the same subject A *symposium interview* is a story based on interviews of several people.

sync 1 SYNCHRONIZATION 2 [film] the linking of picture and sound; also called *dead sync, edit sync, editorial sync, level sync,* or *parallel sync*

synchronic of or concerned with language or other subjects at a specific time, without regard to the antecedents, as opposed to DIACHRONIC, which refers to changes over an extended period of time

synchronization the coordination of elements, such as audio and video *Synchronized,* or correctly related, elements are *in synchronization,* or *in sync.* The SYNC MARK is the signal on the audio and video tracks to correlate the two.

synchronization rights permission to use existing recorded music, such as for background in an animation film In television, sync rights are granted by a music publisher in behalf of a composer; in addition, performance rights must be obtained from the performer.

synchronizer a device that produces operation in unison In photography, it trips the camera shutter simultaneously with the illumination from a FLASH or lighting unit. In computers, it compensates for a difference between two or more devices in the rate at which information is processed.

synchronous simultaneous; having the same period between movements In *synchronous data communications,* streams of individual bits are transmitted at equal time intervals. A *synchronous transmission* does not use synchronous timing and simply defines the beginning and end of each BYTE.

syncing [film] SYNCHRONIZING, particularly of picture and sound *Syncing dailies* is the arrangement of daily workprints so that picture

and sound are *in sync.* The synchronizing process is called *syncing up.*

syncopate to shorten a work; to shift the accent in a poem or musical composition *Syncopation* is the process of syncopating, such as in syncopated rhythm.

syncope the omission of a letter or letters from the middle of a word; a poetic or literary technique, sometimes indicated by an apostrophe, as in *o'er* for *over,* or the dropping of a sound from the middle of a word, as in pronouncing *Gloster* for *Gloucester* An *elision* is a syncope (pronounced SIN-ka-pee).

sync punch [film] a hole, or *sync mark,* punched on the film leader to synchronize it with the soundtrack or other pieces of film, or on the soundtrack as an audible cue for SYNCHRONIZATION with the picture or other soundtracks

synd. SYNDICATE

syndetic connecting or connected, as with conjunctions A *syndetic index* includes the relationships between headings, as with "see also" and other cross-references in accordance with a *syndetic structure;* it is used in a *syndetic catalog* or *connective catalog.*

syndicate (synd.) a service that provides articles, columns, cartoons, or other items distributed to newspapers and other subscribers The same concept is used to syndicate radio and TV programs, whose producer often is called a *syndicator* or *packager* rather than a syndicate. A *self-syndicator* is a columnist or broadcaster who distributes independently rather than turning over the material to a syndicate.

syndicated mailing [direct marketing] a mailing of items provided by different advertisers, such as coupons from various manufacturers

syndicated study a survey conducted by a market research firm or another third party and sold to several customers, in contrast to a single-client study done exclusively for the sponsor

syndicate store a low-price variety chain store

syndication the process or business of distributing a newspaper column, radio or TV program, or other material *First-run syndication* refers to programs produced for initial release to individual stations; *off-network syndication* is broadcast first on a network and then offered to individual stations.

syndicator in direct mail, a company that produces a sales sheet for an item or an entire catalog of items and provides the sales materials to others for imprinting and mailing to consumers

synecdoche a figure of speech in which a part of something is used to signify the whole or the whole for the part, such as hands for workers, mouths for people, or bread for food A common journalistic practice, particularly by newspaper headline writers, is to use the capital of a state or country to refer to the entire entity, such as Washington for the United States and Bonn for West Germany. It may be shorter, but, for example, Pretoria for South Africa can be confusing, particularly to readers who are poor in geography.

synectics a technique designed to encourage creative solutions to problems by uncritically using lateral or free association to provide new insights; also called *brainstorming*

synergy combined or cooperative action; also called *synergism*, an action of two or more substances or organisms to achieve an effect of which each is individually incapable Synergy is a word that has been adopted by communicators who use, overuse, or misuse it, generally to mean the mutual strengthening of two or more elements in a campaign to achieve a *synergistic effect* (always favorable).

synesthesia in literary composition, the description of one kind of sensation in terms of another, such as attributing color or odor to sounds, as with the color green evoking the smell of grass; also called *sense transfer* or *sense analogy* The word is from physiology and means a sensation felt in one part of the body when another part is stimulated.

synonym a word with the same or similar meaning as another word

synonymy the study of synonyms; a list of synonyms; the quality of being synonymous, as Johnny Carson is with the National Broadcasting Company

synopsis an outline; an abstract; a summary

synoptic presenting a general view, summary, or synopsis A *synoptic chart* or *synoptic map*

provides a broad view, particularly of atmospheric conditions over a wide area. A *synoptic journal* prints only summaries of articles. A *synoptic/microform journal* prints summaries of articles and also publishes the full articles in a *microfiche* edition.

syntax 1 sentence structure; the branch of grammar dealing with the systematic way in which words are put together to form phrases and sentences 2 [computers] the rules governing the construction of a computer machine language

synthesizer an electronic device with filters, oscillators, and amplifiers capable of producing speech and musical sounds, including the sound of musical instruments The *Moog synthesizer*, which often is used for musical effects, was invented by Robert A. Moog (b. 1934). The name rhymes with vogue.

sysop a computer systems operator; pronounced SIS-op

system a group of interacting, interrelated, or interdependent elements; a method; a network The *systems approach* or *systems analysis* examines all components of a problem. In computers, system has many definitions depending on whether it is applied to software or hardware or from the viewpoint of the machine or its applications to users.

systematic sampling a PROBABILITY SURVEY method in which a name is selected randomly from a population list and then, using that as a starting point, every Nth name (such as every 100th name) is selected for the survey This technique is related to RANDOM SAMPLING.

systems cue a signal for local station identification; a prearranged word, phrase, sound, or image

T

T TABLE; TIME In papermaking, *T* refers to *trimming* or cutting; paper trimmed on all four sides is *T4S*.

TA TOTAL AUDIENCE; THEATRE AUTHORITY INC.

tab 1 a small flat loop, strap, or flap; a projecting piece of a card, particularly an index file folder; a label, marker, or indicator 2 [computers] A tab is located at either or both ends of a medium, such as a tape. *Tabbing* is the moving of a cursor or printer head to a specified column on the screen or paper. A *tab command* shifts the cursor to the next *tab stop*. 3 [newspapers] short for TABLOID A theme supplement, such as a back-to-school, auto show, or fall fashion supplement, generally is published as a tabloid, inserted in a full-size newspaper, and referred to as a *school tab, car tab, fashion tab*, etc. 4 [typography] short for TABBING, *tabulation*, or *tabular material* A tab is the point marking the beginning of a column in which *tabular* material is to appear.

tabbing 1 [computers] a process of shifting a cathode-ray-tube CURSOR or a printing head to a prespecified column on the screen or paper 2 [typography] the insertion of QUADS or spaces on lines in a table (*tabular lines*) to fill out each line to the column measure

table an orderly arrangement or list of items, such as a *table of contents*, a list of chapters, articles, sections, or other components of a book or other publication The abbreviation is *T.*, generally followed by a number or letter.

tableau a striking dramatic scene or picture, particularly a stationary grouping of performers or figures (a more contemporary word is *frieze*); also, an elaborate stage presentation, generally involving groupings of silent, posing performers, called *tableau vivant* or living tableau

tabloid a newspaper of less-than-standard size, generally about 1,000–1,200 AGATE lines on a page that is 14 inches high and has four or more columns, about 12 inches in width Originally published for mass appeal, tabloids featured large sensational headlines on the front page and developed a disreputable reputation. Today, tabloids are an important part of journalism and include the *Christian Science Monitor* and

Newsday, as well as the *National Enquirer* and other large-circulation weeklies. Preprinted advertising supplements generally are tabloid-size, for insertion in all sizes of newspapers. For example, *The New York Daily News* has a tabloid page of six advertising columns, each 9.6 picas or $1^1/_{16}$ inch wide and 202 agate lines deep, totaling a type-space area of $14^3/_8'' \times 9^3/_4''$.

tabloid fold a longitudinal fold; also called *first parallel fold*

tabloid-style TV program a program that uses the popular style of combining news and features associated with tabloid newspapers

tabular matter type set in a TABLE or statistical form *Tabular work* is the typesetting of a table, typically two or more columns of data, such as a financial table in a newspaper.

tabulation the production of a collection of data; a TABLE

tachistoscope an instrument to measure recognition of a message, such as advertising, or perception of a package by evaluating the response time, in fractions of a second, of eye movement; also called *t-scope*

tack the adhesive quality of a medium in printing, the stickiness or pulling force of an ink—the degree to which the ink pulls between the paper and the inking surface; sometimes spelled *tac Tacky* is sticky paper or other material that is slightly adhesive or gummy. A *tacky ink* has a high *pulling* force and can split a weak paper. A *tackoscope* or inkometer measures the stickiness or tack of an ink. The degree of adhesion is indicated by *high tack* or *low tack*.

tactics methods and actions to achieve objectives; different from *strategy*, which is the plan that precedes the execution or tactics

tag 1 a key phrase; the final line of an act or scene; also called *tag line* 2 [advertising] the slogan or phrase accompanying a LOGO; the bottom line in a print ad or the last line in a commercial A local live addition to a recorded commercial is called a tag or *tagalong*. 3 [journalism] a closing mark at the end of a story or news release, such as -30- A tag line, or tag-line, is a brief caption or comment; it is also a line preceding or following an article, particularly in a newspaper, indicating its source, such as a wire service. **4** [music] an extension to a song; also called CODA **5** [writing] In a novel or other work, a character can be identified with a specific mannerism or trait, called a *character tag*, such as an *action tag* (a physical trait or mannerism), *background tag* (a stereotypical demographic trait), *name tag* (a name with a geographical, ethnic, or other connotation), or *speech tag* (a dialect or speech mannerism). Actors such as Robert DeNiro and Jack Nicholson are expert in adapting character tags, as are many writers, directors, and others.

tagging a process of coating postage stamps with an invisible phosphorous additive that glows when exposed to ultraviolet light Mail-processing machines recognize the *tagged* stamps and automatically FACE the envelopes to cancel them.

tail the last sequence of a show, commercial, or recording

tail-light display an advertisement on the outside rear of a bus or other vehicle; also called *rear-end display*

tailpiece a small typographical ornament or illustration placed at the end of a block of text, used by *Fortune* and other publications; a concluding article in a publication or the last report on a TV news program

tails out unrewound film or tape with the *tail* or end outermost; also called *tails up* Its opposite is HEADS UP, which has the front or beginning outermost.

take **1** to catch, hit, obtain, perform, seize, or win The verb has many other idiomatic usages, including *take a picture* (to photograph), *take a level* (to test to determine audio level), *take a meeting* (to meet), *take it from the top* (to begin again), and *take five* (to have a coffee or rest break of about five minutes). **2** [film] a scene, shot, or other single uninterrupted component Each time the scene is repeated is another take with a different numerical designation. A *selected take* is one that has been approved. A *take list* or *take sheet* is a sheet of film or tape takes. A *long take* generally lasts longer then one minute. **3** [journalism] a page of news copy or a short length of copy, such as a section sent at one time to the composing room *Take now* is commonly used by a variety of media people to mean a version, as of an article. **4** [photography] all of the pictures of an assignment **5** [typography] part of a larger typesetting job *Take back* is an instruction to move one or more lines to a previous column or page. *Take over* is an instruction to move one or more lines to the next column or page. An ink that *takes* is effective. **6** [television] a direction to move from one camera or video source

to another *Take camera* is an instruction to a performer to turn toward the camera. *Take it* is to print a take. **7** [theater] a performer's physical reaction, such as of surprise A *double take* is two reactions, the second more emphatic; a *slow take* is a delayed reaction; a *body take* involves the head. To *take a scene* or *take the stage* is to draw attention to oneself. To *take a bow* (or *call a hand*) is to acknowledge audience applause. To *take a count* is to delay reaction by timing a pause. *Take it away!* is a direction to begin, such as to open the curtain or start an act, though it also can mean to remove. *Take down* is to decrease, as with the intensity of a light, or to dismantle scenery. *Take the veil*, which literally means to become a nun, is theatrical slang for leaving show business.

take a 42 an announcement of a 42-minute meal break for a film production crew, as specified in union contracts

takeaway a coupon or other item removed from a pad attached to a transit CAR CARD or point-of-sale display

take-bar [television] a device that records and stores cuts, mixes, and other effects and then automatically produces them from memory for use in editing when a bar is pressed

take it away a broadcast-engineering cue, such as "Take it away New York," indicating a transition to a studio or location in New York

takeoff an adaptation; a variation; a caricature

take-one pad a pad of coupons or other promotional materials affixed to a CAR CARD, display, shelf, or other surface so that a consumer can tear off and take one

takeout **1** an extract; an excerpt **2** [radio] a complete report by a reporter from outside the studio; also called *wrap, wraparound, wrapper,* or *package* **3** [theater] to raise or remove scenery; to dim or turn off lighting **4** [writing] an impression, an article or other work based on something already in existence A *takeout book*, on the other hand, is a very successful book, so successful that it takes out or reduces the probability of success by other books of the same type or on the same subject.

take rate in pay-per-view television, the percentage of subscribers who purchase the specific programs offered during a particular period, generally a month The average take rate is 20 percent, which means that the average subscriber accepts 20 percent of the total available programs.

take 2 the second TAKE, slang for a reprint or rebroadcast

take-up reel package reel for processed film; the receiving reel on a REEL-TO-REEL tape player, the *B-reel* The input reel is the *A-reel* or *feed reel.*

taking it home giving a rousing finale, as in a jazz music performance

taking lens [film] the lens, among several lenses on a turret, that is actually used for a specific TAKE

tale a story, particularly an exotic or adventurous narrative; malicious gossip or a lie

talent performers and other creative people, such as writers and directors

talent coordinator a person who auditions and schedules performers and guests on TV talk shows, the equivalent of a *casting director* in films Generally, the performers are paid and the guests, if they are not union members and are not performing, are not paid. There are several talent coordinators at such programs as *The Tonight Show,* where their power with regard to publicists and performers is awesome.

talkback 1 a communications system within an audio or video studio linking the control room with people in the studio 2 [television] a brief sequence at the end of a live REMOTE news report in which the ANCHOR asks one or more questions of the reporter

talkies old-fashioned slang for sound films, particularly in the early days—the late 1920s and early 1930s—of pictures with sound

talking book a recorded version of a book in which the text is spoken, primarily for use by the blind

talking head [television] a person shown merely speaking, presented in a dull or unimaginative way

talk show a radio or TV show with interviews, telephone conversations with listeners, and other talk or chatter

talk station a radio station that broadcasts all or mostly news, interviews, and sports

talk turkey to talk candidly and directly

tall copy a specially prepared book that is longer than others of the same edition The upper and lower margins are wider, generally as a result of less trimming of the leaves or by printing on larger paper.

tally light a red light on an *active camera;* a *cue* light indicating that the camera is in use

TALO TOTAL AUDIENCE LISTENING OUTPUT

T and A tits and ass, a movie or other work featuring female anatomy

T and E travel and entertainment

T & M time (labor) and materials (expenses)

tank development film processing in a tank

tank-shot [film] the filming of action on or under water, using a large container of water—a *studio tank*

tap an electrical or other connection, often used to overtly or secretly divert a signal; a place in a circuit where a connection can be made

tape to record on audio and/or videotape; a ribbon or band of paper, cloth, plastic, or other material, such as a magnetic strip for audio or video recording and playback Plastic tape, acetate, mylar, or polyester is impregnated on one side with iron oxide or chromium oxide that retains a variable magnetic charge. Tape widths include $1/4$, $1/2$, $3/4$, 1, and 2 inches. Tape speeds include $1 1/8$, $3 3/4$, $7 1/2$, and 15 inches per second. Tapes are supplied on *reels* or *cassettes* (*cartridges*). A *pure* tape is error-free. A tape cartridge or cassette contains an endless loop of magnetic tape and is used in dictation and other recording and playback on various types of tape recorders and players. A symbol for a computer tape is ⌑. A variety of *pressure-sensitive* tapes with adhesive backs used in graphic arts include glossy- and matte-finish tapes, transparent and opaque tapes, and pattern tapes with ruled lines and other borders and patterns for use in displays. In bookbinding, strips of paper or cloth are pasted on sewn (*sewn-on* tapes) to the covers to strengthen the binding.

TAPE television *audience program evaluation,* a technique of evaluating viewer reaction

tape deck a device to play tapes, sometimes including a *recorder* but without speakers, a component in an audio or video system A *tape library* is a collection of tapes.

tape delay system on call-in radio programs, a procedure used to tape a phone call and delay it for a few seconds prior to broadcast so that obscenities can be deleted or the call cut off prior to broadcast

tape log a list of contents or sequences on an audio or videotape

tape picking the use of tape to lift—*pick*—self-adhesive letters from the surface on which they have been positioned

tapping the track a process of marking a soundtrack or tape—*tapping the tape*—for use in editing

tare the weight of a container deducted from the total weight to determine the weight of the contents or load In printing, the *tare weight* includes the carton and anything else that is not the contents, such as packing material and SKIDS.

target 1 a recipient of a communication, such as a magazine or other medium, or the specific audience sought by the communicator The primary or most important group often is called the *target audience. Targeted* or *selective media* are specific communication channels that can deliver a message to specific audiences. **2** a small circular piece of material to shade a camera lens

Target Group Index (TGI) a market research report provided by Axiom Market Research Bureau in Melville, NY, based on a survey of selected media audiences and including DEMO-GRAPHICS and information about usage of products and services

target language in a bilingual dictionary, the language of the definitions The entry words are in the SOURCE LANGUAGE.

target marketing a strategy aimed at a specific audience, as compared to broad or mass marketing *Target market coverage* (T.M.C.) is a campaign or media designed to reach a specific audience or area.

Tass the Soviet news agency owned by the government

tat [theater] costumes, particularly old costumes, kept in a *tatbox*

tautology a redundant word or words; the unnecessary repetition of an idea in different words; also called *pleonasm* It is sometimes used as an intentional RHETORICAL device, for emphasis.

TAX international telex abbreviation: "what is the charge" or "the charge is"

taxi-top an advertising panel, generally BACKLIT, on the roof of a taxicab The advertisements affixed to the roofs or rears of cabs are called *taxi displays.*

TBA 1 to be announced, used in broadcasting when the name of a program or other information is not available **2** a class of automotive trade that refers to tires, batteries, and accessories

T.B.D. to be determined, as of an unchosen time period for a TV program

TBE time base corrector, a device to stabilize the picture in a videotape recorder

T core a plastic spool, or core, that is relatively small, two inches in diameter, and holds up to 400 feet of 16mm film

T.C.U. TIGHT close-up

T.D. TECHNICAL DIRECTOR

TDD TELECOMMUNICATIONS FOR THE DEAF

T.E. TELEGRAPH editor at a newspaper

teardown to dismantle, as with an exhibit

tearing the irregular horizontal synchronization of a TV picture

tearjerker a movie or other work that is sad, sentimental, maudlin, and evocative of tears

tears TEAR SHEETS

tear sheet or **tearsheet** a page or pages from a publication consisting of an article, advertisement, or other material A *tear-sheet book* is a publication composed entirely of previously printed material. Standard & Poor's, a company in New York, publishes reports about publicly owned companies that stockbrokers sometimes tear from their binders and send to customers; the sheets thus are called tear sheets. In film, a tear sheet or *breakdown sheet* is prepared for each scene during the production, with considerable information about the location, equipment, cast, and other details.

tear strength the degree of resistance of a paper to tearing or ripping

tease 1 advertising, publicity, or promotion to develop curiosity about a forthcoming campaign; also called *teaser* **2** [broadcasting] a bit of news preceding the newscast; an announcement of an upcoming story to whet interest; also called teaser or *hooker* **3** [journalism] a word or brief headline appearing above the main headline, also called teaser or *kicker*; text or art on the cover of a magazine to develop interest in an article or feature *Teaser copy* is advance material or part of a letter or other item designed to whet curiosity, to tease or *hook* the reader. **4** [theater] a horizontal piece of flat scenery above two vertical pieces called TOR-MENTORS, used to frame a stage opening

tea-wagon slang for a sound-mixing console

techie or **tekkie** theatrical slang for a technician; also, someone versed in computers or technical equipment

technical director (T.D.) the director of the technical facilities in a television studio He or she generally sits next to the director in the control room and operates the switcher (see SWITCH).

technical pen a type of drawing pen with a round point that produces a precise, controlled flow of ink

Technicolor a trademarked color motion-picture process Originally, all color movies involved equipment from Technicolor Corp., including a camera that makes three negatives, one for each of the primary colors, from which a Technicolor composite print was processed. Other subsequent color processes include Eastman Color. Formed in 1915 as the Technicolor Motion Picture Corporation, the company, now called Technicolor Inc., is headquartered in North Hollywood, CA.

technique a systematic procedure; a skill or style, particularly of an artist or musician

tech reqs technical requirements of a TV or other production, pronounced "tek-reks"

tee the letter *T* or anything shaped like a *T*, such as the tee used as a support for the legs of a camera TRIPOD, also called a *wheeled tee*, *spreader*, or *spider* and sometimes shaped like a *Y* (a triangle)

t.e.g. TOP-EDGE gilt

tel. *telegram*; TELEGRAPH; *telegraphic*; TELEPHONE

telco a telephone company In broadcasting, a *telco line* is telephone cable, commonly used to transmit radio and TV broadcasts. The plural is *telcos*.

telecast a broadcast on television

telecide slang for an unsuccessful TV program or a TV performer who fails, a contraction of television and suicide

telecine a film-and-slide projection system or department of a TV station The second part of the word is from the French *ciné* or *cinema*, and the pronunciation is French: tel-i-sin-ay. A telecine is also a machine that converts film into a format suitable for TV transmission, also called a *film scanner*. Types of telecine machines include a *film chain* and *flying spot*.

telecommunication electronic transmission by cable, computer, radio, satellite telegraph, telephone, or television, or the message itself; also used as a plural noun, *telecommunications* Associations include the International Association of Satellite Users in McLean, VA, International Communications Association in Washington, DC, and North American Telecommunications Association in Washington, DC.

telecommunications device for the deaf (TDD) a typewriterlike device with an acoustic coupler that fits into a phone receiver so that hearing- or speech-impaired people can type and receive messages transmitted via telephone lines A specific TDD is the Teletypewriter (TTY). TDD listed after a subscriber's name in a telephone directory indicates that the subscriber has a TDD.

Tele-Communications, Inc. one of the largest operators of cable-TV systems and other broadcasting companies, headquartered in Denver, CO

telecommuting use of a cellular telephone, personal computer, or other device connected via telephone lines to conduct business from a car, home, or other place that is not a conventional office

teleconference a meeting held at more than one site with the sites joined by audio and/or video links The process is *teleconferencing*. The term is also used for a computerized method of linking students with professors and other experts.

Telecopier a facsimile transceiver made by the Xerox Corporation, Dallas, TX

tele-extender an optical device placed between a PRIME LENS and the film plane to lengthen the effective focal length of the lens; also called *teleconverter* A 2X tele-extender doubles the focal length of a lens so that, for example, a 135mm lens is converted to a 270mm lens.

telefilm a motion picture produced for television

TeleFrance USA a cable network in New York that transmits French films and other French programs

telegenic visible personal characteristics that create an attractive physical appearance on television; the TV counterpart of *photogenic*

telegraph an apparatus or system for transmitting messages by coded electronic signals by wire or cable A *telegrapher* is a person who transmits or receives telegraphic messages—*telegrams*. *Telegraphy* is communication by telegraph. At newspapers, the *telegraph editor* (*T.E.*) is in charge of telegraph news, including The Associated Press and other wire news. The telegraph editor may supervise the newspaper's correspondents, particularly foreign correspondents, or may be limited to editing copy received on the wires. The term *telegraph editor* has generally been replaced by *wire editor*. To telegraph is to transmit a telegraphic message, or to unintentionally make known in advance, as with a hint or clue in a story or play about a forthcoming development.

telemarketing selling via the telephone

Telematique a French TELETEXT system

telemetry a process of detecting and gathering information at one location and transmitting it, particularly via radio, to another The instrument or device for determining the distance is a *telemeter*.

telephone an instrument or system for electronic transmission of acoustic source signals Originally, telephonic transmission was of voice or other sound via wire; now it includes data and other waves and is not limited to wire. A *telephone book* is a directory of telephone subscribers. The major telephonic trade association is the United States Telephone Association in Washington, DC.

telephone agency a company that specializes in using the telephone for research and promotions—TELEMARKETING—or in handling large numbers of telephone inquiries and other incoming and outbound telephone calls

telephone auction a fund-raising technique used by many public broadcasting stations in which listeners or viewers call on the telephone to bid on products and services that have been donated

telephone coincidental a telephone survey of viewers or listeners, conducted during a program

telephone program a recorded message, such as prayers, jokes, or pornography, available to callers of special numbers, generally for a premium charge

telephone sales representative (TSR) a person who sells via the telephone

telephone survey a survey conducted by telephone rather than by mail or in person

telephone tag the process of one person telephoning another who is out or on another call and leaving a "call me" message When the call is returned, the original caller is out or on another call, and a "returned your call" message is left. This vexing cycle sometimes goes on for days.

telephony the science of telephone transmission; the making or operation of telephones; the name of a trade publication, *Telephony*, based in Chicago; pronounced tell-LEF-o-nee

telephoto 1 a camera lens to photograph objects or action at a distance; also called *long lens* or *narrow-angle lens* 2 a photograph transmitted by wire

telephotography the art or process of photographing distant objects by using a *telephoto lens*, a camera lens designed for this purpose, or by using a telescope with a camera; the science or process of transmitting images over distances by converting light rays into electric signals that are sent over wire or radio channels Communications satellites use this technique to transmit television pictures.

telepic a feature-length motion picture made for television

teleplay a play written or adapted for television

teleport a site—*port*—with a collection of telecommunications facilities, generally linked via optical fiber to a nearby cluster

teleprinter a TELETYPEWRITER

teleprocessing transmitting data over telephone lines; computer service via terminals remote from the central computer

teleprompter a trademarked visual prompting device for speakers and television performers that reproduces the current portion of the script in enlarged letters, originally made by a New York-based company no longer in business Its device, attached to the TV camera so that performers can look into the camera, was called a TelePrompTer, which has become a generic term for a teleprompter, also called a *teleprompt*. To teleprompt is to use such a device.

In the United Kingdom, a teleprompter is called an *autocue*. See also PROMPTER.

telepublishing ELECTRONIC PUBLISHING

Tele-Research Item Movement Inc. (TRIM) a market research firm in Los Angeles specializing in SCANNER data

telescope to condense or shorten, as one does with the tubes of a collapsible telescope; to overlap speeches, such as when two performers unintentionally speak at the same time

telescoping a process of compressing or shortening, as in the editing of taped commercials to omit silent spots or other material in order to reduce them to 30 seconds or another desired length

teleselling TELEMARKETING; use of the telephone for promotion

teletex a telecommunications system for the sending and receiving of messages via word processors and other electronic equipment It is an upgraded version of *Telex* and is not the same as TELETEXT.

teletext one-way transmission of newspapers, newsletters, data, timetables, advertisements, and other "pages" of printed and graphic material onto a TV screen, such as in a home or office The text is transmitted on the *vertical blanking interval*, which is sometimes seen as a black bar on the TV screen when the picture rolls. Thus, teletext can be transmitted with regular programs and can be viewed only with a *decoder* attached or built in to the TV set. *Broadcast teletext* is sent over the air. *Cable teletext* or *cabletext* is transmitted by cable or satellite to cable systems. Teletext is a form of VIDEOTEX. It is not the same as TELETEX.

telethon television marathon, a long TV program to raise funds from viewers

Teletype a trademarked name of the Teletype Corporation of New York for a TELETYPEWRITER leased-line service The term is commonly used generically—*teletype*—for a data or text transmission system; for the device itself, consisting of a keyboard and printer; and as a verb, meaning to transmit via such a system.

teletypewriter a device that is a combination of a telegraph and a typewriter; abbreviated as TTW or, more commonly, TTY The receiver prints messages typed on a keyboard. Teletypewriters are used by hearing-impaired people to communicate via teletypewriters in their home.

teletypewriter exchange (TWX) an electromechanical typewriter system for two-way communication that transmits and receives news and messages carried by TELEGRAPH or telephone wires

televangelist an evangelist who preaches on television

television (TV) the transmission of visual images (*video*), generally with accompanying sound, as with electromagnetic waves transmitted by a TV station and received by TV sets The sets in homes (*television homes* or *TV households*) are used as the basis for TV audience ratings of the number of *televiewers*. Televiewer may have a more specific definition, such as a person who watches at least six minutes of a 30-minute program.

television black not pitch black, with about 3-percent *reflectance*

Television Bureau of Advertising (TvB) a promotion and research organization, based in New York, to promote TV as an advertising medium

television receive-only in satellite broadcasting, an earth station that can receive but not transmit, consisting of an antenna and equipment; commonly called a *TVRO terminal* or *satellite terminal*

television recording (TVR) a film of a TV commercial or program as it is broadcast; also called *film transfer, transfer, kinescope recording,* or *kine* No longer common, it generally has been replaced by *videotape recording* (VTR).

television white not pure white, having about 60-percent *reflectance* (about 60 percent of light is reflected from the TV screen) The TV camera cannot reproduce pure white or pure black.

Telex a contraction of *teletypewriter* and *exchange*, a Western Union communications system of teletypewriters; to transmit via Telex or, generically, via any keyboarding system using telephone lines

Telidon a two-way interactive videotex system developed by the Canadian government

tell-all book a publication in which the subject, generally the author, candidly describes what his or her experience was really like, such as to have been in the White House

tell story a news report read by a radio or TV announcer or reporter without accompanying tape or film

tell-tale an identification system used in dictionaries and other reference books with a headline that has the first word on the left page and the last word on the right page

telly British slang for television

Telly Awards a prize—a statuette—for outstanding TV commercials that were not broadcast on the three major networks; started in 1979 by Telly Awards in Cincinnati

telop *telopticon*, a device for projecting small cards on TV for announcements The term is also used to describe the slides used with a *Balopticon*, though these actually are BALOPS.

Telstar the first microwave communications satellite, placed in orbit on July 10, 1962

tempera a painting medium in which pigment is mixed with water-soluble materials or egg yolk; opaque watercolor paint In spite of the egg yolk, it's not tempura and is not edible.

template or **templet** a guide, usually plastic or metal, containing a pattern or drawing and other graphic arts A *lettering template* is a sheet, generally plastic, with letter forms that can be traced by moving a drawing tool along the edges of the openings. A template may also be a cutout, generally metal, used on a spotlight or scenery to create the outline of a shape; this is usually called a *cookie.*

tempo the pace or rate of activity, particularly of music *In tempo* is conforming to the speed at which a musical composition was written, the opposite of *out of tempo*. To *step up the tempo* is to increase the speed.

Tempo a cable network featuring home shopping, headquartered in Tulsa, OK; formerly Satellite Program Network

temp track [film] a soundtrack with existing recorded music, such as classical music, used during the production of a film, to be replaced during post-production with new music on a new soundtrack

ten a ten-second commercial

ten-add details of an article written or transmitted before the beginning—the lead or top—is written The procedure is used when an obituary or biography is written before a person dies or when late-breaking news developments, such as the outcome of a sports event or election, are awaited. The phrase refers to the practice of marking pages after the first page as one-add (addition), two-add, etc. On the assumption that the forthcoming material will be several pages but not more than nine-add, the material written *in advance* is started with ten-add, thus distinguishing it from the material written subsequently.

ten codes codes commonly used in radio transmission by ham operators, dispatchers, police, and others *Ten-4* usually means "O.K." or "message received"; *ten-33* usually signals an emergency.

ten-K 1 10,000, as in a 10,000-watt spotlight **2** a report filed by a public company with the Securities and Exchange Commission (SEC) with additional information not included in its annual reports to shareholders

tenlight a lighting unit with ten bulbs, generally in a rectangular housing and used as a STRIPLIGHT along the floor to provide even illumination over a wide area

tenner a 10,000-watt spotlight, with a FRESNEL lens

ten percenter an agent, such as a performer's or literary agent, though the commission now is generally more than 10 percent

10-point column a phrase used at *The Wall Street Journal* for its Business and Finance column (page one, column two), which is set in 10-point type, slightly larger than the rest of the news material

tentative cut a portion of a film, tape, or script that can be eliminated in the final editing; also called *provisional cut*

tent card a display card printed and folded to be legible from two directions, often used on restaurant tables

tentpole [film] a series of sequels and spinoffs emanating from one company and serving as the foundation of its revenues

tent-pole [broadcasting] the time slot or position of a popular program that is preceded or followed by a weak one In HAMMOCKING, a weak program is scheduled between two popular programs, which have the outside or tent-pole positions, in an attempt to bolster it.

10XXX a telephone code in which the caller dials 1, then 0, then a three-digit (XXX) code to reach a specific carrier, such as 288 to reach AT&T; pronounced ten-triple-X For long-distance calls, the caller dials 1, then the area code and the seven-digit telephone number.

tera a trillion (10 to the 12th power or, in computers, 2 to the 40th power, which actually is more than a trillion)

term a word or phrase with a special meaning in a specific field, such as art or journalism In library science, a term is a subject heading in an index.

term dictionary common words, technical phrases, or other items stored in a word processor that can be called from memory with a minimum of keystrokes

terminal a point at which a current may be connected to an electric circuit; a device or location at which data feeds in or out of a computer

terminal area in newspapers, the lower right portion of a page

terms of sale the time and type of discounts and other aspects of payment

terper VARIETY slang for a dancer, from Terpsichore, the Greek muse of the dance

terrestrial feed radio, TV, or other transmission via land lines such as telephone, or direct (without lines); different from SATELLITE FEED

terrestrial interference (T.I. or TI) interference in broadcast transmission due to something on earth, such as other transmitters, in contrast to atmospheric interference

tertiary color a hue produced by a mixture of secondary colors, such as green, orange, and violet It is generally dull or dark.

test an examination, trial, standard, or criterion A *test pattern* is transmitted by a TV station to determine broadcast reception quality. A *test group* is a collection of individuals who are surveyed. *Testing* is examining, as in the administration of market research or other surveys. In photography, a *test strip* is a piece of paper already exposed at several different exposures that is used as a standard to determine printing time.

TEST international telex abbreviation: please send a test message

test-fly to try out

testimonial a statement testifying to a truth or fact; an affirmation of character or worth A *testimonial campaign* is the use of a person, generally but not necessarily prominent, to assert personal use or endorsement of a product or service. A *testimonial event* is an occasion, usually a lunch or dinner, at which individuals declare their support of or pay tribute to the person being honored.

test market an area in which a product is sold to gauge its appeal and/or for which advertising, public relations, and other techniques are utilized to determine their effectiveness with regard to broader distribution *Test-market translation* is the conversion of a national market plan to test market dimensions or, conversely, a projection of test-market results to a larger area.

tête-bêche a book with one text starting at the front and another text, generally a translation or another version of the same work, starting at the back, with each inverted to the other; also called *inverted pages* Postage stamps sometimes are printed in error with one inverted to the other. From the French, the term describes two people in a bed with the head of one at the feet of the other. It is different from *dos-à-dos*, in which two books are bound together and open in opposite directions with a covered board between them.

text 1 editorial material, as differentiated from advertising or artwork; the body of a printed work exclusive of preface, index, and other front and back matter; the exact words or the theme or topic of a speech or other work The word is from the Latin *textus*, or "fabric," so any script or work that is woven or fabricated is a text. An accurate version of a manuscript or other work is a *good text* and a poor or unreliable version is a *corrupt text*. 2 [computers] that part of a message that contains the information to be conveyed A *text editor* is a program that makes it possible to alter text that is stored. **3** [typography, publishing] body matter set in type (*body type*) as text; a class of BLACK-LETTER type, such as Old English, as used in various printed versions of the *Scriptures* (the text); a type of high-quality paper, generally 60- or 70-lb. and commonly used in books and other printing A *text edition* is an edition of a book for school use, usually at a lower price than the TRADE edition and sometimes with special material or an accompanying teacher's manual. A *textbook* or *text* is a book used for study, either prepared solely for instruction or a text edition of another book. A *text-fiche* is a book with microfiches, generally inserted in a pocket inside the front or back covers.

textual literal; word-for-word; conforming to a TEXT *Textual criticism* is the scientific investigation of literary documents to discover their history and origin.

Textura a formal, GOTHIC, BLACK-LETTER typeface used in early bibles; also called *lettre de forme* The name relates to the ornate look of a woven texture on the page.

texture the arrangement or character of the threads or components of fabric or paper Highly textured or uncoated papers generally have a strong feel or tactile appearance but tend to diffuse light so that colors may be less bright and accurate, whereas coated or smooth papers with less texture have sharper definition, greater color fidelity, and more durability. However, a coated paper may cost more and reflect light and thus sometimes tires the eye or seems too dazzling. Texture also refers to the composition, graininess, and feel or structural quality of a medium, generally a work of art but sometimes a work in another medium. For example, a sound engineer can describe a recording as having a great texture.

T.F. to fill, an instruction to a typesetter to set type to fill an indicated space; TILL FORBID, an instruction from an advertiser indicating that the advertising is to be repeated until further notice *TFN* means "until further notice."

theater a building or other place where films, operas, plays, and other works are presented; a lecture hall, auditorium, or other place in which shows or other presentations are given; a region or place where events take place, such as the *Southeast Asian theater* or other military designations; drama; the theatrical world, people engaged in theatrical activity, the *legitimate theater* of plays and similar live productions, as opposed to film and television; the technique involved in producing a play or similar work, or a reference to its effectiveness, as in a play that

is *good theater* A *theatergoer* is a person who attends a playhouse or other theater, usually quite often. Types of theaters include *outdoor theater*, *playhouse*, and *tent theater*. *Theaterland* is the theatrical district in a city, such as Broadway in New York, or the world of theatrical people.

Theater Communications Group a nonprofit organization in New York that provides fund-raising, public relations, and other services, primarily to nonprofit theater groups

theater of the absurd an experimental theatrical style that came into prominence in the 1950s and '60s with the *avant-garde* plays of Samuel Beckett, Jean Genêt, Eugene Ionesco, Harold Pinter, and others whose work was characterized by absurd or pointless situations and existential themes of isolation and frustration The term is sometimes capitalized as Theater of the Absurd; prose works of the same genre are called *Literature of the Absurd.*

theater party a special performance, particularly for the benefit of a charity or other group, and the audience who attends this performance

theatre alternate spelling, particularly in British countries, for *theater* It is sometimes mispronounced, for comic effect, the-AY-ter.

Theatre Authority (TA) an organization in New York and Hollywood that has jurisdiction over benefit performances by members of its participating unions and guilds

Theatre Development Fund (TDF) a New York organization to promote the theater that sells half-price tickets on days of performance at booths in Times Square and elsewhere

Theatre Guild a theatrical producing organization in New York whose projects includes a subscription service for touring plays

theatrical having to do with the theater, sometimes referring to a performance that is overly dramatic or histrionic To *theatricalize* is to make theatrical. *Theatricals* are performances of stage plays, particularly by amateurs. *Theatrics* are done or said for dramatic or histrionic effect.

theatrical box office revenue from films shown in theaters or motion-picture theaters themselves, as distinct from home video

theatrical movie a full-length motion picture The term originally referred to films shown in movie theaters but now refers to all types of feature films, which are also called *theatrical films* or *theatricals.*

thematic merchandising a selling promotion, such as in a retail outlet, in which products are jointly promoted in accordance with a central theme or focus, such as a holiday or season

thematic montage a film-editing technique to create a mood or establish or repeat a theme

theme the general subject, message, point of view, or idea of a broadcast program, publication, project, or campaign In show business, theme, or SIGNATURE, also means the principal melody, musical passage, or other identification of a specific program, performing group, or personality.

theme line a phrase, akin to a slogan, that appears in a prominent place in an advertisement, such as at the top or bottom, often below or adjacent to the name of the company or product

therefore mark a symbol used in mathematics as part of the proof of a theorem, consisting of three dots in the configuration of a triangle (∴) indicating hence, therefore, or, in Latin, *ergo*

thermal process heat or thermal copying, a nonreversing copying process that uses thermal energy, or heat, on heat-sensitive copy paper or film

thermography a LETTERPRESS printing process, similar to but cheaper than engraving, that produces slightly raised letters on paper such as letterheads or calling cards by adding a powder to the ink and then baking (*therm* means "heat")

thermomechanical pulp wood pulp that is steamed prior to and during its processing to produce a paper, such as high-quality newsprint, that is stronger than that from regular groundwood pulp

thesaurus a book of synonyms or definitions of specialized words, as in a particular field The best-known reference book of this type originally was compiled by Peter Mark Roget, an English physician (1779–1869), and still is published as *Roget's Thesaurus.*

thesis a proposition maintained or defended in argument; an unproven statement assumed as a premise; a research paper written in partial fulfillment of an academic degree The plural is *theses*, pronounced thee-sieze. The origin is a Greek word for "position" or "proposition." Since a thesis was a putting down, the ancient Greek poets referred to an accented syllable (indicated by the lowering of the hand or foot) as a thesis, the opposite of *arsis*, the raising or unaccented syllable. In classical Greek poetry, a thesis was the long or accented syllable of a group of syllables. However, in Latin usage and in later poetry, the meanings of thesis and arsis were reversed and a thesis became the lowering of the voice, as on a short, unaccented, unstressed syllable or syllables. Syllables sometimes are referred to as *in thesis* or *in arsis.*

thesis play a drama about a social problem, generally with a solution; sometimes called a *problem play* This type of play originated in France in the 19th century and was called *pièce à thèse.*

thespian having to do with drama or the theater; a performer The word derives from Thespis, a Greek poet, playwright, and actor and an originator of the TRAGEDY form of drama in the sixth century B.C., and now often is used to describe an overly dramatic or pretentious performance.

the trades the business—*trade*—publications in a specific field For example, a performer refers to *Variety, Hollywood Reporter,* and other show-business publications as "the trades."

theyism the habit of blaming someone else for a problem "They ought to drive more carefully," grumbles a *theyist* motorist as he drives through a red light.

thimble printer a direct-impression or -impact printer that uses a print head with two-character spokes radiating from a hub

thin weak, ineffective, without substance, as with a sound without resonance or an article without details In typesetting, a THIN SPACE is usually about 2 *points* in width.

thingamajig slang for any device, particularly a gadget, the name of which is not known or forgotten, as in "hand me that thingamajig"; also called *thingamabob*

thinking part theatrical slang for a role without dialogue

think piece an analytic article expressing opinions of the writer

thinner an additive, such as turpentine, mixed with ink, paint, rubber cement, or another substance to reduce viscosity and promote flow and ease of application

thin space the narrowest space between words, less than standard space

third-class mail a postal designation for printed matter and merchandise under a pound, including most of the bulk mail sent by direct-mail companies Third-class mail that meets size and other specifications is sent at rates considerably lower than those for FIRST-CLASS mail. If it is undeliverable, third-class mail is not returned to the sender unless it bears the notation *Return Postage Guaranteed* or *Address Correction Requested*, which is available to mailers at an extra fee.

third cover (3C) the inside back cover of a periodical

third generation a device or system that is significantly more advanced than the preceding second-generation models, such as a third-generation computer introduced in the 1960s with greater speed and increased storage and a third-generation typesetter whose character image is formed by a photographic or DIGITAL record on the face of a cathode-ray tube Fourth-generation computers were introduced in the 1980s.

third-number call   a telephone call charged to a number that is neither the calling nor receiving number and requires operator assistance; also called *bill-to-third-number call*

third party   a person other than the principals It is not the same as *third person,* which is *he, she, it,* or *they,* or a third-person narrative that is impersonal or less personal than a first-person narrative. In communications, the *first party* is the speaker or source and the *second party* is the listener or recipient. In public relations, an intermediary is used as a communications vehicle: the source, or first party, communicates with the audience, or second party, via an intermediary *third party*—a newspaper, radio station, TV station, magazine, or other medium. Because the third party exercises journalistic standards, it provides an endorsement by conveying the message from the first to the second party. Another usage of third party refers to an outside expert or other individual not directly connected to the first party who conveys his approval, a *third-party endorsement.*

third-party referral   [direct marketing] a technique of offering an incentive to customers or members who refer new customers or members

third stick   a direction to set type one-third the width of a newspaper column, as in a TABULATION The origin is the composing stick, or type holder, used by printers in the days of metal type.

thirty   1 [broadcasting] a 30-second radio or TV commercial, written as :30 2 [journalism] the number used to signify the end of a story, as in a newspaper dispatch, written as -30- The origin may be the Roman numerals for 30, XXX, which were used by telegraphers as a sign-off. Another theory is that at the time when it was common practice for telegraphers to end a message by indicating the number of words it contained, the first telegraphed message to a press association during the Civil War ended with the number 30, which then became the standard sign-off. The 30 symbol, called a TAG, has been replaced by many writers with -END- or a series of DOUBLE DAGGERS, generally three (‡‡‡). A *30-bar* is a heavy rule without a number used to end an article. A *30-dash* is several dash marks used for the same purpose; several *asterisks* comprise a *30-mark.*

thirty by forty   a poster about 30 inches wide and 40 inches high, generally called a *one-sheet* and commonly used in theater lobbies and elsewhere

Thirty-Day Rule   a regulation of the FEDERAL TRADE COMMISSION that requires direct market-

ers to notify customers if ordered products cannot be delivered within 30 days of the receipt of the order and to offer a refund or cancellation The full title is the *30-Day Delayed Delivery Rule.*

thirty-five   35-millimeter film, written as 35mm, with no periods and the *mm* adjacent to the number

Thirty Rock   the headquarters building of the National Broadcasting Company (NBC) at 30 Rockefeller Plaza in mid-Manhattan

thirty sheet   an outdoor advertising poster about 22 feet wide and 10 feet high

thirty-twomo   a page size, about $3\frac{1}{2}'' \times 5\frac{1}{2}''$, resulting from a printer's sheet about $19'' \times 25''$ folded into 32 leaves (64 pages), or a book or other publication of this size; pronounced 32 mo, abbreviated and generally written as 32mo, plural: *32mos* or *thirty-twomos*

Thomson Newspapers Ltd.   a major publisher of newspapers in the United States and Canada, headquartered in Toronto, Ontario The *International Thomson Organisation* owns many publications throughout the world. In 1989, the two companies merged to form Thomson Corp., one of the world's largest media companies.

Thoth Award   annual awards for public relations campaigns presented by the Washington, DC, chapter of the PUBLIC RELATIONS SOCIETY OF AMERICA

thread   a strand or filament; a continuing line, such as the thread of a story; to form a thread, as in to *thread* or *thread up* a film or tape to pass through a projector or other device

Three Bees   the BETTER BUSINESS BUREAU, a non-profit organization based in Washington, DC, that promotes ethical business practices, including advertising

3C   the inside back cover, or third cover, of a periodical; three-color printing

3-D TV   three-dimensional television: a system of simulating a three-dimensional picture by adding depth to a two-dimensional picture, requiring special glasses for viewers A new process called *Visidep* operates without glasses.

three o'clock   [film] the time that a *call sheet* generally is posted to announce the next day's schedule of production

three-point lighting   a standard photographic arrangement, consisting of the KEY, FILL, and *back* lights—the three points—plus the *base light*

three-quarters back   [film, television, theater] the position of a performer who is facing the rear at a 45-degree angle away from the audience; midway between *full back* and *profile,* a 90-degree angle

three-quarters front [film, television, theater] the position of a performer who is facing the audience at a 45-degree angle; midway between *full front* and *profile*, a 90-degree angle; also called *one-quarter position*

three-quarter view a camera angle, such as in a portrait photo when the head is tilted slightly—one-fourth—to the side, so that it is not a full view

three-sheet a poster commonly used for transit advertising and outside stores, about 7 feet high and 3½ feet wide

three-shot or **three shot** a film or TV picture of three performers, generally from the waist up, as at a news desk

three slot a pay telephone with three separate coin slots for nickels, dimes, and quarters It is obsolete now that one slot accepts all.

three-star edition a designation for a specific edition that appears on the DATELINE atop page one of a daily newspaper At *The Wall Street Journal*, the three-star edition is the second or late edition and is *locked up* at about 10 P.M.

three-to-em space [typography] one-third of an EM, generally abbreviated as *3-em space*

three-wall set a movie or other *set* with three walled sides and a fourth open side where the camera is located

threnody a poem or song of lamentation; an editorial or other work that deplores, mourns, or regrets It is pronounced THREN-a-dee.

throughput 1 net speed or production over a period of time The throughput of a computer-typesetting system is expressed as lines of type per minute or hour. Throughput reflects *input*, processing, and *output*, each of which may be different, so the throughput is limited by the slowest component of the system. 2 [marketing] the movement of merchandise through dealers or retailers to the consumer The manufacturer attempts to pre-sell an item to the consumer so that it moves through the dealer and does not depend on retail sales personnel.

through-the-lens (TTL) a system of viewing the subject through the lens of a camera instead of through a separate VIEWFINDER, as in the optical viewing system of a 35mm single-lens reflex camera or a simplified video camera A more elaborate video camera has an electronic viewfinder (EVF).

throw to move, connect, or engage, as to *throw a light*, a stage term for turning on a light; to deliver in an offhand manner, as to *throw a line* of dialogue; the distance something is tossed or thrown, such as the distance between the lens of a film projector and the screen

throw a cue to give a hand signal as a *cue*

throwaway 1 a HANDBILL, an advertising circular, or a type of publication, generally a weekly newspaper, that is distributed free to apartment houses and individual residences Some of these publications contain no editorial matter, while others publish MATS and other editorial material. Sometimes a throwaway is called a *pennysaver* or *shopper*. 2 [theater] dialogue lines that are underplayed by a performer

throw line in broadcasting, a live lead-in, or introduction, to a tape

throwout a leaf with a map or other reference material mounted on another leaf—a *guard* or *guard leaf*—so that it can be opened and consulted as the book is read

THRU international telex abbreviation: you are connected to a telex position

thrust a general direction or tendency, as in a *campaign thrust*

thrust stage a stage that extends out into the auditorium so that part of the audience sits on its sides A thrust stage differs from the traditional *proscenium stage*, with the entire audience sitting in front, and an *arena stage*, or *theater in the round*, which is surrounded by the audience.

thumb index a series of rounded indentations cut into the front edges of book leaves imprinted with letters or subjects to facilitate turning to the desired section, common in dictionaries and reference books; to prepare this type of index

thumbnail sketch a small, rough drawing or layout, generally called a thumbnail; an outline or brief description of a biography or history A *thumbnail photo* is a small photo, perhaps a half-column wide; it is also called a *porkchop*.

thumbsucker journalism jargon for a superficial or ponderous article resulting in reader discomfort that is alleviated by thumb sucking; an article about speculation, as compared to a factual report In the United Kingdom, an off-the-record backgrounder or unofficial press conference is called a thumbsucker.

Thurstone scale in market research, an attitude-measurement technique in which respondents are given several statements, generally seven, expressing different attitudes about the same subject and are asked to select with a circle or check the one with which they are in agreement; developed by *L.L. Thurstone* in England in 1928 A Thurstone scale differs from the LIKERT SCALE.

thyrister an electronic device that converts *alternating current* (*AC*) to *direct current* (*DC*), such as a solid-state semiconductor used in photography

T.I. TITLE INFORMATION; TERRESTRIAL INTERFERENCE

ticketed call a telephone call for which a record is made of the called and calling numbers, time, duration, and other data, a procedure formerly used by telephone companies and still used by operators in some private systems

ticking off the process of determining the length of a proposed headline

tickler a reminder; also called *tickle* A *tickler book* or *tickler file* is used by salespeople and others for reminders about follow-up calls. A tickler file is used at newspapers and other media to list anniversaries, forthcoming events, and other reminders for news or feature coverage.

tick mark a short, fine line used for various purposes, particularly as a printing indication of the location of characters on a matrix or other image master used in phototypesetting

ticky-tack a rough model, commonly used in developing a POINT-OF-PURCHASE display

tie a cord, ribbon, string, or other item that unites objects; in bookbinding, a narrow strip of material attached to the edge of book covers to hold the front and back covers together

tie back [journalism] a summary of preceding events

tied letter a LIGATURE; two (a *double letter*) or three letters or characters tied together with one or more strokes in common, such as ffi

tie-down a chain device used to secure a camera TRIPOD, such as when it is on a moving vehicle or an angled or unstable surface A tie-down is sometimes called a *spreader*, which is a different device with three arms that also is attached to the legs of a tripod for support.

tie-in a connection; an auxiliary or coordinated promotion; a product or project of two or more participants A *tie-in advertisement* announcement or promotion makes reference to another advertisement or advertiser or another product or service of the same advertiser. A *tie-in sale* literally links two products, as in "buy one and get the other at a reduced price." A *tie-in commercial* can be a local live addition to a recorded commercial, as for a local retailer; it is also called a TAG. In journalism, a tie-in is a story or part of a story connected with another, such as a local aspect of a national survey, or a work issued in two or more media, such as a *novelization* of a film.

tie-in reissue a previously published book with a new look related to a TV show, movie, or play, such as Victor Hugo's *Les Misérables* in paperback with cover artwork based on the Broadway play

tie line a direct connection between two telephones or other links in a communications or other system

tier one of a series of rows placed one above another, as in a concert hall In cable TV, a tier is the level of service—the number and type of channels—available to a subscriber.

tiering charging a cable-TV subscriber extra for pay-TV channels and other TIERS, often at a package price

Tiffany a SERIF typeface

tight close, as with a *tight line* with little space between words or a cramped layout with little or no space around a subject A *tight close-up* (*T.C.U.*) is an exceptionally close-in scene; to *tighten up* is a direction to a photographer or artist to move in closer or to reduce the space around a person or subject. A program, publication, or schedule on a *tight budget* has little leeway or is close to its allocation. A *tight negative* is overexposed and/or underdeveloped to produce a sharp print. A *tight loudspeaker* is relatively free of *hangover*, sound that continues after the signal input stops. A *tight recording* has very little extraneous sound, such as due to *close miking* or close placement of the microphone to the sound source.

tight-back a book with its cover SPINE glued directly to the BACKBONE with no space, as distinguished from a higher-quality HOLLOW-BACK book in which the spine is loose so that it bows outward

tighten to reduce the space, as in a layout In film, the tightening of a shot by coming closer to remove unnecessary background is called a *pull-up*.

tight joint in bookbinding, a type of inside strip or hinge (a *joint*) in which the cover boards are fitted tight against the spine; also called *closed joint*, different from a free-swinging *open joint* or *French joint*

tight on an instruction to a television camera operator for a close shot of a specific person or object, as in "tight on (name of performer)"; also called *close on*

tight two shot a direction to a TV camera operator for a close-up of the heads of two people

tilde a mark used over a letter to indicate nasalization, as in Spanish over the letter *n* (señor) and in Portuguese over vowels (*lã*); pronounced TILL-deh It is also used as a symbol in mathematics and other vocabularies, such as in the computer field, where it means approximate.

Tilley, Eustace a distinguished-looking character, sometimes called Regency Dandy, who has become the mascot or symbol of *The New Yorker* magazine The drawing was created by Rea (pronounced Ray) Irvin, the magazine's first art director, and appeared on the cover of the first issue, dated February 21, 1925. It is the only piece of original art owned by the magazine (artists sell *The New Yorker* one-time usage of their work), and reproductions from the original are used on anniversary issue covers.

till forbid or **'til forbid (TF, T.F.)**   an instruction to continue to publish an ad at specified intervals, broadcast a commercial until told to stop, or continue a subscription or other order until notified to the contrary; also called *till forbidden*

tilt   a direction to move a camera up or down; a vertical PAN

time   **1** [broadcasting] the period available for a program or commercial   A *time buyer* purchases broadcast time, perhaps with a *time contract* and at a *time discount*, a reduced price for quantity and/or frequency, from a *time card* that indicates a different *time charge* for each *time class* or *classification* (such as *prime time* or *drive time*) or *time slot* (a specific time period). The time may come from a *time bank* (a reserve of *spot commercial time*, often obtained by barter) via a *time buying service*. To *clear time* is to make time available, as for a program or commercial.   **2** [journalism] short for *any time*, as with an article that is not dated and can be used at any time   **3** [photography] *Time to clear* refers to the time a print remains in the fixing bath, or *hypo*, to remove any milky appearance.

time freeze   an interval or period of time, particularly in relation to a specific program or event

Time Inc.   one of the world's largest media companies, headquartered in New York   It publishes *Fortune, Life, Money, People, Sports Illustrated, Time*, and other magazines and owns HBO and other companies. In 1989, Time Inc. and Warner Communications merged to form the world's largest media and entertainment company, Time Warner Inc.

time lapse   a technique of filming a motion or a development, such as the blossoming of a flower, over a period of time, by photographing at intervals and then putting together the sequences

time line   a list of events in chronological order

time lock   a dramatic device in a film or other work in which a predetermined action is set to take place at a specific moment, such as a bomb that is set to explode

time peg   an aspect of a news release or article with relevance to a particular day, season, or other time of the year that makes it newsworthy

timer   [film] a technician in a film laboratory who examines a negative and makes adjustments with regard to exposure or color intensity; called a *grader* in the United Kingdom

Since most films now are made in color, a key person is the *color timer*, who works with the DAILIES—the TAKES from each day's shooting—using filters and other equipment, and then with the entire film to produce the *answer print*. The color timer is assisted by one or more lab technicians.

time-series analysis or **forecasting**   the use of previous sales or other past data to make projections

time sheet   a daily record of employee hours, generally arranged by client, project, or job, used for cost-accounting and billing   A *time buy sheet* or *buy sheet* is a record of broadcast advertising purchases. A *timing sheet* or *rundown sheet* is a list of film or TV scenes in chronological order, generally with the time of each and the total time.

time signal   an announcement of the time, as on a broadcast, indicated with a beep, sometimes accompanied by a commercial announcement   For many years, the time signal on radio stations was sponsored by Bulova and called *Bulova watch time*. A producer or other person in radio or TV program production gives a time signal to indicate the time remaining in a program or program segment by displaying a card with the number of minutes or raising the appropriate number of fingers.

Times Mirror Co.   one of the country's largest media companies   Headquartered in Los Angeles, Times Mirror publishes the *Los Angeles Times, Baltimore Sun, Newsday*, and other newspapers and *Broadcasting, Field & Stream, Popular Science*, and other magazines; it also owns TV stations and cable-TV systems.

time spent   the number of minutes of reading time spent by an average reader of a single issue of a publication; the number of hours of listening or viewing time spent over a specific period by an individual or household

Times Roman   a typeface with upright SERIF letters designed for and named after the English newspaper *The Times* of London

timetable   a schedule, a list of events arranged in sequence

timing   the regulation of speed; the moment of occurrence, such as the timing or scheduling of an announcement; the measurement of time; the pacing of a performer or performance to achieve a desired tempo, as in the criticism "his timing was off"   In photography and other procedures, *correct timing* is essential. In film labs, recommendations for corrections of a film to be reprocessed are listed on a *timing card*.

Tin Pan Alley   publishers, writers, and others associated with popular music   The phrase refers to those people wherever they are geographically and also to any area where there are many songwriters and publishers, such as the Times Square area of Manhattan. In the early 20th century, many music publishers were located on West 28th Street between Fifth and Sixth avenues in Manhattan. Some of their upright pianos had paper behind the steel strings, resulting in a tinny sound akin to a tin pan.

tinseltown slang for HOLLYWOOD in the unreal, glittering era of the 1930s and subsequently

tint a slight trace of color. Various colors of ink are shown on a *tint chart, color chart,* or *tint block* used to print colors; the density of the basic color is the standard, so that a 50-percent tint is half as "strong" as the full color. A tint block is a solid-color area on a printed piece or a panel of color on which text or art is printed. A *tint plate* prints an even or flat area of color with no design. *Tinted paper* is lightly colored. The coloring process is *tinting. Tinted stock* is film with a light-absorbing color added to its base to prevent halation, or light reflection from the base to the emulsion.

tintype a ferrotype, an old kind of photograph taken directly as a positive print on a sensitized plate of enameled tin or iron

TIO Television Information Office, a group of TV stations and networks, based in New York

tip a hint; advance or inside information, such as a *news tip* or lead provided to a reporter

tip-in a preprinted card, page, or other item inserted in a publication, generally as an advertisement in a magazine or special illustration in a book. The insertion process is *tipping in.*

tip-on an item glued, generally only on one edge, to a printed piece, such as a coupon, reply card, product sample, or fragrance swatch affixed to an advertisement

tipping the process of attaching an item (a TIP-IN or TIP-ON) to a sheet, either outside a SIGNATURE (*outside tipping*), which can be done mechanically, or inside a signature (*inside tipping*), which is more expensive because it is done by hand

tip sheet a press-advisory or assignment memo; a letter or sheet that generally includes the *five W's*—who, what, when, where, and why—about an event or occasion to which media people are invited

tipster a person who provides inside information or other TIPS, free (as to the media) or for a fee (as by a horse-race handicapper or someone with confidential information about a stock)

tiring room the attiring room or dressing room in 17th-century English theaters. The dresser was called a *tireman* or *tirewoman* (or *tiring-man* or *tiring-woman*). Also called a *tireroom,* it often was decorated in green, a relaxing color, or

had green walls, and may be the predecessor of the Green Room for performers and guests on TV programs.

tissue a rough layout or sketch made on translucent or semitransparent paper or a translucent sheet with such a sketch. The sheet may function as a cover for finished art or other materials or be used to note corrections. Tissue also is used in books and other publications, particularly to cover an illustration to prevent ink transfer onto the facing page.

titan a person or thing of great power. A *titan arc* is a 350-ampere carbon arc lamp used at premieres and other events.

title (tit.) **1** a name, as of a book. A *title entry* is a library catalog card or index listing referring to the title of a publication. *Title information (T.I.)* is a card or sheet with the name of the author, publisher, and other data about a book or other publication. **2** a heading, including film credits, *subtitles* in a foreign film, and other film and TV explanations, sometimes accompanied by *title music.* A *title background* is a scene that appears behind the titles. A *title card* or *title board* is a card or cel with titles printed on it that is then photographed on a *title stand* (a support for the camera and title cards) or *titler.* A *title designer* creates the opening and closing credits, which often are quite creative, involving animation or live action, generally produced by a *title company* and including *title music* and sometimes a *title song.* Titles may appear in crawl-like succession—*title crawl, title roll,* or *creeping title*—because they're often mounted on a roll. Credits may be in the *main titles* at or near the start or in the *end titles.* Their size and order may be determined by contract, as in *star title position,* or by union regulation, such as that the director's name appear last among the main titles. In advertising for movies and other attractions, the *artwork title* is the main title and is larger then the *billing block title,* also called the *regular title* or *follow title,* which precedes the list of credits, or *billing block.* Major credits that precede the artwork title are called *above the title,* as compared to those *below the title.*

title page the first full page of a book, bearing its name and that of the author and publisher. A *part title* or *half title* is the title of a section of a book and generally appears on a separate right-hand page preceding the text. The leaf bearing the title page is the *title leaf.* The *title sheet* or *title signature* is the first SIGNATURE of a book, often without a SIGNATURE MARK, containing the title leaf and other front matter. The conventional arrangement of a book is to start with the half-title page, followed on a verso (left-hand) page with the *fact title,* a list of books by the same author or other books in a series, and on the next recto (right-hand) page the title page.

title verso (T/V) the page to the left of the title page of a book

titling the typesetting of large capital letters, sometimes ornate, as in a book title

tix show-business jargon for *tickets*

TK to come, an indication that material will follow

TM TRADEMARK

T.M.C. target market coverage (see TARGET MARKETING); TOTAL MARKET COVERAGE

t-number a *t-stop* number, a designation for light transmission through a camera lens

TNX wire-service jargon: thanks

T/O TURNOVER

to be announced (TBA) a term commonly used in broadcasting when the name of a program or other information is not currently available

to-be-sure graf *Wall Street Journal* jargon for a paragraph in an article that indicates exceptions to the generalizations stated in the NUT GRAF or an earlier paragraph, sometimes beginning with "To be sure"

toenails printer's slang for *parentheses*

token [direct marketing] a stamp, tear-off piece, or other involvement DEVICE or ACTION that the consumer places on an order card

toll call a long-distance phone call for which there is a charge beyond the local rate A *toll-free call*, as to an *800* number, is free to the caller.

tombstone an *all-text* print advertisement for an announcement and/or to meet legal requirements, generally small-size, dull-looking, and lifeless (hence the name)

tombstone heads headlines of the same structure in terms of typeface, size, and width of line, akin to cemetery tombstones They are used in TOMBSTONE and other advertisements

tomesis the separation of the syllables of a word by an intervening word or words, such as unbe-damn-lievable Pronounced ta-MEE-sis, it is derived from the Greek for a "cutting."

tone a vocal or instrumental sound or its quality, pitch, or modulation; the relative height of pitch with which words are pronounced; a manner of speaking or writing that expresses a particular meaning, feeling, or attitude; the prevailing style or character of a place or period; a quality or value of color, tint, or shade The value of a color is indicated on a scale called *tonal range*, with whiteness the highest value (*high tonal key* or *high key*) and darkness the lowest value (*low tonal value* or *low key*). A

film can reproduce over 100 tones between black and white. *Cold tones* (bluish) and *warm tones* (reddish) are used to describe black-and-white as well as color photos. Paper, which has a limited tonal range, can reproduce from about 15 to 60 tones. In broadcasting, a tone is the musical sound that indicates a precise time, identified by an announcement such as, "At the tone, the time will be 7:30."

tone poem a musical composition that interprets poetic ideas; also called *symphonic poem* A lyrical tribute in any form to a person or other entity sometimes is called a tone poem, since tone refers to the author's attitude to the subject and/or the audience.

toner carbon particles, dry or suspended in a liquid, used to produce an image in electrostatic copying and duplicating machines

tones and bars a test pattern that precedes a TV program, consisting of sound tones and color bars or stripes

tongue to move a crane-mounted camera horizontally while aiming it at a single subject in a tonguelike manner The crane boom itself sometimes is called a tongue. The command is *tongue left* or *tongue right*.

toning the process of chemically converting a black-and-white image to a color image The greater the concentration of exposed silver crystals, the darker the tone and deeper the color.

tonnage [advertising] slang for *heavy linage* (many AGATE LINES) or a very big audience

tony or **toney** high-toned; luxurious; stylish It derives from TONE; the comparatives are *tonier* and *toniest*.

Tony Award annual awards to Broadway performers and others, created in 1947 by the AMERICAN THEATRE WING and presented by the American Theatre Wing and The League of American Theatres and Producers The Tony Award is named after Antoinette (Tony) Perry (1888–1946), who was the executive director of the American Theatre Wing.

tool in bookbinding, the hard stamp or heated implement used to apply or impress pigment, metal foil, or other decoration on a book cover or *spine* The process and also the decoration itself is called *tooling*.

toon short for CARTOON

tooth 1 a small notched projection or sprocket, as on a film projector 2 [photography] the degree to which a film surface is receptive to RETOUCHING 3 [printing] the roughness of a paper surface A *toothy paper* or a paper *with tooth* is slightly rough, not smooth or slick, and receives ink more readily than glossy paper.

top 1 the beginning, as in *top of the script* or *top of the story* Thus, a film, tape, or reel starts *at the top* and ends *at the bottom*. The *top deck* is the main part of a headline. **2** uppermost, as in *top billing* for a *top performer* at the top of an advertisement or program For a performer, to *top a line* is to execute a line of dialogue at greater intensity or with greater effect than the preceding line. To *top a laugh* is to outdo the preceding joke.

TOP temporarily out of print, regarding a book

top banana a TOP performer, particularly the star comedian in a vaudeville show; an important person The probable origin is the banana-shaped soft club used by some comedians and clowns to slap another performer. The straight man, or secondary comedian, is the *second banana*.

top box score [market research] a method of interpreting a list of ratings by highlighting only the top score—for example, on a scale of one to ten, interpreting only the top score or perhaps the top two scores (*top two box score*)

top-down planning a business planning system in which top management sets goals and plans for lower levels; different from *bottom-up planning* and *goals down-plans up planning*

top-edge gilt (t.e.g.) a book with gold leaf or simulated gold affixed to the upper ends of its pages

top-end display a transit advertisement in a premium position, such as above a door (*overdoor display*)

top forty a radio-station format playing mostly the current 40 most-popular records as determined by *Billboard* magazine or other trade sources; also called *contemporary hit* radio Some stations broadcast programs, generally weekly, with the *top 10*, *top 20*, or other selections of current hit records.

top hat a camera mount for low-angle photography; a lighting control unit shaped like a top hat commonly used in overhead installations

Topic A the first or top-priority category in a list of subjects

topic box [television] a visual inserted in a window—a *box*—on the screen, generally to the right of a newscaster, to identify the subject of a news report; also called a *box, frame, squeeze,* or *theme identifier*

top lighting illumination from above

top line or **topline** [film, television, theater] star billing, the listing of a performer's name on the top line of an advertisement, poster, or program The term is more common in the United Kingdom, as is *top liner*, a performer who receives *top lining*. The U.S. equivalent is *headliner*.

top of mind a high level of awareness, as with the first name, brand, or campaign that comes

to a respondent's mind in connection with awareness and attitude research

topping a theatrical technique in which each performer displays a greater speed, pitch, or intensity than the preceding performer

top-sizing to add more absorbent material, called SIZE, to a paper

top-staining to add dye—*stain*—to the top trimmed edge of a book

torm TORMENTOR

tormentor [theater] a piece of scenery or a curtain on the side of a stage to conceal the wings and backstage area, generally behind the TEASER; together, the teaser and tormentors form an inner PROSCENIUM or stage opening Thus, a tormentor is called a *proscenium wing*. A *tormentor spot* is a spotlight mounted on the side of the stage, perhaps on a *tormentor tower* in the *tormentor position* upstage of the tormentor. Tormentors and tormentor lights often are called *torms*.

TOS temporarily out of stock, regarding a book or other item

toss [broadcasting] one or more words spoken by a newscaster in a newscast that serves as a transition to a colleague, such as a reference to the forthcoming news report and/or the colleague's name; for example, "And now for a report on just how hot it really was today, here's Frank Field" A *split story toss* is a reading of part of a news report by one newscaster followed by a continuation of the same story by another.

total advertising the aggregate space devoted to advertising in a publication for a single issue or specific period of time, generally expressed as the number of AGATE lines—*linage*—for newspapers and the number of pages for other publications

total audience (TA or **T.A.)** gross audience: the entire readership of a periodical or net unduplicated households tuned to a radio or TV program for at least one minute if the program is under 10 minutes, and at least five minutes for longer programs *Total audience impressions* is the total number of exposures to a specific number of issues of a periodical or group of periodicals. A *total audience plan* (*TAP*) is a schedule of commercials to reach the entire audience of a station throughout its broadcast day.

total audience listening output (TALO) a radio-station audience-survey technique of ARBITRON RATINGS CO. In a TALO, the number of listener diaries in which a station is mentioned is tallied by market or other area.

total bus a purchase of all advertising space in a bus or other vehicle by a single advertiser

total circulation the aggregate numbers of copies of a publication, including all types of free and paid distribution *Total net paid circulation* is the total number of purchases of one issue of a periodical.

total cost fixed cost plus variable cost

total distribution saturation distribution of a product

total-in, total-out [advertising] a system of scheduling advertising, particularly broadcast, for a week or short period (total-in) and then suspending it (total-out); also called BLINKERING, *blinking,* or FLIGHTING

total market coverage (T.M.C.) distribution to every household in an area; a saturation campaign, as with a comprehensive mailing or door-to-door distribution of circulars

Total Prime Time (T.P.T.) the actual recollection by viewers of TV commercials as compared with the potential total audience of the prime-time programs on which they were shown, as measured by GALLUP AND ROBINSON

total program a comprehensive advertising campaign

Total Survey Area (T.S.A.) the geographical area of counties that account for 98 percent or more of the net weekly audience circulation of a television station, as defined by Arbitron The term is used by other research firms and includes the METRO SURVEY AREA plus nearby counties.

touch & seal envelope an envelope with an application of a specially formulated latex that allows the flap to be sealed merely by pressing it into place

touchscreen the display area of a computer terminal that receives commands from the user by physical contact with instructions displayed on the screen, commonly used in automatic teller machines in banks A touchscreen is *user-friendly.*

touchtone [telephone] pushbutton dialing, as opposed to the use of a ROTARY dial Actually, Touchtone is a trademark of AT&T, though it is used generically for pushbutton phones.

touch type to type without having to look at the keyboard

touchy-feely an advertisement or other work that evokes a warm emotional response related to touching and feeling

tour escort a publicist or other professional person who accompanies a SPOKESPERSON on a media tour or other activity A *tour guide* helps with logistics and also serves as a counselor and escort.

tower a vertical layout

Towne-Oller, Inc. a market research firm in New York that audits food-store deliveries of health and beauty-aid products

townline a headline at the top of or within a newspaper page indicating the point of origin of the news below it, used on the state or suburban page or section of some daily newspapers

t.p. TITLE PAGE

TPR international telex abbreviation: teleprinter or TELETYPEWRITER

tr, tr., or trs a proofreader's symbol or instruction to a printer to TRANSPOSE a character or copy block, as in "tr to galley 2"

T.R. turn rule, an instruction to a typesetter to turn a RULE—a thin line—or SLUG upside down in the GALLEY to indicate that an addition—a pickup or insert—or change is to be made at this place The rule itself is called a *rule for insert* or *rule for pickup.* The instruction T.R. or *rule* when written on copy means that the printer should be on the alert for changes to come.

T/R an earth station equipped to transmit and receive

trace a mark or small amount; to follow a course; to locate, as with a *tracer,* a person or instrument; to copy, as with TRACING or TRANSPARENT paper

TRACE a system of testing TV commercials in selected cable homes, developed by MarketVision, a company in Cincinnati

traceable expenditure reported spending; space or time advertising listed by medium and advertiser; gross cost

traceoline a transparent film with a granular surface used for drawing

tracing 1 a reproduction, such as one made by superimposing a transparent sheet over an original and drawing over the lines In architecture, engineering, and other technical fields, a translucent blue-line sheet is used by draftsman to make a tracing. *Tracing paper,* which is commonly used by artists, is ONIONSKIN paper that is highly transparent. 2 the section on a library catalog card that lists other headings under which the book or other work is listed

track 1 a mark; a path or route; a sequence of items; a band; to follow or observe, as in tracking the course or progress of a component of a study 2 [broadcasting] a part of a reporter's narration from outside the studio, with each track numbered to precede each section of the interview or "activity," so that track 1 is the introduction, track 2 is between the first and second *bites,* and track 3 precedes the third bite 3 [computers] that part of a magnetic drum, tape, or disk that passes under a reading head position; abbreviated as *T, TK, TR,* or *TRK* Specific tracks include the *address track, card track,* *clock track, feed track, magnetic track,* and *regenerative track. Track pitch* is the distance between corresponding points of adjacent tracks. *Track density* is the number of adjacent tracks per unit of distance on a magnetic tape, disk, or other storage unit, as indicated, for example, by *tracks per inch (tpi)*. **4** [film] A *tracking* or *trucking shot* is one in which the camera platform moves along tracks to follow the action. To move the camera closer to the subject is to *track in* or *track forward;* to move away is to *track out* or *track back.* A *buzz track* is a recording on a set or elsewhere without dialogue or action made to obtain *room tone* to be used in subsequent editing, as between passages of dialogue. **5** [recording] a single line of recorded sound In making a record, each microphone produces a separate track that then is mixed with others. A track is also an audio component, such as a *movie track* or *voice track,* which are mixed to produce the total *soundtrack* or *magnetic track* of a film. A single *cut* or piece of music on a record also is called a track.

track ball in computer graphics, a movable ball used as a locator device to control and make changes on a video screen; also called *control ball*

tracking following a path; monitoring; recording data An example is the targeting of a signal source, such as of a communications satellite by a *tracking station* and the following of that source in a process called a *lock-on.* A tape that wobbles and does not follow its path has a *tracking problem;* this notation sometimes appears on rented VCR videos.

tract a paper, pamphlet, or short treatise, particularly on a philosophical, political, or religious subject

tractor feed a sprocketed feed mechanism to advance and position paper on a line printer

trade advertising advertising to wholesalers, retailers, or other distribution channels in a particular trade or industry, generally the TRADE PRESS, such as the FAIRCHILD publications

trade area an area in which a product or service is sold, or *traded* For example, a regional BRAND has a specific trade area, as compared to a national brand.

trade association an organization representing companies or individuals in a specific industry, as distinguished from a professional association representing teachers, physicians, and other professionals

trade book **1** a business periodical for people in a specific industry, or *trade;* also called *trade journal* or *trade publication* **2** a book distributed through the book trade's retail outlets,

such as bookstores, as distinguished from a *textbook* A *trade edition* is a trade book or a trade version of a book. A *trade paperback* is a paperbound book that is higher-priced and of better quality than standard paperbacks.

trade card a small card with advertising, popular in the 19th century, printed by manufacturers of food, drugs, and other products and distributed free by retailers The cards often had charming drawings and witty headlines.

trade channel a route or sequence through which products or services move from producer to consumer; also called *channel of distribution*

trade character a depiction of a person, animal, or other object that is identified with a BRAND or line of products, such as the animated characters on cereal boxes

trade discount a reduction from the retail or regular price made by a supplier to a retailer or someone else along the distribution route as a professional courtesy; also called *functional discount*

trade dress a color or colors associated with a company, such as the red on Marlboro cigarette packs and the yellow, red, and black on Kodak film packages

trade fair a major commercial exhibition, such as an international exposition

trade list [publishing] a catalog or other list of titles available for sale to book retailers

trademark (TM) a symbol, LOGOTYPE, motif, word, words, or combination of these that is legally registered with the federal government for exclusive use by a manufacturer or other company to identify and protect the registered item (the company's product or services covered by the trademark); to make such registration A *descriptive trademark* provides information about a product, such as Diet Coke or Pepsi Lite.

trade name a name by which a product, process, or service is generally known or identified in its industry, not its TRADEMARK or technical description; the name under which a company operates and is known

trade-off an exchange

trade out an exchange of advertising space or time; a *barter* arrangement in which, for example, a magazine receives free time to advertise itself on a radio or TV station in return for advertising space provided to the station to advertise itself in the magazine

trade press publications that deal with specific industries, such as chemical, retailing, and others; sometimes referred to as *specialized business press, the trades,* TRADE BOOKS, or *trade papers*

trade printer a printer who works only for other printers, such as one who does engraving or other specialized services

trade promotion promotion efforts to encourage wholesalers, retailers, and others *in the trade* rather than direct promotion to the consumer

trade show a commercial exhibition conducted by a TRADE ASSOCIATION or other exhibition manager for wholesalers, retailers, and others in a specific industry or related industries

trade-up a sale or purchase of a more expensive or more "fashionable" item

trading area one or more counties in which residents transact the majority of their retail purchases; the primary market in which a company sells its goods or services

trading stamps stamplike coupons offered as PREMIUMS with purchases, redeemable for specific products

Traffic Audit Bureau an organization, based in New York, of outdoor advertisers and outdoor advertising plants that functions as the official bureau of circulation verification and audits of out-of-home advertising

traffic builder a product promotion or activity designed to attract customers—*traffic*—into a store, exhibit, or other place

traffic count the number of people passing a specific point within a specific time, sometimes charted on a *traffic flow map*

traffic department a department in an advertising agency, broadcast station, printer, or other service business that maintains production schedules to keep work "moving" on schedule, sometimes with a *traffic system* The traffic department in a radio or TV station, headed by the *traffic manager* or *traffic director*, maintains the daily BROADCAST LOG.

traffic pattern the time and frequency of shopping by customers of a store or area

tragedy a serious play or other work, generally with an unhappy or disastrous ending

tragicomedy a play or other work with tragic and comic elements, generally with a happy ending

trailer a short, blank strip at the end of a reel of tape; a promotional announcement at the end of a radio or TV program about a forthcoming program; a commercial attached to the end of a program or another commercial; a short film promoting a forthcoming theatrical motion picture The original trailers, called *coming attractions*, followed the feature movie (hence the name) and were shown between the movies of a *double feature*. Now, trailers generally precede the feature film.

trailing edge the last part of a roll of paper, tape, or other material The first part is the *leading edge*.

tranny British slang for a TRANSPARENCY

trans. transaction; transitive; translated; translation; transpose; transposition; transverse

transaction **1** a business deal or agreement, such as a purchase, so that the time immediately prior to and following it is called the *pre-* and *post-transactional* period **2** a record of a meeting (the *proceedings*) The published papers and reports presented at a meeting of a scientific society or other organization often are part of the title of the published work, such as *Transactions of the American Mathematical Society.*

transaction provider (TP) [videotex] a company or organization that provides a service enabling subscribers to make reservations or purchase products and services directly through a VIDEOTEX or TV station *Transactional* services include banking and shopping.

transceiver a radio transmitter and receiver

transcribe to write or type copy; to transfer from one medium to another, as from a dictation tape to a typed sheet; to record for later broadcast; to adapt or arrange a musical composition for a voice or instrument

transcription an adaptation of a musical composition; a reproduction of a soundtrack on disc or tape A *transcribed program* or *syndicated program* is a prerecorded broadcast sold—*syndicated*—by a packager—*syndicator*—to individual stations. A *transcript* is a typed copy, as of the text of a broadcast, speech, or testimony.

transducer a device that transmits energy from one system to another or converts energy from one form to another, such as from acoustic, magnetic, or mechanical energy into electrical energy in a microphone, loudspeaker, or other equipment

transfer to make a film copy; a DECAL, film, or sheet—*transfer sheet*—containing an image to be moved, or *transferred* Transfer-Key is a trademarked process of the *3M Company* for preparing color-separation proofs. *Transfer letters* include Visi-Type and other brands.

transfer drawing a drawing or watercolor transferred from one sheet to another The process, as used by Paul Gauguin (1848–1903) and other artists, involves placing a piece of paper over an inked sheet and drawing on the top sheet, thus transferring the drawing to the reverse side of the top sheet.

transfer ink a liquid emulsion applied to a LITHOGRAPHIC plate to form an image; also called TUSCHE

transfer process a contact copying method that involves mechanical transfer, as in a *gelatin* *transfer process*, or chemical transfer, as in a *diffusion transfer process*

transfer type letters on transparent plastic sheets that are pressed on—*transferred*—to a layout or other surface Each sheet generally has a complete FONT of type with extras of the vowels and other frequently used letters, numerals, and punctuation marks as well as lines and common symbols. A common brand used by artists is Letraset, made by Letraset USA Inc. of Paramus, NJ.

transient *transitory*, as with an electrical disturbance

transient advertising rate a noncontractual rate for one-time or *transient* advertisers

transit advertising posters, CAR CARDS, and other advertising placed inside or outside vehicles and their stations; also called *transportation advertising* or *transit* *Transit radio* is radio broadcasting in public transit vehicles and facilities. A *transit spectacular* is an advertisement of exceptionally large size, such as running close to the full length of the inside or outside of a public transit vehicle.

Transit Advertising Association an organization in New York that promotes advertising space in public transit vehicles and facilities

transition an audio or visual effect leading from one scene or shot to the next

transition time the time between broadcast periods, generally referring specifically to the time immediately before or after *prime time*; also called *fringe time*

translate to convey meaning, literally or figuratively; to change form or give form, as from ideas to substance TEST-MARKET results can be *translated* into a national projection; conversely, a *test translation* is the simulation of a national campaign in a test market or the production of a sample or test model.

translation 1 the conversion of one language or form of expression into another; the process itself or the result—the *translated* version The conversion may be literal and automatic, as in a computer that converts from one language to another, or it may be an explanation to clarify, explain, or analyze. 2 [advertising] A translation is the simulation of a national media plan in a TEST MARKET. 3 [publishing] An *annotated translation* includes FOOTNOTES or other comments and explanations by the *translator* or editor. The American Translators Association is located in Ossining, NY.

translator [broadcasting] a station that *rebroadcasts* signals of other stations and does not originate its own programming

Translite a Kodak film used to make a black-and-white transparency with a *translucent* base, such as for a display

transliteration the process of writing or spelling in the corresponding characters of another alphabet, or the new *transliterated* version itself It is not the same as TRANSLATION, as the *transliterator* simply represents the sounds of one language spelled with another alphabet, sometimes as an aid to a speaker.

translucency a photographic or printed copy of an advertisement or other item used in backlighted displays Something *translucent* permits light to pass through it.

Trans-lux a trademarked short-focus rear-screen projector for films or slides, made by the Trans-Lux Corporation of New York

transmit 1 to convey; to send, as with a signal A *transmission* is the act of conveying or the item, such as a message, transmitted. A *transmitter* is a telegraphic instrument, telephone, or electronic equipment that generates, amplifies, and conveys signals. 2 [photography] to allow to pass through, as with blue light transmitted through a blue filter A *transmission copy* is a TRANSPARENCY or other item photographed by light transmitted through it rather that reflected from it. 3 [publishing] A *transmittal meeting* is a conference at which the production details of a manuscript are determined before it is put into production.

transmittal sheet [publishing] a form accompanying a manuscript sent for typesetting or other production, with a list of items in the package ("herewith") and items "to come"

transparency a transparent positive photograph in color or black-and-white, in contrast to a NEGATIVE It is often viewed by *transmitted* light.

transparent clear, diaphanous, capable of *transmitting* light as if there were no intervening material *Transparent ink*, such as process inks, allow colors underneath to show through. A *transparent proof* is a copy of text or artwork made on acetate or cellophane.

transponder a RECEIVER that transmits signals when activated by a specific signal For example, a *satellite transponder* picks up signals from earth, translates them into a new FREQUENCY, amplifies them, and transmits them back to earth. The word originates from transmitter and responder.

transport in computers, recording, and other fields, a mechanism that moves magnetic or paper tape past reading or recording heads; more generally called a *drive*, as with a *magnetic tape drive*; also called *tape transport* or *tape transport mechanism*

transportables in satellite communications, earth stations that are portable and can be moved to various locations

transportation advertising advertising in public transportation vehicles

transportation coordinator [film, television] an individual who supervises the moving of equipment and personnel to the set or on location and sometimes is in charge of the *transportation department*, which maintains and operates all vehicles, or reports to the *transportation captain*, who is the department chief

transpose (tr, tr., or trs) **1** [graphic arts] to put in a different place, such as to change or move art or text adjacent to other characters, words, lines, or other matter **2** [music] to write or perform in a different key

transposition **1** the act of reversing or interchanging, as in the improper placement of adjacent words in typesetting **2** [music] the changing of the key of a song or composition, such as to accommodate the vocal range of a singer; see also TRANSPOSE

trap **1** a receptacle, such as for catching or holding **2** [printing] the overlap allowed for two colors to be printed on the same sheet without white space between them *Trapping* is the ability to print over previously printed material. *Dry trapping* is printing wet ink over dry ink; *wet trapping* is printing wet ink over wet ink. *Poor trapping* or *undertrapping* occurs when too little ink is transferred. **3** [theater] a TRAP DOOR or opening in a stage floor through which performers can enter or exit

trap door a hinged or sliding door in a ceiling or floor; also called TRAP In a theater, a trap door enables performers to enter or exit. The record number of trap doors in a play is in the Broadway production of *The Phantom of the Opera*, which has 12 major trap doors and 97 smaller traps for the candles.

traveler **1** [publishing] a sales representative who calls on bookstores, colleges (a college traveler), or other customers **2** a stage-set curtain that opens horizontally

traveling display any type of advertisement on or within a moving vehicle, though generally a poster panel on the outside of a bus

traveling matte printing a film-printing process in which a mask silhouette or matte on a strip of film, called the traveling matte, moves through the printer with the print film and blocks out an area, thus creating a light area or space into which new material or a special effect can be introduced

traveling shot filming or taping in which the camera moves and follows the movement of a performer

travelog a lecture, film, or other work about travel

trayed mail metered and other mail not requiring cancellation of postage stamps, placed in trays furnished by the Postal Service It is used by large mailers for efficiency, because it bypasses some of the handlings at the post office.

tray pack a carton that can be converted into a shelf-sized display unit by removing its top

treatment **1** the general handling, approach, or tone of an article, advertisement, or campaign; the general way in which a book or other prose is converted into a script **2** a prose account of a story outline, sometimes prepared by a *treatment writer* It precedes the actual script and shows how the writer proposes to treat the story as a screenplay or full script. For a full-length screenplay, a treatment is about 50 pages. A shorter version is a *treatment outline*, generally written in outline form rather than in full sentences.

tree a framework or structure, such as an arrangement of computer data in hierarchical form Since the lower levels contain more detailed information, it really is an *inverted tree.*

trenching the digging of a hole—a *trench*—in a floor for performers to stand in to appear shorter, to hold a camera in order to achieve a desired height or angle, or for other purposes

trend a general inclination, tendency, or direction, as predicted by a *trend spotter*, who observes *trendsetters*, forerunners of actions and options prior to general acceptance and usage Such people are *trendy*, reflecting the newest fads or fashions.

Trendex a New York firm that provides syndicated media research services, particularly TV ratings

trendline a mark, line, or other indication of a direction, trend, or tendency, as of conditions, events, opinions, or other data

triad a group of three, such as an arrangement in a long poem of groups of three stanzas or a musical chord of three tones

trial a test of a product or service, perhaps of a *trial size*, or *sample*, or on a *trial basis* (reduced price or special offer)

trial balloon an action or statement designed to test opinion on an issue or to try out a planned campaign

Tribune Company one of the country's largest media companies, headquartered in Chicago It publishes the *Chicago Tribune, New York Daily News*, and other newspapers and owns several radio and TV stations, including WGN in Chicago.

trifold a piece of scenery consisting of three sections, sometimes used in a television studio as the three walls of a room

triggyback a 20-second commercial sold for about one-third the price of a 60-second commercial

trim 1 [advertising, marketing, theater] a border or frame, as of an outdoor advertisement; an ornament or decoration; to decorate, as to *trim* or *dress a set* or to trim a store window with *window trim* or *display trim* 2 [film] an unused or deleted segment, including OUTTAKES Trims are not discarded on the cutting-room floor. The parts cut out of a take or trimmed during the editing are hung from pins on a *trim rack* over a container, generally cloth-lined to minimize abrasion, called a *trim bin*. 3 to cut the edge of pages of a publication to a predetermined size Folded or *untrimmed* printed sheets are trimmed to open the pages. (Sometimes, a few of a book's pages are unintentionally left untrimmed.) To *cut flush* or *trim flush* is to make the cover the same size as the inner pages. The *trim size* is the actual size after trimming. *Trimmed edges* are pages that have been cut (actually, leaves, since a page is one side of a leaf).

trim 4 an instruction to trim all four sides of a sheet

trim mark [printing] a line placed on the copy to indicate the edge of the page

triple-decker lead the beginning or introduction of an article written as a three-paragraph entity

triple-duty envelope a mailing piece consisting of an envelope from an advertiser, a reply envelope for the recipient, and an order form

triple-spotting the presentation of three commercials within a single station break or at one time within a program

triplexing the placement of three type styles with identical ESCAPEMENT or width values on the same phototypesetting MATRIX or image master

tripod 1 [photography] a three-legged object, such as the adjustable stand and support used for a camera The *tripod head* is the device on the tripod to which the camera is mounted. 2 [journalism] A tripod head is a three-line headline configuration in which one line in large type appears on the left and two lines of smaller type appear on the right. This layout is used on the covers of weekly TABLOIDS and other flashy periodicals.

triptych an ancient hinged writing tablet consisting of three panels of wood or other material

triviality unimportant news; a *trivial* thing

tri-vision [advertising] a display with a triangular *louver* for three messages shown in sequence

trochaic a verse or other literary composition with a stressed or long syllable followed by an unstressed or short syllable; also called *trochee*

trombone a long, curved BRACKET shaped somewhat like the musical instrument, to which lights are attached

trompe l'oeil a painting or other art that creates an illusion, such as a painting of windows on a solid wall that gives the illusion of actual windows; a French term for "trick of the eye," pronounced trump-loy

trope a figure of speech *Tropus* is Latin for "turn"; tropes are words with a change or turn of their literal meaning, so to trope is to use a word in a figurative sense, to use a figure of speech or figurative language.

trouble box a container with a variety of tools and supplies kept to avert trouble, as at an exhibition; also called *gang box*

troupe a troop or group of performers A *trouper* is a member of such a group; it is also an experienced performer.

trpl. triplicate

TRT total running time; in broadcasting, a common notation for the time in minutes and seconds from the beginning to the end of a recorded tape Time under a minute is preceded by a colon, as in :40 (40 seconds). See also TST.

truck to move a camera sideways, generally on a mobile cart called a DOLLY; to follow a moving object in a *truck* or *trucking shot*

true authentic A *true work* is a legal term for a nonfiction book. A *true-life story* corresponds to reality.

tru-line rate the milline rate of a newspaper based on the circulation in its trading area only

Trump a SERIF typeface; named after Georg Trump, a German designer The main text of this book is set in *Trump Medieval*.

truncate to cut off a part; to shorten In typesetting, to truncate is to break a word at the end of a line without a hyphen and continue it on the next line; the hyphen is omitted due to lack of space. A truncated line should be followed by a line beginning with a hyphen. A lengthy decimal sometimes is truncated for reasons of space or readability by dropping one or more of the digits at the end.

trunk the main service wire of a wire service A *trunk line* is the main line of a telephone system.

trunk show a fashion show held by a designer at department stores The apparel being shown is shipped in *wardrobe trunks*.

tryout an audition, such as a *voice tryout* for singers or *dance tryout* for dancers A play or other work that is performed prior to its opening to test audience reaction is called a tryout.

try story   a phrase used at *The Wall Street Journal* and elsewhere to indicate a medium-grade news priority, to be printed *if room*

ts   tab set, a typesetting command

TSA   TOTAL SURVEY AREA

t-scope   TACHISTOSCOPE

T-setting   [photography] a time-exposure setting of longer than one second

TSL   time spent listening; see also TTSL

tsm publishing   technical, scientific, and medical publishing

T square or **tee square**   a T-shaped ruler commonly used to draw lines or as a base against which other drafting shapes are placed

TSR   TELEPHONE SALES REPRESENTATIVE

TST   total story time; in broadcasting, the time in minutes and seconds of a "story" or report, from the start by the announcer or newscaster to the end, including any tape or other material within TRT, Total Running Time, refers to the time of the taped portion of the TST.

t-stop   a designation of the transmission of light through a camera lens   The *t-stop number* (the *t* stands for transmission) indicates the exact amount of light reaching the film, whereas the F-STOP number indicates the amount of light reaching the lens. T-stops thus are more precise than f-stops, though they generally are not used.

TTL   THROUGH-THE-LENS

TTSL   total time spent listening   In radio, the TTSL is the number of quarter-hours of listening to a radio station by the population group being measured, such as the market or listening area. The TTSL divided by the cumulative audience equals the Time Spent Listening (TSL).

TTY   TELETYPEWRITER

tubby   referring to a low-frequency sound; also called *boomy*

tube   a cylinder or duct that may be open or sealed, such as a toothpaste tube; also short for *electron tube*, a sealed enclosure in which electrons move between electrodes, or *vacuum tube*, an electron tube with most of the air removed   The screen of a TV set, which is the outside surface of an electron tube, is called a *picture tube* or tube. TV viewing is called watching *the tube. Down the tube* or *tubes* is a cancellation or failure.

tub sizing   the process of immersing paper in a container or tub that holds a solution of glue, often used for good-quality paper

tubthumping   promotion by a *tubthumper* or *drumbeater*, such as a publicist   The term dates from the era when performers literally

went through the streets beating tubs or drums to call attention to their shows.

tubular back   in bookbinding, a publication with a flexible cylindrical piece of fabric that is glued to the BACKBONE and to the cover SPINE, so that the back is flexible and can curve outward when the publication is opened. Its quality is better than that of a TIGHT-BACK.

tuck envelope   an envelope with no adhesive application on the flap   The contents are retained in the envelope by tucking the flap into the envelope body.

tucker blade   a part of a paper folder on a web-fed printing press   Its fold is called a *tucker fold, jaw fold,* or *parallel fold.*

tuck-in   a layout in which the text starts under a headline and continues under a photo to the right

tulip crane   a camera platform, or DOLLY, mounted on a movable crane 8 to 16 feet long for high-angle filming

tumbling   [computer graphics] a technique of modifying a two-dimensional image of an object so that the object appears to be rotating on an axis, enabling the viewer to see all of it, as if it were in three dimensions

tummeler   a lively, prankish person, such as a social-activities director at a BORSCHT BELT resort hotel   The word is from the Yiddish, which is from the German *tummeln,* "to bustle about."

tune   a melody; correct musical pitch; harmony, agreement, as in *in tune*

tune in   to adjust a radio or TV receiver to receive signals at a particular FREQUENCY   The *tune-in audience*—the number of listeners or viewers intentionally tuned in to a particular network, station, program, or commercial—is measured in various ways. *Tune-in advertising* time or space may be purchased to promote interest among listeners or viewers.

tungsten   a metallic element with a high melting point used in filaments of electric lamps   *Tungsten light* is artificial light, as contrasted with natural light, so *tungsten films* have characteristics different from daylight films.

tuning out   perceptual blocking; the reduction of conscious awareness of sound or other stimuli

tunnel radio   broadcasting only in tunnels to car radios, a system now operating in several cities

turkey   a failure, particularly in show business   An alleged origin is inept productions that opened on Thanksgiving in expectation of benefiting from holiday-season business, generally good for all shows.

turn 1 [marketing] the frequency of sale of a product within a time period, called the *stock turn* A product may have a daily, weekly, or monthly turn and a fast or slow turn. 2 [photography] processing that is too dark, as with a *turned-out negative* 3 [publishing] text continuing on another page, as in a *turn column*, often without a headline if the continuation is on an adjacent page 4 [theater] an act that appears as part of a schedule Its place on the program is its turn.

turnaround the length of time required to produce a job or complete a function, from *time in* to *time out* A film or other project that is terminated prior to completion is *in turnaround* during the time it is being revised or submitted to a new producer.

turnaway [theater] a sold-out performance for which people are turned away from the box office *Turnaway business* is a sign of success.

turndown a rejection

turned commas inverted commas or quotation marks

turned letter [typography] a piece of metal type inserted upside down in the FORM If done intentionally, it indicates that the letter, perhaps a special character of unavailable size, is to be inserted, as shown in the PROOF with two heavy parallel horizontal lines.

turned rule a thick black line, formed by an upside-down rule or metal strip when using letterpress or generated in computerized typesetting, sometimes used below the headline in obituaries of prominent people

Turner Broadcasting System, Inc. an Atlanta, GA, company that operates Cable News Network and other broadcasting companies

turn-in [book production] the portion of the covering material that folds over onto the three inside edges of the front and back BOARDS

turnout a gathering of people A *good turnout*—large numbers or desired numbers of people—is the opposite of a *poor turnout*. In theater, to *turn out* is for a performer to turn away from the center of the stage and face the audience.

turnover 1 [broadcasting] the frequency with which a program's audience changes over a period of time, the ratio of the net unduplicated cumulative audience over several time periods to the average audience for one time period; also known as *audience turnover*, a measure of the program's holding power 2 [film] a direction—*turn over*—given by a director to turn on the power of the camera 3 [marketing] the rate at which a product sells; the number of times in a year that it *turns*, when all stock is sold out and new stock is reordered 4 [publishing] the lines

of a headline or title after the first line; an arrow, pointer, or other symbol at the bottom of a page, requesting the reader to turn over the page to continue the story

turn rule (T.R.) an instruction to a typesetter to turn a rule, a thin line or slug, upside down in the GALLEY to indicate that an addition—a pickup or insert—or change is to be made at this place The rule itself is called a *rule for insert* or a *rule for pickup*. The instruction *T.R.* or *rule* written on copy means that the typesetter should be on the alert for changes to come.

turnsort type turned upside down with a mark made on it by the typesetter, thus indicating that the character is to be replaced because it is defective

turntable a rotating circular platform that carries a phonograph record or other disc A *turntable hit* is a record that is popular on radio stations but not necessarily in retail sales.

turret a rotating structure, such as a circular mount for a camera lens; also called *rack* or *rack mount* A *divergent turret, divergent lens mounting*, or *divergent-axis turret* holds three or more lenses in different—divergent—positions.

turtle a metal truck to transfer a LETTERPRESS FORM from the composing room to the printing press In the days of letterpress, the turtle truck or table was quite common and quick-moving. Turtle referred to a curved container into which a type form was locked.

turtle graphics an easy-to-use computer program, such as for children, to draw graphics on a screen

tusche a black substance used for drawing in LITHOGRAPHY and also as a resistant coating on nonprinting areas The soft or liquid emulsion ink is applied to lithographic plates to form an image and also used in silk screening. It is pronounced TOOSH-uh, from the French *toucher*, "to touch," and is sometimes called *transfer ink*.

tutorial a class or demonstration; a case history; a detailed study or report; instruction pertaining to operating equipment or a station, particularly computer hardware or software

TV TELEVISION

TV assignment the allocation by the FCC of a *channel*—or *carrier frequency*—to a station

TvB TELEVISION BUREAU OF ADVERTISING

TV black in television, a very dark color but not pure, absolute black

TV board a cardboard, such as *poster board* or *mat board*, generally gray, used for TITLE cards and other artwork No longer common, it generally has been replaced by computerized graphics and other computerization.

TV HH television households

TV mat a black card with rectangular openings, commonly used for the STORYBOARD of TV commercials and other video

TV pad a pad, with sheets imprinted with one or more rectangles shaped like TV screens, used as layout paper for the FRAMES of TV commercials and other video   Beneath each rectangle is a panel, so that the art or image is drawn or printed in the upper area and the action or dialogue appears below. The area around each frame is perforated so that it can be removed from the sheet.

TvQ qualitative ratings of network and syndicated programs conducted by Marketing Evaluations Inc. in Port Washington, NY   The *TvQ reports* provide *TvQ scores* based on ratings of favorite programs from mail questionnaires provided to a panel of viewers.

TVRO TELEVISION RECEIVE-ONLY earth station

TV safety the central area of a TV scene that is seen on most sets   The peripheral area (a perimeter of about 10 percent) sometimes is not seen on the screen and is called *outside TV safety.*

TV screen [graphic arts] a rectangular SHADOW BOX to frame an illustration

TV white [television] an off-white color that is not pure white and that reflects light shone on it   TV white has a reflective value of about 60 percent.

twang box a sound-effects device with one string of piano wire

tweak to pinch   **1** [broadcasting] to adjust to perfection   A common tweaking process involves adjusting an electronic circuit to enhance its sensitivity, also called alignment   **2** [graphic arts] to twist, distort, or modify

tweenie [film] slang for a spotlight with a 600-watt bulb   It is between 500 and 1,000 watts.

tweeter a loudspeaker that reproduces high-pitched sounds with accurate or high fidelity

12–14 unit a truck used for REMOTE TV news, with a microwave transmitter-receiver, called a *dish,* mounted on its roof   It transmits at 12 GIGAHERTZ and receives at 14 gigahertz. The KU-BAND is 12 to 14 gigahertz, and these trucks also are called KU TRUCKS.

twelvemo a page size of a book, about 5″ × 7³/₄″, formed by folding a printer's sheet, about 19″ × 25″, into 12 leaves (24 pages) or a book of this page size; also called *duodecimo*   Pronounced twelve mo, it is abbreviated and generally written as 12mo. The plural is 12mos, twelvemos, or duodecimos.

12–12–12 the maximum number of stations that can be owned by one company: 12 TV stations, 12 AM radio stations, and 12 FM radio stations   This rule of the FEDERAL COMMUNICATIONS COMMISSION replaces the longtime limitation of 7–7–7.

20th Century-Fox Film Corporation a major film and TV company in Los Angeles, formed in 1935 from the merger of Fox Film Corporation and Twentieth Century Pictures   Note that the numeral is not spelled out and the name is hyphenated. The company is called 20th Century-Fox, or simply Fox.

twenty a 20-second commercial

twenty-footer an exhibit space that is 20 feet wide and 10 feet deep, a common size

twenty-fourmo a page size about 5³/₄″ high resulting from a printer's sheet, about 19″ × 25″, folded into 24 leaves (48 pages), or a publication of this page size   Pronounced twenty-four mo, it is abbreviated and generally written as 24mo; the plural is 24mos or twenty-fourmos.

24-sheet poster the standard outdoor advertising space, about 8¹/₂ feet high and 19¹/₂ feet wide or long, originally covered with 24 separate sheets—*one sheets*—but now generally covered with 10 sheets   The structure holding the posters is larger, generally about 12 feet high and 25 feet long.

twice-up art art that is twice the width that it will appear when reproduced

twig books specialized publications (twigs of broader disciplines)   *Twigging* is the proliferation of publications in specialized fields, particularly scientific and scholarly ones.

twinkle an anecdote, amusing remark, or other entertaining comment in an interview

twin-lens [photography] a system of two lens compartments, as in a *twin-lens reflex camera (TLR)*, in which the top lens is a VIEWFINDER and used for focusing and the bottom lens transmits the light and takes the picture

twin pack two attached products, such as toothpaste and a toothbrush, sold as a promotion at a discounted price

twin-wire binding a style of mechanical binding with a double-wire coil passed through slots or holes in the edge of the leaves   When the publication is opened, the facing pages are aligned, more exactly than with spiral binding.

twix See TWX.

two along [book production] the hand-sewing of two sections at a time, generally thin sections, to reduce the thickness in the back of the book; also called *two on* or *two sheets on*

two-by-four a piece of lumber 2 inches thick and 4 inches wide, commonly used in theatrical and other construction; sometimes called a *two by*

two-by-six rule a system of setting up a room for optimum use of an overhead projector The distance from the screen to the first row of seats should be two times the width of the screen; the distance from the screen to the last row of seats should be six times the width of the screen.

2C second cover, the inside front cover of a periodical

twofer [marketing, theater] a reduced-price item or ticket: "buy two and pay for one"

twofold a piece of scenery consisting of two sections, often V-shaped

two-rhyme FEMININE RHYME

2S two sides, as of a paper coated on both sides, as compared to *1S*, or one side

two's the filming of two identical frames of animation instead of one There are 24 frames per second in a sound film.

two-sheet detector a device on a sheet-fed printing press to detect if more than one sheet at a time is being fed through the press; also called *two-sheet caliper* or choke (it shuts off automatically)

two-shot a photograph, motion picture, or close-up TV scene that focuses on two persons or objects In the 1930s and 1940s, the two-shot was commonly used in Hollywood films; some European filmmakers called it the *American shot.*

two-star edition a designation on the DATELINE atop page one of a daily newspaper for the second edition At *The Wall Street Journal*, two stars designate the early edition, which is *locked up* at about 7 P.M., and three stars indicate the late edition.

two-tone a paper with a different color on each of its sides

two-tone head a headline with two weights of letters in the same line

two-up/one-down a teleconference format with two or more origination points and one reception point

two-way capability [television] the ability of a cable system to handle subscriber-to-HEADEND signals in addition to the conventional one-way transmission to the subscribers

two weeks under, one week out slang for a clause in a theatrical contract that gives the theater owner or an employer the right to terminate a show that goes under a specified revenue during a two-week period by giving one week's notice

two-wire circuit the conventional circuit for local telephone communications A more sophisticated *four-wire circuit* permits talking and listening simultaneously.

TWX teletypewriter exchange, an automatic teletypewriter switching service akin to TELEX; pronounced TWIX

TY wire-service jargon: thank you

tying in [broadcasting] a procedure for a local station to pick up or to join a network program after it has started

Tyler mount a sturdy ball-balanced platform installed in an airplane to hold a camera with minimum vibration; also called *Tyler helicopter mount*, though it can be used in other planes

tympan [printing] packing or padding of paper or cloth placed on the *platen* or cylinder of a printing press to provide support for the sheet being printed

typamatic key a key on a keyboard that when depressed keeps repeating its character or function until released

type 1 a group of persons or things with common habits or characteristics Advertising, publications, products, and programs are classified by type. 2 [typography] a small block of metal or wood bearing a raised letter or character or a collection of such pieces; printed or typed characters or representations of such characters, as in photocomposition, in which there is no physical type See also TYPEWRITE.

type area part of a page, sheet, or layout set up to contain typeset material rather than artwork

typebar the part of a typewriter with the characters, punctuation marks, and symbols

typecasting the selection—*casting*—of a performer to conform to an *archetype* or a character established in previous roles of the same type

type character a character or role in a play, novel, or other work who is typical or representative of a general class of people; sometimes also called a *stock character*, who is a familiar figure or role, though not necessarily typical of a group

type comprehensive a layout with type components in place

type C print a color print made directly from a color negative

type dress the complete range of styles and sizes of type regularly used by a publication

typeface the surface of a piece of type that makes the impression; the size or style of a character or the full range of type of the same design The original, unique copyrighted design of a set of characters is called a *true typeface* to distinguish it from a *cheater typeface*, which is an imitation. The same design typeface is manufactured by different *type founders* in varying widths and sometimes with design variations. The four basic forms of typefaces are *italic, roman, script,* and *text.* Most modern typefaces are roman. Examples of typefaces are *Baskerville, Bodoni, Caslon, Clarendon, Garamond, Helvetica,* and many others that are named after the designer and therefore capitalized. Older definitions of typeface, when there were fewer, refer to these designs as TYPE FAMILIES.

type family variations of a typeface, including *roman, italic, bold, bold italic, condensed, expanded,* and other permutations of the basic design

type font a complete assortment of any one size and style of a specific TYPEFACE

type founder a company that designs and produces type

type group several TYPE FAMILIES with common characteristics The largest group of typefaces is roman, which includes most of the *serif* styles—typefaces with serifs, or small hairlines, crossing the main stroke or at the end of the stroke, thus producing a contrast between the thick (heavy) and thin (light) strokes. Older styles, such as *Caslon, Janson,* and *Garamond,* have more contrast than more recently designed typefaces, such as *Clarendon, Consort,* and *Fortune.* A popular modern roman typeface is *Bodoni.* The term *type group* has generally been replaced by *type style.*

type-high as high as the standard height of metal type, slightly less than an inch

type library the entire collection of TYPEFACES available from a *typographer,* printer, or other source

type louse a fictional insect Actually, ink drops between characters of metal type. Apprentice printers sometimes were asked to look for type lice.

type metal an alloy of tin, lead, antimony, and sometimes copper, used in printing type

typeover in word processing, a revision obtained by typing over existing text

type page the printed area on a page The area around the type page is the *margin.* The margin adjacent to the FOLD is the *gutter.*

typescript typewritten text

type series a TYPE FAMILY Not a common term, it originally referred to the different sizes of the same typeface.

typeset to set in type, or COMPOSE, as by a *typesetter,* a compositor or person who sets type, or by a machine

type spec type specification, an indication of TYPE STYLE, size, and other instructions to the *typesetter* for use in working with the manuscript or copy

type style a basic form of TYPEFACE Another way of grouping typefaces is to break them out into additional classes, such as *Modern* (an example is *Times Roman,* which also is in the roman class), *Ornate* (an example is *Davida*), and *Text* or *Black-letter* (an example is *Old English*).

typewrite to write with a TYPEWRITER; usually shortened to *type* The process is *typewriting* (or *typing*).

typewriter a machine for producing printed characters Christopher Latham Sholes (1819–90) patented the first U.S. typewriter in 1868. One of the earliest typewriters, the Remington No. 1, had only uppercase, or capital, letters. The Remington No. 2, introduced in 1878, had both uppercase and lowercase letters. The early machines were operated manually by pressing keys on a keyboard to raise metal hammers that strike an inked ribbon and make an impression on a sheet of paper. Contemporary typewriters are manual and electric, portable and full-size, with various kinds of ribbons and key systems, movable and nonmovable carriages, and self-correcting and other features. The abbreviation *typw.* refers to typewriter, typewritten, or typeset.

typo a mistake made by a *typesetter* when reproducing copy, also called *typographical error;* a typing error

typography (typog.) the process of setting material in type for printing A *typographer* is someone who specifies and sets type or a designer—a *type director*—who specifies the type to be set.

typositor a machine that produces high-quality DISPLAY type one line at a time

U

u or **U** upper (also *up*); upstage; ULTRAHIGH FRE-
QUENCY *U* also is a symbol, usually appearing
within a circle, much like the TRADEMARK registration symbol, on the label of a food product to
indicate that it has been prepared in accordance
with the Kosher certification standards of the
Kasruth Division of the Union of Orthodox Jewish Congregations of America, headquartered in
New York.

U & LC   UPPER- and LOWERCASE

uc, u.c., or **UC**   **1** up center, a portion of the
stage (see also AREAS)   **2** UPPERCASE, the capital
letters of the alphabet; also called *CAPS*   The
proofreading symbol for capitalization is three
lines under the letter to be capitalized.   **3** urban
contemporary format of radio stations

UCC   uniform commercial code: state laws regulating the buying and selling of goods and services

UE   upper entrance, a stage notation

UFB   unfit for broadcast

UGT   telegraphic abbreviation for urgent

UHF   ULTRAHIGH FREQUENCY

UL   up left, a portion of a stage; see also AREAS
ULC is up left center.

ultrafiche   *microfiche* with images that have
been greatly reduced (reduction ratio of 90X or
more)

ultrahigh frequency (UHF)   limited-range wave
bands for television channels (14 to 82) that
transmit from 470 to 890 megaHertz (mHz),
with lower power and over a smaller area than
low-band (channels 2 to 6) or high-band (7 to 13)
very high frequency (VHF) stations

ultraviolet   an invisible range of radiation wavelengths, shorter and just beyond violet light
This part of the SPECTRUM produces exposure of
light-sensitive photographic emulsions.

umbra   a shade or shadow, or the blackest area
of a shadow   A penumbra is a partial shadow.

umbrella   a name or theme that is unifying and
encompasses several elements; actual umbrel-
las or umbrella-shaped reflectors that are used
in photography   The reflecting umbrella is
sometimes called a *photographer's umbrella*;
when mounted on a small platform so that it

can be swiveled, it is called an *umbrella and
stand.*

umbrella brand   a family brand, a group of products with the same name

umbrella pricing   the practice of establishing
the same or similar prices by competing companies in a field, also called *price leadership*, in
which one company sets a price and others follow, as in the airline industry

unaided recall   the ability of a reader, viewer, or
listener to remember the name of an advertiser
24 hours (or another time period) after having
been exposed to the advertisement with no
prompting or hints from a researcher; also
called *unaided brand recall* or *unaided recall
interview*   If the test is conducted the day after
a broadcast, it is called *day-after-recall on-air.*

unb.   unbound; also abbreviated as *unbd.*

unbleached   not oxidized   Unbleached paper
has a light-brown color.

uncial   a large rounded letter, as used in Greek
and Latin manuscripts; from the Latin *uncialis,*
"of an inch"   *Half-uncial* was a handwriting
style in the 5th to 9th centuries in which the
uncial style took on cursive (connected) characteristics, including the use of LIGATURES.

uncoated book paper   a paper used for a variety
of printing jobs that has smooth finishes applied
on the machine rather than with lacquering or
enameling   Uncoated book paper is made in
four finishes: antique (rough), machine or ma-
chine-finished (medium smooth), English
(smoother), and SUPERCALENDERED (smoothest).

uncut edges   the leaves of a book or other publication that have not been trimmed; not the
same as UNOPENED

undated   not dated   An *undated story* lacks a
date, intentionally or in error, or a DATELINE,
such as a roundup or other story originating
from several places

under   to lower, as in a direction to reduce the
sound, the development time of a film (*un-
derdevelop*), or the light

underact   to perform weakly or without intensity, perhaps intentionally

undercrank [film] to operate a camera at a slower-than-standard speed, so that the resulting film, when projected at the standard 24 frames per second, appears to be in fast motion Its opposite is *overcrank.*

undercut to make a depression; to diminish effectiveness In printing, a plate that is over-etched, so that it is usable directly but not for molding duplicates, is undercut.

under-dash material an article prepared in advance about an impending event, such as an obituary of a dying person When the event (such as the death) occurs, an UPDATE is written followed by a *jim dash* or *dinky dash* (a line with a few dashes) and the prepared material. Under-dash material or *underdash matter* also may be a late development; it is printed after a preceding story and separated by a series of short dash marks.

underexposed describing a film that has received insufficient light, or a book or other work that has not been widely seen

underground unconventional, perhaps avant-garde; experimental; noncommercial; radical, as with underground media, including the *underground press* (alternative publications) and *underground film* and *television* (independent, low-budget productions)

underlay [printing] the placement of paper or other packing under the type form or press plate to support it on the bed of the printing press and raise it to the proper height

under-lighting in film animation, illumination from under an animation table that illuminates the artwork; also called *back lighting* or *bottom lighting*

underlighting dim lighting, perhaps intentional

underline to draw a line under, or UNDERSCORE; to emphasize There are several proofreader's marks for creating emphasis. One line under a letter is an instruction to set it in *italic* type; two lines indicates SMALL CAPITAL LETTERS. Emphasis also can be achieved by capitalizing (indicated by three lines under the letter), using larger type or BOLDFACE (indicated by a wavy underline), indenting, and other techniques. A combination of straight and wavy underlines indicates boldface italic. A broken underline—or STET—indicates that the item is to be left unchanged. A horizontal line through characters indicates that they are to be deleted. Two horizontal lines also can be an instruction to correct the alignment. The caption below an illustration sometimes is called an underline.

underplay to perform a role with restraint or less than the usual emphasis

underprinting the printing of editorial matter beneath and related to an advertisement, such as sports scores as part of a SCOREBOARD ADVERTISEMENT in a newspaper

underrule a line or rule placed under characters

underrun a shortage in the quantity ordered, as in printing

underscore a rule set below characters for emphasis; also called UNDERLINE

underset a line with insufficient characters, resulting in excessive spacing between letters or words

understudy a person who studies or is trained to do the work of another, as in a theatrical production

undertone a low tone of sound or voice; an underlying quality or element; a faint or subdued color, particularly one seen through other colors, as in some glazes or a thin film of printing ink

underwriting in public television, the granting of money by companies (*underwriters*) who receive identification on the program, as with the sponsorship by Mobil of "Masterpiece Theatre" and other Public Broadcasting Service programs

unduplicated audience the total number of individuals or households that listen to or view a specific radio or TV commercial, program, or series over a period of time, generally one to four weeks; also called *accumulated audience, cume, cumulative audience, net unduplicated audience,* or *reach*

unearned discount a discount taken by a customer who has not met the payment terms or an advertiser who has not fulfilled the quantity or frequency specified in a contract

unedited not changed, altered, or revised, as in an early stage of production of a manuscript, film, or other work A movie that is shown uncut may be marked "unedited."

unglazed paper uncoated paper, without luster

uniform commercial code (UCC) state laws regulating the buying and selling of goods and services

uniform edition one or several volumes containing the complete works of an author; also called *author's edition*

unimatch a combination of two type styles on a page

union catalog cards with the holdings of a group of libraries, such as the branches of a system or the members of a cooperative

unipole an advertisement erected on a single steel pole or column, as in a shopping mall or a transportation terminal; also called *monopole*

unique selling proposition (USP or U.S.P.) an aspect or feature of a product or service that is unusual or superior and thus can be the basis of an advertising or other campaign The concept was originally developed by the Ted Bates advertising agency, now Backer Spielvogel Bates, in New York

unit   **1** the smallest element, as of a sales territory; a standard volume equivalent by which a single sale is measured; a single copy of an advertisement or a medium   **2** [film, television] a group of production people involved in a specific technical area, such as a *special effects* unit, or assigned to a specific location   A *unit manager* handles the financial and other business concerns of a crew on location. The *unit director* may be the director or assistant director. The *first unit*, the group with the principal actors, works under the director. The *second unit* involves special locations; the *second-unit director* may be an assistant director. An *insert unit*, headed by an *insert-unit director*, produces one or more shots, such as of a map or other unmoving objects, that are inserted into a scene. **3** [typography] A *relative unit* is a measure of space related to the specific *point* size of the type, generally expressed as units of an em, such as 18 units per em, stated simply as 18. A *machine unit* is the smallest distance that a typesetter's spacing or escapement mechanism can move, usually one relative unit in the smallest point size.

unit cost   the total variable or fixed cost of a single unit

unit-count font   typefaces with identical widths, such as those used in wire-service copy

United Scenic Artists (USA)   a labor union, headquartered in New York, of about 2,000 SCENIC ARTISTS and designers, costume and lighting designers, and others in film, television, and theater   USA is a local unit of the International Brotherhood of Painters and Allied Trades.

unitization   **1** [marketing] the combination of several cases of merchandise into a single containerized unit to fit evenly into standard warehouse or shipping space and to reduce damage, theft, and cost   **2** [typography] determination of the width of the characters and specification of the *width units* based on the em or SET SIZE of the FONT

unit pricing   prices quoted on the basis of a standard measure, such as per ounce, liter, or pound

unit publicist   [film] a person in charge of publicizing a specific film before, during, and after its production   The unit publicist is not the same as a *unit director* or other personnel involved with secondary locations, or units, during the filming

unit set   [theater] a basic set that can be modified for all of the scenes of a play

unit split   the division of a radio or television commercial into two parts, each of which is called a *piggyback*

unity   oneness, as in an arrangement of parts in a work that produces a single, harmonious effect   The *unities* of dramatic construction are the principles that a play or other work require: *unity of action* (a unified plot, in which all elements are connected, usually by a cause-and-effect relationship), *unity of time* (all action confined to one day or in a specific period with no break in time), and *unity of place* (all action in the same place).

Universal Copyright Convention (UCC)   an international agreement on copyrights signed in Geneva in 1952 and subsequently accepted by the United States and most Western countries

universal desk   a section of a newspaper that handles all general copy, excluding specialized departments such as business and sports

Universal Product Code (UPC)   a coding system now used on many products and publications, particularly those sold in supermarkets, so that visual SCANNERS at checkout counters can record price and other information for automatic tabulation of the bill and for inventory control

universe   the total population from which a SAMPLE is drawn

university press   a publishing operation owned by or affiliated with an educational institution or group that publishes scholarly and other works, including TRADE BOOKS

UNIX system   a set of programs that control a variety of computer hardware and software, developed in 1969 by Bell Laboratories of Murray Hill, NJ

unjustified composition   typesetting that is not aligned at the margin   It generally refers to the uneven right margin as compared to the left margin, which is almost always justified, or aligned, so that lines of copy are even (FLUSH).

unload   to sell merchandise expeditiously, such as at a considerable discount

unobtrusive measures   a research technique in which the researcher does not intrude on the behavior of the individuals being studied, such as collecting data from records and other archival sources

unopened   paper that has been folded but not cut, either intentionally, as with a GATEFOLD or other special size, or unintentionally, as sometimes happens with the top or bottom edges of the leaves of a book

unrestricted sample   a random SAMPLE, not predetermined as in a QUOTA SAMPLE

unretouched photograph a photo not altered by retouching, either the original or an exact facsimile

unspool to project or *unreel* a film Unspool and unreel are slang words.

unwired network a group of radio or TV stations, akin to a network, on which an advertiser places a specific program and/or commercials

up greater intensity, pitch, or volume, as in *turning up* the sound; high, as in *moving up* a component in a layout; euphoric or exciting, as in being "up" A newspaper is up when it is printed. Common show-business directives are *bring up the lights* and *up the music*. A performer who forgets lines is said to be up. To *go up* is to falter or forget or to move UPSTAGE.

-up [printing] *two-up, three-up*, and other numbers that refer to imposition of material to be printed on a larger size sheet to take advantage of full press capacity

UP *United Press International*, a major wire service formed by the merger of *United Press* and *International News Service*; also abbreviated as UPI Formerly owned by *Scripps-Howard*, it was sold in 1982. Its headquarters was moved in 1983 from New York to Washington, DC.

up-and-over a direction to a sound engineer or music conductor; to increase music or other sound as speech fades or ends; the opposite of *down-and-under Up-and-under* is a direction to bring in music and then lower it below the dialogue or other sound.

upbeat 1 optimistic 2 an unaccented beat of music, especially the last beat of a measure

upcut [television] an editing error that results in the audio ending after the video and conflicting with the next audio segment

upcutting [broadcasting] the elimination of part of a network or syndicated program by a radio or TV station to leave more time for local announcements, as in *triple spotting* Upcutting is generally considered unethical or fraudulent.

update to bring up to date; a revision

upfront at the beginning; in advance, as in an *up-front payment* or an advance on royalties paid to a writer or other person at the inception of the project In broadcasting, *upfront buying* is an advance commitment or prepayment early in the buying season or planning period, such as a commitment to sponsor a program long before it is broadcast In contrast, *scatter buying* is done close to airtime.

up full a direction for audio to be heard at full volume

uplink [telecommunications] the portion from the ground source up to the satellite The balance of the circuit is the *downlink*.

upload the transmission of text, such as a news article, from a keyboard terminal to the computer

up-market pertaining to a high socioeconomic group The term is often used in positioning a product.

upper and lower (U&L, U & LC, uc/lc, or c/lc) an instruction to a printer for conventional use of capital (*uppercase*) and noncapital (*lowercase*) letters

uppercase capital or uppercase letters; also called SHIFT, as in the shift position to produce uppercase characters on a standard typewriter As two words, upper case is the case itself that contains the capital letters and special characters. (However, these cases are becoming uncommon with the increased use of photocomposition instead of metal type.)

upper rail (UR) the upper section of matrices in a phototypesetting system, generally for ITALIC or BOLDFACE The primary position is the *lower rail (LR)*.

uprating a process of increasing the recommended speed of a film by using a different developer or increasing the immersion time of the film in the developer; also called *pushing*

upright 1 a book that is greater in height than width and thus is the conventional or standard size 2 a vertical support, called a STANDARD, of a sign

upscale describing high income, higher education, or other characteristics on the upper end of the DEMOGRAPHIC scale

upset price a reserve or floor price at which an item is withdrawn from a sale or from the market, as at an auction

up shot a camera shot from below the subject It is different from *upshot*, which is the final outcome or result.

Upson board a fiberboard used in exhibits

upstage away from the audience or camera; the rear of a stage; to lessen the effect of another performer by calling attention to oneself, such as by moving to the rear of the stage so that the performer at the front (who is *upstaged*) may have to turn toward the rear, away from the audience

upstream in interactive or two-way TV, the signals, or reaction, from the subscriber to the primary distribution point, or the HEADEND of a cable system

upstyle a typographic style with emphasis on capitalization; the opposite of *downstyle*

up-to-speed the regular flow of action

UR up right, a portion of a stage; see also AREAS URC is up right center.

urban contemporary a music format of radio stations, primarily for black audiences

urge line [advertising] the closing portion of an advertisement with the key point or request to buy

u.s. abbreviations for the Latin *ubi supra* ("where mentioned above") and *ut supra* ("as above"), used in lists of citations and other references

US abbreviation for LUMINOSITY

USA UNITED SCENIC ARTISTS

USA Network a cable network based in New York

user fee money collected from users of specific services, such as toll roads or pay-per-view television

user-friendly [computers] describing a system that is easy to access and nonantagonistic to the human who is interacting with it

user ID a number or code used by a computer or other system to identify the user or customer

userid user identification, generally a number, entered by a user to commence operation of a computer system

use-the-user plan a sales program in which a referral premium is used as an incentive to recommend other customers

USIA the United States Information Agency in Washington, DC, which operates Voice of America and other communication activities outside the United States

USP UNIQUE SELLING PROPOSITION

USPS United States Postal Service

US SPRINT See SPRINT

UUUU [radio] a research notation for unidentified, as describing listeners who were surveyed but could not be designated as listening to a specific station The four *U*s are to make sure there is no confusion with other *U* words.

UV ULTRAVIOLET UV inks are printing inks that dry by exposure to ultraviolet light.

V

v. verb; verse; version; VERSO; versus; vertical; voice; volume; vowel

V vertical; VERY HIGH FREQUENCY (VHF)

VAC Viewer and Consumer Ratings, a system of Quantiplex (a subsidiary of John Blair Co. in New York) that characterizes audiences in the Primary Buying Area (PBA) and Regional Buying Area (RBA) and correlates product purchases with specific TV programs and newspapers

vacuum frame in offset printing, a suction device to hold material during exposure

vacuum-seal a packaging process used in tamper-resistant packages with air-tight foil or a plastic seal covering the product or sometimes part of a product, such as a bottle cap

valance a drapery, decorative board, metal strip, or other ornamental item mounted across the top of a store window or door; a roll-on strip for advertising or identification along the upper edge of a window, door, wall, counter, or other area of a store

Valentine an article that is favorable to a person or an organization

valley [computers, typography] in OPTICAL CHARACTER RECOGNITION, an indentation in a stroke

VALS Values and Lifestyles Program, developed by SRI INTERNATIONAL to measure audience quality In this system, which is used by SIMMONS and other market researchers, the U.S. population is divided into nine groups: survivors and sustainers (need-driven); belongers, emulators, and achievers (outer-directed); the individualistic, experimental, and societally conscious (inner-directed), and the integrated. For example, the societally conscious tend to be responsible, mission-oriented, mature, and successful and to lead single lives, watch public TV, and consume various types of products and services that are often different from the other groups' choices. In 1989, the VALS-2 system was introduced, with eight groups: actualizers, fulfillers, achievers, experiencers, believers, strivers, makers, and strugglers.

value fair price; usefulness; merit; principle; relative duration of a musical tone or rest; relative lightness or darkness of a color Black has the lowest value and white the highest value, so as a hue lightens, its value increases, as indicated on a numerical scale. The usual retail price of a product, its fair price, sometimes is referred to as *value price.*

value-added network a private telephone-communications company that leases services from AT&T or other common carriers and then combines or adds features for resale to end users

value-added tax [marketing] a tax added at various stages of the movement of a product based on the difference of value at each successive stage Exported products frequently are exempt from value-added tax to make their prices more competitive.

value analysis a cost-reduction method based on determining which components of a product or service can be produced more cheaply or efficiently

value judgment [market research] an action or decision based on the comparison of alternatives

vamp **1** to improvise, particularly musically, as by an orchestra before a performance commences **2** a seductive woman, a type of actress or character; from the word *vampire*

vampire video a bizarre or attention-getting device in a TV commercial

vanda a telephone connection combining *video and audio*

Van Dyke a printing proof in the form of a positive print on inexpensive photosensitive paper made from a film negative; also called *brownprint, brownline,* or *Van Dyke print* Generally, dark-brown color is used in the areas to be printed, whereas a *blueline* is typically blue. Sometimes spelled Vandyke or vandyke, this type of print was invented in India by a British army engineer named Vandyke.

vanilla ordinary; dull; not customized *Plain vanilla* is really dull.

varactor a variable capacitance diode used in the electronic tuning of radio and TV receivers; from variable reactance The process is called *varactor tuning.*

variable inconstant, changing In word processing and direct mail, *variables* are the individual parts that change with each letter, such as name, address, and salutation.

variable-area soundtrack [film] an optical soundtrack on film stock with a width that varies in accordance with different sound waves This narrow transparent area also is called a *bilateral soundtrack* or *bilateral track*, because the sound modulations run symmetrically on each side of a longitudinal axis down the length of the track.

variable cost the range of cost in materials, labor, and other components that change with various levels of output

variable document one of two documents in a typing-merge procedure, containing the names or other information to be inserted in the standard, or primary, document; also called *secondary document*

variable mike a microphone with several ports, or openings, in it so that it has a directional pickup pattern, such as a shotgun or long-shafted mike The Variable-D mike is a super-cardioid microphone manufactured by Electro-Voice, Buchanan, MI.

variance tendency to change, degree of change, or discrepancy In market research, variance is the square of the standard deviation, used to measure the actual differences among the scores of a SAMPLE.

variant something deviating from the standard or more common form, such as a word with a different spelling or pronunciation or a book with variations on the binding or other differences from books produced at the same printing

Variety a weekly tabloid newspaper covering film, broadcasting, and all areas of show business Founded in 1905 by Sime Silverman and now owned by Cahners Publishing Company in New York, it is famous for its coinage of words and abbreviations, such as *B.O.* (box office) and *deejay* (disc jockey), and its puns, inimitable journalistic jargon, and show-biz style. It avoids some words, such as money, which it prefers to call *coin.*

variorum an edition of a book with several versions of the text or notes by scholars, such as a variorum edition of Shakespeare; from the Latin *cum notis variorum,* "with notes of various persons"

Varitronics a typesetting system commonly used in desktop publishing, manufactured by Varitronic Systems, Inc., of Minneapolis

VariTyper one of the earliest electric typewriters that produces reproducible copy, has a large selection of interchangeable typefaces, and justifies lines A line of digital typesetters currently is made by VariTyper of East Hanover, NJ, a division of AM International.

varnish paint or another preparation made of resins dissolved in oil or alcohol, used to finish wood, metal, paper, or other surfaces; the shiny protective coating resulting from varnish *Varnishing* is the process of applying varnish and also another word for varnish.

Vaughn Grid [market research] a device to determine whether there is high or low involvement on the part of the person purchasing a product and whether the decision to buy is a thinking decision or an emotional one Basically, the grid is divided into four quadrants, one of which will contain a point indicating high or low personal involvement and another with a point showing an intellectual or emotional decision. A product or service placed on the grid in this way helps to target the buyers. Developed in 1978 by Richard Vaughn, research director of the Los Angeles office of Foote, Cone & Belding, it is also called the *FCB Grid.*

VCR videocassette recorder

v.d. abbreviation for *various dates,* as used in BIBLIOGRAPHIES

V disc Victory disc, an acetate record with popular music distributed during World War II to U.S. military personnel, recorded from radio programs or specially recorded

VDR videodisk recorder

VDT VIDEO DISPLAY TERMINAL

VDU visual display unit, more commonly called a visual or video display terminal

Veblenian model a marketing concept of the consumer as a product of environmental conditioning Thorstein B. Veblen (1857–1929) was an American political economist and social scientist. *Veblen pricing* refers to increasing the price to increase the demand.

vector [computer graphics] the use of lines, rather than the RASTER technique of dots, to create images

Veeder a trademarked device that measures film length, used on movie cameras and editing equipment made by Veeder-Root, of Simsbury, CT

veejay video disc jockey

vegetables printer's marks

vehicle a device, technique, or medium; a role to display the special talents of a performer or group; a substance such as oil in which pigments are mixed for paint or ink

veiling a soft, fuzzy density that sometimes appears between the large dots of a HALFTONE

vellum a fine parchment made from calfskin or the skin of other young animals, from *vellm,* an old English word pertaining to a calf Vellum originally was used for the binding and pages of very fine-quality books. Today, it still is a heavy, off-white, all-rag, translucent paper that resembles parchment and has a rough, dull surface (*vellum finish*) that absorbs ink quickly. Vellum paper is used to make copies in a type of duplicating machine called WHITEPRINT. *Tracing vellum* is a transparent paper used by artists for tracing; it is not *tracing paper*, which is lower-priced transparent ONIONSKIN paper.

velocitator a mobile carrier for a camera with a small crane to elevate the camera and seats for a camera operator and assistant Intermediate in size between a *dolly* and a *boom*, it is usually pushed by hand but sometimes is motorized. It is commonly used in film, and can be quickly elevated and moved (hence the name, from *velocity*).

velocity the relative speed with which a specific retail item is sold; also called *stock turn*

velour a fabric like velvet with a soft nap *Black velours* are nonreflective black drapes used as TV backdrops.

Velox a print made on photographic chloride paper from a HALFTONE screen; pronounced VEE-lox Retouching may be done without marring the original, and the Velox itself can be used for reproduction. The word should be capitalized (though it generally is not), as it is trademarked by the Eastman Kodak Company, of Rochester, NY.

velveting sound a process of cleaning a film soundtrack by moving it between two pieces of soft cloth; also called *gloving sound*

veneer an overlay; gloss

venue a place Originally a legal term, it is now used in show business for a theater, nightclub, or other site of a performance. That's appropriate—*venue* is a French verb form of "to come."

verbal pertaining to words, in contrast to actions Verbal includes written words, though it generally refers to spoken words, as in *verbal contract* (technically, and more properly, an oral contract, as different from a written contract).

verbatim using exactly the same word or words, or a literal transcription; from the Latin *verbum*, "word" *Verbatim* is also the name of a newsletter about language, published by Laurence Urdang in Essex, CT. *Verbatim et literatim* is Latin for "word for word" (verbatim) and "letter for letter" (literatim), which indeed is a faithful transcription.

verbiage wordiness; excess words

verbose wordy; using or containing excess words

Vericolor a KODAK film Vericolor print film is used to make positive transparencies and slides from color negatives.

verisimilitude the appearance of being true or real, a characteristic of realistic or historical novels, DOCUDRAMAS, or other work

vernacular language that is indigenous to or characteristic of a specific area or group, such as slang or idiomatic words It is less formal than literary language.

vernier a short graduated scale running parallel to a longer scale and used to measure a part of the longer scale; an auxiliary device to facilitate adjustments on a precision instrument *Vernier tuning* refers to the continuous fine tuning of a radio receiver.

verse writing arranged in a rhythmic pattern, as in poetry or song; a section of such a composition

verso (vo) a left-hand page, which always has an even number; the opposite of RECTO

versus (v, vs, or vs.) in contest against; in contrast with

vert. vertical

vertex 1 an apex, or highest point 2 [typography] the point at which the stems of a letter meet, such as the bottom of a *V*

vertical arrangement a retail shelf arrangement in which similar or related items are placed from top to bottom, generally in a limited or separate section In a supermarket, for example, jams and jellies may be arranged horizontally in the conventional manner while elsewhere there may be a vertical unit for gourmet or specialty jams and jellies. A vertical layout or sign has a height greater than its width.

vertical blanking interval a portion of a TV signal between waves Coded CLOSED CAPTIONING for hearing-impaired viewers and TELETEXT are transmitted in this interval for viewing with a decoder attached to the TV set.

vertical buy an advertising schedule designed to reach audiences with similar characteristics

vertical camera a camera used in color-process reproduction in which the bellows extends vertically instead of in the conventional horizontal position Thus, the camera is positioned above the item to be photographed.

vertical cume the *cumulative rating* for two or more programs broadcast on the same day

vertical discount a discount for purchase of broadcast time during a week or other specific period

vertical file a collection in filing drawers arranged in the conventional manner, with each cabinet in sequence in an upright or vertical column

vertical half-page half the entire width of the full height of a periodical page

vertical integration channel integration of a *vertical marketing system* (*VMS*): common ownership of most or all of the stages in the distribution chain by a manufacturer or a single company, such as a company that owns or controls its suppliers and also owns or operates its retail stores Vertical marketing systems are of three types: *corporate VMS* (company-owned, such as Sherwin-Williams); *contractual VMS* (wholesaler-sponsored voluntary chains, such as Independent Grocers' Alliance or IGA; retailer cooperatives, such as Associated Grocers'; and franchise organizations, such as McDonald's); and *administrative VMS*, such as Procter & Gamble, which coordinate stages of production and distribution through size, importance, and power rather than actual ownership or contract.

vertical interval signal [television] a signal inserted outside the regular picture area and transmitted in the vertical interval period between frames *Vertical interval reference signals* (*VIRS*) provide reference data, such as identification of the time and origin of the program; *vertical interval test signals* (*VITS*) provide transmission and other monitoring checks.

vertical music the simultaneous sounds that form harmonies, called *verticals*, as opposed to the successive sounds that form melodies

vertical press publications within a specific industry, as differentiated from the *horizontal press*, the broader-based business or professional media; also called *vertical publications*

vertical rotation distribution of broadcast SPOTS at different times within the same day

vertical saturation concentrated advertising by an advertiser during a single broadcast day

vertical selling selling to buyers in a limited range of industries

vertical spacing [typography] the space between lines, which consists of horizontal areas, though *horizontal spacing* is the space between characters or words

vertigration integration of the advertising and promotion efforts of a retail dealer, franchiser, or licensee into the broader advertising and promotion plans of a manufacturer or licensor, to permit greater impact and efficiency

very high frequency (VHF or V) long-range television stations broadcasting on channels 2 through 13 (54 to 216 megaHertz) There are over 550 commercial and over 100 noncommercial VHF stations in the United States.

Very Promotable Item (VPI) a product that is easy to sell; a *hot product*

vesicular process a dry photographic process using heat to create tiny vesicles, or blisters, which then produce images on the exposed vesicular film; developed by the Kalvar Corporation, Minneapolis

vest-pocket supermarket a bantam store; a convenience store; a superette

vet to examine, investigate, or evaluate; from veterinarian, a doctor who examines (vets) an animal A publisher vets a manuscript by sending it for review by an outside expert (a *vetter*).

VET VIDEO EDITING TERMINAL

VGA video graphics array See VIDEOGRAPHICS.

VHF VERY HIGH FREQUENCY

VH-1 Video Hits One, a cable programming service of MTV Network, Inc., in New York VH-1 offers *adult contemporary* music rather than the rock music of the company's MTV channel.

VHS trademark for video home system, a type of ½-inch videocassette recorder made by Matsushita, RCA, and other companies It is not compatible with the BETA format.

v.i. abbreviation for *vide infra*, Latin for "see below," used to indicate a FOOTNOTE or other reference

V.I. volume indicator

Viacom a television company in New York that produces network and syndicated programs, operates the Showtime pay-TV service, and owns TV stations and cable systems

vice versa (v.v.) conversely; with the order or meaning reversed; from the Latin for "the position being reversed"

victory type extremely large type, as that used to announce a battle victory

vidclip an excerpt—*clip*—from a film or TV production, used on TV for news or promotion

vide Latin for "see"; a direction to a printer or reader to call attention to a particular page or other reference

video the visual portion of a broadcast or film; a synonym for television A *video credit* identifies a performer or other person or thing shown on television. A *videophile* is a TV-lover (a super-viewer). *Videophone* is a trademarked telephone equipped for audio and video transmission and playback. *Videoscan* is a trademarked method for machine character recognition of words or other material using a video camera that recognizes shapes and matches them with shapes in the machine's storage.

video alteration a process of changing a TV image, such as is done with computer graphics or other techniques in which a picture is altered or combined with another picture or artwork; also called *image processing* or *video manipulation*

video assist a system consisting of a videotape camera, recorder, and playback unit attached to a film camera to permit viewing on a monitor during shooting and subsequent viewing on videotape (called *instant dailies*); also called *video playback* or *video tap*

video billboard a large screen with an electronic display, such as the advertising signs in New York's Times Square

videoconferencing the linking of two or more groups via closed-circuit satellite-transmitted television

video display terminal (VDT) a cathode-ray tube linked with a keyboard to make it a computerized typewriter, or any machine or workstation with a display screen; formerly called *cathode-ray tube (CRT)* or *video display tube*

video editing terminal (VET) a cathode-ray tube with a keyboard (a VIDEO DISPLAY TERMINAL) specifically designed for editing text; a *word processor*

video feedback a kaleidoscopic artistic optical effect achieved by aiming a TV camera directly at its monitor so that it tapes its own image

videogenic describing a person or thing that looks attractive on television

videographer a user of a video camera, particularly a portable unit, such as a CAMCORDER

videographic display computerized graphics, charts, pictures, movable objects, and other items drawn by computer using dots or lines

videographics the electronic manipulation of pictures, as in *computer graphics*, in which pictures are created with dots or lines and then manipulated A *videograph* is a high-speed cathode-ray printer. *Video Graphics Array (VGA)* is a color graphics system for personal computers that includes a VGA board or display card.

video-in a jack through which a video signal is fed into a TV set or other receptacle; also called *line-in*

video jockey the TV counterpart of DISC JOCKEY

video layout terminal (VLT) a VIDEO DISPLAY TERMINAL specifically designed for arranging graphic elements, now used for many publications

video manipulation See VIDEO ALTERATION.

video monitor a TV set with no channel selector, used in broadcasting control rooms and studios and for linking with videotape machines for playback It sometimes lacks audio.

video operator [television] a control-room engineer who operates the monitors and camera control units to switch from one camera to another and maintain color, contrast, and other visual qualities The video operator reports to the *technical director.*

video-out a jack from which a video signal is fed out of a videotape recorder; also called *line-out*

video playback See VIDEO ASSIST.

Video Storyboard Tests a market research company in New York specializing in surveying TV viewers about which commercials they recall and like best

video tap See VIDEO ASSIST.

videotape magnetic tape for recording sound and picture, recorded and/or played on a *videotape machine* such as a *videocassette recorder (VCR)* for showing on a TV set Unlike films and records, which can be duplicated quickly, videotapes are duplicated individually and mass production takes a longer time. The laboratories that produce videotapes for home video have hundreds of *slave machines* linked to a master. And unlike film editing, videotape editing does not involve cutting and splicing—it is done electronically by a *videotape editor.* The width of the tape varies from $1/4$ inch to $1/2$ inch for home use, to $3/4$ inch for most common professional uses, to 1 inch and 2 inches, formerly for *super-professional* use. A *videocassette* is a videotape recording contained in a cassette; a *videodisc* is a recording on a record or disc for playback on videodisc players in homes. A *video engineer* is responsible for the video portion of a TV program. *Videotape transfer* is a videotape recording of a film, whereas *videotape duplication* is the replication of a videotape. Unlike film, all videotape has color capability.

videotex a communications medium connecting a home TV or terminal with a central computer via telephone, enabling the home or office user to receive data on the TV screen and interact or respond to it, such as by ordering products or services (*two-way TV cable*) TELETEXT is *one-way videotex* service; *viewdata* is the videotex system linked with a computer keyboard so that it is instantly interactive. The original and correct name is *videotext*, but videotex now is more common. Types of videotex include *business-to-business videotex*, generally from a company to its dealers or directly to customers for business products and services; *corporate videotex*, such as electronic mail used internally by a company or organization; *public access videotex*, interactive services that provide information to passersby at terminals and elsewhere; and *home videotex*, used at home for sending messages, obtaining information, and purchasing products and services. Associations include the International Videotex Information Provider's Association in Tilburg, the Netherlands and the Videotex Industry Association in Roslyn, VA.

video up a directive to brighten the TV picture, sometimes used in editing VIDEOTAPE

video wallpaper a TV background or visual effects that are dull

videozine a magazine in a video format

vide post Latin for "see after," a notation to see later material in the text

vide supra Latin for "see above," a notation to see earlier material in the text

vidicon a small television-camera tube that uses the principle of photoconductivity to form an image over a surface The word is from video and iconoscope. The vidicon, which has an antimony trisulphide target, was widely used in the early days of TV and still is used in closed-circuit TV systems and for other purposes calling for low cost and simplicity. A one-inch vidicon has a target area that is one inch in diameter.

vidiot a video idiot, a zealous video amateur

view camera a professional camera for still photography in a studio, with a large ground glass for viewing and many lens and rotation features

viewdata the British version of VIDEOTEX, an interactive cable-TV system in which a TV set is linked to a computer keyboard so that electronic text can be received and the viewer can respond The first viewdata system was Prestel, developed by the British Post Office and introduced in 1979.

viewer 1 a person who watches, particularly television; also called a *televiewer*, sometimes called a *listener* Technically, the rating services have specific criteria, such as the number of minutes of viewing, before a person is established as a viewer of a specific program. *Viewer characteristics* are demographic descriptions of a viewer or typical viewer. Viewers are measured and characterized in many ways, such as viewers per set, per household, and per viewing household. 2 a light box for looking at still picture transparencies 3 a device for looking at motion-picture film

viewers per set (VPS) the average number of individuals in a household listening to or watching a program

viewfinder an optical device on a camera showing the operator or photographer the area of the scene covered by the camera from that angle and distance

viewpoint 1 a point of view, or opinion 2 a position of a camera with regard to the subject (also called *camera angle*)

viewport 1 [computer graphics] a part of the display space; more commonly called WINDOW 2 [telecommunications] a scheduled time slot on a satellite; also called *space segment* or window

vignette 1 a short story, scene, or incident 2 a decorative design at the beginning or end of a book or chapter or along the border of a page, an unbordered illustration or photograph that blends into the surrounding area (a *soft vignette*) 3 a camera lens mask that gives a *vignette effect* to a shot by blurring the edges 4 to describe in a brief way or to soften the edges of a picture, generally a portrait

violin piece [journalism] the lead story in a magazine or other publication, which sets the tone for the publication

virgin unused or unprocessed, as with virgin film or tape

virgin medium a tape or other medium that has never been used

virgule a slanted bar used in fractions or expressions, such as "and/or"; also called SHILLING BAR, SOLIDUS, or SLANT SLASH

VIRS VERTICAL INTERVAL reference SIGNALS, used in television

virtuoso a person with great skill in music or other arts, as demonstrated by a *virtuoso performance* The origin is the Latin *virtuosus*, "worth" or "virtue," which also is the origin of *virtuous*.

viscosity the thickness of ink, which determines its flow rate

visible distribution the measured extent to which a product is visible and readily accessible to customers of retail stores; also called *visual distribution* The *visual inventory* excludes warehouse or storeroom inventory.

VistaVision a trademarked system of making wide-screen films that can be shown by standard 35mm movie projectors, developed by PARAMOUNT PICTURES

visual of, connected with, or used in seeing or sight; visible In graphic arts, a preliminary sketch sometimes is called a visual.

visual aids films, slides, posters, charts, and other devices or material involving sight The term, as used in schools, libraries, and elsewhere, excludes books and other publications.

visual center a point on a page that appears to be the center, having the illusion that it is a bit above the actual geometric center

visualizer paper a transparent or translucent paper, generally ONIONSKIN or bond, used by artists for layouts and sketches; sometimes called *layout paper*

visual line focus [theater] a technique in which performers scattered about a stage face toward and direct their attention to the principal performer, thus encouraging the audience to focus on him or her It is different from *actual line focus*, in which the performers are arranged in a straight line with the principal performer at the front.

visual machine a photolettering machine on which the operator can see type (or its representation) being set, which is not possible on a *blind machine*

visual tag an identification that is human-readable at the beginning (*leader*) of a machine tape The identification or *visual tag line* is spelled out with perforations.

visual time code a numerical reference, or time code, on a videotape; also called *viz-code* A *visually coded cassette*, or viz-coded cassette, has a window, or area, on which the time appears, often visible only with a *time-code reader* used in editing.

vita a biography, generally brief Pronounced VEE-tuh, it is Latin for "life" and short for *curriculum vitae*, though the full term most often is used in academic circles. The plural is *vitae*, pronounced vee-tee.

Vitagraph a major film company in the silent-film era, sold in 1925 to Warner Bros. Its stars included Adolphe Menjou, Norma Talmadge, and Rudolph Valentino, and its facilities included a large studio on Avenue M in the Flatbush section of Brooklyn that was used in recent years for the production of "The Cosby Show" on TV.

Vitaphone a subsidiary of Warner Bros. that developed one of the first sound film systems, used in 1927 for the film *The Jazz Singer* The system actually was sound on disc synchronized with the film, which was replaced a few years later with sound on film.

VITS VERTICAL INTERVAL test SIGNALS, used in television

viz or viz. that is; namely No longer commonly used, it has been replaced by *i.e.* *Viz* is from the Latin *videlicet*, which is from *videre licet*, "it is permitted to see."

viz-code VISUAL TIME CODE

vizmo a rear-projection device used to insert a background into a TV broadcast

VLT VIDEO LAYOUT TERMINAL

VNU Business Information Services, Inc. a New York company, owner of CLARITAS, SCARBOROUGH, LNA/Media Records and other marketing information companies

VO VOICE-OVER

VOA VOICE OF AMERICA

vogueing a styled version of modeling, as on fashion-show runways, based on poses from *Vogue* magazine The models are referred to as *voguers*.

vogue word a word or phrase that is coined or emerges from obscurity and becomes popular in a short period The phrase was coined by Henry Watson Fowler (1858–1933), the English lexicographer who wrote *Modern English Usage*.

voice sound made through the mouth, or a sound like a vocal utterance; the characteristic quality of an individual or entity, or its opinion or tone, as in the *voice of the people*, or the *voice of a columnist*; a spokesperson or representative, such as the *voice of the government*; a characteristic of verbs indicating the relation of the subject to the action of the verb as agent (*active voice*) or recipient (*passive voice*); a musical sound made with the mouth, the quality of a person's singing (as in a *good voice*); the part of a musical composition that is sung (indicated on the music sheet as voice)

voice grade suitable for transmitting a signal of a human voice, in the range of 300 to 3,400 Hz

voice-grade service a class of telephone service for transmission of voice or data at relatively slow speeds

Voice of America (VOA) a radio service operated throughout the world (outside the United States) by the U.S. Information Agency, based in Washington, DC

voice-over (VO) the sound of an unseen narrator on a TV program or film; a reading by a TV announcer while a videotape is shown *Voice-over credits (V.O.C.)* are audio identifications of sponsors, cast, or other credits, such as at the beginning or end of a TV program. The TV *voice-over story*, in which a newscaster reports while a tape is shown, is very common.

voicer an on-the-spot report of an event by a radio or TV reporter, sometimes read by a reporter who is not necessarily at the news scene

voice-slate to call off information about a film shooting, particularly the number of each TAKE, into a recording microphone

volume 1 a book, or one of the books in a set 2 a series of issues of a periodical All the issues of a periodical for a specific period, generally but not necessarily a year, are bound together in a volume designated by a number. Following are representative styles of indicating the volume number. *The New Yorker* issue of January 10, 1983, was designated on the contents page as Vol. LVIII, No. 47. This magazine started its volume-number system on its first day of publication and changes it annually on its anniversary date. The style, which is the most common, is to use Roman numerals for the volume number and Arabic numbers for the issue number with a colon or comma between. *Fortune* of January 10, 1983, was designated on its contents page as Vol. 107, No. 1. *Fortune* has its own reference numbering system; the volume number does not indicate its founding year (1930). *The New York Times* of January 10, 1983, was designated atop page one as Vol. CXXXII. . . . No. 45,554. Founded in 1851, *The Times* changes its volume number annually but uses consecutive numbering for its issues. Each time it stops its presses for an editorial change or change within an edition, a dot is removed. Thus, the later editions have two, one, or no dots after the volume number as compared with the first or earliest four-dot edition. *The Chicago Tribune* has simplified the system considerably. Its issue of January 10, 1983, was stated atop page one, 136th Year-No. 10. *American Way*, the monthly magazine of *American Airlines*, omits the linking hyphen, colon, or comma and simply stated VOL. 16 NO. 1 on the contents page of its January 1983 issue. **3** the amplitude or loudness of sound A *volume indicator (V.I.)* is a meter for measuring sound volume. **4** size, extent, or amount, such as *sales volume*. A *volume discount* is given for quantity purchases, such as advertising volume. A *volume-merchandising allowance contract* is an agreement in which a manufacturer provides cash or free merchandise to a retailer who agrees to promote the large quantities of the product that were purchased.

voluntary chain a group of independent stores that are affiliated and operate under the same name; also called *voluntary association, voluntary group,* or simply *voluntary* An independent retailer belonging to such a chain is called a *voluntary store*. Several examples exist in the food, hardware, and automotive supply fields; a well-known one is IGA (Independent Grocers Alliance). In this way, small local stores can compete with regional and national chains by purchasing in larger quantities and at lower prices than they could independently and also by combining to advertise together.

voluntary pay a system of delivery of newspapers to home recipients who have the option of paying the delivery person

VOR voice-operated relay, a dictation device to stop the forward movement of a tape or other recording medium during silence It is initiated with the sound of a voice and stops during pauses.

vortex [typography] the bottom junction of two STEMS of a character, such as the two vortex points in *W*

VO/SOT a VOICE-OVER combined with *sound-on-tape:* a studio voice, such as a newscaster's, over a taped segment with a SOUNDBITE, a common format in TV news; pronounced VOH-SOT Two successive sequences are indicated in a TV script as VO/SOT/VO; three successive sequences are indicated as VO/SOT/VO/SOT/VO.

vox pop the abbreviation of *vox populi*, Latin for "the voice of the people"; public opinion In journalism, vox pop is slang for random or *man-on-the-street* interviews.

VPI VERY PROMOTABLE ITEM

VPS viewers-per-set: the number of viewing individuals within a demographic group divided by the number of television sets in use It is most often expressed as viewers per 100 viewing households.

vs. VERSUS; against

VSAT very small aperture terminal, a communications system used by large companies and other private subscribers for high-frequency satellite transmission A VSAT system enables telephone, facsimile, video, computer, and other data to be transmitted to many sites, such as branch offices and stores, via an outdoor VSAT that transmits and receives signals from an orbiting satellite.

VT videotape

VTR videotape recorder

VU volume unit, a measure of audio signal level, common in broadcasting A *VU meter* measures volume units, such as of a tape recorder.

vulgate popular or common speech A Latin version of the Bible, prepared in the 4th century and still used, is called the *Vulgate Bible*.

vulnerability relations the alleged or actual weaknesses in a company or other entity that affect its dealings with various publics

VU meter a meter on a control board showing the intensity (VOLUME) of sounds

v.v. VICE VERSA, or conversely

v.y. abbreviation for *various years*, as used in BIBLIOGRAPHIES

W

w watt; week; weight; weekly; wide; width; wife; with

w/ with

W the first letter in the call letters of almost all U.S. radio and TV stations east of the Mississippi On invoices and purchase orders, *W* means "will advise shortly."

WACK [broadcasting] *w*ait before transmitting *ack*nowledgment, an instruction indicating that a station is not ready to receive a transmission

w.a.f. with all faults, meaning an item may be defective and is sold "as is"

wagon a four-wheeled vehicle or platform used to move scenery

wagon stage [theater] a set on wheels that can be pushed onstage to facilitate a scene change

wagon-wheel effect in cinematography, an optical illusion in which the spoked wheels of a moving vehicle seem to be moving counterclockwise instead of clockwise

wagon wholesaler a *jobber* or other intermediary who delivers and sells from his own trucks Obviously, the origin is from the horse-and-wagon days. Perishable items such as baked goods often are supplied to retailers by such brokers.

waistline [typography] the top of a *nonascender lowercase* letter such as *a, c, e, g, i, m, n, o, p, q, s, u, v, w, x, y,* or *z,* so called because these letters rise only to about the middle of the line, or the waistline; also called *meanline*

waist shot a photograph, or shot, of a person from the waist up

waiting time the period in which a messenger has to stay on the premises until an item is available or other periods of delay of service personnel for which an extra charge is levied

wait order an instruction to a medium to hold an advertisement until told to run it

walkaway an easily won victory; a successful production (though not as successful as a *runaway success*)

Walker Research a market research company in Indianapolis formed in 1939 by Mrs. Tommie Walker Anderson

walkie-talkie a small portable radio transmitter and receiver

walk-in business sales to customers who walk into a store or walk up to a BOX OFFICE or ticket office without advance reservations

Walkman a trademarked portable stereo cassette player with earphones, often combined with a radio, manufactured by the Sony Corporation, headquartered in Japan The product has become a part of our culture, particularly visible attached to the ears of young adults in the street. Since its introduction in 1979, over 42 million units have been sold throughout the world, including about 10 million in 1988.

walk-off the fading out or deterioration of an image while on the printing press during printing

walk-on a minor part in a performance, generally with no dialogue

walk-on pass a ticket or identification that permits the bearer to enter a film studio, stadium, or other place, generally through a gate; also called *gate pass*

walk-through [theater] an early rehearsal

walkup *Wall Street Journal* jargon for an article that is published before an anticipated event; also called *curtainraiser*

walla-walla a murmuring noise in a crowd scene, as by extras in a film scene, produced by repetition of the word; see also RHUBARB

wall banner a hanging advertisement or poster in a retail store

Wallenda a senior editor or other high-ranking person, an in-house term used at *Newsweek*, referring to the Wallenda family of circus aerialists

wallet flap a style of envelope with a wide, straight flap generally extending below the center of the envelope

wall media posters and other material affixed to walls of interior spaces, such as in the reception rooms of doctors' offices and in student and employee lounges

wallpaper video [television] slang for generic visuals, graphics, or other stills or tape that can be used as introductions or backgrounds, or that can be inserted in a WINDOW on the screen They are commonly used in newscasts.

wall power standard current from a wall socket, which in the United States is 60-cycle, 110-volt alternating current

wall-to-wall filled; having no room for space, time, or material to be added to an advertisement or program

the Walnut the nickname at *The New York Times* for its Western edition, printed in Walnut Creek, CA, near San Francisco

J. Walter the nickname of the J. Walter Thompson Company in New York, one of the world's largest advertising agencies

wand [computers] a handheld optical rod used in supermarkets and elsewhere to read information encoded on packages and other items

wandering aisle a store layout with movable fixtures, as in apparel departments

W & F work and flop, a printing method also called WORK-AND-TUMBLE

W&T WORK-AND-TURN

wannabe a person who wants to be something else, such as a movie star or an athlete; pronounced WAN-na-bee

want ad a classified advertisement of a need or desire (a want), as in a newspaper or periodical Some publications have lower rates for personal, as compared to commercial, want ads.

want list items needed or desired for purchase

wardrobe a closet, room, or area (*wardrobe department*) where clothes are kept; a collection of clothes or costumes A *wardrobe mistress* (or *wardrobe girl, woman, man, master,* or *supervisor*) is responsible for the care of costumes in a theatrical production but is not the costume designer. In film, this function is handled by the *key wardrobe,* who sometimes is also the costume designer, reports to the art director or production manager, and supervises a *dresser* or *fitter* and an assistant called a *costumer*. A *wardrobe plot* or *costume schedule* is a detailed list of costumes for each scene and performer. Costumes sometimes are transported in a *wardrobe box* on wheels or in a *wardrobe trunk,* which also contains garment-repair equipment. A *wardrobe call* is a directive to a performer for a costume fitting.

warehousing storing, as with products for distribution to retailers; in film, the storage or shelving of motion pictures so that they cannot be shown In 1977, the warehousing practice of commercial TV networks, in which they bought films so that they could not be shown on pay television, was ruled illegal.

warm and wonder [journalism] an upbeat feature story

warm color a color with a yellowish or reddish cast, akin to that of the sun

warm start the start of a computer station at the beginning of the work period It is not the same as a *hot start,* which occurs after a *crash* or unplanned interruption.

warm-up a brief period before an actual broadcast in which the studio audience is put in a responsive mood, sometimes by a *warm-up announcer*

Warner Communications, Inc. one of the world's largest companies in film, TV, records, and other media; based in New York The renowned Warner Bros. studio is in Burbank, CA. In 1989, Warner acquired Lorimar Telepictures Corporation and also merged with Time Inc. to form Time Warner Inc.

warning light a red light on a TV camera indicating that it is *live* and in use

warpaint cosmetics; makeup; GREASEPAINT

wash 1 [photography] the film-processing stage in which the developing and fixing chemicals are removed, generally with water, in a process called *washing* 2 a type of painting made with a thin, watery layer of paint, such as a watercolor wash drawing

washboard a film defect, as in rotary-camera microfilming when a varying illumination or faulty film advance creates bands (akin to a washboard) perpendicular to the film edge

wash drawing art using watercolor or ink, generally with tints or shaded tones rather than lines, which are diluted with the wet medium; also called a WASH Thus, WASHED OUT describes weak, dissipated, or diluted color.

washed out describing a photo print or other item that is too light

Washington Journalism Review (WJR) a monthly magazine published in Washington, DC, owned by the University of Maryland College of Journalism

Washington Post Co. one of the country's largest media companies, headquartered in Washington, DC It publishes *The Washington Post* and *Newsweek* and owns TV stations and cable-TV systems.

washout a type of optical transition between scenes in which the images change to white; the opposite of a *fade-out* to black

washup the cleaning of a printing press after a job

was-is pricing a retailing system of stating two prices, "was" and "now is," to indicate a legitimate sale or a phony markdown from a fictitious inflated price

wastebin a storage container for scrap film discarded by editors or other technicians

waste circulation readers or others in an audience who are not prospective customers because of demographics, unavailability of the product in the area, or other circumstances; also called *circulation waste*

watch a SHIFT, particularly at night, such as the *late watch*, the period at a newspaper when a skeleton staff remains to handle the late or last edition At an afternoon-newspaper or a broadcast-news operation, the *early watch* precedes the regular shift.

watercolor water-soluble paint, especially a type intended for use on paper, or a painting made with such paint

water haul wasted or unproductive writing or other effort

waterleaf paper that is *unsized*, with no material added to affect its ink or water absorbency

watermark a faint marking pressed into paper during manufacture that consists of letters, words, or designs used as a papermaker's trademark or a prestigious symbol of the purchaser

water spot a defect on a negative due to water on it during the drying process

WATS *w*ide *a*rea *t*elephone *s*ervice, a system permitting unlimited use nationally or in a specific area for a flat fee rather than charging per call

wave a swinging or undulatory movement, generally with the hand or arm Crowds in a stadium often move in unison in a rhythmic motion called *giving the wave.*

wave-form monitor (WFM) an oscilloscope used to test and adjust audio or video signals In television, it is a small oscilloscope tube with a wavy line display that traces the variations of the video signal.

waveguide in satellite broadcasting, a metallic conductor that carries microwave signals into and out of antennas

wave-in an individual admitted free to a nightclub or other place with a wave or signal to the person at the entrance by the owner or person in charge

wave plan cyclical or intermittent advertising or other activity

wave postings in outdoor advertising, moving a concentration of posters or other showings through different areas of a market

wavy edges paper with expanded or warped edges

wax a resinous substance The first records were wax cylinders, invented in 1888 by Thomas Alva Edison; to *wax a record*—to make a recording—is an expression still used. In letterpress printing, a wax engraving, such as an impression of a line drawing, map, or chart, is made by cutting lines into a wax surface that is backed by a thin copper sheet. In offset printing, a *waxing machine* is used to apply wax instead of rubber cement to the back of material to be pasted up for photography. In film, wax sometimes is applied, in a process called *waxing,* to the edge of prints to facilitate passage through the projector.

WCRS Group one of the world's largest advertising and public relations companies, headquartered in London It owns Della Femina, McNamee WCRS and Creamer Dickson Basford, both in New York.

wds wire-service jargon for "words"

wearout the point at which an advertisement loses its sales effectiveness, generally due to excessive exposure

weasel word a word that sounds important but is empty, hollow, or ambiguous—an allusion to the weasel, which allegedly sucks the inside from an egg, leaving an empty shell

The Weather Channel an all-weather cable network based in Atlanta, GA

weave a ripple or horizontal side-to-side movement, such as a *picture weave* in which the film frames move horizontally while being projected

web **1** a complex network, as spun by a spider **2** VARIETY's word for a broadcasting network **3** a large, continuous roll of paper, such as newsprint, that can be cut or fed (*web-fed*) into a rotary printing press (a WEB PRESS) *Web printing* or *roll-fed printing* uses rolls of paper instead of flat or cut sheets. The *web process,* or *web flow,* is continuous and therefore high-speed. A tension-control device maintains the proper *web tension* of the roll of the paper as it is fed to the press (*incoming web*) and while it is on the press (*ongoing web*).

web break a tear in the paper roll that requires stopping the presses Printers constantly try to avert breaks or patch them with the speed of a racing-pit crew.

web lead the amount of paper in a rotary or web press when it's completely threaded and ready to run Lead is pronounced leed.

web press a rotary printing press with curved plates (hence, *rotary*) that print on rolls (WEBS) of paper, particularly for newspapers and other large-run, high-speed jobs; also called *web-fed press*

wedge a tapered V-shaped piece of metal, wood, or other substance inserted in a narrow crevice for leverage, splitting, or tightening; a concept or event that divides or splits a group Because a wedge is solid and its point gets "to the heart," the term *advertising wedge* sometimes is used to describe the unique or primary characteristic of a product or service on which an advertising campaign is based—its UNIQUE SELLING PROPOSITION.

weeding removing and discarding unsuitable or unwanted items In the affixing of self-adhesive letters, as in signmaking, weeding is the removal of the vinyl or other backing.

weekly (wkly.) a weekly publication, generally a newspaper but also a magazine or other publication Newspapers published two or three times a week usually are grouped with once-a-week newspapers and are called weeklies.

weenie slang for a gimmick, such as a trick device in a plot or an object that motivates action, perhaps a stolen treasure dangled in front of someone to tantalize, like a wiener or frankfurter Alfred Hitchcock called it a *MacGuffin*, which is more enigmatic.

weight 1 a measure of heaviness; an object used as a measurement standard; to hold something down, or counterbalance; a burden or influence 2 [advertising] the amount of advertising or other effort in support of a campaign, expressed as size of audience (impressions or rating points) and budget (spending levels) 3 [market research] a set of numbers assigned as multipliers to quantities to be averaged to indicate the relative importance of each quantity's contribution to the average 4 [typography] the relative darkness of a typeface (lightface or boldface) 5 the heaviness or thickness of paper based on the weight of a REAM of a specific size

weighted average a statistical procedure in which numbers are assigned specific values or weights, frequently used as the basis for *index numbers* Similarly, a *weighted sample* is given a specific bias prior to study, as opposed to a *random sampling.*

welded joined together by heat, a term generally referring to metals In bookbinding, *welded binding* is a technique developed by Sendor Bindery, Inc. in New York that uses heat, infrared light, high-frequency sound, or another high-energy source to bind *welded paper* specially coated with a resin without glue or thread.

well-made skillfully constructed or contrived, as with a *well-made plot* Well-made play is a term for a type of play that originated in France in the 19th century (called in French *pièce bien faite*), with a formula in which a secret known only to one or a few characters was revealed at the climax of the basic plot rather than abstract ideas or an offbeat plot.

went up [theater] forgot, particularly lines of dialogue, as by a performer who *went up*

west the left side, as of a drawing

Westar a communication satellite system owned by the Western Union Telegraph Company, Saddle River, NJ

WESTAT Inc. a market research company in Rockville, MD, formed in 1961, that acquired the Crossley Surveys, a pioneer in telephone interviews, in 1983 Most of its work is for U.S. government agencies.

West End a fashionable residential section in the western part of London, England, in which several theaters are located West End thus means London theater, akin to New York's Broadway.

Western a film, novel, or other work about life in the American West An *adult Western* is less simplistic, perhaps artier or with a philosophical theme.

Western Publications Association a Los Angeles organization of periodical publishers that presents annual *Maggie* awards to outstanding magazines

Western Union International (WU) a New York communication company that provides a variety of services, including telegrams, Mailgrams, and international cablegrams In the 19th and early 20th century, out-of-town news reports were transmitted almost entirely via the Western Union Telegraph Company, now based in Saddle River, NJ, and many telegrapher's abbreviations and terms still are used by today's journalists.

Western Writers of America an organization based in Sheridan, WY, of authors of Western novels and stories It presents annual Saddleman and Spur Awards.

Westgate Research, Inc. a market research company in St. Louis that operates On-Air Lab for testing TV commercials

wet printing a printing process in which successive colors are printed before the preceding colors are dry

wet sound a sound or recording with excessive reverberation; the opposite of *dry sound*

wet-strength paper a printing paper that retains more than 15 percent of its dry strength when completely wetted with water

wet stripping a process in *photolithography* in which the base, or stripping, layer of a film is removed, or stripped, after the film has been processed but while it still is wet

wf or w.f. wrong FONT, a character from one size or style of type mixed in with characters from another

WFM WAVE-FORM MONITOR

wh. white

wham a blow or impact Whammo is an exclamation to express startling action; it is sometimes used as show-business slang to refer to a smash hit show.

wheelie   slang for a wheeled device such as a T- or Y-shaped support for a camera TRIPOD; also called *wheeled spreader, wheeled tee,* or *wheeled tie-down*

wheeze   an overworked or trite remark or joke that elicits a wheeze, gasp, or whistling sound

when room   a newspaper term for "to be used anytime" or "can go over" (C.G.O.)

whetstone   an abrasive stone, such as carborundum, commonly used to sharpen knives, drawing and drafting instruments, and various metal tools   Commercial artists generally use a two-sided whetstone with a coarse surface on one side and a fine surface on the other. The origin of the word is the Middle English *whetston. Whetten* means "to make keen."

whip pan   a camera shot in which the camera is moved, or *panned,* very rapidly sideways from one scene to the next to create a blurred image for a transitional effect; also called *zip pan, swish, whip shot,* or *whiz*

whirly   slang for a movie-camera crane that whirls around

white area   [radio] the area or population that does not receive interference-free primary service from an AM station or a specified minimum signal strength from an FM station

white audit   an official, verified report about a publication, printed on white paper, issued by the AUDIT BUREAU OF CIRCULATIONS   A PUBLISHER'S AUDIT, or publisher's statement, is on colored paper.

whiteboard   an electronic device on which text can be written and one or more copies printed using optical sensors   The material can be transmitted over telephone lines and viewed on a TV set, so that a whiteboard can be part of a teleconference.

white bread   in advertising and other fields, a campaign that is bland

white camera tape   white tape put around film cans to prevent light leaks, keep cans together, and allow marking

white clipping   [television] a video control circuit that regulates, or clips, the top level, or *white level,* of the picture signal so that it does not appear on the transmitted picture

white-coat rule   a Federal Trade Commission rule that prohibits, in TV commercials and other advertisements, the use of performers in white laboratory coats or in other ways resembling physicians or other professionals unless properly identified to avoid deception

white envelope   [direct marketing] an envelope of any color with a DIE-CUT, open or covered

with a transparent material, through which is visible the name and address of the recipient as printed on a letter, reply card, or other enclosure

white goods   a type of product, specifically, among alcoholic beverages, gin and vodka; among household appliances, refrigerators and washing machines; and among home furnishings, bed and bath items or household linens, including those not colored white

white label   [recording] a prerelease copy of a record sent to media prior to the affixing of a printed label

white-level set   a control for the luminance level of a color TV camera, also called *white set*

white-light district   a theatrical area, such as Times Square in mid-Manhattan

white line   [typography] a space between lines of type equal in size to one line

white mail   correspondence from consumers in their own envelopes instead of business reply envelopes or envelopes provided by a marketer

white-out   a popular name for the correction fluid used to cover typed material with a whiteness akin to the paper   A common brand is Liquid Paper, made by the Liquid Paper Corporation, Boston.

white pages   a telephone directory with alphabetical listings of subscribers to the local telephone company, as opposed to the *yellow pages,* which have display advertisements and commercial listings

white paper   a document prepared as an argument on behalf of an organization on a given issue   It may be more argumentative than a *position paper.*

whiteprint   a duplicating process using light-sensitive dyes (*diazo process*) to produce black lines on a white background   A dry copy made by this process is called a *diazo print* or whiteprint. The original is on translucent or transparent material, such as VELLUM or parchment paper.

white radio   radio that is government-subsidized or reflects a government source, such as Voice of America

whites   highlights of a photoprint

white sale   a sale of household linens, or WHITE GOODS

white space   an unprinted area in a publication or advertisement

white-space skip   in facsimile transmission, an editing feature that excludes margins, space between lines, or other nontext areas, thus reducing transmission time

white way   a theatrical area, such as the Broadway area in mid-Manhattan

whodunit a detective or mystery book, movie, or other work in which the reader or audience attempts to guess who committed the crime or other action

wholesaler a person or organization that sells goods at a discount to a RETAILER or sometimes directly to the consumer, as at a wholesale outlet store; also called *distributor* or *jobber*

WICI WOMEN IN COMMUNICATIONS INC.

wicket a short two-line headline to the left of a single large headline This type of layout is used on the covers of weekly TABLOIDS and flashy magazines.

Wickey a Wall Street nickname for Warner Communications, Inc., NY

wide-angle lens a camera lens that covers a larger area of a scene with deeper perspective than a standard lens

wideband [broadcasting] the transmission of audio signals with a wide frequency deviation, resulting in a low signal-to-noise ratio It is common in FM broadcasting.

widow [typography] less than half of a typeset line, as at the end of a paragraph Some editors believe that this WHITE SPACE is undesirable, while other editors appreciate it. *Kill the widow* is a proofreader's term meaning to eliminate the line or fill it.

width the measurement from side to side In stating dimensions, width generally precedes height. The standard letterhead sheet, 8½″ × 11″, is 8½ inches wide and 11 inches high. However, measurements sometimes are given as height by width, as in billboards.

width card in computerized typesetting, a card, box, or panel consisting of a circuit board with read-only memory of individual widths of characters of a typeface that can be inserted into a typesetter or typesetting keyboard to determine the spacing (*escapement values*); also called *width plug*

width tape magnetic or perforated tape with encoded information about the unit widths of type characters, used in phototypesetting

wienie a gimmick or trick device; see also WEENIE Disney refers to highly visibile, attractive structures in its theme parks as *wienies*.

wigwag a moving SEMAPHORE signal, perhaps with flashing red lights, placed on a barrier to indicate a warning, such as that film production is taking place nearby A flashing red light outside a studio, particularly a film sound stage, indicates that no one is to enter.

wilco an affirmation, "I will comply with your request," commonly used in radiotelephony by pilots and others

wild **1** uncontrolled, as in to *shoot wild*, in which a camera operator or photographer photographs without a script, as at a news event **2** [film] A *wild camera* shoots silently, as it is not connected with a sound recorder; *wild lines* are unsynchronized lines of dialogue added POSTPRODUCTION; a *wild picture* or *wild shot* is a picture without sound. **3** [journalism] A *wild story* is one that can appear on any inside page. A *wild picture* is a photo not accompanied by an article.

wild motor a film-camera motor with adjustable speeds, not set to be in exact synchronization with the sound recording; also called *variable sound motor*

wild posting the affixing of political, entertainment, and other posters (*bills* or small *billboards*) on walls, boarded-up buildings, lampposts, and other sites The space for this extensive *wild advertising* is free. The posting is done by volunteers or professionals. The largest company in movie posters is National Promotion and Advertising in Los Angeles.

wild shot a motion-picture or television shot without an accompanying recording of sound

wild sound background noise, ambient or natural sound, in contrast to *sound effects* or the recording of such sound without an accompanying picture; also called *wild recording*

wild spot a commercial, generally a SPOT announcement for a national or regional advertiser, that can be used in station breaks, within programs, or at other unscheduled times (hence, wild)

wild track a soundtrack recorded separately and not synchronized with the visual images, or perhaps made without reference to a specific scene; a basic instrumental or *sound-effects* track to which voice and other soundtracks can be added, also called a *wild recording*

wild wall a wall that can be removed from a film or TV set, usually for the placement of one or more cameras; different from a *practical set* with real walls

Winchell paragraph a paragraph starting with an *ellipsis* (three dots), a style popularized by newspaper columnist *Walter Winchell* (1897–1972), whose breezy column included incomplete sentences and many gossip items

wind gag [film] a cover around a microphone to muffle the sound of the wind in an outdoor location; see also WINDSCREEN

wind machine a large fan used in film, stage, and TV production to create the effect of wind It is sometimes used with a *wind howler*, a sound-effects device emulating wind sounds.

window 1 an opening in a building or a period of time, such as a *window of opportunity*; a rectangular insert or other predefined area, as on a computer or video screen 2 [film] the time between release of a title in one medium, such as theater or TV, and its release in another; also called *clearance time* 3 [printing] a clear area or opening; a *die-cut* opening, sometimes covered with clear paper, that reveals the paper below, as in a *window envelope* that shows the name and address of the recipient as typed or printed on a letter or other enclosure 4 [telecommunications] a scheduled time slot on a satellite; also called *space segment* or VIEWPORT 5 [television] brief local programming within a network or syndicated program, such as a 60-second news update, called a *news envelope*

window flat a flat piece of scenery (a FLAT) that resembles a window

windowing [television] the tape slippage that sometimes results from a loosely wound spool; also called *clinching*

windowpane a transparent negative, or a blank, rare among professional photographers

window streamer a banner or strip, generally long and narrow, pasted or taped to a store window A *window poster* is larger and generally vertical instead of horizontal.

winds [film] the last stage; pronounced with a long *i*, as in to *wind up*

windscreen a piece of metal mesh placed over a microphone to muffle the sound of wind in an outdoor location; also called *windshield* A common type is the *zeppelin windscreen*, with a cylindrical or zeppelin shape.

wing a part or section, as of a building or organization; the side of a stage (the *wings*) not visible to the audience; to improvise—to *wing it*

wing mailer a semi-automatic device for applying mailing labels

Winona Research a Minneapolis market research company specializing in shopping-mall and telephone interviews Formed in 1953, it owns the *Research Information Center* in Phoenix.

WIP work in progress, a term used by the *Wall Street Journal* and other media for articles and projects in various stages of completion

wipe 1 [film, television] to clean or *wipe off* the screen in preparation for the next frame, which is done on a computer console The optical effect of the transition can be achieved with a *wiper*, a moving line in the form of an expanding or contracting circle (a *rotating wipe*) that forms a boundary between the two shots. Wipes are created with *wipe blades* in an optical printer or by a TRAVELING MATTE. Types of wipes include a *circle* or *iris wipe*, in which a new image appears as an increasingly larger circle while the old image shrinks; *clock wipe*, in which images shift in a clockwise or counterclockwise motion; *diagonal* or *closing-door wipe*, in which an image moves in from both sides of the screen; *flip wipe*, in which images turn over; *horizontal wipe*, in which images move from top to bottom or vice versa; *hard-edge wipe* (sharply in focus); and *soft-edge wipe* (fuzzy or out of focus). A *burst wipe* or *explosion wipe* is of an irregular geometric shape and is a common technique in silent films. 2 [recording] to remove recorded signals from magnetic tape; to erase a tape

wire a long, thin, circular thread of metal, as used in wire binding or wire stitching; a *news wire*, such as The Associated Press; a telegraph or telegram *Wireless* is without wires, as in radio or wireless telegraphy. A *wiretap* eavesdrops on a telephone wire. To *pull wires* is to use influence. The wire on a papermaking machine is a screen that conveys the water and fiber suspension. The wire side of the sheet is next to the wire.

wire act acrobats or other performers who balance on a wire; also called *high-wire act*

wire code strip a device used at newspapers that receive a tremendous amount of material from news WIRE SERVICES (particularly stock prices and sports scores) that enables the removal of justifying spaces and line-ending codes so the text can be edited

wired city a city or area with a high percentage of cable-TV homes

wired for sound describing a performer who is permitted to speak on camera because of membership in the Screen Actors Guild or other union

wired home a household linked to a cable-TV system

wire editor the person at a newspaper or other medium in charge of all incoming material from *The Associated Press* and other *news wires*

wire frame VECTOR ANIMATION, the use of lines instead of dots to create images

wire house a stock-brokerage firm linked to its branch offices and correspondent firms by private communications wires It is different from a *news wire*, though they share a few terms, such as *flash*, which is a bulletin.

wireless telegraphy by radio and without wires; a message sent with electromagnetic waves A *wireless microphone* uses a small radio transmitter to replace the connecting cable and thus provides greater mobility.

wireless cable a new type of television service in which a TV signal for free and pay-TV programming services is received from a satellite and retransmitted to a viewer's rooftop antenna on a superhigh-frequency microwave channel Thus, a viewer can receive cable-TV channels without subscribing to a cable-TV service.

wire-lines closely spaced parallel lines on LAID PAPER; also called *wire marks* In machine-made paper, wire-lines are produced by the weave of the DANDY ROLL; in handmade paper, the lines are produced by the wires of the mold. The thicker crosslines are called *chain lines.*

Wirephoto a system trademarked in 1934 for electronically transmitting photographs over telephone wires; also, the photo itself The system was used exclusively by The Associated Press but now has been supplanted in many cases by LASER. The equivalent system used by United Press International and other wire services is called Telephoto. Wirephoto and Telephoto machines are not compatible.

wire printer a matrix printer in which each character is represented by a pattern of dots; also called *dot printer*

wire service a news service, such as The Associated Press or United Press International, that transmits primarily by wire The Wire Service Guild in New York is an AFL-CIO union affiliated with the Newspaper Guild.

wire side in papermaking, the side of a sheet of paper that has rested on the wire or screen of the mold or papermaking machine and bears the indentations The other side is the *felt side.*

wire stripping removing *end-of-line* codes from wire-service tape so that a newspaper or other subscriber can change the width of the line or other typographic parameters

wireway an enclosure that holds cables and other wires; also called *raceway*

with story a *side story* accompanying a bigger story and providing a summary, sidelights, or a related story

witness points [film] in computer animation, the insertion of live-action reference points into the computer so that the computer can duplicate the live-action camera moves

wizzywig the pronunciation of W.Y.S.I.W.Y.G., "what you see is what you get"

WJR WASHINGTON JOURNALISM REVIEW

wk. week Weekly is *wkl.*

w/o without

wobbler a lightweight point-of-purchase display that is hung from the ceiling or other place and turned by air currents

W.O.M. WORD-OF-MOUTH

woman [market research] a female 18 years old or older

Women in Communications Inc. (WICI) a professional society headquartered in Arlington,

VA, with about 9,000 members, that provides annual Clarion Awards to outstanding women in communications It was called Theta Sigma Phi until 1972.

women's page a page or section of a newspaper devoted to fashion, food, and other subjects likely to interest women In recent years, the term has been replaced, primarily by *lifestyle* but also by *living, style, family, view,* and other words that are nonsexist and more contemporary. The women's page was produced by a *women's department* headed by a *women's editor.* In some newspapers, the *society department,* headed by a *society editor,* was (and still is) separate from the women's department.

woodcut an engraving or carving on the face of a wooden block or a print made from such a block; sometimes called *wood engraving*

wooden board an old type of book cover made of wood covered with leather

Wooden Indian annual awards for merchandising presented by the Point-of-Purchase Advertising Institute, Englewood Cliffs, NJ

woodshedding 1 practicing on a musical instrument The word originates from the use of a woodshed as an isolated place in which to practice. The verb sometimes is used by performers to indicate going off alone to practice music, dialogue, or other actions. 2 [broadcasting] marking a script to indicate pauses and voice inflections, as with a SLASH mark for a pause, a double slash for a long pause, an UNDERLINE for emphasis, and a double underline for heavier emphasis

woof 1 a technician's synonym for acceptance 2 an engineering direction to stop

woofer an assembly of two or more loudspeakers or one large speaker for reproducing low-frequency sounds The origin is the woof or bark of a dog. A woofer is different from a *tweeter,* which is a smaller speaker for reproducing high-frequency sounds.

woo-woo tone a tone on a telephone line that indicates the number is not available or there is no such number The sound is akin to the whirling sound, woo-woo, and is not related to lovemaking.

word 1 a sound or combination of sounds, or its written or printed representation, that communicates a meaning; a brief remark or pithy saying 2 [computers] a set of BITS comprising the smallest unit of addressable computer memory and occupying a single storage location Types of words include *alphabetic word, doubleword, halfword, index word, instruction word, machine word, numeric word, parameter word,* and *reserved word.*

word book a dictionary, thesaurus, or other reference book with definitions or information about individual words, generally listed alphabetically

word count the number of words in a manuscript or other work Each separate word, numeral, or other item is counted as a word, and the total appears at the end of wire-service transmissions. Many computers automatically tally and insert the word count. Sometimes the word count appears on each page, or take, followed by a hyphen and the total word count.

word-of-mouth (W.O.M.) personal communication

word pair two words that are linked with a conjunction, such as "blond and beautiful"

word processing (WP) the use of automated equipment to process (input, revise, and output) textual information, as distinguished from *data processing*, in which the systems have broader capabilities in manipulating information that is mostly expressed numerically The original word processing systems facilitated secretarial tasks, notably automatic typing of fill-in letters, maintaining mailing lists, and editing and typing reports. This still is a major use in advertising and public relations offices, specifically the storage, manipulation, and retrieval of large quantities of text material. The basic components of a WP system include an input keyboard akin to a typewriter, a storage medium, and a computer. The typing features include the ability to easily add, delete, or correct a letter, word, line, or paragraph. Today, WP systems are standard equipment in the offices of thousands of newspapers and other media. The major development is the evolution from stand-alone single-user systems to clustered multi-user systems that share text and data from the storage medium, often using only the display units and omitting paper. Thus, word processing and data processing (DP) now are combined in office information systems with an ever-increasing variety of add-ons, including telecommunications, typesetting, and linkage with databanks, newswires, and other services.

words [theater] lines of dialogue, as in, "Do you know your words?"

wordsmith a facile writer

word space or **wordspace** the space between two words; to justify a line of type by increasing or decreasing the space between words

word wrap a WORD PROCESSING feature that produces automatic carryover of characters to the next line; also called *wraparound*

wordy using more words than necessary

work 1 toil; employment; occupation; task An item that is the product of creative effort often is called a work, such as a *work of art* or the *collected works* of an author. 2 to move, participate, or perform, as in to *work a room* (move about it, as in a political campaign), *work a show* (participate in its production), or *work downstage* (move slowly or unobtrusively closer to the audience, the opposite of *work upstage*)

work-and-tumble a printing method in which the second side of a sheet is printed by turning it over, left to right, retaining the same GRIPPER EDGE; also called *print-and-tumble* or *work-and-flop (W & F)*

work-and-turn a printing method in which the FORMS for both sides of the sheet are set side by side, to print first on one side of the sheet, which is then turned over left to right, using the same edge of paper as gripper, for printing on the other side, thus reducing total press time; also called *print-and-turn*, *work-and-twist*, or work-and-tumble (W & T) It is obvious and easy to appreciate only when you actually see it, so here's another description. The front and back sides of a printed sheet are printed side by side on the first pass through the press. Turning the sheet over and feeding it through the press again completes the printing for both sides; the front backs up the back and the back backs up the front. (If both fronts were printed "two up" and then backed up with two backs, an extra printing plate would be necessary.)

workbook a learning guide, generally containing tests and exercises based on a textbook or course; a record of work done or planned

worked material that has been processed, such as *worked mail*, which is sorted mail ready to be dispatched or distributed *Working material* is printing, mail, or other items that are being processed, as in a *workroom*.

work-for-hire a legal category describing freelance writing or other activity for which a payment is made but the worker does not own the copyright The original term was "work made for hire."

working alive, in use, as with a *working light*

working papers notes and drafts used in the preparation of a more finished work *Working drawings* are made for the guidance of architects and others working on a project.

working story an article that is *in the works*, or being developed

work light [theater] a lamp on a stand or suspended from the ceiling, used in rehearsal to provide illumination

work marks reference lines used in layout positioning

work order a specification sheet, particularly in printing and other production

work print [film] the first positive print, made in the early stage of editing from the master negative and used to assemble a *rough cut*

works collected writings, such as the works of Shakespeare Anything that is produced, particularly a book, play, or other creative effort, is referred to as a work. A *work in progress* is a painting or other creative effort in the process of creation. The Library of Congress Copyright Office defines several types of works. *Joint works* involve the efforts of more than one author. *Collective works* are anthologies. *Works made for hire* are produced by freelancers or others who are paid, even when they are not the copyright owner. *Anonymous works* and *pseudonymous works* are produced by authors whose names are not revealed.

work sheet a sheet of paper on which records, notes, practice tests, and other material are written; a computer business program, also spelled *worksheet* and more commonly called SPREADSHEET

workstation a person's work area, particularly one that includes a computer terminal or microcomputer

work-up a letterpress printing defect due to SLUGS or other spacing material working up to the height of type and thus making an impression

World Institute of Black Communications a New York organization designed to broaden opportunities for blacks in communication fields and promote the black consumer market to advertisers It presents annual *CEBA* awards for communications excellence to black audiences.

worm's-eye view the viewpoint of the participant, especially a worker or person on a low level; a scene painted, photographed, or produced as if observed from a point below it

wove paper a paper with a finish that resembles textile mesh; different from LAID PAPER

wow a distortion in the pitch fidelity of reproduced sound, usually a slowing as a result of irregular movement of a mechanical part of a record or tape player, particularly irregular speed of the record turntable

WP weather permitting (used in events schedules); WORD PROCESSING; word processor

wpm or **w.p.m.** words per minute

WPP Group PLC one of the world's largest communication companies, headquartered in London It includes the J. WALTER THOMPSON CO., OGILVY GROUP (acquired in 1989), HILL & KNOWLTON, and RESEARCH INTERNATIONAL. The company name derives from Wire and Plastic Products, a British manufacturer of wire shopping baskets.

wrap 1 a cover; a summary; completion; a show-business term to indicate completion of a scene; also called *insert, package, takeout,* WRAPAROUND, or *wrapper* The *wrap-up signal* to end a program quickly is one hand rotating in a circular motion. 2 [broadcasting] a news report that combines the voice of the announcer, the voice of the newsmaker, and background sound 3 [journalism] the completion of an article or a transmission of text to the typesetting or printing department; two or more related stories or segments tied together under one format A *wrap-up* is the completion of all copy for an edition or a final summary, as at the end of a news program. To *wrap in* is to combine a previous article with a revision. To *wrap copy* is to continue text from one column to the next. At the wire services, when the computer writes over, or revises, a story, about 48 hours after it was recorded, the new item is a wrap.

wraparound 1 a promotional band around a magazine or product 2 [broadcasting] the introductory and concluding segments of a program or series; the live portion before and after a taped segment In a wraparound on TV news, a reporter at the scene introduces a previously taped report and then provides additional information or an update. 3 [computers] the automatic carrying over of characters to the next line; also called *word wrap*

wraparound commercial a radio or television commercial with noncommercial material wrapped around it, such as a question about a past sports event at the beginning and the answer at the end; sometimes called an *insert,* as when it is inserted within a movie surrounded by questions about the movie

wrap party a party to celebrate the completion, or WRAP, of a motion picture or production

wrapper paper or other matter that partially or completely covers or encircles a product, such as a book wrapper, magazine wrapper, or other printed or unprinted sheet that serves as a protection for the publication; also called *wrappers* A *dust wrapper* is the paper jacket or cover folded over a bound book.

write to inscribe on a surface; to communicate, as by an author; to transcribe data into a computer or other medium

write down to write disparagingly or in a pointedly simple style

Writers Guild of America a union of staff and freelance broadcast and movie writers, consisting of about 4,000 members in two units, Writers Guild of America East (WGAE or WGAE) and Writers Guild of America West (WGAW or WGAW)

writethru   a label, or slug, at the beginning of the transmission by a newswire service of a breaking, or developing, story Each take, or segment, about a subsequent development in the story is labeled writethru, such as 2nd Ld Writethrus, which is a second lead (Ld) or beginning of a continuing news story.

write-up   **1** a written report, generally favorable, such as an article in a publication; also spelled writeup   **2** [broadcasting] the live *lead-in* or *intro*, the sentence preceding a tape; also called the *throw line* or WRAPAROUND

writing ink   a thin fluid containing a dye, generally black or blue, specifically prepared for use on paper It differs from printing inks and art inks, such as *drawing ink*.

writing paper   a paper with a smooth surface to prevent the absorption of ink

wrong font (wf)   [typography] a character from one size or style of type incorrectly mixed in with characters from another

wrong set   [film] a term indicating that a set no longer is needed, either because of a change of plans or because shooting on that set has been completed

WRU   who are you, a symbol used in computers, telegraphy, and other fields to ask the identity of the sender of a transmission by using the *WRU character*, *WRU signal*, or *inquiry character*

WU   WESTERN UNION

WWD   a daily trade publication, the bible of the women's-wear industry, published by Fairchild Publications in New York; formerly called *Women's Wear Daily*

W.Y.S.I.W.Y.G.   what you see is what you get, a phrase used in printing, computers, and other fields to indicate that the way an item looks in proof or on a computer screen is the way it will look in final form or hard copy; pronounced wizzywig

X

x a symbol or abbreviation used alone or in a variety of words by newspaper editors and others who are oriented to telegraphese. For example, *xmit* means "to submit." The letter *x* can also mean "by," as in *5 x 7* or other dimensions; power of magnification, as in *10x* or *10X*, indicating a magnification of 10 times; or cross or erase, as in *x-out* (past tense, *x-ed*). It is a symbol for broken type, an unknown number or person, or anything unknown; an algebraic variable; and an indication of the length of a line (line measure), such as *x 25* for 25 *picas*.

X a script notation for DISSOLVE; an indication of a location (X marks the spot); abbreviation of extra; a notation for italic; the mark or signature of an illiterate person; a representation of Christ or Christian; a proofreader's symbol or printer's instruction to remove the indicated item; the first letter of radio-station call letters in Mexico. In film, *X* is an abbreviation for a single exposure of film or a single frame. In identifying a film scene or take, each scene is numbered. When an *insert shot*, such as a close-up of a person or object to be added somewhere within the scene, is taken, the take is labeled (take number) – *X*. If another such shot is taken, it is labeled (take number) – *Y*.

X-Acto knife a cutting tool, used in printing and other fields, that consists of a handle and an insertable blade; made by Hunt X-Acto Inc., a subsidiary of the Hunt Manufacturing Company in Philadelphia, PA.

xbld extrabold type

X coordinate a horizontal location on a graph or layout

XCU extreme close-up; more commonly written as *ECU*

x-dissolve *cross-dissolve*, a film technique

xenon a colorless, odorless gaseous element used in stroboscopic (STROBE) and other lamps. Pronounced ZEE-non, the origin is the Greek *xenos*, "stranger." It is not a trademark and not capitalized. A *xenon lamp* is a high-intensity lamp with xenon gas between two tungsten electrodes, commonly used as the bulb in a film projector instead of a carbon arc lamp. Such a projector is called a *xenon projector* or *xenon arc projector*. A *xenon print*, sometimes called a *TV print*, is specially balanced to run in a xenon projector, though it also can be used in a carbon arc projector and for television transmission.

xerography a dry photographic or photocopying reproduction process in which powdered ink is distributed electrostatically so that a negative image is formed on an electrically charged plate and then electronically transferred and thermally fixed as a positive on pages or other material; from the Greek *xeros* ("dry") and *graphos* ("writing"). It is made permanent by the application of heat. The XEROX CORPORATION, headquartered in Stamford, CT, makes trademarked *xerographic* copying and duplicating machines and other equipment.

Xerox Corporation a major manufacturer based in Stamford, CT, of photocopying (XEROGRAPHY) machines and other office equipment. Since the invention has become ubiquitous, the word often is used as a verb (to xerox a page) and generic noun (to make a xerox).

x-height the standard height of lowercase letters in a given FONT, measured by the height of the letter *x*; also, the length of a type character between its WAISTLINE and *baseline*

XIS a film or TV shot that is over or across (X) the shoulders of a performer; also called *O.S.* (over shoulder)

XL extra large; extra long

X-lighting a lighting technique in which two performers or areas receive key lighting, so that the key light for one also is the back light for the other; more commonly called *double-key lighting*

XLS extra-long shot

XMT telegraphese for transmit

X-off, X-on transmitter off, transmitter on, an abbreviation in telecommunications

XR CROSS-REFERENCE

X-rated the classification for a motion picture unsuitable for viewing by persons under 17, as determined by the Code and Rating Administration of the Motion Picture Association of America. The term is generally used for pornographic films or other works.

x-ray   slang for a strip of lights above a set

X-ray border [theater] a strip of lights in a trough hung above the front area of the stage; also called *first border* or *teaser border*

X's *crosses stage*, a stage direction

XS across shoulder; see OVER-THE-SHOULDER SHOT

X-sheet directions for the exposure of animation film

Y

y year; also abbreviated as *yr*.

Y second in a series in which *X* is first and *Z* is third, as in the labeling of insert scenes in the filming of a single take; the luminance portion of a color video signal; yellow

yagi an antenna commonly used for reception in weak-signal areas, consisting of a basic dipole antenna supplemented by several parallel reflector and director elements You've seen these antennas on rooftops—they definitely are not rabbit-ear antennas. They were named after *Hidetsugu Yagi*, a Japanese engineer.

yak slang for excessive or idle chatter, also called *yakety-yak*; a loud laugh or a joke that evokes a laugh, also spelled *yock* or *yuk*

Y & R YOUNG & RUBICAM INC.

Yankelovich the name of several survey and market research techniques associated with Daniel Yankelovich, one of the pioneers in this field He now heads the WSY Consulting Group in New York and is not associated with Yankelovich Clancy Shulman, a major market research firm headquartered in Westport, CT and owned by SAATCHI & SAATCHI.

yapp a type of flexible book binding with extended edges that bind over the pages of the book, invented about 1860 by William Yapp, a London bookseller, for use with Bibles and prayer books; also called *divinity circuit* or *circuit edges*

yardstick a benchmark, a criterion for measurement

yawner a boring show or program

YCM yellow, cyan, and magenta, the primary colors

Y coordinate a vertical location on a graph or layout

year 365 days (366 days in leap year) Many companies operate on a *fiscal year*, most commonly starting April 1, instead of a calendar year starting January 1. Some industries operate on different schedules. For example, in retailing, many department stores begin the year on February 1.

yearbook an annual publication that reviews events of the preceding year

yellowback a low-priced novel bound in yellow board, popular in England in the 19th century

yellow card [theater] the use of local unionized stagehands in a touring show

yellow goods products such as appliances that are seldom consumed and replaced, require high levels of service, and are not as broadly distributed as food (*red goods*) and clothing (*orange goods*) They have a relatively high profit margin.

yellow journalism exaggerative, exploitative, sensational, "cheap" articles designed to attract a mass audience The origin is the use of yellow ink to print "The Yellow Kid," a troublemaker in a comic strip in the *New York World*, a free-wheeling sensationalist newspaper. Subsequently, William Randolph Hearst was called the *Yellow Kid*, and the term became derogatory, implying irresponsible journalism.

Yellow Pages a classified telephone directory, arranged alphabetically within categories of businesses and other classifications, including paid advertisements In 1988, the American Association of Yellow Pages Publishers and the National Yellow Pages Service Association merged to form the Yellow Pages Publishers Association, based in Troy, MI.

yellow sheet a *goldenrod*-coated masking paper on which negatives are taped and positioned prior to offset printing

YNR? international telex abbreviation: what is your telex number?

yock a loud laugh; also spelled *yak* or *yuck*

yoke an arch-shaped frame or bar, such as the U-shaped bracket commonly used to hold a luminaire in a theater or on a set

Young & Rubicam Inc. a major advertising and communications company headquartered in New York

Y signal a color-television signal of a specific intensity, 4.5 MHz (megahertz) or 4.5 million watts

yuk a loud laugh; also spelled *yak* or *yock*

yuppie young urban professional, a designation coined in the 1980s for upscale or on-the-way up individuals

Z

z. zero; zone

Z the 26th letter of the modern English alphabet; an indication of the third item in a series, following *X* and *Y*, akin to *ABC*; abbreviation for IMPEDANCE When used in handwritten copy, the letter *Z* often is crossed with a small line (standard in Europe) to avoid confusion with the numeral 2.

zap [television] the use of a remote-control device to change stations during commercial messages; the use of a device to blip out commercials, as with a pause button in videotaping; also called *zapping*

Zapf, Hermann a West German type and book designer (b. 1918) who created over 175 typefaces, including Melior, Optima, Palatino, and Zapf International Demi

Zap Mail a trademarked service of Federal Express of Memphis, TN, in which letters and other documents were transmitted by facsimile machine The service was dropped in 1986.

Z.B. an instruction to a camera operator to zoom back

Z core a plastic spool on which 16mm film is wound

Zelda a mannequin, generally just the head and shoulders, used to focus film or TV cameras

Zenger, John Peter an early American printer (1697–1746) whose trial in 1735 helped to establish the American tradition of a free press Proper names sometimes are used as verbs, so to *zenger* is to criticize the government.

zeppelin a long, perforated tube, shaped like a zeppelin, attached to a long microphone in outdoor scenes to minimize noise from the wind

zero nothing; the lowest point In data communications, to *zeroize* or *zero fill* is to add zeros to fill an area. For example, if a customer or document has a four-digit number such as 5936 and the system is set up for eight digits, perhaps in anticipation of expansion, the number is zeroized to become 00005936.

zero-based planning a procedure for developing a budget or other plan for a year or other specific period in which all aspects are considered

anew and justified each time, not merely revised from the previous period

zero spacing a typing or typesetting feature that permits a character to be typed over another character without erasing it, such as a SLASH through a letter

zero suppression the elimination of insignificant zeros at the left of a number

zeugma a figure of speech in which a single word, usually a verb or adjective, is related to two or more other words but is logically or grammatically related to only one of them A zeugma can be an unintentional error and often is amusing, particularly in newspaper headlines in which there is a desire to reduce the number of words. The origin is the Greek *zeugma,* "yoke" (something that connects).

Z-fold accordion or fan-fold paper, continuous sheets often perforated and folded in a zigzag manner with each fold in the opposite direction to the previous one It is commonly used in computer printers.

Z-height the height of the body of a lowercase letter, exclusive of *ascender* and *descender;* also called X-HEIGHT

zinc a LINE CUT etched on a zinc plate The process is obsolete, though the phrases *zinc etching* and *zinc halftone* sometimes are used.

zincograph a print made from a zinc plate, such as prints on yellow paper made by Paul Gauguin (1848–1903), the French artist who lived in Tahiti

zine a special-interest publication, generally produced by amateurs for other hobbyists, buffs, or fans; from *magazine,* though it often refers to newsletters Zines are often typed and reproduced in small quantities as photocopies. A *prozine* is such a publication that includes articles by professional writers.

ZI or **Z.I.** an instruction to a camera operator to ZOOM in

zip-ad a miniature sealed booklet affixed to a package at the factory

Zip-A-Tone a trademarked photochemical material used as a shading medium, applied to artwork to create gray values without a second color or the use of a half-tone screen, made by Zipatone Incorporated in Hillside, IL, a graphic-arts manufacturer It is similar to the BEN DAY process and CRAFTINT, a chemically treated drawing paper.

ZIP Code the abbreviation of *Zoning Improvement Plan Code*, the designations of areas by the U.S. Postal Service In the five-digit ZIP Code, the first digit refers to a region, starting in the East (0 for the New England states) and moving westward (9 for California). The nine-digit ZIP Code (*ZIP +4*) provides more precise information, such as a ZIP Code exclusively for one office building.

zip marketing selling by postal ZIP CODE segmentation

zip pan a rapid movement of the TV or film camera; also called *blur*, *whip*, or *whiz*

zipper an electronic billboard with lights that flash on and off to give the effect of moving letters, used for news bulletins and advertising on the outside of buildings and in terminals

zipping television-commercial avoidance during playback accomplished by *fast forwarding* through taped commercials

zit a blemish in printed material

Zoetrope a device that used a revolving drum with a strip of drawings to create the illusion of continuous motion, based on an 1834 invention by British mathematician William George Horner (1786–1837) It was similar to the 19th-century Stroboscope (also called *wheel of life*), a device based on persistence of vision. In Greek,

zoe is "life" and *trope* is "something that turns or changes."

zone an area or region A *zoned edition* of a newspaper or other periodical includes editorial and/or advertising for a specific neighborhood of a city or other area.

zoom an optical effect in television and motion pictures produced by shifting quickly from one camera angle to another, such as from a close-up to a long shot A *Zoomar* lens has adjustable focal lengths that can be changed rapidly. To *zoom in* is to move a camera in quickly for a close-up without changing shots; it is also called *forward zoom*. The opposite is *zoom out (ZO)*, *backward zoom*, or *back zoom (ZB)*. A *zoom shot* is made with a *zoom lens*. A *crash zoom* is a very rapid zoom shot.

Z-page the first page of a newspaper section other than the first section

Z pattern 1 a writing technique that starts with the background and then moves (zigzags) to more detail or literally moves from the background area to the foreground area **2** [advertising] a layout with the headline in the upper left and the advertiser's name or slogan in the lower right, so that the reader's eye moves in a *Z*

Zulu time Greenwich Mean Time, the worldwide reference time based on the time at the Greenwich observatory near London, England, commonly used by broadcasters and other communicators Greenwich is located at 0° (zero degrees) longitude, and zulu is a word for zero or *z*.